Protected Areas of the World

A review of national systems

Volume 2: Palaearctic

IUCN – THE WORLD CONSERVATION UNION

Founded in 1948, IUCN – The World Conservation Union – is a membership organisation comprising governments, non-governmental organisations (NGOs), research institutions, and conservation agencies in over 100 countries. The Union's mission is to provide leadership and promote a common approach for the world conservation movement in order to safeguard the integrity and diversity of the natural world, and to ensure that human use of natural resources is appropriate, sustainable and equitable.

Several thousand scientists and experts from all continents form part of a network supporting the work of its Commissions: threatened species, protected areas, ecology, environmental strategy and planning, environmental law, and education and communication. Its thematic programmes include forest conservation, wetlands, marine ecosystems, plants, the Sahel, Antarctica, population and natural resources, and Eastern Europe. The Union's work is also supported by 12 regional and country offices located principally in developing countries.

WCMC – THE WORLD CONSERVATION MONITORING CENTRE

The World Conservation Monitoring Centre (WCMC) is a joint venture between the three partners who developed the World Conservation Strategy: IUCN – The World Conservation Union, UNEP – United Nations Environment Programme, and WWF – World Wide Fund For Nature (formerly World Wildlife Fund). Its mission is to support conservation and sustainable development through the provision of information on the world's biological diversity.

WCMC has developed a global overview database that includes threatened plant and animal species, habitats of conservation concern, critical sites, protected areas of the world, and the utilisation and trade in wildlife species and products. Drawing on this database, WCMC provides an information service to the conservation and development communities, governments and United Nations agencies, scientific institutions, the business and commercial sector, and the media. WCMC produces a wide variety of specialist outputs and reports based on analyses of its data.

Protected Areas of the World

A review of national systems

Volume 2: Palaearctic

Compiled by the World Conservation Monitoring Centre

in collaboration with

The IUCN Commission on National Parks and Protected Areas

for the

IVth World Congress on National Parks and Protected Areas,
Caracas, Venezuela, 10-21 February 1992

with the support of

The British Petroleum Company p.l.c.

IUCN – The World Conservation Union

November 1991

Published by: IUCN, Gland, Switzerland and Cambridge, UK,
                   with the financial support of The British Petroleum Company p.l.c.

Prepared by: The World Conservation Monitoring Centre, Cambridge, UK

                   A contribution to GEMS – The Global Environment Monitoring System

WORLD CONSERVATION
MONITORING CENTRE

Citation: IUCN (1992). *Protected Areas of the World: A review of national systems. Volume 2: Palaearctic*.
                   IUCN, Gland, Switzerland and Cambridge, UK. xxviii + 556 pp.

ISBN: 2-8317-0091-4

Printed by: Page Bros (Norwich) Ltd, UK

Cover photos: The Malvern Hills, UK: Jeremy Harrison; Sand dunes in the Oman desert: RGS/Wahiba Sands
                   Project; Limestone pinnacles of Guilin, China: Royal Geographical Society

Produced by: IUCN Publications Services Unit, Cambridge, UK, on desktop publishing equipment purchased
                   through a gift from Mrs Julia Ward

Available from: IUCN Publications Services Unit,
                   219c Huntingdon Road, Cambridge, CB3 0DL, UK

The designations of geographical entities in this book, and the presentation of the material, do not imply the expression of any opinion whatsoever on the part of IUCN, WCMC or BP concerning the legal status of any country, territory, or area, or of its authorities, or concerning the delimitation of its frontiers or boundaries.

TABLE OF CONTENTS

	Page
Foreword	vii
Introduction	viii
Acknowledgements	ix
Managing information on protected areas at WCMC	xi
Country accounts: guidelines to their contents	xiii
Maps and Lists (explanation of)	xiv
Internationally designated sites	xv

PALAEARCTIC – Asia

China, People's Republic of	1
Japan	19
Korea, Democratic People's Republic of	43
Korea, Republic of	47
Mongolia, People's Republic of	55
Portugal – Macao	61
United Kingdom – Hong Kong	63
Union of Soviet Socialist Republics	69

PALAEARCTIC – Europe

Albania, Republic of	83
Andorra	89
Austria	91
Belgium	103
Bulgaria, Republic of	109
Czechoslovakia	117
Denmark	125
Denmark – Faroe Islands	135
Estonia, Republic of	137
Finland	141
France	149
Germany, Federal Republic of	165
Greece	185
Holy See (Vatican City State)	193
Hungary	195
Iceland	203
Ireland	209
Italy	217
Latvia, Republic of	231
Liechtenstein	235
Lithuania, Republic of	239
Luxembourg, Grand Duchy of	243
Malta, Republic of	249
Monaco, Principality of	253
Netherlands	255

Norway 263
Poland, Republic of 275
Portugal 287
Romania 295
San Marino 301
Spain 303
Sweden 319
Switzerland 331
Ukraine 341
United Kingdom of Great Britain and Northern Ireland 345
United Kingdom – Channel Islands 365
United Kingdom – Gibraltar 367
United Kingdom – Isle of Man 371
Yugoslavia 373

PALAEARCTIC – North Africa and Middle East

Afghanistan 385
Algeria 391
Bahrain, State of 399
Cyprus 403
Cyprus ("Turkish Republic of Northern Cyprus") 409
Egypt 413
Iran, Islamic Republic of 425
Iraq 435
Israel 439
Jordan 447
Kuwait 455
Lebanon 465
Libyan Arab Jamahiriyah 469
Morocco, Kingdom of 475
Morocco – Saharan Provinces 487
Oman, Sultanate of 491
Qatar 501
Saudi Arabia, Kingdom of 505
Spain – North African Territories 517
Syrian Arab Republic 521
Territories of the West Bank and Gaza Strip 527
Tunisia 531
Turkey 539
United Arab Emirates 547
Yemen, Republic of 551

FOREWORD

The inspirational and aesthetic values of fine examples of the beauty and bounty of nature lay behind the establishment of many national parks and other types of protected areas. More recently there has been increasing recognition of the range of the value of protected areas and of their contribution to meet the needs of society by conserving the world's natural and physical resources. These values range from protection of representative samples of natural regions and the preservation of biological diversity, to the maintenance of environmental stability in surrounding country. Protected areas can also facilitate complementary rural development and rational use of marginal lands, and provide opportunities for research and monitoring, conservation education, and recreation and tourism.

Over the past thirty years, since the *First World Conference on National Parks* was held in Seattle, Washington (1962), our view of the world, and our impact on the world, has changed significantly. Throughout this time, and despite the mounting pressures of expanding human populations, the number of protected areas established has continued to rise. Since the centennial of national parks was commemorated at the time of the *Second World Conference on National Parks* at Yellowstone and Grand Teton, Wyoming in 1972, the "human" element of protected areas has come more and more into focus. They are no longer seen as being "locked up" or "set apart". Rather, they are seen as being integral to strategic approaches to resource management, a concept enshrined in the *World Conservation Strategy* (1980) based on managing natural areas to support development in a sustainable way.

The fundamental contribution of protected areas to sustainable management was reaffirmed by participants at the *World Congress on National Parks* held in Bali, Indonesia (1982), and for the last decade the *Bali Action Plan* has focused attention on a range of actions necessary for promoting and supporting protected areas. These actions were further focused in regional action plans subsequently developed by members of the IUCN Commission on National Parks and Protected Areas, covering the Afrotropical, Indomalayan, Neotropical and Oceanian regions.

More recently, two significant, and widely accepted documents have stressed the very vital roles that protected areas play. The report of the *World Commission on Environment and Development* was published in 1987, and more recently a new strategy *Caring for the World* was launched in 1991. This latter strategy, which has its roots in the *World Conservation Strategy*, clearly identifies the functions and benefits of protected area systems, what they safeguard, and why they are important for development opportunities.

Many countries have declared extensive systems of protected areas, and are continuing to develop and expand them. The systems and the sites they contain vary considerably from one country to another, depending on national needs and priorities, and on differences in legislative, institutional and financial support. Consequently, protected areas have been established under many different national designations to provide for a spectrum of management objectives, ranging from total protection to sustainable use: from strict nature reserves to lived-in landscapes.

IUCN – The World Conservation Union has been involved in protected areas issues for many years, and has published a significant body of information on the subject. The IUCN Commission on National Parks and Protected Areas was set up both to ensure that the appropriate expertise was available to advise the Union, and to bring together professionals to share information and experience. IUCN and CNPPA have together had a very strong hand in developing the programme for the *IV World Congress on National Parks and Protected Areas* in Caracas, Venezuela (1992).

For more than 10 years, IUCN and CNPPA have worked closely with what is now the World Conservation Monitoring Centre, to help in building an information resource on protected areas. The information is of value to the Commission in developing its own programmes, in identifying priorities, and for a wide range of other purposes such as supporting international initiatives in World Heritage, wetlands and biosphere reserves. It is also important to both IUCN and the Commission that such information is made available to others, so that the roles and values of protected areas are more widely recognised, appreciated and respected.

The three volume *Protected Areas of the World: A review of national systems* is being published for the World Parks Congress by WCMC and IUCN in cooperation with British Petroleum, and aims to provide a standard format "overview" of the world's protected area systems. While this product has gaps, and no doubt inaccuracies, it does illustrate very clearly the range of protected areas activities around the world, and gives an indication of the protected areas estate under the stewardship of our managers. This product, in combination with the protected areas reviews being prepared for the Congress by the CNPPA Regional Vice-Chairs, will also provide a benchmark against which to measure our achievements over the next decade.

P.H.C. (Bing) Lucas
Chair
IUCN Commission on National Parks and Protected Areas

INTRODUCTION

Participants at the *Third World National Parks Congress* held in Bali, Indonesia, in 1982, clearly recognised that the availability of comprehensive, good-quality information on the world's protected areas was essential to a wide range of international organisations, governments, protected area managers, voluntary bodies and individuals. Such information is a prerequisite for assessing the coverage and status of protected areas from regional and global perspectives, and is key to the development of regional and global priorities and strategies. Monitoring protected areas is vital to ensure that those areas allocated to conserve the world's natural resources meet the needs of society.

The World Conservation Monitoring Centre (WCMC) is expanding its capabilities as an international centre for information on the conservation of biological diversity. Working closely with the IUCN Commission on National Parks and Protected Areas (CNPPA), WCMC continues to compile an extensive database on the world's protected areas, which is being used more and more frequently as a source of information.

One result of WCMC's work as an information centre is the ability to draw material together into publications which provide background information on protected areas and protected area systems. At the previous congress in 1982, two publications from the protected areas database were available, the *1982 UN List*, and the *IUCN Directory of Neotropical Protected Areas*. Since then, the Centre has collaborated with CNPPA and others on a wide range of publications, including two subsequent *UN Lists* in 1985 and 1990, directories of protected areas for Africa, Oceania, South Asia, and the mountains of central Asia, and various publications on eastern Europe. A full list of publications on protected areas (including those published by others with information provided by WCMC) is available from the Centre.

The present work, *Protected Areas of the world: A review of national systems*, is the first attempt by WCMC to compile a world-wide survey of protected area systems. The book is organised into national (or occasionally sub-national) accounts, each comprising a description of the national protected areas system, accompanied by a summary list and map of protected areas. The book is divided into three volumes, with volume one covering the Indomalayan, Oceanian, Australian and Antarctic realms, volume two the Palaearctic and Afrotropical realms, and volume three the Nearctic and Neotropical realms.

Publication of such a book serves two purposes. First, it provides extensive background information on the protected area systems of the world, relevant to several plenary sessions and workshops at the *IV World Congress on National Parks and Protected Areas*. In particular, it is a contribution to the third plenary session *The Contributions of Protected Areas to Sustaining Society: A Global Review*. Secondly, and perhaps more significantly, it is also part of the process of information collection and verification. Feedback from protected areas professionals, and others familiar with protected areas, is therefore both welcomed and encouraged, because only by a continual process of review and update can we present a true picture.

Jeremy Harrison
World Conservation Monitoring Centre

ACKNOWLEDGEMENTS

Preparation of a directory of this magnitude is only achieved through a tremendous amount of effort and cooperation. Over the years, protected areas professionals throughout the world have reviewed or compiled material for us, or provided new information. Quite simply, without their cooperation this book could not have been completed, and we greatly appreciate their support.

This assistance has been facilitated in part by the IUCN Commission on National Parks and Protected Areas, and the support of the Commission and its past and present officers is gratefully acknowledged. In particular we would like to thank the present chair P.H.C. (Bing) Lucas of New Zealand, and his predecessor Harold Eidsvik of Canada. Work has also been supported by the staff of the IUCN Protected Areas Unit, and in particular James Thorsell and Jeffrey McNeely.

This particular publication is the product of two projects. The *British Petroleum Company plc* has provided support for the preparation of part of the text and maps (for those areas not covered by the second mentioned project), and have provided funds for publishing the book and distributing it at the World Parks Congress in Caracas, Venezuela. At the same time, the *British Overseas Development Administration* has supported review of information on tropical and sub-tropical countries, as part of a project contributing to the FAO Forest Resources Assessment 1990. Thanks are due to both organisations for their support.

A number of past and present staff of WCMC have been involved in preparing this directory, which includes material published in several earlier directories. Compilation of country accounts has been the responsibility of: Patricia Almada-Villela, Daphne Clark, Graham Drucker, Harriet Gillett, Michael Green, Donald Gordon, Jeremy Harrison, Zbigniew Karpowicz, Sara Oldfield, James Paine and Mark Spalding. Assistance with the preparation of maps has been provided by Mike Adam, Clare Billington, Simon Blyth and Gillian Bunting.

Notwithstanding the significant contributions of the many individuals who have provided information to WCMC and CNPPA, errors and omissions must remain the responsibility of the compilers.

This directory is not intended to be a final statement but a review of the world's protected area systems. If WCMC is to continue to carry out its mission, there is a continual need to maintain and update this information as national protected areas systems change and as more information becomes available. Therefore, with this directory goes a plea for corrections, comments and additional material to help WCMC carry out its mission as effectively as possible. By the same token, the information that WCMC collects and manages is available to others to support their work and programmes.

World Conservation Monitoring Centre
219 Huntingdon Road, Cambridge, CB3 ODL, United Kingdom
Tel: (44) 223 277314
Fax: (44) 223 277136
Tlx: 817036 SCMU G

MANAGING INFORMATION ON PROTECTED AREAS AT WCMC

Many individuals and organisations need basic information on protected areas systems, lists of protected areas with certain features, or analyses of protected areas statistics, yet it is unlikely that they will have the time or resources to collect, compile and analyse all of the information for themselves. Such information also needs to be kept up-to-date, as properties are added or extended, and as legislation or administrative regimes change. Users may also require details about the major protected areas within national systems, such as physical features, vegetation and fauna, or on other aspects such as management status and constraints.

It is to meet these needs that the WCMC Protected Areas Data Unit (PADU) was founded. This service enables users to obtain quickly information on protected areas from a single source, be it for purposes of analysis and assessment, or as briefing material. It is not intended that this service should by-pass any need for users to contact or visit the relevant national authorities for such information, but use of PADU's resources enables users to be well informed prior to making such approaches and in a better position to ask the right questions when so doing.

Institutional background

IUCN – The World Conservation Union has been closely involved in protected areas issues for many years. As early as 1960, it established a Commission on National Parks and Protected Areas (CNPPA) to serve as the "leading international, scientific and technical body concerned with the selection, establishment and management of national parks and other protected areas". CNPPA has always emphasised the need for information on which to base effective conservation planning and management, and has been very active in collecting and disseminating information on protected areas.

As the world's network of protected areas has expanded and its management improved, information on national protected areas systems and individual protected areas has proliferated. This led CNPPA to set up PADU in 1981 to manage this increasing volume of information. Establishment of this Unit was supported by the United Nations Environment Programme (UNEP), as part of its Global Environment Monitoring System (GEMS). Originally part of the IUCN Conservation Monitoring Centre, PADU is now a unit within the World Conservation Monitoring Centre (WCMC), restructured in July 1988 and jointly managed by IUCN, the World Wide Fund for Nature (WWF) and UNEP.

Objectives

WCMC aims to provide accurate up-to-date information on protected area systems of the world for use by its partners (IUCN, WWF and UNEP) in the support and development of their programmes, and by other international bodies, governmental and non-governmental organisations, scientists and the general public. Such information covers the entire spectrum of protected areas, from national parks and sanctuaries established under protected areas legislation or customary regimes to forest reserves created under forestry legislation. It also includes privately-owned reserves in which nature is protected.

Specific objectives are to:

- maintain a comprehensive and up-to-date database of the world's protected areas;
- compile definitive, standard-format accounts summarising national protected areas systems;
- hold maps of protected areas systems and digitise them;
- compile definitive, standard-format accounts covering individual protected areas, particularly the major properties in tropical countries and those of international importance;
- accumulate current and historical information on protected areas; and
- provide support to regional and international activities, programmes and conventions relating to protected areas.

Information capture, management and compilation

Information is collected from official sources, namely national agencies responsible for administering protected areas, and other sources through a global network of contacts ranging in profession from policy-makers and administrators to land managers and scientists. It is also obtained from published and unpublished literature. Regional CNPPA meetings and other relevant scientific and technical meetings provide valuable opportunities for making new contacts and collecting fresh information. This material in itself is a major asset of the Centre.

Information, ranging from books, reports, management plans, scientific papers, maps and correspondence, is stored as hard copy in manual files. Basic data on individual protected areas are extracted and, after verification, entered in a protected areas database, which currently holds some 26,000 records. This computerised database can be used for generating lists of protected areas meeting pre-defined criteria, together with summary statistics, as well as performing more complex tasks. In addition, maps of protected areas are gradually being digitised, using a Geographic Information System, in order to generate computerised graphic output.

The information is also used to produce accounts of protected areas systems and individual protected areas. These accounts are compiled according to standard formats developed over the years by WCMC in collaboration with CNPPA.

Dissemination of information

In keeping with its primary objective, WCMC aims to make available good quality information on protected areas to a wide range of users, including international organisations, governments, protected area managers, conservation organisations, commercial companies involved in natural resource exploitation, scientists, and the media and general public. Information may be provided or consulted by arrangement.

Material may be prepared under contract: for example, WCMC regularly provides UNEP with summary data on protected areas for its biennial *Environmental Data Report*. WCMC is experimenting with providing outside users with direct access to its protected areas database. Trials have been ongoing with the US National Park Service since 1986 and it is hoped to be able to extend this service to other users shortly.

Compiled information is periodically published in the form of regional or thematic directories and lists. Directories comprise sections on individual countries, each with a protected areas *system information sheet*, a *list* of protected areas and accompanying *location map*, and a series of *site information sheets* covering at least the more important properties. Prior to releasing or publishing documents, draft material is circulated for review by relevant government agencies and experts to help ensure that compiled information is accurate and comprehensive.

Major lists and directories published to date are as follows:

— *United Nations List of National Parks and Protected Areas* (1982, 1985, 1990)

— *IUCN Directory of Neotropical Protected Areas* (1982)

— *IUCN Directory of Afrotropical Protected Areas* (1987)

— *IUCN Directory of South Asian Protected Areas* (1990)

— *Protected Areas in Eastern and Central Europe and the USSR* (1990)

— *IUCN Directory of Protected Areas in Oceania* (1991)

— *Nature Reserves of the Himalaya and the Mountains of Central Asia* (1992)

— *Information System: Biosphere Reserves: Compilation 4* (1986)

— *Biosphere Reserves: Compilation 5* (1990)

— *Directory of Wetlands of International Importance* (1987, 1990)

— *Protected Landscapes: Experience around the World* (1987)

In addition, numerous draft directories, reports papers and reviews have been produced. A list of these is available from WCMC.

WCMC also disseminates information through the *CNPPA Newsletter* and *Parks* magazine. In the case of the latter, WCMC has assumed responsibility for compiling *Clipboard* in which world news on protected areas is featured.

Special services

WCMC has a very close working relationship with CNPPA. While the Commission provides expert advice and support through its network of members, WCMC supports many of the Commission's activities through provision of technical information. WCMC has a particular responsibility for managing information on natural properties designated under international conventions and programmes, namely the *Convention concerning the Protection of the World Cultural and Natural Heritage* (World Heritage Convention), *Convention on Wetlands of International Importance especially as Waterfowl Habitat* (Ramsar Convention), and the Unesco *Man and the Biosphere Programme*. Thus, WCMC cooperates closely with the Division of Ecological Sciences, Unesco, in maintaining information on biosphere reserves and World Heritage sites accorded by the MAB Secretariat and World Heritage Committee, respectively. Likewise, it works closely with the Ramsar Bureau with respect to managing information on Ramsar wetlands.

The rest of the World Conservation Monitoring Centre

Protected areas is only one aspect of the programme of the World Conservation Monitoring Centre, which also covers information on plant and animal species of conservation concern, important natural habitats and sites of high biological diversity, wildlife utilisation, and the international trade in wildlife.

To monitor the impact of man on nature is a major task. This requires close collaboration between agencies, and between agencies and individuals, and the development and exchange of information. WCMC acts both as an information centre, and as a facilitator of information management and exchange. WCMC has now embarked on an ambitious programme to promote improvements in the availability of information, and to develop its database capabilities and information services. Information on the distribution and status of the world's protected areas is an essential component of this programme.

COUNTRY ACCOUNTS: GUIDELINES TO THEIR CONTENTS

In general, there is an account for each country, divided up into a series of sections with standard headings. The following notes summarise the type of information included in each section where it is available. In certain cases, accounts have been prepared for areas which are parts of countries, usually where the area concerned is geographically separate from the "parent" country.

Country

Full name of country or political unit, as used by the United Nations (United Nations *Terminology Bulletin* on Names of Countries and Adjectives of Nationality).

Area

Total area according to the latest volume of the *FAO Production Yearbook* prepared by the Statistics Division of the Economic and Social Policy Department, FAO, unless otherwise stated (with full reference). Terrestrial and marine components are distinguished, if appropriate.

Population

Total population and its mean annual rate of growth according to the latest issue of *World Population Prospects*, published by the United Nations Population Division. Year of census or estimate is indicated in parentheses. If another source has to be used, it is cited.

Economic Indicators

Gross domestic product and gross national product per capita in US dollars (or net material product in the case of centrally planned economies), with year in parentheses. These figures are according to the latest issue of *National Accounts Statistics: Analysis of Main Aggregates* (prepared by the United Nations Statistical Office) and *The World Bank Atlas*.

Policy and Legislation

Information on aspects of the constitution that are relevant to nature conservation and protected areas.

Summary of national policies that relate to nature conservation, particularly with respect to the protection of ecosystems. This may include reference to policies relating to environmental impact assessments, and national/regional conservation strategies.

Brief chronological account of past and present national legislation and traditions that relate to the establishment of the protected areas system, with names (in English), dates and numbers of acts, decrees and ordinances. Legislation covering forestry and other resource sectors is included, in so far as it provides for protected areas establishment. Procedures for the notification and declassification of protected areas are summarised.

Outline of legal provisions for administering protected areas

National designations of protected areas are cited and their range of provisions outlined. Their legal definitions, together with the names of the authorities legally responsible for their administration, are summarised in an Annex (see below).

Reviews of protected areas policy and legislation are noted, with any identified deficiencies in prevailing provisions highlighted.

International Activities

Participation in international conventions and programmes (World Heritage and Ramsar conventions, MAB Programme, UNEP Regional Seas Programme) and regional conventions and agreements (such as the African, ASEAN and Berne conventions, the FAO Latin American/Caribbean Technical Cooperation Network, South Asian Cooperative Environmental Programme and the South Pacific Regional Environment Programme) relevant to habitat protection is summarised.

Outline of any international, multilateral and bilateral cooperative programmes or transfrontier cooperative agreements relevant to protected areas.

Administration and Management

All authorities responsible for the administration and management of protected areas are named and described, with a brief history of their establishment, administrative organisation, staff structure, budget and any training programmes. Authorities responsible for different types of protected areas are clearly distinguished.

Outline of the role of any advisory boards.

Cooperative agreements between management authorities and national or foreign universities and institutes, with details of any research underway or completed.

Names and brief details of non-governmental organisations concerned with protected areas. Reference to any national directories of voluntary conservation bodies is included.

Effectiveness of protected areas management is noted where information has been provided. Attention is drawn to any sites registered as threatened under the World Heritage Convention, or by the IUCN Commission on National Parks and Protected Areas.

Systems Reviews

Short account of physical features, biological resources, and land use patterns (with percentages if available), including the extent and integrity of major ecosystems.

Brief review of the development of nature conservation programmes, so far as it relates to the establishment and expansion of the national protected areas network. Emphasis is given to any systems reviews or comprehensive surveys of biological resources, with details of major recommendations arising from such studies.

Threats to the protected areas system beyond the control of the management agencies are outlined.

Other relevant information

Tourism and other economic benefits of the protected areas system, if applicable

Other items, as appropriate

Addresses

Names and addresses (with telephone, telex and fax numbers, and cable) of authorities responsible for administering protected areas. Names are given in the original language or transliterated, with English translation in brackets as appropriate, and followed by the title of the post of the chief executive.

Names and addresses (with telephone, telex and fax numbers, and cable) of non-governmental organisations actively involved in protected areas issues. Names are given in the original language or transliterated, with English translation in brackets as appropriate, and followed by the title of the post of the chief executive,

References

Key references (including all cited works) to the protected areas system, in particular, and nature conservation, in general, are listed.

ANNEX
Definitions of protected area designations, as legislated, together with authorities responsible for their administration

The annex includes the following sections:

Title: Name and number of law in the original language or transliterated, with the English translation underneath, as appropriate.

Date: Day, month and year of enactment, followed by dates of subsequent major amendments

Brief description: Summary of main provisions (often this is stated at the beginning of the legislation)

Administrative authority: Name of authority responsible for administering the law, given in the original language or transliterated, with the English translation underneath as appropriate. This is followed by the title of the post of the chief executive.

Designations: National designation of protected area in the original language or transliterated, followed in brackets by the English translation as appropriate. For each designation this would be followed by: definition of designation (if given in legislation), summary of activities permitted or prohibited, outline of penalties for offences, and, where relevant, reference to subsequent legislation relating to the original law.

Source: This may be "original legislation", "translation of original legislation" or a referenced secondary source.

MAPS and LISTS

The descriptive sections are followed by lists of protected areas, and maps showing their location. In most cases, the lists comprise all of those areas qualifying for inclusion in IUCN management categories I-VIII, which have an area of over 1,000 hectares. However, forest and hunting reserves qualifying for IUCN Management Category VIII have been largely omitted, because our information is not comprehensive. Also, size has been ignored for island nations. Note that in certain cases, nationally designated areas (such as some national parks) will not appear in the lists, as they do not meet the criteria. World Heritage sites, biosphere reserves and Ramsar sites are also listed.

Categories and management objectives of protected areas

I   *Scientific Reserve/Strict Nature Reserve*: to protect nature and maintain natural processes in an undisturbed state in order to have ecologically representative examples of the natural environment available for scientific study, environmental monitoring, education, and for the maintenance of genetic resources in a dynamic and evolutionary state.

II   *National Park*: to protect natural and scenic areas of national or international significance for scientific, educational and recreational use.

III *Natural Monument/Natural Landmark*: to protect and preserve nationally significant natural features because of their special interest or unique characteristics.

IV *Managed Nature Reserve/Wildlife Sanctuary*: to assure the natural conditions necessary to protect nationally significant species, groups of species, biotic communities, or physical features of the environment where these require specific human manipulation for their perpetuation.

V *Protected Landscape or Seascape*: to maintain nationally significant natural landscapes which are characteristic of the harmonious interaction of man and land while providing opportunities for public enjoyment through recreation and tourism within the normal life style and economic activity of these areas.

VI *Resource Reserve*: to protect the natural resources of the area for future use and prevent or contain development activities that could affect the resource pending the establishment of objectives which are based upon appropriate knowledge and planning.

VII *Natural Biotic Area/Anthropological Reserve*: to allow the way of life of societies living in harmony with the environment to continue undisturbed by modern technology.

VIII *Multiple-Use Management Area/Managed Resource Area*: to provide for the sustained production of water, timber, wildlife, pasture, and outdoor recreation, with the conservation of nature primarily oriented to the support of economic activities (although specific zones may also be designed within these areas to achieve specific conservation objectives).

Abridged from IUCN (1984). Categories and criteria for protected areas. In: McNeely, J.A. and Miller, K.R. (Eds), *National parks, conservation, and development. The role of protected areas in sustaining society*. Smithsonian Institution Press, Washington. Pp. 47-53

INTERNATIONALLY DESIGNATED SITES

In the field of nature conservation there are two international conventions and one international programme that include provision for designation of internationally important sites in *any* region of the world. These are the World Heritage Convention, the Ramsar (Wetlands) Convention, and the Unesco Man and the Biosphere (MAB) Programme. While there is a wide range of other international conventions and programmes, these cover only regions, or small groups of countries.

Both World Heritage sites and Ramsar sites must be nominated by a State that is party to the relevant convention. While there is an established review procedure for World Heritage sites (and nomination is no guarantee of listing), all nominated Ramsar sites are placed on the List of Wetlands of International Importance. Biosphere reserves are nominated by the national MAB committee of the country concerned, and are only designated following review and acceptance by the MAB Bureau.

Each Contracting Party to the Ramsar (Wetlands) Convention is obliged to nominate at least one wetland of international importance. However, a country can be party to the World Heritage Convention without having a natural site inscribed on the List, and may participate in the MAB programme without designating a biosphere reserve.

World Heritage Sites

The Convention Concerning the Protection of the World Cultural and Natural Heritage was adopted in Paris in 1972, and came into force in December 1975. The Convention provides for the designation of areas of "outstanding universal value" as World Heritage sites, with the principal aim of fostering international cooperation in safeguarding these important areas. Sites, which must be nominated by the signatory nation responsible, are evaluated for their World Heritage quality before being inscribed by the international World Heritage Committee. Only natural sites, and those with mixed natural and cultural aspects, are considered in this publication.

Article 2 of the World Heritage Convention considers as natural heritage: natural features consisting of physical and biological formations or groups of such formations, which are of outstanding universal value from the aesthetic or scientific point of view; geological or physiographical formations and precisely delineated areas which constitute the habitat of threatened species of animals and plants of outstanding universal value from the point of view of science or conservation; and natural sites or precisely delineated areas of outstanding universal value from the point of view of science, conservation or natural beauty. Criteria for inclusion in the list are published by Unesco.

The following States Party to the Convention lie at least partially within the regions covered by this volume:

Afghanistan
Albania
Algeria
Bulgaria
Belarus, Republic of
China
Cyprus
Czechoslovakia
Denmark
Egypt
Finland
France
Germany
Greece
Holy See
Hungary
Iran
Iraq
Italy
Jordan
Lebanon
Libyan Arab Jamahiriya
Luxembourg
Malta
Monaco
Mongolia
Morocco
Norway
Oman
Poland
Portugal
Qatar
Romania
Saudi Arabia
Spain
Sweden
Switzerland
Syrian Arab Republic
Tunisia
Turkey
Ukraine
United Kingdom
USSR
Yemen
Yugoslavia

The following natural and mixed natural/cultural World Heritage sites lie within the regions covered by this volume:

Bulgaria

Pirin National Park
Srébarna Nature Reserve

China
Mount Huangshan
Mount Taishan

France
Cape Girolata, Cape Porto and Scandola Nature
    Reserve (Corsica)
Mont-St-Michel

Greece
Meteora
Mount Athos

Poland
Bialowieza National Park

Spain
Garajonay National Park (Canary Islands)

Turkey
Göreme National Park
Hierapolis-Pamukkale
Mount Athos

United Kingdom
Giant's Causeway
St Kilda

Yugoslavia
Durmitor National Park
Kotor
Ohrid
Plitvice Lakes National Park
Skocjan Caves

Ramsar Sites

The Convention on Wetlands of International Importance especially as Waterfowl Habitat was signed in Ramsar (Iran) in 1971, and also came into force in December 1975. This Convention provides a framework for international cooperation for the conservation of wetland habitats. The Convention places general obligations on contracting party states relating to the conservation of wetlands throughout their territory, with special obligations pertaining to those wetlands which have been designated to the "List of Wetlands of International Importance".

Each State Party is obliged to list at least one site. Wetlands are defined by the convention as: areas of marsh, fen, peatland or water, whether natural or artificial, permanent or temporary, with water that is static or flowing, fresh, brackish or salt, including areas of marine waters, the depth of which at low tide does not exceed six metres.

The following States Party to the Convention lie at least partially within the regions covered by this volume:

Algeria
Austria
Belgium
Bulgaria
Czechoslovakia
Denmark
Egypt

Finland
France
Germany
Greece
Hungary
Iceland
Iran
Ireland
Italy
Japan
Jordan
Liechtenstein
Malta
Morocco
Netherlands
Norway
Poland
Portugal
Romania
Spain
Sweden
Switzerland
Union of Soviet Socialist Republics
United Kingdom
Yugoslavia

The following wetlands which lie within the region have been included in the List of Wetlands of International Importance:

Algeria
Lac Oubeïra
Lac Tonga

Austria
Donau-March-Auen
Lower Inn reservoirs
Neusiedlersee
Pürgschachen Moor
Rheindelta, Bodensee
Untere Lobau

Belgium
Kalmthoutse Heide
Le Blankaart
Le Marais d'Harchies
Le Zwin
Les Schorren de l'Escaut à Doel et à Zandvliet
Les Vlaamse Banken dans les eaux côtières

Bulgaria
Arkoutino
Atanassovo Lake
Durankulak Lake
Srébarna

Czechoslovakia
Cicov "dead arm"
Lednice fish ponds
Modrava peatbogs
Novozámecky and Behyn ponds
Paríz marshes
Senné fish ponds

Šúr
Trebon fish ponds

Denmark
Anholt Island sea area
Ertholmene Islands east of Bornholm
Fiilsø
Hirsholmene
Horsens Fiord and Endelave
Karrebæk, Dybsø and Avnø Fiords
Læsø
Lillebælt
Maribo Lakes
Nakskov Fiord and Inner Fiord
Næreå Coast and Æbelø area
Nissum Bredning with Harboøre and Agger
    Peninsulas
Nissum Fiord
Nordre Rønner
Præstø Fiord, Jungshoved Nor, Ulfshale and Nyord
Randers and Mariager Fiords (part)
Ringkøbing Fiord
Sejerø Bugt
South Funen Archipelago
Stadil and Veststadil Fiords
Stavns Fiord adjacent waters
Ulvedybet and Nibe Bredning
Vadehavet (The Waddensea)
Vejlerne and Løgstør Bredning
Waters south-east of Fejo and Femo Isles
Waters off Skælskør Nor and Glænø
Waters between Lolland and Falster, including
    Rødsand, Guldborgsund, Bøtø Nor

Egypt
Lake Bardawil
Lake Burullus

Estonia
Matsalu Bay

Finland
Aspskär
Björkör/Lagskär
Koitilaiskaira
Krunnit
Maartimoaapa-Lumiaapa
Ruskis
Signilskär
Söderskär/Langoren
Suomujärvi-Patvinsuo
Valassaaret/Björkögrunden
Viikki

France
La Brenne
La Camargue
Etang de Biguglia
Etang de la Champagne Humide
Etang de la Petite Woëvre
Golfe du Morbihan
Marais du Cotentin et du Bessin (Baie des Veys)

xvii

Rives du Lac Léman

Germany
Ammersee
Berga-Kelbra Storage Lake
Bodensee
Chiemsee
Diepholzer Lowland Marsh and Peat Bogs
Dümmersee
Elbe water-meadows between Schnackenburg and
    Lauenburg
Galenbecker See
Ismaning Reservoir and fish-ponds
Krakower Obersee
Lech-Donau Winkel
Lower Havel River and Gülper See
Lower Inn between Haiming and Neuhaus
Lower Elbe, Barnkrug-Otterndorf
Müritz See (eastern shore)
Nationalpark Hamburgisches Wattenmeer
Oder Valley near Schwedt
Ostfriesisches Wattenmeer & Dollart
Peitz Ponds
Rhine between Eltville and Bingen
Rieselfelder Münster
Rügen/Hiddensee and eastern part of Zingst
    Peninsula
Starnberger See
Steinhuder Meer
Unterer Niederrhein
Water-meadows and peat-bogs of Donau
Wattenmeer, Jadebusen & Western Weser Mouth
Wattenmeer, Elbe-Weser-Dreieck
Weserstaustufe Schlüsselburg

Greece
Amvrakikos Gulf
Axios-Aliakmon-Loudias Delta
Evros Delta
Kotichi Lagoon
Lake Kerkini
Lake Mitrikou and adjoining lagoons
Lake Visthonis and Porto Lagos Lagoon
Lakes Mikra Prespa and Megali Prespa
Lakes Volvis and Langada
Mesolonghi Lagoons
Nestos Delta and Gumburnou Lagoon

Hungary
Bodrogzug
Hortobágy
Kardoskut
Kis-balaton
Kiskunság
Lake Balaton
Lake Fertö
Mártély
Ócsa
Pusztaszer
Szaporca
Tata Old Lake
Velence-Dinnyés

Iceland
Part of Mývatn-Laxá Region
Thjorsarver

Iran
Alagol, Ulmagol and Ajigol Lakes
Amirkelayeh Lake
Anzali Mordab Complex
Bandar Kiashahr Lagoon and mouth of Sefid Rud
Deltas of Rud-e-Gaz and Rud-e-Hara
Deltas of Rud-e-Shur, Rud-e-Shirin/Rud-e-Minab
Gavkhouni Lake and marshes of the lower Zaindeh
    Rud
Hamoun-e-Saberi
Khuran Straits
Lake Gori
Lake Kobi
Lake Oroomiyeh
Lake Parishan and Dasht-e-Arjan
Miankaleh Peninsula, Gorgan Bay and
Lapoo-Zaghmarz Ab-bandans
Neiriz Lakes and Kamjan Marshes
Shadegan Marshes and tidal mud-flats of Khor-al
    Amaya and Khor Musa
Shur Gol, Yadegarlu & Dorgeh Sangi Lakes
South end of Hamoun-e-Puzak

Ireland
Baldoyle Estuary
Castlemaine Harbour
Clara Bog
Coole/Garryland
Easkey Bog
The Gearagh
Knockmoyle/Sheskin
Lough Barra Bog
Meenachullion Bog
Mongan Bog
North Bull Island
Owenboy
The Owenduff Catchment
Pettigo Plateau
Pollardstown Fen
Raheenmore Bog
The Raven Nature Reserve
Rogerstown Estuary
Slieve Bloom Mountains
Tralee Bay
Wexford

Italy
Bacino dell'Angitola
Corru S'Ittiri Fishery-Stagno di San Giovanni e
    Marceddi
Diaccia Botrona
Il Biviere di Gela
Isola Boscone
Lago di Burano
Lago di Caprolace
Lago di Fogliano
Lago di Mezzola-Pian di Spagna
Lago di Monaci

Lago di Nazzano
Lago di Sabaudia
Lago di Tovel
Lago di Villetta Barrea
Laguna di Orbetello (Northern part)
Le Cesine
Marano Lagunare-Foci dello Stella
Ortazzo and adjacent territories
Palude Brabbia
Palude di Bolgheri
Palude di Colfiorito
Paludi di Ostiglia
Pialassa della Baiona
Punte Alberete
Sacca di Bellochio
Salina di Margherita di Savoia
Saline di Cervia
Stagno di Cabras
Stagno di Cagliari
Stagno di Mistras
Stagno di Molentargius
Stagno di Pauli Maiori
Stagno di Sale Porcus
Stagno S'Ena Arrubia
Torbiere d'Iseo
Torre Guaceto
Valle Averto
Valle Bertuzzi
Valle Campotto e Bassarone
Valle Cavanata
Valli residue del Comprensorio di Comacchio
Valle di Gorino
Valli del Mincio
Valle Santa
Vincheto di Cellarda
Riserva naturale Vendicari

Japan
Izu-numa and Uchi-numa
Kushiro-shitsugen
Kutcharo-ko
Utonai-ko

Jordan
Azraq Oasis

Liechtenstein
Ruggeller Riet

Malta
Ghadira

Morocco
Khnifiss Bay or Puerto Cansado
Lac d'Affennourir
Merja Sidi-Bourhaba
Merja Zerga

Netherlands
De Biesbosch (part)
De Boschplaat
De Griend
De Groote Peel

De Weerribben
Engbertsdijksvenen
Het Naardermeer
Oosterschelde
Oostvaardersplassen
Wadden Sea
Zwanenwater

Norway
Åkersvika
Dunøyane
Forlandsøyane
Gasøyane
Ilene and Presterødkilen
Isøyane
Jæren
Kongsfjorden
Kurefjorden
Nordre Øyeren
Øra
Ørlandet
Stabbursneset
Tautra and Svaet

Poland
Kara Lake
Luknajno Lake
Siedem Wysp
Słońsk
Swidwie Lake

Romania
Danube Delta

Spain
Complejo Intermareal O Umia-Grove, La Lanzada,
    Punta Carreirón y Lagoa
Bodeira
Doñana
L'Albufera de Valencia
Laguna de Fuentapiedra
Laguna de la Vega o del Pueblo
Lagunas de Cadiz
Lagunas del Sur de Cordoba
Lagunas de Villafáfila
Las Tablas de Daimiel
Marismas del Odiel
Pantano de el Hondo
Prat de Cabanes-Torreblanca
Rías de Ortigueira y Ladrido
S'Albufera de Mallorca
Salinas del Cabo de Gata
Salinas de Santa Pola
Salinas de la Mata y Torrevieja

Sweden
Ånnsjön
Åsnen
Dättern Bay
Falsterbo-Bay of Foteviken
Gammelstadsviken
Getterön

Helga River
Hjälstaviken
Hornborgasjön
Hovran Area
Isles off Gotland
Kilsviken Bay
Klingavälsån-Krankesjön
Kvismaren
Laidaure
Lake Östen
Coastal areas of Öland
Ottenby
Persöfjärden
River Umeälv Delta
Sjaunja-Kaitum
Stigfjorden Bay
Stockholm Outer Archipelago
Store Mosse and Kävsjön
River Svartån
Tåkern
Tärnasjön
Tavvavouma
Tjålmejaure-Laisdalen
Träslövsläge-Morups Tånge

Switzerland
Baie de Fanel & le Chablais
Bolle di Magadino
Kaltbrunner Riet
Lac artificiel de Klingnau
Lac artificiel de Niederried
Les Grangettes
Rade de Genève et Rhône en aval de Genève
Rive sud du Lac de Neuchâtel

Ukraine
Sivash Bay
Karkinitski Bay

Union of Soviet Socialist Republics
Intertidal Areas of the Dounai/Yagorlits and
  Tendrov Bays
Issyk-kul Lake
Kandalaksha Bay
Kirov Bay
Kourgaldzhin and Tengiz Lakes
Krasnovodsk and North-Cheleken Bays
Lake Khanka
Lakes of the lower Turgay and Irgiz
Volga Delta

United Kingdom
Abberton Reservoir
Alt Estuary
Bridgend Flats
Bridgwater Bay
Bure Marshes
Cairngorm Lochs
Chesil Beach and the Fleet
Chichester and Langstone Harbours
Claish Moss
Cors Fochno and Dyfi

Derwent Ings
Din Moss – Hoselaw Loch
Eilean Na Muice Duibhe (Duich Moss)
Esthwaite Water
Fala Flow
Feur Lochain
Glac-na-Criche
Gladhouse Reservoir
Gruinart Flats
Hickling Broad and Horsey Mere
Holburn Moss
Irthinghead Mires
Leighton Moss
Lindisfarne
Llyn Idwal
Llyn Tegid
Loch-an-Duin
Loch Eye
Loch Leven
Loch of Lintrathen
Loch Lomond
Loch of Skene
Lochs Druidibeg, a'Machair and Stilligary
Lough Neagh and Lough Beg
Martin Mere
Minsmere – Walberswick
North Norfolk Coast
Ouse Washes
Pagham Harbour
Rannoch Moor
Redgrave and S. Lopham Fens
Rockcliffe Marshes
Rostherne Mere
Rutland Water
Silver Flowe
The Dee Estuary
The Wash
The Swale
Upper Severn Estuary
Walmore Common

Yugoslavia
Ludaško Lake
Obedska Bara

Biosphere Reserves

The designation of biosphere reserves differs somewhat from that of either of the previous designations in that it is not made under a specific convention, but as part of an international scientific programme, the Unesco Man and the Biosphere Programme. The objectives of a network of biosphere reserves, and the characteristics which biosphere reserves might display, are identified in various documents, including the Action Plan for Biosphere Reserves (Unesco, 1984).

Biosphere reserves differ from World Heritage and Ramsar sites in that they are designated not exclusively for protection of unique areas or significant wetlands, but for a range of objectives which include research, monitoring, training and demonstration, as well as conservation. In most cases the human component is vital to the functioning of the biosphere reserve, something which is not always true for either World Heritage or Ramsar sites.

The following biosphere reserves are located within the region:

Algeria
El Kala
Parc national du Tassili

Austria
Gossenkollesee
Gurgler Kamm
Lobau Reserve
Neusiedler See-Österreichischer Teil

Belarus, Republic of
Berezinsky Zapovednik

Bulgaria
Parc national Steneto
Réserve Alibotouch
Réserve Bistrichko Branichté
Réserve Boatine
Réserve Djendema
Réserve Doupkata
Réserve Doupki-Djindjiritza
Réserve Kamtchia
Réserve Koupena
Réserve Mantaritza
Réscrve Maritchini czcra
Réserve Ouzounboudjak
Réserve Parangalitza
Réserve Sréharna
Réserve Tchervenata sténa
Réserve Tchoupréné
Réserve Tsaritchina

China
Bogdhad Mountain
Changbai Mountain Nature Reserve
Dinghu Nature Reserve
Fanjingshan Mountain
Fujian Wuyishan Nature Reserve
Shennongjia
Wolong Nature Reserve
Xilin Gol Natural Steppe Protected Area

Czechoslovakia
Krivoklátsko Protected Landscape Area
Palava Protected Landscape Area
Polana
Slovensky Kras Protected Landscape Area
Sumava
Trebon Basin Protected Landscape Area

Egypt
Omayed Experimental Research Area

Estonia
West Estonian Archipelago

France
Iroise
Mont Ventoux
Réserve nationale de Camargue
Parc national des Cévennes
Vallée du Fango
Vosges du Nord

Germany
Bayerischer Wald National Park
Berchtesgaden Alps
Middle Elbe
Rügen
Rhön
Schorfheide-Chorin
Spreewald
Vessertal-Thuringen Forest
Waddensea of Schleswig-Holstein

Greece
Gorge of Samaria National Park
Mount Olympus National Park

Hungary
Aggtelek
Hortobágy National Park
Kiskunság
Lake Fertö
Pilis

Iran
Arasbaran Protected Area
Arjan Protected Area
Geno Protected Area
Golestan National Park
Hara Protected Area
Kavir National Park
Lake Oromeeh National Park
Miankaleh Protected Area
Touran Protected Area

Ireland
Killarney National Park
North Bull Island

Italy
Collemeluccio-Montedimezzo
Forêt Domaniale du Circeo
Miramare Marine Park

Japan
Mount Hakusan
Mount Odaigahara & Mount Omine
Shiga Highland
Yakushima Island

Korea, People's Democratic Republic of
Mount Paekdu

Korea, Republic of
Mount Sorak

Mongolia
Great Gobi

Netherlands
Wadden Sea

Norway
North-east Svalbard Nature Reserve

Poland
Babia Gora National Park
Bialowieza National Park
Lukajno Lake Reserve
Slowinski National Park

Portugal
Paul do Boquilobo

Romania
Pietrosul Mare Nature Reserve
Retezat National Park
Rosca-Letea Reserve

Spain

Canal y los Tiles
Doñana
El Urdaibai
La Mancha Humeda
Las Marismas del Odiel
Las Sierras de Cazorla y Segura
Parque Natural del Montseny
Reserva de Grazalema
Reserva de Ordesa-Vinamala
Sierra Nevada

Sweden
Lake Torne Area

Switzerland
Parc national Suisse

Tunisia
Parc national de Djebel Bou-Hedma
Parc national de Djebel Chambi

Parc national de l'Ichkeul
Parc national des Iles Zembra et Zembretta

Ukraine
Askaniya-Nova Zapovednik
Chernomorskiy Zapovednik

Union of Soviet Socialist Republics
Astrakhanskiy Zapovednik
Chatkal Mountains
Kavkazskiy Zapovednik
Kronotskiy Zapovednik
Lake Baikal Region
Laplandskiy Zapovednik
Oka River Valley
Pechoro-Ilychskiy Zapovednik
Repetek Zapovednik
Sayano-Shushenskiy Zapovednik
Sikhote-Alin Zapovednik
Sokhondinskiy Zapovednik
Tsentral'nochernozem Zapovednik
Tsentral'nolesnoy Zapovednik
Tzentralnosibirskii
Voronezhskiy Zapovednik

United Kingdom
Beinn Eighe National Nature Reserve
Braunton Burrows National Nature Reserve
Caerlaverock National Nature Reserve
Cairnsmore of Fleet National Nature Reserve
Claish Moss National Nature Reserve
Dyfi National Nature Reserve
Isle of Rhum National Nature Reserve
Loch Druidibeg National Nature Reserve
Moor House-Upper Teesdale
North Norfolk Coast Biosphere Reserve
Silver Flowe-Merrick Kells
St Kilda National Nature Reserve
Taynish National Nature Reserve

Yugoslavia
Réserve écologique du Bassin de la Rivière Tara
Velebit Mountain

Internationally Designated Sites – World Heritage Convention

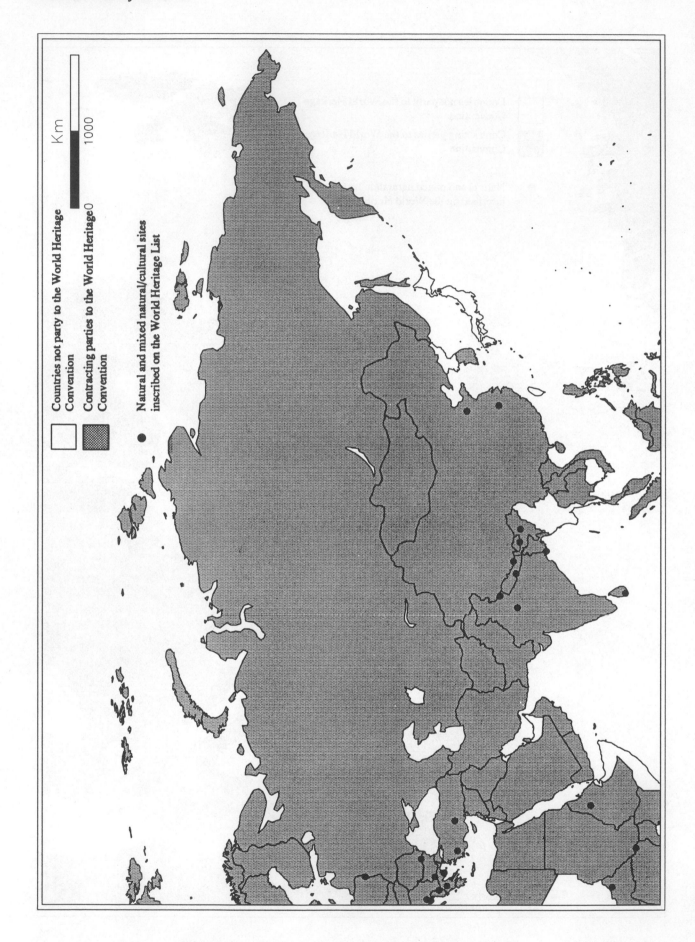

Internationally Designated Sites – World Heritage Convention

Internationally Designated Sites – Biosphere Reserves

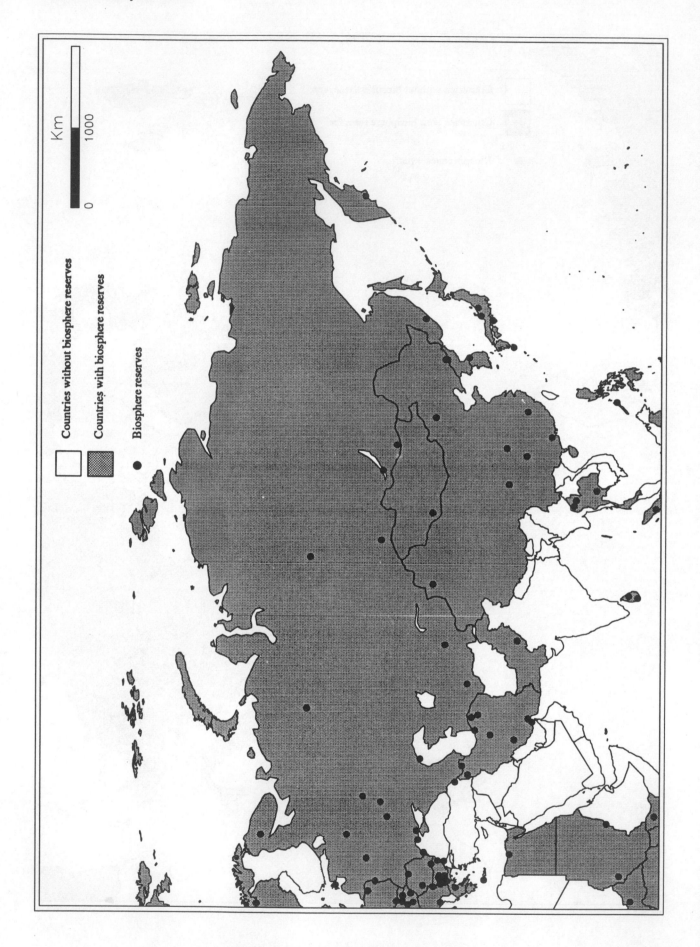

Internationally Designated Sites – Biosphere Reserves

Internationally Designated Sites – Ramsar (Wetlands) Convention

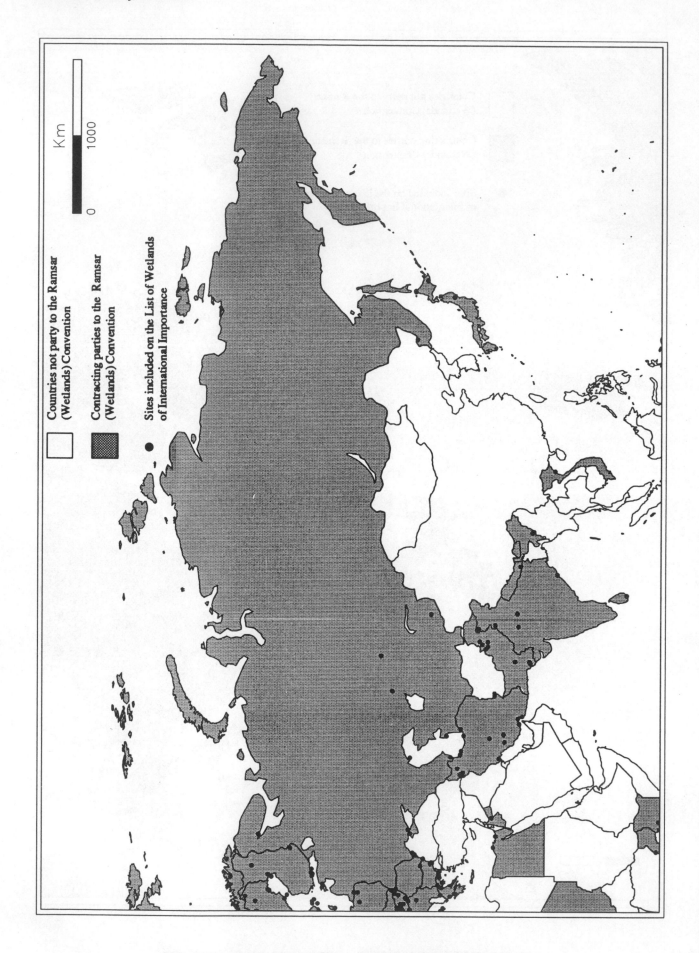

Internationally Designated Sites – Ramsar (Wetlands) Convention

PEOPLE'S REPUBLIC OF CHINA

Area 9,597,000 sq. km

Population 1,133.7 million (1990)
Natural increase: 1.4% per annum

Economic Indicators
GDP: US$ 236 per capita (1987)
GNP: US$ 300 per capita (1987)

Policy and Legislation Nature conservation is incorporated in Articles 9, 10, 22 and 26 of the new Constitution adopted on 12 December 1982, in which it is stipulated that "The State protects the environment and natural resources and prevents and eliminates pollution and other hazards to the public". The Constitution and national legislation covers the four local administrative levels: 22 provinces, three government-controlled municipalities and five autonomous regions (as well as the 1,936 counties).

China is one of the world's oldest civilizations, having founded an agricultural civilization 5,000 years BP. China's recorded history dates back some 3,600 years to the Shang Dynasty. Ancient thinking on conserving nature and natural resources was known at least in the Golden Age of Classical Learning 2,000 years BP, in works of such scholars as Confucius and Lao Zi from the Han dynasty. The concept of nature and nature protection embodies the philosophies of Confucianism, Taoism and Buddhism, which illustrated the awareness of relationships between conservation and utilisation of natural resources and human survival (Ji *et al.*, 1990; Richardson, 1990; Wenhua and Xianying, 1989; Xianpu, 1991). The values of forests have been recorded for at least 2,500 years, leading to the establishment of temple gardens, restricted hunting areas and landscape forests, each of which has contributed towards species protection.

Temple gardens epitomise the needs for naturalness, and wilderness of nature and, through the three philosophies, the sacred position held by society for mountains and rock has led to *de facto* protection of many high places and their surrounding landscapes (FAO, 1982). The first Imperial gardens were established during the Xia Dynasty almost 4,200 years BP, after which temple gardens came into being, many being designated subsequently under the county or provincial park system.

The Environmental Protection Law, adopted in principle as Decree No. 2 at the 11th meeting of the Standing Committee of the Fifth National People's Congress on 13 September 1979, was passed on 26 December 1989 by the National People's Congress (Anon., 1990). The law comprises seven chapters and 33 articles covering nature conservation areas, forests, grasslands, historic sites and scenic spots. In Article 15 is noted the need to protect, develop and rationally utilise wildlife and wild plant resources, and protection is extended to rare

animals and precious trees. Articles 6 and 7 of the law make provision for environmental impact assessments to be instigated by the Environment Protection Bureau and other relevant departments.

The first nature reserves were declared in 1956 under Proposal No. 92, passed at the Third Conference of the First National People's Congress (Yuging, 1987). Under this proposal both the central government (State Council), and the provinces and autonomous regions may designate nature reserves. National and provincial nature reserves are classified into six types according to the administrative system, ecological character of the area and the objectives of protection (see Annex).

There is a differentiation between national nature reserves and provincial nature reserves, the latter being created at the provincial level of government (Lucas, 1987). National nature reserves are covered under the jurisdiction of the National Environmental Protection Agency, Ministry of Forestry and other relevant competent authorities, entitling them to obtain central government funding. National nature reserves can be zoned into core, buffer and experimental areas.

Articles 4, 11, 20 and 21 of the Forest Law of 1979 provide for the establishment of forest reserves (see Annex), management and administration of forests and prevention of hunting in forests (Richardson, 1990).

In 1982, a Marine Environmental Protection Law was adopted, covering a wide range of issues and is administered by the Environmental Protection Agency under the State Council. In 1983, proposals or coastal zone protection legislation existed to conserve mangrove forests in south-east China (UNEP/IUCN, 1988).

Legislation tends to be inadequate, protected areas are ill-defined and boundaries are nor absolute. The poor legislation has led to extensive conflict between conservation and production (Xianpu, 1991).

International Activities The Convention concerning the Protection of the World Cultural and Natural Heritage (World Heritage Convention) was ratified on 12 December 1985 and three natural sites have since been inscribed on the World Heritage List. There are currently seven biosphere reserves designated under the Unesco Man and the Biosphere (MAB) Programme; three designated in 1979, one in 1986, two in 1987 and one in 1990. Cooperative efforts in nature conservation were agreed between the US and China under a special protocol signed in 1986. Earlier, in 1979, the World Wide Fund for Nature (WWF) signed an agreement on cooperative activities including natural resources management, environmental policy and legislation. There is also a bilateral agreement (1981) covering migratory species between China and Japan. China and Nepal have both established protected areas on their respective sides of Mount Everest (Sagarmatha/ Qomolangma). Management plans are being formulated under cooperative agreements with the Woodlands Mountain Institute in the case of both countries.

Administration and Management   Under the State Council, unified coordination is through the National Environmental Protection Agency, based on decentralised management in the autonomous provinces and counties. The Ministry of Urban and Rural Reconstruction and Environmental Protection (an amalgamation of various offices and commissions, including the Environmental Protection Agency) has shared responsibility with the Ministry of Forestry for the administration of all nature reserves (Ratcliffe, 1982).

The Environmental Protection Agency (also referred to as the Environmental Protection Bureau or Office) was set up by the State Council under the Environmental Protection Law in 1979 (revised 1989) and covers nature conservation and protected areas, while the Bureau of Surveying and Mapping deals with research. The Environmental Protection Agency supervises the implementation of legislation concerning environmental protection as well as having scientific and educational roles. In 1986 it had 10 divisions, with bureaux in 324 cities, employing 30,000 people, of which 7,000 were research workers (Thornback, 1986). The Chairman of the Environmental Protection Agency is the Vice-President of the Republic. The Commission for Nature Conservation (a part of the Environmental Protection Agency) is responsible for the coordination of national and international conservation activities, and for reviewing nature conservation resources.

The local governments of the 22 provinces, five autonomous regions and three municipalities are obliged to establish Environmental Protection bureaux by Law. In the counties, autonomous counties and prefectures, environmental protection organisations may be set up (Anon., n.d.). Procedures for identifying and designating new sites follow a number of stages. The initial stage is that the local government officially applies to its provincial government following some basic scientific investigation at the proposed sites. After approval by the provincial government under the Environmental Protection Law of 1989, the sites are designated and recognised as provincial nature reserves. The second stage is then for the provincial government to select a department to administer, manage and fund the newly-declared protected areas. If the provincial government deems that the sites are of national nature reserve quality, it is necessary to get the approval of the State Council, through the auspices of an expert committee within the National Environment Protection Agency. County and municipal authorities have rights to designate sites as county or municipal nature reserves, the central and provincial government can also directly propose sites to the relevant local departments. The level of funding and staff is reflected in the different degrees of importance and protective requirements of the various sites.

The Ministry of Forestry retains responsibility for coordinating protection of all protected areas located on forest land (estimated to be 90% of the total). The Ministry of Forestry functions as an economic ministry operating at state level below the planning and economic commissions. The Ministry is responsible for research (through the Academy of Forestry), education (at three universities and four colleges), and the administration of state forestry throughout China. It administers nature reserves, forest parks and "forest farms" (through the Forest Department) covering 50 million ha. The provincial arm of the Ministry replicates that at the national level, including research and training activities, which is maintained in simplified form at district (prefecture and county) levels. In Heilongjiang, forest production is overseen by a quasi-autonomous Forest Industries Bureau (Richardson, 1990).

Other ministries involved in protected area administration and management include the Ministry of Construction with responsibility for scenery; Ministry of Agriculture, Husbandry and Fisheries responsible for wetlands, steppe, desert and agricultural land; Cultural Ministry for historic heritage, culture and landscape; Ministry of Geology and Mineralogy for geological sections and natural monuments; and the Ocean Agency for coastal and marine protected areas (Xianpu, 1991). At present the number of professional conservationists is over 6,000 and the number indirectly participating in work of protected areas exceeds 20,000. Each responsible department annually conducts training courses sometimes in association with Unesco MAB, IUCN, UNEP, WWF, bilateral and international bodies. Private institutions include such bodies as the Society of Ecology and the Academia Sinica. They have no direct role in protected area administration but are very important in protected areas research. Much of the work associated with developing the protected areas network has been carried out at the local level through universities or local branches of the National Academy (Lucas, 1987).

Management of protected areas tends to vary between provinces and across the country. In some there is effective wardening and management plans, whilst in others there is little protection on the ground. Master plans have been prepared for the entire 29,500 sq. km range of the giant panda (MacKinnon *et al.*, 1989) and management plans for major reserves under a WWF/China joint agreement, which also provides training for Chinese reserve staff. In addition, there is specialist training in wetland management and education project work. Nature reserves are maintained in near natural conditions as far as possible and are extensively used for research and as resources of plant genetic material (Ratcliffe, 1982), but many lack adequate funding and trained personnel (MacKinnon, 1989).

To counteract current management problems in protected areas, responsible departments are taking the following steps: a) enacting national protected area management regulations and criteria for protected areas designations; b) formulating the procedure for establishing reserves of different classes, and making regular inspection of established reserves; c) convening a series of meetings, discussions how to find funds from different sources, carrying out the effective management and strengthening international cooperation; d) keeping close contact with international conservation organisations; e) setting up effective training systems (Xianpu, 1991).

Datian Nature Reserve was added to the IUCN Commission on National Parks and Protected Areas List of Threatened Protected Areas of the World in November 1990 due to the declassification of 25% of the reserve for cattle ranching purposes. Fu Tien Nature Reserve was removed from the list in 1988 after the proposal for a new airport had been dropped. There is a widespread lack of coordination between management agencies, close contact is lacking between the resource and development ministries and bodies concerned with nature conservation, apparently causing many unnecessary conflicts (Xianpu, 1991). These authorities are widely regarded as not having enough understanding of the functions of protected areas and do not recognise them as a necessary part of the national economic and social development. Therefore, there tend to be no special protected area funds, and sites lack effective management and regular inspection for their development (Xianpu, 1991).

Systems Reviews   China's topography ranges from high mountains, undulating plateaux and rolling hills to broad basins and plains. In the west, the relief is high and steep, while in the east it is low and flat. The Qinghai-Tibet plateau in the west comprises a series of east-west aligned mountains, ranging in altitude between 5,000m and 8,848m, and includes the Himalaya of which Qomolangma (Mount Everest) is a part. The three main rivers flowing across China are the Yellow (Huang), Yangtze (Chang) and Amur (Heilong). Much of the country experiences a monsoon climate due to its proximity to the Pacific Ocean, but conditions become much drier in the west (Ji *et al.*, 1990).

Tropical evergreen rain forest occurs in the lowlands of Yunnan and Guangdong provinces and on the eastern side of Hainan Island. Along the southern coast are mangrove forests. Temperate deciduous forests and subtropical broad-leaved deciduous forests exist on limestone in the tropical and sub-tropical zones of the south. Various types of subarctic coniferous forests (taiga) and cold temperate mixed forests are found in the north. The most extensive tracts of natural forest are in the north-east and in the south-western provinces of Sichuan and Yunnan. Much of western China, the vast plains of the north-east and Inner Mongolia, is arable land. Northern Dongbei is mostly steppe grassland. Fuelwood cutting, overgrazing and deforestation has left little primary forest, even in remote areas and steep terrain. In 1980, forests and woodlands accounted for 58 million ha; grassland and pasture 778 million ha; and croplands 134 million ha (Repetto, 1988). According to FAO (1988), natural forest covers 115,047,000ha (12% of total land area). Smil (1983) estimates that China has lost 24% of its forested area since 1949. Other comparisons between natural forest cover in the 1950s and the 1980s reflect decreases from 52% to 35% in north-eastern provinces; from 54% to 21% in southern Yunnan Province; and from 20% to 12.5% in mid-western Sichuan Province (ADB, 1987).

Since the founding of the People's Republic of China in 1949, three nationwide forest inventory surveys have been conducted. A fourth inventory started in 1983 was completed in 1987.

The first protected areas were established in 1956 when 40 reserves were designated. Initiatives to establish a wildlife preservation programme were interrupted during the Cultural Revolution from 1966 to 1976, when conservation practices were abandoned and protected areas misused. The protected areas network has expanded progressively from 45 nature reserves in 1979 (Wang Hucn-pu, 1980), to 73 in 1981 and 273 in 1984 (Boswell, 1983). According to Forest Department statistics, by 1986 there were 333 nature reserves covering a total area in excess of 19,330,000ha (2.0%). In some provinces protected areas have occupied up to 5% of land area (Xianpu, 1991). Of these, 31 were "key" national nature reserves. By the end of 1989, there were 600 protected areas of various kinds, including 60 national nature reserves, with a total land area of 40,000,000ha (4% of the country) (Chongqi, 1991; Xianpu, 1991).

Some of the major problems in protected areas include: a) inadequately defined boundaries, which lead to lack of legal protection; b) illegal hunting and forest felling; c) unrestricted and damaging tourism; d) construction and land reclamation, through constructing buildings and roads; e) excavation, notably mining for minerals; f) excessive over-grazing; g) influences of fire; h) overpopulation pressures. In addition, there tends to be a lack of effective protected area management bodies, lack of scientific management, no clear management aims, lack of funds and training and poor relationships with local residents (Xianpu, 1991). General environmental problems include soil erosion, with 50 billion tons of soil washed away annually due to the degradation of the natural vegetation. An associated problem is desertification, which is increasing at a rate of 6,660 sq. km per year. Another problem facing China is pollution from improper discharge of waste water, waste gas and industrial residues (Ji *et al.*, 1990). Acid rain in the south is being caused by coal burning (Smil *et al.*, 1982). A comprehensive national plan to improve land management and increase afforestation, drafted in 1985, has led to extensive planting schemes covering nearly 4 million sq. km in the border desert regions (Richardson, 1990).

Other Relevant Information   In order to promote forest tourism, the Ministry of Forestry invested over yuan RMB 40 million in creating forest parks during the period 1980-1986. Forest tourism has attracted over 10 million visitors, and yielded visible economic benefits. For example, Zhangjiajie State Forest Park in Hunan province earned Yuan RMB 7,396,000 from 1980 to 1985, equivalent to 94.2% of the total state investment for that site over the same period (Anon., 1987).

Addresses

Division of Nature Conservation (Director), National Environmental Protection Agency, Ministry of Urban and Rural Construction and Environmental Protection, 115 Xizhimennei Nansciaojie, BEIJING (Tel: 1 8992211; Tlx: 22477)

Forest Department (Director), Ministry of Forestry, Hepingh, BEIJING (Tel: 1 22237)

State Oceanic Administration, No. 1 Fuxingmenwai Avenue, BEIJING (Tel: 7283)

Chinese Academy of Sciences, PO Box 767, BEIJING (Tel: 446551; Tlx: 4844)

Provincial Addresses

Anhui Forestry Bureau, Hefei City, Anhui Province

Forest Research Institute, Beijing Municipality

Forestry Research Institute of Fujian, Fuzhou, Fujian Province

Natural Resource Protection Division of Gansu Environment Protection Bureau, 123 Gao Lan Road, Lanzhou, Gansu Province (Tel: 418866)

Forestry Research Institute of Guangdong, Guangzhou, Guangdong Province

Forestry Research Institute of Guangxi, Nanning, Guangxi Zhuang Autonomous Region

Forestry Research Institute of Guizhou, Guiyang, Guizhou Province

Forestry Research Institute, Harbin, Heilongjiang Province

Forestry Research Institute of Henan, Zhengzhou, Henan Province

Forestry Research Institute of Hubei, Wuchang, Hubei Province

Forestry Research Institute of Hubei, Shijiazhuang, Hubei Province

Forestry Department of Hunnan Province, Liangshei City, Hunnan Province

Shandong Forestry Department of Hunnan Province, Liangshei City, Hunnan Province

Forestry Research Institute of Jiangxi, Nanchang, Jiangxi Province

Department of Forestry of Jilin Province, Changchun, Jilin Province (Tel: 22583/24927)

Research Institute of Forest Management, Benxi, Liaoning Province

Forestry Department of Inner Mongolia, Huhehot P.R., Nei Monggol Autonomous Region (Tel: 41801)

Ningxia Forestry Department, Yinchuan City, Ningxia Autonomous Region

Forestry Research Institute of Qinghai Academy of Agriculture and Forestry, Xining, Qinghai Province

Shanghai Museum of Natural History, 260 Yanan Road East, Shanghai Municipality

Forestry Research Institute of Shaanxi, Taiyuan, Shaanxi Province

Forestry Research Institute of Shaanxi, Xian, Shaanxi Province

Forestry Research Institute of Sichuan, Chengdu, Sichuan Province

Tianjing Municipality: no information

Forestry Institute, Wulumuqi, Xinjiang Autonomous Region

Xizang Uygur Zizhiqu Autonomous Region: no information

Yunnan Provincial Forestry Bureau, Kunming, Yunnan Province

Forestry Research Institute of Zhejiang, Hangzhou, Zhejiang Province

References

ADB (1987). *Environmental and natural resources briefing profile, People's Republic of China*. Asian Development Bank, Manila. 11 pp.

Anon. (n.d.). *The Environmental Protection Law of the People's Republic of China (For Trial Implementation)*. Booklet. 32 pp.

Anon. (1987). Forestry Development in China. The Thirteenth Session of the Asia-Pacific Forestry Commission 30 March 3 April 1987, Beijing. 17 pp.

Anon. (1990). Governments: China. *Brundtland Bulletin*. P. 33

Boswall, J. (1983). *Visit to China*. Unpublished report. 10 pp.

Chongqi, L. (1991). Nature reserves in China. *Tiger Paper* 18: 2-5.

FAO (1982). *Forestry in China*. FAO, Rome. 305 pp.

FAO (1988). An interim report on the state of forest resources in the developing countries. FAO, Rome. 18 pp.

Ji, Z., Guangmei, Z., Huadong, W. and Jialin, X. (1990). *The Natural History of China*. Collins, London. 224 pp.

Jing, Z. (1989). Nature conservation in China. *Journal of Applied Ecology*, 29: 825-833.

Keswick, M. (1978). *The Chinese Garden*. Rizzoli International Publications Inc., New York. 216 pp.

Lucas, B. (1987). Notes on trip to China. IUCN, Gland, Switzerland. Unpublished report. 4 pp.

MacKinnon, J. (1989). *National conservation management plan for the giant panda and its habitat*. China Alliance Press, Hong Kong. 157 pp.

MacKinnon, J. (1989). The selection of nature reserves in China. Paper prepared for Beijing Pheasant Symposium. 4 pp.

Ratcliffe, D.A. (1982). Philosophy and practice of nature conservation in China. Nature Conservancy Council, London. Unpublished report. Pp. 34-44.

Repetto, R. (1988). *The forest for the trees? Government policies and the misuse of forest resources.* World Resources Institute, Washington, DC. P. 4.

Richardson, S.D. (1990). *Forests and forestry in China.* Island Press, Washington, DC. 352 pp.

Smil, V., Goodland, R. and Toh, G. (1982). *The People's Republic of China: Environmental Aspects of Economic Development.* The World Bank, Washington, DC. 76 pp.

Smil, V. (1983). Deforestation in China. *Ambio* 12: 226-231.

Thornback, J. (1986). Report of a visit to China 22 June-5 July. IUCN Conservation Monitoring Centre, Cambridge, UK. Unpublished. 7 pp.

UNEP/IUCN (1988). *Coral Reefs of the World. Volume 3: Central and Western Pacific.* UNEP Regional Seas Directories and Bibliographies.

IUCN, Gland, Switzerland and Cambridge, UK/UNEP, Nairobi, Kenya. 378 pp.

Wenhua, L. and Xianying, Z. (1989). *China's nature reserves.* Foreign Languages Press, Beijing. Pp. 11-16.

Xianpu, W. (Huen-pu, W.)(1980). Nature Conservation in China: the present situation. *Parks* 5(1): 1-10.

Xianpu, W. (1991). Review report on the course of protected areas in China. Document prepared for the Palaearctic Asia Regional Review to be presented in the Congress on World Parks and Protected Areas at Caracas, Venezuela, February 1992.

Xuezhi, X. (1987). *Wildlife management in China.* Paper presented at International Conference on Wildlife Conservation in China, 14-19 July, Beijing. Pp. 153-161.

Yuging, W. (1987). Natural conservation regions in China. *Ambio* 16: 326-331.

ANNEX
Definitions of protected area designations, as legislated, together with authorities responsible for their administration

Title : Environmental Protection Law (Proposal No. 92 passed at the Third Conference of the First National People's Congress, incorporated into the Environmental Protection Law)

Date: 26 December 1989. Protected areas element originally covered under Proposal No. 92 passed in 1956

Brief description: Provides for the declaration and classification of nature reserves

Administrative authority: Division of Nature Conservation, National Environmental Protection Agency, Ministry of Urban and Rural Reconstruction and Environmental Protection. Also local, provincial, municipal or county authorities

Designations:

National nature reserve Preserves the flora and fauna in their original state

Designated by the State Council. The first nature reserves were declared in 1956 under Proposal No. 92 passed at the Third Conference of the First National People's Congress. Under this proposal both the State Council, and the provinces and autonomous regions may designate nature reserves, and declare zones divided into core, buffer and experimental areas.

Classified into six types according to the administrative system, ecological character of the area and the objectives of protection. The criteria used in the selection of nature reserves include the degree of naturalness, biological diversity, rarity and size of the area.

The first type is directed towards preservation of natural ecosystems; the second towards protection of rare or endangered fauna; the third towards protection of rare relict plants and special types of vegetation; the fourth towards conservation of natural landscapes; the fifth towards preservation of special geological sections and geomorphological features; and the sixth towards protection of the natural environment and natural resources of the coastline

Many reserves have hunting areas and closed seasons within them

Provincial or autonomous region nature reserve Designated by the provincial or autonomous region government as a natural region with typical significance at the provincial level

Classified into six types according to the administrative system, ecological character of the area and the objectives of protection (see above).

Municipal nature reserve Designated by the municipal government as a natural region with typical significance at the municipal level

Classified into six types according to the administrative system, ecological character of the area and the objectives of protection (see above).

County nature reserve Designated by the county government as a natural region with typical significance at the county level

Classified into six types according to the administrative system, ecological character of the area and the objectives of protection (see above).

Source: Yuging, 1987

Title: National Forestry Law

Date: 1979, amended 20 September 1984

Brief description: Provides for the establishment and administration of forest reserves under Article 16-21

Administrative authority: Forest Department, Ministry of Forestry

Designations:

Forest reserve (see Article 20) Designated for the protection of typical forest ecosystems and forests of great value. Forests for special use: for defence, environmental protection and scientific experimentation purposes, scenic forestry and natural preservation zones.

Regulations include forbidding cutting and gathering in forests, unless with permission from the competent forestry departments of the province, autonomous region or municipality. It is forbidden to hunt wild animals, opening up land for agriculture or farmland, excavate, dig sand and earth or to gather seeds.

Reserve Designated areas for the protection of rare and precious animals, as well as their habitats and breeding grounds.

Forest park Set up in order to promote forest tourism

Sources: Anon, 1987; Richardson, 1990

SUMMARY OF PROTECTED AREAS

Map† ref.	*National/international designations* Name of area	IUCN management category	Area (ha)	Year notified
	BEIJING MUNICIPALITY			
	Nature Reserves			
1	Baihua Mountain	IV	1,700	1985
2	Song Mountain	IV	6,667	1985
	ANHUI PROVINCE			
	Nature Reserves			
3	Guniuxiang	IV	6,433	1982
4	Huangfu Mountain	IV	3,587	1982
5	Huangzangyu	IV	2,333	1980
6	Mazongling	IV	3,490	1980
7	Qingliangfeng 2	IV	1,038	1979
8	Qingliangfeng	IV	3,000	1986
9	Shengjin Lake	IV	33,333	1986
10	Yangtze Alligator	IV	1,500	1977
	Protected Landscape			
11	Mt Huangshan Scenic Beauty and Historic Int. Site	V	15,400	1982
	FUJIAN PROVINCE			
	Nature Reserves			
12	Daiyun Mountain	IV	9,731	1985
13	Jiangshi	IV	1,187	1986
14	Mandarin Duck, Macaque	IV	1,039	1984
15	Meihua Mountain	IV	22,133	1985
16	Wuyi Mountains	IV	56,527	1977
17	Xinkou	IV	1,126	1964
	GANSU PROVINCE			
	Nature Reserves			
18	Annanba	IV	390,000	1982
19	Anxi Gobi Desert Meadow	IV	340,000	1985
20	Baishu River	I	95,292	1963
21	Changling Mountain	IV	3,670	1980
22	Dongda Mountain	IV	4,921	1980
23	Gahai	IV	3,500	1982
24	Great Suhai Lake	IV	3,500	1982
25	Guozhagou	IV	2,509	1982
26	Hei River	IV	4,200	1982
27	Kontong Mountain	IV	1,089	1982
28	Liangucheng	IV	14,000	1982
29	Lianhua Mountain	IV	6,855	1982
30	Maicaogou	IV	3,567	1982
31	Shoulu Mountain	IV	11,060	1980
32	Tou'ersantan	IV	31,937	1982
33	Xinglong Mountain	IV	2,219	1982
34	Yanchiwan	IV	424,800	1982
	GUANGDONG – HAINAN ISLAND			
	Nature Reserves			
35	Algae	IV	4,400	1983
36	Bawangling	IV	2,000	1980
37	Changhang Bawanglin	I	2,000	1980

Map† ref.	National/international designations Name of area	IUCN management category	Area (ha)	Year notified
38	Coral Reef	IV	32,400	1986
39	Datian	IV	2,500	1976
40	Diaoluo Mountain	IV	4,002	1984
41	Dongzhaigang	IV	2,601	1980
42	Fanjia	IV	5,336	1984
43	Fuwan Reservoir	IV	3,333	1975
44	Ganshiling	IV	2,000	1985
45	Huishan	IV	5,336	1984
46	Jianfengling	IV	1,600	1960
47	Jianling Managed	IV	2,600	1984
48	Jiaxi	IV	8,671	1982
49	Jiaxin Managed	IV	2,667	1984
50	Lingaojiao	IV	3,467	1986
51	Liulianling	IV	2,200	1981
52	Nanlin Managed	IV	4,400	1984
53	Nanxi	IV	15,341	1983
54	Piyelingshui	IV	1,380	1986
55	Qinglangang	IV	2,000	1982
56	Qizhi Ridge	IV	3,000	1983
57	Shangxi Managed	IV	2,134	1984
58	Shellfish	IV	4,400	1983
59	Stellate-Hair Vatica Forest	IV	1,666	1980
60	Tongghu Ridge	IV	1,333	1986
61	Wencheng Mangrove Forest	IV	2,000	1981
62	Wuzhi Mountain	IV	18,664	1985

GUANGDONG PROVINCE

Nature Reserves

63	Babao Mountain	IV	3,200	1984
64	Baishuiling	IV	4,000	1984
65	Chebaling	IV	7,545	1982
66	Chengjia	IV	7,867	1983
67	Dadong Mountain	IV	8,000	1985
68	Dapingdong	IV	2,667	1983
69	Dinghu Mountain	IV	1,140	1956
70	Guanyin Mountain	IV	3,000	1985
71	Gutian	IV	4,300	1984
72	Heishiding	IV	4,000	1979
73	Luofu Mountain	IV	2,400	1985
74	Mangrove Forest	IV	3,733	1982
75	Nankun Mountain	IV	2,000	1984
76	Qingpilin	IV	1,066	1980
77	Qingxidong	IV	3,133	1976
78	Xisha	IV	330	1980
79	Zhaoging Dinghushan	I	1,133	1956

GUANGXI AUTONOMOUS REGION

Nature Reserves

80	Baidong River	IV	36,000	1982
81	Buliu River	IV	45,300	1982
82	Chengbi River	IV	16,200	1980
83	Chongzuo	IV	35,000	1981
84	Chuandong River	IV	11,600	1982
85	Chunxiu	IV	5,000	1982
86	Conserving Water Hsienmu Forest	IV	10,600	1982
87	Dahong River	IV	18,100	1982
88	Daming Mountain	IV	58,200	1980

Map† ref.	National/international designations Name of area	IUCN management category	Area (ha)	Year notified
89	Daping Mountain	IV	20,400	1982
90	Dawangling	IV	19,200	1980
91	Daxin	IV	29,900	1980
92	Dayao Mountain	IV	13,500	1982
93	Dehou	IV	12,200	1980
94	Dengbi River	IV	59,300	1982
95	Dizhou	IV	6,000	1982
96	Dugong	IV	200,000	1986
97	Fusui	IV	10,000	1981
98	Gulong Mountain	IV	20,400	1982
99	Gupo Mountain	IV	7,100	1982
100	Haiyang Mountain	IV	106,700	1982
101	Heqiao Ridge	IV	67,000	1982
102	Huagong	IV	15,700	1982
103	Huaping	IV	17,400	1961
104	Huashuichong	IV	12,000	1982
105	Jinxiu	IV	185,000	1982
106	Jinzhong Mountain	IV	22,100	1982
107	Jiuwan Mountain	IV	44,400	1982
108	Laoshan	IV	14,500	1982
109	Longgang	IV	8,000	1979
110	Longrui	IV	2,100	1980
111	Maojie Birds	IV	8,800	1982
112	Miao'er Mountain	IV	45,100	1976
113	Nalin	IV	6,100	1982
114	Nazuo	IV	41,600	1982
115	Nongxin	IV	10,500	1980
116	Qinglong Mountain	IV	15,100	1982
117	Qingshitan	IV	35,500	1982
118	Sanpihu	IV	4,200	1982
119	Shangyue Camellia	IV	2,600	1986
120	Shiwandashan	IV	26,700	1980
121	Shoucheng	IV	65,000	1982
122	Taiping Mountain	IV	17,800	1982
123	Wufubaoding	IV	6,400	1982
124	Xialei	IV	7,900	1982
125	Xiling	IV	14,600	1982
126	Yinding Mountain	IV	21,000	1982
127	Yinzhwaoshan	IV	1,900	1982
128	Yuanbao Mountain	IV	8,100	1982
129	Yueyu	IV	2,300	1982
	GUIZHOU PROVINCE			
	Nature Reserves			
130	Caohai	IV	5,334	1985
131	Cathay Silver Fir	IV	4,600	1984
132	Hongfeng Lake	IV	11,000	1981
133	Jiulongkou	IV	1,333	1985
134	Leigong Mountain	IV	50,000	1982
135	Mount Fanjing	IV	41,902	1978
136	Precious Birds	IV	1,870	1983
	HEBEI PROVINCE			
	Nature Reserves			
137	Lesser Wutai Mountain	IV	22,000	1983
138	Wuling Mountain	IV	14,580	1983

Map† ref.	National/international designations Name of area	IUCN management category	Area (ha)	Year notified
	HEILONGJIANG PROVINCE			
	Nature Reserves			
139	Agate	IV	1,352	1987
140	Dahei Mountain	IV	2,100	1986
141	Dapingtai	IV	25,000	1985
142	Fenglin	IV	18,400	1958
143	Five Joined Lakes	IV	70,000	1980
144	Heilonggong	IV	3,600	1982
145	Hong River	IV	16,333	1984
146	Huma River	IV	30,000	1982
147	Huzhong	IV	194,000	1983
148	Jingpo Lake	IV	120,000	1980
149	Kuerbin	IV	250,000	1985
150	Liangshui	IV	6,394	1980
151	Mudan Peak	IV	40,000	1981
152	North-east Black Bee	IV	270,000	1980
153	Peony Peak	IV	40,000	1980
154	Qixinglazi	IV	33,000	1980
155	Shatian Garania	IV	13,333	1986
156	Songfeng Mountain	IV	1,465	1984
157	Wild Animals Raising And Hunting	IV	21,491	1980
158	Xingkai Lake	IV	16,537	1986
159	Xunbiela River	IV	14,000	1982
160	Yueya Lake	IV	5,133	1986
161	Zhalong	IV	210,000	1979
	HENAN PROVINCE			
	Nature Reserves			
162	Baotianman (Henan)	IV	3,333	1982
163	Baotianman (Neixiang)	IV	4,200	1980
164	Dongzhai	IV	9,333	1982
165	Giant Salamander (Lushi)	IV	65,000	1982
166	Jigong Mountain	IV	3,000	1982
167	Jingangtai	IV	4,200	1982
168	Laojieling	IV	15,333	1982
169	Laojun Mountain (Henan)	IV	2,000	1982
170	Lesser Qinling Mountain	IV	4,000	1982
171	Liankang Mountain	IV	2,000	1982
172	Longchiman	IV	7,502	1982
173	Rhesus Macaque	IV	10,667	1982
174	Shiren Mountain	IV	1,333	1982
175	Taibaiding	IV	3,533	1982
176	Taihang	IV	2,000	1982
177	Xiaoqin Ridge	IV	4,000	1982
	HUBEI PROVINCE			
	Nature Reserves			
178	Huping Mountain	IV	13,333	1982
179	Jiugong	IV	3,995	1983
180	Shennongja	IV	77,333	1978
181	Wild Wintersweet	IV	2,800	1985
182	Xiao River	IV	60,000	1981
183	Xingdou	IV	2,880	1981
	HUNAN PROVINCE			
	Nature Reserves			
184	Badagong Mountain	IV	20,000	1982

Map† ref.	*National/international designations* Name of area	IUCN management category	Area (ha)	Year notified
185	Bamian Mountain	IV	20,000	1982
186	Damiaokou	IV	11,333	1982
187	Dawie Mountain	IV	6,300	1982
188	Dayuanyuankou	IV	9,866	1982
189	Dong-tin Lake	IV	184,300	
190	Gaozeyuan	IV	8,000	1982
191	Huangsang	IV	15,700	1982
192	Jou-li Mountain	IV	5,700	1982
193	Jun Mountain	IV	84,000	1982
194	Mang Mountain	IV	6,667	1982
195	Nanyue	IV	13,333	1982
196	Qianjiadong	IV	5,300	1982
197	Shunhuang Mountain (Dong'an)	IV	10,000	1982
198	Shunhuang Mountain (Xinling)	IV	3,000	1982
199	Suoxiyu	IV	5,333	1982
200	Taoyuandong	IV	10,000	1982
201	Tianzi Mountain	IV	3,340	1982
202	Xiaoxi	IV	10,000	1982
203	Yangming Mountain	IV	2,800	1982
204	Yun Mountain	IV	3,333	1982
205	Zhang-jia-jic State Forest	IV	5,000	
206	Ziyunwanfeng Mountain	IV	22,840	1982

JIANGSU PROVINCE

Nature Reserves

207	Chaihe Reservoir	IV	30,300	1987
208	Nanusilia	IV	4,000	1986
209	Suzihe	IV	360,000	1987
210	Yancheng	IV	40,000	1983

JIANGXI PROVINCE

Nature Reserves

211	Guan Mountain	IV	6,467	1976
212	Jinggang Mountains	IV	15,873	1981
213	Jiulian Mountain	IV	4,067	1976
214	Lu Mountain	IV	30,493	1981
215	Poyang Lake	IV	22,400	1984
216	River Mussel	IV	22,833	1980
217	Taohongling	IV	4,500	1981
218	Wuyi Mountain	IV	5,333	1981
219	Xiazhuang	IV	2,000	1984
220	Yan Mountain	IV	5,333	1977

JILIN PROVINCE

Nature Reserves

221	Chagan Lake	IV	48,000	1986
222	Changbai Mountains	IV	190,582	1961
223	Songhua Lakc	IV	354,098	1982
224	Xianghai	IV	105,467	1981
225	Yaojingzi Praire	IV	23,800	1986
226	Yitong Volcanic Complex	IV	64,100	1984
227	Zuojia	IV	6,008	1982

LIAONING PROVINCE

Nature Reserves

228	Baishilazi	IV	6,667	1981
229	Bali Indian Azalea	IV	12,000	1984

Map† ref.	*National/international designations* Name of area	IUCN management category	Area (ha)	Year notified
230	Fenghuang Mountain	IV	2,600	1981
231	Glabrous Leaf Epaulette Tree Forest	IV	2,580	1985
232	Gushan	IV	7,000	1987
233	Haitang Mountain	IV	3,156	1986
234	Huakun-Sunjiagou	IV	3,333	1981
235	Hunhe	IV	23,000	1986
236	Immortal's Cave	IV	1,733	1981
237	Laohu Cave	IV	11,000	1986
238	Laotudingzi	IV	6,000	1981
239	Liupaoshougou	IV	2,000	1981
240	Mongolian Scotch Pine Seed Stand	IV	1,314	1981
241	Nanliuzhangzi	IV	1,333	1984
242	Nianzigou	IV	1,133	1984
243	Old Baldy Summit	IV	5,930	1981
244	Phoenix Mountain	IV	3,900	1981
245	Pi Mountain	IV	3,333	1981
246	Qianshan	IV	4,500	1985
247	Shaguogou	IV	1,200	1984
248	Shajintai Praire	IV	12,900	1986
249	Shuangtaizi Estuary	IV	7,000	1985
250	Snake Island and Laotieshan	IV	190,000	1980
251	Tanghe	IV	42,000	1986
252	Xipin	IV	1,466	1984
253	Yiwulu Mountain	IV	14,000	1981

NEI MONGGOL ZIZHIQU AUTONOMOUS REGION

Nature Reserves

254	Aibugai River	IV	1,000	1984
255	Bamao River	IV	31,000	1984
256	Bayanaobao	IV	6,737	1980
257	Dalai Lake	IV	400,000	1986
258	Daqinggou	IV	8,183	1980
259	Hanma	IV	135,187	
260	Helam Mountain	IV	10,350	1980
261	Maoienaobao Wetland Birds	IV	134,000	1985
262	Nudeng	IV	28,040	1983
263	Nuomin Virgin Forest	IV	149,770	
264	Xilin Gol Prairie	IV	1,078,600	1985

NINGXIA AUTONOMOUS REGION

Nature Reserves

265	Helan Mountains	IV	61,000	1982
266	Liupan Mountain	IV	7,000	1982
267	Luo Mountain	IV	8,900	1982
268	Qingtongxia	IV	3,333	1984
269	Shapotou	IV	12,000	1983
270	Yunwu Mountain	IV	1,300	1982

QINGHAI PROVINCE

Nature Reserves

271	Bird Island (Niao Dao)	IV	53,550	1975
272	Longbao	IV	10,000	1984
273	Mengda	IV	9,544	1980
274	Qinghaihu Waterfowl Island	IV	7,850	1975

Map† ref.	*National/international designations* Name of area	IUCN management category	Area (ha)	Year notified
	SHAANXI PROVINCE			
	Nature Reserves			
275	Crested Ibis	IV	5,000	1983
276	Foping	IV	35,000	1978
277	Golden Monkey	IV	54,700	1980
278	Sanmenxia Waterfowl	IV	39,000	1980
279	Savin Juniper	IV	7,666	1976
280	Stiff-leaf Juniper	IV	6,354	1961
281	Taibai Mountains	IV	54,103	1965
282	Zhashui Takin	IV	1,600	1980
	SHANDONG PROVINCE			
	Nature Reserves			
283	Ai Mountain	IV	5,333	1984
284	Cha Mountain	IV	2,667	1984
285	Changdao	IV	5,250	1986
286	Dagu River	IV	463,100	1984
287	Dujia Mountain	IV	6,667	1984
288	Fu Mountain	IV	60,700	1984
289	Huanglei River	IV	65,200	1984
290	Huangshui River	IV	98,300	1984
291	Jia River	IV	200,000	1984
292	Longshan	IV	6,667	1984
293	Muzhu River	IV	127,800	1984
294	Nansi Hu	IV	126,600	1982
295	Qingdao Bird	IV	1,065,400	1982
296	Rizhao	IV	40,000	1982
297	Rushan River	IV	95,400	1984
298	Tanyang	IV	10,000	1984
299	Wang River	IV	7,600	1984
300	Weide Mountain	IV	6,667	1984
301	Weihai	IV	39,800	1984
302	Wulong River	IV	265,200	1984
303	Ya Mountain	IV	6,667	1984
304	Yi Mountain	IV	3,200	1982
305	Yuan Mountain	IV	1,000	1985
306	Zhaohu Mountain	IV	6,667	1984
307	Zhifu	IV	22,750	1984
	SHANXI PROVINCE			
	Nature Reserves			
308	Li Mountain	IV	24,800	1983
309	Luya Mountain	IV	21,453	1980
310	Mang River	IV	5,600	1983
311	Pangquangou	IV	10,446	1980
312	Wutai Mountain	IV	3,333	1986
	SICHUAN PROVINCE			
	Nature Reserves			
313	Dafengding Panda	IV	30,000	1978
314	Fengtongzai	IV	40,000	1978
315	Gar Qu	IV	20,000	1963
316	Huanglongsi	IV	40,000	1983
317	Jinyun Mountain	IV	1,400	1979
318	Laba River	IV	12,000	1963
319	Mabian Dafengding	IV	30,000	1978
320	Meigudafengding	IV	16,000	1978

Map† ref.	*National/international designations* Name of area	IUCN management category	Area (ha)	Year notified
321	Tangjia River	IV	28,000	1978
322	Tiebu	IV	23,000	1965
323	Wanglang	IV	27,700	1963
324	Wolong	IV	200,000	1975
325	Xiaozhaizigou	IV	6,700	1979
	XINJIANG UYGUR ZIZHIQU AUTONOMOUS REGION			
	Nature Reserves			
326	A Er Jin Shan (Arjin Mountains)	IV	4,512,000	1985
327	A Er Jin Shan Ye Luo (Arjin)	IV	15,125	1986
328	Bayanbulak	IV	100,000	1980
329	Bulgan River	IV	5,000	1980
330	Bunge Ash	IV	1,400	1983
331	Chinese Walnut	IV	1,180	1983
332	Fuhai Jengsetas	IV	9,767	1986
333	Ganjia Lake	IV	1,042,000	1983
334	Hanas	IV	250,000	1980
335	Huocheng	IV	35,000	1983
336	Kalamaili Mountain	IV	1,700,000	1982
337	Lake of Heaven	IV	38,069	1980
338	Mount Tomur	IV	100,000	1980
339	Naz-Quelute	IV	16,400	1986
340	Qitai	IV	12,333	1986
341	Schrenk Spruce	IV	28,000	1983
342	Tacheng	IV	1,500	1980
343	Tarim	IV	387,900	1980
344	Taxkorgan	IV	1,500,000	1984
345	Tianchi NatR	IV	38,063	1980
346	Urumqi Geological	IV	200,000	1986
	XIZANG ZIZHIQU AUTONOMOUS REGION			
	Nature Reserves			
347	Gang	IV	4,600	1985
348	Jiangcun	IV	34,060	1985
349	Medog	IV	62,620	1985
350	Qomolangma	IV	3,500,000	1989
351	Zayu	IV	101,400	1985
352	Zham	IV	6,852	1985
	YUNNAN PROVINCE			
	Nature Reserves			
353	Ailao Mountain	IV	50,360	1986
354	Baima Mountain	IV	180,000	1983
355	Bitahai	IV	14,133	1984
356	Cangshan Erhai	IV	70,000	1981
357	Dawei Mountain	IV	10,533	1982
358	Daxue Mountain	IV	15,787	1986
359	Erhai Lake	IV	24,976	
360	Fenshuiling	IV	10,760	1986
361	Gaoligong Mountain	IV	123,333	1983
362	Haba Mountain	IV	21,907	1984
363	Haiziping	IV	2,780	1984
364	Heaven Lake	IV	6,667	1983
365	Huanglian Mountain	IV	13,835	1983
366	Jiache	IV	8,287	1984
367	Jizu Mountain	IV	2,000	1983
368	Kunming	IV	143,000	1981

Map† ref.	*National/international designations* Name of area	IUCN management category	Area (ha)	Year notified
369	Laiyang River	IV	7,000	1986
370	Laojun Mountain (Yunnan)	IV	4,507	1986
371	Lugu Lake	IV	8,127	1986
372	Mengla	IV	100,000	1958
373	Mengluen	IV	9,000	1958
374	Mengyang	IV	90,000	1958
375	Nangun River	IV	7,000	1980
376	Napahai	IV	2,067	1984
377	Nu River	IV	375,433	1986
378	Shibalianshan	IV	1,213	
379	Songhuaba	IV	60,000	1981
380	Stone Grove	IV	9,000	1981
381	Tianchi (Yunlong)	IV	7,000	1983
382	Tongbiguan	IV	34,160	1986
383	Weiyuan River	IV	7,780	1983
384	Wuliang Mountain	IV	23,353	1986
385	Xiaomengyang	IV	86,666	1958
386	Xiaoqiaogou	IV	1,894	1986
387	Xishuangbanna	IV	207,000	1958
388	Yaoshan	IV	10,213	1984
389	Yulong Mountain	IV	26,000	1984
	ZHEJIANG PROVINCE			
	Nature Reserves			
390	Baishanzu	IV	1,333	1985
391	Fengyang Mountain	IV	4,667	1975
392	Gutian Mountain	IV	1,333	1962
393	Jiulong Mountain	IV	2,000	1983
394	Longwang Mountain	IV	1,200	1985
395	Nanjilie Islands	IV	1,600	1986
396	West Tianmu Mountain	IV	1,000	1962

	Biosphere Reserves			
	Bogdhad Mountain	IX	217,0001	1990
	Changbai Mountain Nature Reserve	IX	217,235	1979
	Dinghu Nature Reserve	IX	1,200	1979
	Fanjingshan Mountain	IX	41,533	1986
	Fujian Wuyishan Nature Reserve	IX	56,527	1987
	Shennongjia	IX	147,467	1990
	Wolong Nature Reserve	IX	207,210	1979
	Xilin Gol Natural Steppe Protected Area	IX	1,078,600	1987
	World Heritage Sites			
	Mount Huangshan	X	29,600	1985
	Mount Taishan	X	n/a	1987

†Locations of most protected areas are shown on the accompanying maps.

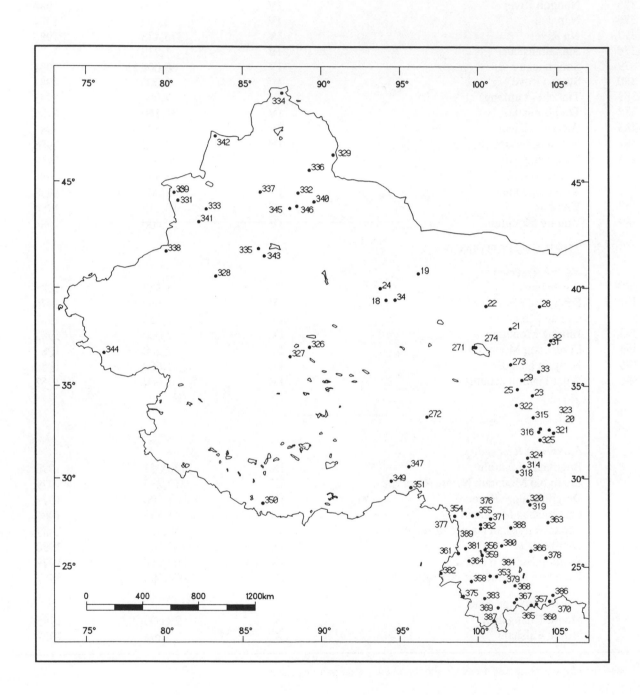

Protected Areas of China

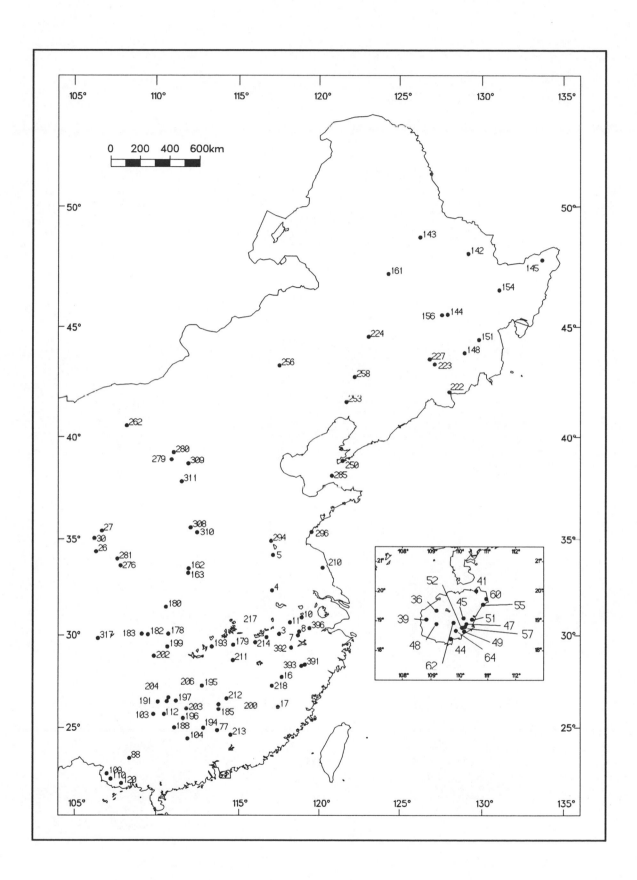

Protected Areas of China

JAPAN

Area   376,520 sq. km

Population   123,460,000 (1990)
Natural increase: 0.39% per annum

Economic Indicators
GDP: US$ 19,471 per capita (1987)
GNP: US$ 15,770 per capita (1987)

Policy and Legislation   Throughout its history, the role of religion in the protection of the natural environment has been important in Japan: this can be dated back to the animist religions and their development into the Shinto religion in the 5th and 6th centuries AD. Buddhism, which arrived in the 6th century, not only reveres all forms of life, but the wide areas covered under the jurisdiction of shrines afford sacred protection to numerous forests and holy mountains (Oyadomari, 1989). One of the first references to wildlife conservation dates from the 7th century AD when the Emperor organised a "bird hunting and preservation section" in his government (Church, 1979).

During the Meiji period (1868-1911), when Japan modelled its government on that of western countries, many of the traditional values of nature were discounted. It was during this period that a western-type of conservation philosophy was first introduced and the first conservation laws were imposed (Oyadomari, 1989). The basis of modern conservation laws, the Imperial Game Law of 1892, ensured regulation of hunting preserves (Church, 1979). Many rare or endangered "non game" classified species were listed as prohibited for hunting. The present constitution dates from 1947.

The first modern legislation, whose primary purpose was the conservation of the natural environment, was the National Parks Law passed by the government in 1931 (Law No. 36/1931). The chief objective of this law is the preservation of the natural landscape on public and private land for public enjoyment and recreation.

A comprehensive series of protected area categories now exists, with sites declared for their conservation importance and/or recreational value. The most important of the current laws concerning protected areas are the Natural Parks Law, 1957 and the Nature Conservation Law, 1972. Protected areas may be declared by national or regional/local authorities. There are 47 regions or prefectures (*Todufuken*) in Japan, each with a democratically elected governor (*Chiji*); within these prefectures there are some 3,268 local authorities.

The new natural parks system, based on the Natural Parks Law (Law No. 161) of 1 June 1957, superseded the 1931 Law and provided a system of three categories of park, with grades ranging from nationally important sites (national parks) to regionally important sites (quasi-national parks and prefectural natural parks), each area being designated irrespective of land ownership. Provisions exist for the zonation of natural parks by the creation of special areas within these categories, and further special protection areas within them. The 1957 Act declares that natural parks are national assets, designated because of their scenic beauty, and also to provide a cultural and recreational asset for the public. In 1970 the law was revised to allow the creation of marine parks within natural park areas (16 May 1970). State purchase of private land within national parks and quasi-national parks has been undertaken since 1972 and 1975, respectively, especially in areas where thorough protective action cannot be taken if it remains in private hands. The definitions of the different categories of natural park are given in the Annex.

The Nature Conservation Law (Law No. 85) of 22 June 1972 was enacted to provide a framework for all legal measures concerning the natural environment and nature conservation. It also provides for the designation of protected areas – wilderness areas, nature conservation areas and prefectural nature conservation areas – that are primarily declared to preserve the original characteristics of an environment for nature conservation, and where recreation is consequently of secondary importance and may be restricted. Another important section (Article 5) requires that "the state shall endeavour to conduct at five-year intervals surveys of the topography, geology, flora and fauna as necessary for the planning of measures to be taken for the conservation of the natural environment". These National Surveys of the Natural Environment, or "green censuses", have been undertaken regularly since 1973.

Areas and objects of conservation importance may also be protected under the 1919 Law for Preserving Scenic Historic and Natural Monuments, under which the Ministry of Education is empowered to designate national historical monuments, places of scenic beauty and natural monuments. National historical monuments generally have little or no value for nature conservation; places of scenic beauty and natural monuments are designated from those gardens, valleys, mountains and animals, plants and minerals which have a high value from an academic or a visual viewpoint (Environment Agency, 1982).

Forestry legislation is centred around the Basic Forestry Law (Law No. 161) of 26 June 1964. This law is based on the development of the forestry industry and the controlled exploitation of forest resources and is, therefore, of little relevance to conservation issues, although Article 4 Paragraph 2 mentions that efforts shall be made to ensure the more efficient use of any national forest land which fulfils such functions as conservation and which provides other public benefits.

Certain categories of protected area can also be declared under the Wildlife Protection and Hunting Law (Law No. 32) of 4 April 1918, amended 22 June 1972 (Law No. 85), and related laws. These laws describe wildlife protection areas (sanctuaries), special protection areas (special sanctuaries), game areas and hunting prohibited areas. The purpose of wildlife protection areas is to ensure wildlife protection and the breeding of game species: such areas may be designated by the Director General of the Environment Agency (national wildlife protection areas) or by the governor of the prefecture concerned (prefectural wildlife protection areas). Further details of these categories are given in the Annex.

In February 1973 the Cabinet published the New Economic and Social Development Plan, the 7th post-war economic plan, which advocated the formulation of a Long-Range Conservation Plan and incorporated target environmental levels to be achieved ten years after implementation in 1975. Following on from this, in October, the cabinet adopted the Natural Environmental Conservation "Basic Principle" which stated that "all land-use projects must be appropriately controlled and directed towards creating a rich environment". The Nature Conservation Council of the Environment Agency were involved in producing a more detailed conservation strategy. Natural parks were affected by the "Basic Principle" which required the improvement and expansion of the natural parks system (Church, 1979).

A number of sites are protected under more than one piece of legislation this is particularly notable for wildlife protection areas, some of which are designated at both the prefectural and the national level. It is not known to what degree this category overlaps with other protected areas such as natural parks.

International Activities Japan is one of the few Asian countries to have ratified the Convention on Wetlands of International Importance especially as Waterfowl Habitat (Ramsar Convention) (17 June 1980) with three sites listed. Four sites were accepted as biosphere reserves under the Unesco Man and Biosphere Programme in 1980.

In March 1988 Japan and the Republic of Korea called upon UNEP to extend its Regional Seas programme to cover the north-west Pacific. Such a programme, if adopted would cover five countries: the USSR, China, Japan, North Korea and South Korea.

Administration and Management The Environment Agency is in charge of executing most of the protected areas legal system, under the powers of the Director General, by coordinating related governmental agencies. The Agency was established in 1971, with many of its staff coming from the Environmental Hygiene Bureau of the Ministry of Health and Welfare, and others from the Ministry of Agriculture and Forestry (Church, 1979). The relevant Environment Agency departments include

a) the Nature Conservation Council which consists of various committees and advisory bodies on conservation of the natural environment, natural parks and wildlife protection and b) the Nature Conservation Bureau which is the main body administering the protected areas covered under the Natural Parks Law, the Nature Conservation Law and the Wildlife Protection and Hunting Law.

The Nature Conservation Bureau consists of five divisions, those of planning and coordination, natural parks planning, conservation and management, recreational facilities and wildlife protection. Directly answerable to the planning and coordination division are the national park offices and ranger stations. In 1985, the parks were administered by 107 rangers located in the various parks, with 30 ranger stations under 10 national park offices (Nature Conservation Bureau, 1985, 1988). The Environment Agency is obliged to formulate a national park management scheme for each park. The first priority of these schemes is the protection and preservation of outstanding ecosystems; construction of visitor facilities can also be included, as can be a number of other services such as guided tours and educational programmes. These schemes are supposed to be reviewed every five years in consultation with the national government organisations, the local government and local communities concerned (Akai, 1991). Nature conservation areas and wildlife protection areas are established and managed either by the Environment Agency or prefectural governments concerned.

The designation and conservation of forestry areas and protected forests is the responsibility of the Ministry of Agriculture, Forests and Fisheries.

The designation, administration and management of national historical monuments, places of scenic beauty and natural monuments is the responsibility of the Department of Cultural Properties in the Culture Agency of the Ministry of Education.

There are a large number of local and national non-governmental conservation organisations, some of which own or manage their own private protected areas (Oyadomari, 1989). The Wild Bird Society of Japan established its "sanctuary movement" in 1981 to encourage the creation of private wildlife sanctuaries by individuals, citizen's groups, universities or local public bodies. These are areas where wildlife and the natural environment is strictly protected, but also areas where environmental education is of major importance. There are now over 10 sanctuaries in Japan: the Wild Bird Society of Japan is involved in the management of seven, and was involved in surveying and planning stages of five. Sanctuaries are on average 20-60ha or larger in size (Anon., 1989). The Nature Conservation Society of Japan is involved in a wide range of activities, including campaigns for the declaration and the safeguarding of existing protected areas (Anon., 1981). A dragonfly sanctuary is managed by the Tombo no kai Dragonfly

Society (Moore, *in litt*, 1987.). Other leading non-governmental organisations include the Nature Conservation Society of Japan, the World Wide Fund for Nature in Japan, the National Parks Association and the National Parks Beautification and Management Foundation. They all promote research, public relations and nature tours. The Nature Conservation Society of Japan particularly concentrates on identifying wildlife and habitats in need of protection as well as funding ecological research.

Management difficulties arise from parks being created in areas that cannot be adequately protected, even though legislation exists to prevent harmful activities, as is the case when they are located adjacent to major industrial complexes or where pollution originates beyond the park boundary – Seto Naikai Inland Sea Park is a case in point. Many of these nationally important protected landscapes are not discreet entities and may consist of a series of isolated blocks separated by many kilometres (some over 100km), yet still administered under a single park authority with an already overstretched park warden system. Parks composed of single blocks appear to have more adequate control with successfully defended buffer, restricted access and core area zones. Thus, while in theory the natural park system adequately protects much of the country's landscape, the pressure from lack of resources and staff, unwieldy park sizes and conflict from multi land-use are currently causing serious threats to the effectiveness of this designation (Sakurai, 1984).

The National Park Management Schemes should be reviewed and revised every five years, but in fact this process is not easily achieved, because of a lack of time, manpower and budget. As a result, the original goals are often lost and become meaningless (Akai, 1991).

Systems Reviews Japan consists of more than 3,800 islands many of which are clustered around the four main islands of Hokkaido, Honshu, Shikoku and Kyushu. These four islands make up 97% of the total land area. The archipelago extends from the Sea of Okhotsk near Russia, 2,800km southwards to the Ryukyu Islands near Taiwan. It ranges from latitude 45° in the north to 21° in the south, with climates ranging from Siberian and sub-arctic to tropical. The islands all lie on the north-west of the Pacific "ring of fire'; they are largely of volcanic origin and there are many volcanoes, extinct, dormant and active. Seismic activity is common, occasionally producing destructive tsunamis (tidal waves) on all coastlines. Geothermal activity is also common. The country is essentially mountainous with only 20% of the surface area comprising low-lying plains formed by alluvial deposition, such as river valleys, coastal areas and plains, typically separated by mountain ridges. Hence, the majority of the population inhabits only 3% of the country and as much as 80% of the population lives in urban areas.

Japan has a particularly large range of natural ecotypes, and a high diversity of flora and fauna. This is largely due to the wide range of latitude covered by the country,

coupled with the wide altitudinal ranges to be found at most latitudes. Originally almost the entire country was forested, but now almost all of the plains and low-lying lands have been cleared for agriculture or the expansion of urban areas.

Forests still cover some 66.9% of the land area, although some 40% of this is commercial plantation (Stewart-Smith, 1987). In Hokkaido, the natural forest is mostly sub-arctic coniferous forest; further south much of Japan is dominated by deciduous broad-leaved woods of beech, oak, birch and chestnut; the south-west is dominated by broad-leaved evergreen forest and the southern Ryukyu Islands by tree ferns, Pandanaceae and mangroves. An alpine zone of scrub, grassland and rocky desert is present in the mountains of the north. Farmland occupies some 15% of the country (9% rice paddies; 6% other), inland waters occupy some 3%, urban areas, wasteland and other categories make up the remainder (Environment Agency, 1983).

During the 8th century AD, the introduction of Buddhism from China enhanced the conservation of wild birds and animals. Between 710 and 730 AD, the Emperor took measures to prevent the despoliation of forests and made private ownership of wildlands illegal (Church, 1979). By the 1600s deforestation had become a problem, although by this time there had been widespread growth and institutionalisation of village rights to common land and, with this, the development of thousands of highly detailed regulations for the conservation of forests and the use of all commons (Marsh, 1987). The first modern game laws in the late 19th century were produced as a result of the wide spread of hunting to different sectors of the population (Church, 1979).

Following the passing of the National Parks Law in 1931, the first national park was declared in March 1934, and a further five in December of that year. By 1936 there were 12 national parks and others were added, although "with the outbreak of the Pacific War, the administration was practically suspended and, at the time of Japan's surrender in 1945, these national parks existed only in name" (Marsh, 1987). At the end of March 1991 there were 28 national parks covering 2.05 million ha (5.43% of the total land area), 55 quasi-national parks covering 1.33 million ha (3.53%) and 299 prefectural natural parks covering 1.95 million ha (5.15%): in total, therefore, natural parks cover 5.33 million ha, some 14.11% of the total land area. A breakdown of these figures shows that, within national parks, special areas make up 70.9% of the total national park area (12.5% of this is special protection areas) while ordinary areas make up the remaining 29.1%; in quasi-national parks special areas make up 93.2% of the area (5.0% of this is special protection areas) while ordinary areas make up the remaining 6.8%; in prefectural natural parks special areas comprise 32.8% of the total area (there are no special protection areas) while ordinary areas make up the remaining 67.2% of the area. Eight marine parks were designated when the 1970 Amendment to the

Natural Parks Law was first introduced and by 1991 the figure had risen to 28 in national parks and 30 in quasi-national parks. Marine park areas total 2,419ha (Nature Conservation Bureau, *in litt.*, 1991).

By March 1991 areas protected under the Nature Conservation Law totalled some 85,586ha; with five nature conservation areas covering some 5,631ha; wilderness areas covering 7,550ha and prefectural nature conservation areas covering some 72,405ha. Between them these categories adequately protect areas ranging from marine and coastal sites through primary forest to montane ecosystems. As at the end of 1991 sites designated under the Law for Preserving Scenic, Historic and Natural Monuments consisted of 256 places of scenic beauty, 914 natural monuments and 1,300 national historical monuments (Nature Conservation Bureau, *in litt.*, 1991).

In terms of the area covered, the national and prefectural wildlife protection areas are undoubtedly very important categories: by the end of 1980 there were some 438 national wildlife protection areas covering some 1,141,000ha and some 2,618 prefectural wildlife protection areas covering some 1,899,000ha: the combined area covering over 8% of the total land area of the country (Environment Agency, 1982).

The natural conservation strategy is based on the National Surveys of the Natural Environment required under Article 5 of the 1972 Nature Conservation Law to be carried out every five years. So far, surveys by the Environment Agency have been undertaken in 1973, 1978/79, from 1983-1987 and the Fourth Survey is underway at present. The purpose of these studies has been to a) identify the present state of the natural environment, b) identify changes on a five-year basis and c) utilise the survey results as basic information for environmental impact assessment and conservation programmes. The present survey is partially supported by a widespread participation of volunteers and non-governmental organisations (Environment Agency, 1989).

As a result of high visitor pressure, there is a major overloading of time spent controlling tourism. Tourism at present levels seriously affects the environment through erosion, pollution, demands on water resources (whilst staying at the park accommodation) and increasing the need for visitor facilities and other buildings (Sakurai, 1984).

Following the end of the Pacific war in 1945, there was a long period when national priorities were devoted entirely to economic recovery and industrial development on a massive scale. This led to widespread environmental disruption both directly, through land clearance, and, more importantly, indirectly through air and water pollution and industrial waste (Church, 1979). Pollution continues to be a massive threat to ecosystems and protected areas, as well as to human life. Industry, however, is an extremely powerful body and, acting through the Ministry of International Trade and Industry, the Ministry of Construction and the Ministry of Transport, has so far prevented proposals by the Environment Agency to create environmental legislation from even reaching parliament. Forms of pollution include toxic waste disposal, water pollution and air pollution (Miyamoto, 1991).

Other Relevant Activities Tourism has always been a major reason for creation of parks in Japan, and in 1986 there were 363 million visitors to the national parks (908 million to all the natural park categories) (Nature Conservation Bureau, 1988). These figures alone represent at least one annual visit by every single person in Japan and represent some of the highest park visitor figures in the world.

Addresses

Nature Conservation Bureau, Environmental Agency, 1-2-2 Kasumigaseki, Chiyoda-ku, TOKYO 100 (Tel: 33 581 3351/FAX: 33 595 1716/Tlx: 33855)

Ministry of Agriculture and Forestry, 2-1-1, Kasumigaseki, Chiyoda-ku, TOKYO (Tel: 3 502 8111)

Ministry of Education, 2-2-3 Kasumigaseki, Chiyoda-ku, TOKYO (Tel: 3 581 4211)

Agency of Cultural Affairs, 3-2-2 Kasumigaseki, Chiyoda-ku, TOKYO

Wild Bird Society of Japan, Aoyama Flower Building, 1-1-4 Shibuya, Shibuya-ku, TOKYO 150 (Tel: 3 406 7141)

World Wide Fund for Nature-Japan, Nihonseimei Akabanebashi Bldg. 7F, 3-1-14 Shiba, Minato-ku, TOKYO 105 (Tel: 03 769 1711; FAX: 03 769 171; Tlx: 02428231 WWFJPN J)

Nature Conservation Society of Japan, Toranomon-Denki Bldg. 4F, 2-8-1 Toranomon, Minato-ku, TOKYO 105 (Tel: 03 503 4896, FAX: 03 592 0496)

References

Akai, I. (1990). Protected area management and community development in Japan. *Regional expert consultation on management of protected areas in the Asia-Pacific Region*. FAO Regional Office for Asia and the Pacific, 10-14 December 1990, Bangkok, Thailand.

Akai, I. (1991). Protected Area management and community development in Japan. *Tiger Paper*. April-June, 1991. Pp.11-14.

Anon. (1965). Japan, Law No. 161. The Basic Forestry Law. *Food and Agricultural Legislation* 14(1), 13(1). Food and Agricultural Organisation, Rome. Pp. 1-7.

Anon. (1981). Nature Conservation Society of Japan. Unpublished report. 7 pp.

Anon. (1986). Concern for Japan's forests. *Oryx* 4(20): 256.

Anon. (1987). Japan's new efforts for wildlife. *Oryx* 2(21): 119.

Anon. (1989). *Sanctuary for Coexistence of Wildlife and Human Beings*. Wild Bird Society of Japan, Tokyo. 17 pp.

Bruns, D.R. (1975). *The National Parks system of Japan*. Boulder, Colorado.

Church, J.R. (1979). *Environmental administration and wildlife protection policies in Japan*. Research paper to the Faculty of Graduate School, University of Oklahoma. Degree of Master of Public Administration.

Environment Agency (1978). *Environmental laws and regulations in Japan*. (IV). Nature, Tokyo.

Environment Agency (1979). *Outline of Nature Conservation Policy in Japan*. Tokyo.

Environment Agency (1982). *Quality of the Environment in Japan*. Tokyo.

Environment Agency (1983). *The Birds and Terrestrial Mammals of Japan*. Tokyo.

Environment Agency (1989). *Aspects of Nature*. National Survey on the Natural Environment, Environment Agency, Tokyo. 18 pp.

Marsh, J.S. (1987). *Marine Parks in Japan*. Report for Contract No. 84-143. Environment Canada, Parks – Ottawa.

Miyamoto, K. (1991). Japan, environmental problems and environmental policy in Japan after the second world war. In: Cutrera, A. (Ed.), *European Environmental Yearbook*. DocTer International UK, London. Pp. 665-676.

Nature Conservation Bureau (1985). *Nature Conservation Administration in Japan*. Environment Agency, Tokyo. 45 pp.

Nature Conservation Bureau. (1988). *Nature Conservation in Japan*. Environment Agency, Tokyo. 45 pp.

National Parks Association (1952). *Chronological history of the national parks of Japan*. Tokyo. 27pp.

National Parks Association (1956). *National Parks of Japan*. Tokyo. 17 pp.

National Parks Association (1966). *National Parks in Japan, 1963-66*. Tokyo.

National Parks Association (1975). *Beautiful Nature of Japan, National Parks and Quasi-National Parks*. Tokyo. 16 pp.

Oyadomari, M. (1989). The rise and fall of the nature conservation movement in Japan in relation to some cultural values. *Environmental Management* 13(1): 23-33.

Sakurai, M. (1984). Adjustment between nature and human activity in National Parks in Japan. In: McNeely J.A. and Miller, K.R. (Eds), *National Parks Conservation and Development*. Pp. 479-485.

Scott, D.A. (in prep.) *A Directory of Neotropical Wetlands*. IUCN Cambridge and IWRB Slimbridge, UK.

Stewart-Smith, J. (1987). *In the shadow of Fujisan, Japan and its wildlife*. Viking/Rainbird Publication Co., London.

Suzuki, M. (1990). *Wetland Conservation in Japan: a Grassroots Perspective*. Friends of the Earth Japan and World Wide Fund for Nature, Tokyo. 33 pp.

Tamura, T. *et al.* (1966). *Marine Parks in Japan*. Nature Conservation Society of Japan. 34 pp.

ANNEX
Definitions of protected area designations, as legislated, together with authorities responsible for their administration

Title : Natural Parks Law (Law No. 161)

Date: 1 June 1957, with amendments in 1962, 1970, 1971, 1972, 1973, 1978 and 1990

Brief description: To protect places of scenic beauty, and also, through the promoted utilisation thereof, to contribute to the health, recreation and the culture of the people.

Administrative authority: Environment Agency (Director General), prefectural authorities (Prefectural natural parks)

Designations:

Natural Park

National park, quasi-national park or prefectural natural park A revision of the law in 1970 provided for the designation of marine parks within the national parks and quasi-national parks. The law also carries details of penal provisions associated with violations of the Law.

Kokuritsu koen (National park) Landscape areas of national importance, "areas of the greatest natural scenic beauty" designated by the Director General of the Environment Agency after seeking the opinions of the Council on Nature Conservation.

Specific regulations are drawn up for the protection of each site and signed by the Director General.

Zoning occurs to restrict activities harmful to the landscape of the park:

Ordinary area Zones where a number of activities are restricted, including the erection, rebuilding or extension of large buildings, the reclamation of land or sea through drainage programmes, mineral mining and changes of water level. Forestry is permitted and there is apparently no control on tourist development and few restrictions on commercial and industrial activities.

Special area The following activities may not be carried out without permission from the Director General: the erection, rebuilding and extension of structures, the felling of trees and bamboos, mining and the removal of stones and soils, horse-riding, off-road driving, the use of motor boats, the landing of aircraft, activities leading to the increase or decrease of water resources, the discharge of sewage, reclamation of water and land area by drainage and the gathering of alpine and other plants. The special area classification may be subdivided into three categories: in Class I the erection of structures is prohibited; in Class II structures that are in keeping with the environment may be permitted, as well as facilities and activities required for the daily life of inhabitants; in Class III special areas all the above is permitted and, with forestry, clear cut felling is allowed.

Special protection area Core areas which are kept strictly free from any development and may include zones of "floral and faunal phenomena of particular interest, special topographical and geological features or scientific, historical or archaeological sites of particular significance". All the restrictions of the above categories apply, in addition to the following restrictions: the planting of trees and bamboos, the pasturing of cattle, lighting of fires, the collection of plant and animal material including fallen leaves and branches, riding horses or driving cars off the road, the use of motor boats and the landing of aircraft. If any restricted and listed activities occur at the time of designation, then these must be registered but are permitted to remain in existence (Articles 17, 18-2, 20).

Marine park

Areas designated within national parks and quasi-national parks, established for the purpose of preserving the "marine natural scenic beauty". Restrictions are as for the other zones but also inhibit the collection or capture of fish, coral, seaweed and other animal life, sea reclamation, the mooring of boats, and discharge of polluted water. Changing the features of the sea bed, and mining and the removal of soil or stones is prohibited within 1km of marine park areas.

Kokutei koen (Quasi-national park) Described as "places of great natural scenic beauty next to the national parks". They are designated by the Director General on the request of the prefecture concerned, after seeking the opinions of the Council on Nature Conservation. These protected areas have lesser status than national parks and are selected and designated only at the request of a prefectural governor. All planning controls and restrictions for national parks are applicable to this category of protected area.

Todofukenritsu shizen koen (Prefectural natural parks) Representative prefectural landscapes of local importance. Special areas may be designated within them for the purpose of preserving the scenic beauty of these areas, however there is no provision for special protection areas. Necessary regulations are to be prescribed by prefectural ordinance, in accordance with the provisions of Section 4 (which broadly describes the restrictions in the different zones of all natural parks). The prefecture shall make compensation for loss occurring as a result of declaration. The Natural Parks Law does not allow for the declaration of any special protected areas or marine parks within their boundaries.

Sources: Environment Agency, 1978; Nature Conservation Bureau, 1988

Title : Nature Conservation Law (Law No. 85; amended by Law No. 73, 1973)

Date: 22 June 1972 (Major amendment: 1973)

Brief description: "Aims to set forth the basic concept of conservation of the natural environment and other basic matters relating to the conservation of the natural environment, and, together with the Natural Parks Law and other laws relating to the conservation of the natural environment, to provide comprehensive promotion of the proper conservation of the natural environment and thereby to contribute to ensuring the health and cultural life of the people, both now and in the future" (Article 1).

Administrative authority: Environment Agency (Director General), prefectural authorities (Prefectural nature conservation areas)

Designations:

Wilderness area Designated on land owned by the state or local public bodies, where the natural environment has been preserved in areas with little or no human influence. Sites are designated by the Director General of the Environment Agency after seeking the advice of the Nature Conservation Council and the governor of the prefecture concerned, these bodies shall also be involved in the drawing up of a conservation plan for wilderness areas. The following acts are restricted unless a permit is obtained from the Director General for scientific research or otherwise for the public good:

all construction work; land clearance; alteration of
the topography; removal of minerals, stones or soil;
land drainage or reclamation; alteration of the water
levels of rivers, lakes or marshes; felling or otherwise
damaging trees or bamboos; collection of plants,
other than trees, including fallen leaves and
branches; planting of trees or bamboos; capturing of
animals or collection of eggs; grazing of cattle;
lighting of fires; use of vehicles, powered boats,
horses and landing of airplanes and other acts likely
to influence the conservation of the natural
environment within the wilderness area (Article 17).
Restricted entry districts may be established within
wilderness areas, no person may enter these districts
without a permit except under exceptional
circumstances, to undertake conservation or
management work, or with a permit from the
Director General.

Nature conservation area Designated in areas in
which conservation of the environment is especially
needed in the light of natural and social conditions.
These areas include natural forests, alpine
communities, coasts, wetlands, coastal and marine
sites, land with unique topography or geology and
other sites with native plants, wild animal habitats or
unique natural features. Sites are designated by the
Director General after seeking the advice of the
Nature Conservation Council and the Governor of
the prefecture concerned, these bodies shall also be
involved in the drawing up of a conservation plan for
nature conservation areas. These areas should not fall
within natural parks covered under the Natural Parks
Law. The conservation plan drawn up for each of
these sites should contain a description of the site and
details of a zone of land within the site to be specially
conserved as a "special area" or a sea zone, a "special
marine area'; the plan should also contain details of
the regulations to apply to site and facilities for the
conservation of the site. The methods and limitations
on the felling of trees within a special area shall be
decided in consultation with the Minister of
Agriculture and Forestry; other limitations to be
imposed within special areas include many of the acts
restricted in wilderness areas (above). In special
marine areas the following activities are restricted:
all construction work; alteration of the topography of
the seabed; removal of minerals soil or stones;
drainage of the seashore or infilling of the sea; the
removal of tropical fish, coral, seaweed or other
animals and plants and the mooring of vessels: some
of these restrictions do not apply to fishing vessels
and activities (Article 27). Where there is a special
need for the protection of specific wild animals and
plants within a special area, the Director General may
designate a "wild animal and plant protection
district" where the capture and collection of wild
animals and plants is prohibited. Areas outside the
aforementioned zones, but within the nature
conservation area are termed "ordinary areas", there
are fewer restrictions within ordinary areas, although

prior notification must be given to the Director
General before undertaking any of the following:
construction work; land clearance for residential
purposes; other work that will change the topography
of the land; removal of minerals, stones or soil; land
drainage or the infilling of lakes; alteration of the
water level in wetlands. The Director General may
prohibit or restrict such acts if this is considered
necessary for the conservation of the natural
environment.

Prefectural natural conservation area Equivalent
to nature conservation areas, but designated by the
prefectures themselves. They may also be zoned,
with special areas and wild animal and plant
protection districts. The framework for regulations to
be applied to these areas is the same as for the nature
conservation areas.

Source: Environment Agency, 1978

Title : Wildlife Protection and Hunting Law
(Law No. 32, 1918, final amendment Law No. 85, 1972);
**Cabinet Order for the implementation of the
Wildlife Protection and Hunting Law** (No. 254,
1953, final revision No. 37, 1973);
**Implementation Ordinance of the Wildlife
Protection and Hunting Law** (Ministry of
Agriculture and Forestry Ordinance No. 108, 1950, final
revision No. 44, 1975)

Date: Law No. 32, 4 April, 1918; Law No. 85, 22
June, 1972 Cabinet Order No. 254, 31 August 1953;
Order No. 37, 31 March 1973 Ordinance No. 108, 30
September 1950; Ordinance No. 44, 5 May 1975

Brief description: To protect and propagate game,
and to allow hunting for the purpose of the
improvement of the living environment and to
contribute to the promotion of agriculture forestry
and fisheries

Administrative authority: Environment Agency
(Director-General)

Designations:

Game area May be declared by the state or by local
public bodies, accompanied by the provision of
specific regulations for the site. A site will not be
approved unless it has the consent of the owner of the
land. The term of existence of game areas shall not
exceed ten years. The administration and
management of these sites, which may involve
activities for the protection and propagation of game,
may be entrusted to certain state or prefectural
bodies. The declaration of an area also requires the
submission of a report which, among other things,
contains details describing the name and location of
the area, the terms of its existence, the procedure for
application for a hunting permit and details of the
fees required for such a permit, conditions to be

observed by hunters and other matters related to the maintenance and control of the game area. These other matters may include details of the establishment of necessary facilities for the breeding and propagation of game, and the stocking of the area with artificially reared species, restrictions on the methods of hunting and quotas for the number of individuals that may be taken. The total number of hunters allowed into a site and the number of days that a site may be open in a year may also be restricted.

Wildlife protection area (Sanctuary) To be declared by the Director-General of the Environment Agency (national wildlife protection area), or the prefectural governor (prefectural wildlife protection area) where it is deemed necessary for the protection and propagation of game. No game may be taken from these sites. The owners, or persons with rights on the land or its trees or bamboo, may not oppose the creation of nesting facilities, water supplies or feeding by the relevant authorities considered necessary for the breeding and propagation of game. Land reclamation, the felling of standing trees and bamboos and the building of major structures requires permission from the Director-General of the Environment Agency, or the prefectural governor. The state or prefecture are required to pay compensation for losses incurred as a result of declaration of such sites. Sanctuaries may not be established until their terms of existence have been fixed: the term of existence shall be less than 20 years. In designating a wildlife protection area a report must be submitted which contains, among other things, a description of the site, the condition of the wildlife, and details of how to protect and propagate the game, and other details of rules and regulations and information on the expenses required for the establishment and maintenance of the area. Application for the alteration or abolition of a wildlife protection area, shall be made by submission of a document, stating the reasons for the changes, to the Director-General of the Environment Agency.

Special wildlife protection area (Special sanctuary) These may be declared by the Director-General of the Environment Agency, or the prefectural governor within the aforementioned wildlife protection areas where this is deemed especially necessary for the protection and propagation of game. All the rules and restrictions which apply to sanctuaries thus also apply to special sanctuaries, although no further details are given in the relevant legislation.

Temporary hunting prohibited area These are areas to be declared by the prefectural governor, in places where the game is decreased and it is deemed necessary to increase such game. Such areas are to be declared for a limited period of not more than three years. No game shall be taken from such areas.

Source: Environment Agency, 1978

Title : Law for Preserving Scenic, Historic and Natural Monuments

Date: 1919 (No information on exact date or dates of amendments)

Brief description: Provides for the designation of national monuments, national historic monuments and places of scenic beauty

Administrative authority: Department of Cultural Properties, Culture Agency, Ministry of Education

Designations:

National historic monument Historic sites, such as ancient middens, tumuli and ancient castle sites. In these areas any change of state is restricted; sites may be privately owned although, if necessary the Minister is empowered to have them procured by the government. These sites may not be of ecological importance.

Place of scenic beauty Designated from those gardens, valleys, mountains and animals, plants and minerals which have a high value from an academic or a visual view point.

Natural monument Designated for the same reasons as places of scenic beauty (Environment Agency, 1982). They may also include areas of major importance for conserving animals and their habitats which may have a high scientific value. Particularly important natural monuments are designated as special natural monuments: reasons for the declaration of these may include their containing: 1) noted endemic species and their habitats; 2) noted non-endemic species in need of preservation and their habitats; 3) unique wildlife, individuals and in groups, in their natural environment and 4) noted animals, except livestock, which were brought from abroad and now live in a wild state, as well as their habitats.

Sources: Church, 1979; Environment Agency, 1982

SUMMARY OF PROTECTED AREAS

Map† ref.	National/international designations Name of area	IUCN management category	Area (ha)	Year notified
	National Parks			
1	Akan	II	90,481	1934
2	Ashizuri-Uwakai	V	10,967	1972
3	Aso-Kuju	V	72,680	1934
4	Bandai-Asahi	II	187,041	1950
5	Chichibu-Tama	V	121,600	1950
6	Chubu-Sangaku	II	174,323	1934
7	Daisen-Oki	V	31,927	1936
8	Daisetsuzan	II	230,894	1934
9	Fuji-Hakone-Izu	V	122,686	1936
10	Hakusan	II	47,700	1962
11	Iriomote	II	12,506	1972
12	Ise-Shima	V	55,549	1946
13	Joshinetsu Kogen	II	189,062	1949
14	Kirishima-Yaku	II	54,833	1934
15	Kushiro Shitsugen	II	26,861	1987
16	Minami Arupusu (Minami Alps)	II	35,752	1964
17	Nikko	V	140,164	1934
18	Ogasawara	II	6,099	1972
19	Rikuchu-Kaigan	V	12,348	1955
20	Rishiri-Rebun-Sarobetsu	II	21,222	1974
21	Saikai	V	24,653	1955
22	Sanin-Kaigan	V	8,763	1963
23	Seto-Naikai	V	62,828	1934
24	Shikotsu-Toya	II	98,332	1949
25	Shiretoko	II	38,633	1964
26	Towada-Hachimantai	II	85,409	1936
27	Unzen-Amakusa	V	28,289	1934
28	Yoshino-Kumano	V	59,798	1936
	National Wildlife Protection Areas			
29	Asama	IV	32,247	1951
30	Daisen	IV	6,025	1957
31	Gamo	IV	7,790	
32	Hakusan	IV	35,912	1969
33	Ina	IV	1,173	1989
34	Ishiduchisankei	IV	10,858	1977
35	Izunuma	IV	1,450	1982
36	Kiinagashima	IV	7,452	1969
37	Kirishima	IV	1,400	1975
38	Kitaarupusu	IV	110,323	1975
39	Kominato	IV	4,515	1971
40	Kushiro Marsh	IV	29,084	1935
41	Kushirositsugen	IV	10,940	1958
42	Lake Hamatonbetsu-kuccharoko	IV	2,803	1983
43	Moriyoshiyama	IV	6,062	1973
44	Nakaumi	IV	8,462	1974
45	Ogasawarashotoh	IV	5,899	1980
46	Ohdaisankei	IV	18,054	1972
47	Ohtoriasahi	IV	38,285	1984
48	Seinan	IV	1,561	1979
49	Sendaikaihin	IV	7,790	1987
50	Shimokitaseibu	IV	5,300	1984
51	Shiretoko	IV	43,172	1982
52	Towada	IV	39,163	1953

Map† ref.	*National/international designations* Name of area	IUCN management category	Area (ha)	Year notified
53	Tsurugiyamasankei	IV	10,139	1989
54	Yagachi	IV	3,680	1976
55	Yakushidae	IV	1,377	1979
	Wilderness Areas			
56	Hayachine	I	1,370	1975
57	Oigawa-Genryubu	I	1,115	1976
58	Onnebetsudake	I	1,895	1980
59	Tokachigawa-genryubu	I	1,035	1977
60	Tonegawa-genryubu	I	2,318	1977
61	Wagadake	I	1,451	1981
62	Yakushima	I	1,219	1975
	Prefecture Wildlife Protection Areas			
63	Adachiyama	IV	1,903	1963
64	Aduma	IV	6,169	1982
65	Aitakayama	IV	3,848	1982
66	Ajara	IV	1,945	1972
67	Ajisu	IV	1,116	1962
68	Akagiyama	IV	2,066	1955
69	Akan	IV	5,373	1981
70	Akanko	IV	8,809	1959
71	Akikawakyuryo	IV	2,235	1974
72	Akiyoshidai	IV	2,285	1972
73	Akkeshiko	IV	3,223	1964
74	Amagi	IV	5,267	1980
75	Amakimi	IV	1,320	1971
76	Amatsu	IV	1,920	1966
77	Ampal	IV	1,058	1985
78	Aoshima	IV	1,090	1970
79	Araya	IV	1,160	1957
80	Ariake	IV	6,234	1972
81	Ariakechoh	IV	1,270	1974
82	Arikawa	IV	1,907	1967
83	Arimafuji	IV	1,050	1988
84	Asahi	IV	1,190	1980
85	Asahigaoka	IV	1,850	1982
86	Asaicho	IV	2,912	1981
87	Asama	IV	20,313	1981
88	Asamushi	IV	1,860	1966
89	Ashikita	IV	1,700	1985
90	Ashitsu	IV	2,407	1972
91	Ashiyasiurayama	IV	1,193	1962
92	Ashizurimisaki	IV	2,787	1953
93	Asoh	IV	2,500	1954
94	Asohturi	IV	2,535	1965
95	Azuchiyama	IV	1,150	1974
96	Azumayamanamen	IV	1,140	1964
97	Batsukawa	IV	3,661	1981
98	Biwa	IV	69,546	1981
99	Biwako	IV	69,546	1971
100	Bizentakadasi-oizuru	IV	1,040	1985
101	Chausuyama	IV	1,035	1973
102	Chiba	IV	1,078	1965
103	Chibashi	IV	2,256	1970
104	Chichiburenpoh	IV	15,150	1965
105	Chimikeppuko	IV	1,411	1962
106	Chohbohsan	IV	1,025	1969

Map† ref.	National/international designations Name of area	IUCN management category	Area (ha)	Year notified
107	Chohyoh	IV	1,580	1968
108	Daibosatsu	IV	1,400	1964
109	Daijohji	IV	1,449	1988
110	Dainichisan	IV	1,950	1987
111	Daisen	IV	6,014	1957
112	Daishi	IV	2,670	1972
113	Daitohsankei	IV	2,549	1989
114	Daitsurugahantoh	IV	1,925	1968
115	Darumayama	IV	1,300	1982
116	Dohgosan (Hiroshima Prefecture)	IV	1,739	1962
117	Dohgosan (Shimane Prefecture)	IV	3,000	1984
118	Dohgosen	IV	3,999	1962
119	Dohheizan	IV	1,303	1967
120	Dohi	IV	1,157	1982
121	Doigahama	IV	1,150	1975
122	Eiheiji	IV	1,150	1970
123	Enakyo	IV	1,860	1964
124	Enshunada	IV	5,261	1972
125	Esashisi-matsunagane	IV	1,085	1984
126	Fujisan	IV	4,331	1983
127	Fujisankita	IV	15,430	1988
128	Fujisanminami	IV	12,447	1983
129	Fukukayama	IV	1,080	1983
130	Fukuohji	IV	1,249	1983
131	Fukuokashi	IV	26,708	1961
132	Fukurengi	IV	1,490	1967
133	Funagata	IV	5,489	1979
134	Funaoka	IV	3,220	1976
135	Furenko	IV	6,462	1973
136	Furiuchi	IV	1,172	1983
137	Furutokoroyama	IV	2,530	1959
138	Fusano	IV	2,536	1983
139	Fushimi	IV	1,000	1965
140	Futamata	IV	1,193	1967
141	Futani	IV	1,260	1974
142	Genkai	IV	1,202	1989
143	Gonohe	IV	1,298	1966
144	Gorohdake	IV	1,275	1990
145	Goshikidai	IV	2,990	1964
146	Goshoura	IV	2,163	1987
147	Goshoyama	IV	1,049	1986
148	Gotohrenpoh	IV	1,924	1983
149	Gowa	IV	3,755	1988
150	Goyohsan	IV	3,255	1973
151	Goyohsan-ookuboyama	IV	2,489	1980
152	Gozenyama	IV	1,990	1970
153	Gyobashi	IV	1,255	1977
154	Hachimantai (Akita Prefecture)	IV	10,913	1980
155	Hachimantai (Iwate Prefecture)	IV	16,229	1980
156	Hachimizo	IV	1,088	1972
157	Hadachokurokawa	IV	2,434	1965
158	Hagi	IV	4,216	1971
159	Hahahata	IV	1,271	1973
160	Hakone (Kanagawa Prefecture)	IV	9,985	1979
161	Hakone (Shizuoka Prefecture)	IV	1,353	1979
162	Hakuhatsudake	IV	2,037	1975
163	Hakuhoh	IV	20,450	1964

Map† ref.	National/international designations Name of area	IUCN management category	Area (ha)	Year notified
164	Hanamagariyama	IV	3,738	1964
165	Hananokoh	IV	1,042	1959
166	Hanaseyama	IV	1,836	1986
167	Handayama	IV	1,612	1969
168	Haramachi	IV	1,622	1967
169	Harunayama	IV	1,290	1955
170	Hashikami	IV	1,150	1968
171	Hatori	IV	2,357	1960
172	Hayachinesan	IV	6,563	1988
173	Hibayama	IV	3,233	1986
174	Hichisenyama	IV	1,196	1989
175	Hidehikoyama (Fukouka Prefecture)	IV	3,000	1955
176	Hidehikoyama (Ooita Prefecture)	IV	1,150	1986
177	Hidekumo	IV	1,294	1981
178	Hieizan	IV	1,558	1964
179	Higashi	IV	5,028	1971
180	Higashine	IV	1,610	1959
181	Higashiyama	IV	2,616	1967
182	Higashiyamaguchi	IV	1,350	1971
183	Hijiriyama	IV	1,674	1961
184	Himekami	IV	1,341	1964
185	Hinosumi kintachi	IV	1,754	1987
186	Hirakawa	IV	1,250	1973
187	Hirohara	IV	3,228	1978
188	Hitsujigaoka-shirohatayama	IV	2,368	1976
189	Hiuchiyama	IV	2,516	1984
190	Hobashirayama	IV	3,600	1957
191	Hohdensan	IV	2,188	1967
192	Hohshi	IV	1,851	1961
193	Hokkaido Univ. -nakagawa enshurin	IV	18,075	1987
194	Hokkaido Univ. -tomakomaienshurin	IV	2,745	1985
195	Hokogadake	IV	1,265	1977
196	Hokotate	IV	2,590	1977
197	Hongoh	IV	1,250	1965
198	Hontanikatamukisan	IV	1,761	1966
199	Hontaniyama	IV	1,156	1990
200	Horoman	IV	1,332	1984
201	Hosono	IV	1,798	1972
202	Houraiko	IV	1,900	1976
203	Hyomikaigan	IV	6,905	1972
204	Hyonosen (Hyogo Prefecture)	IV	2,710	1982
205	Hyonosen (Tottori Prefecture)	IV	2,285	1972
206	Ichienoyama	IV	1,020	1989
207	Ichifusa	IV	1,359	1965
208	Ichinose	IV	1,500	1964
209	Ieshima	IV	1,150	1965
210	Igawako	IV	2,810	1963
211	Iidesan	IV	11,436	1984
212	Iidume	IV	1,197	1982
213	Iitakachohase	IV	4,668	1983
214	Iitakachomiyamae	IV	2,202	1986
215	Iitakachomori	IV	3,109	1988
216	Ikaho	IV	1,961	1958
217	Ikedakounagiike	IV	1,713	1974
218	Ikoma shingisan	IV	2,050	1964
219	Imazucho	IV	1,180	1964
220	Inawashiro	IV	10,933	1954

Map† ref.	*National/international designations* Name of area	IUCN management category	Area (ha)	Year notified
221	Inohana	IV	2,193	1987
222	Inutappu	IV	1,150	1980
223	Irabe	IV	10,933	1984
224	Irako	IV	2,200	1966
225	Iritani	IV	1,510	1979
226	Ishidohyama	IV	1,804	1965
227	Ishiduchisankei	IV	1,356	1982
228	Ishigatanikyo	IV	1,080	1989
229	Ishikama	IV	1,297	1967
230	Ishimineyama	IV	1,850	1964
231	Ishishiroyama	IV	1,110	1964
232	Isumi	IV	5,306	1972
233	Itsutsugeyama	IV	1,450	1967
234	Iwadohdamu	IV	1,680	1967
235	Iwami	IV	2,590	1971
236	Iwanai	IV	2,078	1974
237	Iwatemachi	IV	3,890	1970
238	Izumigadake	IV	1,940	1968
239	Jinbetsu	IV	2,831	1968
240	Jinyoshi	IV	1,245	1973
241	Johkohji	IV	1,300	1972
242	Johzankei	IV	1,695	1981
243	Juniko	IV	1,077	1964
244	Jusanko	IV	2,497	1965
245	Kagoshima-kenminnomori	IV	1,000	1983
246	Kaikoma	IV	3,950	1966
247	Kakiokahigashi	IV	1,240	1975
248	Kamafusa	IV	2,470	1967
249	Kamaishi	IV	1,480	1967
250	Kamakura	IV	3,953	1959
251	Kamanashi	IV	1,227	1973
252	Kamedake ookushi	IV	2,510	1960
253	Kameishisoda	IV	1,015	1966
254	Kameyamashichubu	IV	1,483	1987
255	Kamimura	IV	1,045	1985
256	Kaminuro	IV	5,143	1986
257	Kamisiro	IV	1,135	1966
258	Kamo	IV	1,180	1958
259	Kamuikotan	IV	1,531	1985
260	Kanayamako	IV	1,303	1981
261	Kanegasakichoh-rokuhara	IV	1,413	1962
262	Kanmuriyama	IV	1,630	1988
263	Kannonyama	IV	1,024	1984
264	Kanumaiwayama	IV	1,120	1973
265	Karanuma	IV	1,619	1964
266	Karasawayama	IV	2,015	1953
267	Karasuyama	IV	1,173	1962
268	Kariyasu	IV	1,175	1971
269	Karumaichohkarumai	IV	1,727	1984
270	Kasahori	IV	3,809	1983
271	Kasatoshima	IV	1,200	1972
272	Kashima	IV	1,600	1956
273	Kasuga	IV	1,950	1965
274	Kasumigaura	IV	5,290	1972
275	Kawabatashimo	IV	2,957	1979
276	Kawaguchi (Kumamoto Prefecture)	IV	2,415	1967
277	Kawaguchi (Saitma Prefecture)	IV	1,074	1968

Map† ref.	National/international designations Name of area	IUCN management category	Area (ha)	Year notified
278	Kawamata	IV	1,409	1971
279	Kayanokohgen	IV	1,100	1968
280	Kazan	IV	2,650	1977
281	Kenminnomori (Aichi Prefecture)	IV	1,021	1966
282	Kenminnomori (Miyagi Prefecture)	IV	1,430	1968
283	Kenminnomori (Yamanashi Prefecture)	IV	1,073	1968
284	Kesamaruyama	IV	1,302	1964
285	Kesennuma	IV	1,979	1977
286	Kibohgaoka	IV	1,043	1969
287	Kichiyama	IV	2,917	1979
288	Kikuchisuigen	IV	1,290	1979
289	Kikushika	IV	2,223	1984
290	Kinhokuyama	IV	1,822	1979
291	Kitaarupusu	IV	26,727	1968
292	Kitadaitoh	IV	2,188	1974
293	Kitamatadake	IV	9,184	1980
294	Kitazawa	IV	1,750	1978
295	Kiyotsukyo	IV	1,276	1980
296	Kodomari	IV	3,125	1979
297	Koganesawa	IV	1,480	1964
298	Kogasayama	IV	2,507	1980
299	Koguchigawa	IV	1,871	1969
300	Kohbe	IV	1,017	1984
301	Kohbohyama	IV	2,030	1955
302	Kohdohyama	IV	1,440	1952
303	Kohgen	IV	1,740	1964
304	Kohgenyama	IV	2,459	1953
305	Kohkohseiymanomura	IV	4,328	1982
306	Kohno	IV	1,030	1972
307	Kohrayama	IV	1,186	1958
308	Kohyasan	IV	2,375	1983
309	Koiwainohjoh	IV	2,600	1962
310	Kojimako	IV	1,000	1977
311	Kokiso	IV	2,090	1967
312	Komagadakc	IV	2,567	1980
313	Komaganekohgen	IV	3,626	1984
314	Kominehara	IV	1,100	1967
315	Komuke	IV	1,516	1987
316	Konahichitohkaiiki	IV	36,380	1984
317	Kongohkuzushiro	IV	4,184	1976
318	Konpohsan (Kumamoto Prefecture)	IV	4,835	1962
319	Konpohsan (Nagano Prefecture)	IV	2,970	1983
320	Kooriyama	IV	10,212	1960
321	Kosaishiootomonami	IV	1,000	1976
322	Kosaka	IV	2,406	1979
323	Kosanike	IV	1,160	1960
324	Koshibudamushuhen	IV	2,297	1972
325	Kotanigawa	IV	1,500	1977
326	Kuchisakamoto	IV	1,740	1986
327	Kuju oofune	IV	1,527	1978
328	Kumanoshikaiganbu	IV	3,650	1982
329	Kunisakihantoh	IV	3,635	1966
330	Kurikoma (Akita Prefecture)	IV	10,948	1973
331	Kurikoma (Miyagi Prefecture)	IV	18,625	1975
332	Kurodake	IV	1,580	1973
333	Kurokamiyama	IV	2,202	1984
334†	Kurokohchi	IV	2,661	1980

Map† ref.	*National/international designations* Name of area	IUCN management category	Area (ha)	Year notified
335	Kurotaki	IV	1,580	1980
336	Kurotaki-taihohsankei	IV	10,694	1965
337	Kurumayama-shirakabako	IV	1,390	1982
338	Kusano	IV	1,093	1986
339	Kusatsu	IV	3,387	1953
340	Kushihiki	IV	1,686	1984
341	Kussharoko	IV	8,315	1974
342	Kuwahatayama	IV	2,600	1972
343	Kuzumakichoh-sotokawa	IV	1,110	1989
344	Kuzuryudamu	IV	1,120	1969
345	Kyoto Univ. -enshurin Shibecha	IV	1,436	1979
346	Kyuboteiyama	IV	2,942	1975
347	Kyusenbuyama	IV	1,042	1984
348	Kyushu Univ. -enshurin	IV	3,736	1979
349	Maenikkoh	IV	1,448	1975
350	Maeoni	IV	1,033	1978
351	Maizuruwan	IV	2,481	1958
352	Makinoto	IV	2,200	1986
353	Makiyama (Miyagi Prefecture)	IV	1,262	1967
354	Makiyama (Miyazaki Prefecture)	IV	1,720	1964
355	Mankogawa	IV	1,650	1967
356	Mantarohyama	IV	4,162	1980
357	Marunuma sugenuma	IV	3,750	1967
358	Maruoka	IV	1,500	1965
359	Mataniyama	IV	2,600	1982
360	Matoya	IV	1,109	1983
361	Matsushima	IV	12,262	1983
362	Mayasan	IV	2,560	1980
363	Mayuyama	IV	1,604	1970
364	Meiwacho	IV	1,445	1981
365	Michikawa	IV	1,200	1965
366	Midorigawa	IV	1,070	1977
367	Mikawa	IV	1,059	1984
368	Mikuradake	IV	1,306	1990
369	Minamata	IV	1,450	1977
370	Minamiarupusu	IV	10,827	1979
371	Minamidaitoh	IV	17,957	1974
372	Minamiiso	IV	1,992	1964
373	Minamikanitani	IV	1,070	1965
374	Minamishima-ukurahantoh	IV	1,915	1983
375	Minamitateshina	IV	1,250	1986
376	Mineokayama	IV	1,170	1965
377	Mineyama	IV	2,015	1987
378	Minogoh	IV	1,070	1959
379	Misatoyama	IV	1,180	1960
380	Mishima (Chiba Prefecture)	IV	1,864	1970
381	Mishima (Kagoshima Prefecture)	IV	2,743	1982
382	Mitake	IV	2,330	1962
383	Mitakeyama	IV	1,085	1988
384	Mito	IV	1,500	1962
385	Mitohenzaigoh	IV	1,690	1980
386	Mitohkaigan	IV	1,390	1973
387	Miyajima	IV	4,397	1961
388	Miyakoshi	IV	1,360	1979
389	Miyakoshisakiyama	IV	1,089	1980
390	Miyamorimura-tomoriyama	IV	1,453	1966
391	Miyanan	IV	1,400	1982

Map† ref.	*National/international designations* Name of area	IUCN management category	Area (ha)	Year notified
392	Miyatsuwan	IV	3,243	1986
393	Miyazaki	IV	1,430	1970
394	Miyoshi	IV	3,111	1987
395	Mizuishiyama	IV	1,332	1960
396	Mogami	IV	1,732	1983
397	Mokotoyama	IV	1,224	1986
398	Moritanitoride	IV	1,790	1973
399	Morokamiyama	IV	3,158	1968
400	Motomiya	IV	1,630	1974
401	Murotomisaki	IV	1,545	1964
402	Mutsumi	IV	1,150	1987
403	Myohgi	IV	2,051	1964
404	Myohkohsan	IV	13,881	1984
405	Naebayama	IV	4,188	1980
406	Naga	IV	1,280	1956
407	Nagamine	IV	1,510	1971
408	Naganoyama	IV	1,230	1982
409	Nagashima	IV	4,500	1978
410	Nagawa	IV	3,265	1984
411	Nakafusa	IV	1,992	1984
412	Nakakeijokaigan	IV	2,345	1972
413	Nakaumi	IV	8,800	1984
414	Nakura	IV	6,378	1975
415	Nanatsuka	IV	2,010	1983
416	Nansechoiseji	IV	1,140	1987
417	Nansechounankai	IV	2,230	1986
418	Naruko	IV	2,280	1981
419	Nasugoyohtei	IV	1,185	1967
420	Nejime	IV	1,153	1966
421	Nichinanko	IV	1,453	1974
422	Nihonrain	IV	6,320	1975
423	Niigatatsunoda	IV	4,818	1971
424	Niijima	IV	10,800	1971
425	Niikappushuchiku-bokujo	IV	1,713	1983
426	Niisatomurakariya	IV	1,369	1968
427	Nijohsan	IV	1,123	1983
428	Nikkoh	IV	28,066	1951
429	Ninoheshi-kamitomai	IV	1,265	1970
430	Nirayama-kokuritsukohen	IV	1,400	1964
431	Nishiho	IV	1,010	1974
432	Nishimiyasi-omoteyama	IV	2,112	1962
433	Nishiooashi	IV	2,467	1954
434	Nishisakurajima	IV	1,865	1972
435	Nogi	IV	1,510	1973
436	Nopporo	IV	1,958	1985
437	Norikura	IV	5,557	1980
438	Nosori	IV	1,365	1972
439	Notoroko	IV	5,934	1978
440	Numetokonarigawa	IV	2,292	1983
441	Ochiaikaigan	IV	1,273	1979
442	Odafukayama	IV	1,421	1983
443	Ogasawarashotoh	IV	5,899	1980
444	Ogawairi	IV	1,152	1983
445	Ohjiyama	IV	1,257	1964
446	Ohohtsukunomori	IV	1,055	1986
447	Ojika	IV	5,030	1975
448†	Okazaki	IV	6,450	1968

Map† ref.	National/international designations Name of area	IUCN management category	Area (ha)	Year notified
449	Okazakitohbu	IV	1,110	1973
450	Okuchichibu	IV	6,040	1984
451	Okudohgo	IV	1,348	1964
452	Okuhishima	IV	1,670	1984
453	Okunanaumi	IV	1,457	1962
454	Okuni	IV	2,475	1954
455	Okuniikappu	IV	1,029	1985
456	Okunoto	IV	3,175	1972
457	Okushiri	IV	14,331	1986
458	Okusodebana	IV	3,315	1964
459	Okusodebanakyo	IV	2,200	1974
460	Okutama	IV	2,576	1984
461	Okutateshina	IV	1,827	1983
462	Omikominamiarupusu	IV	1,029	1971
463	Oninamidayama	IV	1,620	1983
464	Ontake (Gifu Prefecture)	IV	1,366	1983
465	Ontake (Nagasaki Prefecture)	IV	1,756	1971
466	Ontake (Yamanashi Prefecture)	IV	4,200	1958
467	Oodaisankei	IV	2,083	1961
468	Ooharako	IV	3,127	1962
469	Oohata	IV	4,369	1985
470	Oohira	IV	1,258	1957
471	Ooigawakakoh	IV	1,590	1976
472	Ooitachubu	IV	8,380	1976
473	Ookamigahana	IV	1,270	1954
474	Ookasa	IV	1,634	1968
475	Ookohchi	IV	1,000	1973
476	Ookura	IV	1,969	1985
477	Ookuradamu	IV	1,500	1976
478	Oonuma (Hokkaido Prefecture)	IV	15,825	1982
479	Oonuma (Yamagata Prefecture)	IV	1,019	1980
480	Oosawa	IV	1,850	1975
481	Ooshiro	IV	1,059	1983
482	Ootaki (Chiba Prefecture)	IV	1,200	1970
483	Ootaki (Nagano Prefecture)	IV	4,683	1983
484	Ootanishiyama	IV	1,490	1953
485	Ootogoku	IV	1,608	1975
486	Ootsujiyama	IV	1,877	1990
487	Oowashi	IV	1,536	1975
488	Ooyabu	IV	1,078	1965
489	Ooyano	IV	1,100	1975
490	Ooyu	IV	1,045	1966
491	Osorezan	IV	2,824	1980
492	Osuzuyama	IV	2,826	1965
493	Owaseshisagaru	IV	2,750	1989
494	Oyama	IV	1,425	1966
495	Oze (Fukushima Prefecture)	IV	6,378	1961
496	Oze (Gunma Prefecture)	IV	10,590	1951
497	Rakanyama	IV	1,381	1965
498	Randairahontani	IV	3,395	1974
499	Rebun	IV	6,510	1986
500	Riga	IV	1,100	1967
501	Rishiri	IV	17,544	1985
502	Rokkohsan	IV	5,440	1963
503	Ryochisan	IV	1,271	1972
504	Sada	IV	1,600	1972
505	Saitoh	IV	1,482	1984

Map† ref.	National/international designations Name of area	IUCN management category	Area (ha)	Year notified
506	Sakamoto	IV	1,828	1979
507	Sakumi	IV	1,375	1982
508	Same	IV	3,520	1971
509	Sandankyo	IV	1,306	1984
510	Sanhohkai	IV	2,875	1965
511	Sanmen	IV	2,138	1984
512	Sanpeisan	IV	2,475	1964
513	Sarugamori	IV	1,070	1965
514	Satamisaki	IV	1,153	1982
515	Sawauchimura-wagadake	IV	1,451	1983
516	Seburiyama	IV	1,963	1983
517	Seikaitoh	IV	7,810	1964
518	Seinan	IV	1,561	1979
519	Sekidohmaruyama	IV	1,038	1973
520	Sekiyama	IV	2,571	1970
521	Senba	IV	1,300	1973
522	Sendai	IV	14,500	1972
523	Sennokurayama	IV	1,419	1980
524	Sennosen (Hyogo Prefecture)	IV	3,498	1982
525	Sennosen (Tottori Prefecture)	IV	2,470	1972
526	Sentoh mizukubo	IV	29,619	1984
527	Sentohmizukubo	IV	1,484	1984
528	Setagaya	IV	1,920	1969
529	Setogawa	IV	1,555	1983
530	Shakadake	IV	1,433	1974
531	Shakamine	IV	1,200	1977
532	Shiawasenooka	IV	1,080	1977
533	Shigakohgen	IV	3,402	1959
534	Shijigawa	IV	1,303	1978
535	Shikanogawa-damushuhen	IV	1,216	1960
536	Shikaribetsu	IV	1,803	1983
537	Shikotuko	IV	22,228	1986
538	Shikura	IV	1,629	1983
539	Shima	IV	1,360	1969
540	Shiminnomori	IV	1,225	1978
541	Shimizuyudosan	IV	1,250	1972
542	Shimoichi	IV	1,640	1975
543	Shimotsuma	IV	2,002	1958
544	Shinji	IV	8,800	1982
545	Shinjiko	IV	8,800	1972
546	Shinrinkohen	IV	1,290	1962
547	Shinzoh	IV	1,507	1986
548	Shiobara	IV	4,135	1961
549	Shiomine	IV	1,882	1955
550	Shioya	IV	1,155	1970
551	Shirahama	IV	1,657	1965
552	Shirakawa (Nagano Prefecture)	IV	1,496	1983
553	Shirakawa (Yamagata Prefecture)	IV	1,960	1974
554	Shirikoma	IV	1,326	1986
555	Shiroishi	IV	1,390	1978
556	Shiroishiyama	IV	6,025	1971
557	Shiroshimakohgen	IV	4,900	1976
558	Shiroumamura	IV	1,268	1965
559	Shiroumarenge	IV	7,875	1980
560	Shitenohji	IV	1,785	1968
561	Shitodaira	IV	1,000	1973
562	Shizukuishichohi	IV	2,280	1971

Map† ref.	*National/international designations* Name of area	IUCN management category	Area (ha)	Year notified
563	Shojiyama	IV	1,050	1984
564	Shukumohwan	IV	1,552	1964
565	Shumon	IV	2,787	1980
566	Shunbetsu	IV	2,322	1984
567	Sobari	IV	1,437	1973
568	Sobokatamukisankei	IV	5,173	1986
569	Soboyama	IV	1,117	1966
570	Sodeura	IV	1,732	1983
571	Sohbudake	IV	3,704	1965
572	Sohsekisan	IV	1,848	1969
573	Sugagawa	IV	1,050	1968
574	Sugimizu	IV	1,100	1973
575	Suidoh	IV	1,535	1990
576	Suzakiwan	IV	2,336	1965
577	Suzuka-kokuteikohen	IV	5,641	1970
578	Suzukakokuteikohen	IV	7,395	1983
579	Tadami	IV	15,817	1971
580	Tagawa	IV	1,048	1964
581	Tainai	IV	3,360	1984
582	Taishi	IV	1,750	1973
583	Tajimakaiganchubu	IV	2,446	1964
584	Takagoyama	IV	2,626	1978
585	Takai	IV	5,058	1971
586	Takakusayama	IV	2,366	1981
587	Takamiyama	IV	3,102	1966
588	Takamoriyama	IV	1,150	1987
589	Takanosu	IV	1,078	1984
590	Takao	IV	4,414	1982
591	Takaoka	IV	4,265	1953
592	Takatohge	IV	3,404	1977
593	Takisawa	IV	1,053	1988
594	Takochoh	IV	1,051	1949
595	Tama River Estuary	IV	5,310	1986
596	Tamagawa	IV	4,607	1986
597	Tamano	IV	1,700	1974
598	Tamanourawan	IV	2,560	1959
599	Tamugimata	IV	1,498	1985
600	Tanabe	IV	1,389	1969
601	Tanigawadake	IV	4,039	1966
602	Tanotaira	IV	1,013	1987
603	Tanzawadaisen	IV	15,812	1983
604	Taradake (Nagasaki Prefecture)	IV	6,803	1957
605	Taradake (Saga Prefecture)	IV	2,405	1984
606	Tashiro	IV	1,052	1967
607	Tashirodake	IV	1,392	1981
608	Tatesatoarakami	IV	2,458	1966
609	Tateshina	IV	1,380	1964
610	Tatokoyama	IV	1,127	1964
611	Tazawako	IV	4,478	1964
612	Teine	IV	2,227	1984
613	Tengubohsan	IV	1,606	1964
614	Tenryugawaisai-enshunada	IV	3,219	1979
615	Terao	IV	1,290	1979
616	Togakureyama	IV	4,582	1983
617	Tohfutsuko	IV	2,051	1982
618	Tohgoh	IV	1,300	1966
619	Tohkaishizenhodoh-haruno	IV	6,500	1972

Map† ref.	National/international designations Name of area	IUCN management category	Area (ha)	Year notified
620	Tohkaishizenhodoh-kawane	IV	2,630	1973
621	Tohkaishizenhodoh-shita	IV	1,898	1974
622	Tohkaishizenhodoh-tatsuyama	IV	1,107	1973
623	Tohkaisizenhodoh-hokuen	IV	1,550	1975
624	Tohkaisizenhodoh-shizuoka	IV	5,935	1972
625	Tohshima	IV	8,400	1974
626	Tohyako	IV	7,132	1974
627	Tokyo Univ. -hokkaidoenshurin	IV	11,066	1985
628	Tokyokoh	IV	12,000	1987
629	Tomansan	IV	1,200	1965
630	Tomogashima	IV	1,200	1983
631	Tonoyama-daitokuzan	IV	1,260	1975
632	Tsuhata	IV	1,600	1973
633	Tsukui	IV	2,100	1981
634	Tsukushimori	IV	1,012	1966
635	Tsunagionsen	IV	1,150	1973
636	Tsurugahantoh	IV	1,800	1957
637	Tsurugiyamasankei	IV	1,809	1989
638	Tsutsukishima	IV	1,300	1984
639	Uenonuma	IV	1,880	1961
640	Uhyohko	IV	1,525	1973
641	Ujoh	IV	2,394	1964
642	Uku	IV	2,671	1976
643	Urabandai	IV	17,957	1961
644	Uratowan	IV	2,854	1959
645	Ushibori	IV	1,120	
646	Ushihorichisaki	IV	1,120	1962
647	Ushikunama	IV	1,244	1957
648	Ushimi	IV	1,690	1983
649	Utano	IV	1,181	1972
650	Utatsuyama	IV	1,450	1973
651	Utsukushigagara	IV	2,203	1968
652	Utsunomiya	IV	2,192	1960
653	Utsunomiya-suidohzana	IV	1,050	1971
654	Wakasugiyama	IV	2,160	1976
655	Yagen	IV	1,132	1983
656	Yagoyama	IV	1,210	1982
657	Yahiko	IV	2,911	1964
658	Yakegaku	IV	1,125	1974
659	Yakeishirenpoh	IV	7,193	1989
660	Yakuraizan	IV	1,330	1971
661	Yakushidake	IV	1,377	1979
662	Yamadera	IV	2,308	1953
663	Yamagatamura-yamagata	IV	1,390	1974
664	Yamanakako	IV	1,360	1987
665	Yamanakaonsen	IV	1,420	1957
666	Yamatoyama	IV	2,110	1971
667	Yashiro	IV	1,340	1981
668	Yatsugatake	IV	6,850	1958
669	Yogoshiyama	IV	1,505	1970
670	Yokokawa	IV	3,602	1984
671	Yokonami	IV	1,292	1988
672	Yonagawan	IV	1,608	1981
673	Yoneyama	IV	2,257	1972
674	Yoroi kabutodake	IV	1,110	1965
675	Yoshinoyama	IV	3,490	1960
676	Yudoh	IV	3,855	1972

Map† ref.	National/international designations Name of area	IUCN management category	Area (ha)	Year notified
677	Yudosan	IV	1,100	1970
678	Yuhoh	IV	7,500	1965
679	Yukuruwakasakanai	IV	4,692	1970
680	Yunosato	IV	1,007	1970
681	Yunotani-okutadamiko	IV	21,222	1983
682	Zaoh	IV	6,208	1984
683	Zaohrenpoh	IV	27,702	1984
684	Zuibaiji Estuary	IV	26,708	1986
	Quasi National Parks			
685	Abashiri	VIII	37,412	1958
686	Aichi Kogen	VIII	21,705	1970
687	Akiyoshidai	VIII	4,502	1955
688	Amami-Gunto	VIII	7,861	1974
689	Biwako	VIII	98,144	1950
690	Chokai	VIII	28,373	1963
691	Echigo-Sanzan-Tadami	VIII	86,129	1973
692	Echizen-Kaga Kaigan	VIII	8,992	1968
693	Genkai	VIII	10,561	1956
694	Hayachine	VIII	5,463	1982
695	Hiba-Dogo-Taishaku	VIII	7,808	1963
696	Hida-Kisogawa	VIII	18,075	1964
697	Hidaka-Sanmyaku-Erimo	VIII	103,447	1981
698	Hyonosen-Ushiroyama Nagisan	VIII	48,803	1969
699	Ibi-Sekigahara-Yoro	VIII	20,219	1970
700	Iki-Tsushima	VIII	11,950	1968
701	Ishizuchi	VIII	10,683	1955
702	Kita Kyushu	VIII	8,249	1972
703	Kitanagato Kaigan	VIII	8,021	1955
704	Kongo-Ikoma	VIII	15,564	1958
705	Kouya-Ryujin	VIII	19,198	1967
706	Kurikoma	VIII	77,137	1968
707	Kyushu-Chuo-Sanchi	VIII	27,096	1982
708	Mikawa Wan	VIII	9,443	1958
709	Minami-Boso	VIII	5,685	1958
710	Minamisanriku Kinkazan	VIII	13,902	1979
711	Muroo-Akame-Aoyama	VIII	26,308	1970
712	Muroto-Anan Kaigan	VIII	7,216	1964
713	Myougi-Arafune-Sakukogen	VIII	13,123	1969
714	Nichinan Kaigan	VIII	4,542	1955
715	Nippo Kaigan	VIII	8,506	1974
716	Niseko-Shakotan-Otaru Kaigan	VIII	19,009	1963
717	Nishi Chugoku Sanchi	VIII	28,553	1969
718	Noto Hanto	VIII	9,672	1968
719	Oga	VIII	8,156	1973
720	Okinawa Kaigan	VIII	10,208	1972
721	Okinawa Senseki	VIII	3,127	1972
722	Onuma	VIII	9,083	1958
723	Sado-Yahiko-Yoneyana	VIII	29,464	1950
724	Shimokita Hanto	VIII	18,728	1968
725	Shokanbetu-Teuriyagishiri	VIII	43,559	1990
726	Sobo-Katamuki	VIII	22,000	1965
727	Suigo-Tsukuba	VIII	34,309	1959
728	Suzuka	VIII	29,821	1968
729	Tanzawa-Oyama	VIII	27,572	1965
730	Tenryu-Okumikawa	VIII	25,756	1969
731	Tsugaru	VIII	25,966	1975
732	Tsurugisan	VIII	20,870	1964

Map† ref.	*National/international designations* Name of area	IUCN management category	Area (ha)	Year notified
733	Wakasa Wan	VIII	21,091	1955
734	Yaba-Hita-Hikosan	VIII	85,023	1950
735	Yamato-Aogaki	VIII	5,742	1970
736	Yatsugatake-Chushin Kogen	VIII	39,857	1964
737	Zao	VIII	40,089	1963
	Biosphere Reserves			
	Mount Hakusan	IX	48,000	1980
	Mount Odaigahara and Mount Omine	IX	36,000	1980
	Shiga Highland	IX	13,000	1980
	Yakushima Island	IX	19,000	1980
	Ramsar Sites			
	Izu-numa and Uchi-numa	R	559	1985
	Kushiro-shitsugen	R	7,726	1980
	Kutcharo-ko	R	1,607	1989
	Utonai-ko	R	510	1991

†Locations of most protected areas are shown on the accompanying map.

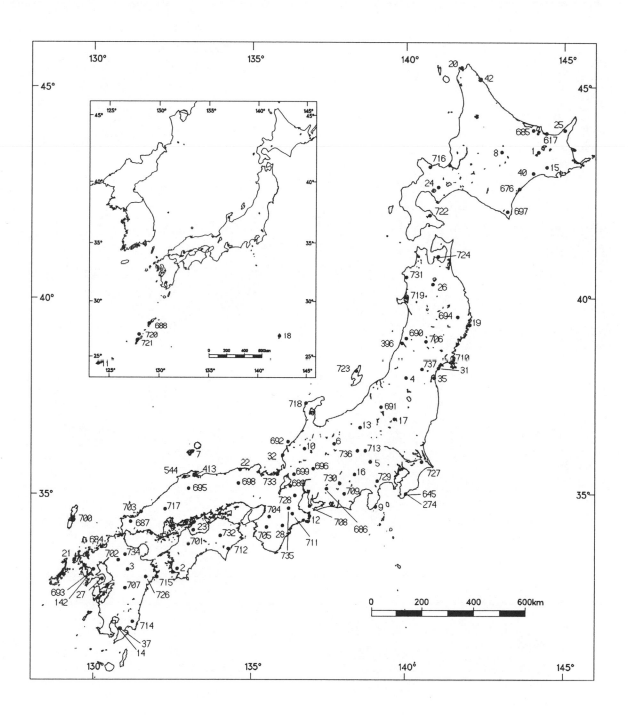

Protected Areas of Japan

DEMOCRATIC PEOPLE'S REPUBLIC OF KOREA
(NORTH KOREA)

Area 120,540 sq. km

Population 21,733,000 (1990)
Natural increase: 1.92% per annum

Economic Indicators
GDP: US$ 799 per capita (1987)
GNP: US$ 1,180 per capita (1985) (Paxton, 1989)

Policy and Legislation Korea has a very long history of nature conservation. For example, in the reign of King Chinsi (540-576 AD) of the Sinra Dynasty the "Hwarang" system of government stressed the importance of scenic areas and included in its "Five Rules of Practice" that people should "cherish all living things". During the seventh year of King Sejo's reign (1461) of the Yi Dynasty an article in the Royal Chronicles prohibited the random felling of pine trees, and listed strict punishments.

In April 1946, the government passed the necessary legislation to create natural monuments and designated the first sites. Since then, relevant legislation has included the following: Cabinet Decisions No. 29 of February 1959 and No. 17 of May 1961 concerning the protection and breeding of useful animals and plants; Cabinet Decision No. 93 of May 1961 concerning the conservation and management of scenic areas and natural monuments; and Presidential Orders No. 1 of July 1973 and No. 7 of October 1976 which further strengthened the preservation of natural monuments. These may be established around important colonies of plants, animals and geographical and geological features such as lakes, waterfalls, hot springs and mineral springs (Scott, 1989).

Detailed legislative information is not available to describe the different protected areas in North Korea. Scott (1989), however, lists the following categories: nature protection areas, animal protection areas, breeding seabird protection areas, aquatic resources protection areas, strict nature reserves, forest reserves, experimental and scientific reserves, protected landscapes, and natural monuments.

International Activities One biosphere reserve has been nominated but not yet designated under the Unesco Man and the Biosphere Programme. North Korea is not a party to the Convention on Wetlands of International Importance especially as Waterfowl Habitat (Ramsar Convention) nor to the Convention concerning Protection of the World Cultural and Natural Heritage (World Heritage Convention).

In March 1988 Japan and the Republic of Korea called upon UNEP to extend its Regional Seas programme to cover the north-west Pacific. Such a programme, if adopted would cover five countries: the USSR, China, Japan, North Korea and South Korea.

Administration and Management The Academy of Sciences has ministerial status and is responsible for deciding whether areas should be afforded protection (Poore, 1986). Several divisions are responsible for carrying out research into the country's wildlife and natural resources: the institutes of Botany, Zoology, Forestry and Environmental Protection. The actual management of nature reserves is the responsibility of the Department of Forestry Management.

Another government organisation is the Union for Nature Conservation of the Democratic People's Republic of Korea. This is an umbrella organisation incorporating the Animal, Plant, Gardening and Aquatic Resources Society. It was first founded as the Korean Gardening and Forestry Society in November 1959.

There do not appear to be any non-governmental organisations concerned with conservation or nature protection (Scott, 1989).

Systems Reviews North Korea makes up the northern half of Peninsular Korea. To the south it has a border with the Republic of Korea, to the north it shares a long border with China, much of it running along the Yalu and Tumen rivers in fairly mountainous terrain; it also shares a short border with the USSR in the north-east. Much of west coast faces the Korea Bay at the northern end of the Yellow Sea, while the east coast drops steeply down to the Sea of Japan. Most of the country is mountainous, especially in the north where there are many peaks over 2,000m. Only in the south-west are there extensive areas of lowland. The mountains are of igneous and volcanic origin. The slopes on the east coast down to the Sea of Japan are steep and abrupt, giving a rugged coastline. Those to the west are less abrupt, sloping down to the Yellow Sea.

The natural vegetation is mixed deciduous coniferous forests between 700m and 1,700m. The uplands are dominated by "taiga" forest, which resembles that of northern Japan. Alpine vegetation is found above 2,000m (Davis *et al.*, 1986; Dudley Stamp, 1957). The only large wetland areas are situated on the west coast and the numerous offshore islands, where there are numerous estuaries, with extensive areas of mudflats, and also large areas of salt-pans. There are over a hundred natural lakes, and over 1,000 man-made storage reservoirs. In the northern highlands there are some mountain bogs of great botanical interest. No known reviews exist of plant or animal species for North Korea, but Lee (1976) lists 2,898 vascular plant species for the Korean Peninsula as a whole, of which 107 are endemic to North Korea (Lee, 1983). Although originally forested, most of the lowlands are now farmed. There are, however, still important coastal estuaries, marshes and islands, some of which have been designated as protected areas (Davis *et al.*, 1986; Ginsburg, 1958; Scott, 1989).

In January 1987 the total number of protected areas was 47. Included in this figure are seven nature protection areas, covering more than 75,000ha; 15 animal protection areas, 6 breeding seabird protection areas, and four aquatic resources protection areas established to protect populations of marine invertebrates and fish. In 1980 there were 394 natural monuments. The 68 geographical natural monuments include natural lakes, 14 waterfalls and 11 scenic stretches of coastline; the 48 geographical 10 hot springs and 4 other mineral springs. There are 192 plant natural monuments and 86 for animal natural monuments: these consist of protected species rather than specific sites (Scott, 1989).

The border between the People's Democratic Republic of Korea and the Republic of Korea, along the 38th parallel, has an UN-designated no-access zone some 4km wide. South Korea maintains an additional 10km-wide strip to which access is severely restricted. This area is uninhabited and a very important refuge for wildlife, covering, as it does, a broad range of pristine habitats right across the country. Numerous species, including large mammals extinct elsewhere in the region, maintain stable populations in this area (Poole, 1991).

There is little information available regarding threats to natural areas. Nature conservation issues received little attention in Korea under the Japanese colonial rule from 1910 to 1946. World War II and the Korean War (1950-1953) led to the devastation of large areas of the country. The need for agricultural land is leading to the reclamation of large areas: the methods used for this are usually labour intensive and unmechanised. In addition to the damage this may be causing to coastal wetlands, it has been reported that some of the rocks being used for this reclamation are being obtained by blasting offshore

rocky islets, which have a very important conservation value (Poole, 1991).

Addresses

Academy of Sciences, Taesong District, Pyongyang (for Botany, Zoology and Forestry institutes)

Institute of Environmental Protection, Academy of Sciences, Central District, Pyongyang

Ministry of Forestry, Pyongyang

Natural Conservation Union of the Democratic People's Republic of Korea, No. 220-93-7-24 Dongsong Street, Central District, Pyongyang

References

Brush, J.E., McCune, S., Philbrick, A.K., Randall, J.R., and Wiens, H.J. (1958). *The pattern of Asia.* Prentice-Hall Inc., Englewood Cliffs, New Jersey.

Davis, S.D., Droop, S.J.M., Gregerson, P., Henson, L., Leon, C.J., Lamlein Villa-Lobos, J., Synge, H., and Zantovska, J. (1986). *Plants in danger: what do we know?* IUCN, Gland, Switzerland, and Cambridge, UK. 461 pp.

Dudley Stamp, L. (1957). *Asia, a regional and economic geography.* Methuen & Co Ltd., London. 726 pp.

Lee, T.B. (1976). Vascular plants and their uses in Korea. *Bull. Kwanak Arboretum* 1. 137 pp. (Unseen)

Lee, T.B. (1983). Endemic plants and their distribution in Korea. *Bull. Kwanak Arboretum* 4: 71-113. (Unseen)

Paxton, J. (1989). *The Statesman's Yearbook.* The Macmillan Press Ltd., London and Basingstoke, UK. 1691 pp.

Poole, C. (1991). The gift of a no-man's-land. *BBC Wildlife.* September. Pp. 636-639.

Poore, D. (1986). Report of a mission to the Democratic People's Republic of Korea. Unpublished report for United Nations Educational, Scientific and Cultural Organisation.

Scott, D.A. (Ed.) (1989). *A directory of Asian wetlands.* IUCN, Gland, Switzerland and Cambridge, UK. 1,181 pp.

SUMMARY OF PROTECTED AREAS

Map ref.	*National/international designations* Name of area	IUCN management category	Area (ha)	Year notified
1	*National Park* Kumgang Mountain	II	43,890	
2	*Protection Area* Paekdu Mt Nature	IV	14,000	1976
	Biosphere Reserve Mount Paekdu Biosphere Reserve	IX	37,430	1982

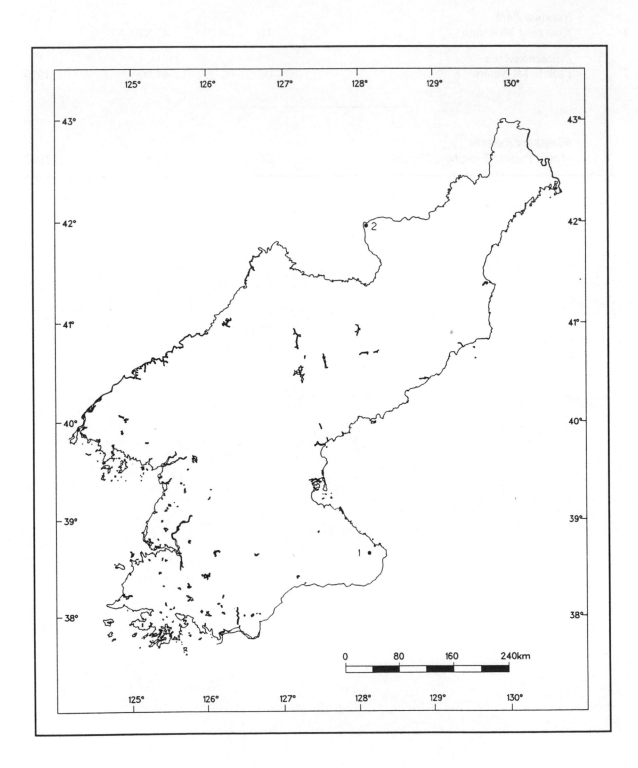

Protected Areas of North Korea

REPUBLIC OF KOREA (SOUTH KOREA)

Area 99,020 sq. km

Population 42,793,000 (1990)
Natural increase: 0.85% per annum

Economic Indicators
GDP: US$ 2,880 per capita (1987)
GNP: US$ 2,690 per capita (1987)

Policy and Legislation The present constitution dates from 1963 (amended in 1980). Korea has a very long history of nature conservation. For example, in the reign of King Chinsi (540-576 AD) of the Sinra Dynasty, the "Hwarang" system of government stressed the importance of scenic areas and included in its "Five Rules of Practice" that people should "cherish all living things'. During the seventh year of King Sejo's reign (1461) of the Yi Dynasty, an article in the Royal Chronicles prohibited the random felling of pine trees, and listed strict punishments. There are now numerous categories of protected areas covered under a wide range of laws.

The Natural Park Law of 4 January 1980 (formerly the Park Law of 1967) provides for the designation, establishment and management of three categories of protected areas: national park, provincial park and county park (see Annex). Under this law the Ministry of Construction has been appointed as the National Park Authority, with its division of Parks responsible for the designation of national parks. Provincial and county parks come under the control of regional authorities. In 1981 miscellaneous laws and decrees relating to national parks were incorporated into the Natural Park Law, ensuring a more favourable and more powerful parks administration (Anon., 1982). From early 1991, the Ministry of Home Affairs has been responsible for the administration of all three categories of natural park (Woo, *in litt.*, 1991).

The Cultural Properties Protection Act of 10 January 1962 provides for the establishment of scenic beauty areas, historic sites, nature reserves and natural monuments, which may include both sites and species (see Annex). Protected areas covered under this Act are designated by the Office of Cultural Properties in the Ministry of Culture (previously the Ministry of Culture and Information).

Article 9 of the Environmental Protection Law of December 1981 provides for natural ecological system protected areas, while the National Land Use and Management Law of December 1982 provides for the establishment of natural environment protection regions, larger areas within which it was suggested that natural ecological system protected areas should be established. The Environmental Protection Law also provides for the protection of "specific protected wildlife/plants", which may receive special protection in "protected areas for specially designated wildlife/plants" (see Annex) (Woo, 1990). The Environmental Protection Law was repealed in July 1990 and replaced by the Basic Law for National Environmental Policy, enacted on 1 August 1990 (Woo, *in litt.*, 1991).

The Law Concerning Protection of Wildlife and Game of 30 March 1967 is concerned with the protection of wildlife and makes provisions for the designation of wildlife sanctuaries, special wildlife sanctuaries and also game reserves where hunting is permitted subject to regulations (see Annex) (Woo, 1990).

The Forest Act of 27 December 1961 (amended in 1980 and 1990) requires that forest land be classified into reserved forests and non-reserved forests. Various categories of reserved forests are described, notably protection forests, seed production stands, nature protected forests and natural recreation forests. Included in the category of nature protected forests are protected trees (see Annex) (Woo, 1990).

Environmental impact assessment is given a statutory basis under the Environment Conservation Law (Law No. 3078) of December 1977. Under this Law, most major construction projects are subject to environmental impact assessment and must undergo consultation with the Environment Administration (now the Ministry of Environment) (Anon., n.d.; Kim, 1988). Environmental policy issues are covered under a long-term environmental preservation plan for 1987-2001 which contains basic environmental policy directions, specific policy directions and financial plans (Anon., 1990a).

Forestry policy and planning are centred around the five-year socio-economic development plans and ten-year forest development plans that have been instigated through these. The second of these forest development plans ran until 1989. Among the activities encouraged through the plans are reforestation programmes, the setting aside of areas for protection from erosion and the maintenance of the ecological balance in certain forests (Forestry Administration, 1987).

International Activities Korea became a party to the Convention concerning the Protection of the World Cultural and Natural Heritage (World Heritage Convention) on 14 September 1988; no natural sites have been inscribed on the World Heritage list. One site has been declared a biosphere reserve under the Unesco Man and the Biosphere Programme.

In March 1988 Japan and the Republic of Korea called upon UNEP to extend its Regional Seas programme to cover the north-west Pacific. Such a programme, if adopted, would cover five countries: the USSR, China, Japan, North Korea and South Korea.

Administration and Management   There is no ministry or lower level body exclusively assigned to the administration of all protected areas. Instead, various ministries are involved in different aspects. Until 1991, the Ministry of Construction had overall responsibility for the designation of natural parks: national, provincial and county parks. The National Parks Authority, which was originally established under this Ministry in 1987, was transferred to the Ministry of Home Affairs in early 1991. It is responsible for the management of national parks, under the leadership of a chairman. It has four divisions, covering Planning, Operations, Administration and Facilities, and also an Office of Audit and Inspection, which work in cooperation with 23 regionally based park offices which collect admission fees used to fund the construction of park facilities (Lee, 1990; Woo, *in litt.*, 1991). The Authority works in cooperation with the nature preservation honourary inspector system organised by the Korean Central Council for the Preservation of Nature (Woo, 1990).

One of the three divisions of the Office of Cultural Properties in the Ministry of Culture is responsible for the establishment and administration of natural monuments, nature reserves and other sites covered by the Cultural Properties Protection Act. These are normally designated in consultation with the Committee for Cultural Properties Protection, an advisory organisation comprised of zoologists, botanists and geologists who, where necessary, conduct field surveys and make proposals for nature conservation measures. Woo (1990) suggests that the financial resources, based on the government budget, are insufficient: there are no field offices nor officials working in any of the nature reserves.

Natural ecological system protected areas and "protected areas for specially designated wildlife/plants" fall under the management and administration of the Ministry of Environment. There is some civilian involvement, notably with the nature preservation honourary inspector system (Woo, 1990). The Ministry of Environment is a new ministry, upgraded from its former position of Environment Administration on 1 January 1990 (Anon., 1990a).

The Forestry Administration of the Ministry of Agriculture, Forestry and Fisheries has overall responsibility for wildlife protection and game. It is also responsible for establishing the "basic management plans" for sites designated under the Law Concerning Protection of Wildlife and Game: wildlife sanctuaries, special wildlife sanctuaries and game reserves. The Forest Administration has an administrator, a deputy administrator, a planning and coordinating officer and three director generals. Also under the Forest Administration there are two research institutions, three national forest stations and one forestry training institute. Detailed management plans are the responsibility of the provincial governors (Forestry Administration, 1987). Wildlife protection officers should be employed in the field by the provincial authorities (Woo, 1990). The

designation of nature-protected forests under the 1961 Forest Act, and also the removal of such protected status, is by decision of the relevant governor, mayor and/or the director of the relevant national forest station, while the Forestry Administration prepares detailed regulations for the management of such areas (Woo, 1990).

The Ministry of Home Affairs is largely responsible for coordinating the environmental protection movement and interacting between the state and the non-governmental organisations, including those organisations which are involved with protected areas (Woo, 1990).

There are various non-governmental organisations in Korea which are concerned with conservation. The National Parks Association of Korea, created on 27 October 1971, was set up to "ensure the sound development of attractive natural scenic areas', including national, provincial and county parks, and other tourist sites. It is responsible for guidance, planning and design of tourist and cultural uses of national parks; management of park facilities and resources as requested by the agency in charge of park administration; research and study on resources of scientific value within park areas and on the ideal development and operation of parks and is involved in exchange with other national park associations outside Korea (Anon., 1982). The Korean Commission for the Conservation of Nature was established in 1963, and renamed the Korean Association for the Conservation of Nature in 1974. This group is a non-governmental, but very influential conservation organisation, involved with research, education and the management of some protected areas. The Korean Central Council for Nature Conservation, established in 1977, is involved in civil campaigning for nature conservation and also has a role in education and research. It also nominates nature preservation honourary inspectors, volunteers at the local and regional level, who work in close cooperation with the Ministry of Home Affairs in the inspection of protected areas (Woo, 1990). Other groups include the Korean Association for Wildlife Protection and the Korean Association for Bird Protection, which may also have some involvement in protected areas. The Department of Forestry in Seoul National University has done considerable work analysing the protected areas system.

Much of the forest area is privately-owned, and a public body, the Forest Association Union, plays an important role in the implementation of forestry programmes by aiming to protect and manage private forests effectively and to improve the socio-economic situation of the members, forest owners and villagers (Forest Administration, 1987).

According to the present legislation, the government or concerned authorities responsible for the designation of the various protected areas should pay compensation to the landowners if the land is privately owned. There appear to be problems concerning compensation, however, due to the low budget of these authorities, and due to difficulties of evaluation (Woo, 1990). Other problems arise from the fact that local governments, as well as the National Parks Authority, cannot afford to employ technical staff (Woo, 1991).

Systems Reviews The Republic of Korea occupies the southern half of the Korean Peninsula and its numerous offshore islands. It is bounded by the Sea of Japan to the east and the Yellow Sea to the west. About two-thirds of the country is hilly or mountainous. In general, the western and southern slopes are gentle, with many well-developed river basins, relatively broad coastal plains, extensive estuarine systems and many offshore islands. Low-lying areas ideally suited to human habitation and cultivation constitute only 3.8% of the country.

The natural vegetation along southern coasts and offshore islands is warm-temperate, broad-leaved evergreen forest with oak, camellia and bamboo, although much of this has now been cleared for agriculture and urban development. Also in the south, away from the coast, are temperate forests containing oak, hornbeam and *Pinus densiflora*. To the north, and at higher elevations, oak/fir forest and cold-temperate fir/birch forest are found (Davis *et al.*, 1986). Forest areas in total cover 65,310 sq. km or 66% of the total land area.

The border between the People's Democratic Republic of Korea and the Republic of Korea, along the 38th parallel, has an UN-designated no-access zone some 4km wide. South Korea maintains an additional 10km-wide strip to which access is severely restricted. This area is uninhabited and a very important refuge for wildlife, covering, as it does, a broad range of pristine habitats right across the country. Numerous species, including large mammals extinct elsewhere in the region, maintain stable populations in this area (Poole, 1991).

Nature conservation issues received little attention under Japanese colonial rule from 1910 to 1946. World War II and the Korean War (1950-1953) resulted in the environmental devastation of large areas of the country. Afforestation programmes have been in operation since 1947 and these continued throughout the Korean War. Thus, in 1953, the forested area was 13% higher than in 1949 (Li Jip, 1987). Public concern for other conservation issues, for the protection of the land and its wildlife, resurfaced in the 1960s, with a conference in 1963 which proposed a plan for academic research into nature preservation issues. The Natural Parks Law, 1967 laid the foundations for a protected area system. In December 1967, Mount Chiri National Park was declared. Two more national parks were declared in 1968, giving a total protected area of 111,821ha. By 1990, 20 national parks had been designated covering 644,045ha, 378,667ha of land and a further 265,378ha of sea, the land figure representing 3.8% of the country's total land area (Nak San Lee, *in litt.*, 1987; Woo, *in litt.*, 1991). The first three natural ecological system protected areas were designated in 1989: they cover a total area of 5,546ha. In 1990 there was a total of 478 wildlife sanctuaries covering some 109,580ha and a further 65 special wildlife sanctuaries covering 1,979ha. Also in 1990 the total area covered by protection forests was 247,000ha; there were 127 nature protected forests covering 11,047ha (Woo, in litt., 1991) and 9,292 protected trees in the country, designated for their aesthetic, historic or religious value (Woo, 1990).

Large numbers of visitors are reportedly causing extreme damage to the natural parks, and the National Parks Authority is considering the introduction of schemes to restrict visitor numbers (Woo, 1990). The country has a very high population density, and the total population is still rising fairly rapidly. In recent decades there has been a great expansion of urban and industrial areas with consequent loss of agricultural land. Agricultural self-sufficiency has fallen greatly, but, in an effort to reverse this trend, a major programme of land reclamation has begun: 155 estuaries and bays were identified for this purpose by the government in 1984. It is estimated (Scott, 1989) that reclamation of all these sites will result in the loss of some 66.5% of coastal wetlands in the south and west of the Republic, including some within protected areas. Marine pollution is also a major threat to some of the marine national parks (Anon., 1990b).

Other Relevant Information In 1975, 7,470,000 visitors used the national parks. By 1985 this figure had reached 26,430,000, and by 1989 there were 36,661,000 visitors (Anon. 1982; Lee, 1990).

Addresses

Ministry of Environment, 7-16, Sincheon-dong, Songpa-gu, SEOUL 138-240

Ministry of Construction, Government Planning Building(2), 1 Joongang-Dong, Kwacheon-Shi, Kyonggi-Do, SEOUL 427-010 (Tel: 2 593 1393)

National Parks Authority, Kunsolhoikwan, 71-2, Nonhyun-dong, Kangnam-gu, SEOUL 135-010 (Tel: 2 540 5619)

Ministry of Culture, Office of Cultural Properties, Sejong-no, Chongno-gu, SEOUL 110-050

Ministry of Home Affairs, Division of Nature Conservation, Government United Building, 77 Sejong-no, Chongno-gu, SEOUL 110-050

Forestry Administration, 207 Cheongyangni-Dong, Tongdaemun-gu, SEOUL 130-010

National Parks Association of Korea, Sahak Building, Room 706, 19 Naeja-Dong, Chongno-gu, SEOUL 110-053 (Tel: 2 736 9656)

Korean Association for the Conservation of Nature, c/o Forest Research Institute, 207 Cheongryangni-dong, Tongdaemun-gu, SEOUL 131-012

National Institute of Environmental Research, 280-17 Pulkwang-dong Eunpyung-gu, SEOUL 122 (Tel: 2 385 5711; Fax: 2 384 6177; Tlx: 25783 ENVIROK)

National Academy of Sciences of the Republic of Korea, Socho-dong, Socho-gu, SEOUL 137-070

Department of Forestry, College of Agriculture, Seoul National University, SUWON 441-744 (Tel: 331 290 2324)

References

Anon. (n.d.). Republic of Korea. In: *Environmental Legislation and Administration: briefing profiles of selected developing member countries of the Asian Development Bank*. ADB Environment Paper No. 2. Asian Development Bank, Manila, Philippines. Pp. 30-32.

Anon. (1982). *National Parks Association of Korea*. Seoul, Korea.

Anon. (1990a). Republic of Korea. *Brundtland Bulletin*. Centre for Our Common Future. September/December 1990. P. 39.

Anon. (1990b). Major reclamation schemes threaten south Korean wetlands. *WWF News* 64. March/April.

Davis, S.D., Droop, S.J.M., Gregerson, P., Henson, L., Leon, C.J., Lamlein Villa-Lobos, J., Synge, H., and Zantovska, J. (1986). *Plants in danger: what do we know?* IUCN, Gland, Switzerland, and Cambridge, UK. 461 pp.

Forestry Administration (1987). *Forestry in Korea*. National Progress Report on Forestry, 1984-1985. Ministry of Agriculture, Forestry and Fisheries. 29 pp.

Johnson, H and Johnson, J.M. (1977). *Environmental policies in developing countries*. Erich Schmidt Verlag, Germany.

Kim, Y.H. (1988). Environmental Impact Assessment in Korea. In: *Papers of the 1st Korea-US Cooperative*

Symposium on Clean Environment. Environment Administration, US Environmental Protection Agency and World Health Organisation. Pp. 299-320.

Lee, S.Y. (1990). *Korea National Parks Authority*. Office of PR, Korea National Parks Authority, Seoul. 61 pp.

Lee, T.B. (1976). Vascular plants and their uses in Korea. *Bull. Kwanak Arboretum* 1: 137. (Unseen)

Lee, T.B. (1979, 1982). *Illustrated Flora of Korea*, 2 volumes. Hyangmunsa, Seoul. (Unseen)

Li Jip (1987). Forest resources and their protection, concern for forests. *Korea Today* 3: 7-11.

Poole, C. (1991). The gift of a no-man's-land. *BBC Wildlife*. September. Pp. 636-639.

Won, P.O. (1979). Nature Conservation in Korea. *Theses collection*, Kyung Hee University 9: 501-516. Seoul.

Won, P.O. (1981). *Red data book of the Republic of Korea*. Korean Association for the Conservation of Nature, Seoul.

Won, P.O. and Lee, Y.N. (1973). *Wildlife and flowering plants*. Korea Background Series, Korean Overseas Information Service, Seoul.

Woo, B.M. (1990). Status of management of the protected areas in the Republic of Korea. Paper No. 13, delivered at FAO Conference: Regional expert consultation on management of protected areas in the Asia-Pacific Region, 10-14 December 1990, Bangkok, Thailand. 43 pp.

Woo, B.M. (1991). Status of the Management of the Protected Areas in the Republic of Korea. *Tiger Paper* 18(2): 14-20.

ANNEX
Definitions of protected area designations, as legislated, together with authorities responsible for their administration

Title : Natural Park Law which replaced the Park Law (Law No. 1909)

Date: 3 March 1967 (Park Law), 4 January 1980 (Natural Park Law), last amended 30 June 1987

Brief description: Provides for the designation, establishment and management of: national parks, provincial parks and county parks. Appoints administrative authority.

Administrative authority: National Parks Authority in the Ministry of Home Affairs (*Naemoobu*) (previously in the Ministry of Construction) (for national parks); City or Provincial Office (*Do*) (for provincial parks); City or County Office (*Gun*) (for country parks)

Designations:

Jayeongongwon (Natural park)

Gookripgongwon (National park) Large areas containing representative areas of scenic heritage. Management plans should incorporate a zoning system based on the following:

Nature conservation area Has the highest degree of protection; minimal parks facilities may be installed; scientific research is permitted; military facilities may be installed; and Buddhist temples may be restored and used for services. Limited afforestation and silvicultural practices may be permitted, including the building of forest roads.

Natural environment area In addition to the activities permitted in the previous category, primary land-based industries, such as agriculture and forestry, are permitted, providing they do not alter the present state of the land, silvicultural facilities may also be installed.

Village area A residential area is allowed to function without strict controls. Some expansion is allowed and the development of cottage industry provided there is no pollution.

Mass facility area The development of facilities for tourism and recreation are permitted.

Parks protection area Buffer zone found around some national parks, where such acts as littering and obstructing park entrances are not permitted.

Doripgongwon (Provincial park) Detailed management plans are determined by the provincial governor working with the provincial parks committee. Typically these parks may be zoned in a similar manner to the national parks.

Gunripgongwon (County park) Detailed management plans are determined by the county governor working with the county parks committee.

Source: Woo, 1990

Title : Cultural Properties Protection Act

Date: 10 January 1962, last amended 31 December 1984

Brief description: Provides for the designation, establishment and management of natural monuments, nature reserves, scenic areas and historic sites. A natural monument may be either a site or a species.

Administrative authority: Office of Cultural Properties (*Moonwhabu*) in the Ministry of Culture (*Moonwhajae-gwanriguk*) (previously Ministry of Culture and Information) (MOCI)

Designations:

Natural monument Natural monuments may simply be plants, animals or minerals, or they may be sites of scenic or ecological importance. These sites are small and designated under one or more of the following criteria: unique plants or animals and their natural environment; geomorphological features such as caves, sand dunes and waterfalls; individual trees of scientific or historical importance; representative areas of wilderness and natural habitats.

Chonyeonbohoguyok (Nature reserve) A type of natural monument, designated over larger areas, where the whole area has natural monument status or contains many smaller natural monuments. These may exist within national parks. The aim of nature reserves is to achieve the absolute preservation of nature without any form of disturbance.

Scenic beauty area Designated for their unusual natural beauty

Historic site Area of historical significance: prehistoric dwellings; ancient middens (shell mounds), fortresses, battle grounds, historic kiln sites, ancient tombs and temples and confucian schools and shrines.

Sources: Woo, 1990; *in litt.*, 1991

Title : National Land Use and Management Law

Date: December 1982, last amended 1990

Brief description: Provides for the establishment of natural environment protection regions

Administrative authority: Ministry of Construction

Designations:

Natural environment protection region Declared because of the natural habitat value, or because of characteristic topography, or because they contain threatened animals, plants or ecosystems

Restrictions include prohibition of house-building, cutting of trees, land reclamation, changes in land use, livestock grazing and the capture of wild animals.

Sources: Scott, 1989; Woo, 1990; *in litt.*, 1991

Title : Environmental Protection Law
Basic Law for National Environmental Policy

Date: December 1981 Environmental Protection Law, repealed in 1990, provisions now included in the Basic Law for National Environmental Policy of 1 August 1990

Brief description: Provides for the establishment of natural ecological system preservation areas within natural environment protection regions and also for the establishment of protected areas for specially designated wildlife/plants.

Administrative authority: Ministry of the Environment (*Whankyongcheo*) (formerly Environment Administration)

Designations:

Jayeonsaengtaegeobojonjigu (Natural ecological systems preservation area) Areas within a national environment protection region which require further special protection

Hunting is not permitted.

Protected area for specially designated wildlife/plants

Collection or damage to wild plants is strictly prohibited and hunting is forbidden.

Sources: Scott, 1989; Woo, 1990

Title : Law Concerning the Protection of Wildlife and Game

Date: 30 March 1967, last amended 13 January 1990

Brief description: Concerned with the preservation of certain wildlife species, particularly birds and mammals, and with the regulation of hunting and game

Administrative authority: Forestry Administration (*Sanrimcheong*) in the Ministry of Agriculture, Forestry and Fisheries (*Nongrimsoosambu*), Provincial authorities/National Forest Stations

Designations:

Josoobohogu (Wildlife sanctuary) Construction work and the cutting of trees is restricted.

Game reserve Controlled hunting is permitted, although often only on a rotational basis around a seven-year period. Hunting fees should be paid by people hunting in these areas. Wildlife protection officials should be employed to cover these sites.

Special wildlife sanctuary Distinguished from others because they contain rare or important species. Wildlife protection officials should be employed to cover these sites.

Source: Woo, 1990

Title : Forest Law

Date: 27 December 1961 (replacing the Forest Law of 1908); entirely amended on 4 January 1980; last amended 13 January 1990

Brief description: Provides for the classification and management of all forest areas

Administrative authority: Forestry Administration (Forest Service) (*Sanrimcheong*), Ministry of Agriculture, Forestry and Fisheries (*Nongrimsoosanbu*)

Designations:

Boanrim (Protection forest) Designated by either by the provincial governor or by the director of regional national forest stations

Selected for one or more of the following purposes: the prevention of soil erosion, landslides or the drifting of sand dunes; the protection of watersheds and river catchment areas; the protection of fish habitats (coastal forests) and maintenance of areas because of their value to human health, or because of their aesthetic value

The cutting of trees, grazing of livestock and the collection of forest products is not permitted unless approval is obtained from the provincial governor or the director of regional national forest stations.

Cheonyeonbohorim (Nature protected forest) Areas of forest of more than 1ha, protected because of their value as sites of virgin forest, alpine forest or forests containing "rare, precious or useful" plant species

Also included in this category are trees, protected for their aesthetic, historic or religious value and experimental forests.

Chaejongrim (Seed production stand) Designated by the mayor of a city, province governor and/or the director of national forest offices, with the approval of the Forestry Administration

Used for the collection of tree seeds (Woo, 1990)

Natural recreation forest Can be designated by the Director General of the Forestry Administration

Primary purpose is for recreation, education and to bring in income for the forest owners who may collect an entrance fee (Woo, 1990)

SUMMARY OF PROTECTED AREAS

Map[†] ref.	*National/international designations* Name of area	IUCN management category	Area (ha)	Year notified
	National Parks			
1	Ch'iak Mt	V	18,209	1984
2	Chiri Mt	V	44,045	1967
3	Chuwang Mt	V	10,558	1976
4	Halla Mt	V	14,900	1970
5	Kaya Mt	V	79,235	1972
6	Kyeryong Mt	V	6,112	1968
7	Kyongju	V	13,816	1968
8	Naejang Mt	V	7,603	1972
9	Odae Mt	V	29,850	1975
10	Puk'an Mt	V	7,845	1983
11	Pyonsan Bando Peninsula	V	15,700	1988
12	Sobaeksan	V	32,050	1987
13	Songni Mt	V	28,340	1970
14	Sorak Mt	V	37,300	1970
15	Togyu Mt	V	21,900	1975
16	Wolch'ulsan	V	4,188	1988
17	Worak Mt	V	28,450	1984
	Marine National Parks			
18	Hallyo-Haesang Sea	V	47,862	1968
19	T'ae-an-hae-an Seashore	V	32,899	1978
20	Tadohae-Haesang Sea	V	234,491	1981
	Nature Reserves			
21	Daeamsan-Daewoosan	I	3,070	1973
22	Hallasan	I	8,300	1966
23	Hyangrobong-Kunbongsan	I	8,330	1973
24	Soraksan	I	16,340	1965
	Natural Ecological System Preservation Areas			
25	Chirisan Virgin Forest Original State	I	2,020	1989
26	Nakdonggang River Mouth Migratory Bird	I	3,420	1989
	Biosphere Reserve Mount Sorak	IX	37,430	1982

[†]Locations of most protected areas are shown on the accompanying map.

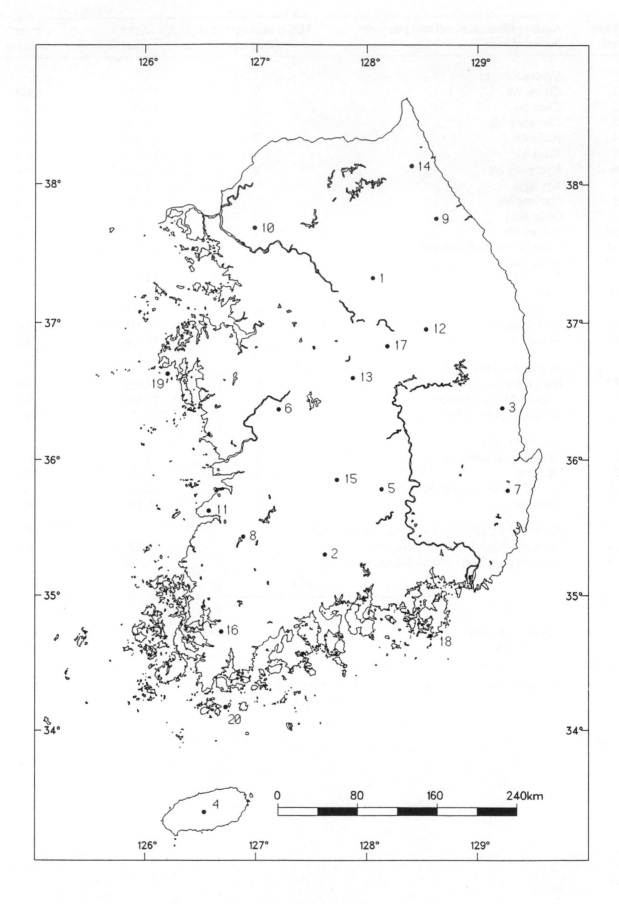

Protected Areas of South Korea

MONGOLIAN PEOPLE'S REPUBLIC

Area 1,566,500 sq. km

Population 2,190,000 (1990)
Natural increase: 2.67% per annum

Economic Indicators
NMP: US$ 803 per capita (1987)
GNP: no information

Policy and Legislation   Under the present constitution, which dates from 1960, all land, forests and water, and the wealth they contain, are the property of the state and hence of the people: this nationalisation of the land took place at the start of the people's revolution in 1921. State ownership of the land legally consolidates the right of the Mongolian people to use the pasture lands and other natural wealth (Jigj, 1986).

The tradition for protecting nature goes back to the 13th century when many forested hills were protected as holy areas. Kublai Khan, grandson of Ghengis Khan, extended protection to forests in general and also decreed a law in the 13th century forbidding hunting of any game during the summer months, under penalty of death. The introduction of buddhism from Tibet in the 16th and 17th centuries provided further protection for animals and for the establishment of the first protected areas in the late 1700s (Nowak, 1970).

The Decree on the Rational Utilization of Natural Resources and the Protection of the Natural Environment was passed by the Great Horal (Parliament) on 30 June 1972. This law requires every person to act for the good of nature and for the protection of natural resources (Borisov *et al.*, 1985; Kosmider, 1985).

Legislative texts concerning environmental issues are reviewed by the Great Horal and the Main Forest Administration before being issued by the Council of Ministers. In the early 1970s a number of laws were introduced including a second Law on Land Use (1971); a Law on Hunting (6 January, 1972) (originally drawn-up in 1934, revised in 1944, issued in 1962); a Law on Water and a Law on Forests (1974) (Jigj, 1982). In 1972, the 6th Session of the Great Horal of the 7th Convocation discussed the rational use of natural resources and environmental protection with special reference to the protection and use of forests, hunting and trapping, which resulted in the creation of a Commission on Nature Conservation with branches at all levels of the administration. Together with the new Law concerning Reserve Protection, this resulted in the declaration of new nature preserves and the preparation of a Red Data Book (Jigj, 1982, 1986).

The first reserve, Bogdo-ula, was declared in 1778; others were declared by separate decrees in 1957 (two sites), 1965 (eight sites), 1977 (one site) and 1978 (one site). One national park, Great Gobi National Park, was established in 1975 and given legal status under Decree No. 283 of 1976; a second national park was created in the southern part of Ar Toul Game Reserve in 1984 and two hunting reserves in 1983 and 1984. It appears that there is no overall enabling legislation covering these different categories of protected area and that sites are designated individually, with specific regulations drawn up for each site.

The 1972 Law on Hunting strictly controls hunting, this being the responsibility of the Hunting Section of the Main Forest Administration which administers the open season and the hunting licence scheme. Licences are organised on aimag (province) residence basis. This Law also administers wood felling and collection of medicinal herbs and other plants in nature reserves. There are suggestions that restrictions be imposed on the numbers of shepherds and livestock using certain hunting preserves, but that controlled and limited hunting (of named species) takes place.

There is a further law concerning the designation of game management areas. This law specifies ten sites and also suggests that every aimag should have a game management area near its town to cater for urban hunters. These are sites where the conservation and utilisation of game is the primary land use (see Annex) (Anon., n.d. a).

The main law concerning forestry is the Law on the Protection and Utilisation of Forests of March 1957. Under this Law, all forests are the property of the state, under the constitution, and cannot become private property. Other laws include the Law on the Settlement of Forest Use (Law No. 112) of March 1964 and the Law on Certain Measures Preventing Forest and Steppe Fire of April, 1967 (Parewicz *et al.*, 1972).

International Activities   Mongolia became a party to the Convention concerning the Protection of the World Cultural and Natural Heritage (World Heritage Convention), accepting the terms of the Convention on 2 February 1990, but no sites have been declared. One site has been accepted as a biosphere reserve under the Unesco Man and the Biosphere Programme. Mongolia is not party to the Convention on Wetlands of International Importance especially as a Waterfowl Habitat (Ramsar Convention).

There has been some international involvement in the preliminary work leading to the establishment of protected areas in Mongolia. One important group has been the International Foundation for the Conservation of Game, and there have been a number of Polish expeditions in particular, working with Mongolian counterparts, that have contributed significantly to the establishment of protected areas.

Administration and Management Responsibility for protected areas used to lie with the Academy of Sciences

(IUCN, 1971). Several organisations concerned with conservation issues were established by the government in 1972: a Wildlife Management Department was established within the Ministry of Forestry and Forest Industries; the Department for Nature Protection was brought into being within the Council of Ministers State Committee of Science and Technology by the Council of Ministers; and a Wildlife Management Section was initiated in the Forest Research Institute (Anon., n.d. b). At the local level, legislation is supervised by the aimag (province) and somon (district) authorities.

Currently, responsibility for protected areas lies with the Department for Nature Protection (Borisov *et al.*, 1985).

The scientific and educational roles within protected areas and elsewhere are the responsibility of the Mongolian Society for Nature Conservation and Environmental Protection, set up in 1975. Although it has been described as a voluntary body, the Society has close links with the government. It has some 320,000 members, and provides all-round assistance in promoting the observance and authorisation of the statutory texts concerning the protection, renewal and rational use of soils, water, mineral resources, forests, flora and fauna protection and the use of meadows and grazing lands. For this purpose, it is divided into a number of commissions including the Commission for Nature Reserves, the Commission on Natural Monuments and the Commission on Landscape Protection, which were established by the Presidium of the Great Horal, and have sections in the peoples' deputies at aimag, somon, and city levels. The Society plays an important role in public education and also in initiating public activities relating to nature conservation issues. It has also initiated the creation of a number of protected areas (Jigj, 1986; Kosmider, 1985).

Increasing environmental problems and increasing public awareness of these, coupled with the necessity to coordinate at national level the measures aimed at protecting nature and rationally utilising its resources, led to the creation of the Ministry of Nature and Environment Protection in the late 1980s. This body is involved in writing proposals to improve existing legislation and formulate new legislation on the protection of nature and the environment. It is also responsible for soil reclamation projects and reafforestation projects which are starting up in some areas (Mavlet, 1988). The Ministry is also involved in the support of Nature and Environment Protection Months, month-long campaigns which take place twice a year to raise environmental awareness and support environmental activities such as afforestation projects (Bayer, 1988).

Forestry activities are under the control of the Department of Forestry and Forest Industries. In 1962 this Department was organised into four divisions: forestry, forest industry, wildlife and economics. Within the Forestry Division, administration of forest areas is divided into eleven inspectorates and five ranges. The inspectorates correspond to those aimags in which the major forests occur, while the ranges correspond to those aimags where there is limited forest activity. In 1972, a typical inspectorate staff consisted of three-five fully trained staff (Director, manager/engineer and technicians) and about forty rangers and permanent workers; range staff would typically consist of one technician and eight rangers (Parewicz *et al.*, 1972).

Financial aid is being granted to the Mongolian Hunters Association by the International Foundation for the Conservation of Game, to study the development of optimal uses of wildlife in reserves. In addition, technical help and scientific equipment will be provided.

Systems Reviews The People's Republic of Mongolia is a land-locked country, which borders the USSR to the north and the People's Republic of China to the south. It makes up the majority of the total area of Mongolia, an east-central Asian region divided in two by the Gobi Desert. Inner Mongolia, to the south of the Gobi Desert, lies within the People's Republic of China. Physically, the country is a high altitude plateau, the lowest points being some 500m above sea level, almost all of the country lying above 1,000m. There are a number of mountain ranges, notably in the north and west of the country. The Altai Massif occupies the western borders; as this range runs south-eastwards, it fades into a series of isolated fault blocks known as the Gobi Altai. The highest peak lies in this range and is some 4,231m above sea level. The centre of the country is occupied by the Khanggai (Hangayn) Mountains, while the Khentai (Hentiyn) Mountains run from just east of the centre up to the USSR border. Most of the southern borders run through the Gobi Desert, a large desert of relatively low relief.

The country is divisible into four main phytogeographic zones: mountain forests/taiga (which cover some 7% of the surface area) are found in the high altitude regions in the north of the country and are dominated by larch, cedar, pine and birch; there are also areas of natural forest on the edges of the Gobi Desert found along river banks, dominated by poplars and tamarisk. Steppe (51% of the surface area) occupies a broad swathe across the country from east to west; arid steppe/semi-desert (27% of the surface area) lies in a line to the south of this on the borders of the Gobi Desert, and desert (15% of the surface area) on the southern border with China. The steppe category may be subdivided into mountain steppes with sparse forests (25% of the total surface area) and grassy steppes (26%) (Nowak, 1970). Forest cover of all types totals 15 million ha or 10% of the country.

Wetlands are an important habitat type – standing water covers some 15,000 sq. km and there are some 50,000km of rivers. These wetlands are also extremely diverse, ranging from cold, deep ultra-oligotrophic lakes to temporary saline lakes. Many of the rivers have extensive floodplains (Scott, 1986).

Mongolia has a very low population density and this is unlikely to change very rapidly despite the high population growth rates, as one-third of the population lives in the capital Ulan Bator. Traditionally, a large proportion of the economy was centred around livestock herding by the large numbers of nomadic people. Government efforts to transform the economy have led to the expansion of settled agriculture, and to the development of industry. In response to the dramatic declines in wildlife during the 1930s and 1940s, conservation measures were enacted in the 1950s and 1960s (Hibbert, 1964) and, according to the resolution of the 17th Congress of the Mongolian Peoples Republic Party and the national economic and cultural development guidelines for 1976 to 1980, the five-year and annual plans include sections on conservation and environmental protection. The five-year plan section contained 140 projects and had a budget of 700 million tugriks. Projects carried out in the five-year plan to 1980 included pollution control, forest regeneration, forest belt planting, soil conservation and wild animal breeding. There are also longer-term schemes for environmental protection and scientific programmes to 1990 and to 2000.

Since 1975, two months, called Nature and Environment Protection Months, have been held annually (starting on 15 April and on 15 September for one month). These are supported by the Ministry of Nature and Environment Protection and are devoted to nature conservation related activities on any number of themes, such as protection of steppes and forests against fire, water conservation and so on. In 1980 a nature palace, which houses a museum and nature exhibitions, was opened in Ulan Bator.

Threats to ecosystems are generally limited in extent and severity. A number should be mentioned, however. Mining, especially open cast, is on the increase and is causing soil erosion and pollution in some areas. There is little or no environmental control. Open cast phosphorite mining 100km from Lake Huvsgul (Khovsgol) threatens to cause eutrophication of the delicate ecosystems of this important oligotrophic lake which is an integral part of the Lake Baikal (USSR) basin (Anon., 1988; Mavlet, 1988). Over-utilisation of water resources is causing a problem in some urban and industrial areas and many rivers are apparently growing shallow (Mavlet, 1988). Deforestation is also taking place. Some 14,000ha of forest are cleared every year, while only 5,000ha are replanted (Mavlet, 1988).

Other Relevant Information The possibility of establishing organised hunting for tourists has been discussed by various bodies and could become an important source of hard currency in the future. It has been reported that foreign currency revenues from tourist hunting parties in reserves could be as much as US$ 500,000 annually (Anon., 1977, 1982).

Addresses

Department for Nature Protection, Director, State Committee for Science and Technology, Council of Ministers, Government House, ULAANBAATAR

Mongolian Association for the Conservation of Nature and Environment, President, Sambuugiin gud 17, ULAANBAATAR 11 (Tel: 26330)

References

Anon. (n.d. a). Mongolian People's Republic Protected Game Management Areas. English translation of the law concerning the establishment of these areas (incomplete).

Anon. (n.d. b). Establishment of the "Mongolian-Altai Wildlife Reserve". Draft project outline. Unpublished. 9 pp.

Anon. (1977). Forestry development and wildlife management. FAO report. Unpublished. 5 pp.

Anon. (1982). Hunting, conservation and development in Mongolia. International Foundation for the Conservation of Game. *Bulletin* 10/11: 2-3.

Anon. (1988). Journalists hold "ecological" round table. *News from Mongolia* 13(61): 1-7.

Alexandrowicz, Z. (1984). Nowe dane o ochronie przyrody w Mongolii. *Chronmy Przyrode Ojczysta* 40 z.1.: 55-58.

Bayer, R. (1988). Nature protection month. *News from Mongolia* 8: 16.1 April.

Borisov, V.A., Belousova, L.S., and Vinokurov, A.A. (1985). *Okhranyaemye prirodnye territorii Mira*. Moskva Agropromizdat.

Brzezniak, E. (1977). Obszary chronione w Mongolskiej Republice Ludowej. *Chronmy Przyrode Ojczysta* 33 z.1.: 79-82.

Hibbert, R.A. (1967). Wildlife protection in Mongolia. *Oryx* 9(3): 196-210.

IUCN (1971). *United Nations List of National Parks and Equivalent Reserves*. 2nd Ed. Hayez, Brussels.

Jigj, S. (1982). Ochrana prirody w Mongolskicj Narodnej Riespublice. In: *Komitet po nauczno-techniczeskomu sotrudniczestwu, wklad stran-czlenow CEW w ochranu okruzajuszczej sredy*. Moscow. (Unseen)

Jigj, S. (1986). *Report of activity of environmental protection of nature and use of natural resources in the MPR*. Unpublished.

Kosmider, J. (1985). Mongolskie Towaszystwo Ochrony Przyrody. *Przyroda Polska* 7/8. 46 pp.

Mavlet, U. (1988). Ensuring harmony between interests of man and nature. *News from Mongolia* 6(54): 1-3.

Nowak, E. (1970). The waterfowl of Mongolia. *Wildfowl* 21: 61-68.

Parewicz, R., Rudzki, K., Szaniawski, A. and Walther, S. (1972). Report to the Government of Mongolia on Forestry, Forest Industries and Wildlife Survey. United Nations Development Programme, No. TA 3093. FAO, Rome.

Scott, D.A. (Ed.) (1986). *A directory of Asian wetlands*. IUCN, Gland, Switzerland and Cambridge, UK. Pp. 1-30.

ANNEX
Definitions of protected area designations, as legislated, together with authorities responsible for their administration

Title : Law concerning the designation of game management areas (no information concerning the exact title)

Date: No information

Brief description: Provides for the designation of game management areas and contains specific regulations for ten sites

Administrative authority: Ministry of Forestry and Forest Industries

Designations:

Game management area Areas where game conservation and utilisation shall be the primary land use. Other economic uses, such as the grazing of domestic stock and forestry, may be permissible provided they are compatible with the primary objectives. The need for the creation of game management areas arises from increasing pressure on the land and increasing competition between domestic animals and economically valuable game species; further reasons for establishment are to guarantee the integrity of some sites where human populations are presently low or absent and to allow scientific management programmes to be set up for each area to establish maximum limits for game hunting and to set permissible limits for other economic activities. It is deemed important that local populations should profit from game management areas as they might from any other form of land use. "Reputable hunters" from local hunting associations may be given the title of "honourary warden" of specific sites and be made responsible for the enforcement of regulations concerning the owning and carrying of firearms and ammunition. Specific regulations are also given for some of the ten sites specifically mentioned in this Law. Statistics will be kept for each area concerning the amounts of game taken and, where applicable, the numbers of domestic stock using the site. The carrying of guns, ammunition and traps in these areas is restricted to registered persons under special licence. There is a restriction on the number of licences issued. Enforcement of these regulations is the responsibility of the local hunters association and of the Ministry of Forestry and Forest Industries and its agents.

Source: Anon., n.d. a

SUMMARY OF PROTECTED AREAS

Map[†] ref.	National/international designations Name of area	IUCN management category	Area (ha)	Year notified
	National Parks			
1	Ar-Toul	II	93,560	1984
2	Dzungarian	II	550,000	
3	Great Gobi Desert	II	5,300,000	1975
	Reserves			
4	Batkhan	I	2,000	1957
5	Bogdkhan	I	4,080	1978
6	Bogdo-ula	I	54,100	1778
7	Bulgan-gol	I	2,700	1965
8	Bulgan-ula	I	4,800	1965
9	Khasagt-Khayrkhan	I	33,600	1965
10	Khorgo	I	20,000	1965
11	Lkhachinvandan-ula	I	75,000	1965
12	Nagalkhan	I	2,000	1957
13	Tulga-togo-Zhallavch-ula	I	3,000	1965
14	Uran-ula	I	3,000	1965
15	Yolyn-am	I	20,000	1965
	Hunting Reserves			
16	Ar-Toul	VI	799,360	1984
17	Khuhtsyrh	VI	90,900	1977
	Biosphere Reserve			
	Great Gobi	IX	5,300,000	1990

[†]Locations of most protected areas are shown on the accompanying map.

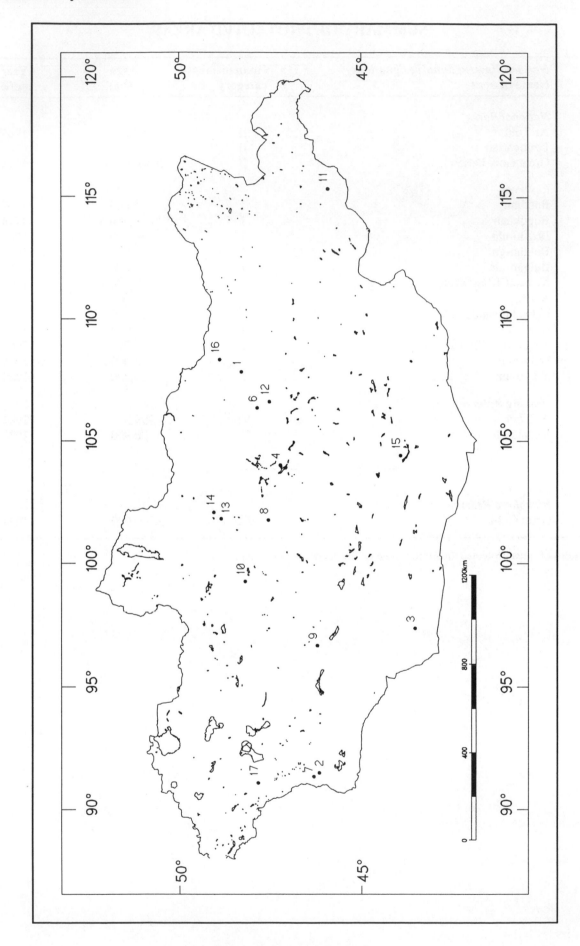

Protected Areas of Mongolia

PORTUGAL – MACAO

Area 6.05 sq. km

Population 440,000 (1990)
Natural increase: 1.3% per annum

Economic Indicators
GDP: no information
GNP: no information

Policy and Legislation By agreement with China in 1974, Macao is a Chinese territory under Portuguese administration based on the original Sino-Portuguese treaty of 1 December 1887. Agreements with the People's Republic of China between 1986-87 will lead to China taking over administrative authority in 1999 (Hunter, 1991).

The statute published on 17 February 1976 defined the territory as "*Pessoa colectiva*" (collective entity), with internal legislative authority which is subject to Portuguese Constitutional laws. The Portuguese Constitution, dating from 1976, gives a high profile to environmental matters. Article 9 states that nature and environmental defence, and the preservation of natural resources, are some of the main tasks of the state. Article 66 states that everyone has the right to an ecologically well-balanced environment, and the duty to defend it (Jonaz de Melo, 1987).

As far as is known there is no specific protected area legislation for Macao.

International Activities Foreign relations are dealt with by Portugal. Portugal ratified the Convention concerning the Protection of the World Cultural and Natural Heritage (World Heritage Convention) on 30 September 1980. No natural sites have been inscribed in Macao. The Convention on Wetlands of International Importance especially as Waterfowl Habitat (Ramsar Convention) was ratified on 24 November 1980 but no sites have been inscribed in Macao. Although Portugal is bound by the terms of the European Community Wild Birds Directive, Macao is not included.

The 1988 initiative to extend the UNEP Regional Seas Programme to cover the north-west Pacific would encompass the territory of Macao. Such a programme, if adopted would cover five countries: the USSR, China, Japan, North Korea and South Korea, and it is not known if Macao or Portugal would be represented.

Administration and Management Until 1975, the government departments of Agriculture, Forestry and Fisheries were responsible for nature conservation in their respective sectors and introduced legislation on hunting, forestry and fisheries in Portugal. Conservation matters in Portugal ultimately fall under the control of the Ministry of Planning and Land Management

(*Ministério do Plano e Administraçao do Territorio* (MPAT) (for further information read entry on Portugal).

The Forestry and Agricultural Service of Macao (*Sevicos Florestais e Agricolas de Macau*) undertakes forestry administration and management and would be the main body with responsibility for natural resources and nature conservation matters (Noguera, 1984).

Systems Reviews Lying at the mouth of the Canton River, and consisting of land and islands in the South China Sea, Macao is largely a rocky peninsula linked to the mainland of China by a narrow sandy isthmus. The area lies within the subtropical evergreen and monsoon forest zone, but natural forest is almost non-existent, having been greatly modified by fuelwood collecting and timber cutting. Although the peninsula consists largely of urban development and maritime construction, there still remain areas of secondary scrub and grassland. Limited figures for size of native flora and number of plant endemics are available, although work undertaken by the Forestry and Agricultural Service has identified over 380 plant species (Noguera, 1984). One globally threatened plant species has been recorded (Davis *et al.*, 1986).

According to available information there are no protected areas and no areas proposed for future establishment.

Some environmental problems have included coastal land reclamation on the east of Macao (Stamp, 1957).

Other Relevant Information Tourism is an important element of the Macao economy. In 1987 there were 5.1 million visitors to the territory (Hunter, 1991). The level of ecotourism is unknown.

Addresses

Forestry and Agricultural Service of Macao (*Sevicos Florestais e Agricolas de Macau*), Macao

General Directorate of Forestry, Ministry of Agriculture, Fisheries and Food, Av. Joas Crisostomo 28, 1000 LISBON, Portugal

References

Davis, S.D., Droop, S.J.M., Gregerson, P., Henson, L., Leon, C.J., Lamlein Villa-Lobos, J., Synge, H., and Zantovska, J. (1986). *Plants in danger: what do we know?* IUCN, Gland, Switzerland, and Cambridge, UK. 461 pp.

Edmonds, R.L. (1989). *Macau*. Oxford and Santa Barbara.

Hunter, B. (Ed.) (1991). The Statesman's Year Book 1991-92. The Macmillan Press Ltd, London and Basingstoke, UK.

Joanez de Melo, J. (1987). *European Environmental Yearbook, 1987.* DocTer International UK, London.

Noguera, A.C. de Sa (1984). *Catalogo descritivo de 380 especies tanicas da Colonia de Macau.* Sevicos Florestais e Agricolas de Macau, Julho. 181 pp.

Stamp, L.D. (1957). *Asia, a regional and economic geography.* Methuen, London.

UNITED KINGDOM – HONG KONG

Area 1,090.29 sq. km (Government of Hong Kong, 1989)

Population 5.8 million (1989)
Natural increase: 0.8% per annum

Economic Indicators
GDP: US$ 9,642 per capita (1988)
GNP: US$ 8,260 per capita (1987)

Policy and Legislation Hong Kong Island and the southern tip of Kowloon Peninsula were ceded by China to Britain after the Treaty of Nanking in 1842 and the Convention of Peking in 1860. Northern Kowloon was leased to Britain for 99 years by China in 1898 under the second Convention of Peking on 9 June 1898. Hong Kong continues to be under British administration, but following the Joint Declaration of 19 December 1984 sovereignty of the entire colony will be transferred to China from 1 July 1997. Hong Kong will then be established as a Special Administrative Region of China, retaining its own legislature and judiciary, as embodied in the Basic Law of 1990, for a further 50 years (Hunter, 1991).

External affairs are dealt with by the United Kingdom. Domestic administration is in the hands of a Governor, aided by an Executive Council and Legislative Council.

Alarmed by the rapid rate of urbanisation threatening to destroy the countryside in the 1960s, it was proposed that forestry policies be revised to accommodate the recreational demands of an increasingly urban population (Daley, 1965). The concept of establishing a system of parks zoned for varying intensities of recreational use, as outlined in several reports (Daley 1964a, 1964b; Phillips and Marshall, 1965; Scott, 1964), was strongly endorsed in a review of the conservation of the countryside undertaken for the Department of Agriculture and Fisheries by IUCN (Talbot and Talbot, 1965). The government was further stimulated into action by a report on the civil disturbances of 1965-1966 pressing, *inter alia*, for recreational outlets for the young (Hong Kong Government, 1967). Following the establishment of a Provisional Council for the Use and Conservation of the Countryside in 1967, a number of recreational (country parks) and conservation (nature reserves) areas were proposed (Wholey, 1968). A pilot country park scheme was initiated in the Shing Mun Reservoir area in 1971 and, by June 1972, the first five-year country park development programme was approved.

The Country Parks Ordinance was enacted in 1976 to provide a legal framework for the designation, development and management of country parks and special areas, in order to conserve and, where appropriate, open up the countryside for the greater enjoyment of the population. Whereas country parks may be developed for recreational purposes, public access to special areas is largely restricted and recreational facilities are not provided because of their high conservation value, be it geological, floral, faunal or cultural (see Annex). An exception is Tai Po Kau Special Area, where access for study and appropriate recreational activities is permitted. Provisions within the Country Parks Ordinance do not specifically extend to the sea bed. Thus, country parks and special areas with a coastline do not afford protection to marine elements within their boundaries (UNEP/IUCN, 1988).

Under the Wild Animals Protection Ordinance, 1976, access to an area specified in the Sixth Schedule may be restricted for a defined period, as specified in the Schedule (see Annex). Mai Po Marshes and Fung Shui Wood behind the village of Yim Tso Ha are currently listed in the Sixth Schedule. The Governor may amend the Schedule by order published in the *Gazette*. Amendments may include changes to existing areas or the addition of new areas.

The concept of sites of special scientific interest (SSSIs) (see Annex) was first adopted in 1973 by the Advisory Committee for Recreational Development and Nature Conservation, since when the Hong Kong government has established a register of sites. Although listing of an area does not confer any legal protection, it does mean that its conservation value has to be considered in the government planning process. The Country Parks Authority is responsible for SSSIs and promoting their importance within all government departments likely to be involved in developments that may threaten their existence (Thrower, 1984). Despite such provisions, a number of developments have taken place, and some sites have been lost or damaged (Scott, 1989).

Present conservation policy is, *inter alia*, to conserve the countryside by the effective protection and management of its landscape, vegetation and wildlife for the benefit of present and future generations. Principal objectives with respect to country parks are: to manage this estate on a multiple-use basis for water conservation and compatible types of recreation; to protect the vegetation against fire; to control development within country parks; to keep country parks clean and tidy; and to care for the vegetation as a natural heritage by promoting better understanding of the countryside and its value as a resource for recreational, educational and scientific purposes (Lee, 1990).

Other relevant legislation includes the Forests and Countryside Ordinance, 1937, which provides for the general protection and management of vegetation and for special protection of certain native plant species. It also provides for the establishment of prohibited areas in order to protect afforestation operations (see Annex). This Ordinance is due to be revised in the near future. Although activities in coastal waters may be regulated by a variety of ordinances, there are no legal provisions for the protection of coastal marine habitats (UNEP/IUCN 1988).

International Activities The United Kingdom extended its ratification of the Convention on Wetlands of International Importance especially as Waterfowl Habitat (Ramsar Convention) to Hong Kong on 10 September 1979. Similarly, the United Kingdom ratification of the Convention concerning the Protection of the World Cultural and Natural Heritage (World Heritage Convention) applies to Hong Kong. No sites have been inscribed under either convention, but it has been recommended that Mai Po/Inner Deep Bay be designated as wetlands of international importance under the Ramsar Convention (Anon., 1989; Scott, 1989).

In March 1988 Japan and the Republic of Korea called upon UNEP to extend its Regional Seas programme to cover the north-west Pacific, which would encompass all the countries of the region and Hong Kong (Anon., 1989).

Administration and Management The Conservation and Country Parks Branch of the Department of Agriculture and Fisheries is responsible for protecting and, where appropriate, managing woodlands and vegetation cover on hillsides, the latter contributing significantly to the effective maintenance of water catchment areas. Planning for multiple land use is promoted and resources are managed to provide sustainable benefits. Services include protecting and, where necessary, restoring the countryside, with continual surveillance of floral and faunal habitats, especially those designated as SSSIs (Lee, 1990).

Within the Conservation and Country Parks Branch, headed by an Assistant Director, there are three divisions: Conservation, Country Parks and Countryside Development. Each division is headed by a senior officer. In March 1988, the total number of staff within the Branch was 1,276, distributed as follows: Conservation Division 80; Country Parks Division 1,179; and Countryside Development Division 15. While the Conservation Division is responsible for the conservation of flora and fauna, the Country Parks Division is responsible for the protection, development and management of the country parks estate. The Countryside Development Division deals with planning, facility design and control of development in country parks, and also with the management of certain newly established woodlands around new towns. The three divisions work closely together and are extending their operations to selected lands outside the country parks system.

Under the Country Parks Ordinance, the Country Parks Authority is headed by the Director of Agriculture and Fisheries, who is responsible for the protection, management and development of country parks and special areas. A Country Parks Board was appointed in August 1976 to advise the Authority on policy and programmes and to consider objections raised against the establishment of protected areas. The three main objectives of the Country Park Development Plan are to

provide for conservation, recreation and education. Park management is based on a system of zonation providing for three categories of land use, namely: recreation zones, which are located in accessible areas subject to heavy visitor use; wilderness zones, which provide the scenic background to recreation zones; and conservation zones, which are SSSIs and to which access by visitors is not encouraged. Now that most potential sites have been established, the emphasis of the country park programme has shifted to maintaining and upgrading facilities, as well as encouraging countryside interpretation through provision of visitor centres, information boards and nature trails. Other tasks include provision of litter collection and fire-fighting services throughout the country park estate (Jim, 1987; Lee, 1990; Thrower, 1984).

The Country Parks Development Programme has been financed in two stages. Initially funds were provided for the establishment of a protected area system, an operation lasting from 1976 to 1981. Subsequent expenditure follows standard government procedures and is based on five-year budgets, with detailed estimates of approved projects each year (Thrower, 1984). The current programme (1988/1989-1992/1993) is directed towards meeting the expected growth in demand for facilities and services in various country parks (Lee, 1990).

The most significant of the-non governmental conservation bodies is the World Wildlife Fund for Nature-Hong Kong, which was incorporated as a registered charity in 1981 (Anon., 1990). Its main activity is the management and development of the Mai Po marshes as a *de facto* nature reserve with educational facilities. The Conservancy Association is an older society which has been involved in environmental education (Oldfield, 1987). Both the Hong Kong Bird Watching Society and Hong Kong Natural History Society are non-governmental organisations actively involved in conservation. With the transfer of administration to China in 1997, WWF-Hong Kong is attempting to strengthen long-term non-governmental organisation involvement in conservation in the territory and to link shared management of wetland sites straddling the border between China and Hong Kong into current or near future transboundary proposals (UK Forum, *in litt.*, 1991).

Systems Reviews Lying on the south-east coast of China, Hong Kong comprises an area of mainland (Kowloon and the New Territories) and 235 offshore islands, of which Hong Kong and Lantau are the main ones. Much of Hong Kong is hilly with deeply incised submerged coastal features. Approximately 80% of the territory is over 100m above sea level. Urban development (16.5% of the land area) and agriculture (9% of the area) are concentrated in the lowlands and, in coastal regions, land has been extensively reclaimed to provide for development. Oak-laurel forest *Fagaceae-Lauraceae* covered Hong Kong up to 1,000 years ago, when there were few inhabitants apart from aboriginal coastal traders and scattered garrisons of the Tiangs. Yoa tribesmen are reported to have lived in the forests and probably practised shifting cultivation. Later, in the Sung dynasty, the descendants of the Han began to settle in the valleys and were followed by the Hakka, or guest people, also predominantly farmers. Vast areas of forest were burnt to provide agricultural land and pasture, and to discourage the more dangerous wildlife (Marshall and Phillips, 1965). Remnants of the original forest cover are now restricted to ravines (Ismail, 1987). Native pines *Pinus massoniana* and exotics, notably Australian Brisbane box *Tristania conferta*, have been widely planted in Hong Kong, largely to protect the catchment areas of the many reservoirs constructed to meet the territory's water requirements. Many plantations were established in the late 1940s and early 1950s, following the devastation of much of the vegetation during the Japanese occupation in World War II (Thrower, 1984).

Reclamation of marshlands began with early human settlers converting areas for paddi, salt pans and, more recently *gei wais*. By 1985, about 3,250ha of land had been reclaimed. The spread of paddi farming has increased the amount of freshwater habitat even if reclamation of coastal marshes reduced intertidal habitat diversity. By 1986, only one sq. km of coastal brackish swamp and mangrove remained, both mostly around Deep Bay. The largest remaining wetland is Mai Po marshes (325ha) and the associated tidal flats of Deep Bay. Further details of the wetlands are given in Scott (1989).

Offshore, there are no true reefs, but coral communities are found growing on any hard substrate along the narrow coastal fringe on the eastern and south-eastern hard shores and in oceanic waters. In suitably sheltered bays, with clear water, relatively rich communities with 100% cover are present (UNEP/IUCN, 1988).

The development of the nature conservation programme in Hong Kong following the enactment of the Country Park Ordinance, led to an accelerated crash programme resulting in the establishment of a comprehensive network of 19 country parks, covering 37.5% (40,833ha) of the territory, over a three-year period (1977-1981) (Anon., 1990). Some 14 special areas have also been established: all but three (Tai Po Kau, Tsiu Hang and Tung Lung Fort) lie within country parks (Jim, 1987; Thrower, 1984). In addition, over 47 SSSIs have been designated to ensure that their conservation importance is taken into account by government departments concerned with developments in or near such sites (Lee, 1990). Access to two of these SSSIs (Mai Po and Yim Tso Ha) is restricted under the Wild Animals Protection Ordinance. Forests (mixed broad-leaf woodland) presently cover about 22,112ha, or 21% of the total land area, of which 13,210ha lie in country parks and the rest outside (Hong Kong Government, 1989). No coastal or marine reserves have yet been established, but the entire coastline of the north and eastern regions has been recommended for marine reserve status (UNEP/IUCN, 1988). Mai Poi Marshes, located on the southern shore of deep bay, is the most important area in Hong Kong for

international wildlife conservation (Anon., 1989). Hoi Ha Wan, presently an SSSI, is being recommended for marine reserve status and two other sites (Cape D'Aguilar and Mirs Bay) are under consideration as potential marine reserves (Anon., 1990; WWF-Hong Kong, pers. comm., 1990).

Pressure from the dense population, construction and rapid economic growth threatens the territory's natural resources. Considerable industrial and residential expansion has taken place in the New Territories, until recent decades a rather isolated rural area. Such developments have been conceived largely as isolated urban schemes with little integrated regional planning. The importance of developing a symbiotic relationship between urban and rural areas has hardly entered into official planning and policy-making (Dwyer, 1986). The very high population density and poor quality of the urban environment makes the requirements for countryside recreation imperative for physical and mental health. The country park programme has been successful in encouraging and satisfying this demand, but the ever-increasing visitor numbers are not being matched by a corresponding increase in the management resource base. Over the last decade the number of visitors to country parks has risen greatly. Concomitantly, the amount of litter collected annually has increased from 446 to 4,000 tonnes. The most popular sites are now heavily over-used, excessive trampling having decimated the grass cover (Jim, 1987b, 1987c). Fires damaged some 5,415ha in 1985/86. Over the past 16 years the number of trees killed by fire (5.42 million) has exceeded that planted (4.84 million). Besides affecting a more equitable spatial-temporal visitor distribution in future, low impact pursuits need to be encouraged to off-load some of the pressure on over-used areas. Drastic new management approaches are needed to contain the widespread damage from fire and litter (Jim, 1987a).

Other Relevant Information   Over the decade 1975/76-1985/86 the number of visitors to country parks has risen from 2.0 to 9.46 million per year, representing an increase from 0.45 to 1.76 visits per capita per year (Jim, 1987b, 1987c). In 1987/1988, country parks received a total of 8.8 million visitors. This is slightly less than for the previous year, possibly due to easier access to neighbouring areas (e.g. Macau and Shenzhen Special Economic Zone) following the introduction of the "Easy Travel Scheme". Visitor use is greatest (65% of the annual total) in the drier and cooler months from October to April, but it has been increasing in the summer in recent years. Weekends (Saturdays and Sundays) account for 57% of visitor use (Anon., 1990; Lee, 1990; Yim, 1989).

Addresses

Agriculture and Fisheries Department, Canton Road Government Offices, 393 Canton Road, 12th Floor, KOWLOON (Tel: 3 733 2136; FAX: 3 311 3731; Cable: AGFISH HONG KONG)

World Wide Fund for Nature-Hong Kong, GPO Box 12721, The French Mission, Battery Path, Central, HONG KONG (Tel: 5232316/ 5264473/5261011-6; FAX: 8452734; Tlx: 66711 WWFHK HX; Cable: PANDAFUND)

References

Anon. (1989). Mai Po Marshes A second future? *Forum News*, January. P. 2

Anon. (1990). Hong Kong, Special Issue. *Forum News*, September. 4 pp.

Daley, P.A. (1964a). National parks. A note prepared by Forestry Officer, Agriculture and Fisheries Department, Hong Kong. Unpublished report. 4 pp.

Daley, P.A. (1964b). The use of renewable resources in Hong Kong. Agriculture and Fisheries Department, Hong Kong. Unpublished report. 23 pp.

Daley, P.A. (1965a). Forestry and its place in natural resource conservation in Hong Kong – a recommendation for revised policy. Agriculture and Fisheries Department, Hong Kong. Unpublished report.

Dwyer, D.J. (1986) Land use and regional planning problems in the New Territories of Hong Kong. *The Geographical Journal* 152: 232-242.

Hong Kong Government (1967). *Kowloon disturbances. Report of the Commission of Enquiry*. Government Printer, Hong Kong.

Hong Kong Government (1989). *Geotecs Map 8 – vegetation*. Geotechnical Control Office, Civil Engineering Services Department.

Hunter, B. (Ed.) (1991). *The Statesman's Year Book 1991-92*. The Macmillan Press Ltd, London and Basingstoke, UK.

Ishmail, A. (1987). *Hong Kong 1987*. Government Printer, Hong Kong. 364 pp.

Jim, C.Y. (1987a). Country park usage and visitor impacts in Hong Kong. *Parks* 12(1): 3-8.

Jim, C.Y. (1987b). Camping impacts on vegetation and soil in a Hong Kong country park. *Applied Geography* 7: 317-332.

Jim, C.Y. (1987c). Trampling impacts of recreationists on picnic sites in a Hong Kong country park. *Environmental Conservation* 14: 117-127.

Lee, L.H-Y. (1990). Agriculture and Fisheries annual departmental report 1987-1988. Government Printer, Hong Kong. 64 pp.

Marshall, P.M. and Phillips, J.G. (1965). Plans for conserving the wildlife of Hong Kong. *Oryx* 8: 107-112.

Oldfield, S. (1987). *Fragments of Paradise. A guide for conservation action in the UK Dependent Territories*. Pisces Publications, Oxford. 192 pp.

Scott, P. (1964). Report on a brief visit to Hong Kong in October, 1964. Hong Kong University. Unpublished. 3 pp.

Scott, D.A. (Ed.) (1989). *A directory of Asian wetlands*. IUCN, Gland, Switzerland and Cambridge, UK. 1,181 pp.

Talbot, L.M. and Talbot, M.H. (1965). *Conservation of the Hong Kong countryside*. Government Printer, Hong Kong. 34 pp.

Thrower, S.L. (1984). *Hong Kong country parks*. Government Printer, Hong Kong. 216 pp.

UNEP/IUCN (1988). *Coral Reefs of the World. Volume 2: Indian Ocean, Red Sea and Gulf. UNEP Regional Seas Directories and Bibliographies*. IUCN, Gland, Switzerland and Cambridge, UK/UNEP, Nairobi, Kenya. 440 pp.

Wholey, J.W. (1968). *The countryside and the people: report of the Provisional Council for the Use and Conservation of the Countryside*. Government Printer, Hong Kong.

Yim, C.Y. (1989). changing patterns of country-park recreation in Hong Kong. *The Geographical Journal*. 155 (2): 167-178

ANNEX
Definitions of protected area designations, as legislated, together with authorities responsible for their administration

Title: Country Parks Ordinance (Chapter 208)

Date: 16 August 1976 (No. 10)

Brief description: To provide for the designation, control and management of country parks and special areas, the establishment of the Country Parks Board, and for purposes connected therewith.

Administrative authority: Country Parks Authority (Director of Agriculture and Fisheries)

Designations:

Country park An area approved by the Governor in Council, following the submission of map showing the proposed country park together with such facilities are services as considered appropriate.

It is the duty of the Authority to encourage its use and development for purposes of recreation and tourism; to protect the vegetation and wildlife; to preserve and maintain buildings and sites of historic or cultural significance but without prejudice to the Antiquities and Monuments Ordinance; and to provide facilities and services for public enjoyment. These provisions apply equally to special areas.

The Authority is empowered to discontinue or modify any use or proposed use of any leased land within a country park which would substantially reduce its enjoyment and amenities.

Special area An area of Crown land (defined as land which is not leased) either within or outside a country park designated by the Governor.

Provisions for its use and development are the same as those for a country park (see above).

Title: None

Date: n/a

Brief description: n/a

Administrative authority: Country Parks Authority (Director of Agriculture and Fisheries)

Designations:

Site of special scientific interest (SSSI) Area recognised by the Country Parks Authority as being of special interest and value by reason of its geological, floral, faunal, cultural or archacological features (Thrower, 1984).

Title: Wild Animals Protection Ordinance (Chapter 170)

Date: 23 January 1976 (No. 5), last revised 1980 (No. 58)

Brief description: To make provision for the conservation of wild animals, and for purposes connected therewith

Administrative authority: Agriculture and Fisheries Department (Director)

Designations:

Restricted area An area specified in the Sixth Schedule to which entry or presence is restricted for a given period.

No person, other than an authorised officer, may enter such an area except in accordance with a written permit granted by the Director of Agriculture and Fisheries.

A person who lawfully enters a restricted area may not be in possession of any hunting appliance or hunt any wild animal.

The government may amend any schedule by order published in the *Gazette*.

Title: Forests and Countryside Ordinance

Date: 30 July 1937 (No. 11), last revised 1974 (No. 82)

Brief description: To consolidate and amend the law relating to forests and plants, and to provide for the protection of the countryside

Administrative authority: Agriculture and Fisheries Department (Director)

Designations:

Prohibited area Area declared by the Governor in Council for the protection of afforestation operations.

Entry by any person without lawful authority or excuse is an offence.

SUMMARY OF PROTECTED AREAS

Map ref.	National/international designations Name of area	IUCN management category	Area (ha)	Year notified
	Country Parks			
1	Lam Tsuen	V	1,520	1979
2	Lantau North	V	2,200	1978
3	Lantau South	V	5,640	1978
4	Ma On Shan	V	2,880	1979
5	Pat Sin Leng	V	3,125	1978
6	Plover Cove	V	5,224	1978
7	Sai Kung East	V	4,477	1978
8	Sai Kung West	V	3,000	1978
9	Shing Mun	V	1,400	1977
10	Tai Lam	V	5,330	1979
11	Tai Mo Shan	V	1,440	1979
12	Tai Tam	V	1,585	1977

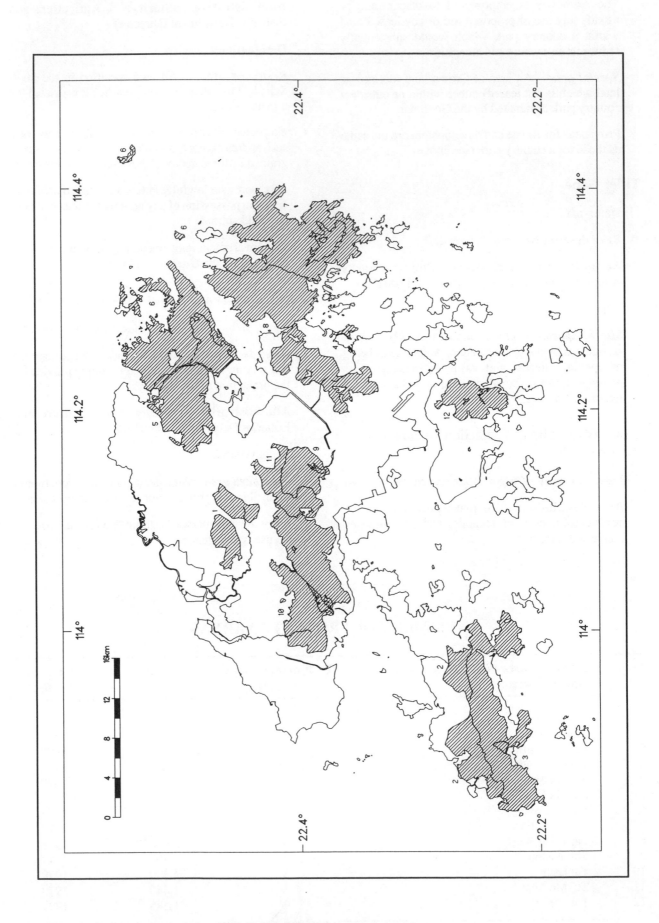

Protected Areas of Hong Kong

UNION OF SOVIET SOCIALIST REPUBLICS*

Area 22,402,200 sq. km

Population 288,595,000 (1990)
Natural increase: 1.0% per annum

Economic Indicators
GNP: US$ 8,375 per capita (1988)

Policy and Legislation Several articles in the 1977 Constitution reflect the growing importance given to environmental protection. Under Article 18 it is a primary duty of the state to protect and make scientific use of natural resources, and to ensure air and water quality, while under Article 67 all Soviet citizens are obliged to protect nature and conserve its riches. This is augmented by the 1985 Decree on the enforcement of nature conservation laws and the rational use of natural resources. A draft law to update and encompass all forms of environmental protection was prepared and submitted to the Council of Ministers in 1989 (Anon., 1988). The draft Treaty on the Union of Soviet Sovereign Republics (USSR) is now under discussion and may have a bearing on the administration of environmental protection (Dobrynina, *in litt.*, 1991).

Legislation relevant to the protection of areas appeared in Imperial Russia during the 1880s in the form of hunting, land use and forestry regulations (Karpowicz, 1988), followed by the first conservation measures in 1909. The first legislation of an environmental nature, however, was adopted as early as the 11-12th centuries: the core of the Beloveshskaya Pushia was set aside in the 13th century and forests along the southern boundaries of the Russian state were granted protection in the 14-17th centuries (Dobrynina, *in litt.*, 1991). Protected areas legislation appeared in 1921 in the form of a decree of the Council of People's Commissioners entitled "Protection of Natural Monuments, Gardens and Parks" and signed by V.I. Lenin. In 1957 a series of acts addressing conservation was passed in the wake of the Conservation of Nature Act in Estonia. This was followed in 1968 by the Principles of Land Legislation of the USSR and Union Republics. In 1972 a decree was passed by the Central Committee of the Communist Party of the Soviet Union and the Council of Ministers to strengthen nature conservation and improve the use of natural resources.

The current Law on Wildlife Protection and Use is based on the state regulations of 25 June 1980 (coming into force on 1 January 1981). This law includes regulations on protected natural areas and measures to ensure wildlife protection (Articles 21-26) approved by the State Planning Committee and the State Committee for Science and Technological USSR Council of Ministers (Karpowicz, 1988; Kolbasov, 1981). In 1985 the decree of the Supreme Soviet covered nature conservation legislation and rational use of natural resources.

The legislative status of state nature reserves (*Zapovedniki*) is based on Article 21 (Section 6 on creating preserves and reserves) and Article 25 (on protection of animals in preserves, reserves and other protected areas) of the 1981 Law on Wildlife Protection and Use, following the earlier two acts of the Supreme Soviet: Principles of Land Legislation of the USSR and Union Republics (adopted on 13 December 1968) and Principles of Water Legislation of the USSR and Union Republics (adopted on 10 December 1970). Under the Principles of Land Legislation, any activity disturbing natural ecosystems within state nature reserves, or threatening the conservation of natural objects of special scientific or cultural value is prohibited both within state nature reserves and their surrounding protected zones. The state regulations entitled The Status of State Nature Reserves, enacted by the Council of Ministers on 27 November 1951 together with the relevant regulations of the Republics, has been revised in the 1981 Act.

Laws on soil, water, forest, mineral and fauna as well as individual republic laws cover protection of zones and natural objects. There is no overall law governing conservation areas and other areas under special protection (Weisenburger, 1991), but the state environmental protective programme (1991-1995) envisages such legislation being prepared, and a draft "Basis of Law of the USSR and the Republics on Specially Protected Natural Areas" has been prepared (Nikol'skii, 1991). Special regulation covering environmental and nature protection in the far north was passed by decree of the Supreme Soviet on 26 November 1984. A framework law on nature conservation, which is intended to apply throughout the union, is being drawn up (Weisenburger, 1991).

There are approximately 60 different categories of protected area which provide for nature conservation to varying extents. The six main categories of nature

---

*This information is correct at the time of going to press, but is likely to be overtaken by events which could alter the legislative, administrative and management structure of protected areas throughout the region. As of September 1991 the constituent republics of the former Soviet Union included: Armenia, Azerbaijan, Belorussia (Bielorussia or Belarus), Georgia, Kazakhstan, Kirgizia, Moldavia (Moldova), the Russian Republic (RSFSR) and its Baltic enclave of Kalingrad, Tadzhikistan, Turkmenistan, Ukraine and Uzbekistan.

conservation areas, represented both at national and republic levels are: state nature reserve (*Zapovednik*), national park (*Natsional'nyi park*), nature sanctuary or partial reserve (*Zakaznik*), national hunting reserve (*Zapovedno-okhotnich'ye khozyastvo*) and nature reserve or natural monument (*Natsional'nyi pamyatnik*). The principal category, and the most rigorously protected, is the state nature reserve. In addition, there are protected seashore areas, sea islands and sea shelves, set up to protect the environment, conserve gene pools, and provide for the restoration of resources, recreation and education. State forests and forest reserves protect watersheds, provide windbelts and control erosion. There are also green zones and forest parks which tend to be protected green belts around cities and health resorts. They have limited nature conservation values, usually being managed landscapes with a high recreation priority (Borodin *et al.*, 1984). In matters of forestry conservation, it is unclear as to the exact responsibilities of the environment administration and that of the forestry authorities (Weisenburger, 1991).

The current laws tend to be general and are considered to have weak sanctions for infringement and hence have little impact (Weisenburger, 1991). Similarly, the protection of forests is also considered inadequate, with over-felling and destruction of valuable areas (Silviancedar).

International Activities   In a *Pravda* article entitled "The Reality and Guarantee of a Safe World", President Mikhail Gorbachov identified the need to develop a global strategy for environmental protection and rational use of natural resources. This highlights present policy within the Soviet Union towards international conservation (Anon, 1989). In 1988, the USSR participated in 55 international conventions and agreements concerning environmental protection, several of which related to protected areas (Anon., 1989).

A network of wetlands of international importance has been established under the Convention on Wetlands of International Importance especially as Waterfowl Habitat (Ramsar Convention), which was ratified by the USSR on 11 October 1976. By 1990 12 sites had been listed. A further 16 have been proposed, which would add 8,000,000ha to the existing network. The USSR is also actively involved in developing a network of biosphere reserves under the Unesco Man and the Biosphere programme, 19 sites having been established by 1990. The USSR signed the Convention Concerning the Protection of the World Cultural and Natural Heritage (World Heritage Convention) on 12 October 1990. No natural sites have yet been inscribed on the World Heritage List. International cooperation between USSR and USA has extended to the twinning of biosphere reserves for comparative research and management purposes. Negotiations are underway with the USA and Finland to establish transfrontier parks on the shores of the Bering Straits and adjacent to Kostomukhskiy, respectively.

Multilateral cooperation between the members of the Warsaw Pact was implemented within the framework of a Permanent Commission on Cooperation in Environmental Protection. This ceased to exist after the Pact was disbanded in 1991. Cooperation with Sweden has been implemented within the framework of a Joint Working Group on Environmental Protection under the Soviet-Swedish Intergovernmental Commission on Economic and Scientific and Technical Cooperation. Among the primary areas of cooperation is the conservation of ecological systems and individual floral and faunal species (Anon., 1989).

Administration and Management   Until 1988 the supreme authority for broad and comprehensive environmental issues (executive and management roles in nature conservation) was the central government's Council of Ministers, and its representatives within each republic. Administration was handled by 16 ministries and state committees such as: the State Committee for Hydrometeorology and Natural Environmental Control (concerned with nature conservation, forestry and game management), the State Committee for Forestry (*Goskomles*) and the USSR Agro-Industrial Trust (formerly USSR Ministry of Agriculture) with committees at republic level.

In January 1988 the administrative bureaucracy was streamlined and simplified by the creation of the USSR State Committee for Nature Conservation (*Goskompriroda*), which was responsible for coordinating conservation activities throughout the entire USSR. *Goskompriroda* has offices at the Republic level, further divided into 200 *oblast* (district) offices, each with some 200 staff. Its main tasks include: monitoring the use and conservation of natural resources (including hunting activities); management of nature reserves; registration of threatened fauna and production of the USSR red book; and dissemination of information about the environment. In 1991 the structure was revised with the creation of the USSR Ministry of Nature Use and Environmental Protection (*Minpriroda*) (Dobrynina, pers. comm., 1991). The relationship between this Ministry and the republican authorities will only be defined once the Treaty on the Union of Sovereign States (USSR) has been agreed. Nine republics signed the Treaty by mid-1991. However, the *Minpriroda* ceased to function in autumn 1991 (IUCN-EEP, *in litt.*, 1991) and, although for a brief period administration was organised in a similar fashion at Union and republic levels in the future, perhaps only transboundary issues will require central coordination (Weisenburger, 1991). In late 1991, there was a suggestion to establish an inter-republican Council for protected area management (Nikol'skii *et al.*, 1991).

From 1 January 1975 state nature reserves were under the direct or indirect supervision of the Department of Nature Conservation, and Game Management of the USSR Ministry of Agriculture. The majority of state nature reserves were managed by the departments or committees of nature conservation in the republics, but some fell under the supervision of the USSR Academy of Sciences. The establishment of state nature reserves required final approval from the State Planning Committee, *Gosplan* (Braden, 1986). By 1988 most state nature reserves had come under the administration of the Chief Administration for Nature Conservation, Nature Reserves, Forestry and Game Management (*Glavpriroda*). By 1990, 124 state nature reserves were under *Gosmopriroda* (27 USSR State Committees, 97 under Republic State Committees), 20 under *Goskomles*, and 19 under USSR Academy of Sciences and other bodies (Nikol'skii *et al.*, 1991; Weisenburger, 1991). Fifteen national parks remain under the USSR State Committee for Forestry, three under republic state committees and three under other authorities. The 700 nature sanctuaries in RSFSR are subordinated to the Hunting Department (Nikol'skii *et al.*, 1991). Most state nature reserves have five to 20 scientific staff, additional research being undertaken by the Academy of Sciences, universities and other institutions (Braden, 1986). In 1990, total staff level was 8,250 (3,470 in national parks, and 4,780 in nature reserves), with perhaps an additional 2,000 in nature sanctuaries (Nikol'skii, 1991). There are no special training centres for protected area professionals. In the RSFSR, national hunting reserves are administered by the Chief Administration for Hunting and Nature Reserves (*Glavokhota*). Until recently, financial arrangements and provision of material and technical equipment was centrally organised (Nikol'skii *et al.*, 1991). Rangers (3,000 in total) are responsible for controlling poaching, and hunting is limited to sustainable levels.

In 1985 roubles 4.4 million were spent on national parks and roubles 27.8 million on the state nature reserve system by 28 different administrative bodies employing over 1,000 specialists. In 1988 a budget of roubles 10 billion was earmarked for use by the state for environmental protection, as compared with a total of roubles 60 billion spent during the previous decade (Karpowicz, 1988). Total investment in protected areas increased by 1990 to roubles 54.9 million (Nikol'skii *et al.*, 1991), averaging roubles 282,000 per protected area. A long-term programme for environmental protection and rational utilisation of natural resources has been formulated for the 13th Five-Year Plan (1991-1995) and up to the year 2005 by the former USSR State Committee for Nature Protection and other key institutions. Total investment for the period 1991-2005 is estimated at roubles 240-335 billion, increasing from roubles 48-55 billion for the 13th Plan to roubles 120-180 billion for the 16th Plan (IUCN, 1991), of which 3 billion are directly for establishment of protected areas (Weisenburger, 1991).

The oldest and largest nature conservation organisation is the All Russian Society for Nature Conservation. Founded in 1924, it is reputed to be the largest in the world, with 38 million members active in local groups, collectives and state farms, factories, offices and schools. In all Soviet republics there are national nature conservation societies which work within the framework of the peace council of the USSR. Other societies include the USSR Geographical Society, USSR Theriological Society and the USSR Ornithological Society. The basis of nature conservation is taught both in schools and in universities and other institutions of higher education (Knystautas, 1987). A union of environmental protection societies was set up in early 1989.

Systems Reviews The USSR is the world's largest country covering one-sixth of the globe's land surface. For the most part it is lowland, with only 5% lying above 1,500m. There are four distinct vegetation zones: tundra, forest (broad-leaf woodland and coniferous taiga), steppe and desert. The deserts and semi-deserts (Central Asia) fringing the southern borders give way to steppe and temperate grasslands, which in turn are replaced by a great zone of broad-leaf woodland and conifer taiga forest stretching for more than 11,250km east-west, and by treeless cold desert and tundra along the northern coasts. Forests now cover 7.47 million sq. km (33% of total land area), with vast areas of virgin forest remaining in the far north, parts of Siberia and in the high mountains. The main centres of plant diversity include the Carpathian mountains, southern shores of the Crimea, western and eastern Transcaucasus region, western Kopet, Tien-Shan, Pamirs and Primorskiy region (Davis *et al.*, 1986).

Protected areas play an important role in the conservation of rare faunal species, containing 39% of mammal species, 55% of bird species, 56% of fish species, 68% of reptile species, and 90% of amphibians listed in the USSR Red Book. Moreover, they have proved to be vital for the conservation of a number of species such as tiger and Bactrian deer (Anon., 1989). Strict protection is afforded to about 1.5% of total land area under the existing network of national parks and state nature reserves (24 national parks and 172 nature reserves in 1991). The inclusion of 1,958 nature sanctuaries raises the coverage to 4.1% of the surface area, of which 700 are administered at the republic level in 1991) (Nikol'skii *et al.*, 1991). The majority of protected areas are located on the Russia plateau, and in the Caucasian and Middle Asian mountains, with 60% in European USSR. There are plans to establish between 40 and 50 national parks over the next 10 years, mainly in the Far East, as well as 110 state nature reserves (IUCN, 1991; N. Zabalina, pers. comm., 1991). Overall, the protected areas network will be extended to 2% of total land area by 1995, 4% by 2000, and to at least 6% by 2005 (IUCN, 1991). The network would greatly expand the coverage of Arctic islands, northern taiga and tundra, mountainous steppe and forest steppe (Nikol'skii *et al.*, 1991). These figures are part of the plan for future investment as specified by USSR Supreme Forest Decision Act of 27 November 1984 "On Urgency Measures for Ecological Rehabilitation of the Country".

The protected area system is used extensively for research by national and international groups (Minister Vorontsov specifically invited foreign scientists to set up studies in the Soviet Baltic Republics) organised in Regional Scientific Councils and coordinated by the Commission on Coordination of Scientific Research in Nature Reserves of the Academy of Sciences. All nature reserve bodies publish status reports (Nikol'skii, 1991). Monitoring stations have been established in 10 biosphere reserves (Nikol'skii, 1991).

In the past, even designated protected areas were not completely secure from short-term economic exploitation, with reserves temporarily removed from the system. A total of 88 state nature reserves was thus removed by a reform in 1951, with subsequent surface area reduced from 12.5 million ha to 1.5 million ha. In 1961, 16 of the existing 85 state reserves were removed (Weisenburger, 1991). The protected areas system has been threatened over time by a number of activities such as oil prospecting, livestock grazing, over-fishing, uncontrolled tourism, illegal building schemes and hunting by the privileged few (Braden, 1986; Karpowicz, 1988). Aerial pollution, soil contamination and dust and gas damage have been recorded (Nikol'skii *et al.*, 1971). Dneprovsko-Teterevskoe National Hunting Reserve lies partly within Zone A (total evacuation) of the Chernobyl reactor accident site and extensive nuclear contaminants have inevitably been recorded here and elsewhere within the region.

Other Relevant Information   Tourism is largely underdeveloped, with only 320,000 visitors recorded in 1989/90 to 27 state nature reserves (Nikol'skii *et al.*, 1991).

Addresses

USSR Minpriroda Ministry of Nature Use and Environmental Protection, Nezhdanovoi St 11, Moscow 103 009 (Tel: 95 229 5759; Tlx: 411258 zerno su)

USSR Research Institute for Nature Conservation and Reserve Management, P/o Vilan, Znamerskoye-Sadki 113 628, Moscow

References

Anon. (1988). Resolution on the formation of USSR State Committee for the Protection of Nature. *Pravda* 17 January.

Anon. (1989). *Report on the state of the environment in the USSR, 1988*. USSR State Committee for the Protection of Nature, Moscow. 151 pp.

Bannikov, A.G. (1969). (Ed.). *Zapovedniki Sovetskogo Soyuza*. Kolos, Moscow. 552 pp.

Borodin, A.M., Isakov, Y. and Krinitsky, V.V. (1984). The system of natural protected areas in the USSR: biosphere reserves as part of this system. In: *Conservation, science and society*. Unesco, Paris. Pp. 221-228.

Borodina, A.G. and Syroechkovskogo, I.Y.Y. (Ed.) (1983). *Zapovedniki SSSR*. Lesnaya Promyshlennost', Moscow. 248 pp.

Braden, K. (1986). Wildlife reserves in the USSR. *Oryx* 20: 165-169.

Cerovsky, J. (1988). *Nature conservation in the socialist countries of East Europe*. East-Europe Committee, IUCN Commission on Education/Ministry of Culture of the Czech Socialist Republic, Prague.

Davis, S. D., Droop, S. J. M., Gregerson, P., Henson, L., Leon, C. J., Lamlein Villa-Lobos, J., Synge, H., and Zantovska, J. (1986). *Plants in danger: what do we know?* Threatened Plants Unit. IUCN, Gland, Switzerland and Cambridge, UK. 461 pp.

IUCN (1991). *Environmental Status Report 1990*. Volume Three. USSR. IUCN East European Programme, Gland, Switzerland and Cambridge, UK.

Karpowicz, Z.J. (1988). Conservation and environment protection. In: M.J. Berry (Ed.), *Science and technology in the USSR*. Longmans, London. Pp. 361-379.

Kolbasov, O.S. (1981). Two new environmental laws. *Environmental Policy and Law* 7: 79-100.

Knystautas, A. (1987). *The natural history of the USSR*. Century, London. 224 pp.

Nikalaevskiy, A.G. (1985). *Natsional'nye parki*. Agropromizdat, Moscow. 189 pp.

Nikol'skii, A., Bolshova, L.I. and Karaseva, S.E. (1991). *Palaearctic-USSR Regional Protected Areas Review*. Paper prepared for IV World Parks Congress Caracas, February 1992. USSR Ministry of Natural Resources Management and Environmental Protection, Moscow.

Sokolov, V.Y. and Syroechkovskogo, Y.Y. (Eds). (1985). *Zapovedniki SSSR*. 11 volumes. Mysl, Moscow.

Weisenburger, U. (1991). Nature conservation in the Soviet Union. In: *Nature Conservation in Austria, Finland, Norway, Sweden, Switzerland, Bulgaria, Czechoslovrakoia, Hungary, Poland, Romania, Yugoslavia and the Soviet Union* (European Parliament Director-General for Research). Environment, Public Health and Consumer Protection Series 17. EN-9-1991. Pp. 140-149.

ANNEX
Definitions of protected area designations, as legislated, together with authorities responsible for their administration

Title : Law on Wildlife Protection and Use

Date: 25 June 1980 (entered into force 1 January 1981)

Brief description: No information

Administrative authority: *Goskompriroda* (USSR State Committee for Nature Conservation)

Designations:

Zapovednik (State nature reserve) Typical or unique plot of natural land used by "scientific institutions...and studied for its natural complexes and established on land excluded from economic utilisation" sites. Both protect threatened flora and fauna, and serve as an outdoor laboratory for field study. As far as possible, they are maintained in their natural condition unchanged by man.

Prohibited activities include building construction, any economic activities, such as agriculture or industry, and unrestricted entry.

Main management objectives include: (1) protection of wildlife and its habitats, including maintenance of entire ecosystems; (2) scientific research; and (3) strictly limited recreational activities or, in some cases, controlled tourism.

Surrounded by an area of semi-protected land which provides a buffer to the adjacent countryside. Existing economic activities are allowed to continue, providing they are not harmful.

Natsional'nyi park (National park) Protected natural area established in natural wilderness or altered landscapes (including arable land), although mainly on state forest property. Designated for recreation as well as nature protection and, as in the case of a protected lakeshore, differs from a state nature reserve in that tourism is allowed.

Legislation for national parks is complex. Parks are zoned into: areas in which economic activities are controlled; nature reserves, containing the finest examples of original natural habitat, where economic activities and public entry is forbidden; nature sanctuaries where tourists are allowed but economic

activities are strictly prohibited; and peripheral buffer areas of economic activity, where habitation and sustainable levels of exploitation of natural resources (including fishing) are permitted.

Zakaznik (Nature sanctuary or partial reserve) Natural area partly withdrawn from economic utilisation because of its outstanding landscape, rare plants, or breeding colonies of threatened species. Controlled hunting is sometimes allowed.

Established to enable certain floral and faunal populations to recover within a specified time period. Exploitation is prohibited during this period, unless it does not interfere with management objectives.

May only be fully protected in certain seasons when all economic activities and entry is banned. Status and administration varies in the different republics of the USSR.

Zapovedno-okhotnich'ye khozyastvo (National hunting reserve or reserved hunting unit) Highly protected, and provides vital refuges for wildlife. Numbers of some game species is regulated by controlled hunting.

Natsional'nyi pamyatnik (Nature monument or national monument) Limited area surrounding isolated natural features such as geological sites or exceptionally old trees.

Sources: Braden, 1986; Cerovsky, 1988; Kynstautas, 1987

Title : Law on Forestry

Date: No information

Brief description: Provides for the designation of forest reserves

Administrative authority: *Goskomles* (Forest Administration)

Designations:

Forest reserve No information

Source: Weisenburger, 1991

SUMMARY OF PROTECTED AREAS

Map[†] ref.	*National/international designations* Name of area	IUCN management category	Area (ha)	Year notified
	ARMENIA SSR			
	National Park			
1	Sevan	II·	150,000	1978
	State Nature Reserves (Zapovedniki)			
2	Dilizhanskiy	I	24,232	1958
3	Khosrovskiy	I	29,680	1958
4	Shikaokhskiy	I	18,000	1975
	AZERBAYDZHAN SSR			
	State Nature Reserves (Zapovedniki)			
5	Ak-Gel'skiy	I	4,400	1978
6	Geigel'skiy	I	7,131	1926
7	Girkanskiy	I	2,904	1969
8	Ilisuinsky	I	9,345	1987
9	Ismaillinskiy	I	5,778	1981
10	Karayazskiy	I	4,155	1978
11	Kyzylagachskiy	I	88,360	1929
12	Pirkulinskiy	I	1,520	1968
13	Shirvanskiy	I	17,745	1969
14	Turianchaiskiy	I	12,634	1958
15	Zakatal'skiy	I	23,843	1930
	BYELORUSSIAN SSR			
	State Nature Reserves (Zapovedniki)			
16	Berezinskiy	I	76,201	1925
17	Prypyatskiy	I	62,213	1969
	State Hunting Reserves (Zakazniki)			
18	Belovezhskaya Pushcha	IV	87,577	1940
19	Telekhanskoye	IV	10,947	1977
	GEORGIA SSR			
	National Park			
20	Tbilisskiy	II	19,410	1973
	State Nature Reserves (Zapovedniki)			
21	Adzhametskiy	I	4,848	1957
22	Akhmetskiy	I	16,297	1980
23	Algetskiy	I	6,000	1965
24	Borzhomskiy	I	18,048	1959
25	Kazbegskiy	I	8,707	1976
26	Kintrishskiy	I	13,893	1959
27	Lagodekhskiy	I	17,818	1912
28	Liakhvskiy	I	6,385	1977
29	Mariamdzhvarskiy	I	1,040	1959
30	Pitsyundo-Myusserskiy	I	3,761	1966
31	Pskhu-Gumistinskiy	I	40,819	1976
32	Ritsinskiy	I	16,289	1957
33	Saguramskiy	I	5,247	1946
34	Vashlovanskiy	I	8,034	1935
	KAZAKHSTAN SSR			
	National Park			
35	Bayanaul'sky	II	45,500	1985

Map† ref.	*National/international designations* Name of area	IUCN management category	Area (ha)	Year notified
	State Nature Reserves (Zapovedniki)			
36	Aksu-Dzhabagly	I	75,094	1927
37	Alma-Atinskiy	I	73,342	1961
38	Barsakel'messkiy	I	18,300	1939
39	Kurgal'dzhinskiy	I	237,138	1968
40	Markakol'skiy	I	75,040	1976
41	Naurzumskiy	I	87,694	1934
42	Ustiyurtskiy	I	223,300	1984
	KIRGHIZIA SSR			
	National Park			
43	Ala-Archa	II	19,400	1976
	State Nature Reserves (Zapovedniki)			
44	Besh-Aral'skiy	I	116,732	1979
45	Issyk-Kul'skiy	I	18,999	1948
46	Narynskiy	I	18,260	1983
47	Sary-Chelekskiy	I	23,868	1959
	MOLDAVIA SSR			
	State Nature Reserves (Zapovedniki)			
48	Kodry	I	5,177	1971
49	Redenskiy Les	I	5,664	1976
	RSFSR			
	National Parks			
50	Bashkiriya	II	98,134	1986
51	Losinyy Ostrov	II	10,058	1983
52	Mariy Chodra	II	36,600	1985
53	Pribaikalskiy	II	412,750	1986
54	Priel'brusskiy	II	101,000	1986
55	Samarskaya Luka	II	128,000	1984
56	Sochinskiy	II	190,000	1983
57	Zabaikalskiy	II	269,300	1986
	State Nature Reserves (Zapovedniki)			
58	Altaiskiy	I	881,238	1968
59	Astrakhanskiy	I	63,400	1919
60	Azas	I	337,290	1985
61	Baikal'skiy	I	165,724	1969
62	Baikalo-Lenskiy	I	659,919	1986
63	Barguzinskiy	I	263,200	1916
64	Bashkirskiy	I	79,609	1930
65	Bassegi	I	19,422	1982
66	Bol'shekhekhtsizskiy	I	45,123	1963
67	Bryanskiy Les	I	11,778	1987
68	Bureinskiy	I	358,444	1987
69	Dagestanskiy	I	19,061	1987
70	Dal'nevostochnyy	I	64,316	1978
71	Darvinskiy	I	112,630	1945
72	Dauzsky	I	631,300	1986
73	Il'menskiy	I	30,380	1920
74	Kabardino-Balkarskiy	I	74,099	1976
75	Kandalakshskiy	I	58,100	1932
76	Kavkazskiy	I	263,277	1924
77	Kedrovaya Pad'	I	17,897	1916
78	Khinganskiy	I	97,836	1963
79	Khoperskiy	I	16,178	1935

Map[†] ref.	National/international designations Name of area	IUCN management category	Area (ha)	Year notified
80	Kivach	I	10,460	1931
81	Komsomol'skiy	I	63,866	1963
82	Kostomukhskiy	I	47,457	1983
83	Kronotskiy	I	1,099,000	1967
84	Kuril'skiy	I	65,365	1984
85	Laplandskiy	I	278,436	1930
86	Lazovskiy	I	116,524	1957
87	Les na Vorskle	I	1,038	1979
88	Magadanskiy	I	883,805	1982
89	Malaya Sos'va	I	92,921	1976
90	Mordovskiy	I	32,148	1935
91	Nizhne-Svirskiy	I	40,972	1980
92	Okskiy	I	22,911	1935
93	Olekminskiy	I	847,102	1984
94	Ozenbuzgskiy	I	21,653	1989
95	Pechoro-Ilychskiy	I	721,322	1930
96	Pinezhskiy	I	41,244	1975
97	Pozonaiskiy	I	56,669	1988
98	Prioksko-Terrasnyy	I	4,945	1948
99	Putozanskiy	I	1,887,251	1988
100	Sayano-Shushenskiy	I	390,368	1976
101	Severo-Osetinskiy	I	28,999	1967
102	Shul'gan Tash	I	22,531	1986
103	Sikhote-Alinskiy	I	347,052	1935
104	Sokhondinskiy	I	211,007	1973
105	Stolby	I	47,154	1925
106	Taimyrskiy	I	1,348,708	1979
107	Teberdinskiy	I	84,996	1936
108	Tsentral'nochernozemnyy	I	4,847	1969
109	Tsentral'nolesnoy	I	21,380	1931
110	Tsentralno-Sibirskiy	I	972,017	1985
111	Ussuriyskiy	I	40,432	1932
112	Ust'Lenskiy	I	1,433,000	1986
113	Verkhne-Tazovskiy	I	631,308	1986
114	Visimskiy	I	13,750	1971
115	Vitimskiy	I	585,021	1982
116	Volzhsko-Kamskiy	I	8,034	1960
117	Voronezhskiy	I	31,053	1927
118	Vrangel Island	I	795,650	1976
119	Yuganskiy	I	648,636	1982
120	Yuzhno-Uzalskiy	I	254,914	1978
121	Zavidovskiy	I	125,442	1972
122	Zeyskiy	I	82,567	1963
123	Zhigulevskiy	I	23,140	1966
	TADZHIKISTAN SSR			
	State Nature Reserves (Zapovedniki)			
124	Dashti-Dzhumskiy	I	19,700	1983
125	Ramit	I	16,168	1959
126	Tigrovaya Balka	I	49,700	1938
	TURKMENISTAN SSR			
	State Nature Reserves (Zapovedniki)			
127	Amu-Dar'inskiy	I	50,506	1982
128	Badkhyzskiy	I	87,680	1941
129	Kaplankyrskiy	I	570,000	1979
130	Kopetdagskiy	I	49,793	1976

Map[†] ref.	National/international designations Name of area	IUCN management category	Area (ha)	Year notified
131	Krasnovodskiy	I	262,037	1928
132	Kugitangskiy	I	27,100	1986
133	Repetekskiy	I	34,600	1928
134	Syunt-Khasardagskiy	I	29,700	1976
	UZBEKISTAN SSR			
	National Park			
135	Uzbekistan People's Park	II	31,503	1978
	State Nature Reserves (Zapovedniki)			
136	Baday-Tugay	I	5,929	1971
137	Chatkal'skiy	I	35,686	1947
138	Gissarskiy (Kyzylsuyskiy and Mirakinskiy)	I	87,538	1983
139	Kitabskii	I	5,378	1979
140	Kyzylkumskiy	I	10,141	1971
141	Nuratinskiy	I	22,537	1975
142	Suzkhanskiy	I	28,014	1986
143	Zaaminskiy	I	15,600	1959
144	Zeravshanskiy	I	2,352	1975
	Biosphere Reserves			
	Astrakhanskiy Zapovednik	IX	63,400	1984
	Chatkal Mountains	IX	71,400	1978
	Kavkazskiy Zapovednik	IX	263,477	1978
	Kronotskiy Zapovednik	IX	1,099,000	1984
	Lake Baikal Region	IX	559,100	1986
	Laplandskiy Zapovednik	IX	278,400	1984
	Oka River Valley	IX	45,845	1978
	Pechoro-Ilychskiy Zapovednik	IX	721,322	1984
	Repetek Zapovednik	IX	34,600	1978
	Sayano-Shushenskiy Zapovednik	IX	389,570	1984
	Sikhote-Alin Zapovednik	IX	340,200	1978
	Sokhondinskiy Zapovednik	IX	211,000	1984
	Tsentral'nochernozem Zapovednik	IX	4,795	1978
	Tsentral'nolesnoy Zapovednik	IX	21,348	1985
	Tzentralnosibirskii	IX	5,000,000	1986
	Voronezhskiy Zapovednik	IX	31,053	1984
	Ramsar Wetlands			
	Issyk-kul Lake	R	629,800	1976
	Kandalaksha Bay	R	208,000	1976
	Karkinitski Bay	R	37,300	1976
	Kirov Bay	R	132,500	1976
	Krasnovodsk and North-Cheleken Bays	R	188,700	1976
	Lake Khanka	R	310,000	1976
	Lakes of the Lower Turgay and Irgiz	R	348,000	1976
	Volga Delta	R	650,000	1976

[†]Locations of some protected areas are shown on the accompanying maps.

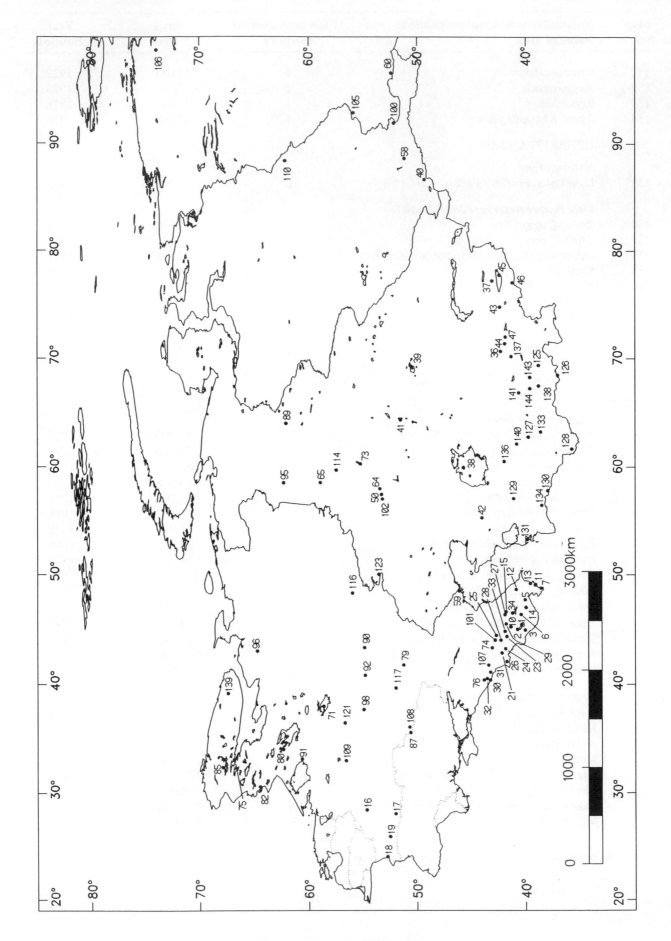

Protected Areas of the USSR

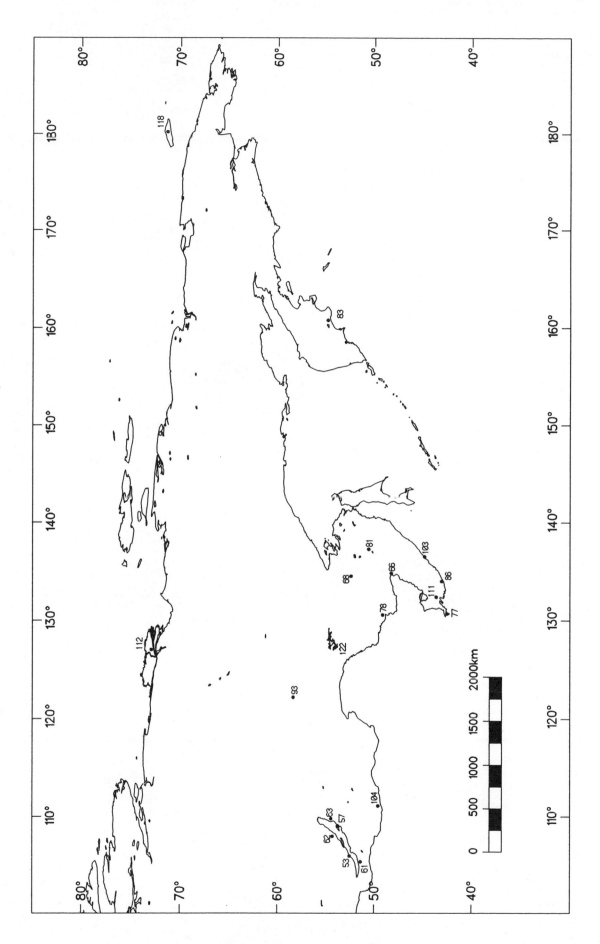

Protected Areas of the USSR

Palaearctic – Europe

REPUBLIC OF ALBANIA

Area 28,752 sq. km

Population 3,200,000 (1989)
Natural increase: 2.1% per annum (1980-1986)

Economic Indicators
GNP: US$ 1,217 per capita

Policy and Legislation   The Albanian Constitution of December 1976 proclaims that "The protection of the land, the natural resources and the waters from damage and pollution is a duty of the state and of all public and economic organizations, as well as of all citizens". All land and natural resources are legally in the public domain, making all protected areas state property. Two relevant pieces of legislation are the Law on Forest Protection, No. 3349 of 3 October 1963, which was superseded by a subsequent law of 1966 and another in 1968 (Crockford *et al.*, 1991), and the Law on Hunting, No. 1351 of 1 November 1951 (Borisov *et al.*, 1985; IUCN, 1967). The enabling legislation designated three categories: *Parqet nationale* (national park) where tourism is encouraged (IUCN, 1971); integral reserve which is strictly protected for nature conservation; and oriented reserve providing for traditional human activities (Bogliani, 1987).

A number of designated types of protected forest zone have been created by the Ministry of Forestry (Crockford *et al.*, 1991). A new law covering forestry, hunting and nature protection is currently being drafted, linked to new legislation on land ownership and agriculture (Crockford *et al.*, 1991).

International Activities   Albania is party to the World Heritage Convention which it ratified on 10 July 1989. No natural sites have yet been inscribed on the World Heritage list. It also became party to the UNEP Regional Seas Programme (Barcelona Convention concerning the Mediterranean) in the same year, and to the Specially Protected Areas Protocol and the Mediterranean Action Plan. Proposals for the inclusion of six coastal sites under the Convention are being considered (de Grissac, *in litt.*, 1990).

Administration and Management   A state body with responsibility for nature protection (Nowak, 1974) was part of the Ministry of Forest and Water Resources, established in 1948 (Borisov *et al.*, 1985; IUCN, 1971). By 1990 the management of the environment was shared between the Ministry of Agriculture and Fisheries and the Ministry of Forestry. The Ministry of Health, Department of Hygiene and Environmental Protection, was responsible for regulating environmental matters (IUCN, 1991). From 1991 the Ministry of Forestry administers national parks and all matters relating to nature protection (Crockford *et al.*, 1991). The Ministry is subordinate to the Ministry of Agriculture in all matters. The Ministry of Forestry has a Department of Forestry and a Forest Scientific Station. The Commission for Protection of the Natural Environment was set up in 1990 and, most recently, a Ministry of Communal Works and Environmental Protection was established which is part of the Commission (Crockford *et al.*, 1991). The Ministry of Agriculture was responsible for wetland conservation until June 1989 when this function was taken over by the Ministry of Forestry (Crockford *et al.*, 1991).

Within national parks, funds are allocated to cover salaries, as well as reafforestation, other forestry programmes, civil engineering works, construction of pioneer camps, villas and infrastructure such as electricity and water supplies. National parks are state controlled, with little human activity permitted. From 1988, tougher measures were introduced especially with regard to hunting, fishing and protection of threatened species. However, reports in 1991 suggest that grazing, forestry and other activities are not controlled and that only six protected areas exist in practice (J. Chytil, *in litt.*, 1991). An ecology party (known as the Green Party) was set up in March 1991, as well as the Albanian Nature Conservationists Union, although their interest in protected areas is not clear (IUCN, 1991; IUCN (in press)).

Most integral reserves have either been destroyed, severely degraded or are now managed as hunting refuges, mostly situated along the coast, where shooting is controlled in winter (Crockford *et al.*, 1991).

Systems Reviews   According to Markgraf (Davis *et al.*, 1986), there are four natural vegetation zones, from west to east across the country, beginning with a narrow coastal strip in the west, now largely agricultural, but with some maquis, phrygana and secondary steppe. This coastal zone is approximately 60km wide and cut by numerous rivers. To the east lies a broad Mediterranean and transitional deciduous forest zone, south of the Orum Valley, with limestone mountains and valleys. European deciduous montane forests of beech *Fagus sylvatica* dominate the eastern mountain belt between the Drin and Osman valleys, with scattered patches of Macedonian pine *Pinus peuce*. Finally, in the highest elevations over 2,000m, along the Yugoslavian border, is a subalpine and alpine zone, north of the River Drin. The latter zone occupies approximately 14% of the territory (IUCN, 1991a). The coast, which appears to be the least altered part of the country, is 472km in length and physically diverse. Four large lakes (between 6,000ha and 35,000ha) are shared with Yugoslavia and/or Greece. All had significant waterfowl populations in the past, but their importance has greatly diminished as a result of extensive land reclamation and drainage.

Some 43% of the country's surface area is forested, the most common trees including beech *Fagus sylvatica*, black pine *Pinus nigra*, and oak *Quercus* sp. Of all newly planted species (some 16 million trees were planted in 1983), 75% are conifers, the rest deciduous. Forests are used for honey and silkworm production, with only small amounts of wood exported (Ellenberg and Damm, 1989). The mountainous forested terrain (50% of land surface is forest and bush) has allowed the bear population to thrive, although the threat of deforestation for agriculture is becoming more significant as land is privatised (IUCN, 1991a). The forests, which are divided into 367 units in 26 districts, are nominally controlled by a ranger. Local people, however, are now using the forests indiscriminately (Crockford *et al.*, 1991).

A major management proposal in 1987 was to combat erosion by further forestry development, involving a national undertaking to expand and improve the forests. During December 1987 over 9 million saplings were to be planted, about 2,400ha of forest improved and 12,000 sq. km of mountainous land protected (Anon., 1987). Tree planting is concentrated in the Puka, Shkodra, Librazhd, Kukes and Fier districts (IUCN, 1991a). One quarter of each of the country's 26 districts is designated as hunting refuge, governed by the Hunting Law and administered by the Forestry Engineering Department (Crockford *et al.*, 1991). Protected forest areas cover 120,476ha (Crockford *et al.*, 1991), divided into: land protection zones (75,000ha); cultural zones (15,671ha); and areas of scientific importance (28,991ha, including biogenetic reserves which cover 5,671ha). Biogenetic reserves consist of (i) natural monuments (1,556ha); (ii) research areas (96ha); (iii) forest occurring outside their normal phytoclimatic zone (1,599ha); (iv) forests protected for their rare and vulnerable species (769ha); (v) forests with medicinal uses (308ha); (vi) rare scrub and endemic plants (90ha) and (vii) biogenetic reserves (1,226ha); forests with special social and medicinal values (748ha). The remaining protected areas include seven national parks and a series of integral and oriented reserves (Crockford *et al.*, 1991).

Strong pressure to convert land for agricultural purposes, coupled with a drive against malaria, have led to the drainage and reclamation of extensive areas of coastal marshes and lagoons. Between 1966 and 1970, 20% of all capital investment was devoted to major hydrological projects. Drainage had already started in 1946 with Maliq Lake and marshes. Between 1946 and 1974 some 60,000ha of wetlands were drained and a further 170,000ha were "improved" for agricultural production; it was proposed that some 18,000ha of the remaining 30,000ha of coastal plains would be developed for future agricultural projects and intensive fisheries. Concern has been expressed (Imboden, *in litt.*, 1990) over several new projects for soil improvement and land reclamation. Three of these overlap or adjoin coastal wetlands considered by the ICBP and IWRB to be of international importance (Kusse and Winkels, 1990).

Water pollution is affecting fisheries and possibly flora and fauna; in the coastal plains the more important rivers are visibly polluted by industrial waste and the establishment of "river parks", similar to those in Greece, has been suggested (Prigioni *et al.*, 1986). Many rivers in the coastal belt have been regulated and canalised. The extensive wetland modification and destruction of habitats is thought to have had a negative effect on many species (IUCN, 1991). A report in 1991 suggests that many nature reserves have been destroyed or severely damaged, leaving only six national parks (Dajti, Divjaka, Llogora, Lvra, Thethi and Bredhi i Drenover) and two forest parks (Voskopoja and Qafshtama) within the protected areas network (Crockford *et al.*, 1991). The major causes for the destruction of nature reserves are clearing for arable land, forest fires, drainage, over-grazing, over-hunting, military use and felling (Crockford *et al.*, 1991).

Addresses

Ministry of Forestry, TIRANA

Central Commission for Environmental Protection, The Council of Ministers, TIRANA

Tirana University, Fakulteti Shkencave Natyre, TIRANA

References

Anon. (1987) ATA in English 0900 gmt 5 Dec 1987.

Bogliani, G. (1987). C'è del verde in Albania – riscopriamo una nazione che cambia. *Airone* 74. June. Italy.

Borisov, V.A., Belousova, L.S. and Vinokurov, A.A. (1985). *Okhranyaemye prirodnye territorii Mira. Natsional'nye parki, zapovedniki, rezervaty.* Moskva, Agropromizdat.

Carp, E. (1980). *Directory of wetlands of international importance in the Western Palaearctic.* IUCN/UNEP/WWF, Gland, Switzerland.

Cobani, J. (1988). Problems of state in protection of the atmospheric environment. (Abstract). *Balkan Scientific Conference*, Environmental protection in the Balkans. Varna, Bulgaria, 20-23 September 1988. (Unseen)

Crockford, N.J. and Sutherland, W. (1991). *Albania: environmental status.* Unpublished report.

Davis, S.D., Droop, S.J.M., Gregerson, P., Henson, L., Leon, C.J., Lamlein Villa-Lobos, J., Synge, H., and Zantovska, J. (1986). *Plants in danger, what do we know?* IUCN, Gland, Switzerland, and Cambridge, UK. 461 pp.

Ellenberg, H. and Damm, K. (1989). *Albanien 1989.* Institut für Geografie, Technische Universität Berlin. 384 pp.

IUCN (1967). *Liste des Nations Unies des parcs nationaux et réserves analogues.* IUCN, Brussels.

IUCN (1971). *United Nations list of national parks and equivalent reserves.* Second edition. Hayez, Brussels. (Translation from the French edition, 1967).

IUCN (1990). *1990 United Nations list of national parks and protected areas.* IUCN, Gland, Switzerland and Cambridge, UK. 284 pp

IUCN (1991). *The environment in Eastern Europe: 1990.* IUCN East European Programme Environmental Research Series 3.

IUCN (1991a). *Environmental status reports: 1990 Volume Two: Albania, Bulgaria, Romania and Yugoslavia.* IUCN East European Programme.

IUCN (in press). Albania. *East European Newsletter* 1.

Karadimov, I. (1989). *Balkan mayors on the environment.* Sofia Press, Bulgaria. (Unseen)

Kusse, P.J., and Winkels, H.J. (1990). Remarks on desalination and land reclamation in the coastal area of the Peoples Socialist Republic of Albania. Dutch Ministry of Agriculture, Nature Management and Fisheries. Unpublished report.

Mara, H. (1988). Des problèmes de l'état et de la protection de l'environnement naturel en RPS d'Albanie. *Environmental Protection in the Balkans.* Balkan Scientific Conference. Varna, Bulgaria, 20-23 September 1988.

Nowak, E. (1976). Albania. In: Smart, M. (Ed.), *Proceedings of the International Conference on Conservation of Wetlands and Waterfowl, Heiligenhafen, Fed. Rep. of Germany, 2-6 December 1974.* IWRB, Slimbridge, UK. Pp. 67-72.

Prigioni, C., Bogliani, G., and Barbieri, F. (1986). The otter *Lutra lutra in Albania. Biological Conservation* 36: 375-383.

Wirth, H. (Ed.) (1979). *Nature reserves in Europe.* Edition Leipzig, Leipzig, German Democratic Republic. 331 pp.

ANNEX
Definitions of protected area designations, as legislated, together with authorities responsible for their administration

Title : Law on Hunting No. 1351

Date: 1 November 1951

Brief description: Legally provides for designation of hunting refuge, governed by the Hunting law and administered by the Forestry Engineering Department

Administrative authority: Forestry Engineering Department

Designations:

Parqet nationale (National park) Has the dual role of providing for public access, recreation and education, and protecting the landscape.

No permanent human occupation or exploitation is permitted. Hunting is prohibited and ancient grazing rights have been withdrawn, although villagers from neighbouring settlements are allowed to gather dead wood.

Tourism is encouraged. Each national park has a forest lodge for accommodation and vehicular access is permitted.

Rezervat gjuetie kategorie A (Integral reserve) Strictly protected for nature conservation. A total protection regime is imposed, with no entry, occupation or exploitation permitted. Hunting is prohibited and ancient grazing rights have been withdrawn.

Rezervat gjuetie kategorie B (Oriented reserve) Provides for traditional human activities, education and protection of the landscape or wildlife. Recreational fishing is permitted.

The system of integral reserves has been largely replaced by hunting refuges, with controlled shooting in the winter, which are situated along the coast.

Sources: Bogliani, 1987; Crockford *et al.*, 1991; IUCN, 1967; IUCN, 1971

Title : Law on Forest Protection No. 3349, superseded by acts of 1966 and 1968

Date: 3 October 1963, 1966 and 1968

Brief description: Legally provides for designation of protected forest areas and administered by the Forestry Engineering Department.

Administrative authority: Forestry Engineering Department, Ministry of Forestry

Designations:

Protected Forest Area Divided into a series of designated types of protected forest zone, by Ministry of Forestry regulations:

Land protection zone to prevent soil erosion and protect water catchments

Cultural zone protected for traditional use by local residents

Area of scientific importance including biogenetic reserves comprising (i) natural monument; (ii) research area; (iii) forest occurring outside normal phytoclimatic zone; (iv) forest protected for their rare and vulnerable species; (v) forests with medicinal use (*Tilia* for lime blossom tea); (vi) rare scrub and endemic plants and (vii) biogenetic reserve.

Forest with special social and medicinal value

Sources: Bogliani, 1987; Crockford *et al.*, 1991

SUMMARY OF PROTECTED AREAS

Map[†] ref.	*National/international designations* Name of area	IUCN management category	Area (ha)	Year notified
	National Parks			
1	Dajt	II	4,000	1966
2	Divjaka	II	4,000	1966
3	Llorgara	II	3,500	1966
4	Lures	II	4,000	1966
5	Thethit	II	4,500	1966
6	Tomori	II	3,000	1956
	Nature Reserves			
7	Berzane	IV	1,000	
8	Cangonj	IV	3,000	
9	Fushe-Senje (Kuqe Negel Patok)	IV	4,200	
10	Karaburum	IV	2,000	
11	Kuturman	IV	4,000	
12	Pishe-Poro	IV	5,500	
13	Rushkull	IV	1,800	

[†]Locations of most protected areas are shown on the accompanying map.

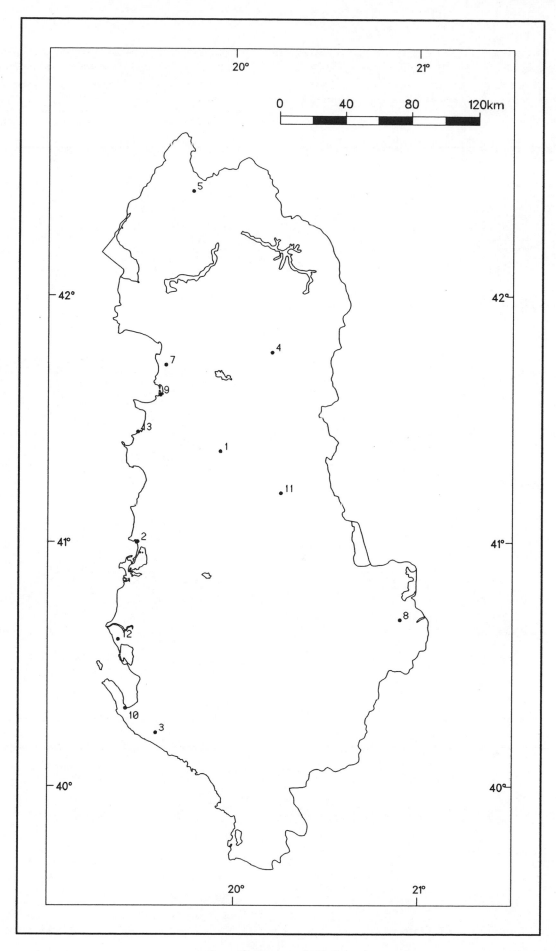

Protected Areas of Albania

ANDORRA

Area 450 sq. km

Population 51,400 (1988) (Hunter, 1991)
Natural increase: 2.76% per annum (Anon., 1990)

Economic Indicators
GDP: No information
GNP: US$ 8,408 per capita (Anon., 1990)

Policy and Legislation The principality of Andorra was formed by a treaty in 1278. Constitutionally, the sovereignty of the country is vested in two Co-Princes, the President of the French Republic and the Spanish Bishop of Urgel. Administrative and legislative powers have been vested in the General Council of the Valley. Since 1982, executive powers were separated from the Council and an Executive Council established.

No specific nature reserve legislation appears to relate to Andorra and no legally designated protected areas were identified in the 1990 *United Nations List of National Parks and Protected Areas*. Specified reserve areas are set aside with three-year temporary hunting bans, under the authority of the General Council (Agriculture and Natural Heritage). Generally hunting restrictions identify game species and hunting seasons, and in addition all birds of prey have been protected by law since February 1988 (Grimmett and Jones, 1989; Hunter, 1991).

International Activities Andorra is not a member of the European Community (although has negotiated trade agreements) or of the Council of Europe, nor has it signed any major international nature conservation treaties. Its foreign affairs are conducted by the Republic of France.

Administration and Management Under the General Council of the Valley, the administrative and management powers relating to the environment are vested in the Council for Agriculture and Natural Heritage (*Conselleria d'Agricultura*) which has responsibility for agriculture, forestry, reafforestation and hunting. Forests are managed for timber production and as an aesthetic resource. Hunting is controlled by issuing permits, by identifying closed seasons and by establishing and administering non-hunting areas. Some species, such as chamois *Rupicapra pyrenaica* require hunting permits during an eight day "season" in September.

The major non-governmental organisation is the Association for the Defence of Nature (*Associacio per a la Defensa de la Natura*).

Systems Reviews Andorra is located on the southern slopes of the eastern Pyrenees, between France and Spain. It contains many mountain peaks, narrow valleys and gorges, which range in altitude from 860m to 2,946m. More than 33% of the country is classed as forest, with pine, fir, oak and birch. Alpine meadows are also well represented. In 1988, there were some 1,000ha of arable land, 10,000ha of forests and 25,000ha of pasture (Grimmett and Jones, 1989; Hunter, 1991).

Andorra has been described as "one of the best centres for exploring the Pyrenean plant world" (Polunin and Smythies, 1973); over 1,000 plant species (including many that are endemic or threatened) have been described (Losa Espana and Montserrat, 1947). Migrating birds use the high passes *en route* between northern Europe and the south and include such species as *Ciconia* and *Pernis apivorus* (Grimmett and Jones, 1989).

Forest land has been classified. To maintain game species hunting is prohibited for three-year periods in non-hunting areas. In 1989, only one such site was in existence (established in 1987). Presently, hunting is prohibited until 1992 in one reserve. Recommended areas of botanical importance include the floristically diverse areas of Pic de Casamanya, Arinsal and Ordinbo (Anon., *in litt.*; Davis *et al.*, 1986; Grimmett and Jones, 1989). Only one ornithological site, Pirineo de Andorra, is listed in the *Important Bird Areas of Europe* (Grimmett and Jones, 1989).

Prior to 1930 there were no paved roads connecting Andorra to France or Spain, and access was largely by mule or on foot. Since then Andorra has developed rapidly. Threats to the land arise from increased human pressure in the form of agriculture, the development of mass tourism, skiing and the use of four-wheel drive vehicles, scrambling motorbikes and skidoos. Hunting and the use of poisoned baits is also a major problem (Carrick, 1988; Fowler, pers. comm., 1991).

Other Relevant Information Tourism is the main economy of the principality with an estimated 10 million tourists per year in 1990 rising from 6 million in 1982 (Hunter, 1991). There are 7 ski resorts, 240 hotels and 26 campsites. Many visitors are further attracted by the duty free status (Carrick, 1988; Hunter, 1991).

Addresses

Conselleria d'Agricultura, Edifui CASS 5e pis, Larrer Maragall S/N, Andorra La Vella
Associacio per a la Defensa de la Natura, Apartat de Correus Espanyols, no. 96, Andorra La Vella

References

Battagel, A (1980). *Pyrenees Andorra Cerdagne a guide to the mountains for walkers and climbers*. Gastons – West Col Publications.
Carrick, N. (1988). *Lets Visit Andorra*. The Macmillan Press Ltd, Basingstoke, UK.

Davis, S.D., Droop, S.J.M., Gregerson, P., Henson, L., Leon, C.J., Lamlein Villa-Lobos, J., Synge, H., and Zantovska, J. IUCN (1986). *Plants in Danger: What do we know?* IUCN, Gland, Switzerland and Cambridge, UK.

Grimmett, R.F.A. and Jones, T.A. (1989). *Important Bird Areas of Europe. International Council for Bird Preservation, Cambridge, UK.*

Hunter, B. (Ed.) (1991). *The Statesman's Year Book 1991-92.* The MacMillan Press Ltd, London and Basingstoke, UK.

Losa Espana, M. and Montserrat, P. (1947). Aportaciones para el conocimiento de la flora del val de Ordesa. *Collect. Bot.* (Barcelona), I. (Unseen)

Losa Espana, M. and Montserrat, P. (1950). Aportacion al conocimiento de la flora de Andorra. *Primo Congreso Internacional del Pirineo del Inst. Est. Pirenaicos*, 53. (Unseen)

Paxton, R. (Ed.)(1989). *The Statesman's Yearbook.* The Macmillan Press Ltd, London and Basingstoke, UK. Pp. 79-80.

Polunin, O. and Smythies, B.E. (1973) (reprinted 1989). *Flowers of south west Europe, a field guide.* Oxford University Press, Oxford.

AUSTRIA

Area 83,848 sq. km

Population 7.6 million (1990)
Natural increase: 0.1% per annum

Economic Indicators
GDP: No information
GNP: US$ 11,970 (1987)

Policy and Legislation The Federal Republic of Austria recovered its sovereignty and independence from the wartime allied forces on 27 July 1955. According to Article 15 Section 1 of the constituted law of 1 October 1920, which was restored on 27 April 1945, matters of nature conservation, hunting and fishing are placed under the jurisdiction of each of the nine state (Länder) governments. However, water and forestry legislation is the domain of the federation. For this reason, Austrian conservation legislation is very complicated, leading to nine sets of legal codes issued by each of the provincial governments for their own territories alone (Anon., 1987; Wegscheider *et al.*, 1991).

One of the first pieces of legislation regarding the environment was the Forestry Act of 1852 which was only repealed in 1975 with a new federal forest law (Mang, 1990). The earliest environmental legislation covering all provinces was enacted in 1938 when the German Nature Conservation Law was extended to Austria and remained in force as the *Reichsnaturschutzgesetz* until the new provincial laws, based on this earlier legislation, took force following World War II (Mang, 1990).

The basic legal principles for all nature conservation matters are laid down in the provincial laws (*Landesgesetze*); further details on wildlife protection are set out in ordinances (*Verordnungen*), whilst their administration is dealt with in specific regulations (*Verwaltungsvorschriften*). A special ordinance is issued for the establishment of each protected area, designating the area and its boundaries and permitting or restricting land uses or other activities.

The main conservation laws for the provinces are included in the Annex; different definitions and regulations occur in the various states: Burgenland – Nature Protection Act of 27 June 1961 (amended 1974); Oberösterreich – Nature and Landscape Protection Act No. 80/1982 of 1982); Niederösterreich – Nature Protection Act No. 3/1977 of 11 November 1976 (amended in No. 3/1985); Salzburg – Nature Protection Act No. 86/77 of 3 July 1977 (amended No. 76/1986); Steiermark – Nature Protection Act No. 65/1976 of 30 June 1976 and No. 79/1985; Tirol – Nature Protection Act No. 15/1975 of 28 November 1974; Vienna – Nature Protection Act No. 6/1985 of 1985); Vorarlberg – Nature Protection Act No. 36/69 of 1969 and Landscape Protection Law No. 1/1982 of 1982; Kärnten – Nature Conservation Law No. 5/1986 of 1986 and Landscape Law No. 49/69 of 30 June 1969.

According to the "Definitions for Nature Conservation" set up by the Working Group of the Conference of provincial officials responsible for nature conservation (Anon., 1975), the following main categories of protected areas are distinguished: nature reserve (*Naturschutzgebiet*); protected landscape (*Landschaftsschutzgebiet*); natural monument or site (*Naturdenkmal*); nature park (*Naturpark*) and national park (*Nationalpark*), although definitions can vary from province to province. While the 1975 classification defines nature reserves as one category, the laws of Burgenland, Kärnten, Niederösterreich, Salzburg and Vienna distinguish two sub-categories, namely: strict nature reserve (*Vollnaturschutzgebiet*), and partial nature reserve (*Teilnaturschutzgebiet*) (Poore and Gryn-Ambroes, 1980; Mang, 1990).

Other aspects of conservation are covered in the provincial hunting laws which not only authorise the hunting of game but also identify a number of species which have a "closed season throughout the year". In addition, the laws governing forestry, fisheries, physical planning and water include regulations for the conservation of nature. In general, the conservation content of these laws consists simply of a basic provision that the objectives of nature conservation and landscape management must be considered in physiographic and land use planning, insofar as this is compatible with social planning and economics (Anon., 1987; Poore and Gryn-Ambroes, 1980).

The Federal Forest Act of 3 July 1975 (repealing the Act of 1852) refers to protection of forests and regulations defining the forms of protection throughout the entire country. The Forest Act defines forest land suited for the purposes of exploitation, protection, environmental influence and recreation. Throughout Austrian legislation, in all categories of protected area, hunting and fishing might be allowed (Grimmett and Jones, 1989).

The legal provision for administering procedures for notification states that once an area is selected, the proposal has to be displayed for public scrutiny. Discretionary decisions are made to change and designate the area through an act of administration. Although the land is then ultimately under sovereign authority, restrictive regulations and ownership may not necessarily be governmental. The degree of protection as well as the range of exemptions from protected status are laid down in a specific ordinance for each protected area. The ordinances provide for general rules, mainly repeating the regulations covered under the law, as well as providing very detailed regulations (see Annex). If an area is purchased, either by the conservation administration or by a private conservation organisation, the price for the land is subject to voluntary negotiation. According to the laws of some provinces, land can be expropriated with compensation to establish a nature reserve but this has never been applied in practice.

A review of protected areas policy and legislation has been undertaken (for details see Mang, 1990). Deficiencies have been identified, indicating that the stated goals of nature conservation legislation have not yet been achieved, and that existing conservation instruments are "inadequate" (Mang, 1990). The problems of protected areas are regarded in some reports as the result of poor legislative, administrative, and policy-making institutions. Existing legislative regulations in provincial nature conservation laws contribute to these problems through: a) lack of clearly defined objectives for each category of protected area; b) lack of enforceable requirements to protected areas; c) lack of categories to adequately protect biotic communities, natural areas connecting the protected areas; nationally significant and represent areas; d) lack of enforceable regulations to protect habitats of endangered species; e) lack of regulations that require the protection of the proper size and shape of protected areas; f) split authority between the nine provinces with no mechanisms for inter-provincial coordination and no consideration of nationwide conservation tasks; g) selection and management are not linked in a comprehensive manner, due to lack of protection objectives; h) general permission for agriculture, forestry, hunting and fishing in protected areas which is detrimental to its protection (Mang, 1990).

International Activities Austria is a member of the Council of Europe: 18 Council of Europe biogenetic reserves have been declared (end-1990). In 1967 one site in Salzburg was awarded the Council of Europe European Diploma. Austria has signed and ratified the Bern Convention on the Conservation of European Wildlife and Natural Habitats. Austria is party to the Convention on Wetlands of International Importance especially as Waterfowl Habitat (Ramsar Convention), ratified on 16 December 1982, and five sites had been inscribed up to 1990. Four areas have been approved as biosphere reserves under the Unesco Man and Biosphere Programme. Austria is not a member of the European Community, but has applied for membership. A decision on integration cannot be expected before the year 1993. Should Austria become a member, guidelines covering the protected area systems of EC countries will be binding for Austria.

In 1952 the Commission Intérnationale pour la Protection des Régions Alpines (CIPRA) was formed, with responsibility for the protection of the Alps. In 1974, IUCN and the Italian Alpine Club jointly organised a major conference in Trento, which produced an action plan for "The Future of the Alps", covering planning, management and use of resources, protection of nature and natural resources. This was followed in 1976 by the Strasbourg Ecological Charter for the Mountainous Regions of Europe, which has led to attempts at integrating community development and nature conservation. In September 1988 a meeting in Voding of invited CIPRA and IUCN experts was commissioned to draft jointly an Alpine Convention which would protect nature and culture in the region.

Transfrontier projects exist for bilateral protected areas with West Germany and Hungary (Firnberg, 1972; Thorsell and Harrison, 1990).

Administration and Management Protected forests and hunting reserves throughout the country are administered and managed by the Federal Ministry of Agriculture and Forestry and managed on a day-to-day basis by personnel of the Department of Forestry. Local forestry administrations establish guidelines for forest areas, particularly those in nature reserves, as well as rules for game management in those protected areas under the auspices of the forestry administration.

There is no administrative organisation responsible for nature conservation at the federal level, although the Ministry for Environment, Youth and Family (*Bundesministerium für Umwelt, Jugend und Familie*) has an advisory role. Provincial nature conservation agencies have authority over the administration of protected areas, which covers the operational demands of planning, designation and management (see address list and Annex for details at the provincial level).

The conservation administration in the provinces is part of the general administration undertaken by the Office of the Provincial Government (*Amt der Landesregierung*), or, in Vienna, the municipal authority (*Magistrat*). Day-to-day responsibility is given to different departments in different provinces (Departments of Agriculture, Cultural Affairs, Physical Planning and Justice). There are apparently no special administrative bodies at the district or local level, where the execution of conservation laws is part of the general administration. However, most of the executive work lies with the district administration (*Bezirksverwaltungsbehörde*), whereas the provincial authorities are responsible for general concepts and conservation policy, initiatives in legislation, release of ordinances and the establishment and abolition of reserves. At provincial level there is an honourary council (*Beirat*) for nature conservation; at district level an honourary adviser (*Konsulent*) has to be appointed by the provincial government. Members of the provincial council are elected from different groups, such as the board of agriculture (*Landwirtschaftskammer*), board of labour (*Kammer für Arbeiter und Angestellte*), boards for the economy, natural history, forestry, tourism, hunting and fisheries (Poore and Gryn-Ambroes, 1980).

Permanent staff are not specifically assigned to administration or management of protected areas and the only qualified full-time employees are those in the Office of the Provincial Governments (*Amt der Landesregierungen*).

In Oberösterreich, AS 20 million were allocated for nature conservation and recreation in 1974 of which AS 2 million were earmarked for the management of nature reserves, and other general nature conservation activities. In Niederösterreich, also in 1974, a total of AS 800,000 was made available for nature conservation (including acquisition of land, management of reserves, publications), and a further AS 4.2 million for nature parks and recreation. In both examples, staff salaries were not included (Poore and Gryn-Ambroes, 1980). Additional sources of funds for nature conservation in general and reserves in particular are sometimes available in other branches of administration, for example, the forestry administration or the provincial museums. The museum authorities are involved in public relations campaigns, while the forest department has a similarly active interest in the management of any nature reserve containing substantial amounts of woodland or forest (Anon., 1987; Poore and Gryn-Ambroes, 1980).

Guidelines are generally not prepared for reserve management nor are there management plans for particular areas (the exceptions include Hohe Tauern National Park and the Neusiedlersee area). Some reserves with particularly urgent management problems have specific regulations, for example, reed-cutting, maintenance of peatbogs and grasslands and the mowing of sedge-meadows (Poore and Gryn-Ambroes, 1980). Normally the conservation branch of the provincial government is responsible for the management and control of nature reserves; but in forest areas this is generally left to the forestry administration in agreement with the conservation administration.

Normally, when the landowners or public body in charge of the land (like the Federal or State Forestry Administration or a community) is not willing to submit to restrictions on their land, some compromise is found, such as establishing a partial nature reserve instead of an intended full nature reserve or by zoning the reserve (Poore and Gryn-Ambroes, 1980).

Responsibility for scientific research rests with the conservation administration of the provinces and the degree of activity differs from one province to another. Close cooperation exists between the provincial administration and certain biological institutions whose research includes conservation management problems. The former Austrian Institute for Nature Conservation and Landscape Management (*Institut für Naturschutz und Landschaftspflege*) of the *Österreichischer Naturschutzbund* (ÖNB), renamed the Institute for Environmental Sciences and Nature Conservation (*Institut für Umweltwissenschaften und Naturschutz*) undertakes research in existing protected areas, on areas regarded as requiring protection, as well as undertaking work on the improvement and greater effectiveness of conservation management (Poore and Gryn-Ambroes, 1980).

The private acquisition of land to ensure the protection of nature is done mostly by the more established organisations such as the Austrian section of WWF, the *Naturschutzbund* and *Österreichischer Alpenverein*. WWF owns two areas totalling over 1,200ha and the *Naturschutzbund* owns 16 areas totalling 99.2ha. The Alpenverein started to purchase alpine areas in 1918 to protect them from development and for recreation purposes. Presently about 34,020ha in the alpine region are owned by this body (Mang, 1990). The above mentioned NGOs, including ÖNB, have played an important role as pressure groups for improvement of reserves as well as in the management and landholding of reserves.

The administration of protected area management is presently regarded to be not sufficiently performed, due to the following:

- no time limit for the administrative procedure to establish protected areas;
- insufficient data and scientific research on natural resources and conservation issues;
- conservation agencies share their authority with conflicting powerful agencies that have mandates promoting utilisation of natural resources.

It is regarded by some bodies that environmental groups have limited personnel and monetary resources, limited access to the political arena and no opportunity to participate legally in the management of protected areas.

Systems Reviews Located in Central Europe, much of land-locked Austria is above 500m. The country consists of three major landscape divisions; the Alps, granite and gneiss highlands and forelands and basins, of which 60% is alpine. The south-west is dominated by the Alps mountain massif which generally exceeds 3,600m; 925 glaciers are located in the central Alps. The Alps have an oceanic climate with a total annual precipitation of up to 3000mm. Ten per cent of the country consists of the granite and gneiss division, a landscape of rolling and moderate slopes. The Forelands and basins division, consists of sedimentary rock in the east, which is in the south there is a is humid continental climate, and in the east a dry continental annual precipitation up to 880mm. Rivers cover a total length of 90,000km and there are over 9,000 lakes and ponds. Major rivers include the Danube (Donau), which divides the north-east of the country, and the March that runs along the border with Czechoslovakia.

The different forms of land use cover include 38.6-42.4% forests and woodland (80% conifers), 33.1-46.9% arable and pasture land and 5-12.8% built-up areas (Mang, 1990; Poore and Gryn-Ambroes, 1980). Forests are largely alpine and subalpine temperate European forest types of oak *Quercus*, fir *Abies* and spruce *Picea*, with oak and chestnut *Castanea* in the lowlands. Extensive tracts of riverine forest still occur along the major river systems. Only remnants survive of the formally extensive moorland and Pannonian forest steppe (Davis *et al.*, 1986; Grimmett and Jones, 1989). About 85% of the forest is set aside for timber production. Surveys have resulted in a list of threatened natural torrents and waterways, including waterways of symbolic national importance (Anon., 1990). Surveys, however, have been going on in most provinces since 1965 to find out which habitats and which areas should be set aside as nature reserves, natural monuments or as protected landscapes (Poore and Gryn-Ambroes, 1980).

Vegetation and phytogeography maps on a scale of 1:100,000 were published in 1971 (Wagner, 1971). There are 2,873 species of fern and flowers and 959 mosses identified (Mang, 1990). In addition, there are 30,000 animal species, 409 vertebrates, 83 mammals, 219 birds, 12 amphibians, 13 reptiles and 73 fish species (Mang, 1990).

The first seminar on nature and national parks throughout Austria took place in May 1986 in Grebenzen Nature Park, Styria. The joint organisers were the Nature Park Administration and CIPRA (Nature and National Parks, 1986). There is now a policy to establish larger reserves in order to ensure a higher extent of representation of the major geo-ecological regions. As in other countries where no national parks or other extended protected areas existed before 1945, nature parks have been established to safeguard outstanding landscapes for recreation and proposals have been made for national parks (Poore and Gryn-Ambroes, 1980; Mang, 1990).

There has been a rise of 20.5% in the number of protected areas, from 116 sites before 1959, to 567 by 1988 (53 designated in the years 1960-69 and 193 in 1970-79) (see Mang, 1990 for details). Up to 23.1% of Austria's surface was protected in 1988 (567 sites) – 3.5% of nature reserves (280 sites), 17.1% of protected landscapes (246 sites), 0.06% protected landscapes - sections (12 sites), 1.0% nature parks (925 sites) and 1.5% national parks (3 sites). Coverage varies from one province to another; nature reserve coverage ranged from 0.3% of a province's land surface (Burgenland) to 12.5% (Vorarlberg) (Mang, 1990).

A comprehensive evaluation of the protected areas has not been conducted, so the suggested revisions have never been put into context (Mang, 1990). Recommendations were forwarded in 1990 for reform of the protected areas system, largely by incorporating the IUCN category system for conservation areas (see details in Mang, 1990). Details included the following: a) an evaluation of protected areas, including an identification of the present failure in legislation, administration and policy for protected areas, an assessment of suggested revisions and an assessment of the protected areas systems in other countries; b) a review of the status and categories of existing areas; c) an assessment of the connection between Austria's protected areas and other conservation and environmental protection strategies; d) an assessment of

the relationship of its categories to those of IUCN (Mang, 1990).

Environmental problems which affect the protected areas system range from aerial pollution to habitat loss through changing agriculture. Currently, 31% of the forested area is damaged by air pollution. The predicted loss of forest cover, is anticipated as endangering vast areas of the country, by making them susceptible to erosion, adding to the already 0.8 million ha under threat from erosion (Mang, 1990). Some of the most serious environmental concerns at present include threats to the Lech, Brandenberger Ache and Gesaüse where there are projects to install hydro-electric power stations (Anon., 1990). Protected area visitor pressure is generally high, and antagonised by local inhabitants, mainly landowners, in rural areas not being sympathetic to the establishment of new reserves or of improving the conservation status of existing reserves (Poore and Gryn-Ambroes, 1980). In the past 10 years an average of 24.8ha has been developed per day for agricultural purposes. In the past century wetlands have been reduced to 10% of their original size due to drainage, buildings or hydrological structures for flood prevention (Mang, 1990).

Addresses

Federal

Bundesministerium für Land-und Forstwirtschaft als Wasserrechts, oder Forstbehörde, 1010 VIENNA

Bundesministerium für Verkehr als Eisenbahnbehörde, VIENNA

Bundesministerium für Bauten und Technik für Angelegenheiten der Bundesstraßen, VIENNA

Bundesministerium für Umwelt, Jugend und Familie (Ministry for Environment, Youth and Family), Radetzky Strasse 2., 1030 VIENNA

(Forestry Department), Federal Ministry of Agriculture and Forestry, Stubenring 1, A-1010 VIENNA

Institut für Umweltwissenschaften und Naturschutz (Institute for Environmental Sciences and Nature Conservation), Österreichischen Akademie der Wissenschaften, Heinrichstrasse 5, 8010 GRAZ

Österreichische Gesellschaft für Natur-und Umweltschutz (Austrian Society for Nature and Environmental Protection), Hegelgasse 25, 1010 VIENNA (Tel: 0222/5132962)

Österreichischer Naturschutzbund, ÖNB (Austrian Nature Protection Union), Arenbergstrasse 10, 5020 SALZBURG

Österreichischer Alpenverein (Austrian Alpine Club), Wilhelm Greilstrasse 15, 6020 INNSBRUCK (Tel: 0512/59547)

WWF-Austria, Österreichischer Stiftverband für Naturschutz, Ottakringer Strasse 114-116/9, Postfach 1, 1162 VIENNA (Tel: 022 2/461463)

Provincial

Burgenland Amt der Burgenländischen Landesregierung, Abt V/I, Landhaus, A-7000 EISENSTADT

Kärnten Amt der Kärntner Landesregierung, Abt. 2, (Verfassungsdienst und Abt. 20, (Landesplanung), Wulfengasse 11, A-9020 KLAGENFURT

Niederösterreich Amt der Niederösterreichischen Landesregierung, Abt. 11/3, Herrengasse 11, A-1014 VIENNA

Oberösterreich Amt der Öberosterreichischen Landesregierung, Promenade 31, A-4020 LINZ

Salzburg Landesgruppe Salzburg, Arenbergstraße 10, 5020 SALZBURG (Tel: 0662/74371)

Amt der Salzburg Landesregierung, Abt. 7, Michael Pacher Straße 36, A-5020 SALZBURG

Steiermark Amt der Steiermärkischen Landesregierung, Abt. 6, A-8010 GRAZ-burg

Tirol Amt der Tiroler Landesregierung, Abt Umweltschutz, Michael-Gaismayr-Straße 1, A-6010 INNSBRUCK

Vienna Magistrat der stadt Wien, Magistratsabt, 22-Umweltschutz, Ebendorferstraße 4, A-1082 VIENNA

Vorarlberg Amt der Vorarlberger Landesregierung, Abt. 11c, Montfort Straße 12, A-6900 BREGENZ

References

Anon. (1975). Naturschutz – Begriffsdefinition, verfasst und zusammengestellt vom Arbeitsausschuss der Konferenz der beamteten Naturschutzreferenten. Manuscript.

Anon. (1984). *Naturschutz Salzburger Report.* Schriftenreihe des Landespressebüros, Salzburg Information Nr. 36. 118 pp.

Anon. (1986a). Nature Conservation policy in the Austrian provinces of Salzburg. *Nature and National Parks* 24: 32.

Anon (1986b). Austria. *Nature and National Parks* 24: 91. 35 pp.

Anon. (1987). Austria. *European Nature Conservation.* Council of Europe, European Committee (Environment Protection and Management Division) for the Conservation of Nature and Natural Resources. Strasbourg.

Anon. (1990). Austria: Threatened waterways. Council of Europe. *Naturopa* 11: 3-4

Anon. (n.d.). Austria - Federal Act to regulate the forest sector (Forest Act 1975). *Food and Agriculture Legislation.* 25: 73-74.

Davis, S.D., Droop, S.J.M., Gregerson, P., Henson, L., Leon, C.J., Lamlein Villa-Lobos, J., Synge, H. and Zantovska, J. (1986). *Plants in danger: what do we know?* IUCN, Gland, Switzerland and Cambridge, UK. 461 pp.

Firnberg, H. (1972). Transfrontier Natural Parks. *Nature in Focus* 11: 2-4.

Gluck, P. (1984). State action in the ecology crisis. *Allgemeine-Forstzeitung* 95: 125-128.

Grimmett, R.F.A. and Jones, T.A. (1989). *Important Bird Areas in Europe.* International Council for Bird Preservation, Technical Publication No. 9, Cambridge, UK.

Hartl, H., Sampl, H. and Unkart, R (1982). *Kleinode Kärntens, Naturschutzgebiete, Landschaftsschutzgebiete and Naturdenkmal.* Kärtner Druck-und Verlagsgesellschaft mbH, Klagenfurt.

Kux, S., Kasperowski-Schmid, E. and Katzmann, W. (1981). *Naturschutz-Empfehlungen zur Umweltgestaltung und Umweltspflege II.* Österreichisches Bundesinstitut für Gesundheitswesen. Vienna. 125 pp.

Mang, J. (1990). Evaluation of Austria's Protected Area System and IUCN's contribution to improve this system. M.Sc. Thesis, University of Michigan. 75 pp.

OROK (1988). *Naturschutzrechtliche Festlegungen in Österreich.* Österreichische Raumordnungskonferenz (OROK) Schriftenreihe Nr. 68. Wien. 23 pp.

Poore, D. and Gryn-Ambroes, P. (1980). *Nature Conservation in Northern and Western Europe.* UNEP-IUCN-WWF, Gland, Switzerland.

Stüber, E. (1986). *Aspekte zur Umweltsituation im Land Salzburg.* Landesanwaltschaft für Ökologie und Landschaftsschutz. 168 pp.

Thorsell, J. and Harrison, J. (1990). Parks that promote peace: a global inventory of transfrontier nature reserves. In: Thorsell, J.W. (Ed.), *Parks on the Borderline: Experience in Transfrontier Conservation.* IUCN, Gland, Switzerland and Cambridge, UK. Pp. 3-12.

Wagner, H. (1971). Natürliche Vegetation. In: Bobek, H. (Ed.), *Atlas der Republik Österreich.* Map IV/3. Österreich Akad. d. Wissensch. Freytag-Berndt & Artaria.

Wegscheider, H., Sokoloff, S. and Haslinger, M. (1991). Nature Conservation in Austria. *Nature Conservation in Austria, Finland, Norway, Sweden, Switzerland, Bulgaria, Czechoslovakia, Hungary, Poland, Romania, Yugoslavia and the Soviet Union.* European Parliament, Directorate-General for Research. Environment, Public Health and Consumer Protection Series, 17. Pp. 9-18.

Wolkinger, F. (1981). *Die Natur- und Landschaftsschutzgebiete Österreichs.* Österreichische Gesellschaft für Natur- und Umweltschutz. Bohmann Druck und Verlag, Vienna.

ANNEX
Definitions of protected area designations, as legislated, together with authorities responsible for their administration

Title: There is no federal nature conservation law (see provincial details)

Date: See provincial details in text

Brief description: There is no federal law encompassing protected area legislation throughout the country. Existing nature conservation legislation was originally based on the German Nature Conservation Law of 1938 which was incorporated into separate legislation in each of the nine provinces (Bundesländer), and on the 1975 classification according to the "Definition for Nature Conservation" of the working group of the Conference of provincial officials responsible for nature conservation. See original provincial legislation for specific information.

Administrative authority: Exists at the provincial level (see address list in text)

General Designations:

This section will focus on the common content of the provincial laws (specific details and laws are listed in Poore and Gryn-Ambroes, 1980; Mang, 1990).

Naturschutzgebiet (Nature reserve) (category provided for in all provincial laws) an area which is distinguished by its highly natural character, by its diversity of fauna or flora and which acts to protect rare or endangered animals, plants or biocenoses. The general criteria for selection of nature reserves are laid down in the conservation laws of the provinces and in the 1975 terminology paper.

— in general all activities which conflict with the specific conservation objectives of the nature reserve are forbidden;
— when public interests in economic exploitation are superior to those of nature conservation, exemptions can be granted from this general line of protection;
— in nearly all privately-owned reserves, it is usual to keep the *status quo*, i.e. economic activities can usually be continued as they were before the establishment of the reserves; forestry, hunting and fishing are not or only partially controlled;
— in all reserves on public lands, forestry, hunting and fishing are normally allowed, as well as the collecting of mushrooms and wild berries; but it is generally forbidden to remove any other plants from a reserve (special regulations dealing with mushroom-gathering are often provided in plant reserves).

Landschaftsschutzgebiet (Protected landscape or landscape protected area) (category provided in all provincial laws) An area of special beauty or importance for public recreation, operations which would change the appearance of a landscape are forbidden, although alterations in the type and land use are generally permitted. There is no general prohibition of human activities. However, some activities such as construction of buildings and other activities with major impacts on ecosystems, are listed in the acts required to get an approval of the administrative agency.

Geschutzer Landschaftsteil (Protected landscape-sections) (category provided by four provincial laws) designated small parts of land containing natural elements, forming unity with buildings, of local climatic, cultural or ecological importance. Permitted activities vary between provinces.

Naturdenkmal (Natural monument or site) (category provided in all provincial laws) a natural feature of scientific or cultural interest or of unique character, aesthetic value or rarity, or a significant feature characteristic of the land- or townscape. No human activities are allowed. The owner of the land is required to maintain the monument or site.

Naturpark (Nature park) (category provided by four provincial laws) an area, open to the public, of special recreational or educational value for the interpretation of nature and landscape. The recreational or educational values of the parks are managed and developed for the public. There is no general restriction of activities, but specifications for each particular area is possible.

Nationalpark (National park) (category provided by six provincial laws) The establishment of a national park requires the enactment of its own national park law. It is an area of representative national value because of its characteristic geomorphological features, its fauna and flora, and of scientific and recreational interest and are open to the public. The area must be protected through legal measures and must be divided into a core zone (of the rank of a "nature reserve") and a fringe zone of the rank of a "protected landscape". It must have a continuous administration and must be under scientific control.

General protection of waters and shores, bogs and fens, alpine regions, glaciers, specific types of ecosystems that are sensitive to human influences receive general protection throughout the provinces. No further particular designation by an act of administration is required. The protection includes prohibition of listed activities and requirements for specific projects for approval by the provincial agencies.

Source: Mang, 1990; Poore and Gryn-Ambroes, 1980

Title: Forest Act

Date: 3 July 1975, repealing sections 1-21 of the Forest Act of 1852

Brief description: Federal act to regulate the forest sector

Administrative authority: Federal Forestry Research Institute

Designations:

Protection forest There are detailed provisions prohibiting and regulating different activities and providing a general public right of access for recreational purposes (Part III).

Source: Mang, 1990

SUMMARY OF PROTECTED AREAS

Map[†] ref.	National/international designations Name of area	IUCN management category	Area (ha)	Year notified
	National Parks			
1	Hohe Tauern (Karnten)	V	27,263	1986
2	Hohe Tauern (Salzburg)	V	66,719	1983
3	Nockberge	V	24,000	
	Nature Reserves			
4	Altausseersee	V	1,050	1959
5	Arnspitze	IV	1,250	1942
6	Auhirschen	IV	1,400	1980
7	Bazora	IV	1,146	1959
8	Blockheide Eibenstein	V	1,400	1964
9	Bodensee – Sattenbachtal	IV	1,400	1982
10	Dachsteingebiet	V	20,000	1964
11	Eisenerzer Reichenstein-Krumpensee	IV	1,000	1973
12	Gadental	IV	1,336	1987
13	Gesause und anschliessendes Ennstal	IV	13,700	1958
14	Grossglockner-Pasterze mit Gamsgrube	IV	3,698	1935
15	Grundlsee mit Toplitzee, Kammersee u. Teile.	IV	9,700	1959
16	Gurkursprung	IV	1,497	1981
17	Hochifen u. Gottesackerwande	IV	2,956	1964
18	Hohe Kugel-Hoher Freschen-Mellental	IV	7,500	1979
19	Horfeld	IV	2,166	1987
20	Inneres Pollatal	IV	3,200	1973
21	Kaisergebirge	V	10,200	1963
22	Kalkhochalpen	IV	24,600	
23	Karwendel (LGB1 15/75)	IV	54,326	1989
24	Karwendel	V	72,000	1933
25	Keutschacher See-Tal	V	2,532	1970
26	Klafferkessel	IV	1,200	1980
27	Krakauhintermuhlen	IV	6,200	1987
28	Lainzer Tiergarten	V	2,300	1941
29	Loser-Brunning-Zinken	IV	1,750	1974
30	Marchauen-Marchegg	IV	1,150	1973
31	Muttersberg	IV	1,146	1959
32	Nasskohr	IV	1,000	1971

Map[†] ref.	*National/international designations* Name of area	IUCN management category	Area (ha)	Year notified
33	Nenzinger Himmel	IV	1,051	1958
34	Neusiedler See u. seine Umgebung	V	49,100	1980
35	Neydhartinger Moor	IV	1,238	1979
36	Niedere	IV	1,283	1974
37	Nordwestlicher Teil des Gemeeinde Ramsan am Dach.	IV	1,288	1972
38	Patscherkofel	IV	1,200	1947
39	Rellstal und Lunerseegebiet	IV	3,328	1966
40	Rheindelta	IV	1,959	1976
41	Rosanin	IV	1,100	1977
42	Schobergruppe-Nord	IV	10,380	1964
43	Seekar-Barental	IV	1,100	1981
44	Sengsengbirge	IV	3,400	1976
45	Sonntag	IV	4,977	1968
46	Steirische Nockberge	IV	2,074	1988
47	Tennengebirge	IV	4,400	1982
48	Tiefenwald-Staffel	IV	1,156	1974
49	Untere Marchauen	IV	1,166	1987
50	Valsertal	V	3,300	1941
51	Vandans-Tschagguns	IV	4,062	1963
52	Villacher Alpe	IV	1,902	1967
53	Vilsalpsee	V	1,510	1957
54	West- und Ostabhange des Zirbitzkogels	IV	2,314	1966
55	Wildalpenar Salzatal	IV	51,460	1958
56	Wolayersee und Umgebung	IV	1,939	1973
	Landscape Protected Areas			
57	Achental-West	V	3,812	1989
58	Amering-Stubalpe	V	22,000	1956
59	Ausseres Pollatal	V	1,730	1973
60	Barenkopf	V	1,300	1989
61	Bernstein-Lockenhaus-Rechnitz	V	25,281	1972
62	Bisamberg	V	2,000	1965
63	Bohmerwald	V	96,000	
64	Bundschuhtal	V	2,250	1973
65	Dachstein-Salzkammergut	V	54,000	1956
66	Dobersberg	V	1,600	1978
67	Donau-March-Thaya-Auen	V	20,500	1982
68	Ennstaler Alpen-Eisenerzer Alpen	V	47,740	1956
69	Enzerfeld-Lindabrunn-Hernstein	V	7,000	1967
70	Eppzirl	V	3,341	1989
71	Falkenstein	V	3,500	1980
72	Felbertal, Amertalod, Dorferod	V	9,500	1980
73	Forchenstein-Rosalia	V	3,732	1968
74	Forstheide	V	1,250	1983
75	Friesingwand u. Enge v. St.Peter-Freienstein	V	1,060	1956
76	Gamstein-Voralpe	V	4,845	1987
77	Gasteiner Tal	V	13,850	1978
78	Gemeinschaftsalmen	V	1,153	1989
79	Geras und Umgebung	V	3,250	1970
80	Gleichenberger Kogel	V	5,280	1956
81	Goll, Hagengebirge, Hochlonig Steinernes Meer	V	4,200	1980
82	Grossfragant	V	1,115	1973
83	Grossglochner Hochalpenstrasse	V	1,200	1984
84	Habachtal	V	20,000	1960
85	Haltschlger Talschlusse	V	6,350	1978
86	Hefferthorn-Fellhorn-Sonnenberg	V	6,800	1983
87	Herberstein-Klamm, Freienberger-Klamm	V	2,160	1956
88	Hochalpe	V	7,140	1956

Map[†] ref.	National/international designations Name of area	IUCN management category	Area (ha)	Year notified
89	Hochschwab-Zeller Staritzen	V	37,080	1956
90	Hohe Wand-Durre Wand	V	12,800	1955
91	Huttschlager Talschlusse	V	6,350	
92	Johannisbachklamm	V	2,000	
93	Kamptal	V	35,000	1955
94	Katselberg-Budesstrasse	V	1,710	1959
95	Keutschacher Sea-Tal	V	2,532	1970
96	Konigsleiten	V	3,600	1964
97	Koralpe	V	3,200	1956
98	Lantschfeldtal, Oberes Zederhaustal, Ob.Murtal	V	25,400	1958
99	Leiserberge	V	7,000	1970
100	Lobau	V	1,000	1954
101	Lungauer Nockgebiet Kalkogel	V	7,770	1983
102	Mariazell-Seeberg	V	23,460	1956
103	Martinswand-Solstein-Reither Spitze	V	4,773	
104	Millstatter See-Sud	V	1,984	1970
105	Mittleres Ennstal	V	5,120	1956
106	Murauen Graz-Werndorf	V	1,480	1956
107	Murauen Mureck-Radkersberg	V	11,280	1956
108	Murauen im Leibnitzer Feld	V	1,380	1956
109	Niedere Tauern	V	20,000	
110	Nord Kette	V	1,846	1989
111	Nordliches u. ost. Hugelland v. Graz	V	11,670	1956
112	Nosslachjoch-Obernberger See-Tribulaune	V	9,200	1984
113	Oberes Ennstal	V	7,400	1956
114	Oberes Pulkautal	V	3,500	1973
115	Obertauern	V	3,714	
116	Otscher-Durrenstein	V	80,000	1955
117	Otztaler Alpen	V	39,600	1981
118	Pack-Reinischkogel-Rosenkogel	V	23,480	1956
119	Palten-und Liesingtal	V	3,900	1956
120	Peggauer Wand-Lurgrotte	V	1,140	1956
121	Plesch-Walzkogel	V	6,600	1956
122	Pleschaitz-Puxberg	V	2,400	1956
123	Pollauer Tal	V	12,100	1979
124	Postalm	V	1,405	1975
125	Priedrof	V	1,650	1986
126	Rax-Schneeberg	V	71,500	1955
127	Reiting-Eisenerzer Reichenstein	V	10,280	1956
128	Rottenmanner-Triebener u. Seckauer Alpen	V	53,260	1957
129	Salzberg-Sud	V	1,248	1975
130	Sausal	V	6,200	1974
131	Schafberg-Salzkammergutseen	V	5,769	1981
132	Schladminger Tauern bis Solker Pass	V	52,280	1956
133	Schlossberg bei Leutschach	V	2,120	1956
134	Schockl-Weizklamm-Hochlantsch	V	30,660	1956
135	Schonberg-Gfollerriegel	V	1,680	1956
136	Serles-Habicht-Zuckerhutl	V	18,000	1984
137	Sierningtal	V	3,100	1978
138	Soboth-Radlpass	V	10,660	1956
139	Spertental-Rettenstein	V	4,100	1984
140	Strudengau u. Umgeburg	V	12,600	1955
141	Stubaier Alpen	V	35,220	1983
142	Stuhleck-Pretul	V	9,180	1956
143	Sudbegenlandisches	V	14,272	
144	Tennengebirge	V	2,500	1965
145	Thayatal	V	2,900	1955

Map[†] ref.	*National/international designations* Name of area	IUCN management category	Area (ha)	Year notified
146	Trumer Seen	V	2,300	1986
147	Turracherhohe-Eisenhut-Frauenalpe	V	26,620	1956
148	Untersberg	V	4,242	1953
149	Veitsch-Schneealpe-Raxalpe	V	23,560	1956
150	Villacher Alpe	V	3,904	1970
151	Vorberg	V	2,450	1989
152	Vornbacher Enge	V	3,000	
153	Wachau und Umbegung	V	46,300	1955
154	Waldbach-Vorau-Hochwechsel	V	20,120	1956
155	Waldheimat	V	5,640	1956
156	Warscheneck-Gruppe	V	13,880	1956
157	Weissensee	V	7,648	1970
158	Westliches Berg- und Hugelland von Graz	V	5,792	1956
159	Wienerwald	V	105,000	1955
160	Wildegg-Speikkogel	V	9,000	1956
161	Wildgerlostal, Krimmler, Achental, Oberes.	V	5,000	1958
162	Wollanig-Oswaldiberg	V	1,120	1970
163	Wolzertauern von Solkerpass bis G. Windlucke	V	22,880	1956
164	Zirbitzkogel	V	9,200	1956
	Lake Protection Areas			
165	Aber oder Wolfgangsee	IV	1,904	1971
166	Grabensee und Trumerseen	IV	2,300	1971
167	Waller oder Seekirchrer See	IV	1,412	1971
	Nature Parks			
168	Eichenhain	V	3,500	1983
169	Eisenwurzen	V	4,845	1987
170	Fohrenberge	V	6,600	1974
171	Grebenzen-Furtnerteich	V	6,600	1982
172	Hohe Wand	V	2,000	1973
173	Jauerling-Wachau	V	3,600	1983
174	Kamptal Schonberg	V	1,515	1986
175	Leiserberge	V	4,500	1970
176	Otscher-Tormauer	V	9,000	1970
177	Pollauer Tal	V	12,100	1982
178	Solktaler	V	28,800	1982
	Biosphere Reserves			
	Gossenkollesee	IX	100	1977
	Gurgler Kamm	IX	1,500	1977
	Lobau Reserve	IX	1,000	1977
	Neusiedler See-Österreichischer Teil	IX	25,000	1977
	Ramsar Wetlands			
	Donau-March-Auen	R	38,500	1982
	Lower Inn reservoirs	R	870	1982
	Neusiedlersee	R	60,000	1982
	Pürgschachen Moor	R	62	1982
	Rheindelta, Bodensee	R	1,960	1982
	Untere Lobau	R	1,039	1982

[†]Locations of most protected areas are shown on the accompanying map.

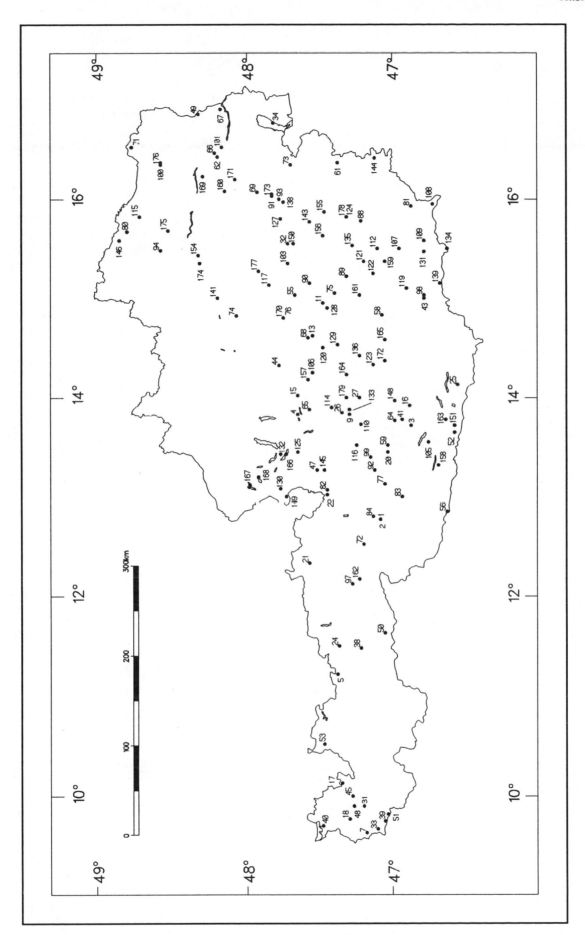

Protected Areas of Austria

BELGIUM

Area 30,512 sq. km

Population 9,845,000 (1990)
Natural increase: 0.0% per annum

Economic Indicators
GDP: US$ 14,387 per capita (1987)
GNP: US$ 11,360 per capita (1987)

Policy and Legislation The Kingdom of Belgium was formed as an independent state from the Netherlands under the decree of 4 October 1830. The Constitution dates from 1831.

The administrative and legal structure, as it relates to protected areas, is complex. Five public bodies are covered under the legislative framework. First, there is the National State, with legislative power. Next, there are three regions, Flanders (the Flemish Region), the Walloon Region and the Brussels Region. These have regional councils made up of regional members of parliament and are capable of passing legally binding decrees; the Regional Executive is elected by the Regional Council, where the different political parties are proportionally represented. Next, there are three language communities (French, Flemish and German), each with a Council and an Executive, with a composition and function similar to those of the regional bodies. There are nine provinces, each of which has a democratically elected Provincial Council, and also a non-constitutional Regional Delegation which is often entrusted by law with certain duties, including matters of the environment. Finally, there are some 600 communes (municipalities), each with a democratically elected municipal Council responsible for municipal regulations (Cutrera, 1991).

The 1957 Act, establishing the Council for Nature Conservation (as part of the Ministry of Agriculture), allowed for the creation of nature reserves and the formulation of a national policy for nature conservation. This Act was superseded by the Law on Nature Conservation of 12 July 1973, which is intended to safeguard the character, diversity and integrity of the natural environment by measures protecting flora and fauna, their communities and their habitat, as well as the soil, sub-soil and air. It states that areas may be set aside as nature reserves either under full protection or of the specialised type, such as forest reserves and nature parks. Within the nature reserve category it allows for privately-owned approved reserves (réserves agréées), subject to an agreement between the regional Minister responsible for nature conservation and the landowner (see Annex). This law actually contains very few provisions suitable for immediate implementation (Cutrera, 1987).

The Law of Institutional Reforms of 8 August 1980 has led to the three regions being vested individually with responsibility for nature conservation. Thus, the 1973 Law now falls under regional jurisdiction (Jadot and Serusiaux, 1987; Poore and Gryn-Ambroes, 1980).

The Walloon Region approved a Nature Parks Decree on 16 July 1985 which gives details of the definition and establishment of nature parks, and also covers management, planning, modification, declassification, and penalties concerning these parks (Anon., 1986), although this only applies to sites in Walloon.

The Forestry Code was approved by the law of 19 December 1854, while details of its implementation were covered under the Royal Ordinance of 20 December 1854. Most of the regulations, which are now the responsibility of the regions, are concerned with public forests. Some of these regulations are aimed at forest conservation, for example the obligation to manage woodland and to limit tree felling. A law of 28 December 1931 gives further details of the protection of woods and forests. This is also now administered regionally, and gives further protection to privately-owned forests where these are greater than 10ha. It allows the relevant authority to object to the clearing of trees in areas where conservation is considered to be in the public interest (Cutrera, 1991).

The Law on the Conservation of Monuments and Natural Sites of 7 August 1931 covered the conservation of monuments and places of cultural importance. This Law originally empowered the Ministry of National Education and Culture to protect areas against modification, using a relatively efficient and simple procedure, although it did not provide for management of such areas. Under the 1980 Law of Institutional Reforms, cultural heritage was entrusted to the separate language communities, although since the 1988 reforms this has changed and responsibility now falls to the regions. Existing legislation thus includes national, community and regional texts. Although the sites, monuments and areas designated under these laws largely protect the cultural and archaeological heritage, some of the legislative texts include reference to works of nature and sites, the preservation of which is important for scientific reasons.

An EC Directive concerning environmental impact assessments (EIAs) was adopted on 27 June 1985. EIAs must take into account a number of factors including, among other things, flora, fauna, soil, water, and the landscape. Belgium has indicated that it intends to implement the EC Directive under a separate new law. So far, it has not, however, prepared any legislation on the national level. In the Walloon Region an EIA decree was passed in September 1985, while a separate ordinance providing for the enforcement of these rules has been effective since January 1988. In the Flemish Region EIA regulations, notably to control the granting

103

of mining licences, exist within the framework of the Decree of June 1985 on anti-pollution measures, although regulations on the procedures to make the decree operative have yet to be passed. There are no EIA regulations in the Brussels Region (Coenen and Jörissen, 1989; Cutrera, 1991).

The authorisation process for nature reserves is complex and there is no legislation concerning what sites may or may not be given this title. In nature parks the need for a management plan to incorporate the conservation, planning and development goals of sites and to incorporate the needs of the local population is essential, although so far only one site has such a management plan (Cutrera, 1991).

International Activities   Belgium became a party to the Convention on Wetlands of International Importance especially as Waterfowl Habitat (Ramsar Convention) in March 1986. Six sites are listed under this Convention.

Belgium has signed The Convention on the Conservation of European Wildlife and Natural Habitats (Bern Convention). It is a member of the European Community and hence is bound by its environmental directives: 36 sites have been designated as EC special protection areas under the Wild Birds Directive (1991). The country is also a member of the Council of Europe: 18 sites have been declared as Council of Europe biogenetic reserves. In addition, one site has been awarded the Council of Europe European Diploma.

There are two important transboundary protected areas: Hautes-Fagnes Eifel Park and Nordeifel Nature Park in Germany; and the Belgium-Luxembourg Nature Park.

Administration and Management   Prior to 1980, the 1973 Nature Conservation Act was under the authority of the Water and Forests Administration (Administration des Eaux et Forêts) of the Ministry of Agriculture. The Water and Forests Administration has two directorates: one concerned with general matters, hunting and fishing; the other concerned with public, communal and private forests. This latter has seven divisions, of which the Nature Conservation Service (Le Service de la Conservation de la Nature, Dienst voor Natuurbehoud), set up by Royal Decree on 18 May, 1976, has responsibility for the establishment and management of nature reserves (Anon., 1980; Poore and Gryn-Ambroes, 1980).

Under Article 6 of the Law of Institutional Reforms of 8 August 1980, most state control of environmental issues was delegated to the regions with their Directorates for Nature Conservation. This included urban and regional planning, green belts, parklands, forests, hunting and fishing (Cutrera, 1987). A further reform, passed under the Law of 8 August 1988 (in force since January 1989), lays down the new constitutional framework for environmental policy in Belgium. The regions have been awarded new powers and the financial means at the disposal of the federal agencies have been increased. The local authorities, particularly the municipalities, are responsible, in principal, for all matters related to the management of environmental issues within their respective localities. Problems have arisen in the past from legislation decreed by higher authorities which has effectively deprived the municipalities of part of their authority in this area. More recently, there have moves to hand back to the municipalities a number of specific powers (Cutrera, 1991).

Since decentralisation as a result of the 1980 reforms, nature conservation services within the competent regional administration departments have been responsible for the acquisition and management of state-owned nature reserves. State-owned reserves, however, make up only part of the reserve network; they cover some 45% of the reserve area in the Walloon Region and about 35% of the reserve area in the Flemish Region the remainder are managed by non-governmental organisations NGOs). In every region the Upper Council for Nature Conservation (Le Conseil Supérieur de la Conservation de la Nature, Hoge Raad voor Natuurbehoud) is consulted with regard to new reserves or similar projects for nature protection. This Council was originally nominated by Royal Decree; it has representatives from government, universities and private nature conservation bodies. Since 1987, management commissions, or advisory committees, composed of scientific experts, have assisted in the management of state-owned nature reserves (Anon., 1980; Cutrera, 1991; Poore and Gryn-Ambroes, 1980).

In the Flemish Region the Directorate for Nature Conservation is a part of the Administration for Land Management and Environment. The Nature Conservation Institute (*Institut voor Natuurbehoud*) has been created within this administration to undertake specific research and give scientific advice. In the Walloon Region the Directorate for Nature Conservation is a part of the Administration of Natural Resources and Environment. In the Brussels Region the Water and Forests Service now administers the Nature Conservation Act. These authorities are responsible for all matters of nature conservation, including drafting new decrees, coordination of advisory committees and regional nature conservation councils, all matters relating to purchase of reserves and public relations (Anon., 1987a, 1990).

The administration and management of public forests is under the control of regional forestry departments, whose structure varies from region to region. The national territory is divided into inspectorates and cantons headed by engineers in charge of administering and supervising forest land. Private forests are entirely managed by their owners, who are under no obligation with regard to management practices, but equally receive no government aid, subsidy nor other incentive for improvement (Cutrera, 1991).

Concerning the cultural heritage, the Royal Commission for Monuments and Sites (Commission Royale des

Monuments et Sites), established in 1835, decided what was to be designated a monument or site by Royal Order. Under a 1931 Law all requests for the classification of sites had to be placed through the Commission, which came under the Ministry for National Education and Culture (Anon., 1980; Poore and Gryn-Ambroes, 1980). Following the 1980 Law of Institutional Reforms the managing of the cultural heritage fell to the language communities. This was changed again, however, under the 1988 reforms, and responsibility now falls to the regions. There is a Royal Commission for Monuments and Sites for each region, while separate regional administration also exists (Cutrera, 1991).

The transfer of sovereign powers in environmental matters has led to some confusion, both in matters of understanding of responsibility and in matters of legal interpretation of the 1980 Act. A further problem arises from the lack of a regional definition of the relationship between the regional and the community authorities. Thus, disputes have arisen between regional policies concerning conservation and town and country planning and community policy concerning protection of the cultural heritage (Cutrera, 1991).

A number of NGOs own or manage nature reserves; in all they manage about 60% of the reserve area and 88% of the reserves themselves. Most of these organisations belong to a coordinating body, "Inter-Environment", which also acts as their spokesman with the central authorities. Some of the most important NGOs which own and manage protected areas include Entente national pour la protection de la nature, L'Association des réserves naturelles et ornithologiques de Belgique, Ardennes et Gaume and De Wielewaal (Duffey, 1982; Cutrera, 1991). In 1980 the financial support given by the state to NGOs was FrB 3 million, while FrB 10 million was made available for the management of state nature reserves (Duffey, 1982).

Systems Reviews   Belgium is mostly a low-lying country bordering the Netherlands, Germany, Luxembourg and France. It is dominated by the basins of the rivers Escaut/Schelde and Meuse, and the basin of the river Ijzer; the only high ground is in the south-east where the Ardennes rise to 694m. The coast is low and sandy with a line of dunes running along it. This area is largely built up, while behind it lies a 10-15km wide fertile plain that has been reclaimed and is intensively farmed. Inland are more plains and hilly regions.

Heathland is found in the Kempen region, but in many places this has been replaced by *Pinus* plantations. Remnants of oak and oak/beech woods with birch are found in the north and east. Further south, the river lowlands of Sambre and Meuse are densely populated and have large industrial areas. Between the river lowlands and the Ardennes is a region where the soils are rather poor for intensive agriculture and where, as a result, some dry grassland and forest still remains. In the Ardennes the slopes are largely covered by deciduous forest or coniferous plantations, while on the highest plateaux there are a number of peat bogs (Davis *et al.*, 1986; Grimmett and Jones, 1989). In 1985, woodland covered some 20% of the country, while some 47% of the land was cultivated. These figures were little changed from the figures in 1970 (Anon., 1987).

The first protected areas were all under private ownership and date back to 1945. It was not until 1957, when the Council for Nature Conservation was founded, that the first two state reserves were founded (Duffey, 1982). By 1970 Belgium had 54 nature reserves, covering 11,839ha; this figure included both state and private (though not necessarily "authorised") nature reserves, which covered a similar area at the time. This number had virtually doubled by 1977, although the average size of the reserves had decreased enormously, such that the area under protection only increased by 16%. In the subsequent six years, the state's financial support rose by only 2%, while private organisations increased their assistance by 59%. The area covered by protected areas increased to 17,719ha by 1983-4 (Jadot and Serusiaux, 1987). In 1987 there were 98 private reserves in the Walloon Region, 130 in the Flemish Region and 1 in the Brussels Region (Anon., 1987a). There is only one national nature park at present, Hautes-Fagnes Eifel Park established by Decree on 21 March 1984. There are 12 nature parks planned for the Walloon Region and four for the Flemish Region. The initiators behind these include NGOs, provinces and inter-commune consortia (Cutrera, 1991).

Private reserves greatly exceed state reserves both in number and, to a lesser degree, in area covered; *L'Association des réserves naturelles et ornithologiques de Belgique*, for example, owns 100 reserves covering some 4,000ha (Anon., 1987b). It is not possible, under existing legislation, for these reserves to obtain state recognition (as authorised nature reserves) in Walloon, and the authorisation procedures for state recognition in Flanders are lengthy and complex. As a result, it is difficult to quantify and categorise the majority (Jadot and Serusiaux, 1987). A further inconsistency in Flanders and Walloon has arisen from the fact that anyone in these regions can call an area a nature reserve, so there is little or no consistency in the meaning of this title when applied to unrecognised private reserves (Cutrera, 1987).

The forested area is divided amongst over 100,000 landowners, 69% of whom own less than 1ha. This fragmentation, largely the resulting from the inheritance laws, creates major difficulties with regard to the effective management of forest areas. There as an increasing predominance of coniferous forest areas, often at the expense of deciduous forest, which is being encouraged by the political authorities. The planting of exotic spruce trees in the Ardennes has developed unchecked; in the Walloon Region direct government subsidies are available for forest clearance. It is estimated that the coniferous forest area is increasing at the rate of 2,000ha a year (Cutrera, 1987).

In the Walloon Region an inventory of sites of major biological interest has been prepared and is continuously updated by the NGO Inter-environnement Wallonie.

Many of the large protected areas are under increasing pressure for recreational use. As more and more people move off the paths so disturbance to the wildlife is increasing in Haute Fagnes Eifel Nature Park mandatory trails have been marked out, surveillance has been increased and access permits are now required (Cutrera, 1991).

Addresses

Administration de la Recherche Agronomique, Ministère de l'Agriculture, Manhattan Centre, 7ème étage, Av. du Boulevard 21, 1210 BRUSSELS (Tel: 2 211 7211; Tlx: 22033 Agrilla; Fax: 2 211 7216)

Administration des eaux et forêts, Ministère de l'Agriculture, Chaussée d'Ixelles 29-31, 1050 BRUSSELS

Inter-Environment Wallonie, rue d'Arlon 25, 1040 BRUSSELS (Tel: 2 512 3010)

Entente nationale pour la protection de la nature, rue de la Paix 83, 6168 CHAPPELLE-LEZ-HERLAIMONT (Tel: 64 443303)

L'Association des réserves naturelles et ornithologiques de Belgique, rue Vautier 31, 1040 BRUSSELS (Tel: 2 648 3746)

Ardennes et Guame, Square Marguerite 1, 1040 BRUSSELS (Tel: 2 733 9151)

References

Anon. (1980). *Protected Areas in the European Community, an approach to a common classification.* Environment and Consumer Protection Service, Commission of the European Communities.

Anon. (1986). XIX/4 – National Parks and Nature Reserves, Belgium. *Food and Agricultural Legislation* 35: 92-93.

Anon. (1987a). *Management of Europe's natural heritage, Twenty-five years of activity.* Environment Protection and Management division, Council of Europe, Strasbourg.

Anon. (1987b). Short news. *Nature and national parks* (25): 35.

Anon. (1990). *Directory of wetlands of international importance.* Ramsar Convention Bureau, Gland, Switzerland. 796 pp.

Coenen, R. and Jörissen, J. (1989). *Environmental impact assessment in the member countries of the European Community, implementing the EC-Directive: an overview.* KfK 4507 B, Kernforschungszentrum, Karlsruhe, Germany. 42 pp.

Cutrera, A. (1987). *European environmental yearbook 1987.* DocTer International UK, London. 816 pp.

Cutrera, A. (1991). *European environmental yearbook.* Institute for Environmental Studies. DocTer International UK/London. 897 pp.

Davis, S.D., Droop, S.J.M., Gregerson, P., Henson, L., Leon, C.J., Lamlein Villa-Lobos, J., Synge, H., and Zantovska, J. (1986). *Plants in danger: what do we know?* IUCN, Gland, Switzerland, and Cambridge, UK. 461 pp.

Duffey, E. (1982). *National parks and reserves of Western Europe.* Macdonald and Co. (Publishers) Ltd., London and Sydney. 288 pp.

Grimmett, R. F. A. and Jones,T. A. (1989). *Important bird areas in Europe.* International Council for Bird Preservation, Cambridge, UK.

Poore and Gryn-Ambroes (1980). *Nature conservation in Northern and Western Europe.* UNEP/IUCN/ WWF, Gland, Switzerland. Pp. 103-116.

ANNEX
Definitions of protected area designations, as legislated, together with authorities responsible for their administration

Title: *Loi sur la conservation de la nature* (Law on Nature Conservation)

Date: 12 July 1973

Brief description: Provides for the establishment of three types of protected area for conservation purposes (supersedes the 1957 conservation act).

Administrative authority:
Brussels Region: Water and Forests Service
Flemish Region: Directorate for Nature Conservation, within the Administration for Land Management and the Environment
Walloon Region: Directorate for Nature Conservation, within the Administration of Natural Resources and the Environment

Designations:

Réserve naturelle (Nature reserve) Subdivided into those that are "fully protected", where the natural systems are allowed to exist and evolve without human influence, and those termed "specialised" nature reserves, where certain aspects of the flora and fauna are managed, or where modified habitats are to be restored. Generally, these reserves are state-owned.

There is also a provision for "authorised nature reserves", privately-owned and managed, which may be eligible for government subsidies towards administration and management. These have been recognised in the Flemish and Walloon regions, where regulations have been established which control the concession of authorisations and subsidies.

In all nature reserves, hunting and the felling of trees is prohibited. A Ministerial Decree of 25 October 1975 established rules on surveillance, policing and traffic in the state-owned nature reserves. There are also particular laws dealing with motorised vehicles, camping and leaving litter.

Réserve forestière (Forest reserve)   Forests, or parts of forests, protected for their distinctive or important indigenous tree species. The regional authority may, at the request of the Minister, turn an area of forest which is under its jurisdiction into a forest reserve.

A Royal Decree of 24 April 1979 sets forth the rules and regulations regarding the management, stipulating that the owners of any territory that is to be turned into a forest reserve must draw up a management plan. It also contains a series of laws concerning construction, litter and camping sites. In some instances silvicultural exploitation and hunting may be permitted.

Parc naturel (Nature park)   Areas governed by special arrangements designed to conserve the environment, the indigenous flora and fauna, the air, water and soil. The law makes a distinction between national nature parks and regional nature parks. National nature parks can only be established by a regional authority, through an official decree (only one exists to date). Regional nature parks can be established by any other authority.

In the Walloon Region nature parks are established under a decree of 16 July 1985 which defines their main objectives as the conservation of the character, diversity and scientific values of the environment and of the natural flora and fauna whilst acknowledging their importance for recreation and tourism. They have a minimum size of 5,000 ha, are multiple use areas (with some restrictions on human activities) and contain villages and local industries.

Sources: Cutrera, 1991; Duffey, 1982

SUMMARY OF PROTECTED AREAS

Map ref.	*National/international designations* Name of area	IUCN management category	Area (ha)	Year notified
	State Nature Reserve			
1	Hautes Fagnes	IV	3,975	1957
	Nature Park			
2	Hautes-Fagnes-Eifel	V	67,854	1985
	Ramsar Sites			
	Le Blankaart	R	2,160	1986
	Kalmthoutse Heide	R	4,045	1986
	Le Marais d'Harchies	R	535	1986
	Les Schorren de l'Escaut à Doel et à Zandvliet	R	417	1986
	Les Vlaamse Banken dans les eaux côtieres	R	1,900	1986
	Le Zwin	R	550	1986

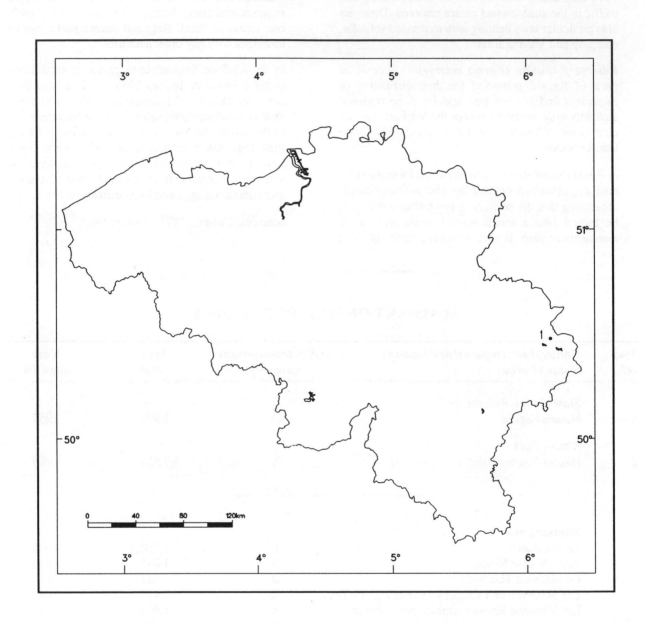

Protected Areas of Belgium

REPUBLIC OF BULGARIA

Area   110,911 sq. km

Population   9,000,000 (mid-1989 estimate)
Natural increase: 0.1% per annum

Economic Indicators
GDP: No information
GNP: US$ 7,129 per capita (Anon., 1990)

Policy and Legislation   On 5 October 1908 Bulgaria declared its independence from Turkey and in September 1946 a People's Republic was proclaimed. The Constitution refers to nature conservation under Article No. 31 (1971). In Articles 22 and 23, proposals for designation of protected natural sites can be submitted by enterprises, institutions, organisations and by individuals. The new Constitution, enacted in 1991, treats the matter of the environment in a single text – Article 15 (Spiridonov *et al.*, 1991).

Countryside protection dates from 1928 (Carter, 1977), when a "union for nature protection", the Council for the Protection of the Countryside, was formed. The first Conservation of Nature Act was issued in 1936 (Decree on protection of native nature) (Cerovsky, 1986; Spiridonov *et al.*, 1991). It established four categories of protected area and introduced species protection measures (Spiridonov *et al.*, 1991). Little more was achieved during the war of 1939-45 nor in the ten years that followed. A nature protection decree was formulated on 27 August 1960 and brought into force by rules published on 5 June 1961, with the legislation applying equally to reserves and national parks (Article 7 of the Rules) (IUCN, 1971).

The 1967 Law on Nature Protection covers the preservation, restoration, rational use of nature and natural resources, monuments, historical sites, development of science and scientific research. This Law, and the 1969 Regulations for the Administration of the Law of Nature Protection, effectively repealed the Ordinance related to the protection of nature, and the Decree of 1960 (Spiridonov, 1991). According to the 1967 Law, there are five categories of protected area: nature reserve, national park, nature sanctuary, protected site and historical site. Buffer zones are managed according to Directive No. 4 (1980) of the Committee on Environmental Protection on the Council of Ministry (now the Ministry of Environment). Suggestions for establishment of protected areas can be made both by private bodies and by state organisations. The law determines the temporary protective status, defines the bodies responsible, research programmes and public support (Spiridonov *et al.*, 1991).

The duties of all organisations and agencies in the field of flora, fauna and habitat protection are further defined in a number of acts, including the Law on Protection of Air, Water and Soil against Pollution (1963), Nature Protection Law (1967), Water Law (1969), Law on protection of Cultivated Lands and Pastures (1973) Territorial and Settlement Organisation Law (1973), Hunting Enterprise Law (1982) and Fishing Enterprise Law (1982) (Spiridonov *et al.*, 1991). Some other acts may also include relevant sections (ECE, 1986).

The *Komitet za opazvane na prirodnata sreda* (KOPS) (Committee for Environmental Protection) of the Council of Ministers was established under state legislation in 1976. KOPS declares a locality or an object under protection, by order of the Committee's President, after consultation with the Academy of Science's Institute of Ecology and interested departments on whose territory the objects are located. These orders are published in the *State Gazette*.

In 1977, a new document entitled "Guidelines for the Protection and Reproduction of the Environment in the People's Republic of Bulgaria" was approved by State Council (Cerovsky, 1986). This document covers environmental preservation, restoration and management policies and now plays a central role in formulating state environmental policy (Stoilov *et al.*, 1981). Another major policy document written in the early 1980s was the General Plan of the People's Republic of Bulgaria. This treats the environment as a complex integrated system. In particular, the sections dealing with "Recreation" and "Standard Regional Planning Measures" refer to the important role played by legally protected areas (Mladenova and Paychev, 1985). Resources needed for protection measures are provided for in five-year and annual plans adopted by the government and People's Assembly (parliament) (ECE, 1986).

All land is state-owned and reserve boundaries are marked with symbols and occasionally fenced. Existing legislation in the field of nature protection is felt to be inadequate and inefficient. A draft Protected Area Act 1991 has been prepared and submitted by the Green Party (G. Spiridonov and L. Mileva, *in litt.*, 1991). Other legislation at the discussion stage includes the Ecological Policy Law, Control of Pollution Law and two bills on Forestry Law (Spiridonov *et al.*, 1991). A Natural Heritage Charter has also been prepared and submitted by the Green Party (G. Spiridonov and L. Mileva, *in litt.*, 1991).

International Activities   The Convention concerning the World Natural and Cultural Heritage (World Heritage Convention) was signed on 7 March 1974 and two natural sites inscribed in 1983. The Convention on Wetlands of International Importance especially as Waterfowl Habitat (Ramsar Convention) was signed on 24 September 1975 and the Paris Protocol instrument was signed on 27 February 1986; four Ramsar sites have been designated. Seventeen sites, covering 25,201ha, were accepted in 1977 as biosphere reserves under the Unesco Man and the Biosphere Programme. The Berne Convention was ratified in 1991 principally as an instrument to conserve populations in protected areas (Spiridonov *et al.*, 1991). The Institute of Ecology is active in international environmental conservation activities organised by Unesco, UNEP, FAO and CMEA.

Progress is reported to have been made on the preparation of a Treaty for Environmental Protection of the Balkans (IUCN, 1991) and the first international meeting on the biodiversity of the Balkans Massif is to be held in 1992 (IUCN-EEP, *in litt.*, 1991).

Administration and Management   In 1971 the Ministry of Forests and Environmental Protection was established; it largely concentrated its attention on natural sites, establishing new reserves and improving those already in existence (Stoilov *et al.*, 1981). In 1972 the Research and Coordination Centre for Preservation and Restoration of Environment of the Bulgarian Academy of Sciences was established (Cerovsky, 1986)(see Annex).

KOPS is the main governmental, inter-departmental coordinating and controlling body, the President is of ministerial rank and the Committee has 16 regional inspectorates and one scientific centre (Cerovsky, 1986). It had a staff of 400 and operated on one-year and five-year plans with a budget of 4,120 billion leva (1971-1981) with 500 million leva in 1989 destined specifically for nature protection (IUCN, 1991a). It had the task of controlling, coordinating and implementing the policy and decisions of the Central Committee of the Bulgarian Communist Party, the National Assembly, the State Council and the Council of Ministers on questions of environmental protection and restoration and water resource utilisation. The committee elaborates state plans on nature protection, as well as plans for research and development (ECE, 1986). The committee was also directed to establish a system to provide scientific data for matters relating to environmental protection. The Unified National System for Observation and Information on the State of the Environment was set up, which includes a subsystem of "Protected Natural Sites and Objects". A card index on protected natural sites has been prepared by the committee, as well as sets of methods for a comprehensive study of protected natural sites and objects (Stoilov *et al.*, 1981).

In December 1986 a ministerial council was set up at the Council of Agriculture, but abolished in 1987 when the Ministry of Agriculture and Forests was created (Ashley, 1988). At the party congress of April 1986, the Bulgarian Communist Party committed itself to a new "National Programme for Environmental Protection to the Year 2000 and Afterwards", a long-term ecological programme which largely concentrated on the control and reduction of pollution control. In May 1988 a Politburo decision recommended that KOPS be merged with the Ministry of Agriculture and Forests to create the new Ministry of the Land, Forests and Environmental Protection (Ashley, 1988).

At the beginning of 1990, the Committee of Environmental Protection was replaced by the new Ministry of Environment (IUCN, 1991). Local elections and the general election of October 1991 will allow radical restructuring of administration, with the subsequent preparation of framework laws on environmental policy and protected areas (introducing IUCN categories into national legislation) (IUCN, 1991). The Institute of Ecology, formerly known as the "Research and Coordination Centre for the Conservation and Renewal of the Environment" (NKCOVOS), at the Academy of Sciences, has worked alongside KOPS in designating protected areas. It is a research institute with a staff of 60 which coordinates ecological research within the Academy of Sciences and with other scientific research establishments and universities (Cerovsky, 1986). It is also active in international environmental conservation activities. It maintains lists and data describing protected areas (Fisher, 1990), and has prepared a programme on the scientific base and development of the protected areas system which proposed two-thirds of the existing reserves and two new national parks (Spiridonov *et al.*, 1991). An Environmental Commission within parliament also deals with protected areas (Spiridonov *et al.*, 1991).

Direct administration of protected areas falls to a number of bodies with varying levels of responsibility. Foremost is the Ministry of the Environment which carries out research, elaborates proposals and declares new protected areas, including document preparation, category assignment, boundary definition, financing basic and restoration research. The management body on "Conservation of Forestry and protected natural sites" is a department within the Ministry (Spiridonov *et al.*, 1991). An Environmental Monitoring Centre is responsible for the control of regulations and coordination of management plans, through 16 regional inspectorates for environmental protection (Spiridonov, 1991). Others include Ministry of Forests and Forest Industry, Ministry of Architecture and Works, Balkan Tourist, Academy of Sciences, Nature Protection Commission, Ministry of Education, Committee of Arts and Culture, Academy of Agricultural Sciences and the Union of Hunters and Fishermen. The Committee of Forestry, municipal councils, agricultural and other authorities also are engaged in the direct management and protection of protected areas working closely with the land owners (Spiridonov, 1991). On-the-ground supervision of reserves is the responsibility of the Committee for Forestry and is carried out on a part-time basis by forest rangers. The local state forestry administration maintains individual protected areas, while large national parks have directorates. Over 90% of protected areas are managed by the Forestry Committee. These areas in the agricultural fund are entrusted to local municipalities and research institutes (Spiridonov *et al.*, 1991).

The control of reserves has been improved. Over 1,200 checks were carried out in 1977 and 160 violations were notified, falling in 1978 to 1,121 checks and 144 violations (Stoilov *et al.*, 1981). Vertebrate fauna, threatened and rare species have been studied in 12% of nature reserves and in almost all national parks. Special attention has been given to research on wetland bird fauna and of higher plants on the Balkan Range reserves, under a joint ten-year programme by the Bulgarian Academy of Sciences and the Polish Academy of Sciences (IUCN, 1991a). Research stations have been established at Srebarna and Atanasovsko reserves (IUCN, 1991a).

Until 1990, voluntary environmental conservation groups were organised in the framework of the Patriotic Front, through a system of Committees for Nature Conservation at the Patriotic Front Councils on all levels. These were centralised in the All-National Committee for Nature Conservation at the National Council of the Patriotic Front, *Obshchenarodniya Komitet za zashchita na prirodata*, which promoted environmental awareness.

The Union of Hunters and Fisherman was active in the field of conservation, while the Hiker's Union publicises natural sites within the country and promotes their care (Stoilov *et al.*, 1981). "Ecoglasnost", a non-governmental organisation set up in early 1989 with a particular interest in ecological problems, has most recently transformed itself into a political forum, the Green Party (IUCN, 1991). It was a very influential movement involving a number of anti-pollution campaigns. In its "Charter '89", Ecoglasnost devotes considerable space to its policies on protected areas, which it suggests should be greatly expanded, with numerous new areas being designated in all biogeographical regions. Ecoglasnost is made up of local groups, about 50 in Sofia and 30 in the rest of the country. There is a possibility that it will become more involved in party politics in the future (Fisher, 1990). Recently, the Wilderness Fund, another non-governmental organisation, was set up. It aims to further the conservation of natural areas and to facilitate the self-recovery of areas that have suffered human alteration (Ivanov, 1989). Groups concerned with specific areas, such as the Rhodope Mountains, have also been created (IUCN-EEP, *in litt.*, 1991). Other prominent non-governmental organisations included the Bulgarian Society for the Protection of Birds, the Union for Nature Protection, the Association of Bulgarian Ecologists, Association Ecoforum, the Green Society Foundation, the National Ecological Club, the Ecos Foundation, the Ecoforum for Peace and the Scout Organisation of Bulgaria.

Systems Reviews The country straddles the boundary between Continental and Mediterranean climates. It can be divided approximately into five regions: the fertile Danube plain in the north running along the border with Romania; the Stara Planina Mountains, a large 600km mountain chain running east-west, dividing the country;

the central plain and valleys of the River Maritsa immediately south of the Stara Planina; the mountains of the Rila Planina, Pirin Planina and Rodopi Planina in the south-west; and the relatively flat areas along the Black Sea coast (Grimmett and Jones, 1989). These approximate to the five recognised phyto-geographic regions of the country, namely the European broad-leaved forest region (Balkan province, Euxinian province, and Macedonian province), the Euro-Asian steppe and forest steppe provinces and the Mediterranean sclerophyll region (IUCN, 1991a). Lowlands (0-200m) cover 31% of the total surface area of the country; hills (200-600m) cover 41%; highlands (600-1,600m) cover 25% and mountains (over 1,600m) cover 3%. The climax vegetation is *Quercus* up to 1,000m, *Fagus* between 1,000m and 1,500m and coniferous woodland up to 2,200m, with some especially well-developed stands of *Pinus peuce* in the Rila, Pirin and Rodopi mountains.

Under the initiative of the 1928 Council for the Protection of the Countryside, a number of bills and decrees were published and the first reserve was established in 1933, followed by the first national park, Mount Vitosha, in 1934. After this date few new areas were established until the 1960s. The total number of protected sites has risen from 50 in 1940 to about 130 in 1973 and to 3,922 in 1989. Most reserves (covering 33,000ha in total) were created between 1978 and 1985 on the recommendation of the Ecological and Environmental Centre of the Academy of Sciences, whilst three-quarters of the national parks were established in the period 1974 to 1988 (IUCN, 1991a). Three quarters of the reserves are over 1,000ha, with buffer zones. Some 82% of reserves and 89% of national parks are in mountainous areas (IUCN, 1991a). In 1989 these areas covered 195,155ha, or nearly 2% of the country (Anon., 1989), of which 30% are strict nature reserves (65,000ha) (IUCN, 1991). It was planned to increase this figure to 3% by the year 2000 (ECE, 1986), although current thinking is for an increase closer to 8% (IUCN, 1991). On 30 July 1991, there were 10 national parks (105,000ha), 96 reserves (66,500ha), 2,135 natural monuments (23,250ha), 79 protected areas (17,150ha), 973 historical places covering 12,200ha, giving a total of 224,000ha (Spiridonov *et al.*, 1991). Zoogeographically, 77% of reserves belong to the Balkan and the Rila-Rhodopi Range. An inventory has been carried out of representative ecosystems covering areas over 1,000ha in separate reserves – over 20 forest formations have been catalogued. In 1982 forests covered 38,590 sq. km (35% of the land surface). More than 25% of forests are under special protection (ECE, 1986). More recent figures show that 34% of the country is under forests (35% conifers) in two categories, 71% commercial and 29% protection forests (IUCN, 1991a).

The main wetlands lie along the Danube and the Black Sea coast. Many of the marshes and coastal lakes have been drained, largely for agriculture, and the remainder are particularly important for migratory bird species. The north-eastern part of the Black Sea coast has some remnant steppe areas. The lowlands have largely been converted to agricultural land, and in the uplands large areas have been devastated by grazing, mostly by sheep. Tourism and especially skiing are a potential threat to the remaining, less disturbed upland areas (Grimmett and Jones, 1989). In certain regions (sea coasts and mountains) the number of visitors to protected areas has grown as a result of urbanisation, road construction and the increase in motor traffic and access to sites. Nature trails are popular and are being constructed first of all in protected areas. Threats arise partly from the lack of sufficiently severe penalties, and from the non-application of governmental decrees. Cattle grazing is still allowed in some nature reserves, and poaching (hunting/fishing) continues to be prevalent in others. The major problems include: outdated legislation (new draft of protected areas law has been prepared, sponsored by the Green Party), inadequate administration, lack of qualified staff, insufficient funds for management and research: lack of a database, lack of training, and public education programmes. The future development of a protected areas system depends on the adoption of a law on protected areas, creation of an Agency for Management of Protected Areas, associated with the Ministry, the establishment of a Nature Conservation Fund and the creation of training and education programmes (Spiridonov, 1991).

Addresses

Ministry of the Environment, "William Gladstone" str. No. 67, SOFIA 1000 (Tel: 876151; FAX: 521634; Tlx: 22145 KOPS)

Institute of Ecology, Academy of Science, Department of Protected Areas and Genetic Pool, ul. Gagarin 2, 1113 SOFIA (Tel: 720459; FAX: 705498)

Committee of Forestry, Ar. No 17, Sofia Wilderness Fund, c/o Institute of Ecology, Academy of Science, Department of Protected Areas and Genetic Pool, ul Gagarin 2, 1113 SOFIA (Tel: 720459; FAX: 705498)

Society for the Conservation of the Rhodopi Mountains, 2 Gagarin St, SOFIA 1113

References

Anon. (1989). Protected natural sites: invaluable national heritage. Committee for the Protection of the Environment with the Council of Ministers of the People's Republic of Bulgaria. *ECO facts and figures*. Sofia Press, Bulgaria.

Anon. (1990). *PC Globe Inc.*. Tempe, Arizona, USA.

Ashley, S. (1988). Politburo Announces "New" Ecological Policy. *Radio Free Europe* 13(21): 9-13.

Carter, F.W. (1978). Nature reserves and national parks in Bulgaria. *L'Espace Géographique* 1: 69-72.

Cerovsky, J. (1986). *Nature Conservation in the Socialist Countries of East Europe*. East-Europe Committee, IUCN Commission on Education. Administration of the Krkonose (Giant Mountains) National Park, Vrchlabi.

Cerovsky, J. (1988). *Nature conservation in the Socialist countries of East Europe*. East-Europe Committee, IUCN Commission on Education. Ministry of Culture of the Czech Socialist Republic, Prague.

ECE (1986). Meeting Finland 25-29 August. ENV/SEM. 16/R.1.

Fisher, D. (1990). Environmental Politics in Bulgaria. Report on a visit to Bulgaria 24-28 February 1990. Ecological Studies Institute, London.

IUCN (1971). *United Nations list of national parks and equivalent reserves* 2nd Ed. Hayez, Brussels.

IUCN (1991). *The environment in Eastern Europe: 1990*. Environmental Research Series 3. IUCN East European Programme, Cambridge, UK.

IUCN (1991a). *Environmental Status Report: 1990. Volume Two: Albania, Bulgaria, Romania, Yugoslavia*. IUCN East European Programme, Cambridge, UK.

Ivanov, L. (1989). Memorandum of Association of the Wilderness Fund. Sofia, Bulgaria. Unpublished.

Johnson, H. and J.M. (1977). *Environmental policies in developing countries*. Erich Schmidt Verlag.

Mladenova, M. and Peychev, V. (1985). Concept of the General Plan of the Peoples Republic of Bulgaria on Legally Protected Areas. In: Nedialkov, S. (Ed.), International Symposium "Conservation of Natural Areas and of the Genetic Material They Contain". Project 8, MAB-Unesco 23-28 September. Blagoevgrad, Bulgaria. Collection of reports. Three volumes. Jurautor, Sofia.

Profirov, L. (1989). Internationally recognised nature reserves. In: Gerassimov, P. and Staleva, M. (Eds), *Bulgaria, Special Issue*. Sofia Press, Bulgaria.

Spiridonov, J. (1977). *Oazisi na divata priroda*. Zemizdat, Sofia. (In Bulgarian)

Spiridonov, J. and Juras, A. (1991). Nature Conservation in Bulgaria. In: *Nature conservation in Europe*. European Parliament Directorate-General for Research, Environment, Public Health and Consumer Protection Series 17. EN-9-1991.

Stoilov, D., Noshtev, V., Gerasimov, S., Velev, V. (1981). *Protected natural sites in the People's Republic of Bulgaria*. Jurautor, Sofia.

ANNEX
Definitions of protected area designations, as legislated, together with authorities responsible for their administration

Title: The Law of Nature Protection; The regulations for the Administration of the Law of Nature Protection

Date: 1967, 1969 (regulations)

Brief description: Provides the legal regulation of protected areas and defines them

Administrative authority: Komitet za opazvane na prirodnata sreda (KOPS) (Committee for Environmental Protection) (Ministry of the Environment)

Designations:

Rezervat (Strict nature reserve) Strictly protected areas containing rare plant and animal communities, threatened by depletion or extinction and used for scientific research.

Economic exploitation, including any agricultural and industrial activities, is prohibited. Admittance to, and movement in reserves are restricted to defined roads and paths.

A special directive was adopted designating the creation of buffer zones around reserves. In exceptional circumstances clear felling is allowed for forest protection reasons.

Naroden park (National park) Includes natural parks, which are comparatively large areas suitable for short-term recreation and tourism and for research. Other categories of protected areas may be included within the boundaries of national parks.

Tourism development is encouraged especially by state enterprises such as Balkan Tourist. Entry is free and unrestricted. Tourism may be well developed in the form of road networks, tourist chalets, resthouses, restaurants, cable cars and camping sites. These areas have general protection throughout, with no settlement or exploitation allowed; hunting, fishing and flower-picking is forbidden.

Some are zoned into a scientific zone (no exploration, visitors restricted to certain paths), a tourist zone (accommodation, tree-felling and afforestation) and a commercial forest zone.

Natural monument Specific natural formation protected for its aesthetic and scientific significance, preserved for public interest due to national, geographic or scientific values as well as phenomena of aesthetic, natural or historical value, which includes single items, such as trees and rocks.

Protected site Specific location with picturesque landscapes or characteristic habitats suitable for recreation.

Historic site Site of major historical event, or historical monument or grave, as well as protected specific natural feature of the landscape, and their surrounding area. Certain sites are protected jointly by KOPS and the Committee for Culture and the Institute for the Monuments of Culture.

Sources: IUCN, 1971; Stoilov *et al.*, 1981

SUMMARY OF PROTECTED AREAS

Map[†] ref.	*National/international designations* Name of area	IUCN management category	Area (ha)	Year notified
	National Parks			
1	Balkan Central	II	73,262	1991
2	Choumensko plato	IV	3,930	1980
3	Melnishki Piramidi	III	1,165	1960
4	Pirin	II	40,067	1963
5	Roussenski Lom	III	3,259	1970
6	Sinite kamani	IV	6,685	1981
7	Vitocha	IV	25,485	1934
8	Vratchanski balkan	V	26,772	1988
9	Zlatni pyassatsi	IV	1,320	1943
	Buffer Zones			
10	Djendema Reserve	IV	4,699	1983
11	Rila Monastery Forest Reserve	IV	2,402	1986
12	Steneto Reserve	IV	2,522	1983
	Botanical Reserves			
13	Tchervenata stena	IV	3,029	1962
14	Tissata (Tissova Bartchina)	IV	1,452	1949
	Reserves			
15	Alibotouche	I	1,628	1951
16	Atanasovsko ezero	IV	1,650	1980
17	Baevi doupki-Djindjiritsa	I	2,873	1934
18	Bistrichko branichte	I	1,062	1935
19	Boatin	I	1,597	1948
20	Djendema	I	4,220	1953
21	Doupkata	I	1,211	1956
22	Foret du Monastere de Rila	I	3,446	1986
23	Goliam Skakavets	I	4,180	1985
24	Ibar	I	1,701	1985
25	Kamenchtitsa	I	1,018	1984
26	Kongoura	I	1,312	1988
27	Koupena	I	1,086	1961
28	Mantaritsa	IV	1,082	1968
29	Maritchini ezera	I	1,509	1951
30	Oreliak	IV	1,228	1985
31	Parangalitsa	I	1,508	1933
32	Peechti skali	I	1,465	1979
33	Severen Djendem	I	1,610	1983
34	Sokolna	I	1,250	1979
35	Srebarna	IV	1,143	1948
36	Stara reka	I	1,975	1981
37	Steneto	I	3,579	1980
38	Tajansko jdrelo	IV	1,290	1985
39	Tchervenata stena	I	3,029	1962
40	Tchouprene	I	1,440	1974
41	Tsaritchina	I	3,274	1949
42	Uzdini ezera	IV	1,150	1985
43	Veleka	IV	1,271	1989
44	Vratchanski karst	I	1,439	1983
	Forest Reserves			
45	Beli Lom	IV	1,051	1980
46	Kamtchia	IV	1,445	1951
47	Ourdini ezera	IV	1,150	1985

Map[†] ref.	*National/international designations* Name of area	IUCN management category	Area (ha)	Year notified
48	Ouzounboudjak	I	2,530	1956
49	Persin (iles de)	IV	1,715	1981
50	Tissovitsa	IV	1,251	1990
	Biosphere Reserves			
	Parc national Steneto	IX	2,889	1977
	Réserve Alibotouch	IX	1,628	1977
	Réserve Bistrichko Branichté	IX	1,177	1977
	Réserve Boatine	IX	1,281	1977
	Réserve Djendema	IX	1,775	1977
	Réserve Doupkata	IX	1,210	1977
	Réserve Doupki-Djindjiritza	IX	2,873	1977
	Réserve Kamtchia	IX	842	1977
	Réserve Koupena	IX	1,084	1977
	Réserve Mantaritza	IX	576	1977
	Réserve Maritchini ezera	IX	1,510	1977
	Réserve Ouzounboudjak	IX	2,575	1977
	Réserve Parangalitza	IX	1,509	1977
	Réserve Srébarna	IX	600	1977
	Réserve Tchervenata sténa	IX	812	1977
	Réserve Tchoupréné	IX	1,440	1977
	Réserve Tsaritchina	IX	1,420	1977
	Ramsar Wetlands			
	Arkoutino	R	97	1975
	Atanassovo Lake	R	1,050	1975
	Durankulak Lake	R	350	1975
	Srebarna	R	600	1975
	World Heritage Sites			
	Pirin National Park	X	40,060	1983
	Srebarna Nature Reserve	X	600	1983

[†]Locations of most protected areas are shown on the accompanying map.

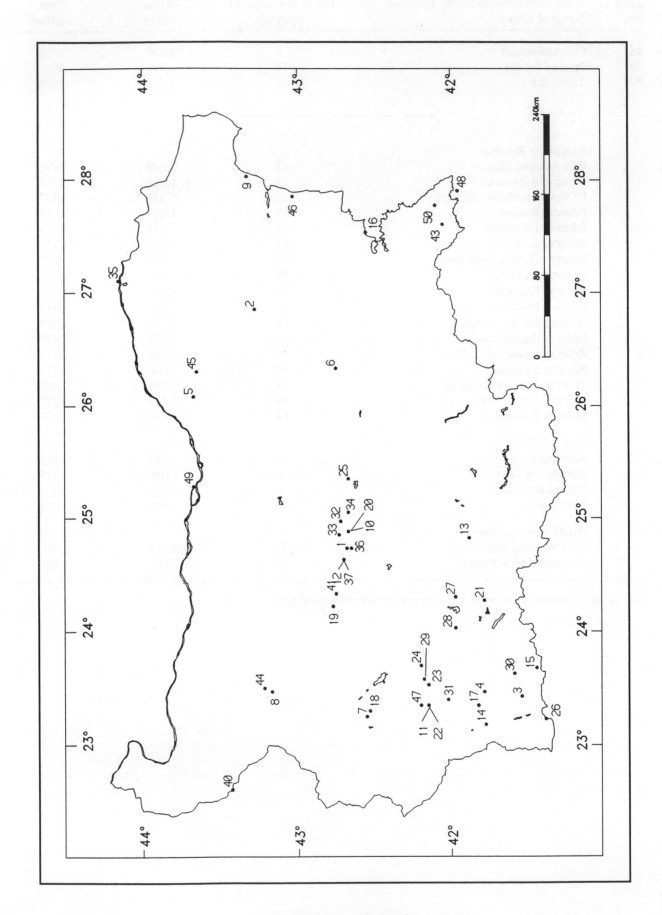

Protected Areas of Bulgaria

CZECHOSLOVAKIA
(CZECH AND SLOVAK FEDERATIVE REPUBLIC)

Area 127,870 sq. km (78,860 sq. km of the Czech Republic and 49,010 sq. km of the Slovak Republic)

Population 15,600,000 (1989 estimate)
Natural increase: 0.2% per annum

Economic Indicators
GNP: US$ 9,472 per capita (Anon., 1990)

Policy and Legislation The Czechoslovak state was created on 28 October 1918 following the dissolution of the Austria-Hungarian Empire. Czechoslovakia is a federal republic consisting of two nations of equal rights: the Czech republic (the Czech lands, previously Bohemia, Moravia and parts of Silesia) and the Slovak republic (Slovakia) (Hunter, 1991). A law of 12 December 1990 defines the respective jurisdiction of the two republics and devolves most of the former federal administrative and economic authority to them (Hunter, 1991). The relevant section of the Constitution, relating to protected areas, is Law No. 100/1960, Article 15. The first conservation of nature acts were introduced in 1955 and 1956.

The first recorded establishment of protected areas was in 1838 when two forest reserves were created in south Bohemia, followed by additional reserves in 1858 and 1884 and two in Slovakia in 1895. An ordinance giving protection to natural monuments was decreed in Slovakia in 1900 (Cerovsky, 1988).

The two republics have separate laws dealing with conservation: the State Nature Conservancy Act of 1955, Law No. 1/SNR 1955 for the Slovak Republic, and the State Nature Conservancy Act of 1956, Law No. 40/1956 for the Czech Republic. In 1986 the Czech and Slovak national councils enacted Laws Nos 65/1986 and 72/1986, respectively, to impose penalties for offences against the State Nature Conservancy decrees of 1956. Republic acts are brought together and integrated by federal legislation, which is preparing a law dealing with the environment. In June 1990 a Commission for the Environment was set up at the federal level, which is preparing law dealing with environment. The integration of natural resource conservation with economic activities is dealt with by sectors such as forestry, water management, agriculture, mineral surveys, mining, industrial production and construction.

At republic level the State Nature Conservancy acts define nature conservation as the preservation, renewal, enhancement and use of natural wealth and the special protection of important areas and natural features. These laws are supplemented by separate republic guidelines issued in 1978 and 1980 dealing with nature conservation development. The overall objective is to integrate conservation and use of natural resources and to apply principles of ecosystem conservation. The main categories defined in the law include: *Narodni parky* (national park), *Chranene Krajinne Oblasti* (CHKO) (protected landscape area), *Statni Prirodni Rezervace* (SPR) (national nature reserve). A further five categories of protected areas are also used: *Chranene Studijni Plochy* (CHSP) (protected study area), *Chranene Prirodne Vytvory Krasove Javy* (CHPV) (protected natural feature), *Chranene Parky a Zahrady* (CHPZ) (protected park and garden), and *Chranene Naleziste* (CN) (protected habitats) and *Chranene Prirodne Pamatky* (CHPP) (protected natural monument) (IUCN, 1971; Marsakova and Skrivanek, 1982; Povolny, 1986; Skrivanek, 1982; Wiltowski, 1979; Hromas, *in litt.*, 1991) (see Annex).

Protected areas are declared according to the State Nature Conservation Acts of the Czech Ministry of Environment and by the Slovak Commission for Environment, with the exception of national parks which have to be enacted by the governments of the republics, and protected nature monuments and protected natural features which are declared by district councils (previously protected areas were established under the 1955 and 1956 acts by the respective Ministries of Culture) (Marsakova and Skrivanek, 1982; Hromas, *in litt.*, 1991).

In the Czech Republic, respective district national committees declare, in accordance with territorial plans, "quiet areas" where motor vehicles, camping and other recreational activities are prohibited.

A set of new laws is in draft stage and includes a nature and landscape conservation law, agricultural soil protection law, land-use planning law, environmental impact assessment law and others. Nature conservation is also included in the Building Code and Land-Use Planning Act No. 50/1976 5b where all new investments require an assessment of their impact on the environment (Atkinson *et al.*, 1991).

International Activities The Convention on Wetlands of International Importance especially as Waterfowl Habitat (Ramsar Convention) was acceded to on 2 July 1990; eight sites have been designated. Six sites have been accepted as biosphere reserves by Unesco under the Man and the Biosphere Programme, the latest two in 1990. The Czech and Slovak governments signed the Convention concerning the World Cultural and Natural Heritage (World Heritage Convention) in 1990 and tentative lists of nine sites for nomination are in the process of being drawn up by the republics.

Krkonose National Park is listed by IUCN as a globally threatened protected area.

Administration and Management In 1904 the Trust for Enhancement and Protection of Native Country was founded in Prague. The State Institute for Protection of Monuments and Conservation of Nature was established in Prague in 1958; in Slovakia the Institute was established in Bratislava in 1951. Administration of protected areas was the responsibility of the respective Ministry of Culture in each republic, with the central conservation authority within these ministries being the Department for Nature Conservation. From 1988, a new Ministry of Interior and Environment was established in each republic. This was the central authority for management of the environment, as well as for coordination and control of the environmental functions of other ministries.

In June 1990 a federal level State Commission for the Environment was set up, headed by the Federal Environment Minister. There are four departments: legislation and landscape planning, policy, projects and international cooperation. At the republic level, a Czech Ministry was established by Act No. 173/1989 of the National Assembly, and was defined as the highest state control authority in environmental protection. It is responsible for water, air and nature protection as well as land protection aspects of agriculture and forestry and mineral resource protection. A Slovak Commission was established by Act No. 96/1990 of the Slovak National Assembly in March 1990. It exercises state executive rights for designation and protection of the environment, including nature conservation, protection of water quality and use, physical planning, planning orders and energy conservation (Hromas, *in litt.*, 1991). It does not administer forestry, land use and mineral resource issues.

The republican ministries will concentrate on executive and inspection functions, while the federal commission will concentrate on forward planning and strategy. A 13-member Federal Committee for the Environment, headed by the Federal Environment Minister, was also set up in 1990 which meets regularly to discuss environmental matters (Fisher, 1990; Karpowicz, *in litt.*, 1991).

Before 1990, at the federal level, the environment was controlled by the State Committee for Scientific, Technical and Investment Development (*Stani Komise Provedecky, Technicky a Investicni Rezvej*), acting through the Czech Centre for State Protection of Monuments and Nature Conservation (*Statni ustav Pamatkové Péce a Ochrany Prirody*) (SUPPOP) and the Slovak Centre for State Nature Conservation (*Ustredie Statnej Ochrany Prirody*) (USOP) (Cerovsky, 1988). There were eleven regional centres for Protection of Monuments and Conservation of Nature which had representatives present from the nature protection departments (IUCN, 1971). A Council for Environment acted as an advisory and consultative body for both republics and dealt with the key problems of natural resource conservation (Cerovsky, 1988; Marsakova and Skrivanek, 1982). A key exercise was the preparation and revision every ten years of a special planning

document, the "territorial project of nature conservation" which was elaborated for all national parks and protected landscape areas (Cerovsky, 1988; Povolny, 1986).

In June 1990, responsibility for environment was given to the Federal Committee for the Environment (*Zivotni prostredi*), represented in the two republics by the Czech Ministry of Environmental Protection (*Ministerstvo Zivotniko prostredi Cesky republiky*) and the Slovak Commission for Environmental Protection (*Slovenska komisepio Zivotni prostredi*) (IUCN, 1991) with regional offices and district administrations (Atkinson *et al.*, 1991). Nature conservation inspectorates have been proposed. From 1990, SUPPOP was restructured as the Czech Institute for Nature Conservation (*Cesky Ustav Ochrany Prirody*) with seven regional offices. At the same time an equivalent Slovak Institute for Nature Conservation (*Slovensky Ustav Ochrany Prirody*) (SUOP) replaced USOP in Slovakia. The main aim of the two institutes continues to be the selection, management and use of protected natural components. They are also likely to continue to carry out wide-ranging research on threats to protected areas, monitoring and basic inventory work for each protected area and prepare management plans (Marsakova and Skrivanek, 1982). The Czech Institute provides a professional training house for 25 participants each year in nature conservation. In addition, two education centres at Rychovy (Czech) and Cibelary (Slovak) provide in-service training careers, and regional centres, concerned with protected landscape areas administration and management of the Czech and Moravian caves (Hromas, *in litt.*, 1991). The total numbers employed in protected areas management and administration are *c.* 1,200 in the Czech Republic and 1,400 in the Slovak Republic (including foresters from Tatransky National Park) (Kucera, 1991).

The Ministry of Forest and Water Management and Timber Industry is responsible for water and atmospheric conservation, pollution control, forest management and conservation.

The administration and management of national parks tends to undertaken by the park authorities themselves, although it can vary from site to site. The authorities are answerable directly to the Czech Ministry of the Environment and to the Slovak Commission of Environment. Exceptions are High Tatra National Park which is under the direct responsibility of the Slovak Ministry of Forest and Water Management, and Krkonosze National Park which is subordinate to the East-Bohemian Regional National Committee. Many frontier national parks and protected areas are organised on a bilateral basis with neighbouring countries (Drucker, *in litt.*, 1990).

Protected landscape areas are administered by separate offices for each area which deal directly with the local and regional authorities (Wiltowski, 1979; Karpowicz, *in litt.*, 1991). They employ an average of four to ten professional staff, who are principally involved in planning, management, monitoring and educational work. Research in CHKOs is conducted by the Academies of Science or by the research institutes of the competent ministry. In the Czech Republic protected landscape areas are likely to be supervised by the Institute for Nature Conservation (Cerovsky, *in litt.*, 1990). In the Slovak Republic, protected landscape areas are administered by the Slovak Institute for Nature Conservation.

In the Czech Republic, national parks receive KCS 30,872 million and protected landscape areas KCS 19,102 million; in the Slovak Republic, 67,432 million and 6,659 million, respectively (Kucera, 1991). The total for Slovakia is KCS 69,6 million in 1991 (Berko, 1991).

Land is in the most part under state ownership, but where private enclaves occur in protected areas, the owners are obliged to conform to legal requirements.

In 1958, the National Museum Society, the first non-governmental nature conservation organisation was founded but later disbanded and subsequently replaced in 1979 by the Czech Union of Nature Conservation (*Cesky svaz ochrancu prirody*) (CSOP). In 1969 the Slovak Union of Nature and Landscape Conservationists (*Slovensky svaz ochrancov prirody a krajiny*) (SZOPK) was founded with 14,000 individual members, over 400 collective members, 260 local groups and more than 600 youth groups with 11,000 members; CSOP was founded ten years later with 24,000 individuals, over 350 collective members and 768 local groups (Cerovsky, 1988). These groups often take responsibility for the management of nature reserves and monuments (Atkinson *et al.*, 1991).

Systems Reviews   Most of the Slovak Republic is mountainous, as are the northern and southern boundaries of the Czech lands, the highest peak being Gerlach (High Tatra) at 2,655m. Much of the remaining area of the country is covered by forest, with broad-leaved deciduous forest (and extensively reafforested areas of *Picea* and *Pinus*, equally about 80% of all woodland at lower altitudes, giving way to mixed coniferous and deciduous woodland at higher altitudes, and *Pinus* in subalpine zones (IUCN, 1990). The forests, particularly in the north-west, are among the worst affected by air pollution in Europe, some 470,000ha in the Czech Republic and 30,000ha in Slovakia (IUCN, 1990). In warmer areas close to the Hungarian border there are remains of steppe-woodland and steppe-grassland vegetation (Grimmett and Jones, 1989). Vascular plant species number approximately 3,500 and there are some 60,000 animal species including 600 vertebrates (Hromas, *in litt.*, 1991). Agricultural land covers 69,000 sq. km (54% of the land area), of which 48,000 sq. km are arable, 8,000 sq. km are meadow and 8,000 sq. km are pasture.

On the basis of the June 1990 document *The Environment in Czechoslovakia*, a "Draft Concept of State Ecological Policy" was produced (Vavrousek, 1990; Vavrousek *et al.*, 1990a). This was followed in July 1990 by the document *Ecological Programmes and Projects, Czech and Slovak Federative Republic* which added more details to the draft policy and described specific objectives, including the development of national and international parks (Vavrousek *et al.*, 1990b).

The Czech Ministry of Environment, through its state nature conservation bodies, has an advisory input to discussions on state and republic plans, agricultural and water management and energy projects, and all types of physical planning. It produced the Blue Book and Rainbow Book (*Environment of the Czech Republic 1991*) a comprehensive survey of the country's environmental situation and programme of environmental protection (Hromas, *in litt.*, 1991).

In response to environmental crises, a national plan – "the ecoprogramme" – was being developed, aimed at integrating ecological and economic activities. A national conservation strategy was also being prepared and contains a Species Preservation Strategy for the Czech Republic (Cerovsky, 1986). As yet unresolved is the question of the return of land to its former private owners (under the Restitution Law) which might result in the break-up of larger protected areas (Atkinson *et al.*, 1991).

Total protected area coverage is 1,930,000ha or 15% of the country (IUCN, 1990) is divided into 10,869 sq. km in the Czech Republic (13.8%) and 8,163 sq. km in the Slovak Republic (16.7%) (Cerovsky, 1988). The first recorded forest reserves were established in 1838. The first national park was created in the mountainous High Tatras in 1948, and the first protected landscape area in 1955. In 1988, there were four national parks (198,483ha), 34 protected landscape areas (1,626,557ha), 831 state nature reserves (96,286ha) and 123 protected habitats (1,453ha) (IUCN, 1990). By 1991, there were eight national parks (three in the Czech republic, five in Slovakia), and one proposed; five are located on international borders and have close management relations with adjoining park authorities. Other protected areas in the Czech Republic include 40 protected landscape areas and 149 protected areas of other categories (Hromas, *in litt.*, 1991). The total protected area in the Czech Republic is given as 12,121 sq. km and 8,810 sq. km in the Slovak Republic (Hromas, *in litt.*, 1991). Four more border parks are proposed (Kucera, 1991).

A plan for the development of the protected area network to the year 1990 envisages an increased area of 490,000ha, or an addition of 10% to the surface area (Wiltowski, 1979). In addition to protected areas, a new designation, "elements of ecological stability" (EES), has been created. It is yet to attain legal status. They aim at the protection of remnants of habitats in largely agricultural landscapes (Atkinson *et al.*, 1991). Further protected areas are planned to safeguard the remaining

Danube flood plain and a trilateral natural area shared between Slovakia, Poland and Ukraine (Berko, 1991).

Major environmental threats range from acid precipitation and agricultural mechanisation to tourism and recreation (for full details see IUCN, 1990).

Other Relevant Information Special governmental decisions were passed in 1976 and 1978 regarding environmental education, which was to be promoted at all levels in both republics. In the Czech and Slovak republics new universities offer courses on "Protection of the Natural Environment". In the Slovak Republic a conservation training centre operates in Gbelany near Zilina and in the Czech Republic there is an establishment in the Krkonose National Park. Since 1982 the Centre for Nature Conservation Development in Bratislava has published *Chranene uzemia Slovenska-spravodajca*, a yearbook on protected areas in Slovakia, and the journal *Pamiatky a priroda* (*Monuments and nature*) (also published in the Czech Republic. Tourism is a major element of national park interests. Selected protected areas are used very extensively for educational purposes and have visitor centres and nature trails.

Addresses

Federal
Federal Committee for the Environment, Slezska 9, 120 29 PRAGUE 2 (Tel: 256488/FAX: 2152659/Tlx: 121427)

Czech Republic
Ministerstvo Zivotniko Prostredi (Ministry of Environment CR), Lazarska 7, 110 00 PRAGUE 1 (Tel: 712111; FAX: 731 357)
Cesky Ustav Ochrany Prirody (Czech Institute for Nature Conservation), Slezska 9, 12 029 PRAGUE 2 (Tel: 215 1111; FAX: 215 2810)

Slovak Republic
Slovak Commission for Environment, Hlboka 2, 812 35 BRATISLAVA (Tel: 492 451)
Slovak State Centre for Nature Conservation, Hejrovskeho 1, 841 03 BRATISLAVA-Lamac

References

Atkinson, R., Kos, J. and Moldan, B. (1991). Nature Conservation in Czechoslovakia. *Nature conservation in Austria, Finland, Norway, Sweden, Switzerland, Bulgaria, Czechoslovakia, Hungary, Poland, Romania, Yugoslavia and the Soviet Union.* European Parliament Directorate-General for Research. Environment, Public Health and Consumer Protection Series 17. EN-9-91.

Cerovsky, J. (1986). *Nature conservation in the Socialist countries of East-Europe.* East-Europe Committee, IUCN Commission on Education, Administration of the Krkonose (Giant Mountains) National Park. Vrchlabi.

Cerovsky, J. (1988). *Nature conservation in the Socialist countries of East-Europe.* East-Europe Committee, IUCN Commission on Education, Ministry of Culture of the Czech Socialist Republic, Prague.

Cerovsky, J and Petricek, V. (1985). *Rukovet ochrance prirody* (Handbook of Nature Conservationists). Ministry of Culture of CSR, Prague.

Fisher, D. (1990). Environmental policy in central Europe: some notes on a visit in July 1990. Unpublished report.

Grimmett, R.F.A., and Jones, T.A. (1989). *Important bird areas in Europe.* International Council for Bird Preservation, Cambridge, UK. 888 pp.

Hunter, B. (Ed.) (1991). *The Statesman's Year Book 1991-92.* The MacMillan Press Ltd, London and Basingstoke.

IUCN (1971). *United Nations list of national parks and equivalent reserves.* (2nd Ed.). Hayez, Brussels.

IUCN (1990). *Environmental status reports: 1988/1989.* Volume One: *Czechoslovakia, Hungary, Poland.* IUCN-East European Programme, Cambridge, UK.

IUCN (1991). *The environment in Eastern Europe: 1990.* IUCN-EEP Environmental Research. Series 3.

Marsakova, M. (Ed.) (1983). *Statni ochrona prirody v CSR* (State Nature Conservancy in the CSR). SUPPOP, Prague. (Unseen)

Marsakova, M. & Skrivanek, F. (1982). *Conservation of nature and natural environment in the Czechoslovak Socialist Republic.* OBIS SUPPOP, Prague.

Marsakova-Nemejcova, M., Mihalik, S. *et al.* (1971). *Narodni parky, rezervace a jiha chranena uzemi prirody v Ceskoslovensku (National parks, reserves and other natural protected areas in Czechoslovakia).* Academia, Prague. (Unseen)

Vavrousek, J. (1990). *The environment in Czechoslovakia.* UTEIN, Praha. Vavrousek, J., Moldan, B., Ondrus, V. *et al.* (1990a). Draft concept of state ecological policy. Unpublished document.

Vavrousek, J., Moldan, B., Tirpak, I. *et al.* (1990b). *Ecological Programmes and Projects, Czech and Slovak Federative Republic. State Commission for Science, Technology and Investments.* Ministry of Environment of the Czech Republic and Slovak Commission for Environment, Prague and Bratislava.

Wiltowski, J. (1979). Ochrana przyrody w Slowacji. *Chronmy Przyrode Ojczysta.* R. 35 z.1. Pp. 46-52.

ANNEX
Definitions of protected area designations, as legislated, together with authorities responsible for their administration

Title: State Nature Conservancy Act, Law 1/SNR 1955 (Slovak)
State Nature Conservancy Act, Law No. 40/1956 (Czech)

Date: 1955 (Slovak), 1956 (Czech)

Brief description: Dealing with conservation of nature, that is preservation, renewal enhancement and use of natural wealth and the special protection of important areas and natural features.

Administrative authority: Ministry of Culture (Slovak and Czech)

Designations:

Narodni parky (National park)   Areas with very valuable natural resources, little influenced by human activity, with great climatic, health and recreational importance.

Have complete protection, except for some forest exploitation which is strictly controlled. Parks are zoned with a "controlled area" for recreational development, including villages, holiday homes, sanitaria, camp sites and other facilities. Hunting is prohibited.

Are fully open to visitors with the exception of access to strict nature reserves within them. Tourism is regarded as a main objective.

Chranene Krajinne Oblasti (CHKO) (Protected landscape area)   Areas of lower natural values but with significant scenic and aesthetic qualities. They represent the harmonious interaction between natural components and traditional human activities, and aim to protect all values and typical features of the landscape and encourage rational use of natural resources. They are also used extensively for recreation.

The most valuable areas are strictly protected as nature reserves or natural features. Although they are not excluded from further exploitation, all economic activities are carried out in accordance with the understanding of the republic-level nature conservation bodies.

Projects dealing with water management, forest management, agriculture, industry, transportation, building, tourism and recreation, as well as exploitative activities such as mining, must be conducted in accordance with the goals of the protected area and territorial planning is conducted, discussed and revised accordingly.

All CHKOs in the Slovak Republic have buffer zones.

Statni Prirodni Rezervace (SPR) (National nature reserve)   Areas where the complete ecosystem is subject to conservation management and are strictly protected areas of great scientific and research importance.

Chranene Studijni Plochy (CHSP) (Protected study area)   Small protected sites designated for research and teaching purposes.

Chranene Parky a Zahrady (CHPZ) (Protected park or garden)   Parks or gardens of historical or dendrological interest (also protected under the Cultural Monument Act).

Chranena Naleziste (Protected habitat)   Are sites in which the occurrences of one or more plant or animal species are subject to preservation.

Chranene Prirodni Vytvory (CHPV) (protected natural feature)   Are natural geological features, especially karst areas, as well as individual selected trees, or groups of trees.

Chranene Prirodni Pamatky (CHPP) (protected natural monument)   Are natural geological features documenting human activities or associated with historical events.

Sources: IUCN (1971); Wiltowski (1979); Marsakova and Skrivanek (1982); Skrivanek (1982); Povolny (1986).

SUMMARY OF PROTECTED AREAS

Map[†] ref.	*National/international designations* Name of area	IUCN management category	Area (ha)	Year notified
	National Parks			
1	Krkonose	V	36,300	1963
2	Mala Fatra	II	22,630	1988
3	Nizke Tatry	II	81,095	1978
4	Pieninsky	II	2,125	1967
5	Podyji	II	6,300	1991
6	Slovensky raj	II	19,763	1988
7	Sumava	II	68,520	1991
8	Tatransky	II	74,111	1948
	National Nature Reserves			
9	Adrspassko Teplicke skaly	IV	1,772	1933
10	Choc	IV	1,428	1982
11	Dropie	IV	9,218	1955
12	Dumbier	IV	2,043	1973
13	Janska dolina	IV	1,696	1984
14	Karlstejn	IV	1,547	1955
15	Kokorinsky dul	I	2,097	1953
16	Modravske slati	I	3,615	1989
17	Prameny labe	I	2,884	1980
18	Prameny upy	I	4,280	1980
19	Salatin	I	1,193	1982
20	Stara Reka	IV	1,197	1956
21	Tlsta	IV	3,066	1981
22	Vltavsky Luh	IV	1,845	1989
	Protected Landscape Areas			
23	Beskydy	V	117,319	1973
24	Biele Karpaty	V	43,519	1979
25	Bile Karpaty	V	71,291	1980
26	Blanik	V	4,057	1981
27	Blansky les	V	21,235	1989
28	Broumovsko	V	41,000	1991
29	Cerova vrchovina	V	16,280	1989
30	Ceske stredohori	V	107,113	1976
31	Cesky kras	V	12,458	1972
32	Cesky raj	V	8,646	1955
33	Horna Orava	V	70,333	1979
34	Jeseniky	V	73,689	1969
35	Jizerske hory	V	35,002	1967
36	Kokorinsko	V	26,726	1976
37	Krivoklátsko	V	63,346	1978
38	Kysuce	V	65,462	1984
39	Labske Piskovce	V	32,474	1972
40	Latorica	V	15,620	1990
41	Litovelske pomoravi	V	9,600	1990
42	Luzicke Hory	V	26,441	1976
43	Male Karpaty	V	65,504	1976
44	Moravsky kras	V	8,545	1956
45	Muranska planina	V	21,931	1976
46	Orlicke hory	V	20,410	1969
47	Palava	V	8,017	1976
48	Podyji	V	10,300	1978
49	Polana	V	20,079	1981
50	Ponitrie	V	37,665	1985
51	Poodri	V	8,150	1991

Map[†] ref.	*National/international designations* Name of area	IUCN management category	Area (ha)	Year notified
52	Slavkovsky les	V	61,896	1974
53	Slovensky kras	V	36,166	1973
54	Stiavnicke vrchy	V	77,630	1979
55	Strazovske vrchy	V	30,979	1989
56	Sumava	V	99,752	1963
57	Trebonsko	V	70,695	1979
58	Velka Fatra	V	60,610	1973
59	Vihorlat	V	4,383	1973
60	Vychodne Karpaty	V	66,810	1977
61	Zahorie	V	27,522	1988
62	Zdarske vrchy	V	70,881	1970
63	Zelezne hory	V	38,000	1991
	Natural Areas			
64	Demanovske jaskyne	III	1,517	1972
65	Udoli Oslavy a Chvojnice	IV	1,002	1975
	Biosphere Reserves			
	Krivoklátsko Protected Landscape Area	IX	62,792	1977
	Palava Protected Landscape Area	IX	8,017	1986
	Polana	IX	20,079	1990
	Slovensky Kras Protected Landscape Area	IX	36,165	1977
	Sumava	IX	167,117	1990
	Trebon Basin Protected Landscape Area	IX	70,000	1977
	Ramsar Wetlands			
	Cicov dead arm	R	135	1990
	Lednice fish ponds	R	553	1990
	Modrava peatbogs	R	3,615	1990
	Novozámecky and Behyn ponds	R	923	1990
	Paríz marshes	R	141	1990
	Senné fish ponds	R	442	1990
	Šúr	R	984	1990
	Trebon fish ponds	R	10,165	1990

[†]Locations of most protected areas are shown on the accompanying map.

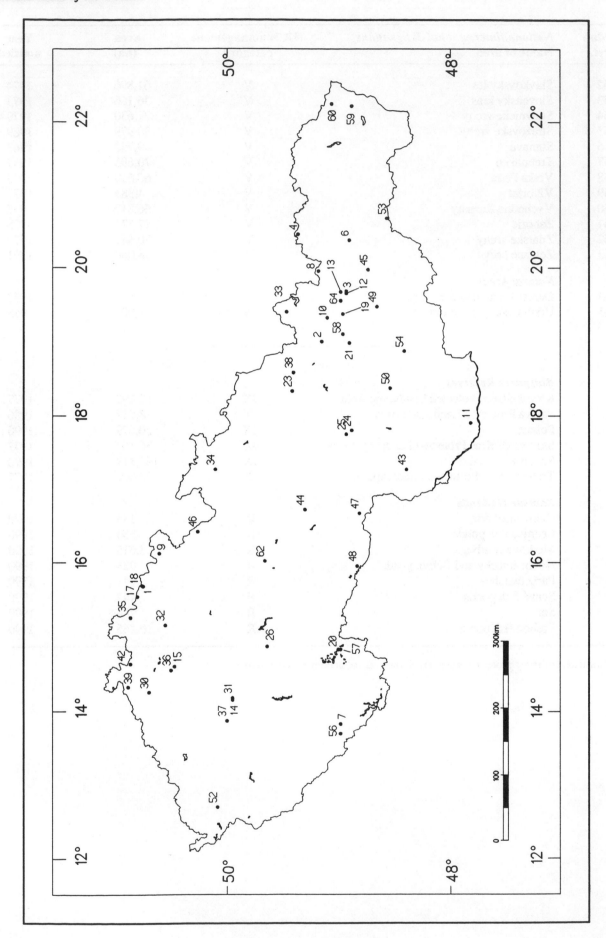

Protected Areas of Czechoslovakia

DENMARK

Area 43,070 sq. km

Population 5,143,000 (1990)
Natural increase: 0.06% per annum

Economic Indicators
GDP: US$ 19,881 per capita (1987)
GNP: US$ 15,010 per capita (1987)

Policy and Legislation The present constitution was established in 1953. Conservation is based on a broad philosophy of long-term planning and protection. Legislation on protected areas does not operate within the formalised structure of national parks and equivalent reserves. Thus, it is not possible to categorise reserves in the same way as in many other countries. Although specified protected areas do exist, equally large areas are covered by legislation relating to the protection of specified biotopes. There are also strict controls on physical planning throughout the rural environment. Special legal courts handle conservation matters, and conservation boards function under a Supreme Conservation Board (Poore and Gryn-Ambroes, 1980).

The earliest pieces of protected areas legislation were the 1805 Decree concerning the improvement, maintenance and conservation of forests (see below) and the Act concerning State Parks (*Lov af 12/3 om Statshaverne*) passed in 1852. There are several current laws relevant to the protected areas system. The Conservation of Nature Act (*Lov nr. 314 af 18/6 om Naturfredning*), passed on 13 June 1969 (amended 1975, 1978 and 1984/530) and its precursor passed in 1917, have served two main purposes: to preserve and protect nature on scientific, educational and cultural grounds and to open nature up to the general population for outdoor recreation (Koester, 1984). The present Act bases the conservation of nature around two kinds of measures: individual conservation orders and general conservation measures. Individual conservation orders, with a very detailed set of rules, may be applied to a particular area with the object of protecting such an area against, for example, further cultivation or the use of chemical insecticides, or to open it up for outdoor recreation purposes. Categories protected under individual conservation orders may be termed nature reserves, major conservation areas, or areas of national biological importance (see Annex) (sites given the latter title are designated by the National Forest and Nature Agency). Typically, the aim of these areas is to maintain and preserve them in their existing condition, in which case they are protected under "status quo" conservation orders. The Minister for the Environment may, by Order, impose conservation measures on areas of the country's territorial waters; this provision has enabled protection of the tidal flats of the Wadden Sea area. All ancient monuments and sites are automatically protected under Articles 48 to 53 of the Conservation of Nature Act.

Under a 1984 amendment this includes wrecks of ships lost more than a century previously; there are some 26,000 ancient monuments and sites (Cutrera, 1987, 1991; Koester, 1984).

A number of scientific reserves were established pursuant to legislation now repealed, but are still maintained as reserves. Very limited public access is permitted to these sites; egg collecting and hunting are prohibited (Koester, 1980).

General conservation measures are also provided by the Conservation of Nature Act, which include buffer zone strips around certain features and protected biotopes. In the former category, all land within 100m of protected monuments is protected. A similar 100m protected strip, measured from the beginning of land vegetation, runs along the entire coastline. Restrictions within these areas are fairly strict, although cultivation and agricultural buildings are largely permitted. All construction, planting, digging and fencing are forbidden (Cutrera, 1987; National Forest and Nature Agency, *in litt.*, 1991). There are also protected strips of land along the banks of some of the larger rivers and lakes. Construction, except for agricultural purposes, is forbidden within 300m of public forests and the larger private forests this protection was first enforced in 1937. The Act rules that approval of the conservation authorities must be obtained for the building of roads and the erection of electricity pylons in the countryside (Koester, 1984).

Biotope protection was a major feature of the 1969 Act, although no biotopes were specified for protection at that time. Amendments to the Act in 1972 gave the nature conservation authorities more control over the protection of public lakes and watercourses, while the Danish Society for Nature Conservation was given the right to appeal against decisions by the regional conservation authorities, thus providing a public voice. Further amendments in 1978 extended this protection to cover private watercourses, and also bogs and moors. The right to appeal was also extended in 1978 and is now widely used by local committees of the Ornithological Association, local naturalists clubs, anglers associations and other small groups. Amendments proposed in 1983, which entered into force in 1984, extended the protection of biotopes. The present list of protected biotopes consists of: watercourses (public and private), lakes (over 500 sq. m), bogs (over 5,000 sq. m), heaths, salt meadows and salt marshes (Cutrera, 1987; Koester, 1984).

The Nature Management Act (Act No. 339) of 24 May 1989 sets out to promote endeavours to: conserve and tend landscape amenity and cultural heritage values; preserve or improve conditions for wild plant and animal life; increase the forest area; and to improve the general public's opportunities for recreational activities.

Through the Nature Management Act, funds are to be made available for the acquisition of property and the management of this property (including afforestation); such funds are also to be available for loans to counties, municipalities and other non-profit organisations for property purchase and management activities. The Act also provides the Minister for the Environment with an option to purchase on properties in rural zones or weekend cottage areas, and, where such properties are of essential importance for the implementation of the Act, they may be expropriated for this purpose (Ministry of the Environment, 1991). A new Act merging certain elements of this Act with the Conservation of Nature Act is being prepared (National Forest and Nature Agency, *in litt.*, 1991).

The Hunting and Wildlife Administration Act (*Lov nr. 221 af 3/6 om Jagt- og viltforvaltning*), 1967 (amended 1983/57 and 1984/297), is largely concerned with hunting restrictions and the protection of birds and mammals, but also provides for the creation of wildlife reserves (also sometimes nominated as game reserves or bird reserves). Wildlife reserves can be established in marine territory as well as on land and in inland waters (see Annex).

The protection of forests has been a part of Danish legislation since the 1805 Royal Decree concerning the improvement, maintenance and conservation of forests (*Forordning af 27/9 om Skovenes udskiftning, vedligeholdelse og fredning*), when it was decided that all areas then under forest would have to be kept under forest in perpetuity, and that the owners would be responsible for the maintenance and improvement of these forests (Koester, 1984). The Forestry Act of 1935 supersedes the 1805 Decree, ensuring that a large proportion of the country remains under forest by imposing a special maintenance obligation on the greater part of forests in the country. These obligatory forest areas must remain under forest and may not be converted to other land uses without special permission from the forest authorities. Such permission is usually only given only on condition that another area be afforested. A replacement Forestry Act was passed in 1989 which maintains the system of obligatory forest areas, where the land must be covered with trees which form, or will form within a certain time span, a closed high forest (these forests are often commercial and may have very little conservation value). This Act provides an even greater emphasis on preservation and protection than its predecessors, although a major part of the Act is still concerned with ensuring a large and valuable wood production (Plum and Honoré, 1988; Wulff, 1991). The 1969 Conservation of Nature Act provides general measures permitting public access to all private and public woodland. More detailed regulation of public access to forests has also been provided: Statutory Order 123 of 19 April 1972 covers state, local authority and church forest; Statutory Order 373 of 15 August 1979 covers private woodland: all private forests larger than 5ha are open to the general public if connected by a public road or path. State compensation for conservation measures applied to private woodlands is covered in the 1977 Act concerning Subsidies to Measures in Private Forests (*Lov nr. 476 af 14/9 om Tilskud til foranstaltninger i private skove*, latest amendment, 1985/524) (Cutrera, 1987). In regional plans (see below) special afforestation areas are laid out where both public and private landowners are encouraged to plant trees, largely for commercial purposes, although grants can be obtained to promote the growth of deciduous species (Wulff, 1991).

The conservation of nature and the establishment of protected areas is a major feature of overall town and country planning. A major planning element is incorporated into the 1969 Conservation of Nature Act. Plans for nature conservation are proposed after three phases: mapping, analysis and evaluation. The plans produced specify overall aims for the protection, care and use of the region's natural areas. Areas protected by conservation orders play an important role in conservation planning, as do other protected areas: internationally designated sites such as Ramsar sites and EC special protection areas.

The National and Regional Planning Act (*Lov nr. 375 af 13/6 om Lands-og regionplanlaegning*) of 13 June 1973 (amended 1982/735) provides for comprehensive physical planning on a national and a regional scale. This Act is based on an integrated evaluation of Denmark's areas and natural resources. It does not aim to produce a single integrated plan for the entire nation, but to make sure that the viewpoints and directives of central government are incorporated into the planning of the regions and municipalities. Regional plans are required, among other things, to provide directives for the conservation of nature and the designation of areas with particular natural assets; for the reservation of areas for recreation; and for the control of pollution of rivers lakes and the sea. Local planning, which takes place in conformity with the Local Planning Act of 1977, must also provide directives of the type mentioned above. The Urban and Rural Zones Act (*Lov nr. 315 af 18/6 om By-og landzoner*) of 18 June 1969 (amended 1985/446) is another important act. This Act divides the country into three zones: urban zones, where urban development can take place; summer house areas, within which new summer houses may be located; and rural zones, covering by far the greatest proportion of the land area, where construction is strictly limited. It is among the explicit aims of this Act and the associated planning legislation that landscape values and nature conservation interests are safeguarded and recreational facilities are provided. Another important planning directive laid out by the government, which is binding on regional and municipal authorities, dictates that no further holiday housing areas may be laid out in zones along and near the coast. County councils are also required to produce sector plans, including a plan for the conservation of nature: the legal basis for this lies in the Conservation of Nature Act (Cutrera, 1991; Primdahl, 1991).

The Act Concerning Purchase of Property for Leisure Purposes (*Lov nr. 230 af 7/6 om Erhvervelse af ejendom til fritidsformaal*), 1972 may also have some relevance to nature conservation as it provides the means by which the state has purchased areas of land for recreational purposes (Koester, 1980).

The Environmental Protection Act (*Lov nr. 372 of 13/6 om Miljoebeskyttelse*) of 13 June 1973 (most recently amended 1985/86) aims to "safeguard physical environmental qualities essential to the health and recreational aspects of human life and to the maintenance of the diversity of plants and animals" (Poore and Gryn-Ambroes, 1980). An EC Directive concerning environmental impact assessments (EIAs) was adopted on 27 June 1985. EIAs must take into account a number of factors including, among other things, flora, fauna, soil, water, and the landscape. There is no one legal text implementing the Directive, however, regulations with similar objectives certainly exist elsewhere in the country's legal framework: the National and Regional Planning Act (mentioned above) and the Urban Planning Act of 1975 require the inclusion of environmental matters in their regional, local and town plans, and all development takes place within the framework of these acts. Large construction projects also require a permit from the environmental authorities under the terms of the Environment Protection Act (Coenen and Jörissen, 1989; Cutrera, 1991).

Larger landscapes of interest for conservation and recreation are usually safeguarded by a combined administration of the above mentioned acts (see below under "Other Relevant Information").

In June 1987 parliament presented a statement on an integrated strategy for marginal agricultural land, concentrating on four major topics: the conservation of peatland and agricultural land around lakes and streams; the re-establishment of small biotopes in intensively cultivated agricultural land; the afforestation of poorer, marginal agricultural land; and the improvement of the possibilities for recreation and tourism in open land. In the same year the Minister for Agriculture presented a statement on future agriculture policy which included, among its four major objectives, increasing the environmental and recreational value of forests (Plum and Honoré, 1988).

Potential problems exist regarding the protection of biotopes, notably those caused by the difficulties of providing strict legal definitions of biological systems. These definitions have, however, become relatively well established over the years and restrictions have frequently been tightened, but rarely relaxed. The need for specific conservation orders still remains, notably for the protection of those biotopes not covered under specific conservation orders, but also for the provision of public recreational areas. As a rule, compensation is not paid in respect of restrictions imposed by the general conservation measures of the Conservation of Nature Act. The maintenance of areas covered by general conservation orders, notably protected biotopes, by the conservation authorities may be a problem if an agreement with the local landowner cannot be reached. In such areas, specific conservation orders may have to be imposed simply to secure access. This is regarded by some as an untenable situation and may well be changed in the future (Cutrera, 1987; Koester, 1984).

International Activities   Denmark acceded to the Convention on Wetlands of International Importance especially as Waterfowl Habitat (Ramsar Convention) on 2 September 1977. Twenty-seven sites have been nominated (with a further eleven sites in Greenland). The Convention concerning the Protection of the World Cultural and Natural Heritage (World Heritage Convention) was ratified on 25 July 1979, but no sites have been inscribed. Denmark is a participant in the Unesco Man and the Biosphere programme: there are no biosphere reserves in the country (although there is one in Greenland).

The Convention on the Conservation of European Wildlife and Natural Habitats (Bern Convention) was signed on 1 January 1983. Denmark is a member of the European Community and hence is bound by its environmental directives: 111 sites have been designated as EC special protection areas under the Wild Birds Directive (April, 1991). Although Denmark is a member of the Council of Europe and therefore participates in the identification of European biogenetic reserves, none has been nominated in Denmark itself, nor have any sites been awarded the Council of Europe European Diploma. Denmark is a party to the Convention on the Protection of the Marine Environment of the Baltic Sea (Helsinki Convention) which it signed on 22 March 1974 and which entered into force in 1980; this Convention deals with a wide range of issues, from the protection of seals to pollution control measures.

In 1982 the three Wadden Sea states of the Netherlands, Germany and Denmark signed the "Joint Declaration on the Protection of the Wadden Sea". This declaration provides protection by the full and coordinated application of international legal instruments by the states and countries concerned. Such decisions are made at the Trilateral Governmental Conference on the Protection of the Wadden Sea. The fifth meeting took place on 17 November 1988 at Bonn, where agreements were reached concerning the implementation of Ramsar, the Convention on the Conservation of European Wildlife and Natural Habitats (1982), the Convention on the Conservation of Migratory Species of Wild Animals (1979) and the EC Bird Directive (79/409/EC) (Anon., 1988).

The Nordic Council, of which Denmark is a member state, is involved in a number of environmental protection issues: the Nordic Council of Ministers has run a series of four to five-year environmental protection programmes, the current programme beginning in 1988. These programmes cover a wide range of activities which include, among other things, bringing greater attention to nature conservation in connection with planning activities. The Council has encouraged the registration of valuable landscapes in the Nordic area, the concentration of conservation efforts towards the preservation of particularly important habitat types and the use of natural areas by the wider public for recreation purposes. It has also encouraged the development of standardised data collection for monitoring environmental quality (Nordic Council of Ministers, 1983). On 5 October 1976 Denmark became a party to the Nordic Environmental Protection Convention, which requires authorities to take into account the environmental consequences to all other parties before granting permits for environmentally damaging activities (Nordic Council of Ministers, 1978).

Administration and Management   A number of public authorities are involved in nature conservation: the Ministry of the Environment (*Miliøministeriet*) (including secretariat and Ministerial staff); the Environment Appeal Board; the National Environment Protection Agency (*Miliøstyrelsen*); the National Forest and Nature Agency (*Skov- of Naturstyrelsen*); the National Agency for Physical Planning (*Plantstyrelsen*); and the National Institute for Food (*Staten Levnedsmiddelinstitute*); the Geological Survey of Denmark and the environmental sections of the regional authorities (of which there are 14), municipal authorities (227) and the conservancy boards (26). Three of the agencies mentioned above are subordinate to the Minister of the Environment and act on his instructions; the National Environment Protection Agency, the National Forest and Nature Agency and the National Agency for Physical Planning (Anon., 1987; Cutrera, 1991). The Ministry of Agriculture is also involved in the administration of some protected areas.

After passage of the 1973 Environmental Protection Act, the Ministry of the Environment was made responsible for national and regional planning, preservation of architecturally and/or historically important buildings, the protection of natural and recreational areas and the management of forests. Under a 1977 amendment, decisions on countryside conservation and planning, as well as the management of all the protected areas within each region, were transferred from separate conservation planning committees to the regional authorities themselves in each of the 14 counties (Poore and Gryn-Ambroes, 1980; National Forest and Nature Agency, *in litt.*, 1991).

The National Environment Protection Agency deals largely with control of pollution, such as toxic emissions, pesticides, industrial release of chemicals and recycling. In the 1985-1990 Five-year Environmental Protection Programme three main tasks were outlined for this Agency: the preservation of human life (pollution control); the conservation of flora and fauna and the protection of natural resources (Cutrera, 1991).

The National Forest and Nature Agency was formed in 1987 by the merger of the National Forestry Service and the National Agency for the Protection of Nature, Monuments and Sites in a move designed to give more weight to the ecological aspect of the management of state land. The National Forest and Nature Agency has to decide under the Forestry Act which forest areas are to be subject to stricter protection. The Agency acts as the supervisory authority over the national forestry system, which consists of more than 30 local forestry districts (Cutrera, 1991). The Agency is responsible for monitoring work in areas of national and international importance (for instance, nature reserves, Ramsar sites, EC special protection areas). It is further responsible for the management of wildlife (game) reserves and the declaration of areas of national biological importance. Within Ramsar sites and EC special protection areas biotope protection is weak and agricultural use of the land is not restricted (Cutrera, 1987).

There is a total of 26 Nature Conservation Boards, legally created under the Conservation of Nature Act, which are independent of the Ministry. They are composed of a chairman with a legal background, appointed by the Minister, and two local representatives, one elected by the municipal authorities, the other by the regional authorities. In effect, they are courts concerned exclusively with conservation matters and administration of the Conservation of Nature Act. They are responsible for placing areas under conservation orders and also have powers for protection of beach conservation areas. The Supreme Conservation Board is the final administrative authority concerning the conservation of nature. This board consists of members of parliament and judges of the Supreme Court; it is equivalent to a high court of justice (Cutrera, 1991; Poore and Gryn-Ambroes, 1980; National Forest and Nature Agency, *in litt.*, 1991). In cases where the Ministry of Agriculture, or other government or non-governmental organisations, stand as the owners of particular protected areas, they are responsible for the administration and management of these areas (National Forest and Nature Agency, *in litt.*, 1991).

Overall environmental expenditure in 1988 was some Danish Kroner 6 billion. Public expenditure on environmental policy measures was then 7.5% of all national expenditure. In other sectors plans for public expenditure are generally made every four years. Due to the long-term character of environmental expenditure, however, this period has been increased to six years. The present environmental expenditure plan was proposed by the government in April 1989 and will run from 1989-1994: Kroner 33 billion have been set aside for this period. The plan is divided into four areas; water, nature protection, air and waste (Cutrera, 1991).

The most active and powerful non-governmental organisation is the Danish Nature Conservation Society. It frequently takes cases to the conservation boards, and its members play an important role in preventing infringements on protected areas and biotopes. It also puts funds towards purchasing sites that cannot be protected by conservation orders (Poore and

Gryn-Ambroes, 1980). Other groups, such as local committees of the Ornithological Association (*Ornithologisk Forening*), also play an important role as watchdogs over protected areas and biotopes (Cutrera, 1987).

Systems Reviews   Denmark is the southernmost of the Nordic countries. It is a physically complex country, largely shaped by the most recent Pleistocene glaciations, lying in the mouth of the Baltic. There are no less than 500 islands, and numerous smaller islands, shoals and banks; the coastline is very long with a high degree of indentation, and an abundance of fjords, bays, straits and peninsulas. Mainland Denmark itself is a peninsula with only a narrow connection to the rest of Europe at its border with Germany. Most of the country comprises lowland or gently undulating plains, with the highest point reaching 150m. The west coast is made up of sand bars and lagoons backed by lagoons and fenland. The centre is underlain by sandy soils, while the ground towards the east is covered by thick, gently undulating glacial deposits including outwash materials and moraines.

Unlike the other Nordic countries, almost all landscapes are, or have been, influenced by man's activities (excluding Greenland and the Faroes), the only exceptions being the west coast salt marshes and some scattered patches of inland heath (Duffey, 1982). About 12% of the country is forested – this figure has been as low as 2%, but has increased since the first Forestry Act in 1805. About 66% of the present forest cover is in the form of coniferous plantations. Much of the remainder is made up of deciduous forest, including some small stands of natural or semi-natural forest; most of this forest is dominated by beech *Fagus sylvatica* (Heiss, 1987). The Ministry of the Environment aims to double the area under woodland in the next 80-100 years. In the last 50 years the area under coniferous forest has increased rapidly, while the area of broad-leaved woodland has decreased by 7-8%. About 10% of public forests are protected areas (Cutrera, 1991). Wetlands, especially coastal wetlands, are an extremely important habitat type in Denmark: coastal sites include salt marshes, reed swamps, meadows, mud flats and dunes systems is long and mostly low-lying with numerous fjords, inlets and islands.

Rural land is protected by the strict application of existing land-use and environmental protection legislation. In addition, a number of areas on land and at sea are protected under the Conservation of Nature Act. Much of the preparatory work behind the Act was undertaken by a committee established in 1961 to study nature conservation legislation. It produced a comprehensive report in 1967 which supported the protection of specified biotopes as one of the key tools to nature conservation legislation. Biotope protection was thus a major feature of the 1969 Act, and, with the subsequent amendments providing for the protection of specified biotopes, it is now an essential feature of conservation in Denmark.

The Ramsar sites and the EC special protection areas are largely overlapping; in 1987 they covered 9,500 sq. km, 2,500 sq. km of which was land (5.6% of the total land area). Over one-fifth of this land area is further protected under specific conservation orders. For the remainder, protection is minimal, although it is expected to be increased by strict application of general conservation measures and the further creation of many more specific conservation orders (Cutrera, 1987). Several thousand areas, covering some 3.5% of the area of the country, are protected under individual conservation orders. They range in size from 2,000ha down to tiny sites which may be simply a few distinctive trees or an individual geological formation (Cutrera, 1991). The National Forest and Nature Agency has declared over 90 areas of national biological importance under the Conservation of Nature Act. There are also nine scientific reserves (covering 1,400ha of land and 13,000ha of sea). By the end of 1985 a total of 86 wildlife reserves covered over 100,000ha, 85% in wetlands and 42 within Ramsar sites (National Forest and Nature Agency, *in litt.*, 1991). A detailed overview of protected areas, with maps and details of all sites, is given in Dahl (1988).

Other Relevant Information   Figures given for the protected areas coverage may appear to be somewhat misleading. Frequently sites which are protected under separate conservation orders adjoin one another; adjoin obligatory forest areas; or are only separated by minor features such as roads. In other cases single conservation orders cover sites that may be split into several unconnected units. Wider areas protected under a number of different legal texts are sometimes considered as single units a protected landscape where the different categories give a form of zonation; in other places sites are not considered in relation to others, although they may still form part of a continuum; while in places where a single designation covers a number of distinct and separate areas these are usually written as a single site (Dahl, 1988; National Forest and Nature Agency, *in litt.*, 1991).

Addresses

Ministry of the Environment, The National Forest and Nature Agency, Slotsmarken 13, DK-2970 HORSHOLM (Tel: 276 5376; FAX: 276 5477)

National Environment Protection Agency, Strandgade 29, DK-1401 COPENHAGEN (Tel: 1 578310)

Danmarks Naturfredningsforening (Society for the protection of Nature in Denmark), Norregarde 2, DK-1165 COPENHAGEN K (Tel: 1 871101)

References

Anon. (1982). Unpublished document on protected areas, produced by the National Agency for the Protection of Nature Monuments and Sites in the Ministry of the Environment.

Anon. (1987). National Activities, Denmark: reorganisation. Council of Europe. *Naturopa* 5: 3.

Anon. (1988). Fifth trilateral governmental conference on the protection of the Wadden Sea. Communique. Bonn, 17 November.

Björkland, M.I. (1974). Achievements in marine conservation: 1. Marine parks. *Environmental Conservation* 1(3).

Coenen, R. and Jörissen, J. (1989). *Environmental impact assessment in the member countries of the European Community, implementing the EC-Directive: an overview.* KfK 4507 B, Kernforschungszentrum, Karsruhe, Germany. 42 pp.

Cutrera, A. (1987). *European Environmental Yearbook 1987.* Institute for Environmental Studies. DocTer International UK/London. 815 pp.

Cutrera, A. (1991). *European Environmental Yearbook.* Institute for Environmental Studies. DocTer International UK/London. 897 pp.

Dahl, K. (1988). *Fredede omrader og statsskove.* 2 volumes: Jylland and Øerne. Danmarks Naturfredningsforening Skov- og Naturstyrelsen. Copenhagen. 280 pp and 189 pp.

Duffey, E. (1982). *National parks and reserves of Western Europe.* Macdonald and Co. (Publishers) Ltd., London and Sydney. 288 pp.

Grimmett, R.F.A. and Jones, T.A. (1989). *Important bird areas in Europe.* International Council for Bird Preservation, Cambridge. 888 pp.

Heiss, G. (1987). Inventory of natural (virgin) and ancient seminatural woodlands within the councils member states and Finland. European Committee for the Conservation of Nature and Natural Resources. Unpublished.

Koester, V. (1980). *Nordic countries' legislation on the environment with special emphasis on conservation,* a survey. IUCN Environmental Policy and Law Paper No. 14. IUCN, Gland, Switzerland. 44 pp.

Koester, V. (1984). Conservation Legislation and General Protection of Biotopes in an International Perspective. *Environmental Policy and Law* 12: 106-116.

Ministry of the Environment (1991). The Nature Management Act. Translation. National Forest and Nature Agency, Ministry of the Environment, Horsholm. 4 pp.

Nordic Council of Ministers (1978). *The Nordic Environmental Protection Convention, with a commentary.* Nordic Council of Ministers, Stockholm. 14 pp.

Nordic Council of Ministers (1983). *Programme for Nordic cooperation in environmental protection for 1983 to 1987.* Nordic Council of Ministers, Stockholm. 37 pp.

Plum, P.M. and Honoré, B. (1988). Forest Policy and Legislation. *Environmental policy and law* 18 (4): 111-115.

Poore, D. and Gryn-Ambroes, P. (1980). *Nature conservation in Northern and Western Europe.* UNEP/IUCN/WWF, Gland, Switzerland. Pp. 116-129.

Primdahl, J. (1991). Countryside Planning. Introduction to Environmental Management. In: Hansen, P.E. and Jorgensen, S.E. (Eds), *Developments in environmental modelling* Series No. 18. Elsevier. Pp. 8.1-8.28.

Wulff, H. (1991). Danish Environmental Law. Introduction to Environmental Management. In: Hansen, P.E. and Jorgensen, S.E. (Eds), *Developments in environmental modelling* Series No. 18. Elsevier. Pp. 10.1-10.25.

ANNEX
Definitions of protected area designations, as legislated, together with authorities responsible for their administration

Title: Conservation of Nature Act

Date: 13 June 1969, with major amendments in 1975, 1978 and 1984

Brief description: Provides for the conservation of nature and for the recreational requirements of the population, through individual conservation orders on specific sites and through general conservation measures, notably concerned with the protection of specific biotopes.

Administrative authority: Regional authorities, ie. county councils
Designation of sites is by independent regional conservation boards.

Designations:

Nature reserves/major conservation area Each area is protected under an individual conservation order, on a case-by-case basis. Protection might be imposed for scenic, scientific, historical, cultural or recreational reasons, or for a combination of these, hence the degree of protection varies widely, both between areas and within them. There several thousand such conservation orders. Regulations are drawn up specifically for each area but in general existing uses including farming, forestry and hunting may well continue and farming methods are usually not restricted. Typical regulations could ban: cultivation, planting, disturbance or destruction of flora and fauna, changes in landforms, extraction of raw materials such as clay, chalk, sand and gravel and construction work. These areas are usually well protected from industrial activities, water and road developments, and the establishment of power lines. Regulations are also set down for the management of these areas; they can close, restrict or open a site for public access; they can also enforce the removal of plantations or other vegetation or the removal of buildings and other constructions. Conservation orders can also demand the expropriation of private land for the establishment of a protected area although this right is rarely used.

Area of national biological importance Established in a similar fashion to the above under conservation orders, these sites are singled out by the National Forest and Nature Agency for their biological importance on a national scale (prior to 1987 they were declared by the National Agency for the Protection of Nature, Monuments and Sites).

Protected biotope A major part of the Act concerns the protection of nature through the designation of protected biotopes. No biotopes were listed in the original legislation, however, under a series of amendments, a number have since been designated. Specific areas are not mentioned in these amendments, the biotopes covered are described in the main text.

Sources: Grimmett and Jones, 1989; Koester, 1980; Poore and Gryn-Ambroes, 1980; National Forest and Nature Agency, *in litt.*, 1991

Title: The Hunting and Wildlife Administration Act

Date: 1967, amendments in 1983 and 1984

Brief description: The major law concerned with the protection of birds and mammals and the imposition of hunting regulations, it also provides for the designation of game reserves.

Administrative authority: Minister of Agriculture Wildlife Reserve Committee of the Wildlife Administration Council

Designations:

Game reserve/wildlife reserve/bird reserve These may be established on land, in freshwater areas and in territorial waters where necessary for the purpose of preserving the country's stock of wildlife including migratory birds. Sites shall be established by the Minister of Agriculture, following negotiations with the Wildlife Reserve Committee of the Wildlife Administration Council.

Individual sites should be designated through an Order issued by the Minister of Agriculture; this should contain details of the delimitation of the site as well as regulations which shall apply to hunting access and traffic in the area, for the purpose of protecting and building up the stock of wildlife. Full compensation shall be paid for any restrictions of ownership, although if no agreement can be reached a figure will be fixed by an Agricultural Commission.

Source: Original legislation

131

SUMMARY OF PROTECTED AREAS

Map[†] ref.	*National/international designations* Name of area	IUCN management category	Area (ha)	Year notified
	Scientific Reserve			
1	Vejlerne	I	5,000	1960
	Nature Reserves			
2	Esrum Soe and Gribskov	IV	7,280	
3	Flyndersoe and Stubbergaard Soe	IV	1,670	
4	Hansted	IV	6,500	
5	Skagen	IV	4,300	
6	Tipperne/Valeinengene (Bird Reserve)	I	3,020	1936
7	Tisvilde	IV	2,000	
	Major Conservation Areas			
8	Aalvand Klithede and Foerby Soe	V	1,200	1977
9	Agger Tange	IV	6,100	1984
10	Anholt	V	1,856	1939
11	Bognaes, Kattinge Vig	V	1,200	1969
12	Borris Hede	V	1,830	1902
13	Bulbjerg, Lild Klit and Hjardemaal Klit	V	1,500	1947
14	Egtved and Vejle River Valleys	V	1,025	1980
15	Esrum Soe and Surrounding Areas	V	1,900	1952
16	Fanoe	V	1,400	1964
17	Flyndersoe and Stubbergaard Soe	V	1,670	1934
18	Hanstholm Reserve	IV	4,800	1972
19	Harbooere Tange	V	2,400	1984
20	Hesseloe Sea Area	V	5,000	1982
21	Hoeje Moen	III	2,090	1980
22	Hulsig Klit	IV	2,144	1940
23	Kaergaard Klitplantage-Loevklitterne-Lyngbos	V	1,670	1955
24	Kongenhus Hede	V	1,300	1953
25	Ledreborg Gods	V	1,800	1973
26	Lyngby, Lodbjerg, Flade Soe	V	3,327	1976
27	Maribo Soerne	V	1,195	1957
28	Mols Bjerge	V	2,750	1972
29	Noerre Hvalsoe and Kisserup Area	V	1,132	1980
30	Nord-Bornholm	V	2,500	1970
31	North Coast of Vejle Fjord	V	1,004	1949
32	Rabjerg Mile/Rabjerg Stene	III	4,200	1962
33	Rands Fjord	V	1,047	1968
34	Roemoe	IV	2,500	1947
35	Roennerne	V	1,496	1980
36	Ryegaard Gods, Tempelkrog and Bramsnaes Vig	V	1,515	1940
37	Salten Langsoe, Vissingkloster, Mossoe	V	3,950	1971
38	Saltholm	V	1,600	1983
39	Skagen Klitplantage, Grenen	IV	2,175	1921
40	Skallingen and Langli	IV	2,400	1980
41	Soevind, Sondrup, Aakaer and Vorsoe	V	2,200	1974
42	Stavnsfjord	V	1,525	1984
43	Stigsnaes Peninsula	V	1,215	1978
44	Store Vildmose	V	2,100	1973
45	Sydlige Fanoe	V	1,400	1985
46	Toendermarsken	V	5,650	1988
47	Tranum Area	V	2,160	1956
48	Tystrup-Bavelse Soerne	V	3,750	1957
49	Ulfborg-Vind Area	V	1,300	1949
50	Ulvedybet og Nibe Breding	V	20,304	1930
51	Vadehavet Naturereserve	V	95,000	1985

Map[†] ref.	National/international designations Name of area	IUCN management category	Area (ha)	Year notified
52	Vaernengene	V	2,600	1977
53	Valloe Gods	V	1,383	1981
54	Veststadil Fjord and Husby Klit	V	1,465	1969
55	Vorupoer-Stenbjerg	V	2,270	1954
	Bird Reserves			
56	Ertholm	I	1,257	
57	Hirsholmene	I	2,000	1948
58	Ronner (Laeso)	IV	2,923	1980
59	Stavnsfjord	IV	16,320	1984
60	Totten	I	2,100	
61	Vadehavet	V	120,000	1979
	Protected Region			
62	Selso-Lindholm-Bognaes	V	1,990	
	Other areas			
63	Farum	IV	5,000	
64	Gudenaens	IV	6,500	
65	Ulvshale, Nyord	IV	1,130	
	Ramsar Wetlands			
	Anholt Island sea area	R	12,720	1977
	Ertholmene Islands east of Bornholm	R	1,257	1977
	Fiilsø	R	4,320	1977
	Hirsholmene	R	480	1977
	Horsens Fiord and Endelave	R	43,200	1977
	Karrebæk, Dybsø and Avnø Fiords	R	19,200	1977
	Læsø	R	67,840	1977
	Lillebælt	R	37,330	1977
	Maribo Lakes	R	4,400	1977
	Nakskov Fiord and Inner Fiord	R	8,960	1977
	Næreå Coast and Æbelø area	R	13,800	1977
	Nissum Bredning with Harboøre and Agger peninsulas	R	13,280	1977
	Nissum Fiord	R	11,600	1977
	Nordre Rønner	R	2,923	1977
	Præstø Fiord, Jungshoved Nor, Ulfshale and Nyord	R	25,960	1977
	Randers and Mariager Fiords (part)	R	41,440	1977
	Ringkøbing Fiord	R	27,520	1977
	Sejerø Bugt	R	42,560	1977
	South Funen Archipelago	R	39,200	1977
	Stadil and Veststadil Fiords	R	7,184	1977
	Stavns Fiord adjacent waters	R	16,320	1977
	Ulvedybet and Nibe Bredning	R	20,304	1977
	Vadehavet (The Waddensea)	R	140,830	1987
	Vejlerne and Løgstør Bredning	R	45,280	1977
	Waters between Lolland and Falster, including Rødsand, Guldborgsund, Bøtø Nor	R	36,800	1977
	Waters off Skælskør Nor and Glænø	R	17,120	1977
	Waters south-east of Fejo and Femo Isles	R	32,640	1977

[†]Locations of most protected areas are shown on the accompanying map.

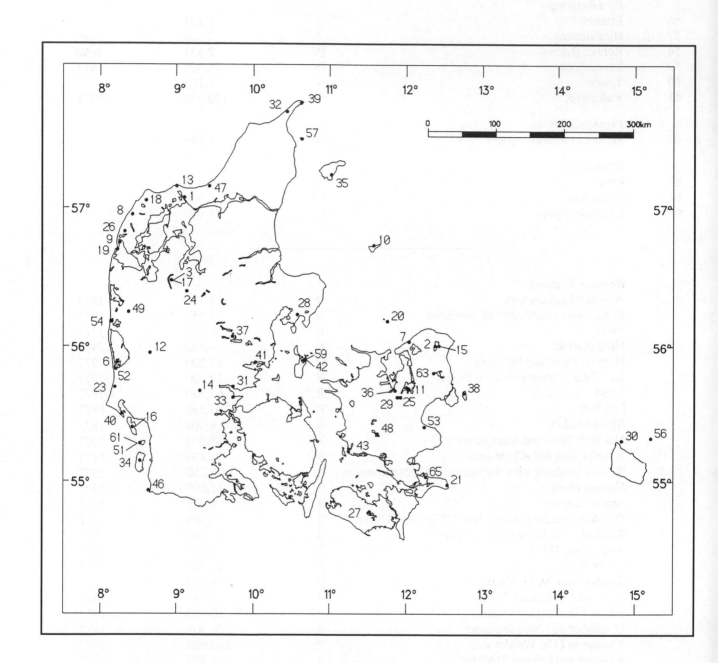

Protected Areas of Denmark

DENMARK – FAROE ISLANDS

Area 1,400 sq. km

Population 47,663 (1988) (Hunter, 1989)
Natural increase: No information

Economic Indicators
GDP: No information
GNP: No information

Policy and Legislation   The Faroes have been self-governing, semi-autonomous islands (with home rule) of Denmark since 1852. There is no protected areas legislation as such, the mainland legislation does not apply. According to the Game Legislation, most birds are protected within the 200 nautical miles fishing limit (named species, however, can be hunted year round, or during restricted periods).

A recommendation for new game legislation is being discussed, which may bring improved conservation legislation to certain areas (Grimmett and Jones, 1989).

International Activities   As part of Denmark, the Faroes are covered by the Ramsar Convention, although no sites have been designated (Denmark acceded to the Ramsar Convention on 2 September 1977). Unlike mainland Denmark, the Faroe Islands are not covered by the World Heritage Convention, the Bern Convention, nor the EC Wild Birds Directive (they are not a part of the EC).

Administration and Management Not applicable

Systems Reviews   The Faroe Islands are a group of 18 main islands in the north-east Atlantic, 300km from the Shetland Isles (UK) and 675km from Norway. They are dominated by mountains, rising to a height of 882m. The base rock is basalt, only partly covered by a thin and stony soil. Vegetation is mostly dwarf scrub, with bog and grassy heath communities. Above 300m alpine tundra covers the mountainous North Islands, and the north-facing peaks of the Central Islands group (Davis *et al.*, 1986). There are a few small woods. There are 262 native vascular plant species on the islands (Hansen, 1972). The islands are an important centre for seabirds:

the cliffs, slopes and screes facing the sea provide important nest sites for about 50 regularly breeding species, which feed in the productive waters around the islands. Sheep are grazed throughout the islands, and some areas are also grazed by cattle in the summer (Grimmett and Jones, 1989). On 17 of the islands are inhabited and some 2% of the land surface area is cultivated, the main crop being potatoes (Hunter, 1991). During the next few years hydrocarbon exploration will be carried out in Faroese waters which may affect the important bird populations of the islands (Grimmett and Jones, 1989).

Other Relevant Information   The Faroe Islands were a Norwegian province from 1380-1789. Their parliament was restored in 1852. Since 1948 they have been a self-governing region of the Kingdom of Denmark (Hunter, 1991).

Addresses

Museum of Natural History, 3800 TORSHAVN
Government Offices (includes Ministries of Fisheries and Agriculture), PO Box 64, TORSHAVN (Tel: 42 11080)

References

Davis, S.D., Droop, S.J.M., Gregerson, P., Henson, L., Leon, C.J., Lamlein Villa-Lobos, J., Synge, H., and Zantovska, J. (1986). *Plants in danger: what do we know?* IUCN, Gland, Switzerland, and Cambridge, UK. 461 pp.

Grimmett, R.F.A. and Jones, T.A. (1989). *Important bird areas in Europe*. ICBP, Cambridge, UK.

Hansen, K. (1972). Vertical vegetation zones and vertical distribution types in the Faroes. *Saertryk Bot. Tidssk.* 67. Pp. 33-63. (Unseen)

Hunter, B. (Ed.) (1991). *The Statesman's Yearbook*. The Macmillan Press Ltd., London and Basingstoke, UK. Pp. 425-427.

Rutherford, G.K. (Ed.) (1982). *The physical environment of the Faroe Islands*. The Hague. (Unseen)

REPUBLIC OF ESTONIA

Area 45,215 sq. km

Population 1.5 million (1990)
Natural increase: no information

Economic Indicators
GNP: No information
GDP: No information

Policy and Legislation Immediately following the failure of the August 1991 coup, the country became independent from the USSR and was recognised by the United Nations.

Until 1991 there was no overall law governing conservation areas and, in its absence, it is highly probable that new laws will be drafted (Weisenburger, 1991). Existing republic laws on land (Land Code of the Estonian SSR, 1970), water (Water Code of the Estonian SSR, 1972), forest (Forest Code of the Estonian SSR, 1978), minerals (The Mineral Wealth Code of the Estonian SSR, 1976), air (On the Protection of the Atmospheric Air, 1981), fauna (On the Protection the Utilization of the Animal Kingdom, 1981) and specific regulations will need to be adjusted to the new legislation (Weisenburger, 1991). These are now being revised (Kaasik, 1991), in advance of which a new law on Lahemaa National Park was passed in March. In June 1991, a working group was set up to prepare a bill on protected areas, species protection and the classification of protected areas (Kaasik, 1991).

The designation of nature reserves and the administrative and scientific institutions were covered until recently by the 1957 Law on the Protection of Nature in the Estonian SSR. The Nature Conservancy Board at the Ministry of Forest Management and Nature Protection was the body responsible for protected area regulations, whilst the Commission of Nature Protection and Rational Utilization of Natura Resources at the Supreme Soviet of the Estonian SSR was charged with supervision of legal enforcement (Varep, 1988).

International Activities The country is active in the Unesco Man and the Biosphere Programme and has proposed the West Estonian Archipelago Biosphere Reserve for acceptance. The Convention concerning the World Cultural and Natural Heritage (World Heritage Convention) and the Convention on Wetlands of International Importance especially as Waterfowl Habitat (Ramsar Convention) apply to the country under original USSR ratification.

On 17 April 1991 the Association of Baltic National Parks was established and the statutes signed on 22 June. The Association comprises five national parks, with a Board of Directors and a secretariat in Lahemaa National Park (A. Kaasick, pers. comm., 1991).

Administration and Management The management of protected areas is undertaken by the state authorities. On 6 June 1991 the Union of the Protected Areas of Estonia was set up for 13 national protected areas, as well as a regional information centre. The centre is the repository for information on protected areas in the Baltics. Scientific research was carried out by the Academy of Sciences, as well as by the Tarta State University branch of the Hydrometeorology and Natural Environment Control Committee, and the Scientific Research Institute of Forest Management and Nature Conservation (founded in 1969) (Varep, 1988).

Non-state financial support for national parks is in the form of funds supported by numerous organisations and individuals. For example, in 1990 the budget of 609,000 roubles for Lahemaa National Park comprised 155,000 roubles from the state and 454,000 from other sources, including private sources (Nikol'skii et al., 1991). The investment in protected areas increased steadily from 394,000 roubles in 1975 to 1,244,000 in 1989, but dropped to 634,000 roubles in 1990 (Nikol'skii et al., 1991).

The Estonian Nature Conservation Society, founded in 1966, with 21,000 members in 50 branches, takes an active interest in the education aspects of protected areas (Varep, 1988).

Systems Reviews Bounded by the USSR to the east, Gulf of Finland to the north and the Baltic Sea to the west, the country has a 4,000-year history of human occupation, giving rise to a mosaic of forests, agricultural land and bogs (11,800ha in total, covering 20% of the country). The landscape is essentially flat and sandy, with limestone, dotted with small, deep, clear lakes and bogs. The forest is a mixture of boreal and deciduous, representing the West European *taiga* and Boreanemoral. The northern coastal zone has an unique ecosystem, the "alvar" juniper-studded grassland (Kaasik et al., 1983). The *Red Data Book* lists 155 plant species in the country, in addition to 13 mammals, 73 birds, 4 amphibians, 1 reptile, 9 fish, 2 mollusc, 1 insect and 1 leech species, protection all of which cost 0.7 million roubles in 1988 (including supervision of hunting)(Weisenburger, 1991).

Rational land-use planning provides for "compensation zones" such as river lowlands, lake basins, steep slopes etc. (Nikol'skii et al., 1991). The earliest example of a protected area, set up between 1910 and 1916, includes the Vaika Islands. By 1940 there were 47 nature reserves. Work was revived by the Nature Conservation Commission of the Academy of Sciences of Estonia in 1955, with four national reserves and 28 local reserves being created by 1957 (Varep, 1988). In the mid-1960s, the protected area network was increased rapidly (Nikol'skii et al., 1991), followed by the creation of a national park at Lahemaa (64,900ha). In May 1991 there were five nature reserves (totalling 62,600ha) and one national park, covering 2.83% of the area of the country (Nikol'skii *et al.*, 1991), as well as 15 landscape reserves, 1 geological reserve, 3 botanical/faunal reserves, 2 ornithological reserves and 29 peatbog reserves (Varep, 1988).

In 1989 the establishment of West Estonian Archipelago Biosphere Reserve was proposed, to include the islands of Miiumma, Saaremaa and Muhu and surrounding waters, totalling 1,560,078ha.

Addresses

Baltic Protected Areas Regional Information Centre, 202 128 Viitna, Laane-Vivumaa

References

Kaasik, A. and Kask, E. (1983). *Lahemaa Rahvuspark - Lahemaa National Park*. Eesti Ramat Publisher, Tallinn. 182 pp.

Nikol'skii, A., Bolshova, L.I. and Karaseva, S.E. (1991). *Palaearctic-USSR Regional Protected Areas Review*. Paper proposed for IV World Parks Congress on National Parks and other Protected Areas. USSR Ministry of Natural Resources Management and Environmental Protection, Moscow.

Varep, E. (1988). The network of nature reserves in the Estonian SSR. In: Punning, J.M. (Ed.), *Estonia: geographical researches*. Academy of Sciences of the Estonian SSR/Estonian Geographical Society, Tallinn. 164 pp.

Weisenburger, U. (1991). Nature conservation in the Soviet Union. *Nature Conservation*. European Parliament Director-General for Research, Environment, Public Health and Consumer Protection Series 17. EN-9-1991. Pp. 140-149.

ANNEX
Definitions of protected area designations, as legislated, together with authorities responsible for their administration

Title: On the Protection of Nature in the Estonian SSR

Date: 7 June 1957

Brief description: Basis of nature conservation and establishment of nature reserves, as well as defining administrative, scientific and social institutions

Administrative authority: Nature Conservancy Board at the Ministry of Forest Management and Nature Conservation. The Board and its local offices and representative ensure effective preservation of all protected areas, reserves, sanctuaries, parks and various other natural objects. It also deals with air and water pollution and landscape degradation.

Designations:

Rahvuspark (National park) see separate act (below)

Looduskaitscalad (Zapovedniki, state nature reserve) as for *Zapovedniki* in the USSR

Source: Varep, 1988

Title: Act of the Republic of Estonia on the Lahemaa National Park (Resolution of the Supreme Council of the Republic of Estonia)

Date: 27 March 1991

Brief description and designation:

Rahvuspark (National park) Thirteen-paragraph Act dealing with the national park: definition, jurisdiction, activities, protection regulations, tasks, timetable of activities, rights and powers, and land tenure.

Source: Varep, 1988

138

SUMMARY OF PROTECTED AREAS

Map[†] ref.	National/international designations Name of area	IUCN management category	Area (ha)	Year notified
	State National Park			
1	Lakhemaa	II	64,911	1971
	Nature Reserves			
2	Aela-Viirika (Mire)	IV	2,602	1981
3	Agusalu (Mire)	IV	7,675	1981
4	Avaste (Mire)	IV	4,188	1981
5	Emajoe-Suursoo (Mire)	IV	18,425	1981
6	Endlaskiy	I	8,162	1985
7	Kaina Bay (bird)	IV	1,280	1971
8	Keava (Mire)	IV	1,577	1981
9	Kikepera (Mire)	IV	4,700	1981
10	Kuresoo (Mire)	IV	11,927	1981
11	Laanemaa-Suursoo (Mire)	IV	9,713	1981
12	Laukasoo (Mire)	IV	2,141	1981
13	Marimetsa (Mire)	IV	4,190	1981
14	Matsaluskiy	I	39,697	1957
15	Meelva (Mire)	IV	1,827	1981
16	Meenikunnu (Mire)	IV	1,757	1981
17	Muraka (Mire)	IV	12,274	1957
18	Natsi-Volla (Mire)	IV	9,772	1957
19	Nigulasskiy	I	2,771	1957
20	Ordi (Mire)	IV	5,043	1981
21	Parika (Mire)	IV	1,472	1981
22	Sami-Kuristiku (Mire)	IV	1,339	1981
23	Sirtsi (Mire)	IV	2,853	1981
24	Tuhu (Mire)	IV	2,771	1981
25	Valgeraba (Mire)	IV	2,486	1981
26	Vil'sandiyskiy	I	10,689	1910
27	Virtsu-Laelatu-Puhtu Botanical	IV	3,609	1957
28	Viydumyaeskiy	I	1,194	1957
	Landscape Protected Areas or Landscape Reserves			
29	Haanja	V	9,163	1979
30	Islets near Hiiumaa Island	IV	313	1971
31	Karula	IV	10,318	1979
32	Korvemaa	V	21,270	1957
33	Kurtna	IV	2,541	1987
34	Otepaa	V	23,031	1979
35	Paganamaa	IV	1,107	1979
36	Vooremaa	IV	9,900	1964
	Landscape			
37	Ahja River Valley	IV	1,040	1957
	Biosphere Reserve			
	West Estonian Archipelago	IX	1,560,000	1990
	Ramsar Wetland			
	Matsalu Bay	R	48,634	1976

[†]Locations of most protected areas are shown on the accompanying map.

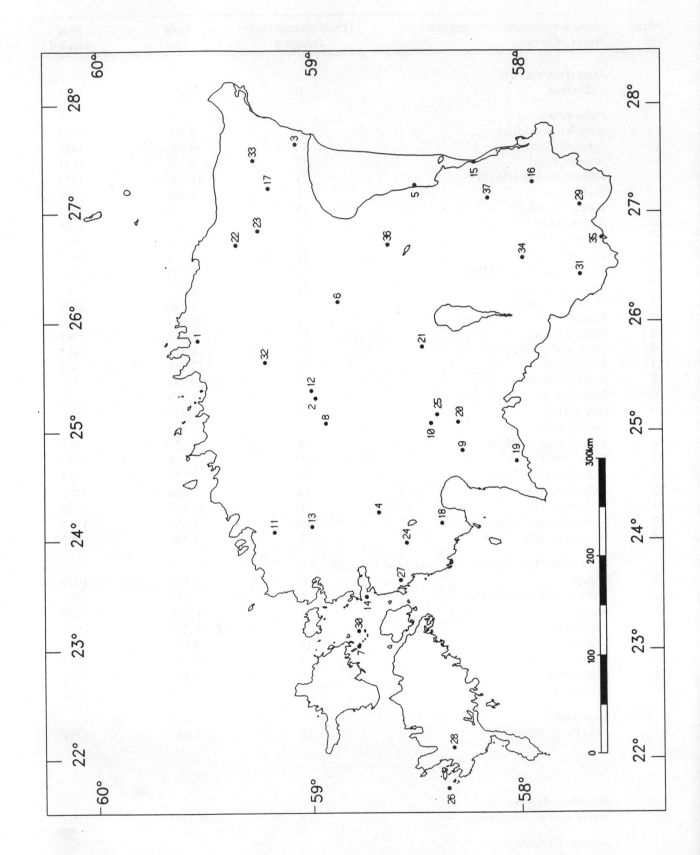

Protected Areas of Estonia

FINLAND

Area 338,130 sq. km

Population 4,975,000 (1990)
Natural increase: 0.22% per annum

Economic Indicators
GDP: US$ 18,110 per capita (1987)
GNP: US$ 14,370 per capita (1987)

Policy and Legislation Finland became independent of Russia in 1917 and the constitution was enacted on 17 July 1919.

The principal legislation concerning nature conservation is the Nature Protection Act No. 71/1923 of 23 February 1923, which entered into force on 1 July 1923. There have been several subsequent amendments, including some major changes in 1991. Five protected area categories are covered under this Act: *luonnonpuisto* general or strict nature reserve where human impact is minimal; *kansalispuisto* special reserve or national park; *naturminne* natural monument where small natural features such as trees or geological formations are given specific protection; *muut luonnonsuojelualuet* other special reserve, similar to national park, but given a different designation because of its small size or other reasons; and peatland reserve, created under a 1981/2 amendment (see Annex) (Haapanen, 1983; Forest Research Institute, *in litt.*, 1991). Like peatland reserves, a number of other biotopes are subject to conservation programmes established by the government (see Administration and Management): biotopes include certain wetlands, forest groves and eskers. They are usually protected under existing categories of protected area under the Nature Protection Act.

In 1981 an amendment was made to the Act, whereby a landowner can receive compensation for those economic losses he or she may sustain when a nature reserve is established on private land. For the designation and establishment of national parks or special reserves exceeding 500ha on state-owned land, specific legislation has to be enacted and cross-referenced to the Act. Reserves can also be designated on private land, subject to a decision of the relevant provincial authority. Reserves of less than 500ha are designated by statute. Natural monuments of less than 1ha are established by a resolution of the National Board of Forestry or the Forest Research Institute, also under provision of the Act. Both institutes hold state-owned land (Forest Research Institute, *in litt.*, 1991).

The provincial governments may declare reserves on private land, on application by the owner with the approval of the State Counsellor of Nature Conservation in the Ministry of Environment. The sites are created by resolution of the Ministry of Environment, under the Nature Protection Act (Forest Research Institute, *in litt.*,

1991). The Ministry is also empowered by the Act to purchase land for conservation purposes.

There are a number of other Acts which provide for the designation of certain areas. The Wilderness Act, 1991 defines wilderness areas, mostly found in Lapland, which cover approximately 5% of the country. The Act presupposes the creation of certain totally protected zones, but in most of these wilderness areas the land may be used for recreation, natural methods of forestry, and the general living and occupation of the Lapps. A government permit is required for the construction of roads and other establishments. The Ancient Relics Act, 1963 prohibits the movement of, or damage to, relics such as archaeological sites, old buildings and shipwrecks such sites are often now part of the natural environment. The Recreation Act, 1973 regulates the establishment of (municipal) recreation routes, the creation of (state) hiking areas in places that could not be protected under the Nature Conservation Act and the control of privately owned camping grounds. The Waterfalls (Rapids) Protection Act, 1987 was passed as a supplement to the Water Act, naming certain watercourses where permission may not be given for the construction of power plants (Hollo, 1991).

In Finland, public access to nature, the so-called *allemandsret*, is founded in common law, whereby everybody has the right, subject to certain limitations, to cross other individual's property and to remain there for short periods. This principle of common law is now quoted in the preamble of the Nature Protection Act.

The Hunting Act, 1962 (revised in 1969) specifies game species and their hunting seasons. It also provides for the designation by provincial government resolution of areas classed as game bird reserves on private land.

The 1922 Forest Zones Protection Act is aimed at the prevention of erosion of northern forest areas, where the different species of trees are at their northernmost limits and hence where regeneration would be difficult. Vast areas of Lappland are thus protected, with a view to maintaining traditional forestry practices in the area (Hollo, 1991; Koester, 1980). The Act provides for the establishment of protected forest zones in the archipelago, along the coastline and in all areas where the forest has, until now, been a shelter for settlement and agriculture against wind erosion. It also states that it is forbidden to cut trees close to the shores of lakes, rivers and the sea if such woods are seen as important for breeding fish (Hollo, 1991). The Fishing Act, 1957, the Building (Planning) Act, Water Management and Protection Legislation all have some relevance to nature conservation.

The autonomous county (*landskap*) of Åland has a council of one chamber, headed by a provincial governor with a county board which has executive powers in matters within the field of the autonomy of the county. An independent Nature Conservation Act No. 41/77 for Aland entered into force in 1977. Provisions also exist for protection of the cultural heritage of the Aland islands.

Provisions for the protection of beaches were introduced in 1969, affording possibilities for building control to safeguard scenic values. They are regarded as inadequate as instruments for general coastal protection (Koester, 1980). Although there is a Building Act dated 1958/1974, there is no regulation to prevent, for example, holiday houses being scattered all over the open country (Koester, 1980).

In order to conserve various specific biotopes, ecosystems or geomorphological formations, there have been a number of conservation programmes initiated by the government. The first of these was the national peatland preservation programme established by a Council of Ministers Decision, in 1981. Other schemes have been a national eutrophic wetland preservation programme (*Valtakunnallinen Lintuvesiensuojeluohjelma*) which was initiated in 1981 by the Ministry of Agriculture and Forestry; a national esker (glacially deposited ridge) preservation programme; and a wild river and waterfall preservation programme (Haapanen, 1983). Two more conservation programmes have since been ordered by the Ministry of Environment: the Forest Groves Protection Programme, initiated in 1989, and the Shore Protection Programme, initiated in 1991 (Forest Research Institute, *in litt.*, 1991). This latter programme seeks to protect some 5% of Finland's 200,000km of lake shore. It aims to prohibit building, but allow some logging in these areas and has met with considerable resistance from private landowners (Anon., 1991).

Limited types of hunting and fishing are allowed under permit by local inhabitants in several protected areas, including some strict nature reserves. In general, within strict nature reserves the above activities, together with firewood collecting, gathering of plants, berries, fungi and molluscs, are generally forbidden or very restricted. The general policy is to exclude industrial installations and other activities, such as hydro-electric schemes, from protected areas, but the 1923 Act makes exception for activities of the National Geological Survey (Poore & Gryn-Ambroes, 1980). Cultivation is still allowed in two of the national parks, and in reserves by coastal villages livestock husbandry is confined to reindeer. Based on common law, the public has access without question or permit to all protected areas except game bird reserves and strict nature reserves, although even in the latter there are rights-of-way. In the north, the Lapps' reindeer have unrestricted access to their rangeland in all protected areas including national parks.

International Activities The Convention concerning the Protection of the World Cultural and Natural Heritage (World Heritage Convention) was ratified on 4 March 1987, although no sites have been inscribed. The Convention on Wetlands of International Importance especially as Waterfowl Habitat (Ramsar Convention) was ratified on 28 May 1974, and 11 sites have been designated. The country has not designated any biosphere reserves under the Unesco Man and the Biosphere Programme, although the Programme has undertaken studies for the proposed establishment of a number of sites (Rajasärkkä, 1987).

Finland is not a member of the EC nor of the Council of Europe, and hence is not bound by their environmental agreements. It has, however, signed and ratified the Bern Convention on the Conservation of European Wildlife and Natural Habitats. The Nordic Council, of which Finland is a member state, is involved in quite a number of environmental protection issues: the Nordic Council of Ministers has run a series of four to five-year environmental protection programmes, the present programme beginning in 1988. These programmes cover a wide range of activities which include, among other things, bringing greater attention to nature conservation in connection with planning activities. The Council has encouraged the registration of valuable landscapes in the Nordic area, the concentration of conservation efforts towards the preservation of particularly important habitat types and the use of natural areas by the wider public for recreation purposes. It has also encouraged the development of a standardised data collection for monitoring environmental quality (Nordic Council of Ministers, 1983). Finland is also a party to the Nordic Environmental Protection Convention, which requires authorities to take into account the environmental consequences to all other parties before granting permits for environmentally damaging activities (Nordic Council of Ministers, 1978).

The most important transboundary protected area is Lemmonjoki National Park which shares a border with Ovre Anarjokka National Park in Norway. Negotiations are underway between the USSR and Finland to establish a transborder park adjacent to Kostomukhskiy.

Administration and Management The Ministry of Environment, established on 1 October 1983, is the highest authority responsible for protected areas (prior to this date responsibility fell to the Ministry of Agriculture and Forestry). It prepares all acts and statutes relating to protected areas. It is directly responsible for the two offices that hold protected areas: the Finnish Forest Research Institute (METLA) (*Metsantutklmuslaitos*) and the National Board of Forestry (*Luonnonsuojelualuetoimisto*). The Ministry of Environment works closely with the Ministry of the Interior and the Ministry of Agriculture and Forestry and much of the practical work of the two forest offices is done through the latter Ministry. The provincial governments are responsible for the designation of reserves on private land. Much of their work is coordinated through the Ministry of the Interior. The Nature Conservation Bureau was placed under the Ministry of Environment, being established as the main body concerned with environmental and nature conservation matters (previously responsibility lay with the Council of Natural Resources).

In practice, most management planning is carried out by the National Board of Forestry in the Office of National Parks (*Metsähallitus*) and the Forest Research Institute. Forest and peatland protected areas are normally established by National Forestry Board resolution. The Finnish Forest Research Institute is the oldest state owner of protected areas in the country. It administers three national parks, strict nature reserves and a number of other special reserves. This institute also conducts its own research in these areas, including studies on the development of unmanaged and timberline forests; the impact of recreation on the natural environment; the needs of visitors; landscape analysis; and vegetation research, while protected areas also provide a valuable control for comparing the results obtained from studies of managed forest (Forest Research Institute, *in litt.*, 1991).

The Finnish Association for the Protection of Nature (*Suomen Luonnonsuojelluliitto*) is the largest non-governmental organisation, with some 40 regional branches. This body is involved in management and research in state and private protected areas. WWF-International and WWF-Finland are also involved in protected areas management. WWF-Finland is involved in the management of the dune area of Svanvik and the nearby Gulf of Täktom, whilst WWF-International has helped in the establishment and management of the South-east Archipelago (Project No. 1467).

Systems Reviews   Finland faces the Gulf of Bothnia in the Baltic Sea in eastern Scandinavia and is bounded by Norway, Sweden and the Soviet Union. Approximately 20% of the country lies within the Arctic Circle, a rugged terrain with high-level plateaux and deep river valleys which cut into the ancient rocks of the Fenno-Scandian shield. Central and southern Finland is rather low-lying (rarely exceeding 200m above sea level) with a complex coastline and series of thousands of islands and islets reflecting the change in sea level in relationship to land movements. Recent glaciation has resulted in a network of lakes which number over 60,000. Tracts of natural coniferous taiga forest cover about 65-70% of the land surface, open mires about 10% and treeless alpine areas 5% (Heiss, 1987). Extensive areas of peat bog (30% of the country) border pine and spruce forests; Scandinavia possesses 80% of Europe's peatland (Davis *et al.*, 1986; Rassi, 1983). Pine, heathland and herb-rich meadows are found in the south of the country (Davis *et al.*, 1986). Agricultural land represents 10.9% of the country and 0.9% is covered by towns and other settlements, leaving extensive tracts of land with no permanent human occupation (Anon., 1987).

Proposals for the establishment of protected areas date from those of A E Nordenskiöld in 1880, followed by a proposal of the *Societas pro Fauna et Flora Fennica* to the Council of Ministers that a nature conservation act was needed (Haapenen, 1983). The first nature reserve on private land was established in 1925. Many important private reserves were established in the 1920s and 1930s, but the most active period of designation began in the late 1960s. The first national park was established in 1938. In 1956 seven national parks and 12 strict nature reserves were designated, followed in 1961 by one reserve and in 1982 by the declaration of 11 national parks and five strict nature reserves. In 1983 a further two national parks were established. In addition, 59 and 43 peatlands were placed under protection in 1982 and 1985, respectively (Anon., 1988). In the early 1970s there were nine national parks, covering 238,800ha, all other protected areas totalling 1,905,000ha (Anon., 1975). In 1991 there were 27 national parks covering 701,978ha (31,450ha of which was water); 19 strict nature reserves covering 151,689ha; 173 peatland reserves covering 404,060ha; 28 other special reserves covering 36,878ha and 884 private protected areas covering 58,862ha (40,283ha of which was water). In total these protected areas thus cover some 4% of the total land area (Forest Research Institute, *in litt.*, 1991). Lemmenjoki National Park alone, at 280,000ha, is one of the largest national parks in Europe and, together with the adjacent Ovre Anarjokka National Park in Norway, covers some 420,000ha and forms the largest protected wilderness in Europe (Udvardy, 1983).

The natural environment is being altered at an increasing rate. A common trend is the impoverishment of ecosystems. The natural forests have been extensively changed by silvicultural activities which favour two species of conifer (spruce and pine), with the loss of deciduous trees. The loss of old-growth forest is continuing. The National Board of Forestry has plans to cut around 100,000ha including most of that in the Kessi region, an important area of wilderness in the north of the country. Such forestry activities also threaten the livelihoods of the indigenous peoples of the area. Forest roads already dissect some of the last extensive wilderness areas. One of the greatest habitat losses has been that of peatland which is largely drained for forestry. Nearly 6 million ha, over 60% of the total natural peatland area, have already been drained throughout the country. In the south, almost 90% of the original peatlands have been drained for forestry, this drainage leading to greatly increased nutrient and humus loads in the waterways and wetlands, and consequent reductions in fish populations. Drainage also causes higher rates of decomposition of the organic material in peat leading to the release of massive levels of carbon dioxide into the atmosphere (Grimmett and Jones, 1989; Isomäki, 1991; Ruuhijärvi, 1983). Acid deposition, notably sulphur deposition, originating from Finland itself and from the USSR, is causing problems in areas across the country, and is affecting numerous lake communities as well as forest and bog ecosystems (Kämäri *et al.*, 1991; Ministry of Environment, 1987).

Addresses

Ministry of the Environment, Eteldesplanadi 18A, PL 399, 00121 HELSINKI (Tel: 358 0 19911/FAX: 358 0 1991 399)

Metsähallitus (Office of National Parks) (National Board of Forestry), Luonnonsuojelualuetoimisto, Erottajan Katu, PL 233, 00121 HELSINKI (Tel: 358 0 906 1631)

Metsantutklmuslaitos (METLA) (Finnish Forest Research Institute) Unioninkatu 40A, 00170 HELSINKI (Tel: 358 0 90857051; Fax. 358 0 625308; Tlx. 125181 hyfor sf attn: metla)

Ålands Landskapsstyrelse, PB 60, 22101 MARIEHAMN (Tel: 358 928 15000)

Suomen Luonnonsuojelulitto (Finnish Association for Nature Protection), P O Box 169, 00151 HELSINKI (Tel: 358 0 642881)

Finnish Forestry Association, Salomonkatu 17A, 00100 HELSINKI 10

References

Alexander, M.B. and Dube, D.E. (1985). Fire management in wilderness areas, parks and other nature reserves. In: Wein, R.W. and Maclean, D.W., *The role of fire in northern Circumpolar ecosystems.* Scope 18. John Wiley and Sons, Chichester.

Anon. (1975). *National parks of Finland.* National Board of Forestry.

Anon. (1985). *Strict nature reserves of Finland.* National Board of Forestry. 7 pp.

Anon. (1986a). *Finnish national parks.* National Board of Forestry. Helsinki. 68 pp.

Anon. (1986b). *The National parks of Finland.* Office for National Parks, National Board of Forestry, Helsinki. 16 pp.

Anon. (1987). Finland (Suomi). In: *Management of Europe's natural heritage, twenty-five years of activity.* Environment Protection and Management Division. Council of Europe, Strasbourg.

Anon. (1988). *Protected areas on state-owned land.* The Finnish Board of Forestry, Helsinki. 6 pp.

Anon. (1991). Shore protection opposed. *Oryx* 25 (1): 7.

Davis, S.D., Droop, S.J.M., Gregerson, P., Henson, L., Leon, C.J., Lamlein Villa-Lobos, J., Synge, H., and Zantovska, J. (1986). *Plants in danger: what do we know?* IUCN, Gland, Switzerland, and Cambridge, UK. 461 pp.

Finnish National Board of Forestry. (1991). *Protected Areas on State-owned land.* Pamphlet, Metsähallitus/ The Finnish National Board of Forestry, Helsinki.

Grimmett, R.F.A. and Jones, T.A. (1989). *Important bird areas in Europe.* ICBP Technical Publication No. 9. International Council for Bird Preservation, Cambridge, UK.

Haapanen, A. (1983). The Finnish nature reserve system. In: *The Finnish- Soviet Symposium on National Parks and Nature Reserves, Luonnonvarainhoitotormiston, Julkaisuya 7.* Pp. 15-25.

HAPRO (1987). *Acidification in Finland.* Finnish Research Project on acidification (HAPRO) Secretariat. Helsinki.

Heiss, G. (1987). *Inventory of natural (virgin) and ancient semi-natural woodlands within the councils' member states and Finland.* European Committee for the Conservation of Nature and Natural Resources. 462 pp.

Helminen, M. (1983). Management of the national parks and other protected areas in Finland. In: *The Finnish-Soviet Symposium on National Parks and Nature Reserves, Luonnonvarainhoitotormiston, Julkaisuya 7.* Pp. 87-89.

Hollo, E.J. (1991). Nature Conservation in Finland. *Nature Conservation in Austria, Finland, Norway, Sweden, Switzerland, Bulgaria, Czechoslovakia, Hungary, Poland, Romania, Yugoslavia and the Soviet Union.* European Parliament, Directorate-General for Research. Environment, Public Health and Consumer Protection Series, 17. Pp. 21-27.

Isomäki, R. (1991). Paper, pollution and global warming, unsustainable forestry in Finland. *The Ecologist* 21 (1):14-17.

Kämäri, J., Forsius, M., Kortelainen, P., Mannio, J. and Verta, M. (1991). Finnish Lake survey: present status of acidification. *Ambio* 20 (1):23-27.

Koester, V. (1980). *Nordic Counties' Legislation on the Environment with special emphasis on conservation, a survey.* IUCN Environmental Policy and Law Paper No. 14. IUCN Gland, Switzerland. 44pp.

Ministry of Environment (1987). *Acidification in Finland.* Ministry of Environment, Ministry of Agriculture and Forestry, Helsinki. 4pp.

Nordic Council of Ministers (1978). *The Nordic Environmental Protection Convention, with a Commentary.* Nordic Council of Ministers, Stockholm. 14 pp.

Nordic Council of Ministers (1983). *Programme for Nordic Cooperation in Environmental Protection for 1983 to 1987.* Nordic Council of Ministers, Stockholm. 37 pp.

Poore, D. and Gryn-Ambroes, P. (1980). *Nature conservation in northern and western Europe.* UNEP/IUCN/WWF, Gland Switzerland. Pp. 130-150

Rajasärkkä, A. (1987). *Establishing a biosphere reserve in Finland.* Report of the symposium. Finnish National MAB Committee/Academy of Finland, Helsinki. 92 pp.

Rassi, P. (1983). Planning of protected areas in Finland. In: *The Finnish- Soviet Symposium on National Parks and Nature Reserves, Luonnonvarainhoitotormiston, Julkaisuya 7.* Pp. 55-62.

Ruuhijärvi, R. (1983). Protected areas and ecological research in Finland. In: *The Finnish-Soviet Symposium on National Parks and Nature Reserves, Luonnonvarainhoitotormiston, Julkaisuya 7.* Pp. 63-68.

Udvardy, M.D.F. (1983). Finland expands its protected areas. *Parks* 7(4): 1.

ANNEX
Definitions of protected area designations, as legislated, together with authorities responsible for their administration

Title: Nature Protection Act

Date: 1 July 1923 amended in 1941, 1962, 1964, 1981, 1983 and 1991

Brief description: Provides for the establishment under law of nature reserves, over 50ha in size, protection of natural monuments and protection of animal and plant species (Anon., 1975; Helminen, 1983)

Administrative authority: National Forestry Board; Finnish Forest Research Institute

Designations:

Luonnonpuisto (General reserve or strict nature reserve) Sites reserved mainly for research work, they are not tourist sites or outdoor recreation areas. Where their protection and research goals permit they also endeavour to promote nature conservation. All access is prohibited without written permission, and this is only granted for specific projects. Some reserves have marked trails where access is permitted, although the leaving of these trails is prohibited.

Kansalispuisto (Special reserve/national park) Sites reserved as "public sights of nature", representing the most valuable and typical natural landscapes in Finland. Nature conservation is the main purpose of national parks, but they also serve scientific research, because they offer almost irreplaceable opportunities for comparison and monitoring; teaching and general knowledge about nature; recreation. The public has free access within these areas.

Each park has its own by-laws setting out regulations necessary for the specific requirements of individual parks, although there a number of general principles that apply. Disturbing and causing damage to nature is forbidden. Camping and lighting fires is only permitted at specific sites except in some of the larger Lappish national parks in the north of the country which have wilderness zones where restrictions are less severe. Visitors may pick berries and collect edible mushrooms. Hunting is usually prohibited, although visitors may fish in some parks provided they obtain a licence from the National Board of Forestry.

Muut luonnonsuojelualuet (Other special reserve) Areas that, because of their small size or other reasons, cannot be called national parks. They are protected by law or statute like national parks and have similar regulations. A number of these sites are designated for the specific biotopes covered under the various State protection programmes.

Naturminne (Natural monument) A natural feature such as an historic or ancient tree, a group of trees, geological feature or other special natural element of the landscape. These designations are possible on private land with the owner's agrement, and there are certain provisions for expropriation.

Peatland reserve Regulations are weaker than those applied to the former categories. The chief objective is the preservation of peatland nature certain types of "landscape friendly" forestry may be permitted within the reserves. Free access, berry and mushroom picking, hunting and fishing rights are only curtailed when they jeopardize the conservation goals of a reserve. Drainage is not permitted.

Sources: Anon., 1975; Finnish National Board of Forestry, 1991; Forest Research Institute, *in litt.*, 1991

Title: Act on the Preservation of Woodlands (Orders of the National Board of Forestry on State-owned Land)

Date: 1922

Brief description: Provides for the establishment of forest protected areas on state-owned land, established by Decision of the National Board of Forestry and the Finnish Forestry Research Institute

Administrative authority: National Forestry Board; Finnish Forest Research Institute

Designations:

Luonnonhoitometsä (Protected woodland) Lappland areas declared with a view to maintaining traditional forestry practices

Special conservation forest areas established on grounds of social, scenic or biological values, and which may include zonation of differing levels of management, through zones of untouched habitat, scenic managed areas to production forest sections.

Source: Anon., 1975; Koester, 1980; Poore and Gryn-Ambroes, 1980

SUMMARY OF PROTECTED AREAS

Map[†] ref.	*National/international designations* Name of area	IUCN management category	Area (ha)	Year notified
	National Parks			
1	Helvetinjaervi	II	2,100	1982
2	Hiidenportti	II	4,000	1982
3	Isojaervi	II	1,900	1982
4	Itainen Suomenlahti	II	800	1981
5	Kauhaneva-Pohjakangas	II	3,150	1982
6	Lauhanvuori	II	2,650	1982
7	Lemmenjoki	II	280,000	1956
8	Linnansaari	II	3,820	1956
9	Oulanka	II	20,170	1956
10	Pallas-Ounastunturi	V	50,000	1938
11	Patvinsuo	II	8,800	1982
12	Pyhae-Haekki	II	1,350	1956
13	Pyhaetunturi	II	4,100	1938
14	Riisitunturi	II	7,600	1982
15	Salamajaervi	II	5,530	1982
16	Seitseminen	II	3,060	1982
17	Skargaardshavet	II	3,000	1983
18	Tiilikkajaervi	II	2,050	1982
19	Urho Kekkonen	V	252,000	1983
	Strict Nature Reserves			
20	Jussaro	I	2,400	1956
21	Kevo	I	71,000	1956
22	Koivusuo	I	2,100	1982
23	Malla	I	2,950	1938
24	Maltio	I	14,700	1956
25	Olvassuo	I	6,000	1982
26	Paljakka	I	2,660	1956
27	Pelso	I	1,800	1982
28	Pisavaara	I	5,000	1956
29	Runkaus	I	7,150	1956
30	Salamanpera	I	1,270	1956
31	Sompio	I	17,600	1956
32	Sukerijaervi	I	1,900	1982
33	Ulvinsalo	I	2,500	1956
34	Vaerrioe	I	11,000	1982
35	Vaskijarvi	I	1,140	1956
	Ramsar Wetlands			
	Aspskär	R	369	1974
	Björkör/Lagskär	R	5,760	1974
	Koitilaiskaira	R	34,400	1974
	Krunnit	R	4,600	1974
	Maartimoaapa-Lumiaapa	R	7,400	1974
	Ruskis	R	235	1974
	Signilskär	R	11,600	1974
	Söderskär/Langoren	R	9,632	1974
	Suomujärvi-Patvinsuo	R	9,400	1974
	Valassaaret/Björkögrunden	R	17,700	1974
	Viikki	R	247	1974

[†]Locations of most protected areas are shown on the accompanying map.

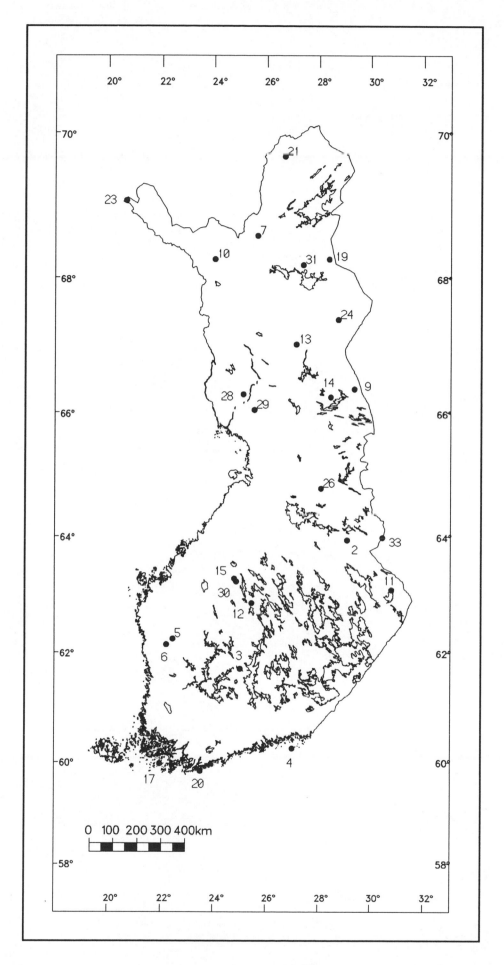

Protected Areas of Finland

FRANCE

Area 551,500 sq. km

Population 56,138,000 (1990)
Natural increase: 0.35% per annum

Economic Indicators
GDP: US$ 15,854 per capita (1987)
GNP: US$ 12,860 per capita (1987)

Policy and Legislation The Constitution of the Fifth Republic, superseding that of 1946, came into force on 4 October 1958. It has 92 articles (2) and gave rise to the current conservation legislation.

France has a long history of habitat protection for forestry and hunting purposes, with some areas specified in texts going back to the Middle Ages. Parts of the Forest of Fontainebleau have been protected for a number of centuries; from 1853 the areas within this forest were protected as reserves, and by 1904 reserves covered one-tenth of the entire area of the forest (Rackham, 1980).

One of the first modern laws of relevance to the protection of areas of conservation importance was the Law of 2 May 1930 relating to the protection of natural monuments and sites of artistic, historical, scientific, romantic or scenic interest, inspired by a previous Law of 1913 concerning historic monuments. A major law augmenting the 1930 law was approved on 1 July 1957 (No. 57/740). Two classifications described in the 1930 Law remain of relevance to nature conservation: classified site and registered site (see Annex) (such sites are occasionally referred to as nature reserves, but they remain distinct from those covered under the 1976 Act described below) (Cutrera, 1991).

The general framework for establishing protected areas is provided by the Law Relating to the Creation of National Parks No. 60.708 of 22 July 1960 and its enforcement Order No. 61.1195 of 31 October 1961, primarily defining and establishing the framework for the enabling acts for national parks (parcs nationaux) (see Annex). The Law provides for flexible application of its protective measures from one national park to another. In principle, this is for ecological reasons, but also in practice for political and economic reasons (Saussay, 1980). Following consultation on national park designation, the final decision is expressed by decree which lays down the applicable regulations and arrangements for the level of development and management, the level of protection, and lists of activities permitted. Decree No. 77-1299 simplified the procedure applicable to breaches of regulations in national parks. National parks usually have some degree of zonation, comprising of a central zone (zone centrale) which is quite strictly protected, and a peripheral zone (zone périphérique), otherwise known as a preparc, with fewer restrictions. There may also be nature reserves within national parks, providing an even more strictly protected zone.

The Nature Conservation Act No. 76 629 of 10 July 1976 includes provision for the general framework for defining, designating and establishing nature reserves (réserves naturelles). These may be designated by the state, or volunteered for designation, in which case they are termed voluntary nature reserves (see Annex). There are several decrees, passed in 1977, which cover the implementation of various articles within this Act. Nature reserves tend to provide a stricter form of protection, and are designated for the conservation of specific aspects of the natural environment. Individual sites are passed under separate decrees. The Decree passed on 25 November 1977 implementing articles 4 and 5 of the 1976 Act is largely concerned with the protection of species. There is, however, a provision in this decree which empowers the prefects (préfets, representatives of the central government in the départments) to make orders for the protection of habitats that are necessary for the survival of protected species: this general obligation has been used with discretion by the Prefects to protect particular areas where these species occur – the orders for protection are called biotope protection orders (arrêtés de protection de biotope) (see Annex) (Cutrera, 1991).

The criteria for establishment and designation of regional natural parks (parcs naturels régionaux) were set out in Decree No. 67-158 of 1 March 1967 and updated by Decree No. 75-983 of 24 October 1975. This latter Decree has been replaced by Decree No. 88-443, 1988 relating to regional natural parks. The purpose of regional natural parks is not strictly speaking the protection of natural areas. They are generally established in territory with a fragile balance and a rich natural and cultural heritage, designation is intended to protect this, while, at the same time to contributing to the economic and social development of the site. In 1978 a new generation of regional parks, sometimes referred to as regional natural areas (espaces naturels régionaux), were established, the first of which was Nord-Pas-de-Calais Park created in 1978. This type of park is essentially the same as the parc naturel régional but consists of many fragmented sections. The 1988 Decree substantiates the decentralising aim of the original Decree and local bodies are now closely involved in their installation (see Annex) (Anon., 1988b; Cutrera, 1991).

A Ministerial Order of 19 May 1982 provides for the designation of national hunting reserves (réserves nationales de chasse). These reserves cover a large area and play an important role in the protection of threatened species. They are also used for scientific and technical research and for training and education purposes (see Annex) (Tesson, 1990).

The protection of forests is also provided under some of the forestry legislation, notably the Law of 28 April 1922 relating to protected forests, and the Forest Code (Decree No. 79-114) of 25 January 1979 and Law No. 85-1273 of 4 December 1985. Under the Forest Code, forests in need of protection, for reasons of public interest, may be set aside if their "conservation is deemed necessary for the maintenance of land situated on mountain summits or slopes, for protection against landslides, erosion, flooding and destabilisation of sand, woods and forests near urban areas, or in areas where conservation is necessary for ecological reasons or for the welfare of the community (Anon., 1923?; Cutrera, 1991).

Marine environmental protection relies on a whole series of legal instruments governing the occupation and utilisation of the marine environment (for fishing, mining, sea transport and industrial pollutant discharge). Wholly marine protected areas may be declared under the Law on Maritime Hunting of 24 October 1968, although these are essentially only declared for the protection of waterfowl (see Annex). Protective fisheries are set up by permit or lease of occupation of the marine public domain on the basis of decrees of 9 January 1852 and 21 December 1915. They are renewable every 25 years (non-mobile establishment) and five years (mobile establishment). Fishery preserves (fish reserves) are governed by ministerial Decree of 4 June 1963. These are sites of edible species conservation and for experimental restocking schemes, and include protected areas for shellfish and a fish conservation area off Corsica. Regulations are governed by specific Orders, and by definition they include no onshore territory. Marine nature parks may be created by a legal management body which can be one of the following; a foundation, departmental administration, a joint syndicate or an association subject to a 1901 Act. There is no specific marine element in the legislation pertaining to the designation of regional natural parks. However, Article 1 of the 1960 Law Relating to the Creation of National Parks states that national parks may "extend into the maritime public domain", while nature reserves created under the 1976 Act may be wholly or partly marine (Augier, 1981; Saussay and Prieur, 1980).

The Coastline and Lakeshore Conservancy (Conservatoire de l'espace littoral et des rivages lacustres (CELRL) was established under a Law of 10 July 1975: it has an important role in the acquisition and protection of coastal sites, sometimes known as scheduled management zones (zones d'aménagement différés), sensitive areas (périmètres sensibles) or sensitive natural areas (espaces naturels sensibles). The latter category is largely used by the departments, some of which have their own departmental conservatories. Some designated areas are also given "additional protection" against camping, building and enclosure. Areas that are acquired, managed and opened to the public by the departmental authorities are financed by a departmental tax (taxe départmentale des espaces naturels sensibles), which was established by a Law of

31 December 1976 and modified by that of 18 July 1985 (Anon., 1988a; Cutrera, 1991). Additional protection for coastal areas is covered under the Coastline Law No. 86-2 of 3 January 1986, relating to protection planning and development of the littoral zone. This prohibits offshore dumping of substances likely to interfere with the conservation of marine resources and also regulates onshore development and prohibits construction work on a 100m wide strip of coastline (Cutrera, 1991). Marine reserves may be declared under the Law on Maritime Hunting of 1968, established by order of the Minister responsible for Hunting and the Minister responsible for the merchant navy (Saussay and Prieur, 1980).

An EC Directive concerning environmental impact assessments (EIAs) was adopted on 27 June 1985. EIAs must take into account a number of factors including, among other things, flora, fauna, soil, water, and the landscape. France has had EIA legislation incorporated into its statutes for a number of years: it was introduced in the framework of the 1976 Nature Protection Act and a further Decree of 1977. Around 4,000 to 5,000 projects require EIAs annually (Coenen and Jörissen, 1989).

A national plan for the environment was drawn up by the government in 1990. The plan puts the long-term social viability of the country as its central aim; it considers environmental issues on a global, European and national level. Proposals include the increased implementation of EC regulations and guidelines for landscape protection and specify increasing the land area designated for special protection under the existing "Birds" Directive and also under the forthcoming "Habitats" Directive, in addition to entering into management agreements with farmers under the provisions of Article 19 of the EC Regulation No. 1760/87 in order to preserve landscape. Another specific policy orientation concerns environmental protection measures in the overseas dominions and territories, particularly by reinforcing regional participation in existing international structures, such as the UNEP Regional Seas Programmes. The Plan mentions increasing the protection of natural areas, and particularly coastline preservation. There is also a specific policy orientation towards the protection of the Mediterranean Basin, again stressing the importance of action through regional programmes such as the Mediterranean Action Programme of UNEP: particular actions mentioned include forest protection, the creation of a professional network for managers of national and regional natural parks as well as national nature reserves and biosphere reserves, and the launching of a coastal land conservancy following the model of the Coastal and Lakeshore Conservancy (Nowicki, 1990).

Domestic sectoral objectives of the plan are listed under several headings which include: marine and coastal environment, landscape and nature conservation, and urban ecology. The policy sector concerning landscape management and nature protection is one of the most comprehensive in the plan: it suggests a reform in the whole approach to nature protection, turning it from a position of defensive protection, to a dynamic policy of not only maintaining, but also increasing and re-establishing biodiversity. A number of specific measures are described under the section for ecosystems, under Systems Reviews.

General measures for the implementation of these proposals include changes in the taxation system to encourage the ecologically secure management of the land, changes in planning guidelines and administrative changes, including the increasing of staff in the Ministry of the Environment. The plan also contains budget proposals for the next ten years, figures are given both in real terms and as a proportion of the GNP (Nowicki, 1990).

Although regional natural parks are doubtless of some value to nature conservation, their purpose, according to some sources, is not the protection of natural areas, while their aim to further "the recreation, education and relaxation of people, and tourism" and of general socio-economic development has been said to be incompatible with the protection of an ecologically fragile territory (Cutrera, 1991).

The zoning system used in national parks has created a certain amount of conflict between objectives in the two main zones. According to the law, buffer zones (or preparcs) were intended to act as transitional areas between the natural wilderness in the central zone and the outside world. Interpretation of this Law has led to these zones being used as "compensation areas". Considerable investment is often made in these areas, seen perhaps as compensation for the inconvenience to the local authorities and population resulting from the designation of the national park. The buffer zones themselves thus may put considerable pressure on the central zones. The central zones, too, appear to under pressure from economic developments, including the building of skiing facilities and roads in these areas. Such developments require the approval of the public authorities, but this appears to have been given at least in some cases. A further problem in national parks arises from the fact that there are few means of restricting the activities of the National Forestry Office, which do not always take into account ecological issues and hence can disturb and damage areas. There is also no control over military activities which may take place in parks (Cutrera, 1991). The establishment procedure is often extremely slow: in Mercantour National Park there was heated local opposition and the consultation period lasted some five years.

International Activities   France accepted the World Heritage Convention on 27 June 1975. One natural site (in Corsica) has been inscribed, while Mont-Saint-Michel and its Bay has been inscribed as a mixed natural/cultural site. The Convention on Wetlands of International Importance Especially as Waterfowl Habitat (Ramsar Convention) was ratified on 1 October 1986, eight sites have been declared. Seven biosphere

reserves have been declared under the Unesco Man and the Biosphere Programme (five on the mainland, one on Corsica and one in the Tuamoto Islands, French Polynesia).

France is a signatory to the Convention on the Conservation of European Wildlife and Natural Habitats (Bern Convention), although it has not yet enforced this Convention (Cutrera, 1991). As a member of the European Community, France is bound by EC regulations, including the Directive (79/409/EEC) on the Conservation of Wild Birds, which, in Article 4, requires member states to designate important areas as special protection areas. As of April 1991, 61 special protected areas had been declared. It is also a member of the Council of Europe, and has declared 35 Council of Europe biogenetic reserves (1991). Five sites have been awarded the Council of Europe European Diploma (1991). The Convention for the Protection of the Mediterranean Sea against Pollution (Barcelona Convention) was formally adopted by France in February 1976. The contracting parties to the Convention adopted the Protocol concerning Mediterranean Specially Protected Areas on 2 April 1982, which entered into force on 23 March 1986 and has been subsequently ratified by France: nine sites which have been declared as Mediterranean specially protected areas, and an additional 61 declared CELRL areas, covered under the same classification. France has also ratified the Convention for the Protection and Development of the Marine Environment of the Wider Caribbean Region, the Convention for the Protection, Management and Development of the Marine and Coastal Environment of the Eastern African Region and the Convention for the Protection of the Natural Resources and Environment of the South Pacific Region. The importance of many of these regional international agreements has been stressed under the National Plan for the Environment which was drawn up in 1990 (see Policy and Legislation).

There are a number of transboundary agreements between those bodies managing border protected areas in France and equivalent bodies in neighbouring countries managing adjacent protected areas. These include: Pyrenées Occidentales National Park and the Spanish Ordesa and Monte Perdido national parks (cooperative agreement signed); Vanoise National Park and the Italian Gran Paradiso National Park (formal twinning in 1972); Vosges du Nord Regional Nature Park and the German Pfälzerwald Nature Park; Mercantour National Park and the Italian Argentera Regional Nature Park. Discussions are also underway to examine the feasibility of a "tri-national park" around Mont Blanc, involving France, Italy and Switzerland (Anon., 1989).

Administration and Management   Administrative responsibility for nature conservation lies with the Ministry of the Environment (Ministère de l'Environnement) which was established in 1971, but whose present structure is defined by the Decree of

21 July 1987 (No. 87-564). This Ministry was set up as a small office dealing exclusively with the environment, including protection of nature, prevention of pollution and management of the rural or urban environment. It combined with the Ministry for Public Works, and is complemented at national level by coordinating structures and advisory bodies. Bodies involved in this central organisation include the Agency for the Quality of Life (Délégation à la qualité de la vie), the Directorate for Water and the Prevention of Pollution Risks (Direction de l'eau et de la prévention des pollutions et des risques), the Directorate for Nature Conservation (Direction de la protection de la nature), and the High Committee for the Environment (Haut Comité de l'Environnement). There are several semi-autonomous bodies which fall under the supervision of the Ministry of the Environment, including the National Hunting Office (Office national de la chasse), the Higher Council for Fishing (Conseil supérieur de la pêche), the national parks and the Coastal and Lakeshore Conservancy (Conservatoire de l'espace littoral et des rivages lacustres) (CERL). A law of 7 January 1983 has led to the decentralisation of much of the authority of the higher bodies and local authorities now share administrative responsibilities with the central government. This reform did not, however, bring radical changes to the distribution of powers for environmental policy which still remains in central government hands; it does establish the principle of coresponsibility between the state and the decentralised authorities "for the protection of the environment and the improvement of the quality of life". At the present time, the only powers delegated to the local authorities are the designation of regional natural parks by the regions and the acquisition, management and opening to the public of sensitive natural areas by the departments (Cutrera, 1991).

The Agency for the Quality of Life is responsible for the definition and coordination of environmental policies. It ensures that environmental issues are incorporated into administrative decisions; is also has a role in environmental impact assessments. It maintains contacts with associations for nature protection. It is also responsible for liaison between the central administration and the decentralised services of the state.

The Directorate for Water and the Prevention of Pollution Risks deals with problems related to the physical environment, air, water and soil: it has a major involvement in the monitoring of this environment.

The Directorate for Nature Conservation is responsible for the policy and the measures relating to the conservation of the natural heritage. Its work has two objectives; the protection of landscapes and the protection of specific animal and plant species. This Directorate is thus responsible for the creation and management of a system of protected areas and also for the more general restoration and protection of the landscape. It is responsible also for hunting and fishing policies and regulations. The hunting lobby is large and

powerful and frequently comes into conflict with conservation issues – the powers of the Directorate as regards hunting and fishing have largely been transferred to the hands of the prefects (Cutrera, 1991). There are three departments within the Directorate of Nature Conservation: the Department of Hunting which controls the National Hunting Office; the Department of Fisheries and Hydrobiology, which controls the Fisheries Council; and the Department of Parks and Reserves. The Department of Parks and Reserves includes four bureaux responsible for national parks, nature reserves, fauna and flora, and information and education. This Department acts as a coordinating body for the establishment and management of national parks and nature reserves. It is responsible for all decisions not taken locally, for the supervision of reserves, for implementing agreements concluded between the Ministry and the managing body and for producing reports on new areas. The Department is advised by the National Council for the Protection of nature which usually meets about four times a year at the request of the Directorate of Nature Conservation (Poore and Gryn-Ambroes, 1980).

The High Committee for the Environment is a consultative organisation which gives advice on all big projects of national interest and on legislative material. Its composition was modified under a decree of 28 May 1982, and it now has 55 members, including representatives from unions, agriculture and elected members under the chairmanship of the Minister for the Environment (Cutrera, 1991).

The Ministry of Regional Planning has responsibility for land-use planning and is closely concerned in the elaboration of the zone périphérique of national parks.

Cutrera (1991) indicates that public administration expenditure on protecting the natural heritage is the only environmental sector in which public expenditure regularly declines, particularly capital expenditure this trend may well change with the implementation of the 1990 national plan for the environment. The total expenditure for this sector in 1987 was FF 6,386 million (including expenditure in regional parks, parks and gardens, other green spaces, centres for nature education, the improvement of the surroundings of monuments, the acquisition of green forestry spaces, forestry development and developing fishing and hunting) (Cutrera, 1991).

In addition to ministerial and affiliated bodies there is an Inter-Ministerial Committee on the Quality of Life, attached to the Prime Minister's office. Its function is to define, activate and coordinate the government policies conducted concerned with environmental quality. It also decides about the use of the "funds for improving the quality of life" (Fonds d'intervention pour la qualité de la vie), which are typically used to favour experimental or innovatory projects conducted by different ministerial departments. Such projects might include those to protect the natural environment, or to raising public awareness. The composition of the Committee varies, but in 1982, 24 of the 44 government ministries in office were represented there by right, and others could be called upon to participate, depending on the questions to be dealt with (Cutrera, 1991). Other groups represented on the Committee include conservation societies, agricultural interests, hunters and scientists (Cutrera, 1991)

The Law Relating to the Creation of National Parks of 1960 classifies national parks as public institutions (although most of the land is owned either privately or by local communities) which fell under the Ministry of Agriculture until 1971, when responsibility was transferred to the Ministry of the Environment. For the creation of a national park a draft project by the Ministry of the Environment is presented to local authorities for opinion (such bodies as municipal councils, rural authorities, chamber of agriculture, commerce and industry in the relevant departments, the National Nature Conservation Council and the Interministerial Committee on National Parks) and then passed to national advisory bodies. If agreed by the Head of State it is passed back again to the local consultants for an obligatory survey. The final decision is expressed by decree.

Each national park has a Board of Directors with the total membership fixed by decree. Their members are drawn from civil servants (representing the various ministries); "conseils d'administration" (other administrative boards); "conseillers généraux" (county councillors and mayors); two representatives of the National Nature Conservation Council, one from the National Museum of Natural History and one from the National Centre for Scientific Research. The total number varies between national parks (from 27 to 50) (Poore and Gryn-Ambroes, 1980). The central authorities issue no general instructions on management. In each national park the Board of Directors decides, in principle, how the park is to be administered, managed and regulated. The executive director is, however, responsible for day-to-day administration. The core zone of the national park is managed by the director and his staff with the protection of wildlife as its first objective. The peripheral zone is administered at national level by the Ministry of Regional Planning, and at the local level by a Departmental Committee, headed by the préfet concerned. Coordination of scientific research is entrusted to the Scientific Committee which has a purely advisory status, but prepares yearly and five yearly research programmes. The Directorate of Nature Conservation has established a working group to coordinate the research done in all national parks. Since national parks are public institutions, almost all the operating expenses, capital investment and research costs are borne by the State (Ministry of the Environment). The Park Director and the administrative council do not come under hierarchical authority of the Minister. Staff numbers in national parks vary from 24 to 70. There is a certain lack of coordination in the peripheral zone where Public Works, Agriculture and the Delegation for Territorial Management carry out improvement programmes without coordination or participation of the park administration.

Nature reserves are established, under local initiative, with the owner's consent and with the approval of the Ministry of the Environment. Management of these areas is entrusted by the state to qualified bodies, usually a nature conservation society, sympathetic owners, local authorities or non-profit making, organisations with the necessary advisory, management and scientific boards also established. The state normally covers the management costs (within the budget for the Ministry for the Environment) but financial assistance of the local authority (region, department, municipality) is also sought regularly. The Directorate of Conservation can initiate research for the purposes of nature reserve establishment and works in consultation with the National Nature Conservation Centre.

The whole purpose of regional natural parks was that their designation, administration and management should be the responsibility of the regions. However, until 1975, administrative "regions" had not been set up, hence the creation of regional natural parks depended upon ministerial decree, although the state assumed less than half of the operating and investment costs. The 1975 Decree on regional natural parks implied that they should be administered by organisations separate from the authorities which created them: most regional natural parks are thus managed by a Board composed of representatives of the municipalities, the departments and professional organisations. The Director in charge of administration carries out duties delegated to him by the Board. Membership of the associations controlling the park is voluntary and, although most of the stimulus and enthusiasm for the park comes from the department level, most decisions have to be implemented by rural communes with their approval. The Decree of 1988 concerning these parks has now largely completed the decentralisation of administration and management. Various local bodies are thus involved, from the communes, departments and regions, including the local authorities, trade and industry and regional associations, while the Ministry of the Environment still maintains an important role. Although preliminary studies of regional natural parks are largely self-financing, the cost of most of the parks facilities is borne by the local communities assisted by state subsidies. Management costs are calculated to be twice that of national parks. As an example, in Parc Naturel et Régional d'Amorique, the Department of Finistère bears all capital costs and 70% of the running costs, the balance coming from 27 constituent rural communes which contribute 20%, and the City of Brest giving the remaining 10%.

Forestry issues are covered by the Ministry of Agriculture. The creation of the National Forestry Board and also of 17 regional centres for forests property in the 1960s was seen as an attempt to separate forest policy management from forest administration. Since July 1984 there has been a separate Secretary of State for Forests under the Ministry of Agriculture. The Departmental Directorate for Agriculture and Forests (Direction départmentale de l'Agriculture et de la Forêt) was established under a Decree (No. 84-1911) of 28 December 1984; and is the ministerial body responsible for the implementation of public projects designed to safeguard and enhance forest areas as well as for the development of forest and timber industries. This Directorate also exercises powers on behalf of the Ministry of the Environment, notably for matters concerning nature conservation. The National Forestry Office (Office National des Forêts), was set up in 1964 under Article 1 of the Law of 23 December. It is a public body of an industrial and commercial nature, which administers and provides for state forests, and, when requested, for privately-owned and local authority forests. It has a board of management, a Director and 19 regional directorates covering the whole of France (Cutrera, 1991).

CELRL works to safeguard sea and lake shores from urbanisation, through acquisition, either by negotiation, compulsory purchase, or preemption. In its purchasing policy, CELRL gives priority to sites of national importance and sites which need protection for ecological reasons. It is funded by regional and national government and by donations and legacies, in the last 15 years it has purchased over 30,000ha and opened these to the public, about 70% of this land borders the Mediterranean (Tesson, 1990).

Coastal planning largely falls into general regional planning. Regional coastline strategic schemes (Schémas régionaux du littoral) are drawn up by the regions, the departments and state authorities but have no legal status. More important for the conservation of nature are the marine development schemes (Schémas du mise in valeur de la mer) originally provided for under the Decentralisation Act of 7 January 1983. These schemes must establish the essential guidelines for coastal protection, use and management: they determine the overall aims of various coastal zones (Cutrera, 1991).

The 1990 national plan for the environment proposes the creation of an Institute for the Environment to collect and make available a reliable and complete array of data concerning the environment and to have the capacity to interpret that data. It proposes that this body should be independent but should use the resources of other specialised bodies (Nowicki, 1990).

There are a small number of non-governmental organisations involved in the establishment or management of private protected areas. The most effective of these is the National Society for the Protection of Nature (Société Nationale de Protection de la Nature), whilst the oldest is the Society for the Study and Protection of Nature in Brittany, where the majority of private nature reserves are to be found. The French Federation of Nature Conservation Societies (FFSPN) incorporates most of the country's numerous local and regional nature conservation societies. Some societies have established and manage nature reserves and may receive government funding (Duffey, 1982). The French Natural Park Federation (Fédération des Parcs Naturels de France) is established to support the implementation and development of local authority policies towards natural parks, to represent public interests, to provide information and to promote the natural parks nationally and internationally and to provide technical assistance to the authorities.

For the designation of nature reserves, the government has preferred to seek agreement with local landowners and not purchase land and this has resulted in delays in the designation of important sites. One site, Vanoise National Park, was placed on the IUCN Commission on National Parks and Protected Areas list of threatened protected areas in 1984, as a result of proposals for hydro development.

Systems Reviews France is one of the largest Western European countries, with borders on the Atlantic Ocean, the English Channel, the North Sea and the Mediterranean. It shares its south-western borders with Spain and Andorra, while to the east it has common borders with Belgium, Luxembourg, Germany, Switzerland and Italy. It encompasses the terrestrial border of the Principality of Monte Carlo, and also includes the large Mediterranean island of Corsica. Most of the north and west of the country is relatively low-lying, dominated by a number of large river basins: the Seine, flowing into the English Channel, the Loire flowing into the northernmost end of the Bay of Biscay and the Dronne, Dordogne and Garonne flowing into the Gironde estuary, also in the Bay of Biscay. There are a number of mountainous areas: in the south of the country there is a large ancient mountain block, the Massif Central; to the north-east, close to the border with Germany, is another chain of old mountains, the Vosges; the Jura Mountains and the Alps lie close to and traverse the borders with Switzerland and Italy; the border with Spain and Andorra runs along the line of another younger mountain range, the Pyrenees. The highest peak in France, Mont Blanc, is 4,807m and lies on the border with Italy. The other large river in France, the Rhône, runs between the Alps and the Massif Central, into the Mediterranean. Corsica is a mountainous island, north of the Italian island of Sardinia and just over 150km from the south-east corner of mainland France – the highest peak on the island is Mount Cinto, at 2,170m.

Four main vegetation zones are recognised in France. The mountain zone includes formations of *Pinus* and alpine grasslands. The Mediterranean zone is found in the southern low-lying parts of the country and on much of lowland Corsica. It is a floristically rich zone; in most areas the climax vegetation is dominated by *Quercus ilex*, although in the Departments of Var, Alpes-Maritimes and Corsica this is replaced by *Q. suber*, while *Q. pyrenaica* and other species are found in some areas. Most of this zone has been replaced or degraded to pine forest, grasslands, and maquis on silaceous soil and garigue on calcareous soil. The Atlantic zone is located along the Atlantic coast and in Normandy, notably in the silaceous zones where it is occupied by heathland, with *Erica cinerea*, *Genista anglica* etc. The final zone is the Central European zone which occupies the east of France and the Massif Central. It is dominated by forests of *Quercus* and montane forests of *Fagus* and *Abies* (Grimmett and Jones, 1989).

Much of the landscape is now agricultural, especially in the north and west-central areas: agriculture and grazing pastures occupy around 60% of the total land area. Forests occupy over 25% of the land area, two-thirds are deciduous broad-leaved (two-thirds of which are coppiced) and one-third evergreen. On the south coast there is a Mediterranean influence in the forests, and garigue and areas of maquis are also found, although the area covered by the latter is diminishing. France also has a large and important area covered by dry grassland, notably in the Jura, pre-Alps, Quercy and Causses regions. The montane areas support a notable alpine flora (Anon., 1987; Davis *et al.*, 1986; Grimmett and Jones, 1989).

There are a number of important wetlands: those of the Atlantic coast are on one of the main migration routes of Palaearctic. The shallow bays and estuaries, with their extensive mudflats which are exposed at low tide, offer excellent feeding and roosting sites for large numbers of waterfowl and waders; the Camargue on the Mediterranean coast is an internationally important site for breeding, migrating and wintering waterfowl and waders. Inland the most important wetland sites include the Rhine valley and the shores of Lake Geneva (Ramsar Convention Bureau, 1990).

Formulation of conservation legislation was fairly slow and the first nature reserves were created by private societies, the first reserves not appearing until 1961 and the first national park not until 1963 (Duffey, 1982).

The concept of regional natural parks was advanced in the early 1960s by DATAR, an agency responsible for establishing regional planning policy, and the first park, St Amand-Raismes, was created in 1968 (Nowicki, 1983). By 1990 there were 26 regional natural parks (including sites in the dominions and overseas territories) which together cover 6.4% of the total land area of France. Up to 1973 nature reserves were established on a case-by-case basis, but in that year a nature reserve programme was formulated based on a national stocktaking covering 350 sites. The present system is incomplete, being strongly in favour of mountains. A seven-year programme was launched and 100 sites were given priority rating and approved by the inter-Ministerial Action Committee on Nature and the Environment (CIANE) in December 1973, intended to be implemented throughout the 6th Plan and the beginning of the 7th Plan. To 1977, 36 sites covering 41,000ha had been selected and 59 by the end of 1977. By 1990 there were 100 nature reserves (including those

in overseas territories and dominions) covering over 110,000ha, or 0.2% of the total land area. In 1982, the Directorate of Nature Conservation launched a campaign to compile an inventory of natural zones of ecological, faunistic and floristic interest (ZNIEFF).

All the national parks were established on the mainland between 1963 and 1979: there are six in total, with central zones covering 346,133ha and peripheral zones covering a further 957,600ha. A seventh national park was established on the Caribbean island of Guadeloupe in 1989. A new park is being discussed in the Haute-Ariège.

A number of specific measures for the future protection of natural areas are given in the section for ecosystems in the 1990 national plan for the environment. All remaining coastal dune systems will be protected, and 40% of the remaining non-urbanised coastal land, particularly through the acquisition of 20,000ha by CELRL. Two-thirds of the existing wetlands will be strictly preserved and managed through the creation of 2 national parks, 40 nature reserves, the acquisition of 30,000ha by CELRL, financial assistance to the regional conservancies, and agricultural management agreements covering 750,000ha. Woodland and forest management will be conducted in a more ecological manner, while stands of particular importance will be preserved through the creation of a national park, 40 nature reserves, 100 biological domainal reserves, and the intervention of the regional conservancies and the regional natural park authorities. The protection of aquatic ecosystems is also stressed, with the creation of an integrated policy for the ecological management of the major rivers, and with the creation of five riverine regional natural parks. Marine ecosystems will receive further protection with the creation of 2 marine national parks, 4 nature reserves and 50 protected sites in French territorial waters; fishing methods will also be further regulated. National parks and protected areas will also be created in the dependent territories and dominions: national parks in French Guiana, and Reunion, and contractual agreements for ecological management to cover over 1 million ha of private forests; caverns and geological sites are to be protected through the creation of 60 nature reserves (Nowicki, 1990).

There are a number of threats to protected areas and to the natural heritage in general: some 10,000ha of wetlands are drained each year. Urban areas are expanding at a rate of 50,000ha a year and are threatening some important habitats, such as mountains and coastal areas. Hunting is extremely popular and it is difficult to protect individual species of bird and mammal outside of protected areas (Anon., 1987). The dry grasslands are poorly protected and large areas are being ploughed up and converted to cereal crops each year (Wolkinger and Plank, 1981).

Other Relevant Information In addition to mainland France, there are a number of overseas departments and territories closely allied to France to which most of the national legislation and administration applies. Separate country information sheets have been written for these although, for much of the legislative and administrative information, it may be necessary to refer back to this document. The following have departmental status: French Guyana (South America); Guadeloupe (Caribbean); Martinique (Caribbean); Mayotte (Indian Ocean); Reunion (Indian Ocean); and St Pierre and Miquelon (North Atlantic, off the coast of Newfoundland). Of these, French Guiana, Guadeloupe, Martinique and Reunion were all granted greater powers of self government in 1982. The following are described as overseas territories: French Polynesia (consisting of the South Pacific island groups of the Society, Tuamoto, Gambier, Tubuai and the Marquesas Islands); New Caledonia (west Pacific); the Wallis and Futuna Islands (central Pacific) and the Southern and Antarctic Territories.

Addresses

Direction pour la Protection de la Nature, Ministère de l'Environnement, 14 Boulevard du General Leclerc, 92524 NEUILLY-SUR-SEINE (Tel: 14 758 1212; FAX 14 745 0474/2360; Tlx: 620602 denvir f)

Ministère de l'Environnement, 45 Avenue Georges-Mandel, 75116 PARIS

Service des Fôrets, Ministère de l'Agriculture, 1-ter Avenue de Lowendal, 75700 PARIS

Office national de la Chasse, 85 bis Avenue de Wagram, 75017 PARIS (Tel: 14 227 8175)

Société Nationale de Protection de la Nature, BP 405, 75221 PARIS Cédex 05

Fédération Française des Societés de Protection de la Nature (FFSPN), 57 rue Cuvier, 75005 PARIS

Fédération des Parcs Naturels de France, 45 rue de Lisbonne, 75008 PARIS

References

Anon. (1923?). *International Yearbook of Agricultural Legislation*. Chapter IV, Legislation on Forestry and Forest Products, translation of the Decree containing public administrative regulations determining the conditions of application of the law of 28 April, 1922, relating to protected forests. Pp. 330-336.

Anon. (1982). Biotopes of Significance for Nature Conservation. Site Register XI/94/83.

Anon. (1987). *Management of Europe's natural heritage. Twenty-five years of activity*. Council of Europe, Strasbourg. Pp. 81-83.

Anon. (1988a). Les conservatoires départmentaux. *Espaces pour Demain. Revue trimestrielle* 17(3): 9-10.

Anon. (1988b). National parks and nature reserves, France. *Food and Agricultural Legislation* 37: 226.

Anon. (1989). Proposed National Park for Mont Blanc. *Nature and National Parks* 27: 35.

Anon. (1990). *100 réserves naturelles prennent l'air de la fête*. Journées mondiales de l'environnement.

Package of documents and pamphlets prepared by the Conférence Permanente des Réserves Naturelles.

Augier, H. (1981). Stage d'écologie sur les parcs marins en Europe, les réserves sous-marines françaises. Unpublished paper from a conference on Zakynthos Island, Greece, organised by the European Committee for the Conservation of Nature and Natural Resources. Strasbourg.

Baccar, H. (1977). A survey of existing and potential marine parks and reserves in the Mediterranean region. IUCN/UNEP.

Carp, E. (1980). *Directory of wetlands of international importance in the Western Palearctic*. UNEP-IUCN.

Coenen, R. and Jörissen, J. (1989). *Environmental Impact Assessment in the Member Countries of the European Community, Implementing the EC-Directive: an Overview*. KfK 4507 B, Kernforschungszentrum, Karlsruhe, Germany. 42 pp.

Commission of the European Communities. (1979). Protected Areas in the European Community. An approach to a common classification. Environment and Consumer Protection Service.

Cutrera, A. (1991). *European Environmental Yearbook*. International Institute for Environmental Studies, DocTer UK Ltd, London. 897 pp.

Davis, S.D., Droop, S.J.M., Gregerson, P., Henson, L., Leon, C.J., Lamlein Villa-Lobos, J., Synge, H. and Zantovska, J. (1986). *Plants in danger: what do we know?* IUCN, Gland, Switzerland and Cambridge, UK. 461 pp.

Duffey, E. (1982). *National Parks and Reserves of Western Europe*. Macdonald and Company, London, UK. 288 pp.

Gerfau (1979). *Réserves naturelles de France*. Ministère de l'environnement et du Cadre de vie.

Gryn-Ambroes, P. (1980). *Preliminary annotated lists of existing and potential Mediterranean protected areas*. UNEP/IUCN. UNEP/IG. 20/Inf.5.

Grimmett, R.F.A. and Jones, T.A. (1989). *Important bird areas in Europe*. Technical Publication No. 9. International Council for Bird Preservation, Cambridge, UK.

Nowicki, P.L. (1983). National and natural park protection in France. *Parks* (2): 4-6.

Nowicki, P.L. (1985). Overview: protected areas in Europe. In: *Proceedings of the Twenty-Fourth Working Session of IUCN's Commission on National Parks and Protected Areas, Madrid, Spain*. 3-4 November 1984. IUCN.

Nowicki, P.L. (1990). *The National Plan for the Environment: a Summary*. Ministry of the Environment, Paris. 34 pp.

Poore, D. and Gryn-Ambroes, P. (1980). *Nature conservation in Northern and Western Europe*. UNEP/IUCN/WWF Gland, Switzerland.

Rackham, O. (1980). Forêt de Fontainebleau (Seine-et-Marne). *Ancient woodland, its history, vegetation and uses in England*. Edward Arnold, London. P. 303-304.

Ramsar Convention Bureau (1990). *Directory of wetlands of international importance.* Ramsar Convention Bureau, Gland, Switzerland. 796 pp.

Saussay, Ch. du (1980). Legislation on wildlife, hunting and protected areas in some European countries. *Legislative Study* No. 20. FAO, Rome.

Saussay, Ch. du and Prieur, M. (1980). *Survey of national legislation relevant to marine and coastal protected areas.* Intergovernmental Meeting on Mediterranean Specially Protected Areas, Athens, 13-18 October 1980. United Nations Environment Programme UNEP/IG.20/INF.3, restricted distribution. 60 pp.

Spagnesi, M. (1982). Proceedings of the conference on the conservation of wetlands of international importance especially of waterfowl habitat (24-29 November 1980, Cagliari, Italy). *Supplemento alle Ricerche di Biologia della Selvaggia.* Vol. VIII Numero Unico.

Tesson, J.-L. (1990). Les mesures de protection applicables aux zones humides françaises. Office National de la Chasse, *Bulletin Mensuel* 152: 32-36.

Wirth, H. (1979). *Nature reserves in Europe.* Edition Leipzig.

Wolkinger, F. and Plank, S. (1981). Dry grasslands of Europe. Council of Europe, Strasbourg. *Nature and Environment Series* No. 21. 56 pp.

ANNEX
Definitions of protected area designations, as legislated, together with authorities responsible for their administration

Title: Act of 28 December 1967 (supersedes Article 8-bis of the Act of 2 May 1930 (concerning sites of natural beauty and historical archaeological or natural monuments) which was superseded by the Act of 1 July 1957, the Act of 28 December 1967 and the Decree of 13 June 1969)

Date: Act on 28 December 1967 (Decree on 13 June 1969)

Brief description: Provides the general framework for defining, designating and establishing sites of natural beauty and historical archaeological or natural monuments

Designations:

Classified site (Site classé) Major developments are restricted in these areas which are of artistic, historic, scientific or landscape value. These sites may be neither destroyed nor changed from their present state and appearance without special authorisation given by the Préfet or the Minister of the Environment. Camping and outdoor advertising are prohibited.

Inscribed site (Site inscrit) Designation of sites is for their preservation in their existing state. This is not major protective measure, but serves to alert the authorities of the importance of the site and hence it's place in future regional or national planning. The owners of these sites are obliged to notify the public administration of their intention to undertake work other than those of "current practise" and "normal upkeep" of rural properties.

Sources: Cutrera, 1991; Tesson, 1990

Title: Loi No. 60/708 rélative a la création de parcs nationaux (Law No. 60/708 Relating to the Creation of National Parks) and Décret No. 61-1195: pris en application de la loi du 22 juillet 1960 instituant les parcs nationaux (Decree No. 61-1195: for the enforcement of the law of 22 July 1960 for the establishment of national parks)

Date: 22 July 1960; 31 October 1961, amended in 1989 (Decree No. 89-6)

Brief description: Provide the general framework for establishing national parks.

Administrative authority: Ministry of the Environment (prior to 1971: Ministry of Agriculture)

Designations:

National park (Parc national) The open wording of Article 2 of the 1960 Law has resulted in flexible application of its protective measures from one national park to another. A site may be declared "when the conservation of its flora, fauna, subsoil, climate, waters, and its natural environment in general is of special interest and when it is important to preserve this environment from all effects of natural degradation and to screen it from all artificial intervention capable of changing its appearance, composition and evolution".

Sites are declared by individual decree in the Council of State. Prior to designation, the Ministry of the Environment conducts preliminary studies and consultations, which are then put before the Prime Minister: this is followed by a public enquiry and the drafting of the decree. The limits of the territory declared under the decree may include national maritime waters.

The legislation allows for the establishment of a buffer zone or preparc around the park itself (which is sometimes referred to as the central zone), where none of the protective constraints apply this is intended to act as a transitional area between the natural wilderness in the park itself and the outside world.

The Decree of 1989 lists the behaviour and activities which are to be restricted and which carry penalties corresponding to five classes of contravention, according to their degree of seriousness. The individual decrees for the different parks draw from this list as befits the need of the individual park: hunting (but not fishing) is in principle banned from all the parks as is the interference with the flora and fauna, film-making, professional photography, publicity and the usurpation of the "national park" label. There are generally restrictions on commerce and industry, public and private works, mining, water-use, and, to some extent, public access. In reality for these latter restrictions there is usually a complex system of prohibitions and exemptions based on each individual decree of classification. Forestry and agricultural activities are generally continued although they are closely monitored to ensure that they do not come into conflict with the main purpose of the park.

Sources: Cutrera, 1991; Saussay, 1980

Title: Loi No. 76/629 relative à la protection de la Nature (Nature Conservation Act No. 76 629); and decrees relating to the implementation of this Act (including nos. 77/1141; 77/1295; 77/1296; 77/1297; 77/1298; 77/1300)

Date: 10 July 1976

Brief description: A wide ranging Act, covering "the protection of natural areas and the countryside, the preservation of animal and plant species, the maintenance of biological equilibrium through the protection of natural resources against all causes of degradation". This Act includes framework provisions for the definition, designation and establishment of nature reserves, voluntary nature reserves and biotope protection orders.

Administrative authority: Directorate for Nature Conservation

Designations:

Nature reserve (Réserve naturelle) "Those parts of the land of one or more communes...where the conservation of the fauna, flora, subsoil, water, mineral and fossil deposits and, in general, the natural surroundings is of particular importance or which require the suspension of all artificial intervention that might lead to their degradation".

Classification of sites pay include areas of the "le domaine public maritime" or French territorial waters.

Factors taken into consideration include: preservation of species and habitats in danger of disappearing from part or all of the national territory; restoration of animal or plant populations in their natural habitats; conservation of botanical gardens or arboretums which form reserves of rare plant species or those under threat of disappearance; preservation of biotopes and formations of geological, geomorphological or speleological interest; preservation or creation of stop-over points on major migration routes; scientific or technical studies indispensable to the development of human knowledge; sites of particular interest for the study of evolution.

Established with the approval of the Ministry of the Environment under an agreement of a contractual nature. Subject to the owner's consent the decision to establish a reserve is issued in the form of a decree after the local authorities have been consulted and the scientific authorities (National Nature Conservancy Council) have given their opinion. If the owners object, publication is followed by a survey and the reserve is designated by a Council of State decree which sets out details of the activities which are permitted and takes into account the maintenance of traditional activities and if compatible, their development. To avoid these objections, the Decree of 25 November 1977 requires that the request is accompanied by an agreement from the owners or title holders of the land (Article 17).

The legislation stipulates that approval may not be granted for reserves incompatible with management and urbanisation laws, but once given the approval constitutes the act binding interested parties. The approval for a nature reserve on private property is valid for a six-year period renewable by tacit agreement. The owner may interrupt the process, but only with a notification period of two years before termination. The State very rarely purchases land for nature reserves; it may compensate an owner after the value is fixed by mutual agreement or by the Expropriations Judge.

Regulations in nature reserves are modulated according to the function of the site in question. Alterations of any sort may only be made following special authorisation from the Minister.

Penalties for breaking any of the regulations are stipulated, they include fines of up to FF 80,000.

Voluntary nature reserve (Réserve naturelle volontaire) These are covered by Article 24 of the

1976 law, and regulated by Articles 17-25 of the Decree No. 77-1298 of 25 November 1977.

Privately owned land may be established as voluntary nature reserves by mutual agreement with the owners.

The length of the agreement and the general regulations concerning the reserve is covered under an individual decree. Penalties for breaking any of the regulations in state-owned nature reserves apply equally to voluntary nature reserves.

Biotope protection order (Arrêté de protection de biotope) Intended to protect the habitat of endangered species of flora and fauna, individual orders are declared by the préfet after consultation with the farmers' professional organisation (Chambre départmentale d'agriculture). Regulations vary but typically restrict human activities, particularly agricultural practises such as the use of pesticides and the burning of vegetation.

Sources: Anon., 1990; Cutrera, 1991; Nature Conservation Act, 1976; Poore and Gryn-Ambroes, 1980

Title: Décret No. 67-158 rélatif aux parc naturel régionaux (Decree No. 67-158 relating to regional natural parks) and subsequent decrees (Nos. 75-983 and 88-443)

Date: 1 March 1967, 24 October 1975, 25 April 1988

Brief description: Provide the criteria for the establishment and designation of regional natural parks. The 1975 Decree gave more responsibility to the regions concerning the designation of these areas, a move that was strengthened by the 1988 Decree which replaced it.

Administrative authority: Separate administrative organisations are established for each park (see main text).

Designations:

Regional natural park, regional nature park (Parc naturel régional) Under the Decree of 1988 a territory with a fragile balance and a rich natural and cultural heritage may be given this classification if this would include: protection of this heritage, particularly through careful management of the natural environment; contribution to the social and economic development of the area; promotion of facilities for public recreation, education and information; and the performance of experiments or demonstrations in the aforementioned fields, and a contribution to research programmes. Earlier definitions gave less emphasis to nature conservation

their purpose was given as to further "recreation, education, and relaxation of people, and tourism" this has been described as a more accurate portrayal of the existing situation.

Each park is governed by a Charter drawn up by common agreement between the regions and the interested local communities. Classification is declared by the Minister for the Environment following the recommendation of the Commission for Regional Natural Parks. The Charter covers five main points: administrative organisation; plan of work; park facilities; legal measures to be taken; and arrangements for financing the provision of facilities and management. These points effectively become the park's bye-laws once it is established under existing regulations (without requiring a specific Act of Parliament). Various bodies (town council civil and military administrations, department commissions, local hunting organizations) are consulted up to a maximum of four months. During the approval period modifications to statutes and boundaries can only be carried out by agreement with the parties, but central authorities can extend the powers of managers and the regulatory measures of the Conservation Police. Approval may be withdrawn by the Ministry of Environment. In regional natural parks (as in national parks) compensation is collective with indemnification for losses suffered by the communes in the park itself.

Each park has a special development plan, aimed at maintaining and preserving the traditional landscape. This plan is codified in the Charter, accompanied by a budget for investment and operating costs for the last few years. A public or private body is designated by the Charter with responsibility for the management of the park.

Since 1988 classification of a park has carried a time limit, and has been renewable every 10 years.

Sources: Anon., 1988b, Cutrera, 1991

Title: Arrêté Ministériel (Ministerial Order)

Date: 19 May 1982

Brief description: Provides for the designation of national hunting reserves

Administrative authority: Office National de la Chasse (National Hunting Office)

Designations:

National hunting reserve (Réserve nationale de la chasse) No information

Title: Law No. 19-918 on Maritime Hunting

Date: 24 October 1968

Brief description: Provides for the designation of marine reserves

Administrative authority: Minister responsible for Hunting and the Minister responsible for the merchant navy

Designations:

Marine reserve (Réserve marine)   Declared under Article 11. Reserves may be established at sea, within territorial waters, salt pools or other bodies of salt water...and in the maritime public domain. Protection only extends to the protection of wildfowl.

Under Article 9 of the 1972 Decree, these reserves are created by Order of the Minister responsible for hunting and the Minister responsible for the merchant navy for a period of not less than six years.

Source: Saussay and Prieur, 1980

SUMMARY OF PROTECTED AREAS

Map[†] ref.	*National/international designations* Name of area	IUCN management category	Area (ha)	Year notified
	National Parks			
1	Cevennes	V	84,800	1970
2	Ecrins	II	91,800	1973
3	Mercantour	II	68,500	1979
4	Port Cros	II	2,494	1963
5	Pyrenees Occidentales	II	45,700	1967
6	Vanoise	II	52,839	1963
	Pre-parcs			
7	Cevennes	V	228,000	1970
8	Ecrins	V	178,600	1973
9	Mercantour	V	200,000	1979
10	Pyrenees Occidentales	V	206,000	1967
11	Vanoise	V	145,000	1963
	Nature Reserves (Natural Reserves)			
12	Aiguilles Rouges	IV	3,279	1974
13	Baie de Bourgneuf	IV	4,200	
14	Camargue	I	13,117	1975
15	Cherine	I	1,987	
16	Contamines-Montjoie	IV	5,500	1979
17	Foret dominiale de Cerisy	IV	2,124	1976
18	Gorges de l'Ardeche	IV	1,572	1980
19	Grande Sassiere	IV	2,230	1973
20	Haut Plateaux du Vercors	IV	16,661	1985
21	Ile St Aubin	IV	2,500	
22	Lac de Grandlieu	IV	2,695	1980
23	Lac de la Foret d'Orient	IV	2,300	
24	Mantet	IV	3,028	1984
25	Moeze	IV	6,700	1985
26	Mont Ventron	IV	1,647	1989
27	Montjoie et Passy	IV	2,000	1980
28	Neouvielle	IV	2,313	1968
29	Nohedes	IV	2,137	1986
30	Passy	IV	2,000	1980
31	Prats de Mollo	IV	2,185	1986
32	Py	IV	3,929	1984
33	Sixt-Passy	IV	9,200	1977
34	Val d'Isere/Bonneval-sur-Arc	IV	1,491	1963
35	Ventron Massif	IV	1,647	1989

Map[†] ref.	National/international designations Name of area	IUCN management category	Area (ha)	Year notified
	Marine Reserves			
36	Abers du Leon	IV	2,020	
37	Archipel de Glenon	IV	3,800	
38	Baie de Seine and marshes	IV	7,800	
39	Etang de Bages and Sigean	IV	1,700	
40	Fiers d'Ars and Fosse de Loix	IV	1,300	
	Coastline and Lakeshore Conservancy (CELRL) Sites			
41	Etang de Vic	IV	1,338	1975
42	La Cote Bleue	IV	3,070	1975
43	Les Agriates	IV	3,933	1975
	Marine Nature Parks (Marine Natural Parks)			
44	Beaulieu-sur-Mer	VIII	8,825	1968
45	Cote Bleue	V	3,070	1982
	Regional Nature Parks (Regional Natural Parks)			
46	Armorique	V	110,000	1969
47	Ballons des Vosges	V	308,000	1989
48	Brenne	V	166,000	1989
49	Briere	V	40,000	1970
50	Brotonne	V	45,000	1974
51	Camargue	V	85,000	1970
52	Foret d'Orient	V	70,000	1970
53	Haut Languedoc	V	145,000	1973
54	Haut-Jura	V	62,088	1986
55	Haute Vallee de Chevreuse	V	22,000	1985
56	Landes de Gascogne	V	206,000	1970
57	Livradois-Forez	V	300,000	1986
58	Lorraine	V	205,000	1974
59	Luberon	V	130,000	1977
60	Marais Poitevin	V	205,000	1979
61	Marais du Cotentin et du Bessin	V	113,000	1991
62	Montagne de Reims	V	50,000	1976
63	Morvan	V	173,000	1970
64	Nord-Pas-de-Calais	V	146,000	1986
65	Normandie-Maine	V	234,000	1975
66	Pilat	V	65,000	1974
67	Queyras	V	60,000	1977
68	Vercors	V	155,000	1970
69	Volcans d'Auvergne	V	393,000	1977
70	Vosges du Nord	V	118,000	1975
	CORSICA			
	Nature Reserves (Natural Reserves)			
1	Casabianda	IV	1,760	1978
2	Foret domaniale du Fango	IV	6,410	1977
3	Iles Lavezzi	IV	5,170	1982
4	Scandola	I	1,670	1975
	Regional Nature Park (Regional Natural Park)			
5	Corse	V	300,000	1972
	Fishery Preserves (Fish Reserves)			
6	Calvi	IV	1,075	1978
7	Porto-Vecchio	IV	1,615	1978
8	Saint Florent	IV	2,440	1977
9	Tuccia-Sagone-Cargese	IV	1,620	1978
10	Ventilegne	IV	1,000	1977

Map[†] ref.	*National/international designations* Name of area	IUCN management category	Area (ha)	Year notified
	Biosphere Reserves			
	Camargue	IX	13,117	1977
	Cevennes	IX	323,000	1984
	Vallee du Fango	IX	25,110	1977
	Mont Ventoux	IX	72,956	1990
	Iroise	IX	21,400	1988
	Vosges du Nord	IX	120,000	1988
	Ramsar Sites			
	La Camargue	R	85,000	1986
	Etang de Biguglia	E	2,000	1986
	Etang de la Champagne Humide	R	135,000	1986
	Etang de la Petite Woëvre	R	5,300	1986
	Golfe du Morbihan	R	20,000	1986
	La Brenne	R	140,000	1986
	Marais du Cotentin et du Bessin (Baie des Veys)	R	32,500	1986
	Rives du Lac Léman	R	3,335	1986
	World Heritage Site			
	Cape Girolata, Cape Porto and Scandola	X	12,000	1983

[†]Locations of most protected areas are shown on the accompanying maps.

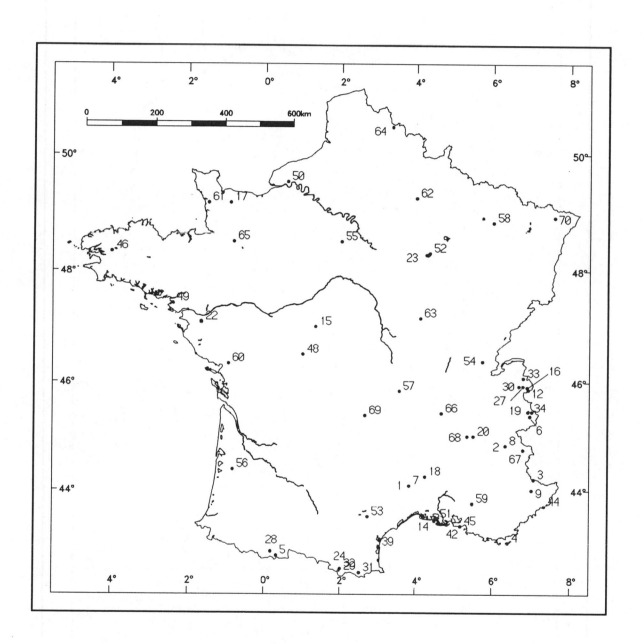

Protected Areas of France

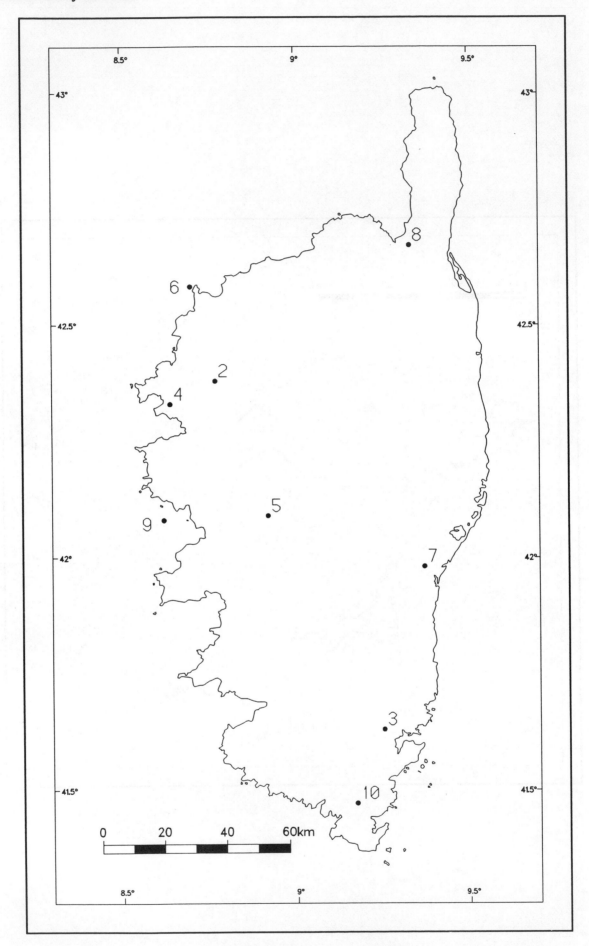

Protected Areas of France – Corsica

GERMANY
(FEDERAL REPUBLIC OF GERMANY, FRG)

Area 356,840 sq. km

Population 77,483,000 (1990)
Natural increase: – 0.06% per annum

Economic Indicators
GDP: US$ 18,354 per capita (former FRG) (1987)
GNP: US$ 14,460 per capita (former FRG) (1987)
(No information for the entire country since unification)

Policy and Legislation The Treaty on the Final Settlement with Respect Germany was signed by the Federal Republic of Germany, the German Democratic Republic (GDR) and the four former wartime allies (France, the UK, the USSR and the USA) on 12 September 1990, and ratifed by the relevant German parliaments (Volkskammer, Bundestag and Bundesrat). On 3 October 1990, the two Germanies, divided since the end of World War II in 1945, unified. Prior to this date, monetary union had occurred and, of direct relevance to protected areas, legal precedence rested with the laws of the Federal Republic.

Once Germany was densely covered in forest, but gradually it was cleared away by man over the centuries. In mediaeval times numerous hunting reserves were set up, and forest and game species were protected by strict legislation. Forestry management dates back at least to the mediaeval period when forests were being increasingly exploited for the growing forest industries, and needed to be protected from over-exploitation by woodland management and by law. Large and regularly-planned forest villages (Waldehufendorfer) were established at an early date (Mayhew, 1976). In the 19th century areas such as the present Berchtesgarden National Park were Royal hunting reserves set up for the Bavarian kings. Detailed forest stand surveys were undertaken as long ago as 1850 in many of the areas now protected for nature conservation (Bibelriether and Schreiber, 1989). In more recent times one of the first protected areas was established in 1852 at "Teufelsmauer" (Devil's Wall) near Quedlinburg, then, in 1904, the first objectives were drawn up to protect natural monuments. The first nature reserves this century were set up under private initiative, such as Luneburg Heath in 1906 (Cerovsky, 1988; IUCN, 1987; Drucker, *in litt.*, 1987).

One of the first laws of this century directly concerned with the protection of nature for conservation purposes was the Law on the Conservation of Nature of 1935 (this law applied to the German Reich, including the whole of present-day Germany). Currently, protected area categories, establishment procedures and responsibilities for nature conservation are largely defined in the nature conservation legislation at the state (Länder) level. There are, however, general legislative provisions for conservation at the federal (Bund) level, as the Bund has the right to establish acts as a framework for Länder legislation, for example in the field of nature and landscape protection and species protection (Holzner, 1986).

Perhaps the most important piece of federal legislation concerning protected areas is the Federal Nature Protection Act of 20 December 1976 (adopted by the new federal Länder in July 1990). This Act provides the framework legislation for the Länder (Reiss and Bibelreither, 1984). Section I lays down general provisions and states that nature conservation and environmental protection should be sought as a basis for man's existence and as a prerequisite for recreation in natural areas: specific points are laid down including the conservation, preservation, development and restoration of habitats and biotopes for wild flora and fauna and the designation of areas for recreational purposes. Section II covers countryside planning. It specifies Länder landscape programmes, regional landscape development plans, local landscape plans, and their respective contents. General measures are set out in Section III for the protection, maintenance and development of nature and landscape. These measures also define which general activities and land uses are considered to be in conflict with nature and landscape.

Section IV deals directly with protected areas. It names various categories of protected area: nature reserve (Naturschutzgebiet), national park (Nationalpark), landscape reserve or landscape protected area (Landschaftsschutzgebiet), nature park (Naturpark), natural monument (Naturdenkmal) and protected part of landscape (Geschützter Landschaftsbestandteil) (see Annex), and authorises the different Länder to designate and register these areas for protection. Section V deals broadly with the protection of species. Article 20c covers the conservation of specific biotopes, and lists over 20 such biotopes which must be protected from any action that may lead to the destruction or major or lasting impairment of these.

Section VI covers access to nature and landscapes for the purposes of recreation: rights of access to private land are to be laid down in greater detail by the appropriate Länder, while federal, Länder, regional and local authorities may appropriate large areas of public land for recreation purposes. Other sections give the right to recognised associations to examine reports and make comments on plans and decisions (Article 29); penalties and the rights of some authorities are also covered (Cutrera, 1987). The Länder have adopted their legislation on nature conservation and physical planning in conformity with this Act (Holzner, 1986).

At present, existing or potential areas of nature or landscape interests are identified in the regional landscape development plans. These plans are based on complex negotiations, sometimes lasting up to ten years or more between public authorities, institutions, interested groups and experts. The plans are enacted by Länder government orders. National parks and nature parks are established by the Länder; nature reserves or landscape reserves by the counties; exceptionally small sites may be designated by the districts. Conservation orders are enacted which describe the site and its demarcation, and the reasons for its designation; they contain a set of prohibitions, and list the activities for which permission is required and for which exceptions are granted. Depending on the type of conservation area, there are various restrictions on agriculture. These may preclude drainage, removal of landscape features, intensification, the construction of buildings or other permanent facilities, fencing and so on. Usually there are no compensation payments, but there may be grants for active conservation works. Creation of reserves under the Nature Conservation Law does not exclude hunting and separate declarations of controlled hunting areas or non-hunting areas must be made under the Hunting Laws (Holzner, 1986).

The main piece of legislation concerning hunting at the federal level is the Federal Hunting Act (Bundesjagdgesetz) of 1 October 1976. This Act is largely concerned with hunting activities, although it does consider game conservation as being concomitant with the right to hunt. It also provides for the suspension of hunting on land which does not belong to any hunting district and in any areas designated as sanctuaries no futher details are provided concerning sanctuaries in this framework legislation (Federal Hunting Act, 1976).

The legislation of the former GDR relating to conservation issues no longer plays any role. Prior to 1990 the most important environmental legislation was the Landeskulturgesetz of 14 May 1970, coupled with an Ordinance covering species protection linked to habitat conservation (flora and fauna), which was passed on 1 October 1984. Until 1990 there were three main categories of protected area in Eastern Germany: natural nature reserve of protected area (Naturschutzgebiet) (NSG); landscape protected area or reserve (Landschaftschutzgebiet) (LSG); and natural monument (Flächennaturdenkmal). Of these categories there has had to be little or no change to the natural nature reserves of the landscape protected areas, as these relate closely to the categories of the Federal Nature Protection Act.

At the Länder level, the relevant nature conservation legislation has been largely covered under the following acts (Anon., 1987):

Baden-Württemberg The Act governing the Conservation of Nature, the management of the landscape and the provision of recreational facilities in the countryside of 21 October 1975.

Bavaria The Act governing the conservation of nature, the management of the landscape and recreation in the natural environment of 2 July 1973, promulgated in its amended form on 10 October 1978, last amended by law on 6 December 1983.

Berlin The Nature Conservation and Landscape Management Act of 30 January 1979

Bremen The Nature Conservation and Landscape Management Act of 17 September 1979

Hamburg The Hamburg Nature Conservation and Landscape Management Act of 2 July, 1981

Hessen The Hessian Nature Conservation and Landscape Management Act of 19 September 1980

Lower Saxony The Lower Saxony Nature Conservation Act of 20 March 1981

North-Rhine/Westphalia The Act governing the protection of the ecological balance and the development of the landscape of 18 February 1975, promulgated in its amended form on 26 August 1980

Rhineland-Palatinate The Nature Conservation and Landscape Management Act of 14 June 1975, promulgated in its amended form on 5 February 1979

Saarland The Act governing the conservation of nature and the management of the landscape of 31 October 1979

Schleswig-Holstein The Nature Conservation and Landscape Management Act of 16 April 1973, promulgated in its amended form on 19 November 1982.

Brandenburg, Mecklenburg-Vorpommern, Saxony, Saxony-Anhalt and Thuringia No acts have been established to date.

The most important piece of forestry legislation at the federal level is the federal forestry law of 2 May 1975. Among the general provisions is that forests should be maintained "for the sake of their economic use...and for the environment, especially where the sustained productive potential of the ecological system, climate, hydrology, clean air, soil fertility, landscape, agricultural and other infrastructures, and recreation...are concerned" (Anon., 1976). Chapter 2 of this Law makes provision for the framework legislation for the Länder; Section I covers the framework planning for forests, while Section II covers the maintenance and management of forests, and afforestation. Article 9 of this section states that forests may not be subject to clearance and conversion to a different land use without the approval of the highest competent authority. Such approval should be refused particularly if the forest in question is of importance for productive potential of the ecological system, forest production or recreation. Article 12 covers protection forests which are to be declared particularly for such purposes as protection against water and wind erosion, drought, harmful run-off of precipitation and avalanches. Article 13 covers recreation forests which may be declared "if the welfare of the general puplic demands that forest areas be protected, conserved or otherwise arranged for recreational purposes". Article 14 covers access to forests; access is formally permitted to forests for recreational purposes, although access may be restricted, with good reason, by individual Länder legislation (Anon., 1976). Protection and recreation forests are described in the Annex.

An EC Directive concerning environmental impact assessments (EIAs) was adopted on 27 June 1985, and gives member states three years in which to incorporate certain requirements into their own national legislation. The main elements are that for public or private development projects, which are likely to have a significant effect on the environment, information on the project and its environmental effects should be submitted to the competent authority, which must then take into consideration both the information and opinions it receives before authorising the project. EIAs must take into account people, flora, fauna, soil, water, air, climatic factors, the landscape, material assets and the cultural heritage.

Some provisions for environmental impact assessment were incorporated into Germany's legislation in the 1975 law entitled "environmental impact assessment basic regulations – principles for testing the environmental compatability of public measures of the government of the Federal Republic of Germany". The existing legislation does not meet the minimum requirements of the EC-Directive, although a further "article law" and a corresponding legislative proposal have been prepared. Article 1 determines some basic principles of environmental impact assessment, while subsequent Articles amend other relevant environmental and planning laws (Coenen and Jörissen, 1989).

International Activities   The Convention on Wetlands of International Importance especially as Waterfowl Habitat (Ramsar Convention) was ratified on 26 February 1976 (the former GDR ratified in 1978): 29 sites have now been designated. The Convention concerning the Protection of the World Natural and Cultural Heritage (World Heritage Convention) was signed on 23 August 1976 (the former GDR signed in 1988), but no natural sites have yet been listed. Nine biosphere reserves have been designated under the Unesco Man and the Biosphere Programme.

Germany is also party to the Convention on the Conservation of European Wildlife and Natural Habitats (Bern Convention). As a member of the European Community Germany is bound by EC regulations, including the EC Wild Birds Directive: some 398 EC special protection areas have been declared (none of these are in the Länder of the GDR, it may be expected that a number of futher areas will be declared in these Länder in the near future). Germany is also a member of

the Council of Europe. No sites have been declared as Council of Europe biogenetic reserves, however eight sites have been awarded Council of Europe European diplomas.

Germany, with Luxembourg, was one of the first countries in Europe to use the idea of trans-border parks; establishing the German-Luxembourgeois Nature Park between the Grand Duchy of Luxembourg and the German Land of the Rhineland-Palatinate under the treaty of 17 April 1964. Nordeifel Nature Park was officially twinned with Hautes Fagnes-Eifel Nature Park in Belgium in 1971. In 1982 the three Wadden Sea states of the Netherlands, Germany and Denmark signed the "Joint Declaration on the Protection of the Wadden Sea". Several trilateral governmental conferences on the protection of the Wadden Sea have taken place since (Anon., 1988). Discussions have been undertaken between the Bavarian and the Czech authorities on the formation of a trans-border national park, uniting Bayerischer Wald National Park in Bavaria with Sumava Protected Landscape Area (Anon., 1990). Proposals have also been put forward for trans-border parks with Austria, both at the Unterer Inn Nature Conservation Area and Ramsar site and at Berchtesgaden National Park, and with France to link Pfälzerwald Nature Park with Vosges du Nord Regional Nature Park.

Administration and Management   In 1904, the first set of objectives and tasks for the care of natural monuments was formulated and in 1906 the first government nature conservation authority, the Prussian (later Central German) Board for Care for Natural Monuments, was established in Danzig (Cerovsky, 1988).

The various responsibilities for environmental legislation and administration are shared between the federal government (Bund), the federal states (Länder), the counties or districts (Kreise) and the large towns outside these districts (Kreisfreie Städte). The federal government actually plays quite a major role in environmental issues. It shares legislative power with the Länder in a number of sectors, including waste disposal, energy, fisheries, the promotion of agricultural and forestry production and the protection of flora and fauna. Furthermore, the federal government is empowered to issue general rulings concerning water management, nature protection, landscape conservation, hunting and land-use planning. The Länder participate in federal legislation *via* the Federal Council (Bundesrat). They can supplement the general legislation of the federal government, and also have legislative power to expand on the national framework laws provided these do not clash with federal laws. Municipalities and administrative districts are autonomous with regard to local matters, provided their decisions do not clash with federal or Länder legislation (Cutrera, 1987).

At the federal level, the Ministry of Environment, Nature Protection and Nuclear Safety (Bundesminister für Umwelt, Naturschutz und Reaktorsicherheit) is responsible for administration of nature conservation together with scientific and technical agencies. This new Ministry was established on 5 June 1986, and incorporated the Environment Division of the Ministry of the Interior, the Nature Protection Division of the Ministry of Food and Agriculture and the divisions on the Protection of People and Foodstuffs of the Ministry of Youth, Family and Health. The new Ministry has three divisions: the Division of Environmental Protection, the Division of Nature Protection and Environment and the Division for the Safety of Nuclear Facilities and Radiation Protection. The Environmental Protection Division has three subdivisions dealing with basic environmental protection policy, water and waste management and emissions control and international cooperation. The Nature Protection and Environment Division has two subdivisions, one dealing with nature protection and landscape planning, the other with environment, soil protection and chemicals (Cutrera, 1987).

None of the ministerial bodies at the Federal level has direct responsibility for protected areas, rather this is the duty of the Länder ministries. The administrative structure at the Länder level varies from Land to Land, but within each administration is at three levels; the ministerial, the regional offices (Regierungspräsidenten) and the lower authorities of the administrative districts (Kreise) and the municipalities (Gemeinde). The ministerial authorities in the different Länder responsible for nature protection and protected areas are as follows:

Baden-Württemberg: Minister for the Environment (Minister für Umwelt)

Bavaria: State Minister for Territorial Development and Environmental Problems (Staatsminister für Landesentwicklung und Umweltfragen)

Berlin: Minister of Town Planning and Environmental Protection (Senator für Stadtentwicklung und Umweltschutz)

Brandenburg: Minister for the Environment, Nature Protection and Land Planning (Minister für Umwelt, Naturschutz und Raumordnung)

Bremen: Minister for Environmental Protection and Town Planning (Senator für Umweltschutz und Stadtentwicklung)

Hamburg: Environment Authority (Umweltbehörde)

Hessen: Minister for Territorial Development, Housing, Land Protection, Forestry and Nature Protection (Minister für Landesentwicklung, Wohnen, Landwirtschaft, Forsten und Naturschutz)

Mecklenburg-Vorpommern: Minister for the Environment (Minister für Umwelt)

Lower Saxony: Minister for the Environment (Umweltminister)

North-Rhine/Westphalia: Minister for Environment, Nature Protection and Land Planning (Minister für Umwelt, Naturschutz und Raumordnung)

Rhineland Palatinate: Minister of the Environment and Health (Minister für Umwelt und Gesundheit)

Saarland: Minister for the Environment (Minister für Umwelt)

Saxony: State Minister for the Environment and Land Development (Staatsminister für Umwelt und Landesentwicklung)

Saxony-Anhalt: Minister for the Environment and Nature Protection (Minister für Umwelt und Naturschutz)

Schleswig-Holstein: Minister for Nature, the Environment and Land Development (Minister für Natur, Umwelt und Landesentwicklung)

Thuringia: Minister for the Environment (Minister für Umwelt)

Attached to these Länder ministries are institutions or councils for Nature Conservation and Landscape Management, which work at local, district, and Länder level, and act as advisory bodies to the authorities concerned with the administration and management of protected areas. National parks are administered by park authorities responsible to their respective Länder governments or district authorities. Nearly all nature reserves are established on private land and in most some form of land use continues. In relatively few sites (mostly bird reserves) are staff specifically employed for nature conservation purposes, their expenses tend to be paid from a general budget.

The Federal Research Centre for Nature Conservation and Landscape Ecology (Bundesforschungsanstalt für Naturschutz und Landschaftsökologie) (formerly the Federal Institute for Vegetation Research, Nature Conservation and Landscape Management) operates under the auspices of the Ministry for the Environment, Nature Conservation and Nuclear Safety. It undertakes research in a number of fields, including nature conservation and landscape management, ecology and planning. In this role it acts as an advisory body to federal and Länder authorities. Within this organisation are three institutes: the Institute for Vegetation Ecology; the Institute for Nature Conservation and Animal Ecology; and the Institute for Landscape Management and Landscape Ecology. The latter maintains information on protected areas (Anon., n.d.).

Forestry and forestry policy matters are the responsibility of the Federal Ministry for Food, Agriculture and Forests (Bundesministerium für Ernährung, Landwirtschaft und Forsten). Forest interests, forest owners groups and professional associations are represented by the National Council for

Forest Management (Deutscher Forstwirtschaftsrat). This organisation aims to protect the financial interests of these groups, and to deal with relevant social and political issues. The different Länder have their own forestry laws, which are largely based on the federal Forestry Law. The titles of the different Länder ministries responsible for forestry administration vary, but generally forestry comes under the ministries of agriculture, environment, forest economy, water management, viticulture, food, finance and/or economy. Within the Länder, trade unions and other relevant institutions also play a part in formulating forest policy and legislation (Cutrera, 1991).

In the former GDR, the supreme authority for nature conservation, including protected areas, was the Ministry of Agriculture, Forest Management and Food, with the regional authorities being the forest management departments of the regional councils in all 15 Bezirke. Research and advice was provided by the Institut für Landschaftsforschung und Naturschutz (Institute for Landscape Research and Nature Conservation) of the Academy of Agricultural Sciences, created in 1953 with five regional branches at Dresden, Greifswald, Halle, Jena and Potsdam. The state nature conservation bodies often actively cooperated with voluntary bodies in programmes of species protection (Cerovsky, 1988). In late 1989, a Ministry of Environment was created, to be replaced in 1990 by a Ministry for the Environment, Nature Conservation, Energy and Nuclear Safety. The GDR ministerial bodies no longer exist; the Institute for Landscape Survey and Nature Conservation continued its work after unification. However it was due to terminate its duties at the end of 1991.

In 1904 the Bund Deutscher Heimatschutz (German Trust for Protection of the Native Country) was founded and continued to exist (in Saxony only) until the end of World War II. The Verein Naturschutzpark (VNP) (Nature Conservation Society) was one of the first bodies to acquire protected areas, when in 1906 it purchased Luneburg Heide, which later formed the basis of the present nature reserve (IUCN, 1987). There are now a vast number of non-governmental organisations concerned with nature conservation; a number of these own nature reserves, or parts of nature reserves, or have taken over management or wardening of reserves (especially bird reserves) (Ant and Engelke, 1973; Holzner, 1986). Most of the largest and most important of these organisations are recognised by the Länder in accordance with Article 29 of the federal Nature Protection Act. About three to four million people belong to one or more of these recognised societies, which have spread into the former Länder of the GDR (Cutrera, 1991). One of the most important non-governmental organisations in the former GDR was the Gesellschaft für Natur und Umwelt im Kulturbund der DDR (the Society for Nature and Environment in the Cultural Union of GDR), founded in 1980 and with 60,000 members (1991).

Systems Reviews   Germany is one of the largest central European countries. To the north it has a coastline on the Baltic Sea and the North Sea, separated by a short border with Denmark. To the west it has borders with the Netherlands, Belgium, Luxembourg and France; to the south there are borders with Switzerland and Austria; and to the west with Czechoslovakia and Poland. The Baltic coastline in the north is generally flat, with numerous bays, peninsulas and islands, as well as large areas of shallow water and intertidal mudflats. The North Sea coast comprises the German sector of the Wadden Sea, with extensive areas of saltmarshes and mudflats, as well as islands and some important estuaries. Away from the coast lies the North German Lowland (Norddeutsches Tiefland) characterised by fens, sandy uplands and natural alluvial plains and marshland: most of the northern half of the country, including most of the former GDR, is low-lying. Much of central Germany is made up of medium altitude hills and mountains. In the south-western corner is the plain of the River Rhine and the adjacent Black Forest, while along the borders with Switzerland and Austria is the German section of the Alps. There are also some large lakes in the south of the country.

Nearly 60% of the land area of is used for agriculture, mostly arable, while forests cover some 27-30% and lakes and rivers a further 2%. Much of the country is a patchwork of agricultural land, woodland, fens and marshes. To the north, oak *Quercus* and beech *Fagus* and pine *Pinus* sp. comprise the main natural woodland cover, although much of this has been replaced with conifer plantations. In the south there is a vertical zonation of oak and hornbeam *Carpinus* forest, which gives way to montane beech forests, and above 500m forests of beech, fir and spruce (Davis *et al.*, 1986; Grimmett and Jones, 1989).

Natural vegetation has largely been replaced by agriculture, urban and industrial sprawl and forestry: large areas are now given over to plantations of pine and spruce (two-thirds of the former FRG), while riverine woodlands have been widely replaced by poplar plantations and meadows. Most of the remaining natural or semi-natural vegetation is to be found in the uplands and in the south. Other important ecosystems which are disappearing include peatlands in the north threatened by exploitation, drainage and military exercises, and also grasslands, being drained and afforested and hedges being cleared (Grimmett and Jones, 1989; Heiss, 1987).

One of the first protected areas was established in 1852 at "Teufelsmauer" (Devil's Wall) near Quedlinburg (Cerovsky, 1988). Until the end of the 1960s there was no central organisation for the establishment of protected areas and the reserves which were declared, from about 1910, were selected more or less by chance through the efforts of individuals or private organisations.

Most of the summary data concerning protected areas is still only available in pre-unification form. In the former FRG, the first national park was declared in 1969, and by 1990 there were five national parks. In 1977 landscape reserves occupied 20.4% of the total area of the country. In 1980 this figure was 24.9%, while by 1988 it had risen to 29.5%. The 64 existing nature parks (1987) occupy about 20.7% of the national territory. Nature reserves cover a much smaller area; in 1980 they covered 0.83% of the land area, in 1987 they covered 1.22%, and by 1990 there were some 3,288 reserves covering 1.48% of the land area (Cutrera, 1991; Reiss and Bibelriether, 1984; Federal Research Centre for Nature Conservation and Landscape Ecology, *in litt.*, 1991). In the former GDR the total area protected in 1988 was 2,068,000ha, which is more than 19% of the surface area of the country, classified as 766 natural protected areas, covering 104,000ha (of which 6,980ha were strict reserves); 404 landscape protected areas, covering 1,964,000ha; and 9,500 natural monuments, covering over 4,000ha (Cerovsky, 1988; for 1980 lists see Jesche *et al.*, 1980). Nature reserves equivalent to those in the former FRG numbered 825 in 1990, covering some 0.98% of the total land area. On 12 September 1990, five national parks, three nature parks, and six biosphere reserves were designated by the Volkskammer (GDR parliament), the Bundesländer will complete the designations (Anon., 1990).

Threats to the environment are largely from industrial and agricultural development. Although the protected areas system of East Germany was extensive, many sites have been degraded through use for military and economic purposes. The former GDR is also littered with waste dumps, and has the highest emissions of sulphur dioxide per capita in Europe. Most of its lignite-fired power stations have little or no adaptions to clean up emissions (Björkland, 1989). Acidification of the environment is a major problem facing the entire country. Effects are produced through acid rain, acid mists and dry deposition, with the main pollutants being sulphur dioxide and nitrogen dioxide. Forests have been particularly badly affected, including those in protected areas (Bibelriether, 1984). Much of the air pollution has been related to emissions from coal-fired industries, notably power stations. This led to the passing of a law concerning the emissions from large combustion plants in 1983 (the Grossfeuerungsanlagen-Verordnung) which requires all large power plants to be fitted with flue gas cleaning equipment; since 1983 most major electricity suppliers have cut their sulphur emissions by 70-75% and had plans to cut their nitrogen oxide emissions by the same amount (Björkland, 1989). There is evidence that car emissions are also playing a major role in air pollution (Greenberg, 1985). By 1985 foresters reported that 52% of the nation's trees were damaged in some way, one-fifth of them seriously (Pearce, 1986).

Other Relevant Information   Tourism is a major element of the economy. In 1989 alone there were 155.3 million overnight stays by tourists in accommodation in FRG. Protected areas play an important part in the tourism of the country; Bayerischer Wald National Park had 1.5 million tourists per year in the mid-1980s

(Bibelriether, 1989; Reiss and Bibelreither, 1984; Bibelreither, pers. comm., 1990).

Addresses

Federal (Bund)

Bundesminister für Umwelt, Naturschutz und Reaktorsicherheit, Kennedyallee 5, W-5300 BONN 2 (Tel: 228 30 50)

Bundesforschungsanstalt für Naturschutz und Landschaftsökologie (Federal Research Centre for Nature Conservation and Landscape Ecology), Konstantinstrasse 110, D-5300 BONN 2 (Tel: 0228 84910)

Länder

Baden-Württemberg: Minister für Umwelt, Kernerplatz 9, W-7000 STUTTGART 10 (Tel: 71 112 600)

Bavaria: Staatsminister für Landesentwicklung und Umweltfragen, Rosenkavalierplatz 2, W-8000 MÜNCHEN 80 (Tel: 89 92141)

Berlin: Senator für Stadtentwicklung und Umweltschutz, Lindenstr. 20-25, W-1000 BERLIN 61 (Tel: 30 25 86 0)

Brandenburg: Minister für Umwelt, Naturschutz und Raumordnung, Heinrich-Mann-Allee 107, 0-1560 POTSDAM (Tel: 30 80 22196)

Bremen: Senatorin für Umweltschutz und Stadtentwicklung, Ansgaritorstr. 2, W-2800 BREMEN 1 (Tel: 421 36 11)

Hamburg: Umweltbehörde, Steindamm 14a-22, W-2000 HAMBURG 1 (Tel: 40 24 86 0)

Hessen: Minister für Landesentwicklung, Wohnen, Landwirtschaft, Forsten und Naturschutz, Hölderlinstr. 1-3, W-6200 WIESBADEN (Tel: 611 81 71)

Mecklenburg-Vorpommern: Ministerin für Umwelt, Schlosstr. 6-8, 0-2750 SCHWERIN (Tel: 84 780)

Lower Saxony: Umweltministerin, Archivstr. 2, W-3000 HANNOVER (Tel: 511 1040)

North-Rhine/Westphalia: Minister für Umwelt, Raumordnung und Landwirtschaft, Schwannstr. 3, W-4000 DÜSSELDORF 30 (Tel: 211 45660)

Rhineland Palatinate: Minister für Umwelt und Gesundheit, Kaiser-Friedrich- Str. 7, W-6500 MAINZ (Tel: 6131 16 1)

Saarland: Minister für Umwelt, Hardenbergstr. 8, W-6600 SAARBRÜCKEN 1 (Tel: 681 5011)

Saxony: Staatsminister für Umwelt und Landesentwicklung, Ostra-Allee 23, 0-8010 DRESDEN (Tel: 51 48 62 235)

Saxony-Anhalt: Minister für Umwelt und Naturschutz, Olvenstedter Str. 1-2, 0-3010 MAGDEBURG (Tel: 91 382 2330)

Schleswig-Holstein: Minister für Natur, Umwelt und Landesentwicklung, Grenzstr. 1-5, W-2300 KIEL 14 (Tel: 431 21 90)

Thuringia: Minister für Umwelt, Joh. Seb. Bach-Str. 1, 0-5085 ERFURT (Tel: 61 37 244)

References

Anon. (n.d.). Federal Research Centre for Nature Conservation and Landscape Ecology. (Pamphlet).

Anon. (1976). XIII/1 – General Forest Legislation, Germany (Federal Republic). *Food and Agricultural Legislation* XXV. Pp. 60-66.

Anon. (1987). Sweden. *Management of Europe's natural heritage, twenty-five years of activity.* Council of Europe, Environment Protection and Management Divison, Strasbourg. Pp. 110-111.

Anon. (1988). Fifth trilateral governmental conference on the protection of the Wadden Sea. Communique. Bonn, 17 November.

Anon. (1990). National parks for Germany, material for building a common European home. *European Bulletin* 28(107): 10-11.

Ant, H. and Engelke, H. (1973). *Die Naturschutzgebiete der Bundesrepublik Deutschland. Bundesanstalt für Vegetationskunde, Naturschutz und Landschaftspflege.* Bonn-Bad Godesberg.

Bibelriether, H. (1984). Bayerischer Wald National Park threatened by Air Pollution. *Parks* 9(2): 1-3

Bibelriether, H. (1989). Die Nationalparke der Bundesrepublik Deutschland. In: (Eds.) Bibelriether, H. and Schreiber, R.L., *Die Nationalparke Europas.* Suddeutscher Verlag, Pro Natur GmbH, Frakfurt/Main. Pp. 37-45.

Bibelriether, H. and Schreiber, R.L. (1989). *Die Nationalparke Europas.* Suddeutscher Verlag, Pro Natur GmbH, Frankfurt/Main. 240 pp.

Björkland, S. (1989). West German coal and lignite power stations come clean. *Acid Magazine* 8: 12-21.

Cerovsky, J. (1986) (Ed.). *Nature Conservation in the Socialist Countries of East-Europe.* Administration of the Krkonose National Park, Vrchlabi.

Cerovsky, J. (1988) (Ed.). *Nature Conservation in the Socialist Countries of East-Europe.* East-Europe Committee, IUCN Commission on Education. Ministry of Culture of the Czech Socialist Republic, Prague.

Charlton, P. and Stiles, R. (1974). Landscape work in the countryside. *Landscape Design* 124: 17-25. (Unseen)

Coenen, R. and Jörissen, J. (1989). Environmental impact assessment in the member countries of the European Community: implementing the EC-Directive: an Overview. KfK 4507 B, Kernforschungszentrum, Karsruhe, Germany. 42 pp.

Cutrera, A. (1987). *European Environmenal Yearbook 1987.* Institute for Environmental Studies. DocTer International UK/London. 815 pp.

Cutrera, A. (1991). *European Environmental Yearbook.* Institute for Environmental Studies. DocTer International UK/London. 897 pp.

Davis, S.D., Droop, S.J.M., Gregerson, P., Henson, L., Leon, C.J., Lamlein Villa-Lobos, J., Synge, H., and Zantovska, J. (1986). *Plants in danger: what do we know?* Threatened Plants Unit. IUCN, Gland, Switzerland, and Cambridge, UK. 461 pp.

Erz, W. (1979). *Katalog der Naturschutzgebiete in der Bundesrepublik Deutschland.* Institut fur Naturschutz und Tierökologie, Bonn.

Erz, W. (1980). Naturschutz Grundlagen, Probleme und Praxis. In: Buchwald, K. and Engelhardt, W., *Handbuch für Planung, Gestaltung und Schutz der Umwelt. Vol. 3 Die Bewertung und Planung der Umwelt.* BLV Verlag, München/Wien/Zürich. Pp. 560-637.

Grimmett, R.F.A. and Jones, T.A. (1989). *Important bird areas in Europe.* International Council for Bird Preservation, Cambridge, UK.

Greenberg, D.S. (1985). Germany's dilemma, fast cars and sick trees. *International Wildlife.* July-August. Pp. 22-24.

Haarmann, K. and Pretscher, P. (1976). *Die Feuchtgebiete Internationaler Bedeutung in der Bundesrepublik Deutschland.* Kilda-Verlag, Greven. (Unseen)

Haarmann, K. and Pretscher, P. (1988). Naturschutzgebiete in der Bundes-republik Deutschland, Übersicht und Erläuterungen. *Naturschutz Aktuell* 3. Kilder Verlag, Greven. 182 pp.

Heiss, G. (1987). Inventory of natural (virgin) and ancient seminatural woodlands within the councils member states and Finland. Unpublished report. European Commitee for the Conservation of Nature and Natural Resources.

Holzner, J. (1986). Nature Conservation in the Federal Republic of Germany. *Ecos* 7(4): 13-18.

IUCN (1987). *Protected landscapes: Experience around the World.* IUCN, Gland, Switzerland and Cambridge, UK. 432 pp.

Kaule, G. 91986). *Arten- und Biotopschutz.* Ulmer Verlag, Stuttgart. 461 pp.

Jesche, L., Klafs, G., Schmidt, H and Starke, W. (1980). *Handbuch der Naturschutzgebiete der Deutschen Demokratischen Republik. Band* 1-5. Urania-Verlag, Leipzig, Jena and Berlin.

Kube, G. (1983). Interpretation in Germany's visitor centres. *Parks* 8: 5-7. (Unseen)

Mayhew, A. (1976). *Rural settlement and farming in Germany.* Batsford, London.

Offner, H. (1976). *Unsere Naturpark: Gepflegte Landschaften und Statten der Erholung, Band 1: Schleswig-Holstein, Hamburg, Niedersachsen, Nordrhein-Westfalen.* DRW-Verlag, Stuttgart.

Poore, D. and Gryn-Ambroes, P. (1980). *Nature conservation in Northern and Western Europe.* UNEP/IUCN/WWF, Gland, Switzerland. Pp. 103-116.

Pearce, F. (1986). The strange death of Europe's trees. *New Scientist* 4 December. Pp. 41-45.

Reiss, W. and Bibelreither, H. (1984). Administration and management of protected areas in West Germany. Proceedings of the 24th Working Session of IUCN: CNPPA. Madrid, Spain, 3-4 November. 4 pp.

Röser, B. (1990). *Grundlagen des Biotop- und Artenschutzes.* Ecomed Verlag, Landsberg. 176 pp.

Rösler, M., Schwabe, E. and Lambrecht, M. (1990). *Naturschutz in der DDR*. Economia Verlag, Bonn. 305 pp.

Schoenichen, W. (1935/37). *Urdeutschland Deutschlands Naturschutzgebiete in Wort und Bild*. Two volumes. Neumann Verlag, Neudamm. 319, 349 pp.

Steinberg, K-H. (1990). Country address. GDR Minister for the Environment, Nature Conservation, Energy and Nuclear Safety. Action for a Common Future conference 14-16 May 1990. Bergen, Norway.

Sword, K. (1990). (Ed.). *The Times guide to Eastern Europe: the changing face of the Warsaw Pact*. Times Books, London, UK. 270 pp.

Weinitschke, H. (Ed.). (1980). *Handbuch der Naturschutzgebiete der DDR* (Handbook of Natural Protected Areas of GDR). 5 volumes. Urania Verlag, Leipzig/Jena/Berlin. 2nd revised ed. 1980-1985. In German. (Unseen)

Weinitschke, H. (1982). *Naturschutz gestern, heute, morgen* (Nature conservation yesterday, today, tomorrow). Urania Verlag, Leipzig/Jena/Berlin. In German. 104 pp. (Unseen)

Weinitschke, H. (1986). *Landnutzung und Naturschutz* (Land use and nature conservation). VEB Gustav Fischer Verlag, Jena. In German. 400 pp. (Unseen)

WWF (1986). Naturschutzgebiete. *WWF Journal* 2/86: 5-12. (Unseen)

ANNEX
Definitions of protected area designations, as legislated, together with authorities responsible for their administration

Title: Bundesnaturschutzgesetz (Federal Nature Protection Act)

Date: 20 December 1976, amended June 1980 and December 1986, adopted by the Länder of the former GDR in July 1990

Brief description: A federal law giving framework legislation for nature conservation for the Länder

Administrative authority: Bundesministerium für Umwelt, Naturschutz und Reactorsicherheit (Ministry for the Environment, Nature Conservation and Nuclear Safety)

Designations:

Nature reserve (Naturschutzgebiet) Designated in order to conserve biocenoses or biotopes of certain species of wild flora and fauna, or for reasons of science, natural history or natural heritage, or because of the areas' uniqueness, or particular beauty. All actions which may lead to destruction of, cause damage to, or induce changes in, a nature reserve or which may be a source of major disturbance for a nature reserve, shall be prohibited, subject to further specific provisions. Where this is compatible with the purpose of protection, nature reserves may be accessible to the general public.

National park (Nationalpark) This category provides uniform protection to the areas concerned, which are large and of singular character; criteria defined for nature reserves apply to the greater part of the area of a national park; the area has not been affected by human intervention at all, or to a limited extent only, and, helps to conserve the greatest possible variety of native fauna and flora species. The Länder shall ensure that, taking into account

exceptions imposed by the large size of areas or the presence of population centres, national parks enjoy the same protection granted to nature reserves. Where this is compatible with the purpose of protection, national parks shall be accessible to the general public.

Landscape reserve or landscape protected area (Landschaftsschutzgebiet) Designated in order to preserve or restore the balance of nature, or preserve or restitute usability of nature's resources; for the diversity, singularity, or beauty of landscapes, or, for an area's special importance for recreation. All actions which alter the character of landscape reserves or are not compatible with the purpose of their protection shall be prohibited, and subject to further specific provisions.

Nature park (Naturpark) Specifically designated for uniform development and maintenance of the balance of nature. Nature parks are typically to be large in size and to consist mainly of landscape or nature reserves; such areas are particularly suitable for recreational purposes, due to their landscape assets. Sites are designated, in accordance with the principles and objectives of area planning and of regional planning by Länder, either as a recreational area or as a tourist destination area. Nature parks shall be planned, structured and developed in accordance with their recreational purpose.

Natural monument (Naturdenkmal) Designated to conserve areas for reasons of science, natural history or national heritage; for their uniqueness, singularity or beauty; the area designated may also include the surrounding area necessary to conserve the natural monument concerned. The removal of natural monuments, as well as any action which may lead to their destruction, defacement or alteration, or which may cause major disturbance to the monument or its protected surrounding area, shall be prohibited, subject to further specific provisions.

Protected part of landscape (Geschützter Landschaftsbestandteil) Sites or objects designated as specifically protected parts of nature or of landscapes in order to safeguard the balance of nature; to improve, structure or preserve the scenery of a local community or landscape or to protect the area from deleterious influences. In some areas this category may apply to trees, hedges or other parts of the landscape. The destruction, defacement, removal or alteration of these sites shall be prohibited subject to more specific provisions. Where plant populations are reduced, the Federal Länder may rule that substitute vegetation be planted where this is appropriate and reasonable.

Sources: Anon, 1976; Cutrera, 1991

Title: Bundeswaldgesetz (Federal Forestry Law)

Date: 2 May 1975

Brief description: A federal law giving framework legislation for forestry in the Länder. Specified aims include the conservation of forests for their economic value and their environmental significance.

Administrative authority: Bundesministerium für Ernährung, Landwirtschaft und Forsten (Federal Ministry for Food, Agriculture and Forests)

Designations:

Protection forest or protective forest reserve (Schutzwald) Any forest may be declared a protection forest if it is necessary to carry out or desist from specified forestry measures for defence or protection of the general public from hazards, a major disadvantage or nuisance. They may be declared for protection against such undesirable environmental effects as water and wind erosion, drought, harmful run-off of precipitation and avalanches. Clear felling or thinning shall require approval from the appropriate authority under Länder law. Detailed regulations should be provided under specific Länder law.

Recreational forest (Erholungswald) Any forest may be declared a recreation forest if the welfare of the general public demands that forest areas be protected, conserved or otherwise arranged for recreational purposes. The Länder shall provide detailed regulations, including provisions concerning: the management of the forest in a manner consonant with its nature; restrictions on the practise of hunting for the safety of visitors; the obligations of forest owners to allow the construction or upkeep of roads, benches, shelters and equipment, and the removal of such things; the conduct of visitors to forests (Anon., 1976).

Sources: Anon, 1976; Cutrera, 1991

SUMMARY OF PROTECTED AREAS

Map[†] ref.	*National/international designations* Name of area	IUCN management category	Area (ha)	Year notified
	National Parks			
1	Bayerischer Wald	II	13,100	1970
2	Berchtesgaden	V	21,000	1978
3	Hamburgisches Wattenmeer	V	11,700	1990
4	Hochharz	V	6,000	1990
5	Jasmund	V	3,000	1990
6	Muritz	V	31,000	1990
7	Niedersachsisches Wattenmeer	V	240,000	1986
8	Sachsische Schweiz	V	9,200	1990
9	Schleswig-Holsteinisches Wattenmeer	V	285,000	1985
10	Vorpommersche Boddenlandschaft	V	80,000	1990
	Nature Reserves			
11	Alter Stolberg	V	4,520	1970
12	Ammergebirge	IV	28,850	1963
13	Anklamer Stadtbruch	IV	1,200	1967
14	Baerguendle, Oytal mit Hoefats	IV	3,850	
15	Barnbruch	IV	1,200	
16	Bucher Brack-Bolsdorfer Haken	IV	1,008	1978
17	Der Bock und Hohe Duene Pramort	IV	1,832	1957
18	Die Lucie	IV	1,800	
19	Dollart	IV	2,140	
20	Eggstaett-Hemhofer Seenplatte	IV	1,008	
21	Federsee	IV	1,400	1939
22	Feldberg	IV	3,231	
23	Fischteiche in der Lewitz	IV	1,732	1967
24	Galenbecker See	IV	1,015	1967
25	Grosser Winterberg und Zschand	IV	1,069	1961
26	Grosses Moor	IV	2,720	
27	Hadelner und Belumer Aussendeich	IV	1,283	
28	Hahnheide	IV	1,450	
29	Hasledorfer Binnenelbe mit Elbvorland	IV	2,056	
30	Haunstetter Wald und Stadtwald Augsburg	IV	1,804	
31	Helgolaender Felssockel	IV	5,138	
32	Hinrichshagen	IV	1,124	1967
33	Hoher Ifen	IV	2,430	
34	Insel Oie und Kirr #1	IV	418	1967
35	Insel Pulitz	IV	149	1937
36	Insel Usedom	V	37,500	1966
37	Inseln Bohmke und Werder	IV	118	1971
38	Inseln Oie und Kirr #2	IV	450	1967
39	Inseln im Senftenberger See	IV	899	1981
40	Isarauen Zwischen Schaefrlorn und Bad Toelz	IV	1,663	
41	Jasmund	IV	1,500	1935
42	Karwendel und Karwendelvorgebirge	IV	19,100	1959
43	Krickenbecker Seen	IV	1,240	
44	Kuehkopf-Knoblochsaue	IV	2,369	
45	Laacher See	IV	2,100	
46	Lange Rhoen	IV	2,657	
47	Langeoog	IV	600	
48	Luneburger Heide	IV	19,720	1920
49	Muendung der Tiroler Achen	IV	1,250	
50	Murnauer Moos	IV	2,355	
51	Neuwerker und Scharhoerner Watt	IV	7,260	

Map[†] ref.	National/international designations Name of area	IUCN management category	Area (ha)	Year notified
52	Nord-Sylt	IV	1,796	1969
53	Obere Wuemmeniederung	IV	1,385	
54	Oberharz #1	IV	7,030	1954
55	Oberharz #2	IV	1,980	1967
56	Oestliche Chiemgauer Alpen	IV	9,500	
57	Osterseen	IV	1,086	
58	Ostufer der Muritz	IV	4,832	1967
59	Peenemunder Haken, Struck und Ruden	IV	1,870	1925
60	Peenetal-Moor	IV	1,478	1981
61	Rehdener Geestmoor	IV	1,085	
62	Retterschwanger Tal mit Daumen	IV	2,100	
63	Saupark	IV	2,480	
64	Schachen und Reintal	IV	4,000	
65	Schliffkopf	IV	1,380	
66	Seegrund Ahlbeck	IV	1,166	
67	Serrahn	IV	1,817	1961
68	Siebengebirge	IV	4,200	
69	Spiekeroog Ostplate	IV	885	
70	Stechlin	IV	2,140	1938
71	Steckby-Loedderitzer Forst	IV	3,550	1961
72	Taubergiessen	IV	1,601	
73	Tinner und Staverner Dose	IV	3,200	
74	Uhlstaedter Heide	IV	1,082	1981
75	Untere Mulde	IV	1,137	1961
76	Vessertal	IV	1,649	1939
77	Vogelinsel Heuwiese und Freesenort	IV	250	1961
78	Wahner Heide	IV	2,630	
79	Westdarsz und Darszer Ort mit Bernsteininsel	IV	1,130	1957
80	Wurzacher Reid	IV	1,387	
	Landscape Reserves (Landscape Protected Areas)			
81	Aga-und Elstertal	V	2,796	1968
82	Allgauer Hochalpenkette	V	19,680	1972
83	Altmuhltal mit Nebentalern #1	V	3,322	1961
84	Altmuhltal mit Nebentalern #2	V	1,240	1961
85	Altmuhltal mit Nebentalern #3	V	25,850	1967
86	Ammersee mit Ufer- und Moranenlandschaft	V	9,910	1972
87	Ammerthal und Hainsberg	V	1,084	1965
88	Amperauen	V	9,750	1968
89	Amperauen und Mooslandschaft nordostlich	V	1,801	1983
90	Amperland sudlich Furstenfeldbruck	V	3,575	1979
91	Auerbachtal mit Soinkargebiet	V	4,815	
92	Augustusburg-Sternmuhlental	V	1,487	1968
93	Auwald beiderseits der Iller	V	1,641	1968
94	Bachmuhlbachtal und Paintner Forst #1	V	1,967	1971
95	Bad Freienwalde	V	4,340	1965
96	Barlebener-Jerslebener See mit Elbniederung	V	3,548	1964
97	Bibert- und Metlachtal	V	2,047	1967
98	Bleicheroder Berge	V	4,103	1970
99	Blumberger Forst	V	1,960	1965
100	Bodeniederung	V	7,200	1975
101	Boxberg-Reichwalder Wald-und Wiesengebiet	V	1,157	1968
102	Brandenburger Wald-und Seengebiet	V	16,270	1966
103	Briesetal und Muhlenbecker See	V	3,175	1966
104	Burgrain, Kaltenbrunn und Barmsee	V	1,434	1976
105	Burgsteinlandschaft	V	2,808	1968
106	Calau-Altdobern-Reddern	V	4,800	1968
107	Chiemsee, seine Inseln und Ufergebiete #1	V	2,224	1986

Map† ref.	National/international designations Name of area	IUCN management category	Area (ha)	Year notified
108	Chiemsee, seine Inseln und Ufergebiete #2	V	10,466	1986
109	Choriner Endmoranenbogen	V	16,500	1957
110	Colditzer Forest	V	4,600	1963
111	Colmberg-Sulzbachtal	V	2,236	1968
112	Dahlener Heide	V	16,700	1963
113	Dammuhlenteich	V	1,036	1974
114	Deisenhofener Forst	V	2,156	1970
115	Dillberg-Heinrichsberg	V	1,836	1964
116	Dippoldiswalder Heide und Wilisch	V	2,420	1974
117	Dobbertiner Seen usw	V	12,100	1964
118	Dobbin-Zietlitzer Feldmark	V	2,000	1938
119	Dolgener und Hohensprenzer See	V	1,500	1961
120	Donauauen ostl. Neuburg mit Branst	V	2,163	1987
121	Donautal mit Seitentalern	V	11,850	1986
122	Dreigleichen	V	1,698	1960
123	Dresdener Heide	V	5,876	1971
124	Dubener Heide	V	11,380	1961
125	Duen-Helbetal	V	5,600	1963
126	Durnbucher Forst	V	6,388	
127	Ebersberg und Bohlgrund	V	1,676	1966
128	Ebersberger Forst	V	7,548	1984
129	Egartenlandschaft um Miesbach	V	10,396	1955
130	Eisenberger Holzland	V	1,828	1983
131	Elbaue Martinskirchen-Muhlberg	V	1,490	1968
132	Elbhange Dresden-Pirna und Schonfelder Hoch.	V	3,540	1974
133	Elbsee bei Aitrang	V	1,536	1955
134	Elbtal nordlich von Meissen	V	2,320	1960
135	Elsteraue	V	10,000	1937
136	Elsteraue und Teichlandschaft usw	V	1,860	1968
137	Elsteraue zwischen Herzberg und Ubigau	V	2,160	1968
138	Elsterniederung usw	V	19,650	1968
139	Endmoranenzug Brohmer usw	V	5,000	1962
140	Fahner Hohe	V	4,950	1970
141	Fahrenberg-Zottbachtal	V	2,300	1965
142	Faulenbacher Tal, Lechtal und Alpseeraum	V	1,185	1956
143	Feldberger Seenlandschaft	V	7,000	1962
144	Fischland-Darss-Zingst	V	15,000	1966
145	Flaming	V	38,670	1961
146	Flemsdorf	V	1,720	1965
147	Forggensee und benachbarte Seen	V	6,050	1956
148	Forstenrieder Park und Furstenrider Wald	V	4,921	1963
149	Frankenalb	V	17,230	1966
150	Frankenwald #1	V	7,381	1986
151	Frankenwald #2	V	33,279	1984
152	Frankenwald #3	V	3,340	1984
153	Frankische Schweiz-Flussgebiet der Wiesent	V	3,509	1955
154	Freiberger Mulde-Zschopau	V	7,000	1963
155	Freisinger Moos und Echinger Gfild	V	4,204	1977
156	Freudenberg-Wutschdorf-Etsdorf	V	1,621	1965
157	Friedewald und Moritzburger Teichgebiet	V	5,565	1977
158	Furth	V	1,629	1976
159	Gambachtal und Reithenauer Bachtal	V	2,000	1986
160	Gamengrund	V	2,390	1965
161	Gebiet um Bad Wilsnack	V	2,700	1964
162	Gebiet um die Wies	V	3,013	1971
163	Geichburg, Gugel und Wurgauer Tal	V	1,770	1953
164	Gelandestr. langs d. Bundesautobahn Berlin-Munchen	V	1,500	1954

Map† ref.	National/international designations Name of area	IUCN management category	Area (ha)	Year notified
165	Gelandestreifen langs der B85	V	1,000	1970
166	Geraer Stadtwald	V	1,575	1972
167	Glonntal	V	1,273	1974
168	Gotzer Berge	V	2,325	1966
169	Grabentour	V	2,864	1968
170	Grosser See bei Furstenwerder	V	1,200	1962
171	Grosser und Kleiner Gleichberg	V	1,988	1939
172	Grosssteinberg-Ammelshain	V	2,440	1963
173	Grunau-Grunheider Wald-und Seengebiet	V	21,700	1965
174	Grunten und Wertacher Hornle	V	7,650	1972
175	Gubener Fliesstaler	V	3,200	1968
176	Gulitzer Endmorane und Kummerower See	V	9,000	1962
177	Haffkuste	V	12,500	1962
178	Hainleite	V	5,976	1970
179	Hakel	V	1,425	1939
180	Harbke-Allertal	V	22,770	1975
181	Hardtlandschaft und Eberfinger Drumlinfelder	V	5,814	1985
182	Harz	V	154,700	1960
183	Hauptsmoorwald #2	V	2,350	1952
184	Hausener Tal	V	1,240	1985
185	Havelquellseen Kratzeburg	V	2,600	1962
186	Hciligcnstadter Stadtwald	V	3,025	1960
187	Helmestausee	V	1,717	1970
188	Herzogenaurach	V	1,462	1986
189	Hesselberg	V	1,460	1985
190	Hiddensee	V	1,860	1955
191	Hienheimer Forst	V	3,796	1970
192	Hildburghauser Wald	V	5,250	1978
193	Hirschbachtal	V	1,638	1971
194	Hirschbachtal mit Schwarzem Brand u. Lehenbachtal	V	1,946	1970
195	Hirschberg, Kerschlager Forst	V	1,488	1970
196	Hofoldinger und Hohenkirchner Forst	V	4,955	1971
197	Hogenbachtal	V	2,282	1970
198	Hohburger Berge	V	2,000	1963
199	Hohes Holz-Saures Holz mit ostlichem Vorland	V	7,240	1964
200	Illerdurchbruch	V	1,517	1976
201	Ilmtal	V	19,850	1960
202	Innerer Bayerischer Wald #1	V	32,298	1967
203	Innerer Bayerischer Wald #2	V	22,466	1967
204	Innerer Bayerischcr Wald #3	V	4,100	1967
205	Inntal	V	6,725	
206	Insel Usedom	V	37,500	1966
207	Inselsee und Heidberg	V	1,300	1964
208	Isarauen	V	1,547	1964
209	Isartal	V	1,840	1969
210	Isartal und -auen	V	2,925	
211	Jessener Berge	V	1,025	1968
212	Kahl a. M. und Alzenau	V	2,580	1978
213	Kleinseenplatte Neustrelitz	V	12,000	1962
214	Klocksiner Seenkette	V	20,000	1962
215	Knappensee	V	1,100	1968
216	Koferinger und Vils-Tal mit Hirschwald #2	V	8,736	1965
217	Kohrener Land	V	17,000	1959
218	Konigshainer Berge	V	4,855	1974
219	Korbaer Teich und Lebusaer Waldgebiet	V	2,258	1968
220	Kothener See	V	1,790	1966
221	Krakower Seenlandschaft	V	2,350	1955

Map[†] ref.	National/international designations Name of area	IUCN management category	Area (ha)	Year notified
222	Kreuzberg und Semberg	V	1,332	1954
223	Kreuzlinger Forst mit Pentenrieder Schlag #1	V	2,293	1985
224	Kreuzlinger Forst mit Pentenrieder Schlag #2	V	2,293	1985
225	Kuhberg-Steinicht	V	1,377	1968
226	Kuhlung	V	14,000	1966
227	Kyffhauser	V	7,722	1941
228	Kyritzer Seenkette	V	1,600	1958
229	Landschaftsstreifen beiderseits	V	1,550	1956
230	Landschaftsteile um Rothenburg	V	10,690	1955
231	Lattengebirge	V	2,870	
232	Lausitzer Grenzwall zwischen usw	V	14,235	1968
233	Lauta-Hoyerswerda-Wittichenau	V	2,920	1968
234	Lauterachtal #1	V	5,215	1962
235	Lechtal	V	2,386	
236	Lehniner Wald- und Seengebiet	V	2,525	1966
237	Leinleitertal mit Nebentalern	V	1,254	1955
238	Leipziger Auewald	V	5,700	1959
239	Leitzachtal	V	3,304	1955
240	Leuchtenberg-Luhetal	V	1,743	1965
241	Lewitz	V	12,000	1959
242	Lindenthaler Forst	V	4,070	1975
243	Lindhorst-Ramstedter Forst	V	5,996	1964
244	Linkselbische Taler usw	V	2,355	1974
245	Ludwigsluster Schlosspark usw	V	1,500	1955
246	Lychen-Boitzenburg	V	7,500	1962
247	Madlitz-Falenhagener Seengebiet	V	1,030	1965
248	Mainhohe	V	1,042	1968
249	Malchiner Becken	V	6,000	1962
250	Markische Schweiz	V	3,800	1957
251	Merzdorf-Hirschfelder Waldhohen	V	2,060	1968
252	Mittelelbe	V	48,200	1957
253	Mittelheide	V	2,500	1969
254	Mittlere Frankenalb nordlich Neumarkt	V	3,598	1964
255	Mittlere Mulde	V	9,700	1963
256	Mittlerer Strelasund	V	2,300	1966
257	Mittleres Saaletal	V	19,150	1972
258	Mittleres Warnowtal	V	8,500	1964
259	Mittleres Zschopautal	V	1,487	1968
260	Mockern-Magdeburgerforth	V	29,140	1975
261	Muhldorfer Hart	V	1,100	1979
262	Muhlhauser Stadtwald	V	3,496	1970
263	Muldental-Chemnitzal	V	11,471	1968
264	Muritz-Seen-Park	V	30,000	1962
265	Naabtal zwischen Perschen und Wolsendorf	V	1,364	1962
266	Naabtal zwischen Wernberg und Pfreimd	V	1,298	1962
267	Nauen-Brieselang	V	3,225	1966
268	Naunhof-Brandiser Forst	V	2,750	1963
269	Neisseaue im Kreis Forst	V	1,330	1968
270	Neuendorfer See	V	1,600	1968
271	Neuruppin-Rheinsberg usw	V	80,200	1966
272	Noitzscher-und Prellheide	V	1,500	1963
273	Nordlicher Riesrand	V	8,000	1973
274	Nordliches Harzvorland	V	13,506	1961
275	Ober-Uecker-See	V	5,400	1962
276	Obere Saale	V	21,240	1965
277	Oberer Bayerischer Wald	V	10,214	1969
278[†]	Oberes Alztal	V	1,065	1956

Map[†] ref.	*National/international designations* Name of area	IUCN management category	Area (ha)	Year notified
279	Oberes Vogtland	V	17,100	1968
280	Oberes Westerzgebirge	V	17,015	1981
281	Oberes Zschopautal	V	8,207	1968
282	Oberlausitzer Bergland	V	30,730	1963
283	Oberpfalzer Wald #1	V	2,700	1972
284	Oberpfalzer Wald #2	V	16,250	1972
285	Osterseen	V	1,266	1955
286	Osterzgebirge	V	55,025	1968
287	Ostmarkstrasse-nordlicher Teil #1	V	2,000	1967
288	Ostrand der Arendseer Hochflache	V	7,210	1964
289	Ostrugen	V	47,500	1966
290	Parthenaue-Machern	V	1,300	1963
291	Peitzer Teichlandschaft mit Hammergraben	V	2,040	1968
292	Perlacher und Grunwalder Forst	V	3,400	1970
293	Petersberg	V	1,730	1961
294	Pfreimdtal	V	2,956	1962
295	Pfreimdtal-Goldbachtal-Michlbachtal	V	4,123	1965
296	Pfuhler-, Finninger- und Bauern-Ried	V	2,072	1961
297	Plauer See	V	3,500	1957
298	Plothener Teichgebiet	V	1,896	1961
299	Potsdamer Havelseengebiet	V	16,250	1966
300	Pressnitztal	V	2,300	1984
301	Rabensteiner Wald-Pfaffenberg	V	1,280	1962
302	Rambower und Rudower See	V	1,500	1960
303	Rathenower Wald-und Seengebiet	V	17,325	1966
304	Regental	V	2,886	1986
305	Rennsteigstreifen	V	3,900	1940
306	Rinne-Rotenbachtal	V	6,976	1970
307	Rippachtal	V	2,880	1968
308	Roderaue	V	1,720	1960
309	Rotehofbachtal	V	2,444	1964
310	Rotwand	V	4,412	1987
311	Saale	V	28,550	1961
312	Saaletal #2	V	2,534	1982
313	Sachsische Schweiz	V	36,810	1956
314	Saidenbachtalsperre	V	4,490	1962
315	Salzachtal	V	1,035	1977
316	Salzwedel-Diesdorf	V	13,310	1975
317	Schaalsee und Heckenlandschaft Techin	V	2,500	1958
318	Schambachtal	V	1,436	1961
319	Scharmutzelsee-Storkower usw	V	10,600	1965
320	Schellenberg bei Waldkirch	V	1,002	1965
321	Schlaubetal	V	6,490	1965
322	Schleibheimer Forst, Scholbpark	V	1,578	1970
323	Schliersee	V	1,544	1955
324	Schwarzach- und Auerbachtal	V	6,100	1962
325	Schwarzachdurchbruch und Aschabergland #2	V	8,100	1972
326	Schwarzachtal mit Nebentalern	V	3,597	1970
327	Schwarze Laber #2	V	3,554	1962
328	Schwarzholzl mit Wurmkanal und Baggersee	V	1,135	1964
329	Schweriner Seenlandschaft	V	4,300	1938
330	Schwielochsee	V	4,440	1965
331	Seendreieck bei Furstensee	V	3,200	1962
332	Seengebiet Warin-Neukloster	V	7,500	1938
333	Seenkette bei Comthurey	V	1,200	1962
334	Sempt- und Schwillachtal	V	1,550	1986
335	Sewekow	V	2,850	1966

Map[†] ref.	National/international designations Name of area	IUCN management category	Area (ha)	Year notified
336	Simssee	V	2,253	1963
337	Spitzingsee	V	1,632	1955
338	Spree-und Teichgebiet sudlich Uhyst	V	1,210	1968
339	Spreeniederung	V	1,850	1974
340	Spreewald	V	28,700	1968
341	Sprottetal	V	1,100	1984
342	Stadtwald Berlin	V	7,548	1972
343	Staffelsee	V	2,545	1955
344	Starnberger See und westliche Uferlandschaft	V	9,421	1987
345	Starnberger See-Ost	V	3,200	1979
346	Staubeckenlandschaft Brasinchen-Spremberg	V	2,925	1968
347	Steigerwald	V	1,188	1970
348	Steinachtal mit Nebentalern #2	V	1,492	1984
349	Steinsee-Brucker Moos	V	2,550	1987
350	Steinwald	V	8,500	1974
351	Stepenitztal	V	1,600	1958
352	Strausberger und Blumenthaler	V	6,120	1965
353	Striegistaler	V	4,233	1968
354	Sudlich von Zwickau	V	6,200	1968
355	Sudlicher Dromling	V	2,556	1967
356	Sulzberg-Schneeberg	V	1,091	1965
357	Susser See	V	3,820	1954
358	Sylvensteinsee bei Fall	V	5,000	1983
359	Tal der Frankischen Rezat mit Seitentalern #2	V	2,244	1967
360	Tal der Wassernach #1	V	1,166	1966
361	Tal der Wilden Weisseritz	V	1,415	1960
362	Talsperre Kriebstein	V	1,162	1968
363	Talsperre Pirk	V	1,432	1940
364	Talsperre Pohl	V	2,300	1962
365	Talsperre Quitzdorf und Kollmer Hohen	V	4,417	1974
366	Tegernsee mit Sutten und Weissachtal	V	14,532	
367	Templiner Seenkreuz	V	11,500	1962
368	Teupitz-Koriser Seengebiet	V	23,317	1966
369	Thanner Grund	V	2,200	1972
370	Tharandter Wald	V	5,440	1974
371	Thummlitzwald	V	11,500	1984
372	Thumsee	V	1,100	1986
373	Thundorfer Weihergebiet	V	1,165	1962
374	Thuringer Wald	V	151,613	1963
375	Thuringische Rhon	V	61,500	1989
376	Tollense-Becken	V	10,000	1962
377	Torgelower See	V	3,000	1962
378	Triebischtaler	V	1,940	1974
379	Uchte-Tangerquellen	V	6,681	1975
380	Untere Havel	V	21,940	1967
381	Untere Isar	V	3,336	1973
382	Unteres Naabtal	V	4,800	1962
383	Veldensteiner Forst	V	4,708	1966
384	Volkacher Mainschleif	V	1,132	1969
385	Volkacher Mainschleife #1	V	3,235	1969
386	Vorderer Bayerischer Wald #1	V	33,140	1966
387	Vorderer Bayerischer Wald #2	V	19,611	1964
388	Waginger-und Tachinger See	V	2,349	1972
389	Walchensee	V	1,640	1955
390	Wald- und Berglandschaft um Cham	V	34,214	1967
391	Wald- und Restseengebiet Dobern	V	1,850	1968
392	Wald-u.Seengeb.z.Schwielochsee, Libe.u.Spree	V	3,850	1968

Map[†] ref.	National/international designations Name of area	IUCN management category	Area (ha)	Year notified
393	Walder u. Forste mit Ossinger und Breitenstein	V	4,000	1969
394	Walder um Greiz und Werdau	V	5,525	1961
395	Waldgebiet Huy	V	1,561	1939
396	Waldgebiet bei Crivitz u. Barniner See	V	1,000	1964
397	Waldgebiet des Fallstein	V	1,375	1939
398	Waldmunchen	V	23,050	1970
399	Wallensteingraben	V	2,000	1966
400	Wandlitz-Biesenthal-Prendener Seegebiet	V	5,600	1965
401	Webellinsee-Grimnitzsee	V	3,790	1965
402	Weidatalsperre	V	1,680	1961
403	Weissensee bei Pfronten	V	1,466	1963
404	Weissmain #2	V	2,973	1954
405	Wellheimer Donautrockental	V	2,004	1984
406	Wermsdorfer Forst	V	13,000	1963
407	Westlausitz	V	29,070	1974
408	Westlicher Teil des Landkreises Starnberg	V	16,270	1972
409	Wetterstein mit Vorbergen	V	12,300	1976
410	Wiesen-und Teichgebiet Eulo und Jamno	V	1,440	1968
411	Wiesen-und Teichlandschaft Kolkwitz-Hanchen	V	2,020	1968
412	Wiesent mit Nebentalern	V	1,570	1955
413	Wissinger und Bachhaupter Laber	V	3,638	1961
414	Wolletzseengebiet	V	7,000	1965
415	Wurmtal	V	3,646	1984
416	Zeitzgrund	V	1,291	1958
417	Zichtauer Berge und Klotzer Forst	V	10,800	1964
418	Zittauer Gebirge	V	6,270	1958
419	Zuwachs-Kulzauer Forst	V	5,040	1975
	Nature Parks			
420	Altmuhltal	V	290,800	1969
421	Augburg-Westliche Walder	V	117,500	1974
422	Bayerische Rhon	V	124,000	1967
423	Bayerischer Spessart	V	171,000	1963
424	Bergstrase Odenwald	V	162,850	1960
425	Dummer	V	47,210	1972
426	Fichtelgebirge	V	100,400	1971
427	Franken Wald	V	97,170	1973
428	Frankenhohe	V	110,450	1974
429	Frankische Schweiz-Veldensteiner Forst	V	234,600	1988
430	Hasberge	V	80,400	1974
431	Hessenreuther und Manteler Wald	V	27,000	1975
432	Hoher Vogelsberg	V	38,447	1958
433	Nordeifel	V	175,116	1960
434	Oberpfelzer Wald	V	72,385	1971
435	Pfalzerwald	V	179,850	1959
436	Schonbuch	V	15,564	1974
437	Siebengebirge	V	4,200	1959
438	Solling-Vogler	V	52,750	1966
439	Steigerwald	V	128,000	1971
440	Steinwald	V	23,300	1970

	Biosphere Reserves			
	Bayerischer Wald National Park	IX	13,100	1981
	Berchtesgaden Alps	IX	46,800	1990
	Middle Elbe	IX	43,000	1979

Map[†] ref.	*National/international designations* Name of area	IUCN management category	Area (ha)	Year notified
	Rhön	IX	130,488	1991
	Rügen	IX	22,800	1991
	Schorfheide-Chorin	IX	125,891	1990
	Spreewald	IX	47,600	1991
	Vessertal-Thuringen Forest	IX	12,670	1979
	Waddensea of Schleswig-Holstein	IX	285,000	1990
	Ramsar Wetlands			
	Ammersee	R	6,517	1976
	Berga-Kelbra Storage Lake	R	1,360	1978
	Bodensee	R	1,077	1976
	a) Wollmatingen reed-bed with north-eastern part of Ermatingen Basin			
	b) Giehren marsh with Bay of Hegne on the Gnadensee			
	c) Mindelsee near Radolfzell			
	Chiemsee	R	8,660	1976
	Diepholzer Lowland Marsh and Peat Bogs	R	15,060	1976
	Dümmersee	R	3,600	1976
	Elbe water-meadows between			
	Schnackenburg and Lauenburg	R	7,560	1976
	Lower Elbe, Barnkrug-Otterndorf	R	11,760	1976
	Galenbecker See	R	1,015	1978
	Water-meadows and peat-bogs of Donau	R	8,000	1976
	Ismaning Reservoir and fish-ponds	R	900	1976
	Lower Havel River and Gülper See	R	5,792	1978
	Lower Inn between Haiming and Neuhaus	R	1,955	1976
	Krakower Obersee	R	870	1978
	Lech-Donau Winkel	R	230	1976
	a) Feldheim Reservoir on the Lech			
	b) Bertoldsheim Reservoir on the Donau			
	Müritz See (eastern shore)	R	4,830	1978
	Oder Valley near Schwedt	R	5,400	1978
	Ostfriesisches Wattenmeer and Dollart	R	121,620	1976
	Peitz Ponds	R	1,060	1978
	Rieselfelder Münster	R	233	1983
	Rhine between Eltville and Bingen	R	475	1976
	Rügen/Hiddensee and eastern part of Zingst Peninsula	R	25,800	1978
	Starnberger See	R	5,720	1976
	Steinhuder Meer	R	5,730	1976
	Unterer Niederrhein	R	25,000	1983
	Nationalpark Hamburgisches Wattenmeer	R	1,170	1991
	Wattenmeer, Elbe-Weser-Dreieck	R	38,460	1976
	Wattenmeer, Jadebusen and Western Weser Mouth	R	49,490	1976
	Weserstaustufe Schlüsselburg	R	1,550	1983

[†]Locations of most protected areas are shown on the accompanying maps.

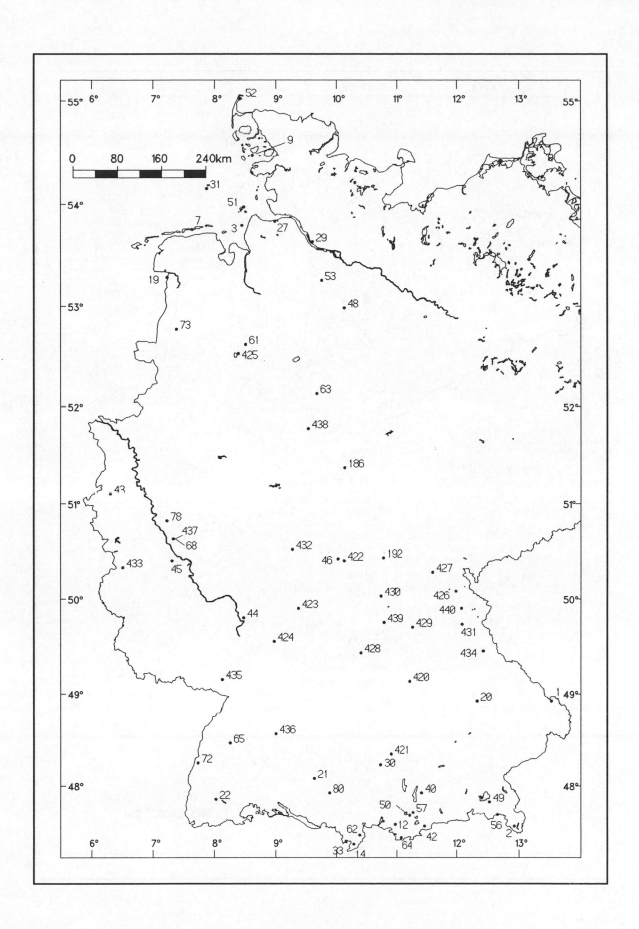

Protected Areas of Germany

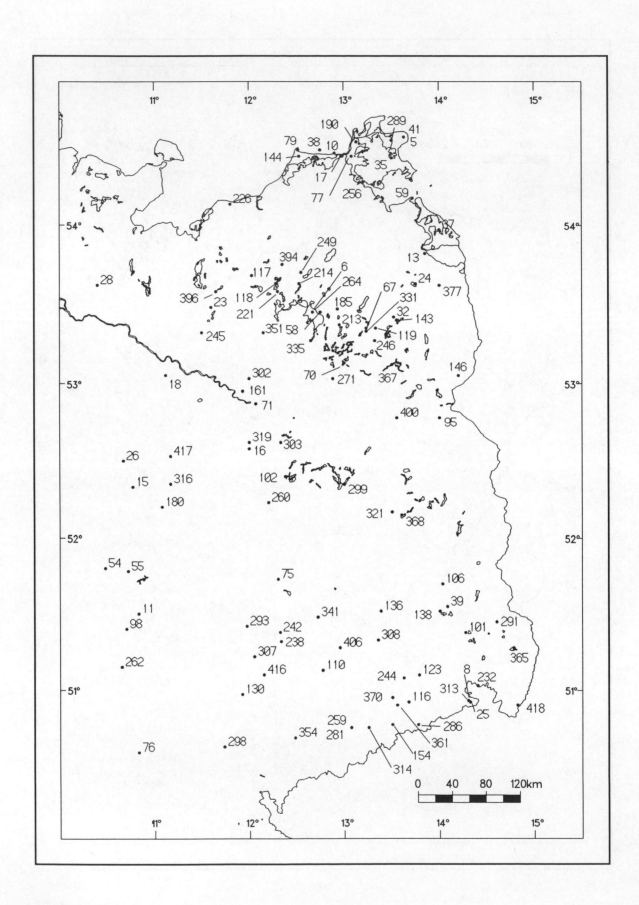

Protected Areas of Germany

GREECE

Area 131,990 sq. km (islands account for 25,042 sq. km)

Population 10,047,000 (1990)
Natural increase: 0.15% per annum

Economic Indicators
GDP: US$ 4,722 (1987)
GNP: US$ 4,350 (1987)

Policy and Legislation   Greece gained its independence from the Ottoman Empire of Turkey in 1821-29. The Greek Republic is at present governed according to the Constitution passed in 1975. Article 24 of the Constitution requires the state to protect the natural and cultural environment and Articles 24 and 117 refer particularly to the protection of forests and forest lands. Article 105 of the Constitution confirms the special status of Monastic Republic of Mount Athos, an autonomous form of government composed of 20 monasteries and their land (Mount Athos is listed under the World Heritage Convention).

Ancient Greece was the cradle of one of the great ancient civilisations of the Mediterranean and has over the millennia been settled by Phoenicians, Carthaginians and Romans. A detailed understanding of the environment was well known 5,000 years ago during the classic Greek period. Between 370-285BC Theophrastus of Erosos was the first great botanical writer of classical antiquity and is regarded as the intellectual "grandfather" of modern botany, having studied amongst others with Plato and Aristotle. At that time he became the chief of the Lyceum in Athens and of its gardens. His 200 credited works indicate a deep knowledge of botany, plant ecology and the environment.

One of the first pieces of protected areas legislation enacted in this century was the Forest Code (Law No. 4173/1929) of 1929 which called for special measures to be taken in the management of certain areas to be known as protected forests in order not only to protect their soils and other natural and man-made features and works, but also to preserve wildlife and amenity values for the benefit of people (Kassioumis, 1990). Another important piece of early legislation giving protected status to certain areas was the Antiquities Law No. 5321, 1932 which is still valid; this protects archaeological features and an area of 500m radius around them. All antiquities are automatically protected by law and do not need special designation. This legislation was extended in 1950 (Law No. 1469/1950) to modern monuments and landscapes of natural beauty, the latter now forming a separate category of protected area which are established by ministerial decision, published in the Official *Gazette* (Kassioumis, 1987a).

Referring particularly to nature conservation, Law No. 856, 1937 must be mentioned, proposing the creation of five national parks, each not less than 3,000ha in area with a buffer zone of 4,000ha. The areas designated according to this law as national parks are Olympus, Parnassus, Parnes, Ainos and Samaria) (Ministry of Agriculture, *in litt.*, 1991).

National parks, aesthetic forests and protected natural monuments can now be established by the Forest Service under Law Decree No. 996/1971 which is an amendment of Law Decrees Nos 856/1937 and 86/1969 (see Annex). These are part of the Forestry Code which deals with national parks and other protected areas as well as hunting legislation and faunal, floral and habitat protection. Each of the above new protected areas is declared by Presidential Decree, having been proposed by the Council of Ministers on the advice of the Technical Council on Forests. The same Presidential Decree also fixes the size and boundaries of such areas. Changes to the status of protected areas or to boundaries are declared in the same way (*Government Gazette of Greece*, Section A, No. 192/6.10.71). The Forest Service, which is also the authority controlling hunting, can also establish protected areas, under the Forest Code, as game refuges, game breeding stations and controlled hunting areas these are designated for game management under Law No. 177/1975 (Article 254) and Presidential Decree No. 453/1977 (Kassioumis, 1987a).

Law No. 360 of 18 June 1976 on Physical Regional Planning and the Environment issued by the Ministry of Coordination deals with regional planning and the environment, including marine areas: Article 1.5 defines the environment as embracing land, sea, flora, fauna and natural resources. It also sets out the institutional and procedural mechanisms for the preparation of national and regional plans as well as specialised plans covering particular sectors or activities, and specifies that these are to be integrated with economic and social development programmes (Gryn-Ambroes, 1980). It also controls the use of certain defined zones and allows their protection, restoration and general improvement of the environment.

Protective status is extended to wetlands by Public Law No. 998/1979 issued to cover forest and forest land protection and under Decree No. 67/1981 which covers protection to fauna and flora, whilst wetland game reserves can be established by the Ministry of Agriculture under the hunting legislation. There are no special laws on marine protected areas but decisions of the National Council for Planning and the Environment (Nos. 2659(2)/1980 and 11 and 12/1981) proposed a protected status for a sea turtle nesting area in Zakynthos and a marine park in the Northern Sporades.

The establishment of a protected area by a local authority is exceptional. Protection measures have, however, been issued, including hunting prohibition and nature protection, in an order by the Prefect of Evros, of 8 December 1978, in the Evros Delta. This was possible under application of Articles 251 and 267 of the Forestry Code (Gryn-Ambroes, 1980).

A new institutional law on the environment, designed to eliminate deficiencies in previous legislation, was submitted to parliament by the cabinet as a framework bill on 4 June 1986, to be implemented in detail by a series of presidential decrees (European Environmental Review, 1986). This was ratified by parliament (Law No. 1650/1986), but requires further clarification by decrees, and until this stage is passed the existing laws will remain valid (Kassioumis, 1987a). The new law includes a special section covering the protection of natural resources and landscapes. It also introduces certain changes in existing laws, especially Law No. 1469/1950 concerning landscapes of natural beauty and Law No. 996/1971 Article 78 on national parks, aesthetic forests and protected natural monuments; the main changes are that five new categories of protected area are recommended: absolutely protected natural area; protected natural area; national park; protected natural monument; protected landscape and element of landscape; and area for ecodevelopment (Kassioumis, 1987a). Three ministries, Agriculture, Environment Planning and Public Works, and Manufacture Energy and Technology, are responsible for initiating the establishment of new reserves in these categories. Individual areas will be designated by special presidential decrees that will also specify which authorities are to be responsible for administration of each area and the necessary means and measures for their protection (Ministry of Agriculture, *in litt.*, 1991).

Legislation regarding the management of each national park is separate from its establishing legislation and is via a statute, issued by decision of the Minister of Agriculture and published in the *Government Gazette*. This regulates the organisation, operation and administration of each national park (*Government Gazette of Greece*, Section A, No. 192/6.10.1970). National park administration has been the responsibility of the Forest Service since 1937 (Law No. 856/1937). Under Law No. 996/1971, aesthetic forests and protected natural monuments are to be administered by the Forest Service.

Environmental legislation is considered to be advanced but is poorly understood and barely implemented (IUCN, 1987). Current legislation has several negative features, including lack of public involvement, insufficient sanctions and administrative difficulties. Two decisions of the National Council for Planning and the Environment (No. 2659/1980 and Nos. 11 and 12/1981) list 23 sites with recognised status for becoming protected areas. These decisions do not provide protective legislation enforcements; some of these sites have, however, been covered by other relevant legislation for protected areas (e.g. L.D. 996/1971 or hunting legislation) and/or are also covered

under international conventions (e.g. Ramsar) (Kassioumis, 1987a).

International Activities The Convention Concerning the Protection of the World Cultural and Natural Heritage (World Heritage Convention) was ratified on 17 July 1981: two sites have been inscribed as mixed natural/cultural sites, their importance arising from the man/nature interaction rather than from natural features alone. The Convention on Wetlands of International Importance especially as Waterfowl Habitat (Ramsar Convention) was acceded to on 21 August 1975 with 11 sites listed (1991). Two sites have been designated as biosphere reserves under the Unesco Man and the Biosphere Programme.

The Protocol Concerning Mediterranean Specially Protected Areas of 1982 (Barcelona Convention) was ratified on 25 February 1987 (Cutrera, 1991): eight Mediterranean specially protected areas have been designated. As a member state of the European Community, Greece is a party to the 1979 Wild Birds Directive, under which 16 EC special protection areas have been designated (Grimmett and Jones, 1989). It is also a member of the Council of Europe: 16 sites have been designated as biogenetic reserves and one site has been awarded the Council of Europe, European Diploma. Greece ratified the Convention on the Conservation of European Wildlife and Natural Habitats (Bern Convention) on 1 October 1983.

There are two transboundary parks in Greece: Mikra Prespa National Park and Galicia National Park in Yugoslavia, and Evros Delta Reserve and the Gala Golu Proposed Reserve in Turkey. There is little or no interaction or cooperation between the countries in either of these areas.

Administration and Management Two ministries have responsibility for nature conservation. Originally, it was administered solely by the Ministry of Agriculture further controlled by regional forestry departments and locally by forest inspectorates and game wardens. In 1978 the National Council for Regional Planning and the Environment was established, governed by law 360/1976, but although not abolished, most of its responsibilities were taken over by the Ministry of Regional Planning, Housing and the Environment, itself created in 1980 (later renamed the Ministry of Environment, Regional Planning and Public Works).

Overall environmental activity is thus now coordinated by the Ministry of Environment, Physical Planning and Public Works (IUCN, 1987). National parks, aesthetic forests and protected natural monuments are administered by the Forest Service of the Ministry of Agriculture. The actual protection and management of these areas is the responsibility of district forest offices, supervised, at a national level, by the Section of Parks and Aesthetic Forests. This section was renamed and exists today as the Section for the Forest Environment National Parks and Forest Recreation. It is one of five sections reporting to the Directorate for Aesthetic Forests, Parks and Game Management, which is one of seven under the Forest Department of the Ministry of Agriculture. The National Parks Section is headed by a forester with a staff of one other forester, one forest technologist and two support staff (Ministry of Agriculture, *in litt.*, 1991). In addition to its management function, the National Parks Section is responsible for applying criteria for the selection as well as management of national parks. It is also responsible for conservation work carried out by the district forest officers (Duffey, 1982). Of the ten national parks, only one has staff and active management, but work is being carried out to produce general management plans for all ten national parks and towards establishing natural history museums in each of them. Recreation is not considered to be a main objective, unlike education, landscape protection and scientific research (Wade, 1987).

The Game Management Section of the Directorate General of Forests and Forest Environment controls game reserves and controlled hunting areas. Responsibility for administration and management of historic places lies with the Ministry of Culture, but responsibility for landscapes of natural beauty was transferred from that Ministry in 1984 to the Ministry of Environment, Planning and Public Works (Kassioumis, 1987a). Wetland conservation is the initiative of the Ministry of Planning, Housing and the Environment, which is now in the process of establishing boundaries based on the results of study projects which have been completed for each wetland (ICBP, 1985). All registered wetlands are administered in collaboration with respective authorities and services responsible for particular sectors or activities. For example, Mikra Prespa National Park is administered by the district Directorate of Forests based at Florina. In several cases the local authorities are responsible for fishing and hunting regulations. The Forest District Office responsible for each national park appoints one forester and one forest technologist per park. Since 1983, most parks have had two permanent wardens and other (temporary) game staff.

The EC is supporting the establishment of a biological station on Allonisos, part of the Sporades group, specifically to study monk seal. The Greek organisation Elliniki Eteria (EE) has established a biological research station in Prespa National Park to study the ecology of the area, which supports the richest community of fish-eating birds in Europe (Hoffmann, 1988).

One of the most important non-governmental organisations concerned with protected areas and nature conservation is the Hellenic Society for the Protection of Nature, founded in 1951, which focuses on supporting the establishment of protected areas and nature conservation. Other societies include the Hellenic Ornithological Society, the Hellenic Botanical Society, the Hellenic Zoological Society, the Union of Greek Ecologists and the Friends of the Forest Association. The Society for the Protection of Nature and Ecodevelopment was formed to operate regional nature conservation schemes; the Greek Society is primarily involved with protecting the country's cultural and natural heritage; the Panhellenic Centre of Environmental Studies, founded in 1979, is concerned with promoting policies to ensure ecological balance and with research and education. On 27 June 1991 the first meeting of the Advisory Committee of the Greek Wetland Centre was held at the Goulandris Museum in Athens (funded by the EC and contributions by WWF); it is intended that the Centre will advise the government on conservation matters, and particularly wetland matters such as define the boundaries of identified wetlands (for the Wetlands Action Plan for Greece) listed in the 1989 Thessaloniki wetlands seminar (1991).

Protected areas management faces various problems. Only one of the ten national parks has active management and full-time staffing; even Mount Olympos National Park has no full-time staff. Enforcement of the prohibition of activities in the core areas of national parks is therefore limited. Although all national parks contain areas of considerable natural beauty, at least two (Sounion and Mount Parnassos, near Athens) have many problems and obstacles weakening their value as national parks; Parnes and Prespa also suffer from tourism pressure and man-made landscapes, lowering the quality and value of their natural areas. Of the eleven wetlands listed under the Ramsar Convention, only one is so far subject to legal and administrative protection as a result of becoming a national park in 1974 (Cutrera, 1987). Local opposition has caused difficulties in protecting some areas fully and there is a lack of education to raise public awareness. There are also problems with organisational and institutional aspects of management and a rather limited political commitment to conservation (Kassioumis, 1987b). The National Parks Service is aware of many of these management problems but is hampered by lack of resources (Duffey, 1982; Ministry of Agriculture, *in litt.*, 1991).

Systems Reviews Despite its relatively small surface area compared with other European countries, Greece has one of the longest coastlines in Europe, of about 15,000km, about half of which is on the mainland and the rest on islands, the whole coastline being extremely indented. The mainland shares borders with Albania, Yugoslavia, Bulgaria and Turkey. Much of Greece is mountainous, the ancient hard, crystalline rocks of the east and north-east having been shaped by large-scale earth movements into a rugged topography while in the rest of the country there are much younger rocks which have been heavily folded. The highest point is the legendary Mount Olympus, 2,917m high, which is part of a national park. Limestone rocks dominate the whole landscape resulting in steep slopes, ravines and caves (Duffy, 1982). Wetlands are widespread and 11 of the larger ones are now Ramsar sites; however, only one is a national park and many medium-sized and small sites are unprotected. Reduction in water level is a serious threat to most sites (Anon., 1990).

Greece has one of the richest floras in Europe with about 5,500 different species and subspecies of which 20% are endemic (Davis, *et al.*, 1986). Of these, Presidential Decree N0. 67 of 1981 lists some 800 species as protected (Cutrera, 1987). Over 1,000 of these are endemic to the country with endemism being concentrated in the mountains and islands of the Ionian and Aegean seas; Crete alone has 150 endemic species (Grimmett and Jones, 1989). All of Greece was once well wooded but forest clearance, fire and centuries of overgrazing by sheep and goats has created vast areas of scrub and semi-desert (Duffey, 1982). Maquis and garrigue cover 25% of the country and phrygana 15% (Council of Europe, 1987). The country is not particularly deforested compared with other EC states; the total remaining forested area is 2.5 million ha, 19% of the country's area. Of the non-managed forest, 35,000ha are legally protected against exploitation. The only remaining virgin forest is limited to three sites: Barougas, Paranesti and Trahoni-Xanthi) of small area but much larger areas of ancient seminatural forest remain. In addition, 95% of the total forest area is composed of native tree species (Heiss, 1987). Over half the forest area is for timber production and over two-thirds of the forested area is coniferous (Grimmett and Jones, 1989). On some of the highest peaks there is an alpine plant community above the treeline, which occurs at about 2,500m (Duffy, 1982).

The fauna is also remarkably rich and includes numerous species of large birds of prey which are scarce in Europe. Several seriously endangered raptors occur near the Evros River in north-eastern Greece and will benefit from the recently-established Dadia-Lefkimi-Soufli Nature Reserve. Wolf and jackal still survive in reasonable numbers. There is also a small population of brown bear *Ursus arctos* which is threatened by poaching and disturbance. Crete is the only place in Europe where the Bezoar goat, or agrimi *Capra aegagrus cretica*, has survived. The numerous estuaries and lakes provide wintering grounds for large numbers of migrant birds and also support a number of residents species. In the early 1960s the 13 largest wetlands in Greece harboured up to 1.5 million wintering waterfowl, 25-50% of those wintering in the Mediterranean and Black Sea area. Since then, three of these have been drained completely and five others greatly reduced in area, lowering the total carrying capacity by over half. Further drainage plans are under consideration (Hoffmann, 1988). Greece is also one of the remaining retreats of monk seal *Monachus monachus* and there is an important breeding colony of loggerhead turtle *Caretta caretta* on Zakynthos island. Seven marine reserves have been suggested, but only one, Lindos Marine Park, is has been considered seriously (Baccar, 1977).

Greece now has ten national parks covering 68,742ha, the oldest of which, Mount Olympos and Parnassos, were set up in 1938, the rest being established in the 1960s and early 1970s (Cutrera, 1987). There are also 19 aesthetic forests established from 1973 to 1980, covering 33,107ha. An area of 16,625ha is protected around natural monuments and historic trees, although the vast majority of this (15,000ha) comprises one area. Only one marine park, covering 100,000ha, has been established, in 1986. The National Council for Regional Planning and the Environment created 20 protected areas in March 1980 and February 1981. This figure included 13 wetland sites and the protected forests of Dadia and Paranesti. Greece has a vast wealth of archaeological sites which come under the jurisdiction of the Ministry of Culture. Existing laws are aimed primarily at protecting the physical integrity of the antiquities themselves and boundaries are too narrowly defined and do not protect the surroundings sufficiently.

The Forest Service has had the responsibility for protecting wild flora and fauna for over 100 years (Kassioumis, 1987b). Under the hunting legislation, within the Forest Code, more than 500 areas have been designated as game refuges, where hunting is prohibited, covering about 800,000ha in habitats ranging from estuaries to forests and mountain peaks. Twenty-one game breeding stations, covering about 13,000ha, have also been set up and eight controlled hunting areas cover about 120,000ha (Kassioumis, 1990).

There is considerable pressure on forested lands from agriculture, while forest fires also destroy between 25,000ha and 120,000ha each year (Cutrera, 1987). A new law, passed in 1988, referring to grazing activities, has caused much concern as it permits the clearance of large areas of forest for grazing purposes. Some sources suggest that up to 61% of forest is open to destruction as a direct result of this law, or have suggested that the total forest cover may drop from 19% to 13% of the country's area (Anon., 1989; WWF, 1988).

Information dated 1985 suggested that the major threats to protected areas include road construction, tourism development and forest exploitation. It has been estimated that over 70% of the population, 90% of tourism and recreation and over 80% of industrial activities are concentrated in a narrow coastal strip. Urbanisation came late, occurring most rapidly between 1951 and 1981, but was not accompanied by sufficient infrastructure to alleviate the environmental problems it caused. Overgrazing by sheep and goats is a problem in most forested areas. Wetlands are threatened by drainage, tourism and uncontrolled hunting. There are over 300,000 active Greek hunters *plus* many Yugoslavians and Italians who hunt in Greece (Cutrera, 1987).

Other Relevant Information   Greece earns the largest part of its foreign exchange from tourism, with about seven million visitors per year (Cutrera, 1987). Only a small proportion of the total figure is for ecotourism or visits to protected areas.

Addresses

Ministry of Agriculture and Forestry, National Parks Section, 3-5 Ippokratous Street, ATHENS (Tel: 1 363 7659)

Ministry of Agriculture and Forestry, Department of Forest Research and Education, Terma Alkmanos Ilisia, GR-115 28 ATHENS (Tel: 1 778 4850)

Ministry of Physical Planning, Public Works and the Environment, Directorate of the Environment, Poulion 8, GR-115 23 ATHENS (Tel: 1 646 1189; Tlx: 222088)

Ministry of Energy and Natural Resources, Zalokosta 1, GR-106 71 ATHENS (Tel: 1 360 9320)

Ministry of Environment, Physical Planning and Public Works, Environmental Planning Division, Nature Management Section, Trikalon 36, 115 26 ATHENS

Greek Academy of Sciences (Akademia Athinon), 28 Panepistimiou Street, GR-106 79 ATHENS

Panhellenic Centre of Environmental Studies (PAKOE), 7 Sufliou Street, Ampelokopi, GR-115 27 ATHENS

Friends of the Forest Association, 3 Place Mitropoleos, ATHENS (Tel: 1 322 1337)

Hellenic Society for the Protection of Nature, 24 Nikis Street, GR-105 57 ATHENS (Tel: 1 322 4944)

Society for the Protection of Nature and Ecodevelopment, PO Box 47, GR-642 00 HRYSOUPOLIS

References

Anon. (1980). New Nature Reserves in Greece. *Unasylva* 32(129): 34.

Anon. (1988). Greece: Forests and the Law. Council of Europe. *Naturopa* 88(3): 3

Anon. (1990). Greek wetlands 1990. The other half of the truth. Elliniki Etaria. Unpublished. 6 pp.

Augier, H. (1985). *Protected marine areas. The example of France: appraisal and prospects*. European Committee for the Conservation of Nature and Natural Resources. Council of Europe, Strasbourg.

Baccar, H. (1977). *A survey of existing and potential marine parks and reserves in the Mediterranean region*. IUCN/UNEP.

Cassios, C.A. (1980a). *Greece*. IUCN/CNPPA Meeting 1-8 June 1980 Perth, Scotland. Unpublished manuscript.

Cassios, C.A. (1980b.) National parks and nature reserves in Greece. *Nature and national parks* 67(18): 9-10.

Council of Europe (1987). *Management of Europe's natural heritage*. Strasbourg.

Cutrera, A. (1987). *European environmental yearbook 1987*. DocTer International UK, London. 816 pp.

Davis, S.D., Droop, S.J.M., Gregerson, P., Henson, L., Leon, C.J., Villa-Lobos, J.L., Synge, H. and Zantovska, J. (1986). *Plants in danger: What do we know?* IUCN: Gland, Switzerland and Cambridge, UK.

Duffey, E. (1982). *National parks and reserves of Western Europe*. Macdonald and Company, London. Pp. 262-272.

European Environmental Review (1986). *Greece: Draft environment law* 1(1): 28.

Grimmett, R.F.A. and Jones, T.A. (1989). *Important bird areas in Europe*. International Council for Bird Preservation, Cambridge, UK. Pp. 271-308.

Gryn-Ambroes, P. (1980). *Preliminary annotated list of existing and potential Mediterranean protected areas*. UNEP/IUCN report. UNEP/I.G. 20/INF.5

Heiss, G. (1987). Inventory of natural (virgin) and ancient seminatural woodlands within the Council's member states and Finland. European Committee for the Conservation of Nature and Natural Resources. Unpublished report.

Hoffmann, L. (1988). WWF's new strategy in Greece. *World Wildlife Fund News* 51: 5.

ICBP (1981). *Important bird areas in the European Community*. Report.

ICBP (1982). Biotopes of significance for nature conservation. Site Register XI/94/83.

ICBP (1985). 81 bird species in Council of Europe countries. Draft report to Council of Europe.

ICBP (1985b). National section reports. Unpublished manuscript. Gland and Cambridge, UK.

IUCN (1987). *Directory of wetlands of international importance*. IUCN, Switzerland and Cambridge, UK. Pp. 148-162.

Kassioumis, K. (1987a). Nature conservation in Greece (legislation and administration of parks and reserves). Unpublished manuscript.

Kassioumis, K. (1987b). Conservation of natural heritage – protected areas in Greece. Balkan Scientific Conference, Varna, Bulgaria, 20-23 September 1988.

Kassioumis, K. (1990). Greece. In: Allin, C.W. (Ed.), *International Handbook of National Parks and Nature Reserves*. Greenwood Press, New York, Westport and London. Pp. 157-174.

Malakon, M. (1985). *I. Alyki Kitrous*. I. Fusis March: 10-13, 37.

Saussay, Ch. du and Prieur, M. (1980). *Survey of national legislation relevant to marine and coastal protected areas*. Intergovernmental Meeting on Mediterranean Specially Protected Areas, Athens, 13-18 October, 1980. United Nations Environment Programme UNEP/IG.20/INF.3, restricted distribution. 60 pp.

Stein, J. (1981). The Kentriki Primary Forest in the Rhodope Mountains North Greece. *Nature and national parks* (19)73/74: 10/12.

Wade, J.W. (1987). *Report. An assessment of the organization, staffing and training in the national parks of Greece*. Project 3789. World Wide Fund for Nature.

Waycott, A. (1983). *National parks of Western Europe*. Inklon Publications, Southampton.

Wirth, H. (Ed)(1979). *Nature reserves in Europe*. Edition Leipzig. 331 pp.

WWF. (1988). Greek forests burn for cattle. *WWF News* 51: 1.

ANNEX
Definitions of protected area designations, as legislated, together with authorities responsible for their administration

Title: Law Decree No. 996/1971

Date: 1971

Brief description: Governing the declaration of national parks, aesthetic forests and protected monuments and their protection

Administrative authority: Forest Service of the Ministry of Agriculture. Designation of particular sites is undertaken by the Council of Ministers by recommendation of the Technical Council of Forestry

Designations:

National park A forest area presenting special interest from the viewpoint of conservation of its wild flora and fauna, its geomorphology, its subsoil and atmosphere, its waters and generally its natural surroundings, whose protection seems necessary, as well as the conservation and improvement of its constitution and form and natural beauties, for aesthetic, psychological and healthy recreation and for carrying out all kinds of scientific research (Article 78, Section 1.a). The core area must be no smaller than 1,500ha, except on islands, where it can be smaller, and must be fully protected. The peripheral zone must be at least as large as the core and its exploitation controlled so as to leave the core undisturbed. If complete protection of the core area is possible by other means, a peripheral zone can be omitted (Article 79).

The following activities are prohibited in the core area: private ownership of land; mining, quarrying or removal of minerals; excavation of earthworks which would destroy the natural beauty; placing any noticeboards not approved by the Minister of National Economy; all industrial activity; installation of any building not essential to the protection and operation of the park or scientific research; woodcutting and uprooting plants; grazing; hunting, except of pest species; and fishing in lakes and mountain streams (Article 80, Section 3). The peripheral zone is regulated in the same way as an aesthetic forest (see below).

Aesthetic forest A forest or natural landscape which does not possess all the characteristics of a national park, but has a particular aesthetic, health or touristic significance together with characteristics which demand the protection of their flora, fauna and particular natural beauty (Article 78, Section 2).

Certain activities are permitted in aesthetic forests (and peripheral areas of national parks) to be carried out by the relevant forestry service. They include: increase or reduction of wild flora and fauna by various means; technical preservation of geomorphological features; installing game reserves, fisheries and plant nurseries or forest enclosures to increase species' numbers; the construction of necessary roads and huts for personnel and scientists; installations for camping, tourism and sport; and uprooting plants or capturing animals for scientific purposes with approval of the Minister of National Economy (Article 80). The ownership of aesthetic forests can be public, private or municipal.

Protected natural monument An area not meeting the characteristics of an aesthetic forest but which presents special palaeontological, geomorphological and historical significance (Article 78, Section 3). They cannot be privately-owned (Article 80).

Sources: Cutrera, 1987; Ministry of Agriculture, *in litt.*, 1991

SUMMARY OF PROTECTED AREAS

Map[†] ref.	National/international designations Name of area	IUCN management category	Area (ha)	Year notified
	National Parks			
1	Ainos	II	2,862	1962
2	Mount Oita	II	7,210	1966
3	Mount Olympos	II	3,998	1938
4	Parnassos	II	3,513	1938
5	Parnitha	II	3,812	1961
6	Pindos	II	6,927	1966
7	Prespes	II	19,470	1974

Map[†] ref.	*National/international designations* Name of area	IUCN management category	Area (ha)	Year notified
8	Samaria	V	4,850	1962
9	Sounio	V	3,500	1974
10	Vikos-Aoos	II	12,600	1973
	Game Refuge			
11	Dadia-Lefkimi and Soufli Forest	IV	7,200	1986
	Natural Monument			
12	Petrified Forest of Lesbos Island	III	15,000	1985
	Other Protected Areas (Law 1650)			
13	Zakynthos	VI	3,500	1986
14	Northern Sporades	VI	100,000	1986
	Aesthetic Forests			
15	Kalavrita	V	1,750	1977
16	Kavala	V	2,816	1979
17	Nestos	VI	2,380	1977
18	Ossa	VI	16,900	1977
19	Patras	VI	1,850	1974
20	Skiathos Island	III	3,000	1977
21	Tembi Valley	V	1,762	1974
	Controlled Hunting Areas			
22	Dias Island	IV	1,250	1977
23	Gioura Island (Game Refuge)	IV	1,000	1979
24	Island of Antimilos (Game Breeding)	IV	745	1963
25	Island of Sapienza	IV	880	1977

	Biosphere Reserves			
	Gorge of Samaria National Park	IX	4,840	1981
	Mount Olympus National Park	IX	4,000	1981
	Ramsar Sites			
	Amvrakikos Gulf	R	25,000	1975
	Axios-Aliakmon-Loudias Delta	R	11,000	1975
	Evros Delta	R	10,000	1975
	Kotichi Lagoon	R	3,700	1975
	Lake Kerkini	R	9,000	1975
	Lakes Mikra Prespa and Megali Prespa	R	8,000	1975
	Lake Mitrikou and adjoining Lagoons	R	3,800	1975
	Lake Visthonis and Porto Lagos Lagoon	R	10,000	1975
	Lakes Volvis and Langada	R	2,400	1975
	Mesolonghi Lagoons	R	13,900	1975
	Nestos Delta and Gumburnou Lagoon	R	10,600	1975
	World Heritage Sites			
	Meteora Group of Monasteries	X	375	1988
	Mount Athos	X	n/a	1988

[†]Locations of most protected areas are shown on the accompanying map.

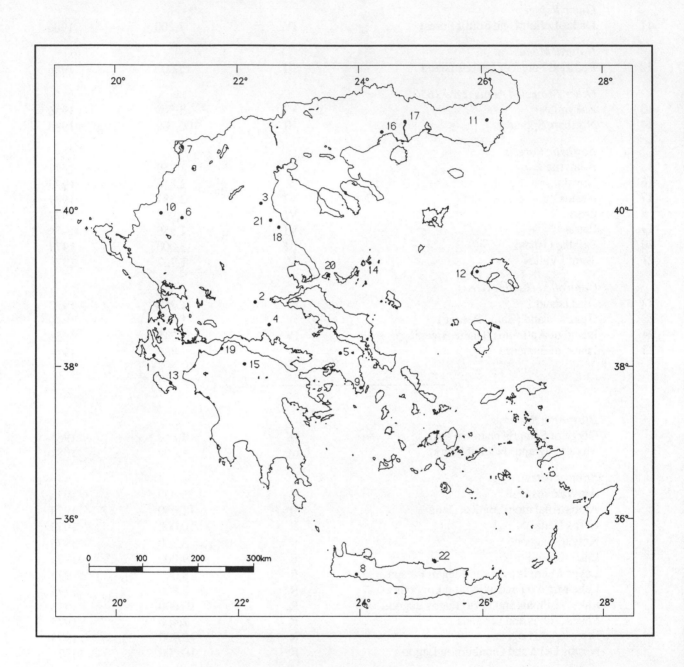

Protected Areas of Greece

HOLY SEE
(VATICAN CITY STATE)

Area 0.44 sq. km

Population 1,000 (1989)(Hunter, 1991)
Natural increase: No information

Economic Indicators
GDP: No information
GNP: No information

Policy and Legislation   On 11 February 1929 the Treaty with Italy recognised the full and independent sovereignty of the Holy See in the City of the Vatican. A revised Concordat between the Italian Republic and the Holy See was subsequently signed in 1984 and came into force on 3 June 1985 (Hunter, 1991). The Vatican City State is governed by a Commission appointed by the Pope, which acts as the government of the Roman Catholic Church. The Pope exercises authority and has absolute legislative, executive and judicial powers. The central administration of the Roman Catholic Church is carried out by a number of permanent committees called Sacred Congregations (Hunter, 1991).

Under the Assisi Declarations of 1986, the Christian declaration on nature states: "many are the causes of the ecological disaster which mankind faces today ... Christians repudiate all ill-considered exploitation of nature which risks destroying it and, in turn, to make man the victim of degradation." The declaration urged ecumenical dialogue on the goals of scientific research and on the environmental consequences of the use of its finding (Anon., 1986).

International Activities   In its diplomatic relations with foreign countries the Holy See is represented by the Secretariat of State. It maintains permanent observers to the United Nations and to Unesco and FAO, although it has not ratified the Convention on the World Cultural and Natural Heritage (World Heritage Convention) nor has it an Unesco Man and Biosphere National Committee.

On 26-29 September 1986 the unique Assisi (Italy) Declaration and Alliance was forged between conservation and five of the world's great religions, in cooperation with and marking the 25th Anniversary of the WWF (World Wide Fund For Nature) (Anon., 1986). By 1990 there were eight faiths in the New Alliance of Conservation and Religion: the Baha'i faith, Buddhism, Christianity, Hinduism, Islam, Jainism, Judaism and the faith of the Sikhs (Anon., 1990b).

Administration and Management   The main body involved in environmental study and research is the Pontifical Academy of Sciences which was revived in 1936 with 70 members (Hunter, 1991). The Roman Catholic Church, through the Pontifical Council of Justice and Peace, in 1990 accepted the WWF offer to be its consultant in programmes concerning nature conservation, effectively appointing WWF as the Pontifical See's Conservation Advisor. The first WWF-Vatican working group met during the summer of 1990 (Anon., 1990a).

Systems Reviews   Located as an enclave within the Republic of Italy, the Holy See is found largely within the urban development of the city of Rome on the Italian peninsula. Extra-territorial rights outside Rome include the land of the Pope's summer villa at Castel Gandolfo (Hunter, 1991). Less than 1% of the total land area of the Holy See is even semi-natural, approximately 99% consists of buildings or other constructions. The only undeveloped area is planted with grass lawns, ornamental shrubs and trees.

Addresses

Scientific Committee, Pontifical Academy of Sciences, The Vatican, Holy See

Conservation Advisor to the Pontifical See, Ethics and Conservation Officer, WWF (World Wide Fund for Nature) International, CH-1196, Gland, Switzerland

References

Anon. (1986). Extracts from the Assisi Declarations. *The New Road, the Bulletin of the WWF Network on Conservation and Religion*. Issue No. 1 Winter 86/87. P. 2

Anon. (1990a). WWF and Catholic Church cooperate to protect nature *The New Road, Bulletin of the WWF Network on Conservation and Religion*. 14: 2

Anon. (1990b). Jains to be eighth faith in new alliance. *The New Road, Bulletin of the WWF Network on Conservation and Religion*. 15: 1

Hunter, B. (Ed.) (1991). *The Statesman's Year Book 1991-92*. The Macmillan Press Ltd, London and Basingstoke, UK.

HUNGARY

Area 93,032 sq. km

Population 10,600,000 (1989 estimate)
Natural increase: -0.2% per annum

Economic Indicators
GNP: US$ 2,240 per capita

Policy and Legislation The first legal measure for environmental management and protection was the Hungarian Forest Act which came into force in 1879 (the territory was at that time part of the Austro-Hungarian Empire). The Forests and Nature Conservation Act (No. IV/1935) was the first comprehensive act on nature conservation, and laid the foundation for the preservation of scientifically valuable areas, wildlife communities, natural features and species. The 1935 Act was subsequently updated after World War II as a consequence of fundamental changes in social and economic conditions and the increasing awareness of nature conservation. The most important of these was an ordinance adopted in Law Decree No. 18/1961 (updated in 1971). The Nature Conservation Act, 1961 made provisions for a national supreme body for the management of nature conservation. This role is currently filled by the Ministry for Environment and Regional Policy (*Környezelvédelmi Minisztérium*). The governmental decree enacted in 1971 enabled the establishment of national parks, the first created at Hortobagy in 1973. The increased need for stronger enforcement and nature conservation control led to the Environmental Act II, on the Protection of Human Environment, which was endorsed by Parliament in 1976. It was the first legislative act to provide comprehensive protection for the whole range of the environment, synthesising all earlier legislation.

Nature conservation legislation was based on Bill No. IV of 1982 and Cabinet Decree No. 8/1982 on Conservation of Nature. These were introduced by the National Authority for Environmental Protection and Nature Conservation and supersede all former acts on nature conservation. The basic objectives included: the assessment of natural assets and the declaration of protected areas; the determination of methods for maintaining areas under protection (balancing nature conservation operations with economic activities); acquiring ownership rights for protected areas, most notably those sites threatened by economic activities, and the protection and management of nature reserves.

Protected areas are designated at the national or local level, according to their degree of importance. Those of national (and in some cases international) importance, declared under the 1982 legislation, are: national parks, landscape protection areas and nature conservation areas party to the Convention on the Conservation of European Wildlife and Natural Habitats (Bern Convention) (see Annex). In addition, caves form a special category and all caves are placed under national protection. Sites of local importance are placed in two categories: county nature protection areas and natural monuments. For certain special biotopes of some threatened species, areas of intensive protection are defined within protected areas. They are only used for scientific research and are closed to the public (caves also receive this special protection) (IUCN, 1989). The category natural monument (*Védett*) is represented by specific formations of nature (individual trees, copses, rocks, and geological sections).

Conservation legislation also provides for *in situ* protection of important fauna and flora resources. The safeguarding of habitats of the most valued protected species is one of the primary objectives for the designation of protected areas. More than 90% of the total number of vascular plant species, and 100% of the protected animal species benefit from *in situ* protected area designation (ECE Finland, 1986). Legislation states that it is forbidden to destroy, damage or change the character of natural landscapes, areas and objects declared protected. Utilisation of agricultural lands in declared protected areas can only be ensured in conformity with the category of protection, except in strictly protected areas where agricultural land may be withdrawn from use in the interest of nature conservation (Kallay *et al.*, 1987).

International Activities Bill No. IV of 1982 on Conservation of Nature stated that nature conservation should be incorporated within the framework of international conventions and protocols. Hungary acceded to the Convention on Wetlands of International Importance especially as Waterfowl Habitat (Ramsar Convention) on 11 April 1979; 13 sites were listed in 1989. It accepted the Convention concerning the World Natural and Cultural Heritage (World Heritage Convention) in July 1985; no natural sites have yet been inscribed. In 1982 five sites covering 128,000ha were accepted as biosphere reserves under the Unesco Man and the Biosphere Programme, two of them transboundary; Aggtelek with Czechoslovakia and Lake Fertö with Austria (Neusiedlersee). Most recently, the country became a contracting party to the Bern Convention in 1989 (IUCN, 1991; Szilassy, *in litt.*, 1991).

Administration and Management The first nature protection authority, the National Nature Preservation Council, was founded in 1939 under the auspices of the Ministry of Agriculture. It was replaced in 1961 by the National Authority for Nature Protection, an independent authority acting directly under the Cabinet. In 1977 this authority extended its power to cover coordination and supervision of nature and the protection of environment and was renamed the National Authority for Environment Protection and Nature

Conservation (*Orszagos Környezet és Természetvedelmi Hitaval*) (OKTH). Under the provisions of the 1982 Cabinet Decree, administrative tasks, supervision, coordination and control of nature conservation activities were the duties of the President of OKTH. On 1 January 1988, the OKTH was merged with the National Office of Water Management to establish the Ministry for Environmental Protection and Water Management (*Környezelvédelmi és Vizgazdalkodasi Minisztérium*) (KVM) and subsequently replaced by the Ministry of the Environment and Regional Policy (*Környezelvédelmi Minisztérium*) (KTM).

Until recently, the KTM had a network of twelve regional directorates, as well as four directorates for national parks. The Ministry embodied 17 separate technical or operational units among which are those for air protection, water protection, river regulation and nature preservation. At the national level, KVM had eight departments, including the Department of Nature Conservation, which was divided into four constituent parts including the Division of Landscape Protection. The latter had seven inspectorates which actually carry out management. National parks are managed by their own directorates. Aspects of the environment still remained under the control of other senior authorities: the Ministry of Agriculture and Food which supervised the conservation of soils and forests and the protection of landscapes not declared to be protected from the point of nature conservation, the Ministry for Construction and Town Development dealt with the urban environment, and the Ministry for Industry and its Central Authority for Geology protects mineral resources. Through the network of regional directorates, the KVM supervised and controlled nature conservation activities,such as the organisation and promotion of scientific research and law enforcement in protected areas.

At the local level, tasks within the regional responsibility of the KVM were carried out jointly by its local organisations, the inspectorates for environment protection and nature conservation and the national park directorates. The structure described above is now being superseded by new administrative organisations whose final configuration is yet to be decided. Within the framework of the KTM, the newly-established National Authority for Nature Conservation was set up on 1 January 1991 as a part of the Ministry. It has two departments and eight regional directorates (including the national park directorates) (Szilassy, *in litt.*, 1991). The directorates are responsible for the management of areas of national importance whilst the national park directorates manage their specific areas. They employ nature conservancy guards to safeguard and prevent damage to protected areas (National Authority for Environment Protection and Nature Conservation, 1983, 1984). County committees for environmental protection and nature conservation need to act as advisory and controlling bodies, their work including maintenance of protected areas. They report to central authorities.

Although the democratic elections held in April 1990 have resulted in a reorganisation of the KVM, the new Ministry of the Environment and Regional Policy will have a similar *modus operandi*.

Between 1976-1980 forints 0.5 billion (of a total environment budget of 41.2 billion forints) were spent on nature conservation and landscape protection (Cerovsky, 1988; Sasvari, 1982). The KVM spent approximately forints 400 million annually on environmental protection research in the institutes of the Academy of Sciences and other institutions of higher education (IUCN, 1989).

Of the numerous non-governmental organisations (NGOs), the Green Parties, and the traditional hunting, fishing and animal protection societies are particularly active in the field of conservation. The Hungarian Ornithological Society, founded in 1974, is the largest voluntary organisation, with about 10,000 members. The first private reserve to be created (a wetland of 7,000ha) is owned by an NGO called *Somogy Természetrédalmi Szervezet*. Other areas created locally have also been recognised officially, such as the private reserve of the Hungarian Ornithological Society (Atkinson *et al.*, 1991; Kallay, *in litt.*, 1990). There are various voluntary national park friendship circles (with members being drawn into park management), such as the Friends of Bukk National Park which grew into the Environmental Protection Association of the County of Borsod. The Speleological Institute supervises the protection of Hungary's caves (IUCN, 1988).

Systems Reviews The majority of Hungary is lowland, bisected by the rivers Danube and Tisza. There are low mountains in the north, reaching a maximum altitude of 1,015m. Protected areas include examples of the four main natural vegetation types: a) mountain bog on peat; b) mountain meadows, also containing important alpine flora; c) steppe or puszta; and d) broad-leaved and coniferous woodland. Other protected habitats include lakes (Lake Balaton is the largest lake in central Europe and an important bird migration area), soda lakes, volcanic mountains and extensive cave systems. The climax vegetation of the Great Hungarian Plain used to be steppe-woodland, dominated by *Quercus*. However, most of this was removed during the 16th and 17th centuries, and has been replaced by steppe-grassland, or puszta, an alkaline and very saline grassland rich in annuals (Davis *et al.*, 1986; Grimmett and Jones, 1989).

Hungary is densely populated with an agriculturally dominated economy. Forests still cover 17% of the land (increased from 12.4% in 1945), while meadows cover 5.4% and arable and grazing land covers 67.7% (Cerovsky, 1986; Grimmett and Jones, 1989). Although the total forest area is increasing, this is largely due to afforestation by commercial species. Recently, a "forest moratorium" was enacted and a law on forest management is in draft form (Atkinson *et al.*, 1991).

The first protected area was the Forest of Debrecen, which was designated in 1939. By 1970 the total protected areas system covered only 15,000ha. In less than ten years from 1970 it was increased to exceed 400,000ha. In 1987, protected areas covered 550,000ha, or 5.9% of the country (IUCN, 1989), increasing by 1991 to cover 630,000ha or approximately 6.8% of total land area (Szilassy, *in litt.*, 1991) and consisted of five national parks, 43 landscape protection areas, 135 nature conservation areas and 900 local sites (Atkinson *et al.*, 1991). Up to 92 caves receive special protection (IUCN, 1989). National parks are to be exempt from privatisation and new ones are proposed in the northern Balaton region (Atkinson *et al.*, 1991).

The puszta steppes are threatened by agricultural intensification, and most recently, land use and ownership changes. Other major threats and problems include soil erosion, threats of floods and the proposed Gabcikova/Nagymaros Danube river barrage system (GNRBS), which threatened to disrupt water levels along the Danube; work on this project has been halted on the Hungarian side since May 1989. Previous military training areas (zone within protected area) were used as firing ranges and ammunition dumps.

Addresses

Ministry for the Environment and Regional Policy, 1011 BUDAPEST I., Fö u. 44-50 (Levélcim: 1394 Budapest, Pf 351) (Tel: 1 562133; FAX: 1 757457; Tlx: 226115)

References

Anon. (1983). *Nature Conservation legislation in Hungary.* National Authority for Environment Protection and Nature Conservation, Budapest. 55 pp.

Atkinson, R., Miro-Kiss, I. and Csapo, A. (1991). Nature Conservation in Hungary. In: *Nature Conservation in Austria, Finland, Norway, Sweden, Switzerland, Bulgaria, Czechoslovakia, Hungary, Poland, Romania, Yugoslavia and the Soviet Union.* European Parliament. Directorate-General for Research, Environment, Public Health and Consumer Protection Series 17. EN-9-91.

Borhidi, A and Janossy, D. (1984). Protected Plants and Animals in Hungary. *Ambio* 13(2): 106.

Cerovsky, J. (1986) (Ed.). *Nature conservation in the socialist countries of East Europe.* East Europe Committee, IUCN Commission on Education. Ministry of Culture of the Czechoslovak Socialist Republic, Prague.

Cerovsky, J. (1988). *Nature conservation in the socialist countries of East Europe.* East-Europe Committee, IUCN Commission on Education. Ministry of Culture of the Czech Socialist Republic, Prague.

Davis, S.D., Droop, S.J.M., Gregerson, P., Henson, L., Leon, C.J., Lamlein Villa-Lobos, J., Synge, H., and Zantovska, J. (1986). *Plants in danger: What do we know?* Threatened Plants Unit, IUCN-CMC, Kew, UK.

ECE Finland (1986). Environment seminar 16/25-29 August 1986 . ENV/SEM 16/R1. 28 pp.

Glenny, M. (1988). Hungarian Greens with the Danube Blues. *New Scientist* 18 August. Pp. 28-29

Grimmet, R. and Jones, T. (1989). *Important bird areas in Europe.* International Council For Bird Preservation, Cambridge. 888 pp.

IUCN (1987). *Directory of wetlands of international importance.* IUCN, Gland, Switzerland and Cambridge, UK. 460 pp.

IUCN (1988). *Environmental protection profile of Hungary.* East European Programme Working Document No. 3. IUCN East European Programme, Cambridge, UK. 29 pp.

IUCN (1989). *Environmental status reports: 1988/1989, Volume One: Czechoslovakia, Hungary, Poland.* IUCN East European Programme, Cambridge, UK. 127 pp.

IUCN (1991). *The environment in Eastern Europe: 1990.* Environmental Research Series 3. IUCN East European Programme, Cambridge, UK. 64 pp.

Kallay, G. *et al.* (1987). *Saving the birds welcome to Hungary.* Hungarian Ornithological Society, Visegrad, Hungary.

Kopasz, M. (n.d.). *Environmental education in Hungary's universities and high schools.* Pp. 31-33

Laszio, E. (1984). The state of the environment in Hungary. *Ambio* 13(2): 93-108.

National Authority for Environmental Protection and Nature Conservation (1983). *Nature conservation legislation in Hungary.* National Authority for Environmental Protection and Nature Conservation/Department for International Relations, Budapest.

National Authority for Environmental Protection and Nature Conservation (1984). Management of national parks and other protected areas in Hungary. National Authority for Environmental Protection and Nature Conservation/Department for International Relations, Budapest.

Sasvari, A. (1982). Environmental protection in Hungary 1972-1982. Information from the National Authority for Environment Protection and Nature Conservation, Budapest.

Tolgyesi, I. (1984). Nature conservation in Hungary: presentation of a national park. *Parks* 8(4).

ANNEX
Definitions of protected area designations, as legislated,
together with authorities responsible for their administration

Title : Bill and Order on Nature Conservation (Bill No. IV and Cabinet Decree No. 8/1982 on Conservation of Nature)

Date: 1982

Brief description: Assessment of natural assets, declaration of protected areas, balancing nature conservation with economic activities, acquiring ownership rights and protection and management of nature reserves.

Administrative authority: National Authority for Environment Protection and Nature Conservation (Ministry for the Environment and Regional Policy)

Designations:

Nemzeti Park (National park) Large areas of land essentially of an unchanged natural state, where the landscape, fauna, flora or geological formations are of outstanding national importance. These areas are of value for public education and recreation.

Zonation ensures that strictly protected areas exist where nature conservation is the prime management objective.

Tajvédelmi Körzetek (Landscape protection area) Large areas of special scenic value, that are protected to safeguard and maintain nature conservation values as well as landscape features.

Protection extends to natural landscapes, regions and objects whose preservation and maintenance is of importance for science, culture or other public interest.

Természfetvédelmi Terület (Nature conservation areas) Established to preserve and maintain small areas of importance for nature conservation. They are divided into two categories, those of national significance and those of local importance, the latter being declared by county councils only.

The Nature Conservation Act has guaranteed the protection of all caves since 1961.

Source: Tölgyesi, 1984

SUMMARY OF PROTECTED AREAS

Map[†] ref.	National/international designations Name of area	IUCN management category	Area (ha)	Year notified
	National Parks			
1	Aggteleki	II	19,708	1985
2	Bukki	II	38,815	1976
3	Ferto-tavi	II	12,543	1991
4	Hortobagyi	II	52,213	1973
5	Kiskunsagi	II	35,859	1974
	Nature Conservation Areas			
6	Agotapuszta	IV	4,700	1973
7	Nagybereki Feherviz	IV	1,537	1977
8	Pusztakocsi mocsarak	IV	2,815	1973
9	Tiszadobi arter	IV	1,000	1977
10	Tiszafuredi madarrezervatum	IV	2,500	1973
11	Tiszatelek-Tiszaberceli arter	IV	1,263	1978
	Landscape Protection Areas			
12	Badacsonyi	V	7,028	1965
13	Barcsi Osborokas	V	3,417	1974
14	Beda-Karapancsai	V	6,498	1989
15	Biharugrai	V	7,899	1990
16	Borsodi Mezosegi	V	9,168	1989
17	Borzsonyi	V	17,897	1978
18	Budai	V	10,234	1978
19	Devavanyai	V	12,144	1975
20	Gemenci	V	17,779	1977
21	Gerecsei	V	8,617	1977
22	Godolloi Dombvidek	V	11,817	1990
23	Hajdusagi	V	5,681	1988
24	Hansagi	V	7,086	1976
25	Kali-medence	V	9,111	1984
26	Karancs-Medves	V	6,709	1989
27	Kecskeri puszta	V	1,226	1990
28	Kelet-Cserhat	V	6,916	1989
29	Kelet-Mecsek	V	9,248	1977
30	Kesznyeteni	V	4,070	1990
31	Keszthelyi	V	2,711	1984
32	Kis-Balaton	V	14,745	1986
33	Koszegi	V	3,987	1980
34	Kozep-Tiszai	V	7,670	1978
35	Lazberci	V	3,634	1975
36	Martelyi	V	2,232	1971
37	Matrai	V	11,863	1985
38	Ocsai	V	3,576	1975
39	Orgovanyi	V	2,953	1976
40	Orsegi	V	37,911	1978
41	Pilisi	V	23,323	1978
42	Pitvarosi pusztak	V	3,156	1989
43	Pusztaszeri	V	22,151	1976
44	Sarreti	V	2,211	1986
45	Soproni	V	4,905	1977
46	Szabadkigyosi	V	4,773	1977
47	Szatmar-Beregi	V	22,246	1982
48	Szentgyorgyvolgyi	V	1,916	1976
49	Szigetkozi	V	9,158	1987
50	Tihanyi	V	1,532	1952
51	Tokaj-Bodrogzug	V	4,242	1986

Map[†] ref.	National/international designations Name of area	IUCN management category	Area (ha)	Year notified
52	Vertesi	V	15,035	1976
53	Zempleni	V	26,496	1984
54	Zselicsegi	V	9,042	1976
	Biosphere Reserves			
	Aggtelek	IX	19,247	1979
	Hortobágy National Park	IX	52,000	1979
	Kiskunság	IX	22,095	1979
	Lake Fertö	IX	12,542	1979
	Pilis	IX	23,000	1980
	Ramsar Wetlands			
	Bodrogzug	R	3,782	1989
	Hortobágy	R	15,000	1979
	Kardoskut	R	488	1979
	Kis-balaton	R	14,745	1979
	Kiskunság	R	3,903	1979
	Lake Balaton*	R	59,800	1989
	Lake Fertö	R	2,870	1989
	Mártély	R	2,232	1979
	Ócsa	R	1,078	1989
	Pusztaszer	R	5,000	1979
	Szaporca	R	257	1979
	Tata Old Lake*	R	269	1989
	Velence-Dinnyés	R	965	1979

*Designations only apply from 1 October to 30 April.

[†]Locations of most protected areas are shown on the accompanying map.

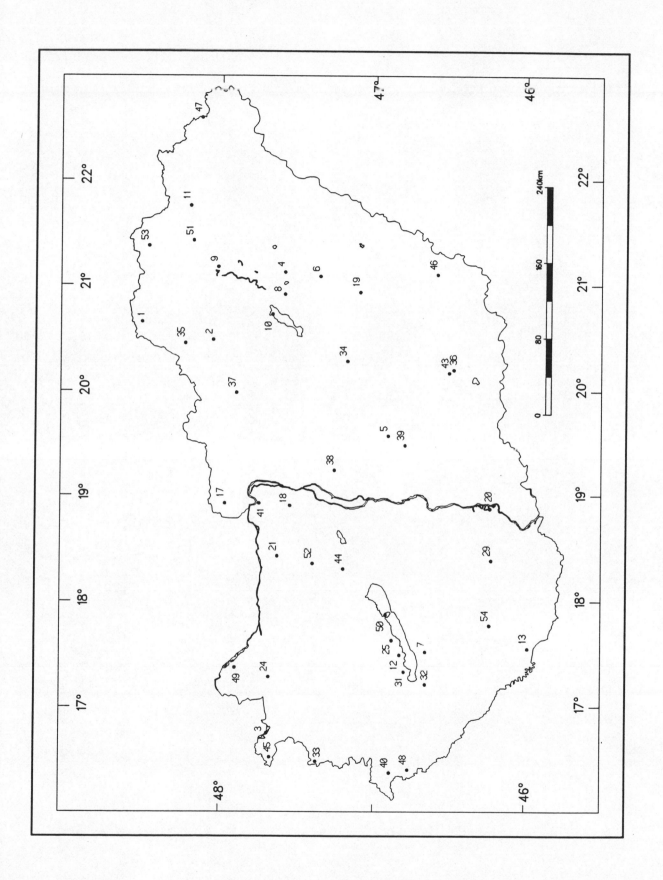

Protected Areas of Hungary

ICELAND

Area 103,000 sq. km

Population 253,000 (1990)
Natural increase: 0.83% per annum

Economic Indicators
GDP: US$ 21,617 (1987)
GNP: US$ 16,670 (1987)

Policy and Legislation   Since 1 December 1918 Iceland has been acknowledged as an independent state, being united with Denmark through a common sovereign until it was proclaimed an independent republic on 17 June 1944.

The principal legislation concerning environmental protection is the Nature Conservation Act No. 47/1971 of 16 April 1971 (Act No. 48 of 7 April 1956, the original act on nature conservation, was invalidated by the 1971 Act). The 1971 Act covers all aspects ranging from the fight of public access to nature and public conduct (Articles 11-21), the Declaration of Protection of Natural Phenomena and Establishment of Recreation Areas (Articles 22-27) to Implementation of Declaration of Protection (Articles 28-33). The aim of the legislation is to ensure the protection of the diversity of habitats and landscapes, flora and fauna, and "to encourage the intercourse of Man and Nature in such a way that life or land use be not needlessly wasted, nor sea, fresh water or air polluted" (Article 1). Protection is afforded to areas of exceptional value. Care of the countryside as a whole is exercised through consultation in the planning process. Under the Act there are four main categories of protected area, all entail some restrictions on exploitation and development: national park (pjödgardur), nature reserve (fridland), natural monument (natturuvaetti), and recreation area or country park (folkvangur) (see Annex).

Under the Nature Conservation Act of 1971 (Article 28), the Nature Conservation Council (NCC) identifies and compiles a register of sites of special interest, natural features considered important and deemed worthy of protection. Registration is seen as a declaration of intent and serves as a basis and a first step in negotiations for their protection. Sites of special interest include areas suitable for recreation, areas of outstanding beauty, areas of unusual diversity in terms of nature or landscape, and areas of special scientific interest. The procedures for eventual protection are slow and hence registration does not imply imminent protection. This inventory is revised and published at three to four year intervals. The first inventory edition was published in 1975 (Natturuverndarrao, 1988).

Details of general activities permitted or prohibited under the 1971 Nature Conservation Act include the following: the public right of access to nature, which includes privately-owned land; prohibiting off-road driving where this can cause damage to the environment; and care be taken to avoid unnecessary damage to wildlife, vegetation and water. Where buildings and other constructions have been left in neglect the owner is requested that they do not blemish the scenic value of the surroundings. Local authorities can prohibit any mining on private land if it will disturb exceptional landscape or noteworthy natural phenomena.

The first conservation legislation in 1928 involved the designation of Thingvellir National Park under Law No. 59/1928, special legislation protecting this one site "as the common heritage of the Icelandic nation", which remains in force despite the subsequent introduction of the Nature Conservation Act No. 47/1971. This park is sometimes referred to as a special national park, it is administered by a parliamentary committee (the Thingvellir Committee). This was followed by separate laws No. 36/1974 designating Myvatn-Laxa Reserve. These two sites are still not covered under the Nature Conservation Act of 1971 which is concerned with all other major protected areas.

Law No. 3/1955 and No. 22/1966 relate to forestry and forest conservation. Certain areas may be declared protected forests: here the introduction and exploitation of conifers is usually not allowed in protected natural woodlands. These may have been set aside either for ecological studies or for amenity purposes, leading to different management practices within the general conservation framework. No information is available concerning the legislation relating to this category. Additional legislation relating to protected areas includes Law No. 17/1965 on soil conservation and Law No. 33/1966 on bird protection, hunting and hunting reserves. Under the Bird Act the seasons when hunting is restricted for specified areas are defined.

International Activities   Accession to the Convention on Wetlands of International Importance especially as Waterfowl Habitat (Ramsar Convention), took place on 2 December 1977: two Ramsar sites have been designated. Iceland is a member of the Council of Europe, but no sites have been classified as Council of Europe biogenetic reserves. Furthermore, no sites have been awarded the Council of Europe European Diploma. The Nordic Council, of which Iceland is a member state, is involved in a number of environmental protection issues: the Nordic Council of Ministers has run a series of four to five-year environmental protection programmes, the present programme beginning in 1988. These programmes cover a wide range of activities which include, among other things, bringing greater attention to nature conservation in connection with planning activities. The Council has encouraged the registration of valuable landscapes in the Nordic area, the concentration of conservation efforts towards the preservation of particularly important habitat types and the use of natural areas by the wider public for recreation purposes. It has also encouraged the development of a standardised data collection for monitoring environmental quality (Nordic Council of Ministers, 1983).

Administration and Management In accordance with Article 29 of the Nature Conservation Act, the Nature Conservation Council (NCC) (Natturuverndarrao) shall execute nature conservation measures as set forth in the Act (Article No. 7) and is regularly consulted in connection with all major projects which may affect conservation. The authorisation of the Council is required before any construction or development proceeds. The Council shall take the initiative in public instruction about conservation, such as through publications, schools and mass media and maintain close cooperation with voluntary conservation organisations. The NCC comes under the Ministry of Education and Cultural Affairs (Menntamalaraouneytio) which is in charge of all matters regarding the conservation of nature. Decisions taken by the NCC concerning protection or declaration of protection do not come into force until approved by the Ministry and published in the *Law and Ministerial Gazette*. The Ministry has the authority to expropriate land, constructions and rights in order to execute conservation measures provided for in the Act. The expenses of the NCC are paid by the State Treasury (Poore and Gryn-Ambroes, 1980; Reynisson, 1976).

The administration of nature conservation and protected areas is outlined in the legal provisions of the Nature Conservation Act No. 47/1971 (Articles 2-8). Day-to-day management of protected areas is undertaken by the NCC in cooperation with local communes, volunteers from conservation societies and the Icelandic Tourist Association (see below). In 1982 the three national parks and Myvatn-Laxa Reserve had one superintendent, one warden, and 13 seasonal assistants. Running costs for these sites totalled £134,000 of which £20,000 was for maintaining the field station at Myvatn-Laxa (IUCN, *in litt.*, 1982). Recreation areas are maintained by municipalities which work in consultation with the NCC.

The ministries responsible for land-use are primarily the Ministry of Agriculture (Landbunaoarraouneytio) and the Ministry of Social Affairs. Under the former come the agencies for soil conservation, forestry and rural planning. State lands are administered by the Ministry of Agriculture. The Urban Planning Authority comes under the Ministry of Social Affairs. The State Forestry Service (Skograekt Rikisins) has jurisdiction over forest land.

The Icelandic Environment Union (Landvernd) was established in 1969 and is the most influential non-governmental environmental body. Member societies number over 60, including youth, sports and travel organisations, conservation associations, farming and labour unions. Landvernd is active in promoting soil conservation, reclamation, education and information on

environmental matters (Duffey, 1982). It advises the NCC on local environmental issues and participates in policy-making and recommendations for future protected areas to be listed in the Register of protected areas. Other non-governmental organisations include the Association of Icelandic Nature Conservation Societies. Conservation societies are involved in part-time wardening and supervision of government-declared protected areas, in association with local communes and the Icelandic Tourist Association.

Systems Reviews Iceland is the second largest island in Europe, 1,000km from Norway in the North Atlantic. It is located just south of the Arctic Circle on the mid-Atlantic Ridge and is influenced by the North Atlantic drift of the Gulf Stream. Arctic pack-ice is found within 50-100 nautical miles north-west of the country. Over 70% of Iceland lies above 300m in altitude; lava plains, now cut by rivers and glaciers, form valleys and fjords separated by mountain ranges. The bedrock is mostly volcanic basalt, with an active volcanic zone running through the island from the south-west to the north-east. Permanent ice fields cover 12,000 sq. km (about 11.5% of the total area).

Lowlands are dominated by mixed heathland, grassland and sedge bogs and minute remnants of birch woodland, the latter representing the original lowland cover (now representing only 1.2% of the country). Above 600m, in the high alpine zone, an Arctic/Alpine tundra of mosses and herbs dominates the terrain. The vegetation is heavily influenced by man and livestock; cutting and burning of vegetation and heavy grazing cause considerable soil loss (Grimmett and Jones, 1989; IUCN, 1986). About 27% of the total area of the country lies below 200m altitude, the majority being under cultivation.

Thingvellir was the first national park, declared in 1928. In 1978, 49 areas were protected by law, with a total area under protection of 700,020ha, including three national parks (totalling 69,200ha) and seven landscape reserves (Anon., 1987; Duffey, 1982). In the 1988 edition of the NCC *Gazette*, the number of protected areas had risen to 69 (Natuuruverndarrao, 1988).

The fourth edition of the list of protected areas was published in 1984, and the latest, the fifth, in 1988. It is divided into two parts, the first containing all sites legally designated and the second including all sites of special interest sites that are considered important, but which cannot presently be brought under protection. In 1978, 150 sites were registered on the latter list, rising to 266 in 1984 and 273 in 1988 (Natturuverndarrao, 1988).

Factors affecting conservation include: sheep grazing on enclosed land often leading to considerable erosion; drainage grants for farmers towards land improvement, where wetland conflict may arise; generally fairly weak planning control both in terms of "structure plans" and development control; possible demands for development projects linked with the generation of hydro or geothermal electricity; increasing road communications leading to increased pressure on the very fragile terrain (Reynisson, 1976).

Other Relevant Information Ecotourism is becoming an increasingly important element of the tourist industry. In 1989 there were 130,498 visitors to Iceland. The Icelandic Tourist Association works in association with the conservation societies and the NCC to warden and supervise government-declared protected areas (Hunter, 1991).

Addresses

Natturuverndarrao (Nature Conservation Council), Hverfisgata 26, 101 REYKJAVIK (Tel: 1 22520)

Skograekt rikisins (State Forestry Service), Ranargata 18, 101 REYKJAVIK

Landvernd (Environmental Union), Skolavordustigur 25, 101 REYKJAVIK

References

Anon. (1987). *Management of Europe's natural heritage: twenty-five years of activity.* Council of Europe, Strasbourg, France. 127 pp.

Carwardine, M. (1986). Iceland: nature's meeting place. *Iceland Review.* (Unseen)

Davis, S.D., Droop, S.J.M., Gregerson, P., Henson, L., Leon, C.J., Lamlein Villa-Lobos, J., Synge, H. and Zantovska, J. (1986). *Plants in danger: what do we know?* IUCN, Gland, Switzerland and Cambridge, UK. 461 pp.

Duffey, E. (1982). *National parks and reserves of Western Europe.* Macdonald and Co (Publishers) Ltd., London and Sydney. 288 pp.

Grimmett, R.F.A. and Jones, T.A. (1989). *Important bird areas of Europe.* International Council for Bird Preservation, Cambridge, UK. Pp. 325-340

Hunter, B. (Ed.) (1991). *The Statesman's Year Book 1991-92.* The Macmillan Press Ltd, London and Basingstoke, UK. 1692 pp.

Koester, V. (1980). Nordic countries' legislation on the environment with special emphasis on conservation: a survey. *IUCN Environmental Policy and Law Paper* 14. 44 pp.

Natturuverndarrao (1988). Natturuminjaskra, fridlyst svaedi og adrar skradar natturuminjar. 5. utgafa. Natturuverndarrad, Reykjavik. 60 pp. (English summary).

Nordic Council of Ministers (1983). *Programme for Nordic Cooperation in Environmental Protection for 1983 to 1987.* 37 pp.

Poore, D. and Gryn-Ambroes, P. (1980). *Nature conservation in northern and western Europe.* Pp. 205-215

Reynisson, A. (1976). Survey of western and northern European parks and equivalent reserves. Unpublished report.

ANNEX
Definitions of protected area designations, as legislated, together with authorities responsible for their administration

Title: Nature Conservation Act (47/1971)

Date: 16 April 1971

Brief description: The principal legislation covering all aspects of environmental protection, including public access to the countryside, the protection of flora and fauna and protected areas

Administrative authority: Nature Conservation Council
Local authorities (country parks)

Designations:

Pjödgardur (National park) May be established by the NCC in areas considered outstanding in landscape, flora or fauna, or having special historic significance. They can only be established on state-owned land. Public access is facilitated by marking trails and providing necessary visitor facilitates and information. The Council also has an educational role in furnishing general information concerning the natural history of the parks. Public access is provided in accordance with specified rules necessary sanitary facilities shall be erected in national parks, as well as camping sites footpaths and other facilities which render easier public usage of the area and prevent damage.

Fridland (Nature reserve) According to Article 25, the NCC may protect areas considered important because of their landscape, flora or fauna. Common to all reserves is protection of their nature and landscape and a restriction on development. The degree of protection and limitation on development, however, varies substantially and are defined in each particular instance: restrictions may include those on traffic and public rights of access, and also uses of the area for hunting and fishing. The declaration may also contain details of actions to be undertaken in a reserve, such as the building of paths, erection of fences, etc. The owner or tenant of the land is equally bound by the restrictions imposed on a nature reserve.

On some small reserves, there are severe restrictions on visitors and a few may even be closed to human traffic. In large reserves, there are restrictions on development and buildings, but most reserves are open to the public all the year round, sometimes with certain restrictions.

Natturuvaetti (Natural monument) Under Article 22 unique natural monuments and monuments of outstanding beauty or scientific interest may be protected. Natural monuments include waterfalls, volcanic sites, caves, rock formations, as well as beds containing fossils or rare minerals. The area around a natural monument shall be preserved, as necessary for its appreciation this area must be clearly described when the site is designated and clearly marked at the site itself. Natural monuments may not be destroyed, damaged or changed, except on instructions from the NCC.

Folkvangur (Public recreation area or Country park) These are declared through the NCC by one or more municipalities, who are responsible for drawing up the boundaries and regulations. The parks vary in size and landscape. Management policies may also vary, although disturbance of vegetation or soil is generally prohibited or subject to consent by the local authorities or the NCC. Sites are declared in the *Official Gazette*, after which owners and other members of the public have eight weeks to raise any objections.

Sources: Nature Conservation Act, 1971; Natturuverndarrao, 1988

SUMMARY OF PROTECTED AREAS

Map† ref.	National/international designations Name of area	IUCN management category	Area (ha)	Year notified
	National Parks			
1	Jokulsargljufur	II	15,100	1973
2	Skaftafell	II	160,000	1967
3	Thingvellir	II	5,000	1928
	Nature Reserves			
4	Fjallabak	V	47,000	1979
5	Flatey	IV	100	1975
6	Geitland	III	11,750	1988
7	Herdisarvik	V	4,000	1988
8	Kringilsarrani	IV	8,500	1975
9	Miklavatn	IV	1,550	1977
10	Surtsey	I	270	1965
11	Thjosarver	IV	37,500	1981
	Natural Monuments			
12	Alftaversgigar	III	3,650	1975
13	Askja i Dyngjufjollum	III	5,000	1978
14	Lakagigar	III	16,000	1971
15	Skogafoss	III	2,204	1987
	Nature Reserves (Landscape)			
16	Esjufjoll	V	27,000	1978
17	Herdubreidarfridland	V	17,000	1974
18	Hornstrandir	V	58,000	1975
19	Hvannalindir i Krepputungu	IV	4,300	1973
20	Lonsoraefi	V	32,000	1977
21	Vatnsfjorour	V	20,000	1975
	Conservation Area			
22	Myvatn Laxa (Landscape)	V	440,000	1974
	Country Parks			
23	Blafjoll	VIII	8,400	1973
24	Reykjanesfolkvangur	VIII	30,000	1975
	Ramsar Wetlands			
	Part of Mvatn-Laxá Region	R	20,000	1977
	Thjorsarver	R	37,500	1990

†Locations of most protected areas are shown on the accompanying map.

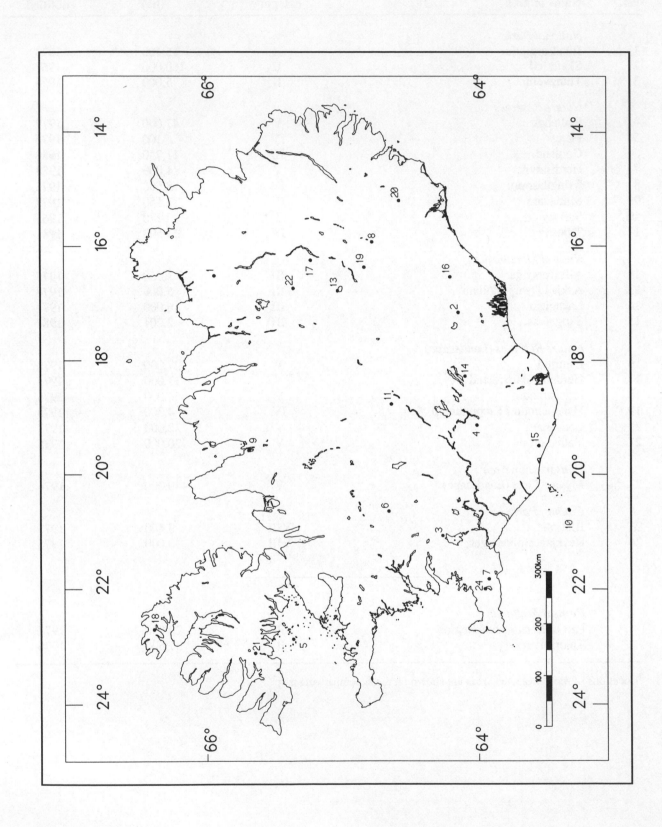

Protected Areas of Iceland

IRELAND (EIRE)

Area 70,280 sq. km

Population 3,720,000 (1990)
Natural increase: 0.95% per annum

Economic Indicators
GDP: US$ 7,808 per capita (1987)
GNP: US$ 6,030 per capita (1987)

Policy and Legislation   Ireland is a sovereign independent republic. The republic was first proclaimed in April 1916, and on 6 December 1921 a treaty was signed between Ireland and Great Britain by which Ireland accepted dominion status subject to the right of Northern Ireland to opt out. This right was exercised and the border fixed and ratified in December 1925. The Republic of Ireland Act, 1948 came into operation on 18 April 1949 (Hunter, 1991). The present Constitution dates from 1 July 1937. The National Policy for environmental protection has been enacted and is the responsibility of the Minister for the Environment.

Parks have been in state ownership since 1860, when Phoenix Park was entrusted to the Commissioners of Public Works. Protected area legislation began with the Bourn Vincent Memorial Park Act in 1932 which enabled this park, now part of Killarney National Park, to be set up. The State Property Act, 1954 enabled the setting aside of land for subsequent national parks. This Act gave the Commissioners of Public Works (Office of Public Works) responsibility of managing, for state purposes, any land vested in them (Cutrera, 1991).

A number of general legislative acts relate partly to protected areas, including the 1946, 1961 and 1983 Turf Development Acts; the 1963 Coast Protection Act; the 1956 Forestry Act; and the 1980 Ombudsman Act and 1984 amendment. The 1963 Local Government (Planning and Development) Act makes provision for local authorities to make Special Amenity Area Orders (SAAO) and conservation orders. The first SAAO was made recently in respect of part of the Liffey Valley near Dublin city (1991).

The current legislation for establishing protected areas, other than national parks, and protecting flora and fauna is the Wildlife Act, 1976 which repeals the Game Preservation Act and Wild Birds Protection Act, 1930. Under Section 15 and 16 it lays down the legislative basis for the protection of fauna and flora. This includes: provision of an adequate legal framework for wildlife conservation; providing better protection for wild flora and fauna; providing the machinery for protecting areas of specific wildlife value; regulating the development of game resources; and improving land acquisition powers. This is achieved by subordinate legislation in the form of statutory orders and regulations. It is administered by the National Parks and Wildlife Service of the Office of Public Works (Cutrera, 1991; Grimmett and Jones, 1989).

Categories of protected area covered under the 1976 Act include nature reserve, refuge for fauna and no-shooting area (wildfowl sanctuary). Provisions under the Act also prohibit hunting, except under licence on state-owned foreshore and state-owned lakes. The 1976 Act does not provide a statutory basis for national parks (Grimmett and Jones, 1989; Poore and Gryn-Ambroes, 1980) (see Annex).

Areas of scientific interest (ASIs) are listed, mapped and notified to various land-use agencies and planning authorities, although no legal protection is provided as yet. The intention is for them to be covered by the 1976 Act (Grimmett and Jones, 1989).

The Forestry Act of 1946 (1988) covers state forest, which includes regulations for recreational use and establishment of forest parks (Anon., 1979, 1987; Cutrera, 1991).

Legislation is currently being drafted to provide a statutory basis for national parks and certain other categories of protected area not covered by present legislation, and to amend the Wildlife Act in various ways, including providing statutory procedures for the designation of areas of scientific interest (Office of Public Works, in litt., 1991). A new type of country side park may be developed, through agreement between local authorities and tourism interests. However, the single existing site, Slieve Bloom Environment Park, has had little statutory basis since its inception in 1988 (Cutrera, 1991). Other proposed categories include heritage zone, a combination of landscape, natural heritage and monuments (Cutrera, 1991).

An EC Directive concerning environmental impact assessments (EIAs) was adopted on 27 June 1985. EIAs must take into account a number of factors including, among other things, flora, fauna, soil, water, and the landscape. The 1976 Local Government (Planning and Development) Act lays down provisions for environmental impact assessment. This, however, only applies to certain types of large-scale private projects and does not apply to public projects (Anon., 1987; Coenen and Jörissen, 1989).

Legislation has been presented to parliament in order to establish an Environment Protection Agency.

International Activities   The Convention on Wetlands of International Importance especially as Waterfowl Habitat (Ramsar Convention) was ratified on 15 November 1984: 21 sites have been declared. Two sites have been approved as biosphere reserves under the Unesco Man and the Biosphere Programme. The Convention on the Conservation of European Wildlife and Natural Habitats (Bern Convention) was signed on 1 August 1982. Ireland is a member of the European Community and hence is bound by its environmental directives: 20 sites have been designated as EC special protection areas under the Wild Birds Directive. Ireland is also a member of the Council of Europe: 14 sites have been classified as Council of Europe biogenetic reserves, but no sites have been awarded the Council of Europe European Diploma (1991).

Administration and Management Responsibility for management of national parks and other protected areas is vested in the Office of Public Works (Oifig Na nOibreacha Poibli), a semi-autonomous part of the Department of Finance established in 1932. In 1987 the former Forest and Wildlife Service was split, and its wildlife responsibilities were transferred to the Office of Public Works. In 1991, the nature conservation functions of that office were reorganised and brought together as the National Parks and Wildlife Service of the Office of Public Works.

The Office of Public Works (Commissioners of Public Works) was first entrusted with parks in 1860. The State Property Act, 1954 gave the Commissioners responsibility for managing, for state purposes, any land vested in them, including parks. The Office provides wardening to the parks, however, management objectives have not been completely documented as only one national park has a management plan (others are under preparation). Since 1981 the Office of Public Works has maintained a list of over 1,500 ASIs. These are taken into account by planning authorities and development agencies, particularly where EC grants for agricultural and forestry development are sought.

Under Section 15/16 of the Wildlife Act, 1976, nature reserves, refuges for fauna and no-hunting wildfowl sanctuaries are under the jurisdiction of the Office of Public Works, as are state-owned foreshore and state-owned lakes.

Under the 1988 Forest Act, 90% of all state forest assets were transferred in 1989 to a new commercially-orientated state forestry board (Coillte Teoranta), the remainder continuing to be covered under the 1946 Act and administered by the Irish Forest Service. The 1946 Act covered state forest parks which have been set up for recreational use. Other bodies involved in protected area management include Dublin Corporation, which owns and manages North Bull Island. New types of countryside park include the single environment park at Slieve Bloom, which has been set up by agreement between local authorities and tourism interests Cutrera, 1991). Expenditure during 1989 for forestry, fisheries and tourism totalled IP£56 million, dropping to IP£54 million in 1990 (Hunter, 1991).

The Department of the Environment is responsible for environmental protection generally, including pollution control and the National Environmental Policy. The Wildlife Act provides for a Wildlife Advisory Council, but there is no Council in office at present. The National Heritage Council, set up initially on a non-statutory basis, provides advice to government on a broad range of matters relating to the national heritage (Office of Public Works, *in litt.*, 1991).

A number of non-governmental bodies are involved in nature protection. A small number of reserves are owned by voluntary organisations such as An Taisce (National Trust for Ireland) and Irish Wildbird Conservancy (the leading voluntary wildlife organisation in the Republic with over 5,000 members). The Irish Peatland Conservation Council, in conjunction with the Dutch Foundation for the Protection of Irish Bogs, acquired Scragh Bog in 1984 for nature conservation and planned to buy more peatland with the help of WWF-Netherlands. The Irish Wildlife Federation is concerned primarily with education, and Earthwatch has been established more recently (Whilde, 1988).

Systems Reviews The Republic of Ireland has a land border with Northern Ireland, which is part of the United Kingdom. Ireland has the most humid, maritime climate in the British Isles due to its westerly position bordering the Atlantic Ocean. The topography of peripheral mountains and hills around a central limestone plateau also tends to concentrate the rainfall (Whilde, 1988). The central plateau is largely drained by the River Shannon and its tributaries and there are over 4,000 lakes and ponds greater in size than 1ha. Another characteristic landscape is the bare limestone expanses of the Burren in County Clare, where a national park is being established. The coastline is extremely indented and includes a great variety of coastal habitats including dunes, saltmarshes and estuaries (Grimmett and Jones, 1989).

Flora and fauna is reduced in comparison with continental Europe and there are few endemics, most of which are at the subspecific level. There are also a number of amphi-atlantic plants with American affinities (Anon., 1987). Some animals and plants, such as strawberry tree *Arbutus unedo*, which has an otherwise Mediterranean distribution. Other plants found otherwise only occur in Alpine areas (Whilde, 1988). A Flora Protection Order (1987) under the Wildlife Act lists 68 species of vascular plant as protected. Only a few mountain summits and parts of the seashore can be considered to be in pristine condition; most woodland is recent semi-natural oakwood with birch and holly; little of the original extensive oak woodland still remains (Whilde, 1988). The largest area of oakwoods are within Killarney National Park (Craig, 1987). The total remaining area of semi-natural forest is 2,000ha, of which 1,500ha is oak (Heiss, 1987). The woodlands also have a great variety of bryophytes due to the moist climate (Heiss, 1987).

Many thousands of wintering waterfowl and waders utilise the varied wetland habitats (Poore and Gryn-Ambroes, 1980). Many of the apparently natural blanket bogs probably have a partly anthropogenic origin. In 1984 only one-fifth of the original area of raised bog remained and this may virtually disappear by the early 1990s (Anon., 1990). Ireland has the last remaining areas of raised bog in Europe (MacLochlainn, 1988). The area of blanket bog has not yet been so extensively depleted as it is more difficult to cut. Commercial forestry may also result in the acidification of streams and upset the nutrient balance of nearby blanket bogs (Anon., 1987). About 5% of the country has been afforested with exotic conifers, much of this on blanket and raised bogs.

The Irish Peatland Conservation Council, founded in 1982, has drawn up a list of 40 sites covering about 100,000ha which they regard as the minimum necessary to conserve the range of peatland variation existing in Ireland. This was accepted by the European parliament in its "Resolution on the Protection of Irish Bogs" adopted in April 1983. Due to Ireland's low population density and slow intensification of agriculture, environmental awareness was slow to develop until the late 1980s. In the 1970s EC-funding speeded up agricultural intensification and peat extraction increased. In the 1980s industrial fish farming increasing considerably; these trends accelerated the exploitation of natural resources and set the scene for the emergence of a conservation lobby. This developed from two main sources: established organisations, such as the Irish Wildbird Conservancy and An Taisce, and also from more recent organisations such as Earthwatch (Whilde, 1988).

Parks have been in state ownership since 1860. The first national park was established through a donation to the nation in 1932, as Bourn Vincent Memorial Park, which has since been expanded to become Killarney National Park. Since the enactment of the Wildlife Act in 1976, progress in establishing nature reserves was slow for the first few years and largely confined to forest land already owned by the state. More recently, there has been substantial progress, particularly in acquisition of peatlands. In the 1980s there were over 50 nature reserves with a total area of 12,000ha and by 1991 up to 68 nature reserves had been established, covering a total area of over 15,000ha (Cutrera, 1991; Office of Public Works, *in litt.*, 1991). By 1991 there were three national parks, Killarney, Glenveagh, Connemara Letterfrack covering 22,309 ha (Cutrera, 1991). Two additional national parks, Wicklow Mountains and Burren, have now been officially listed and both will be fully notified by 1993, by which time over 30,000ha will be protected in the five national parks (Office of Public Works, *in litt.*, 1991). Areas of scientific interest numbered over 1,500 in 1991. Recreational use of state forests has increased considerably over the past decade and a half and 300 forests are now open to the public (1991). In the early 1980s 12 sites had been developed into forest parks (Anon., 1979, 1987; Cutrera, 1991).

Several major problems threaten the integrity of protected areas. One major drawback to peatland protection is that the three activities which threaten it

most, peat cutting, forestry and agriculture, are exempt from planning control (MacLochlainn, 1988). A much-studied problem is the spread of the introduced rhododendron *Rhododendron ponticum* which spreads rapidly on acidic soils and threatens to destroy oak woodlands in Killarney and Glenveagh national parks (Craig, 1979). Pollution of estuaries and loughs by run off containing fertilisers is becoming more extensive (Carp, 1980).

Other Relevant Information   In the publication of the *Plan for National Recovery*, there are proposals to double the earnings from tourism, inferring total future earnings of some IP£ 500 million per year and providing 25,000 new jobs (cf revenue from tourism above). Protected areas were regarded as part of this tourism "product" and a series of developments including expanding the national park network and designation of new categories (including environment parks and heritage zones) has been considered (Cutrera, 1991). In state forest and forest parks there were some 600,000 visitors in 1980 and an estimated 1.5 million visitors annually in the late 1980s (Anon., 1979, 1987).

Addresses

National Parks and Wildlife Service, Office of Public Works, 51 St Stephen's Green, DUBLIN 2 (Tel: 613111; Tlx: 90160; FAX: 610747)

Department of Energy, Clare Street, DUBLIN 2 (Tel: 715233)

Department of the Environment, Custom House, DUBLIN 1 (Tel: 742961; Tlx: 31014)

Coillte Teoranta, Leeson Lane, DUBLIN 2 (Tel: 615666; Tlx: 90253; FAX: 789527)

An Taisce (The National Trust for Ireland), The Tailor's Hall, Back Lane, DUBLIN 8 (Tel: 783940)

Irish Wildbird Conservancy, Rutledge House, 8 Longford Place, MONKSTOWN, Co. Dublin (Tel: 804322)

Irish Wildlife Federation, 132a East Wall Road, DUBLIN 3 (Tel: 366821)

References

Anon. (1987). *European Environmental Yearbook.* Docter UK Ltd., London. 897 pp.

Carp, E. (1980). *A directory of wetlands of international importance in the Western Palaearctic.* IUCN, Gland, Switzerland.

Coenen, R. and Jörissen, J. (1989). *Environmental impact assessment in the member countries of the European Community, implementing the EC-Directive: an overview.* KfK 4507 B, Kernforschungszentrum, Karsruhe, Germany. 42 pp.

Craig, A. (1979). The national parks of Ireland. *Parks* 17: 10-13.

Cutrera, A. (1991). *European Environmental Yearbook.* Institute for Environmental Studies. DocTer International UK, London. 897 pp.

Davis, S.D., Droop, S.J.M., Gregerson, P., Henson, L., Leon, C.J., Lamlein Villa-Lobos, J., Synge, H. and

Zantovska, J. (1986). *Plants in danger: what do we know?* IUCN, Gland, Switzerland and Cambridge, UK. 461 pp.

Duffey, E. (1982) *National parks and reserves of Western Europe.* Macdonald and Co. (Publishers) Ltd, London and Sydney. 288 pp.

Grimmett, R.F.A. and Jones, T.A. (1989). *Important bird areas in Europe.* Technical Publication No. 9. International Council for Bird Preservation, Cambridge, UK. Pp. 350-374

Heiss, G. (1987). Inventory of natural (virgin) and ancient seminatural woodlands within the council member states and Finland. European Committee for the Conservation of Nature and Natural Resources. Unpublished report.

Hunter, B. (Ed.) (1991). *The Statesman's Year Book 1991-92.* The Macmillan Press Ltd, London and Basingstoke, UK. 1692 pp.

MacLochlainn, C. (1988). The battle of the bogs. *Environment Now* 11: 15-17.

Poore, D. and Gryn-Ambroes, P. (1980). *Nature Conservation in Northern and Western Europe.* IUCN/WWF, Gland, Switzerland. 408 pp.

Whilde, T. (1988). An Irish Perspective. *ECOS* 9(2): 14-17.

ANNEX
Definitions of protected area designations, as legislated, together with authorities responsible for their administration

Title: Wildlife Act, Section 15 and 16 (repealing Game Preservation Act and Wild Birds Protection Act of 1930)

Date: 1976

Brief description: Lays down the legislative basis for the protection of fauna and flora

Administrative authority: National Parks and Wildlife Service, Office of Public Works

Designations:

Nature reserve Section 15 of the Act allows the establishment of statutory nature reserves on state land. Section 16 allows the establishment of nature reserves in privately owned areas. In the latter case the owner is required to manage the land in accordance with a management plan drawn up the National Parks and Wildlife Service. Nature reserves are established to conserve species, communities, habitats, or ecosystems which are of scientific interest, and which are likely to benefit from the designation.

Refuge for fauna Designated where species require special measures to protect their habitat. Land ownership does not affect designation. Limitations on land-use may be ordered, but there is provision for the payment of compensation.

No-hunting area (Wildfowl sanctuary) Area where hunting is prohibited

Provisions under the 1976 Wildlife Act also prohibit hunting, except under licence on state-owned foreshore and state-owned lakes.

Sources: Cutrera, 1991; Grimmett and Jones, 1989; Poore and Gryn-Ambroes, 1980

Title: The State Property Act (National Park)

Date: 1954

Brief description: Enables the setting aside of land for subsequently notified national parks. This Act also gives the Office of Public Works (Commissioners of Public Works) responsibility of managing, for state purposes, any land vested in them. Incorporates the Bourn Vincent Memorial Park Act of 1932.

Administrative authority: National Parks and Wildlife Service, Office of Public Works

Designations:

National park Established either by special Act of Parliament or under the State Property Act 1954. Relatively large sites over 2,000ha owned by the state.

Permitted activities include grazing and other agreements negotiated with local people. Forestry and small-scale peat cutting occurs (but is being phased out).

Management is undertaken, visitor access is permitted and education is an important element (land for Glenveagh national park was acquired in 1975 but it was not opened to the public until 1984).

Sources: Cutrera, 1991; Office of Public Works, *in litt.*, 1990

Title: Forestry Act of 1946 and 1988 (repealing Acts of 1919 and 1928)

Date: 1946; 1988

Brief description: Under the 1988 Act 90% of all state forest assets have been transferred to the Coillte Teoranta, the remainder is covered under the 1946 Act and administered by the Irish Forest Service.

Administrative authority: Irish Forest Service and the Coillte Teoranta (Irish Forestry Board Limited)

Designations:

Forest park The Forestry Act of 1946 covers state forest, which includes regulations for recreational use and establishment of forest parks. Overnight stays are not permitted except in one park.

Sources: Anon., 1979, 1987; Cutrera, 1991; Poore and Gryn-Ambroes, 1980

Title: Local Government (Planning and Development) Act

Date: 1963 and 1976

Brief description: Requires the inclusion in the development plan of each local authority provisions for the use of land as: open spaces; public parks and recreation areas; and game and bird sanctuaries. It also enables local authorities to designate areas of outstanding natural beauty and of nature conservation value.

Administrative authority: Department of the Environment

Designations:

Open space see above

Public park and Recreation area see above

Game and bird sanctuary see above

Area of outstanding natural beauty and of nature conservation value see above

Sources: Cutrera, 1991; Office of Public Works, *in litt.*, 1991; Poore and Gryn-Ambroes, 1980

213

SUMMARY OF PROTECTED AREAS

Map ref.	*National/international designations* Name of area	IUCN management category	Area (ha)	Year notified
	National Parks			
1	Connemara	V	2,699	1980
2	Glenveagh	V	9,667	1984
3	Killarney	V	10,129	1932
	Nature Reserves			
4	Glendalough Valley	IV	1,958	1988
5	Knockadoon Head and Capel Island	IV	127	1985
6	Slieve Bloom Mountains	IV	2,230	1986
	Ramsar Wetlands			
	Baldoyle Estuary	R	203	1988
	Castlemaine Harbour	R	923	1990
	Clara Bog	R	460	1988
	Coole/Garryland	R	364	1990
	Easkey Bog	R	607	1990
	Knockmoyle/Sheskin	R	732	1987
	Lough Barra Bog	R	176	1987
	Meenachullion Bog	R	194	1990
	Mongan Bog	R	127	1988
	North Bull Island	R	1,436	1988
	Owenboy	R	397	1987
	Pettigo Plateau	R	900	1986
	Pollardstown Fen	R	130	1990
	Raheenmore Bog	R	162	1988
	Rogerstown Estuary	R	195	1988
	Slieve Bloom Mountains	R	2,230	1986
	The Owenduff Catchment	R	1,382	1986
	The Gearagh	R	300	1990
	The Raven Nature Reserve	R	589	1986
	Tralee Bay	R	861	1989
	Wexford	R	194	1984

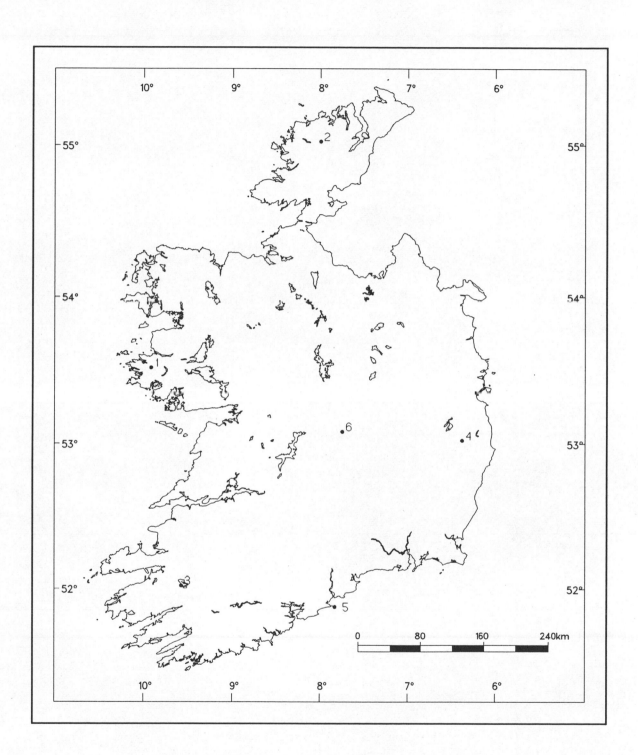

Protected Areas of Ireland

ITALY

Area 301,270 sq. km

Population 57,061,000 (1990)
Natural increase: 0.02% per annum

Economic Indicators
GDP: US$ 13,205 per capita (1987)
GNP: US$ 10,420 per capita (1987)

Policy and Legislation   The present Constitution came into force on 1 January 1948. Article 116 of the Constitution provides for the establishment of five "special statute" autonomous regions and 15 "ordinary statute" autonomous regions. Each region has its own parliament and government with its own legislative and administrative functions (these include Piemonte, Valle d'Aosta, Lombardia, Trentino-alto Adige, Veneto, Friuli-Venezia Giulia, Liguria, Emilia Romagna, Toscane, Umbria, Marche, Lazio, Abruzzi, Molise, Campania, Puglia, Basilicata, Calabria, Sicilia and Sardegna). The coordination of regional activities and national policies is the responsibility of a government commission. Article 9 of the Constitution stipulates that, amongst other responsibilities, the Republic shall protect the landscape and the historical and artistic heritage of the nation (Poore and Gryn-Ambroes, 1980).

A detailed understanding of the environment was well known 2,000 years ago during the classic Roman period. Caius Plinius Secondus (Pliny the Elder) wrote the *Natural History*, of which 37 volumes survive, recording everything known about the world. At that time throughout the Roman Empire there were forest administration structures, delimited forests, wardening systems and programmes of tree planting, along with areas set aside for wildlife (Drucker, *in litt.*, 1985; Mallett, *in litt.*, 1991). In the 19th century royal hunting reserves were established and in 1922 the first national park was set up.

The main categories of protected area in existence include national park (parcho nazionale), state reserve (riserva di stato), regional park (parcho regionale), regional reserve (riserva regionale), marine reserve (riserva marina) and wetland zone (zona umida) (also see below and the Annex) (Ministero dell'Ambiente, 1991).

Most protected areas are covered under regional legislation; one category, widespread in almost every region, is regional park (also known as regional nature park or natural park). Similarly, most regions have legislation for the establishment of nature reserves. There is little or no consistency between the different regional definitions of these parks, making it extremely difficult to relate the variety of regional parks to specific international definitions and classifications on anything higher than a case-by-case basis. This situation remains despite a long list of proposals to introduce such legislation that have been placed before parliament at

regular intervals since 1964 (Cutrera, 1991). Other regional categories of protected area, which are less widespread, include: "area system" (in Piedmont and Lombardia); "biotope" (Alto Adige, Trentino); "protected area" (Liguria); "equipped area" (Piedmont); "suburban park" and "urban park" (Latium); "metropolitan belt park" (Lombardy) and "equipped park" (Abruzzo, Puglia) (National Council of Research, *in litt.*, 1991).

The Presidential Decree No. 616 of 24 July 1977 transferred to the ordinary statute regions the administration of agriculture, forestry, hunting, fishing in inland waters, and the protection of nature, nature reserves and nature parks. National parks and nature reserves of national importance have remained under central control, although more recently some of the responsibilities for national parks have also been devolved. A separate law of 31 December 1979 defines the relevant regulations and the division of responsibility between the state, regions and the "communitá montane" (mountain communities) (Poore and Gryn-Ambroes, 1980). The 1977 Decree maintained the right of the central authorities to designate new areas as national parks and nature reserves, provided they are of inter-regional interest. In special statute regions (Valle d'Aosta, Trentino-Alto Adige, Sicily, Sardinia Friuli-Venezia Giulia) these matters are governed by regional constitutions and legislation (IUCN, 1987; Poore and Gryn-Ambroes, 1980).

The four major national parks were each created under separate legislation, enacted between the 1922 and 1935, to protect fauna and flora, to preserve geological formations, to safeguard the beauty of the landscape and, with one exception (Gran Paradiso), to promote tourism (IUCN, 1987). The fifth and last national park was designated in 1968. Each park has its own constitution, amended and completed by enabling regulations which define the individual institutions which exist in that protected area (see Annex) (Saussey, 1980).

In addition to the national park legislation, some landscape protection has been given under Law No. 1497 of 29 June 1939 concerning the protection of the landscape and all natural assets: this Law has been administered by the Ministry of Culture and Environmental Heritage since this Ministry was established in 1975, although Decree No. 616 of 1977 led to the decentralisation to the regions of most of these responsibilities. This Law has been utilised effectively by nature conservation organisations to restrict developments in areas bordering national parks (Cutrera, 1991; Poore and Gryn-Ambroes, 1980).

A law was passed on 8 August 1985 concerning the protection of natural sites of particular value (Law No. 431). This Law underlines the great necessity and urgency of issuing decrees for the protection of a wide range of biotopes: coastal areas within 300m of the shore, including raised coastlines; lakeshore areas within 300m of the shore; rivers, streams and watercourses; mountain areas over 1,600m in the Alps and 1,200m in the Appenines; glaciers and glacial cirques; national and regional parks and reserves; areas covered by forests and woods, including routes through the forests and forests that have been damaged by fire; areas threatened by public use; wetland areas; volcanoes and areas of archaeological use. The Law largely calls on the increased application of existing legislation for the protection of these biotopes. Specific aspects of this law relate to forest and coastal protection (see below) (*Official Gazette* No. 197).

A number of laws at the national level relate to forestry and forest conservation in Italy. Law No. 3627 of 30 December 1923 is still the only comprehensive framework legislation on forestry issues: it established the existing hydrological-geological based restrictions in an attempt to stop forest deterioration. Tax concessions and financial incentives are provided to reduce the burden of such restrictions, and to encourage owners to implement forest improvement and replanting schemes. Law No. 991, 1952 relates to forestry issues in mountain areas. Law No. 1102 of 1971 still determines public policy in mountain areas and established the mountain communities as a form of local authority. Law No. 431, 1985 regulates forest management, providing for "controlled harvesting, afforestation, reafforestation, improvement schemes, fire regulations, and conservation measures, as allowed by existing laws". This Law also requires regions to draw up territorial development plans or landscape plans which may include rules and restrictions governing forest management – so far few regions have complied with this requirement. A national inventory of forests was completed in 1986/7; at the same time the outline for a national forest plan (piano forestale nazionale) was drawn up. This latter was completed in 1988, as required under the Pluriennial Law for Programmed Intervention in Agriculture No. 752, 1986. The national forest plan is the first comprehensive forestry policy in post-war Italy. It analyses the present situation of forests and forestry and the role of forestry in the economy and the environment. It sets out a number of proposals and measures to expand the forest industry, to increase the total area under forest (there are probably 2.5 million ha of abandoned farmland in Italy); great emphasis is also placed on encouraging the technical, environmental, administrative and economic aspects of forest research (Cutrera, 1991).

Prior to 1982 there was no single legal text concerning marine protected areas. However, some important sites had been designated on the basis of special texts: regional laws such as those applied for the designation of at least one nature park in Tuscany; decrees based around Law No. 963 of 14 July 1965 on fishing (which have been used to establish four protected areas at the

decision of the Minister for the Navy); the classification of sites under international treaties (Ramsar) and the designation of sites by special concession. Miramare Marine Park fell into this latter category. It was set up in 1973 by a concession by the harbour master of Trieste under the Navigational Code (the site is now a marine reserve and biosphere reserve) (Saussay and Prieur, 1980).

The Marine Protection Act No. 979/82 of 31 December 1982 is the first systematic law on sea protection. The law has a wide range of aims which include the designation of marine reserves: a framework description of a marine reserve is provided (see Annex), to be instituted by the Minister for the Environment. A list of 25 proposed marine reserves is given. The Act also requires the formulation of general policy plan for the prevention of marine and coastline pollution and for the protection of the marine environment, but to date such a plan is still pending implementation. The Law provides for the designation of a network of monitoring stations all along the coast, to be staffed by Central Institute for the Scientific and Technological Research into Maritime Fishing. A subsequent Law, No. 431 of 8 August 1985, specifies measures for the protection of the coastline: it follows the provisions of Law No. 1497, 1939 and subjects all land within 300m of the water's edge to landscape restrictions, calling upon the regions to make specific landscape plans that limit or ban building in these zones. Few of the regions have so far imposed these restrictions. Law No. 349, 1986 gives the Minister of the Environment, in consultation with the respective regions, the power to declare certain areas as "environmentally high-risk areas" if the balance of the water, soil or air in these sites is severely altered (Cutrera, 1991).

The Ministry of the Environment (Ministero dell'Ambiente) was created under the terms of Law No. 349 of 8 July 1986. This event marked, to some degree, the beginning of a recentralisation of authority over certain environmental issues. In October 1989 the Minister of the Environment confirmed that a second generation of national parks was about to be created. Through Law No. 350, passed in August 1989, containing the Three-year Programme for Environmental Protection, parliament expressed the need to establish seven new national parks in the immediate future (Cutrera, 1991), none of which has been established to date. Part of the impetus behind this has undoubtedly arisen from a campaign established by the World Wide Fund for Nature and the Italian Committee for National Parks and Equivalent Reserves (see Administration and Management).

A detailed database containing up-to-date copies of all national and regional legislation relating to the environment has been established in the Computer Documentation Centre of the High Court of Justice by the study group of Ecology and Territory (Cutrera, 1991). The Ministry of Environment Decree on 10 June 1991 led to the publishing of the Register of Italian protected areas (Registro delle Aree protette Italiane, rubrica dei dati riassuntivi articolati per regione e per totale nazionale) prepared by the Nature Conservation Service (Servizio Conservazione della Natura) in June 1991 (Ministero dell'Ambiente, 1991).

The failure of the government to establish any national legislation concerning the designation of protected areas has been widely criticised: as already mentioned, numerous bills have been proposed to change this situation, none of which has succeeded in completing its course through parliament. One reason is undoubtedly the indistinct division of responsibility between the central government and the regions on this issue. It was hoped that establishment of the Ministry of the Environment in 1986 might lead to some changes, but, despite growing public awareness of conservation issues and a vociferous campaign by non-governmental conservation organisations, parliament has been reported to delay the issue (Cutrera, 1991; CPNRA/WWF, *in litt.*).

International Activities The Convention concerning the Protection of the World Cultural and Natural Heritage (World Heritage Convention) was ratified on 23 June 1978, but no natural sites have been inscribed on the list. The Convention on Wetlands of International Importance especially as Waterfowl Habitat (Ramsar Convention) was ratified on 14 December 1976: 18 sites were designated on ratification and 46 are now listed. Three sites have been declared biosphere reserves under the Unesco Man and the Biosphere Programme.

Italy has participated in and ratified the UNEP sponsored Barcelona Convention and Mediterranean Action Plan of the Regional Seas programme, notably the Protocol Concerning Mediterranean Specially Protected Areas of 1982 which Italy ratified on 23 March 1986 (Cutrera, 1991): ten Mediterranean special protected areas have been listed. As a member state of the European Community, Italy is a party to the 1979 Wild Birds Directive, under which 74 EC special protection areas have been designated. Italy is also a member of the Council of Europe: 37 sites have been designated as biogenetic reserves and three sites have been awarded the Council of Europe, European Diploma. Italy ratified the Convention on the Conservation of European Wildlife and Natural Habitats (Bern Convention) on 1 June 1982.

There are a number of transboundary agreements between Italy and neighbouring states concerning the management of adjacent border parks: Gran Paradiso National Park was formally twinned with Vanoise National Park in France in 1972, in an action that led to the expansion of their common borders from 6 to 14km. A further agreement was signed in 1981. Argentera Regional Nature Park was formally twinned with Mercantor National Park in France in 1987. Stelvio National Park shares a common border with Swiss National Park in Switzerland, although no formal agreement has been signed between them; discussions

are also taking place concerning the proposals for an international (three-nation) park around Mont Blanc, with France and Switzerland, to incorporate the proposed Italian site of Carlaveyron Nature Reserve.

Administration and Management Law No. 349 of 8 July 1986 created the Ministry of the Environment (Ministero dell'Ambiente), which was structured, under this law, to ensure "the promotion, conservation and restoration of environmental conditions which safeguard the fundamental interests of the community and the quality of life". More specifically, the duties of the Ministry, as listed under this Law include: pollution issues; the protection of nature, parks and nature reserves (transferred from the Ministry of Agriculture); environmental impact assessment; the establishment of environmental improvement plans for areas of "high environmental risk"; and the production of a twice yearly report to parliament on the state of the environment. Regulations for the organisation of the Ministry were approved by Presidential Decree No. 306 of 19 June 1987. They divide the Ministry into three services associated with specific areas of responsibility: prevention of pollution and environmental clean-up; nature conservation; and environmental impact assessment and information services. In addition, there are two services of an instrumental, general nature (general affairs and personnel; cooperation with affiliated bodies). The Geological Service (Servicio Geologico) is also (temporarily) affiliated to the Ministry of the Environment. Regarding technical assets, the Ministry is able to use the state and local technical services, while the "ecological operations unit" of the Carabinieri (police) is functionally responsible to this Ministry.

Two other bodies are closely affiliated to the Ministry: the Scientific Advisory Committee, which is composed of experts designated by the various ministries, of members of the other state advisory bodies and of experts appointed by the Ministry of the Environment itself; and the National Council for the Environment (Consiglio nazionale per l'Ambiente), which is composed of representatives of the regions as well as town and country associations, scientific and energy bodies and representatives appointed by the Ministry from short-lists submitted by 18 national environmental organisations. In some areas the Ministry of the Environment is required to carry out its functions in concert with other relevant ministries; for example, with the Ministry of the Merchant Navy and with the Ministry of Cultural and Environmental Heritage. In its present, relatively new, form, the Ministry is not particularly powerful. A number of previously existing ministries have retained control of sectors normally associated with environmental ministries. Prior to the creation of the Ministry of the Environment, national parks fell under the control of the State Forestry Agency in the Ministry of Agriculture and Forestry (Cutrera, 1991).

Nature reserves are established and managed by the state, the regions or privately.

The Ministry of Cultural and Environmental Heritage cooperates with Ministry of the Environment in the field of environmental impact assessment. It also has powers concerning landscape protection, which it has used for the protection of the natural as well as the cultural environment. The Ministry is advised by the National Council for Cultural and Environmental Heritage (Consiglio Nazionale per i Beni Culturali e Ambientali) (Cutrera, 1991).

Each region has an environmental or territorial council (Assessorato all'Ambiente o al Territorio) which is involved in environmental issues at a regional level. The regional councils occur in each of the regions. There are about 100 provinces which are also in charge of some environmental controls and therefore have their own environmental councils (Assessorati all'Ambiente). There are also some 8,000 municipalities, of which some larger have their own environmental offices, mostly involved in pollution control, but also in providing information services (Cutrera, 1991).

Forest management originally came under the Ministry of Agriculture and Forests (Ministerio dell'Agricoltra e delle Foreste) through the State Forestry Agency. Presidential Decree No. 11 of 1972 (modified by Decree No. 616 of 1977) led to the transfer of all administrative functions in forestry to the regions, with the Ministry simply retaining control of policy and coordination. In some provinces, forestry tasks are carried out by specific boards; in many cases these tasks have been delegated to the provinces, districts, mountain communities and municipalities. In other regions these tasks have been divided between a number of different boards (e.g. soil protection, environment, production).

Research on forestry is carried out by agencies of the Ministry of Agriculture and Forests, as well as by universities and by various other public bodies. In 1987 the General Directorate of Mountain and Forest Economics (Direzione Generale economie montane e foreste) published the results of the national inventory of forests, which was compiled by the State Forestry Agency (Cutrera, 1991).

The Ministry of the Merchant Navy is largely responsible for the designation of marine reserves and for wider issues of marine and coastal protection, and the fight against pollution. In this regard, the Central Institute for the Scientific and Technological Reseach into Maritime Fishing carries out periodic checks on the marine environment, collecting a wide range of data from the network of monitoring stations along the coastline. Reserves themselves are instigated by individual decree by the Minister for the Environment, acting in agreement with the Minister for the Merchant Navy, in consultation with the Council for Sea Protection. They may be administered directly through boards operating within the Harbourmaster's Offices, which are subject to the Central Inspectorate for Sea Protection, or indirectly through the appointment of public bodies, scientific institutions, or recognised

associations. These latter appointments are made by the Ministry of the Merchant Navy and the Ministry of the Environment.

If a reserve borders on a national park or a state nature reserve, the decree for its designation is issued jointly with the Ministry of Agriculture and Forestry. There is a long list of areas mentioned in the law as worthy of protection, most of which have not been designated (Cutrera, 1991).

Three of national parks, Stelvio, Circeo and Calabria, continue to be administered and managed by the Forest Service in the Ministry of Agriculture and Forestry, which appoints the park directors. The parks' specific advisory commissions are composed of representatives of ministries, local communities, institutions and others. Gran Paradiso and Abruzzo national parks are administered by independent park agencies (Enti). They have sole responsibility for administration and management and their membership consists of scientists, local community members and representatives of ministries (IUCN; 1987; Poore and Gryn-Ambroes, 1980; Ministry of the Environment, *in litt.*, 1991).

The Investment and Employment Fund (Fonds Investimentie Occupazione) has played an important role in the financing of environmental issues. This fund, which is included in the draft budget of the state, is largely assigned to the Ministry of Financing and Economic Programming for "operations of high economic interest within the country, in agriculture, in building...and for safeguarding environmental and cultural assets". In 1986, of a total of 643 applications for project funding, 293 were for the safeguarding of the environment. The total environmental expenditure charged to the state budget, the Investment and Employment Fund and to the regions was close to lire 8,000 billion, or 0.85% of the GDP: this figure was 0.82% in 1985; 0.67% in 1984 and 0.82% in 1983 (Cutrera, 1991). The budgets for national parks are fixed by law and in the case of Abruzzo and Gran Paradiso can only be changed with Parliament's consent. Those of Stelvio and Circeo are augmented by the Azienda. The total national park budget in 1975 and 1976 was lire 1,180,000 but in the case of Gran Paradiso a heavy proportion went towards employing the 60-65 park wardens. Each national park has two to eight executive and administrative staff and between seven and 65 wardens (Poore and Gryn-Ambroes, 1980).

Private reserves and wildlife refuges and protection "oases" can be set up privately by voluntary bodies and by universities. WWF-Italia is the most active environmental body which manages wildlife habitats, while there are ten reserves totalling 7,000ha which have been set up by the universities. Voluntary bodies such as Italia Nostra, the Italian Botanical Society and the Consiglio Nazionale delle Ricerche, have all made efforts to promote nature conservation, including compiling inventories for areas needing protection (Poore and Gryn-Ambroes, 1980). Eighteen of the larger non-governmental organisations in Italy are represented in the National Environmental Council, an organ of the Ministry of the Environment, and hence have at least some direct influence on the government. These include: the Italian Touring Club (TCI), the Italian Mountaineering Association (Club Alpino Italiano), WWF-Italia, the Environmental League (Lega per l'Ambiente) (LIPU), the Environmental Research Group (GRE), the Italian Environmental Fund (Fondo Ambiente Italiano), Agriturist, Work and Environment (Ambiente e Lavoro), Pro Natura, ANIA, Italia Nostra, Friends of the Earth (Amici della Terra) and Greenpeace. A number of environmental associations, headed by WWF-Italia and the Italian Committee for National Parks and Equivalent Reserves (Comitato Parchi Nazionali e Riserve Analoghe – Italia) (CPNRA), have been running a campaign since 1990 centred on establishing protection for 10% of the country. 1990 was declared "the year of the parks", and the campaign was run under the slogan "a land of green parks and a sea of blue parks": recommendations have been made for the establishment of 25 new national parks. It may be partly a result of this campaign that the government is now considering the designation of a number of new sites (CPNRA, *in litt.*, 1991)

Problems arising from the legislation relating to national parks have included the ambiguity between conservation and tourism objectives which has contributed to the development of conflicts. This may be linked to decentralisation and regionalisation: whereby local authorities are more susceptible to vested interests such as hunters, timber enterprises and tourism development: and continue potentially damaging activities in protected areas such as promoting tourism, and allow public works (highways and ski lifts) to be developed (Commission of the European Communities, 1979; Framarin, 1984). A further problem is that the first four national parks were created in the inter-war period without any prior consultation with local authorities and without adequate compensation to the local community. As a result neither the national parks nor the laws which created them are highly respected or upheld by the inhabitants of the area concerned (IUCN, 1987; Poore and Gryn-Ambroes, 1980; Saussey, 1980). Local opposition to proposing national parks in the past has almost completely stopped the establishment of these areas.

National parks had been undergoing regionalisation for more than 10 years in an attempt to ensure more local representation on their management committees (Framarin, 1984). The process of regionalisation has caused the administrative split of Stelvio National Park between central and regional authorities. Only some 25% of national park land is state-owned and there apparently has always been a shortage of government money to run these areas, despite increasing numbers of visitors and management needs (Poore and Gryn-Ambroes, 1980).

Stelvio National Park has been on the IUCN Commission on National Parks and Protected Areas list of threatened sites since 1986 due to a proposal by the authorities for a 50% reduction in size to allow for additional forestry and hunting activities.

Systems Reviews   To the north, Italy shares borders with France, Switzerland, Austria and Yugoslavia – for the majority of its length this border passes through the Alps, although the eastern border with Yugoslavia crosses a low plain before reaching the coast at Trieste. The highest mountain in Europe, Mont Blanc, lies on the border with France, at 4,807m. Italy's largest river, the Po, drains a wide area, flowing from the Alps to the Adriatic; this river effectively separates the continental landmass of Italy from the larger area, the "spine" of Italy, a long peninsula running south-east into the Mediterranean Sea. The eastern coast of Italy, and the Gulf of Venice leading round to the border with Yugoslavia, form the northern and western edges of the Adriatic Sea; to the south there is the Ionian Sea. To the north of the French island of Corsica, where the leg of Italy joins the main continental landmass, lies the Ligurian Sea and the Gulf of Genoa. The Appennines are a lower mountain range running down most of the length of the peninsula of Italy. There are two very large Mediterranean islands: Sicily to the south-west and Sardinia to the west; between these islands and the western coast of the mainland lies the Tyrrhenian Sea with a myriad of minute islands and islets. Both of the large islands are also fairly mountainous: Mount Etna on Sicily rises to 3,323m and is the largest active volcano in Europe.

Much of Italy is modified by agriculture. Some central European vegetation remains in the foothills of the Alps, with broad-leaved and coniferous forests, with pines *Pinus sylvestris* and *P. cembra*, oaks and beech. Alpine meadows and cushion vegetation are abundant above the treeline up to 4,000m, many of them grazed in summer. Large areas of the Appennines have maintained their cover of natural deciduous forest, predominantly oak *Quercus*, sweet chestnut *Castanea sativa* and beech *Fagus*, although other areas have been widely deforested for agriculture. The original lowland and coastal cover of sclerophyllous forests, dominated by pine *Pinus halepensis*, is largely degraded or converted to agriculture: in places it has been replaced by coastal maquis with oak *Quercus ilex* scrub. Little natural vegetation remains on Sicily or Sardinia, especially around the coastline. Inland, on Sardinia, a zone of holm oak *Quercus ilex* is dominant, although much has been replaced by dry pasture or degraded to garigue. In Sicily forest cover was once almost continuous in the north, dominated by Sicilian fir *Abies nebrodensis*, but now only fragments remain; some broad-leaved forests remain elsewhere, including on the slopes of Mount Etna, although degradation is now widespread (Davis *et al.*, 1986; Grimmett and Jones, 1989).

The area covered by wetlands has been in decline since Roman times, and now only a tiny proportion remains. There remain, however, a number of important wetland sites, including a few relict sites along the Po, and others along the north-west shores of the Adriatic. A few wetland sites of importance are situated along the Tyrrhenian coast, a number of which have protected status (IUCN, 1990). Between 1982 and 1984 some 41% of Italy was under cultivation, and a further 17% was pasture land (Grimmett and Jones, 1989). Forests cover 29% of the total land area, or 8,675,100ha: some 42% of this is coppice woodland and 25% is high forest. There are numerous tracts of forest on private land: the National Forest Plan lists 1.2 million privately-owned tracts and 14,500 held by municipalities and local public bodies. A detailed annual survey on the deterioration of forests has been undertaken since 1984 by the State Forest Agency. There has been a decline in human encroachment on mountains and hills in recent decades and this has favoured an increase in the quality and quantity of forest biomass (Cutrera, 1991).

A full list of the protected areas of Italy has most recently been produced in June 1991 by the Servizio Conservazione della Natura of the Ministry of the Environment, the Registro delle Aree protette Italiane, rubrica dei dati riassuntivi articolati per regione e per totale nazionale (Ministero dell'Ambiente, 1991).

Italy's first protected areas were the four national parks established in 1922, 1923, 1934 and 1935. These were enlarged by a total of 53,000ha in the 1970s, but despite this the total was still below 1% of total surface area (Framarin, 1984). The first nature reserves were established by the Ministry of Agriculture and Forestry in 1959, although the first legally gazetted reserve, Carso Triestino, was not established until 1968 (under an individual decree) (Poore and Gryn-Ambroes, 1980). The current situation may be summarised as follows. National designations: 5 national parks covering 273,086ha; 140 national nature reserves covering 107,029ha; 5 marine reserves covering 6,496ha and 46 Ramsar sites covering 53,885ha, giving a total of 194 nationally designated sites, covering a total of 427,012ha or 1.47% of the total land area. Regional designations: 80 regional natural parks covering 1,310,036ha; 148 regional nature reserves covering 75,187ha and 170 other areas covering 29,135ha, giving a total of 398 sites covering 1,403,607ha or 4.66% of the total land area. Combining national and regional protected areas the total, including areas managed by private institutions, there are 602 sites with a combined area of 1,805,717ha, some 5.99% of the total land area (although some of these sites overlap, the land areas have in no case been counted more than once) (National Council of Research, *in litt.*, 1991). By the first half of 1991 the official total number of reserves was 627 with a combined area of 2,226,754ha, some 7.4% of the total land area (Ministero dell'Ambiente, 1991). If the 20 new national parks proposed by the conservation organisations are adopted, the total area covered by national parks will be some 970,000ha. In order to attain their desired level of protection for 10% of total land area, it has been recommended that the area protected under regional, local and private categories will also have to be expanded considerably (CPNRA, *in litt.*, 1991). The National Council of Research maintains a database describing both national and regional protected areas in Italy, and also undertakes analyses of this information (Napoleone and Palladino, 1990).

Of the total surface area covered by forests, some 89% have a limited form of protection under the hydrological-based restrictions of the 1923 Forestry Law, 5% are covered under other restrictions, and 5% are free of restrictions (Cutrera, 1991).

Fragmentation of farmland is a major problem: in 1980, 76% of agricultural holdings were less than 5ha and only 2% were greater than 50ha: this clearly presents problems when it comes to designating new protected areas and managing sites that are not on state-owned land. Agricultural methods are still fairly traditional and labour intensive, especially in the south and in the mountainous regions, although mechanisation and intensive monoculture are on the increase. Huge areas of natural value have been destroyed in recent years through agricultural, industrial and touristic developments, often aided by EC grants. Many wetland areas have been drained, while many of the steppic type areas of southern Italy, Sicily and Sardinia have been replaced by cultivation over the last 100 years. Tourism is largely concentrated on the coasts and offshore islands, where large natural areas are being destroyed (Grimmett and Jones, 1989).

Pollution is a problem in a number of rivers, and also along large stretches of the coastline: during the summers of 1988 and 1989 stretches of the upper Adriatic were subject to extreme forms of environmental pollution. This sea in particular receives a large quantity of fresh water input, with associated human waste, from a number of rivers, as well as a direct human waste input from the various settlements along the coast. Extreme eutrophication has led to algal proliferation and, in 1989, a layer of mucilaginous material formed on the water surface, with adverse consequences both for the marine life and the tourist industry. As a result, the government declared an emergency situation in the area and efforts are being made to bring the situation under control. Clearly, this is an extreme case, but it serves to illustrate the threat facing huge areas of the heavily populated and polluted Italian coastline. The State Forest Agency survey, Indagine sul deperimento delle foreste, has shown an increase in the incidence of damaged trees, with the highest incidence found among the pine and fir species: 11.1% of oak trees show some sign of damage, although for beech populations this figure is only 5.6%. This damage may be related to air pollution: while the problem has not reached the same scale as in regions of central Europe, the overall figure of 10% of trees showing some signs of damage should not be ignored. Forest fires too have increased considerably in the last 20 years, although the increase in area covered affected is less dramatic (Cutrera, 1991).

Other Relevant Information   In 1989, up to 55.1 million foreign visitors went to Italy spending up to lire 16,443,99 million. In 1979/1980 there were estimates of 300,000 visitors to Stelvio and 500,000 to Gran Paradiso alone.

Addresses

Ministerio dell'Ambiente, Servizio Conservazione della Natura (Director General), Piazza Venezia 11, 00187 ROME (Tel: 6 679 7124)

Ministry of Agriculture and Forestry, Direzione Generale per l'Economia Montana e le Foreste, Division 11, 5. via Caducci 00100 ROME (00187 ROME)

National Council of Research, Via Lancisi 29, 00161 ROME

Comitato Parchi Nazionali e Riserve Analoghe, Viale delle Medaglie d'Oro 141, 00136 ROME (Tel: 6 3496993; Tlx: 242550 NAT PAR I; FAX: 6 3497594)

Commissione per la Conservazione della Natura, e delle sue Risorse del Consiglio Nazionale, delle Rich Ricerche, 7 Piazzela delle Scienze, 00158 ROME

Addresses also available for bodies within each of the following regions: Piemonte, Valle d'Aosta, Lombardia, Trentino-alto Adige, Veneto, Friuli-Venezia Giulia, Liguria, Emilia Romagna, Toscane, Umbria, Marche, Lazio, Abruizzi, Molise, Campania, Puglia, Basilicata, Calabria, Sicilia and Sardegna

References

Anon. (1985). Rapporto di Campo dei Fiori. Sulla salvaguardia dell'Ambiente in Lombardia. Regione Lombardia – Settore Ambiente Ecologia.

Anon. (1987). *Management of Europe's Natural Heritage, twenty-five years of Activity*. Council of Europe, Environment Protection and Management Division, Strasbourg. 128 pp.

Augier, H. (1985). *Protected marine areas. The example of France: appraisal and prospects*. European Committee for the Conservation of Nature and Natural Resources, Strasbourg.

Baccar, H. (1977). A Survey of Existing and Potential Marine Parks and Reserves in the Mediterranean Region. IUCN/UNEP.

Barducci, G. (1979). The Nature Parks of South Tirol. *Nature and National Parks* 66(17): 13.

Barducci G. (1978). The National Parks of Italy. *Nature and National Parks* 62(16): 11-12.

Commission of the European Communities (1979). Protected Areas in the European Community. An approach to a common classification. Environment and Consumer Protection Service. ENV/311/80.

Cutrera, A. (1991). *European Environmental Yearbook*. Institute for Environmental Studies. DocTer International UK, London. 897 pp.

Davis, S.D., Droop, S.J.M., Gregerson, P., Henson, L., Leon, C.J., Lamlein Villa-Lobos, J., Synge, H. and Zantovska, J. (1986). *Plants in danger: what do we know?* IUCN, Gland, Switzerland and Cambridge, UK. 461 pp.

Duffey, E. (1982). *National parks and reserves of Western Europe*. Macdonald and Company, London.

Framarin, F. (1984). Small is a can of vermicelli. *Parks* (9)1: 16-17.

Grimmett, R.F.A. and Jones, T.A. (1989). *Important bird areas in Europe*. International Council for Bird Preservation, Technical Publication No. 9, Cambridge, UK.

Gryn-Ambroes, P. (1980). Preliminary Annotated Lists of Existing and Potentially Mediterranean Protected Areas. IUCN.

ICBP (1985). Draft report to Council of Europe 81 bird species in Council of Europe countries.

ICBP (1982). Biotopes of significance for Nature Conservation. Site Register XI/94/83.

IUCN (1987). *Directory of wetlands of international importance*. IUCN. Gland, Switzerland and Cambridge, UK.

IUCN (1990). *Directory of wetlands of international importance*. Ramsar Convention Bureau, Gland, Switzerland. 796 pp.

Ministero dell'Ambiente (1991). *Registro delle aree protette Italiane, rubrica dei dati riassuntivi articolati per regione e per totale nazionale*. Servizio Conservazione della Natura, Ministero dell'Ambiente. 249 pp.

Napoleone, I. and Palladino, S. (1990). Aree naturali protette in Italia: stato delle conoscenze ed esigenze di ricerca. 2nd Workshop, Progetto Strategico Clima, Ambiente e Territorio nel Mezzogiorno. Parchi Naturali e Aree Protette, S. Marina Salina (Isole Eolie), 28-30 Maggio, 1990. 18pp.

Palladino, S. (1987). *Lista delle aree naturali protette in Italia*. Centro di studio sulla genetica evoluzionistica del CNR. Roma.

Pavan, M. (1985). *Appunti e documenti sulla situazione del patrimonio naturaliscico italiano. Territori protetti. Minacce sulla fauna, flora e vegetazione*. Instituto di Entomologia dell 'Universita di Pavia.

Poore, D. and Gryn-Ambroes, P. (1980). *Nature conservation in Northern and Western Europe* UNEP/IUCN/WWF, Gland, Switzerland.

Ray, C. and McCormick, P.A.G. (1976). Critical marine habitats: list of areas. IUCN/WWF Project No. 39/4-1037

Saussey, C. du (1980). *Legislation on wildlife, hunting and protected areas in some European countries*. Legislative study No. 20. FAO, Rome.

Tassi, F. (1982). Comitato Parchi: Un Lustro d'Attività.

UNEP (1980). *Survey of national legislation relevant to marine and coastal protected areas*. Report IG.20/Inf 3. GE. 80-2585 by the legal office of the Food and Agriculture Organisation of the United Nations based on the works of C. du Saussey and M. Prieur.

Wirth, H. (1979). *Nature reserves in Europe* Edition Leipzig.

ANNEX
Definitions of protected area designations, as legislated, together with authorities responsible for their administration

Title: Individual laws related to the designation of individual national parks: Gran Paradiso National Park Royal Decree Law No. 1584; Abruzzo National Park Royal Decree No. 257 and Law No. 1511; Circeo National Park Law No. 285; Stelvio National Park Law No. 740 and Calabria National Park Law No. 503

Date: 3 December 1922 (Gran Paradiso); 11 January 1923 and 12 July 1923 (Abruzzo); 25 January 1934 (Circeo); 25 April 1935 (Stelvio); and 2 April 1968 (Calabria)

Brief description: Individual laws covering the designation and regulations for each national park

Administrative authority: State departments in the Ministry of the Environment and the Ministry of Agriculture and Forestry; and also regional and local authorities

Designations:

Parcho nazionale (National park) Commercial activities, including agriculture and forestry, still continue in the national parks with forestry plans prepared by the Forest Service and the level of exploitation varying from park to park. Under Law No. 968 of 1977, hunting was declared illegal in national parks, but could have been authorised by special permit.

Currently there is pressure to reintroduce hunting into the national parks; heavy fines are imposed to prevent hunting (typically some five times the value of the animal concerned).

Some regions issue large numbers of hunting permits. Fishing is permitted, as is fruit and fungi collection. There is open access to national parks, with tendencies for extremely high visitor numbers for short break or longer stay vacations in the numerous hotels, "pensions" and campsites.

Land is generally in the ownership of local authorities or private individuals and tends to consist of a mosaic of relict primary unspoilt ecosystems along with plantations, grazing and agricultural land. As in the case of Abruzzo National Park a buffer zone around national parks may be established under Article 2 of the establishment Act and hunting is prohibited under Article 14 of the 1923 regulations. Stelvio National Park has produced a zonation plan; another exists for Abruzzo. The legal requirements for building construction vary from park to park, and in some depend on regional building laws and local

communities authorisation, whilst in others are controlled by the park authorities. The control on building schemes outside of urban areas is provided by Act No. 1497 of 29 June 1939 on "Protezione delle Bellezze Naturali" administered by the Cultural and Environmental Heritage Ministry and by the regional authorities. All proposals are referred to the relevant local authorities or "soprintendenze". Some parks have closed down roads, whilst others have developed new ones and winter sport facilities are also present.

Sources: Duffey, 1982; IUCN, 1987; Poore and Gryn-Ambroes, 1980; Saussey, 1980

Title: No specific legislation

Date: Different dates for each decree

Brief description: Natural reserves established under national or regional legislation or by individuals or private organisations.

Administrative authority: Authorities at the state, regional and municipal level. Regions authorities are found in each of the following regions: Piemonte, Valle d'Aosta, Lombardia, Trentino-alto Adige, Veneto, Friuli-Venezia Giulia, Liguria, Emilia Romagna, Toscane, Umbria, Marche, Lazio, Abruizzi, Molise, Campania, Puglia, Basilicata, Calabria, Sicilia and Sardegna

Designations:

Riserva naturale (Natural or nature reserve) There is no strict definition and rules and regulations vary enormously. Many reserves tend to lack basic legislation, although there are notable regional variations. The designation of some nature reserves follows a classification typology adapted by the Council of Europe, these reserves include: a) strict nature reserves (riserve naturali integrali); b) managed nature reserves (riserve naturali orientate); c) partial reserves, including five divisions ranging from geological to botanical, zoological, biological and anthropological reserves (riserve parziali); d) special reserves, including four divisions ranging from natural reserve area, natural monument, forestry reserve to vegetation/animal or biogenetic reserve (riserve speciali). Visitors to nature reserves tend to need permits for entry

Many nature reserves were established on state land by order of ministerial decrees. Those on private property were established either by parliamentary authorisation, by the regional governments or on the initiative of the land owners. Other nature reserves have been established under authorisation of special statute regions and by universities (such as Pavia and Comerino).

Sources: Palladino, 1987; Pavan, 1985; Poore and Gryn-Ambroes, 1980

Title: Various regional laws

Date: Individually declared

Brief description: Declared under regional legislation

Administrative authority: Regional and local authorities. Regions authorities are found in each of the following regions: Piemonte, Valle d'Aosta, Lombardia, Trentino-alto Adige, Veneto, Friuli-Venezia Giulia, Liguria, Emilia Romagna, Toscane, Umbria, Marche, Lazio, Abruizzi, Molise, Campania, Puglia, Basilicata, Calabria, Sicilia and Sardegna

Designations:

Parcho regionale (Regional park)   Also known as regional park or recreational park, these areas have been established for a combination of nature conservation, recreation purposes and safeguarding important landscape features and local traditional land use practices. Although created under a wide range of different legislation, they have a number of features in common: their proximity to large conurbations; the tendency to permit the development of existing economic activities, even those of an industrial nature (such as mining and quarrying) if these can be made compatible with the aims of nature conservation; the tendency to encourage agricultural and forestry activities; the possibility of providing recreational and other facilities for the local inhabitants within the sites; and the possibility of providing educational responsibility and service for local schools and wildlife organisations. These sites are typically under the management of local administrations, sometimes in conjunction with local authorities.

Sources: Commission of the European Communities, 1979; Cutrera, 1991; Palladino, 1987; Pavan, 1985

Title: Marine Protection Act (No. 979)

Date: 31 December 1982

Brief description: A wide ranging Act covering the protection of the coastline, including the designation of marine reserves.

Administrative authority: Ministry of the Environment

Designations:

Riserva marina (Marine reserve)   These are defined as marine environments consisting of the sea water, sea bed and stretches of the sea coast that are of special interest because of their natural, geomorphological, physical and biochemical features, particularly with respect to the marine and coastal flora and fauna and their scientific, ecological, cultural, educational and economic importance. Sites are declared by the Minister for the Environment by individual decree, in consultation with the Minister for the Merchant Navy in Consultation with the Council for Sea Protection. Restrictions vary, but might include a ban or restriction on movement, access, or mooring of vessels of any kind; bathing, fishing, and hunting along the coast; the dumping of waste; and any kind of activity which might disrupt the animal or vegetable life of the marine environment.

Source: Cutrera, 1991

225

SUMMARY OF PROTECTED AREAS

Map[†] ref.	*National/international designations* Name of area	IUCN management category	Area (ha)	Year notified
	National Parks			
1	Abruzzo	II	43,950	1923
2	Arcipelago Toscano	II	67,500	1989
3	Calabria	II	15,894	1968
4	Circeo	V	8,622	1934
5	Dolomiti Bellunesi	II	31,000	1990
6	Gran Paradiso	II	70,000	1922
7	Sibillini	II	65,200	1990
8	Stelvio	V	148,271	1935
	Nature Reserves			
9	Abbadia di Fiastra	IV	1,808	1985
10	Area piu alta del Massiccio del Pollino	IV	3,000	
11	Badia Prataglia	IV	1,631	1977
12	Bosco della Mesola	IV	1,058	1977
13	Bosco e Laghi di Palanfre	V	1,050	1979
14	Camaldoli	IV	1,168	1977
15	Campigna	IV	1,191	1977
16	Cavagrande del Cassibile	IV	2,696	1984
17	Faggeta Madonia	IV	2,949	1984
18	Fara S. Martino-Palombaro	IV	4,202	1983
19	Feudo Ugni	IV	1,563	1981
20	Foce del Crati	IV	1,490	1990
21	Foresta Demaniale del Circeo	IV	3,070	1977
22	Foresta di Monte Arcosu	IV	3,205	1985
23	Foresta di Sabaudia	IV	3,070	1978
24	Foresta di Tarvisio	IV	23,294	1980
25	Foresta di Vallombrosa	IV	1,300	1977
26	Gole del Raganello	IV	1,600	1987
27	Grotticelle	IV	21,422	1971
28	Isola di Caprera	IV	1,575	1980
29	Isola di Lampedusa	IV	275	1984
30	Isole dello Stagnone di Marsala	IV	2,012	1984
31	Laghi Lungo e Ripasottile	IV	1,948	1985
32	Lago di Campotosto	IV	1,600	1984
33	Lago di Mezzola-Pian di Spagna	IV	1,586	1983
34	Lago di Vico	V	3,240	1982
35	Lama Bianca di S. Eufemia a Maiella	IV	1,407	1987
36	Larna Branca di S. Eufemia a Maiella	IV	1,300	1987
37	Marchesale	IV	1,257	1977
38	Montagne della Duchessa	IV	3,000	1988
39	Montagne delle Felci e dei Porri	IV	1,521	1984
40	Monte Mottac	IV	2,410	1971
41	Monte Navegna e Monte Cervia	IV	1,350	1988
42	Monte Pelmo-Modeval-Passo Giau	IV	4,670	1990
43	Monte Quacella	IV	2,010	1984
44	Monte Rotondo	IV	1,452	1982
45	Monte Rufeno	IV	2,840	1983
46	Monte Soro	IV	4,396	1985
47	Monte Velino	IV	3,550	1987
48	Montecristo Island	IV	1,039	1971
49	Monti del Sole	IV	3,035	1972
50	Mt. d. Felci e Dei Porri d. Isole di Salina	IV	1,600	1984
51	Oasi Faunistica di Vendicari	IV	1,512	1984
52	Oasi del Simeto	IV	1,859	1984

Map[†] ref.	National/international designations Name of area	IUCN management category	Area (ha)	Year notified
53	Piani Eterni-Errera-Val Falcina	IV	5,463	1975
54	Pineta di Vittoria	IV	3,531	1984
55	Poverella-Villaggio Mancuso	IV	1,086	1977
56	Salina di Margherita di Savoia	IV	3,871	1977
57	Schiara Occidentale	IV	3,172	1975
58	Somadida	IV	1,676	1972
59	Sorgive di Bars	IV	1,100	1987
60	Stornara	IV	1,456	1977
61	Tarsia	IV	1,510	1990
62	Tirone-Alto Vesuvio	IV	1,019	1972
63	Torrente Prescudin	IV	1,670	
64	Toscane	IV	1,039	
65	Val Tovanella	IV	1,040	1971
66	Val di Farme	IV	4,500	
67	Valle del Fiume Argentina	IV	3,980	1987
68	Valle del Fiume Lao	IV	5,200	1987
69	Valle dell'Orfento	IV	2,606	1971
70	Valli del Mincio (regional)	IV	1,081	1983
71	Valli del Mincio (state)	IV	1,300	1977
72	Vallombrosa	IV	1,270	1977
73	Vette Feltrine	IV	2,764	1975
74	Voltigno e Valle d'Angri	IV	5,172	1989
75	Zingaro Regional	IV	1,600	1981
76	Zompo lo Schioppo	IV	1,025	1987
77	Zona tra Monte Mia ed Erbezzo	IV	1,300	1990
	Marine Reserves			
78	Isola di Ustica	IV	4,280	1986
79	Isole Tremiti	IV	2,116	1989
80	Montecristo	IV	1,035	1979
81	Secche della Meloria	IV	120,000	1982
	Nature Monument			
82	Campo Soriano	III	1,500	1985
	Regional Nature Parks/Regional Parks			
83	Adamello (Lombardy)	V	48,100	1983
84	Adamello-Brenta (Trentino-Alto Adige)	V	61,864	1967
85	Adda Nord	V	5,580	1983
86	Adda Sud	V	23,600	1983
87	Alpe Devero	V	6,588	1990
88	Alpe Veglia	V	4,135	1978
89	Alpi Apuane	V	60,000	1985
90	Alpi Giulie	V	10,000	1990
91	Alta Valle Pesio	V	3,955	1978
92	Alta Valsesia	V	6,435	1979
93	Alto Appennino Modenese	V	9,026	1988
94	Alto Appennino Reggiano	V	8,868	1988
95	Alto Garda Bresciano	V	38,269	1989
96	Argentera	V	25,883	1980
97	Boschi di Carrega	V	1,270	1982
98	Campo dei Fiori	V	5,400	1984
99	Capanne di Marcarolo	V	11,800	1979
100	Colli Euanei	V	15,000	1989
101	Colli di Bergamo	V	4,979	1977
102	Corno alle Scale	V	3,030	1988
103	Crinale Romagnolo	V	15,887	1988
104	Dolomiti d'Ampezzo	V	11,000	1990

Map[†] ref.	National/international designations Name of area	IUCN management category	Area (ha)	Year notified
105	Dolomiti di Sesto	V	11,635	1981
106	Etna	V	50,000	1987
107	Fanes-Sennes-Braies	V	25,680	1980
108	Fiume Serio	V	7,570	1985
109	Gessi Bolognesi e Calanchi Abbadessa	V	3,000	1988
110	Gran Bosco di Salbertrand	V	2,005	1980
111	Groane	V	3,445	1976
112	Gruppo di Tessa	V	33,430	1976
113	La Mandria	V	6,470	1978
114	Lessinia	V	8,000	1990
115	Lucretili	V	18,000	1989
116	Madonie	V	35,000	1989
117	Maremma	V	9,800	1975
118	Migliarino-San Rossore-Massaciuccoli	V	22,000	1979
119	Mincio	V	13,708	1984
120	Mont Avic	V	3,500	1989
121	Monte Corno	V	6,660	1980
122	Monte Fenera	V	3,365	1987
123	Montevecchia e Valle del Curone	V	1,598	1983
124	Monti Simbruini	V	38,000	1983
125	Oglio Nord	V	14,170	1988
126	Oglio Sud	V	12,800	1988
127	Orobie Bergamasche	V	84,000	1989
128	Orobie Valtellinesi	V	44,000	1989
129	Orsiera-Rocciavre	V	10,928	1980
130	Paveneggio-Pale di San Martino	V	19,097	1967
131	Pineta di Appiano Gentile e Tradate	V	4,597	1983
132	Po Delta	V	60,000	1988
133	Pollino	V	77,000	1986
134	Prealpi Carniche	V	25,000	1990
135	Prescudin	V	1,647	1974
136	Puez-Odle	V	9,210	1977
137	Sciliar	V	5,850	1974
138	Serio	V	7,570	1985
139	Sirente Velino	V	50,000	1989
140	Val Troncea	V	3,280	1980
141	Valle del Lambro	V	6,452	1983
142	Valle del Ticino (Lombardia)	V	90,640	1974
143	Valle del Ticino (Piemonte)	V	6,250	1978
144	Vendrette di Ries	V	20,581	1988

	Biosphere Reserves			
	Collemeluccio-Montedimezzo	IX	478	1977
	Forêt Domaniale du Circeo	IX	3,260	1977
	Miramare Marine Park	IX	60	1979
	Ramsar Wetlands			
	Bacino dell'Angitola	R	875	1989
	Corru S'Ittiri Fishery-Stagno di San Giovanni e Marceddi	R	2,610	1979
	Diaccia Botrona	R	2,500	1991
	Il Biviere di Gela	R	256	1988
	Isola Boscone	R	201	1989
	Lago di Burano	R	410	1976
	Lago di Caprolace	R	229	1976

Map[†] ref.	National/international designations Name of area	IUCN management category	Area (ha)	Year notified
	Lago di Fogliano	R	395	1976
	Lago di Mezzola-Pian di Spagna	R	1,740	1976
	Lago di Monaci	R	94	1976
	Lago di Nazzano	R	265	1976
	Lago di Sabaudia	R	1,474	1976
	Lago di Tovel	R	37	1980
	Lago di Villetta Barrea	R	303	1976
	Laguna di Orbetello (Northern part)	R	887	1976
	Le Cesine	R	620	1977
	Marano Lagunare-Foci dello Stella	R	1,400	1979
	Ortazzo and adjacent territories	R	440	1981
	Palude di Bolgheri	R	562	1976
	Palude Brabbia	R	459	1984
	Palude di Colfiorito	R	157	1976
	Paludi di Ostiglia	R	123	1984
	Pialassa della Baiona	R	1,630	1981
	Punte Alberete	R	480	1976
	Riserva naturale Vendicari	R	1,450	1989
	Sacca di Bellochio	R	223	1976
	Salina di Margherita di Savoia	R	3,871	1979
	Saline di Cervia	R	785	1981
	Stagno di Cabras	R	3,575	1979
	Stagno di Cagliari	R	3,466	1976
	Stagno di Mistras	R	680	1982
	Stagno di Molentargius	R	1,401	1976
	Stagno di Pauli Maiori	R	287	1979
	Stagno di Sale Porcus	R	330	1982
	Stagno S'Ena Arrubia	R	300	1976
	Torbiere d'Iseo	R	325	1984
	Torre Guaceto	R	940	1981
	Valle Averto	R	200	1989
	Valle Bertuzzi	R	3,100	1981
	Valle Campotto e Bassarone	R	1,363	1979
	Valle Cavanata	R	243	1978
	Valle di Gorino	R	1,330	1981
	Valle Santa	R	261	1976
	Valli residue del Comprensorio di Comacchio	R	13,500	1981
	Valli del Mincio	R	1,082	1984
	Vincheto di Cellarda	R	99	1976

[†]Locations of some protected areas are shown on the accompanying map.

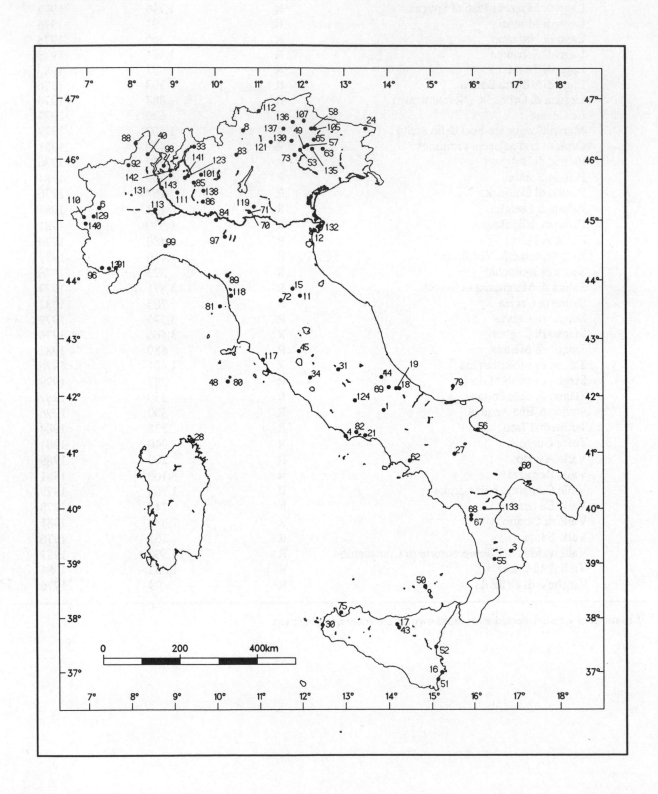

Protected Areas of Italy

REPUBLIC OF LATVIA

Area 63,700 sq. km

Population 2,681,000 (Paxton, 1991)
Natural increase: no information

Economic Indicators
GNP: No information
GDP: No information

Policy and Legislation Following the abortive coup of August 1991, Latvia declared its independence from the USSR and was recognised by the international community, receiving its seat at the United Nations. No overall law on protected areas was prepared before the date of independence, and therefore a new law is likely to be required. Past republic laws on soil, water and forests, on mineral extraction and faunal protection, as well as specific regulations, are likely to be superseded by new national legislation (Weisenburger, 1991).

Based on past Republic laws, there are 13 categories of protected area: reserve, complex nature sanctuary, botanical sanctuary, wetland sanctuary, peat reserve, ornithological sanctuary, geological-geomorphological object, national park, nature park, landscape protection area, natural monument, park, other protected area (Melluma, 1982).

International Activities The first biosphere reserve is now proposed as part of continued participation in the Unesco Man and the Biosphere Programme. The Convention concerning the World Cultural and Natural Heritage (World Heritage Convention) and the Convention on Wetlands of International Importance Especially as Waterfowl Habitat (Ramsar Convention) continue to apply following independence from USSR.

In April 1991 the Association of Baltic National Parks was established and started work after the statute was signed on 22 June 1991. Membership comprises five national parks and the secretariat is based in Estonia.

Administration and Management Protected areas are administered and managed by state authorities. Budgets for protected areas increased rapidly from 1975 to 1985 (245,000 roubles to 1,116,000) and have since remained steady to 1990 (1,188,000 roubles) (Nikol'skii *et al.*, 1991). The administrative budget for the Environmental Protection Committee was 150,000 roubles (Berzins *in litt.*, 1991).

Non-state financial support for national parks is in the form of funds which are provided by numerous organisations and individuals. For example, the 1990 budget for Gaua National Park was 756,000 roubles, 230,000 from the state and 526,000 from other sources (Nikol'skii *et al.*, 1991).

Systems Reviews Latvia is one of the three former Baltic Republics of the USSR. To the west it has a coastline on the Baltic Sea; in the north-west this coastline sweeps round into the deep bay of the Gulf of Riga. It borders Estonia in the north, the Russian Soviet Socialist Republic in the east and the Byelorussian Soviet Socialist Republic and Lithuania to the south. Most of the country is low-lying, although there are a few hills rising to over 200m in the centre and east.

Land-use planning allows for the retention of so-called "compensation zones" which are untouched reserve areas (Nikol'skii *et al.*, 1991). The idea of conserving natural areas was promoted by the Riga Society of Nature and in 1912 protection had extended to the Moriczala area (Kondratowicz *et al.*, 1983). The 1960s saw a rapid expansion of the nature reserve system (Nikol'skii *et al.*, 1991) and the creation of the first national park at Gaya in 1973. The first biosphere reserve has been proposed in the Northern Vidreme Regional Nature Protection Complex, established in 1990 and covering 400,000ha (Berzins in litt., 1991). As early as 1982 perspective plans for the development of a multi-functional system of protected objects had been proposed (two national parks, fifteen nature parks, including two river parks and four landscape protection areas) (Melluma, 1982). In 1982, 13 categories of protected areas were listed; one national park, five nature parks, four reserves, 148 sanctuaries, five protected landscapes, 73 geological objects and 173 parks. In May 1991, five nature reserves covered 38,7000ha, and one national park 83,800ha, comprising 1.93% of total land area (Nikol'skii *et al.*, 1991). In total some 10% of the country is covered by protected areas (Berzins, *in litt.*, 1991).

Addresses

Northern Vidzeme Regional Nature Protection Complex, Smilson str. 22-2, Salacgriva, Limbazu Distr., Latvia

References

Cerovsky, J. (1988). *Nature conservation in the socialist countries of East Europe*. East-Europe Committee, IUCN Commission on Education/Ministry of Culture of the Czech Socialist Republic, Prague.

Kondratowicz, R. and Czekalski, M. (1985). Lotewski Park Narodowy "Ganja". *Chronmy Przyrode Ojczysta*. R.XLI. 2.4.

Melluma, A. KL., Rungule, R. KL, and Emsis, I.V. (1982). *Otdykhna priorode kak pripodookhrannaya problema*. Riga: Zinatne 1982. P. 157.

Nikol'skii, A., Bolshova, L.I. and Karaseva, S.E. (1991). *Palaearctic-USSR Regional Protected Areas Review*. Paper proposed for IV World Parks Congress on National Parks and other Protected Areas. USSR Ministry of Natural Resources

Management and Environmental Protection, Moscow.

Weisenburger, U. (1991). Nature conservation in the Soviet Union. *Nature Conservation*. European Parliament Director-General for Research, Environment, Public Health and Consumer Protection Series 17. EN-9-1991. Pp. 140-149.

ANNEX
Definitions of protected area designations, as legislated, together with authorities responsible for their administration

Title: USSR Law on Wildlife Protection and Use

Date: 25 June 1980 (entered into force 1 January 1981)

Brief description: Following the Latvian declaration of independence in 1991, the previously legislation is being maintained until promulgation of the new law. Past republic laws on soil, water and forests, on mineral extraction and faunal protection, as well as specific regulations are likely to be superseded by new national legislation.

Administrative authority: Northern Vidzeme Regional Nature Protection Complex

Designations:

Zapovednik (State nature reserve) Typical or unique plot of natural land used by "scientific institutions...and studied for its natural complexes and established on land excluded from economic utilisation" sites maintained in their natural condition unchanged by man.

Prohibited activities include building construction, any economic activities, such as agriculture or industry, and unrestricted entry.

Main management objectives include: protection of wildlife and its habitats, including maintenance of entire ecosystems; scientific research; and strictly limited recreational activities or, in some cases, controlled tourism.

Natsional'nyi park (National park) Protected natural area established in natural wilderness or altered landscapes (including arable land), although mainly on state forest property. Designated for recreation as well as nature protection and, as in the case of a protected lakeshore, differs from a state nature reserve in that tourism is allowed.

Parks are zoned into: areas in which economic activities are controlled; nature reserves, containing the finest examples of original natural habitat, where economic activities and public entry is forbidden; nature sanctuaries where tourists are allowed but economic activities are strictly prohibited; and peripheral buffer areas of economic activity, where habitation and sustainable levels of exploitation of natural resources (including fishing) are permitted.

Zakaznik (Nature sanctuary or partial reserve) Natural area partly withdrawn from economic utilisation because of its outstanding landscape, rare plants, or breeding colonies of threatened species. Controlled hunting is sometimes allowed.

Established to enable certain floral and faunal populations to recover within a specified time period. Exploitation is prohibited during this period, unless it does not interfere with management objectives.

May only be fully protected in certain seasons when all economic activities and entry is banned. Status and administration varies in the different republics of the USSR.

Zapovedno-okhotnich'ye khozyastvo (National hunting reserve or reserved hunting unit) Highly protected, and provides vital refuges for wildlife. Numbers of some game species is regulated by controlled hunting.

Natsional'nyi pamyatnik (Nature monument or national monument) Limited area surrounding isolated natural features such as geological sites or exceptionally old trees.

Sources: Cerovsky, 1988; Weisenburger, 1991

SUMMARY OF PROTECTED AREAS

Map ref.	*National/international designations* Name of area	IUCN management category	Area (ha)	Year notified
	National Park			
1	Gauya	II	83,750	1973
	Nature Reserves			
2	Grini	I	1,477	1957
3	Krustkalny	I	2,902	1977
4	Slitere	I	15,037	1921
5	Teychi	I	19,047	1982

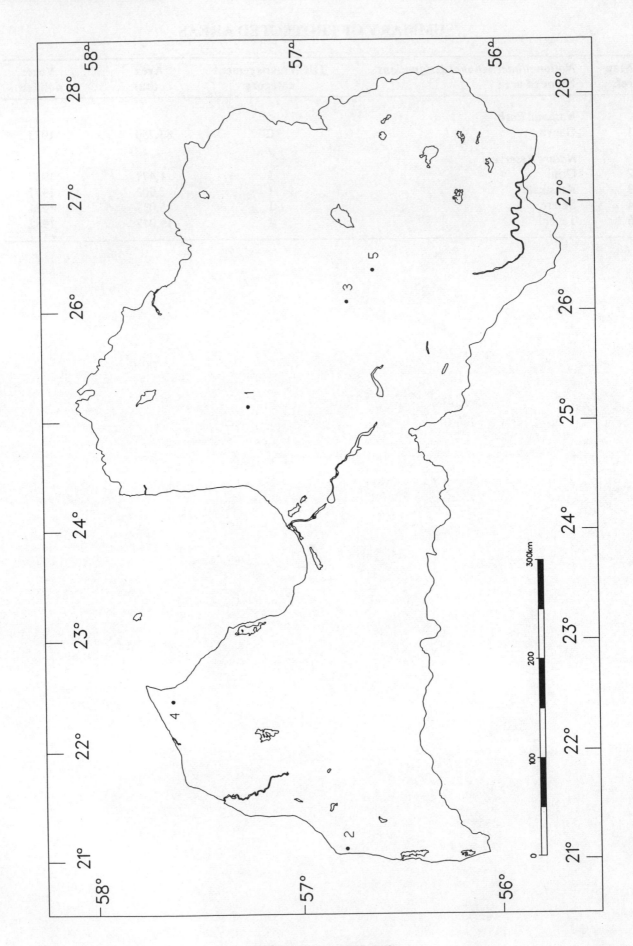

Protected Areas of Latvia

LIECHTENSTEIN

Area 160 sq. km

Population 28,181 (1988)
Natural increase: 0.89% per annum

Economic Indicators
GDP: No information
GNP: US$ 16,643 (1987)

Policy and Legislation The first law relating specifically to nature conservation was the Protection of Nature Act which came into force in 1933, with a number of amendments in subsequent years. The aim of the Act was to preserve and care for natural monuments, landscape and living space, flora and fauna and their natural habitats (Broggi, 1987). In 1952, the first site, Malbrun Valley, a plant protection area, was designated specifically for nature conservation. In 1961, the first nature reserve was created. The categories of protected areas covered by the Act include: nature reserves, conservation reserves and protected landscapes (Naturpark). The specific objectives of these protected areas include research, recreation, education and conservation, with priority given to the latter (Broggi, 1988). Under the Ordinance of 17 May 1989 (Verordnung vom 17.5.1989) some 6,000ha was given legal status as a floral mountain protection area (Liechtensteinische Gesellschaft für Umweltschutz, *in litt.*, 1990).

A government decree in 1968 ordered the coordination of all types of land use by means of an integral redevelopment of mountain districts, introducing the idea of linking landscape management with nature conservation (Broggi, 1977). In 1989, a bill was passed for the conservation of sparse grassland (including dry meadows, mown and damp meadows), offering grant payments based on surface area to farmers and landowners (Anon., 1989).

Conservation policies and legislation specific to forestry appeared during the last century. In 1865, a policy implementing forestry planning was introduced (Broggi, 1977). In 1895 the Forest Preserve Law was passed setting a legal precedent for landscape conservation (Broggi, 1977). A more specialised law passed in 1944 gave legal protection to all trees and shrubs in the northern parts of the Rhine Valley (Broggi, 1977). The government extended its legislation to the encouragement and support of tree-planting projects drafted for all "valley villages" (Anon., 1988). In the past 25 years one million trees and shrubs have been planted (Broggi, 1977).

International Activities Liechtenstein ratified the Bern Convention and most recently, on 6 August 1991, the Convention on Wetlands of International Importance especially as Waterfowl Habitat (Ramsar Convention) which will enter into force on 6 December 1991. The country is not party to the Convention concerning the Protection of the World Cultural and Natural Heritage (World Heritage Convention). No biosphere reserves have been listed under the Unesco Man and the Biosphere Programme. Liechtenstein is a member of the Council of Europe, however no biogenetic reserves have been declared and no sites have been awarded the Council of Europe European Diploma. It is a member of CIPRA (Commission Intérnationale pour la Protection des Régions Alpines), a regional commission, in conjunction with IUCN, responsible for protection of the Alps (documenting the survival of species, assisting in the process of establishing protected areas, gathering information on legal systems and promoting education, training and public awareness). In its Berchtesgaden Declaration of 1981, CIPRA invited all Alpine nations to create and ensure protection of large protected areas in the region.

Administration and Management The authority responsible for the administration and management of protected areas is the Ministry of Agriculture, Forestry and Environment. About 2% of the state budget is made available annually for the redevelopment and coordination of land use and restoration of vegetation in mountain areas (Broggi, 1977).

Various non-government organisations have provided important stimuli, encouragement and support for the cause of nature conservation. CIPRA, an association of organisations and institutions founded in 1952, of which Liechtenstein has been a member since 1988, concerns itself with the problems of nature and countryside protection, and with the maintenance and management of protected areas (Broggi, 1977) and land specifically in alpine areas. Since 1952 the Warden Service of the Alpine Club has been given responsibility for enforcing regulations in the Malburn Valley. Other organisations include five ornithological associations, the Society for the Protection of Animals, The Game Protection Society of Liechtenstein Sangan Wedenberg and the Liechtenstein Society for Environmental Protection (Broggi, 1977).

Systems Reviews The small, land-locked Principality of Liechtenstein is situated between Switzerland and Austria. One-third of the country lies in the Rhine Valley, which runs along the western border of the country, the rest is mountainous, rising to 2,595m (Grimmett and Jones, 1989). There are three main physical regions: the alluvial flood plains of the Rhine, now largely used for agricultural and human settlement; the slopes of the Rhine Valley, of which 40% is wooded; and the high mountain areas. Native deciduous woodland formerly dominated the Rhine Valley slopes. However, coniferous forests now occupy a larger area. The slopes are also widely used for human settlement. The high mountain areas are situated in the south-east, covering one-third of the country, and are characterised by north-south oriented mountain ridges and valleys, with forest and alpine pastures. These areas are used for livestock grazing, forestry and tourism (Grimmett and Jones, 1989). Land use subdivisions may be summarised as follows: village and development areas 13%; open agricultural areas 25%; alpine pastures 16%; forests 34%; and unproductive alpine areas 12% (Anon., 1987). The remnants of extensive boglands, once used for commercial reed production, also exist in the Rhine Valley (Broggi, 1989).

Within the forest category 84% is high forest, coppice woodland makes up a further 13%. Approximately 50% of the total forest area is unmanaged. No untouched virgin forest remains in Liechtenstein, however, 65% of the forest stands are over 100 years old and 75% of the total forest area is composed of native tree species (Heiss, 1987).

Nature conservation efforts have been concentrated mainly on the Rhine Valley area. It is here that the greatest conflicts arise with commercial development. Conservationists have been seeking the establishment of a national park, or a large nature reserve, for many years (Broggi, 1977). In 1989, Liechtenstein, the seat of CIPRA's headquarters, declared a floral mountain protection area of 6,000ha (37.5% of the total land area) and proposed another, Garselli-Zigerberg (Alpengebiet) (950ha) (5.9% of the total land area). Other protected areas include nine small nature reserves covering about 1% of the total land area (Broggi, 1977).

There has been a drastic decline in wetlands, as a consequence of drainage due to agricultural intensification. In 1900 wetlands covered 60% of open areas (Anon., 1988); the current figure is 4%. A similar decline of dry grasslands has occurred due to agricultural intensification and village expansion.

Addresses

Gesellschaft für Umweltschutz, Heiligkreuz 52, 9490 VADUZ (Tel: 41 75 25262)

References

Anon. (1987). Liechtenstein: soil in a sorry state. *Naturopa* 87-9: 3.

Anon. (1988). Liechtenstein: the state of the forests. *Naturopa* 88-1: 2.

Anon. (1989). Liechtenstein: conservation of sparse grasslands. *Naturopa* 89-1: 2.

Broggi, M. (1977). Nature conservation and landscape management in Liechtenstein. *Parks* 2(3): 14-15.

Broggi, M. (1977). Nature conservation and land management in the Principality of Liechtenstein. *Nature and national parks* 15(55): 15-17.

Broggi, M. (1988). An extensive alpine reserve for Liechtenstein. *Nature and national parks* 26(100): 29-30.

CoE (1987). *Management of Europe's natural heritage. Twenty-five years of activity.* Environmental Protection and Management Division, Council of Europe, Strasbourg.

Davis, S.D., Droop, S.J.M., Gregerson, P., Henson, L., Leon, C.J., Lamlein Villa-Lobos, J., Synge, H. and Zantovska, J. (1986). *Plants in danger: what do we know?* IUCN, Gland, Switzerland and Cambridge, UK. 461 pp.

Grimmett, R.F.A. and Jones, T.A. (1989). *Important bird areas in Europe.* International Council for Bird Preservation/International Waterfowl and Wetlands Research Bureau. 880 pp.

Heiss, G. (1987). Inventory of natural (virgin) and ancient seminatural woodlands within the Council's member states and Finland. Unpublished report for the European Committee for the Conservation of Nature and Natural Resources. Pp. 311-313.

IUCN (1989). *The Alps: a system under pressure.* IUCN, Gland, Switzerland. 113 pp

Paxton, J. (Ed.) (1989). *The Statesman's Yearbook 1989-90.* The Macmillan Press Ltd., London, UK. 1691 pp.

ANNEX
Definitions of protected area designations, as legislated, together with authorities responsible for their administration

Title: Protection of Nature Act

Date: 1933, last amended 1989

Brief description: To preserve and care for natural monuments, land and living space, flora and fauna and their natural habitats

Administrative authority: Ministry of Agriculture, Forestry and Environment

Designations:

Nature reserve Designed to afford more protection to such "natural formations" as waterfalls, geological structures, habitats of rare flora and fauna.

SUMMARY OF PROTECTED AREAS

	National/international designations Name of area	IUCN management category	Area (ha)	Year notified
1	*Unclassified* Floral Mountain Protected Area	V	6,000	1989

REPUBLIC OF LITHUANIA

Area 65,200 sq. km

Population 3,690,000 (1989, Paxton, 1990)
Natural increase: no information

Economic Indicators
GNP: No information
GDP: No information

Policy and Legislation In August 1940 Lithuania was admitted to the USSR but its independence continued to be recognised by the international community. Following the abortive coup of August 1991, Lithuania declared its independence and became a member of the United Nations. Up to October 1991, no overall law on protected areas had been prepared, although this was envisaged in the environmental programme for 1991-1995, and it seems likely that a new national law will be drafted in the near future. Past republic laws (on soil, water, forest, minerals, fauna) and regulations may form the basis of the new state legislation (Baskyte, *in litt.*, 1991; Weisenburger, 1991). A Law on Environmental Protection has been presented to Parliament. The laws on natural resources utilisation and pollution taxation have been in effect since July 1991.

The protected area system, carried over from the former republic status, includes strict nature reserves, managed nature reserves, national parks and regional parks and natural monuments. The national parks have the following attributes: they represent the most characteristic and valuable landscape types and/or ethno-cultural regions; and contain stable ecological situations. Regional parks exhibit scientifically valuable landscapes, recreational potential and geo-ecological integrity.

International Activities There are no biosphere reserves, but membership of the Unesco Man and the Biosphere Programme continues following independence, as does that of the Convention concerning the World Cultural and Natural Heritage (World Heritage Convention) and the Convention on Wetlands of International Importance especially as Waterfowl Habitat (Ramsar Convention).

Administration and Management Protected areas are administered and managed by the state authorities. Budgets for protected areas increased from 58,000 roubles in 1975 to 190,000 in 1986, dropping in the years 1987/88 and rising to 248,000 roubles in both 1989 and 1990 (Nikol'skii *et al.*, 1991).

In April 1991 the Association of Baltic National Parks was established and started work after the Statute was signed on 22 June 1991. Membership comprises five national parks and the secretariat is based in Estonia.

Systems Reviews Lithuania is the southernmost of the three former Baltic Republics of the USSR; to the west it has a coastline on the Baltic Sea. To the north it shares a border with Latvia; with the Byelorussian Soviet Socialist Republic to the east; with Poland to the south; and with an isolated European enclave of the Russian Soviet Socialist Republic in the south-west. Most of the country is low-lying, although rising slightly in the south-east and east.

Under a land-use planning system, "compensation zones" are retained to ensure genetic variety in the landscape. The 1960s witnessed an extension of the nature reserve system (Nikol'skii *et al.*, 1991). This was followed in 1974 by the first national park (Aukstaitija National Park). In late 1991, four new national parks were created (Dzukija, Kursin Nerija, Trakai and Zemaitija) which, with Aukstaitija, account for 34% of all protected areas. In total, 25 regional parks are planned; to date, one (Pavilniai) has been created. The process of land privatisation is seen as a particular problem to the protected areas system (Baskyte, *in litt.*, 1991).

In May 1991, there were three nature reserves covering 17,000ha and one national park of 30,000ha, equal to 0.73% of the total land area (Nikol'skii *et al.*, 1991). In October 1991 there were four strict nature reserves covering 20,800ha, five national parks covering 33,300ha, one regional park of 1,800ha, 248 managed nature reserves covering a total of 259,600ha and 688 natural monuments. The total number of protected areas is 946, covering 415,500ha or 6.0% of total land area (Baskyte, *in litt.*, 1991).

Threats to the environment include livestock grazing, over-fishing, inappropriate building schemes and hunting. Atmospheric pollution, soil contamination and dust and gas damage have been recorded (Nikol'skii *et al.*, 1991). Water pollution also is considerable. The annual amount of sewage discharged into recipients is 450 million cu.m. Only 11.7% is treated in accordance with existing regulations.

Addresses

Lithuania Republic Environmental Protection Department, Juozapavichus str. 9, 232600 VILNIUS

References

Cerovsky, J. (1988). *Nature conservation in the socialist countries of East Europe*. East-Europe Committee, IUCN Commission on Education/Ministry of Culture of the Czech Socialist Republic, Prague.

Nikol'skii, A.A., Bolshova, L.I. and Karaseva, S.E. (1991). Palaearctic-USSR Regional Protected Areas Review. Paper proposed for IV World Parks Congress on National Parks and other Protected

Areas. USSR Ministry of Natural Resources Management and Environmental Protection, Moscow 1991.

Weisenburger, U. (1991). Nature conservation in the Soviet Union. *Nature Conservation.* European Parliament Director-General for Research. Environment, Public Health and Consumer Protection Series 17. IN-9-1991. Pp. 140-149.

ANNEX
Definitions of protected area designations, as legislated, together with authorities responsible for their administration

Title: USSR Law on Wildlife Protection and Use

Date: 25 June 1980 (entered into force 1 January 1981)

Brief description: Following the Lithuanian declaration of independence in 1991 the previously legislation is being maintained until promulgation of the new law. Past republic laws on soil, water and forests, on mineral extraction and faunal protection, as well as specific regulations are likely to be superseded by new national legislation.

Administrative authority: Lithuania Republic Environmental Protection Department

Designations:

Zapovednik (State nature reserve) Typical or unique plot of natural land used by "scientific institutions ... and studied for its natural complexes and established on land excluded from economic utilisation" sites maintained in their natural condition unchanged by man.

Prohibited activities include building construction, any economic activities, such as agriculture or industry, and unrestricted entry.

Main management objectives include: protection of wildlife and its habitats, including maintenance of entire ecosystems; scientific research; and strictly limited recreational activities or, in some cases, controlled tourism.

Natsional'nyi park (National park) Protected natural area established in natural wilderness or altered landscapes (including arable land), although mainly on state forest property. Designated for recreation as well as nature protection and, as in the case of a protected lakeshore, differs from a state nature reserve in that tourism is allowed.

Parks are zoned into: areas in which economic activities are controlled; nature reserves, containing the finest examples of original natural habitat, where economic activities and public entry is forbidden; nature sanctuaries where tourists are allowed but economic activities are strictly prohibited; and peripheral buffer areas of economic activity, where habitation and sustainable levels of exploitation of natural resources (including fishing) are permitted.

Zakaznik (Nature sanctuary or partial reserve) Natural area partly withdrawn from economic utilisation because of its outstanding landscape, rare plants, or breeding colonies of threatened species. Controlled hunting is sometimes allowed.

Established to enable certain floral and faunal populations to recover within a specified time period. Exploitation is prohibited during this period, unless it does not interfere with management objectives.

May only be fully protected in certain seasons when all economic activities and entry is banned. Status and administration varies in the different republics of the USSR.

Zapovedno-okhotnich'ye khozyastvo (National hunting reserve or reserved hunting unit) Highly protected, and provides vital refuges for wildlife. Numbers of some game species is regulated by controlled hunting.

Natsional'nyi pamyatnik (Nature monument or national monument) Limited area surrounding isolated natural features such as geological sites or exceptionally old trees.

Sources: Cerovsky, 1988; Weisenburger, 1991

SUMMARY OF PROTECTED AREAS

Map[†] ref.	*National/international designations* Name of area	IUCN management category	Area (ha)	Year notified
	National Parks			
1	Aukstaitija	II	30,300	1974
2	Dzukija	II	55,500	1991
3	Kursiu nerija	II	18,800	1991
4	Trakai	II	8,200	1991
5	Zemaitija	II	20,500	1991
	Nature Reserves			
6	Chapkyalyay	I	8,477	1975
7	Kamanos	I	3,650	1979
8	Viesvile	I	3,200	
9	Zhuvintas	I	5,457	1946
	Regional Park			
10	Pavilniai	V	1,800	1991

[†]Locations of most protected areas are shown on the accompanying map.

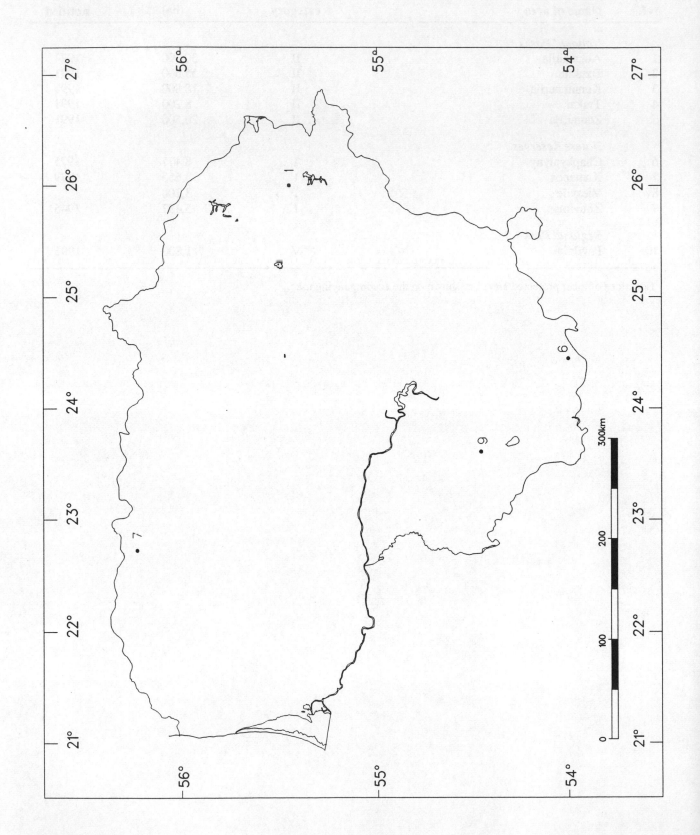

Protected Areas of Lithuania

GRAND DUCHY OF LUXEMBOURG

Area 2,587 sq. km

Population 373,000 (1990)
Natural increase: 0.18% per annum

Economic Indicators
GDP: US$ 16,285 per capita (1987)
GNP: US$ 15,860 per capita (1987)

Policy and Legislation The constitution dates from 17 October 1868, and has been revised many times, most recently in 1989.

The Law of 29 July 1965 on the conservation of nature and natural resources deals, in Section One, with general landscape conservation measures. This section states, among other things, that no buildings may be erected outside built-up areas, or closer than 100m to a wood of a size greater than 10ha, or extending along the banks of a watercourse, without ministerial permission. This same Act binds bodies involved in mining operations to do everything possible to restore sites to their original condition. The Act also gives certain powers to the Service for Nature Conservation, including powers to regulate construction and forestry, but is not empowered to establish nature reserves (Duffey, 1982). Bill No. 1729, tabled in 1973, modified this Act, making it necessary to gain ministerial permission for all schemes involving the draining, dredging and rechanelling of watercourses, and, outside built-up areas, for other modifications such as the building of transport and communication facilities, power-lines, liquid or gas pipelines, and the removal of top-soil from any site larger than 20,000 sq. m (Poore and Gryn-Ambroes, 1980).

A new Law concerning the protection of nature and natural resources was passed on 11 August 1982 broadening the application of the 1965 Law. It contains a section giving general measures for the protection of the environment: wide areas of the country are classified as green zones where, through regional development plans, the environment must be protected. More specific measures are also given for the protection of the flora and fauna (including banning the destruction of natural habitats and biotopes such as ponds, reed-marshes, hedges and copses), and of the natural environment. Protected areas are described as one means of safeguarding the natural environment, and the Law authorises the Ministry of Planning and the Environment to designate sites in consultation with the local authorities, and with a full public enquiry. Such sites must be designated through specific Grand-Ducal regulations, passed by the State Council. These regulations must specify restricted and forbidden activities under a number of headings. The Water and Forests Administration is given responsibility under this law for the establishment and implementation of management plans for these "classified sites" (Anon.,

1982): this legal document has close links with the policy document of 1981, described below.

The major government document, which provides the basis for the protection of areas is the Partial Development Plan Concerning the Natural Environment (Plan d'aménagement partiel concernant l'environnement naturel). This plan, with its "Declaration of general intention" was officially adopted by government in Council on 24 April 1981 and was published in the *Memorial*, the official journal of the Grand-Duchy. It lists a wide range of motives for the protection of the natural environment, going some way to fulfil Articles 1 and 2 of the Land Management Act of 20 March 1974, which require the "harmonious development of the land and use of its resources" and the protection of nature and the safeguarding of its natural resources. Although the document itself does not have legal authority, it lists the relevant acts and decrees which relate to the protection of the natural environment, and it points out the lack of legislative apparatus and special legislation that would allow the creation of protected areas, suggesting that producing this legislation should be a priority. The plan suggests that the entire area of the country should be classified according to the utilisation of the land, and that certain "priority zones" where land use is considered to be of particular importance should be identified: such areas include "nature protection areas", and also "peaceful zones near towns, holiday areas and groundwater protection areas" (Anon., 1981).

Areas to be protected for their natural value are also listed and categorised in the 1981 Declaration. They are defined under a number of headings: natural park (parc naturel), protected recreational area (zone de protection à vocation récréative), interurban protected green zone (zone verte interurbaine protégée), site and natural monument (site et monument naturel), protected landscape (paysage protégée), forested area of particular interest and plateau forest (surface forestière d'un intérêt particulier et massif forestier), and nature or natural reserve (réserve naturelle) (Anon., 1981). A number of potential sites are listed under each category. Within the nature reserve category, the original inventory lists 113 potential sites, which, it was proposed, should be given protected area status progressively under specific Grand-Ducal regulations. A new inventory of sites to be classed as nature reserves was released in 1989/1990, updating the original 1981 list and including 137 sites. These nature reserves are subdivided into 20 forest reserves (réserves forestières) (containing parts of rare or exceptional woodlands); 81 wetlands areas (zones humides); 13 dry grasslands (pelouses sèches); and 23 diverse habitats (habitats divers) (Anon., 1987; Kremer, 1988; Ministère de l'Aménagement du Territoire et de l'Environnement, *in litt.*, 1991). The different recommended categories, together with the restrictions

243

that would be imposed within these categories, are given in the Annex.

The 1981 Declaration is widely recognised as one of the most important texts concerning protected areas and this alone may provide a limited form of protection for a number of the sites listed. Other sites have subsequently received legal recognition under individual regulations. Nine nature reserves have legally binding regulations to date, and a further seven sites are currently undergoing the classification procedure. None of the three natural parks has legal definition, although the 1964 treaty with Germany concerning the German-Luxembourgeois Nature Park is considered to give some legal status to Our Natural Park in Luxembourg (Ministère de l'Aménagement du Territoire et de l'Environnement, *in litt.*, 1991).

Act No. 9 of 7 February 1986 makes provision for subsidies to be available for works that favour the conservation, character and beauty of the countryside and forests and are carried out on land located in green zones, as defined in the 1982 amendments to the Act on the Conservation of Nature and Natural Resources.

The guiding programme of land management decreed on 6 April 1978 also considers the environment. Directive 54 of this Act mentions both the prevention of pollution of air and water and the protection of nature, the countryside, monuments and sites. In the chapter on the environment, this Act mentions the necessity of protecting certain categories of protected area, and it lists certain categories; it also mentions the protection of other natural elements in the countryside, such as hedges, isolated trees, and small clumps or avenues of trees, and the protection of individual animal and plant species (Anon., 1981).

The Act of 12 August 1927, completed and amended by the Act of 20 February 1966 on the conservation and protection of national sites and monuments, allows the scheduling of sites whose landscape or scientific value is such that their conservation is in the public interest. Once a site is scheduled it is fully protected by law. If a site is on private land, the government informs the owner of the intention to schedule (see Annex) (Poore and Gryn-Ambroes, 1980).

Other legislation with some relevance to protected areas includes the Act of 20 March 1974 on land management, designed to promote the optimum use and development of the country's resources. This acknowledges the need to protect nature and conserve natural resources (Poore and Gryn-Ambroes, 1980).

Also, the Act of 28 June 1976 regulates inland fishing, making it compulsory to obtain authorisation before: clearing river bank vegetation; effecting the water flow or harming aquatic fauna and flora; and forbids planting of conifers less than 4m from the bank of a water course.

Although there is considerable legislation concerning nature conservation and protected areas in general, there are remarkably few sites which currently have any form of legal protection. The numerous sites and categories listed in the 1981 Declaration are proposed sites which, with no actual protection, may well be open to damage or destruction.

International Activities   The Grand Duchy of Luxembourg has ratified the Convention concerning the Protection of the World Natural and Cultural Heritage (World Heritage Convention) on 28 September 1983. No natural sites have yet been inscribed. It does not participate in the Convention on Wetlands of International Importance especially as Waterfowl Habitat (Ramsar Convention).

The Convention on the Conservation of European Wildlife and Natural Habitats (Bern Convention) was signed on 1 June 1982. Luxembourg is a member of the European Community and hence is bound by its environmental directives: four sites have been designated as EC special protection areas under the Wild Birds Directive (April, 1991). It is also a member of the Council of Europe and one site has been designated as a Council of Europe biogenetic reserve; no sites been awarded the Council of Europe European Diploma.

Luxembourg was one of the first countries in Europe to use the concept of trans-border parks by establishing the German-Luxembourgeois Nature Park between the Grand Duchy and Germany's Rhineland-Palatinate under the treaty of 17 April 1964.

Administration and Management   The authorities responsible for the administration and management of the proposed protected areas are specified under the 1982 Law concerning the protection of nature and natural resources. The Ministry of Planning and the Environment (Ministère de l'Aménagement du Territoire et de l'Environnement) is responsible for the initial stages in the designation of sites, in consultation with the local authorities. Sites must be approved under a Grand-Ducal Regulation, by the State Council (Conseil d'Etat). The Water and Forests Department (Direction des Eaux et Forêts) is given responsibility under this Law for the establishment and implementation of management plans for these recognised protected areas (Anon., 1982). The Nature Conservation Council (Service Conservation de la Nature), within the Water and Forests Department, is widely involved in the preliminary investigations and in the subsequent management of sites, although final management decisions rest with the Directorate of the Department of Water Resources and Forestry. The physical implementation of the final decision is carried out by wardens. The methods used in each reserve are different and are determined by the conditions prevailing. The Water and Forests Department has direct responsibility for most other aspects of conservation, as well as hunting and fishing, it also manages state-owned forests (Poore and Gryn-Ambroes, 1980).

The Minister of Cultural Affairs is responsible for execution of the Acts (12 August 1927, amended 20 February 1966) on protection of national sites and monuments.

The Luxembourg League for the Study and Protection of Birds and Nature (Ligue Luxembourgeoise pour l'Etude et la Protection des Oiseaux et de la Nature) is a non-governmental organisation which embraces a large number of affiliated nature conservation organisations. The League owns and manages a number of small reserves, most around 10ha in size, and is subsidised by the state. In 1982 the League had some 100,000 members and in 1980 its governmental subsidy was some BFrs 5 million (Duffey, 1982).

Systems Reviews Luxembourg is a small land-locked country which shares borders with France, Germany and Belgium. Most of the south and central parts of the country are dominated by agriculture. Further north there is a strip of very steep heavily wooded valleys which is part of the Eifel/Ardennes massif. In the north-west there is a cultivated plateau which has some remnant areas of marshes and bogs (Grimmett and Jones, 1989).

In all, agriculture covers some 56% of the land area, woodland 37%, while urban and industrial areas cover a further 7% (Ministère de l'Aménagement du Territoire et de l'Environnement, *in litt.*, 1991). In the south of the country there is a small area of iron ore deposits which supports a declining, but still important iron and steel industry. Luxembourg actually has the highest density of woodland in the European Community (Kremer, 1988), although most of this is modified to some degree. Of the forested area, 46% is deciduous, 30% coniferous, and most of the rest is coppiced or pollarded oak *Quercus*. An inventory of private woodland carried out in 1985 revealed that a large amount of reforestation was being carried out, although most of this was with coniferous trees, modifying and in some cases reducing the value of the natural woodland. The lack of infrastructure and the extreme fragmentation of private woodlands is seen as an obstacle to rational management (Anon., 1987).

Despite the thoroughness of the partial management plan of 1981, most of its recommendations have not yet been realised. By 1989, nine of the 137 proposed nature reserves had official protection: these nine sites have a total of 520ha, the total area covered by all the sites mentioned in this inventory is 5,856ha, with a further 15,834ha of buffer zones. None of the other sites mentioned in the plan has received national, statutory protection. Our Nature Park, although originally established under the bilateral treaty of 1964, has received no further statutory protection, which is considered necessary by some (Kremer, 1988): the three natural parks mentioned in the 1981 Declaration cover 64,900ha. It is not clear to what degree the proposed protected areas are protected prior to official statutory designation. Some sources describe an extensive protected areas network in Luxembourg (such as Poore and Gryn-Ambroes, 1980), which may indicate that proposed sites already have some degree of non-statutory protection. If this is not the case, however, there may be cause for concern that the proposed sites may be degraded before their eventual designation.

A nationwide survey of forests to assess the impacts of acid rain in Luxembourg suggested that about 19% of trees showed signs of damage and that 4% were badly damaged. The worst affected sites were stands of mature trees where almost 30% of trees were damaged; among the worst hit tree species were beech, oak, spruce and pine (Anon., 1985).

Addresses

Ministère de l'Aménagement du Territoire et de l'Environnement (Ministry of Planning and the Environment), 5A rue de Prague, L-2918 LUXEMBOURG (Tel: 488002; Tlx: 2536 MINENV-LU; FAX: 400410)

Service Conservation de la Nature (Nature Conservation Council), Direction des Eaux et Forets, BP 411, L-2014 LUXEMBOURG-Ville (Tel: 402201; FAX: 485985)

Ligue Luxembougeoise pour l'Etude et la Protection des Oiseaux et de la Nature (Luxembourg League for the Study and Protection of Birds and Nature), BP 709, LUXEMBOURG-Ville (Tel: 2 486137)

Musée d'Histoire Naturelle de Luxembourg, Marché-aux-Poissons, 2345 LUXEMBOURG

References

Anon. (1981). *Memorial, Journal Officiel du Grande-Duché de Luxembourg, administratif et economique* B-69: 1271-1299.

Anon. (1982). *Memorial, Journal Officiel du Grande-Duché de Luxembourg, recueil de legislation.* A-69: 1486-1494.

Anon. (1985). Luxembourg deciduous trees most affected. *Acid News* 1: 8.

Anon. (1987). *Management of Europe's natural heritage. Twenty-five years of activity.* Council of Europe, Strasbourg.

Carp, E. (1980) *Directory of wetlands of international importance in Western Palaeaearctic.* UNEP/IUCN.

Duffey, E. (1982) *National parks and reserves of Western Europe.* Macdonald and Co. (Publishers) Ltd., London and Sydney. 288 pp.

Grimmett, R.F.A. and Jones, T.A. (1989). *Important bird areas in Europe.* Technical Publication No. 9. International Council for Bird Preservation, Cambridge, UK.

Davis, S.D., Droop, S.J.M., Gregerson, P., Henson, L., Leon, C.J., Lamlein Villa-Lobos, J., Synge, H. and Zantovska, J. (1986). *Plants in danger: what do we know?* IUCN, Gland, Switzerland and Cambridge, UK. 461 pp.

Kremer, P. (1988) The natural environmental and nature conservation in the Grand Duchy of Luxembourg. *Nature and National Parks* 26(99): 20-22.

Poore, D. and Gryn-Ambroes, P. (1980). *Nature conservation in Northern and Western Europe.* UNEP/IUCN/WWF, Gland, Switzerland.

ANNEX
Definitions of protected area designations, as legislated, together with authorities responsible for their administration

Title: Plan d'aménagement partiel concernant l'environnement naturel (Partial Management Plan Concerning the Natural Environment

Date: 24 August 1981

Brief description: A framework decree giving various proposals for the protection of the natural environment, including detailed descriptions of a proposed protected area system, which, in the most part, has yet to be implemented.

Administrative authority: Chef du Service Conservation de la Nature, Direction des Eaux et Forêts

Designations:

Parc naturel (Natural park) A region or part of a region designated to protect the character, beauty and diversity of the countryside, its cultural and/or scientific value, its flora and fauna, the purity of the air and water, and to favour leisure and tourism. All activities are subject to a management plan: industry, commerce, forestry, agriculture, leisure and tourist activities and anything else that would alter the natural balance or the beauty or the character of the park. Current practices of agriculture and forestry within a park are not subject to regulations and are allowed to continue.

Zone de protection à vocation récreative (Protected recreational area) These areas are situated outside natural parks. They are also areas which have particular interest because of their natural or cultural value. They are zoned, with part set aside for landscape protection and other parts open for public recreation. Plans for the protection and the development of these areas are based on the 1974 law on land management.

Zone verte interurbaine protégée (coupure verte) (Interurban protected green zones) Rural areas in the immediate vicinity of urban areas. They have an essential role in providing a balance with urban areas and their high populations; they are peaceful, natural areas. The rural character of these zones must be maintained or improved, where woodland is concerned, while agriculture must remain important.

Paysage protégée (Protected landscape) Large areas of land, less important than a natural park, subject to certain legislation to protect the natural resources and characteristic features, to control tourism and recreation and to prevent activities that would alter the landscape. Such sites are declared based on ecological considerations – construction is forbidden except where necessary for agriculture or forestry.

Surface forestière d'un intéret particulier et massif forestier (forested area of particular interest and plateau forest)

The importance of all forests is noted for their role in the hydrological cycle, the purification of air and the production of oxygen, the reduction of noise, their natural ecological value and their value for tourism and recreation. Protection of forests in general is covered by the forestry legislation, but in these areas it is suggested that there should be strict controls over road construction and the extension of industrial zones or of the agricultural land area.

Réserve naturelle (Natural reserve) A protected area, where elements of the natural environment, including the diversity of flora and fauna, as well as the characters of soil and vegetation, are to be conserved. A natural reserve is a part of the territory exempt from intervention by man and managed by public bodies for conservation and protection, as opposed to an area exploited more freely by man. Four categories of these reserves are proposed, site are chosen as representative areas, and reserves of principal types of animal or plant community, common or rare, typical or unusual, or sites which contain interesting physical characteristics. Access to these sites should be restricted.

Réserve forestière (Forest reserve) Certain woods or parts of forests may be declared natural reserves because of their exceptional beauty, specific features, diversity or rare vegetation types. These elements are subject to special protection status for management and exploitation.

Zone humide (Wetland) All transition zones between water and dry land are considered to be wetlands. They are characterised by a high water level producing wide species variety. Ecosystems formed by natural means, such as abandoned river beds, ponds and pools, meres, water bodies and lakes with riverine vegetation, temporary swamps, emergent swamps and peatbogs, are included as wetlands. Artificial ditches, peatbogs, pools and accumulation basins constructed by man are also considered to be wetlands. As wetlands are ecosystems in the process of evolution, intervention through management plans based on scientific data is required to direct the necessary developments.

Pelouse sèche (Dry grassland) Zones which, because of the nature of their sub-soil and exposure to the sun, only support xerophilic and thermophilic

246

vegetation and fauna. Special protection status should prevent urbanisation, use of fertilisers and penetration of these threatened biotopes, which are of great beauty and scientific interest.

Réserve naturelle diverse (Diverse natural or nature reserve) Zones of great scientific and aesthetic interest which cannot be classified under the definitions above, or which contain several different biotopes.

Source: Anon., 1981

Title: Loi sur la conservation et la protection des sites et monuments nationaux (Law on the conservation and protection of national sites and monuments)

Date: 12 August 1927, modified by the Law of 20 February 1966

Brief description: Provides for the designation and protection of sites whose landscape or scientific value is such that their conservation is in the public interest

Administrative authority: Ministry of Cultural Affairs

Designations:

Site et monument naturel (Natural site and monument) Sites are generally larger picturesque landscapes, while natural monuments are small areas or objects which, in view of their rarity, beauty or scientific value, need to be conserved. These include geological rarities or exceptional landscape features.

Source: Anon., 1981

SUMMARY OF PROTECTED AREAS

Map ref.	*National/international designations* Name of area	IUCN management category	Area (ha)	Year notified
1	*Nature Park* Parc Germano-Luxembourgeois (Our)	VIII	36,000	1965

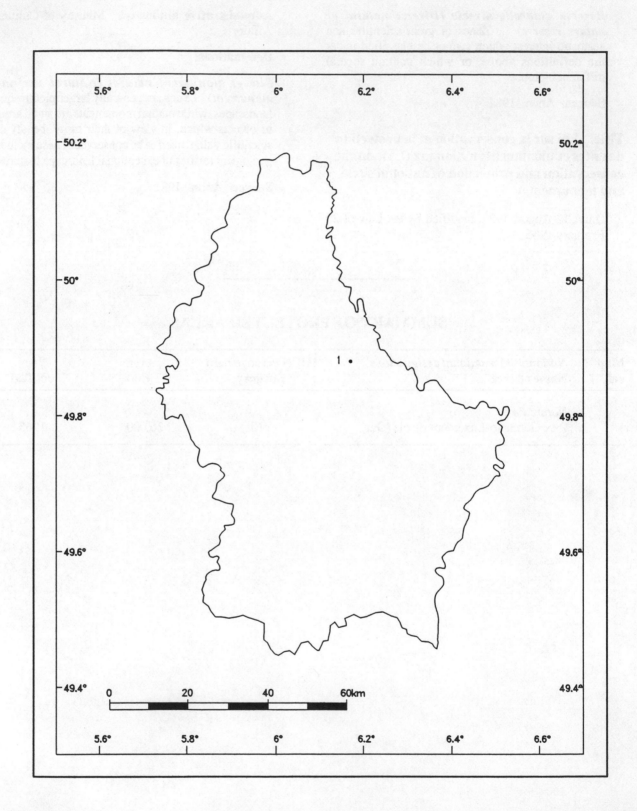

Protected Area of Luxembourg

MALTA
(REPUBLIC OF)

Area 320 sq. km

Population 353,000 (1990)
Natural increase: 0.40% per annum

Economic Indicators
GDP: US$ 5,292 per capita (1987)
GNP: US$ 4,010 per capita (1987)

Policy and Legislation The islands were annexed to the British Crown by the Treaty of Paris in 1814 and became independent on 21 September 1964 under the Malta Independence order of 1964. The Constitution makes provision for the protection of fundamental rights and freedom of the individual, and for freedom of conscience (Hunter, 1991).

The territory has over the millennia been settled by Phoenicians, Carthaginians, Romans and early Arabs, inheriting many elements of traditional nature protection. The origins of Buskett Woodland Garden goes back to the mid 16th century (1636-1657) when it formed part of a hunting lodge estate (Borg, 1991). More recently the Antiquities Act of 1933 (Article 3) provided protection for trees under a government notice in the Malta Government *Gazette* of 19 July 1933. The notice includes trees over 200 years old which are considered as having antiquarian importance, lists of specified trees and groups of trees (Borg, 1991; Davis *et al.*, 1986; Sultana, pers. comm., 1989).

The most important nature conservation legislation is the Bird Protection Act (1980), Act No. XV of 1988 and edicts of the Ministry of Agriculture. In a number of specific sites considered to be of most importance, shooting and trapping are prohibited. Sites may include natural or semi-natural habitats such as plantation or woodland gardens. No species other than birds are protected within these sanctuaries and neither are the habitats within their bounds (Schembri, 1988). The Bird Protection Act and Regulations also gives protection to all breeding birds, all birds of prey and large numbers of migrant species. The closed season extends from 22 May to 31 August (Sultana, *in litt.*, 1988).

Nature reserves (national nature reserve) are established by specific acts for each site. The first, the saline marshland at Ghadira Wetland Reserve, was established in 1978 by Legal Notice No. 126, 1978, Protection of Birds (Amendment) Regulations (Carp, 1979; Schembri, 1988). Assistance came from the WWF, the International Council for Bird Preservation and the DBV of the Federal Republic of Germany towards its establishment and for a comprehensive management plan approved by the government (Sultana, *in litt.*, 1988). A specific act was required to set up the protected area at Filfla, The Filfla Nature Reserve Act No XV, which

was passed by the House of Representatives on 10 May 1988. Regulations state that nothing may be killed, captured, collected, trapped, commercially exploited or removed from the reserve except with the written permission of the Minister. Camping is not permitted and written permission of the Minister responsible for the environment is required for access, and then only on educational and scientific grounds (Act No. XV, 1988; Anon, 1988).

Presently, various bodies, including the Environmental Office for Conservation in the Environmental Division of the Ministry of Education, are working on a list of new areas to be declared nature reserves (Schembri *et al.*, 1987; Schembri, 1988; Sultana, *in litt.*, 1988).

In 1990 a white paper on environment protection was issued by government. A draft Bill on Environment Protection is currently being considered by Parliament (1991). Part 7 of the bill relates solely to the protection of flora and fauna; the concept of tree preservation orders has been incorporated into the bill. A "national park" was inaugurated in September 1990 which will receive more formal protection when the Environment Bill is passed, although it should be noted that the site has little or natural value and is largely used for sports, agriculture and tourism (Borg, 1991).

The Protection of Trees Notice under the Antiquities Act of 1925 is not widely known or enforced (Borg, 1991).

International Activities Malta acceded to the Convention on Wetlands of International Importance especially as Waterfowl Habitat (Ramsar Convention) on 30 September 1980, and one site has been inscribed. The Convention concerning the Protection of the World Cultural and Natural Heritage (World Heritage Convention) was signed in 1980 but no natural sites have been declared.

Malta has participated in, and ratified, the UNEP Mediterranean Regional Seas sponsored Convention for the Protection of the Mediterranean Sea against Pollution (Barcelona Convention) and its Protocol Concerning Mediterranean Specially Protected Areas of 1982: two Mediterranean specially protected areas have been designated. Malta is also a member of the Council of Europe: two sites have been designated as biogenetic reserves. However, no sites have been awarded the Council of Europe, European Diploma.

Administration and Management The authority responsible for nature conservation is the Environmental Division of the Ministry of Education (Environmental Office for Conservation), which administers and manages nature reserves. Bird sanctuaries are administered by the Department of Agriculture and

Fisheries (Dipartiment ta' L-Agrikoltura u Sajd). The national park is administered by a number of departments including the Department of Agriculture and Fisheries.

A WWF project (No. 1505) in 1981 granted US$ 10,000 towards the establishment of Ghadira Wetland Reserve (WWF, 1982), for which a comprehensive management plan had been prepared and approved in principle by the Ministry (Carp, 1979). This envisaged the enlargement of the pool by dredging and the construction of a perimeter ditch, which would carry water from a permanent reservoir, to be constructed at the western end of the area. Hides and educational facilities have been planned, as well as a tree planting scheme (1991).

The Malta Council for Science and Technology was established in 1988 in order to launch an effective national policy for science and technology. Within this Council the Biological Diversity and Genetic Resources Network was established in 1990. Within this network is the Biodiversity Inventory and Monitoring Working Group which is responsible for promoting research to assess and document local species of plants and animals and their habitats, as well as monitoring changes in ecosystem diversity and function due to human activities. A project has been started to establish a National Database on the Biodiversity of the Maltese Islands (Malta Council for Science and Technology, *in litt.*, 1991).

The most important voluntary and non-governmental organisations include the Malta Ornithological Society (MOS), which has in recent years pursued a vigorous educational and anti-hunting campaign; the Society for the Study and Conservation of Nature; and Zaghazagh ghall-Ambjent (Youths for the Environment), a new, small but active environmental group (Sultana, *in litt.*, 1988).

Systems Reviews   Situated in the centre of the Mediterranean Sea on the submarine ridge, which extends 90km from the Ragusa Peninsula of Sicily southward to the African coasts, 200km east south-east of Cap Bon in Tunisia. The islands consist of Malta, Gozo and Comino, and several islets including Filfla, where there is a scheme to establish a marine protected area around the existing nature reserve (Augier, 1985; Sultana, *in litt.*, 1988).

Malta has a long history of settlement dating back to 5,000BC. The settlers introduced sheep and goats whose grazing activities prevented tree regeneration; this process of deforestation has continued and resulted in the almost total destruction of native forests and trees; all present day wooded areas have been planted by man in relatively recent times (Schembri, 1988). Remaining vegetation is characterised by the four remnants of natural holm oak *Quercus ilex* forest at Buskett, Ballut tal-Wardija, Il Bosk, Ballut ta l-Imgiebah and Ta'Baldu/Wied Hazrun; by garigue, steppic grassland and coastline communities (Schembri, 1988; Schrembri *et al.*, 1987).

Built up areas represent *c.* 16% of the island of Malta and *c.* 10% of the island of Gozo; registered agricultural land covers *c.* 38% of the islands' area (Schembri, 1988). Land conversion from agricultural use has mainly resulted in an increase in urban and touristic development, whilst hunting pressure is severe.

Presently, various bodies, including the Environmental Office for Conservation in the Environmental Division of the Ministry of Education, are working on a list of new areas to be declared nature reserves, as given in *Localities with conservation value in the Maltese islands* (Schembri, 1988; Schembri *et al.*, 1987; Sultana, *in litt.*, 1988).

The first forms of protection were for protected trees in 1933 and for nature reserves in 1978 (Ghadira Pool Reserve of 6ha); the only other nature reserve is Filfla island (6ha). There are a limited number of bird sanctuaries which are all small in area. The single national park, Ta'Qali, was inaugurated in September 1990 and covers 80ha. There is one inscribed Ramsar wetland site, two Mediterranean specially protected areas under the Barcelona Convention and two Council of Europe biogenetic reserves (Borg, 1991; Davis *et al.*, 1986; Sultana, pers. comm., 1989).

Most natural ecosystems are under threat from human activities, of which the most important are building development, road construction, quarrying and dumping of domestic and building waste. Additional threats include excess pressure to wildlife from *c.* 13,500 registered hunters (1986) and an unknown number of trappers (estimated at *c.* 12,000); all sand dune ecosystems are degraded due to the heavy use of the few existing local sandy beaches by large numbers of visitors; afforested areas are under threat from fires (accidental and deliberate) during the dry period; the very few saline marshlands are all are under threat from a variety of anthropomorphic causes, except one; sandy beaches, which constitute only 2.4% of the coastline, are under high pressure from the continued expansion of tourism and hotel development. The Maltese islands are situated in close proximity to the main Mediterranean sea routes which puts them at special risk from major pollution disasters (Schembi, 1988). In the reserves and sanctuaries there are problems with tourism, agricultural encroachment and poaching, and in Buskett Gardens Bird Sanctuary on one day alone in September 1986 up to 369 shots were fired at birds (Anon, 1986a; Anon, 1986b; Carp, 1979).

Other Relevant Information   Tourism is the major foreign currency earner. In 1989, up to 828,3111 tourists produced earnings of LM 135 million. Estimated number of tourists rose from 170,853 in 1970 to 864,000 in 1990. Tourism is an important element of Ta'Qali and Buskett parks (Borg, 1991; Hunter, 1991).

Addresses

Department of Agriculture and Fisheries, 14, M.A. Vassalli Street, VALLETTA (Tel: 224941/2; Tlx: 1790 MPDEV MW)

Environment Officer/Conservation, Ministry of Education, BELTISSEBH

References

Anon. (1986a). Maltese bird slaughter continues. *Oryx* 20(3): 187.

Anon. (1986b). Profiles in action, Joe Sultana. *ICBP World Birdwatch*. International Council for Bird Preservation. P. 12.

Anon. (1988). Filfla Nature Reserve visits. *Malta Times*, Monday, June 20.

Augier, H. (1985). *Protected marine areas. The example of France: appraisal and prospects*. European Committee for the Conservation of Nature and Natural Resources. Council of Europe, Strasbourg.

Borg, J. (1991). Malta's national parks and protected areas. A 1991 report for the World Conservation Monitoring Centre. Department of Agriculture and Fisheries, Valletta, Malta. (Unpublished). 2 pp.

Carp, E. (1979). *Directory of wetlands of international importance in the Western Palaearctic*. IUCN-UNEP. 506 pp.

COE (1984). *European nature conservation. Twenty years of activities*. Environment and Natural Resources Division. Council of Europe, Strasbourg. 127 pp.

Davis, S.D., Droop, S.J.M., Gregerson, P., Henson, L., Leon, C.J., Lamlein Villa-Lobos, J., Synge, H., and Zantovska, J. (1986). *Plants in danger: what do we know?* IUCN, Gland, Switzerland, and Cambridge, UK. 461 pp.

Hunter, B. (Ed.) (1991). *The Statesman's Year Book 1991-92*. The Macmillan Press Ltd, London and Basingstoke.

Schembri, P.J. (1988). IUCN islands directory entry for the Maltese islands. Unpublished report for the Department of Science, University of Malta. 26 pp.

Schembri, P.J., Lanfranco, E., Farrugia, P., Schrembri, S and Sultana, J. (1987). *Localities with conservation value in the Maltese islands*. Environment Division, Ministry of Education. 27 pp.

World Wildlife Fund (1982). *Year-Book 1982*. Pp. 128-129.

PRINCIPALITY OF MONACO

Area 1.95 sq. km

Population 29,876 (1990) (Hunter, 1991)
Natural increase: no information

Economic Indicators
GDP: No information
GNP: US$ 13,552 per capita (1990)

Policy and Legislation On 17 December 1962 the Constitution was promulgated, maintaining the hereditary monarchy. Executive power is exercised by the Head of State and a four-member Council of Government. The judicial code is based on that of France (Hunter, 1991).

The only protected area legislation is that for underwater reserves notified under Royal Order. The first reserve was decreed on 11 August 1976, amended and augmented by the Sovereign Order of 25 April 1978 and the Offences Act of 29 December 1978. The second site was established by Ordinance on 18 August 1986.

International Activities Monaco ratified the Convention concerning the Protection of the World Cultural and Natural Heritage (World Heritage Convention) on 7 November 1978, but no sites have been inscribed on the list. The Convention for the Protection of the Mediterranean Sea against Pollution (Barcelona Convention) was formally adopted in February 1976. The contracting parties to the Convention adopted the Protocol concerning Mediterranean Specially Protected Areas on 2 April 1982, which entered into force on 23 March 1986: two protected areas have been declared as Mediterranean specially protected areas.

Administration and Management Administration is undertaken by the Monaco Society for Nature Conservation (*Association Monegasque pour la Protection de la Nature* (AMPN), with most of the finance provided by private donation. Reserve boundaries are marked out offshore. A number of activities are prohibited including sports diving, all forms of fishing (including spear fishing) and the use of powered boats of any kind. Permanent surveillance is undertaken by the police service of the Principality and a team appointed by the governing board of the AMPN. The AMPN also supports scientific research in the reserves.

Systems Reviews The Mediterranean coastline is 0.9km long; inland the Principality is completely surrounded by French sovereign territory (Alpes Maritimes region). The Italian frontier is 10km to the east. The entire land area is an urban landscape, although there are some ornamental parks and gardens. The norther frontier rises steeply towards the limestone hills of the maritime alps. Offshore the marine benthos is of note, with a variety of substrates including sand, sea grass meadows, silt, gravel and rock. Many species of Mediterranean fish are found, and there are also some important populations of red coral *Coralium rubrum*. Artificial reefs have been created in Larvotto Reserve.

The only protected areas are Monaco Underwater Reserve "Larvotto" (50ha) and Red Coral Reserve (1ha). The former was established in 1976, the latter by ordinance on 18 August 1986.

Potential environmental threats include pollution from the adjacent port and land reclamation. Some 22ha have been reclaimed from the sea at Foutvielle for future office and residential development (Hunter, 1991).

Other Relevant Information There is a yearly average of 250,000 visitors to the Principality, with 245,146 in 1989 (Hunter, 1991).

Addresses

Association Monegasque pour la Protection de la Nature, Secretariat, 7 rue de la Colle, MC 98000 Monaco (Tel: 93 302107)

References

Anon. (1988). *Association Monegasque pour la Protection de la Nature: compte-rendu des activités 1986/7*. Monaco. 40 pp.

Augier, H. (1985). *Protected marine areas. The example of France: appraisal and prospects*. European Council for Conservation of Nature and Natural Resources, Strasbourg.

Hunter, B. (Ed.) (1991). *The Statesman's Year Book 1991-92*. The Macmillan Press Ltd, London and Basingstoke, UK. 1692 pp.

NETHERLANDS

Area 37,330 sq. km

Population 14,951,000 (1990)
Natural increase: 0.6% per annum

Economic Indicators
GDP: US$ 14,792 (1987)
GNP: US$ 11,860 (1987)

Policy and Legislation The latest revision of the 1814 Netherlands Constitution dates from 1983. In recent years environmental issues have been a major feature of election campaigns. Local government is often responsible for the acquisition of land and the enforcement of environmental legislation and policy.

Nature conservation began in 1905 with the formation of the *Vereniging tot Behoud van Natuurmonumenten* which established the first nature reserve, Naardemeer, in 1906. Presently, the most common way of protecting natural areas is by purchasing land for nature reserves. This is done by both the state and public bodies, and some sites receive additional protection through legislation. All state-owned nature reserves are areas where agriculture, industry and settlement are forbidden. Access to many smaller reserves of scientific importance is prohibited.

One of the principal acts giving increased protection to nature reserves and other ecologically valuable areas is the Nature Conservation Act, 1967 under which the central government can designate protected natural monuments on private property and state natural monuments on state property (see Annex). This Act also contains some of the main texts concerning the protection of species (Cutrera, 1991).

A less stringent form of protection may be provided under the Physical Planning Act, 1962 which deals with general planning, issuing general directives for the development of management plans, rules for land-use, and approves municipal and regional zoning plans. A municipality can designate land as a nature area under this Act. Such land may not be used for other purposes, but the Act may not be used to expropriate land for conservation purposes. Under the same Act flora and fauna on farmland can be given limited protection through the provision of licences for such activities as the digging of ditches and construction of new roads and tracks (Cutrera, 1991; Poore and Gryn-Ambroes, 1980).

A number of other acts, decrees and regulations exist which further support the protection of nature. The Areas of Natural Beauty Act, 1928 includes the possibility of tax concessions as compensation for nature conservation measures undertaken on private estates. The Land Consolidation Act, 1954 and the Forestry Act, 1961 contain a number of clauses which are applicable to nature conservation issues. A number of environment protection acts and other decrees and regulations may be used by national and provincial governments for nature conservation outside protected areas (Cutrera, 1991).

A number of the most important categories of protected area are not defined under existing legislation: protection is dependent on a combination of the aforementioned acts and on the cooperation of government and public owners of these areas. Since the 1970s it has been government policy to create units of land of over 1,000ha for conservation purposes, to be managed by the concentrated application of existing legal instruments. Four main categories of protected area can be distinguished: national parks, national landscapes, large landscape zones and large nature zones (see Annex). Although these are not legally defined, they are recognised and established by the government and treated in much the same way as protected areas in other countries (Cutrera, 1991).

The most important piece of forest legislation is the Forest Act, 1961, one of the principal aims of which is to conserve the existing forest and woodland in the Netherlands. This Act requires that all forest felling must be declared and areas felled must be replanted. The main aim of government forestry and silvicultural policy, as outlined to the year 2000, include: maintaining the existing forest; increasing timber production; extending the forest area and enhancing natural qualities of the country's forest (Cutrera, 1991).

In June 1990, the Dutch government proposed a major new policy initiative, the Nature Policy Plan, the objectives of which are the sustainable development and restoration of ecological and landscape values. This policy also interfaces with the National Environmental Policy Plan and the Third National Policy Document on Water Management the three plans are considered essential for the overall success of nature conservation policy. The Nature Policy Plan deals with species protection, public involvement in environmental problems, and integrating nature conservation policy with other policy areas. Certain characteristic ecosystems are highlighted for special attention, while overall the plan calls for: the creation of a sustainable structure for nature conservation through a "national ecological network"; the development of new areas of high ecological value; the stimulation of social support for the nature conservation policy; and the reinforcement of landscape conservation. The national ecological network consists of a network of core areas, nature development areas (sites with potential for habitat creation and restoration) and ecological corridors (zones designed to enable the movement of wildlife between areas in the network). The government intends to provide a legal basis for this plan in the Nature Conservation Act (Ministry of Agriculture, Nature Management and Fisheries, 1990).

An EC Directive concerning environmental impact assessments (EIAs) was adopted on 27 June 1985. EIAs must take into account a number of factors including, among other things, flora, fauna, soil, water, and the landscape. The General Environmental Act (WABM), 1979 was supplemented in 1986 by a new EIA law which represents a central legal regulation, incorporating all major aspects of EIAs (Coenen and Jörissen, 1989).

International Activities Accession to the Convention on Wetlands of International Importance especially as Waterfowl Habitat (Ramsar Convention) took place on 23 May 1980 with 11 sites listed (a further six sites are listed in the Netherlands Antilles). The Dutch section of the Wadden Sea was accepted as a biosphere reserve under the Unesco Man and the Biosphere (MAB) Programme in October 1986. The Convention on the Conservation of European Wildlife and Natural Habitats (Bern Convention) was signed on 1 June 1982. The Netherlands is a member of the European Community and hence is bound by its environmental directives: nine sites have been designated as EC special protection areas under the Wild Birds Directive (April, 1991). The Netherlands is also a member of the Council of Europe: 18 sites have classified as Council of Europe biogenetic reserves, in addition, one site has been awarded the Council of Europe European Diploma.

In 1982 the three Wadden Sea states of the Netherlands, Germany and Denmark signed the "Joint Declaration on the Protection of the Wadden Sea". This declaration provides protection by the full and coordinated application of international legal instruments by the states and countries concerned. Such decisions are made at the Trilateral Governmental Conference on the Protection of the Wadden Sea. The fifth meeting took place on 17 November 1988 at Bonn, where agreements were reached concerning the implementation of Ramsar, the Convention on the Conservation of European Wildlife and Natural Habitats (1982), the Convention on the Conservation of Migratory Species of Wild Animals (1979) and the EC Bird Directive (79/409/EC) (Anon., 1988). Other transboundary protected areas are being considered under the National Nature Policy Plan, in an effort to link the Dutch ecological network with nature areas across the borders with Belgium and Germany (Ministry of Agriculture, Nature Management and Fisheries, 1990).

Administration and Management Since 1982, the Ministry of Agriculture, Nature Management and Fisheries (Ministerie van Landbouw, Natuurbeheer en Visserij), which includes the Directorate for Nature Conservation, Environment and Fauna Management, has been the main government body concerned with protected areas and nature conservation. The Ministry receives advice from the Nature Conservancy Council (Natuurbeschermingsraad) concerning the designation of natural monuments and environmental impact assessments for large and potentially threatening projects.

The National Forest Service (Staatsbosbeheer) is part of the Ministry of Agriculture, Nature Management and Fisheries. It was reorganised in 1988, with the objective of separating policy tasks from the management of state-owned forest and nature areas. The National Forest Service is now only responsible for the latter, which includes the management of all state-owned nature reserves, while the policy tasks are now the responsibility of the Government Agency for Forestry and Landscape (*Directie Bos-en Lanschapsbouw*) both organisations remain within the Ministry of Agriculture, Nature Management and Fisheries. The Nature Conservation Inspectorate and the Research Institute of Nature Management is a part of the National Forest Service. Working for the Inspectorate is a nature conservation officer assisted by a biologist in each province. In each district, a district officer is assisted by a biologist, a physical planner and an administrator. The private organisations, which own a substantial proportion of the nature reserves in the country, are responsible for their own management, however they receive a high degree of government subsidy for much of their land purchase and management costs. The 1990 Nature Policy Plan states that substantial increases in finance will be required for the acquisition of land, management, nature development and other sectors. It proposed the allocation of DFL 41 million in 1990, rising to DFL 155 million in 1994, of which over two-thirds has been provisionally allocated towards policy on environmental sensitive areas and on national parks (Ministry of Agriculture, Nature Management and Fisheries, 1990).

When taking decisions concerning issues of nature conservation, the Ministry is usually required to work with the Ministry of Housing, Town Planning and Environmental Policy (Ministerie van Volkshuisvesting, Ruimtelijke Ordening en Milieu) and many policy statements have to be produced jointly.

In 1975 the government established a policy which aimed at establishing 21 national parks in areas designated as "potential national parks". The Provisional National Parks Commission (Voorlopige Commissie Nationale Parken) was set up at the national level. It has no legal powers, and investigates the problems facing potential parks and the willingness of local communities and landowners to have such parks established. Consultation groups are set up, and the Minister of Agriculture, Nature Management and Fisheries can then give a park the status of "national park in formation". After a development and management plan has been established and approved by all involved, the park can be officially designated as a national park (Cutrera, 1991).

Research is currently being undertaken by the Royal Institute for Nature Management (Rijksinstituut voor Natuurbeheer), which is assisting the Ministry in all matters related to nature conservation and management (Poore and Gryn-Ambroes, 1980).

Non-governmental organisations play a crucial role in the protection of areas. The Association for the Conservation of Natural Monuments (Vereniging tot Behoud van Natuurmonumenten) has more than 250,000 members and owns more than 50,000ha of nature reserves. Other big private owners include the Provincial Landscape Boards (Provinciale Landschappen), one in each province, organisations include the Royal Forest, National Park Foundation "De Kennemerduinen", National Park Foundation "De Hoge Veluwe", Foundation Gooil Natuurreservaat, Foundation "Twicket" and the "Huis Bergh" Foundation. Also there is a foundation for the Conservation of the Provincial Landscape, owning a total of 26,400ha and managing a further 6,000ha. Most of the private organisations come together under the Foundation for Nature and the Environment (Stichting Natuur en Milieu) which has a major influence in government and public circles (Cutrera, 1991).

The protection of small nature reserves has proved to be very difficult because the surrounding areas are often intensively farmed. It is partly for this reason that the four categories of large protected areas were proposed, although these too have suffered problems. The policy for the designation of national landscapes was protested vigorously by many farmers, to such an extent that, in 1984 the government withdrew its subsidies for these areas, in spite of objections from the provinces and private organisations. Little is heard about this category and only one site remains and is actively promoted (Cutrera, 1991).

Systems Reviews   The Netherlands is a very low-lying, open country in north-west Europe. It has a long coastline facing the North Sea which is dominated in the south-west by the delta complex of the rivers Schelde, Maas and Rijn (Rhine). In the north-east there is a continuous narrow belt of dune topography, and in the north the major intertidal wetlands and barrier islands of the Wadden Sea. Inland, the country borders Germany to the east and Belgium to the south.

The population density is the highest of any European country. The natural vegetation has been modified by agriculture, forestry and urban development. About 40% of the land surface is man-made, the result of reclamation from the sea (some 30% lies below sea level). Despite the drainage of large marsh and peat bog regions (the polders) in the west, valuable wetland flora still exists in places. Much of the forest cover had been removed by the mid-19th century. There are a number of areas of floristic interest, such as the Wadden Sea area, the dunes along the North Sea, especially the Isle of Voorne, the relict heathlands of the Velusue and the Biesbos Delta. In Limburg district in the far south the terrain is high rocky calcareous sandstone moorland, rising to 350m and supporting an isolated central European flora. The flora is predominantly of an Atlantic type, with no endemics. Inlets along the coast and between the islands of Zuid-Holland and Zeeland have been closed off by dykes. Inland, there are a number of freshwater lake complexes and deep water holes along river banks formed by dyke falls. Untouched areas include the low fenlands, such as Noord-West Overijssels and the Wadden Sea, an area of flat lowlands and intertidal mudflats. The largest land-user is agriculture which accounted for more than 70% of total land area in 1978.

Expansion of the protected areas network is planned through the establishment of natural landscape parks. A programme of national parks was begun in 1975, with the first one established in 1984 and another 20 proposed. Protected areas covered 3.5% of total land area in 1987.

Threats to protected areas beyond the control of the management agencies mainly come from pollution and gas exploitation. Pollution in the form of acid rain has led to the death of half of the country's forests, according to a government report, requiring new government measures. The Wadden Sea, an area of international importance, is threatened by pollution from various sources of pollution and immediate action is required. The newly designated national parks are threatened with disturbance due to the comprehensive road systems which facilitate access by car. Other threats, all of which could be prevented, come from hunting, forestry and sport fishing which in itself causes severe erosion of river banks and shore lines.

Other Relevant Information   Visitor numbers to protected areas are on the increase. Access is free to state nature reserves. However, membership of the association concerned is often required for access to private nature reserves.

Addresses

Directoraat-General, Landelijke Gebieden en Kwaliteitszog, Directie Natuur, Milieu en Faunabeheer, Ministerie van Landbouw en Visserij, Postbus 20401, Bezuidenhoutseweg 73, 2500 EK 's GRAVENHAGE (Tel: 70 793911; FAX: 70 793600; Tlx: 32040 lavinl/Telegrams: Landvis)

National Forest Service, Postbus 20020, 3502 LA UTRECHT

Ministry of Cultural Affairs, Recreation & Social Welfare, Steenvoordelaan 370, RIJSWIJK

Ministry of Agriculture, Nature Management and Fisheries, PO Box 20401, 2500 EK 's GRAVENHAGE (Tel: 70 379 2057/379 2062)

Landelijke Vereniging tot behoud van de Waddenzee, Postbus 90, HARLINGEN (Tel: 5178 5541)

Nederlandse Vereniging to Bescherming van Vogels, Driebergseweg 16b, ZEIST (Tel: 3404 25406)

Stichting Natuur en Milieu, Donkerstraat 17, UTRECHT (Tel: 030 331328)

Vereniging tot behoud van Natuurmonumenten in Nederland, Noordereinde 60, 's GRAVENHAGE (Tel: 35 62004)

Wereld Natuurfolds Nederland, Postbus 7, 3700 AA ZEIST (Tel: 3404 22164)

References

Anon. (1978). *Nature and landscape conservation in the Netherlands*. Ministry of Cultural Affairs, Recreation and Social Welfare.

Anon. (1987). *Directory of wetlands of international importance*. Ramsar Canada Conference.

Anon. (1988). Fifth trilateral governmental conference on the protection of the Wadden Sea. Bonn.

Anon. (1989). Netherlands Environmental Policy Plan-Plus. 12 pp.

Adriaanse, A., Jeltes, R. and Reiling, R. (1988). Towards a national reference center for environment information in the Netherlands: a review. *Environmental Management* 12(2): 145-149.

Boer, A. (1978). A system of national parks in the Netherlands. *Parks* 3(1): 9-11.

Boer, A. (1988). Some experiences with national parks in the Netherlands. *Nature and National Parks Bulletin* 26(100): 34-37.

CoE (1984). *The Netherlands*. European Nature Conservation. Council of Europe, Environment and Natural Resources Division, Strasbourg. Pp. 81-82.

CoE (1986). *Convention on the conservation of European wildlife and natural habitats.* 7 November. Pp. 16.

CoE (1986). *Convention on the conservation of European wildlife and natural habitats.* 20 November. Pp. 2.

CoE (1989). Netherlands: the national environment plan is to be brought before Parliament. *Naturopa*. Council of Europe.

Coenen, R. and Jörissen, J. (1989). *Environmental impact assessment in the member countries of the European Community, implementing the EC-Directive: an overview.* KfK 4507 B, Kernforschungszentrum, Karsruhe, Germany. 42 pp.

Cutrera, A. (1991). *European Environmental Yearbook*. Institute for Environmental Studies. DocTer International UK, London. 897 pp.

Davis, S.D., Droop, S.J.M., Gregerson, P., Henson, L., Leon, C.J., Lamlein Villa-Lobos, J., Synge, H. and Zantovska, J. (1986). *Plants in danger: what do we know?* IUCN, Gland, Switzerland and Cambridge, UK. 461 pp.

ECE (1986). *ENV/Sem. 16/l.2*. 25-29 August. ECE Finland. Pp. 10, 20-21, 39-40.

Gelder, T. van (1989). The biological survey and monitoring programme at the Dutch National Forest Service. National Forest Service.

Gersie, J. (1987). The Netherlands. *European Environmental Yearbook: parks and nature reserves.* Pp. 394-396.

Ministry of Agriculture and Fisheries (n.d). *National parks, National park policy in the Netherlands*. The Hague. 12 pp.

Ministry of Agriculture, Nature Management and Fisheries (1990). *Nature policy plan of the Netherlands*. The Hague. 103 pp.

Paxton, J. (1990). *The Stateman's Yearbook*. Pp. 901-903.

Roderkerk, E.C.M. (1980). Nature conservation in the Netherlands. *Nature and National Parks* 18: 11.

Wolters, A.R. (n.d.). New features in the nature policy of the Netherlands. *Naturopa* 89: 4. Environment features. Council of Europe.

Zwiemk, K. van der (1987). Internal protection – Wadden Sea. Convention on Wetlands of International Importance Especially as Waterfowl Habitat. Unpublished document.

ANNEX
Definitions of protected area designations, as legislated, together with authorities responsible for their administration

Title: Natuurbeschermingwet (Nature Conservation Act)

Date: 1967

Brief description: Provides, among other things for the designation of natural monuments

Administrative authority: Ministry of Cultural Affairs, Recreation and Social Work

Designations:

Bescherrmde natuurmonumenten (Protected natural monument)

Staatnatuurmonumenten (State natural monument) Designated by Ministerial announcement. Actions harmful to the natural or scientific interest of the designated area are prohibited, however, some activities are allowed under permit. By law, the Minister is required to devise a management plan for each protected area.

Sources: Cutrera, 1991; Poore and Gryn-Ambroes, 1980

Title: Individual acts relating to national parks, national landscapes, large landscape zones and large nature zones

Date: Various

258

Brief description: Four categories of protected area which are probably the most important categories in the country, and which are established through the application of policy and protected under a range of Acts, decrees and regulations.

Administrative authority: Ministry of Agriculture and Fisheries

Designations:

Nationale parken (National park) Areas that cover at least 1,000ha and consist of natural features such as rivers, lakes and/or woods/forests having a special scientific character and flora and fauna. Such areas should provide adequate opportunities for the inclusion of restricted zones for the limited recreational use.

Should contain little or no cultivated land. Management objectives are to preserve and/or to develop their natural ecological, geomorphological and aesthetic features. Opportunities should be provided for public enjoyment and appreciation of these areas.

For the purpose of planning and management, preference shall be given, in principal, to the preservation, maintenance and restoration of the natural, scientific and scenic value of these areas over and above all other developments. Each national park is also a large nature zone (below).

Nationale landschappen (National landscape) Wider areas, of at least 10,000ha, which incorporate nature reserves and agricultural land and settlements. The entire area then presents a large landscape of natural and cultural value. The possibilities for outdoor recreation should be exploited and further developed in these areas.

Can include one or more national parks and other large nature and large landscape zones.

Grote landschseenheden (Large landscape zone) Similar to national landscapes but may be smaller (less than 10,000 but over 5,000ha). Less important for outdoor recreation and the financial support that is available to national landscapes is not available for these areas.

Grote eenheden natuurgebied (Large nature zone) Cover at least 1,000ha and have similar regulations to national parks, but outdoor recreation is not to be encouraged in these areas.

Sources: Cutrera, 1991; Ministry of Agriculture and Fisheries, 198?

SUMMARY OF PROTECTED AREAS

Map† ref.	National/international designations Name of area	IUCN management category	Area (ha)	Year notified
	National Parks			
1	De Biesbosch	IV	7,100	1987
2	De Groote Peel	IV	1,320	1985
3	De Hamert	IV	1,460	1989
4	De Meijnweg	IV	1,600	1990
5	De Weerribben	IV	3,450	1986
6	Dwingelderveld	IV	3,600	1986
7	Hoge Veluwe	IV	5,450	1935
8	Schiermonnikoog	II	5,400	1989
9	Veluwezoom	IV	4,720	1930
10	Zuid-Kennemerland	IV	2,090	1990
	Nature Reserves			
11	Alde Feanen	IV	1,850	
12	Ameland	IV	4,500	
13	Amsterdamse Waterleidingpuinen	IV	3,370	
14	Ankeveense-Kortenhoefre-Loosdrechtre Plassen	IV	1,450	1969
15	Bargerveen	IV	2,100	
16	Berkenheuvel	IV	1,000	1956
17	Boswachterij Schoorl	IV	2,000	1894
18	De Geul en Westerduinen	I	1,681	1926
19	Diependal	IV	1,310	
20	Duinen Terschelling	IV	9,500	
21	Duinen Texel	IV	2,300	
22	Duinen Vlieland	IV	3,910	
23	Eierlands Gat Zeehondenreservaat	IV	20,000	1947
24	Fochteloerveen	IV	1,715	1972
25	Goois	III	1,500	1987
26	Haarler-Holterberg	IV	1,600	
27	Hardenberg	IV	1,190	
28	Haringvliet Forelands	IV	3,600	
29	Jisperveld	IV	1,516	1961
30	Kootwijkerzand/Garderen	IV	1,500	
31	Lauwersmeer	IV	2,500	
32	Leuvenhorst and Leuvenumse Bos	IV	1,855	
33	Loonse and Drunense Duinen	IV	1,730	
34	Meijendel	IV	1,280	
35	Meijnweg (incorp. into National Park)	IV	1,015	
36	Nieuwkoopse Plassen	IV	1,500	1968
37	North Veluwe	IV	2,850	1954
38	Oerd en Steile Bank	I	1,200	
39	Oostvaardersplassen	III	5,600	
40	Planken Wambuis	IV	1,965	
41	Schouwen Duinen	IV	3,064	1980
42	Slikken van Flakkee	IV	3,700	
43	Strabrechtse Heide	IV	1,020	1951
44	Stroomdallandschap Drentsche Aa	IV	1,250	1965
45	Tjonger- and Lindevallei and Rottige Meenthe	IV	1,353	
46	Varkensland and Waterland	IV	1,010	
47	Wassenaarse Duinen	I	1,330	
	Natural Monuments			
48	Berkheide	III	1,000	1990
49	Boschplaat	III	4,400	1974
50	Deurnse Peel	III	1,500	1980
51	Dollard	III	5,000	1977

Map[†] ref.	*National/international designations* Name of area	IUCN management category	Area (ha)	Year notified
52	Eemmeer	III	1,200	1976
53	Engbertsdjiksvenen	III	1,000	1985
54	Gras- and Rietgorzen Haringvliet	III	1,030	1971
55	Kop van Schouwen	III	2,200	1978
56	Krammer-Volkerak	III	3,430	1988
57	Kwelders Friesland	III	1,370	1982
58	Kwelders Groningen	III	1,230	1982
59	Mariapeel	III	1,100	1964
60	Markiezaatsmeer Zuid	III	1,860	1982
61	Mispeleindse -/Landschotse Heide	III	1,135	1983
62	Oosterschelde	III	24,000	1990
63	Schorren van de Eendracht	III	1,000	1982
64	Ventjagersplaten and Slijkplaat	III	1,090	1980
65	Verdronken Land van Saeftinghe	III	3,500	1976
66	Waddenzee	III	154,800	1981
67	Zwarte Meer	III	1,650	1990

Biosphere Reserve			
Waddensea Area	IX	260,000	1986

Ramsar Wetlands			
De Biesbosch (part)	R	1,700	1980
De Boschplaat	R	4,400	1980
De Griend	R	23	1980
De Groote Peel	R	900	1980
De Weerribben	R	3,400	1980
Engbertsdijksvenen	R	975	1989
Het Naardermeer	R	752	1980
Oosterschelde	R	38,000	1987
Oostvaardersplassen	R	5,600	1989
Wadden Sea	R	249,998	1984
Zwanenwater	R	600	1988

[†]Locations of most protected areas are shown on the accompanying map.

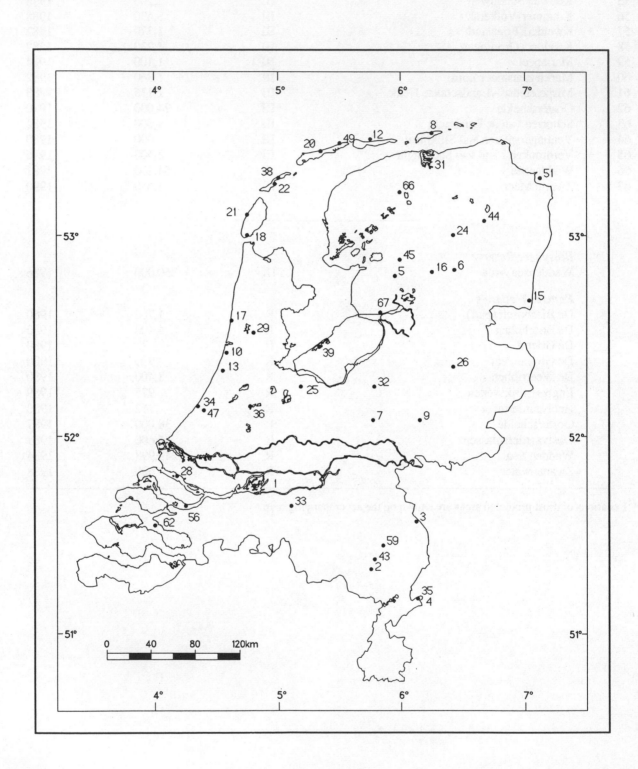

Protected Areas of the Netherlands

NORWAY
(INCLUDING SVALBARD AND JAN MAYEN)

Area 323,900 sq. km (Svalbard 62,051 sq. km, Jan Mayen 380 sq. km)

Population 4,212,000 (1990)
Natural increase: 0.28% per annum
Svalbard 3,646 (1988, 2,579 of these were Soviet citizens) (Paxton, 1990)

Economic Indicators
GDP: US$ 19,895 per capita (1987)
GNP: US$ 17,110 per capita (1987)

Policy and Legislation The first Nature Conservation Act entered into force in 1910, followed by another Nature Conservation Act in 1954. The 1954 legislation was replaced on 19 June 1970 by the Nature Conservation Act No. 63. This Act was most recently amended on 14 June 1985 (The Nature Conservation Act No. 77) and remains the legal basis and main instrument for setting aside and applying protection to all conservation areas. This Act declares nature a national asset which is administered for its long-term preservation and which should only be utilised as part of a long-term comprehensive administration of resources. It gives protection to flora, fauna and natural areas.

Four categories of protected areas are covered by the Nature Conservation Act: national park, landscape protected area, nature reserve, and natural monument (see Annex). The Act provides guidelines for the regulations for the different types of protected area. Specific regulations, however, are drawn up for individual sites. The Act also makes provision for the National Council for the Conservation of Nature to act as an advisory body to the Ministry of the Environment. Conservation legislation is geared to be long-term in operation and Clause 18 gives owners and users of natural resources the right to comment upon activities proposed by specific governmental or provincial agencies, whilst the Ministry of Environment can place the resources under preliminary protection. The Department of Environment Protection is obliged to prevent all development and construction work, pollution and any kind of encroachment. Access is unrestricted, regardless of land ownership, in line with traditional Scandinavian practices. The Act makes provision for the creation of biotope reserves and bird sanctuaries in places which are of major importance to flora and fauna. Such sites do not have to fulfil the main legal requirements of any of the main protected area categories, although they are sometimes considered to be a subdivision of nature reserves in the broad sense. The Act also confers powers for interim protection of sites pending final decisions, such protection being decided by the Directorate for Nature Management, subject to appeal to the Ministry of Environment (Backer, 1991).

Legislation for flora and fauna protection outside national parks is weaker than inside, but is now covered under the Wildlife Act (No. 38) of 19 May 1981 (which entered into force on 2 April 1982). This Act, which completely replaces the Game Management Act, 1951 restricts hunting to certain species and within certain seasons. It also includes provisions for the protection of areas which are of essential value for game (Ministry of Environment, 1982a, 1982b). More broadly, the Wildlife Act prescribes that planning authorities shall give due consideration to the effect on wildlife habitats in their general land-use planning (Backer, 1991).

The Building and Planning Act, 1965 deals with land use planning (physical planning) at the national, provincial and community level and specifies that nature conservation interests must be considered in planning activities "to guide local planners and to harmonise plans among sectors". County plans give attention to conservation problems and coordinate local plans of the community, they are reviewed every four years (Ministry of Environment, 1982b; Poore and Gryn-Ambroes, 1980). Since 1982 this Act has been replaced by a new Planning and Building Act: three paragraphs in the new Act are of particular relevance to nature conservation. Paragraph 17 allows for national political regulations to be made for a defined area or an object such as a river to prevent the destruction of their natural quality. Work has recently been completed in analysing how these regulations might be used to protect rivers from man-made impacts, to replace the existing Norwegian Protection Plan for River Systems. Under Paragraph 20 areas such as wetlands can be given temporary protection for four years where major conflicts of land use arise. Under Paragraph 25 smaller natural areas such as bays and marshes can be regulated for nature conservation purposes at the municipal level. Such areas may be sites that do not qualify for protection under the Nature Conservation Act because of their size, ecological importance or other reasons. So far, few such areas have been designated, probably because of the compensation regulations which apply to the owner under the terms of the Act.

A new set of regulations concerning environmental impact assessment came into force on 1 August 1990 under the Planning and Building Act: prior notification of all major physical projects and projects that require a significant change in the landscape must be provided to the Ministry concerned, together with details of the project and alternatives and a preliminary assessment of its impact. Based on this notification, the Ministry may require the developer to undertake a more thorough environmental impact assessment. In addition to major building schemes, projects requiring environmental impact assessment include mining projects, the development of new agricultural land and large reforestation schemes. Among the impacts to be considered under the new regulations are the environmental impact on plant and animal life, areas of outstanding natural beauty, natural and man-made landscapes; the impact on natural resources including forest resources; and the social impact, including effects on outdoor and recreational activities (Ministry of Environment, 1990).

Other legislation includes the Forest Management Act, 1863, the Forest Protection Act, 1909 and the Forest Production and Protection Act, 1985. This latter Act authorises the designation of specific forest areas of particular importance for nature conservation or open-air recreation. Regulations on forestry practices may also be laid down for these areas. The Directorate for State Forest and Land in the Ministry of Agriculture has established "administrative protection" in some areas, mainly those put aside as forest reserves. Most of these areas are also protected as nature reserves under the Nature Conservation Act as part of a national plan for the conservation of coniferous forest (Backer, 1991; Directorate for Nature Management, *in litt.*, 1991).

The Shore and Mountain Planning Act (No. 103) of 10 December 1971 followed on from a temporary law passed in 1965, prohibiting house building within 100m of the seashore and making all construction along coastal and inland waters conform to land utilisation plans. This Act is now abolished and its provisions have been incorporated into the new Building and Planning Act. Other legislation already enacted or under consideration provides for the protection of 200 watercourses from hydroelectric development (the Norwegian Protection Plan for River Systems) and for restricting the use of off-road or cross-country vehicles. The Act for the Protection of Ancient Monuments, 1951 safeguards areas around natural monuments.

Other peripheral legislation includes the Open-Air Recreation Act, 1957 which deals with the creation and maintenance of recreation areas and states the right of free public access to all uncultivated areas with no buildings. To improve the accessibility of land, for example in built-up areas and along coastlines where there are many holiday homes, the state has purchased a number of areas throughout Norway which are termed public recreation areas. Such areas are not protected under the Nature Conservation Act as their designation is not primarily for conservation purposes. Such sites, however, clearly are of conservation value.

In 1980, a 13-member government-appointed committee, chaired by the President of the Norwegian Parliament, completed a report on national conservation perspectives (Protection of Norwegian Nature St. meld Nr. 68 (1980-81) *Vern av norsk natur*) based on the World Conservation Strategy, resulting in a subsequent report to parliament in 1981 and a proposal for a national conservation policy plan. This report was adopted by parliament as the basis for a Conservation Policy Plan.

The plan requires that all relevant government authorities give greater consideration to nature conservation issues, under guidance from the Ministry of the Environment. It stresses the importance of conservation issues in regional planning, and suggests the creation of many new nature reserves to be based on regional plans. The policy plan also covers pollution, acid rain, species protection and the protection of water courses (Ministry of Environment, 1982a).

Most national parks have been created according to a plan proposed in 1964 and adopted by parliament in 1967. A second plan was put forward in 1986 and is now awaiting submission to parliament (Backer, 1991).

Svalbard came under Norwegian sovereignty at the signing of the Spitzbergen Treaty on 9 February 1920. However, citizens of the contracting parties of the Treaty have equal right to fish and hunt in the area, and to establish commercial operations. This right has been quite widely used by the Soviets. Norwegian civil and penal laws apply. In addition, some laws apply specifically to Svalbard and to Jan Mayen. A Royal Decree of 26 February 1932 established two plant protected reserves; Royal Decrees of 1 June and 11 October 1973 established three national parks, two nature reserves and fifteen bird sanctuaries (Ministry of Environment, 1981). Fairly tight regulations, covered under a Royal Decree of 28 May 1971, apply in Svalbard and Jan Mayen to economic and other activities to control interference with nature. A Royal Decree of 11 August 1978 concerns the management of game and freshwater fishes. Chapter V, Clause 14 of this Decree places restrictions on activities near cliffs used by nesting birds between 1 April and 31 August. All cultural monuments on Svalbard and Jan Mayen are protected by a Royal Decree of 21 June 1974 (Ministry of Environment, 1981).

International Activities   The Convention concerning the Protection of the World Cultural and Natural Heritage (World Heritage Convention) was ratified on 12 May 1977. No natural sites have been accepted, but three sites (Vistenfjord-Vega-Lovund, Kong Karlsland and Hardang-ervidda) have been placed on a tentative list of sites recommended for future consideration by the World Heritage Secretariat. The Convention on Wetlands of International Importance especially as Waterfowl Habitat (Ramsar Convention) was signed without reservation as to ratification on 9 July 1974, and 14 wetlands have been designated as Ramsar sites, five in Svalbard. One site (in Svalbard) has been designated as a biosphere reserve under the Unesco Man and the Biosphere Programme.

Norway is a member of the Council of Europe: 11 sites have been declared as Council of Europe biogenetic reserves. No sites have been awarded the Council of Europe European Diploma (end-1990). Norway, but not Svalbard, is also a party to the Bern Convention on the Conservation of European Wildlife and Natural Habitats, which it signed in 1979. The Nordic Council, of which Norway is a member state, is involved in a number of environmental protection issues: the Nordic Council of Ministers has run a series of four to five-year environmental protection programmes, the present programme beginning in 1988. These programmes cover a wide range of activities which include, among other things, bringing greater attention to nature conservation in connection with planning activities. The Council has encouraged the registration of valuable landscapes in the Nordic area, the concentration of conservation efforts towards the preservation of particularly important habitat types and the use of natural areas by the wider public for recreation purposes. It has also encouraged the development of a standardised data collection for monitoring environmental quality (Nordic Council of Ministers, 1983). Norway is also a party to the Nordic Environmental Protection Convention, which requires authorities to take into account the environmental consequences to all other parties before granting permits for environmentally damaging activities (Nordic Council of Ministers, 1978).

There are a number of transboundary protected areas, the most notable being: Femundsmarka National Park and the proposed Rogen-Langfjallet National Park (currently Rogen Nature Reserve) in Sweden; Rago National Park and Sarek/Padjelanta/Sonfjallet national parks in Sweden; and Ovre Anarjokka National Park and Lemmonjoki National Park in Finland.

Administration and Management   A National Council for Nature Conservation was established in 1955. The first post of Nature Conservation Inspector was created in 1960. In 1965 the Administration of Outdoor Recreation and Nature Conservation was established within the Ministry of Local Government and Labour (Norderhaug, 1985).

The Ministry of Environment (*Miljoverndepartementet*) was created in 1972. It is responsible for the coordination of regional planning and for natural resource management (resource accounting and budgeting for energy, water, land, fish, soils and forests), for pollution control, including oil, and noise abatement, problems of waste disposal, conservation of nature and recreation areas, management of wildlife and freshwater fish, coordination of environmental research and international environmental cooperation, conservation of the country's natural heritage, improvement of residential environments and urban renewal and also the coordination of mapping of land and territorial waters (Ministry of Environment, 1983). It is also responsible for long-term management of natural resources (Norderhaug, 1985). This Ministry consists of five departments: General Coordination Department, Department of Regional Planning and Resource Management, Department of Pollution Control, Department of Natural Resources and Department of Nature Conservation and Open-Air Recreation.

The Department of Nature Conservation and Open-Air Recreation has responsibility for, amongst other things, protected areas and the administration of the provisions of the Nature Conservation Act of 1970. It is divided into eight sections. The First Nature Conservation Division is responsible for protection and conservation in pursuance of the Nature Conservation Act; it covers conservation planning, monitoring, inventories and surveys of areas and species deserving protection, it is responsible for the establishment and administration of protected areas; it also covers conservation on Svalbard, and international cooperation on conservation issues; it has a staff of ten, nine university graduates and one lawyer. The Second Nature Conservation Division covers conservation and recreation in relation to hydro-power development, and the use of watercourses; it has a staff of eight, comprising one lawyer, one forester, one civil engineer, one agronomist, one sociologist and three others. The Third Nature Conservation Division is involved with landscape protection and planning and also with environmental impact assessments. The First Open-Air Recreation Division deals with application of the Open-Air Recreation Act, the right of public access and the expropriation and protection of recreation areas. The Second Open-Air Recreation Division covers planning and research with respect to recreational areas, and also planning pursuant to the Building and Planning Act. The Division of Shore Planning and Administration administers the Shore and Mountain Planning Act. The Wildlife and Freshwater Fish Division covers the Wildlife Act and other legislation dealing with hunting and fishing. The Management Section is responsible for the care and management of protected areas (Ministry of Environment, 1983).

The First Nature Conservation Division also acts as the Secretariat of the National Council for the Conservation of Nature, a state agency affiliated to the Ministry of the Environment. Matters of importance are referred to the Minister, who also appoints two high level inspectors for nature conservation, one for north and central Norway and one for the south. At a local level, each of the 20 counties has an environmental protection department which is responsible, through the County Governor, to the Ministry of Environment. These local departments are responsible in particular for water supply, sewerage, waste disposal and pollution issues, nature conservation and open-air recreation, wildlife and freshwater fish and county mapping (Ministry of Environment, 1983). Wardens are appointed locally or by the appropriate state directorates (Directorate for State Forests). In Svalbard the Governor has overall responsibility for protected areas; he has jurisdictional, police and administrative power throughout the Archipelago (Ministry of Environment, 1981).

There are five Directorates/Institutions under the Ministry of Environment: Directorate for Nature Management, State Pollution Control Authority, Norwegian Polar Research Institute, Norwegian Mapping Authority and Central Office of Historic Sites and Monuments. The Directorate for Nature

Management (*Direktoratetfor Naturforvaltning*) has the most direct involvement with the Department of Nature Conservation and Open-Air Recreation. It was established on 1 September 1985 and is authorised to manage Norwegian nature through various laws and regulations, notably the Nature Conservation Act, the Wildlife Act, the Salmon and Inland Fishing Act and the Open Air Recreation Act; it is also involved in solving other environmental problems by cooperating with, advising and informing other governmental and private bodies. The Directorate is divided into five departments: Outdoor Recreation, Terrestrial Ecology, Aquatic Ecology, Environmental Impact Assessments and Administration. Much of the work undertaken by the Directorate is of a monitoring nature: the effects of acid rain and control measures, pollution, hunting, fish stocks, river management, public planning. It is also involved in the promotion of the aforementioned Acts, international conservation agreements and the promotion of nature to the Norwegian public. Each year it allocates funds for the acquisition and development of recreational areas in the vicinity of towns and built-up areas. At present, the Directorate for Nature Management has around 125 employees (Directorate for Nature Management, *in litt.*, 1991).

In 1982 the Ministry of Environment had a full-time staff of 190 with about 1,000 full-time employees in affiliated institutions. The budget for the Ministry was 517 Mkr (US$ 68.8 million) in 1978, rising to 739 Mkr (US$ 1094.5 million) in 1982, but included affiliated institutions, and for the Department of Nature Conservation and Open-Air Recreation (in 1978) was 28.5 MKr (US$ 3.77 million). The latter figure includes wardening, boundary demarcation, wages, compensations and operations. The Department's budget includes 8.6 Mkr (US$ 1.12 million) for land acquisition and compensation, but most is used for recreation provision (Poore and Gryn-Ambroes, 1980). Technical staff are funded by the Department's budget whilst subordinate members are officially part of the Ministry. Research (inventories, surveys, studies) is funded by the Ministry, and carried out by contracted universities and specialist institutes. The Ministry takes all major management decisions, advice being given by the management authority of the area. On the ground management is the responsibility of the county advisor in the Directorate for State Forests. Management plans are being elaborated for nature reserves. With few exceptions the policy is one of non-intervention; management is passive and limited to activities connected with public use.

The Ministry of Agriculture and the Ministry of Industry consult the Ministry of the Environment, where appropriate, whilst all major development decisions are taken by parliament, administered by the Ministry of Industry. The Forestry Act is administered by the Ministry of Agriculture, while the Water and Watercourses Act is covered by the Ministry of Oil and Energy, which is also responsible for the designation of watercourses to be protected by plenary decision in parliament (Backer, 1991).

The major voluntary society is the Norwegian Union for Nature Protection (*Naturvern forbund*), established in 1964, which has 36,000 members in 18 local associations (1980). It is completely independent, although partially supported by government funds, and was the most important force in Norwegian nature conservation until the National Council for Nature Conservation was established in 1955 (Poore and Gryn-Ambroes, 1980).

Systems Reviews Mainland Norway is a long, narrow country running from approximately 58°N to 71°N. It shares a long eastern border with Sweden, while to the north, in Lapland, it shares borders with Finland and a short border with the Russian Republic of the former USSR. The mainland coastline is over 20,000km long and indented, with over 53,000 islands; the total length of coastline, including islands, is some 53,069km (Ministry of Environment, 1982a). To the north the coastline borders the Arctic Ocean, to the west the Norwegian Sea and, to the south and south-west it borders the Skagerrak Straits and the North Sea. The archipelago of Svalbard lies some 700km north of mainland Norway at its nearest point. It lies between the Barents Sea in the east and the Greenland Sea in the west. The archipelago is surrounded by pack-ice in spring, while the limit of permanent pack-ice lies less than 200km north of the islands. The mainland is mountainous, with the highest peak reaching 2,469m. Its geomorphology is shaped entirely by recent glaciation, with countless, U-shaped valleys, fjords, moraines, erratics and other glacial features. Much of the mountainous area is exposed or sparsely covered with bedrock. Some glaciers remain, but in general the climate is mild, and the coastline, including the significant proportion that lies within the Arctic Circle, remains ice-free throughout the year (Duffey, 1982).

Forests cover about 30% of the country. They are mostly coniferous, and two-thirds of them are exploited commercially. Plant species diversity is highest in the south-east where there are some deciduous forests of oak, elm and lime, up to 550m. These are replaced by widespread pine and spruce forests at higher altitudes and also further north. Along the west coast, forests of birch, oak and alder predominate, together with blanket bogs and mires. Some 9% of the total land area is covered by bogs and other wetland habitats. Lakes and other open freshwater areas cover a further 5% of the country (Ministry of Environment, 1982a), but also important for wetland species is the long rugged coastline with its numerous sheltered bays, small islands and complex water courses. On the central mountains running the length of the country, alpine flora, with dwarf shrubs, predominate from 1,200-1,600m; at higher altitudes plant communities become dominated by cryptogans. In the extreme north and north-east, pine and birch give way to arctic/alpine vegetation: lichen-tundra accompanied by dwarf shrubs, grasses and rushes (Davis *et al.*, 1986). Only 3% of the total land area is under cultivation.

About 20,000 Lapps live in the north of the country. They depend largely on reindeer husbandry for their needs.

Svalbard consists of several large islands, the largest of which is Spitzbergen, and numerous smaller islands. It is partly covered by glaciers. The land is rugged and mountainous, but with a flat coastal plain reaching a maximum width of 10km. The subsoil is permanently frozen, with permafrost reaching to a depth of several hundred metres. The vegetation comprises mainly grasses, mosses and lichens (Grimmett and Jones, 1989). The seas to the west of Svalbard are relatively productive due to a northern branch of the Gulf Stream: plant growth is more productive on the western coasts and there are numerous large seabird colonies. This contrasts strongly with the north and east coasts which are affected by a cold drift-ice stream from the north-east (Ministry of Environment, 1981).

Jan Mayen is a small isolated island positioned centrally between Norway, Greenland, Svalbard and Iceland. It is of volcanic origin, mountainous, reaching a hcight of 2,277m, and partly covered by glaciers. Volcanic activity, which had ceased, restarted in 1970 (Paxton, 1990). The island has a rocky landscape, with thin tundra vegetation, and holds extremely important breeding seabird populations, but has no protected areas.

The arctic explorer, Nordenshrold, first suggested that national parks be established in the Nordic countries in 1880, and in 1902 the first proposal for a national park was presented by Reusch, to be followed by other proposals by the Norwegian Conservation Society (founded in 1914) and the Norwegian Tourist Society. Despite this, the establishment of the park system started later than in other Nordic countries (1962) and even later in Svalbard (planned in 1966 and implemented in 1973). In 1955 the first National Council for Nature Conservation was appointed by the government. In 1962 the Council initiated a systematic nationwide inventory of important habitats, indigenous forest areas of high conservation interest and important botanical and ornithological habitats. They produced the first nationwide plan for national parks in 1964 (this was two years after the first national park was established). The plan covered 16 areas (630,000ha or 2% of the country's surface) although originally this was to be eight national parks and eight nature parks; the latter exclusively protective, the former for public recreation. The national park plan was well-received by parliament and adopted in 1967 as the basis for the establishment of national parks in the country, and has now, in principle, been fully implemented. Work on a second, follow-up strategy has begun. The first national park was established in 1962. By the end of 1990 there were 17 national parks covering 1,230,500ha or 3.80% of the country's surface area; 911 nature reserves covering 143,400ha (0.44%), 70 landscape protected areas covering 432,300ha (1.33%),

280 nature monuments covering 100ha, and 68 other reserves (*andre omradefredninger*) covering 9,500ha (0.03%). The total area of Norway protected under the Nature Conservation Act amounted to 1.79% in 1979, 3.12% in 1984 (CoE, 1984) and 5.6% by the end of 1990. Public recreation areas now cover 43,200ha, including a stretch of islands and peninsulas along the southern coast known as the Archipelago Park (Directorate for Nature Management, *in litt.*, 1991).

The Spitzbergen conference held in 1914 in Oslo discussed nature conservation in Svalbard and a proposal was formulated to establish a large conservation area in North Spitzbergen. In the 1960s the Norwegian Polar Research Institute reactivated the interest and in 1966 a first "study of present problems related to conservation and wildlife management in Svalbard" was completed. In 1967 an inter-ministerial task force was organised to propose practical conservation measures. In 1968, a draft plan for national parks and nature reserves was prepared (Norderhaug, 1987). In 1973, three national parks, two nature reserves and fifteen bird reserves were established (Ministry of Environment, 1981). Support for nature conservation issues in Svalbard also came from the interpretation of Article 3 and Article 8 of thc Svalbard Treaty of 1920 (commercial and economic activities) in relation to Article 2 (nature conservation in Svalbard).

The Ministry of Environment is considering designating additional landscape protected areas as buffer zones around national parks. The Norwegian Society for the Conservation of Nature disagrees with the Ministry on several issues. It believes that national parks should not be restricted to state-owned land (as proposed in the 1964 plan); that there should be no recreation facilities located within national parks as this leads to the alteration of their wild character; it considers that there should be no human interference with these natural ecosystems and hence that hunting, grazing and forestry activities should be prohibited (Poore and Gryn-Ambroes, 1980). The report presented to parliament in 1981, and later adopted by parliament as the National Conservation Policy Plan, suggested the need for a new national park policy resulting in the Ministry of Environment asking the National Council to organise a study on the future of national parks. This is due to include a critical review of existing parks in relation to the biogeographic zoning and a review of areas where new national parks could be located. The most serious shortcomings have been identified as the coastal areas, in general, and the lowland regions of southern Norway.

Protective measures in accordance with the Nature Conservation Act have resulted in county conservation plans being produced by each of the new county environmental protection departments. These plans have tended to concentrate on certain types of areas, for example, wetlands, deciduous forests, mires, seabird colonies. Plans are based on comprehensive surveys and each plan is thoroughly reviewed by all involved parties. Comments are sent to the Ministry of Environment, with the government deciding whether areas should be protected. Similar plans are to be prepared for Quaternary geological phenomena, rare minerals, fossil sites, bird cliffs, lakes and marsh reserves. It is expected that 100-150 new nature reserves will be established annually. Landscape areas of historical and cultural values are also to be protected through regional planning systems. The Ministry of Environment is coordinating with the relevant Norwegian Research Council to launch research to further develop guidelines for the long-term management of protected areas (Ministry of Environment, 1982a, 1982b). The establishment of nature monuments is of low priority in the Ministry, due to the disproportionate amount of work required to protect small areas.

Threats to protected areas and other important natural ecosystems come from numerous sources. The deciduous forests which dominated much of the southern lowlands since the last glaciation have largely been removed by man and replaced by cultivated land and grassland. There has also been a great loss of wetlands due to drainage. From 1966-1976, an average of 100 sq. km was removed every year. In 1976 a total of 4,000 sq. km of bog areas was reclaimed, representing 20% of the total area of bogs in the country. In recent years an average of 70-75 sq. km has been drained annually and subsequently used for cultivation or forestry. The threat to ecosystems, which, perhaps more than any other, has brought conservation issues to the attention of the widest range of the population, has been the development of Norway's water resources for hydro-electric schemes. The building of dams and the loss of river and waterfalls into tunnels threatened almost every large river and watershed in the country: some protected areas have been designated to prevent this, while other protected areas are themselves threatened by hydro-electric schemes (Carp, 1980; Duffey, 1982). A number of watercourses have been fully or partially protected, not by written statute, but under ordinary plenary decisions of parliament, which, although not legally binding, act as an instruction to the administration to dismiss any application for a development license. Acid deposition, notably from acid rain, is also a major problem. A recent survey showed that only 49.7% of the forest is completely free from the damage caused by acid rain. Minor or moderate damage includes 46.3%, whilst 4% is seriously damaged (Anon., 1989).

In Svalbard the natural environment is particularly prone to disturbance due to its typical high arctic features: pollutants and waste are slow to break down, tracks and scars in the land surface may remain unchanged for decades, and such damage may be increased by subsequent freeze-thaw activity. The major economic activity is coal mining, practised in various sites by Norwegian or Soviet companies. Recreation and scientific expeditions have been increasing in numbers in recent years. These generally tend to visit protected areas and pose a threat for the reason outlined (Grimmett and Jones, 1989). Oil exploration too is a potential threat.

In 1973 a total of 1,259 oil claims was issued in Spitbergen, of which 668 were located in areas of high conservation value (Norderhaug, 1987).

Addresses

Nature Conservation Division (Head of Division), Ministry of Environment (Miljoverndepartementet), Myntgaten, PO Box 8013, 0030 OSLO (Tel: 2 349090/419010; FAX: 2 349560; Tlx: 21480 env n)

Department of Forestry, Ministry of Agriculture, Postboks 8007, 0510 OSLO

Directorate for Nature Management (Director), Tungasletta 2, N-7004 TRONDHEIM (Tel: 7 580500; FAX: 7 915433)

Norger Naturvernforbund (Norwegian Society for the Conservation of Nature) Postboks, Hammersborg, OSLO 1

References

Anon. (1986). Copy from a Norwegian report to ECE on strategy for environmental protection.

Anon. (1989). Norway: condition of the forest. Council of Europe. *Naturopa Newsletter* 4: 3

Backer, I.L. (1991). Nature Conservation in Norway. *Nature Conservation in Austria, Finland, Norway, Sweden, Switzerland, Bulgaria, Czechoslaovakia, Hungary, Poland, Romania, Yugoslavia and the Soviet Union.* European Parliament, Directorate General for Research, Environment, Public Health and Consumer Protection Series, 17. Pp. 30-38.

CoE (1984). *European Nature Conservation. Twenty years of activities.* European Committee for the Conservation of Nature and Natural Resources. Council of Europe, Environment and Natural Resources Division, Strasbourg.

Duffey, E. (1982). *National Parks and Resources of Western Europe.* Macdonald and Company, London.

Koester, V. (1980). *Nordic Countries' Legislation on the Environment with Special Emphasis on Conservation. A Survey.* IUCN Environmental Policy and Law Paper No. 14. IUCN, Gland, Switzerland.

Ministry of Environment (1981). *Environmental Regulations for Svalbard.* Ministry of Environment Document T-516, Oslo. 52 pp.

Ministry of Environment (1982a). *Nature Conservation in Norway, Development of a national conservation policy plan.* Ministry of Environment Document T-525, Oslo. 20 pp.

Ministry of Environment (1982b). *Environmental Approaches in Norway.* Ministry of Environment Document T-529, Oslo. 12 pp.

Ministry of Environment (1983). *Norway's Ministry of Environment.* Ministry of Environment Brochure, Oslo.

Ministry of Environment (1985). *The Nature Conservation Act.* Ministry of Environment Document T-558, Oslo. 13 pp.

Ministry of Environment (1989). *Report to the Storting No. 46 (1988-89), Environment and Development, programme for Norway's follow-up of the report of the World Commission on Environment and Development. Ministry of Environment, Oslo.* 74 pp.

Ministry of the Environment (1990). *Environmental Impact Assessment in Norway.* Ministry of Environment Document T-750E, Oslo. 8 pp.

Norderhaug, M. (1985). *National parks and protected areas in Norway, with particular reference to the Arctic.* Presented at the Arctic Heritage Symposium Association of Canadian Universities for Northern Studies, Banff, Canada, 24-28 August.

Nordic Council of Ministers (1978). *The Nordic Environmental Protection Convention, with a Commentary.* Nordic Council of Ministers, Stockholm. 14 pp.

Nordic Council of Ministers (1983). *Programme for Nordic Cooperation in Environmental Protection for 1983 to 1987.* Nordic Council of Ministers, Stockholm. 37 pp.

Paxton, J. (1990). *The Statesman's Yearbook, 1990-1991.* 127th Edition. The MacMillan Press Ltd, London and Basingstoke, UK. Pp. 949-964.

Poore, D. and Gryn-Ambroes, P. (1980). *Nature Conservation in Northern and Western Europe.* UNEP/IUCN/WWF. Pp. 280-290.

Waycott, A. (1983). *National Parks of Western Europe.* Inklon Publications, Southampton.

ANNEX
Definitions of protected area designations, as legislated, together with authorities responsible for their administration

Title: Nature Conservation Act

Date: 19 June 1970 (Act No. 63), last amended 14 June 1985 (Act No. 77)

Brief description: A wide-ranging act covering the protection of landscape and natural environment, flora and fauna, protected areas and also compensation measures

Administrative authority: Department of Nature Conservation and Open Air Recreation, Ministry of Environment

Designations:

Nasjonal park (National park) The first national parks were established under general regulations set out in a Royal Decree (October 1967), which defined them as areas of national value with no or little known human disturbance, in state ownership reserved to "preserve large unspoiled or essentially unspoiled or singular or beautiful tracks". All national parks must be based on large tract of state-owned land but neighbouring privately-owned lands "of the same kind" may be included in a national park. It is suggested that the integrity of national parks has never been infringed. Because access is difficult there is at present no over use. No zonation system has been developed inside national parks or nature reserves, but parks may be closed to public access (seasonally or permanently). No buffer-zones exist around national parks but some areas parks are adjoined by landscape protected areas or state forests.

Specific regulations are drawn up for each national park and are signed by the Head of State. These vary from site to site but have the following common elements: domestic animal husbandry and grazing is forbidden as is the presence of domestic animals and pets (reindeer herding in some areas is permitted). Forestry is prohibited. Areas are open to the public, although parts may be closed from time to time, and access is by foot only; no payment or permits are required; no tourism development is allowed nor organised visits; sport fishing is restricted to special permit; hunting of certain species is allowed under permit, as is firewood and berry collection. All commercial and industrial activities are excluded.

Landskapvernomrade (Landscape protected area) State or private lands reserved to preserve unique or beautiful natural or cultural lands, similar to national parks except that traditional farming, grazing and restricted forestry activities are allowed under control. No activities are permitted which might substantially change the nature and character of the landscape. Further regulations concerning specific sites are drawn up and signed by the Head of State. Typically, regulations for different sites contain the following common elements: construction of buildings, roads and overhead lines, felling of large areas of trees, the clearance of land for agriculture, drainage, dumping, removal of earth and soil, use of chemical fertilisers and pesticides and the release of sewage are prohibited. The changing of forest types for silvicultural purposes is not permitted. Motorised traffic, including low-flying aircraft, is restricted. Administrative authorities may give permission for minor exceptions to these rules, for example for the extension and repair of houses used by reindeer herders on the construction of footpaths or new pistes may be permitted. Management authorities are specified in the site regulations.

They may, in some cases, act as buffer zones close to reserves or national parks.

Naturreservat (Nature reserve) State or private areas "which have unspoilt or virtually unspoilt nature or constitute special types of nature and which have special importance for science or education or which stand out by virtue of their unusual character". No human interference is allowed (with a few exceptions). Creation is based on regional conservation plans, worked out for the most important types of ecosystems or categories of objects: sites may be declared because of their mires, wetlands, deciduous forests, seabird sites or Quaternary geology. The planning is mirrored in the number of reserves established in each category. Such regional planning does not ensure representativeness at the national level. In approximately one third of reserves, public access may be restricted.

Naturminner (Nature monument) "Geological, botanical and zoological features of scientific or historic interest or which are unusual", together with "areas around the feature". Areas may also be protected which are "of special importance as the resort of a number of (protected animal) species". Specific measures concerning the implementation of the protection measures may be drawn up.

Sources: Anon., 1986; Ministry of Environment, 1985; Poore and Gryn-Ambroes, 1980

Title: Provisions for south Spitsbergen National Park, Forlandet National Park, North-west Spitsbergen National Park, North-east Svalbard Nature Reserve, South-east Svalbard Nature Reserve and 15 bird sanctuaries along the west coast of Spitsbergen

Date: 1 June and 11 October 1973

Brief description: Provides descriptions of the boundaries of these sites, details of the regulations covering these different sites, and the authorities involved in their administration

Administrative authority: Ministry of Environment

Designations:

Bird sanctuary Established on Svalbard pursuant to Part 4 of the Svalbard Act of 17 July 1925 (No. 11) of Article 2 of the Treaty concerning Spitsbergen of 9 February 1920, by Royal Decrees 1 June and 11 October 1973.

Regulations prohibit technical interference, construction, mining, oil drilling, quarrying and other activities which interfere with the terrain or disturb the natural environment. The seabed is protected from catching or gathering activities by divers or by the use of bottom trawl or scraper. The dumping of waste is prohibited. All mammals and birds are protected, no new species may be introduced, plants and fossils may not be removed. All traffic, including offshore traffic and aircraft landing is prohibited from 15 May to 15 August. The Government may in consultation with the Ministry grant dispensations.

Source: Ministry of Environment, 1981

Title: Establishment of two plant protected reserves in Svalbard

Date: 26 February 1932

Brief description: Gives regulations and provides detailed descriptions of the boundaries of the two sites

Administrative authority: Ministry of Environment

Designations:

Plant protected reserve All vegetation is protected against collection and destruction.

Regulations shall not prevent the carrying out of mining and other pursuits, but the destruction of plants should, in that case be avoided as far as possible without any particular difficulty or expense. If such destruction is going to be caused by the work the proper State Department should be notified in advance.

Source: Ministry of Environment, 1981

SUMMARY OF PROTECTED AREAS

Map† ref.	*National/international designations* Name of area	IUCN management category	Area (ha)	Year notified
	National Parks			
1	Anderdalen	II	6,900	1970
2	Borgefjell	II	110,650	1963
3	Dovrefjell	II	25,580	1974
4	Femundsmarka	II	39,030	1971
5	Gressamoen	II	18,150	1970
6	Gutulia	II	1,900	1968
7	Hardangervidda	II	342,200	1981
8	Jotunheimen	II	114,540	1980
9	Ovre Anarjakka	II	139,870	1975
10	Ovre Dividal	II	74,280	1971
11	Ovre Pasvik	II	6,660	1970
12	Rago	II	16,740	1971
13	Reisa	II	80,300	1986
14	Rondane	II	58,010	1962
15	Stabbursdalen	II	9,820	1970
	Nature Reserves			
16	Atnoset	I	1,080	1989
17	Blodskyttodden/Barvikmyran	I	2,650	1983
18	Borgann og Frelsoy	I	1,600	1973
19	Faerdesmyra	I	1,200	1972
20	Flaman	I	2,920	1989
21	Fokstumyra	IV	7,500	1923
22	Froan	I	12,000	1979
23	Grandefjaera	I	2,100	1983
24	Grimsmoen	I	1,440	1989
25	Grovelsjoen	I	1,360	1989
26	Grytdalen	IV	1,600	1978
27	Hanestadnea	I	1,760	1989
28	Havmyran	I	4,000	1982
29	Hogkjolen/Bakkjolen	I	1,131	1990
30	Hukkelvatna	I	1,050	1983
31	Hynna	I	1,547	1990
32	Javreoaivit	I	3,000	1981
33	Karlsoeyaer	IV	1,000	1977
34	Kraakvaagsvaet	IV	1,190	1983
35	Kvisleflaa	I	3,301	1981
36	Litle Soelensjoen	I	1,630	1981
37	Makkaurhalvoeya	I	11,350	1983
38	Myldingi	I	1,240	1989
39	Nekmyrene	I	1,880	1981
40	Nord-Fugloy	I	2,130	1975
41	Nordre Oeyeren	IV	6,260	1975
42	Oera	I	1,560	1979
43	Osdalen	I	4,800	1969
44	Ostmarka	I	1,250	1990
45	Ovdaldasvarri	I	1,430	1983
46	Ovre Forra	I	10,800	1990
47	Rangeldalen	I	2,600	1988
48	Reinoey	I	1,300	1981
49	Semska-Stoedi	I	1,300	1976
50	Skogvoll	I	2,800	1983
51	Smoldalen	I	1,325	1974
52	Stabbursneset	I	1,620	1983

Map[†] ref.	*National/international designations* Name of area	IUCN management category	Area (ha)	Year notified
53	Storlia	I	2,400	1989
54	Storloen	I	1,147	1990
55	Vignesholmane	IV	1,515	1982
56	Vikna	I	2,100	1973
	Landscape Protected Areas			
57	Brannsletta	V	1,880	1983
58	Dovrefjell	V	5,700	1974
59	Favnvassdalen	V	1,390	1983
60	Femundsmarka	V	7,040	1971
61	Froan	V	4,000	1979
62	Gardsjoen	V	2,000	1983
63	Grytdalen	V	1,600	1978
64	Hjerkinn	V	2,440	1974
65	Hovden	V	5,900	1986
66	Indre Vassfaret	V	4,200	1985
67	Innerdalen	V	7,300	1977
68	Jaerstrendene	V	1,608	1977
69	Lusaheia	V	12,200	1991
70	Mosvatn/Austfjellet	V	29,900	1981
71	Osterdalen	V	2,700	1983
72	Raisduottarhaldi	V	8,000	1986
73	Skaupsjoen/Hardangerjokulen	V	55,100	1981
74	Skipsfjorddalen	V	4,200	1978
75	Stolsheimen	V	36,700	1990
76	Strandaa/Os	V	1,670	1983
77	Trollheimen	V	73,050	1987
78	Utladalen	V	31,400	1980
79	Vassfaret and Vidalen	V	20,000	1985
80	Vidmyr-Hovden	V	5,900	1986
	SVALBARD AND JAN MEYEN			
	National Parks			
1	Northwest Spitzbergen	II	356,000	1973
2	Prins Karl's Forland	II	64,000	1973
3	South Spitzbergen	II	530,000	1973
	Nature Reserves			
4	North-east Svalbard	I	1,903,000	1973
5	South-east Svalbard	I	638,000	1973

[†]Locations of most protected areas are shown on the accompanying map.

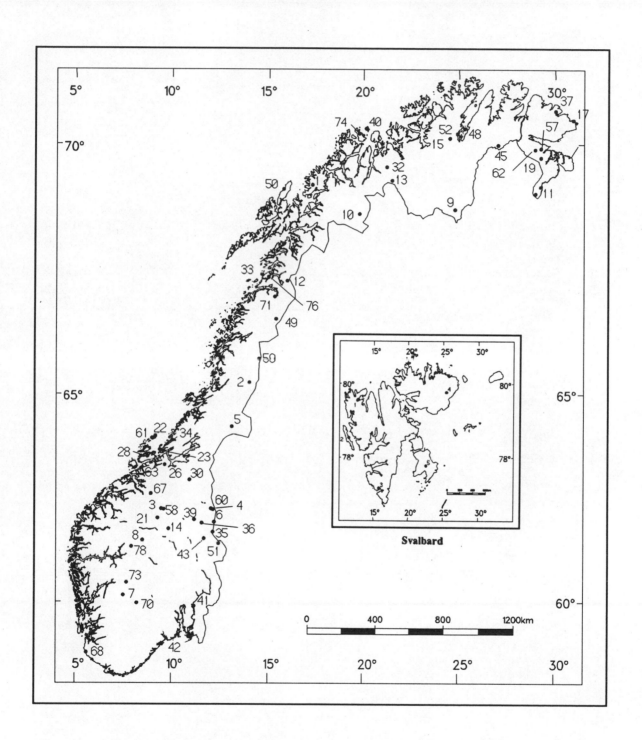

Protected Areas of Norway

REPUBLIC OF POLAND

Area 312,683 sq. km

Population 38,200,000 (1990)
Natural increase: 0.6% per annum

Economic Indicators
GDP: No information
GNP: US$ 1,421 per capita (1991)

Policy and Legislation The National Constitution of 1952 includes sections dealing with nature conservation (Article 8) and the protection and rational development of the natural environment (Article 12, Section 2).

Legal conservation of nature and landscape has a long tradition. Specific nature protection and hunting legislation dates back to the reign of the Piast and Jagiellon dynasties of the 14th century AD. The so-called "Wislice State", edited by King Kazimierz the Great in 1347, defined prohibitions of destructive activity in woodlands, such as pasturing of domestic animals in forests, cutting trees harbouring bees and making fire. The major document dealing with forest nature protection was the Warecki Statute (1420-1423), in which King Wladyslaw Jagiello forbade the felling of yews, prohibited making fire in forests and poaching large animals.

The protection of specific natural objects is covered by a number of legislative acts starting with the Decree of 1918, followed by government ordinances of 1919 (Monitor Polski Nr. 208, poz. 2) and 1925, and culminating in the laws of 1934 (Dz.U.R.P. Nr. 31, poz. 274 Ustawa o ochronie przyrody) and 1949 (Nr. 25, poz. 180. Ustawa o ochronie przyrody), the last amended in 1972 (Amendment No. 49 poz. 317), in 1975 (Amendment No. 17, poz. 94), in 1987 (Amendment No. 33, poz. 180) and in 1990 (Amendment No. 34, poz. 198). The Law on Nature Conservation of 7 April 1949 governs the organisation of nature conservation in general and introduced four protected area categories: national park, nature reserve, natural monument and area protection for fauna and flora species (Anon., *in litt.*, 1991). This Law governs the creation, administration and management of these three types of area. Two further types of protected area, landscape park and area of protected landscape, began to be created in the 1970s. The Law of 1980 concerning Protection and Management of the Environment (Ustawa o ochronie i ksztaltowaniu srodowiska, Dz.U. Nr. 3, poz. 6 amended in 1983 No. 44, poz. 180; 1989 No. 26, poz. 139 and No. 35, poz. 192; 1990 No. 34, poz. 180; and No. 39, poz. 223) (Anon., *in litt.*, 1991) regulates all problems connected with landscape protection. This is a general act, passed in January 1980, to regulate natural resource use in the national planning context and to control pollution levels and apply protection of the landscape in general terms.

In 1979 the State Council for Nature Conservation (Panstwowa Rada Ochrony Przyrody) (PROP) and the Department of Nature Protection in the former Ministry of Forestry and Woodworking Industry prepared an outline draft of a proposed Nature Protection Law. This project, discussed over a number of years, dealt with conservation of nature separately from the Law on Protection and Management of the Environment. One of the aims of the project was to adjust the legislation to the criteria of the International Union for Conservation of Nature (IUCN) and especially to the World Conservation Strategy. However, the project was discontinued and the law as drafted was not passed. Attempts were also made to link the Law of 1949 on Nature Protection with the Law of 1980 on Environmental Conservation into one unified text and simultaneously to redraft the individual laws. The Law on Protection of Arable Land and Forests defines protected forests, where conservation policies are given priority (limiting timber production and construction). All forests in protected areas are classified as protected forests, the uses of which are governed by the Main Board of State Forests (Atkinson *et al.*, 1991).

The new administration which was established in 1990 is preparing a framework law (see Dziennik Ustaw No. 34) covering all aspects of environmental protection, which was presented to and accepted by parliament at the end of 1991. Sector laws will then be developed. At the same time, the parliamentary Committee on the Environment recommenced the preparation of a new Law on Nature Conservation which was enacted by parliament on 19 September 1991.

The most significant shortcoming of the legislation has included a lack of cohesion, conflict of aims with priority being given to achievement of economic goals, the lack of protection given to the marine environment, wide dispersion of provisions among a large number of laws and the mixture of civil and criminal codes (IUCN, 1990). New draft laws on nature conservation may be negatively affected by the passage of other new laws such as that on land development (Atkinson *et al.*, 1991).

International Activities The Convention concerning the World Natural and Cultural Heritage (World Heritage Convention) was ratified in June 1976 when one natural site was designated; the Convention on Wetlands of International Importance Especially as Waterfowl Habitat (Ramsar Convention) was acceded to on 22 November 1977 with one site listed. On 3 January 1984 four more sites were added. There are four biosphere reserves, designated in 1976 under the Unesco Man and the Biosphere Programme. Other conventions signed include the Baltic Convention related to the protection of resources in this sea, and the Bern Convention related to European Natural Heritage.

Administration and Management   The first administrative body dealing with nature conservation, the Temporary State Commission for Nature Protection, was created in Krakow in 1919, by Order of the Minister of Religious Persuasions and Public Enlightenment, and was transformed in 1925 into the State Commission for Nature Protection. The decrees of 1936 (Dz.U.R.P. nr. 94, poz. 660) and 1937 (Dz.U.R.P. nr. 27, poz. 195) created a Permanent Department within the State Council for Nature Conservation (PROP) and five regional nature protection committees. The major activity prior to 1945 was the establishment of national parks and nature reserves. The Law on Nature Conservation, 1949 was followed by a Council of Ministers Order, 1950 (Dz.U. nr. 13, poz. 127) creating the State Council for Nature Conservation and in 1969 (Dz.U. nr.12, poz. 88) by the formation of Conservators of Nature offices in each of the 17 administrative regions (voivodships) of the country. Under Article 9 of the 1949 Law, nature conservation became the responsibility of a Chief Conservator of Nature within the Ministry of Forestry and Timber Industry, but in the 1970s a separate Ministry, the Ministry of Administration, Regional Economy and Environmental Protection (Ministerstwo Administracji, Grospodarki Terenowej i Ochrony Srodowiska) took over the overall control of environmental protection and spatial planning functions. On 12 November 1985 a new law (Dz.U. nr. 50, poz. 262) created the Ministry for Conservation of the Environment and Natural Resources (Ministerstwo Ochrony Srodowiska i Zasobow Naturalnych) which deals with all aspects of environmental protection (air, water, solid wastes, soils), water management, geology and nature conservation and all matters governed by the Law on Nature Conservation of 7 April 1949, except the administration of national parks. The Chief Conservator for Nature was also a Vice-Minister, whilst there was a separate Director who is in charge of the Ministry's Department of Nature Conservation and Soil Management (Departament Ochrony Przyrody i Powierzchni Ziemi). Only the Ministry for Conservation of the Environment, however, had executive control over national parks deciding overall principles of protection and management. Administratively, the complete national park system was managed by the Ministry of Agriculture, Forestry and Food Economy (Ministerstwo Rolnictwa, Lesnictwa i Godpodarki Zywnosciowej) and specifically by its Department of Forestry and National Parks (Departament Lesnictwa i Parkow Narodowych). This section employed specialists in nature conservation and maintained the central register for national parks, nature reserves and landscape parks. However, spatial planning was within the responsibility of the Ministry of Construction and Municipal Economy (Ministerstwo Budownictwa i Gospodarki Komunalnej).

In 1990, overall responsibility was taken over by the newly created Ministry of Environmental Protection, Natural Resources and Forestry (Ministerstwo Ochrony Srodowiska, Zasobow Naturalnych i Lesnictwa) within which a Department for Nature Conservation was created (Anon., *in litt.*, 1991). National parks are supervised by the National Park Service which coordinates and monitors the park activities and allocates budgets from the state.

According to the Laws of 7 April 1949, 31 January 1980 and 23 October 1987, the State Council for Nature Conservation and the State Council for Environmental Conservation are the official advisory bodies, the former on nature conservation matters, and the latter on environmental conservation aspects. Since 1990, the former has been affiliated to the Ministry, the latter to the Council of Ministers (Atkinson *et al.*, 1991). Since 1989, a Parliamentary Commission on Environmental Protection specifically monitors nature conservation legislation. The Minister for the Environment appoints members of both bodies and is their Chairman. The State Council for Nature Conservation gives advice and expert opinions on all projects concerning the creation of national parks, landscape parks and nature reserves and also presents its own initiatives. The State Council consists of a Secretariat, and seven permanent commissions, including the Commission on National Parks and Nature Reserves, the Commission on the Protection of Inanimate Nature and the Commission on the Protection and Management of the Landscape. The Commission on National Parks and Nature Reserves cooperates closely with the councils of specific national parks, with the Voivodship Conservators of Nature and with the Academy of Science's Nature Protection Research Centre (Zaklad Ochrony Przyrody i Zasobow Naturalnych, PAN), with the Nature Conservation Research Centre of the Polish Academy of Sciences (Zaklad Ochrony Przyrody i Zasabow Naturalnych PAN) and with the Forestry Research Institute (Instytut Badawczy Lesnictwa – Zaklad Ochrony Przyrody). The Commission is responsible for the preparation of documentation (or its review) prior to the creation of new national parks and nature reserves and for programmes of protected areas systems as well as research and management.

In 1990, the state budget for the 17 national parks was 27.4 million zloty, with 24.2 million zloty for infrastructure investment. Additional income (tourism, rents, grants, fees) equalled zloty 13.6 million. A report in 1991 provided a financial assessment of the future needs of the national park network. It estimated equipment costs at zloty 17.7 billion (15,000 zloty = 1 US$), building costs at zloty 261 billion, plan preparation zloty 57 billion, land building purchases zloty 60 billion., afforestation zloty 5 billion, rare animal breeding centre zloty 10 billion, environmental protection zloty 450 billion, with the creation of new parks and enlargements of existing ones costing zloty 51 billion. Therefore an ideal budget would amount to zloty 911.7 billion (Polish National Park Service, 1991). The state owns 85% of the area of the national parks, managed by the park authorities, the rest being in private hands, with the exception of water bodies which are owned and managed by the state fishing Farms. Plans exist to reduce private ownership to 5,000ha (3%) over the next 10-20 years (Polish National Park Service, 1991).

Each national park has its own administration, with a director in charge, appointed by the Ministry of Environmental Protection (Polish National Park Services, 1991) on advice of the National Park Service and the State Council of Nature Protection, and between 15-30 supporting staff, with 1-2 individuals employed as scientific workers. Moreover, a scientific council, numbering up to 15 specialists representing varied expertise, is appointed as an advisory body for each park. Ten national parks have museums and two have public education centres (Polish National Park Service, 1991).

Where any proposed developments are likely to damage designated areas, the state authorities are obliged to seek the advice of the State Council for Nature Conservation and to inform the Ministry for Conservation of the Environment and Natural Resources of such actions. At the end of 1990, the total national park staff numbered 1,373 (Polish National Park Service, 1991).

The 1949 Law envisaged wide social and community involvement in nature protection and resulted in the creation of the voluntary Citizen Nature Conservation Guards (Straz Ochrony Przyrody), which is composed of the Nature Conservation League (Liga Ochrony Przyrody) (founded in 1928 and now with 1,600,000 members), the Polish Tourist Society, the Polish Hunters Society, the Polish Anglers Society and the Alpine Club. Among the hundreds of emerging non-governmental organisations the Polish Ecological Club (Polski Klub Ekologiczny created in 1981 and formed of regional sections provides independent advise on protected areas' creation and management. More recent groups include the Polish Ornithological Society (working on wetland conservation), the Society for the Preservation of the Tatra Mountain, the Podlasie Society of Bird Preservation, and Social Committee, acting in specific areas (e.g. Mazurian Lakes, Hel Peninsula) (Atkinson *et al.*, 1991). The first private reserve (8.5ha) recognised by the government was created by the Northern Podlasie Bird Preservation Society (Atkinson *et al.*, 1991).

Continuing difficulties in application of the new pre-ecology policies are due to the inadequate legislation, the need to deal with the catastrophic ecological situation in the country, and the lack of coordination between central, provincial and local government (Atkinson *et al.*, 1991).

Systems Reviews The landscape is dominated by the northern European plain which takes up the majority of the country, (with only 9% of the land over 300m) bordered to the north by the Baltic Sea and to the south by the Carpathian Mountains and surrounded by Germany and Czechoslovakia, as well as the Republics of Lithuania, Byelorussia and Moldavia. There are lake districts in the north-west and the north-east (over 1,000 lakes covering 2% of the country) with some of Europe's

most extensive lowland peatbogs (1.5 million ha) present in the east of the country. Principally an agricultural landscape but with 30% forest cover (with natural elements containing *Quercus* sp., *Tilia* sp., and *Carpinus betulus*; *Picea* and *Pinus* in the mountains) and perhaps 25% with natural and semi-natural vegetation.

The mechanism for monitoring the enactment of the National Spatial Management Plan is the *Protocol of the Sub-Assembly for Ecological Affairs of the Round Table*. This sets as a priority the classification of the country into four management zones; (i) ecologically devastated area (ii) area in severe ecological danger, (iii) area in ecological equilibrium, and (iv) protected area (IUCN, 1991). The National Spatial Management Plan was superseded by the National Programme for Environmental Planning to the year 2010, adopted in November 1990, and the National Conservation Strategy was published in spring 1991 (IUCN, 1991). Since 1990, an inventory of natural sites has been progressing together with evaluation of specific regions such as the north-east of the country, often considered the least degraded of all regions (Atkinson *et al.*, 1991).

The first programme for the creation of a network of reserves was elaborated at the beginning of the 20th century, and by 1918 there were 39 small nature reserves totalling 1,469ha. This number increased to 180 covering 28,478ha by 1937. Simultaneous with the creation of nature reserves, proposals were made to establish national parks. The main attention was paid to the mountain regions such as Tatras, Pieniny, Babia Gora, Gory Swietokrzyskie, and to Bialowieza Primeval Forest in the lowlands. The first proposal to create Tatra National Park was submitted in 1885, only 13 years after Yellowstone National Park in the USA, but complicated property structure meant that the first Polish national park was created not in Tatras but in Bialowieza Forest. At first it was a large reserve created in 1921 and transformed into Bialowieza National Park 11 years later (1932) on the 50th anniversary of Yellowstone. By 1936 five national parks had been created; Bialowieza, Pieniny, Babia Gora, Wielkopolski and Czarnohora (now in the Ukraine), totalling over 10,000ha, but none was given legal recognition. In 1988 the total area protected in national parks and nature reserves amounted to 252,791ha, or 0.8% of the surface area of the country, while the joint area of all types of protected territory, including areas of protected landscape, reached the total of about 5,724,694ha, or 18.3% of the country. This included the then 15 national parks (0.4% surface area) and 900 nature reserves (0.4%). The landscape parks occupied 2.5% of the country's land area and the protected landscape areas, 10% (IUCN, 1990). According to the development plan for nature conservation, the total area of national parks amounted to 230,000ha by 1990 (141,414ha in 1989) by the addition of five new parks and the extension of a few existing parks, while nature reserves increased by c. 600 sites, giving a total area of 180,000ha (111,377ha in 1989). The proposed total area protected is 8,734,500ha or 28% of the surface area of the country. In the 1980s only two national parks were created (Gorce and Wigry), while one park was extended by the addition of a buffer zone. Only four had legally satisfied their spatial management plans, three parks were awaiting extension and six others were in the process of ratification. As of January 1989 there were 15 national parks (141,414ha), 970 nature reserves (111,377ha), 54 landscape parks (1,992,753ha) and 159 protected landscape areas (3,479,150ha). In 1990, there were 17 national parks (165,933ha), 1,001 nature reserves (116,952ha), 68 landscape parks (1,215,445ha) and 214 areas of protected landscapes (4,574,759ha) (IUCN, 1991). By 1991, the national park area had increased to 177,773ha (Polish National Park Service, 1991). The area of national parks is due to increase to cover 1.2% of the country's surface (Polish National Park Service, 1991). By June 1991, there were 68 landscape parks (with a proposal contained in the draft law on protection of natural environment, to classify these as either national or regional), 1,001 nature reserves and areas of protected landscape in 31 voivodships. The draft laws envisages the creation of a new category of protected areas – "area of ecological use" and "natural landscape unit". It also will propose the creation of a National Fund for Environment and Nature Conservation (Atkinson *et al.*, 1991).

The major threats to national parks are a combination of uncontrolled tourism, atmospheric pollution, water pollution and unsuitable forms of economic development. The liberalisation of some property rules has increased the threats to natural resources, especially on the exploitation of peat bogs (IUCN, 1991). Forests cover 28% of the country's surface, but these are very unequally distributed with 25 of the 49 voivodships having less than 25% of their surface under forest and due to logging pressures, they are generally immature with 44% less than 40 years and 18% less than 20 years old (IUCN, 1991). However, some 74% of national park area is covered by forest (Polish National Park Service, 1991). In a 1982 report "State of forests and their management in Poland" the Polish Forest Society reported that in the post-war period (1954-1980) more than 610 million cu. m of wood, about 115 million over the projected limit, were cut down. Each year's wood production averaged 123% and some 111,000 cu. m came from national parks and reserves. A survey in 1983 suggested that two-thirds of the surface area of Poland's forests is in a "state of disaster" and industrial pollution has directly damaged 654,000ha of woodland. In 1990 a new report on the "State of forests and forestry in Poland" was elaborated by the Ministry and the Forestry Research Institute. It was based on inventories carried out in 1988 and showed a decrease in felling volume. At the end of 1990, the area of woodland endangered covered 1,187,000ha while wood production in state-owned forests amounted to 17,290,000 cu.m (106,000 cu.m from national parks). The National Spatial Management Plan until the year 1996 identified

27 regions (11% of the surface area of the country) as ecologically damaged, nine national parks and six landscape parks as severely threatened and 23 health resort areas as threatened. In 1982 the Academy of Sciences published a "State of the Environment" report (nine volumes), and in 1985 four areas were declared "ecological disaster" areas and 23 as of "high ecological risk". The number of visitors, making use of 1,500km of trails, totalled 9 million annually in the mid-1980s, rising to 10.5 million in 1991 (Polish National Park Service, 1991). There are proposals for national parks to be zoned to provide areas for recreation, communications and other uses.

Addresses

Ministerstwo Ochrony Srodowiska, Zasobow Naturalnych i Lesnictwa (Ministry of Environmental Protection, Natural Resources and Forestry), Ul. Wawelska 52/54, 00-922 WARSAW (Tel: 254141/FAX: 253355/Tlx: 817157)

Panstwowa Rada Ochrony Przyrody, Wawelska 52/54, 00-922 WARSAW (Tel: 251114; Tlx: 817157)

Zaklad Ochrony Przyrody i Zasobow Naturalnych, Ul Lubicz 46, 31-512 KRAKOW (Tel: 215144; Tlx: 322414 PAN PL)

References

Atkinson, R. and Kamieniecki, K. (1991). Nature conservation in Poland. In: *Nature conservation in Austria, Finland, Norway, Sweden, Switzerland, Bulgaria, Czechoslovakia, Hungary, Poland, Romania, Yugoslavia and the Soviet Union.* European Parliament. Directorate-General for Research Environment, Public Health and Consumer Protection. Series 17 EN-9-1991.

Cerovsky, J. (1986). *Nature conservation in the Socialist countries of East-Europe.* East-Europe Committee, IUCN Commission on Education, Administration of the Krkonose (Giant Mountains) National Park. Vrchlabi.

Cerovsky, J. (1988). *Nature conservation in the Socialist Countries of East-Europe.* East-Europe Committee, IUCN Commission on Education, Ministry of Culture of the Czech Socialist Republic, Prague.

Denisiuk, Z. (1989). *Protected areas in Poland.* 12 pp.

IUCN (1971). *United Nations List of National Parks and Equivalent Reserves.* (2nd Edition). Hayez, Brussels.

IUCN (1990). *Environmental Status Reports: 1988/1989. Volume One: Czechoslovakia, Hungary, Poland.* IUCN-East European Programme.

IUCN (1991). *The Environment in Eastern Europe: 1990.* Environmental Research Series 3. IUCN-East European Programme.

Karpowicz, Z.J. (1987). *The Polish Park System.* Unpublished PhD thesis. University of Birmingham.

Polish National Parks Service (1991). *National Parks in Poland.* Unpublished report. 25 pp.

ANNEX
Definitions of protected area designations, as legislated, together with authorities responsible for their administration

Title: (Ustawa o ochronie przyrody) Law on Nature Protection (Dz. U.R.P. Nr. 31 poz. 274) 1934, Revised by Law on Nature Conservation (Ustawa o ochronie przyrody) (Nr. 25, poz 180), 1949 and amended by Amendment No. 49 poz. 317 in 1972 and by Amendment No. 17 poz 94 in 1975

Date: 1934, 1949 (1972, 1975) (19 September 1991)

Brief description: Provides protection for specific natural objects, and organisation of nature conservation in general. It covers creation administration and management of national parks, nature reserves and natural monuments. The new Law on Nature Conservation governs general organisation and execution of nature and landscape conservation. Chapter 3 deals with particular forms of nature protection and in Article 13 describes the national system of protected areas (Krajowy System Obszarow Chronionych). In total nine designated area types exist.

Administrative authority: Ministry of Environmental Protection, Natural Resources and Forestry (Ministerstwo Ochrony Srodowiska, Zasobow Naturalnych i Lesnictwa)

Designations:

National park (Park narodowy) The law on Nature Protection of 1934 (Article 9) defines these as "especially beautiful landscape, rich in natural values ... for areas not less than 300 hectares". Current legislation defines:

Areas over 500ha protected for their unique natural values, for their floral and faunal components and their overall landscape features. They were until 1989 created by decree of the Council of Ministers based on the recommendations of the Ministry for Conservation of the Environment and Natural Resources (Ministerstwo Ochrony Srodowiska; Zasobow Naturalnych) and expert advice from PROP.

In practice, areas proposed for conservation as national parks should be over 1,000ha. They are zoned into strict protection areas (24% of total national park area) and partial protection areas, the former excluding all human activity, the latter allowing active conservation management of selected elements. Additionally, several national parks have buffer zones designated around them. Each national park is obliged to have detailed activity plans, such as a reserve management plan, a forest management plan, a scientific management plan, and a spatial Management Plan (the latter is compulsory according to the 1949 law). They are now created by decree of the Council of Ministers based on the recommendations of the Ministry of Environmental Protection, Natural Resources and Forestry (Ministerstwo Ochrony Srodowiska, Zasobow Naturalnych i Lesnictwa) and expert advice from PROP. Where any proposed developments are likely to damage designated areas, the state authorities are obliged to seek the advice of the State Council for Nature Conservation and to inform the Ministry of such action (Anon., *in litt.*, 1991).

Nature reserve (Rezerwat przyrody) Are areas of various sizes (mostly less than 100ha) divided for management purposes into strict (fully protected) reserves and partial (partially protected) reserves. The former are used exclusively for research, the latter are subjected to controlled management activities. Most areas belong to the second group, many are mixed, with strict and partial protection of respective parts).

Created under the 1949 law, by decree of the Ministry for Conservation of the Environment and Natural Resources. Proposals for the creation of reserves are submitted to the Ministry by the Voivodship Conservator of Nature (Wojewodski Konserwator Przyrody) who is responsible for the management of this type of protected area.

Classified into nine basic types, according to the main object of protection, namely: forest reserve, floristic reserve, steppe vegetation reserve, halophytic reserve, peatbog reserve, water reserve, faunal reserve, inanimate nature and landscape reserve. They are administered by the forestry authorities in the sub-forest district in which they occur while ten-year management plans are prepared by the Voivodship Conservator for Nature.

Natural monument (Pomnik przyrody) Areas which may also be included in protected areas. They are mostly single objects, such as large trees, old alleys, cliffs, erratic blocks and rock outcrops. They are declared under the 1949 law by the voivodship authorities and protected by the voivodship Conservator of Nature on all natural monuments against any activity which would change their status. Special documentation on all natural monuments is provided by each region.

Documentative locality (Stanowiska dokumentacyjne) Areas important from scientific and educational points of view, such as geological formations, collections of fossils or minerals and sections of quarries or mines.

Established by the voivodship authorities by special act.

Ecological unit (Uzytki ekologiczne) Sections of the ecosystem containing unique genetic resources and types of habitats such as: natural water reservoirs, field and forest, fragments of undergrowth and groups of trees, swamps, peatbogs, dunes, waste areas, old river beds, geological outcrops, scarp faces and others.

They are included in local spatial management plans and listed in the official land registry.

They are established by voivod decree.

Natural and landscape complex (Zespoly przyrodniczo krajobrazowe) Particularly valuable areas of natural and cultural landscape protected for their aesthetic value.

Set up by order of voivods.

Sources: Anon., *in litt.*, 1991; Denisiuk, 1989, *in litt.*, 1991

Title: (Ustawa o ochronie i ksztaltowania srodowiska) Law on the Protection and Management of the Environment (Dz. U. Nr. 3, prz 6. zn: Dz. U. z. 1983 r. No. 44, prz 20), Law on Nature Conservation

Date: 1980, amended 1983, Law on Nature Conservation (19 September 1991)

Brief description: Regulates the creation of landscape parks and areas of protected landscapes and all problems connected with landscape protection. It also controls natural resource use in national planning and control of pollution levels.

Administrative authority: Regional authority (Voivodship People's Council) (1980 law). Since 1990 passage of law on local bodies of state administration, such areas are established by decision of the voivodship governor.

Designations:

Landscape park (Park krajobrazowy) Combines nature conservation with the needs of recreation and tourism. They represent "areas of exceptional natural values, ... with a predominance of natural landscape ... regarded as non-intervention zones for the development of industry and urban agglomerations and for large recreation centres".

Created by regional authority (Voivodship People's Council) decrees, under the 1980 law, but only a few have their own administration. Since 1990, with the passing of the law on local bodies of state administration, such areas are established by decision of the voivoidship governor.

A spatial management plan is required which defines tourist carrying capacities, forestry and agricultural exploitation, industrial development and urban construction. A number of nature reserves and natural monuments can usually be found within landscape parks. Often a "protective belt" is planned around them, mostly surrounded by a further area of protected landscape (Obszar chronionego krajobrazu). A coordinating committee, appointed by the regional chief executive (voivoda), enforces the orders, restrictions and prohibitions and works within the limits of the spatial management plan for the region.

Area of protected landscape (Obszar chronionego krajobrazu) Also established under the 1980 Law by decision of regional authorities. They are more extensive territories than landscape parks and contain landscape features characteristic of a given region, often with cultural features as well, and are envisaged as major areas for recreation and tourism development. Economic activities (agriculture, forestry, industry) are not subject to serious limitations, but have to conform to certain standards. The areas are delimited in spatial management plans and included in regional voivodship plans. They are created and administered by the voivodship authorities, represented by the Conservator of Nature.

Sources: Anon., *in litt.*, 1991; Denisiuk, 1989, *in litt.*, 1991

SUMMARY OF PROTECTED AREAS

Map† ref.	National/international designations Name of area	IUCN management category	Area (ha)	Year notified
	National Parks			
1	Babia Gora	II	1,734	1933
2	Bialowieza	II	5,317	1932
3	Bieszczady	II	15,337	1973
4	Drawski	II	8,691	1990
5	Gorce	II	6,750	1981
6	Kampinos	II	35,486	1959
7	Karkonoski	II	5,563	1959
8	Ojcow	I	1,592	1956
9	Pieniny	II	2,329	1932
10	Polskie	II	4,903	1990
11	Roztocze	II	6,857	1974
12	Slowinski	II	18,247	1967
13	Swietokrzyski	II	5,906	1950
14	Tatra	II	21,164	1955
15	Wielkopolski	II	5,198	1933
16	Wigierski	V	14,840	1989
17	Wolinski	II	4,844	1960
	Nature Reserves			
18	Czerwone Bagno (Faunal-Peatbog)	IV	11,630	1957
19	Jata (Forest)	IV	1,117	1952
20	Jezioro Dobskie (Landscape)	IV	1,833	1976
21	Jezioro Druzno (Bird)	IV	3,022	1967
22	Jezioro Kosno (Landscape)	IV	1,232	1982
23	Jezioro Nidzkie (Landscape)	IV	2,935	1973
24	Jezioro Siedmiu Wysp (Bird)	IV	1,007	1956
25	Kurianskie Bagno (Floral)	IV	1,714	1985
26	Las Warminski (Forest)	IV	1,798	1982
27	Lasy Janowskie (Forest)	IV	2,677	1984
28	Nadgoplanski Park Tysiaclecia (Landscape)	IV	12,684	1967
29	Paslece (Faunal)	IV	4,116	1970
30	Puszcza Bialowieska (Landscape)	IV	1,357	1969
31	Rzeka Drweca (Water)	IV	1,287	1961
32	Slonsk (Faunal-Peatbog)	IV	4,166	1977
33	Stawy Milickie (Bird)	IV	5,324	1963
34	Stawy Przemkowskie (Bird)	IV	1,046	1984
35	Wielki Bytyn	IV	1,826	1989
36	Wielki (Faunal)	IV	4,116	1970
	Area of Protected Landscapes			
37	Baltowskim	VIII	5,100	1973
38	Bolimowsko-Radziejowski	VIII	66,500	1986
39	Borow Niemodlinskich	VIII	47,350	1988
40	Bory Dolnoslaskie	VIII	5,100	1985
41	Chelmski	VIII	24,500	1983
42	Dolina Biebrzy	VIII	13,448	1986
43	Dolina Bugu	VIII	30,162	1986
44	Dolina Bugu i Nurca	VIII	6,473	1982
45	Dolina Czarnej Wody	VIII	10,303	1982
46	Dolina Narwi	VIII	63,717	1986
47	Dolina Odry	VIII	1,270	1982
48	Dolina Pilicy i Drzewiczki	VIII	70,380	1983
49	Dolina Radwi	VIII	3,560	1975
50	Dolina Wkry i dolnego biegu rzeki Lydyni	VIII	51,400	1977
51	Dolina rzeki Jeziorki	VIII	16,920	1983

Map[†] ref.	National/international designations Name of area	IUCN management category	Area (ha)	Year notified
52	Dolina rzeki Narew	VIII	9,053	1977
53	Dolina rzeki Wkry i Lydyki	VIII	47,160	1977
54	Doliny Bzury	VIII	13,300	1986
55	Drumliny Zbojenskie	VIII	7,085	1983
56	Fragment Borow Tucholskich	VIII	16,632	1981
57	Fragment pradoliny Leby na S od Leborka	VIII	16,731	1981
58	Goplansko-Kujawski	VIII	61,500	1986
59	Gornej Rawki	VIII	8,300	1986
60	Gory Bardzkie i Sowie	VIII	15,131	1981
61	Gory Bystrzyckie i Orlickie	VIII	19,000	1981
62	Gory Izerskie	VIII	43,450	1986
63	Gory Kamienne	VIII	5,920	1981
64	Gorynski	VIII	2,240	1985
65	Grabowiecko-Strzelecki	VIII	29,900	1983
66	Grodziec	VIII	2,180	1982
67	Ilza-Makowiec	VIII	16,650	1983
68	Jeleniowsko-Staszowski	VIII	33,000	1985
69	Jeziora Druzno	VIII	12,950	1985
70	Jezioro Bobecinskie	VIII	3,328	1981
71	Jezioro Gluszynskie	VIII	5,985	1983
72	Jezioro Letowskie	VIII	6,680	1981
73	Jezioro Lubniewickie	VIII	6,995	1984
74	Jezioro Modzerowskie	VIII	1,508	1983
75	Jezioro Skapskie	VIII	10,405	1983
76	Jezioro Szczecineckie	VIII	18,000	1975
77	Kieleckie	VIII	150,500	1973
78	Koneckim	VIII	19,500	1973
79	Kopuly Chelmca i Trojgarbu	VIII	2,785	1981
80	Koszalinski Pas Nadmorski	VIII	48,330	1975
81	Krawedz Doliny Odry	VIII	2,478	1984
82	Krawedz Doliny Warty	VIII	1,274	1984
83	Kwidzynsko-Prabucki	VIII	13,380	1985
84	Lasow Stobrawsko-Turowskich	VIII	183,300	1988
85	Lasu Glubczyckiego	VIII	1,640	1988
86	Lasy Chocianskie	VIII	6,390	1982
87	Lasy Przysusko-Szydlowieckie	VIII	43,580	1983
88	Legu Zdzieszowickiego	VIII	1,640	1988
89	Lipsko-Janowski	VIII	30,000	1985
90	Lochowski	VIII	30,231	1983
91	Lodzki	VIII	34,917	1987
92	Lukowski	VIII	22,890	1983
93	Minski	VIII	29,500	1983
94	Mrogi-Mrozycy	VIII	16,200	1986
95	Nadbuzanski	VIII	55,908	1983
96	Nadwislanski	VIII	21,270	1985
97	Nizina Ciechocinska	VIII	36,814	1983
98	Obszar lesny na poludnie od Lidzbarka i Rybna	VIII	60,000	1975
99	Okolice Kalisza Pomorskiego	VIII	1,580	1975
100	Okolice Lidzbarku, Rybna	VIII	58,984	1977
101	Okolice Mlawy i Ilowa	VIII	4,200	1975
102	Okolice Polanowa	VIII	1,857	1975
103	Okolice Regimina	VIII	3,800	1975
104	Okolice Zydowo-Bialy Boru	VIII	12,350	1975
105	Okolice jeziora Krepsko i Szczytno	VIII	12,428	1981
106	Ostrzyca Proboszczowicka	VIII	1,190	1982
107	Pas Pobrzeza na wschod od Ustki	VIII	3,336	1981
108[†]	Pas Pobrzeza na zachod od Ustki	VIII	7,520	1981

Map[†] ref.	National/international designations Name of area	IUCN management category	Area (ha)	Year notified
109	Pawlowski	VIII	8,000	1983
110	Pilicy	VIII	7,000	1973
111	Pogorze Mysliborskie	VIII	14,440	1982
112	Pojezierze Drawskie	VIII	100,053	1975
113	Pojezierze Lubuskie z dolina Lubuszy i Bobru	VIII	175,231	1985
114	Pojezierze Miedzyrzecko-Miedzychodzkie	VIII	42,043	1984
115	Pojezierze Mysliborsko-Barlineckie	VIII	94,863	1984
116	Pojezierze Slawskie, pradolina Obry	VIII	41,700	1985
117	Poleski	VIII	19,000	1983
118	Powidzko-Bieniszewski	VIII	46,000	1986
119	Pradolina Biebrzy i okolice Rajgrodu	VIII	85,258	1982
120	Pradolina Narwi	VIII	17,890	1982
121	Pradolina Pisy i NE czesc Puszczy Knyszynskiej	VIII	38,085	1982
122	Przemysko-Dynowski	VIII	112,220	1987
123	Puszcza Bialostocka	VIII	89,040	1986
124	Puszcza Drawska	VIII	117,982	1984
125	Puszcza Knyszynska	VIII	123,500	1986
126	Pyzderski	VIII	30,000	1986
127	Radzynski	VIII	3,706	1983
128	Rejon Bukowca	VIII	7,208	1984
129	Rejonu Jeziora Otmuchowskiego	VIII	13,150	1988
130	Rejonu Mokre-Lewice	VIII	8,190	1988
131	Rejonu Wroblina-Maciawakszy	VIII	5,650	1988
132	Rownina Ornecka	VIII	8,210	1985
133	Rozlewisko Slonskie	VIII	44,166	1984
134	Roztoczanski	VIII	56,086	1987
135	Rzeki Bandy	VIII	2,150	1985
136	Rzeki Banowki	VIII	2,630	1985
137	Rzeki Dzierzgon	VIII	4,740	1985
138	Rzeki Pasleki	VIII	10,700	1985
139	Rzeki Waska	VIII	5,805	1985
140	Siedlecko-Wegrowski	VIII	35,840	1983
141	Sieniawski	VIII	52,408	1987
142	Solec n/Wisla	VIII	15,170	1983
143	Srodkowy odcinek na prawnym brzegu Narwi	VIII	6,600	1975
144	Suski	VIII	15,890	1985
145	Szydlowieckim	VIII	2,900	1093
146	Uniejowski	VIII	18,000	1986
147	Wloszczowskim	VIII	4,100	1973
148	Wschodnio-Beskidzki	VIII	162,800	1972
149	Wysoczyzna Gorzowska	VIII	30,264	1984
150	Wzgorza Dalkowskie	VIII	2,630	1982
151	Wzgorza Niemczansko-Strzelinskie i Kielczynskie	VIII	15,158	1981
152	Wzgorza Sokolskie	VIII	40,450	1986
153	Wzgorza Zielonogorskie	VIII	13,000	1985
154	Wzniesien Gorowskich	VIII	9,180	1985
155	Zagnansko-Suchedniowskim	VIII	21,000	1973
156	Zespol jezior Czluchowskich	VIII	1,108	1981
157	Zlotogorski	VIII	31,000	1986
158	Zrodla Skrwy	VIII	5,178	1983
159	Zrodliskowy obszar rzek Brdy i Wieprzy	VIII	11,776	1981
160	Zulaw Wislanych	VIII	5,320	1985
	Landscape Parks			
161	Bolimowski	V	25,900	1986
162	Brodnicki	V	22,240	1985
163	Chelmski	V	23,500	1983
164	Doliny Slupi	V	120,201	1981

Map[†] ref.	National/international designations Name of area	IUCN management category	Area (ha)	Year notified
165	Drawski	V	63,642	1979
166	Gor Opawskich	V	4,830	1988
167	Gory Sw. Anny	V	5,780	1988
168	Gostyn sko-Wloclawski	V	51,344	1979
169	Inski	V	51,843	1982
170	Kaszubski	V	34,544	1983
171	Kazimierski	V	38,670	1979
172	Kozienicki	V	45,535	1983
173	Krasnabrodzki	V	40,184	1988
174	Ksiazanski	V	4,500	1981
175	Lagowski	V	10,070	1985
176	Lasy Janowskie	V	62,950	1984
177	Mazowiecki	V	25,510	1986
178	Mazurski	V	69,219	1977
179	Mierzeja Wislana	V	22,390	1985
180	Nadmorski	V	27,610	1978
181	Narwianski	V	47,915	1985
182	Poleski	V	27,500	1983
183	Popradzki	V	78,000	1987
184	Przedborski	V	31,120	1988
185	Pszczewski	V	57,587	1986
186	Puszcza Knyszynska	V	123,349	1988
187	Puszczy Solskiej	V	115,246	1988
188	Slezanski	V	12,200	1988
189	Snieznicki	V	28,800	1981
190	Sobiborski	V	19,000	1983
191	Stolowogorski	V	13,600	1981
192	Strzelecki	V	10,300	1983
193	Suwalski	V	14,901	1976
194	Szczecinski	V	22,384	1982
195	Trojmiejski	V	33,107	1979
196	Tucholski	V	52,928	1985
197	Wdzydzki	V	17,650	1983
198	Wigierski	V	21,301	1976
199	Wzniesienie Elblaskie	V	33,292	1985
200	Zaleczanski	V	14,278	1979
201	Zespol Jurajskich	V	246,276	1980
202	Zespol Parkow Ponidzia	V	82,648	1986
203	Zespol Swietokrzyskie	V	100,625	1988
204	Zywiecki	V	57,587	1986

	Biosphere Reserves			
	Babia Gora National Park	IX	1,741	1976
	Bialowieza National Park	IX	5,316	1976
	Lukajno Lake Reserve	IX	710	1976
	Slowinski National Park	IX	18,069	1976
	Ramsar Wetlands			
	Lukajno Lake	R	710	1977
	Karas	R	816	1984
	Słonsk	R	4,166	1984
	Siedem Wysp	R	1,016	1984
	Swidwie Lake	R	382	1984

Map[†] ref.	National/international designations Name of area	IUCN management category	Area (ha)	Year notified
	World Heritage Site Bialowieza National Park	X	5,316	1979

[†]Locations of most protected areas are shown on the accompanying map.

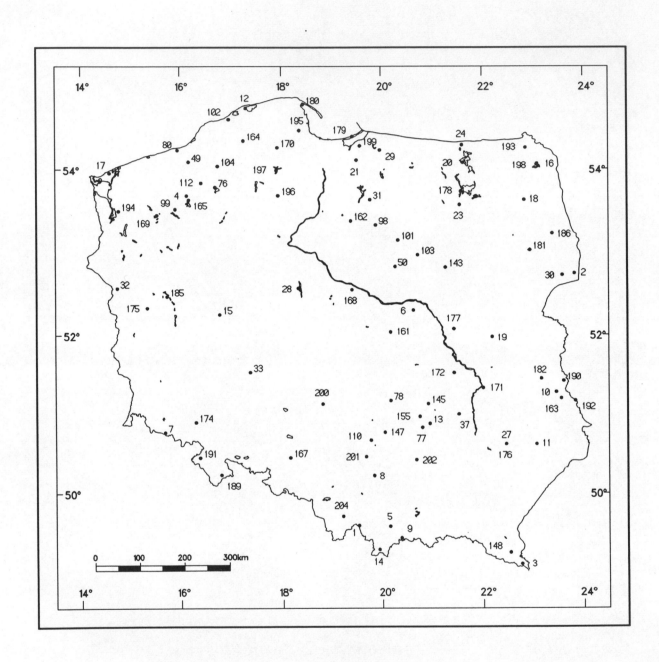

Protected Areas of Poland

PORTUGAL

Area 92,390 sq. km (Azores 2,344 sq km; Madeira 798 sq km)

Population 10,285,000 (1990)
Natural Increase: 0.28% per annum
Azores 250,000 (1981)
Madeira 265,000 (1975)

Economic Indicators
GDP: US$ 3,601 per capita (1987)
GNP: US$ 2,890 per capita (1987)

Policy and Legislation The Constitution, replacing that of 1976, was promulgated in September 1982. The autonomous regions of the Azores and Madeira islands were established in 1976, and have their own legislatures and governments.

Portugal has a long history of environmental legislation which stems back to the classic Roman period. Hunting reserves had been established prior to 1910 when the country was still a Kingdom. The first protected areas legislation was the Act on National Parks and other Reserves (Act 9/70: Dos parques nacionais e outros tipos de reservas) of 8 June 1970. This Act, among other things, lists eleven basic principles, vesting the government with responsibility for nature protection, rational use and conservation of natural resources. Provision is made for national parks, covering four types: strict reserves, nature reserves, scenic reserves and tourist reserves, together with three other "reserves" – botanical, zoological and geological – all subject to full or partial afforestation rules. Provision is also made for the participation of private owners in semi-governmental agencies and for administrative and financial autonomy of these national parks (Anon., 1971).

Further legislation was approved in 1976 (Decree No. 613/76), which, like the 1970 Act, is a major text concerned with the conservation of nature, the protection of landscape and sites, the rational planning and management of natural resources and ensuring the regenerative capacity of the natural environment. This legislation does not officially replace the 1970 Act. Most protected sites, however, now fall into the categories given in this Decree. Under the Decree the Secretary of State for the Environment is authorised to provide the Council of Ministers with the definitions and constitutions of five main categories of protected area: natural reserve (reserva natural) which may be either strict nature reserve (reserva natural integral) or national park (parque nacional). In addition, there are partial natural reserve (reserva natural parcial), recreational reserve (reserva de recreio), protected landscape (paisagem protegida) and classified place, site, complex and object (Lugar, sito, conjunto e objecto classificado) and natural park (parque natural) (see Annex).

The definitions of the different categories of protected areas do not provide detailed restrictions, which are covered under the result of individual site orders and regulations. The management of these areas is to be undertaken by the National Service for Parks, Reserves and Nature Conservation, in collaboration with other groups and local authorities. Article 3 of the Decree gives the Secretary of State for the Environment the right to propose, after consultation with the competent Ministerial Departments, definitions of areas that would especially guarantee the biological equilibrium of regional landscapes four categories are listed: special ecological area (área ecológica especial); special forested or agricultural area (área agricola o florestal especial); degraded area for restoration (área degradada a recuperar); and area of subsoil reserve (área de reserva de subsolo) (Decreto-Lei No. 613/76, 1976).

Act No. 4/78, passed in 1978, covers the organisation of parks and reserves. Act No. 264/79, passed in 1979, provides for the establishment of bird sanctuaries. Act No. 321/83, passed in 1983, delimits the national ecological reserve category, which includes coastal ecosystems and inland lakes, lagoons, river beds and springs.

In 1927, legislation was introduced to limit the depletion of forested areas.

The Game Act regulates the species and quantities of animals that may be killed. It also provides for the designation of areas where hunting is temporarily or permanently banned. Hunting and shooting have also been banned along the entire coast, and around the offshore islands, this protection extending from the cliffs to 1km inland (Anon., 1986b). The Fisheries Act regulates licensed fishing, specified closed seasons and contains provisions for the protection of immature species and spawning beds for certain species (Anon., 1986a).

Two acts in were passed in 1987; The Organic Act No. 10/87 makes provisions for the National Institute for the Environment (Instituto Nacional do Ambiente) (INAMB) to give technical and financial assistance to voluntary associations for the promotion and implementation of measures to protect the environment. The Framework Act on the Environment No. 11/87 establishes the basis of the national environment policy, "which should be directed towards optimising and guaranteeing the permanent utilisation of natural resources both qualitatively and quantitatively, with the view to lasting development". Specific rules should be laid down for the prevention of environmental damage; the rehabilitation of degraded environments and compensation for ecological damage (Anon., 1989a).

Azores The Atlantic archipelagoes of the Azores is an integral part of the Republic of Portugal, although they

287

have their own autonomous governments. Their protected areas systems are based on the same legislation as that of the mainland, notably the 1975 Decree (SNPRCN, *in litt.*, 1991).

Madeira The Atlantic archipelago of Madeira is an integral part of the republic of Portugal, although they have their own autonomous governments. Their protected areas systems are based on the same legislation as that of the mainland, notably the 1975 Decree. In addition, Madeira has two additional categories: geological and high altitude reserve (reserva geologica e de vegetaçao de altitude), which are areas above 1,400m where the flora and fauna are fully protected and hunting, cattle grazing and construction are restricted; and zone of silence and rest (zona de repouso e silencio), which are recreation areas where noise and motorised vehicles are restricted or forbidden (Grimmett and Jones, 1989; SNPRCN, *in litt.*, 1991).

International Activities Portugal acceded to the Convention on Wetlands of International Importance Especially as Waterfowl Habitat (Ramsar Convention) on 24 November 1980: two Ramsar sites have been designated. It acceded to the Convention Concerning the Protection of the World Cultural and Natural Heritage (World Heritage Convention) also on 30 September 1980: no natural site have been inscribed. One site has been designated as a biosphere reserve under the Unesco Man and the Biosphere Programme.

Portugal ratified the Convention on the Conservation of European Wildlife and Natural Habitats (Bern Convention) on 1 June 1982. Portugal is a member of the EC and is party to the 1979 Wild Birds Directive: some 34 EC special protection areas have been designated. It is also a member of the Council of Europe: seven sites have been designated as Council of Europe biogenetic reserves. However, no sites have been awarded the Council of Europe, European Diploma.

Administration and Management Until 1975, the government departments of Agriculture, Forestry and Fisheries were responsible for nature conservation in their respective sectors and introduced legislation on hunting, forestry and fisheries.

Conservation matters now fall under the control of the Ministry of Planning and Land Management (Ministério do Plano de Administraçao do Territorio). Within this Ministry are four secretaries of state. The one most concerned with conservation issues is the Secretary of State for the Environment and Natural Resources (Secretaria de Estado do Ambiente e Recursos Naturais) (SEARN). SEARN oversees several central and regional services; of these, the service most directly involved with the administration of protected areas is the National Service for Parks, Reserves and Nature Conservation (Serviço Nacional de Parques, Reservas e Conservaçao da Natureza) (SNPRCN). Other services covered by SEARN include the General Directorate on Environmental Quality (Direcçao-General da Qualidade

do Ambiente), the General Directorate on Natural Resources (Direcçao-General dos Recursos Naturais) and also the Water Basin Authorities and Air Management Committees (Cutrera, 1987).

The SNPRCN was first set up in 1975 as part of the Environment Secretariat. It is an administrative and financial body, staffed by legal experts, responsible for: (a) drawing up a national nature conservation plan; (b) preparing studies and proposing measures for the conservation of genetic stocks, effective wildlife management and the protection of species; (c) proposing the establishment of nature parks, reserves, protected landscapes and other scheduled areas and taking part in their management; (d) promoting and supervising the preparation of planning measures relating to nature parks, reserves, protected landscapes and other scheduled areas; (e) fostering and participating in scientific and technical research projects in the areas for which it is responsible; (f) carrying out studies and drawing up an inventory of the composition, structure, functioning and productivity of ecological elements and systems; and (g) proposing the conclusion of international agreements and conventions in the field of nature conservation and landscape protection and participating in the activities of international bodies dealing with subjects within the areas for which it is responsible (Anon., 1986a). In addition to the SNPRCN, the Forestry Department, in the Ministry of Agriculture Fisheries and Food, has a section dealing with parks and reserves (Duffey, 1982).

On a regional level, regional governments and municipalities (concelhos) are responsible for the management of protected areas in the areas under their control (Cutrera, 1987). INAMB attempts to increase public awareness of conservation issues by being involved in environmental education and studying present and proposing future government conservation issues.

There are a few, small non-governmental organisations; the League for the Protection of Nature (Liga para a Protecçao da Natureza) (LPN), Portugese Friends of the Earth (Amigos da Terra), the Group of Studies on land Management and the Environment (Grupo de Estudos de Ordenamento do Territorio e Ambiente) (GEOTA) and the Portuguese Ornithological Society, which have some influence on policy. Regional and local conservation groups have also been formed in some areas, notably in Setubal (Projecto Setubal Verde) and Oporto (Quercus). Some of these groups are well organised and have been very successful in certain issues, but it is not known whether they own, or are involved with the management of any private nature reserves (Cutrera, 1987).

Azores The SNPRCN does not operate in the Azores. Protected areas on these islands are the responsibility of the Regional Secretariat for Tourism and the Environment on the Azores (Grimmett and Jones, 1989; SNPRCN, *in litt.*, 1991).

Madeira The SNPRCN does not operate in Madeira, where there is a well developed system of protected areas administered by the Parque Natural da Madeira and Direcçao de Serviços Florestais through the Regional Secretariat of Economics (Grimmett and Jones, 1989; SNPRCN, *in litt.*, 1991).

Systems Reviews Portugal lies in south-west Europe, and together with Spain and Gibraltar it makes up the Iberian Peninsula. To the south and west is faces the Atlantic Ocean, to the north and east it has a border with Spain. Also included in the country are the archipelagos of the Azores and Madeira (described below). The mainland is divided approximately north-south by the River Tejo which dissects Portugal near Lisbon. To the north of the Tejo, the country is mountainous, with some original *Quercus* forest, ericaceous heathland and coniferous cover (including *Pinus* plantations). South of the Tejo, the country is more undulating and farmed more extensively; Mediterranean type forest is found in this region, in natural stands dominated particularly by cork oak *Quercus suber*. Along the coast there are stretches of cliffs and rocky offshore islands, but much of the coast is low-lying and sandy, with large areas of sand dunes and marshes. There are also a number of major estuaries.

In 1907 forests covered 21% of the country. By 1974 forest cover had risen to 55% largely due to an increase in the number of plantations. In addition, other natural ecosystems, with herbaceous or little vegetation, cover a further 12% of the mainland (Anon., 1987). Agriculture covers a further 26% of the land area (Cutrera, 1987).

The protected areas system was slow to become established, with the first parks being created throughout the 1970s. In the years following the establishment of the SNPRCN there was no real conservation policy and there was competition rather than cooperation between the SNPRCN and the Forestry Service. More recently, the SNPRCN has been restructured, the management of protected areas is being entrusted to the regions and a national strategy for conservation of nature is being prepared (Cutrera, 1987).

Threats to the natural ecosystems come from agricultural development, including the draining of meadows and afforestation of marginal land, supported in a number of cases by EC agricultural grants. Since 1982 there has been extensive planting of *Pinus* and *Eucalyptus* (Grimmett and Jones, 1989). The unrestricted development of tourism is a major problem, threatening coastal ecosystems and protected areas, notably in the Algarve region (Grimmett and Jones, 1989). The use of marginal land for agriculture, and other poor agricultural practices, has led to some serious cases of soil erosion, increased water run-off and irregularity of river discharge; in some cases this has led to desertification (Cutrera, 1987).

Azores This volcanic archipelago comprises nine main islands, situated some 1,420-1,563km from mainland Europe. The islands have steep slopes, rising to a peak height of 2,351m. On the main islands there is a cultivated zone along the coasts, with forests and grazing on the upper slopes. More than half of the islands' vascular plants are exotic introductions, some of which are extremely competitive and invasive. Much of the original Macronesian type forest cover has been cleared to create pastures, or has been replaced by exotic plantations. The native laurel *Laurus* forest covers only 2% of the islands (Grimmett and Jones, 1989). Many wetlands are also being cleared to make way for pasture (Anon., 1987).

The protected area system in the Azores is poorly developed, with twelve nature reserves listed in 1989, but only three over 1,000ha. In 1987 the Regional Forestry Service in Ponta Delgada had plans to create Forestry Reserves on a number of islands (Grimmett and Jones, 1989).

Madeira This is a much smaller archipelago than the Azores, with four main islands, again volcanic in origin. It lies 600km from the continent of Africa (Morocco). The slopes of the main islands rise steeply to a maximum height of 1,861m on Madeira. Most of Madeira was forested when it was discovered in 1419. At present, human habitation is most dense around the south coast, where the slopes are cultivated up to 1,200m. To the north of the island there remain large tracts of the original macronesian laurel *Laurus* forest. Natural woodlands cover 15.4% of the islands, and managed or cultivated woodlands a further 22.7% (these figures are only for the two main islands of the archipelago, the others are deserted). The islands of Porto Santo, Desertas and Selvagens are much drier and arid with sparse vegetation. Madeira is important for its endemic flora and fauna, which include 171 endemic species of land molluscs, and 145 endemic plants. Protected areas cover some 33.9% of the total area (Anon., 1987; Grimmett and Jones, 1989).

Addresses

Serviço Nacional de Parques, Reservas e Conservação da Natureza (National Service for Parks, Reserves and Nature Conservation), rua da Lapa 73, 1200 LISBON (Tel: 1 675259; FAX: 1 601048; Tlx: 44089)

General Directorate of Forestry, Ministry of Agriculture, Fisheries and Food, Av. Joas Crisostomo 28, 1000 LISBON

Instituto Nacional do Ambiente, Rua Felipe Folque, 46-2°, 1000 LISBON (Tel: 1 780097)

Secretaria Regional de Turismo e Ambiente, Direcção Regional de Ambiente, Rua Marcelino Lima, 9900 HORTA, Faial-Azores (FAX: (92) 31496)

Secretaria Regional da Economica, Parque Natural da Madeira, Quinta do Bom Sucesso-Caminho do Meio, 9000 FUNCHAL, Madeira (FAX: (91) 20081)

Liga Portuguesa para a Protecção da Natureza (Portugese League for the Protection of the Environment), Estrado do Calhariza a Benfica 187, 1500 LISBON (Tel: 1 780097; FAX: 1 780097)

References

Anon. (1970). Protecção da natureza. *Bol. inform. Liga Prot. Nat.*, N.S. 11

Anon. (1971). XIX/4 – National Parks and Nature Reserves, Portugal – Act No. 9/70 on National Parks and other reserves. *Food and Agricultural Legislation* XX: 99-100.

Anon. (1986a). ECE Finland. 25-29 August 1986. Unpublished report.

Anon. (1986b). *Naturopa* 86(2): 2. Council of Europe.

Anon. (1987). Management of Europe's natural heritage, Twenty-five years of activity. Environment Protection and Management division, Council of Europe, Strasbourg.

Anon. (1989a). Portugal – Act No. 11/87: Framework Act on the Environment. *Food and Agricultural Legislation* 38: 305-307

Anon. (1989b). Portugal's national and nature parks. *European Bulletin* 27(101): 6-8.

Cutrera, A. (1987). *European environmental yearbook 1987*. DocTer International UK, London. 816 pp.

Duffey, E. (1982). *National parks and reserves of Western Europe*. Macdonald and Co. (Publishers) Ltd., London and Sydney. 288 pp.

Grimmett, R.F.A. and Jones, T.A. (1989). *Important bird areas in Europe*. International Council for Bird Preservation, Cambridge, UK.

ANNEX
Definitions of protected area designations, as legislated, together with authorities responsible for their administration

Title: Dos parques nacionais e outros tipos de reservas (Act No. 9/70) (Act on national parks and other reserves)

Date: 8 June 1970

Brief description: The original Act providing for the designation of national parks (four types: strict reserves, nature reserves, scenic reserves and tourist reserves), and also botanical, zoological and geological reserves.

Administrative authority: Serviço Nacional de Parques, Reservas e Conservaçao da Natureza (National Service for Parks, Reserves and Nature Conservation)

Designations:

Reserva integral (Strict reserve) Areas where natural ecological factors are allowed to continue without external intervention. No activities which might alter ecosystem dynamics are allowed. Access is only permitted for administrative or scientific reasons.

Reserva natural (Nature reserve) Areas designated for the protection and conservation, through adequate legislation, of their flora, fauna and scenic interest. These are reserves where flora, fauna, soil, geological and water resources are protected by measures appropriate to their scientific study and use

Reserva de paisagem (Scenic reserve) Areas designated for the protection and conservation of their particular habitats and landscape, as well as for the protection, consolidation, conservation and restoration of sites of ethnic and technical interest. They may be rural or urban areas and many are representative of the culture and customs of the population.

Reserva turistica (Tourist reserve) Areas to be developed according to the needs of the population and of tourism. The promotion of recreation is thus of key importance in these areas, although due account is also taken of the need to protect the natural environment and ecological balance.

Reserva botanica (Botanical reserve) Areas conserved because of their rare flora, the conservation of which is justified because of its scientific and/or educational interest.

Reserva zoologica (Zoological reserve) Areas protected as a refuge for rare species, and species threatened with extinction.

Reserva geologica (Geological reserve) Areas containing geological formations which have a scientific and/or educational interest, which are thus protected against exploitation.

Source: Original legislation

Title: Decreto-Lei no. 613/76 (Decree-Law No. 613/76)

Date: 27 July 1976

Brief description: Provides for the designation of protected areas in addition to those covered under the 1970 Act, and also provides for the definition of wider areas of the country as areas that would specially guarantee the biological equilibrium of the regional landscape.

Administrative authority: National Service for Parks, Reserves and Nature Conservation

Designations:

Reserva Natural (Natural Reserve)

Reserva natural integral (Strict nature reserve) Areas where the protection of all aspects of nature is provided. Activities are restricted which would alter the dynamics of the respective ecosystems admittance to these areas is only permitted for administrative and scientific purposes

Parque nacional (National park)　These are a complex of reserves established for the protection of nature and for education. They may contain strict nature reserves and partial nature reserves, surrounded by other areas of value for protection or recreation. The presence of human settlements is permitted only under special circumstances

Reserva natural parcial (Partial natural reserve) Areas where it is intended to safeguard certain aspects of nature such as fora, fauna, soil, geology and aquatic resources　taking adequate steps that allow for protection, scientific study and utilisation. In this way the following reserves may be established: natural biological, botanical, zoological (ornithological or other), geological, aquatic and marine.

Reserva de recreio (Recreational reserve)　Areas that are particularly suitable to satisfy the needs of the urban population regarding active or passive recreation, and hence where the recreational aspects of the landscape are emphasised.

Paisagem protegida (Protected landscape)　Areas established to safeguard rural or urban regions where characteristic aspects of the culture remain, permitted activities include agricultural, pasture and grazing, and other traditional activities. Designation is orientated towards the social, cultural and economic well-being of the resident populations.

Lugar, sito, conjunto e objecto classificado (classified place, site complex and object) Indispensable measures are proposed to safeguard landscapes with certain natural phenomena and/or places which have cultural, scientific, technical or other interest, such as villages, rural communities, archaeological remains, ruins, exposed geological formations, rocks, individual or groups of trees and characteristic ecological communities.

Parque natural (Natural park)　Areas of land designated for recreation, nature conservation, landscape protection and the promotion of rural populations. These areas can be established on public or private property, zoning establishes the different uses for sectors within the park. Sites may include one or more of the aforementioned categories of protected area, which are integrated within the overall structure.

Source: Original legislation

291

SUMMARY OF PROTECTED AREAS

Map[†] ref.	*National/international designations* Name of area	IUCN management category	Area (ha)	Year notified
	National Park			
1	Peneda-Geres	II/V	71,422	1971
	Nature Reserves			
2	Berlenga	IV	1,020	1981
3	Estuario do Sado	IV	24,000	1980
4	Estuario do Tejo	IV	14,563	1976
5	Lagoa do Fogo (Azores Autonomous)	IV	2,920	1974
6	Sapal de Castro Marim	IV	2,089	1975
7	Serra da Malcata	IV	21,759	1981
	Natural Monuments/Classified Sites			
8	Montes de Barca/Agoluda	III	1,158	1980
9	Penedo do Lexim	III	2,730	1975
	Areas of Protected Landscapes			
10	Arriba Fossil Costa Caparica	VIII	1,635	1984
11	Costa Vicentica e Sudoeste Alentejano	V	60,886	1988
12	Sintra-Cascais	VIII	14,500	1981
	Natural Parks			
13	Alvao	V	7,365	1983
14	Arrabida	V	10,821	1976
15	Montezinho	V	75,000	1979
16	Ria Formosa	V	16,000	1987
17	Serra de Estrela	V	100,000	1976
18	Serra de S. Mamede	V	31,750	1989
19	Serras de Aire e Candeeiros	V	34,000	1979
20	Madeira (Madeira Autonomous)	V	34,000	1979
	Scientific Nature Reserves			
21	Ilhas Selvagens (Madeira Autonomous)	I	3,400	1971
	Biosphere Reserve			
	Paul Do Boquilobo	IX	395	1981
	Ramsar Wetlands			
	Formosa Sound	R	16,000	1980
	Tagus Estuary	R	14,563	1980

[†]Locations of most protected areas are shown on the accompanying map.

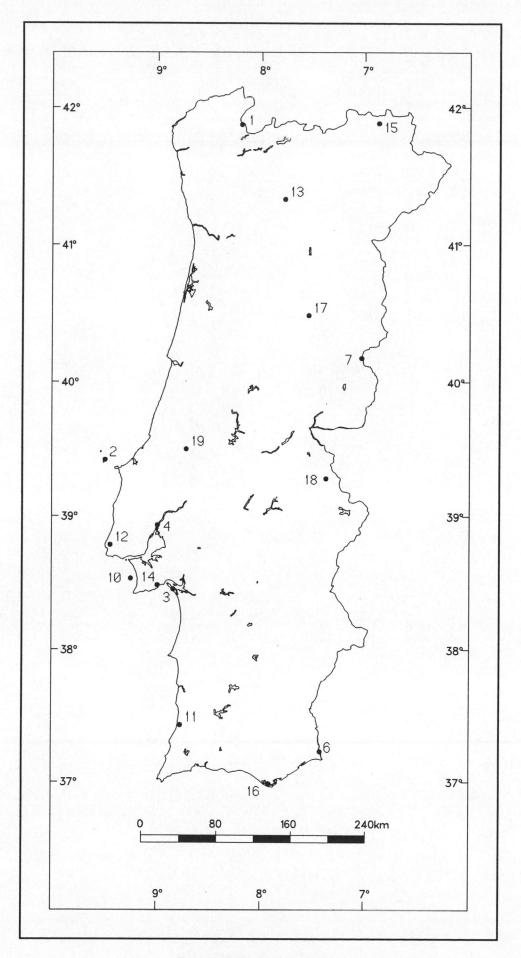

Protected Areas of Portugal

ROMANIA

Area 237,500 sq. km

Population 23,200,000 (1989)
Natural increase: 0.5% per annum

Economic Indicators
GDP: No information
GNP: US$ 6,453 per capita (Anon., 1990)

Policy and Legislation Proposals for the protection of the landscape and natural monuments date back to 1907. The first Nature Protection Act came into force on 7 July 1930. A new Act passed in October 1950 (No. 237) on the Protection of Natural Monuments was complemented by Order of Council No. 518 of 1954. In the same year an Environment Protection Law was introduced, to be replaced by the Environmental Law passed in 1973 (No. 9/1973). Section VI, Article 29 of this Law specifies the official concept governing a national park, the legislative framework and the procedure for creating such protected areas (Oarcea, 1984).

Protected areas are classified into: science reserve or nature reserve (rezervat natural), parcul natural (nature park), parcul national (national park) (see Annex).

Forests are protected by the 1954 Forest Code and the subsequent 1962 Forest Code. In 1976, a national programme to protect and develop forest resources was initiated. Full protection is afforded to about 14% of forest cover (Pop *et al.*, 1965), with a further 36% of forests classified as "protective forest", where restrictions on forest operations, in some cases, result in complete protection. The scientific research category was one established (until 1990) by either the Commission for the Protection of Natural Monuments of the Academy of Sciences or by the Ministry of Forest Economy, whilst areas under the soil conservation category (on slopes over 35°) were subject to total protection, operated jointly by the Commission and the Ministry.

In April 1991, Decree No. 264 established a new ministerial structure consisting of six departments (IUCN, 1991b). The government has also passed a number of decrees (Decree No. 983, 27 August 1990) which created the Danube Delta Biosphere Reserve (of 674,000ha) (IUCN unpublished reports, 1991).

Law No. 9/1980, although not yet mandatory, deals with the preparation of feasibility studies for all projects likely to have an effect on "the preservation of the genetic stock". Approval is given by the Commission for Monuments of Nature of the Romanian Academy.

A new law for environmental protection is drafted. Articles 38, 41, 48 and 49 define the preservation of specific biological diversity through the declaration of nature reserves; the creation of a national network of protected natural areas and monuments of nature; defines biosphere reserves, national parks, nature reserves and natural monuments; the preparation and updating of a catalogue of protected areas and a Red Data Book of plants and animal species; and describes the creation of additional types of protected areas for species protection and use of gene banks (Negoita *et al.*, 1991).

International Activities Romania has been involved in the Unesco Man and the Biosphere (MAB) programme (three areas were declared as biosphere reserves in 1979, with a fourth site added in 1990), and accepted the Convention concerning the World Natural and Cultural Heritage (World Heritage Convention) on 16 May 1990, proposing one site for listing. Romania acceded to the Convention on Wetlands of International Importance especially as Waterfowl Habitat (Ramsar Convention) in 1991 with one site listed on accession.

Administration and Management In 1930, as a consequence of the Nature Protection Act, a Commission for Natural Monuments was established within the Ministry of Agriculture and Landed Estates. In 1950, a new Commission, the Commission for Natural Monuments of the Romanian Academy of Sciences (Comisia pentru Ocrotirea Monumentelor Naturii Academii Republici Socialiste Romania) was created, consisting of a Chairman and eight members. The Commission acted as the main coordinator of research and nature conservation activities, with field projects and monitoring carried out by university biology and geography departments and by other academic institutes. A scientific research base was established at Timisoara.

Up until 1989, the supreme authority for environmental matters was the National Council for Environment Protection (Consiliul National pentru Conservarea Mediului) at the Council of Ministers which came under the National Council for Science and Technology (Consiliul National pentru Stiinta si Tehnologie). It was, however, ineffectual, because it had no budget and relied upon volunteers (IUCN, 1991a). Another influential body was the Academy of Agricultural and Forestry Sciences (Academia de Stiinte Agricole si Silvice) (Cerovsky, 1986).

The nature conservation administration was organised on a regional basis with the three constituent territories of Transylvania, Moldavia and Walachia divided into 40 regions, Bucharest making 41. The Commission parallels this structure with sub-commissions for the Protection of Natural Monuments in Cluj-Napoca (set up in 1933), in Craiova (set up in 1936) and in Iasi (set up in 1938). At the lower administrative level, each region had a local committee (responsible to the People's Council), in charge of wildlife conservation with representatives from forestry, hunting, fishing, agriculture, and education (Cerovsky, 1986; Kirby and Heap, 1984). These were often quite efficient with regard to maintenance and conservation of sites (IUCN, 1991a).

The Commission has a staff of specialists (biologists, forest engineers) and administrative personnel. Its main responsibility is to designate new science reserves (for which proposals are prepared) and to administer reserve areas (including national parks), although it carries out only limited management work. It has the right to intervene in all questions concerning road construction, siting of industrial developments and tourist camps, and any activity which is liable to deteriorate the reserves or degrade the landscape. The regional offices have staffs of approximately 200. Due to the fact that the statutes regulating the organisation and functioning of the park do not provide management guidelines to appropriate authorities, the national park lacks proper administration (IUCN, 1991a).

Each science reserve has at least one warden (guardian), who regulates access and controls grazing rights as well as preventing illegal entry, fishing, and hunting. The reserve guardian may be an employee of the national forest service and as such is often responsible for economic forest land in addition to his duties on the reserve (Kirby and Heap, 1984). Reserves located outside forest lands are administered by the former town and county halls (county popular councils). Often they are poorly protected and have been converted to agriculture on industrial uses (IUCN, 1991a).

Since mid 1990, a new Ministry of Water Management, Forests and the Environment has been set up, which operates through the existing 41 regional offices, namely, survey and environmental protection agencies (Negoita *et al.*, 1991). The national park comes under the administration of the Commission, a function soon to be given to The Ministry's Department of the Environment (Vadineau, pers. comm., 1990). Within the Ministry of Environment, there are departments for water and forests. In April 1991, Decree No. 264 established a new ministerial structure consisting of six departments: departments of Biodiversity and Nature Conservation; Integrated Monitoring; Systems of Research and Impact Assessment; Forestry and Water; Enforcement and Public Relations, and Risk Assessment in Nuclear Plants (IUCN, 1991b). A Commission for the Environment and Ecological Balance was established at the level of the legislative and is attached to the House of Deputies. Its members are all deputies, and it has the support of a team of technical experts in environment. Its primary role is in environmental legislation. Similarly, Commissions for the Protection of the Environment have been formed in the regional town and county halls, consisting of one or two permanent councillors and staffed, at present, by volunteers. These local commissions await confirmation in national laws. There is also a board of inspectors for the environment for each county and a County Agency for the Protection of the Environment (IUCN, 1991a).

The Society for Tourism and Nature Protection was created in 1920, followed in 1922 by another voluntary body, the Mountain Brotherhood (Cerovsky, 1988). Groups formed more recently include the Ecological Movement of Romania (Miscarea Ecologista Din Romana) (MER), which at one time consisted of 112 local groups, had 100,000 members and 29 specialist working parties. It seems to have largely disappeared following the general elections in May 1990 (IUCN, 1991b), the Romanian Ornithological Society (Societatea Ornithologica Romana) and the Ecological-Cultural Party. Each has a general interest in protected areas (Fisher, 1990). In the last year or so, several new several new non-governmental organisations concerned with nature conservation have emerged, such as the Danube Delta Society, which is a nationwide grouping created to support environmental protection throughout the country. It has a staff of 5 to 10 with offices in Bucharest. The other new non-governmental conservation body is "Unesco" Ecological Club, based at the University of Bucharest, with a sub-office in Iasi and is expected to operate as clubs within universities for promotion of environmental education (Vadineanu, pers. comm., 1991).

Systems Reviews The country is divisible into lowlands less than 200m (33%), hills and highlands between 200m and 300m (36%) and mountains averaging 800m (31%). Forests cover between 20% and 27% (Kirby and Heap, 1984; Cerovsky, 1986). There are three main vegetation zones; steppe in the south-east (largely under agriculture), forest-steppe in the centre of the country and montane forests in the Carpathians (Davis *et al.*, 1986). The lowlands are intensively cultivated, as is most of the Danube valley, with nearly all natural and semi-natural vegetation restricted to the mountains where most of the forests are also to be found (IUCN, 1991a). Many of the natural forest stands have been destroyed over the last 300 years with oak woodlands reduced from the original 10 million ha to 1.2 million ha. Some 27.6% of the country is forested with 10% in the lowlands (below 150m), 70% on hill districts (150m-170m) and 60% is the mountain (700m and above). The dominant species is beech (30% of total deciduous cover which amounts to 69%). Of the conifers, 22% of the total is spruce (IUCN, 1991).

Proposals for the protection of the landscape and natural monuments date back to 1907. In the 1980s, the Commission for Protection of Natural Monuments, in collaboration with the General State Forest Management Inspectorate, constructed a concept for the elaboration of a national park system, consisting of at least 12 parks. The study dealt with establishment criteria, organisation and management and preparatory studies covering four new national parks. In the early 1980s there were between 300 and 310 nature reserves covering 0.5% of the country (Alexandrowicz, 1982; Ionescu *et al.*, 1985). By 1986 this had risen to 420 nature reserves and one national park (Cerovsky, 1986) covering 222,545ha (Boscaiu, 1985).

Up to the end of 1989, there was only one designated national park with a further 11 in preparation (Cerovsky, 1988). In 1990, these 11 national parks were declared by forest authorities, but awaits formal recognition, and one further national park, Dracea, has been proposed. Together, those areas cover 664,057ha (2.79% of the country), which includes buffer and pre-park zones and also the proposed extensions to Retezat National Park. By 1991, one national park (21,000ha) and almost 400 science reserves (107,900ha) as well as a further 31 sites (364ha) classified as "monuments of nature" had been designated (IUCN, 1991a). This, however, covers only 0.42% of the country's area. Most recently, the government passed a number of decrees (Decree No. 983, 27 August 1990) which created the Danube Delta Biosphere Reserve (of 674,000ha) (IUCN unpublished reports, 1991). Once declared, all the national parks will cover 154,057ha, and all protected areas 664,057ha which will be 2.74% of the country. The aim is to designate 5% of the country's surface on protected areas (Hopkins, *in litt.*, 1991).

The natural environment is presently threatened by a combination of factors such as industrial pollution, intensification of agriculture (with 30% of arable land affected by soil erosion (IUCN 1991b) and tourism. For example, Rosca-Letea Biosphere Reserve has until recently been threatened by agricultural development plans, which have now been halted. However, the affects from upstream pollution sources are still a threat. Due to excessive felling and inadequate afforestation, young woodlands predominate. Acid rain has changed 5.5% of the forests (IUCN, 1991a).

Addresses

Department of the Environment, Ministry of Water Management, Forests and the Environment, R-Bucharest-Artera Noüa N-S, Tronson 5-6, Sector 5, BUCHAREST (Tel: 316044; Tlx: 10455/10435; FAX: 316199)

References

Alexandrowicz, Z. (1982). Wielkoprzestrzenne obszary rezerwatowe Rumunii. *Chronmy Przyrode Ojczysta* 38(6): 134-137.

Boscaiu, N. (1985). Le dévéloppement d'un système de réserves pour la protection de la flore de Roumanie. In: Nedialkov, S. *et al.* (Eds.) *International Symposium "Conservation of Natural Areas and the Genetic Material they Contain".* Project 8 on the Programme "Man and the Biosphere" (MAB) of Unesco, 23-28.09.1985, Blagoevgrad, Bulgaria. Vol II, BAN, Sofia. Pp. 171-178.

Cerovsky, J. (1986) (Ed.). *Nature conservation in the Socialist countries of East-Europe.* East-Europe Committee, IUCN Commission on Education, Administration of Krkonose National Park, Vrchlubi.

Cerovsky, J. (1988) (Ed.). *Nature conservation in the Socialist countries of East-Europe.* East-Europe Committee, IUCN Commission on Education, Ministry of Culture of the Czech Socialist Republic, Prague.

Davis, S.D., Droop, S.J.M., Gregerson, P., Henson, L., Leon, C.J., Lamlein Villa-Lobos, J., Synge, H., and Zantovska, J. (1986). *Plants in danger: what do we know?* Threatened Plants Unit. IUCN, Gland, Switzerland, and Cambridge, UK. 461 pp.

Fisher, D. (1990). *Developments within the environment movement.* Romania. 10-12 March 1990, 28 March-8 April 1990. Unpublished report.

Horeau, C. and Cogran, I. (1981). *Rezervatii naturale si monumenti ale naturii din judentul Vaslui* (nature reserves and natural monuments). (Unseen)

Ionescu, M. and Condurateanu-Fesci, S. (1985). *Parcuri si Rezervatii Naturale Pe Glob.* Colectia Cristal, Bucuresti.

IUCN (1971). *United National List of National Parks and Equivalent Reserves 2nd Edition.* Hayez, Brussels.

IUCN (1991a). *Environmental Status Reports: 1990 Volume Two: Albania, Bulgaria, Romania, Yugoslavia.* IUCN East European Programme.

IUCN (1991b). *The Environment in Eastern Europe: 1990. Environmental Research Series 3.* IUCN East European Programme.

Kirby, K.J. and Heap, J.R. (1984). Forestry and Nature Conservation in Romania. *Quarterly Journal of Forestry* 78(3): 145-155.

Negoita, R.T. and Juras, A. (1991). Nature Conservation in Romania. In: *Nature Conservation in Austria, Finland, Norway, Sweden, Switzerland, Bulgaria, Czechoslovakia, Hungary, Poland, Romania, Yugoslavia and the Soviet Union.* European Parliament Directorate-General for Research. Environment, Public Health and Consumer Protection, Series 17. EN-9-91. (90% of material straight copy of IUCN, 1991a).

Oarcea, Z. (1984). The evolution of the conception and the principles governing the creation and the setting up of the Retezat National Park. In: Pascu, S. *et al.* (Eds.), *Recherches écologiques dans le Parc National de Rétézat.* Travaux du Symposium du 13 avril 1984. Cluj-Napoca. Pp. 27-31.

Pop, E. and Salageanu, N. (1965). *Nature reserves in Romania.* Meridiane Publishing House, Bucharest.

Resmerita, I. (1983). *Conservarea dinamica a naturii.* Edit Stiinfica si encicilopedica Bucuresti. (Unseen)

Seghedin, T.G. (1983). *Rezervatiile naturale din Bucovina.* Nature reserves in Bukovina. Edit Sport-turism, Bucuresti. (Unseen)

ANNEX
Definitions of protected area designations, as legislated, together with authorities responsible for their administration

Title: Environmental Law (No. 9/1973)

Date: 1973

Brief description: Section VI, Article 29 provides the official concept governing national parks and the legislative framework and procedure for creation of protected areas

Administrative authority: Department of the Environment in the Ministry of Water Management, Forests and the Environment

Designations:

Protected areas are classified into national park, nature park and nature reserve categories:

Science or nature reserve (Rezervat natural) Divided into seven categories classified as mixed forest, botanical, zoological, geological, morphological, palaeontological and speleological. Ecosystems within nature reserves are under complete protection, and access is subject to special authorization, with tourists allowed to enter by special permit only. Several have strictly defined protected areas or scientific research zones, where, house construction and quarrying is not allowed without authorisation.

Nature park (Parcul natural) Would protect large areas of the landscape. These are still at a planning stage and lacking legal guidelines.

National park (Parcul national) Category has three basic functions: scientific, socio-educational and economic, and is divided into two sectors; a strictly protected zone and a protected zone. The strictly protected zone has complete protection with no permanent residence allowed, no pasturing but some biological control of insect pests is permitted. In the protected zone, hunting is forbidden, but fishing is allowed in some lakes, subject to fish stocks. Grazing of domestic stock is also permitted in July and August, and tourism is encouraged (Retezat National Park).

Sources: Alexandrowicz, 1982; Cerovsky, 1988; IUCN, 1971; Oarcea, 1984

Title: Forest Code

Date: 1962 (revision of 1954)

Brief description: Defines types of protection and lays down restrictions on forest operations

Administrative authority: Ministry of Water Management, Forests and the Environment

Designations:

Five categories are defined:

Soil conservation and the reduction of avalanches; the protection of water supplies; the use of forests for recreation; for landscape protection specifically surrounding urban, industrial, tourist and health zones; and as scientific research areas protecting rare fauna, geological and speleological formations.

Source: Kirby and Heap, 1984

SUMMARY OF PROTECTED AREAS

Map[†] ref.	National/international designations Name of area	IUCN management category	Area (ha)	Year notified
	National Parks			
1	Apuseni	V	57,900	1990
2	Bucegi	V	35,700	1990
3	Caliman	V	15,300	1990
4	Ceahliu	V	17,200	1990
5	Cheile Carasului	V	30,400	1990
6	Cheile Nerei-Beusnita	V	37,100	1990
7	Cheile-Bicazului	V	11,600	1990
8	Cozia	V	17,100	1990
9	Domogled-Valea Cernei	V	60,100	1990
10	Piatra Craiului	V	14,800	1990

Map[†] ref.	National/international designations Name of area	IUCN management category	Area (ha)	Year notified
11	Retezat	II	54,400	1935
12	Rodna	V	56,700	1990
	Biosphere Reserve (National)			
13	Danube Delta	IV	500,000	1990
	Nature Reserves			
14	Bicaz (narrow Gorge) and Lacul Rosu	IV	5,369	1955
15	Bucegi	V	3,748	1943
16	Caliman	IV	1,625	
17	Carorman	I	2,250	1990
18	Cheile Bicazului	IV	3,241	1955
19	Cheile Carasului	IV	1,025	1982
20	Cheile Nerei-Beusnita	IV	11,098	1943
21	Cozia	IV	7,284	
22	Grindul Chituc	I	2,300	1990
23	Grindul Lupilor	I	2,075	1990
24	Letea	I	2,825	1990
25	Periteasca-Bisericuta-Portita	I	4,125	1990
26	Piatra Craiului	IV	1,459	1958
27	Pietrile Boghii-Pietroasa	IV	1,737	1971
28	Pietrosu Mare	IV	5,865	1932
29	Raducu	I	2,500	1990
30	Rosca-Buhaiova	I	9,625	1990
31	Sahalin-Zatoane	I	24,250	1990
32	Saritoarea Bohodeiului	IV	1,950	1981
33	Scarisoara-Belioara	IV	6,507	1941
34	Sesul Craiului-Bellcara	IV	6,507	1941
35	Snagov Forest and Snagov Lake	IV	1,768	1952
36	Vatafu-Lungulet	I	1,625	1990
	Nature Park			
37	Gradistea Muncelului-Cioclovina NatP	V	6,030	1979
	Forest Reserves			
38	Ceahlau-Politele cu crini	IV	5,424	1955
39	Domogled-Tesna-Virful lui Stan	IV	5,991	1932
40	Tismana	VIII	1,251	1982
	Other Reserve Area			
41	Bila-Lala	IV	5,135	1973
	Biosphere Reserve			
	Pietrosul Mare Nature Reserves	IX	3,068	1979
	Retezat National Park	IX	20,000	1979
	Rosca-Letea Reserve	IX	18,145	1979
	Ramsar Wetlands			
	Danube Delta	R	647,000	1991

[†]Locations of most protected areas are shown on the accompanying map.

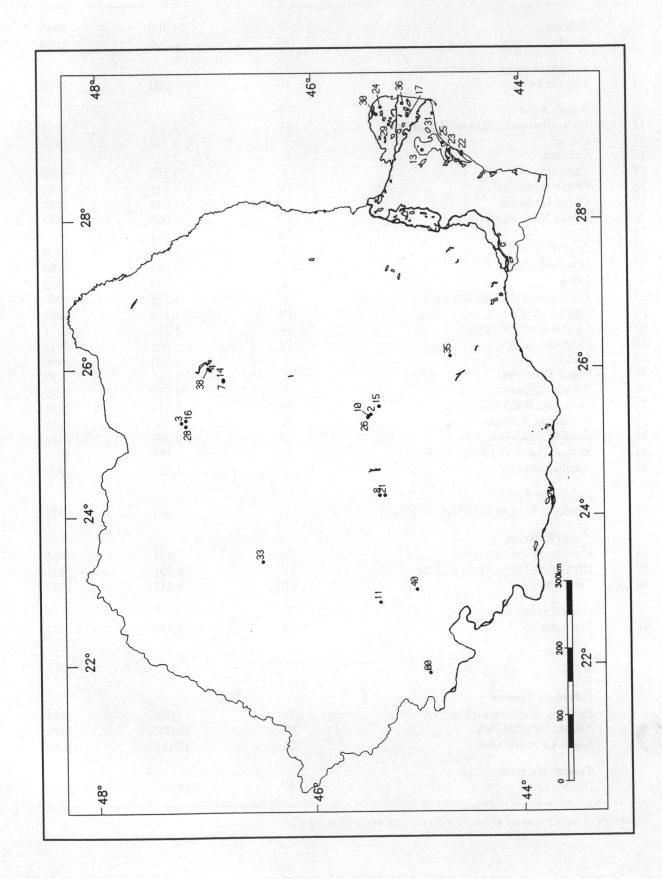

Protected Areas of Romania

SAN MARINO

Area 61.2 sq. km

Population 22,746 (1988) (Hunter, 1991)
Natural increase: No information

Economic Indicators
GDP: No information
GNP: No information

Policy and Legislation   Although founded in 301 AD, the present Constitution of San Marino was written in 1600 based on the original Statuti Comunali of 1300. Administrative and legislative powers are passed from the Arengo parliament to the elected representative assembly, the Grand General Council (Consiglio Grande e Generale). Executive power is exercised by the State Congress, composed of three Secretaries of State and seven deputies; heads of department include those of Territory (Town Planning), Environment and Agriculture (Anon., 1986).

Most of the San Marino landscape is the product of man's interaction with nature; a mosaic of urban development, agriculture, forestry, industry, and other activities. This landscape is long established and protection is achieved through a complicated web of policy and administration such as planning and agricultural legislation. In a statute of 1245, protected forest zones (Gualdarie) were first identified and defined. Currently, the various forms of protected area include forest, hunting and fishing reserves and natural parks (Anon., 1986).

International Activities   The Republic of San Marino is represented by its own mission and delegations in international organisations including the United Nations and Unesco. Recently San Marino instituted diplomatic relations with the EC and is an observer to the Council of Europe. San Marino is not party to any major nature conservation convention.

San Marino has concluded a series of friendship treaties with Italy, the last on 31 March 1939 (amended 1985), which were designed to preserve the independence of this ancient republic.

Administration and Management   Authorities with responsibility for nature conservation and the environment include the Ministry of Town Planning and Environment and Agriculture. Traditional management of the deciduous woodlands continues to be maintained by a coppice regime.

Systems Reviews   An enclave within Italy, the Republic of San Marino is located in the hills of Rimini on the eastern side of the Italian peninsula, 20km from the Adriatic. The republic is dominated by the 750m high limestone slopes of Monte Titano, where the capital city, Cita, is situated. Centuries of man's use of the landscape has led to a distinct lack of natural ecosystems, although there are still areas of semi-natural Mediterranean vegetation and relict flora and fauna communities on the cliffs and slopes of Monte Titano and copses throughout the republic. Of the six major habitat communities recorded in San Marino, the dominant forms are *Ostrya* woodland, *Quercus pubescens* woodland, wood pasture, *Salix* and *Populus* riverine woodland, and grasslands. Woodlands make up 16.1% of the territory and agriculture up to 60% (Valli, 1986).

A mosaic of managed and coppiced woodland is to be found right against the walls of the main town itself. Vineyards, woodland coppice, olive, cereal, cotton fields and cattle pasture are the main cultivated or semi-natural landscapes.

Although there are no recorded globally threatened species, the territory is of regional importance for the limestone Monte plant and animal communities that remain in isolation surrounded by the low Italian plains of the region. Inventories have identified four species of fish, three species of amphibian, nine reptiles, 13 mammals and 137 bird species (Valli and Amadei, 1986). There are over 140 species of plant (Valli, 1986).

Managed woodlands and the cliff habitats are *de facto* nature reserves in San Marino. The classes of protected area are hunting reserve, fishing reserve, natural park and forest reserve (Anon., 1986).

Some of the main environmental threats have included limestone extraction and quarrying, small bird hunting, agricultural improvement and fertiliser run-off since the late 1950s, water and atmospheric pollution (Anon., 1986; Valli, 1986; Drucker, *in litt.*, 1991).

Additional Information   In 1987, three million tourists visited San Marino, but at that time there was no indication of even a small level of ecotourism (Hunter, 1991; Drucker, in litt., 1991).

Addresses

Ministry of Commerce, Tourism and Sports, Via Omaguano, SAN MARINO
Ministry of Town Planning and Environment and Agriculture, Palazzo Begni, Contrada Omerelli, 47031 SAN MARINO

References

Anon. (1986). *Repubblica di San Marino*. Palazzo del Turismo, San Marino.
Hunter, B. (Ed.) (1991). *The Statesman's Year Book 1991-92*. The MacMillan Press Ltd, London and Basingstoke, UK.
Packett, C.N. (1970). *Guide to the Republic of San Marino*. Bradford.

Valli, A.S. (1986). La Flore, lineamenti della vegetazione della Repubblica di San Marino. *Storia Illustrata della Repubblica di San Marino* 1: 2-18. AIEP Editore.

Valli, A.S. and Amadei, V. (1986). La Fauna. *Storia Illustrata della Repubblica di San Marino* 42: 653-668. AIEP Editore.

SPAIN

Area 504,780 sq. km (including Balearic and Canary Islands)
Canary Islands: 7,275 sq. km
Balearic Islands: 5,015 sq. km

Population 39,187,000 (1989)
Natural increase: 0.37% per annum
Canary Islands: 1,614,882 (1986)
Balearic Islands: 754,777 (1986) (Times Atlas, 1990)

Economic Indicators
GDP: US$ 7,432 per capita
GNP: US$ 6,010 per capita

Policy and Legislation The new Constitution came into force on 29 December 1978. This established a semi-federal system of regional administration with the autonomous community (comunidad autonoma) as its basic element. There are 17 autonomous communities, each having a parliament, regional government and exclusive legislative rights to enact their own laws (they include Andalusia, Aragon, Asturias, Baleares, Basque, Canary Islands, Cantabria, Castilla, Mancha, Castilla-Leon, Catalonia, Extremadura, Galicia, Madrid, Murcia, Navarra, Rioja, Almeria, Cadiz, Cordoba, Granada, Huelva, Jaen, Malaga and Sevilla, in addition to the Valencian Community and the municipalities of Ceuta and Melilla (also see entry for Spain – North African Territories). The Constitution envisages much of the control, which used to be central, being delegated to the regions. Article 45 Chapter III of the Constitution, entitled "Guidelines for Social and Economic Policy", embodies principles of conservation including rational use of resources, protection and restoration of the environment. It also suggests that the protection of the environment should not be restricted to local or regional organisation as it is an issue which crosses boundaries in both space and time (Poore and Gryn-Ambroes, 1980).

Spain has a long history of environmental legislation. A detailed understanding of the environment was well known 2,000 years ago during the classic Roman period. At that time throughout the Roman Empire there were forest administration structures, delimited forests, wardening systems and programmes of tree planting, along with areas set aside for wildlife (Drucker, *in litt.*, 1985; Hiyam, *in litt.*, 1991). Spanish hunting reserves were set up at an early date; Doñana having a known history of over 700 years, being a favourite hunting reserve of Spanish Christian kings until established as a national park in 1969. The Moorish kingdoms of southern Spain had a major impact on the landscape which is still apparent today. The Moorish authorities maintained Islamic law, beliefs and customs which included traditional forms of rangeland protection and land management control mechanisms on common land or hereditary lands (agdal, habous, guich) (Child and Grainger, 1990).

The earliest environmental decree dates back to 1837 when the General Directorate of Mountains was established (Poore and Gryn-Ambroes, 1980). In 1859, a "Catalogue of Mountains for Public Utility" was created, listing a total of 6,755,280ha of land; these areas "enjoyed legal protection with proper management" (Rodriguez, 1985). The Mountains Directorate was extended to cover fishing and hunting in 1928 and was incorporated in 1931 into the Ministry of Agriculture (Poore and Gryn-Ambroes, 1980). On 7 December 1916 a General Law of National Parks was passed and enforced by a Royal Decree on 23 February 1917 (Rodriguez, 1985). The first two national parks were established in 1918 under this Law, and several more were declared between 1954 and 1974. A further category of protected area was provided for in the Decree of 7 June 1931 on the Protection of Natural Resources (Protección de los Recursos Naturales). Sites were defined as natural sites of national interest (sitios naturales de interès nacional) – natural areas, equivalent to national parks, but of reduced dimensions, and as such designated for their importance as natural beauty, landscape, geological formations or hydrology. Cultural sites were originally protected under the Law of 13 May 1933 governing the protection of sites of historical and archaeological interest (IUCN, 1987).

In the period between 1941 and 1971, some eight laws relating to mountains and reafforestation and five to hunting had been enacted (Poore and Gryn-Ambroes, 1980). The 1916 Law remained valid until 1957 when a Law of the Mountains was drafted. The Act and its Regulations, approved in 1962, contained two chapters referring to national parks. These included details on protection, establishment by decree, conservation, expropriation, violation and finance (Rodriguez, 1985). The 1957 Act also redefined natural sites of national interest and created a new category, natural monuments of national interest. Such sites were to be promulgated by ministerial decree (practised since 1920). In 1971 the institutional administration of the Ministry of Agriculture was amended by Decree 28 to establish a National Institute for Nature Conservation (Instituto Nacional para la Conservación de la Naturaleza) (ICONA).

Existing protected areas were reclassified under the Law on Protected Natural Areas (espacios naturales protegidos) 15/1975 of 15 May 1975 and given legal status under regulations introduced on 4 March 1977. Four categories of protected area are described in this Law: national park, natural park, natural area of national importance or interest and integral reserve of scientific interest. Precise protection measures are not defined in this general legislation, legal definitions of the different categories of protected area are given in the Annex. A further category was added by Decree No. 3128/82 of 15 October 1982, which defines national biological reserves. The May 1975 Law also provides for boards, planning and regional zoning. It establishes areas of protection classified by the competent authorities as specially protected non-urbanised ground where only traditional uses and exploitation compatible with the parks' objectives are allowed. New activities require the prior approval of the board. Socio-economic influence zones are also set up around each national park in order to link the park with the local population, to maintain traditional activities, population levels, and rational use of resources (Rodriguez, 1985).

A major new piece of legislation was enacted on 27 March 1989: Law No. 4 on the Conservation of Natural Spaces, Flora and Wildlife (Ley de Conservación de los Espacios Naturales, de la Flora y Fauna Silvestres). This law was intended to comply with the 1978 Constitution and lead to the regionalisation of many issues of nature conservation, including those relating to protected areas. The general principles of the law include the maintenance of ecological processes; the preservation of genetic diversity; the rational use of natural resources; and measures leading to benefits for fauna and ecosystems, the restoration of damaged ecosystems and the preservation of the natural beauty of the country. There are several sections to the law, including those on natural resource planning, protected areas and general flora and fauna. The articles on natural resource planning require are important in that, for the first time, they require the drawing up of obligatory management plans: the autonomous communities are required to plan the resource management within their jurisdiction these plans are not simply to be drawn up for certain zones, but are an instrument to be used for all the territory and for all natural resources (Llorens and Rodriguez, 1991).

The 1989 Law specifically states that areas are to be designated for protection when their natural features are of interest and value to the nation and constitute a representative example of the principle ecosystems and natural regions found in the national territory. Protected areas may also include areas of cultural, educational, aesthetic, scientific or recreational importance. Four categories are described in the Law: parks, natural reserves, natural monuments, and protected landscapes. Although definitions of these categories are given (see Annex), in many cases these do not give great detail and are not as clear as those provided under the 1975 Law. For example, the differences between parks and natural reserves are not altogether clear, as their definition lies between natural parks and integral reserves of scientific interest in the 1975 Law. The law also provides for the possibility of establishing peripheral protection zones (buffer zones) around protected areas. The declaration of these protected areas is the responsibility of the autonomous communities which are also responsible for drawing up specific regulations for sites in their region. The state maintains the right to declare and manage natural areas that are a part of the "public domain", for example in marine and coastal areas and inland lakes.

The state may also declare areas that fall under the jurisdiction of two or more autonomous communities (Llorens and Rodriguez, 1991).

Other relevant articles in the 1989 Law give the Ministry of Agriculture, Fisheries and Food responsibility for conducting a national inventory of humid zones and including them in the protected areas system. The National Commission for the Protection of Nature is also established under this Law as a consultant organisation (Llorens and Rodriguez, 1991).

Although the 1989 law replaces the 1975 Law on Protected Natural Areas, at least in terms of nature conservation policy the categories of protected area that were originally covered under this Law remain until such time as these areas are reclassified. There are a number of problems with the implementation of the new law. As already mentioned the definitions of some of the different categories are not particularly clear; furthermore, the clauses that allow for the intervention of central government, in both natural resource planning and in the designation of sites, leave the role of the autonomous communities open to question national parks remain the charge of the state, as do areas in the public domain, and areas that cover more than one community much of the text refers to areas and issues of "national" importance, and yet the law is supposed to be primarily aimed at the autonomous communities. There is some confusion as to which authorities are responsible for which tasks. It has also been suggested that much of the previous experience gained by the state in the designation of protected areas will not necessarily be passed on to the autonomous communities. Some of these issues will only be clarified by the establishment of further decrees at the national and autonomous community level (Llorens and Rodriguez, 1991).

Hunting legislation is also important for the designation of protected areas. Laws concerning the creation of national hunting reserves were declared on 31 May 1966 (Law No. 37/1966), on 4 April 1970 (Law No. 1/1970) and on 17 March 1973. There are three categories of hunting reserves: national hunting reserve, national hunting sanctuary and national hunting refuge (see Annex) (ICONA, *in litt.*, 1988). Faunal sanctuaries can be enacted under Article 11 and 12 of the Hunting Act, following proposals of the Ministry of Agriculture, Fisheries and Food. In general, the legislation omits effective protection of fauna and wetlands (Poore and Gryn-Ambroes, 1980).

The Law on Forestry (Ley de Montes) of 1957, with the 1962 Decree covering regulations for its implementation, contains the main legal provisions governing the forestry sector. Part I, Chapter II of the 1957 Law describes a register of "Forests of Public Importance", and also states that lists shall be made of privately-owned forests, including partly-forested lands and catchment area protective zones. Part II broadly describes conservation measures that are to be applied to these areas. Book I of the 1962 Forest Regulations

Decree classifies several categories of forest, two of which may be of importance for conservation purposes (see Annex). This Decree covers reafforestation and forest conservation measures.

Two further categories of protected area are defined under Law No. 6/1987 of 10 April 1987 of Regional Urban Standards for the Protection and Use of the Territory; these are natural areas and partial nature reserves (see Annex) (ICONA, *in litt.*, 1988).

Although wetlands are not specifically protected, a Wetlands Working Group, comprising ICONA, the Spanish Environmental Committee and others, has been set up. Marine areas are protected under local designations defining zones prohibiting fishing (Zonas de veda de pesca) (Drucker, pers. comm., 1988).

The protection of coastal areas is covered by regulations within the Law on Coasts (Ley de Costas) of 28 July 1988 (Law No. 22/1988). This Law was approved by Royal Decree No. 1471 of 1 December 1989. It lists obligations for the protection of the sea up to 100m offshore (subject to extension); it restricts the number of traffic and access routes to the coast (including pedestrian); it also defines a "zone of influence" which extends 500m from the water line which may affect the land and urban planning; the disposal of solid waste and raw sewage is prohibited in this area (Cutrera, 1991).

One important piece of regional legislation is the Law 1/1984 of 14 March 1984 (Ordenación y Protección do Areas Naturales de Interès Especial) which, in the Balearic Islands, provides for the protection of natural areas of special interest (àreas naturales de interès especial). These sites are declared by the Parliament of the Balearic islands for outstanding natural features including flora, fauna or landscape (ICONA, *in litt.*, 1988).

The policy of the Directorate of Mountains over the last 100 years provided a balance between constant afforestation, maximised production, adequate provision of pasture land, hunting, fishing and recreation (Poore and Gryn-Ambroes, 1980), but prior to the formation of ICONA there were apparently no laws specifically related to nature conservation (IUCN, 1987). In the past the law has provided tax exemption and relief to owners of land within protected areas. It has been proposed that bipartite international commissions should be set up for protected areas crossed by national borders.

Cultural sites were originally protected under Law of 13 March 1933 on historic and artistic heritage (Ley de Patrimonio Historico-Artistico), and the subsequent acts of 16 April 1936; picturesque sites (parajes pintorescos) were defined as historic-artistic monuments which should be preserved from destruction or detrimental reform, being conserved for promotion of their historic-artistic national heritage.

In 1985 the Spanish Historial Heritage Law (Ley de Patrimonio Historico Español) was passed, which provides for the protection of property of cultural interest (bienes de interès cultural) (see Annex).

International Activities   Spain acceded to the Convention on Wetlands of International Importance Especially as Waterfowl Habitat (Ramsar Convention) on 4 May 1982 and 17 sites have been designated. It acceded to the Convention Concerning the Protection of the World Cultural and Natural Heritage (World Heritage Convention) also on 4 May 1982: one natural site has been inscribed (in the Canary Islands). Ten sites have been designated as biosphere reserves under the Unesco Man and the Biosphere Programme.

Spain ratified the Convention on the Conservation of European Wildlife and Natural Habitats (Bern Convention) in September 1986. It has participated in, and ratified, the Barcelona Convention as sponsored by the UNEP Mediterranean Action Plan and Regional Seas programme, notably the Protocol Concerning Mediterranean Specially Protected Areas of 1982, which Spain ratified on 22 January 1988 (Cutrera, 1991): six sites have been designated as Mediterranean specially protected areas. Spain joined the EC in 1986 and is party to the 1979 Wild Birds Directive: some 135 special protection areas have been designated. It is also a member of the Council of Europe, however no sites have been designated as Council of Europe biogenetic reserves, although three sites have been awarded the Council of Europe, European Diploma.

A number of parks are found on international borders. An important transboundary protected area has been established, with a cooperative agreement signed, between Ordesa and Monte Perdido national parks and Pyrénées Occidentales National Park in France.

Administration and Management   The national body responsible for administration of protected areas is the National Institute for the Conservation of Nature (Instituto Nacional para la Conservación de la Naturaleza) (ICONA). This body was set up in 1971 as an amendment to the Institutional Administration of the Ministry of Agriculture, Fisheries and Food (Ministerio de Agricultura, Pesca y Alimentación) (Decree Law of 28 October 1971). Its functions include; the encouragement of renewable resource use and maintenance of ecological balance; the creation and administration of national parks and sites of national interest; and the development and exploitation of inland fishing and hunting assets (Poore and Gryn-Ambroes, 1980). As a result of the decentralisation of the government in 1978, responsibility for many conservation issues was handed over to the 17 autonomous communities this has been further helped by the 1989 Law on the Conservation of Natural Areas, Flora and Wildlife. Some of the work originally performed by ICONA has thus, in subsequent years, been handed over to these authorities. ICONA remains responsible for the administration and management of national parks, while other protected areas including forest sites (Cutrera, 1991) are managed by the autonomous communities, who also have the power to designate new sites, sometimes even using non-standard criteria and nomenclature in the designation of these: the 1989 Law should provide for standardisation of protected areas classified or reclassified in the future. The National Commission for the Protection of Nature (Comisión Nacional de Protección de la Natura) was established under the 1989 law as a consultant organisation, coordinating the activities of the central organisations and the autonomous communities within this Commission is the Committee for Natural Protected Areas (Comité Nacional de Espacios Naturales Protegidos), comprising a representative of each of the autonomous communities and having the Director of ICONA as its President (Llorens and Rodriguez, 1991).

ICONA consists of a central service and provincial network. The central service comprises a General Secretariat and four divisions dealing with fire and ecology, national forests, renewable natural resources and administration, respectively (Duffey, 1982). The renewable natural resources division is responsible for national parks, reserves, hunting grounds, fishing, protection of mountains, fauna and organisation of natural areas, and is itself divided into two services: game, and parks and reserves. Peripheral services are undertaken by 11 regional inspectorates and 50 provincial services. Each consists of a manager, a number of senior and middle-grade technicians and a mobile corps (ICBP, 1985).

Prior to 1971, nature conservation was administered by a series of bodies. In 1837 the General Directorate of Mountains was set up by Royal Decree as a part of the Home Office responsible for all matters relating to nature. In 1928 this Directorate, now in the Ministry of Public Works, also became responsible for fishing and hunting. In 1931, the Directorate of Mountains, Hunting and River Fishing became part of the Ministry of Agriculture where it remained until 1971. At the end of the Spanish Civil War in 1936, there was a great need for wood and the State Forestry Commission was set up. This has since been incorporated into ICONA. In 1939 national parks also became the responsibility of the general Directorate of Mountains in the reorganised Ministry of Agriculture. This was thus the first state body in Europe to undertake responsibility for national parks (Poore and Gryn-Ambroes, 1980).

There was no management planning in national parks prior to the 1975 Act, activities being limited to maintenance and supervision. Only a minimal percentage of lands in a natural state is state property; a greater percentage belongs to the city governments, while the rest is privately-owned (Rodriguez, 1985). The policy is now gradually to acquire lands constituting parks, or, failing this, to enter into use arrangements with the owners. To collaborate with ICONA, as covered under Article 12 of the 1977 Decree, National Park Boards (or Trustee Committee) are established for each

national park, whilst natural parks have a Directory Commission (or Governing Board) in which all interests are represented. The objectives of the National Park Board are numerous but include the promotion of national park interests, financial administration, plan and management provision, the submission of an annual report to the Director of ICONA, the approval of special plans (Article 7), the delegation of functions to People's Commission and the modification of internal park regulations (Anon., 1978; Rodriguez, 1985).

Article 11 of the 1977 Decree, establishing natural parks, also directed ICONA to draw up formats for park plans. These plans are envisaged to cover a number of points including general organisational guidelines, carrying capacity standards, zonation plans, rules and sanctions. The plans must have the approval of the National Park Board, and be valid for four years, after which time they may be revised. As a tool of park management, ICONA also drafts special plans to implement the rules and regulations of the main plan, these too must have the approval of the National Parks Board, their objectives are to establish the means to eliminate exploitation of the parks natural resources, to formulate management activities and research to maintain the existing biological equilibrium and to organise environment education, interpretation and information aimed at visitors (Rodriguez, 1985).

Conservation managers are in charge of each national park and natural area. Each manager has a team of up to ten specialist and outside researchers (Poore and Gryn-Ambroes, 1980). For the socio-economic influence zone, a budget is proposed and the municipalities submit requirements. The Board identifies priorities, submits them to ICONA and releases the funds. Although the administration in national parks is centralised, local representation is still allowed but is limited to submitting opinions only which have no legal means of enforcement (Saussey, 1980).

Marine protected areas come under the Ministry of Agriculture, Fisheries and Food and are managed through ICONA. Protected areas established on state land are administered by ICONA but Article 10 does provide for a management body in each protected area.

The Higher Council for Scientific Investigation (CSIC) is the main state research organisation; it has a scientific advisory committee for nature conservation which advises ICONA (Duffey, 1982).

There are a number of non-governmental organisations concerned with conservation in Spain, some of which are involved in the ownership or management of protected areas. Some of the more important of these organisations include the Association of the Defence of Nature (Asociación para la Defensa de la Naturaleza) (ADENA) which is the branch of the World Wide Fund for Nature in Spain, and the Spanish Ornithological Society (Sociedad Española de Ornitología) (SEO). There are also a number of EUREL reserves in Spain, established under agreement with the European Association for Free Nature Reserves.

Systems Reviews   Spain is one of the largest states in Europe, making up the majority of the Iberian Peninsula, bordering Portugal in the west, Gibraltar in the south and France and Andorra in the north. In the north, the coastline borders the Bay of Biscay and the Atlantic Ocean. The Spanish border then runs inland around Portugal. In the south, west of the Straits of Gibraltar, there is a further short stretch of coastline facing the Atlantic and, east of the Straits, a long stretch of Mediterranean coastline which runs as far as the border with France. This border runs approximately east-west along the Pyrenees and here there is also a short border with Andorra.

Most of the Iberian Peninsula is dominated by the meseta, a vast area of high ground, partly dissected, but with an average height of around 600m. The meseta is a massive block of ancient rock, faulted into a series of plateaux. In addition, there is a series of high mountain ranges, the largest and highest being the Pyrenees in the north-east rising to 3,404m which isolate the Iberian Peninsula from the rest of mainland Europe. Other mountain ranges rising to over 2,000m include the Cordillera Cantabrica in the north-west of Spain and a number of ranges in the central parts of the country; the Sierra de la Demanda, Sierra de Guadarrama, and Sierra de Gredos. In the south, close to the Mediterranean coast, the Sierra Nevada rises to some 3,482m. There are a number of large river systems including the Guadalquivir and the Ebro.

The Balearic Islands lie in the Mediterranean, some 90km east of the mainland. They comprise three main islands – Mallorca, Menorca and Ibiza – and several smaller islands. In general, these islands have a gentle relief, although there are mountains on the north-west coast of the largest island, Mallorca.

The Canary Islands lie some 100km from the south-west coast of Morocco and mainland Africa, and several hundred miles south of the Portuguese island of Madeira. There are seven main islands, comprising: Lanzarote, Fuerteventura, Gran Canaria, Tenerife, La Palma, La Gomera and El Hierro. They are of volcanic origin, and all are mountainous – the highest peak in Spain is the Pico del Teide on Tenerife which reaches 3,718m.

Spain is one of the most floristically-diverse countries in Europe, with nearly 5,000 described vascular species. Originally, much of the country was covered by sclerophyllous forest, although this has been almost entirely removed or degraded into woods or maquis scrub. Some 20-30% of Spain is under forest, although this figure includes plantations: both coniferous and eucalyptus. Along the wetter north coast, there are remnants of a central European type of mixed woodland with oak *Quercus*, beech *Fagus* and Scots pine *Pinus sylvestris*. The rest of Spain is dominated by a Mediterranean climate and flora. Inland, holm oak

Quercus ilex, Pyrenian oak *Q. pyrenaica* and cork oak *Q. suber* were once widespread, although the holm oak forests on the central plateaux are now largely degraded to kermes oak *Q. coccifera* scrub and garigue. Large expanses of dry grassland survive on the slopes of some of the mountain ranges. The original Mediterranean coastal vegetation consisted of aleppo pine *Pinus halepensis*, stone pine *P. pinea* and holm and kermes oak: this has been greatly modified in most places leading to large areas of secondary scrub (maquis) with many introduced exotics, such as palms and cacti (Davis *et al.*, 1986).

Cultivated land takes up some 40% of total land area, while pasture takes up a further 13%. Most of the population is urban, so rural areas tend to have a very low population density (Grimmett and Jones, 1989).

The Balearic Islands have little natural vegetation at low altitudes. Aleppo pine forests and maquis are found in the mountains and along the coast of Mallorca, while Ibiza has perhaps the most extensive aleppo pine forests at higher altitudes (Davis *et al.*, 1986).

The Canary Islands are extremely varied, both physically and biologically. About 2,000 species of native and introduced vascular plant species have been described. There is also a high degree of endemicity, with over 500 endemic plant taxa. Six vegetation types have been described, which show altitudinal zonation: semi-desert succulent scrub (0-700m); juniper scrub (400-600m on southern slopes); tree heath, with *Erica arborea* and evergreen laurel forest (400-1,300m); *Pinus canariensis* savanna (800-1,900m); montane scrub (1,900-2,500m) and subalpine scrub only on the highest peak in Tenerife.

The reclassification of national parks in the 1975 legislation provided an opportunity to extend existing park areas (from some 90,000ha to 156,000ha), but as a consequence required legal provisions with the "Status of Bills" to be submitted to the state Cortes for approval. By 1985, eight of the nine national parks had been approved (Rodriguez, 1985). Protected areas include five national parks (four more in the Canaries), 19 natural sites of national interest, 1 natural park and 36 national game reserves. According to ICONA (1984), the nine national parks cover 123,000ha and the reserves and national game preserves 1,650,000ha.

The possibility of enacting a series of protected marine areas is being studied. ICONA has established two marine parks, one at Cabrera Island (administered by military authorities) and the other at Medas Island (local authority).

The decentralisation of the government in 1978, with the subsequent division of responsibility with respect to protected areas, has led to a somewhat confusing system, whereby new sites have in some cases been designated using non-standard criteria and nomenclature (Lillo, 1988). Further confusion also arises from the fact that there are over 30 agencies with jurisdiction over one or other aspect related to the environment and nature

(Rodriguez, 1985). When the confusion concerning the 1989 Law on the Conservation of Natural Areas, Flora and Wildlife has been resolved, this Law may help to solve a number of these problems.

Loss of natural forests is a major problem. Between 1947 and 1973 as many as 2.1 million ha of native forest had been felled and replaced by 1.2 million ha of eucalyptus plantation, largely for the paper industry (ICBP, 1985). Erosion often occurs in these areas, while pollution from the paper industry apparently disturbs rich fish and mussel grounds (Rudolf de Groot *in litt.*). Acid rain is yet to become a major problem, although it is affecting trees locally in the Valencia region. Forest fires, in contrast, present a much greater threat and it has been suggested that if rates of burning continue at their present levels forests may lose their natural capacity for regeneration. Most fires are intentional and only a small proportion can be attributed to natural causes (Cutrera, 1991). Agricultural developments have also damaged a number of natural ecosystems: there has been a marked increase in irrigated land in recent years and in places this is causing salinification of the soil and encouraging desertification.

Other Relevant Information   Tourism is a major industry and vast areas have been developed, mostly concentrated on the Mediterranean coastline, with over 52 million tourists in 1990. Tourism is a major element of national park philosophy; in many cases areas have become so well visited that they have been damaged. Tourism continues to threaten other areas, both protected and unprotected. Tourist developments in the Coto Donaña area threaten the integrity of this protected area through a multitude of constraints, ranging from visitor pressure to agricultural pollution and excessive water extraction drastically reducing natural water resources from within the park itself.

Addresses

National Institute for Nature Conservation, Instituto Nacional para la Conservación de la Naturaleza (ICONA), Gran Via de San Francisco 35-41, 28005 MADRID (Tel: 1 347 6159/6189; FAX: 1 265 8379; Tlx: 47591 aeico e)

Consejo Superior de Investigaciones Cientificas (CSIC), Serrano 117, 28005 MADRID

Consejo de Pesca Continental Caza y Parques Nacionales, General Sanjurjo 47-30, 28005 MADRID 3

Sociedad Española de Ornitología, Facultad de Biología, Pl.9, 28040 MADRID (Tel: 91 449 3554)

Asociación Defensa de la Naturaleza (ADENA) (WWF-Spain), Santa Engarcia 6, MADRID

Addresses also available for bodies within each of the autonomous communities: Andalusia, Aragon, Asturias, Baleares, Basque, Canary Islands, Cantabria, Castilla, Mancha, Castilla-Leon, Catalonia, Extremadura, Galicia, Madrid, Murcia, Navarra, Rioja, Almeria, Cadiz, Cordoba, Granada, Huelva, Jaen, Malaga and Sevilla in addition to the Valencian Community and the municipalities of Ceuta and Melilla (for the last entry see under Spain – North African Territories).

References

Anon. (1962). XIII/1, Spain, Forest Regulations (Decree No. 485/1962) (Extracts: Preliminary Part and Book I (Forest Property). *Food and Agricultural Legislation*, Vol. XI – No. 2. Food and Agricultural Organisation, Rome. Pp. 1-16.

Anon. (1978). XIX/4 – National Parks and Nature Reserves, Spain – Crown Decree No. 2676/77 approving the Regulation for the enforcement of Act No. 15/1975, of 2 May 1975, on Protected Nature Areas. *Food and Agricultural Legislation*, Vol XXVII. Food and Agricultural Organisation, Rome. Pp. 91-100.

Augier, H. (1985). *Protected marine areas. The example of France and appraisal and prospects.* European Committee for the Conservation of Nature and Natural Resources. Council of Europe, Strasbourg.

Aritio, L.B. (1979). *Parques nacionales españoles.* INCAFO. 192 pp.

Baccar, H. (1977). *A survey of existing and potential marine parks and reserves in the Mediterranean Region.* IUCN-UNEP.

Carp, E. (1980). *Directory of Wetlands of International Importance in Western Palearctic.* UNEP/IUCN. Pp. 346-361.

Child, G. and Grainger J. (1990). *A system plan for protected areas for wildlife conservation and sustainable rural development in Saudi Arabia.* NCWCD, Riyadh, Saudi Arabia. 389 pp.

Cutrera, A. (1991). *European Environmental Yearbook.* Institute for Environmental Studies, Milan. DocTer International, London, UK. 897 pp.

Davis, S.D., Droop, S.J.M., Gregerson, P., Henson, L., Leon, C.J., Lamlein Villa-Lobos, J., Synge, H., and Zantovska, J. (1986). *Plants in danger: what do we know?* Threatened Plants Unit. IUCN, Gland, Switzerland, and Cambridge, UK. 461 pp.

Duffey, E. (1982). *National parks and reserves of Western Europe.* Macdonald and Company, London. Pp. 206-223.

Grunfeld, F.V. (1988). *Wild Spain.* Ebury Press, London, UK. 222 pp.

Gryn-Ambroes, P. (1980). *Preliminary annotated lists of existing and potential Mediterranean protected areas.* IUCN UNEP/IG.20/INF. 5. GE. 80-3092.

ICONA (1984). XVI General Assembly of the IUCN. Conservation in Spain. Summary. 10 pp.

ICONA (1984b). Conservacionismo en España. Información No. 3 *Ambiental.* 47 pp.

ICBP (1985). 81 bird species in Council of Europe countries. Draft report to Council of Europe. International Council for Bird Preservation, Cambridge, UK.

ICBP (1985). Conference of the European Continental Section of ICBP. 22/23 February 1985.

Unpublished. International Council for Bird Preservation, Cambridge.

IUCN (1985). *1985 United Nations List of National Parks and Protected Areas* IUCN Gland and Cambridge. Pp. 175

IUCN (1987). *Directory of Wetlands of International Importance*. IUCN. Gland, Switzerland and Cambridge, UK.

Lillo, A.L. (1988). Protected natural areas in Spain. *Nature and national parks* 26(100): 24-26.

Llorens, V. and Rodriguez, J.A. (1991). *Els espais naturals protegits a espanya, legislació i inventari*. Intitució Valenciana d'Estudis i Investigació, València. 165 pp. (In Catalan).

Medina, F.O. (1977). Spain's national parks policy. *Parks* (2)1: 12-14.

Ortuño, F. and Jorge de la Peña (1976). *Reservas y cotos nacionales de caza. Region Pirenaica Vol. 1, Region Cantabrica, Vol. 2, Region Central, Vol. 3, Region Mediterranean, Vol. 4*. INCAFO, Spain.

Poore, D. and Gryn-Ambroes, P. (1980). *Nature conservation in northern and western Europe*. UNEP/IUCN/WWF, Gland, Switzerland. Pp. 291-314.

Rodriguez, F. (1985). Administration of protected areas in Spain. In: Proceedings of Twenty-fourth Working Session of Commission on National Parks and Protected Areas, Madrid, Spain. 3-4 November 1984. IUCN, Gland, Switzerland.

Saussey, Ch. du (1980). Legislation of wildlife, hunting and protected areas in some European countries. *Legislative Study* No. 20. FAO, Rome.

UNEP (1980). Survey of national legislation relevant to marine and coastal protected areas. Report IG.20/Inf. 3.GE 80-2585 by the Legal Office of the Food and Agriculture Organization of the United Nations based on the work of Ch. du Saussay and M. Prieur.

Wirth, H. (1979) (Ed). *Nature Reserves in Europe*. Edition Leipzig. Pp. 290-293.

ANNEX
Definitions of protected area designations, as legislated, together with authorities responsible for their administration

Title: Ley de Espacios Naturales Protegidos (Law on Protected Natural Areas, Act No. 15/1975, with regulations approved by Crown Decree No. 2676/77)

Date: Act: 2 May 1975; Decree: 4 March 1977

Brief description: To promote nature conservation through the assigning of appropriate special protection status to such areas as stand in need thereof in consideration of their unique significance and interest where nature is concerned.

Administrative authority: National parks: Instituto Nacional para la Conservación de la Naturaleza (ICONA) (National Institute for Nature Conservation);
Other categories: regional authorities

Designations:

Parque nacional (National park) Natural spaces of relatively large area which are declared by law to protect primary ecosystems which have not been substantially altered by exploitation or human occupation. They are sites of outstanding importance for their fauna, flora, cultural heritage, recreational and educational value as well as being areas of natural landscape of outstanding beauty. The Ministry of Agriculture, Fisheries and Food, acting through the National Institute for the Conservation of Nature (ICONA) and as provided in Section 7 of the Act, shall issue a guideline plan prescribing such intervention and measures as are necessary in order to safeguard the characteristics and values justifying the declaration of the national park in question, to facilitate access for the purpose of use, enjoyment and contemplation and the exploitation of the products thereof and to ensure the prevention of any acts that may directly or indirectly result in its destruction, deterioration or defacement.

Parque natural (Natural park) Natural parks shall be those areas which the government, because of their demonstrated natural significance, so declares by decree, on its own initiative or on that of local government authorities, agencies, companies or private persons, with a view to facilitating contact between man and nature (cf. section 5 (1) of the Act). Provision shall be made in the said parks to secure the conservation of their natural value while maintaining the orderly use of their products, including the allowance of access for livestock grazing purposes, while maintaining any such park in a state similar to, or from the evolutionary standpoint concordant with, the state in which it existed at the time of declaration. Such areas may be declared on state, regional or privately-owned land. Independent participation and consultation is allowed for in the legislation, when the protected area relates to the public (Art. 8.2). In the case of communal properties and certain mountainous regions called "montes de comun de vecinos", surveys are organised. The law also provides for the consultation of various professional organisations (corporations, farmers), as well as scientific bodies both in setting up of the protected area and also in the subsequent management.

Reserva integral de interès científico (Integral reserve of scientific interest)   These are natural areas of limited extension which are of exceptional scientific value. Priority is for fauna, flora and physical feature protection and conservation, prohibiting such actions which would result in deterioration, destruction, transformation and disfiguring of the biological communities. The aforesaid reserves may be botanical, zoological or geological reserves as determined by the principal reason justifying their declaration. The precise details of use and regulations, including visitor access, are to be defined based on the specific purpose assigned to such areas. These measures are prescribed in order to obviate any external perturbing influences on the natural environment making up the reserve in question.

May represent individual sites located in otherwise non protected habitats or may form the core or integral reserve area within protected areas such as national parks or natural parks.

Paraje natural de interès nacional (Natural area of national interest)   Tracts of country, sites or single natural features which, being in all cases of limited extension, are declared in view of the important needs necessitated by their specific and unique values. Designation aims to ensure conservation of flora, fauna, geomorphical features, sites of special beauty, or other elements of exceptional natural status. The enjoyment of and visits to such sites together with the exploitation of the products thereof shall proceed in conformity with the rules prescribed by the Ministry of Agriculture and in a manner compatible with the conservation of the values justifying the declaration of the precinct in question.

The designation is more concerned with landscape protection and traditional land use than solely with wildlife protection.

Sources: Anon., 1978; ICONA, *in litt.*, 1988.

Title: Decree No. 3128/82

Date: 15 October 1982

Brief description: Provides for the designation of national biological reserves as an addition to the categories of protected area covered under the 1975 Law on Protected Natural Areas

Administrative authority: Institute Nacional para la Conservación de la Naturaleza (ICONA) (National Institute for Nature Conservation)

Designations:

Reserva biologica nacional (National biological reserve)   These are areas which are necessary the strict management of biological and natural equilibria, conservation of the integrity of existing communities of fauna and flora, as well as the genetic resources implied.

Source: ICONA, *in litt.*, 1988

Title: Ley No. 4 de Conservación de los Espacios Naturales, de la Flora y Fauna Silvestres (Law No 4 on the Conservation of Natural Areas, Flora and Wildlife)

Date: 27 March 1989

Brief description: Largely replaces the Law on Protected Natural Areas of 1975; provides the autonomous communities with the power to designate four categories of protected areas and also covers wider issues of national resource planning and flora and fauna preservation.

Administrative authority: Autonomous communities (Andalusia, Aragon, Asturias, Baleares, Basque, Canary Islands, Cantabria, Castilla, Mancha, Castilla-Leon, Catalonia, Extremadura, Galicia, Madrid, Murcia, Navarra, Rioja, Almeria, Cadiz, Cordoba, Granada, Huelva, Jaen, Malaga and Sevilla).

Institute Nacional para la Conservación de la Naturaleza (ICONA) (National Institute for Nature Conservation)

Designations:

Parque (Park)   Natural areas that have had little or no alteration by man and that are declared for reasons of their interest or value of their natural elements, or because they represent a fine example of the principle ecosystems and natural regions found in the national territory.

Limited exploitation of natural resources is possible, although any exploitation which is incompatible with the purposes of the declaration are prohibited. Permitted activities include tourism.

Administration follows guidelines given in the Principle Plan for Use and Management, which will state regulations and will be periodically reviewed, and are obligatory for each area.

Reserva natural (Natural reserve)   Natural areas that require protection to conserve their ecosystems, communities, or biological elements that are rare, fragile or unique.

Exploitation is limited except when this is compatible with protection objectives.

In order for a park of a natural reserve to be established a management plan must first be approved

Monumento natural (Natural monument) Natural area with elements of singular beauty, including geological formations and archaeological sites.

Paisaje protegido (Protected landscape) Natural or seminatural areas with aesthetic or cultural value

Source: Llorens and Rodriguez, 1991

Title: Ley Foral de normas urbanisticas regionales para protección y uso del territorio (6/1987) (Law of Regional Urban Standards for the Protection and Use of the Territory)

Date: 10 April 1987

Brief description:

Administrative authority: Institute Nacional para la Conservación de la Naturaleza (ICONA) (National Institute for Nature Conservation)

Designations:

Espacio natural (Natural area) Defined as areas with certain ecological or landscape values, declared as such "to ensure their preservation or improvement, so that permitted activities may take place without altering the said values".

Reserva natural parcial (Partial natural reserve) Areas with high ecological values declared as such in order to ensure the preservation and improvement of defined geological formations or phenomena, especially biotopes, communities or ecosystems, and their evolution. Human activities to redress exceptional imbalances or developments are permitted, providing that those elements subject to protection are not compromised or impaired.

Source: ICONA, *in litt.*, 1988

Title: Ley des Montes (Law on Forestry) and Decreto por el que se aprueba el Reglemento de Montes No. 485/1962 (Forest Regulations Decree)

Date: Act: 8 June 1957; Decree: 22 February 1962

Brief description: The Act and Decree together contain the main legal provisions governing most of the forestry sector.

Administrative authority: Institute Nacional para la Conservación de la Naturaleza (ICONA) (National Institute for Nature Conservation) and the governments of the autonomous regions (Andalusia, Aragon, Asturias, Baleares, Basque, Canary Islands, Cantabria, Castilla, Mancha, Castilla-Leon, Catalonia, Extremadura, Galicia, Madrid, Murcia, Navarra, Rioja, Almeria, Cadiz, Cordoba, Granada, Huelva, Jaen, Malaga and Sevilla).

Designations:

Forest of general public utility Declared in public forests and forests used by the public, which may have any of the following characteristics: forests at the headwaters of river basins; forests which may usefully serve to regulate and change the rainfall; forests which hold together soil or sand dunes, prevent landslides or resist erosion; forests which assist in marsh reclamation; forests which ensure the continuance of satisfactory or hygienic economic and social conditions in neighbouring towns and villages or, in general, wooded areas or forest lands whose position or area is such as to make their maintenance or replanting necessary as a result of their national or local economic or physical influence for public health reasons, for improvement of the water system, protection of the land and its fertility for agricultural purposes, or by reason of their usefulness for national defence, upon request by the military authorities.

Protective forest Privately-owned, but may be declared for any of the reasons given above, or as a result of special legislation.

Source: Anon., 1962

Title: Ley sobre Creación de Reservas Nacionales de Caza (Law on the creation of national hunting reserves) No. 37/1966 and Ley de Caza (Law on hunting) No. 1/1970

Date: 31 May 1966 and 4 April 1970

Brief description: Contain the main legal provisions concerning the establishment and subsequent protection of the different categories of hunting reserves.

Administrative authority: Bodies set up in each of the 17 regional governments (Grunfeld, 1988) (Andalusia, Aragon, Asturias, Baleares, Basque, Canary Islands, Cantabria, Castilla, Mancha, Castilla-Leon, Catalonia, Extremadura, Galicia, Madrid, Murcia, Navarra, Rioja, Almeria, Cadiz, Cordoba, Granada, Huelva, Jaen, Malaga and Sevilla).

Designations:

Reserva nacional de caza (National hunting reserve) May be publically or privately owned. They are areas which are considered important as core areas for hunting, and as important sites for the maintenance and regeneration of wild fauna, notably game species. The areas surrounding many of these sites have been destroyed or damaged through uncontrolled exploitation to such an extent that they have reached a critical situation or are in danger of disappearing. Hunting is a very important feature of these reserves, it is often considered a necessary form of management and actively encouraged, although it remains controlled.

Coto nacional de caza (National hunting sanctuary) Essentially very similar to reserves in both the reasons for their designation and the restrictions imposed. Perhaps the major difference is that they may only be declared on nationally owned land. As a result, because there is no third party involved in the designation of sites, the legal formalities involved in declaring a site are less strict and complex.

Refugio nacional de caza (National hunting refuge) Areas where, for biological, scientific or educational reasons, it is necessary to ensure the conservation of determined species of game.

Sources: Ortuño and Peña, 1976; ICONA, *in litt.*, 1988

Title: Ley de Patrimonio Historico Español (Ley 13/1985) (Spanish Historical Heritage Law)

Date: 25 June 1985

Brief description: Largely intended for the protection of cultural sites and, among other things, provides for the designation of property of cultural interest.

Administrative authority: Regional governments and, to a lesser degree, local authorities (Andalusia, Aragon, Asturias, Baleares, Basque, Canary Islands, Cantabria, Castilla, Mancha, Castilla-Leon, Catalonia, Extremadura, Galicia, Madrid, Murcia, Navarra, Rioja, Almeria, Cadiz, Cordoba, Granada, Huelva, Jaen, Malaga and Sevilla).

Designations:

Bien de interès cultural (Property of cultural interest) Elements, movable or immovable, which are considered to be an integral part of the historical heritage. Such objects or sites may be declared because of their artistic, historical, palaeontological, archaeological, ethnographic, scientific or technical interest. This designation could potentially lead to the protection of sites of ecological importance.

Source: Cutrera, 1991

SUMMARY OF PROTECTED AREAS

Map† ref.	National/international designations Name of area	IUCN management category	Area (ha)	Year notified
	National Parks			
1	Aigues Tortes y Lago de San Mauricio	II	10,230	1955
2	Caldera de Taburiente	II	4,690	1954
3	Donana	II	50,720	1969
4	Garajonay	II	3,984	1981
5	Montana de Covadonga	II	16,925	1918
6	Ordesa y Monte Perdido	II	15,608	1918
7	Tablas de Daimiel	II	1,928	1973
8	Teide	II	13,571	1954
9	Timanfaya	II	5,107	1974
	National Biological Reserve			
10	Bosque de Muniellos	V	5,542	1982
	Natural Reserves			
11	Caidas de la Negra	IV	1,926	1987
12	Els Aiguamolls de l'Emporda	IV	4,866	1983
13	Foz de Arbayun	IV	1,164	1987
14	Laguna de Fuentepiedra	IV	1,364	1984
15	Larra	IV	2,353	1987
16	Mas de Melons	IV	1,140	1987
	National Hunting Reserves			
17	Alto Pallars-Aran	IV	94,231	1966
18	Arroyo de la Rocina	IV	1,005	
19	Bahla del Santona	IV	2,893	
20	Benasque	IV	23,750	1966
21	Cadi	IV	27,202	1966
22	Cameros	IV	92,918	1973
23	Cerdana	IV	19,437	1966
24	Cijara	IV	24,999	1966
25	Cortes de la Frontera	IV	12,342	1973
26	Degana	IV	11,914	1966
27	Fresser y Setcasas	IV	20,200	1966
28	Fuentes Carrionas	IV	47,755	1966
29	Islas d'Espalmador, Espardell y Islotes	IV	175	
30	La Buitrera	IV	1,200	1982
31	Las Batuecas	IV	20,976	1973
32	Los Ancares Leoneses	IV	38,300	1973
33	Los Ancares	IV	7,975	1966
34	Los Circos	IV	22,844	1966
35	Los Valles	IV	28,765	1966
36	Mampodre	IV	30,858	1966
37	Montes Universales	IV	59,260	1973
38	Muela de Cortes	IV	36,009	1973
39	Picos de Europa	IV	7,630	1970
40	Puertos de Beceite	IV	30,418	1966
41	Ria de Villaviciosa	IV	1,032	
42	Ria del Eo	IV	2,000	
43	Riano	IV	71,538	1966
44	Saja	IV	180,186	1966
45	Serrania de Cuenca	IV	25,724	1973
46	Serrania de Ronda	IV	21,982	1970
47	Sierra Espuna	IV	13,855	1973
48	Sierra Nevada	IV	35,430	1966
49	Sierra de Gredos	IV	22,815	1970

Map[†] ref.	National/international designations Name of area	IUCN management category	Area (ha)	Year notified
50	Sierra de Tejeda y Almijara	IV	20,398	1973
51	Sierra de la Culebra	IV	65,891	1973
52	Sierra de la Demanda	IV	73,819	1973
53	Somiedo	IV	89,650	1966
54	Sonsaz	IV	68,106	1973
55	Sueve	IV	8,300	1966
56	Urbion	IV	100,023	1973
57	Villafafila	IV	42,000	1986
58	Vinamala	IV	49,230	1966
	Protected Landscapes			
59	Brazo del Este	V	1,336	1989
60	Desfiladero de los Gaitanes	V	2,016	1989
61	Desierto de Tabernas	V	11,625	1989
62	Embalse de Cordobilla	V	1,460	1989
63	Karst de Yesos de Sorbas	V	2,375	1989
64	Ladera de Vallebron	V	2,142	1987
65	Los Ajaches	V	2,876	1987
66	Los Reales de Sierra Bermeja	V	1,236	1989
67	Macizo de Pedraforca	V	1,671	1982
68	Macizo de Tauro	V	1,179	1987
69	Marismas de Isla Cristina	V	2,145	1989
70	Marismas del Odiel	V	7,185	1984
71	Marismas del Rio Piedras y Flecha del Rompido	V	2,530	1989
72	Punta Entina-Sabinar	V	1,960	1989
73	Sierra Alhamilla	V	8,500	1989
74	Sierra Pelada y Rivera del Asserador	V	12,980	1989
75	Torcal de Antequera	V	1,171	1978
76	Valle del Monasterio de Poblet	V	2,477	1984
77	Vertiente sur del Massis de l'Albera	V	2,413	1986
	Natural Areas of National Interest			
78	Albufera des Grau	IV	1,187	1986
79	Cumbre, Circo y Lagunas de Penalara	IV	1,012	1930
80	Es Trenc Salobrar de Campos	IV	1,493	1984
81	Pinar de la Acebeda	IV	1,000	1930
82	Salines d'Eivissa i Formentera	IV	1,180	1985
	Natural Area			
83	Ses Salines de Ibiza, Formentera e Islotes	IV	1,180	1985
	Nature Parks (Natural Parks)			
84	Acantilado y Pinar de Barbate	V	2,017	1989
85	Albufera de Valencia	V	21,000	1986
86	Anaga	V	14,119	1987
87	Ayagaures y Pilancones	V	10,166	1987
88	Bahia de Cadiz	V	10,000	1989
89	Bandama	V	1,508	1987
90	Barranco Quintero, El Rio, La Madera y Dorado	V	1,485	1987
91	Barranco de la Rajita y Roque de la Fortaleza	V	1,788	1987
92	Barranco de las Angustias	V	1,508	1987
93	Barrancos de los Hombres y Fagundo y Acantila	V	1,058	1987
94	Betancuria	V	15,538	1987
95	Cabaneros	V	25,615	1988
96	Cabo de Gata-Nijar	V	26,000	1987
97	Cadi Moixero	V	41,342	1983
98	Canon del Rio Lobos	V	9,580	1985
99	Carrascal de la Font Roja	V	2,450	1987
100	Cornalvo	V	10,570	1988

Map[†] ref.	National/international designations Name of area	IUCN management category	Area (ha)	Year notified
101	Corona Forestal de Tenerife	V	37,173	1987
102	Cuenca Alta del Rio Manzanares	V	37,500	1978
103	Cuenca de Tejeda	V	5,968	1987
104	Cumbre Vieja y Teneguia	V	8,023	1987
105	Cumbres	V	8,929	1987
106	Dehesa del Moncayo	V	1,389	1978
107	Delta del Ebro	V	7,736	1983
108	Despenaperros	V	6,000	1989
109	Dunas de Corralejo e Isla de Lobos	V	2,526	1982
110	El Hierro	V	11,980	1987
111	El Montgo	V	2,700	1987
112	Entorno de Donana	V	54,250	1989
113	Guayadeque	V	1,203	1987
114	Hayedo de Tejera Negra	V	1,641	1978
115	Inagua, Ojeda y Pajonales	V	8,448	1987
116	Islas Cies	V	433	1980
117	Islotes del Norte de Lanzarote y de los Risco	V	8,929	1986
118	Jandia	V	11,938	1987
119	La Geria	V	15,189	1987
120	La Isleta	V	1,258	1987
121	Ladera S. Ursula, Los Organos, Altos del Vall	V	12,114	1987
122	Lago de Sanabria	V	5,027	1978
123	Lagunas de Ruidera	V	3,772	1979
124	Los Alcornocales	V	170,025	1989
125	Macizo de Adeje y Barranco del Infierno	V	2,057	1987
126	Macizo de Pena Cabarga	V	2,588	1989
127	Macizo de Suroeste	V	10,538	1987
128	Majona	V	1,920	1987
129	Monfrague	V	17,852	1979
130	Montana de Montserrat	V	3,630	1987
131	Monte Doramas	V	4,262	1987
132	Monte Lentiscal	V	2,969	1987
133	Monte el Valle	V	1,900	1979
134	Montes de Malaga	V	4,762	1989
135	Montes de los Sauces y Punta Llana	V	3,173	1987
136	Montseny	V	17,370	1928
137	Pozo Negro	V	9,237	1987
138	S'Albufera de Mallorca	V	1,700	1988
139	Saja Besaya	V	24,500	1988
140	Sant Llorenc de Munt i L'Obal	V	9,638	1987
141	Senorio de Bertiz	V	2,040	1984
142	Sierra Nevada	V	140,200	1989
143	Sierra de Aracena y Picos de Aroche	V	184,000	1989
144	Sierra de Baza	V	52,337	1989
145	Sierra de Cardena y Montoro	V	41,212	1989
146	Sierra de Castril	V	12,265	1989
147	Sierra de Cazorla, Segurla y las Villas	V	214,300	1986
148	Sierra de Grazalema	V	51,695	1984
149	Sierra de Hornachuelos	V	67,202	1989
150	Sierra de Huetor	V	12,428	1989
151	Sierra de Maria	V	18,962	1987
152	Sierra de las Nieves	V	16,564	1989
153	Sierras Magina	V	19,900	1989
154	Sierras Subbeticas de Cordoba	V	31,568	1988
155	Sierras de Andujar	V	60,800	1989
156	Somiedo	V	29,122	1988
157[†]	Tamadaba	V	8,010	1987

Map[†] ref.	National/international designations Name of area	IUCN management category	Area (ha)	Year notified
158	Teno	V	7,647	1987
159	Tigaiga	V	1,735	1987
160	Urkiola	V	5,768	1989
161	Valle Gran Rey	V	1,960	1987
162	Volcan de la Corona y el Malpais de la Corona	V	2,690	1987
163	Zona Volcanica de la Garrotxa	V	12,112	1982
	Biosphere Reserves			
	Canal y los Tiles	IX	511	1983
	Doñana	IX	77,260	1980
	Grazalema Reserve	IX	32,210	1977
	Las Sierras de Cazorla y Segura	IX	190,000	1983
	Mancha Humeda	IX	25,000	1980
	Marismas del Odiel	IX	8,728	1983
	Montseny National Park	IX	17,372	1978
	Ordesa-Vinamala Reserve	IX	51,396	1977
	Sierra Nevada	IX	190,000	1986
	Ramsar Sites			
	Complejo Intermareal O Umia-Grove, La Lanzada, Punta Carreirón y Lagoa Bodeira	R	2,561	1989
	Doñana	R	49,225	1982
	Laguna de Fuentapiedra	R	1,355	1983
	Lagunas de Cadiz	R	158	1989
	a) Laguna de Medina			
	b) Laguna Salada del Puerto			
	Lagunas del Sur de Cordoba	R	86	1989
	a) Laguna de Zóñar			
	b) Laguna Amarga			
	c) Laguna del Rincón			
	Laguna de la Vega o del Pueblo	R	34	1989
	Lagunas de Villafáfila	R	2,854	1989
	L'Albufera de Valencia	R	21,000	1989
	Las Tablas de Daimiel	R	1,812	1982
	Marismas del Odiel	R	7,185	1989
	Rías de Ortigueira y Ladrido	R	2,920	1989
	Pantano de el Hondo	R	2,337	1989
	Prat de Cabanes – Torreblanca	R	860	1989
	Salinas del Cabo de Gata	R	300	1989
	Salinas de la Mata y Torrevieja	R	2,100	1989
	Salinas de Santa Pola	R	2,400	1989
	S'Albufera de Mallorca	R	1,700	1989
	World Heritage Site			
	Garajonay National Park	X	3,984	1986

[†]Locations of most protected areas are shown on the accompanying maps.

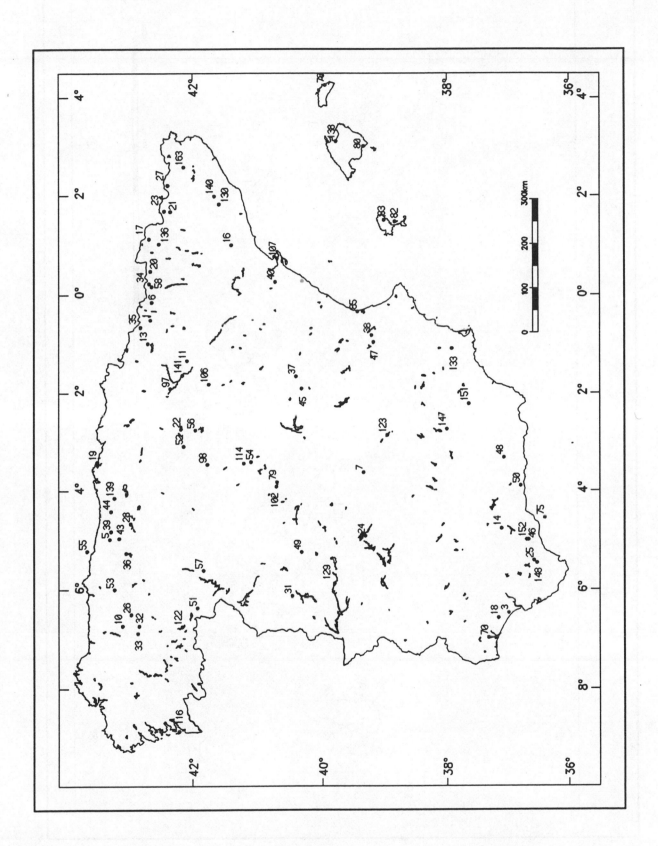

Protected Areas of Spain

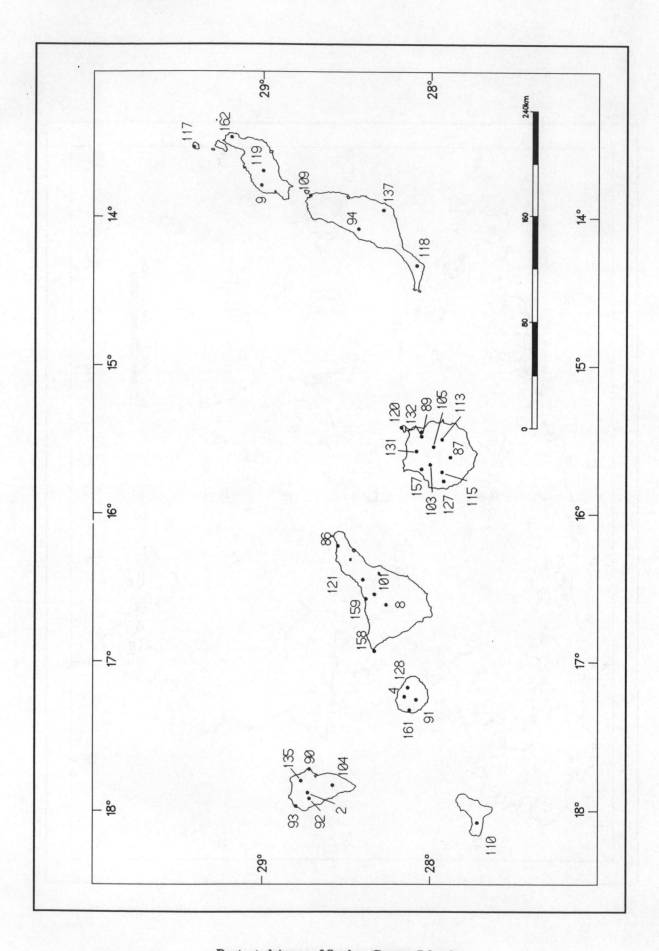

Protected Areas of Spain – Canary Islands

SWEDEN

Area   440,940 sq. km

Population   8,444,000 (1990)
Natural increase: 0.15% per annum

Economic Indicators
GDP: US$ 19,109 per capita (1987)
GNP: US$ 15,690 per capita (1987)

Policy and Legislation   The present constitution came into force in 1975. Sweden was the first European country to enact legislation on national parks. The first conservation act, The Protection of Nature Act, was passed in 1909 and provided for the establishment and protection of national parks, crown reserves (for forests) and natural monuments such as geological features and individual trees. This law is no longer valid and the statutory texts are now largely covered under the Nature Conservancy Act (below) (NEPA, *in litt.*, 1991).

The most important component of protected areas legislation is the Nature Conservancy Act, 1964 (No. 822 in the Swedish Statute Role) with various amendments (notably in 1973, 1976 and 1987). The Act prescribes ways in which national parks, nature reserves and natural monuments are to be established and managed (see Annex), and defines methods by which plants and animals may be afforded protection. A Royal proclamation issued in 1964 lays down ways in which the Act must be implemented and administered. A further proclamation, issued in 1965 and dealing with establishment of wildlife sanctuaries, was incorporated into the Nature Conservancy Act in 1976 (see Annex). In 1974 a further amendment to the 1964 Act provided for the establishment of nature conservation areas (also known as landscape management areas) (see Annex) (Poore and Gryn-Ambroes, 1980). Under Section 14 of the Act the County Board may establish by-laws which restrict activities such as hunting, fishing or even access within specified "protected species areas". This is designed to give additional protection to flora and fauna defined as endangered under the Act. There are a number of islands in the archipelagos and lakes which are declared as endangered bird areas, to which access is prohibited during the breeding season (Michanek, 1991).

Section 18 of the Nature Conservancy Act provides protection for wetlands drainage of wetlands is placed under permit control. In deciding whether to grant a permit, the county board shall balance the ecological value of a site against the advantages of its exploitation. Further to this, the government may identify specific areas where "protection is especially urgent" and prohibit any drainage (Michanek, 1991). The Act provides for non-site specific protection from development of all land and water within 100m of the shores of lakes, rivers and the sea. This legislation is primarily designed to safeguard such areas for recreational use, but there is an obvious benefit to nature conservation. Some county administrations have used powers given them under Section 15 of the Act to extend this zone of protection to 300m (Poore and Gryn-Ambroes, 1980). The Act also provides further conditions for nature conservation by requiring consultation with the county board prior to any activity which may lead to the "significant alteration of nature". Consultation areas are established and by-laws for each of these specify the types of activity (e.g. tree-felling, use of pesticides) which will always require prior consultation, negligence of this duty being a criminal offence. A new, 1991 provision in the Act states that "exploitations and other harmful activities may not be carried out in smaller land or water areas (biotopes) which are habitats for endangered species of flora or fauna or which in other respects are especially worthy of protection", such types of biotopes to be identified in regulations or by-laws. No biotopes have yet been identified (July 1991); biotopes mentioned in the legislation as worthy of protection in the future include alder forests, wetlands, and certain types of cultivated land (Michanek, 1991).

In addition to the protected areas covered under the 1964 Nature Conservancy Act, provisions for nature conservation are also included in forestry legislation. The National Board of Crown Forests and Lands (now known as the Forest Service) has created some 800 crown reserves under the 1909 Protection of Nature Act. In 1974 the Beech Forest Law was passed, strictly regulating the future management of such forest and restricting its felling. The Forestry Act of 7 June 1979 (Act No. 429) contains a provision for "forests difficult to regenerate and protected forests", the cutting of trees within these forests is restricted, and requires permission of the County Forestry Board. A more general requirement of the same law is that conservation interests should be considered by all landowners undertaking forestry activities. In this respect, the National Board of Forestry issued "prescriptions and general advice" for all kinds of forestry operations. It is stated that the limitations should be placed on the area that is to be clear-felled, and that, out of consideration for the wildlife, unproductive forest, as well as small areas of productive forest should be left particular examples are specified. In most cases, adhesion to these guidelines requires the interest and support of the landowners concerned (Larsson, 1990). In 1983 the Deciduous Forests Law was passed.

The Environmental Protection Act, 1969 provides protection for specific areas against pollution. Under Section 8a specified areas of land or water may be designated as "protected environment areas" if protection is especially urgent". By-laws specify the precautions which must be taken to prevent pollution from point-sources or more general sources (such as fertilisers) (Michanek, 1991).

The Natural Resources Act of 1987 provides a limited form of protection to wide areas of the country: it deals with the long-term use of natural resources and attempts to strike a balance between differing interests. Under the Act areas of national importance are designated. Their importance may be for recreation or nature conservation and areas so declared will often obtain a degree of protection for their natural value (see Annex). Areas of national importance may also be declared for other reasons, such as military purposes, fishing and mining (NEPA, *in litt.*, 1991).

In Sweden all people have the right, subject to certain limitations, to cross, at least on foot, other people's property, including protected areas, and to remain there for short periods. This principle of common law is quoted in the preamble to the Nature Conservancy Act, 1964.

The National Environment Protection Agency (*Naturvardsverket*) (NEPA), which plays a major role in the administration and management of protected areas, was established by Statute No. 444 in 1967.

The protection afforded to national parks and to nature reserves is to a large degree dependent on the individual by-laws affecting each site: there are a number of sites which appear to have poor protection, and as a result have been considerably degraded by man's activities since their designation. The National Environment Protection Agency has recommended the downgrading or declassification of a number of these sites (Larsson, pers. comm., 1991).

The legal principle entitling landowners to compensation when their land-use is restricted by the designation of protected area status has been said to be preventing efficient nature conservation in many situations. The adoption of a "polluter pays" principle, covered to some degree in the Environmental Protection Act, and mentioned in the preambles to the 1991 amendments to the Nature Conservancy Act, may reduce this problem when if it is given a wider legal application in the future (Michanek, 1991).

International Activities   Sweden is party to the Convention on Wetlands of International Importance Especially as Waterfowl Habitat (Ramsar Convention), following accession on 18 March 1985. Thirty sites have been listed (1990). It ratified its membership of the Convention concerning the Protection of the World Cultural and Natural Heritage (World Heritage Convention) on 22 January 1985, but no natural sites have been inscribed. One site has been nominated under the Unesco Man and the Biosphere programme.

Sweden is a member of the Council of Europe: ten Council of Europe biogenetic reserves have been declared, and a further 32 sites have been proposed to the Secretariat. Six sites have been awarded the Council of Europe European Diploma. Sweden has signed the Helsinki Convention on the Protection of the Marine Environment of the Baltic Sea. It is not a member of the EC and hence is not bound by its environmental agreements. It has, however, signed and ratified the Bern Convention on the Conservation of European Wildlife and Natural Habitats. The Nordic Council, of which Sweden is a member state, is involved in quite a number of environmental protection issues: the Nordic Council of Ministers has run a series of four to five-year environmental protection programmes, the present programme beginning in 1988. These programmes cover a wide range of activities which include, among other things, bringing greater attention to nature conservation in connection with planning activities. The Council has encouraged the registration of valuable landscapes in the Nordic area, the concentration of conservation efforts towards the preservation of particularly important habitat types and the use of natural areas by the wider public for recreation purposes. It has also encouraged the development of a standardised data collection for monitoring environmental quality (Nordic Council of Ministers, 1983). Sweden is also a party to the Nordic Environmental Protection Convention, which requires authorities to take into account the environmental consequences to all other parties before granting permits for environmentally damaging activities (Nordic Council of Ministers, 1978).

There are a number of transboundary protected areas the most notable being with Norway: the proposed Rogen-Langfjallet National Park (currently Rogen Nature Reserve) and Femundsmarka National Park; Sarek/Padjelanta/Sonfjallet national parks and Rago National Park. Cooperation also exists between the USSR and Sweden within the framework of a Joint Working Group on Environmental Protection under the Soviet-Swedish Intergovernmental Commission on Economic and Scientific and Technical Cooperation. Among the primary areas of cooperation is the conservation of ecological systems and individual species of flora and fauna (Anon., 1989).

Administration and Management   Until 1976 the Forest Service had responsibility for the management of all national parks and most nature reserves. A new ordinance in 1976 led to major changes in organisation and management. The NEPA, established in 1967, is the central administrative authority responsible for the nature conservation of all protected areas. It administers the Nature Conservation Fund, which essentially gives it responsibility for the management of national parks and all state-owned protected areas in consultation with the county administrations; it issues regulations concerning national parks and designates management authorities, in consultation with the county administrations; it formulates management policy and issues instructions regarding management and utilisation. It also supervises research and surveys in protected areas; it is the central authority responsible for information about protected areas and is responsible for the provision of state grants regarding land use/resource management and buildings, landscape conservation and management of beech forests (Larsson, 1977).

There are a total of 24 county administrations (*Länsstyrelse*) across Sweden, each of which with a section responsible for conservation work. These are responsible, at the county level, for establishing and managing nature reserves, nature conservation areas, natural monuments and wildlife sanctuaries in consultation with the NEPA. They issue management regulations and designate management authorities responsible for the day-to-day management of protected areas in consultation with NEPA. They also apply for and allocate grants from NEPA towards the management of protected areas and are responsible for biological surveys and the preparation of management plans and information about protected areas. County administrations may appoint a management council to act as an advisory committee in questions related to management (Larsson, 1977).

The management authorities responsible for the day-to-day management of protected areas in accordance with ratified management plans, and on advice from the management council, vary depending on the type of protected area. The Forest Service is responsible for national parks (subordinated to NEPA) and state-owned protected areas; the county forestry board is responsible for privately owned protected areas; municipalities or local foundations are responsible for municipality-owned protected areas; while, for a limited number of privately owned areas, responsibility falls to certain associations or private persons (Larsson, 1977). From January 1992 the county administrations will be given greater responsibility concerning national parks. From that date they will be responsible for nature management, including issuing permits for different activities. The NEPA still has the right of appeal on decisions taken by the administration (NEPA, *in litt.*, 1991).

There are a number of privately-owned reserves in Sweden. The Swedish Society for Nature Conservation (*Svenska Natursyddsföreningen*) is the largest private conservation organisation, receiving a substantial annual grant from the government to support its work (Duffey, 1982). It owns a number of sites across the country (20 in 1990, covering 3,900ha), and is responsible for the management of a number of others. Around half of these sites have been recognised formally as nature reserves by the appropriate county administration (Poore and Gryn-Ambroes, 1980).

Systems Reviews   Sweden is the largest of the three Scandinavian countries, with a long border shared with Norway, a shorter border shared with Finland and an extensive coastline along the Gulf of Bothnia and the Baltic Sea. Most of the country is underlain by ancient, precambrian rocks, the Fennoscandian shield. Areas of younger rock are very limited in extent and distribution. Most of northern Sweden, and the western side of the country along the border with Norway, is mountainous. Several peaks in the north of are over 2,000m. The landscape has been heavily shaped by the cycle of glacial and interglacial stages during the Quaternary. Thus,

there are many characteristic glacial and peri-glacial features: ground down mountain tops, U-shaped valleys, ribbon lakes, moraines, drumlins, areas of denuded soil cover and other areas of deep glacial drift (Grimmett and Jones, 1989). There are over 90,000 lakes covering some 9% of the country. If other wetland types are considered, this figure rises to some 20-25% (Anon., 1987). About 9% is agricultural land (Poore and Gryn-Ambroes, 1980).

Forests cover some 23.5 million ha, about 57% of the land area. Much of this is in the form of coniferous plantations, but around 25% of the total forest area consists of natural or semi-natural forests over 100 years old. In the south-west coastal fringe the climax vegetation is dominated by such species as European beech, which are able to thrive because of the mild oceanic climate. This beech forest has largely been cleared for agriculture or settlement, and in places land has degenerated to heathland. Much of the rest of southern Sweden is covered by forests which make up the transition between Nemoral and Boreal zones. These are typically mixed forests, with Scots pine *Pinus sylvestris* and Norway spruce *Picea abies*, hazel *Corylus avellana* and oak *Quercus* sp. Most of the remaining parts of the country fall in the Boreal zone, which is effectively a western extension of the Eurasian taiga, with large expanses of low diversity coniferous forests, interspersed with *Sphagnum* bogs and fenlands, and with birch *Betula nana* forests in colder areas. In the highest and northernmost areas there is a alpine zone with arctic alpine species including willow *Cassiope* sp. and lichens. Between 1978 and 1981 a systematic national survey produced an inventory of natural and semi-natural forest (Heiss, 1987). Despite the huge area of forest only 4% remains unmanaged (Davis *et al.*, 1986; Grimmett and Jones, 1989; Heiss, 1987). During recent years the protection of natural/virgin forests has been given high priority. In 1988, 33 areas of northern Sweden were given protection, covering some 730,000ha of forest land. In all about 1 million ha of mountain forest are fully protected (NEPA, *in litt.*, 1991).

Sweden was the first European country to enact national park legislation with the 1909 Protection of Nature Act. In the same year, seven national parks were designated covering some 348,500ha. The protected areas network increased greatly following the 1964 Nature Conservancy Act: by 1978 there were 16 national parks and 1,008 nature reserves, as well as 435 wildlife sanctuaries, 1,185 natural monuments and 750 crown reserves. In 1991 there were some 22 national parks, covering 631,000ha, and 1,381 nature reserves covering just under 2 million ha. In 1991 there were 215 areas of national importance for recreation, covering 10.8 million ha and 1,366 areas of national importance for nature conservation, covering 10.1 million ha, which together cover some 30% of total land area (NEPA, in litt., 1991).

In 1978 the National Environmental Protection Agency was commissioned by the cabinet to initiate a National

Swedish Environmental Monitoring Programme (PMK). PMK took over responsibility for a number of investigations which had already been running for some time, but has also initiated many new investigations, often in cooperation with groups such as the University of Stockholm, the Swedish Environmental Research Group, the Geological Survey of Sweden, the Swedish Meteorological and Hydrological Institute, The Swedish Ornithological Society and the Swedish Museum of Natural History. Much of PMK's work concerns monitoring the terrestrial environment, and the effects of environmental disturbance on the flora, fauna and the physical environment. It work is divided into several sub-programmes, namely: air and precipitation, soil and vegetation, birds and mammals, ground water and drainage water, waterways and lakes, seas and coastal waters and toxic substances in living organisms. PMK performs much of its terrestrial monitoring in some twenty reference areas, for which detailed inventories exist, situated in relatively isolated areas. The total PMK budget was US$ 6.5 million for the financial year 1991/1992 (Anon., 1985a, 1985b; NEPA, *in litt.*, 1991). A computer data base has been set up by the Swedish Museum of Natural History with the National Environmental Protection Agency, which contains much of the information obtained by PMK (Anon., 1985c).

In 1989 radical changes to the national parks system were proposed by the National Environment Protection Agency in the "Plan for New National Parks in Sweden". Twenty new national parks have been proposed; four existing parks should be reconstructed and amalgamated into bigger parks; three existing parks should be expanded and four others should be totally or partially transformed into nature reserves. If these proposals are carried out, the number of national parks will be increased to 33, and the area covered will be 2,257,800ha or 5% of the total land area (Naturvardsverket, 1989).

In 1990 NEPA presented the government with five action programmes to prevent or reduce continuing damage to the environment: these cover air and marine pollution, action on chemical, nature conservation and freshwater conservation. A number of recommendations for the cleaning up of the Baltic are made under the marine pollution action programme (Arby, 1990). Among the proposals in the nature conservation action programme are the introduction of regulations to protect relict habitats within landscapes modified by man; considerable restrictions should be placed on artificial drainage projects and further wetlands should be created or recreated in agricultural areas; and where land is being forested a greater proportion of deciduous trees should be planted (Terstad, 1990). The freshwater conservation action programme addresses the issues of acidification, eutrophication and toxic pollutants (Sandberg, 1990).

Threats to the natural systems, and especially those within protected areas come from many sources. All except four of the major river systems have been destroyed by a series of dams and hydroelectric plants (Curry-Lindahl, 1984). Road building, mining

exploration and deforestation have seriously affected four national parks in Lapland and several Ramsar sites (Curry-Lindahl, 1984). Marine sites are severely affected by pollution in the Baltic Sea, one of the most polluted seas in the world, with high levels of chlorinated hydrocarbons including PCBs, mercury compounds and other toxic chemicals. Pulp mills are also a major source of such pollution. Extensive eutrophication is also a problem, largely caused by nitrogen and phosphate run-off from agricultural areas (Curry-Lindahl, 1984). Acidification of the environment through acid rain and dry deposition, the main pollutants being sulphur dioxide and nitrogen dioxide, is a major problem facing the entire country. A national inventory carried out in 1985 showed that approximately 15,000 lakes have been acidified to the extent that sensitive plant and animal species can no longer survive; 4,500 of these have essentially no fish life, and over 1,800 have no life at all (Hanneberg, 1987). Soils too are thought to be losing minerals at an accelerating rate as a result of acidification, while this, coupled with direct contact of trees with polluted air, is causing major stress in some forests. It is estimated that one spruce in four and one pine in seven have lost over 20% of their needles as a result of acidification (Aniansson, 1988). Efforts to combat acid rain have included drastic cuts in sulphur dioxide emissions, now reduced by two-thirds from the peak values of the early 1970s (Hanneberg, 1989). Major liming schemes are underway in some lakes and streams, while re-stocking of fish also occurs (Thunberg, 1988).

The wildlife and balance of the ecosystems in some areas in northern Sweden may be under threat from the native Lapps as they acquire modern equipment, such as skidoos, which give them access to previously more inaccessible areas (Poore and Gryn-Ambroes, 1980). Similarly, the popularity of off-road driving on snow and bare ground is presenting problems in some protected areas, although a law passed in 1975 produced national restrictions on cross-country driving (Larsson, 1977; NEPA, in litt., 1991).

Addresses

Naturvardsverket (National Environmental Protection Agency), S-171 85 SOLNA (Tel: 8 799 1000; FAX: 8 292382; Tlx: 11131)

National Board of Forestry, S-551 83 JÖNKÖPING (Tel: 36 169400/Tlx: 70358)

Swedish Forest Service, S-791 81 FALUN

Swedish Museum of Natural History, Box 50007, S-10405 STOCKHOLM (Tel: 8 666 4000)

Naturskyddsföreningen (Swedish Society for Nature Conservation), Box 4510, S-10265 STOCKHOLM (Tel: 8 702 6500)

Miljöförbundet (Swedish Association for Environmental Groups), Box 7048, S-40231 GOTHENBURG

References

Aniansson, B (1988). The situation surpasses our worst fears. *Acid magazine* 6: 6-9.

Anon. (1985a). *Monitor 1985, the National Swedish Environmental Monitoring Programme (PMK)*. National Swedish Environmental Protection Agency INFORMS, Solna. 207 pp.

Anon. (1985b). *International evaluation of the environmental monitoring programme, PMK*. National Swedish Environmental Protection Agency REPORT 3090, Solna. 25 pp.

Anon. (1985c). *RUBIN*. National Swedish Environmental Protection Agency INFORMS, Solna. 6 pp.

Anon. (1987). Sweden. *Management of Europe's natural heritage, twenty-five years of activity*. Council of Europe, Environment Protection and Management Division, Strasbourg. Pp. 110-111.

Anon. (1989). *Report on the State of the Environment in the USSR, 1988*. USSR State Committee for the Protection of Nature, Moscow. 151 pp.

Arnby, G. (1990). Joint Action on polluted Baltic. *Enviro* 10: 12-13.

Curry-Lindahl, K (1984). Conservation in Sweden – problems and progress. *Oryx* 18 (4).

Davis, S.D., Droop, S.J.M., Gregerson, P., Henson, L., Leon, C.J., Lamlein Villa-Lobos, J., Synge, H., and Zantovska, J. (1986). *Plants in danger: what do we know?* IUCN, Gland, Switzerland, and Cambridge, UK. 461 pp.

Duffey, E. (1982). *National Parks and Reserves of Western Europe*. Macdonald and Co. (Publishers) Ltd, London and Sydney. 288 pp.

Grimmett, R.F.A. and Jones, T.A. (1989). *Important Bird Areas in Europe*. International Council for Bird Preservation, Cambridge, UK.

Hanneberg, P. (1987). Keeping tabs on acidification. *Acid magazine* 1: 2-5.

Hanneberg, P. (1989). Combatting acidifying emissions – Swedish strategies and policies. *Acid magazine* 6: 25-26.

Heiss, G. (1987). Inventory of natural (virgin) and ancient seminatural woodlands within the council's member states and Finland. European Committee for the Conservation of Nature and Natural Resources. Unpublished report.

Ingelög, T., Thar, G. and Gustafsson, L (Eds), (1984). *Floravard i Skogsbruket. Del 2 – Artdel* (Plant conservation and forestry. Part 2 – Species data, a plant Red Data Book). För fatharna och Skogsstyrelsen, Jönköping. (Unseen)

Koester, V (1980). *Nordic countries' legislation on the environment with special emphasis on conservation, a survey.* IUCN, Gland, Switzerland.

Köpp, H (1979). Environment Protection in Sweden. *Nature and National Parks* European Bulletin 65 (17): 12-14.

Larsson, T. (1977). Nature conservation in Sweden: recent developments and legislative changes. *Biological Conservation* 11: 129-143.

Larsson, T. and Lindahl, H. (1989). *Svenska vatmarker av internationell betydelse, vatmarkskonventionen och CW - listan* (Swedish wetlands of international importance). Naturvardsverket, Solna. 154 pp. (Summary in English).

Michanek, G. (1991). Nature Conservation in Sweden. *Nature Conservation in Austria, Finland, Norway, Sweden, Switzerland, Bulgaria, Czechoslovakia, Hungary, Poland, Romania, Yugoslavia and the Soviet Union.* European Parliament, Directorate-General for Research. Environment, Public Health and Consumer Protection Series 17. Pp. 40-49.

Naturvardsverket. (1989). *Nationalparksplan för Sverige.* Naturvardsverket, Imformerar, Solna, Sweden. Pp. 126. (Summary in English).

Nordic Council of Ministers (1978). *The Nordic Environmental Protection Convention, with a Commentary.* Nordic Council of Ministers, Stockholm. 14 pp.

Nordic Council of Ministers (1983). *Programme for Nordic Cooperation in Environmental Protection for 1983 to 1987.* Nordic Council of Ministers, Stockholm. 37 pp.

Poore, D. and Gryn-Ambroes, P. (1980). *Nature Conservation in Northern and Western Europe.* UNEP/IUCN/WWF, Gland, Switzerland. Pp. 103-116.

Sandberg, H. (1990). Lakes and groundwater at risk. *Enviro* 10: 26-27.

Terstad, J. (1990). Biodiversity at Stake. *Enviro* 10: 24-25.

Thunberg, B (1988). Liming is just a holding operation. *Acid magazine* 7: 8-9.

ANNEX
Definitions of protected area designations, as legislated, together with authorities responsible for their administration

Title: Nature Conservancy Act

Date: 1964, major amendments 1973, 1976, 1987 (national parks and natural monuments were first covered under the 1909 Protection of Nature Act)

Brief description: A wide-ranging act covering all areas of nature conservation and providing the basis for the protected areas legislation

Administrative authority: National parks – Swedish Environment Protection Agency
Nature reserves, wildlife sanctuaries and nature conservation areas – county administrations

Designations:

National park Individual sites must be approved by separate Acts of Parliament in a lengthy administration process, the degree of protection is to some degree dependant on the by-laws drawn up for each site. National parks can only be designated on land owned by the Crown. Although regulations governing their use may vary, there are usually strict controls preventing forest felling, hunting, trapping, damage to soil or other vegetation and camping and lighting fires outside authorised sites. In the seven national parks established in Lapland the Lapps are specifically exempted from certain park regulations. They are able to use parks as ranges for their reindeer to shoot certain species and to fish in the lakes and rivers.

Nature reserve The criteria for selection by county administration are varied: scientific reasons include the protection of well-developed representative biotypes and the protection, within each province, of as wide a range of plant formations as possible. Other reserves are set up more because of their outdoor recreational value or aesthetic beauty, here natural history interest might simply be considered as a "bonus".

May be established on Crown land or privately-owned land. The reason for the designation must be stated and restrictions deemed necessary for protection of the site must be enumerated. Typically, the landowner is forbidden to erect buildings, or to use pesticides, hunting by the landowner may also be restricted or forbidden. There are rules for the public preventing damage or destruction to the natural environment and restricting camping, the use of vehicles (including boats) and the creation of noise. In addition, the public is usually reminded of relevant restrictions in the national legislation. Many nature reserves are managed according to a non-interference policy, but some are actively managed to maintain their scientific interest.

Before designation, the county administrations must consult with persons and organisations whose interests may be affected by the proposals. Owners may be compensated for the restrictions placed on there land and occasionally the county administration may agree to purchase the land from the owner, although it is normally reluctant to use its powers of compulsory purchase.

Natural monument Usually small or very small sites. Many are individual trees, or isolated boulders such as glacial erratics. In recent years more effort has been put into preservation of areas rather than single objects, so the number of sites in this category is slowly decreasing.

Wildlife sanctuary Provide refuge for birds and seals. Persons are not allowed to enter the majority at certain times of the year, while birds and other animals within them are afforded protection against egg collecting, shooting, hunting, photography or other disturbance. There is no general strategy covering the overall policy of wildlife sanctuary designation. They are not normally subject to special management regimes, nor are they specifically protected against exploitation or land use dangers. This category includes bird sanctuaries.

Nature conservation area (Landscape management area) This category was introduced in the 1974 amendment to the Nature Conservancy Act. It provides a less restrictive form of protection. Various management measures can be carried out in agreement with the landowner. No financial compensation is available to landowners as regulations do not significantly hinder current land use activities.

Sources: Koester, 1980; Larsson, 1977; Poore and Gryn-Ambroes, 1980; NEPA, *in litt.*, 1991.

Title: Forestry Act

Date: 7 June 1979

Brief description: Largely concerned with the supervision of silviculture

Administrative authority: County Forestry Board

Designations:

Forest difficult to regenerate and protected forest These are forests difficult to regenerate due to an unfavourable location, or forests needed as protection against sand or soil erosion or which are to be kept to prevent the lowering of the timber line. Cutting of such forests may not take place without the permission of the county forestry board, which may impose certain restrictions. Permission is not required for cleaning or thinning which benefits the development of the forest.

Title: Natural Resources Act

Date: 1987

Brief description: Deals with the long-term use of natural resources and the balance between different interests in society

Administrative authority: National Board of Housing, Building and Planning

Designations:

Area of national importance   There are a number of categories, including areas of national importance for recreation, nature conservation, fishing, mining, and military purposes. Those areas of national importance for recreation and nature conservation are defined and described by the Swedish Environment Protection Board. Such areas should be protected from activities that may be harmful to the area. Large power plants and similar projects may not be located in some coastal areas, and certain watercourses areas protected from hydro-electric exploitation. Activities already existing in these areas are not prohibited.

Sources: Michanek, 1991; NEPA, *in litt.*, 1991

SUMMARY OF PROTECTED AREAS

Map† ref.	National/international designations Name of area	IUCN management category	Area (ha)	Year notified
	National Parks			
1	Abisko	II	7,700	1909
2	Bjornlandet	II	1,130	1909
3	Bla Jungfrun	II	198	1926
4	Djuro	II	2,400	1991
5	Gotska Sandon	II	4,500	1909
6	Muddus	II	49,340	1942
7	Padjelanta	II	198,400	1962
8	Peljekaise	II	15,340	1909
9	Sarek	II	197,000	1909
10	Skuleskogen	II	2,950	1984
11	Sonfjallet	II	2,622	1909
12	Stora Sjofallet	V	127,800	1909
13	Store Mosse	II	7,850	1982
14	Tiveden	II	1,353	1983
15	Tofsingdalen	II	1,615	1930
16	Vadvetjakka	II	2,630	1920
	Nature Reserves			
17	Alajaure	IV	17,000	1980
18	Algon	IV	1,046	1974
19	Almo	IV	880	1987
20	Angso	IV	6,860	1960
21	Arholam-Ido	IV	1,035	1978
22	Arshultsmyren	IV	1,150	1972
23	Arvesjakka	IV	8,000	1988
24	Aspnas	IV	1,560	1973
25	Asvikelandet	IV	1,567	1971
26	Axmor	IV	4,500	1978
27	Barga	IV	4,100	1988
28	Batfors	IV	1,550	1991
29	Billuden	IV	1,930	1979
30	Biskopso	IV	4,000	1983
31	Bjuralven	IV	2,290	1982

Map[†] ref.	National/international designations Name of area	IUCN management category	Area (ha)	Year notified
32	Bjurum-Dagsnas	IV	3,600	1952
33	Blaikfjallet	IV	11,000	1988
34	Braviken	IV	9,160	1968
35	Brommo	IV	955	1987
36	Bullero	IV	4,300	1967
37	Daimadalen	IV	28,400	1990
38	Dellikalven	IV	8,800	1988
39	Djuro Archipelago	IV	320	1980
40	Drakon	IV	1,510	1990
41	Dundret	IV	5,500	1970
42	Fjardlang	IV	2,000	1986
43	Florarna	IV	5,172	1976
44	Fullfjallet	IV	38,060	1973
45	Fulltofta	IV	1,020	1971
46	Gitsfjallet	IV	40,000	1988
47	Glaskogen	IV	28,000	1970
48	Gryt	IV	2,574	1968
49	Gyllbergen	IV	1,020	1982
50	Gysinge	IV	2,260	1975
51	Hall-Hangvar	IV	2,161	1967
52	Haparanda Sandskar	IV	4,256	1961
53	Harjaro	IV	1,130	1975
54	Harmano	IV	1,550	1967
55	Harrejaure	IV	26,700	1988
56	Hartso	IV	5,630	1981
57	Hastholmen-Ytteron	IV	1,160	1975
58	Hedlandet	IV	1,365	1978
59	Hemlingson	IV	1,789	1989
60	Hjalmo-Ladna	IV	1,370	1991
61	Hokensas	IV	5,500	1969
62	Holmoarna	IV	25,000	1980
63	Hornavan	IV	12,000	1988
64	Hovfjallet	IV	1,400	1969
65	Jarflotta	IV	3,225	1968
66	Kaitum	IV	40,100	1988
67	Kallovaratjeh	IV	2,235	1970
68	Karingboda	IV	1,060	1974
69	Kartevare	IV	2,400	1988
70	Klaveron	IV	2,252	1966
71	Klingavalsan	IV	2,128	1968
72	Komosse	IV	1,117	1980
73	Kosteroarna	IV	1,155	1984
74	Kronoren	IV	4,067	1975
75	Kungshamn	IV	1,170	1963
76	Kvado	IV	1,569	1979
77	Lacka	IV	4,898	1978
78	Langfjallet	IV	51,705	
79	Lango	IV	1,590	1980
80	Langsjon	IV	2,200	1988
81	Langvattnet	IV	1,020	1974
82	Langviksskar	IV	2,300	1983
83	Licknevarpefjarden	IV	6,020	1970
84	Likskar	IV	2,362	1969
85	Lilla Husarn	IV	1,000	1981
86	Lina	IV	8,600	1988
87	Listerby	IV	1,015	1981
88	Luro Archipelago	IV	1,500	1967

Map[†] ref.	National/international designations Name of area	IUCN management category	Area (ha)	Year notified
89	Marsfjallet	IV	86,000	1988
90	Millesvik Archipelago	IV	8,000	1980
91	Misterhult	IV	8,500	1967
92	Nallovardo-Storgidna	IV	4,400	1988
93	Nimtek	IV	4,400	1988
94	Njupeskar	IV	1,447	1970
95	Norra Vattens	IV	2,340	1973
96	Nuortap-Antivaratj	IV	7,600	1988
97	Nynas	IV	3,890	1971
98	Osta friluftsreservat	IV	1,080	1973
99	Ostra Jarvafaltet	IV	1,200	1979
100	Oxfjallet	IV	1,700	1988
101	Pakketanjaure	IV	21,000	1988
102	Palja	IV	4,300	1988
103	Palkaive	IV	1,400	1988
104	Parlalven	IV	56,600	1988
105	Perso	IV	4,000	1981
106	Pessinki	IV	51,500	1988
107	Plassa	IV	1,200	1988
108	Rago	IV	1,562	1980
109	Rautusakkara	IV	1,200	1988
110	Reuskar	IV	2,400	1973
111	Rido-Sundbyholm	IV	5,756	1984
112	Ringso	IV	1,825	1980
113	Rodkallen-Sor-Aspen	IV	7,004	1970
114	Rogen	IV	48,700	1976
115	Roro	IV	150	1976
116	Salvorev	IV	62,000	1987
117	Sandsjobacka	V	2,550	1968
118	Sankt Anna inkl. Vanso	IV	1,211	1967
119	Segerstads skorgora	IV	5,000	1979
120	Serri	IV	3,687	1970
121	Sibberon	IV	1,015	1979
122	Sjaunja	IV	285,000	1986
123	Skackerfjallen	IV	46,700	1988
124	Skarsasfjallen	IV	1,200	1990
125	Skokloster	IV	1,790	1972
126	Slado-Askeskar	IV	2,000	1965
127	Slaton-Medholma	IV	1,790	1970
128	Stadjan	IV	20,393	1973
129	Stadsholmen	IV	1,600	1968
130	Stenungssundskusten	IV	2,136	1988
131	Stora Karlso	IV	1,180	1970
132	Stora Nassa	IV	3,000	1965
133	Storasjoomradet	IV	1,058	1985
134	Stordalen	IV	1,000	1980
135	Storo-Bocko-Lokao	IV	5,900	1972
136	Storrebben	IV	2,737	1969
137	Stromsholm	IV	2,584	1979
138	Stubba	IV	8,300	1988
139	Sundby	IV	5,000	1965
140	Svenska Hogarna	IV	2,600	1976
141	Svenskadalen	IV	18,700	1990
142	Sydbillingen	IV	1,750	1981
143	Takern	IV	5,420	1975
144	Tandovala	IV	3,450	1987
145	Tinaset	IV	3,350	1983

Map[†] ref.	National/international designations Name of area	IUCN management category	Area (ha)	Year notified
146	Tjadnesvare	IV	4,000	1988
147	Tjeggelvas	IV	32,100	1988
148	Toro	IV	1,174	1973
149	Tromto	IV	1,242	1982
150	Tyresta-Ava	IV	3,400	1986
151	Uto	IV	4,110	1974
152	Valadalen	IV	117,500	1988
153	Vallo	IV	2,663	1973
154	Vamhuskolen	IV	2,694	1987
155	Varmland	IV	24,300	1980
156	Vastra Asnen	IV	1,228	1986
157	Vattlefjall	IV	1,621	1987
158	Verkean	IV	2,506	1975
159	Vindelfjallen	IV	550,630	1974
160	Vittangi-Soppero	IV	18,800	1988
161	Vrango	IV	5,310	1979
	Wildlife Sanctuaries			
162	Annsjon	IV	1,029	1990
163	Bjarehalvons kust	IV	4,700	1967
164	Enskar	IV	2,670	1984
165	Kallskaren	IV	1,400	1978
166	Klacksten	IV	5,000	1987
167	Klyndrorna	IV	1,065	1974
168	Lessejaure	IV	1,010	1982
169	Lilla and Stora Bommeskar	IV	1,385	1985
170	Lillgrund	IV	1,300	1981
171	Oro Sankor	IV	1,095	1978
172	Tjalmejaure	IV	44,010	1967
173	Vaderon	IV	2,105	1967
174	Vasterbaden	IV	1,540	1976
	Nature Conservation Areas			
175	Agon Krakon	V	1,170	1990
176	Balgo	V	2,200	1988
177	Balson (islands)	V	740	1990
178	Brattforsheden	V	10,000	1984
179	Fegen	V	3,117	1980
180	Gullmarn	V	40,300	1983
181	Hackeberga	V	4,482	1982
182	Halle-Hunneberg	V	4,100	1982
183	Hallsundsudde	V	1,920	1978
184	Kallands Skargardar	V	6,500	1989
185	Kalvoskargard	V	2,190	1986
186	Kinnekulle	V	6,655	1982
187	Malingsbo-Kloten	V	13,500	1981
188	Nordingra	V	6,000	1983
189	Oja-Landsort (islands)	V	500	1985
190	Stenningsundskusten	V	2,136	1988
191	Stigfjorden	V	7,000	1979
192	Svenska Bjorn	V	4,500	
193	Tanumskusten	V	1,224	1988
194	Tullgarn	V	1,755	1985
195	Vrinneviskogen	V	2,075	

Map[†] ref.	National/international designations Name of area	IUCN management category	Area (ha)	Year notified
	Biosphere Reserve			
	Lake Torne Area	IX	96,500	1986
	Ramsar Wetlands			
	Ånnsjön	R	11,000	1974
	Åsnen	R	16,800	1989
	Dättern Bay	R	3,920	1989
	Falsterbo-Bay of Foteviken	R	7,530	1974
	Gammelstadsviken	R	430	1974
	Getterön	R	340	1974
	Helga River	R	5,480	1974
	a) Hammarsjön and Egeside			
	b) Araslövssjön			
	Hjälstaviken	R	770	1974
	Hornborgasjön	R	6,370	1974
	Hovran Area	R	4,750	1989
	Isles off Gotland	R	4,220	1974
	a) Faludden			
	b) Grötlingboholme and Rone Ytterholmen			
	c) Laus holmar			
	d) Skenholmen			
	Kilsviken Bay	R	8,910	1989
	Klingavälsån-Krankesjön	R	3,970	1974
	Kvismaren	R	780	1974
	Laidaure	R	4,150	1974
	Lake Östen	R	1,010	1989
	Ottenby	R	1,610	1974
	Coastal areas of Öland	R	8,460	1974
	a) Stora Ören – Gammalsbyören			
	b) Egby-Kapelludden			
	c) Södviken			
	Persöfjärden	R	3,320	1974
	Sjaunja-Kaitum	R	188,600	1974
	Stigfjorden Bay	R	5,180	1989
	Stockholm Outer Archipelago	R	15,000	1989
	Store Mosse and Kävsjön	R	7,580	1974
	River Svartån	R	1,990	
	a) Lake Gorgen-Nötmyran			
	b) Fläcksjön-Gussjön			
	Tavvavouma	R	28,700	1974
	Tåkern	R	5,650	1974
	Tärnasjön	R	11,800	1974
	Tjålmejaure-Laisdalen	R	21,400	1974
	Träslövsläge-Morups Tånge	R	1,990	1989
	River Umeälv Delta	R	1,040	1989

[†]Locations of some protected areas are shown on the accompanying map.

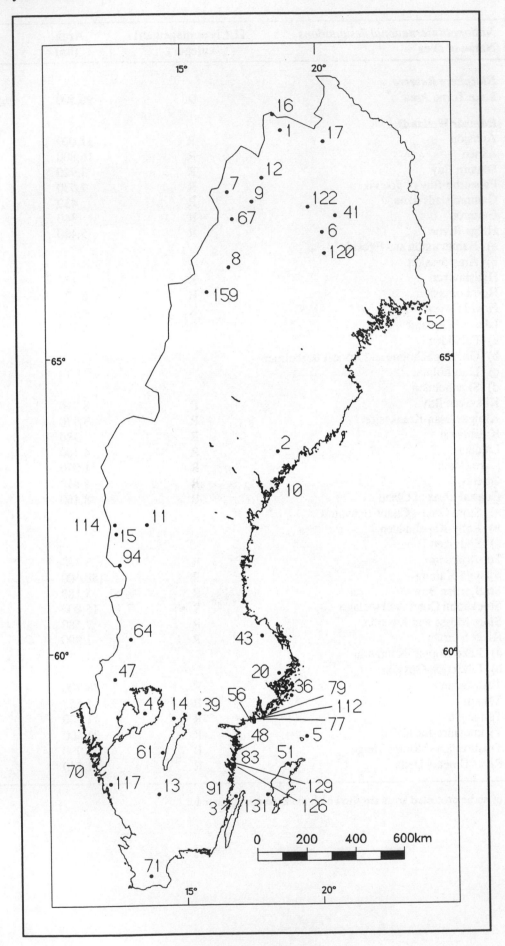

Protected Areas of Sweden

SWITZERLAND

Area 41,290 sq. km

Population 6,609,000 (1990)
Natural increase: 0.22% per annum

Economic Indicators
GDP: US$ 26,155 (1987)
GNP: US$ 21,250 (1987)

Policy and Legislation Switzerland is a federal state composed of 26 cantons (including 6 demi-cantons), in which the federal government has been entrusted with authority concerning public works. Each of the cantons and demi-cantons is sovereign, so far as its independence and legislative powers are not restricted by the federal constitution. All cantonal governments are organised around, and place a high value on, the principle of the sovereignty of the people. The responsibility of the Confederation for the nature and landscape protection is laid down in Article 24 of the Federal Constitution, in the following terms: the protection of nature and preservation of national heritage is a cantonal concern; the Confederation shall, in carrying out its obligations, preserve the characteristic aspects of landscapes and localities, of historical sites and of natural and cultural monuments, and it shall leave them untouched whenever their general interest is predominant; the Confederation may assist efforts to protect nature and landscape by granting subsidies and it may acquire or conserve nature reserves, historical sites and monuments of national importance on a contractual basis, or by means of expropriation; the Confederation may promulgate rules concerning the protection of fauna and flora; mires and mire landscapes of particular beauty and national importance are protected objects. In those areas, construction and the alteration of the soil are not permitted, unless they aid the protection of the site and the agriculture of the area if this was already in existence.

The last point, concerning the protection of mires, is the so-called Rothenthurm Article (named after a small village in the canton Schwyz), which was accepted in a plebiscite in 1987. There is also an amendment which states that the retroaction of this clause goes back to June 1 1983. The rules are extremely strict concerning mires and mire landscapes of national importance.

Nature protection commenced at an early date, the first hunting reserves being established in 1875 and the first national park in 1914, following private initiatives of 1909.

The basic laws concerning all forms of nature and landscape protection are the 'Federal Law on the Protection of Nature and Preservation of National Heritage' (LPN) of 1 July 1966, which entered into force on 1 January 1967, and the 'Ordinance on the Protection of Nature and Preservation of National Heritage' of 16 January 1991, which entered into force on 1 February 1991.

The 1966 Federal Law calls for inventories to be established, as well as regularly revised lists of areas and biotopes of national importance. Once an area has been listed in an inventory as nationally important, it must be preserved in the form specified, unless equal or higher aspects of the public interest oppose such conservation. In case of raised bogs, fens and mire landscapes of national importance and particular beauty, there are no factors which may be considered important enough to oppose their conservation: according to the federal constitution these objects must be preserved. If there is imminent change to a non-listed site, the Confederation can put it under its temporary protection. It can also acquire sites as nature reserves and make cantons, municipalities or non-profit associations responsible for their administration. Most cantons have their own inventories of sites of regional and local importance.

In recent years work on the different inventories has been done more conceptionally and with a improved legal background. Besides the 'Ordinance Concerning the Federal Inventory of Landscapes and Natural Monuments of National Importance' of 10 August 1977 (see Annex), two other federal inventories have been approved: the 'Ordinance Concerning the Inventory of Raised and Transition Bogs of National Importance' of 21 January 1991, and the 'Ordinance Concerning the Inventory of Reserves for Water and Migratory Birds of International and National Importance' of 21 January 1991 (see Annex). In the process of approval are: the 'Ordinance Concerning the Inventory of Fens of National Importance'; the 'Ordinance Concerning the Inventory of Mire Landscapes of National Importance'; and the 'Ordinance Concerning the Inventory of Alluvial Sites of National Importance'. Further to this other inventories are still being compiled, such as the 'Inventory of Glacier Forefields and Alpine Alluvial Landscapes of National Importance'.

Due to an absence of coherent protected areas legislation, a new law or ordinance must be established for each new protected area designated. Many sites have been established at the federal or the canton level, but there is no specific legal definition covering all of these as a single category. The degree of management and the type of regulations regarding the use of protected areas vary from one reserve to another. In most there is a strict prohibition on the collection of fauna and flora, as well as restrictions on public access.

Swiss National Park, situated in the canton of Grisons, was established originally by private initiative in 1909. The Confederation took over responsibility for the park in 1914 (Federal Contracts of 1913, 1914, revised in 1920 and 1959, superseded by the "Federal Law

Concerning the Swiss National Park in the Canton of Grisons of 1980", which entered into force on 15 April 1981).

Areas in which hunting is restricted or totally forbidden can be declared either by the cantons or by the Confederation, based upon the 'Federal Law on Hunting and the Protection of Wild Living Mammals and Birds' of 20 June 1986 and the LPN. This Act notably protects waterfowl wintering sites of international importance. The ordinance concerning water and migratory birds, mentioned above, is also based upon these two laws. The 'Ordinance on Federal Hunting Reserves' of 19 August 1981 has been revised recently and will enter into force in its new form in 1992, providing for the designation of federal hunting reserves (see Annex). A large number of cantonal hunting reserves have also been established, although, once again, there is no general enabling legislation regarding their establishment.

'The Federal Law Concerning the Supervision by the Confederation of the Administration of Forests' of 11 October 1902 (with repeated revisions, the last in 1991/1992) with accompanying ordinances, commonly called the Forest Law, requires that the area of forest within the country should not diminish and that forests should be classified as public forests, private forests, protective forests and non-protective forests. Section V concerns the Conservation and Extension of the Forest Range, and states that the forest range of Switzerland shall be conserved with regard to its extent and regional distribution, in view of the productive, protective and social usefulness of the forest (Anon., 1966).

Other important federal laws or ordinances, essential to nature or environmental protection, are for example: 'The Federal Law on Comprehensive Territorial Planning' (1979), 'The Ordinance on Comprehensive Territorial Planning' (1989), Federal Law on Fisheries of 1973 (which, in Article 22, requires the protection of natural shores and stands of plants), 'The Federal Law to Protect Water from Pollution' (1971), 'The Ordinance on Water Protection' (1971), 'The Federal Law on Regulating Subsidies to Agriculture' (1979), and 'The Ordinance on Regulating Subsidies to Agriculture' 1989 (compensation of ecological contributions).

On the occasion of the 700th anniversary of the Confederation, the Federal Assembly (National Council and Council of States) created a special 'Fund for Conservation and Management of Cultural Landscapes Close to Nature' of SFr 50 million (Federal Resolution of 3 May 1991, entered into force on 1 August 1991 limited to 31 July 2001).

In 1971 a referendum on an amendment to the Constitution on the protection of the environment was voted in and adopted with an overwhelming majority. This rule is the base for the Federal Law on the Protection of the Environment of 1983.

International Activities   The Convention on Wetlands of International Importance especially as Waterfowl Habitat (Ramsar Convention), was ratified on 16 January 1976: eight sites have been inscribed. The Convention Concerning the Protection of the World Cultural and Natural Heritage (World Heritage Convention) was ratified on 17 September 1975, although no natural sites have been inscribed. One biosphere reserve has been designated under the Unesco Man and Biosphere Programme.

Switzerland ratified the Bern Convention in 1981. It is a member of the Council of Europe: nine sites have been designated as Council of Europe biogenetic reserves, while Swiss National Park has been awarded a Council of Europe European Diploma. Switzerland participates actively in CIPRA, the Commission Intérnationale pour la Protection des Régions Alpines formed in 1952, with responsibility for the protection of the Alps. In 1974, IUCN and the Italian Alpine Club jointly organised a major conference in Trento, which produced an action plan for "The Future of the Alps", covering planning, management and use of resources, protection of nature and natural resources. This was followed in 1976 by the Strasbourg Ecological Charter for the Mountainous Regions of Europe, which has led to attempts to integrate community development and nature conservation. In September 1988 a meeting in Voding of invited CIPRA and IUCN experts was commissioned to draft jointly an Alpine Convention which would protect nature and culture in the region (Briand *et al.*, 1989). This Convention will be signed in 1991.

There is one existing transboundary park, where Swiss National Park shares a border with Stelvio National Park in Italy. Although there are no legally binding agreements between the two parks, there is some cooperation. Discussions have also taken place concerning the establishment of a tri-national park around Mont Blanc, with Italy and France, based on a proposal by the Italian Alpine Club (Anon., 1989a).

Administration and Management   At the federal level, responsibility for the protection of nature and the landscape and for Swiss National Park is vested in the Department of the Interior. Within this Department the appropriate office is the Federal Office for Environment, Forests and Landscape: there is a Main Division for Nature and Landscape Protection (Hauptabteilung Natur- und Landschaftsschutz) with two subdivisions (each of them with four sections) concerned with the protection of nature and the landscape. Both the Department and the Main Division are advised by the Federal Commission for the Protection of Nature and Preservation of National Heritage, which was originally founded in 1908.

The federal structure is mirrored to a greater or lesser degree in the cantonal governments. Nature reserves and other types of protected areas of national importance are designated by the federal government. The cantons must establish and manage them. Responsibility for nature reserves and biotopes of regional and local importance falls to the cantons and municipalities.

Non-governmental organisations also manage many nature reserves.

The Swiss League for the Protection of Nature, a leading non-profit association with over 100,000 members, has played an essential role in nature conservation ever since its foundation in 1909. It is one of the partners, with the federal government, in the administration of Swiss National Park, provides three out of the nine members of the Federal Commission responsible for the park and makes considerable contributions to its management and wardening (1 SFr for each member of the association, that means about 7% of the national park's budget). The League acquires nature reserves through substantial subsidies from the federal government and manages large numbers of sites, together with other organisations. In 1991 the League owned or supported approximately 520 nature reserves, covering a total surface of about 80,000ha. The management of these sites costs the League SFr 2 million per year, about 30% of its annual budget (FOEFL, 1991).

Protection is also ensured by planning controls and through land acquisition *via* purchase, lease or agreement. Specially engaged in this field are the League and its cantonal branches; also involved are many local associations and Pro Natura Helvetica (a joint programme of WWF and the League, aimed at the conservation and management of natural areas). It is generally accepted that the League and other non-governmental organisations have a major role in carrying out a large part of the work of nature protection. Decisive achievements to the late 1970s were largely due to the activities of voluntary bodies. In reality, the circumstances can be complicated, e.g. La Pierreuse Reserve is partly owned by the League, the League Vaudoise, the State of Vaud, and a private foundation, with surrounding areas held under agreement between the League and the community (FOEFL, 1991; Poore and Gryn-Ambroes, 1980).

Systems Reviews   Located in the centre of the continent of Europe, Switzerland shares borders with France, Germany, Austria and Italy. The country may be divided into five main natural regions from north to south: the Jura, the Mittelland (Swiss Plateau), the Northern Alps, the Central Alps and the Southern Alps. The mountains of the Central Alps rise to peaks higher than 4,000m. Apart from mountains there are a large number of lakes remaining from the Pleistocene which are characteristic of the country. Forest now covers some 10,519 sq. km, or 25.5% of the total surface: there are few remaining areas of truly virgin forest, however some areas are covered by ancient seminatural forests. Most of the forests are managed to a greater or lesser degree (Heiss, 1987). The climax vegetation of much of the country consists of deciduous beech *Fagus* forests, with oak *Quercus* and maple *Acer* communities at lower altitudes. In the montane zone there are forests of beech mixed with fir *Abies* and in the subalpine zone of the Northern Alps above 1,200-1,400m coniferous forests, dominated by spruce *Picea*. In the subalpine zone of the

Central Alps the climax vegetation is cembra pine *Pinus cembra* and larch *Larix decidua* forest. The alpine timberline lies in the Northern Alps at about 1,800m above sea level and in the Central Alps at about 2,200m. In the lower alpine zone there are mainly alpine meadows. The upper alpine and nival zone consists of sparse and patchy vegetation, boulders and rocks, leading to areas continuously covered in snow and ice throughout the year. The lower part of the Southern Alps belongs to the insubric zone.

About three-quarters of the country is regarded as productive, and is used for agriculture, as arable land, grassland, orchards, vineyards and pasture, as well as for forestry. Cultivation and urban sprawl has changed the landscape drastically over the last 100 years. Since 1850 more than 90% of the fens and bogs have been drained, decreasing in total area from 108.4 sq. km to 57.0 sq. km in the 25 years since 1965. Most of the remaining river courses are now artificial and only minute parts of the original riverine forests remain. Traditional pasture and hedgerow landscapes still exist, although the use of heavy machinery, fertilizers and pesticides is increasingly damaging the rural landscape and its biocenosis.

Under the "Federal Inventory of Landscapes and Natural Monuments of National Interest" (IFP) of 1977 there have, up to now, been two listings (1977 and 1983) covering 119 objects. A third series containing about 45 additional landscapes will be issued in 1992. The inventory accompanying the Ordinance on the Protection of Raised and Transition Bogs of National Importance consists of 514 objects, covering about 1,500ha, which corresponds to 0.03% of the total area of the country. The objects are very unevenly distributed over the different topographical areas and cantons, and two-thirds have been damaged to some degree. The inventory compiled under the Ordinance on the Reserves of Water and Migratory Birds of International and National Importance consists of nine reserves for waterfowl and migratory birds of international importance and of one reserve of national importance (Col de Bretolet; a route for migratory-birds). Seven out of the nine objects of international importance are also Ramsar sites. In addition to the federal inventories for the protection of various aspects of the landscape, there are also some inventories produced by non-governmental organisations, such as the inventory of wetlands of international and national importance for wetland birds, established by the Swiss Institute of Ornithology at Sempach. At present, such inventories have no legal jurisdiction, but may later become a basis for a federal inventory. In this way, the private CPN-Inventory, compiled by three non-governmental organisations, provided the basis for the IFP.

Three institutions are involved with the mapping of nature: the Centre du Réseau Suisse de Floristique, Geneva (flora); the Centre Suisse de Cartographie de la Faune, Neuchâtel (fauna); and the Swiss Federal Institute for Forest, Snow and Landscape Research,

Birmensdorf (biotopes). Official "Red Lists" will be published or approved by the Federal Office for Environment, Forests and Landscape. There are also some red lists published by private organisations, although these have no legal jurisdiction.

The first protected area, Swiss National Park, was established in 1914, followed by such areas as Neeracher Ried Nature Reserve in 1927. In 1991 the list of reserves included about 100 areas of 500ha or more. No more exact information is available than this at the national level, although an Inventory of Legally Designated Nature Protection Areas (IRENA) is currently underway. The nature of these reserves varies considerably, while the number of sites may be expected to change considerably in the near future. Hunting reserves generally have a long tradition. Federal hunting reserves date back to 1875. In 1992, there will be 41 federal hunting reserves covering total about 1,500 sq. km. In 1966 there were 116 cantonal hunting reserves (Tromp, 1966). By 1992 this number will be around 400.

Environmental problems in the Swiss Alpine region involve a wide and complex range of natural, cultural, social, economic and political questions. There are many conflicting interests. Five main problem areas have been identified: threats to the forest, tourist pressure, agriculture and community decline, climate change, and human impact on the water regime through hydropower plants. Atmospheric pollution alone has resulted in more than 50% of conifers exhibiting slight to severe defoliation (Briand *et al.*, 1989). Outside the Alps, the most important problems are intensification of agriculture, over-fertilisation of the soils, expansion of cities and villages, growth of individual motored traffic and impoverishment of nature, especially the decreasing of biological diversity.

Addresses

Main Division, Protection of Nature and Landscape, Federal Office for Environment, Forests and Landscape, Hallwylstrasse 4, CH-3003 BERNE (Tel: 31 618075; FAX: 31 619981)

Federal Office for Environment, Forests and Landscape, Hallwylstrasse 4, CH-3003 BERNE (Tel: 31 619311; FAX: 31 619981)

Department of the Interior, Inselgasse, CH-3003 BERNE

Swiss League for the Protection of Nature, Wartenbergstrasse 22, PO Box, CH-4020 BASEL (Tel: 61 312 7442; FAX: 61 312 7447)

Swiss Association for the Protection of Birds, PO Box, CH-8036 ZURICH (Tel: 1 463 7271; FAX: 1 461 4778)

WWF-Switzerland, Forrlibuckstrasse 66, PO Box, CH-8037 ZURICH (Tel: 1 272 2044; FAX: 1 272 2844)

References

This document was redrafted and considerably expanded by M. Küttel, and others, of the Main Division for Nature

and Landscape Protection in the Federal Office for Environment, Forests and Landscape, who are therefore the major reference for this document. Other references include:

Anon. (1966). XIII/1: Switzerland, B. Ordinance providing for execution of the Federal Act concerning the supervision by the Confederation of the administration of forests. *Food and Agricultural Legislation*, XV (2). Food and Agricultural Organisation, Rome. Pp. 3-13.

Anon. (1988). *SBN: Eine Chance für unsere Natur!* Schweizerischer Bund für Naturschutz, Basel.

Anon. (1989a). Proposed international park for Mont Blanc. *Nature and national parks* 27(89).

Anon. (1989b). *Who is, what does, SLNP.* Swiss League for Nature Protection. Basel, Switzerland. 12 pp.

Briand, F., Dubost, M., Pitt, D. and Rambaud, D. (1989). *The Alps, a system under pressure.* IUCN/International Centre for Alpine Environments, Chambéry, France. 128 pp.

Brugge, E.A., Furrer, G., Messerli, B. and Messerli, P. (Eds) (1984). *The transformation of Swiss mountain ranges.* Haupt, Bern.

FOEFL (1991). Draft country information sheet concerning the protected areas system in Switzerland (provides the basis for the present document), prepared for the World Conservation Monitoring Centre. Federal Office for Environment, Forests and Landscape, Bern. 10 pp.

Federal National Park Commission (1988). *The Swiss National Park, official guide to the trails.* Federal National Park Commission, National Park House Foundation, Zernez. 46 pp.

Gottesmann, J. (1991). Nature conservation in Switzerland. *Nature conservation in Austria, Finland, Norway, Sweden, Switzerland, Bulgaria, Czechoslovakia, Hungary, Poland, Romania, Yugoslavia and the Soviet Union.* European Parliament, Directorate-General for Research. Environment, Public Health and Consumer Protection Series, 17. Pp. 54-59.

Grimmett, R.F.A. and Jones, T.A. (1989). *Important bird areas in Europe.* ICBP Technical Publication No. 9. International Council for Bird Preservation, Cambridge, UK. Pp. 696-706.

Heiss, G. (1987). Inventory of natural (virgin) and ancient seminatural woodlands within the council's member states and Finland. Unpublished report for the European Committee for the Conservation of Nature and Natural Resources. Pp. 287-310.

Messerli, P. (1987). The development of tourism in the Swiss Alps. *Mountain Research and Development* 7(1).

Poore, D. and Gryn-Ambroes, P. (1980). *Nature conservation in northern and western Europe.* UNEP/IUCN/WWF, Gland Switzerland. Pp. 355-364.

Tromp, H. (1966). Wald, Jagd, Fischerei, Naturschutz (Forêts, chasse, pêche, protection de la nature). *Atlas der Schweiz/Atlas de la Suisse.* 1:500,000. Descriptive notes 54.

ANNEX
Definitions of protected area designations, as legislated, together with authorities responsible for their administration

Title: Ordinance concerning the Federal Inventory of Landscapes and Natural Monuments of National Importance (IFP)

Date: 10 August 1977 (entered into force on 21 November 1977)

Brief description: Listing of the objects in an annex. The relation to the CPN-Inventory, compiled by three Swiss non-governmental organisations for the protection of nature and landscape, is written down.

Administrative authority: Department of the Interior, Federal Office of Environment, Forests and Landscape

Designation:

The inventory includes mainly: landscapes and natural monuments unique from a Swiss viewpoint; and typical landscape forms and habitats particularly characteristic of a region. Inclusion of an object in the Inventory reflects that it is particularly worthy of conservation to maintain it in its present state or at least merits the greatest possible care. The inventory constitutes a binding guideline for all federal agencies whose activities have an impact on the existing landscape. Also the objects should be taken into consideration by the comprehensive territorial planning on cantonal level. In the inventory each object is defined by a map-extract and a description of its importance.

Source: FOEFL, 1991

Title: Ordinance on the Protection of Raised and Transition Bogs of National Importance

Date: 21 January 1991 (entered into force on 1 February 1991)

Brief description: Contains the protection rules and a listing of the objects, also in a separate inventory.

Administrative authority: Department of the Interior, Federal Office of Environment, Forests and Landscape

Designation:

All bogs of national importance are protected. They must be strictly conserved. Where they are degraded, they should be restored. The rules are extremely strong, no exceptions are possible. This is partly a consequence of the Rothenthurm-article, an amendment to the federal constitution (see main text).

The accompanying inventory the objects to be conserved.

Source: FOEFL, 1991

Title: Ordinance on the Reserves of Water and Migratory Birds of International and National Importance

Date: 21 January 1991 (entered into force on 1 February 1991)

Brief description: Designation of the objects, protection rules and organisation of the survey, listing of the objects in a separate inventory.

Administrative authority: Department of the Interior, Federal Office of Environment, Forests and Landscape

Designation:

The inventory includes reserves for waterfowl and migratory birds of international importance and of reserves of national importance. According to the Federal Law on Hunting and the Protection of wild living Mammals and Birds, reserves of international importance can be established without the approval of the cantons. Reserves of national importance have to be approved by the cantons. In each description of the objects in the inventory, a list of special measures to be taken for the respective site is given.

Source: FOEFL, 1991

Title: Ordinance on the federal hunting reserves

Date: 19 August 1981 (entered into force on 1 September 1981, a new version will enter into force on 1 January 1992 probably)

Brief description: Prohibition of hunting, organisation of the surveillance, listing of the objects

Administrative authority: Department of the Interior, Federal Office of Environment, Forests and Landscape

Designation:

The original goal of hunting reserves was an increase of stock of wild living mammals, especially of chamois, ibexes, red and roe deer. This goal has now been reached and problems have changed. Partially the stocks of the named animals are too great and that can lead to a severe damaging of forests. On the other hand, species, previously not endangered, such as the capercaillie, rock partridge, partridge, field hare, are now in decline. Therefore the ordinance has been revised and two types of hunting reserves have been created; one giving total protection to all wild living animals and one giving partial protection, where hoofed animals can be regulated according to instructions of the competent authorities. Forty-one federal hunting reserves spread all over the country with detailed regulations will be included in the new inventory.

Source: FOEFL, 1991

Title: Federal Law concerning Swiss National Park in the Canton of Grisons

Date: 19 December 1980 (entered into force on 15 April 1981)

Brief description: Deals with organisation, financing and tasks of the park

Administrative authority: Department of the Interior, Federal National Park Commission

Designation:

National park Nature is left entirely to develop naturally protected from any human activity, except visiting on marked paths and demarcated rest areas and scientific activities. Activities forbidden include: hunting, fishing, collecting plants, flowers, berries or dead wood, killing or disturbing animals, lighting fires, camping, grazing of cattle, taking dogs into the park, making commercial films, skiing and cycling. Shooting of animals for management purposes is admitted. Persons under 15 years of age may only enter the park when accompanied by adults.

Sources: Federal National Park Commission, 1988; FOEFL, 1991

SUMMARY OF PROTECTED AREAS

Map[†] ref.	National/international designations Name of area	IUCN management category	Area (ha)	Year notified
	National Park			
1	Swiss	I	16,887	1914
	Federal Hunting Reserves			
2	Albris	IV	1,016	
3	Aletsch Bietschhorn	IV	19,388	
4	Augstmatthorn	IV	2,116	
5	Bernina-Albris	IV	7,405	
6	Campo Tencia	IV	3,494	
7	Combe-Grede	IV	1,099	
8	Creux-du-Van	IV	1,443	
9	Fellital	IV	4,133	
10	Grand Muveran	IV	5,006	
11	Graue Horner	IV	5,640	
12	Greina	IV	6,013	
13	Hahnen	IV	2,297	
14	Haut de Cry/Derborence	IV	7,244	
15	Hochmatt-Motelon	IV	3,135	
16	Hutstock	IV	5,385	
17	Karpf	IV	10,681	
18	Kiental	IV	8,337	
19	Le Noirmont	IV	2,584	
20	Les Bimis-Ciernes Picat	IV	1,288	
21	Leukerbad	IV	5,395	
22	Mont Pleureur	IV	11,558	
23	Pez Vial	IV	2,203	
24	Pierreuse-Gummfluh	IV	1,029	
25	Piz Beverin	IV	3,309	
26	Piz Ela	IV	3,656	
27	Santis	IV	2,632	

Map[†] ref.	*National/international designations* Name of area	IUCN management category	Area (ha)	Year notified
28	Schilt	IV	1,361	
29	Schwarzhorn	IV	7,671	
30	Silbern-Jagern-Bodmerenwald	IV	10,250	
31	Tannhorn	IV	1,187	
32	Trescolmen	IV	1,965	
33	Turtmanntal	IV	3,781	
34	Urirotstock	IV	2,643	
35	Val Ferret/Combe de l'A	IV	6,613	
36	Weissfluh	IV	2,158	
	Nature Reserves			
37	Binntal	IV	4,650	
38	Combe Grede	IV	1,202	
39	Creux du Van et Gorges de L'Areuse	IV	1,100	
40	Engstlen See-Junigbach-Achtelsass	IV	10,500	
41	Gelten-Iffigen	IV	4,300	
42	Grimsel	IV	10,000	
43	Hohgant	IV	1,504	
44	Holloch Karst	IV	9,240	
45	La Pierreuse	IV	3,255	
46	Val Languard, dal Fain, and Minor	IV	1,750	
47	Val de Bagnes	IV	20,000	
48	Vallee de Joux et Haut Jura Vaudois	IV	22,000	
49	Vallee du Doubs	IV	3,400	
50	Vallon de Nant	IV	1,368	
	Landscape Protected Areas			
51	Aarelandschaft Thun-Bern	V	1,061	
52	Albiskette-Reppischtal	V	4,191	
53	Baselbieter Tafeljura mit Eital	V	4,526	
54	Belchen-Passwang-Gebiet	V	6,557	
55	Bergsturzgebiet von Goldau	V	1,320	
56	Berner Hochalpen and Aletsch-Bietschhorn-Gebiet	V	42,866	
57	Binntal	V	5,084	
58	Campolungo-Campo Tencia-Piumogna	V	5,349	
59	Creux du Van et gorges de l'Areuse	V	2,123	
60	Dent Blanche-Matterhorn-Monte Rosa	V	30,271	
61	Denti della Vecchia	V	2,137	
62	Flyschlandschaft Hagleren-Glaubenberg-Schlieren	V	11,892	
63	Franches Montagnes	V	3,979	
64	Gempenplateau	V	4,458	
65	Glaziallandschaft Neerach-Stadel	V	1,413	
66	Glaziallandschaft zwischen Lorenztobel and Sihl	V	10,904	
67	Glaziallandschaft zwischen Thur und Rhein	V	12,192	
68	Hallwilersee	V	1,903	
69	Hohgant	V	2,275	
70	Irchel	V	2,236	
71	Kesch-Ducan-Gebiet	V	13,760	
72	La Cote	V	1,786	
73	La Pierreuse-Gummfluh-Vallee de l'Etivaz	V	6,282	
74	Lac de Tanay	V	1,503	
75	Lag da Toma	V	1,114	
76	Lagerengebiet	V	2,486	
77	Le Chasseral	V	2,159	
78	Maderanertal-Fellital	V	16,176	
79	Monte Generoso	V	6,203	
80	Monte San Giorgio	V	2,360	
81	Murgtal-Murtschental	V	4,210	

Map[†] ref.	*National/international designations* Name of area	IUCN management category	Area (ha)	Year notified
82	Napfbergland	V	16,352	
83	Oberengadiner Seenlandschaft und Berninagruppe	V	37,523	
84	Pilatus	V	5,052	
85	Piora-Lucomagno-Dotra	V	9,690	
86	Piz Arina	V	4,991	
87	Quellgebiet des Hinterrheins and San Bernardino	V	5,833	
88	Randen	V	7,513	
89	Reusslandschaft	V	6,465	
90	Rive sud du Lac de Neuchatel	V	4,218	
91	Ruinaulta	V	2,044	
92	Schrattenflue	V	4,230	
93	Silberen	V	8,369	
94	Silvretta-Vereina	V	14,376	
95	Tafeljura nordlich Gelterkinden	V	1,847	
96	Thurgauisch-furstenlandische Kulturlandschaft	V	1,297	
97	Untersee-Hochrhein	V	12,827	
98	Val Bavona	V	11,969	
99	Val Verzasca	V	19,932	
100	Val de Bagnes	V	16,869	
101	Val di Campo	V	3,023	
102	Vallee du Doubs	V	3,998	
103	Vallee du la Brevine	V	4,218	
104	Vallon de Nant	V	1,492	
105	Vanil Noir	V	4,931	
106	Vierwaldstattersee mit Kernwald Burgenstock	V	38,447	
107	Wassermatten in den Talern der Langete der Rot	V	1,063	
108	Weissenstein	V	2,989	
109	Zugersee	V	1,601	

	IUCN management category	Area (ha)	Year notified
Biosphere Reserve			
Parc national Suisse	IX	16,870	1979
Ramsar Wetlands			
Baie de Fanel and le Chablais	R	1,155	1976
Bolle di Magadino	R	661	1982
Kaltbrunner Riet	R	150	1990
Lac artificiel de Klingnau	R	355	1990
Lac artificiel de Niederried	R	303	1990
Les Grangettes	R	330	1990
Rade de Genève et Rhône en aval de Genève	R	1,032	1990
Rive sud du Lac de Neuchâtel	R	3,063	1990

[†]Locations of some protected areas are shown on the accompanying map.

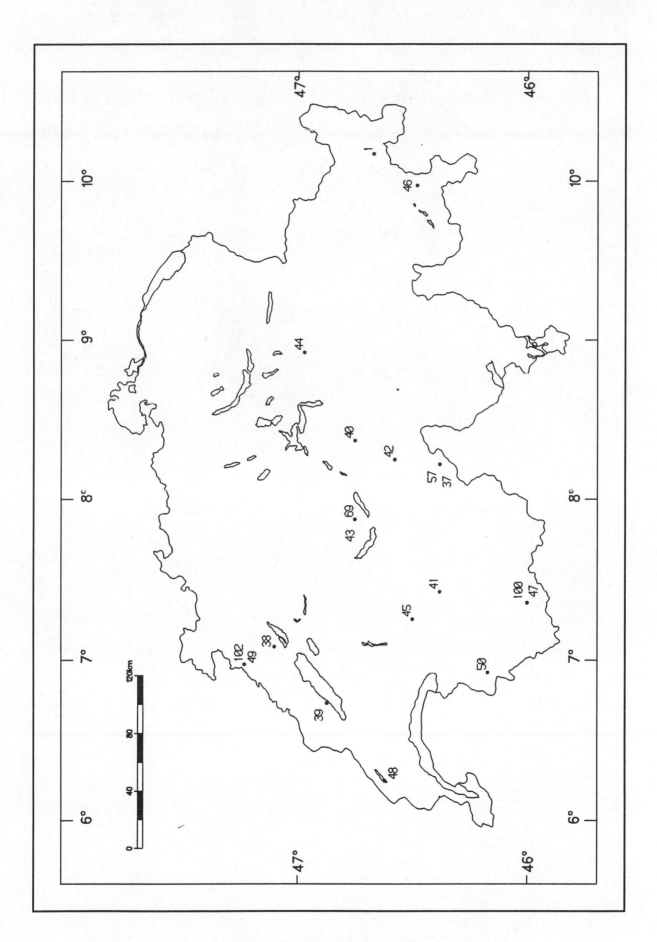

Protected Areas of Switzerland

UKRAINE*

Area 603,700 sq. km (Hunter, 1991)

Population 51,704,000 (Hunter, 1991)
Natural increase: no information

Economic Indicators
GDP: No information
GNP: No information

Policy and Legislation The Ukraine was one of the founding sovereign nations signing the United Nations Charter on 26 June 1945. In July 1990 parliament made a declaration of sovereignty, and on 5 December 1991 the Ukraine officially declared itself no longer part of the Soviet Union, following the referendum vote for independence on the 1 December.

In the 1978 Constitution of the Ukrainian Soviet Socialist Republic general provisions for nature protection were included in Article 65 "citizens ... are obliged to protect nature and to conserve its riches". The unified Environmental Code is specified in the Ukrainian Law on the Protection of Nature of 1960 .

Specific provisions on the protection of flora, fauna and their habitats were made in the Ukrainian Law on the Protection and use of Wildlife of 1981 and the Ukrainian Forest Code of 1979 (Anon., 1986a). The Status of State Nature Reserves enacted by the Council of Ministers of the USSR on 27 November 1951, together with the relevant regulations of the Republics, has been revised in the 1981 Act. The Supreme Soviet Law (also of 1981) includes regulations on protected natural areas and measures to ensure wildlife protection (Articles 21-26). The legislative status of state nature reserves (zapovedniki) is based on Article 21 (Section 6 on creating preserves and reserves) and Article 25 (on protection of animals in preserves, reserves and other protected areas) (see the annex in USSR text).

Some of the first protected areas were set up as Imperial hunting reserves, such as the Crimean State Forest and Hunting preserve in 1913, the same site becoming the first zapovednik of the Soviet State in 1923. Zapovedniki are defined as tracts of land containing natural resources, withdrawn from their original landowner, administered as permanent nature preserves by a state or republic level ministry, for the purpose of preserving floral and faunal resources in their natural habitats (Newcombe, 1985; see legislation text for the USSR).

International Activities A network of wetlands of international importance has been established under the Convention on Wetlands of International Importance especially as Waterfowl Habitat (Ramsar Convention), which was ratified by the USSR on 11 October 1976.

The former Ukrainian SSR was actively involved in developing a network of biosphere reserves under the Unesco MAB programme, two sites having been established in 1984 and 1985, respectively. The USSR signed the Convention Concerning the Protection of the World Cultural and Natural Heritage (World Heritage Convention) on 12 October 1990 but no sites are situated in the Ukraine.

Administration and Management In 1985, as with the whole of the USSR at the time, state protected areas were under the jurisdiction of all-union ministries (see text for the USSR). The Ukrainian SSR Ministry of Forestry governed the main protected areas (Newcombe, 1985). In 1986 a state committee of the Ukrainian SSR on nature protection was formed in the Republic to manage environmental policy and to coordinate activities of other bodies, *inter alia*, for the protection of flora, fauna and their habitats (Anon., 1986).

Systems Reviews The Ukraine, formerly in south-west European USSR, borders Poland, Romania, Czechoslovakia, Hungary, Byelorussia and the Russian Republic. The region largely consists of open plains with low hills, the Carpathian mountains lie in the south-west of the country and the River Dnieper passes through the territory. Steppes and primary forests still occur in many parts of the country, such as in the Carpathians mountains. The Crimea has developed an unique flora and fauna, with over 2,400 plant species, which include numerous endemic species dating back to the Tertiary period. There are important wetlands on the Black Sea coast (Newcombe, 1985; Davis *et al.*, 1986; Cerovsky, *in litt.*, 1991).

Up to 480,000 sq. km of the country is under cultivation.

In 1976 a book of rare and endangered animals and plant species, *A Red Data Book of the Ukraine*, was published; listed organisms include 18 species of insect, four species of amphibian, six species of reptile, 28 species of bird, 29 species of mammal and 151 species of vascular plant (Anon., 1986a).

---

*This information is correct at the time of going to press, but is likely to be overtaken by events which could alter the legislative, administrative and management structure of protected areas throughout the region. As of September 1991 the constituent republics of the former Soviet Union included: Armenia, Azerbaijan, Belorussia (Bielorussia or Belarus), Georgia, Kazakhstan, Kirgizia, Moldavia (Moldova), the Russian Republic (RSFSR) and its Baltic enclave of Kalingrad, Tadzhikistan, Turkmenistan, Ukraine and Uzbekistan.

Protected areas in the 1980s included 5,000 sites under special protection totalling 8% of the Ukraine; this included two national parks totalling 170,694ha, 13 state zapovedniki totalling 159,000ha and 202 hunting reserves (four alone covering over 173,000ha). There are two biosphere reserves representing 121,000ha. Wetlands and important bird sites are protected by 200,000ha of Ramsar wetlands of international importance and 24 important bird areas recognised to be of European regional importance by IWRB and ICBP (Grimmett and Jones, 1989). Among the state nature reserves being set up are new landscape, forest and general zoological subcategories, including the Zhukov Ostrov Forest Area, Turye-Polyansky and Rechansky in the trans-Carpathian region. A proposed national park is located at Dnepro-Desnyanskiy and Verchnednepproskiy; a national park in the Chernobyl fallout zone was being considered in 1988 (Anon., 1986a, 1986b; Gensiruk, 1985: Milne, 1988).

Environmental constraints are varied, ranging from extremely high levels of atmospheric pollution, from coal, chemical, and ore industrial centres, to loss of wetlands (figures indicate a total wetland loss of up to 2.2 million ha); to large scale excavation operations (Hunter, 1991). Dneprovsko-Teterevskoe State Hunting Reserve lies partly within Zone A (total evacuation area) of the Chernobyl reactor accident site and extensive nuclear contaminants have inevitably been recorded here and elsewhere within the region (Anon., 1986b).

Other Relevant Information   The southern Black Sea coast of the Crimean Peninsula prior to independence was one of the busiest resort areas in the Soviet Union.

Addresses

Former State Committee of the Ukrainian SSR on Nature Protection, KIEV

References

Anon. (1986a). Organisation of the preserved territories network in Ukrainian SSR. International Symposium "Protection of Natural Areas and the Genetic Fund they Contain" Project No. 8 on the Programme Man and Biosphere (MAB) of Unesco, 23-28 September 1985, Blavoevgrad, Bulgaria. Pp. 11-17

Anon. (1986b). What reserves were affected by the Chernobyl accident? *Commission on National Parks and Protected Areas Newsletter* 36: 1.

Bannikov, A.G. (1969). (Ed.). *Zapovedniki Sovetskogo Soyuza.* Kolos, Moscow. 552 pp.

Braden, K. (1986). Wildlife reserves in the USSR. *Oryx* 20: 165-169.

Davis, S. D., Droop, S. J. M., Gregerson, P., Henson, L., Leon, C. J., Lamlein Villa-Lobos, J., Synge, H., and Zantovska, J. (1986). *Plants in danger: what do we know?* Threatened Plants Unit. IUCN, Gland, Switzerland and Cambridge, UK. 461 pp.

Hunter, B. (Ed.) (1991). The Statesman's Year Book 1991-92. The Macmillan Press Ltd, London and Basingstoke, UK. 1692 pp.

Knystautas, A. (1987). *The natural history of the USSR.* Century, London. 224 pp.

Milne, R. (1988). Chernobyl disaster zone to become national park. *New Scientist.* 15 September 1988. P. 34

Newcombe, L.F. (1985). Protected natural territories in the Crimea, USSR. *Environmental Conservation* 12(2): 147-155.

Sokolov, V.Y. and Syroechkovskogo, Y.Y. (Eds). (1985). *Zapovedniki SSSR.* 11 volumes. Mysl, Moscow.

Weisenburger, U. (1991). Nature conservation in the Soviet Union. In: European Parliament Director-General for Research *Nature Conservation. Environment, Public Health and Consumer Protection* Series 17. IN-9-1991. Pp. 140-149.

SUMMARY OF PROTECTED AREAS

Map[†] ref.	*National/international designations* Name of area	IUCN management category	Area (ha)	Year notified
	National Parks			
1	Karpatskiy	II	50,303	1980
2	Shatskiy	II	82,500	1983
	State Nature Reserves (Zapovedniki)			
3	Askaniya Nova	I	11,054	1921
4	Chernomorskiy	I	71,899	1927
5	Dunaiskie Plavni	I	14,851	1981
6	Kanevskiy	I	1,035	1968
7	Karadagskiy	I	1,370	1979
8	Karpatskiy	I	18,544	1968
9	Luganskiy	I	1,580	1968
10	Polesskiy	I	20,104	1968
11	Rastoch'e	I	2,080	1984
12	Ukrainskiy Stepnoy	I	1,634	1961
13	Yaltinskiy	I	14,591	1973
	State Hunting Reserves (Zakazniki)			
14	Azovo-Sivashskoye	IV	57,430	1957
15	Dneprovsko-Teterevskoye	IV	37,891	1967
16	Krymskoye	IV	42,957	1957
17	Zalesskoye	IV	35,089	1957
	Ramsar Wetlands			
	Intertidal Areas of the Dounai/Yagorlits and Tendrov Bays	R	128,051	1976
	Karkinitski Bay	R	37,300	1976
	Sivash Bay	R	45,700	1976

[†]Locations of most protected areas are shown on the accompanying map.

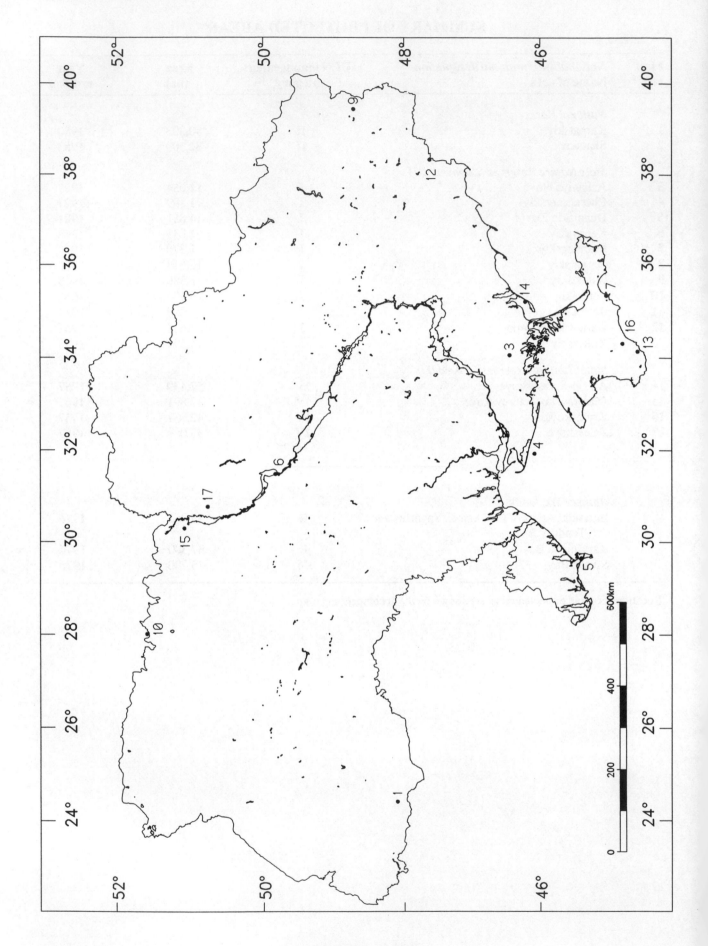

Protected Areas of Ukraine

UNITED KINGDOM OF GREAT BRITAIN AND NORTHERN IRELAND

Area 244,880 sq. km

Population 57,237,000
Natural increase: 0.22% per annum

Economic Indicators
GDP: US$ 12,096 per capita
GNP: US$ 10,430 per capita

Policy and Legislation By the Act of Union, 1801, Great Britain (comprising of England, Scotland and Wales) and Ireland formed a legislative union as the United Kingdom of Great Britain and Ireland (UK). Northern Ireland remained within the Union following separation of the rest of Ireland in 1921. The supreme legislative power is vested in parliament. A Bill has to be passed by both Houses and by Royal Assent before it can become an Act of Parliament and part of Statute law. The UK has no written Constitution; the environment is afforded no fundamental rights. Protection of the landscape is achieved through a complicated web of law, policy and administration at the national and local level. Protected area designations and authorities which administer them vary between the countries. This is particularly true for Scotland and Northern Ireland which, although sharing some protected area categories with the rest of the UK, have largely different legislative and administrative systems. In a number of cases the regional legislation and administration tends to work in parallel with other regions.

The first laws pertaining to natural resource protection were the Forest Laws of King Cnut (Canute) in *c.* 1014, followed by enactments of 1184, 1217 and 1238. The oldest extant protected area, the New Forest, was declared a Royal hunting preserve in 1079, and the oldest in Scotland dates from the 12th century. In the 19th century control of forests was vested in the Commission of Woods and Forests. More recent policy and legislation relating to nature conservation were applied by the British administrators in their overseas territories. Environmental degradation in the dependent territory of St Helena in 1722 is said to have influenced the administration to enact laws to protect the environment in a number of territories: India (British Indian Forest directives of 1855), Mauritius (Game Ordinance of 1869) and Cyprus (Forest Law of 1879). In the UK probably the first areas to be given legal protection for nature conservation purposes were a number of "bird sanctuaries" declared in the 19th Century and the first national park in 1951 (English Nature, *in litt.*, 1991). The establishment of non-statutory reserves by individuals and non-governmental organisations has also played an important role in the early history of nature conservation and protected areas in the UK.

The main current legal texts covering protected areas in the UK are:

> **England, Scotland and Wales** – National Parks and Access to the Countryside Act, 1949; Countryside Act, 1968; Wildlife and Countryside Act, 1981
>
> **Scotland** – Countryside (Scotland) Act, 1967; Town and Country Planning (Scotland) Act, 1972; Natural Heritage (Scotland) Act, 1991
>
> **Northern Ireland** – Nature Conservation and Amenity Lands (Northern Ireland) Order, 1985

These acts cover most protected area designations in the UK, while other categories are not covered, or only partially covered under legislation, or provided for under other schemes (for example, assistance schemes in agriculture, or development planning control). Many protected areas throughout the UK gain further protection as a result of obligations under EC law and/or international treaties. It is necessary to use UK domestic law for their implementation. Environmentally sensitive areas (ESAs), resulting from EC Regulations on Agricultural Structures, are designated using powers in the Agriculture Act, 1986 (see Annex). The programme for the establishment of ESAs is on the point of substantial expansion (Countryside Commission, *in litt.*, 1991).

The legislation, where it does not apply to the entire country, can best be understood by dividing it according to the regions to which it relates:

England, Scotland and Wales The 1949 National Parks and Access to the Countryside Act established the National Parks Commission, responsible for the designation of national parks in England and Wales and for advice on their administration (see Annex).

Three further categories of protected area are also given some degree of statutory recognition under the 1949 Act: area of outstanding natural beauty (AONB), site of special scientific interest (SSSI) and nature reserve (NR) (see Annex). Certain provisions of the Act relating to national parks also apply to AONBs. The sections of this Act concerning national parks and AONBs only apply to England and Wales. Nature reserves were originally declared under Section 17 of the 1949 Act, which provided for their acquisition and establishment by the national and local authorities. Section 21 remains the main legal text for the establishment of local nature reserves (LNRs) which are now distinguished from national nature reserves (NNRs), discussed below (NCC, 1989). The 1949 Act also imposed on the Nature Conservancy Council the duty to designate SSSIs and to notify local planning authorities; this category is now largely covered under the Wildlife and Countryside Act,

1981. Both national parks and AONBs tend to contain within their boundaries large numbers of protected areas of other categories, notably nature reserves and SSSIs.

The Wildlife and Countryside Act, 1981 and the Wildlife and Countryside (Amendment) Act, 1985 have several sections on protected areas, providing for the designation of NNRs, marine nature reserves, SSSIs, limestone pavement orders and nature conservation orders (see Annex). Limestone pavement orders may be placed on areas of wholly or partly exposed limestone where these are considered of particular importance or interest and are considered to be in danger of damage from limestone removal. Nature conservation orders may be imposed by the appropriate Secretary of State on land he/she considers to be of special importance (see Annex). Nature conservation orders under the Wildlife and Countryside Act, 1981 have been used to give further protection to SSSIs where designation under the Ramsar Convention or the EC Birds Directive is required (English Nature, *in litt.*, 1991).

One of the broader requirements of the Countryside Act, 1968 and the Countryside (Scotland) Act, 1967 was that all departments and agencies of the government should "have regard to the desirability of conserving the natural beauty (including flora, fauna and geological features) and amenity of the countryside". Country parks are designated under these acts; they are sites established by local authorities primarily for their leisure and recreation value (see Annex).

The Forestry Commission (FC) was established under the Forestry Act, 1919 originally to promote forest industry, rather than for nature conservation purposes – its powers and duties are now mainly defined under the Forestry Act, 1967. It has affirmed its intention increasingly to promote nature conservation, and some statutory basis is given for this in the 1985 Wildlife and Countryside (Amendment) Act. The FC has recently published a statement of forestry policy for Great Britain. The two aims of the government's policy are: "the sustainable management of the existing woods and forests, and a steady expansion of tree cover to increase the many and diverse benefits that the forests provide" (Forestry Commission, *in litt.*, 1991).

The protection of forests in the UK is provided under a broad range of legislation and policy: there is no clear division between protected and unprotected forest. Specific protection is provided under the national and international protection categories mentioned elsewhere in this section. Individual trees and woodland may be protected under tree preservation orders which are now provided for under the Town and Country Planning Act, 1990. A further degree protection for forests is provided by the general restrictions on the felling of trees: a Forestry Commission licence is required for most tree-felling operations in forested areas, under the Forestry Regulations (notably 1979 and 1987) (Forestry Commission, 1989a).

There are a number of non-statutory designations of forest areas maintained by the Forestry Commission which are also of conservation importance. Forest parks are relatively large areas of forest and open land in which provision for public recreation is a primary management objective. Forest nature reserves are discrete areas of particular nature conservation value, chosen by virtue of their species richness and/or the local, regional or national rarity of the species present; they are chosen to be of sufficient size for the reserve's primary interest to be largely self-sustaining, while management is aimed at conserving and enhancing the wildlife value of the reserves. In addition to these two categories, the Forestry Commission uses the broader term of conservation area to cover all the areas under its management where the primary object of management is nature or archaeological conservation. These areas include all SSSIs on Forestry Commission land (Forestry Commission, *in litt.*, 1991).

From 1985 government policy concerning broad-leaved woodland in Great Britain has attempted to prevent any further loss of this woodland: in most cases, clearance for agricultural purposes will not be allowed; the planting of new broad-leaved woodland on agricultural and waste ground should lead to an increase in the total area covered, while special attention should be paid to the protection of ancient semi-natural broad-leaved woodlands (areas composed of native trees and shrubs which have borne woodland continuously since the year 1600) (Forestry Commission, 1985).

The Environmental Protection Act came into force on 1 November 1990. Part VII of the Act is concerned with the dismantling and reorganisation of the Nature Conservancy Council (NCC, 1991).

England and Wales A further category of non-statutory protection, heritage coast, has been given to sites covering a large area of undeveloped coastline in England and Wales. Heritage coasts generally receive special attention in development planning, and funds can more readily directed towards their management, following CC reports of 1970 and Department of Environment/Welsh Office Circulars (1972) (Poore and Poore, 1987).

Scotland In the 1940s the Scottish National Parks Survey Committee identified five areas for designation as national parks. The 1949 National Parks and Access to the Countryside Act, however, omitted Scotland, and instead the five sites were designated as national park direction areas, which essentially placed planning controls for these areas in the hands of the central government. In 1978 the Countryside Commission for Scotland (CCS) published the results of a comprehensive review of scenic resources in the document entitled Scotland's Scenic Heritage. The 40 national scenic areas covered under the report were given statutory recognition with effect from 1980 through an order made by the Secretary of State for Scotland under the 1972 Town and Country Planning (Scotland) Act. A high proportion of the land in national scenic areas is privately-owned and so protection is largely in the form of development control (see Annex) (Poore and Poore, 1987).

A 1981 amendment to the Countryside (Scotland) Act 1967 Act enabled regional authorities to establish regional parks, in consultation with the CCS, largely for recreational purposes, but covering much larger areas than the aforementioned country parks (see Annex). The CCS also proposed the establishment of a further category of park, a special park, for areas already under substantial recreational pressure, with provisions for a separate park authority for each park. Legislation was not enacted for this category, although the agreement reached concerning Loch Lomond Regional Park, inaugurated in 1988, with its joint park committee, effectively gives this site special park status, but without unified planning or development control powers, and the joint local authority committee participates on a voluntary basis. The Loch Lomond Park Authority is still pursuing the national park issue (CCS, 1988).

The Natural Heritage (Scotland) Act, 1991 provides for the establishment of a new body, Scottish Natural Heritage (SNH) to take over the functions of the CCS and the Nature Conservancy Council for Scotland which is due to take place in April 1992. National scenic areas will remain, however under the 1991 Act, new areas may be designated as natural heritage areas (see Annex). The Act, controversially, provides for the review of all areas notified as SSSIs.

The CCS's Mountain Areas Report was published in 1990, followed by a further document in 1991 after public consultation. The initial report made recommendations concerning conservation, planning and management issues in mountain areas, and strongly advocated that four areas of special importance be given legislative definition as national parks (CCS, 1990, 1991; *in litt.*, 1991).

Northern Ireland The underlying legislation was originally covered under the Amenity Lands Act, 1965 and is now covered under the Nature Conservation and Amenity Lands (Northern Ireland) Order, 1985. This provides for the designation of areas of outstanding national beauty, national parks, nature reserves, areas of special scientific interest, and marine nature reserves (see Annex). The Department of the Environment for Northern Ireland has made a policy decision not to designate any national parks in the foreseeable future (Poore and Poore, 1987).

Areas of special scientific interest (ASSIs) in Northern Ireland are equivalent to SSSIs in England, Wales and Scotland, although there are differences in the Northern Ireland planning system and, hence, the way these are (or are not) safeguarded from development. These are declared by the Department of Environment for Northern Ireland. There are also NNRs which are areas of land of national importance managed primarily for nature conservation purposes, in much the same way as those in the rest of the UK, through ownership by the Department of the Environment for Northern Ireland, or under lease or agreement with the Department, or by an approved body where the Department is assured of the management expertise of that body (see Annex).

Forest parks and non-statutory nature reserves, comparable to those owned by the Forestry Commission in the rest of the UK, have been established in Northern Ireland. These are established and managed by the Forest Service of the Department of Agriculture for Northern Ireland.

UK Dependent Territories Most of the UK dependent territories have their own conservation legislation, although this parallels the central legislation in a number of cases. See the end of this UK section for information concerning the Isle of Man, Channel Islands and Gibraltar, and separate accounts for further information about UK dependent territories in regions outside the Palaearctic.

UK General The administration of Crown Estate land throughout the whole of the UK is covered under the Crown Estate Act of 1961. This is land which is the property of the British Crown, as distinct from the private estates of the reigning monarch and from land owned by government departments and agencies. The Crown Estate comprises a diverse range of land types, including forests and foreshore, the Act does not require the protection of the land for conservation purposes, although the enhancement of the countryside is one of the factors to be considered in the management of this land. Windsor Forest is a notable example.

There are a few individual sites in the UK which are covered under their own unique legislation. The most notable and important of these are the Norfolk and Suffolk Broads and the New Forest. Designation and Administration of the Norfolk and Suffolk Broads is under the Norfolk and Suffolk Broads Act, 1988, which effectively gives the area the same degree of protection as a national park, although it provides important controls over navigation and the use of water space. The New Forest has been a protected landscape for over 900 years. The legal status of the forest is now covered under the New Forest Act, 1877, although the entire site has also been recognised as a NNR (Poore and Poore, 1987). The Countryside Commission has argued that this area, too, needs to be recognised as on a par with national parks, but with a tailor-made administration. Other areas, such as the Forest of Dean, the Malvern Hills, Ashdown Forest and Chichester Harbour, are also protected under special Statutes (Countryside Commission, *in litt.*, 1991).

Non-governmental organisations have an extremely important role in conservation in the UK. A significant proportion of the statutory protected areas mentioned above are owned or managed by these bodies. The National Trust is a large landowner whose activities are to some degree covered by the National Trust Act, 1907. This Act provides for the establishment of the National Trust for Places of Historic Interest and Natural Beauty, and also states that land held by the Trust may be declared inalienable; it cannot be sold or otherwise disposed of without authorisation of an Act of Parliament, although it can be purchased compulsorily for development under specific circumstances. A broadly similar situation applies to the National Trust for Scotland.

The town and country planning system is a large body of law which is only partly concerned with protected areas. There are also specific rules which are aimed at protected areas: for example, the effect of the Town and Country Planning (national parks, AONBs and conservation areas) Special Development Orders 1981 and 1985 is to restrict the categories of development which would otherwise be automatically allowed in these areas. The legislation (now mainly consolidated in the Town and Country Planning Act, 1990) also governs conservation areas (these tend to be built areas) and rules concerning tree preservation (see above). The Planning and Compensation Act, 1991 contains measures that should further strengthen control over development that may threaten protected areas.

In 1990 a major policy statement was released by the government on the environment in its White Paper *This Common Inheritance: Britain's Environmental Strategy* (HMSO, 1990). This document confirmed the government's belief in the importance of the interaction between man and nature that has influenced, over many centuries, the landscape of the UK as it exists today. It suggested that the government intends to further conservation issues by working alongside private landowners and by encouraging the voluntary effort (for many further details see HMSO, 1990). However, the White Paper contained few initiatives which might improve protection of designated areas.

Government policy in relation to the various activities which may affect the countryside including designated areas, is expressed in guidance notes issued by government departments concerned. These are put into effect by the various agencies responsible for the activities in question, e.g. local planning authorities, the Ministry of Agriculture, the Forestry Commission. Two guidance circulars issued by the Department of the Environment are of particular importance in relation to planning decisions in protected areas: Circulars 107/77 *Nature Conservation and Planning* and 27/87 *Nature Conservation.*

International Activities   The Convention concerning the Protection of the World Cultural and Natural Heritage (World Heritage Convention) was ratified on 29 May 1984, three natural sites have been inscribed: one in Scotland, one in Northern Ireland and one at Henderson Island (UK-Pitcairn) in the Pacific. The government submitted the Cairngorms area for inclusion on the tentative list as a potential World Heritage Site in

1990. In October 1991 a working party was also established by the government to consider the Loch Lomond/Trossachs area (Countryside Commission for Scotland, *in litt.*, 1991). The Convention on Wetlands of International Importance especially as Waterfowl Habitat (Ramsar Convention) was ratified on 5 January 1976: 13 sites were designated on ratification and 47 are now listed, with one further site in the Turks and Caicos Islands, a UK Dependent Territory in the Caribbean. Thirteen sites have been accepted biosphere reserves under the Unesco Man and the Biosphere Programme. Membership of the international conventions by the UK central government does not imply automatic membership by the UK dependent territories, although most are mentioned in the original signatory texts. Examples to the contrary include the exclusion of Anguilla, British Indian Ocean Territory and the British Virgin Islands, which were not covered under the original ratification of the Ramsar Convention; the British Indian Ocean Territory was also left out of the World Heritage Convention, while British Antarctic Territory has been excluded from both (Oldfield, 1987). See separate accounts for further information about individual UK dependent territories.

As a member of the European Community, the UK is bound by EC legislation, including the Directive (79/409/EEC) on the Conservation of Wild Birds, which, in Article 4, requires member states to designate important areas as special protection areas. As of April 1991 there were 40 special protected areas in existence. The UK is a signatory to the Convention on the Conservation of European Wildlife and Natural Habitats (Bern Convention). The UK is a member of the Council of Europe: no Council of Europe biogenetic reserves have yet been declared, although 15 sites have been nominated and have been submitted (1991) to the Council (English Nature, *in litt.*, 1991). Five sites have been awarded the Council of Europe, European Diploma. The UK has also ratified the Convention for the Protection and Development of the Marine Environment of the Wider Caribbean Region, and the Convention for the Protection of the Natural Resources and Environment of the South Pacific Region.

Administration and Management   In a similar manner to legislation, the administration and management of protected areas in the UK is undertaken on a number of different levels: with some organisations working at the national level and others working at the regional or local level. In this section the situation is further complicated by the fact that there have been some very recent changes in the structure of some of the most important organisations.

The Wild Life Conservation Special Committee and the National Parks Committee (England and Wales) were established by the government after World War II (1939-1945) to look into nature conservation issues. One of the recommendations arising from the former Committee was for the establishment of a biological service, which came into effect when the Nature

Conservancy was established under Royal Charter in 1949 (NCC, 1984).

In 1973 the Nature Conservancy was split by the Nature Conservancy Council Act: the research arm remained linked to the National Environmental Research Council (NERC) as the Institute of Terrestrial Ecology (ITE), while the remainder was reconstituted as an independent council, the Nature Conservancy Council (NCC): this was to have a degree of autonomy so that it could take a strong and independent line on major issues when necessary. The functions of the NCC were: the establishment, maintenance and management of nature reserves in England, Scotland and Wales through its series of regional offices and wardening system; the provision of advice to government on the development and implementation of policies for or affecting nature conservation; the provision of advice and dissemination of knowledge about nature conservation; and the commissioning or support of relevant research. The NCC was funded through the Department of the Environment; its main function concerning protected areas was with national and local nature reserves, SSSIs, marine reserves, limestone pavement orders and nature conservation orders; it was also involved with the designation of Ramsar sites and EC SPAs (NCC, 1984). Among its duties, the NCC gave substantial grants towards the purchase and management of land: these were nearly always given to the major NGOs in the UK and were normally for the purchase of land that already has some form of statutory classification (notably SSSIs).

In 1990 the Environmental Protection Act was passed which, among other things led to the reorganisation of the NCC on 1 April 1991. Its duties now fall under the responsibility of four bodies: the Nature Conservancy Council for Scotland (NCCS), the Countryside Council for Wales, English Nature and the Joint Nature Conservation Committee (JNCC). The three "country" organisations have largely taken over the role of the former NCC, in the designation and maintenance of protected areas. The JNCC has 11 voting members and altogether approximately 100 staff. Its aims can be summarised as follows: to advise the government on policies for or affecting nature conservation in Great Britain, the UK or internationally; to disseminate information about nature conservation; to establish common standards for monitoring, research and analysis of results; to conduct research into nature conservation; to advise the country councils (Joint Nature Conservation Comittee, *in litt.*, 1991).

The National Parks Commission was set up under the National Parks and Access to the Countryside Act of 16 December 1949; it became the Countryside Commission (CC) under the Countryside Act of 1968, and in 1982 the CC was granted the status of an independent agency funded by the Department of the Environment: a status parallel to that of the former NCC. The Countryside Commission for Scotland (CCS) has a remit similar to that of the CC, but reports to the Scottish

Office. Both the CC and the CCS are responsible for promoting the conservation and enhancement of the natural beauty and scenic amenity of the countryside and encouraging its enjoyment by the public as a recreational asset. Objectives have been achieved by giving advice and grant-aid to local authorities and voluntary bodies for a whole range of conservation tasks, including land acquisition, tree-planting, the establishment of country parks, picnic sites, warden or ranger services and information. The CC is responsible for the designation of national parks and areas of outstanding natural beauty, and also defines heritage coasts: it advises on their administration and on the development of information and interpretation facilities, it also advises on the administration and management of the Norfolk and Suffolk Broads and the New Forest. In Scotland the CCS is responsible in a similar way for national scenic areas. Other activities undertaken by these bodies include sponsoring research and experimental work related to conservation and recreational problems (CC, 1987b; NCC, 1984). CC policy is formed by the Chairman and some 10 commissioners appointed by the secretaries of State for England and Wales. There are seven regional offices in England, while Wales had a separate committee with substantial delegated powers (until 1991). This Committee for Wales advised the Commission on policy matters; its members were appointed by the CC in consultation with the Secretary of State for Wales (CC, 1986). The new Countryside Council for Wales has combined the work of the former NCC and the CC in Wales. The CC is now responsible only for England.

On 1 April 1992 the CCS is due to be merged with the NCCS in Scotland, although the latter was itself only formed in 1991. The new body will be called Scottish Natural Heritage (SNH) and will inherit the duties of both of its predecessors. These will include the requirement to take account of: actual or possible ecological changes to the natural heritage; the needs of agriculture, fisheries and forestry; the need for social and economic development in Scotland; the need to conserve sites and landscapes of archaeological or historical interest; the interests of owners and occupiers of the land and the interests of the local communities. Natural heritage includes fauna and flora, geological and physiographic features, and natural beauty and amenity. It also has powers of compulsory purchase. Like its predecessors it will be a non-departmental government body accountable to parliament through the Secretary of State for Scotland and funded by the Scottish Office (CCS/NCCS, 1991).

The Department of the Environment (DoE) is the main government body concerned with environmental issues: as already mentioned, it provided the funding for the former NCC and for the CC. The Department has an extremely broad remit with regard to land-use policies and seeks to integrate different sectional interests in advising ministers – in this way, conservation does not always appear to be a primary concern. In Scotland the functions of the DoE are undertaken by the Scottish Office Environment Department (formerly the Scottish Development Department) – the Secretary of State for Scotland has an overview on all matters of environmental concern. A similar situation is found in Wales where environmental affairs are dealt with by the Welsh Office and the Secretary of State for Wales. The central DoE also represents the UK on many international conservation matters (NCC, 1984).

The NCC and the CC and their newly designated successors have no role in Northern Ireland where the Department of Environment (Northern Ireland) performs an equivalent function (although, at the request of the Department, the JNCC does maintain some involvement). This Department is responsible for the designation and management of areas of outstanding natural beauty, areas of special scientific interest, national nature reserves and marine nature reserves. The Department is divided into the Environment Service, the Planning Service, Roads Service and Water Service. Within the Conservation Service the Countryside and Wildlife Branch has responsibility for conservation and wildlife issues, while the Historic Monuments and Buildings Branch has responsibility for the cultural heritage (DoENI, 1989).

The conduct of government forestry policy in England, Scotland and Wales is the responsibility of the Forestry Commission (FC) which was established in 1919. The FC has designated a number of sites under the non-statutory categories of forest park, forest nature reserve and conservation area. In Northern Ireland forestry is the concern of the Forest Service, which is part of the Department of Agriculture (Northern Ireland).

Nature conservation and landscape protection in the UK is tightly linked with agricultural practices and hence there is constant interaction between official nature conservation bodies and the Ministry of Agriculture, Fisheries and Food (MAFF) (England), the Scottish Office Agriculture and Fisheries Department, the Welsh Office Agriculture Department and the Department of Agriculture (Northern Ireland). Section 17 of the Agriculture Act 1986 requires these agriculture departments to take into account conservation and environment issues. Outside their role in the designation of ESAs, the agriculture departments have limited powers, under current EC legislation, to take active steps to promote environmental issues through grant schemes. However, opportunities are increasingly being taken, and further powers are being sought through reform of the EC's Common Agricultural Policy (Ministry of Agriculture, Fisheries and Food, *in litt.*, 1991). The administration of ESAs is covered by the divisional and regional agricultural offices – a nominated Agricultural Development Advisory Service project officer for each site acts as the main interface between farmers and the Ministry or department (MAFF, 1989).

In 1991, the CC launched a national pilot scheme, Countryside Stewardship, offering financial incentives to farmers and landowners to undertake conservation work on their land in accordance with a number of prescriptions throughout the English countryside. These relate to the conservation and enhancement of chalk and limestone grassland, lowland heathland, riverside areas, coastal areas and uplands. The programme is expected to incorporate other prescriptions soon (e.g. hedgerow conservation). Funding for Countryside Stewardship is expected to expand during the next few years (Countryside Commission, *in litt.*, 1991).

Each of the national parks in England and Wales is run by its own statutory national park authority. These authorities fall within the local government system: two-thirds of their members are appointed by the local government, a majority by county councils, but with district councils also represented. One-third of the members are appointed by the Secretary of State for the Environment or Secretary of State for Wales. Funding is provided by central government (75%) and local authority sources (25%). Eight national parks are administered by national park committees within county councils of their respective counties. The other two national park authorities are independent authorities in their own right: the Peak Park Joint Planning Board and the Lake District Special Planning Board. National park authorities have a number of responsibilities which include: preparation of a national park plan setting out management policies; working with the NCC and CC on issues of nature conservation; responsibility for ranger services within the park, and the provision of information, interpretation and recreation facilities; they are also responsible to some degree for safeguarding cultural heritage. Typically, national park authorities have a planning and enforcement section, an estate management or upland management service, a ranger or warden service, an information and interpretation section and an administration section (CC, 1987a). Norfolk and Suffolk Broads are administered by the Broads Authority, while the New Forest is largely administered by the Forestry Commission under a specific mandate from the Minister of Agriculture (Poore and Poore, 1987).

With the endorsement of the government, the CC set up a review of national parks of England and Wales at the end of 1989 which reported early in 1991. Its recommendations have since been broadly endorsed by the CC and the CCW. This review, entitled "Fit for the Future", drew a number of conclusions: it recommended closer links between agriculture and conservation; proposed various ways in which the protection of national parks could be strengthened; called for improved arrangements for access to, and quiet enjoyment of national parks; and made suggestions for strengthening information, interpretation and education. Most importantly it recommended that each national park should be run by its own independent authority. It suggested that the New Forest should be formerly recognised as a national park, but with a specifically designed constitution. It stressed the international importance of the English and Welsh national parks as examples of the protected landscapes approach (IUCN Category V). It also called for additional government funding. In an interim response, the government has made clear that it accepts the central proposal that independent authorities should be established for each national park and has significantly increased the funding available to national parks over the next three years (Countryside Commission, *in litt.*, 1991).

There are a number of other bodies in the UK which have a major influence on the environment and are frequently involved in conservation issues. The National Rivers Authority (NRA) was established in 1989 with statutory responsibilities and powers in relation to pollution control, water resources, flood defense, fisheries, recreation, conservation and navigation (NRA, 1991); it also has a statutory duty under the Water Act, 1989 to further conservation. The Ministry of Defence (MoD) is another major landowner: it owns or leases 242,000ha in Britain, including 204 SSSIs and parts of all but one of the national parks. The MoD has employed a conservation officer since 1973 and there are now some 200 MoD conservation groups in the UK and overseas, each of which has a part-time conservation officer. Although damage may occur when military training takes place in these areas, many military sites appear to be better protected for nature conservation than their surroundings, possibly due to reduced public access, agricultural restrictions and conservation management undertaken by the military personnel themselves (Hills, 1991; MoD, 1989-1991).

Non-governmental organisations play a crucial role in nature conservation and many own or lease their own, non-statutory, protected areas. Many are also involved in the management of statutory protected areas designated by official government bodies (for example, 10% of SSSIs in Britain are owned or managed by NGOs, which is roughly equivalent to the figure owned or managed by the NCC and its successors (English Nature, *in litt.*, 1991)). The National Trust is the second largest landholder in the country – it has over 2,200 full-time and part-time staff in 13 regional offices (Environment Council, 1990; National Trust, 1987). The Trust was established to conserve the beauty of England and Wales by acquiring properties "in perpetuity" – in this way it acts to protect both the natural and the cultural heritage. It has been reported in the past not to have paid sufficient attention to nature conservation issues (Chatters and Minter, 1986). In Scotland, the National Trust for Scotland is a similar, although completely separate organisation: established in 1931 it now owns over 100 properties of natural and/or cultural importance and its countryside estate now covers over 40,000ha (National Trust for Scotland, 1991).

Other NGOs which play an important role in the ownership and management of protected areas include: the Royal Society for Nature Conservation (RSNC) Wildlife Trusts Partnership (which is an umbrella organisation for local and county wildlife trusts); the Royal Society for the Protection of Birds (RSPB); the Woodland Trust; and the Wildfowl and Wetlands Trust. The World Wide Fund for Nature UK is one of the largest of the national WWF bodies: it helps to fund hundreds of conservation projects throughout the UK. The British Trust for Conservation Volunteers, together with its sister organisation, Scottish Conservation Projects, is involved in coordinating conservation and countryside management activities in thousands of sites (mostly protected areas) throughout the UK. Important campaigning bodies include: the Council for the Protection of Rural England; the Association for the Protection of Rural Scotland and the Ramblers Association (Environment Council, 1990).

The Environment Council acts as a umbrella body for a large number of the NGOs operating in the UK, it aims to focus attention on major environmental issues and to facilitate cooperation between organisations concerned with the environment. It produces a series of *Who's Who in the Environment* directories, which summarise information about over 1,000 organisations with an environmental interest in the UK (Environment Council, 1990).

The Council for National Parks is a national voluntary organisation whose objectives are to promote the purposes for which the national parks were set up: the conservation of natural beauty and the promotion of the parks for the enjoyment of the public. It was established as an independent organisation in 1977 to take over from the Standing Committee on National Parks which was set up in 1936 to campaign for the designation of national parks. It is composed of over 30 national and local amenity, recreation and wildlife bodies (CC, 1985). A Scottish Council for National Parks was re-established in 1990 to campaign for national parks in Scotland, following the government's decision to take no further action for the present on the parks recommendations of the Countryside Commission for Scotland (Countryside Commission for Scotland, *in litt.*, 1991)

The organisations with statutory responsibilities for the cultural heritage of the country are the Historic Buildings and Monuments Commission for England (commonly known as English Heritage), Historic Scotland and Cadw in Wales. These are the government's official advisers on the conservation of the built environment, including archaeological sites and ancient monuments (Environment Council, 1990).

Amongst some of the chief concerns about administrative and management threats to protected areas within the UK arise from the ineffectiveness of the legal definitions of almost every category of protected area. Protection, in most cases, appears to rely at least as heavily on goodwill and public opinion as it does on the legal framework. Tens or hundreds of cases arise every year of developments such as road building, mineral extraction, housing and other property developments, land drainage and reclamation, agricultural changes, afforestation, hydro-electric schemes, waste disposal and pollution occurring in or being proposed for the country's "protected" areas – for example, in the year leading to March 1991, 127 existing sites suffered short-term damage; 18 had long-term damage and 4 suffered partial loss of their scientific value (which will lead to denotification of part of the site) (NCC, 1991). The law rarely prohibits such activities, and often the only effective control over these cases arises from the vociferous and relatively well-organised NGO movement. Campaigns led by these organisations are by no means always successful and it is clear that, while protected areas are usually better protected than their surroundings, no category of protection really offers full legal protection to these areas. In Scotland the omission of national parks from the protected areas system is seen by some as a major problem (CCS, 1991).

The agricultural bodies in England, Wales, Scotland and Northern Ireland have come under considerable criticism in the past for the environmental damage they have been seen to encourage, largely through the granting of government subsidies and development-aid (NCC, 1984).

The changes to the organisation of the NCC were apparently not welcomed by the old NCC, nor by the majority of non-governmental organisations in the country. It is thought that they will prove extremely costly in terms of both man-power and financing (NCC, 1990a, 1991). Some problems have arisen concerning the designation of marine nature reserves. Byelaws under the 1981 Act are restricted to those functions which are not already the responsibility of another authority, and there have been considerable difficulties in the negotiations with the sea fisheries committees, who are the principal byelaw making authorities in these areas and yet frequently do not see their own vested interest in nature conservation.

National parks were recommended for Scotland as long ago as 1945. The CCS's Mountain Areas Report, published in 1990, was followed by a further document in 1991 after public consultation. Concern was expressed over use of the term national park, which, it was felt, might increase visitor pressure; some other responses indicated opposition to any form of new designation. Despite support from IUCN for the proposals, government reaction to these documents has been to shelve the idea of national parks for Scotland for the time being, although a working party has been established to consider the special action needed for the Cairngorms (CCS, 1990, 1991, *in litt.*, 1991).

Systems Reviews   The United Kingdom of Great Britain and Northern Ireland is divided into two distinct geographical units: the island of Great Britain (further divided, politically, into England, Scotland and Wales) and Northern Ireland, which consists of the north-eastern corner of Ireland, and shares a border with the Republic of Ireland. Britain is separated from the Nordic countries to the east by the North Sea; the English Channel to the south presents a narrow barrier between Britain and

France, while Ireland lies to the west, separated by the Irish Sea. There are many hundreds of islands off the British coast. These include: the Hebrides off the north-west of Scotland (which include the far-flung St Kilda Group); the Orkneys and Shetlands to the north of Scotland; the Isle of Man in the Irish Sea and the Channel Islands in the Channel, physically very close to the coast of France (see separate accounts for the Isle of Man and the Channel Islands). Most of the south and west of Britain is low-lying or has undulating hills. The Principality of Wales in the west is largely mountainous, with the peak of Snowdon reaching 1,085m. The north of England and most of Scotland are also mountainous; the highest peak in the UK is Ben Nevis in Scotland which reaches 1,343m. Most of the country has been shaped by the ice-cap and glaciers during the Pleistocene, when ice covered all but the southern parts of England. In Northern Ireland the landscape is hilly rather than mountainous except for two small areas, the Sperrin Mountains and the Mountains of Mourne.

The UK has an extremely varied coastline, exceeding 7,000km in length, not including offshore islands: communities are found associated with sandy shores, shingle banks, dune systems, extensive estuarine areas, salt marshes, sea lochs (in Scotland and Ireland), flooded river valleys, rocky shores and cliffs.

The countryside and landscape is almost entirely a product of man's interaction with nature. Man has been active in the country for the past few thousand years. Originally, two-thirds of the country was covered by forest, principally of oak, lime, birch and ash giving way to beech in the south, and Scots pine and birch in the north: much of this was cleared in Neolithic times, and the few small areas of ancient forest which remain have mostly been extensively modified by centuries of coppicing and other activities. In total, forests cover about 2.23 million ha or 9% of the total area of the UK: most of this is coniferous plantation forestry, with low numbers of native species. In a survey of sites of ancient semi-natural woodland over 2ha, the NCC has produced the following figures: Wales, 28,851ha; Scotland, 89,846ha; England, 207,915ha: giving a total of nearly 1.5% of total land area. Caledonian pine forests (which once covered over 1.5 million ha of Scotland) mark the transition to sub-Arctic boreal vegetation; the total area now covered by this type of forest is now no more than 12,500ha (Forestry Commission, 1989, *in litt.*, 1991; Heiss, 1987).

In the humid oceanic areas of north and west Britain, as well as large areas of Ireland, some of the most important areas of peatlands in Europe are found. There are numerous other important biological communities, many of which are wholly or partly the result of man's intervention with nature. Where the forest has been cleared many areas are maintained as grasslands by grazing farm animals. Where they are not subjected to intensive agricultural practices, such sub-climactic semi-natural grasslands can support diverse communities. The landscape is frequently diversified by a complex patchwork of small woodlands and hedgerows. Where the soils are too poor to support grassland, the original forests have been replaced by moors and heaths.

Much of what it is now considered to be in need of protection is a result of agricultural and other human activities and consists of sub-climax communities. The policy behind protection of most areas is, therefore, one of constructive coexistence between the natural environment and human activities. It is seen to be as much about the encouragement of practices which maintain the countryside which man has created, as it is about preventing harmful activities. Much of the countryside designated for special protection is also privately owned. Protection, therefore, has to rely heavily upon a voluntary conservation ethic, helped where appropriate by government aid, so that individuals can act in their own economic interests as well as the interests of conservation.

Historically, the New Forest was one of the first protected areas in the UK, having been declared a royal hunting preserve in 1079. In the early years of this century, the establishment of protected areas for conservation purposes was largely the work of the non-governmental organisations. By 1910 the National Trust owned 13 sites with wildlife importance. The Society for the Promotion of Nature Reserves (SPNR) was established in 1910; one of its first tasks was to compile a countrywide list of 251 areas of national importance for wildlife, of which 52 were recommended as nature reserves. The SPNR was also involved in the promotion of nature conservation issues in post-war reconstruction, and recommended the establishment of a Nature Reserves Investigation Committee which brought together leading amateurs and professionals in a movement that was subsequently embraced by the government. The government established the Wild Life Conservation Special Committee which, in 1947, produced a report entitled *Conservation of Nature in England and Wales* recommending the establishment of nature reserves not only for research and experimentation, but also for their educational and recreational value (NCC, 1984). This was followed with an extensive review of "areas of national biological importance", carried out in the 1960s and 1970s and widely known as the Nature Conservation Review (Ratcliffe, 1977).

By 1973 135 NNRs had been established covering 112,723ha. As of March 1991 there were 242 national nature reserves covering a total of 168,107ha; two marine nature reserves, with a further three proposed; 5,671 SSSIs covering 1,778,474ha; there were also some 29 nature conservation orders in force at that date and 241 LNRs (NCC, 1991). Under the original 1949 Act, a NNR could not overlap with a LNR. Other sites do overlap, however – all NNRs and many LNRs are SSSIs. Only two marine nature reserves have been created in ten years. The first four national parks were designated in 1951 – there are now 10 national parks in England and

Wales, the last of which was declared in 1957, covering a total of 1,364,800ha; the Broads, as designated under the Broads Act of 1988, cover a further 28,800ha, and are widely considered equivalent to national parks: the total area covered by these represents over 9% of the total area of England and Wales (National Parks Review Panel, 1991). AONBs vary greatly in size, from a few sq. km (e.g. the Isles of Scilly) to nearly 2,000 sq. km in the case of the North Wessex Downs. There are 39 designated AONBs, which do not overlap with national parks, covering 2,043,900ha, or 13.5% of the total area of England and Wales (CC, 1991). By August 1989, 41 heritage coasts covering nearly 14,00km of coastline had been either completely or laterally defined (HCF, 1989). In Scotland, the 40 national scenic areas cover 1,017,300ha, or 12% of the total land area (CRC, 1988). The first two statutory regional parks were approved in 1986, and there are now four parks designated. In Northern Ireland, there are nine AONBs (DoENI, 1989) and some 44 NNRs (CCC, 1990).

The major non-governmental organisations holding land for nature conservation purposes include the National Trust; the National Trust for Scotland; the 47 local and county wildlife trusts (which together form the Wildlife Trusts Partnership of the RSNC); the Royal Society for the Protection of Birds; and the Woodland Trust. They play a major role in conservation issues – between them these bodies own and/or manage over 407,000ha, or some 1.66% of the total area of the country.

The government, through a joint initiative between the Forestry Commission and the Countryside Commission, is planning to establish nine "community forests" covering more than 400,000ha of land adjacent to cities in England and Wales, in addition to the three such forests announced in 1989. The aims of these forests will include: recreation, landscape enhancement, wildlife conservation and timber production. Forests will be planted on both agricultural and derelict land, and a large proportion will comprise native deciduous tree species. The programme, costing an estimated £70 million, commenced with the CC obtaining £600,000 to finance coordinating committees for each forest (NCC, 1990b). In addition, the government is supporting the establishment of a new national forest in the English Midlands. This will cover over 50,000ha and will be a forested landscape created from land currently in agricultural use or in a derelict state following former mineral workings (Countryside Commission, *in litt.*, 1991). A central Scotland forest project has been developing over a number of years on the plateau between Edinburgh and Glasgow and recent government initiatives are accelerating these developments (Countryside Commission for Scotland, *in litt.*, 1991).

Threats to natural areas arise from many sources. In SSSIs the main threats have been identified as overgrazing, pollution, and what may well be natural succession in sites that have been designated for the protection of their non-climax communities (English Nature, *in litt.*, 1991). The continued expansion of the road network frequently threatens protected areas and unique habitats. Afforestation programmes, often supported in the past by tax incentives, have been criticised, especially where intensive monocultures are replacing important heathland and moorland communities (Tompkins, 1989). Air pollution and acidification appear to be an increasing threat to communities throughout the country, despite the fact that levels of emissions of many gases have stabilised or dropped markedly in recent years. There is considerable evidence that some plant species, including beech and oak, are suffering a decline in health, partly due to air pollution effects, but also due to pest attack and outbreak of disease (Anon., 1989; Dudley, 1987; Forestry Commission, *in litt.*, 1991). Problems are occurring in a large number of protected areas simply due to the vast number of tourists (see Other Relevant Information). Similar problems are occurring in Scotland, particularly in the Cairngorms and at Loch Lomond. Both areas have been urgently recommended for national park designation by the Countryside Commission for Scotland (CCS, *in litt.*, 1991). One major source of conflict at present is over the threat to lowland raised bogs and blanket bogs which are being destroyed over large areas for commercial peat extraction. These communities, influenced as they are by the oceanic climate, are almost unique to Britain and Ireland (Lawson, 1990).

Other Relevant Information   Tourism is a major feature of the national parks of England and Wales and in some of the national scenic areas in Scotland. The latest available figures show that the national parks of England and Wales received a total of 103 million visitor days a year, with the greatest number visiting the Lake District and Peak District national parks, some 20 million visitor days a year each (National Parks Review Panel, 1991).

Addresses

The Countryside Commission, John Dower House, Crescent Place, CHELTENHAM, GL50 3RA (Tel: 242 521 381; FAX: 242 584 270)

The Countryside Commission for Scotland, Battleby, Redgorton, PERTH PH1 3EW, Scotland (Tel: 0738 27921; FAX: 738 30583)

Countryside Council for Wales, Plas Penrhos, Ffordd Penrhos, BANGOR, Gwynedd LL57 2LQ, Wales (Tel: 248 370 444; FAX: 248 355 782)

Department of the Environment for Northern Ireland, Countryside and Wildlife Branch, Calvert House, 23 Castle Place, BELFAST BT1 1FY, Northern Ireland (Tel: 232 230 560

Department of Agriculture (Northern Ireland), Forest Service, Dundonald House, Upper Newtownards Road, BELFAST, BT4 3SB, Northern Ireland (Tel: 232 650 111)

English Nature, Northminster House, PETERBOROUGH PE1 1UA (Tel: 733 340345; FAX: 733 68834)

Forestry Commission, 231 Corstorphine Road, EDINBURGH EH12 7AT, Scotland (Tel: 31 334 0303)

Joint Nature Conservation Committee, Monkstone House, PETERBOROUGH PE1 1JY (Tel: 733 62626; FAX: 733 555948)

Nature Conservancy Council for Scotland, 12 Hope Terrace, EDINBURGH EH9 2AS, Scotland (Tel: 31 447 4784)

Council for National Parks, 45 Shelton Street, LONDON WC2H 9HJ (Tel: 71 240 3603)

Environment Council, 80 York Way, LONDON N1 9AG (Tel: 71 278 4736)

National Trust, 36 Queen Anne's Gate, LONDON SW1H 0AS (Tel: 71 222 9251)

National Trust for Scotland, 5 Charlotte Square, EDINBURGH EH2 4DU, Scotland (Tel: 31 226 5922; FAX: 31 220 6266)

Royal Society for the Protection of Birds, The Lodge, SANDY, Bedfordshire SG19 2DL (Tel: 767 680 551; Tlx: 82469 RSPB; FAX: 767 692 365)

Royal Society for Nature Conservation, The Wildlife Trusts Partnership and WATCH, The Green, Witham Park, Waterside South, LINCOLN LN5 7JR (Tel: 522 544 400)

Scottish Council for National Parks, 15 Park Terrace, STIRLING, FK8 2JT (Tel: 786 65714; Fax: 786 73843)

The Wildfowl and Wetlands Trust, Slimbridge, GLOUCESTER GL2 7BT (Tel: 453 890 333)

The Woodland Trust, Autumn Park, Dysart Road, GRANTHAM, Lincolnshire NG31 6LL (Tel: 476 74297; FAX: 476 590 808)

References

CCS/NCCS (1991). *Natural Partners*. Countryside Commission for Scotland and Nature Conservancy Council for Scotland, Perth and Edinburgh. 4 pp.

Chatters, C. and Minters, R. (1986). Nature Conservation and the National Trust. *ECOS* 7(4): 24-32.

CRC (1988). *The effectiveness of landscape designations in Scotland, a review study*. Report produced for the Countryside Commission for Scotland and the Scottish Development Department. Cobham Resource Consultants Ltd. 100 pp.

CC (1985). *Watch over the National Parks*. Countryside Commission, Cheltenham. Document: CCP 198. 28 pp.

CC (1986). *Your countryside: our concern*. Pamphlet. Countryside Commission, Cheltenham. 12 pp

CC (1987a). *The National Park Authority*. Countryside Commission, Cheltenham. Document: CCP 230. 20 pp.

CC (1987b). *At work in the countryside*. Pamphlet. Countryside Commission, Cheltenham.

CC (1990). *Protected areas in the United Kingdom*. Map. Countryside Commission, Cheltenham.

CC (1991). *Areas of outstanding natural beauty, a policy statement 1991*. Countryside Council for Wales and

Countryside Commission, Cheltenham. Document: CCP 356. 22 pp.

CCS (1988). *A park system and scenic conservation in Scotland*. Countryside Commission for Scotland, Perth. 4 pp.

CCS (1990). *The mountain areas of Scotland, conservation and management*. Countryside Commission for Scotland, Perth. 64 pp.

CCS (1991). *The mountain areas of Scotland, conservation and management, a report on public consultation*. Countryside Commission for Scotland, Perth. 51 pp.

Cutrera, A. (1991). *European Environmental Yearbook*. International Institute for Environmental Studies, DocTer UK Ltd, London. 897 pp.

DoENI (1989). *Mourne, area of outstanding natural beauty, policies and proposals*. Department of Environment (Northern Ireland), Belfast. 52 pp.

Dudley, N. (1987). *Cause for Concern, an analysis of air pollution damage and natural habitats*. A Friends of the Earth Research Report, London.

Environment Council (1990). *Who's who in the Environment in England*. The Environment Council, London. 337 pp.

Forestry Commission (1985). *Guidelines for the management of broadleaved woodland*. Forestry Commission, Edinburgh. 21 pp.

Forestry Commission (1989a). *Control of Tree Felling*. Forestry Commission, Edinburgh. 7 pp.

Forestry Commission (1989b). *Native Pinewoods Grants and Guidelines*. Forestry Commission, Edinburgh. 11 pp.

Heiss, G. (1987). Inventory of natural (virgin) and ancient seminatural woodlands within the councils member states and Finland. European Committee for the Conservation of Nature and Natural Resources. Unpublished report. Pp. 163-204.

HCF (1989). *Heritage Coast Directory*. Heritage Coast Forum, Manchester Polytechnic, Manchester.

Hills, A. (1991). A green Ministry. *Geographical Magazine* 64(5): 16-20.

HMSO (1990). *This Common Inheritance: Britain's Environmental Strategy*. Her Majesty's Stationery Office.

Lawson, T. (1990). Peat in Peril. *Green Magazine* 1(4): 62-65.

MAFF (1989). *Environmentally Sensitive Areas*. Ministry of Agriculture, Fisheries and Food, London. 50 pp.

MoD (1989-1991). *Sanctuary, the Ministry of Defence Conservation Magazine*. Nos. 18,19,20. Ministry of Defence Conservation Office, Chessington, Surrey.

National Parks Review Panel (1991). *Fit for the future: Report of the National Parks Review Panel*. Countryside Commission, Cheltenham. Document: CCP 335. 151 pp.

NRA (1991). *National Rivers Authority, Guardians of the water environment*. Pamphlet. National Rivers Authority, Bristol.

National Trust (1987). *The National Trust, access and conservation*. Pamphlet. London. 4 pp.

National Trust for Scotland (1991). *Guide to over 100 properties*. National Trust for Scotland, Edinburgh. 57 pp.

NCC (1983). *Eighth Report 1 April 1981-31 March 1982*. Nature Conservancy Council, London. 154 pp.

NCC (1984). *Nature conservation in Great Britain*. Nature Conservancy Council, Shrewsbury. 112 pp.

NCC (1989). *Put nature on the map*. Local nature reserves pamphlet. Nature Conservancy Council, Peterborough.

NCC (1990a). *Sixteenth Report 1 April 1989-31 March 1990*. Nature Conservancy Council, Peterborough. 184 pp.

NCC (1990b). Community forests. *Topical issues*. Nature Conservancy Council, Peterborough. P. 1.

NCC (1991). *Seventeenth Report 1 April 1990-31 March 1991*. Nature Conservancy Council, Peterborough. 126 pp.

Oldfield, S. (1987). *Fragments of paradise: a guide for conservation in the UK dependent territories*. British Association of Nature Conservationists, Oxford, UK. 192 pp.

Poore, D. and Poore, J. (1987). *Protected Landscapes: the United Kingdom Experience*. Countryside Commission/Countryside Commission for Scotland/Department of the Environment for Northern Ireland/International Union for the Conservation of Nature and Natural Resources. IUCN, Gland, Switzerland. 86 pp. (This publication is currently being revised for re-issue in 1992.)

Ratcliffe, D.A. (1977). *A Nature Conservation Review*. Cambridge, UK.

Tompkins, S. (1989). Forestry in crisis. *ECOS* 10(4): 16-21.

Woodland Trust (1991). *The Woodland Trust Annual Report 1989/1990*. The Woodland Trust, Grantham. 14 pp.

ANNEX
Definitions of protected area designations, as legislated, together with authorities responsible for their administration

Title: National Parks and Access to the Countryside Act 1949 and related acts

Date: 16 December 1949

Brief description: Provides for the establishment of national parks in England and Wales and a National Parks Commission (now the Countryside Commission); empowered the Nature Conservancy (subsequently the Nature Conservancy Council and now the four nature conservation authorities) and local authorities to establish and maintain nature reserves, areas of outstanding natural beauty, and sites of special scientific interest. Further provisions relate to publics paths and access to the countryside.

Administrative authorities: National parks – National Parks Authorities, Countryside Commission

Areas of outstanding natural beauty and local nature reserves – Local authorities and the four nature conservation authorities

Designations

National park "Extensive tracts of country" in England and Wales which are worthy of protection by reason of their natural beauty and their recreation value. The objective is to preserve the characteristic landscape beauty, to provide access and facilities for public open air enjoyment; and to protect wildlife and places of architectural and historic interest.

Controls on all activities are very strict, although few activities are actually prohibited, established farming use is effectively maintained. Development plans are a statutory requirement, structure plans are prepared by the county councils (except in the case of the Lake District and Peak District where they are prepared by the national park boards); subject plans (e.g. for minerals or recreation), district local plans and metropolitan Borough unitary plans also play a role.

Mineral extraction, and civil engineering projects such as the building of roads, power stations, reservoirs, pumped storage schemes are theoretically permissable, although it is government policy that any such projects should be subject to rigorous examination and should only be approved when they are clearly in the public interest (all of these activities do take place in one or more of the national parks). The Town and Country Planning (Agriculture and Forestry Development in National Parks, etc.) Special Development Order of 1986 requires farmers to consult the authority on the design appearance and siting of farm buildings and farm and forest roads. Use for military training generally predates the designation of the parks themselves and it continues to the present.

Area of outstanding natural beauty (AONB) "Parts of the countryside [of England and Wales] which, while they lack extensive areas of open countryside suitable for recreation and national park status, are nonetheless of such fine landscape quality that there is a national as well as a local interest in keeping them so".

The principal objective of their protection is the conservation of natural beauty. Full regard, however, must still be paid to the economic and social well being of the area. Nature conservation and the provision of recreation are not given explicit reference although "natural beauty" is defined as including a reference to fauna, flora, geology, etc.

Designation is supposed to assist sound planning and development by constituting clear official recognition of the importance of preserving the attractiveness of the areas.

They tend to lack extensive areas of open country suitable for recreation and national park status, but are nonetheless of such fine landscape quality that there is a national as well as a local interest in keeping them so. Government assistance is available to assist local authorities in their expenditure in these areas - assistance leans towards preservation of the beauty of the area rather than public recreation. Designation by the Countryside Commission (and now the new Countryside Council for Wales), with confirmation by the Secretary of State, takes place after consultation with local authorities, publicity, and representations by interest persons.

Local nature reserve (LNR) Declared by local authorities (borough, county, district and regional councils, and special planning boards), in consultation with the Nature Conservancy Council (and now its new successors), wherever they consider it expedient to do so, under Section 21 of the Act. Most are established by agreement between the local authority and landowners. Regulations are laid down for each site.

Site of special scientific interest (SSSI) Most of the provisions for this category are now covered under the 1981 Wildlife and Countryside Act (see below)

Sources: Countryside Commission, 1987a; National Parks and Access to the Countryside Act 1949

Title : Countryside Act 1968

Date: 3 July 1968

Brief description: Provides for the designation of country parks. Enlarged the functions of the national parks commission; conferred new powers on the local authorities and other bodies for the conservation and enhancement of the countryside and recreational use; amended laws related to trees and woodlands, footpaths, bridleways and other public paths.

Administrative authority: Countryside Commission

Designations:

Country park   To provide opportunities for leisure and recreation closer to urban areas than the national parks, which are in most cases quite far from the major conurbations. Country parks are established by local authorities, either on land which they own (there are powers to purchase land compulsorily for the purpose of establishing Country Parks) or by agreement with the owner. The Countryside Commission (and now the new Countryside Commission for Wales) can influence the location and management with powers it has to recommend whether the local authority should be eligible for grant aid from central government. Many contain sites important for conservation and may be managed for this purpose as well as leisure and recreation.

Source: Original legislation

Title: Wildlife and Countryside Act 1981
Wildlife and Countryside (Amendment) Act

Date: 1981, 1985 (Amendment)

Brief description: A wide ranging Act, Part I deals with the preservation of flora and fauna, Part II of the Act is important for protection of natural areas – it deals with sites of special scientific interest, national nature reserves, marine nature reserves, limestone pavement orders and nature conservation orders. Part III deals with public rights of way.

Administrative authority: Nature Conservancy Council – now replaced by the Countryside Council for Wales, English Nature, the Nature Conservancy Council for Scotland and the Joint Nature Conservation Committee, collectively referred to in the following section as the conservation authorities.

The Act also gives the Minister of Agriculture, county or local (in Scotland, district) planning authorities, various duties and functions in relation to countryside management.

Designations:

Site of special scientific interest (SSSI) Designation may apply to any area of land which, in the opinion of the conservation authorities, is of special interest by reason of its flora, fauna, or geological or physiographical features. Designation involves a procedure whereby the conservation authorities notify the owner and occupier of the land, the local planning authority in the area, and the Secretary of State for the Environment of the SSSI status. It specifies the flora, fauna or geological or physiographical features which render the land of special interest, and lists operations likely to damage such flora, fauna, or features.

After notification the owner or occupier cannot carry out potentially damaging operations unless either (i) the conservation authorities have given consent; or (ii) there is an agreement with the conservation authorities regulating the management of the land; or (iii) a period of four months has elapsed after notifying the conservation authorities of intent to carry out the works, or (iv) there is a grant of planning permission in relation to the land; or (v) the operations are carried out in an emergency and the conservation authorities are notified as soon as practicable afterwards.

There is no presumption against granting planning permission for development on SSSI land, although the planning authority must consult the conservation authorities, and the SSSI status will be a material consideration in reaching any decision.

Unless he or she reaches agreement with the conservation authorities, the owner/occupier is at liberty to carry out potentially damaging operations after four months have elapsed. The only available course then to protect the site is for the Secretary of State, in consultation with the conservation authorities, to make a Nature Conservation Order (see below).

National nature reserve (NNR)   Had previously been declared under Section 17 of the 1949 Act – the 1981 Act gave statutory recognition to the term NNR. They comprise land of national importance which is managed as a nature reserve by the conservation authorities, under an agreement with the them or an approved body. Once designated, the conservation authorities may make byelaws for the protection of the reserve. They are managed (as originally described under the 1949 Act) for the purpose of providing special opportunities for study and research and/or for preserving the fauna, flora or geological or landform features of special interest in the area. Restrictions may be placed on public access, although this is not normally the case. All NNRs are also SSSIs.

Marine nature reserve (MNR)   These may be in tidal waters or parts of the sea from the high water mark out to the seaward limits of the territorial sea. Designation is by the Secretary of State on application by the conservation authorities.

Designation may be for the purpose of conserving marine flora or fauna or geological or physiographical features of special interest, or for providing special opportunities for study and research. The conservation authorities manage MNRs and to facilitate this have power to make byelaws, in consultation with other interested bodies, although these are restricted to those functions which are not already the responsibility of another authority.

Limestone pavement order (LPO)   Made by the Secretary of State or the relevant planning authority, on the recommendation of the conservation authorities or Countryside Commission, they are designed to prevent removal or disturbance of limestone pavements, i.e. areas of limestone which lie wholly or partly exposed on the surface of the ground and which have been fissured by natural erosion in situations where the conservation authorities or Countryside Commission consider them of special interest. As with SSSIs, planning permission may allow disturbance of an area even though it is covered by an LPO. The designation is uncommon but is important for protection of rare flora in some areas.

Nature conservation order   Made by the Secretary of State on land he or she considers to be of special importance or where the designation of a site is necessary to comply with an international obligation. Orders are usually made on the recommendation of the conservation authorities, requiring owners and occupiers to give notice to the conservation authorities of any proposal to carry out any operation specified in the order. Once such an order has been made, the conservation authorities have three months in which to respond by offering to acquire an interest in the land or to enter into a management agreement. If an agreement is not reached the owner or occupier is prohibited from carrying out the work for a further nine months, and if, as a last resort the conservation authorities decide to use their powers of compulsory purchase, the period is further extended to prevent damage to the land. Compensation may be paid to those with an interest in land subject an order under Section 29.

Source: Nature Conservancy Council, 1983

Title: Agriculture Act 1986

Date: 25 July, 1986

Brief description: Provides *inter alia* for the designation of environmentally sensitive areas as required under EC regulations

Administrative authority: Minister of Agriculture, Fisheries and Food (England); Scottish Agriculture and Fisheries Department; Welsh Office Agriculture Department; and the Department of Agriculture (Northern Ireland).

Designation:

Environmentally sensitive area (ESA)   Results from EC Regulations on Agricultural Structures (EEC/2328/91 and predecessors). The EC scheme allows member states to introduce aid schemes which contribute towards the introduction or maintenance of farming practices in areas which are particularly sensitive from the points of view of protection of the environment and natural resources or maintenance of the landscape and countryside. They are put into practice through the Agriculture Act 1986.

The Minister of Agriculture Fisheries and Food may designate an area as an ESA if, following consultation with the Secretary of State for the Environment, the Countryside Commission and the conservation authorities, it appears to him that it is particularly desirable to conserve and enhance the natural beauty of the area; or, conserve the flora or geological or physiographical features of the area; or, protect buildings or other objects of archaeological, architectural or historical interest in the area. Maintenance or adoption of particular agricultural methods must be likely to facilitate such conservation, enhancement or protection. There must also be Treasury consent to the designation. The ESA scheme is then put into practice by MAFF making individual agreements with owners and occupiers of land in the area to manage their land in a particular way in return for cash payments.

Title: Town and Country Planning (Scotland) Act 1972

Date: 1972 – the order made through this Act for the designation of national scenic areas took effect from 1980. In 1986 Section 262C was introduced to the Act to provide a statutory basis for national scenic area designation.

Brief Description: Giving statutory recognition to the 40 national scenic areas outlined under the Countryside Commission's report *Scotland's Scenic Heritage*

Administrative Authority: Countryside Commission for Scotland

Designations:

National scenic area (NSA)   Protection is mainly exercised through special development control procedures. Further protection is given by the requirement that local authorities are bound to consult with the Countryside Commission for Scotland where proposed development or changes fall within certain categories, and must then go to the Secretary of State for Scotland if they disagree with the policy and advice given by the Countryside Commission for Scotland. Much has been achieved concerning the protection of these landscapes simply due to the goodwill and increasing sensitivity towards conservation issues of the landowners and authorities. Agriculture and forestry currently lie outside the control of local planning authorities, and are not strictly controlled.

Sources: Poore and Poore, 1987; Countryside Commission for Scotland, *in litt.*, 1991.

Title: Countryside (Scotland) Act 1967

Date: 27 October 1967

Brief description: Provides for better enjoyment of the Scottish countryside, the establishment of the Countryside Commission for Scotland, the improvement of recreational and other facilities, extension of powers of local planning authorities including establishment of country parks, and for regional councils to designate regional parks. It also deals with access to open country, public paths and long distance routes.

Administrative authority: Countryside Commission for Scotland, local and regional authorities

Designations:

Country park Parks or pleasure grounds in the countryside which by reason of their position in relation to major concentrations of population affords convenient opportunities to the public for enjoyment of the countryside or open air recreation. Generally these are small areas, between 10 and 400ha, with fairly intensive countryside recreational use.

Regional park Extensive area of land, part of which is devoted to the recreational needs of the public.

Sources: Countryside Commission for Scotland, 1988; Countryside (Scotland) Act, 1967

Title: Natural Heritage (Scotland) Act 1991

Date: 27 June 1991

Brief Description: Established Scottish Natural Heritage, which will take over (April, 1992) the functions of NCCS and CCS; provides for designation of National Heritage Areas; review of SSSIs; other unrelated matters.

Administrative Authority: Scottish Natural Heritage (SNH)

Designations:

Natural heritage area Natural heritage includes fauna and flora, geological and physiographic features, natural beauty and amenity. SNH has powers, including using compulsory purchase, to prepare proposals with respect to any area for a development project or scheme which is designed to achieve the conservation or enhancement of or which fosters understanding or enjoyment of the natural heritage. National scenic areas remain in force, but new areas will be established as NHAs.

Title: Amenity Lands Act (Northern Ireland) 1965; Nature Conservation and Amenity Lands (Northern Ireland) Order 1985

Date: 31 March 1965

Brief Description: Wide-ranging legislation which includes the provisions for the designation of national parks and areas of outstanding natural beauty. The 1965 Act was superseded in its entirety by the Nature Conservation and Amenity Lands (Northern Ireland) Order 1985.

Administrative Authority: Environment Service of the Department of the Environment for Northern Ireland

Designations:

Area of outstanding natural beauty (AONB) Similar to AONBs in England and Wales. Sites are designated by the Department of the Environment (Northern Ireland), and the Department may also formulate proposals for: conserving or enhancing the natural beauty or amenities of the area; conserving wildlife, historic objects or natural phenomena within it; promoting its enjoyment by the public; and providing and maintaining public access to it. All areas designated under the old Amenity Lands Act are being reviewed and redesignated under the new 1985 legislation, this is based on a change in emphasis away from development control to a broader conservation objective.

National park Although specified in the above legislation, no sites have been designated and there are no proposals for the designation of sites in the immediate future. In practise there is little difference between the conservation effectiveness of the categories of AONBs and national parks defined under this Act.

Area of special scientific interest (ASSI) Equivalent to SSSIs in the remainder of the UK

National nature reserve (NNR) Equivalent to NNRs in the remainder of the UK

Source: Poore and Poore, 1987

SUMMARY OF PROTECTED AREAS

Map[†] ref.	*National/international designations* Name of area	IUCN management category	Area (ha)	Year notified
	National Parks			
1	Brecon Beacons	V	133,400	1957
2	Dartmoor	V	94,500	1951
3	Exmoor	V	68,632	1954
4	Lake District	V	228,000	1951
5	North York Moors	V	143,221	1952
6	Northumberland	V	103,079	1956
7	Peak District	V	142,285	1951
8	Pembrokeshire Coast	V	57,937	1952
9	Snowdonia	V	217,100	1951
10	The Broads	V	28,800	1989
11	Yorkshire Dales	V	176,113	1954
	National Nature Reserves			
12	Abernethy Forest	IV	2,296	1982
13	Beinn Eighe	IV	4,758	1951
14	Ben Lawers	IV	3,974	1962
15	Ben Lui	IV	2,104	1961
16	Ben Wyvis	IV	5,673	1984
17	Blackwater Estuary	IV	1,031	1983
18	Blar Nam Faoileag	IV	2,126	1985
19	Bridgwater Bay	IV	2,559	1954
20	Caenlochan	IV	3,639	1961
21	Caerlaverock	IV	5,585	1957
22	Cairngorms	IV	25,949	1954
23	Cairnsmore of Fleet	IV	1,922	1975
24	Creag Meagaidh	IV	3,948	1986
25	Dengie	IV	2,011	1984
26	Dyfi	IV	2,095	1972
27	Glen Roy	IV	1,168	1970
28	Glen Tanar	IV	4,185	1979
29	Gualin	IV	2,522	1971
30	Holkham	IV	3,925	1967
31	Inchnadamph	IV	1,295	1956
32	Inverpolly	IV	10,857	1961
33	Lindisfarne	IV	3,278	1964
34	Loch Druidibeg	IV	1,677	1958
35	Loch Leven	IV	1,597	1964
36	Loch Maree Islands	IV	200	
37	Monach Isles	IV	577	1966
38	Moor House	IV	3,894	1952
39	Muir of Dinnet	IV	1,415	1977
40	Newborough Warren/Ynys Llanddwyn	IV	1,405	1955
41	North Rona and Sula Sgeir	IV	130	1984
42	North Strangford Lough	IV	1,015	1987
43	Noss	IV	313	1955
44	Rannoch Moor	IV	1,499	1958
45	Rhum	IV	10,794	1957
46	Ribble Marshes	IV	2,302	1979
47	Scolt Head Island	IV	737	
48	Skomer Island	IV	307	1959
49	St. Kilda	IV	853	1957
50	Stackpole	IV	199	1981
51	Strathfarrar	IV	2,189	1977
52	Upper Teesdale	IV	3,497	1963

Map† ref.	National/international designations Name of area	IUCN management category	Area (ha)	Year notified
53	Y Wyddfa-Snowdon	IV	1,677	1964
	Marine Nature Reserves			
54	Lundy Island	IV	2,200	1986
55	Skomer	IV	1,500	1990
	National Scenic Areas			
56	Assynt-Coigach	V	90,200	1980
57	Ben Nevis and Glen Coe	V	101,600	1980
58	Cuillin Hills	V	21,900	1980
59	Deeside and Lochnagar	V	40,000	1980
60	Dornoch Firth	V	7,500	1980
61	East Stewartry Coast	V	5,200	1980
62	Eildon and Leaderfoot	V	3,600	1980
63	Fleet Valley	V	5,300	1980
64	Glen Affric	V	19,300	1980
65	Glen Strathfarrar	V	3,800	1980
66	Hoy and West Mainland	V	14,800	1980
67	Jura	V	21,800	1980
68	Kintail	V	16,300	1980
69	Knapdale	V	19,800	1980
70	Knoydart	V	39,500	1980
71	Kyle of Tongue	V	18,500	1980
72	Kyles of Bute	V	4,400	1980
73	Loch Lomond	V	27,400	1980
74	Loch Rannoch and Glenlyon	V	48,400	1980
75	Loch Sheil	V	13,400	1980
76	Loch Tummel	V	9,200	1980
77	Loch na Keal	V	12,700	1980
78	Lynn of Lorn	V	4,800	1980
79	Morar, Moidart and Ardnamurchan	V	15,900	1980
80	Nith Estuary	V	9,300	1980
81	North Arran	V	23,800	1980
82	North west Sutherland	V	20,500	1980
83	River Earn (Comrie and St Fillans)	V	3,000	1980
84	River Tay (Dunkeld)	V	5,600	1980
85	Scarba, Lunga and the Garvellachs	V	1,900	1980
86	Shetland	V	15,600	1980
87	South Lewis, Harris and North Uist	V	108,600	1980
88	South Uist Machair	V	6,100	1980
89	St Kilda	V	900	1980
90	The Cairngorm Mountains	V	67,200	1980
91	The Small Isles	V	15,500	1980
92	The Trossachs	V	4,600	1980
93	Trotternish	V	5,000	1980
94	Upper Tweeddale	V	12,300	1980
95	Wester Ross	V	145,300	1980
	Areas of Outstanding Natural Beauty			
96	Anglesey	V	21,500	1967
97	Antrim Coast and Glens	V	70,600	1988
98	Arnside and Silverdale	V	7,500	1972
99	Cannock Chase	V	6,800	1958
100	Causeway Coast	V	4,050	1989
101	Chichester Harbour	V	7,500	1964
102	Chilterns	V	80,000	1965
103	Chilterns variations	V	1,000	1990
104	Clwydian Range	V	15,600	1965

Map[†] ref.	National/international designations Name of area	IUCN management category	Area (ha)	Year notified
105	Cornwall	V	93,200	1959
106	Cornwall Extension	V	2,500	1983
107	Cotswolds	V	150,700	1966
108	Cranbourne Chase and West Wiltshire Downs	V	96,000	1983
109	Dedham Vale	V	5,700	1970
110	Dedham Vale Extension	V	1,500	1978
111	Dorset	V	103,600	1959
112	East Devon	V	26,700	1963
113	East Hampshire	V	39,100	1962
114	Forest of Bowland	V	80,300	1964
115	Gower	V	18,900	1956
116	High Weald	V	145,000	1983
117	Howardian Hills	V	20,500	1987
118	Isle of Wight	V	18,900	1963
119	Isles of Scilly	V	1,600	1976
120	Kent Downs	V	84,500	1968
121	Lincolnshire Wolds	V	56,000	1973
122	Lleyn	V	15,500	1957
123	Malvern Hills	V	10,400	1959
124	Mendip Hills	V	20,600	1972
125	Mourne	V	57,012	1986
126	Norfolk Coast	V	45,000	1968
127	North Devon ANOB	V	17,100	1960
128	North Pennines	V	199,800	1988
129	North Wessex Downs	V	173,800	1972
130	Northumberland Coast	V	12,900	1958
131	Quantock Hills	V	9,900	1957
132	Shropshire Hills	V	77,700	1959
133	Solway Coast	V	10,700	1964
134	South Devon	V	33,200	1960
135	South Hampshire Coast	V	7,800	1967
136	Suffolk Coast and Heaths	V	39,100	1966
137	Surrey Hills	V	41,400	1958
138	Sussex Downs	V	98,100	1966
139	Wye Valley	V	32,500	1971
	Other area			
140	New Forest	V	37,500	1079
	Biosphere Reserves			
	Beinn Eighe NNR	IX	4,800	1976
	Braunton Burrows NNR	IX	596	1976
	Caerlaverock NNR	IX	5,501	1976
	Cairnsmore of Fleet NNR	IX	1,922	1976
	Claish Moss NNR	IX	480	1977
	Dyfi NNR	IX	1,589	1976
	Isle of Rhum NNR	IX	10,560	1976
	Loch Druidibeg NNR	IX	1,658	1976
	Moor House-Upper Teesdale	IX	7,399	1976
	North Norfolk Coast	IX	5,497	1976
	Silver Flowe-Merrick Kells	IX	3,088	1976
	St Kilda NNR	IX	842	1976
	Taynish NNR	IX	326	1977
	Ramsar Sites			
	Abberton Reservoir	R	1,228	1981

Map[†] ref.	National/international designations Name of area	IUCN management category	Area (ha)	Year notified
	Alt Estuary	R	1,160	1985
	Bridgend Flats	R	331	1988
	Bridgwater Bay	R	2,703	1976
	Bure Marshes	R	412	1976
	Cairngorm Lochs	R	179	1981
	Chesil Beach and the Fleet	R	763	1985
	Chichester and Langstone Harbours	R	5,749	1987
	Claish Moss	R	563	1981
	Cors Fochno and Dyfi	R	2,497	1976
	Derwent Ings	R	783	1985
	Din Moss-Hoselaw Loch	R	46	1988
	Eilean Na Muice Duibhe (Duich Moss)	R	574	1988
	Fala Flow	R	323	1990
	Feur Lochain	R	384	1990
	Glac-na-Criche	R	265	1990
	Gladhouse Reservoir	R	186	1988
	Gruinart Flats	R	3,170	1988
	Hickling Broad and Horsey Mere	R	892	1976
	Holburn Moss	R	22	1985
	Irthinghead Mires	R	608	1985
	Leighton Moss	R	125	1985
	Lindisfarne	R	3,123	1976
	Loch Eye	R	195	1986
	Loch of Skene	R	125	1986
	Loch-an-Duin	R	3,606	1990
	Loch of Lintrathen	R	218	1981
	Loch Leven	R	1,597	1976
	Loch Lomond	R	253	1976
	Lochs Druidibeg, a'Machair and Stilligary	R	1,780	1976
	Lough Neagh and Lough Beg	R	39,500	1976
	Martin Mere	R	119	1985
	Minsmere-Walberswick	R	1,697	1976
	North Norfolk Coast	R	7,700	1976
	Ouse Washes	R	2,276	1976
	Pagham Harbour	R	616	1988
	Rannoch Moor	R	1,499	1976
	Redgrave and S. Lopham Fens	R	125	1991
	Rockcliffe Marshes	R	1,897	1986
	Rostherne Mere	R	79	1981
	Rutland Water	R	1,339	1991
	Silver Flowe	R	608	1981
	The Wash	R	63,124	1988
	The Swale	R	5,790	1985
	The Dee Estuary	R	13,055	1985
	Upper Severn Estuary	R	1,437	1988
	Walmore Common	R	51	1991
	World Heritage Sites			
	Giant's Causeway	X	70	1986
	St Kilda	X	853	1986

[†]Locations of most protected areas are shown on the accompanying map.

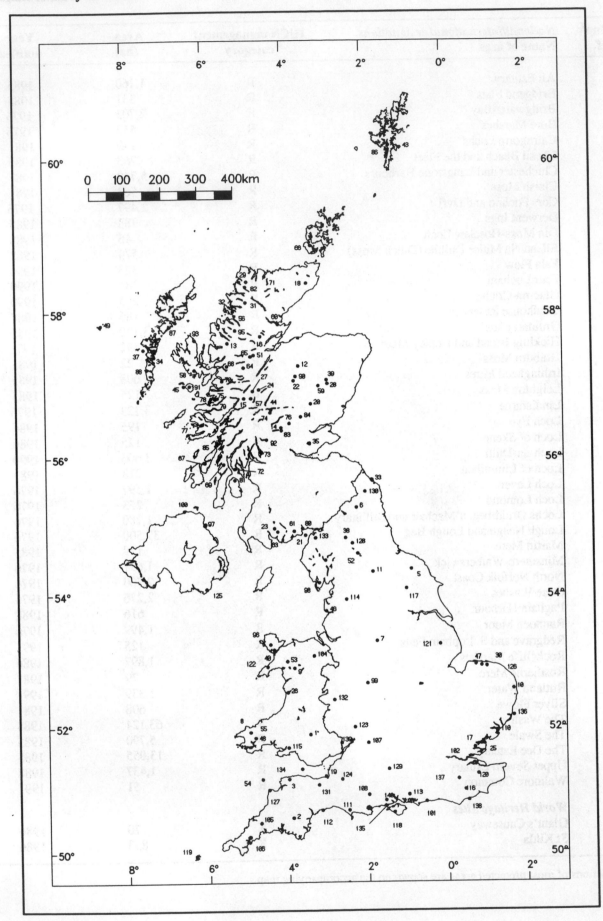

Protected Areas of the United Kingdom

UNITED KINGDOM – CHANNEL ISLANDS

Area 194 sq. km

Population 138,668 (1988)

Economic Indicators
GDP: US$ 12,096 per capita
GNP: US$ 10,430 per capita

Policy and Legislation The Channel Islands are Crown dependencies with their own legislative assemblies; for the states (bailiwicks) of Jersey, Guernsey and Alderney and the Court of Chief Pleas in Sark. Each has their own system of local administration, law and courts. The British government is responsible for international affairs.

The Channel Islands are not covered under UK legislation. Relevant acts include the 1949 Protection of Wild Birds Ordinance (Guernsey), amended in 1974; the 1959 Protection of Wild Birds (Alderney) Ordinance and the 1963 Protection of Birds (Jersey) Law, amended in 1972 (Grimmett and Jones, 1989).

International Activities Jersey is covered by the Convention on Wetlands of International Importance especially as Waterfowl Habitat (Ramsar Convention), but not Guernsey, and both are covered by the Convention concerning the World Cultural and Natural Heritage (World Heritage Convention). No sites have been designated under either convention and no biosphere reserves have been accepted under the Unesco Man and the Biosphere Programme. The Channel Islands are not a part of the EC and are therefore not covered under the Wild Birds Directive.

Administration and Management Environment and nature conservation are the concerns of the planning departments on both Jersey and Guernsey. A conservation officer post exists in Jersey to administer the Protection of the Birds act and for general conservation purposes.

In Guernsey and Jersey there are thriving non-governmental organisations interested in Channel Island heritage: National Trust of Guernsey in St Martins and the National Trust of Jersey in St Mary.

Systems Reviews The Channel Islands consist of five inhabited islands and numerous rocky islets some 130km from the English coast and less than 20km from the French coastline of Normandy. Their coastlines are characterised by cliffs and steep rocky slopes alternating with sandy bays.

Considerable cover of semi-natural vegetation cover is still present, including sand-dune communities, cliff-top heathlands, grassland, wetlands and woodlands. Wooded valleys are largely found on Jersey, and to a lesser extent Guernsey, although they are not widespread on either island. There are about 1,800 vascular plant taxa; 1,340 taxa in Guernsey; over 1,500 species in Jersey (Davis *et al.*, 1986).

A *de facto* bird sanctuary exists as two stacks off the coast of Alderney (Grimmett and Jones, 1989).

Sand dunes and coastal grasslands are increasingly threatened by tourist developments and the few remaining wetlands by drainage schemes (Davis *et al.*, 1986; Grimmett and Jones, 1989).

Addresses

Conservation Officer, Planning Department, South Hill, ST HELIER, Jersey
National Trust of Guernsey, Les Moilpiedes, ST MARTINS, Guernsey
National Trust of Jersey, The Elms, ST MARY, Jersey

References

Davis, S.D., Droop, S.J.M., Gregerson, P., Henson, L., Leon, C.J., Lamlein Villa-Lobos, J., Synge, H., and Zantovska, J. (1986). *Plants in danger: what do we know?* IUCN, Gland, Switzerland, and Cambridge, UK. 461 pp.

Grimmett, R.F.A. and Jones, T.A. (1989). *Important bird areas in Europe*. International Council for Bird Preservation, Cambridge, UK. Pp. 807-808.

Hywel-Davies, J. and Thom, V. (1984). *The Macmillan Guide to Britain's nature reserves*. The MacMillan Press Ltd, London and Basingstoke, UK. 716 pp.

Le Sueur, F. (1976). Changes in the flora of Jersey, 1873-1973. *Bull. Soc. Jersiase.* 2(1):33-40

Le Sueur, F. (1976). *A natural history of Jersey*. Phillimore, London and Chichester, UK. 221 pp.

UNITED KINGDOM – GIBRALTAR

Area 6.5 sq. km

Population 30,689 (1989 estimate)

Economic Indicators
GDP: US$ 12,096 per capita
GNP: US$ 10,430 per capita

Policy and Legislation Gibraltar was ceded to Great Britain by the Treaty of Utrecht, 1713. The Constitution of Gibraltar was approved on 11 August 1969, with provision to transfer legislative authority to the Gibraltar House of Assembly which replaced the former Legislative Council. The Governor appointed by the Crown retains direct responsibility for all external affairs and internal security.

Gibraltar and the surrounding region has a long history of environmental awareness. The region has over the millennia been settled by Phoenicians, Carthaginians, Romans, Moorish Arabs, Spanish and the British. A detailed understanding of the environment was well known 2,000 years ago and many ancient travellers wrote of the wildlife of Gibraltar and nearby Morocco. More recently, after the Moorish invasions of 711AD, great palaces were constructed and wild animals brought to Gibraltar. The Moorish kingdoms of what are now Andalucia and Gibraltar had a major impact on the landscape which is still apparent today. The Moorish authorities maintained Islamic law, beliefs and customs which included traditional forms of range land protection and land management control mechanisms (agdal, habous, guich). Some of the first legislative concern for wildlife on Gibraltar was recorded in military law in the 18th century, the Garrison Orders, when "no hunting areas" were declared. In 1846 Garrison Orders declared that "no person is allowed to shoot, or in any way hurt" Barbary macaque (Gibraltar ape) *Macaca sylvanus*. Concern and military directives have been issued in order to protect this species up to the present day (Drucker, 1988).

The main legislation relevant to nature protection is the Nature Protection Ordinance of April 1991 which provides for the protection of wild birds, animals and plants and for the designation and preservation of protected areas. The two categories of protected area include nature conservation area and marine nature area (see Annex). Many of the legislated ordinances are based on those of the English, Scottish and Welsh systems. The Nature Protection Ordinance, 1991 was drafted using as a model the Wildlife and Countryside Act of 30 October 1981, which provides for the designation within the United Kingdom of national nature reserves, marine nature reserves, sites of special scientific interest and nature conservation orders (see entry for the United Kingdom). Under Part IV Section 20 of the Nature Protection Ordinance, 1991, the Nature Conservancy Council is empowered to enforce the Ordinance and to appoint wildlife wardens.

The Town and City Plan for Gibraltar of 1976 recognised the need for conservation, stating: "animal and plant life, marine life ... ancient monuments ... because of their irreplaceable character, should be conserved" (Cortes, 1978). The upper part of the Rock of Gibraltar, the Upper Rock, has for many decades had Garrison Order prohibitions on shooting, trapping and building, although until recently this has not been enshrined in government of Gibraltar laws for nature conservation (Grimmett and Jones, 1989; Finlayson, pers. comm., 1987).

International Activities The United Kingdom is responsible for the international affairs of Gibraltar. With the United Kingdom, Gibraltar is a party to the Convention on Wetlands of International Importance especially as Waterfowl Habitat (Ramsar Convention), and to the Convention concerning the World Cultural and Natural Heritage (World Heritage Convention). As a member of the European Community, the UK and its dependency, Gibraltar, is bound by EC regulations, including the Directive (79/409/EEC) on the Conservation of Wild Birds, which, in Article 4, requires member states to designate important areas as special protection areas. No special protected areas are in existence in Gibraltar. A recommendation for investigating further the possibility of Gibraltar being recognised under an international conservation convention, such as the World Heritage Convention, was discussed at the Conference "Gibraltar – a small territory as a model in conservation" (Oldfield, *in litt.*, 1990; Cortes, pers. comm., 1991).

In 1987 Gibraltar was still not covered by the Convention on the Conservation of European Wildlife and Natural Habitats (Bern Convention) even though the United Kingdom was a signatory and was taking steps to include Gibraltar (Grimmett and Jones, 1989; Oldfield, 1987). The United Kingdom is a member of the Council of Europe: no Council of Europe biogenetic reserves have yet been declared in either the UK or in Gibraltar. The Convention for the Protection of the Mediterranean Sea against Pollution, usually known as the Barcelona Convention, has not been adopted by the United Kingdom on behalf of Gibraltar. As a consequence, it is not party to the Protocol concerning Mediterranean Specially Protected Areas, with the associated obligation to list representative sites of importance for a Mediterranean network of protected areas.

A transboundary park has been proposed that would incorporate wetland areas for migratory birds, extending from Tetuan in Morocco, to Gibraltar and Spain across the Straits of Gibraltar (Cortes, *in litt.*, 1991).

Administration and Management Administration of the laws of the government of Gibraltar is through the House of Assembly. Funding comes from numerous sources and the Overseas Development Agency (ODA) of the UK continues to administer British aid through the South Atlantic and Gibraltar Department; ODA gross bilateral aid in 1989 amounted to £403,000.

In 1991 a new body, the Nature Conservancy Council, was charged with overall responsibility for nature protection (Part IV Section 20, Nature Protection Ordinance of 1991) and is empowered to enforce the Ordinance. This body will also have the authority to appoint wildlife wardens and honourary voluntary wardens.

Until the creation of the Nature Conservancy Council, there was a diversity of bodies involved in nature protection and general conservation. The Public Health Department had responsibility for pollution control; the Public Works Department responsibility for gardens and the Upper Rock; and the Town Planning Commission exerted an influence on general conservation. Crown estate property and Ministry of Defence land continues to be under the jurisdiction of the Property Services Agency (PSA) of the UK, the British Army and the Royal Navy, although a proportion of Ministry of Defence (MOD) land is gradually being handed over to the care of the government of Gibraltar. Expenditure in 1990 for nature and landscape conservation (including public gardens) amounted to approximately £0.3 million (Cortes, *in litt.*, 1991).

One of the first general attempts to prepare protected area policy and reserve management was completed in 1978 as an independent report presented to the Chief Minister (Cortes, 1978).

In the 1980s the Windmill Hill area on MOD land had been set up as the Windmill Hill Conservation Area, followed by the addition of Jacob's Ladder in 1987. It was, and continues to be, under the management of the Windmill Hill Conservation Group, set up with representation from the Gibraltar Ornithological and Natural History Society (GONHS), the British Army, the PSA and the Royal Navy. The aims of this body are to coordinate improvements to the natural environment of the above-mentioned areas (GONHS, 1990).

In 1987/88 responsibility for investigating the development of protected areas was vested in the Gibraltar Government Tourist Office which commissioned consultants to report on the best way of developing the Upper Rock as a natural park, and to include the historic features within the area (Drucker, 1988; Fa, 1987; Finlayson, *in litt.*, 1988).

In 1991 the first site to be designated under the Nature Protection Ordinance was established on public land on the Upper Rock. Under jurisdiction of the Ordinance wildlife wardens are being appointed to manage the site. Budgetary details have not yet been worked out. Entrance fees are being charged in the touristic part of the park frequented by Barbary macaques (Rock Ape), Queen's Gate region. This self-generating funding is not all dedicated for reinvestment in protected area administration and management (Cortes, *in litt.*, 1991).

Culturally and traditionally, unique management of Barbary macaque continues with the Gibraltar Regiment. The Regiment and its predecessors have maintained the management of the apes without a break since 1915 and periodically before that back to the 18th century (Drucker, 1978, 1988). The cost of establishment of a full network of protected areas has been estimated at between £0.5-1 million (Cortes, *in litt.*, 1991).

The Crown, through the British Army, has for centuries has held jurisdiction over the majority of the dependency. The Upper Rock continues to be Crown estate and is almost solely under the authority of the military and the government of Gibraltar, administered by the British Army, Gibraltar Regiment and the House of Assembly (except in cases where there are agreements with such as GONHS mentioned above). Under ministerial directives, the Ministry of Defence has an obligation to protect the environment. Much of the Upper Rock has been managed sympathetically with the interests of nature conservation in mind, prohibiting certain actions harmful to wildlife. As such, the major part of the Upper Rock is a *de facto* protected area, not having been grazed, hunted, farmed, managed for forestry or built upon in any way for the last 30 to 50 years, thus permitting plant community succession into high maquis and low woodland. The British Army manages a limited number of "firebreak" and other man-made clearings down the west slope of the Rock, which is essential for many species of wildlife including Barbary partridge *Alectoris barbara*; Gibraltar being the only centre of its distribution in Europe (for details of important nature conservation areas on MOD land see GONHS, 1990).

Non-governmental groups have been long interested in nature conservation and the environment. The GONHS has its origins in the Gibraltar Ornithological Society (GOS) founded in 1978. Amongst others, its aims are to safeguard all natural assets, to educate and to work for the improvement and implementation of wildlife and environmental protection. It now has 200 members and includes the former Gibraltar Environmental Group (GEG) which was formed in 1978 with express concerns for the conservation of the environment on the Rock (GEG, 1980). The GONHS runs a field centre within the designated protected area, and there is an active museum based not far away in the main town of Gibraltar which maintains an extensive natural history collection (GONHS, *in litt.*). The field station, which was established in 1990/91, is manned by volunteers and runs on a budget of £2,000 per year (Cortes, *in litt.*, 1991). The newly formed Gibraltar Botanical Gardens at the Alameda intends to undertake extensive plant conservation and threatened plants propagation programmes (Cortes, pers. comm., 1991). Other interested bodies include the Gibraltar Heritage Trust with interests in preservation of the valuable cultural heritage.

Systems Reviews   Gibraltar is a rocky peninsula extending into the Straits of Gibraltar at the entrance to the Mediterranean Sea. It is connected to the southern tip of the Iberian Peninsula of Spain by an isthmus, and is 22km from the coast of Morocco on the African continent across the Straits of Gibraltar. The Rock of Gibraltar is an isolated mass of Jurassic limestone, varied by beds of more recent shale and sandstone. It is made up of numerous cliffs and rocky outcrops, the maximum point reaching a height of 426m on the Upper Rock (see GEG, 1980).

Originally, it was probably covered by natural woodland, however this has been gradually destroyed over the centuries by tree felling and extensive goat grazing. Since the removal of the goats early this century maquis (mattoral) has become the dominant vegetation type. Cliff communities are also important. There are over 600 species of flowering plant, and the existing semi-natural vegetation is dominated by a maquis scrub of *Olea europea, Pistacia lentiscus, Osyris quadripartita* and *Rhamnus alaternus*. There are also areas of pseudo-steppe and garigue. A rich chasmophtyic flora is found particularly on the inaccessible cliffs and ledges of the eastern slopes (for species lists and details see GEG, 1980).

Despite its small size, Gibraltar is of considerable importance for nature conservation, especially for birds, of which over 300 species have been recorded (GONHS, 1990). Up to 0.25 million migrating raptors pass over the Straits of Gibraltar during spring and autumn. The maquis is utilised by passerine migrants in spring, autumn and winter. The Straits are also utilised by seabirds passing from the Mediterranean to the Atlantic. The Rock is home to a number of important bird populations: *Phalocrocorax aristotelis desmarestii* (the only known location on the Iberian mainland) and *Alectoris barbara*. Gibraltar is also renowned for its Barbary macaques, the only population of primates believed to be native to Europe.

There is no longer any agriculture on the Rock, however over half of Gibraltar consists of urban land.

Although there is no system plan as such, the Town and City Plan is of some relevance and numerous reports, scientific research and surveys are of great value to nature conservation. An assessment of the environmental situation, with an appraisal of the problems facing Gibraltar and with a series of recommendations, was given in GEG (1980). Prior to the creation of the Nature Conservancy Council, a scientific committee has been advising the government on environmentally related topics.

Species of particular note include the globally threatened Barbary macaque *Macaca sylvanus*, at its only known location outside north-west Africa (Drucker, pers. comm., 1991), and one endemic plant taxon *Limonium emarginatum*. Gibraltar is also the sole location in the Iberian Peninsula for two bird species/subspecies (GONHS, 1990). Up to 25% of Gibraltar's Mediterranean maquis habitat is contained within protected areas as are 50% of the threatened vertebrate species (Cortes, *in litt.*, 1991).

Most of the important natural sites are Ministry of Defence land, nine of which have been singled out as being of particular conservation value (GONHS, 1990). In 1987 proposals were presented to the MOD for the fencing of Jacob's Ladder as a nature reserve and it was subsequently incorporated into a conservation area (Cortes, 1978). As of October 1991 discussions were underway between government departments and the GONHS leading to the protection of a series of sites of importance. Proposed areas for nature conservation include the Upper rock-southern terraces and Windmill Hill Flats, Upper Rock-east slopes; Governor's Beach and Sea Caves and also southern coastal areas of Europa Point Foreshore (GONHS, 1990; Cortes, *in litt.*, 1991).

The first area to be designated under the Nature Protection Ordinance, 1991 was established in the Upper Rock near the Queen's Gate area, and covers 35ha. Other *de facto* areas include much of the Upper Rock area (Cortes, *in litt.*, 1991). Listed important bird areas, which in the view of ICBP and IWRB require effective protection in Europe, include two sites in Gibraltar, one of 600ha on the Rock of Gibraltar and the other as part of the Straits including land and water under the jurisdiction of the United Kingdom, Spain and Morocco (Grimmett and Jones, 1989).

Environmental constraints inevitably arise with such a high population in such a small area of land. Some of the main problems include: illegal dumping of waste and littering; atmospheric pollution from vehicles and small-scale industry together with that from major industrial complexes across the frontier; excess tourist pressure; expansion of urban development and land reclamation into the sea; direct disturbance of sensitive species such as bats and ground nesting birds; and pollution of the surrounding waters by oil and sewage. Feral cats and rats may have a significant adverse affect upon the wildlife. Minimal management of semi-natural habitats has led to a loss of a certain amount of biodiversity over the decades (GEG, 1980; Grimmett and Jones, 1989; Cortes, *in litt.*, 1991).

Other Relevant Information   The major income is tourism; the number of tourists in 1989 was 3.98 million, the vast majority of whom would have visited the upper Rock and its natural areas.

Addresses

Nature Conservancy Council, Government House, GIBRALTAR

The Gibraltar Ornithological and Natural History Society, The Gibraltar Museum, 18-20 Bomb House Lane, GIBRALTAR (Tel: 74289)

Gibraltar Botanical Gardens, The Alameda, 8/8 Buena Vista Road, GIBRALTAR (Tel: 76818)

References

Anon. (1991). *Third Supplement to the Gibraltar Gazette* No. 2,598 of 7 March 1991. B. 6/91 Nature Protection Ordinance 1991. Gibraltar Chronicle Ltd, Gibraltar. Pp. 19-54.

Cortes, J.E. (1978). Conservation a future?, semi-natural nature reserve Gibraltar. A management plan. Unpublished. 51 pp.

Cortes, J.E., Finlayson, J.C., Garcia, E.F.J. and Mosquera, M.A.J. (1980). *The birds of Gibraltar.* Gibraltar Bookshop, Gibraltar.

Davis, S.D., Droop, S.J.M., Gregerson, P., Henson, L., Leon, C.J., Lamlein Villa-Lobos, J., Synge, H., and Zantovska, J. (1986). *Plants in danger: what do we know?* IUCN, Gland, Switzerland, and Cambridge, UK. 461 pp.

Drucker, G.R. (1978). Population dynamics of the Barbary macaque in Gibraltar. Unpublished report. Royal Holloway College, University of London.

Drucker, G.R. (1988). Feasibility of establishing a free ranging or captive barbary macaque troop on Gibraltar; a natural park for Gibraltar. Report to the Gibraltar Government Tourist Office: natural park consultants to the Government of Gibraltar.

Fa, J.E. (1987). A park for the Barbary macaques of Gibraltar? *Oryx* 21(4): 243-245

Finlayson, J.C., Garcia, E.F.J., Mosquera, M.A.J. and Bourne, W.R.P. (1976). Raptor migration across the Straits of Gibraltar. *British birds* 69: 77-87.

Finlayson, J.C. and Cortes, J.E. (1987). The Birds of the Straits of Gibraltar its waters and northern shore. *Alectoris* 6: 1-74.

GEG (1980). Environmental Conservation in Gibraltar. Report prepared by Bensusan, J., Cortes, J.E., Fa, J.E., Finlayson, J.C. and Mosquera, M.A.J. Gibraltar Environmental Group, Gibraltar. 13 pp.

GONHS (1990). Custodians of wilderness, the wildlife importance of MOD land in Gibraltar. Unpublished report. 9 pp.

Grimmett, R.F.A. and Jones, T.A. (1989). *Important bird areas in Europe.* International Council for Bird Preservation, Cambridge, UK. 888 pp.

Hunter, B. (Ed.) (1991). *The Statesman's Year Book 1991-92.* The Macmillan Press Ltd, London and Basingstoke, UK. 1692 pp.

Oldfield, S. (1987). *Fragments of Paradise: a guide for conservation in the UK dependent territories.* British Association of Nature Conservationists, Oxford, UK. 192 pp.

Wooley-Dodd, A.H. (1914). A Flora of Gibraltar and the neighbourhood. *Journal of Botany* 52. 131 pp.

ANNEX
Definitions of protected area designations, as legislated, together with authorities responsible for their administration

Title : Nature Protection Ordinance 1991

Date: April 1991

Brief description: Legally provides for designation of areas of special interest protected for the purpose of nature conservation under Part III (Section 18-25). In addition, this Ordinance provides for protection of threatened species throughout Gibraltar under Part I (Section 3-17). Under Part IV Section 20 the Nature Conservancy Council is empowered to enforce the Ordinance and to appoint wildlife wardens.

Administrative authority: Nature Conservancy Council, Government of Gibraltar

Designations:

Nature conservation area Areas as defined under Part III. 18 (1). An area of special interest by reason of any of its flora, fauna or geological or physiographical features, or by reason of being the habitat of any wild bird, wild animal or wild plant of any kind specified in this ordinance.

For the purpose of providing under suitable conditions and control, special opportunities for the study of, and research into, matters relating to flora and fauna and the physical features in which they live, or the study of geological and geophysical features of special interest in the area.

Marine nature area Areas as defined under Part III. 18 (2). Land covered (continuously or intermittently) by waters or parts of the sea within territorial waters, is of special interest for conserving marine flora or fauna or geological or physiographical features of special interest in the area.

Providing under suitable conditions and control, special opportunities for the study of, and research into, matters relating to marine flora and fauna and the physical features in which they live, or the study of geological and geophysical features of special interest in the area.

Prohibitions may include the entry into or movement within the area of persons and vessels; the killing, taking, destruction, molesting or disturbance of animals or plants of any description in the area.

Source: Original legislation

UNITED KINGDOM – ISLE OF MAN

Area 572 sq. km

Population 64,282 (1986)

Economic Indicators
GDP: US$ 12,096 per capita
GNP: US$ 10,430 per capita

Policy and Legislation   The Isle of Man is not a part of the United Kingdom, but has been a direct dependency of the British Crown since 1765. It has its own parliamentary, legal and administrative system and thus no UK laws cover the Isle of Man. The legislature, Tynwald, is the oldest parliament in the world in continuous existence.

The first statutory legislation was the Wildlife Act, 1990 which is based closely on the Wildlife and Countryside Act, 1981 of England, Wales and Scotland and provides for the designation of national nature reserves (NNRs) and sites of special scientific interest (SSSIs). It is envisaged that, following promulgation of this Act, the development of conservation will run along similar lines to the UK, with the establishment of a small number of NNRs and a larger number of SSSIs (Department of Agriculture, Fisheries and Forestry, *in litt.*, 1991).

International Activities The Isle of Man is not covered under the Convention on Wetlands of International Importance especially as Waterfowl Habitat (Ramsar Convention). It is covered under the UK in its signature of the Convention concerning the World Cultural and Natural Heritage (World Heritage Convention), although no natural sites on the island are listed. The Island will be asking the UK government to ratify the Ramsar Convention and also the Convention on the Conservation of European Wildlife and Natural Habitats (Bern Convention) on its behalf in the near future (Department of Agriculture, Fisheries and Forestry, *in litt.*, 1991).

The Isle of Man is an associate member of the EC and all international relations are handled through the UK government it is, therefore, not fully covered under the Wild Birds Directive (Grimmett and Jones, 1989).

Administration and Management   Under the Wildlife Act, 1990 conservation is now part of the official remit of the Department of Agriculture, Fisheries and Forestry (Rhynn Eirinys, Eastaght as Keylljyn), through the Wildlife Committee in its Forestry, Amenity and Lands Division. There are as yet no system plans for protected areas, although an ecological survey is currently underway which should lead to the designation of the first statutory protected areas (Department of Agriculture, Fisheries and Forestry, *in litt.*, 1991).

Some important areas are owned and managed by the non-governmental Manx Museum National Trust and the Manx Nature Conservation Trust (Grimmett and Jones, 1989).

Systems Reviews   The Isle of Man lies in the Irish Sea less than 30km from the coast of Scotland and some 50km from the coast of Northern Ireland. It is dominated by a central highland rising to 620m separated by a low valley from further high ground in the south-west. The Calf of Man is a small hilly islet lying 650m from the south-west shore: there are lowlands in the north and a small area of lowland in the south east.

Most of the cultivated area lies below 200m. Arable land accounts for some 11% of the country's area, grassland, 44% and rough grazing 27%. Woodlands account for 4% of the land area, although most of this is coniferous plantations, which are increasing, planted in the moorland zone. The hills tend to be covered in grass and heather. There are some areas of marshland and bogs. Some natural and semi-natural mixed woodlands remain in the valleys and gorges.

In 1991 no sites had yet been designated under the Wildlife Act of 1990. The existing protected areas consist of: eight reserves covering 500ha owned by the National Trust, and five reserves, totalling 100ha, owned by non-governmental organisations. Potential exists for the designation of three NNRs and three marine nature reserves (Department of Agriculture, Fisheries and Forestry, *in litt.*, 1991).

Addresses

Department of Agriculture, Fisheries and Forestry, Forestry, Amenity and Lands Division, Curraghs Wildlife Park, BALLAUGH (Tel: 624 897323)

Manx Museum National Trust, Isle of Man

Manx Nature Conservation Trust, Isle of Man

References

Grimmett, R.F.A. and Jones, T.A. (1989). *Important bird areas in Europe*. International Council for Bird Preservation, Cambridge, UK. Pp. 807-808.

Hunter, B. (Ed.) (1991). *The Statesman's Year Book 1991-92*. The Macmillan Press Ltd, London and Basingstoke, UK. 1692 pp.

ANNEX
Definitions of protected area designations, as legislated, together with authorities responsible for their administration

Title: Wildlife Act

Date: 1990

Brief description: A wide ranging Act based on the UK Wildlife and Countryside Act, 1981. Framework legislation is provided for sites of special scientific interest, national nature reserves and marine nature reserves.

Administrative authority: Department of Agriculture, Fisheries and Forestry (Rhaynn Eirinys, Eastaght as Keylljyn)

Designations:

Site of special scientific interest (SSSI) May apply to any area of land which, in the opinion of the Department of Agriculture, is of special interest by reason of its flora, fauna, or geological or physiographical features (see text for the UK).

National nature reserve (NNR) Land of national importance which is managed as a nature reserve by the Department of Agriculture, under an agreement with the Department of Agriculture or an approved body. Once designated the Department may make byelaws for the protection of the reserves.

Marine nature reserve (MNR) These may be in tidal waters or parts of the sea from the high water mark out to the seaward limits of the territorial sea. Designation may be for the purpose of conserving marine flora or fauna or geological or physiographical features of special interest in the area, or for providing special opportunities for study and research.

Sources: Department of Agriculture, Fisheries and Forestry, *in litt.*, 1991; Nature Conservancy Council, 1983

YUGOSLAVIA*
(SOCIALIST FEDERAL REPUBLIC OF YUGOSLAVIA)

Area 255,803 sq. km

Population 23,700,000 (1989)
Natural increase: 0.6% per annum

Economic Indicators
GDP: No information
GNP: US$ 2,480 per capita (1987)

Policy and Legislation Although environmental protection was written into the federal constitution (*Ustav Socialisticka Federativne Republike Jugoslavije*) of 21 February 1974, it was only recently incorporated into federal development policy as the "Development Policy in 1990 of the SFRY" (Socialist Federal Republic of Yugoslavia). In May 1990, a federal strategy for the environment was drafted, together with an Environmental Law, compliant with EC directives, governing environmental impact assessment (EIA), monitoring and funding activities (IUCN, 1991a). Within the federal legislative framework, each republic and autonomous province has the right to enact specific legislation concerning the protection of the environment and protected areas (IUCN, 1987, 1991; Singleton, 1985).

On 25 June 1991 Croatia and Slovenia proclaimed their independence from the Socialist Federal Republic of Yugoslavia. Both republics demanded the recognition of their borders as international frontier and called for foreign diplomatic recognition. Military conflict and civil war ensued and continues, with the result that the normal legal, administrative and management protected areas activities are in abeyance or seriously affected.

There is no federal legislation with respect to protected areas. All matters of legislation and the creation of protected areas come under the responsibility of the republics (Terselic *et al.*, 1991). The protected area legislation varies from one republic to another, as does the legislation covering the range of activities that can be carried out within protected areas: forestry, hunting, fishing and certain agricultural works (IUCN, 1991). One of the earliest legal measures for nature conservation, the Hunting Act, 1893 was introduced when the country was under the control of the Austro-Hungarian Empire. Among the first laws adopted in 1945, was the Law on the Protection of Cultural

Heritage and Conservation of Natural Rarities. Over 300 federal laws and republican and provincial regulations existed in 1990 together with thousands of decisions at the commune level (IUCN, 1991).

By 1985 there were no specific laws on the creation of marine protected areas. However, general texts on conservation allowed for the establishment of such sites (Singleton, 1985).

Bosnia and Herzegovina The framework law is the Act on the Protection and Use of Cultural Historic and Natural Heritage, 1985 (Zakon o zastiti i koriscenju kulturnoistorijskog i prirodnog nasljedja). The management, operation and protection of national parks are regulated by special statutes: Sutjeska National Park Act 1978 (Zakon o Nacionalnom parku Sutjeska) and Kozara National Park Act 1978 (Zakon o Nacionalnom parku Kozara). Also of importance is the Physical Planning Act 1974 (Zakon o prostornom uredjenju). This Act was amended in 1977, 1981 and 1986 (Terselic *et al.*, 1991).

The main subject of the Act on the Protection and Use of Cultural Historic and Natural Heritage are "heritage goods". "Natural heritage goods of special importance for the republic" are created by the parliament of the republic. Municipal parliaments may create "natural heritage goods" (Terselic *et al.*, 1991). In Article 3, they are defined as nature parks and landscapes (Article 25 lists national parks, memorial landscapes, nature parks and regions of special beauty); nature reserves (strict and special reserves); natural sites and rarities (natural monuments, memorial natural goods, horticultural monuments and rare and endangered plant and animal species). National parks are defined as areas of predominantly authentic nature, with exceptional and manifold natural and other values (Article 26) (Terselic *et al.*, 1991).

Natural sites are designated by a decision of the Institute for Protection of Cultural and Natural Monuments and Natural Rarities No. 683/54, while strict reserves are set up by a decision of the National Institute for the Protection of Historic Monuments and Natural Beauty and, for example, Sutjeska national park was designated by Executive Committee (Baccar, 1977; IUCN, 1971; Mestrovic, 1983).

---

*This information is correct at the time of going to press, but is likely to be overtaken by events which could alter the legislative, administrative and management structure of protected areas throughout the region. Prior to June 1991, the constituent republics and provinces of Yugoslavia included: Bosnia Herzegovina, Croatia, Macedonia, Montenegro, Serbia, Koskova, Vojvodina and Slovenia.

Croatia The framework act on landscape conservation is the Nature Protection Act 1976 (Zakon o zastiti prirode) (Miljanic and Dragonovie, *in litt.*, 1991). In addition, there are two acts on the creation of nature parks and two acts on the creation of scientific reserves. As usual, every national park is created by a specific Act at the level of the republic (one older national park was created by a Federal Act in 1947). Article 16 of the Act defines the following protected nature objects: national parks; scientific reserves; nature parks; nature conservation reserves; forest parks; protected landscapes; natural monuments; horticultural monuments; memorial landscapes and memorial objects; protected plant and animal species. The following statutes also relate to landscape protection: Croatian Penal Act 1977 (Krivicni zakon SR Hrvatske); and the Physical Planning Act 1980 (Zakon o prostornom planiranju i uredjenju prostora) – important amendments were adopted in 1986; Physical Plan of the SR of Croatia 1989 (Prostorni plan Socijalisticke Republike Hrvatske) (Terselic *et al.*, 1991). Parks designated by laws specific to each site include Mljet National Park, designated under the Mljet National Park law published in *"arodne novine"* No. 49/60, 7 December 1960. Nature reserves in Croatia are declared under a decree for the Protection of Natural Rarity No. 221/48 and by proposals of the People's National Liberation Committee No. 05-5056/1 of 1961 (MAB, 1979). All activities within nature reserves in Croatia are restricted by regional by-laws (Singleton, 1985).

Macedonia The framework act is the Protection of Natural Heritage Act 1973 (Zakon za zastita na prirodne retkosti). The following statutes also relate to nature conservation: Agricultural Land Protection Act 1986; Forest Act 1974; Yugoslav Hunting Act 1964; Yugoslav Fishing Act 1965; and the Physical Plan of the Socialist Republic of Macedonia 1982 (Prostoren plan na SRM). In addition, the following statutes are of importance: Protection of Ohrid, Dojran, Prespa Lake Act 1977 (Zakon za zastita na Ohridsko, Prespansko i Dojranski Ezero); National Parks Protection Act 1978 (Zakon za zastita nacionalne parkovi); and Physical Planning Act 1985 (Zakon na sistemot na prostorno i urbanisticko planiranje); Physical Plan of the Socialist Republic of Macedonia 1982 (Terselic *et al.*, 1991).

Article 13 of the Protection of Natural Heritage Act lists the following types of natural sites: natural reserve (these are further specified as national park, strict nature reserve, scientific reserve, characteristic region, characteristic landscape and nature conservation reserve) (see Article 14); rare plant and animal community; natural monument; memorial landscape (Terselic *et al.*, 1991).

Each national park is designated under site specific laws. Only regional parks may be establised by region-wide legislation.

Montenegro The framework act is the Protection of Nature Act of 1977 (Zakon o zastiti prirode). The management of national parks is regulated by the National Parks Act, 1978 (Zakon o nacionalnim parkovima). Skadarsko jezero National Park was created by a special act in 1983 (Zakon o proglasenju Skadarskog jezera nacionalnim parkom). The following statutes are also relevant: Physical Planning Act, 1985 (Zakon o planiranju i uredjenju prostora); Physical Plan of the Socialistic Republic of Montenegro, 1986 (Prostorni plan SR Crne Gora). Key objectives of the Protection of Nature Act is conservation. Article 16 defines the following protected natural objects: nature conservation reserve (in Article 17 they are further specified as national park, regional nature park, strict nature reserve, scientific nature reserve); special nature reserve; natural monument; memorial natural monument; important belvederes; special landscape; rare and endangered plant and animal species (Terselic *et al.*, 1991).

Protected areas are established by enactment of the Conservation Law of 6 August 1952. Plitvice National Park was established by the general act of 1954. Kotor World Heritage Park, an example of the legal complexities of site designation, was enacted by the decision of three organisations: the Republic Institute for Protection of Nature of the Socialist Republic of Montenegro (under General Decree No. 7/1968); Republic Institute for Protection of Cultural Monuments of the SR Montenegro; and the Town Assembly of Kotor (declaration of 14 June 1979).

Serbia This republic follows the example of all others by designating areas under its own legislation. The framework act is the Nature Protection Act, 1988 (Zakon o zastiti prirode). The management of national parks is regulated by the Tara National Park Act, 1981, the Kapaonik National Park Act, 1981 and the Djerdap National Park Act, 1983. Some statutes enacted at republic level deal with conservation at the provincial level. These include the Furska Gora National Park Act, 1965 (Zakon o proglasenju Fruske gore nacionalnim parkom), the Delibatska Pescara Protection Act, 1965 (Zakon o zastiti Delobatske pescara) and the Oplenac Memorial Park Act, 1967 (Zakon o proglasenju Oplenca za prostorni memorijalni park). Also relevant is the Physical Planning Act, 1985 (Zakon o planiranju i uredjenju prostora). The following protected natural objects are defined: area of special importance (further specified as national park, regional national park, strict nature reserve, special nature reserve, forest park, important belvedere, protected landscape and surrounding of cultural heritage); natural site (natural monument and memorial natural monument); natural rarity (rare and endangered animal and plant and its community) (Turselic *et al.*, 1991). A new Environment Protection law (encompassing the Republic of Serbia, and the provinces of Kosovo and Vojvodina) with a nature protection section was issued in October 1991.

Protected areas are established by this legislation (Nikolic, *in litt.*, 1991).

Kosovo The main act in the area of landscape conservation, including the conservation of flora and fauna, is the Nature Protection Act, 1976 (Zakon o zastiti prirode). In the years before the first provincial statutes were adopted, nature conservation in the autonomous province of Kosovo was regulated by Serbian Republic law. The Sar-planina National Park Act, 1986 (Zakon o nactionalnom parku Sar planina) regulates the administration and the operation of the only national park in Kosovo. The Physical Planning Act, 1971 (Zakon o prostornom planiranju) has relevant sections. The protected natural objects are defined as follows: area of special importance (further specified as national park, regional national park, strict nature reserve, special nature reserve, forest park and important belvedere); natural site (natural monument and memorial natural monument); natural rarity (rare and endangered animal and plant and its community) (Terselic *et al.*, 1991).

Vojvodina The main act in the area of landscape conservation, is the Nature Protection Act, 1976 (Zakon o posebnoj zastiti delova prirode). Earlier, Fruska Gora was created as a national park by Serbian law (see above). In 1977 a new Fruska Gora National Park Act (Zakon o nacionalnom parku fruska gora) was adopted. Similarly, new statutes were passed from covering Delibatskoj Pescari Act 1977 (Zakon o elibatskoj pescari); Physical Planning Act, 1976 (Zakon o planiranju i uredjenju prostora); important amendments in 1984; and Regional Physical Plan of Delibatska Pescara, 1981 (Regionalni prostorni plan Delibatske pescare). Natural areas defined in Article 12 are: area of special importance (national park, special nature reserve, scientific reserve, regional park, strict natural reserve, forest park, important belvedere, reserve for protection of rare and endangered plant and animal communities); natural site (natural monument, horticultural monument, memorial landscape and natural historical collection); natural rarity (rare and endangered plant and animal species and its community) (Terselic *et al.*, 1991).

Slovenia The framework act is the Natural and Cultural Heritage Act, 1981 (Zakon o naravni kulturni dediscini). As is the case in other republics, individual parks and reserves are regulated by special acts. National parks are created by special decree under the National Parks Law (Uradni List No. 6, 1959). There are three such acts: Act for the Protection of the Surrounding of the River Soca, 1976 (Zakon o dolocitvi zavarovanje obmocja za reko Soco pritoki); Triglav National Park Act, 1981 (Zakon o Triglavskem narodnem parku); Trebce Memorial Park Act, 1981 (Zakon o Spominskem parku Trebce). Of general relevance is the Physical Planning Act, 1984 (Zakon o urejanju prostora) (Terselic *et al.*, 1991).

A draft for a new Conservation Act, focusing on the protection of natural heritage, has been prepared. In Article 17, the following natural sites are defined: national park, landscape park, regional park, nature reserve, natural monument, protected cultivated feature, endangered plant and animal species (Terselic *et al.*, 1991).

International Activities The World Heritage Convention was ratified on 26 May 1975, with three natural sites inscribed by 1990 (in 1979, in 1980 and 1986). Yugoslavia participates in the Convention on Wetlands of International Importance since 28 March 1977, with two sites listed, and is one of the participating states in the Barcelona Convention (adopted in 1975). Two sites were accepted as biosphere reserves under the Unesco Man and the Biosphere (MAB) Programme in 1976 and 1977. The network of biosphere reserves is linked to World Health Organisation programmes, in a joint effort to establish environmental specimen banks (MAB, 1979). Three conventions are in the process of ratification (the Bonn Convention, CITES and Bern Convention) at the federal level with, at present, Serbia accepting all three (Nikolic, *in litt.*, 1991).

Administration and Management The political instability of the country, resulting in as yet limited civil war, also resulted in declarations of independence by Slovenia, Croatia and Macedonia in 1991, with unforeseen consequences (also see text below). Yugoslavia was until then a federation of six republics and two (previously autonomous) provinces. This has given rise to three levels of administration: federal, republic, autonomous provincial and municipal. The federal administration is responsible for matters relating to areas of interest to the entire country and to matters relating to international cooperation such as conventions (IUCN, 1991). The republics and provinces adopt and implement nature conservation legislation. The municipalities are responsible for the actual execution of nature conservation policy. Coordination at the country level is by the Federal Executive Council's Committee for Environmental Protection and Town Planning (IUCN, 1991). Inasmuch as nature conservation relates to the federation, it is managed by the Federal Ministry of Development (Savezni sekretarijat za razvoj) or, more specifically, by its Department of the Environment (Terselic *et al.*, 1991). Environmental administration is in the form of a decentralised public authority structure in each republic. The republics each has the power to set up a council for the protection of the environment which is charged with coordinating the activities of the various environmental agencies. The councils are federated together in the Jugoslavenski Savez za Zastitu i Unapredivante Covekove Sredine (SAVEZ), which advises on conservation matters (Singleton, 1985). An institute for nature protection exists in each of the six republics (IUCN, 1987). Separate Institutions for Nature Conservation and Protection of Cultural Monuments were established as early as 1947 (IUCN, 1991). In Slovenia, Bosnia and Herzegovina, a single institute combines both nature conservation and cultural protection. Further decentralisation resulted in the establishment of provincial, regional and city authorities with responsibility for nature (IUCN, 1991). The institutes are staffed by biologists, geographers and lawyers, with a director who may be either a civil engineer or a forester (Godiel, 1981; Singleton, 1985). By law each national park must have its own administration, professional staff and funds for effective protection (Godiel, 1981).

In Bosnia and Herzegovina, the Republic Department is responsible for proposing locations for new parks and reserves, their administration their development and monitoring. The management of reserves is handled by reserve administrations which are appointed by the municipal authorities. Suggestions for the protection of a particular area can be made by the department or any nature conservation organisation founded in the republic, as defined in Article 36 of the framework Act. The national parks have their own authorities whilst the nature reserves are administered by "experimental farms" belonging to the Ministry of Agricultural Economy.

In Croatia, the Nature Protection Department (Zavod za zastitu prirode), established in 1946, has developed into one of the strongest nature conservation institutions in Yugoslavia. In 1991, it became a part of the Ministry of Environment, Physical Planning and Construction (Ministarstvo zastite okolisa, prostornog uredjenja i graditeljstva) which was founded in 1990. The Department has legal jurisdiction for all protected areas (Miljanic and Draganovic, *in litt.*, 1991) and proposes locations for new sites as well as compiling studies and monitoring work. Reserves are managed by *ad hoc* reserve administration bodies, which are appointed by municipal authorities at the proposal of the Department. These bodies may be selected from existing forestry, hunters or tourist organisations. Inspection is carried out by the Department and by municipal forestry and hunting inspectors. In one Croatian municipality, there is even a special inspector for nature protection (Terselic *et al.*, 1991). Most national parks are administered by the cultural section of the Secretariat for National Education, Culture and Physical Education, with each park having its own administrative committee, usually its own administrative office and a special management plan. In the case of Lokrum and Krka reserves, the town assemblies are responsible for management under jurisdiction from the urban plan (IUCN, 1971).

In Macedonia, the Department for the Protection of Natural Rarities (Republicki zavod za zastita na prirodne retkosti), as the advisory body, was founded in 1981. From 1949 to 1981, it cooperated with the Department for Cultural Monuments Protection (Terselic *et al.*, 1991). They appoint directors for the parks. The administrators of the natural reserves are appointed by the municipal authorities. The Department of Agriculture and Silviculture, however, retains overall responsibility, with each park having its own governing authority (IUCN, 1971; Singleton, 1985).

In Montenegro, national parks are governed by administrators with their directors appointed by the government of the Republic. Natural reserves and monuments are managed by forestry, hunting or tourist organisations on behalf of the municipal authorities (Terselic *et al.*, 1991). Some national parks such as Biogradska Gora have a special controlling body, while others, including Durmitor and Lovcen, have administrative responsibility vested in the Nature Protection Institute of the Republic or in the Republic Secretariat for Education, Culture and Science. The management is carried out by a local self-management community who elaborate the plans (Singleton, 1985). Responsibility for the management of Kotor World Heritage Site lies with the Town Assembly of Kotor, the Republic Institute for Protection of Cultural Monuments and the Republic Institute for Protection of Nature.

In Serbia, the responsible expert institution is the Republic Department for Nature Protection (Republicki zavod za zastitu prirode). National parks are managed by park adminstrators. All other protected areas are declared and managed by municipal authorities (Terselic *et al.*, 1991). A small Ministry of Environment Protection was created in 1990 consisting of two departments; natural resource protection, and inspection and monitoring. It has to be approved by the Serbia parliament (IUCN, 1991a) (Nikolic, *in litt.*, 1991). There are also three institutes for nature protection (Beograd, Novi Sad and Pristina) (Nikolic, *in litt.*, 1991).

In Kosovo, the responsible expert institution is the Provincial Department for Nature Protection (Pokrajinski zavod za zastitu prirode). The national park is managed by a provincial department. All other protected areas are created and managed by municipal authorities (Terselic *et al.*, 1991).

In Vojvodina, the responsible expert institution is the Provincial Department for Nature Protection (Zavod za zastitu prirode Vojvodine). Fruska Gora National Park is managed by the park administration. Other protected areas are managed by municipal authorities (Terselic *et al.*, 1991).

In Slovenia, the department (at the level of the republic and at the regional office level) is responsible for the expert work and for some administrative duties. Triglav National Park is managed by its own park adminstration consisting of a special commission attached to the Assembly of Radovljica Commune. In the first year after its creation, the administration was dominated by hunters, largely due to the fact that it was a hunting reserve. At present, less than half of the staff is composed of hunters (Terselic *et al.*, 1991). Reserves are administered by the Forestry Service.

Non-governmental organisations tend to be regional. Ecological parties are being formed in some republics, their influence varying greatly, although in Slovenia the Green Party is a major political force (Fisher, 1990). The following associations are worthy of mention: republic nature history associations; Yugoslav and republic entomological societies; republic ornithological

376

associations; the Young Researchers' Movement (Terselic *et al.*, 1991). In Macedonia, for example, voluntary work is carried out by the following nature protection organisations: Macedonian Ecological Association (Dvizenje na ekologistite na Makedonija); Macedonian Ecological Society (Drustvo na ekolozite na Makedonija); Ornithological Society of Macedonia (Drustvo na proucanvanje i zastita ptici vo Makedonija) (Terselic *et al.*, 1991). In Croatia, there are the Croatian Ecological Society (Hrvatsko ekolosko drustvo); Croatian Natural History Association (Hrvatsko prirodoslovno drustvo); Croatian Ornithological Society (Hrvatsko drustvo za zastitu ptica); Croatian Biological Society (Hrvatsko biolosko drustvo); Green Alliance of Croatia (Savez Zelenih Hrvatske).

Systems Reviews   Geographically in the centre of the Balkan peninsula, Yugoslavia has a great diversity of habitats, being under the influence of Mediterranean, alpine and lowland Pannonian climates of central Europe. Deciduous oak woods cover the karst lands of the far north and the far south between 200 and 700m. Oaks *Quercus* spp. dominate at these altitudes, but are replaced by beech *Fagus* spp. at higher altitudes. Many of these forests are ancient and relatively undisturbed. In the central mountains, coniferous forest is dominant, with riverine forests of alder *Alnus* sp., willow *Salix* sp. and ash *Fraxinus* sp. at lower levels. In total, some 37% of the country is forested, with plans to expand the area by 60,000ha annually by afforestation of erosion-prone terrains (IUCN, 1991a). The higher mountain massifs are well represented by relatively undisturbed alpine communities with many endemic plants. Coastal maquis is still widespread, with some patchy forest along the Croatian coast which consists of an offshore string of some 365 islands. The northern Pannonian plain is mostly agricultural, but with some relicts of steppe flora on saline soils (Davis *et al.*, 1986).

Although no unified environmental legislation or strategy exists, preparatory work for coordinating such action at the federal level has been taken, with the publication of the report *Basis of the long-term prospects of the conservation and management of the natural heritage of Yugoslavia* (IUCN, 1991). The first major inventory of protected areas (Inventory of Natural Regions and Natural Monuments) undertaken in 1976, estimated a coverage of 2.2% of the country (IUCN, 1991). This figure had risen considerably by the time a second inventory was undertaken in 1987. For example, the number of protected natural regions and monuments has increased from 1,008 in 1976 to 1,313 in 1987 (IUCN, 1991). Designated national parks had risen from 16 to 22 by 1987, with a total area of 524,784ha (Institute for Nature Conservation of the SR of Serbia, 1988). In 1991, there are 22 national parks, around 150 nature parks and 120 reserves. A further three national parks, 50 nature parks and 120 reserves are planned. By the year 2000, it is planned that protected areas will cover a total of 2,472,403ha (IUCN, 1991a). In Bosnia and Hercegovina there are two national parks and two nature

parks but only 0.5% of the total territory is protected, i.e. the smallest share of all six republics. There is no inventory of the republic's natural heritage (Terselic *et al.*, 1991). In Croatia, 8.1% of the territory, the highest in the country, is now protected. According to the Croatian Physical Plan of 1989, "by the year 2000, the total protected area shall be equal to 14.44% of the Croatian territory". By March 1991, there were 363 areas (Miljanic and Draganovic, *in litt.*, 1991). Some of them, such as Plitvice and Krka were self-supporting and a third one, Brioni, was close to breaking even (Terselic *et al.*, 1991). In Macedonia, the Physical Plan of the republic defines the framework for the protection of landscapes at the level of the republic. The protection of landscapes at the regional level is designed in municipal physical plans. In 1991, 6.4% of the territory is protected. According to the Physical Plan, this share is to increase to 18% by the year 2000 (Terselic *et al.*, 1991). In Slovenia, the Department estimated that currently 20% of the natural heritage of the republic is protected (Spring 1991). More than 50% of Slovenia is covered by forests with resultant high populations of game animals and the creation of hunting reserves. However, recently these have lost their financial support from the government, whilst the hunting reserve administrations were suffering from financial troubles and consequently expressed the wish to have their areas transferred to the category of national parks. Hunting in these parks will probably continue nevertheless. Currently, the regional offices are negotiating with municipalities on the creation of six regional parks in the territories of Karavanke Mountains, River Kolpa, Karst, Pohorje and Kocevski Rog (Terselic *et al.*, 1991). Between 1984 and 1990, 16 new protected landscapes were created, covering a total area in excess of 12,000ha. In Serbia, 3.0% of the territory is protected in a total of 1,016 sites, although the identification of possible protected areas is not yet finished and work on the natural heritage inventory still has to be done (Terselic *et al.*, 1991). In Vojvodina, the inventory of natural heritage is for the most part complete (Terselic *et al.*, 1991). In the country as a whole there are 63 listed sites of importance for birds as defined by the International Council for Bird Preservation (Grimmet *et al.*, 1990).

A relatively low population density has ensured the survival of a number of important ecosystems, notably forest and alpine systems. By contrast, the majority of larger wetland sites have been drained and put under cultivation or pasture since the end of World War II. In several of the wetlands that survive, suitable habitats for breeding waterfowl are seriously degraded or polluted (Duffey, 1982; Institute for Nature Conservation of the SR of Serbia, 1988; IUCN, 1987; Singleton, 1987).

Some of the major threats to protected areas include tourism, water and air pollution (30% of forests were affected by acid rain in 1988), and economic development. Many park authorities have insufficient funds and have to rely on financial assistance from tourism, forestry, sporting and recreational activities.

Sites which are near industrial complexes have also suffered from a lack of concern for environmental issues following rapid industrial expansion in the early 1950s (Duffey, 1982; IUCN, 1987; Singleton, 1985). The following wildlife habitats and national parks are reported to have been affected by the military conflict as a result of the 1991 civil war: Velebit, Biokove, Krka River National Park, Mljet National Park, Plitvice Lakes National Park and World Heritage site and numerous other unique natural monuments. Threats include military manoeuvres in Mljet, fighting and military personnel stationed in Plitvice National Park (tanks are stationed in the park, trees are being felled for road blocks, there are reports of dynamiting the lakes for fish and bears being shot). The technological safety of the nuclear power plant at Krsko (jointly owned by Croatia and Slovenia), however, is reported not to be at risk. Threats by terrorists to mine the nuclear power plant have been rumoured. It has been estimated that 100,000 people would be in danger if a disaster similar to that at Chernobyl were to occur. Oil refineries and oil pipelines are being attacked, and the militia have announced their intention to destroy oil wells in Croatia and oil tankers on rivers and at sea. They set fire regularly to centennial forests in the coastal regions (IUCN-EEP, 1991).

Other Relevant Information   Over the last decade, tourism has become one the main economies of Yugoslavia. The majority of tourists visit Slovenia and Croatia. It has been estimated that Croatia alone is losing US$ 1 billion directly and US$ 5 Billion indirectly from the loss of its tourist business due to the civil war. The revenues from tourism are forecast to be less than 10% of the £3 billion reported for 1990 (IUCN-EEP, 1991). The effects on specific protected area management may be catastrophic in the short-term. For example, in Plitvice National Park alone there were 800,000 visitors in the mid-1980s. Including the average entrance fees (US$ 9 in 1986), the annual visitor income was US$ 2.5 million in 1986, reduced to zero in 1991.

Addresses

Bosnia Herzegovina
Zavod za zastitu spomenika kulkure prirodnih znamenitosti i rijetkosti SR Bosne I Hercegovine (Office for the Protection of Cultural Monuments, Department of Nature Conservation), Obalu 27. jula 11-a, 71000 SARAJEVO, Bosnia and Herzegovina (Tel: 071 653555)

Croatia
Ministarstvo Zastite Okolisa prostornog uredenja igraditeljstra (Ministry of the Environment, Physical Planning and Construction), Ilica 44/II 41000 ZAGREB, Croatia (Tel: 041 432022)

Macedonia
Republicki zavod za zastit u na prirodnite retkosti SR Makedonije (Nature Conservancy), Rudera Boskovica bb, Karpus II, 91000 SKOPLJE, Macedonia (Tel: 091 251133)

Montenegro
Republicki zavod za zastit u prirode SR Crne Gore (Nature Conservancy), Trg., Nikole Kovacevica br. 7, 81000 TITOGRAD, Montenegro (Tel: 081 22992)

Serbia
Republicki zavod za zastit u prirode (Institute of Nature Conservation and Republic of Serbia), Postanskifah 51, Tréci bulevar 106, 11070 N BEOGRAD, Serbia (Tel: 142281/142-165)

Koskova
Pokrajinski zavod zastitu prirode SAP Kosovo (Nature Conservancy), Lenjinova br. 18, 38000 PRISTINA, Kosovo, Serbia (Tel: 038 27027/27026)

Vojvodina
Pokrajinski zavod za zastit u prirode SAP Vojvodine (Nature Conservancy), Petrovaradinska tvrdarva, 21000 NOVI SAD/Petrovasadin tvrdjava, Vojvodina, Serbia (Tel: 021 432200)

Slovenia
Zavod SR Slovenije za varstvo naravne in Kulturne Dedicene (Institute for the protection of monuments and the department of nature conservation), Plecnikov trg.2, 61000 LJUBLJANA, Slovenia (Tel: 213083)

References

Baccar, H. (1977). *A survey of existing and potential marine parks and reserves in the Mediterranean region*. IUCN/UNEP.

COE (1987). Yugoslavia: new structures. *Naturopa* 86(12): 4.

Davis, S. D., Droop, S. J. M., Gregerson, P., Henson, L., Leon, S. J., Villa-Lobos, J. L., Synge, H., and Zantovska, J. (1986). *Plants in danger: what do we know?* IUCN, Gland, Switzerland and Cambridge, UK. 461 pp.

Duffey, E. (1982). *National parks and reserves of Western Europe*. Macdonald and Company, London.

Fisher, D. (1990). Environmental politics in Yugoslavia. *Environmental Policy Review: the Soviet Union and Eastern Europe* 4(2).

Godiel, L. (1981). The protection of rare plants in nature reserves and national parks in Yugoslavia. In: Synge, H. (Ed.), *The biological aspects of rare plant conservation*. John Wiley and Sons Ltd.

Grimmett, R.F. and Jones, T.A. (1990). *Important bird areas in Europe*. International Council for Bird Preservation, Girton, Cambridge, UK. 880 pp.

Gryn, Amroes, P. (1980). *Preliminary annotated list of existing and potential Mediterrranean protected areas*. UNEP/IUCN report. UNEP/IG 20/INF 5.

Institute for Nature Conservation of the SR of Serbia (1988). Report of Yugoslavia. East European Task Force Meeting, Krakow, Poland, October. Institute for Nature Conservation of the SR of Serbia for IUCN East European Programme, Gland, Switzerland and Cambridge, UK.

IUCN (1971). *United Nations List of National Parks and Equivalent Reserves*. 2nd Ed. Hayez, Brussels.

IUCN (1985). *United Nations List of National Parks and Protected Areas*. IUCN, Gland, Switzerland and Cambridge, UK.

IUCN (1987). *Directory of wetlands of international importance*. IUCN, Gland, Switzerland and Cambridge, UK.

IUCN (1991). *Environmental Status Reports: 1990 Volume Two: Albania, Bulgaria, Romania, Yugoslavia*. IUCN East European Programme, Gland, Switzerland and Cambridge, UK.

IUCN (1991a). *The Environment in Eastern Europe: 1990*. Environmental Research Series 3. IUCN East European Programme, Gland, Switzerland and Cambridge, UK.

IUCN-EEP (1991). *The Yugoslav conflict: a summary of reported impacts on the natural values of Croatia and Slovenia*. Unpublished report. IUCN East European Programme.

MAB (1977). Workshop on biosphere reserves in the Mediterranean region: Development of a conceptual basis and a plan for the establishment of a regional network. MAB report series No. 45 Side, 6-11 June. Final Report, Unesco 1979.

Mestrovic, S. (1983). Nature Conservation in Yugoslavia. *Nature and national parks* 21: 27-28.

Movcan, J. (1982). National park development and its economics: experience from Plitvice National Park, Yugoslavia. In: McNeely, J.A. and Miller, K.R. (Eds), *National parks, conservation, and development. The role of protected areas in sustaining society*. Smithsonian Institution Press, Washington, DC.

OECD (1986). *Environmental policies in Yugoslavia*. OECD, Paris. 160 pp.

Singleton, F. (1985). *National parks and the conservation of nature in Yugoslavia*. Paper presented at 3rd World Congress for Soviet and East European Studies, Washington DC, 30 October-4 November 1985.

Singleton, F. (1987). Environmental Protection in Yugoslavia. In: Schreiber, H. (Ed.), *Environmental protection in Eastern Europe*. IIUG, Berlin.

Singleton, F. (1987). Environmental protection in Yugoslavia. Research Unit Environmental Policy, Social Science Centre, Berlin.

Terselic, V. and Juras, A. (1991). Nature Conservation in Yugoslavia. In: *Nature conservation in Austria, Finland, Norway, Sweden, Switzerland, Bulgaria, Czechoslovakia, Hungary, Poland, Romania, Yugoslavia and the Soviet Union*. European Parliament Directorate-General for Research Environment, Public Health and Consumer Protection. Series 17, EN-9-1991. Pp. 118-137.

UNEP/IG 20/Inf. 3 GE-80-2585 (1980). *Survey of national legislation relevant to marine and coastal protected areas*. Report by the Legal Officer of the Food and Agriculture Organization of the United Nations based on the work of Ch. du Saussay and M. Prieur.

UNEP (1987). Yugoslavia. *UNEP Regional Bulletin for Europe* 3: 8.

Wirth, H. (Ed.) (1979). *Nature reserves in Europe*. Edition Leipzig.

ANNEX
Definitions of protected area designations, as legislated, together with authorities responsible for their administration

Title: Varies by republic (see main text)

Date: Varies by republic (see main text)

Brief description: Varies by republic (see main text)

Administrative authority: Varies by republic (see main text)

Designations:

The most important types of protected natural areas have been classified into the following groups:

Nacionalni park or Narodni park (National park) Constitute the largest natural zones of outstanding natural values. Park management varies between republics, many sites being internationally recognised as national parks but others are essentially protected landscapes.

Regionalni park prirode, Krajinski park, Regionalni park (Regional natural park or nature park) Constitute large areas of specific natural value and are of importance as landscape;

Rezervat prirode, Strogi, Naravni rezervat (Natural reserve or nature reserve) Small in size

Established to protect specific natural elements or species

Spomenik prirode, Naravni spomenik (Natural monument) Outstanding geological or animate features, protected for their rarity or specific properties;

Zasticeno rekreaciono podrucje (Recreational zone)   Large area such as sea coasts, lake shores, river banks, mountain resorts or natural features protected specifically for recreation and sports activities

Ostala zasticena podrucja prirode (OZPP) or Karakteristicni pejsazi (Sanctuary of landscape or recreational importance)   Established largely for recreational importance, cultural heritage and characteristic landscape values are of extensive interest to tourism

Memorijalni spomenik (Memorial monument)   Small natural zone established to protect historic features such as important battlegrounds

Spomenik oblikovane prirode or hortikulturni spomenik (Ornate natural monument or horticultural garden)   Notable landscape garden

Source: IUCN, 1991

SUMMARY OF PROTECTED AREAS

Map[†] ref.	National/international designations Name of area	IUCN management category	Area (ha)	Year notified
	National Parks			
1	Biogradska Gora	II	3,400	1952
2	Brioni	V	4,660	1983
3	Djerdap	V	63,500	1983
4	Durmitor	II	33,000	1952
5	Fruska Gora	V	25,398	1960
6	Galicica	II	22,750	1958
7	Kopaonik	II	11,800	1981
8	Kornati	II	22,400	1980
9	Kozara	V	3,375	1967
10	Krka River	II	14,200	1985
11	Lovcen	II	2,400	1952
12	Mavrovo	II	73,088	1949
13	Mljet	II	3,100	1960
14	Paklenica	II	3,617	1949
15	Pelister	II	12,500	1948
16	Plitvice Lakes	V	19,172	1949
17	Risnjak	II	3,014	1953
18	Sara	II	39,000	1986
19	Skadarske jezero	II	40,000	1983
20	Sutjeska	II	17,250	1965
21	Tara	II	19,175	1981
22	Triglav	II	84,805	1981
	Nature Reserves			
23	Bijele i Samarske Stijene	I	1,175	1985
24	Deliblatska Pescara	V	29,352	1965
25	Hajducki i Rozanski Kukovi	I	1,220	1969
26	Jorgov kamen	IV	1,500	1988
27	Kopacki Rit	I	7,200	1967
28	Korab	IV	2,601	1988
29	Kotorsko Risanski Zaliv	V	12,000	1979
30	Malostonski Zaljev	I	10,389	1983
31	Neretva Delta	IV	1,200	
32	Obedska Bara	V	17,501	1968
33	Obedska bara Kod Kupinova III	IV	16,133	1968
34	Ohrid (Ohridsko) jezero	IV	38,000	1958
35	Otok Krk Rta Glavine do Uvale Mala LukaI	V	1,000	1969
36	Planina Vodno	IV	2,840	1970

Map[†] ref.	National/international designations Name of area	IUCN management category	Area (ha)	Year notified
37	Prasuma perucica	IV	1,434	1954
38	Senecka planina	IV	1,953	1988
39	Veliki i Mali Strbac ra Trajonovum tablom	I	1,124	1975
40	Zvijezda	V	2,007	1950
	Natural Monuments			
41	Djalovica Klisura	III	1,600	1968
42	Djavolja varos	I	1,400	1959
43	Dojran	III	2,730	1970
44	Markovi Kuli	III	5,285	1967
45	Ohridsko jezero	III	23,000	1958
46	Prespanske jezero	III	17,680	1977
47	Rugovska klisura	I	4,301	1988
48	Scedro Island	III	750	1968
49	Suma od Krivulj na Jakusici	III	1,000	1970
	Landscape Parks			
50	Robanov Kot	V	1,580	1987
51	Topla	V	1,345	1966
52	Velebit	VIII	200,000	1981
53	Vidova gora	V	1,800	1970
54	Zvecevo na papuku	V	2,586	1966
	Regional Nature Parks			
55	Biokovo	V	19,550	1981
56	Gornje Podunavlje	V	9,996	1982
57	Grmija	IV	1,126	1987
58	Kopacki Rit (Kopacevo Marshes)	VIII	10,510	1976
59	Palic-Ludas	V	6,360	1982
60	Panonija	VIII	3,937	1975
61	Rajac	VIII	1,200	1963
62	Resava	V	10,000	1957
63	Stari Begej	V	1,327	1986
64	Suboticka suma	VIII	4,431	1982
65	Tribevic	V	1,000	1954
66	Visacke planine	VIII	4,177	1982
67	Zahorina	V	2,000	1954
68	Zvijezda na Planini Tara	V	1,893	1971

	Biosphere Reserves			
	Réserve écologique du Bassin de la Rivière Tara	IX	200,000	1976
	Velebit Mountain	IX	150,000	1977
	Ramsar Wetlands			
	Ludaško Lake	R	593	1977
	Obedska Bara	R	17,501	1977
	World Heritage Sites			
	Durmitor National Park	X	492,000	1980
	Kotor	X	n/a	1979
	Ohrid	X	38,000	1979
	Plitvice Lakes National park	X	19,200	1979
	Skocjan Caves	X	200	1986

[†]Locations of most protected areas are shown on the accompanying map.

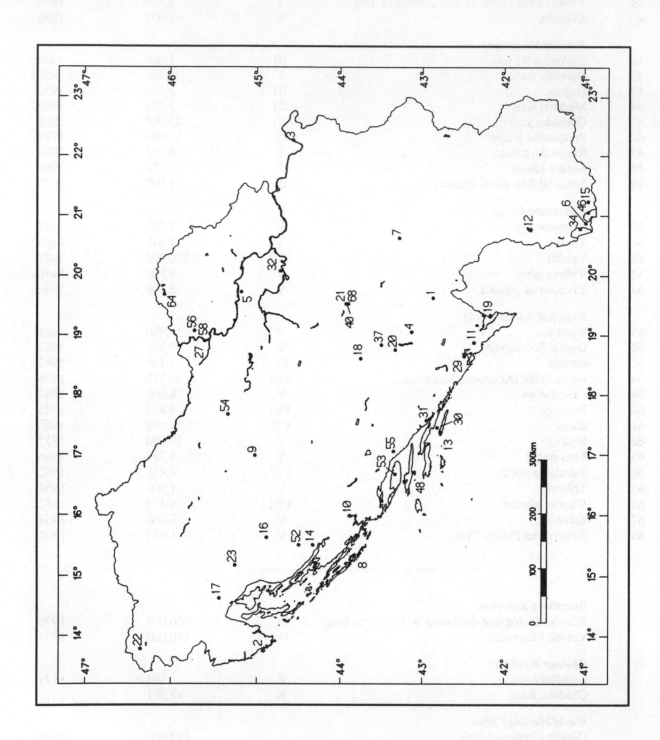

Protected Areas of Yugoslavia

Palaearctic
North Africa and Middle East

AFGHANISTAN

Area 636,265 sq. km

Population 16,557,000 (1990)
Natural increase: 6.68% per annum

Economic Indicators
GDP: US$ 244 per capita (1987)
GNP: US$ No information

Policy and Legislation The Afghanistan republic superseded the former monarchy on 17 July 1973 and a Constitution was approved in November 1987 (Hunter, 1991).

Traditional forms of protection include areas around lakes which have been maintained as hunting grounds since Moghul times. Modern forms of nature conservation began in Afghanistan around the beginning of this century, with the establishment of privileged hunting reserves for use by the royal family, such as at Ajar Valley and Kole Hashmat Khan. During that period a number of protected areas, such as waterfowl reserves or sanctuaries, were individually declared by Royal Decree (Rahim and Larsson, 1978; Shank *et al.*, 1977).

In 1991 there was apparently no overall enabling legislation providing for the establishment and management of protected areas. Previously, the policy adopted for the legal designation of protected areas followed a set procedure. Initially, the site would be established under written order from the Directorate of Wildlife and National Parks. Subsequently, on the basis of legal petitions it would be gazetted by government order signed by the Head of State (Sayer and van der Zon, 1981). The two designation types include waterfowl or wildlife sanctuary and national park. The only national park, Band-e Amir, was declared in 1973 but has not been gazetted. The signing of the June 1977 protocol agreement between the Afghan Tourist Organisation (ATO) and Department of Forests and Range ensured the cooperation for management of the park (FAO, 1978; MacPherson, 1991).

The majority of the declared protected areas have not been published in the official Government Gazette by the Ministry of Justice and, therefore, apparently have no legal status (FAO, 1978; MacPherson, 1991). A draft Law of Forests has been prepared but has not been legislated. It has been proposed that this draft legislation be revised to incorporate provisions for the establishment and management of a system of protected areas, with different management categories clearly defined (Sayer and Van der Zon, 1981).

International Activities Afghanistan ratified the Convention concerning the Protection of the World Cultural and Natural Heritage (World Heritage Convention) on 20 March 1979. To date no sites have been inscribed.

A Treaty of Friendship was signed between the USSR and Afghanistan in December 1978. Based on the Geneva Accord of April 1988 the Soviet military presence was ended by 15 February 1989 (Hunter, 1991).

Administration and Management Prior to military hostilities in 1979, the Department of Forests and Range of the Ministry of Agriculture and Land Reform was responsible for the management and protection of the country's protected areas and wildlife.

The Department was established in 1957 and it formed a Directorate of Wildlife and National Parks in 1973. At that time it was staffed by an administrative officer and two assistants to supervise a number of field officers. It lacked any specific and approved jurisdictional powers (FAO, 1978). On 1 February 1983 an FAO/UNDP project was launched to strengthen the Forestry Department, and still continues to be involved in assistance towards forestry planning and development (MacPherson, 1991).

Authority over the only national park, Band-e Amir, was held by the ATO, which promoted its establishment in 1973. Under the 1977 protocol agreement between the ATO and the Department of Forests and Range, conservation and management became the prerogative of the Department, while all forms of economic utilisation were allocated to the ATO. Since that period, administration and management have been severely restricted, the current situation is largely unknown (FAO, 1978; MacPherson, 1991).

In 1973, the Republican Guard, a cadre of the Afghan army directly linked to the presidential office, was given charge of former royal hunting reserves, such as Ajar Valley and Kole Hashmat Khan. Its management activities were limited but included livestock maintenance (Shank, Petocz and Habibi, 1977).

A training programme for wardens and conservation officers was established through a bilateral agreement with Iran in 1974. Some 34 students were trained prior to this programme being discontinued. In addition, a number of postgraduates were trained in forestry and range management during the 1970s (FAO, 1978).

There is a lack of non governmental organisations concerned with nature conservation. Bodies involved in scientific research and agriculture have included the Science Research Centre of the Afghanistan Academy of Sciences and the Faculty of Agriculture of *Pohantoon-e-Kabul* (Kabul University).

Following the onset of military conflict in 1979, there has been extremely limited activity in the field of conservation and protected areas management and administration (MacPherson, 1991).

Systems Reviews   Situated in central Asia, Afghanistan is a land-locked country with a wide diversity of habitat and terrain, ranging from steppe, semi-desert, riverine forest and lakes to scrubland, mountain woodland and mountain. Rising from the arid plains of Seistan basin, the highest peak is in the Pamir ranges at 7,484m. The natural vegetation of a significant proportion of the country was originally woodland and forest, although over the millenia these have been replaced by the present preponderance of steppe (Sayer and Van der Zon, 1981). According to Sayer and Van der Zon (1981), approximately 54.7 million ha (84%) of the country are rangeland, 7.9 million ha (12%) arable and 2.2 million ha (3.4%) forest. Before 1979 Afghanistan was virtually self-sufficient in agriculture, but by 1989 it was estimated that 33% of land was derelict and abandoned as a consequence of war (Hunter, 1991). It is regarded as almost impossible to obtain an accurate estimate of the current wildlife situation. Access to important wildlife habitat areas is severely restricted due to fighting and/or by the presence of extensive mine fields (MacPherson, 1991).

In the 1970s the state authorities requested the assistance of UNDP and FAO in the conservation and management of its wildlife and natural areas. Under a project running from 1972 to 1979, assistance was given to establish a system of protected areas, strengthening the Department of Forests and Range and contributing towards a conservation strategy (FAO, 1980). Some assistance was also received from the World Wildlife Fund (WWF) for infrastructure developments in Ab-i-Estada and Dashte Nawar waterfowl sanctuaries.

Three wildlife areas and one national park were well protected prior to 1979. However, since that date no activity has been taken in the field of conservation and protected areas. In a 1991 report one national park, Bande Amir, and two waterfowl sanctuaries were listed as protected (MacPherson, 1991). Between February and April 1991 environmental consultants for IUCN The World Conservation Union were contracted to investigate environmental management measures under the auspices of the Office for the Coordination of United Nations Humanitarian and Economic Assistance (UNOCA) Programmes to Afghanistan. The intention of this activity was to seek an overview of the natural resource aspects of current and proposed projects of UN agencies and non-governmental organisations in Afghanistan. It was regarded that inadequate baseline data, the lack of a national institutional framework and the significant constraints of war rendered the development of a national conservation strategy premature at the time (MacPherson, 1991). Recommendations included that in the short-term, existing forestry programmes place a much greater emphasis on social forestry and agroforestry. In the long-term the mission recommended that an attempt be made to protect the remaining natural forests, representative areas being selected initially in areas where security conditions permitted such management.

The mission also recommended that the clearing of land mines from selected key areas of natural forest begin when objectives for mine clearing near settlements had been achieved, and that the planning for the preservation of the remaining natural forests should commence as soon as the security situation permitted. Other recommendations included the need for assessments of damage to protected area candidate sites; strategies for sustainable utilisation of wildlife (projects that were estimated to cost US$ 50,000) and encouragement to join Ramsar and CITES (MacPherson, 1991).

The present preponderance of steppe reflects the degradation of the environment over millenia by grazing, browsing and cutting of wood. Rangeland, on which the majority of Afghans depend directly or indirectly, has been degraded and misused. In more arid regions dry land farming has exhausted soils which has led to erosion. In the early 1980s the few remaining forested areas were being destroyed at an alarming rate to meet the fuel requirements of the major cities, while shrubs and dried herbs have met the needs of the rural population and even those of a number of large towns (MacPherson, 1991; Sayer and Van der Zon, 1981). Military conflict from 1979 onwards caused a breakdown in administration in many areas of the country, of depopulation and abandonment of agricultural land, of laying millions of land-mines throughout the country and of uncontrolled timber and wood use and hunting of wildlife.

Other Relevant Information   Prior to hostilities the ATO was largely responsible for the commercial exploitation of wildlife, first becoming involved in 1968 when it was allowed to set up a commercial hunting programme in Tulibai Valley (Petocz, 1978). The basis for inter-ministerial cooperation on matters of wildlife management and utilisation was defined in a protocol agreement signed in June 1977. In this agreement, conservation and management of wildlife became the prerogative of the Department of Forests and Range, while all programmes of economic utilisation were allocated to the ATO. Any expansion or alteration in the ATO hunting programmes required approval by the Department of Forests and Range. This agreement pertained solely to wildlife (wild animals and birds). Owing to internal political instability there has been negligible tourism since 1979 (Hunter, 1991).

Addresses

General President, Department of Forests and Range, Ministry of Agriculture and Land Reform, Jamal Minja, KABUL (Tel: 408415/411503)

General Director of Wildlife, Ministry of Agriculture and Land Reform, KABUL (Tel: 41151)

Science Research Centre, Afghanistan Academy of Sciences, Sher Alikhan Street, KABUL (Tel: 20350)

Faculty of Agriculture, Pohantoon-e-Kabul (Kabul University), Jamal Mina, KABUL (Tel: 40341)

References

FAO (1978). *National parks and utilization of wildlife resources: Afghanistan.* Project findings and recommendations. UNDP/FAO, Rome. P. 32.

FAO (1980). *National parks and wildlife management: Afghanistan.* Project findings and recommendations. UNDP/FAO, Rome. P. 22.

Hunter, B. (Ed.) (1991). *The Statesman's Year Book 1991-92.* The Macmillan Press Ltd, London and Basingstoke, UK. Pp. 63-67

MacPherson, N. (1991). Opportunities for improved Environmental Management in Afghanistan. Report of an IUCN – The World Conservation Union – mission under contract to the Office for the Coordination of United Nations Humanitarian and Economic Assistance Programmes relating to Afghanistan. 66 pp.

Rahim, A. and Larsson, J. (1978). *A preliminary study of Lake Hashmat Khan with recommendations for management.* UNDP/FAO, Kabul. 17 pp.

Shank, C. C., Petocz, R. G. and Habibi, K. (1977). *A preliminary management plan for the Ajar Valley wildlife reserve.* UNDP/FAO/Department of Forests and Range, Kabul. 35 pp.

Sayer, J.A. and van der Zon, A.P.M. (1981). *National parks and wildlife management. Afghanistan.* A contribution to a conservation strategy. 2 volumes. UNDP/FAO, Rome. 107 and 153 pp.

UN (1991). Operation Salam, programme for 1991. Humanitarian and Economic Assistance Programmes relating to Afghanistan. United Nations Office for the Coordination of United Nations Humanitarian and Economic Assistance Programmes relating to Afghanistan. 158 pp.

ANNEX
Definitions of protected area designations, as legislated, together with authorities responsible for their administration

Title : Individual Government Order Nos. and Petition Nos.

Date: Individually decreed

Brief description: No enabling legislation exists for the protected areas. Each protected area has been individually decreed.

Administrative authority: Directorate of Wildlife and National Parks, Guard-i-Jamhuriat (Republican Guard), Afghan Tourist Organisation (ATO)

Designations:

Waterfowl reserve or sanctuary Originally individually declared by Royal Decree. Gazetted through individual government orders by the Head of State. Following legal protection, management plans are prepared.

Principal objectives include protecting birds from adverse influences of human origin.

National park Long-term objectives are to conserve the natural landscapes through a system of zonation and to develop the tourist potential of the area.

A draft forests law exists but has not been legislated. It has been proposed that this draft legislation be revised to incorporate provisions for the establishment and management of a system of protected areas, with different management categories clearly defined.

Sources: FAO, 1978; MacPherson, 1991; Sayer and van der Zon, 1981

SUMMARY OF PROTECTED AREAS

Map[†] ref.	*National/international designations* Name of area	IUCN management category	Area (ha)	Year notified
	Waterfowl Sanctuaries			
1	Ab-i-Estada	IV	27,000	1977
2	Dashte-Nawar	IV	7,500	1977
	Wildlife Reserves/Areas			
3	Ajar Valley	IV	40,000	1978
4	Pamir-i-Buzurg	IV	67,938	1978
	National Park			
5	Band-e-Amir	VIII	41,000	1973

[†]Locations of most protected areas are shown on the accompanying map.

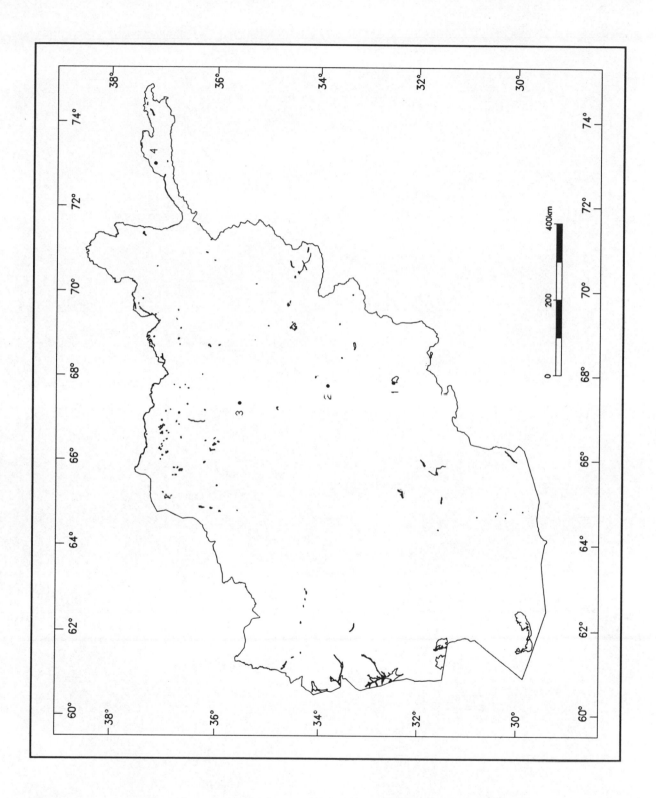

Protected Areas of Afghanistan

ALGERIA

Area 2,381,745 sq. km

Population 24,960,000 (1990)
Natural increase: 2.79% per annum

Economic Indicators
GDP: US$ 2,825 per capita (1987)
GNP: US$ 2,760 per capita (1987)

Policy and Legislation In the Algerian Constitution of 22 November 1976, Article 14 specified that the state "owns for the people the forests, water and all things natural and living in the continental plateau". Constitutional reforms were approved in February 1989 (Hunter, 1991).

There are no major traditional forms of protected area remaining in Algeria, although traditional methods of land management have long maintained irrigation systems, erosion prevention murets and mountain agriculture. Land is under three forms of ownership; state lands such as highlands, forest and water; private ownership largely of agricultural land; and communal lands.

The first conservation legislation and forestry code came into existence in 1912. From 1923 to 1939 a series of national parks was set up by the French administrative authorities. Following independence, the conservation laws and forestry regulations of the French period lapsed. In 1979 a study was instigated to establish a new legal framework intended to cover all aspects of nature conservation and the creation of parks and reserves. In 1982-83 major changes became apparent with the governmental sanctioning of a National Strategy for the Conservation of Fauna on 5 February 1983 in Law No. 83-03. This legislation was based on the Hunting Decree No. 82-10 of 21 August 1982, on Ordinance No. 67-281 of 20 December 1967 on Excavation and Protection of Historic and Natural Monuments and on the General Forests Law No. 84-12 on the general management of forests passed on 23 June 1984. These edicts included new statutes for national park and nature reserve creation and management, pollution control and the protection of non domestic species. Simultaneously, a new Council of Hunting was directed to designate hunting reserves and construct a list of wild species.

\The central law entitled the Law on the Protection of the Environment, Law No. 83-05, governs all environmental topics including the identification of the different classes of protected areas, under Article 17-30. Under this Law, enabling legislation on the designation of protected areas occurs through Decree No. 83-458 of 23 July 1983, entitled Establishing Model Statutes for National Parks. This Law introduced three categories of protected area: réserve naturelle (natural reserve), parc national (national park) and parc régional (regional park) (see Annex). The first protected area designated under the 1983 law was a national park, Tassili N'Ajjer, which had been established previously by the Ministry of Culture as an historic monument in 1972 (Decree No. 72-168); the next four parks were created and governed by Decree No. 83-458 of July 1983 (Decree Nos. 83-459 to 83-462) in accordance with the law (Meziane, 1986). Decree No. 87-143 of 16 June 1987 fixes the regulations and classification of national parks and reserves and Interministerial Act of 9 August 1987 concerns internal organisation of national parks.

Under Act No. 84-12 of the Forest Law of 23 June 1984, it is the duty of each individual to contribute to the safeguarding of the country's forests. Forest areas are classified into production forests where the principal function is that of supplying timber and other forest products; protection forests where the principal function is that of conserving the land; forests and other wooded stands, where the special purpose is that of protecting "rare items and scenic beauties", providing recreation in a natural environment, and scientific research, education and national defence. Under Article 90 of the Forest Law (with due regard to Ordinance No. 67-281 of 20 December 1967 relative to excavations and the protection of historic and nature sites and monuments and in compliance with the Environmental Protection Act) specified portions of the country's forests may be declared national parks and nature reserves. Forest law enforcement is the responsibility of the officers of the Judicial Police and the Corps of Forest Wardens as indicated in Article 63 of the Forest Law.

Ordinance of 23 October 1976 concerns the general administration of fisheries, and provides for the establishment of maritime zones closed to fishing.

Reviews of protected areas policy and legislation dating from the French administrative period led to the reorganised legislation of 1983 and 1984 and the subsequent review and reclassification of the extant protected areas system.

International Activities At the international level, Algeria has entered a number of cooperative agreements and legal obligations. The London Convention on Preservation of Fauna and Flora in their Natural State was accepted in 1933. The African Convention on the Conservation of Nature and Natural Resources was accepted in Algiers in 1968, and ratified on 11 December 1982 (Decree No. 82-440) (see Annex). Algeria is party to the Convention concerning the Protection of the World Cultural and Natural Heritage (World Heritage Convention), which was ratified on 24 June 1974. One natural site has been inscribed to date. Algeria acceded to the Convention on Wetlands of International Importance especially as Waterfowl Habitat (Ramsar Convention) on 4 November 1983, at which time two sites were designated under the terms of the Convention.

Algeria participates in the Unesco Man and the Biosphere Programme and in 1991 there was one site listed. The Convention for the Protection of the Mediterranean Sea against Pollution, usually known as the Barcelona Convention, was formally adopted on 16 February 1976. The contracting parties to the Convention adopted the Protocol concerning Mediterranean Specially Protected Areas on 2 April 1982, which entered into force on 23 March 1986. Four sites have been identified by the Algerian national focal point as being representative of the Mediterranean network. In the Tunis Declaration on the Environment on 19-23 April 1991 (conference of the Ministers of the Environment having in common the use of the French language) Ministers decided to work towards implementing the proposal of devoting at least 5% of their territories to safeguarding their natural heritage, putting the emphasis on the conservation of ecosystems and the diversity of species, within the context of sustainable development (ACCT, 1991).

Under the World Bank Mediterranean Environmental Technical Assistance Programme (CY90-92 METAP), European Investment Bank, United Nations Development Programme and Commission of the European Communities, environmental project preparation included the El Kala National Park management plan and the Tlemcen Coastal Zone management plan (Anon, 1991). The CY91-93 programme includes an institutional support package for environmental management support, training and development of a environmental impact assessment (EIA) unit (Anon., 1991). The World Bank has also been involved in the World Development Indicators on the Environment (see below, Anon., 1990). Representatives from Algeria attended the first meeting of the Mediterranean Protected Areas Network (MEDPAN) meeting on 5-6 October 1990 in Monaco and the first technical meeting to discuss marine protection and economic impacts of protected areas creation was scheduled for September 1991 (Anon., 1991).

Over the past few years, transfrontier cooperative agreements have been investigated with the Tunisian authorities for El Kala and the region between Tabarka and El Feidja National Park. No known cooperative transfrontier initiatives are being planned between Algeria and its other neighbouring countries and provinces; Libya, Mali, Mauritania, Morocco and Niger.

Administration and Management   In the 1960s the Department of Waters and Forests (Département des Eaux et Forêts) of the Ministry of Agriculture and Agricultural Revolution held general responsibility for nature conservation. In the 1970s the Ministry of Land Value and Protection of the Environment (Ministère de la Mise en Valeur des Terres et de la Protection de l'Environnement) was established. Environmental concerns are now the responsibility of the National Agency for the Protection of the Environment (Agence National pour la Protection de l'Environnement).

Throughout the 1980s overall responsibility for protected areas lay with two ministries: the Ministry of Hydrology, Environment and Forestry (Ministère de l'Hydraulique, de l'Environnement et des Forêts (MHEF) and the Ministry of Information and Culture (Ministère de l'Information et de la Culture). The infrastructure within the MHEF consisted of six divisions including the Direction de la Sauvegarde et de la Promotion de la Nature (DSPN) which was concerned with the environment. The DSPN was itself divided into three sections; those concerned with "parcs nationaux et réserves naturelles" et "loisirs et forets" and "environnement". The Sub-directorate for National Parks and Reserves was further subdivided into bureaux of "parcs nationaux", "réserves naturelles" and "faune et flore en disparition".

In 1991 the National Agency for Nature Protection (Agence National pour la Protection de la Nature) of the Ministry of Agriculture (Ministère de l'Agriculture) had already taken over responsibility from the former MHEF for the majority of protected areas, although the two desert national parks continue to be under the jurisdiction of the Ministry of Culture now entitled the Ministère de la Communication et de la Culture.

Under Law No. 83-458 each national park is administered by a resident park director and a management committee or council composed of representatives of the interested ministries and the local authorities concerned. The council is responsible for the organisation and general operation and regulation of the park, the annual programme of work, budget and the programme of scientific research. The decisions of the council are, by law, to be submitted to the supervising ministry for approval. The park director is appointed directly by the Minister and has powers of independent decision and action. Each national park administration has its own budget and is essentially only directly answerable to the Minister. In 1990 there was a total of 56 field staff for all national parks.

Management plans exist for the majority of the parks. The definitive map and management plans of six of the seven national parks in the north have been prepared by the National Bureau of Forest Resources (Bureau National des Etudes Forestières (BNEF). In 1990 a projected collaborative management plan project between the BNEF, University College London and the World Bank was set in motion with Global Environment Facility (GEF) funds. A total of US$ 250,000 has been budgeted for the project. This project is seen as a replicable action that could be applied to reorganise and improve management of other existing protected areas in the country in the future (Anon., 1990). BNEF intends completion of the management plan for the park in 1992, which will include an plan to integrate surrounding land.

Reserves, which are created under the 1983 legislation, are administered by the adjacent national park authorities or by the Forestry Department in the Forest District in which they are situated (Meziane, *in litt.*, 1987).

Regional parks came under the authority of the Wilaya (although they have now been redesignated mainly as reserves or national parks). In principle, each Wilaya has a recreational forest for public use. In those that have been established there are no entry fees, unlike in the national parks.

Under Hunting Law No. 226, a new Council of Hunting was directed to designate hunting reserves and construct a list of wild species. Hunting associations have some 32,000 members and are coordinated by a central national federation. The protection of hunting reserves is strengthened in some cases by being completely surrounded by boundary fencing. Each reserve has a forestry graduate in charge, and a number of sites have management plans. Forestry personnel, such as hunting guards, undertake most of the policing. The direct revenue from hunting is DA 10.8 million per year (1990). Up to 620 tourist hunters, each paying a government subsidised DA 3,000 per day, visited Algeria during the period from October 1989 to March 1990, organised under the auspices of the National Tourism Office (ONAT) and National Tourist Club (CTN).

Research in protected areas is undertaken by a number of governmental and non-governmental scientific bodies. Each park is used extensively for university projects and in 1989 alone 32 research projects were undertaken in one park. These projects are often applied research and tend not to be directly used in protected area management or monitoring, exceptions including bird monitoring at El Kala National Park. One of the most important bodies is the BNEF, which is instrumental in management plan preparation (see above). The Department of Forestry and the Protection of Nature (Département de Foresterie et de Protection de la Nature) is part of the National Institute of Agronomy (Institut National Agronomique, INA). It undertakes an average of 15 conservation or biological theses (theses d'ingenieurs and magisters) in national parks and protected areas per year (Chalabi, *in litt.*, 1991). Other bodies include the Laboratory of Ornithology and Vertebrate Ecology of INA (Laboratoire d'Ornithologie et d'Ecologie des Vertebrates) which undertakes research on threatened species. The National Institute of Forestry Research (Institute National de Recherche Forestière (INRF), which has 17 field stations, is actively involved in research towards forest management. Each of these bodies has cooperative programmes with universities and institutes in Algeria and overseas. Non-governmental citizen groups include the Friends of El Kala National Park, National Federation of Hunters and the Movement of Algerian Ecologists.

The aims of the administrative policy on protected areas is to continue the conservation of native flora and fauna within a framework of a national conservation network and the consolidation of existing protected establishments (namely national parks, nature reserves, forest parks and hunting reserves). Effectiveness of protected areas management has been noted as being well administered although insufficient funds are available for full implementation of management plan programmes, and monitoring is next to non existent. Protection is often enhanced by the areas being surrounded and enclosed by fences and by having an effective wardening system and an independent director and park budget. In the past the multiplicity of organisations involved in protected area establishment, management and research resulted in a recommendation in the FAO report of 1979 (TCP/ALG/6703) for a protocol to ensure coordination between these bodies. The FAO report recommended an ecosystems inventory and the construction of a protected areas list as part of a national plan for a protected areas system (FAO, 1979).

Systems Reviews   The northern part of the country is represented by a Mediterranean type flora and fauna which extends to the southern foothills of the Atlas mountain ranges. To the south of the Atlas and Haut plateaux is steppe land which merges into the Sahara desert. An outlier of Mediterranean vegetation survives on the Hoggar mountains in the extreme south of the country. Northern Algeria has been densely populated even in Roman times, but for centuries the Saharan south has remained under less risk from human disturbance. Algeria has a high level of biodiversity, with 250 endemic plants out of a total list of 3,140 known and over 1,300 plant species identified as nationally threatened. There are also eleven mammals, seven birds and one reptile under global threat of extinction (Zeraia, 1983). Wildfowl on Algerian wetlands have been subject to regular census surveys since 1973; national lists of threatened plant species has been undertaken by the INRF (Zeraia, 1983).

Forests cover 4.7 million ha or 2% of the land area, the greater part representing 3.7 million ha is situated in the northern region (Davis *et al.*, 1986; Hunter, 1991). There were an estimated 7.5 million ha of agricultural land in 1978, of which 6.8 million ha were arable, 31.7 million ha of pasture and scrub and 0.2 million ha of vineyards. In 1987 the government sold back to the private sector land which had been nationalised on the declaration of independence in 1962, a further 0.5 million ha which had been expropriated in 1973 were returned to 30,000 small landowners in 1990 (Hunter, 1991).

In 1989, the systems plan entitled "Development Perspectives to the year 2000 (Perspectives de Développement au Horizon 2000)" was published in two volumes about the activities of the Ministry of Agriculture concerning species and area conservation. The protected area document describes the existing situation, then identifies the short, and medium term requirements for protected areas to 1990 and to 2000, including identification of specific locations. During this ten-year period ten reserves (35,000ha), seven national parks (123,000ha), four hunting reserves, four wetlands and one breeding station have been identified as priority for protection. During the 1990-1994 period five reserves and two national parks were scheduled to be declared. The documentation also indicates budgetary requirements, equipment and manpower needs, and supporting action on research and training. The subsequent five-year development plan from 1990-1994 has incorporated actions from these strategy documents.

A World Bank Watershed Management and Forestry Project, World Development Indicators on the Environment was summarised in 1990/1991 (Anon., 1990). It was recognised that Algeria was probably the most advanced Maghrebian country in nature conservation, had a comprehensive environmental law that included nature conservation; a protected areas system covering 24% of the country, and universities and institutions with specialised training in conservation. However several constraints were identified: a) no national scientific survey had been made to determine the suitability of the projected network of sites; schema-directeur covering administrative rather than scientific needs of protected areas. Project recommendations included: a detailed scientific management plan prepared for one of the larger parks, and funds included in the project for follow up action in other sites; an INRF unit established to undertake research on protected areas with special reference to proposed areas and management of existing sites; bursaries and equipment provided in formal training; meetings and staff training courses (Anon., 1990).

Between 1923 and 1939 a series of 14 national parks was set up by the French administrative authorities. From independence in 1962 to 1983 no new protected areas were established. All current protected areas were gazetted under the Law of 1983 and important previously established sites were regazetted. In the *1990 United Nations List of National Parks and Protected Areas* 19 protected areas were recognised totalling 11,897,687ha; nine national parks covering 11,837,588ha, five nature reserves covering 26,200ha and five major hunting reserves covering 31,784ha.

The population explosion since independence and the rapid economic growth, together with considerable industrial and residential expansion, has had a significant deleterious impact on the environment. The greatest habitat loss in recent years has been through the extensive felling and burning of forests and maquis, of forest encroachment and expansion of agriculture (including conversion of grazing land, especially Atlas steppe, to arable land) and soil erosion. Numerous important wetland sites have also been seriously damaged or completely drained in the last two decades; this has been aggravated by Algerian development projects not taking into account the objectives of nature protection. The relatively recently declared national park at El Kala is perhaps under the greatest threat at present. The lack of cooperation and discussion between the local national park authorities and other ministries has led to the threatened drainage of this wetland area (Drucker, 1987; Chalabi, *in litt.*, 1991). Environmental pollution occurs but is localised and is of lesser significance than the above topics.

Other Relevant Information The first national parks were established under the French administration largely for recreation and tourism. Ecotourism is now an important element of such national parks as Chrea, Djurdjura and Tassili, where extensive visitor facilities exist. The number of tourists in national parks varies enormously. As many as 8,200 people visited Tassili N'Ajjer National Park in 1990, and 4,200 visited the adjacent south-east Tadrart region (Sidhoum Mahrez, *in litt.*, 1991). Entrance fees are charged to enter the parks. Perhaps unique in North Africa and the Middle East has been the visitor questionnaire produced by the Chrea park authorities to determine visitor interests and needs (Anon., n.d).

Addresses

Agence National pour la Protection de la Nature (National Agency for Nature Protection), Ministry of Agriculture, Jardin Botanique, El Hamm, ALGER

Agence National pour la Protection de l'Environnement (National Agency for the Protection of the Environment), BP 154, EL-ANNASER (Tel: 213 771414; Tlx: 65439 enl dz)

Institut National Agronomique, Département de Foresterie et Protection de la Nature (National Institute of Agronomy, Department of Forestry and Nature Protection), Avenue Pasteur, El Harrach, ALGER (Tel: 2 761987; Tlx: 64143 ina dz)

Institut National de Recherche Forestière (National Institute of Forestry Research), BP 37, CHERAGA-ALGER (Tel: 213 849790; Tlx: 61407 cnref dz)

References

ACCT (1991). The Tunis Declaration on the Environment. Première Conférence des ministres chargés de l'environnement des pays ayant en commun l'usage du Français/First Conference of the Ministers of the Environment of Countries having in common the use of the French language. Agence de coopération culturelle et technique, Tunis, 19-23 April 1991. 2 pp.

Anon. (n.d.). Le Parc National de Chrea vous souhaite la bienvenue, pour mieux vous servir, veuillez répondre a ce questionnaire. Parc National de Chrea, Ministère de l'Hydraulique, de l'Environnement et des Forêts. Pamphlet. 2 pp.

Anon. (1990). Algeria, Watershed Management and Forestry Project, Conservation of Nature. World Development Indicators on the Environment. The World Bank, Washington DC. 10 pp.

Anon. (1991). Mediterranean Environmental Technical Assistance Program, Activity Report Spring 1991. World Bank/European Investment Bank/United Nations Development Programme/Commission of the European Communities. 24 pp.

Bougal, N., Djender M., and Thomas J-P. (1976). Projet du Parc National Marin Lacustre Terrestre de El Kala (Annaba) Algerie. Report presented to the UNEP

Expert Consultation on Mediterranean Marine Parks and Wetland, Tunis, 12-14 January 1977. 130 pp.

Chalabi, B. (1987). Exposé sur la protection de la faune et de la flore. Présenté en première année de magister INA, El Harrach. 13 pp.

Carp, E. (1980). *A Directory of Western Palearctic Wetlands.* IUCN-UNEP, Gland, Switzerland. 506 pp.

Chalabi, B., Skinner, J., Harrison, J., et Van Dijk, G. (1984). Les zones humides du Nord-Est Algérien en 1984. Report No. 8. Stichting Werkgroep International Wad- en Watervogelonderzoek, the Netherlands. 45 pp.

De Smet, K. (1984). La nature et sa protection en Algérie. *Réserves naturelles* 3: 29-31.

De Smet, K.J.M. (1989). Studie van de verspreiding en biotoopkeuze van de grote mammalia in Algerije in het kader van het natuurbehoud. Unpublished Thesis. Rijksuniversiteit, Gent.

Drucker, G.R.F. (1987). Protected areas in Algeria. Unpublished report. Sussex, UK. 30 pp.

FAO (1979). Programme de Coopération Technique. Amènagement de l'Environnement rural, notamment des Parcs Nationaux, Algérie. FAO, Rome. TCP/ALG/6703. 18 pp.

Grimmett, R. (1987). *A review of the problems affecting Palearctic migratory birds in Africa.* ICBP, Cambridge, UK. 240 pp.

Gryn-Ambroes, P. (1980). Preliminary annotated lists of existing and potential Mediterranean protected areas. UNEP/IUCN report. IG.20/INF5. 108 pp.

Hunter, B. (Ed.) (1991). *The Statesman's Year Book 1991-92.* The Macmillan Press Ltd, London and Basingstoke, UK. 1692 pp.

Johnson, A.R. and Hafner, H. (1972). Dénombrement de sauvagine en automne sur des zones humides de Tunisie et d'Algerie. Station Biologique de la tour du Valat, le Sambuc, France. 15 pp.

Ledant, J-P. et Jacob, J.P. (1982). Liste rouge des espèces d'oiseaux menacées en Algérie. Rapport préparé pour DPN (Alger)/SEFOR/ICBP/IUCN.

Ledant, J-P and Van Dijk, G. (1977). Situation des zones humides algériennes et de leur avifaune. *Aves* 14: 217-232.

Ledant, J.P., Roux, F., Jarry, G., Gammel, A., Smit, C., Bairlein, F. and Wille, H. (1985). Aperçu des zones de grand intérêt pour la conservation des espèces d'oiseaux migrateurs de la communauté en Afrique. Rapport à la Direction Générale de l'Environnement, de la Protection des Consommateurs et de la Sécurité nucléaire de la Commission des Communautés européennes. Contrat U/84/129.

Maaher Abou Jaafer (1984). *National parks and natural reserves in the Arab World.* Arab League of Education, Culture and Science Organisation (ALECSO). Report order number 80/001/1984/ Science Division, Tunis. (original in Arabic). 112 pp.

Meziane, H. (1986). Textes et Lois et Leurs Applications. *Parc Zoologique et des loisirs d'Alger.* 20-22/09/1986. Pp. 3-8.

MHEF (1983). *Aperçu sur la faune algérienne et la politique engagée pour sa protection et son développement.* Ministère de l'Hydraulique, de l'Environnement et des Forêts. 20 pp.

MHEF (1985). Rapport National sur la Protection de l'Environnement en Algérie. Ministère de l'Hydraulique, de l'Environnement et des Forêts, Alger. 7 pp.

Morgan, N.C. (1982). An ecological survey of standing waters in North-West Africa: II Site descriptions for Tunisia and Algeria. *Biological Conservation* 24: 83-113.

RAC/SPA (1986). Proposed protected areas in the Mediterranean. Special Protected Areas Center, Salammbo, Tunis. 196 pp.

Smart, M. (1974). The wetlands of North Africa and their importance to waterfowl. IWRB, Slimbridge, England. 10 pp.

Touahria, M.A. (1986). Politique nationale Algérienne en matière de conservation de l'environnement. MAB/MEDIT/RB/Florac/ Document No. 12. P. 8.

Van Dijk, G. and Ledant, J-P. (1983). La valeur ornithologique des zones humides de l'est Algerien. *Biological Conservation* 26: 215-226.

ANNEX
Definitions of protected area designations, as legislated, together with authorities responsible for their administration

Title: Law on the Protection of the Environment, No. 83-05; Decree No. 83-458; Decree No. 87-143 and Decree No. 87-144; Interministerial Act of 1987

Date: Law of 5 February 1983; Decree of 23 July 1983; Decrees of 16 June 1987; Interministerial Act of 9 August 1987

Brief Description: Law No. 83-05, governs all environmental topics including the identifying of the different classes of protected areas, under Article 17-30. Under this law enabling legislation on the designation of protected areas occurs through Decree No. 83-458 which provides, under 22 sections, for the legal framework for gazetting protected areas. It is divided into five parts and deals with the establishment and objectives of national parks, their structure and management and their financial administration. Decree No. 87-143 provides for establishing the rules and classification procedures for national parks and natural reserves; Decree No. 87-144 prescribes the procedures for the creation and operation of natural reserves. The Interministerial Act of 9 August 1987 concerns internal organisation of national parks.

Administrative authority: National Agency for Nature Protection (Agence National pour la Protection de la Nature) of the Ministry of Agriculture (Ministère de l'Agriculture); originally placed under the jurisdiction of the Secretary of State for Forests and Land Development, Ministry of Hydrology, Environment and Forestry (Ministère de l'Hydraulique, de l'Environnement et des Forêts MHEF). Two desert national parks are under the authority of the Ministry of Information and Culture (Ministère de l'Information et de la Culture).

Designations:

Parc national (National park) To promote nature protection and recreational activities by a) preserving the whole environment including the fauna and fauna; b) preventing degradation of the environment through human or natural causes; c) developing leisure, sports and tourist infrastructure in the peripheral zones; d) acting as study areas for coordinating scientific research.

Legislation provides for five zones in each park, zone one (integral reserve) to zone five (peripheral zone where tourist installations may be built).

Each park is to be administered by a park director and a council composed of representatives of the interested ministries and the local authorities concerned. Emphasis is placed on the importance of different zones in each national park and at least one protected area, El Kala, has a high profile of maintaining a rural agricultural landscape and economy.

Reserve Naturelle (Natural Reserve)

Divided into two categories dependent upon the degree of nature protection and management. The most important for nature conservation is

Réserve naturelle integrale (Strict nature reserve) Total nature conservation protection is given either to the complete ecosystem or to one or more of its components.

The aim is for conservation of wildlife species and the rehabilitation of their habitats: to protect delicate ecosystems or wildlife and used for scientific and educational purposes (hunting, fishing, mineral extraction and building construction are all prohibited).

Decree No. 87-144 states that every natural reserve should be attached to a national park, within which it shall constitute an independent unit. It shall be managed by the director of the park that it is associated with.

The decree establishing the reserve shall determine its boundaries. A ministerial order is used to define specific regulations.

Parc regional (Regional park) Under the authority of the Wali, they have subsequently been redefined as national parks and wildlife reserves such as the protected areas of Gouraya and Djelfa.

Sources: Journal officiel de la République algérienne démocratique et populaire No. 31, 26 July 1983; MHEF, 1983; Meziane, 1986; Touahria, 1986

Title: Hunting Law No. 82-10

Date: 21 August 1982

Brief description: To secure the protection, and management of species for hunting. A Council of Hunting was directed to create hunting reserves and construct a list of wild species.

Administrative authority: National Agency for Nature Protection (Agence National pour la Protection de la Nature) of the Ministry of Agriculture (Ministère de l'Agriculture); originally placed under the jurisdiction of the Secretary of State for Forests and Land Development, Ministry of Hydrology, Environment and Forestry (Ministère de l'Hydraulique, de l'Environnement et des Forêts) (MHEF)

Designations:

Réserve de chasse and Centre cynégetique (Hunting reserve) Areas where hunting is banned or restricted.

Areas subjected to controlled management activities including restricted grazing regimes and hunting

Source: Journal officiel de la République algérienne démocratique et populaire

Title: General Forests Law No. 84-12

Date: 23 June 1984

Brief Description: To secure the protection, development, expansion, management of forests, together with soil conservation and the control of erosion.

Administrative authority: Previously the Ministry of Hydrology, Environment and Forestry (Ministère de l'Hydraulique, de l'Environnement et des Forêts) (MHEF), currently the Ministry of Agriculture

Designations:

Production forest Where the principal function is that of supplying timber and other forest products

Protection forest Where the principal function is that of protecting the land

Forest and other wooded stand Where the special purpose is that of protecting rare items and scenic beauties, providing recreation in a natural environment, and scientific research, education and national defence.

Under Article 90 of the Forest Law, with due regard to Ordinance No. 67-281 of 20 December 1967 relative to excavations and the protection of historic and nature sites and monuments and in compliance with the Environmental Protection Act, specified portions of the country's forests may be declared national parks and nature reserves.

Forest law enforcement is the responsibility of the officers of the judicial police and the corps of forest wardens as indicated in Article 63 of the Forest Law.

Source: Journal officiel de la République algérienne démocratique et populaire

SUMMARY OF PROTECTED AREAS

Map[†] ref.	*National/international designations* Name of area	IUCN management category	Area (ha)	Year notified
	National Parks			
1	Ahaggar	II	4,500,000	1987
2	Belezma	II	8,500	1985
3	Chrea	II	26,500	1983
4	Djurdjura	II	18,550	1983
5	El Kala	V	76,438	1983
6	Gouraya	II	1,000	1983
7	Tassili N'Ajjer	II	8,000,000	1972
8	Taza	II	3,000	1985
9	Theniet el Had	II	3,600	1983
	Natural Reserves			
10	Akfadou	IV	2,115	
11	Babor	I	1,700	1985
12	Beni-Salah	I	2,000	1985
13	La Macta	I	10,000	1985
14	Mergueb	I	12,500	1985
	Hunting Reserves			
15	Djelfa	IV	20,000	1974
16	Lac Tonga	IV	2,392	1983
17	Mascara	IV	6,000	1985
18	Moulay Ismail	IV	1,000	
	Biosphere Reserves			
	Tassili National Park	IX	7,200,000	1986
	El Kala	IX	76,438	1990
	Ramsar Wetlands			
	Lac Oubeïra	R	2,200	1983
	Lac Tonga	R	2,700	1983
	World Heritage Site			
	Tassili N'Ajjer	X	300,000	1982

[†]Locations of most protected areas are shown on the accompanying map.

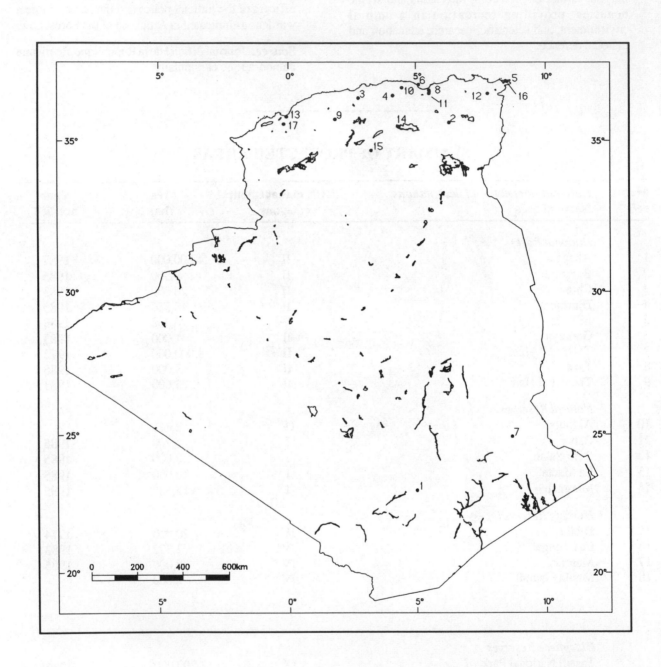

Protected Areas of Algeria

STATE OF BAHRAIN

Area   691 sq. km

Population   0.516 million (1990)
Natural increase: 3.08% per annum

Economic Indicators
GDP: US$ 8,378 per capita (1987)
GNP: US$ No information

Policy and Legislation   From 1882, Bahrain held treaties with Britain which was responsible for Bahrain's foreign relations. Bahrain declared its independence and signed a treaty of friendship on 15 August 1971. The Constitution, ratified in 1973, provided for a national assembly, which was dissolved in 1975 and the country has since been ruled by an Amir.

The legal system subscribes to the Islamic law, *Sharia*, which, as indicated in the Koran, places heavy responsibility on man to guard and protect wild animals and their habitats. Conservation projects are presently attempting to revive the Islamic views of the inter-relationship between man and his environment (Samour *et al.*, 1989). Traditional forms of protected area or range reserves (*Hema*) may have origins over 4,000 years ago in the pre-Islamic period. In their present form they are based on the dictates of the prophet Mohammed who established a legal system that until relatively recently continued to govern these protected areas, preventing hunting and grazing for a period of time and restricting areas to a ruler or tribe (Samour *et al.*, 1989). Between 1976-79, the Crown Prince re-established one site, Al-Areen *Hema*, to become one of the first comprehensive attempts to revive the Islamic views of nature (Clark, 1985; Izzedin, 1980).

Bahrain took the first steps towards effective measures to protect its wildlife on the recommendations of the prime minister. Plans were developed for the establishment of a wildlife park to serve the needs of both conservation and education. National designations of protected areas include wildlife park (*Hema*) and wildlife reserve. The Environmental Protection Committee has divided the protected areas categories into three priorities: priority 1: full protected status; priority 2: conservation status; priority 3: seasonal management status (Environmental Protection Committee, 1989; Vreeland, *in litt.*, 1989) (see Annex). In addition, a degree of protection is given to the southern part of Bahrain Island and the smaller archipelagos, as well as the isolated Hawar islands. In the case of the latter, the government has imposed access restrictions to all but fishermen and those with official permits (UNEP/IUCN, 1988). The government is also taking measures to preserve a significant proportion of the country's coastline, traditional palm grove landscapes and natural pools near Manama. These are being placed under state ownership and form part of the Bahrain green belt programme (Nurun Nabi, 1976).

Reviews of protected areas policy and legislation are not available.

International Activities Bahrain has not acceded to the Convention on Wetlands of International Importance especially as Waterfowl Habitat (Ramsar Convention), nor the Convention concerning the Protection of the World Cultural and Natural Heritage (World Heritage Convention). Bahrain has ratified the Kuwait Action Plan under thed UNEP Regional Seas Progranmme sponsored Convention on the Regional Organization for Protection of the Marine Environment, ROPME. Bahrain is a member of the United Nations, the Arab League, the Gulf Co-operation Council and OPEC.

Administration and Management   The main body concerned with protected area administration and management is the Environmental Protection Committee, which was established in 1980 and supported by the Environmental Protection Technical Secretariat. It is involved in a wide diversity of environmental aspects, ranging from the development of comprehensive environmental legislation to education, research to the establishment of protected areas and protection of individual species such as dugong and turtle (Montague and Bruun, 1987; Vreeland, *in litt.*, 1991). The Council of the State Presidency is considered to be the responsible authority for protecting and developing the reserves and parks in the country (Maher abou Jaafer, 1984). The Al-Areen Wildlife Park Centre acts as a focal point for conservation work in the country, undertakes captive breeding projects of endangered mammals and birds, management of island wildlife projects and undertakes wildlife censuses (Anon., n.d.). The Directorate of Environmental Affairs of the Ministry of Health is responsible for marine and coastal environmental activities. It works with the Bahrain Petroleum Company (BAPCO) on marine pollution and marine environmental affairs (UNEP/IUCN, 1988). The Directorate of Fisheries is concerned with environmental studies and the protection of breeding and nursery areas for fish and shrimp and the establishment of fishing bans in spawning seasons and the development of laws and regulations relating to the protection of the marine environment (Montague and Bruun, 1987). Budaiya Agricultural Experimental Station of the Ministry of Commerce and Agriculture undertakes studies on mammals and plants in coastal and desert areas and is concerned with the impact of water pollution; research includes livestock adaptation and agricultural crops (Montague and Bruun, 1987).

Non-governmental bodies actively concerned with protected areas include the Bahrain Natural History Society (BNHS) which conducts fauna and flora surveys and publishes environmental reports and a monthly journal (UNEP/IUCN, 1988; Richardson, 1990). In the first BNHS report, a number of areas were recommended as nature reserves to ensure survival of threatened wildlife (Hill, *in litt*, 1985). The UBF Stream Wildlife Reserve is managed by the society (Vreeland, *in litt.*, 1989). The park management at Al-Areen has been deeply involved in conservation, not only by keeping and breeding endangered species, but also by cooperating with other conservation projects in the Middle East, particularly for Arabian oryx and houbara bustard. Oryx have been sent to the protected areas of Shaumari in Jordan, to the Jiddat al Harrasis in Oman and various sites in Saudi Arabia. Strong links have been established with the Zoological Society of London and the King Khalid Wildlife Research Centre at Tummammah, Saudi Arabia (Samour *et al.*, 1989).

Effectiveness of protected areas management has not been reviewed in this analysis.

Systems Reviews Consisting of a group of 33 low-lying islands in the Arabian Gulf off Saudi Arabia, Bahrain is largely a land of desert plant communities, with many halophytic species and no known endemics. Coastal lowlands have been classified into loam plains, Khadarah depression, tidal swamps, Nebkha plain and northern sand sheet, Al Areen sand sheet and western and eastern coastal Sabkhas; backslopes include the Hamalah backslope, also the interior basin and the central plateau, jebels and escarpment zone (see text by Virgo, 1980). Other notable habitats include salt marsh, seagrass beds and mangrove swamp, coral reefs and date groves (Phillips, 1988; Fisher, pers., comm., 1991; Vreeland, *in litt.*, 1989).

Numerous environmental surveys have been undertaken: from soils and land classification, to comprehensive studies on plant ecology, vegetation communities, surface material resources survey and its application to regional planning, breeding bird colonies, marine algae, mammals and the lepidoptera of Bahrain (see Virgo, 1980). An ecological study of critical habitats on the coast was undertaken by IUCN in 1975 in cooperation with the Inspectorate of Fisheries and the Directorate of Environmental Protection (IUCN/ROPME/UNEP, 1985). Recommendations included a need for detailed mapping of critical habitats and species of economic or scientific importance as well as an urgent need for environmental education (UNEP/IUCN, 1988). Subsequently, the Environmental Protection Committee undertook an ecological survey of Bahrain based on satellite habitat characterisation imagery, together with information from bathymetric charts and aerial overflights. Thirteen areas recommended for protection, conservation and management were on the basis of their scientific or commercial importance and defined as either classic examples of their type, last remaining representatives or considered particularly vulnerable to disturbance. They were divided into three priorities: priority 1: three sites, priority 2: six sites and priority 3: four sites (Environmental Protection Committee, 1989).

The first major protected area to be designated was Al-Areen Wildlife Park and Reserve established in 1979

which currently totals 800ha. Two further designated areas included UBF Stream Wildlife Reserve (5ha) designated in 1988 and Ras Sanad Mangrove Reserve (50ha) established in 1989 (Phillips, 1988). Manama Town Landscape and Greenbelt Protected Area totals 470ha. Another form of protected area has led to the establishment of a large area of native plants in various habitats at the Arabian Gulf University campus near Sakhir (Philips, 1988). Other sites include various proposed and recommended areas such as Khor al Qaliya and Khor Mugta Tubli reserves, both scheduled for development. The Sitrah, Nabi, Saleh, Al Muharraq and Zida islands region around Khawr Qulay'ah (Khor al Qaliya) was recommended for reserve protection by the Persian Gulf Working Group in 1975 (Anon., 1975). It has been recommended that 10% of the land within the region be set aside for the future and for a revival of the ancient heritage of conservation in the Arab world (Clark, 1985).

The most significant of the environmental problems include the extensive damage and destruction to such critical habitats as seagrass beds, coral reefs, mangrove and mud flats and autumn wader migration feeding grounds through massive urban development programmes and rapid land reclamation programmes (Price *et al*, 1983; Hill, M.R., *in litt.*, 1985). Since oil was first discovered in 1931, many beaches in northern Bahrain have been drastically polluted by oil and potentially there have been serious threats from major oil and chemical spillages such as the Iranian war spills of 1983 (UNEP/IUCN, 1988). Discharge of sewage and industrial effluent as well as dredging has caused damage to the seabed and coral reefs (IUCN/ROPME/UNEP, 1985; Price and Vousden, n.d.).

Other Relevant Information Tourism and education benefits relate to the protected areas system. For example, between October 1983 and April 1984 alone 5,000 school children visited Al-Areen Park (Clark, 1985).

Addresses

Environmental Protection Council, PO Box 26909, ADLIYA (Tel: 973 275792; Tlx: 8511 Health BN; FAX: 973 293694)
Al-Areen Wildlife Park, PO Box 28690, BAHRAIN (Tel: 973 631826; Tlx: 8673 areen bn; FAX: 973 631173)
Bahrain Natural History Society, PO Box 20336, MANAMA

References

Anon. (1975). Reports and recommendations of the working groups. In: Promotion of the establishment of marine parks and reserves in the Northern Indian Ocean including the Red Sea and Persian Gulf. Papers and proceedings of the Regional Meeting held at Tehran, Iran, 6-10 March. *IUCN Publications New Series* 35: 144-163.

Anon. (n.d.) *Al-Areen, wildlife park and reserve.* Al-Areen Wildlife Park and Reserve, Bahrain. P. 22.

Anon. (1989). Sharper lines in Arabia's sands. *The Economist.* 21 January. P. 82.

Clark, A. (1985). In the lion's den. *Aramco World Magazine* 36(1): 36-40.

Good, R. (1955). The flora of Bahrain. In: Dickson, V., *The wild flowers of Kuwait and Bahrain.* Allen and Unwin, London. Pp. 126-140.

Groombridge, B. and Luxmoore, R. (in prep.). The green turtle and hawksbill (Reptilia; Cheloniidae): world status, exploitation trade. A report to the Cites Secretariat. World Conservation Monitoring Centre, Cambridge, UK.

Hill, M. and Webb, P. (1983). Islands of Bahrain. *Wildlife* 25(7): 254-257.

IUCN/ROPME/UNEP (1985). An ecological study of sites on the coast of Bahrain. *UNEP Regional Seas reports and studies* No. 72. United Nations Environment Programme prepared in cooperation with IUCN and ROPME. 70 pp.

Izzedin, F.A. (1980). Al-Areen Wildlife Park and Reserve. *Bahrain Natural History Society, annual reports for 1978-1979.* Bahrain Natural History Society. Pp. 61-63.

Jones, D. J. (1985). Report on intertidal areas. ROPME critical habitat survey of Bahrain 1985. Environment Protection Technical Secretariat, Bahrain. 10 pp.

Maher abou Jaafer (1984). *National parks and nature reserves in the Arab world.* The Arab League Educational, Cultural and Scientific Organization, Tunis. 112 pp.

McCormick, M.G. and Ray, G.C. (1976). Critical marine habitats. IUCN/WWF Project 39/4-1037. 20 pp.

Montague, K. and Bruun, B. (1987). *Biological diversity in North Africa, the Middle East and Southwest Asia; a directory of organizations and institutions.* HLCF, New York, USA. 134 pp.

Nurun Nabi, M. D. (1976). Bahrain. Country Report No. 1. In: Promotion of the establishment of marine parks and reserves in the Northern Indian Ocean including the Red Sea and Persian Gulf. Papers and proceedings of the Regional Meeting held at Tehran, Iran, 6-10 March 1975. *IUCN Publications New Series* 35: 40-42

Ormond, R.F.G. (1980). Management and conservation of Red Sea habitats. *The coastal and marine environment of the Red Sea, Gulf of Aden and Tropical Western Indian Ocean* 2: 137-162.

Phillips, D. P. (1988). *Wild flowers of Bahrain: a field guide to herbs, shrubs, and trees.* Diana Charles Phillips, Manama, Bahrain. Pp. 10-23.

Price, A.R.G. and Vousden, D.H.P. (n.d.). Ecological study of sites on the coast. 2nd Interim Report by IUCN consultants. Unpublished. 5 pp.

Price, A.R. G., Vousden, D.H.P. and Ormond, R.F.G. (1983). An ecological study of sites on the coast of Bahrain with special reference to the shrimp fishery and possible impact from the Saudi-Bahrain causeway under construction. Report of IUCN to UNEP Regional Seas Programme, Geneva. Produced with the support of UNEP, ROPME and IUCN. KA/0503-82-09 (2362).

Richardson, C. (1990). *The birds of the United Arab Emirates.* Hobby Publications, Dubai and Warrington, Cheshire, UK. 204 pp.

Samour, J., Irwin-Davies, J., Mohanna, M. and Faraj, E. (1989). Conservation at Al-Areen Wildlife Park, Bahrain. *Oryx* 23(3): 142-145.

UNEP (1987). Clearing house developments. *Regional Bulletin for Europe* 4: 9.

UNEP/IUCN (1988). *Coral Reefs of the World. Volume 2: Indian Ocean, Red Sea and Gulf.* UNEP Regional Seas Directories and Bibliographies. IUCN, Gland, Switzerland and Cambridge, UK/UNEP, Nairobi, Kenya. 440 pp.

Virgo, K.J. (1980). An introduction to the vegetation of Bahrain. Wildlife in Bahrain. *Annual reports for 1978-1979.* Bahrain Natural History Society. Pp. 65-109.

Vousden, D. and Price, A. (1985). Bridge over fragile waters. *New Scientist* 11 April 1985. Pp. 33-35.

ANNEX
Definitions of protected area designations, as legislated, together with authorities responsible for their administration

Title: Individual declarations

Date: Individually declared

Brief description: Sites have not been covered under any particular extant legislation related to nature protection.

Administrative authority: Environmental Protection Committee, Al-Areen Wildlife Park Authority

Designations:

Hema (Wildlife park) Established under government funds, the single site is designated half as a park and the rest as a wildlife reserve.

Essentially established for visitor use, its object being to increase public awareness in wildlife conservation (artificial lakes, planted trees, and penned exotic game from Africa are represented).

Wildlife reserve Defined as an area left essentially in its natural state, although some Arabian wildlife can be reintroduced to augment existing populations.

Management ensures the minimal planting or spread of exotic or foreign vegetation, and encourages restoration of natural communities.

Public access is prohibited. Entry is restricted to scientific researchers and authorised personnel.

Area of full protected status Priority one areas where no development is permitted without detailed consideration, protective management and monitoring. There is controlled public access to a number of areas. Other management includes reducing the disturbance factor to a minimum.

Area of conservation status Priority two areas which permit strictly controlled small-scale development only; there is protective monitoring, including general supervision to assess any effects from disturbance.

Area of seasonal management status Priority three areas largely ensuring limited development. There is seasonal monitoring and protection, and seasonal control of public access to specific, sensitive areas to reduce disturbance.

Sources: Environmental Protection Council, *in litt.*; Anon, n.d.; Maher abou Jaafer, 1984

CYPRUS

Area 9,251 sq. km (including UK sovereign base areas defined as "99 sq. miles", Marsden, 1990)

Population 701,000 (1990)
Natural increase: 0.90% per annum

Economic Indicators
GDP: US$ 5,223 per capita (1987)
GNP: US$ 6,260 per capita (1988) (Hunter, 1991) (Government controlled area)

Policy and Legislation Cyprus attained independence from the United Kingdom under the Cyprus Act of 1960, having been under British administration since 1878 and prior to that under jurisdiction of the Ottoman empire from 1573. The UK sovereign base areas, Akrotiri and Dhekelia, were established at independence and are considered a part of British sovereign territory under British administration (see below, Marsden, 1990). The constitution was passed in 1960 but was proved unworkable in practice and led to conflict in 1974 (Marsden, 1991).

Following the 1974 crisis, the island was partitioned under military force into two sectors, the legitimate Republic of Cyprus which continues to maintain two-thirds of the island in the south, and the self-proclaimed "Turkish Republic of Northern Cyprus" which controls northern Cyprus. The "Turkish Republic" was declared as illegal by the United Nations Security Council in November 1983 and May 1984. The partition is divided by a neutral zone "Green Line or Attila line" which was established in 1974 and continues to be policed by the United Nations Peace Keeping Force (UNFICYP), under its mandate which was last renewed in 15 June 1990. The Republic of Cyprus does not recognise the claims of the unilaterally proclaimed "Turkish Republic" and continues to state that it is the only legitimate government having rights of jurisdiction over the whole island. At present its administration is not being observed in the "Turkish Republic" occupied areas of northern Cyprus (see below).

The government of Cyprus forest policy is to conserve and develop the forest resources with the following special objectives, namely a) forest reservation: to reserve in perpetuity as protection forests as much as possible of the high level catchment areas and sufficient other land the cultivation of which cannot be justified economically, to ensure a prudent balance of agricultural and forest products; b) water conservation: to prevent flooding and waste, and to regulate the flow of waters by protecting the catchments of streams and other waters; c) soil conservation: to prevent desiccation of the soil and to arrest soil movements caused by water or wind erosion; d) public amenity: to exploit the value of the forests as areas of scenic beauty and amenity for the development of recreation and the expansion of tourist industry; and e) wildlife: to preserve wildlife both fauna and flora, whereby the forests should be areas in which the natural fauna and flora of the territory may be carefully preserved (Ministry of Agriculture, 1991).

The first environmentally related legislation was the Forest Law of 1879, announced the year after Cyprus was placed under British administration. This was reinforced subsequently by the Goat Exclusion laws (forbidding entry of livestock into forests) of 1888 and 1913. The Forest Law was still in effect up to independence in 1960 (Unwin, 1931; Ioannides, *in litt.*, 1982).

The main relevant law on the environment at present is the Forest Law No. 14/1967, which is concerned with protection and management of forests on a sustained yield basis, protection of important ecological features and the establishment of state forest protected areas, specified as permanent forest reserves, national forest parks and nature reserves. The sites are classified according to Part I, Article No. 3 of the Forest Law. The Council of Ministers may, by notice published in the official *Gazette* of the Republic, declare any main state forest, or part thereof, under the three above-mentioned classes (see Annex). The Director of the Department of Forests may, with the approval of the Minister of Agriculture, make regulations in respect of each class of protected area (Art. No. 6 and 7).

The Game and Wild Birds Protection and Development Law No. 39/1974 is concerned with control of hunting and protection of non-game birds. Game reserves are designated under this law (Cap. 98 of 1949 and Cap. 65 of 1959). Under this legislation it is possible to protect game and wild birds by the establishment of temporary or permanent game reserves (Gour-Tanguay, 1977).

The Foreshore Protection Law, 1934 (Cap. 59 and Laws Nos. 22/61, 17/64 and 8/72) provides for coastal zones of exceptional beauty which may be declared off limits to construction of any kind, up to 90m inland; Fisheries Regulations, 1952 (latest in 1989) provide for the protection of important beaches. Under 1989 amendments turtle nesting beaches are protected from 1 June to 30 September each year; the Public Rivers Protection Law (includes Cap. 82 referring to the destruction of the banks or beds of public rivers as an offence). The Town and Country Planning Law No. 90/1972 states that the Minister has the power to issue orders to set up protected areas for natural sites having "special national character" (Anon., 1984; UNEP, 1987). Marine parks are regulated by the Department of Fisheries of the Ministry of Agriculture and Natural Resources. Legal status for the first site was under Regulation 172/89; 273/90.

The Town and Country Planning Law No. 90/1972 is one of the basic environmental laws but is not yet fully in force (Gour-Tanguay, 1977; UNEP, 1987). It provides for an integrated environmental plan for the island and includes chapters on the fixing of "areas of special social, historical, architectural or cultural interest or natural beauty and other subjects of wider or local interest"; for the preparation of plans for protecting areas with special importance including "nature protection areas" and the provision of areas for touristic or other purposes (UNEP, 1987).

British sovereign base areas The United Kingdom retains full sovereignty and jurisdiction over two areas of 99 sq. miles: Akrotiri-Episkopi-Paramali and Dhekelia-Pergamos-Ayios Nicolaos-Xylophagou. The British Administrator of these areas is appointed by the Monarch and is responsible to the Secretary of State for Defence (Marsden, 1990) (for relevant legislation see United Kingdom entry). One protected area is listed as a game reserve, and covered under the Game and Wild Birds (Protection and Development) Ordinance of 1974, which in practice is identical to the Law of the same name issued by the Republic of Cyprus. The reserve was notified under this enabling legislation by the British Administrator in an Act of 3 August 1977, superseded by an Act of 22 October 1979.

International Activities The Convention on International Trade in Endangered Species of Wild Fauna and Flora was ratified by law in 1974. The Convention concerning the World Natural and Cultural Heritage (World Heritage Convention) was ratified on 15 August 1975 but no natural sites have been inscribed. The Bern Convention has been signed but not yet ratified. The Convention for the Protection of the Mediterranean Sea against Pollution, usually known as the Barcelona Convention, was formally adopted by Cyprus in 1976. The contracting parties to the Convention adopted the Protocol concerning Mediterranean Specially Protected Areas on 2 April 1982, which entered into force on 23 March 1986. Two specially protected areas have been identified by the Cyprus national focal point as being representative of the Mediterranean network (one of which is under the jurisdiction of the British Sovereign Areas Authority). Under the Mediterranean Environmental Technical Assistance Programme (CY91-93 METAP) of the World Bank, European Investment Bank, United Nations Development Programme and Commission of the European Communities, it was intended to aid Lara Turtle Conservation Project, but this has subsequently been dropped as a METAP activity for this period.

Cyprus is a member of the Council of Europe and of the British Commonwealth. In 1991 the Council of Europe Secretariat received two new proposals for biogenetic reserves. The Steering Committee for the Protection and management of the Environment and Natural Habitats (CDPE) is currently examining these proposals and deciding whether they should be integrated into the network.

Administration and Management The area under actual administration of the legitimate government of the Republic of Cyprus and that occupied by the self-proclaimed "Turkish Republic of Northern Cyprus" were in 1991 under separate control with no administrative link between the two (see below).

The Department of Forestry (Nature Conservation Service) of the Ministry of Agriculture and Natural Resources is the main body concerned with nature conservation in the Republic of Cyprus. The Cyprus Council for the Conservation of Nature was established in 1969 in order to plan and coordinate the policy making and environmental work of the various governmental departments (Gour-Tanguay, 1977). At that time executive committees for nature conservation were responsible to the Cyprus Council for the Conservation of Nature. They prepared annual work programmes and coordinated nature conservation projects among various ministries and departments. The Forestry Department in 1977 was responsible for the management of all main and minor state forests, and recommended that proposed national forest parks and nature reserves for establishment within State forest land (Gour-Tanguay, 1977). The single marine park is administered by the Department of Fisheries of the Ministry of Agriculture and Natural Resources.

In the 1991 government budget provision of C£ 637,000 (US$ 1,275,000) is made for the establishment, development and conservation of protected areas, and C£ 138,000 (US$ 275,000) for park recreational facilities. Running expenditures vary widely; for Lara Reserve alone costs are US$ 35,000 per year (Antoniou, *in litt.*, 1991).

The establishment of environmental machinery for the protection and preservation of the environment was advanced in February 1988 when the government launching a comprehensive environmental programme to be carried out with the assistance of international organisational and bilateral development aid bodies (UNEP, 1987).

Cyprus Forestry College was established in the 1950s and a research and education division set up in 1954. Following partition in 1974, the College remained under government of Cyprus authority, and forestry personnel continued to train there. In the curriculum there are subjects related to protected areas (10% of the curriculum) (Antoniou, *in litt.*, 1991; Thirgood, *in litt.*, 1987). Since 1988 training courses in turtle hatchery techniques and beach management have been given in Lara Reserve, in the framework of the UNEP Mediterranean Action Plan (Antoniou, *in litt.*, 1991).

Active non-governmental organisations include the Association for the Protection of the Cyprus Environment (APCE), Cyprus Ornithological Society, Cyprus Geographical Association, Society of Cyprus Studies, the Nature Lovers Association and the Pancyprian Association of Foresters. The APCE, together with the pressure group Friends of Akamas, have been pressing the House of Representatives for immediate action to preserve the Akamas coastline as a national park and to block the development of Akrotiri Saltlake Reserve. In 1983 Rotary clubs in Cyprus proposed the establishment of a wildlife park in 10 sq. miles of partly forested land at Listovounos (Theodossiou, *in litt.*, 1983).

British sovereign base areas The single protected area is managed under the authority of the British administrator by the Ministry of Defence (Sovereign Base Areas Administration-Akrotiri) (Marsden, 1990; Abbott-Watt, *in litt.*, 1986; Drucker, *in litt.*, 1982).

Systems Reviews Cyprus, the most easterly of the main Mediterranean islands, is situated 70km off the south-west coast of Turkey and 90km off the coast of Syria. Evidence suggests that in ancient times the island was covered by a dense and extensive forest. However, a flourishing civilisation and subsequent human interference has altered the landscape significantly. The dominant natural vegetation outside agricultural land is heavily grazed Mediterranean garrigue. Remaining forest (17% of land area) is restricted largely to the well-wooded Troodos mountain range with *Pinus brutia* on the lower slopes, *P. nigra* and *Cedrus brevifolia* at higher levels (Anon., 1984; Meikle, 1985; Drucker, pers. obs., 1982). Reforested areas total 13,956ha (98318 dunums). The few remaining wetlands include those at Phasouri and Syrianokhori. The basic policy of the Department of Forestry is "sustained forest yield", yet the majority of state forest land in the mountains (such as Paphos Forest in the troodos massif) is currently not exploited.

Between 20-30% of all threatened plant populations, 80-90% of threatened plant species and 85-90% of threatened animal species are reported to be found in protected areas (Antoniou, *in litt.*, 1991).

The government of Cyprus, as of February 1987, has launched a comprehensive environmental programme as a result of a recently completed environmental profile of the entire island. Emphasis will be placed on an integrated pollution control monitoring system, the conservation and sound development of the proposed national park in the Akamas area, the introduction of an environmental information system, the initiation of environmental impact assessments in development programmes, the creation of an environmental and training programme and the implementation of the Town and Country Planning Law (UNEP, 1987).

Existing protected areas include permanent game reserves totalling 71,689ha, nature reserves totalling 823ha, and national forest parks totalling 19,000ha. The single marine park, Lara-Toxeftra Reserve, has a total area of 550ha marine and 100ha terrestrial. In total, state forests cover 161,820ha (Antoniou, *in litt.*, 1991). The Laona project includes the Akamas peninsula (8,500-9,000ha) designated as a specially protected area with the intention of declaring it a national park in the near future. Other proposed protected areas include the Troodos massif, a forest area of 9,000ha which meets national forest park criteria; a provisional master plan has been already prepared. There are two proposed marine reserves, Cavo Greco and combined sites on the Akamas Peninsula (Antoniou, *in litt.*, 1991).

In the British sovereign areas there is a single protected area, Lake of Limassol (Akrotiri) Game Reserve of 940ha (this site has also been listed as a Mediterranean specially protected area of 2,000ha).

Threats to the environment have been extensive, ranging from the past overstocking of livestock in natural habitats to forest fires and tourism. The fires caused by military action in the 1974 conflict completely destroyed 20% of the island's prime forest. Uncontrolled building development has posed a major threat to the coastal environment, especially as a consequence of the rapid development of industry during the immediate years following the 1974 crisis. It is widely regarded that "misuses" have been extensive in the uncontrolled development of the coastal natural resources for tourism (Ioannides, 1973). Current threatened areas include wetlands such as the Akrotiri saltlake game reserve area which has been threatened by the construction of a sewage treatment plant with funds from the World Bank and the Council of Europe.

Other Relevant Information Tourism is the main growth industry in Cyprus, with over 1.1 million visitors in 1988. In 1989 up to 1.2 million visitors produced C£ 490 million for the country (Hunter, 1991; Marsden, 1990). Ecotourism, and the protected areas system such as at Lara, have played a part in this figure but no details are available.

Addresses

Ministry of Agriculture, Natural Resources and Energy, Department of Forests and Environmental Protection, NICOSIA

References

Anon. (1984). Cyprus. *European Nature Conservation, twenty years of activities*. Environment and Natural Resources Division, Council of Europe, Strasbourg. Pp. 77-78.

Anon. (1987). Environment Day, Government's inaction slammed. *The Cyprus weekly*. 5 June. Nicosia. P. 1.

Anon. (1986). The struggle for Akrotiri: last opportunity or lost cause? *World Birdwatch* 18(3): 1-2.

Gour-Tanguay, R. (Ed.) (1977). Cyprus (republic). *Environmental policies in developing countries*. Beiträge zur Umweltgestaltung. Heft A27. E. Schmitt Verlag.

Hunter, B. (Ed.) (1991). *The Statesman's Year Book 1991-92*. The Macmillan Press Ltd, London and Basingstoke, UK. 1692 pp.

Ionnides, O. (1973). Nature conservation in Cyprus. *Nature in Focus* 14: 6-17.

Leon, C. (1983). *Cyprus: important botanical areas of high conservation value*. Unpublished report. IUCN-Conservation Monitoring Centre, Kew, UK. 20 pp.

Marsden, H. (Ed.) (1990). *Whitaker's Almanack*. 123rd Edition. J. Whitaker and Sons Ltd, London. 1245 pp.

Meikle, R.D. (1977, 1985). *Flora of Cyprus*. 2 vols. Bentham-Mox on Trust, Royal Botanic Gardens, Kew, Surrey, UK. 832 and 1137 pp.

Ministry of Agriculture (1991). Forest Policy, relating to conservation, amenity and recreation. Ministry of Agriculture and Natural Resources. 10 pp.

UNEP (1987). Cyprus. *UNEP Regional Bulletin for Europe* 4.

Unwin, H. (1931). The Cyprus forests and the Forest Department. *Empire Forestry Journal* 10: 218-224.

ANNEX
Definitions of protected area designations, as legislated, together with authorities responsible for their administration

Title: Forest Law 14/1967, forest regulations Section 14

Date: 28 July 1967

Brief description: Concerned with protection and management of forests on sustained yield basis, protection of important ecological features and the establishment of state forest protected areas. Forest regulations classify protected area types under section 14 of the Forest Law. The Director of the Department of Forests may, with the approval of the Minister of Agriculture, make regulations in respect of each class of protected area (Art. No. 6 and 7).

Administrative authority: Department of Forests, Ministry of Agriculture and Natural Resources

Designations:

State forest area

All protected areas under the jurisdiction of the Ministry of Agriculture on declared on state forest land and are classed as:

Permanent forest reserve A main state forest area used mainly for production of timber and other raw material for industry (covered under the 1974 Game and Wild Birds Protection and Development Law).

National forest park A main state forest area that may be declared by the Council of Ministers as a forest to provide amenities and recreation to the general public.

Regulations include prescribing the times and periods during which the public may enter, the fees and the manner collected, protection of forest produce, forest building and any other structure.

Nature reserve A main state forest area that may be declared by the Council of Ministers. A forest appropriated to provide complete and permanent protection of the flora and fauna.

Regulations include those for the protection of the soil, flora and fauna, and fences and any other structures, prohibiting the entry of unauthorised persons.

Source: Original legislation

Title: Game and Wild Birds Protection and Development Law (Cap. 98 of 1949 and Cap. 65 of 1959)

Date: 1974; 1949 and 1959

Brief description: Concerned with protection and management of forests on sustained yield basis, protection of important ecological features and the establishment of state forest protected areas.

Administrative authority: Ministry of Agriculture and Natural Resources

Designations:

Game reserve ("Hunting preserve") Are designated under the Game and Wild Birds Protection Law (Chap. 98 of 1949 and Chap. 65 of 1959). Under this legislation it is possible to protect game and wild birds by the establishment of temporary or permanent game reserves.

Source: Gour-Tanguay, 1977

Title: Fisheries Regulations

Date: 1952; last amended 1989

Brief description: Concerned with protection and management of turtle nesting beaches

Administrative authority: Ministry of Agriculture and Natural Resources

Designations:

Turtle nesting beach From 1 June to 30 September every year, on the beach (inland for 90m) to the 20m isobath offshore, fishing, tourists and boats are forbidden.

SUMMARY OF PROTECTED AREAS

Map ref.	*National/international designations* Name of area	IUCN management category	Area (ha)	Year notified
1	*Game Reserve* Limassol Lake (Akrotiri)	IV	2,000	1963
2	*State Forest Area* Troodos (Paphos)	VIII	9,000	

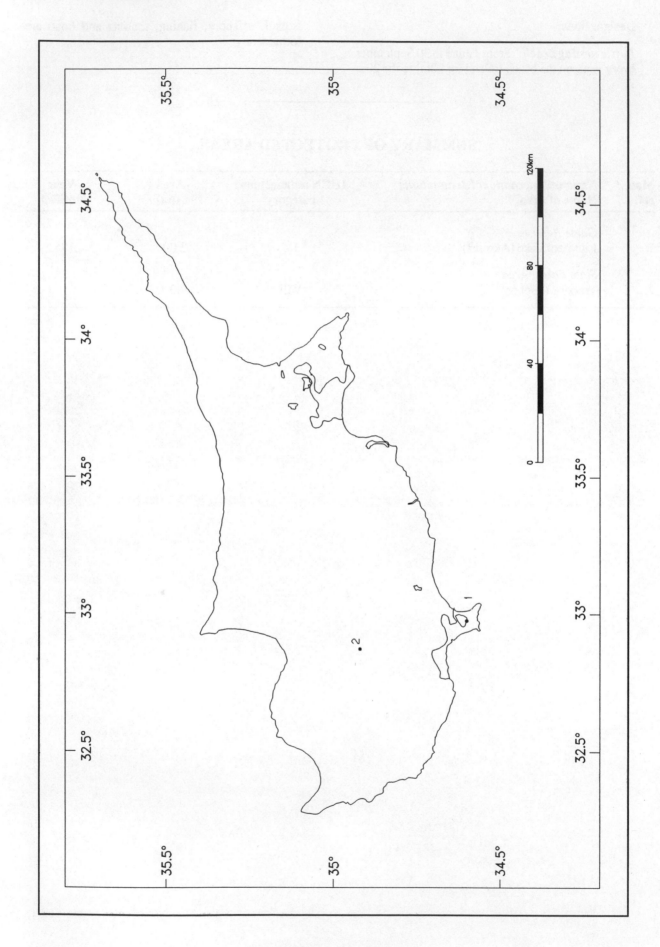

Protected Areas of Cyprus

CYPRUS
"TURKISH REPUBLIC OF NORTHERN CYPRUS"

Area 3,355 sq. km (Hunter, 1991)

Population 165,000 (Hunter, 1991)

Economic Indicators
No information

Policy and Legislation Unilateral declaration of independence of the "Turkish Republic of Northern Cyprus" was proclaimed on 15 November 1983. The Republic of Cyprus lays claim to the whole island and does not recognise the "Turkish Republic of Northern Cyprus", the self-proclaimed House of Representatives nor the laws enacted by that body. The Declaration of the "Turkish Republic" has been condemned by the United Nations Security Council (Hunter, 1991).

The main environmentally-related legislation enacted by the Republic of Cyprus prior to the partition of the island in 1974 remains theoretically in force, although areas in the north are no longer under its control. The Forest Law No. 14/1967 has continued to be the main piece of legislation concerned with the protection of important ecological features and the establishment of state forest areas: namely permanent forest reserves, national forestry parks and nature reserves (see main entry for Cyprus). In northern Cyprus natural forest parks are regarded as forested recreation areas established for recreational and scenic value, whilst natural forest reserves and nature conservation areas tend to be established with forestry and wildlife priorities (Koyuncuoglu, *in litt.*, 1987). Other laws maintained include the Game and Wild Birds Protection and Development Law No. 39/1974, which continues to be concerned with control of hunting and protection of non-game birds, and with the establishment of game reserves (temporary and permanent); the Foreshore Protection Law of 1934 (Cap. 59 and Laws Nos 22/61, 17/64 and 8/72) concerning coastal zones of exceptional beauty which may be declared off limits to construction of any kind; Town and Country Planning Law of 90/1972 whereby the minister has the power to issue orders to set up protected sites for natural areas having "special national character". This last law has not been fully enacted (Council of Europe, 1984; UNEP, 1987; Koyuncuoglu, *in litt.*, 1987).

By-laws ensure prevention of livestock grazing, hunting, timber felling or cutting (including commercial forestry), fires and construction. Stiff penalties are enforced for any infringement of the law.

The legislative process is in hand to designate areas as national parks (Kettaneh *et al.*, 1988; Drucker, pers. comm. 1987; Groombridge, pers. comm. 1988). The Forestry Policy of 1989-1993 includes under Point No. 5 the increase of the "country's" beauty, to meet the public's growing recreational needs by establishing national parks.

In 1987 according to the Department of Forestry and the Environment, there was no effective enforcement of existing and outmoded legislation on environmental protection. What was regarded as the inadequacy of general environmental legislation has resulted in the call for an urgent need to bring in new environment impact assessment laws in view of the increasing threat from uncontrolled construction of tourist hotels. A law is reported to have been passed through parliament to speed up the development of the tourist industry (Koyuncuoglu, *in litt.*, 1987). Partly to rectify the difficulties, the United Nations Development Programme (UNDP) undertook in 1987 surveys for a structure plan to cover the whole island (UNEP, 1987; Koyuncuoglu, *in litt.*, 1987).

International Activities The self-proclaimed "Turkish Republic of northern Cyprus" declaration of November 1983 was condemned by the United Nations Security Council and only Turkey has recognised the new "state" (Marsden, 1990).

The United Nations Peace Keeping Force (UNFICYP), under its mandate which was last renewed in 15 June 1990, patrols the neutral zone. The United Nations High Commission for Refugees continues to liaise between the two Cypriot communities. Since northern Cyprus is not recognised as an independent state by the United Nations, it is not party to any international environmental convention or agreement.

Administration and Management Although the government of the Republic of Cyprus claims the legitimate right to administer and manage the whole island (cf United Nations Security Council resolutions), northern Cyprus is controlled under a completely autonomous Turkish Cypriot administration which has no link with the Republic of Cyprus (see main Cyprus details).

Nature conservation in northern Cyprus is largely under the control of the Department of Forests (previously the Department of Forestry and Environmental Protection) of the Ministry of Agriculture and Forestry, based on the Forest Law, 1967 (Koyuncuoglu, *in litt.*, 1988; 1990). Currently all forest land is in state ownership. The Department of Forests has an obligation to establish, protect and manage these areas for their combined nature conservation, recreation and environmental value. The current programme of the Department is to maintain the existing forest protection areas and at a future date to prepare management plans for each site, as well as undertake detailed surveys of the status of northern Cyprus fauna and flora. All "state-owned" forest land is managed under a ten-year plan, the last was due to be revised in 1990. Most finance is centrally budgeted by the northern Cypriot authorities, with additional assistance from the Turkish General Forest Directorate and the United Nations High Commission for Refugees. In the 1990 fiscal year the authorities spent TL 555 million for civil servants employed in protected areas activities (Kazimoglu, *in litt.*, 1991). To increase the knowledge and protection in the north of the island, the Forest Department undertook a "Survey of the Forests" in 1981, resulting in the classification and division of forest areas into different protection/production zones. Subsequently, in 1987, a UNDP expert was contracted to develop structure plans on the environment for the whole of the island (see also UNEP, 1987).

The Ministry of the Interior is the main body with responsibility for hunting, issuing of permits and declaration of game areas.

A series of important nature conservation areas are under *de facto* protection by being within the perimeter of military restricted areas, such as alongside the main Lefcosa-Magosa road or within proximity of the neutral zone. There are a number of coastal restricted areas in the north-central and east of the country (fencing off a number of hectares of land in each case, which would certainly prevent tourist development within their proximity) (Drucker, *in litt.*, 1987; Groombridge, pers. comm., 1991).

Cyprus Forestry College was established in the 1950s and a research and education division set up in 1954. Following partition in 1974, the College remained under the jurisdiction of the government of the Republic of Cyprus south of the neutral zone. Due to loss of access to the College due to political difficulties, all training by forestry personnel in northern Cyprus has been severely restricted, with short courses available only in Turkey or occasionally in the United Kingdom (Koyuncuoglu, *in litt.*, 1987).

Environmental non-governmental organisations in northern Cyprus were absent in the 1980s. By 1991 there were six environmental groups, with over 2,000 members, under the umbrella of the North Cyprus Environmental Co-ordinating Committee (Cant, *in litt.*, 1991; Kazimoglu, *in litt.*, 1991; Koyuncuoglu, *in litt.*, 1987; Groombridge, pers. comm., 1988).

Due to the current political difficulties, many of the administrative and management bodies in northern Cyprus are under strain from inadequate funding and lack of technical assistance. Funding for forest management and protection has been regarded as of low priority and continues to be severely restricted under the current situation. Liaison between administrative bodies is regarded as totally inadequate; a request has been made for the immediate creation of a Forum or Council to bring together the different interested organisations and ministries in order to ensure the success of environmental programmes (Koyuncuoglu, *in litt.*, 1987).

Systems Reviews Located in the northern part of the Mediterranean island of Cyprus, the area is noted for its conifer forests, cliff and mountain habitats, undisturbed rocky and sandy coastlines and undamaged wetlands. The land fauna is regarded as poor, following many centuries of uncontrolled hunting. The valleys tend to be cultivated, with livestock grazing and burning of man-altered scrub on the hills. The largest land mammals now include wild boar and red fox. Currently, all forest land is in "state" ownership, totalling 70,000ha or 16% of the land area.

Comprehensive surveys of biological resources in recent years include a marine turtle survey in collaboration with WWF. A survey of "state-owned" forest land completed in 1981, divided areas into utilisable forest, natural forest reserves, natural forest parks, nature conservation areas and game protected areas (Koyuncuoglu, *in litt.*, 1987).

The total area of protected land in 1987 was 3,073ha (including 700ha of protected forest nature reserves). By 1991 the protected areas network included one nature reserve established in 1975 and six forest protected areas totalling 8,000ha and one national park, Zafer Burnu, of 5,635ha. There are also proposals dating from 1979 to establish a national park along the Besparmac mountain chain (Kazimoglu, *in litt.*, 1991; Koyuncuoglu, pers. comm., 1987).

Environmental damage has in the past included extensive forest fires resulting from the military conflict in 1974, although subsequent reafforestation has been in part able to rectify much of the damage. Agricultural and building development is reported to have threatened coastal marshes and sand dunes in the mid north such as at Syrianokhori (Leon, 1983; Drucker, *in litt.*, 1987). The tourism threat to Salamis Bay Forest, Yenibogazici, illustrates the potentially increasing threats affecting protected areas throughout the region (Koyuncuoglu, pers. comm., 1987).

Other Relevant Information Tourism is the main growth industry in northern Cyprus with over 0.4 million visitors in 1989, and earnings totalling US$ 130 million (Hunter, 1991; Marsden, 1990). Ecotourism, and the protected areas system, have played a part in this figure but no details are available. Visits to, and recreation within, protected areas is of major importance in northern Cyprus. International tourism is potentially a very important source of foreign exchange earnings for the region and its expansion is imminent.

Addresses

Department of Forestry (Orman Koruma Dairesi), Ministry of Agriculture and Forestry (Tarim ve Orman Bakanligi), Lefkosa (Nicosia), (via) Mersin 10, Turkey (Tel: 74120/71315/71172)

References

Council of Europe (1984). Cyprus *European Nature Conservation, twenty years of activities.* Environment and Natural Resources Division, Council of Europe, Strasbourg. Pp. 77-78.

Foreman, A. (1988). North Cypriots grow weary of special ties with Turkey. *The Guardian.* 16 June. P. 1.

Gour-Tanguay, R. (Ed.)(1977). Cyprus (republic). *Environmental policies in developing countries.* Beiträge zur Umweltgestaltung. Heft A27. E. Schmitt Verlag.

Hunter, B. (Ed.) (1991). *The Statesman's Year Book 1991-92.* The Macmillan Press Ltd, London and Basingstoke, UK. 1692 pp.

Ionnides, O. (1973). Nature conservation in Cyprus. *Nature in focus* 14: 16-17.

Kettaneh, M., Koyuncouoglu, F., Kazimoglu, K. and Nacam, N. (1988). *Zafer National Park (Karpaz Peninsula), Northern Cyprus.* Department of Forestry and Environmental Protection, Nicosia.

Leon, C. (1983). Cyprus: important botanical areas of high conservation value. Unpublished report. IUCN-Conservation Monitoring Centre, Kew, UK. 14 pp.

Marsden, H. (Ed.) (1990). *Whitaker's Almanack, the reference book, the year book.* 123rd Edition. J. Whitaker and Sons Ltd, London. 1245 pp.

Meikle, R.D. (1977, 1985). *Flora of Cyprus.* 2 Vols. Bentham-Moxon Trust, Royal Botanic Gardens, Kew, Surrey, UK. 832, 1137 pp.

UNEP (1987). Cyprus. *UNEP Regional Bulletin for Europe* 4.

ANNEX
Definitions of protected area designations, as legislated, together with authorities responsible for their administration

Title: Individual national park decrees

Date: first act in 1988

Brief description: sites are individually declared by the authorities

Administrative authority: Department of Forestry (Orman Koruma Dairesi), Ministry of Agriculture and Forestry (Tarim ve Orman Bakanligi)

Designations:

National part (Milli park) To be declared on government-owned land.

Designation ensures protection for combined conservation, recreation and tourism together with an effective level of landscape protection.

An entrance charge is envisaged.

Sources: Kazimoglu, *in litt.*, 1991; Koyuncuoglu, *in litt.*, 1987

411

EGYPT

Area 1,002,270 sq. km (including the Sudan Government Administration Area)

Population 52,426,000 (1990)
Natural increase: 2.15% per annum

Economic Indicators
GDP: US$ 1,857 per capita (1987)
GNP: US$ 710 per capita (1987)

Policy and Legislation Egypt was part of the Ottoman Empire from 1517 until 1914 when it became a British Protectorate, and subsequently independent in 1922. The Anglo-Egyptian Condominium of Sudan was proclaimed, a sovereign independent republic in 1956, and the Sudan Government Administration Area (SGAA) between Egypt and Sudan above the 22°N parallel became jointly administered by the two sovereign states. In 1991 Sudanese civil police and the Egyptian army jointly administer the area (see below for Gebel Elba natural protectorate). Egypt merged with Syria in 1958 but the union broke up in 1961. In 1967 Israel occupied the Gaza Strip (previously under Egyptian administration) and invaded the Sinai Peninsula, the latter of which was returned to Egyptian sovereignty in 1982. The Constitution dates from 11 September 1971 (Hunter, 1991).

A detailed understanding of the environment has existed over many millennia as seen on ancient temple inscriptions such as that of Queen Hatsephut of the ancient pharaoh period (1540BC), which illustrates a wildlife expedition to the Land of Punt. Wildlife hunting was frequently illustrated in these ancient depictions and suggests that there was some form of nature protection at a very early date; basic management principles which were followed through by succeeding civilizations: the ancient Greeks, Romans and Ottomans. Traditional forms of protection still exist; a number of areas were regarded as sacred under the traditional law of the local bedouin tribes, such as at Mount Sinai where permanent hunting bans were enforced by the local populace (Hobbs, 1989; Morrow, 1990). At Gebel Elba the nomadic communities maintain restraints, through tribal and religious dictates, on the over exploitation of natural resources (Goodman, 1985). Community protection is also known to exist, as with the "lineage preserves" (Sayaal) where patrilineal descendants have inherited the responsibilities claimed by their ancestors to protect resources in certain wadis. A recent example which still exists is of a preserve set up in 1900 to protect *Acacia* near Jebel Gataar in Khushmaan territory in the Western Desert (Hobbs, 1989). Under Ottoman law, the environmental legislation was covered under the Ottoman civil code within the body of Islamic law (Mejellah). Under Article 1243 it was defined that land and the associated trees growing wild in mountains could not be possessed and should remain ownerless.

The first conservation legislation this century came into being with the creation of the Royal hunting reserve at Wadi Rishrash in 1900. Current interest by the authorities in nature conservation was initiated when a delegation attended the 1955 Unesco meeting on nature protection in Beirut. The first protected site was established at El Omayed and was acquired by the University of Alexandria in 1974 (Baharav and Meiboom, 1981).

The Presidential Decree of 5 March 1980, in expressing concern for environmental matters, established a mechanism for identifying and protecting threatened areas and species through cooperation between provincial governors, the Academy of Scientific Research and the Ministry of Agriculture. Subsequently, Ministerial Decree No. 472 of 5 May 1982 ensured the prohibition of hunting of all birds and animals in a number of sites in the Sinai. Eventually the promulgation of Law No. 102/83, which was passed by the People's Assembly on 20 July 1983, provided for the legal framework upon which the government could establish protected areas throughout the whole of Egypt (see Annex).

The sole category referred to in the Law No. 102/83 is the natural protectorate. Article 1 defines the natural protectorate, its designation and delineation by individual Prime Ministerial decrees, upon recommendation from the Egyptian Environmental Affairs Agency (EEAA). Sub-categories covered under the Prime Ministerial decrees include scientific area, national marine park, conservation area, natural area and protected area (see Annex).

The EEAA is the main administrative body responsible for the enforcement of environmental protection and conservation, and was established under Decree No. 631 of 1982. In 1983 a presidential directive established EEAA offices within each of the Governorate of Egypt. In 1979, the Egyptian Wildlife Service (EWS) was established under the authority of the Ministry of Agriculture Decree No. 349, with responsibility for management of natural protectorates and wildlife research. In 1991 the Minister of Cabinet Affairs and Minister of State for Administrative Development, and the Minister in charge of Environment issued Decree No. 30 for the reorganisation of the EEAA.

Societies for the Protection of the Environment are mentioned under Article 5 of Law No. 102/1983. Some protection is further afforded to a number of hunting preserves through administration by the Ministry of Agriculture or private shooting clubs; areas where uncontrolled hunting or fishing is banned (Verheugt, pers. comm., 1991).

The Ministry of Tourism has, under Article 6 of Law 102/1983, established a special fund entitled "Natural Protectorate Fund", to be used as a means of

413

supplementing the budget of the administration bodies responsible for implementing Law No. 102. The Fund was aimed at being used for projects leading to the improvement of protection of the environment, for environmental research and for law enforcement. The EEAA subsequently prepared a bill for the internal regulation of the Fund. The aim of the bill was to contribute to the improvement of the environment in natural protectorates; the proposal defining funding sources and the formation of a management board to supervise all financial aspects of the Fund. The proposal had been approved by the Ministry of Finance and had been reviewed by the legislative committee prior to submission to the Prime Minister for issue.

Presidential Law No. 101/1985, signed on 3 July 1985 (and Prime Ministerial Decree No. 1488/1985), provides financial assistance for pollution prevention and nature conservation in Egypt, as the "Tourism and Environmental Services Fund". Through this Law a 10% tax was levied on all international air tickets issued in Egypt in local currency by 1991 this percentage had increased to 25% (EEAA, 1991; Hanafy, 1989).

Through the provisions of Law No. 102 of 1983, the Ministry of Justice had issued Decree No. 1611 of 8 March 1989 granting police power to the following: the manager of the EEAA governorate branch in which there is a natural protectorate; the manager of the natural protectorate and to the second protectorate researcher (Hanafy, 1989).

Proposals for new laws include: a) the protection of the marine environment, aiming at protecting all the shores of Egypt, its national marine waters and natural resources. The proposal has been reviewed and approved by the Supreme Administrative Court, and was subsequently under review by the Legislative Committee of the Cabinet, in preparation for submission to the People's Assembly (Hanafy, 1989); b) the EEAA prepared the proposal for a law concerning environmental protection. The situation made necessary the designation and establishment of a Higher Committee for the Protection of the Environment (see below) (Hanafy, 1989)

It has been regarded that the legislation relating to designating natural protectorates, Law No. 102/83, has been inadequate. For example, there has been a lack of legislated provision for management plans, operational budgets and demarcation of protected area boundaries (Verheugt, *in litt.*, 1991). Law No. 102/1983 stipulates that natural protectorates are administered by an executive council. However, as in the case of Zaranikh, this body is regarded as ineffective and has met only once since its creation (Varty and Baha el Din, 1991).

In 1991 there were fundamental, favourable changes in the attitude of the Egyptian government towards environmental protection, resulting in the reorganisation of the EEAA. This new philosophy has led to a drastic change in the way protected areas are considered. They are no longer being considered in isolation, as single isolated units where they cannot survive and achieve their potential if the surrounding areas are left to be degraded. As a result, the authorities have deemed it imperative that a holistic management approach be adopted and implemented. This would be set up in the form of multidisciplinary approaches aimed at resource management and replenishment through environmental impact controls on external factors, coupled with public awareness programmes (also see below) (EEAA, 1991).

A general outline of environmental policies and strategies, as well as a five-year nationwide environmental plan, is being prepared by the Academy of Scientific Research, the National Centre for Research, and universities, with the cooperation of various ministries, under the Global Environment Facility fund (GEF). The plan incorporates many aspects, including the current status of the environment, a partial coverage of the efforts made to address environmental issues, and recommendations for research to solve these problems (Hanafy, 1989). The action plan will be presented at the UNCED Biodiversity Conference in Brazil in June 1992 (*via* Lue Phang, Verheugt, *in litt.*, 1991).

International Activities Egypt has entered a number of cooperative agreements and legal obligations. The International Plant Protection Convention was signed in 1953. The African Convention on the Conservation of Nature and Natural Resources was accepted in Algiers in 1968. Egypt is party to the Convention concerning the Protection of the World Cultural and Natural Heritage (World Heritage Convention), which was ratified on 7 February 1974. No natural sites have been inscribed to date. Egypt acceded to the Convention on Wetlands of International Importance especially as Waterfowl Habitat (Ramsar Convention) on 9 September 1988, at which time two sites were designated under the terms of the Convention. Egypt participates in the Unesco Man and the Biosphere Programme and by 1991 had listed one site as a biosphere reserve. Part of the Fayoum area with a proposed area of 20,000ha was being considered for future listing in 1991 in collaboration with the Tourism Development Unit of the Ministry of Tourism and Al Azhar and Cairo university researchers (Abbas Salleh *via* Verheugt, pers comm., 1991).

The Convention for the Protection of the Mediterranean Sea against Pollution, usually known as the Barcelona Convention, was formally ratified by Egypt on 18 May 1983. The contracting parties to the Convention adopted the Protocol concerning Mediterranean Specially Protected Areas on 2 April 1982, and Egypt ratified the Protocol on 8 July 1983. Four sites have been identified by the Egyptian national focal point as being representative of the Mediterranean network. The Regional Convention for the Conservation of the Red Sea and Gulf of Aden Environment has yet to be signed by Egypt.

The Commission of the European Communities has interests in Egypt through two complementary programmes for the protection of the Mediterranean environment: the Mediterranean Strategy and Action Plan (MEDSAP) which promote community action for the protection of the environment in the region; and the Environmental Regional Programme (ENVIREG), for regional environmental measures undertaken on the initiative of the Commission. The European Community and the Environmental Affairs Agency are currently working on a joint project towards protection and development of Ras Mohammed Marine National Park (Pearson, *in litt.*, 1991).

Under the Mediterranean Environmental Technical Assistance Programme (CY91-93 METAP) of the World Bank, European Investment Bank, United Nations Development Programme and Commission of the European Communities, four activities have been defined for implementation in Egypt, including local environmental management and protected area management (Anon, 1991). Representatives from Egypt attended the first meeting of the Mediterranean Protected Areas Network (MEDPAN) meeting on 5-6 October 1990 in Monaco and the first technical meeting to discuss marine protection and economic impacts of protected areas creation was scheduled for September 1991 (Anon., 1990).

The sole transboundary protected area is Gebel Elba, located in the Sudan Government Administration Area (SGAA) between Egypt and Sudan above the 22°N parallel, an area which is jointly administered by the two sovereign states. In 1991 Sudanese civil police and the Egyptian army jointly administered the area; Egypt has designated Gebel Elba as a natural protectorate under Law No.102/83, whilst Sudan has listed the site as a proposed conservation area (UNEP/IUCN, 1988).

Administration and Management The main administrative body responsible for the enforcement of environmental protection and conservation is the Egyptian Environmental Affairs Agency (EEAA), established within the Prime Minister's Office and set up to act as the umbrella body to coordinate all government activities pertaining to the environment and conservation. It is affiliated to the Council of Ministers and is the competent office for provisions of the law. In 1983 a presidential directive established EEAA offices within each of the Governorate of Egypt, following the creation and success of the independently established Wildlife Office in the Governorate of North Sinai in 1981. Each office is managed by an executive council, which meets at least once every six months, and are regulated by orders of the Prime Minister. The Branch Director is nominated by order of the Governor who undertakes the duties of the council's technical secretary. Management of natural protectorates is under the jurisdiction of EEAA, although in the past the EWS was also a major management agency. Each protected area has a board which is responsible for managing the site. The members of the board are made up of representatives from the EEAA, EWS, Governorate and other officials. Ras Mohammed marine park is administered by the

EEAA and chaired by the South Sinai Governor and membership of representatives from the Ministries of Tourism, Petroleum and Agriculture, as well as the Academy of Science, Research and Technology, along with technical support from the EC. From 1988 an entrance charge was levied at the main park gate. The EEAA also bears responsibility for the daily management of the natural protectorates, as in the case of Lake Qarun and Wadi el Rayan, where two conservators have been appointed for each (Verheugt, pers comm., 1991).

One of the EEAA's chief mandates is to monitor environmental issues and the activities of various other ministries, such that under Decree No. 360/82 the Governorate EEAA offices can require the public or private sector to carry out environmental impact assessments for proposed large-scale physical development schemes. During 1991, under Ministerial Decree No. 30/1991, the EEAA was restructured and a department dealing specifically with protected areas was created. The restructuring was instigated in order to achieve the full participation of concerned ministries and authorities in the preparation and execution of the EEAA action plan. New fields of activities were to include: land protection, afforestation and park development projects; water and coastal areas protection projects; and natural protectorate projects in addition to the establishment of an information and computer centre (EEAA, 1991).

As of 1991 the new policy of the EEAA towards protected areas is as follows: "to construct an efficient network of natural parks, protected areas and managed areas by developing the recently declared sites and selecting new locations; integration of protectorates programme with the social and economic development, to attain sustainable development; conservation of biological resources, its monitoring, surveying, survival and development; to maintain sound management and administration of protected areas projects and enforcing Law No. 102. Priorities in 1991 for developing protected areas include: 1) developing the present successful projects as Ras Mohammed National Park and applying the most effective principles to the management of other protectorates; 2) projects that are integrated with development and that give suitable revenues; 3) research and education on protected areas (EEAA, 1991).

In 1979, the Egyptian Wildlife Service was established under the authority of the Ministry of Agriculture, initially with responsibility for management of natural protectorates and wildlife research. Since 1983, however, management of natural protectorates has been the responsibility of each Governorate EEAA office. The EWS's current mandate is to undertake wildlife management research and conduct flora and fauna inventories (Baha el Din, *in litt.*, 1991). It was initially staffed by 25 full-time scientists and over 20 rangers who had attended courses run by the US-Fish and Wildlife Service. By 1985, there were less than 10 full-time staff. In 1987, the EWS was formally separated from the Giza Zoo and six departments created, including those of wildlife programmes and management, research and data, bird migration, wildlife experimentation, licensing and administration (Anon., 1988; Brunn,1987). Funding in 1989 was E£ 30,000 per year mainly from the Ministry of Agriculture but also from US funds, the PL480 (Baha el Din, *in litt.*, 1989).

In March 1980, the Egyptian government launched the World Conservation Strategy and allocated E£ 80 million for the establishment of natural protectorates in Sinai. Funding for administration and management of Egyptian natural protectorates is channelled through the EEAA from various sources including the Tourism and Environmental Services Fund and the Natural Protectorate Fund. The Natural Protectorate Fund is used for supplementing the budget of the administrative bodies responsible for implementing the provision of Law No. 102, for contributions to the improvement in the protection of the environment, for studies and research and also for law enforcement. The Tourism and Environmental Services Fund has a board which includes the Ministers of Finance, Cabinet Affairs, Tourism, Culture and Local Administration. The EEAA and Tourism board manage these funds for environmental and tourism projects which the national budget is unable to finance and determines their priority. This tax is used to: 1) develop recreational tourist areas and hotels; 2) develop archaeological sites; and 3) finance pollution prevention and nature conservation projects. The budget for the proposed Saharan Natural Protectorate, to be established as part of the Unesco Man and the Biosphere network, has been estimated at US$ 16 million for management and the establishment of a wildlife breeding station (Abbas Saleh, *via* Verheugt, *in litt.*, 1991). Government contributions towards the development of the Ras Mohammed National Park project, from initial phases in 1989 to project completion, will total E£10 million. From 1989-1991 ECU 750,000 have been budgeted, funded with technical support from the EC. The next phase of the development project starting in 1991 is anticipated to involve a budget of ECU 2.5 million (EEAA, 1991).

The Ministry of Tourism through its Tourism Development Unit is concerned with the environment and protected areas. It has been involved in instigating a series of environmental assessments in and around natural protectorates in the Sinai and elsewhere. It is focusing on ecotourism and is providing the local EEAA branches, with detailed zoning and management plans for the conservation of natural protectorates. In general, tourism development is the responsibility of the Ministry of Tourism (see below) (Saleh, pers., comm., 1991). The Ministry of Defence plays an active role in guarding natural protectorates against poaching, in addition to having the authority to issue permits for wildlife hunting in desert areas. The Water Police (Ministry of Defence) of Lake Qarun are entitled to arrest violaters of Prime Ministerial Decree No. 943/89 pertaining to the Natural Protectorate of Lake Qarun (Verheught, *in litt.*, 1991).

Cooperative agreements between the wildlife management authorities and foreign agencies or organisations are extensive, just some of which are mentioned below. The US-Fish and Wildlife Service has supported the work of the EWS since the 1970s. More recent activities include the US-Agency for International Development (US-AID) report prepared in 1988 on the biological resources, with details on status and recommended conservation needs, prepared in association with the Office of Science and Technology, Cairo (US-AID, 1988). Subsequently, it has published environmental profiles for three governorates including Damiette and Fayoum. The World Bank, through its Mediterranean programme, has been funding environmental impact assessments in natural protectorates, such as around Lake Burullus (Varty and Baha el Din, 1991). The International Waterfowl and Wetlands Research Bureau (IWRB) has conducted numerous waterfowl counts in conjunction with the Foundation for Ornithological Research and the EWS. As part of the Eastern Mediterranean wader project, a complete census of waterbirds has been carried out in all Egyptian wetlands. The International Council for Bird Preservation has been running conservation projects in Egypt since 1987, and has been instrumental in establishing a Central Conservation Education Centre, which operates from Giza Zoo staffed by EWS personnel. The Centre has a mobile conservation education unit which has been visiting the various governorates since 1989 (Baha el Din, *in litt.*, 1991; Verheugt, *in litt.*, 1991; Salanthe, pers. comm., 1991).

Non-governmental groups and societies are widespread, and mainly active at the level of research, independent monitoring and education. The Academy of Scientific Research and Technology comprises various expert councils for scientific subjects including nature conservation, it advises the EEAA in natural protectorate management and is represented on the advisory council of a number of the natural protectorates, including Wadi el Rayan and Lake Qarun. Universities have long been undertaking detailed work into environmental and conservation concerns within the established and proposed natural protectorates (Anon., 1988).

With the exception of the traditional community forms of protected area, two universities (Assiut and Alexandria-Omayed) and a number of hunting clubs are the main bodies currently owning private areas for nature protection. However, in addition, a number of universities are actively participating in management of natural protectorates, including Aswan University managing Saluga and Ghazil. El Omayed Biosphere Reserve is rented from local lease holders by the Regional Environmental Management of Mediterranean Ecosystems of Northern Egypt (REMENE). In the mid-1980s, the Egyptian Rotary Club proposed to jointly establish a wildlife peace park with the Rotary Club of Wilmette, Illinois, USA, but a site has yet to be identified (Theodossiou, *in litt.*, 1983). In addition there are number of *de facto* protected areas which are some of the most natural sites in the country, such as restricted access areas owned by oil companies on the Sinai coast (Saleh, *in litt.*, 1991).

The most active citizen pressure groups on matters relating to the environment as a whole include the Society of Natural Resources, Ornithological Society of Egypt, Arab Office of Youth and Environment, National Society for Protection of the Environment and the Tree Lovers Society (Anon., 1988). The Egyptian Wildlife Society was founded early in 1989 to increase public awareness of wildlife and important habitats found in Egypt and to encourage their preservation. It aims to achieve this by 1) establishing wildlife clubs; 2) increase cooperation between Egypt and other nations working to protect wildlife and habitats; 3) set up a headquarters with a library information service; 4) organise awareness days; and 5) develop a system of nature reserves.

There are two principal shooting clubs in Cairo and Alexandria, which operate their own hunting reserves, including one at Lake Qarun. They cooperate with the EWS and Governorate environmental offices responsible for regulating hunting (Baha el Din, *in litt.*, 1989). The Egyptian Shooting Association or Club leases land from the government and owns its own private lakes which are used for hunting. Local shoot controllers are stationed at managed areas such as Lake Karoun (Baha el Din, 1989; Martin, 1990). Funds for management have come from organised hunting excursions through tour companies. For example, in the 1990-91 season an eight-day bird shoot in the Fayoum area was reported to cost US $4,600 and mammal trophy shooting for an eight-day trip between US$ 700-3,300 for individual trophies, budgets which were sufficiently adequate to cover overheads of management, administration and other private protected areas costs (Anon., n.d.; Martin, 1990; Baha el Din, *in litt.*, 1989).

As of 1991, although prime-ministerial decrees have been issued for each site, no reserve borders have been set except for Ras Mohammed and El Omayed reserves. All natural protectorates (except Ras Mohammed) still lack detailed management and annual operational plans and budgets. The administration and management of protected areas is widely regarded as ineffective, barring a few exceptions, and many designated sites do not exist except on paper as management is virtually non-existent. Occasional visits have been made by EWS and EEAA officers to the reserves (cf changes following the success of the Ras Mohammed experience in 1989-1991). By contrast, Omayed Scientific Area, administered by university personnel, is effectively patrolled. Its protection is enhanced by being surrounded and enclosed by fences (Anon., 1988; Sinai Conservation Group, 1985; Baha el Din, pers. comm., 1991; Verheugt, pers comm., 1991). Previously, EWS officers were stationed in natural protectorates but, with the cut back due to lack of funds, staff, and adequate law enforcement, a lack of surveillance is reported to have led to widespread illegal hunting and livestock grazing (Anon., 1988). With the EWS no longer a primary management body, the protection of conservation areas is now almost entirely under the administration of the EEAA and governorate environmental offices which are reported to be severely restricted by totally inadequate funding and expertise (Anon., 1988; Baha el Din, *in litt.*, 1991; Verheugt, *in litt.*, 1991). The conservation management of protected areas is hampered by intensive settlement, continued heavy grazing pressure and illegal hunting of birds and fish by the local population (Anon., 1988; Ghabbour, 1986; Grimmett, 1987). Further conflicts occur as a consequence of high economic returns from activities damaging to protected areas, such as from hunting trophies of globally threatened species in protected areas or elsewhere and of fisheries operations which are worth around E£ 70,000 per year in individual protected areas, for example at Zaranikh (Varty and Baha el Din, 1991). None of the wildlife societies has any direct input into protected area management. They have limited funds and undertake little work outside Cairo (Baha el Din, *in litt.*, 1991; Verheugt, *in litt.*, 1991).

Following the 1991 restructuring of the EEAA, all indications are that a coordinated approach to protection and resource conservation is likely to be successful. Conditions at present are regarded as suitable for donor assistance in this field, levels of awareness in the government sector are increasing, and there is now a general acceptance of the relationship between development and protection. The concept of integrated management is gaining increasing acceptance (EEAA, 1991).

Systems Reviews Egypt is bordered on the north by the Mediterranean Sea, on the east by Israel, on the south by Sudan and west by Libya. Man has been cultivating the Nile Valley since at least 18,000 years BP, in a landscape which has by now largely become a man-made ecosystem. The Nile Valley, the largest desert oasis in the world, still harbours a significant amount of wildlife, not least the great waterfowl flocks of the Nile delta triangle. Biological diversity is illustrated by up to 2,085 plant species, 431 recorded bird species and 150 land mammals. Coastal lakes and lagoons represent 25% of the total Mediterranean wetlands. Since the construction of the Aswan dam additional lake habitats have been created. The northern fringe of Egypt, bordering the sea, is represented by a Mediterranean flora and fauna, whilst inland and away from the Nile Valley there are the eastern and western hyper-arid elements of the Sahara and the Sinai deserts representing over 96% of the country. An extremely rich ecosystem exists around the Red Sea, including coral formations, mangrove stands and many Afrotropical fauna and flora elements. Woodland is practically non-existent except as tree savanna in the steppe habitats and as relict woodland on some mountain peaks such as at Gebel Elba. Intensive cultivation occurs throughout the Nile Valley basin and all along the Mediterranean coast.

No detailed systems reviews have been undertaken for the entire country, although there have been comprehensive surveys of various biological resources. A series of priority sites have been listed by the authorities, in an attempt to arrest habitat loss, if only to protect a few of the most representative examples of each ecosystem type. To date, between two and four sites have been selected in each of the following regions: Sinai, Red Sea/eastern desert, Nile valley and western desert/north-west coast. Furthermore, three reintroduction areas have been selected on a number of islands on the Nile for their botanical interest (Ghabbour, 1986; Amer, *in litt.*, 1988; Springuel, pers. comm.. 1990). Interest in the expansion of the protected areas network is further illustrated by the following example: In March 1991 the Tourism Development Unit of the Ministry of Tourism prepared a master plan for touristic areas in Sinai and Fayoum governorate. It focuses on ecotourism and is providing the local EEAA branches with detailed zoning and management plans for the conservation of protected areas (Baha el Din, *in litt.*, 1990; Rady *via* Verheugt, *in litt.* 1991). In 1986 the Canadian National Agency (CIDA) donated US$ 146,410 to the IUCN-administered Sinai Management Programme whereby a management plan was intended to be submitted to the Egyptian government, involving a resource survey and synthesis of information. This plan was expected to include recommendations for the management of the region to meet the needs of the local population on a sustainable basis, and for the delineation of a buffer zone between biological sensitive areas and areas of development priority (Halle, pers. comm., 1986).

As of 1991 there were 12 recognised natural protectorates. They represented a total of 679,900ha or 0.7% of the country. Scientific reserves totalled 1,000ha, national marine parks 17,100ha (see below), conservation areas 480,000ha, natural areas 107,400ha and protected areas 74,400ha (Amer, *in litt.*, 1989). By 1991 Ras Mohammed National Park had been extended to 19,700ha (EEAA, 1991).

The Environmental Protection Council has recently published three environmental profiles covering the Governorate of Tihama, Al Bayda and Dhamar, undertaken by DHV Consultants, Euroconsult and Darwish Consulting Engineers on behalf of the Netherlands' Directorate General of Technical Cooperation (DGIS) (Verheugt, *in litt.*, 1991). Additional environmental profiles were being prepared in mid-1991 for the Fayoum region and Lake Bardawil (Verheugt, *in litt.*, 1991). Other examples include the 12 volume 1981 Lake Manzala study by MacLaren Engineers, Planners and Scientists Inc produced for the Egyptian Ministry of Development and UNDP. Other studies include an assessment of the likely impact of the North Sinai Agricultural Development project on the region's protected areas, avifauna and their habitats, undertaken by ICBP on behalf of the World Bank (Varty, 1990).

General environmental threats are based in part on the fact that the majority of important habitats are completely unprotected, either by law or by management. Concern is foremost for the network of wetlands, wintering havens for significant numbers of Palaearctic birds, and also for the very fragile Red Sea coral reef ecosystems (Grimmett, 1987; UNEP/IUCN, 1988; Varty and Baha el Din, 1991). The greatest habitat loss in recent years has been a consequence of the construction of the Aswan dam, which has entirely altered the ecology of the River Nile and its deltas; serious effects of the dam construction include the large-scale and off-shore erosion on the Rosetta and Damietta peninsulas, as well as the increased pressure towards reclamation of wetlands (Abu-Fadil, 1986; Kishk, 1986; Mancy, 1981). Overall, the main forms of habitat destruction affecting protected areas and the environment as a whole include: land reclamation of wetlands and steppe, tourist development, pollution and agricultural development or improvement (Anon., 1988). Throughout Egypt, steppe-land habitats are gradually being altered through cultivation and building construction, and even internationally important wetlands are gradually being polluted and destroyed. Specific projects funded or coordinated by international aid agencies are also threatening the environment of the country. Following completion of the Salam Peace Canal, for an irrigation project on the west bank of the Suez canal, an extension will form the core of the North Sinai Agricultural Development Project (NSADP) funded by the World Bank. It will irrigate 0.25 million feddan in North Sinai, and may seriously damage the Bardawil Ramsar site and surrounding natural habitats (Varty, 1990; Varty, pers. comm., 1989). Additional areas are threatened by oil prospecting by international oil companies (Dunnet *et al.*, 1985). Other proposals include mass tourism projects in Sinai to relieve the pressure on traditional tourist attractions elsewhere in Egypt. Under potential threat is St Catherine's Natural Protectorate Wilderness; the Ministry of Housing and Reconstruction wishes to add a cable car, hotels and 500 villas in the area. In December 1989 the Crown Prince of Kuwait is reported to have promised US$ 600 million to build a water pipeline from the eastern branch of the Nile to Sinai resorts, a project which could put further pressure on the natural ecosystems of the region (Bhalla, 1990; Morrow, 1990; Baha el din, *in litt.*, 1990).

Other Relevant Information Some natural protectorates are of major tourism interest. In 1989 30,000 tourists visited Mount Sinai/St Catherine's and 60,000 visited Ras Mohammed (Mishinski, 1989; Morrow, 1990). The figure for St Catherine's may rise to 565,000 if plans are followed for development of the area (Morrow, 1990). Currently revenue collected at Ras Mohammed is US$ 25,000, which will rise to US$ 313,000 in the near future, when proposed plans are put into effect (Mishinski, 1989). To boost funding for protected area management and administration, it has been recommended by independent studies that the various governorates approach the Ministry of Tourism for grants from the Natural Protectorate Fund and Tourism and Environmental Services Fund. Currently, the Ministry of Tourism, in association with the EEAA, is investigating the possibility of developing ecotourism in natural protectorates. Already the local populace in trial areas has shown its enthusiasm for projects (Saleh, *in litt.*, 1991; Varty and Baha el Din, 1991).

Addresses

Environmental Affairs Agency, Council of Ministers, 11 A. Hassan Sabry Street, CAIRO (Tel: 3416546/3416192; Tlx: 93794 wazra un; FAX: 3420768)

Tourism Development Unit, Ministry of Tourism, 21 El Nil Street, Floor 19, CAIRO

National Zoo and Wildlife (Director), Egyptian Wildlife Service, Ministry of Agriculture, GIZA-ORMAN (Tel: 726233)

Ornithological Society of Egypt, Executive Business Service, Cairo Marriott Hotel, PO Box 33, Zamelek, CAIRO (Tel: 344 0953; FAX: 340 6667)

References

Abu-Fadil, M. (1986). Nile Delta under threat. *The Middle East* magazine. Pp. 65-67.

Academy of Scientific Research and Technology. (1988). The Gebel Elba Project. A draft project proposal submitted by the Academy of Scientific Research and Technology, Environmental Research Council.

Anon. (n.d.). Kacca, fl-egittu, 1989-90. Ejjew maghna fir-rizervi taghna. I l-Fayum, il-post idejali ghall-kaccaturi. Pamphlet. P. 2.

Anon. (n.d.). Accomplishments and Activities under the Government of Egypt. US-Fish and Wildlife Service Joint Program of Wildlife Conservation, 1978-80.

Anon. (1980). Annex to the report "The Environment and the Netherlands. Programme for Bilateral Development Cooperation". Country-specific environmental profiles.

Anon. (1988). The status of conservation in Egypt. Unpublished independent report. 16 pp.

Arid Lands Information Center (1980). Draft environmental report on Arab Republic of Egypt. Unpublished report prepared by the Arab Lands Information Centre, Office of Arid Lands Studies, University of Arizona, Tucson, Arizona. National Park Service Contract No. CX-0001-0-0003 with US Man and the Biosphere Secretariat, Washington, D.C.

Ayyad, M.A. and Ghabbour, S.I. (1986). Hot Deserts of Egypt and the Sudan. In: *Hot deserts and arid shrublands*. B. Ecosystems of the World 12B. Elsevier, Amsterdam. Pp. 149-202

Augier, H. (1985). *Protected marine areas*. European Committee for the Conservation of Nature and Natural Resources, Council of Europe, Strasbourg.

Ayyad, M.A. and Ghabbour, S.I. (1986). Omayed Biosphere Reserve: History and future prospects. Mediterranean biosphere reserves workshop. Florac, France, 8-12 September 1986.

Baccar, H. (1977). *A survey of existing and potential marine parks and reserves in the Mediterranean region*. IUCN/UNEP, Gland, Switzerland.

Baha el Din, M. (1988). The status of conservation in Egypt, 1988. Unpublished report. 16 pp.

Baharav, D and Meiboom, U. (1981). The status of the nubian ibex *Capra ibex* nubiana in the Sinai desert. *Biological Conservation* 20: 91-97.

Baldwin, M.F., Ferguson, D., Saterson, K.A. and Wallen, I.E. (1988). The biological resources of the Arab Republic of Egypt, status and recommended conservation needs. US-AID, Cairo. Unpublished draft. (Unseen)

Bhalla, S. (1990). Resort developers prey on Mt Sinai. *The Observer.* 21 January. P. 13.

Boulos, L. (1985). The arid eastern and south-eastern Mediterranean region. In: Gomez-Campo, C. (Ed.), *Plant conservation in the mediterranean area*. Junk, The Hague. Pp. 123-140.

Brunn, B. (1982). Preservation of wetlands and wildlife in the Middle East VII. Report on Activities of the Holy Land Conservation Fund Committee on the Conservation of Wetlands in the Middle East. April 1981 – May 1982.

Brunn, B. (1987). Egyptian wildlife being restructured. *Sinai Newsletter.* (5)1.

Carp, E. (1980). *Directory of Western Palaearctic wetlands*. UNEP/IUCN, Gland, Switzerland. 506 pp.

Dunnet, G.M., Crick, H.Q.P. and Baha el Din, S.M. (1985). Bardawil lagoon baseline environmental studies: 1985 autumn ornithological survey. A report to BP Petroleum Development Ltd, Egypt. Department of Geography, University of Aberdeen, UK.

EEAA (1991). Protected areas in the Arab Republic of Egypt. Paper presented at the Third Man and Biosphere Meeting on Mediterranean Biosphere Reserves and the First IUCN-CNPPA meeting for the Middle East and North Africa, 14-19 October 1991, Tunis (Tunisia). 18 pp.

Fouda, M. (1984). Ras Mohammed: the first national park in Egypt. *Courser* No. 1. The Ornithological Society of Egypt.

Fouda, F.M. and Tahir, I. (1988). A response. Paper written in reply to the draft report by Pearson, M.P. Specification study for the development of a Management Plan for the Ras Muhammad Marine National Park (Technical Cooperation).

Ghabbour, S.I. (1971). Some aspects of conservation in Egypt. *Biological Conservation* 4: 66-67.

Ghabbour, S.I. (1986). Species richness or soil fauna as criteria for priority choices of protected areas. Mediterranean Biosphere reserves workshop. 8-12 September 1986, Florac, France.

Grimmett, R. (1987). *A review of the problems affecting Palaearctic migratory birds in Africa*. International Council for Bird Preservation, Cambridge, UK.

Gryn-Ambroes, P. (1980). Preliminary annotated lists of existing and potential Mediterranean protected areas. IUCN/UNEP report. UNEP/IG 20/INF5.

Goodman, S.M. (1985). Natural resources and management considerations, Gebel Elba Conservation Area. WWF/IUCN Project No. 3612.

Haas, M.H. (1990). Towards management of environmental problems in Egypt. *Environmental conservation* 17(1): 45-50.

Hanafy, H.M. (1989). The administrative and financial organisation of the Environmental Affairs Agency and its branches in the governorate. Document prepared by Hoda Mahmoud Hanafy, Deputy Minister for Information and Supervisor of Administrative and Financial Affairs on the Environmental Affairs Agency. Appendix II. In: Varty, N. and Baha el Din, S. (1991), *A review of the status and conservation of the Zaranik Protected Area, North Sinai, Arab Republic of Egypt and recommendations for its protection.* International Council for Bird Preservation, Cambridge, UK. Pp. 70-76.

Hobbs, J.J. (1989). *Bedouin life in the Egyptian wilderness.* University of Texas Press, Austin, Texas, USA. 151 pp.

Hunter, B. (Ed.) (1991). *The Statesman's Year Book 1991-92.* The Macmillan Press Ltd, London and Basingstoke, UK. 1692 pp.

IFAGRARIA (1984). Lake Burullus Area Development Project. Final Report produced for the Ministry of Development and the Governorate of Kafr el Sheikh, Egypt.

IUCN (1986). Proposal for a natural resources inventory land-use evaluation, and management programme of the south central Sinai mountains. IUCN, Gland, Switzerland. CDC-SG/K2/11/7/86.

Kassas, M. (1971). The River Nile ecological system: A study towards an international programme. *Biological Conservation* 4: 19-25.

Kishk, M.A. (1986). Land degradation in the Nile Valley. *Ambio* 15(4): 226-230.

Larsen, T.B. (1987). The nature of the Nile. *Aramco World* 38: 20-27.

Larsen, T.B. (1988). Siwa: oasis extraordinary. *Aramco World* 39: 2-7.

Ledant, J.P., Roux, F., Jarry, G., Gammell, A., Smit, C., Barlein, F. and Wille, H. (1985). Aperçu des zones de grand intérêt pour la conservation des espèces d'oiseaux migrateurs de la communauté en Afrique. Rapport à la Direction Générale de l'Environnement, de la Protection des Consommateurs et de la Securité nucléaire de la Commission des Communautés européenes. Contrat U/84/129.

Maaher abou Jaafer (1984). *National parks, natural reserves in the Arab World.* Arab League Education, Culture, Science Organization, Tunis.

Mancy, K.H. (1981). The environmental and ecological impacts of the Aswan High Dam. In: H. Slaval. (Ed.), *Developments in arid zone ecology and environmental quality.* Balabau International Science Services, Rehovat.

Martin, B. (1990). Duck on the Nile. *Shooting Times and Country Magazine.* 15-21 February 1990. Pp. 20-23.

Matthews, G.P.J. (1982). International training course on wildlife conservation, Sinai, Egypt. Sinai Conservation Group, UK.

Meninger, P.L. and Mullié, W.C. (1981). *The significance of Egyptian wetlands for wintering waterbirds.* The Holy Land Conservation Fund, New York.

Mishinski, J. (1989). A drop in the ocean. *Cairo Today.* June. Pp. 38-40.

Morrow, L. (1990). Trashing Mount Sinai. *Time* 129. P. 26.

Pearson, M.P. (1988). Draft Report: Specification study for the development of a management plan for the Ras Muhammad Marine National Park (Technical Cooperation). Prepared for the Arab Republic of Egypt, Egyptian Environmental Affairs Agency, December 1988 and financed by the European Commission.

Saleh, M.A. (1987). The decline of gazelles in Egypt. *Biological Conservation* 39: 83-95.

RAC/SPA (1986). *Proposed protected areas in the Mediterranean.* Special Protected Areas Center, Salammbo, Tunis.

Rzoska, J. (1976). *The Nile: biology of an ancient river.* J.V. Junk, The Hague.

Sinai Conservation Group (1985). Sinai Observations, Summer 1985. Report.

Strudwick, N. (1988). A mortifying case of rising damp. *The Geographical Magazine.* November. Pp. 44-48.

UNEP/IUCN (1988). *Coral Reefs of the World. Volume 2: Indian Ocean, Red Sea and Gulf.* UNEP Regional Seas Directories and Bibliographies. IUCN, Gland, Switzerland and Cambridge, UK/UNEP, Nairobi, Kenya. Pp. 333-344.

Unesco (1986). Les lagunes cotières de la Méditerranée du sud (Algérie, Egypt, Libye, Maroc, Tunisie). Description et bibliographie. Rapport de l'Unesco sur les sciences de la mer. No. 34.

US-AID (1988). The biological resources of the Arab Republic of Egypt: Status and recommended conservation needs. Prepared for the US Agency for International Development and the Office of Science and Technology, Cairo. August.

Varty, N. (1990). The ornithological importance of Lake Bardawil, North Sinai and an assessment of the likely impact of the North Sinai Agricultural Development project on the region's avifauna and their habitats. International Council for Bird Preservation report to the World Bank. 78 pp.

Varty, N and Baha el Din, S. (1991). *A review of the status and conservation of the Zaranik protected area, North Sinai, Arab Republic of Egypt and recommendations for its protection.* International Council for Bird Preservation, Cambridge, UK. 78 pp.

WCMC (1988). Draft directory of protected areas in Egypt. Protected Areas Data Unit, World Conservation Monitoring Centre, Cambridge, UK.

ANNEX
Definitions of protected area designations, as legislated, together with authorities responsible for their administration

Title: Presidential Law concerning Natural Protectorates No. 102

Date: 20 July 1983

Brief Description: Promulgated legislation providing for the legal framework for gazetting protected areas entitled natural protectorates. Subsequent prime ministerial decrees are to be issued to designate and delineate individual natural protectorates (1067/83), by decree upon the recommendation of the Egyptian Environmental Affairs Agency.

Administrative authority: EAA and advisory committee of the relevant governorate represented by the Ministry of Agriculture, Ministry of Defence, Ministry of Tourism, Ministry of Housing, Ministry of Interior, Ministry of Information, and representatives of EAA and the Academy of Science and Technology.

Designations:

Natural protectorate The categories covered under separate prime ministerial decrees include:

- *Scientific area*
- *National marine park*
- *Conservation area*

- *Natural area*
- *Protected area*

Defined as any area of land, or coastal or inland water characterised by flora, fauna, and natural features having cultural, scientific, touristic, or aesthetic value.

Under the law, the EAA is empowered to prohibit all activities which destroy, damage or in any way cause the deterioration of the natural environment of the site.

Restrictions include hunting, fishing, transportation of wildlife, killing and disturbance of the fauna and flora. Hunting of mammals, birds of prey and animals useful to agriculture are forbidden within protected areas by ministerial decrees and governorate decrees specific for each site. Fishing or hunting may be authorised subject to the terms and conditions set by the order.

The introduction of non-indigenous species is also prohibited. Damaging activities are forbidden in the region surrounding the protected area. The law gives recommended fines for offences.

Sources: Translation of original legislation; Hanafy, 1989; Varty and Baha el Din, 1991

SUMMARY OF PROTECTED AREAS

Map ref.	*National/international designations* Name of area	IUCN management category	Area (ha)	Year notified
	National Marine Park			
1	Ras Mohammed	II	19,700	1983
	Scientific Area			
2	Omayed	I	7,000	1986
	Natural Protectorates			
3	Ashtoun el Gamil – Tanee Island	IV	1,200	1988
4	Bardawil Lake	IV	60,000	1985
5	St Catherine (Moussa)	IV	45,000	1988
6	Zaranikh (El Arish)	IV	60,000	1985
	Natural Protectorate (Conservation Area)			
7	Gebel Elba	IV	480,000	1986
	Natural Protectorates (Protected Areas)			
8	Qarun Lake (Quaron)	I	20,000	1989
9	Tiran-Sanafir Islands	IV	49,000	1986
	Biosphere Reserve			
	El Omayed Experimental Research Area	IX	1,000	1981
	Ramsar Wetlands			
	Lake Bardawil	R	59,500	1988
	Lake Burullus	R	46,200	1988

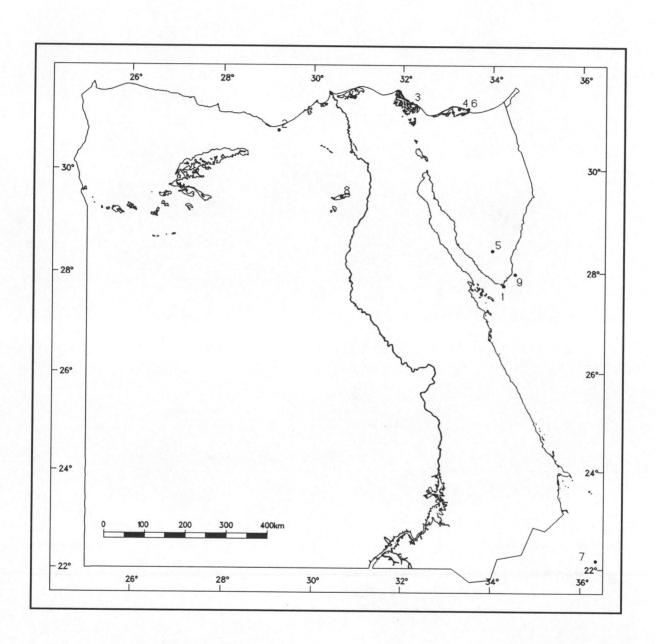

Protected Areas of Egypt

ISLAMIC REPUBLIC OF IRAN

Area 1,648,184 sq. km

Population 54,607,000 (1990)
Natural increase: 2.01% per annum

Economic Indicators
GDP: US$ 3853 per capita (1987)
GNP: No information

Policy and Legislation The country was proclaimed an Islamic Republic on 1 April 1979. Constitutional Act No. 50 states that all citizens are required to honour the conservation of nature and natural resources (Behrouzi-Rad, 1987).

In ancient Persian times areas were protected for hunting. Imperial hunting reserves were established near Tehran sometime between 1792 and 1830, and managed by the Imperial Court for the Royal family. The first wildlife reserves were established in 1927. In 1956 the Game Council was created with a policy to set up hunting centres for the protection of endangered species and the control of hunting (Kopp and Yachkaschi, 1977). In 1967, the Game and Fish Department was empowered by law to declare certain areas for the protection of flora and fauna. In that year the Law of Protection and Exploitation of Forest and Range and the Law on Game and Fish were enacted. The latter was amended in March 1975.

The Environmental Protection and Enhancement Act, 1974 supersedes all previous enabling nature conservation legislation. Four categories of protected natural area are identified under this law, and clauses indicated that any previously designated sites are to be reclassified (Firouz and Harrington, 1976). The protected area categories include national park (wildlife parks were redesignated as national parks in 1974), wildlife refuge, protected area and national nature monument (Firouz and Harrington, 1976). Exceptions in reclassification include Dasht-i-Naz (55ha) and Khoshkedaran (227ha), which would have been reclassified as national parks following the 1974 legislation but were so small that they were reclassified as a wildlife refuge and national nature monument respectively (Firouz and Harrington, 1976). Many other sites changed in name and designation following the 1974 reclassification (for example, Golestan National Park was originally set up in 1956 as Alweh and Ishaki Protected Region and subsequently as Mohammed Reza Shah Wildlife Park in 1964) (IUCN, 1977).

The Law of Protection and Exploitation of Forest and Range was enacted in 1967, and includes specific legislation relating to areas which may be declared as forest parks. They are administered by the Forestry and Range Organisation of the Ministry of Agriculture and Natural Resources and are maintained as parks designated primarily for recreation, although often include important representatives of unique woodland stand types. Other biotic community reserves managed by national organisations include the ex-Imperial Hunting Reserve near Tehran, protected from grazing and unregulated hunting and managed from the 18th century to 1979. Its status was subsequently unclear and the site has not been included in official protected areas lists since that date (Behrouzi-Rad, 1987; Firouz and Harrington, 1976).

The Convention on Wetlands of International Importance especially as Waterfowl Habitat (Ramsar Convention) was ratified on 23 June 1975 and subsequently integrated into the national legislation to enable the designation of national Ramsar sites.

The Game and Fish Law and Regulations were enacted in 1967, and amended in March 1975. The Law represents the basic legal control through which exploitation is curtailed, hunting and shooting are regulated, and game species legally protected. In concert with its regulations, the Law clearly defined the concepts and legal aspects of both wildlife parks and protected areas. It provided legislation to replace the Game Council with an independent governmental organisation named the Game and Fish Department (Firouz et al., 1970). By 1991 it had become legally administered through the Ministry of Agriculture and Natural Resources (Game and Fish Department). Two categories of protection are identified by this Law; protected rivers and wetlands: areas protected from fishing in special protected rivers, in addition to all marshes, wetlands, waterways and bays along the Caspian Sea; fishing refuges or fishing controlled refuges: areas where fishing is banned or restricted (DoE, 1976).

International Activities The Convention on Wetlands of International Importance especially as Waterfowl Habitat (Ramsar Convention) was ratified on 23 June 1975 with 18 sites listed. The Convention concerning the World Natural and Cultural Heritage (World Heritage Convention) was accepted on 26 February 1975, although no natural sites have been inscribed on the World Heritage list. Iran has participated in the Unesco Man and the Biosphere Programme since June 1976 and ratified the Kuwait Regional Convention for Cooperation on the Protection of the Marine Environment from Pollution in the Kuwait Action Plan region of the UNEP Regional seas Programme in 1979. Iran is a member of United Nations, the Colombo Plan and of OPEC. A joint agreement was signed with the USSR in 1973 to combat pollution in the Caspian Sea (Coad, 1980-1981).

Argan International Park (65,750ha) was placed under United Nations patronage at the Ramsar Wetlands Convention meeting in 1971, following recommendations from the then Shah of Iran (IUCN,

1977; Kopp and Yachkaschi, 1977). It was proposed to place the site in trust "to conserve and administer the site for all mankind" (IUCN, 1977; Kopp and Yachkaschi, 1977).

Administration and Management The main administrative and management body is the Department of the Environment, which was established in March 1972 and is divided into a series of divisions dealing with different environmental matters. Under the Environmental Protection and Enhancement Act it superseded the Game and Fish Department in 1974. The latter Department was established in 1967 and had been responsible for the protection of wildlife, hunting, and fishing in inland waters as well as protection of the natural environment. It had succeeded the original Game Council of Iran established in 1956.

The Division of Parks and Wildlife, Department of the Environment is the main body undertaking protected areas management. Generally, the Department undertakes long-term environmental studies and management projects, with responsibilities which include the conservation and enhancement of wildlife resources and the prevention of pollution. It also puts forward regulations on habitat management. Its long-term programmes for the conservation of wilderness sites and wildlife include the cleaning of the Caspian Sea and Iranian rivers and prevention of air pollution in Tehran and Isfahan. The Department has introduced environmental legislation regarding pollution (Behrouzi-Rad, 1987; Sardar, 1982). Recommendations for the establishment of reserves or changes in reserve classification are prepared by the Division of Parks and Wildlife, reviewed by all appropriate divisions of the Department of the Environment, and presented to the High Council of the Environment for approval. The arrangement ensures that all government organisations with jurisdiction over lands proposed for protection have an opportunity to assess the impact on resources administered by their organisations (Firouz and Harrington, 1976). After the proclamation of the Islamic Republic in 1979, the Department of the Environment became responsible for environmental preservation according to a new philosophy, policy aim and strategy, centred on the continued utilisation of environmental resources. Originally, protected areas management was divided between direct control by local Department of the Environment personnel and local councils, including hunters and fishermen as well as departmental personnel. In-service training in the Department of the Environment includes a three-month "environmental guard" curriculum and the two-year "environmental officer" curriculum. A four-year curriculum in environmental conservation has been planned at the University of Tehran and the Department has developed cooperative education programmes with other Iranian universities (Firouz and Harrington, 1976).

Control of grazing and forestry within reserves is determined by regulations adopted jointly by the Forest and Range Organisation of the Ministry of Agriculture and Natural Resources and the Department of the Environment. The Ministry of Agriculture and Natural Resources was created in 1967 and subsequently combined with the revolutionary organisation called the Construction Crusade in 1987/1988. Control of mining, likewise, is determined by agreement between the Department of the Environment and the Ministry of Economy.

Control over water resources must be approved by the Ministry of Energy (Firouz and Harrington, 1976).

Research is conducted in ministries and universities. Almost all ministries have their own research institutes and centres (Coad, 1980-1981). The Faculty of Natural Resources, University of Tehran includes the Department of Forestry and of Forest Economics which conducts studies relating to forest status and protection.

As regards management efficiency, in view of the large size of the country and the limited funds at the disposal of the former Game Council, it was recognised from its inception that if a significant percentage of available resources were allocated to areas of special importance from an ecological point of view, the efficacy and the success of such conservation measures would be greatly enhanced. Thus, the concept of protected regions was born. In those regions hunting was prohibited unless a licence (severely limiting bags) was obtained from the Game Council. Utilisation of range land and forestry incorporated within their confines was subject to restrictions promulgated by that organisation and by the Ministry of Agriculture and Natural Resources, but in principal not excluded. The degree of success in enforcement of these later restrictions was variable, depending mainly on the local stature and initiative of the game officer in charge of a protected region (Firouz *et al.*, 1970).

Systems Reviews Lying as a bridge between four major plant geographical regions (Irano-Turanian, Euro-Siberian, Saharo-Arabian and Sudanian), Iran is one of the largest speciation centres of Holarctic desert flora (Firouz *et al.*, 1970; Tavakoli, 1987). The Irano-Turanian element comprises about 69% of the flora. Euro-Siberian and Sudanian elements make up 5% (Zohary, 1963 cited in IUCN, 1986). Iran borders the Persian or Arabian Gulf and is bounded by Iraq, Pakistan, Afghanistan, USSR and Turkey. Up to 11.5% of the land area is under cultivation, and more than half is classified as uncultivable. Approximately 60% of the country is classified as desert and semi-desert with sparse open scrub of *Acacia*, *Ziziphus* and *Prosopis*. Hot desert in the south-east supports sparse open scrub, on rocky slopes; herbaceous communities with *Atriplex* and *Heliotropium* in sandy depressions; steppe and deserts with *Artemisia* and *Astragalus* occur over most of the centre and east of the country; dry deciduous forests in the west; *Pistacia-Amygdalus* steppe forest in the south-west; *Juniperus* steppe forests in the north; broad-leaved temperate forest in the north up to 2,500m

(Zohary, 1963 cited in IUCN, 1986). There are up to 3.75 million ha of woodland, an estimated 8,900ha of *Avicennia* mangrove, a rich and diverse marine fauna, seagrass beds and coral (Harrington, 1977; Kunkel, 1977, cited in IUCN, 1986; UNEP/IUCN, 1988).

Iran supports some 7,000 plant species of which about 20% are endemic. Most endemics are found in mountains; centres of endemism include the peaks of the Alborz and Zagros massifs, solitary peaks in the central plain, the mountain ridges south of Kashan and Yazd, and to the north of Kerman. The central plateau is species poor (Zohary, 1963, cited in IUCN, 1986). Between 1967 and 1980, 12,000ha of forest plantation had been established and almost 70,000ha of desert lands planted or seeded (Coad, 1980-1981).

At the end of 1965 there were 11 protected regions with a total area of 600,000ha (Kopp and Yachkaschi, 1977). Up to 1976, five rivers had been declared as protected, in addition to all marshes, wetlands, waterways and bays along the Caspian Sea (DoE, 1976). A number of fishing refuges or fishing controlled refuges had also been established by that time. By 1977, the number of protected areas had risen to 69 sites covering a total area of 7,998,168ha or 5% of the country (excluding protected and recreational woodlands). The 11 national parks totalled 1.8 million ha; 4 national nature monuments 12,267ha; 24 protected areas 3.8 million ha and 31 wildlife refuges 2.3 million ha (Kopp and Yachkaschi, 1977). By November 1987, the number of national parks had been reduced to seven due to a change of status. There were 18 national Ramsar sites, 34 protected areas and 26 wildlife refuges (Behrouzi-Rad, *in litt.*, 1987). By April 1989, there were 7 national parks (1,075,300ha), 5 national nature monuments (18,978ha), 26 wildlife refuges (2,585,024ha), 36 protected areas (4,922,718ha) and 18 national Ramsar wetlands (1,350,750ha). The total area protected is currently 10,017,710ha (1991).

Environmental problems include the continued widespread destruction of forests by charcoaling, shifting cultivation and overgrazing by goats (Anon., 1987; Gour-Tanguay, 1977). A sudden relaxation of restrictions and stiff penalties for timber felling, livestock grazing in forest and fishing in 1979 led to widespread abuse (Anon., 1987). Poaching and hunting have increased dramatically and have been largely uncontrolled in the past (Firouz and Harrington, 1976). There are reports of motorised poachers at Kavir National Park and unlicensed sturgeon fishermen dynamiting areas of the Caspian Sea (Anon., 1987). Prior to 1979, felling of trees, charcoal-burning and other exploitation were permitted under a free system (Gour-Tanguay, 1977). Many protected natural areas created prior to establishment of the Islamic Republic were imposed on the local population and, as a result, the enforcement of the game laws and wardening of reserves had not been totally effective (Firouz and Harrington, 1976; Kopp and Yachkaschi, 1977). Throughout the 1970s fixed boundaries were not allotted to a number of

protected areas and they were not zoned nor effectively protected (Kopp and Yachkaschi, 1977).

One of the major environmental threats lasting much of the last decade has been the consequences of the military conflict between Iran and Iraq, although the effects of air pollution from burning Kuwaiti oil wells in the 1990-91 Iraq-Kuwait conflict have also been reported in Iran (WCMC, 1991). In 1983, the Nowruz oil field in the Persian Gulf, north-west of Kharg Island, was damaged, resulting in severe pollution of the sea by oil and gas leakage. As a result of hostilities, Shadegan Marshes and the tidal mudflats of Khor-al Amaya and Khor Musa, a listed Ramsar wetland, was reported to be damaged, the cause being attributed to the use of chemical weapons by Iraq (Ramsar Convention Bureau, 1987). The effects of the 1990-91 military conflict on the same Iranian wetlands (adjacent to the Iraqi frontier) are still largely unknown. Loss of wetlands continues to be one of the most crucial environmental problems. In the 1970s 12 million migratory birds were recorded as seasonal visitors to wetlands. Ten years later the number had fallen to three million, and in the present decade to less than one million, due not only to pollution and hunting, but also to loss of habitat through reclamation of wetlands for agriculture. For example, the internationally important wetland of Anseli Mordab, a designated Ramsar site, has been partially altered by the construction of canals for a locally-conceived reclamation project (Tavakoli, 1987). Many other wetlands are threatened with water loss, ironically because of irrigation schemes. The two Seistan lakes Hamun-e-Hirmand and Hamun-e-Sabari were largely dry during the winter of 1976 because their main water source, the Helmand River, was restricted by the Kajaki dam in Afghanistan. Devegetation, irrigation and industrial pollution and faunal introduction cause dangerous losses of freshwater ecosystems and impact on freshwater fish (Coad, 1980-1981). The petro-chemical industry on the Gulf shore and islands continues to pose a number of threats to the environment, not least pollution. In autumn 1987 flocks of migratory birds are presumed to have mistaken pools of waste oil around Iranian refineries for water and were trapped (Tavakoli, 1987). The movement of oil tankers through the Gulf presents a continued threat to marine life and to the increasingly important Gulf fishery. Associated with expanding industry is a growing coastal population. The population of Banda Abbas, for example, until recently a relatively small port and fish processing centre, is targeted to reach one million by the 1990s (Harrington, 1976).

Other Relevant Information Ruled as an absolute monarchy by the Shahs until the granting of the first Constitution in 1906, Persia was renamed Iran in 1935. Civil unrest in 1979 led to the exile of the Shah and supreme authority passed to a religious leader, the leader of the Shi'a moslems, and the Islamic Republic was declared in 1979. Foreign tourism is virtually non-existent at the present time, although in the past it had some prominence even in protected areas: in the 1970s the Tourist-Consult group recommended marine sites such as Chah Bahar for protection (UNEP/IUCN, 1988). Tourism, and the potential for ecotourism in protected areas, is regarded as being of major significance in the near future (Scott, *in litt.*, 1991).

Addresses

Department of the Environment (Director), PO Box 5181, 15876, TEHRAN (Tel: 1 966441/891261-69; Telex: 215064 DOE CIR)

Forestry and Rangelands, Forestry and Range Organisation (Vice-Minister), Ministry of Agriculture, TEHRAN

References

Anon. (1989). Sharper lines in Arabia's sands. *The Economist.* 21 January 1989. P. 82.

Coad, B.W. (1980-1981). Environmental change and its impact on the freshwater fishes of Iran. *Biological Conservation* 19: 51-80.

DoE (1976). Extract from the Game Laws and Regulations, 1975-1976. Department of the Environment. P. 1354.

FAO (1979). Assistance in wildlife conservation and management. Iran, Project findings and recommendations. Report prepared for the Government of Iran by the Food and Agriculture Organisation of the United Nations acting as executing agency for the United Nations Development Programme. FO: DP/IRA/76/001. Terminal Report. UNDP/FAO, Rome. 26 pp.

Firouz, E. (1974). *Environment Iran.* National Society for the Conservation of Natural Resources and Human Environment.

Firouz, E. and Harrington, F. (1976). Iran: concepts of biotic community conservation. A paper presented at the international meeting on ecological guidelines for the use of Natural Resources in the Middle East and SW Asia. Persepolis, Iran, 24-30 May 1975. *IUCN Occasional Paper* No. 15. IUCN, Morges, Switzerland. 32 pp.

Firouz, E., Hassinger, J.D. and Fergusson, D.A. (1970). The wildlife parks and protected regions of Iran. *Biological Conservation* 3(1): 37-45.

Harrington, F.A. (1975) Iran: surveys of the Southern Iranian coastline with recommendations for additional marine reserves. Country reports No. 4. In: Promotion of the Establishment of Marine Parks and Reserves in the Northern Indian ocean including the Red Sea and Persian Gulf. Papers and proceedings of the Regional Meeting held at Tehran, Iran, 6-10 March 1975. *IUCN Publications New Series* No. 35. Pp. 50-75

Kopp, H. and Yachkaschi, A. (1977). Development and status of protected areas in Iran. *Parks* 2(4): 11-13.

Maher abou Jaafer (1984). *National parks and nature reserves in the Arab World.* The Arab League Educational, Cultural and Scientific Organization, Tunis. 112 pp.

Mohammed Reza, A. (1985). The endangered benthic organisms in effects of oil spilled in Nowruz platform in the Persian Gulf. Symposium on endangered marine animals and marine parks. Cochin, India, 12-16 January 1985.

Montague, K. and Bruun, B. (1987). *Biological diversity in North Africa, the Middle East and Southwest Asia; a directory of organizations and institutions.* HLCF, New York, USA. 134 pp.

Ramsar Convention Bureau (1987) Convention on wetlands of international importance especially as waterfowl habitat (Ramsar, 1971). Third meeting of the conference of the contracting parties. Regina, Saskatchewan, Canada, 27 May 5 June 1987. *Preliminary printing – Conference Report.* Ramsar Convention Bureau, Gland.

Sardar, Z. (1982). Iran. *Science and technology in the Middle East: a guide to issues, organisations and institutions.* Longman, London and New York. P. 121

Tavakoli, E. (1987). Iran environment. Iran Almanak. Pp. 44-48.

UNEP (1987). Clearing house developments. *UNEP Regional Bulletin for Europe* 4. P. 9.

UNEP/IUCN (1988) *Coral Reefs of the World. Volume 2: Indian Ocean, Red Sea and Gulf.* UNEP Regional Seas Directories and Bibliographies. IUCN, Gland, Switzerland and Cambridge, UK/UNEP, Nairobi, Kenya. 440 pp.

WCMC (1991a). Gulf War Environmental Service: impact on the marine environment. World Conservation Monitoring Centre, Cambridge, UK. 37 pp.

WCMC (1991b). Gulf War Environmental Service: impact of atmospheric pollution on the terrestrial environment. World Conservation Monitoring Centre, Cambridge, UK. 37 pp.

ANNEX
Definitions of protected area designations, as legislated, together with authorities responsible for their administration

Title: Environmental Protection and Enhancement Act

Date: 1974

Brief description: The current main law covering nature conservation, the Environmental Protection and Enhancement Act of 1974, supersedes all previous enabling legislation. Four categories of protected natural area can be established and protected; any previously designated sites have been reclassified under this law.

Administrative authority: Department of the Environment

Designations:

National park (Park-e-Melli) (previously designated as wildlife park) Relatively large areas of natural or semi-natural land. They must represent outstanding examples of the nation's geological, ecological, geographic, historical, archaeological and scenic features, to be set aside in perpetuity for their preservation, protection, conservation and recreational potential. Notable requirements include parks possessing unique flora and flora and relatively pristine remnants of the regional flora representative of particular geographical zones.

An area is considered to be of national significance if: it is of sufficient scenic beauty; has unique geomorphological and landscape features; possesses diverse and/or unique examples of biotic communities or ecosystems; and is of sufficient size to permit public use, management, research, zoning and protection.

Management includes minimal measures necessary for the essential conservation of the area, controls being required to limit the damage from visitor use through zoning of recreational areas. Many parks permit human occupation, livestock grazing and agriculture although attempts are being made for them to be phased out. Permitted activities include provisions for culling of wildlife through authorised hunters.

Wildlife refuge (Panahgah-e-Hayat-e-Vahsh) (renamed from wildlife reserve in accordance with the law of 1974) Areas of representative habitat types set aside for conservation and management of native wildlife and the protection and management of its habitat; including breeding, spawning, wintering and other areas. Management practice includes restoration of these resources.

Recreational use by the public is secondary to the purpose of management for wildlife and vegetation restoration. Wildlife refuges include public use zones in which farming, livestock grazing, vegetation cutting or other land use activities are permitted and sometimes encouraged to enhance the wildlife values of the reserves.

Hunting, fishing, trapping, poisoning, or capturing of wildlife and collection of flora is prohibited except were such activities are consonant with management practices. Settlements and human activity are restricted, eliminated or prohibited according to Department of the Environment regulations. Wildlife refuges may include public use zones in which farming, livestock grazing, vegetation cutting or other land use activities are permitted and sometimes encouraged to enhance the wildlife values of the reserves.

Protected area (Maneqe-ye-Hefazat Shode): (previously designated as protected or restricted region) Established to serve various environmental conservation and protection needs. The sites are set up with multiple use and single use objectives, including ecological, scientific, economic, educational, cultural and recreational needs. Selection criteria differentiate 20 categories ranging from protection of unique, unusual or representative flora and fauna, to unusual habitats or species at extremes of their range, to sites where the influence of man on natural ecosystems can be measured. Areas are established to provide conditions conducive to the regeneration and amelioration of representative habitats and/or endangered species. Such regions are also envisaged as centres of breeding stock for the repopulation of wildlife species that are on the decline in adjacent areas.

Unlicensed hunting is prohibited. The utilisation of range-land and forest within the boundaries of protected areas are subject to restrictions promulgated with the co-operation of the Ministry of Agriculture. If livestock grazing, woodcutting or other activities are likely to alter the natural environment they can be curtailed in accordance with legislation of 1974.

Human populations are often present, but in practice an effort has been made to exclude villages and other habitations. Policies include attempts to phase out human settlement, grazing and agriculture. In a number of cases, research and limited tourism occur. Protected areas often act as buffer zones encompassing national parks, ensuring that development can be regulated and limit or avoid management problems.

National nature monument (Asar-e-Tabii-ye-Malli)
Small areas designated for the preservation of special features illustrating typical, unique or unusual phenomena of geological, scientific, historical and/or natural history interest. Prospective sites for this category have no minimum size. To be considered of national significance a site must contain at least one of the following: outstanding geological formations or features illustrating a specific geological process; specialised physiographic areas; aquatic or terrestrial ecosystems containing representative, unique or unusual characteristics; habitats supporting endangered species; examples of scenic grandeur; individual specimens or groups of specimens representing the nation's zoological, botanic, geological or natural history. Such sites may or may not be open to visitors depending on the requirements of the feature for protection and preservation. Management to maintain certain species or to expose features for study is considered acceptable.

Sources: DoE, 1976; Firouz and Harrington, 1976; Firouz *et al.*, 1970

Title: Law of protection and exploitation of forest and range

Date: 1967

Brief description: Legislation connected with forest exploitation

Administrative authority: Forestry and Range Organisation, Ministry of Agriculture and Natural Resources

Designations:

Forest park Designated primarily for recreation, although often including important representative or unique woodland stand types.

Sources: DoE, 1976; Firouz and Harrington, 1976; Firouz *et al.*, 1970

Title: Game and Fish Law

Date: 1967, amended March 1975

Brief description: The Law was amended in March 1975

Administrative authority: Ministry of Agriculture and Natural Resources

Designations:

Protected river Areas designated to protect natural habitats from fishing. Specified areas include protected rivers, in addition to all marshes, wetlands, waterways and bays along the Caspian Sea, all of which are declared protected insofar as fishing is concerned.

Fishing refuge Designated areas set up to act as non-fishing or restricted fishing areas.

Sources: DoE, 1976; Firouz and Harrington, 1976

Title: "National Ramsar wetlands" Law

Date: 1975

Brief description: An international convention, the Ramsar Convention on Wetlands of International Importance especially as Waterfowl Habitat was ratified on 23 June 1975 and subsequently integrated into national legislation providing for the establishment of national Ramsar sites.

Administrative authority: Ministry of Agriculture and Natural Resources

Designations:

National Ramsar wetland Areas which afford protection against hunting and other forms of threat.

Source: DoE, 1976

SUMMARY OF PROTECTED AREAS

Map[†] ref.	National/international designations Name of area	IUCN management category	Area (ha)	Year notified
	National Parks			
1	Bamou	II	48,075	1962
2	Golestan (Mohammad Reza Shah)	II	91,895	1957
3	Kavir	II	420,000	1964
4	Khogir	II	11,570	1982
5	Sorkheh Hesar	II	9,380	1982
6	Tandoureh	II	30,780	1968
7	Uromiyeh Lake	II	463,600	1967
	National Nature Monuments			
8	Alborz-e-Markazi (Central Alborz)	III	4,750	1977
9	Dehloran	III	1,400	1976
	Wildlife Refuges			
10	Amirkelayeh	I	1,230	1971
11	Angoran	I	28,600	1971
12	Bakhtegan	I	327,820	1968
13	Bisotun (Varmangeh)	I	31,250	
14	Dez	I	5,240	1960
15	Dodangeh	I	6,700	1974
16	Gamishlo	I	49,250	1971
17	Karkheh	I	3,600	1960
18	Khab-o-Rochon	I	173,750	1971
19	Khoshyeylag	I	154,400	1963
20	Kiamaky	I	84,400	1974
21	Kolahghazi	I	48,683	1964
22	Mehroyeh	I	7,468	1971
23	Miandasht	I	52,000	1974
24	Miankaleh	I	68,800	1970
25	Shadegan	I	296,000	1972
26	Touran	I	565,000	1973
	Protected Areas			
27	Alborz-e-Markazi	V	399,000	1961
28	Angoran	V	96,130	1971
29	Arasbaran	V	7,240	1971
30	Arjan	IV	52,800	1972
31	Bahramgor	IV	385,000	1973
32	Bahukalat (Gando)	IV	382,430	1971
33	Bazman	IV	324,688	1968
34	Bigar	V	25,000	1971
35	Bisotun	V	50,850	1968
36	Dez	V	10,633	1960
37	Geno	V	27,500	1972
38	Ghorkhod	V	34,000	1971
39	Haftadgoleh	V	82,000	1970
40	Hamoun	V	193,500	1967
41	Hara	V	85,686	1972
42	Hormoud	V	151,284	1976
43	Jahannoma	V	30,600	1974
44	Karkheh	V	9,427	1960
45	Kavir	V	250,000	
46	Lar River	V	28,000	1976
47	Lisar	V	33,050	1970
48	Marakan	V	92,715	1966
49	Mond	V	46,700	1976

Map[†] ref.	*National/international designations* Name of area	IUCN management category	Area (ha)	Year notified
50	Moteh	V	200,000	1964
51	Oshtran Kuh	V	93,950	1970
52	Parvar	V	59,840	1962
53	Salouk	V	16,000	1973
54	Serany	V	17,800	1971
55	Siahkesheim	V	4,500	1967
56	Tandoureh	V	2,300	
57	Tang Sayyad	V	27,000	1971
58	Touran	V	1,295,400	1973
59	Vargin	V	28,000	
	Biosphere Reserves			
	Arasbaran Protected Area	IX	52,000	1976
	Arjan Protected Area	IX	65,750	1976
	Geno Protected Area	IX	49,000	1976
	Golestan National Park	IX	125,895	1976
	Hara Protected Area	IX	85,686	1976
	Kavir National Park	IX	700,000	1976
	Lake Oromeeh National park	IX	462,600	1976
	Miankaleh Protected Area	IX	68,800	1976
	Touran Protected Area	IX	1,000,000	1976
	Ramsar Wetlands			
	Miankaleh Peninsula, Gorgan Bay and Lapoo-Zaghmarz Ab-bandans	R	40,000	1975
	Lake Parishan and Dasht-e-Arjan	R	6,600	1975
	Lake Oroomiyeh	R	483,000	1975
	Neiriz Lakes and Kamjan Marshes	R	108,000	1975
	Anzali Mordab Complex	R	15,000	1975
	Shadegan Marshes and tidal mud-flats of Khor-al Amaya and Khor Musa	R	190,000	1975
	Hamoun-e-Saberi	R	50,000	1975
	Lake Kobi	R	1,200	1975
	South end of Hamoun-e-Puzak	R	10,000	1975
	Shur Gol, Yadegarlu & Dorgeh Sangi Lakes	R	2,500	1975
	Bandar Kiashahr Lagoon and mouth of Sefid Rud	R	500	1975
	Amirkelayeh Lake	R	1,230	1975
	Lake Gori	R	120	1975
	Alagol, Ulmagol and Ajigol Lakes	R	1,400	1975
	Khuran Straits	R	100,000	1975
	Deltas of Rud-e-Shur, Rud-e-Shirin and Rud-e-Minab	R	20,000	1975
	Deltas of Rud-e-Gaz and Rud-e-Hara	R	15,000	1975
	Gavkhouni Lake and marshes of the lower Zaindeh Rud	R	43,000	1975

[†]Locations of most protected areas are shown on the accompanying map.

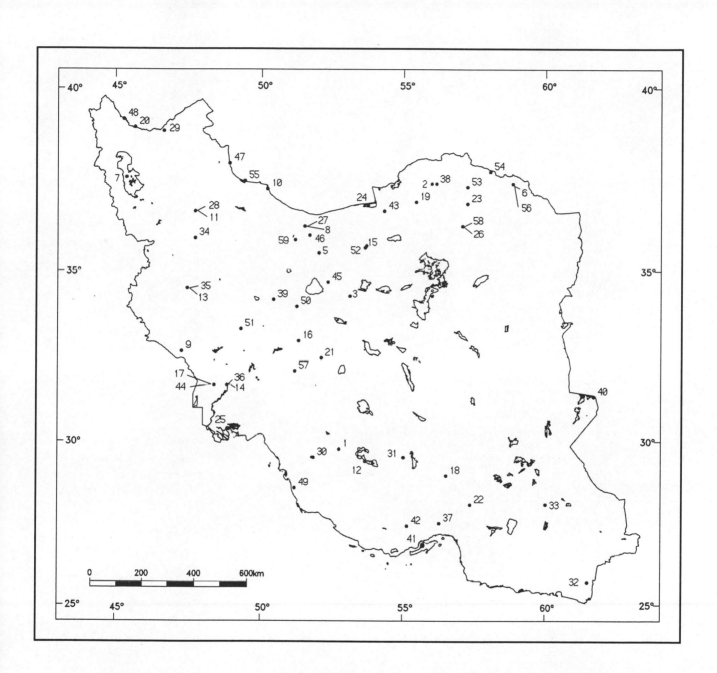

Protected Areas of Iran

IRAQ

Area 434,924 sq. km

Population 18,920,000 (1990)
Natural increase: 3.39% per annum

Economic Indicators
GDP: US$ 2,971 per capita (1987)
GNP: No information

Policy and Legislation Iraq became a kingdom under a League of Nations mandate, administered by Britain in 1921 after four centuries of Ottoman rule. Iraq became independent on 3 October 1932 under the Hashemite dynasty, and subsequently a republic in 1958 (Hunter, 1991). The Constitution was promulgated on 16 July 1970, and all legislation is passed through the highest state authority, the Revolutionary Command Council (RCC) and the National Assembly (1991). Iraq is divided into 18 governorates (liwa), three governorates form the Kurdish autonomous region (1991).

The main extant legislation related to forest protection is the Forestry Law No. 75 of 1955. The legislation ensures forest protection and its demarcation, along with the prohibition of livestock in reserve forests. Ordinance No. 4 of 1958 relates to forest conservation regulations which specify the restriction on the felling of timber and of charcoal burning. One of the main laws reported to protect wildlife is the environment wildlife law of 1981, which is presumed to legislate for wildlife preserves, including those in existence before that date (see Annex) (Abdel-Noor *et al.*, 1991). In 1977 the precursor of the General Directorate of Horticulture and Forestry became responsible for wildlife protection and for this purpose established small wildlife preserves or wildlife breeding stations (Maher abou Jaafer, 1984). Under legal requirements wildlife breeding stations are divided into two categories: those with natural vegetation and native fauna and others with planted habitats and introduced species of fauna and flora (Maher abou Jaafer, 1984). The first were established in 1977/1978.

Other pieces of legislation include the Agrarian Reform Law No. 117 of 1970; Law No. 40 of 1958 on safeguarding and hunting of terrestrial animals; and Law No. 41 of 1958 on protecting and hunting aquatic animals (Gour-Tanguay, 1977). Ordinance No. 1, applying Law No. 41, prohibits fishing in numerous localities throughout the year (Gour-Tanguay, 1977).

Proposed natural protected areas include game parks, nature reserves and bird sanctuaries (Gour-Tanguay, 1977).

A complete lack of adequate enabling legislation has almost certainly contributed towards the lack of protected areas in the country.

International Activities Iraq does not participate in the Convention on Wetlands of International Importance especially as Waterfowl Habitat (Ramsar Convention), but accepted the Convention concerning the Protection of the World Cultural and Natural Heritage (World Heritage Convention) on 5 March 1974. To date no natural sites have been inscribed. The Secretary of the Unesco Man and Biosphere National Committee of Iraq is based at the Scientific Research Council, Baghdad (Clor, 1988). Iraq is a member of the United Nations, Arab League and the Non-Aligned Movement.

Recommendations have been made for a transfrontier initiative in the Zagros mountains, in the Kurdish administrative governorate with neighbouring countries (Herzog, *in litt.*, 1991).

Administration and Management Relevant administrative bodies includes the Secretariat of the Council of Environmental Protection (cf Higher Council for Environmental Protection and Improvement) and the Ministry of Agriculture and Irrigation (Abdel-Noor *et al.*, 1991).

In 1959, a General Administration for Forests and Afforestation was formed (General Commission for Forests, Wild Animal and Bird Breeding Department), together with the Directorate General of Forests and Plantations, Ministry of Northern Affairs. Up until 1991 the General Directorate of Horticulture and Forestry, Ministry of Agriculture and Irrigation, held all responsibility for forests. The Ministry of Agriculture includes numerous other General Directorates (or departments) including the Department of Fisheries with responsibility for fish protection.

The responsibilities of the General Directorate of Horticulture and Forestry includes establishment of protected areas, legislation and enforcement of protection for individual species. The main forms of protected area, wildlife preserves or breeding stations, are managed by forestry personnel. Wardens ensure that hunting ban regulations are enforced (Herzog, *in litt.*, 1991). The administration of breeding stations comprises graduates from universities and institutes, the first of whom received training from Hungary in the 1980s (Maher abou Jafer, 1984).

The Department of Research, Planning and Coordination of the Scientific Research Council, Baghdad undertakes some environmental work. It is divided into various centres; agriculture, biology, building, dates and palms, institutes of applied research on natural resources and petroleum research institute (Sardar, 1982). Some survey research, such as the joint mission with IWRB in 1973, is undertaken by the Iraq Natural History Museum of Baghdad (Koning and Dijksen, 1977). The University of Baghdad has a Natural History Centre which has interests in nature conservation activities. The University of Mosul includes the College of Agriculture and Forestry at Hammam al-Alil with a forestry department undertaking work on forest protection (Sardar, 1982). Scientific investigation of the Hawr al Hammar marshes and their ecosystems is undertaken at the field research station established by the Basra Museum of Natural History in 1975 (Carp, 1980; Scott, *in litt.*, 1991).

There is a complete lack of adequate administration and management of critical sites. Addressing the situation and appointing an effective body to coordinate activities is widely regarded as being imperative.

Systems Reviews Iraq is located in south-west Asia, between Saudi Arabia, Kuwait, Jordan, Syria, Turkey and Iran. Geographically, it is divided into four regions: the mountainous areas of the north-east (with alpine vegetation up to 3,000m); the barren, semi-desert area of the south-west; the desert of the north-west; and the fertile plains and marshes between the Euphrates and Tigris rivers, combining to form the Shatt al-Arab river which flows into the Persian or Arabian Gulf. The vast complex of the Mesopotamian marshes and reedbeds are possibly the largest of their kind in the world, covering about 20,000 sq. km. The climate is generally described as sub-tropical continental, with dry hot summers and cold winters (Irano-Turanian) with certain Mediterranean arid elements. Natural forest covers only 4% of the county. Forest vegetation, largely of oak *Quercus aegilops* and pine *Pinus brutia*, occurs along the borders with Turkey in the Zagros-Taurus mountains (Nasser, 1984).

The cradle of civilisation, Mesopotamia, between the Tigris and Euphrates developed from at least 6,000 years BP. Cultivation actually began 7,000 years BP in the foothills of the northern mountains (Clor, 1988). The Babylonians and subsequent civilisations extensively altered the environment, draining land and constructing complex irrigation systems as long ago as 5,000 years BP (Clor, 1988). By 1991 there was 28 million donams of cultivated land in Iraq (4 donam equal 1ha). In 1990 oil accounted for nearly 50% of total revenue. Date plantations are extensive, the country furnishing about 80% of the world's trade.

There appears to have been little in the way of comprehensive surveys of biological resources in recent decades, reviews include *Systematic List of the Vertebrates of Iraq* (Mahdi and Georg, 1969) and various bibliographies (Allouse, 1954). Limited surveys include that of E. Carp and D. Scott in the mid 1980s, resulting in a national park recommendation for sections of the Mesopotamian marshes submitted to the authorities (E. Carp, pers. comm., 1991). Other areas of natural interest recommended for future protection are situated in the north-east (Zagros mountains) (Herzog, *in litt.*, 1991). A field survey was conducted between 26 August and 4 September 1991 to assess the environmental effects of the Iran-Kuwait military conflict (Abdel-Noor *et al.*, 1991).

In the mid-1980s a total of seven wild animal breeding station protected areas covered 491ha (Montague and Bruun, 1987). There is no known nature conservation strategy for the country.

Major problems to the environment include excess pollution to the Tigris and Euphrates rivers, from organic, agricultural and industrial pollutants. Flood-type irrigation has increased both the ground-water level and salinity of soils, the greatest potential dangers for aquifers throughout the country (Abdel-Noor *et al.*, 1991). In 1950, it was estimated that approximately 60% of agricultural land had been seriously affected by salinity (Clor, 1988). Aerial emissions, such as from the sulphur recovery plant at Kirkuk and the Dora oil refinery near Baghdad, are also reported to include corrosive air pollutants (Gour-Tanguay, 1977). Similar emissions have occurred from other industrial complexes bombed during the Iraq-Kuwait conflict of 1991 The vast wetland areas (total 20,000 sq. km), which are of extreme importance for waterfowl, are under threat from drainage, pollution and irrigation through river control and diversion (Carp, 1980; Koning and Dijksen, 1973). Iraq has recently invested in major land reclamation schemes, with a 10-year plan commencing in 1988 to build a comprehensive network of irrigation canals and land reclamation of 4 million ha. A canalised river is in the process of construction between the Tigris and the Euphrates to flow directly into the Arabian gulf. All activity has been suspended since the 1991 military conflict (Abdel-Noor *et al.*, 1991; Clor, 1988). Destruction of habitats during the Iran-Iraq war (1980-1988) was caused by the reported use of damaging chemical weapons in military conflict areas on the frontier near Basra, and in Kurdish regions such as at Zarivar Lake (Ramsar Convention Bureau, 1987). Reports indicate the use of chemical weapons in the Mesopotamian marshes against refugees following the 1990-1991 military conflict activities (Abdel-Noor *et al.*, 1991). There are unconfirmed reports that a wildlife preserve west of Ramadi was bombed in January 1991 during military activities, killing over 500 deer. Other reports of destruction of wildlife have been reported in the Zagros mountains and Mesopotamian marshes (Abdel-Noor *et al.*, 1991).

Other Relevant Information Territorial rights over the Shatt-al-Arab waterway are disputed with Iran. On 8 August 1990 Iraq declared the annexation of Kuwait as part of the al-Basrah Governorate. It unconditionally withdrew on 28 February 1991 following military action authorised by United Nations Security Council Resolution on 29 November 1990.

There is currently no international tourism in Iraq.

Addresses

General Directorate of Horticulture and Forestry, Ministry of Agriculture and Irrigation, BAGHDAD (Cable: Forestry Baghdad)

Higher Council for Environmental Protection and Improvement, c/o University of Health, P O Box 423, BAGHDAD

General Commission for Forests, Wild Animal and Bird Breeding Department, BAGHDAD

References

Abdel-Noor, L., Al-Khoshman, M. A., Mirkarimi, R. and Picardi, A.P. (1991). Environmental consequences of the war and the impact on Iraqi civilians. Harvard Commission on Civilian Casualties. 39 pp.

Allouse, B.E. (1954). *A bibliography on the vertebrate fauna of Iraq and neighbouring countries.* Iraq Natural History Museum, Baghdad.

Carp, E. (1980). *Directory of Western Palearctic wetlands.* UNEP/IUCN, Gland, Switzerland. 506 pp.

Clor, M. (1988). A land of milk and honey .... and salt. *The Geographical Magazine.* Vol. LX No. 11. Pp. 34-37.

Gour-Tanguay, R. (1977). Environmental policies in developing countries. *Beiträge zur Umweltgestaltung.* Heft A 27. Erich Schmidt Verlag.

Koning, F.J. and Dijksen, L.J. (1977) IWRB Mission to Iraq and Syria, December 1972. *IWRB Bulletin* 35: 57-62.

Mahdi, N and Georg, P.V. (1969). Systematic list of the vertebrates of Iraq. *Iraq Natural History Museum Publication* No. 26.

Maher abou Jaafer (1984). *National parks and nature reserves in the Arab World.* The Arab League Educational, Cultural and Scientific Organization, Tunis. 112 pp.

Montague, K. and Bruun, B. (1987). *Biological diversity in North Africa, the Middle East and Southwest Asia; a directory of organizations and institutions.* HLCF, New York, USA. 134 pp.

Nasser, M.H. (1984). Forests and forestry in Iraq: prospects and limitations. *Commonwealth Forestry Review* 63(4): 299-304.

Ramsar Convention Bureau (1987). Conference report, Third Meeting of the Conference of the contracting parties. Regina, Saskatchewan, Canada, 27 May-5 June.

Sardar, Z. (1982). Iraq. *Science and Technology in the Middle East: a guide to issues, organisations and institutions.* Longman, London and New York. Pp. 152-157

Townsend, C.C. and Guest, E. (1980). *Flora of Iraq.* Ministry of Agriculture and Agrarian Reform, Baghdad. Volume 1. 213 pp.

ANNEX
Definitions of protected area designations, as legislated, together with authorities responsible for their administration

Title: Forestry Law No. 75

Date: 1955

Brief description: The major extant legislation related to forest protection.

Administrative authority: General Directorate of Horticulture and Forestry, Ministry of Agriculture and Irrigation

Designations:

Protected forest Ensures forest protection, demarcation, protection of forest products for the establishment, extension and management of forests and prohibition of cattle in reserve forests.

Source: Gour-Tanguay, 1977

Title: Environment wildlife law

Date: 1981

Brief description: To protect wildlife from poaching by enabling the designation of preserves.

Administrative authority: Ministry of Agriculture and Irrigation (General Directorate of Fisheries and General Directorate of Horticulture and Forestry)

Designations:

Wildlife preserve and breeding station Areas designated to protect wildlife from poachers. The enforcement of this law is aided by government payment incentives to not harm "protected" species including deer. These areas are often fenced and specifically established to protect large native or introduced mammals. Hunting is not permitted within these areas.

Source: Maher abou Jaafer, 1984; Abdel-Noor *et al.*, 1991

Title: Hunting Laws Nos 40 and 41

Date: 1958

Brief description: Relates to protection and hunting of animals; No. 41 concerns aquatic animals and No. 40 regards the safeguarding and hunting of terrestrial animals in specified localities.

Administrative authority: Ministry of Agriculture and Irrigation (General Directorate of Fisheries and General Directorate of Horticulture and Forestry)

Designations:

Fishing restricted area Ordinance No. 1, applying Act No. 41 of 1958 on fisheries protection, prohibits fishing in numerous localities throughout the year.

Source: Gour-Tanguay, 1977

ISRAEL

Area 21,060 sq. km (see below)

Population 4.6 million (1990)
Natural increase: 1.5% per annum

Economic Indicators
GDP: US$ 8,592 per capita (1987)
GNP: US$ 6,810 per capita (1987)

Policy and Legislation In November 1947 the United Nations called for the establishment of both a Jewish and an Arab state (Resolution 242) in the former British mandate state of Palestine (Hunter, 1991). The Jewish community proclaimed the state of Israel on 14 May 1948 but an Arab state was not established. Subsequently, in 1967, the Palestinian areas placed under Jordanian administration in 1950, referred to as the West Bank, became occupied by Israeli military forces (see Territories of the West Bank and Gaza Strip).

A series of fundamental laws, taken together, form the Constitution of the state of Israel. Under Jewish law, in the Torah (Old Testament) and Halakah (parts of the Talmud that concern legal matters), it was specified that certain types of trees should not be destroyed (Book of Deuteronomy Chapter 20: verse 19; Hosea 4: 13). A limited number of sacred forests and trees continue to be protected, including Horshat Ha'arbaim on Mount Carmel and areas in the Dan valley and Tsherkas hill in the Sharon plain (Zohary, 1959; Weitz, 1974). Limited legislation was covered under the Mejellah (Ottoman civil code) Islamic law during the period of Ottoman occupation of Palestine up to the British Mandate period early this century. Article 1243 of the Law defined that land and the associated trees growing wild in mountains were "not to be possessed and should remain ownerless. Under Article 1244 cutting wood on private forests was not permitted unless permission was obtained; infringement resulted in payment of damages (Weitz, 1974).

The enactment of the present Forest Ordinance dates from the 1926 (Palestine Forest Ordinance) British Mandate legislation, and empowered the Ministry of Agriculture (now the Land Development Authority) to declare certain areas as forest reserves, to control these areas and to declare certain types of tree in any part of the country as "protected trees". In 1960, Forest Regulations were introduced under Article 26 of the Forest Ordinance, according to which forest officers would be appointed with regulatory powers (Weitz, 1974). This Law was subsequently strengthened in 1955 by the Plant Protection (Damage by Goats) Law No. 5715-1955, which empowered the Ministry of Agriculture (and its successors) to control and restrict grazing of goats in forested areas. In 1963 the National Parks and Nature Reserves Law No. 5723-1963 was enacted to: create a National Parks Authority (NPA) and Nature Reserves Authority (NRA) for the administration and protection of national parks and nature reserves; empower the Ministry of the Interior to declare protected natural areas; to empower the Ministry of Agriculture to promulgate regulations defining fauna to be given special protection by law (Gour-Tanguay, 1977).

Other relevant environmental legislation includes the Planning and Building Law No. 5725-1965, in which the Ministry of Interior is responsible for planning of sea coastal development; the Water Law No. 5719-1951 which states that all water resources of the state are public property, promotes water conservation and prohibits non marine water pollution; the Wild Animals Protection Law No. 5715-1955 states that all animals and birds are protected, except for pest species and up to 15 listed game animals (enforced by the Nature Reserves Authority). There is also a Protected Natural Values Law (includes the Protected Wild Flowers Law) of 1963-64 (Anon., 1984).

In 1967, Nature Protection laws were reported to have been passed in Sinai by the Israel government, prohibiting the destruction of wildlife. In 1979 the territory came under the administration of Egypt, and Israeli laws lapsed.

Reviews of protected areas policy and legislation have not been not identified in this report.

International Activities At the international level, Israel has entered a number of cooperative agreements and legal obligations. It participates in the Unesco Man and Biosphere Programme and in 1990 there was a National Committee composed of 14 representatives. To date no biosphere reserves have been listed. The Convention for the Protection of the Mediterranean Sea against Pollution, usually known as the Barcelona Convention, was formally adopted in 1976. The contracting parties to the Convention adopted the Protocol concerning Mediterranean Specially Protected Areas on 2 April 1982, which entered into force on 23 March 1986. Seven specially protected areas have been identified by the national focal point as being representative of the Mediterranean network (Jeudy de Grissac, *in litt.*, 1991). It is not party to the Convention concerning the Protection of the World Cultural and Natural Heritage (World Heritage Convention) nor to the Convention on Wetlands of International Importance especially as Waterfowl Habitat (Ramsar Convention).

Possible future cooperation with neighbouring countries includes the bilateral "Jordan Valley Park" between Jordan and Israel in the Zor (Geon-Ha-Yarden) wooded flood plain north of the Dead Sea (Dov Por and Ortal, 1985).

Administration and Management Law No. 5723-1963 of 1963 provided for the establishment of the National Parks Authority (NPA) (Reshut Ha Gannim

Ha-Le'Umi'im) and Nature Reserves Authority (NRA) (Reshut Shmorot Ha-Tev'a). The NPA is attached to the Office of the Prime Minister, Ministry of the Interior, whilst the NRA is part of the Ministry of Agriculture (pre-1965 it was formally called the Nature Conservation Department). In December 1988 the cabinet created the Ministry of the Environment to coordinate environmental topics of concern, which superseded the old Environmental Protection Service (EPS) (Sherut Le-Shmirat Eikhut Ha-Seviva) created by the Ministry of the Interior in 1973 (Anon., 1989). The EPS was originally set up according to requirements laid down in 1963 and 1965 legislation and regulations. It stated that environmental responsibility was the domain of operation of each Ministry and combined activities should involve inter-ministerial forums (Gour-Tanguay, 1977). In cases where there was no expertise, the EPS was used in the role of coordinator (for details of the Service's activities see EPS, 1983). The EPS has been instrumental in funding and coordinating numerous environmental programmes, such as the "Management of the Mediterranean Coast" programme which involved a multi-disciplinary study with the intention of developing a coastal land-use policy, a plan and framework for resources management including that of nature conservation areas (Amir, 1987).

The NRA is responsible for all topics concerning the preservation of nature in Israel and the Occupied Territories. Its tasks include a) setting up and administering reserves; b) protecting designated plants, animals and geological features; c) taking responsibility for hunting licences and supervision. The NRA is based on a regional system, with 36 defined districts each of which has a ranger; the ranger's responsibilities include the development of reserves and the control of poaching and plant collecting in the district. At the local level, each reserve has a small team responsible for estate management and wardening tasks, including site protection and biological survey work. For example, at Eilat Coral Nature Reserve in 1984 there was a staff of five including two wardens (Phillips, *in litt.*, 1986; Shlesinger, *in litt.*, 1984). The headquarters of the NRA is in Jerusalem and provides services for the districts, which include finance, administration and planning. In 1986 there was a total of 250 staff of which 50 were based in the Jerusalem office (Phillips, *in litt.*, 1986). At various nature reserves small entrance fees are charged, partly to restrict public pressure (Shlesinger, *in litt.*, 1984). An auxiliary of the Nature Reserves Authority is the *"Hai-Bar"* organisation whose function is the re-establishment of endangered species in natural habitats. This operation is largely being carried out in several specially equipped nature reserves (Clark, 1990). The NRA maintains a protected area computer database, which includes information on site name, location and size (Anon., 1983; Ashkenazi, 1986; Phillips, *in litt.*, 1986). Other projects include the inland water ecological data base, a combined project of the Hebrew university and the NRA (Phillips, *in litt.*, 1986).

Forest reserves are administered and managed by Land and Forest Reserves section of the Forest Department. This Department is part of the Land Development Authority (Keren Kayemeth Leisrael) which replaced the Afforestation Department of the Ministry of Agriculture which managed the forests from inception in 1926 until dissolution in 1959 (Weitz, 1974). The Department is divided into regional directorates, each with units of forestry management, forestry planning, timber production, fire management and services, these are further subdivided into districts with directors, forest officer, local foresters and workers. In 1989 there was a total staff in the forestry department of 274 professional personnel, 121 technical, 50 vocational and 1,594 workers (Anon, 1990). The overall yearly budget rose from US$ 14.5 million in 1985 to US$ 28 million in 1990. The financing of forestry activities is met mainly by grants and donations from abroad and in country, in addition to income from property, timber export and minor government allocations (Anon., 1990).

A limited number of private reserves exist. In 1983, the Rothschild Foundation commenced cooperation with the Society for the Protection of Nature in Israel (SPNI) (Herva le-haganat ha-teva) in managing the open space of Ramat Hanadiv for nature conservation. Management plans exist together with a detailed programme of research and surveys, education, public awareness and planning, in order to ensure an integrated comprehensive approach (Sagi, 1991b). The SPNI is the largest non-political voluntary organisation in the country, with over 700,000 members. Since establishment in 1953, SPNI has developed education and research techniques to further its aims of conserving landscapes and relics of the past and to protect plant and animal life. This is achieved through collecting data in the field on flora and fauna, setting up research centres in collaboration with universities, hosting seminars, lobbying and supplying information to ensure the creation of new legislation. The SPNI attempts to increase public awareness of nature through education using a network of 25 field study centres, nature tours and community education projects. A study session at SPNI field study centres is now an integral part of the curriculum of high school students and these centres receive some 400,000 visitors a year (Anon, 1983). The annual working budget of SPNI averaged at US$ 10 million per year in the mid 1980s; area impact assessments totalled US$ 60,000 per year and field research and protected area management US$ 8,000. The remainder was largely used for education and teaching (SPNI, n.d.). Contributions to the SPNI are income-tax deductible. Cooperative research has also been undertaken by SPNI in association with WWF International, such as Project No. 3810 on the environmental impact of black goat grazing on maquis, and Project No. 3813 on the survey of cave ecosystems in Mount Sedom (Jungius, *in litt.*, 1988). The Botanical Information Centre, ROTEM, was set up to provide a database on rare and endangered plants, the centre being a joint project of the SPNI and the Hebrew University Department of Botany (Phillips, *in litt.*, 1986).

There is a complex network of environmental organisations, voluntary bodies being coordinated under the auspices of the "Life and Environment" (Hayyim u-Seviva). Associations include the Biological Institute established in 1949 and concerned with botanical gardens and zoos; the Institute for Nature Conservation Research, established in 1974 as part of Tel-Aviv University, a body which undertakes research on the protection of birds of prey and larger mammals including leopard; the Centre for Maritime Studies (University of Haifa) which is concerned with marine life in coastal and marine areas, water pollution and environmental threats (Montague and Bruun, 1987); and the Israel Society for Ecology and Environmental Sciences, a scientific organisation based at the Hebrew University, Jerusalem; Council for a Beautiful Israel (Mo'atza le-eretz Yisrael yaffa), an independent public body concerned with furthering aesthetic cleanliness in public and private areas; Jewish National Fund JNF (Keren Kayemet le-Yisrael) a world-wide Jewish body concerned with land development and afforestation in Israel.

The Nature Reserves Authority was responsible for the nature reserves of Sinai when that region was under Israeli control. These areas are no longer under the NRA's authority following the official handing over of Sinai to Egypt in 1967 (Yehian, *in litt.*, 1980). The Golan Heights of southern Syria continue to be occupied as part of the Israeli Military Administration Zone. Parts of southern Lebanon, the so-called Israeli Occupied Security Zone, are also under Israeli military jurisdiction (1991). It is not known if the environmental organisations of Israel have any administrative role for protected areas in the occupied zone of Lebanon. However, the protected areas in the Golan Heights, together with those in the West Bank and Gaza Strip, are regarded as forming an essential part of the protected areas network of Israel and are under the nature protection jurisdiction of the NRA and NPA; SPNI undertakes field activities within these areas. The Forest Department has no responsibility for administering any forest reserves in the Gaza Strip (Bonneh, *in litt.*, 1990).

Surveys of the effectiveness of protected areas management have been undertaken, although information on the present situation is not available for this report. In the past both the Forest Department and the Soil Conservation Department, of the Land Development Authority, have worked together on land-use projects. Conflict has in the past occurred between the Land Development Authority, the Nature Reserves Authority and the National Parks Authority through differences in purpose and outlook. These organisations state that now the impetus is for open communication and cooperation emphasising a common drive towards conservation (Anon., 1990). Conflict still occurs between the Nature Reserves Authority and the military, which has in the past damaged a number of designated nature reserves. It has been regarded by the SPNI that the protected areas of the country are extremely small in size and therefore insufficient to

preserve the natural values, ecosystems and unique landscape (Sagi, 1991). Since establishment of the Environmental Protection Service, and its successor the Ministry of Environment, there have been marked improvements in certain environmental fields, notably in the control of marine pollution (Anon., 1988).

Systems Reviews   Bounded by Egypt, Jordan, Lebanon and Syria, the region is remarkably diverse for its size, both physically and biologically. Landscapes range from the mountains in the north to the Dead Sea, which is 400m below sea level, one of the lowest points on Earth. Rainfall varies from 1000mm in the north to 20mm in the south (in Eilat), the humidity gradient runs from the Mediterranean region in the north and west over a steppe intermediate zone to the desert regions of the south and east. The Negev desert covers over half of the surface area of the region. In the east, in the Jordanian rift valley, there are "tropical" enclaves (Gour-Tanguay, 1977). The region is the meeting point of the Mediterranean, Irano-Turanian and Saharo-Arabian climatic, phytogeographic and zoogeographical regions. Some 2,317 native plant species have been identified, of which 155 are endemic. In the north and north-west there are areas of deciduous *Quercus/Pistacia* forest. Throughout the Mediterranean region the climax vegetation is that of evergreen forests and maquis, dominated by oak *Quercus*; along the eastern and south-western borders of this region steppe forests become important, dominated by *Pistacia*, *Crataegus* and *Ziziphus*. In the south open dwarf shrub steppes are replaced by the desert communities of the stone deserts and the sand deserts in the western Negev (Davis *et al.*, 1986). At the southernmost part of the country, around Eilat, there is a small section of coastline bordering the Gulf of Aqaba in the Red Sea, which has important fringing coral reef communities. Other areas include the populated coastal Mediterranean conifer and maquis zone and a citrus growing coastal strip. Forests total little more than 115,000ha and consist of plantation, natural woodland as well as maquis scrub. Natural forest is estimated at being a total of 43,000ha. About 2,500 ha of woodland are replanted each year (Anon., 1990).

Reviews of the development of nature conservation programmes have been undertaken and relate to the establishment and expansion of the existing national protected areas network. Comprehensive surveys of biological resources and coastal resources have been undertaken as have land-use and landscape surveys and classifications. Studies have also been undertaken on the distribution and status of animals and plants. During the past three decades 26 species of higher plants, about 1% of the local flora, have been identified as becoming extinct (Dafni and Moshe, 1976). A major list of recommended and proposed nature conservation sites important for the protection of threatened species and ecosystems has been prepared by the Nature Reserves Authority. Officially proposed sites, between 20-30 in number, totalled over 44,000ha (Ashkenazi, 1986;

Glineur, n.d; Nature Reserves Authority, 1983, *in litt.*, 1987).

In order to secure the biodiversity and the visual resources of the country, what has been regarded as a new approach was formulated in the late 1980s in an effort to integrate development and conservation in those areas which had not yet been designated as protected. This followed with the conducting of nature and landscape surveys and evaluations. A model for landscape evaluation has been developed and the aim of mapping the entire unprotected open space landscape in the country has been devised. A preliminary classification identified four categories: protected area, open space landscape area, controlled development area, and building and development area. The aim of this was to incorporate environmentally-sound planning strategies into the overall national planning system (Sagi, 1991) (for details see SPNI, 1991).

Awareness of the need for nature conservation was stressed in the 1950s when researchers listed plant species on the verge of extinction and urged IUCN to assist Israel (Zohary, 1959). The first site to receive nature reserve status was Huleh Reserve in 26 November 1964, followed later that year by Eilat Coral Reef Nature Reserve. A series of nature reserves and national parks was designated at a steady rate across the country from that date onwards. The nature reserves in Sinai, designated under the 1963 Law, were reportedly abandoned when this region was officially transferred to Egyptian authority in 1967 (Yehian, *in litt.*, 1980). As of 1987, 40 areas have been given official legal status as national parks, totalling over 9,000ha, and 280 nature reserves with a total of over 230,000ha. The latter consists of 60,000ha of reserves with woodland (total figures include sites in the territories of the West Bank and Gaza Strip). By 1989 gazetted forest reserves covered a total of 43,000ha (Anon., 1990). Between 1985 and 1990 the increase in area of land protected for forest was only 600ha (Anon, 1990).

The region has been populated since the emergence of the earliest human cultures and the environment has increasingly been altered by man, by felled timber, forest and scrub fires, soil degradation and uncontrolled livestock grazing, as well as by being an arena of wars. The inhabitants of the region cut forest timber, for example on Mount Tabor, as long ago as 2,000 BC, an activity which continued until World War I, when the Ottoman Turks destroyed vast forest areas in order to build rail links to the Suez canal (NRA, 1972). In the early 1990s the region had a mixed economy heavily based on industry and agriculture. The most pressing environmental problem has been the exploitation of its water resources. From the beginning of this century until 1940 practically all the wetlands, totalling about 1,800ha, were drained. By 1948, the only large remaining wetland was Hula Swamp in the Jordan valley (6,000ha), of which only 314ha remained by the late 1980s (Carp, 1980). Between 1985 and 1990 the level of damage to forested protected areas has increased sharply due to forest arson. Fires in September 1989 spread across a major portion of Mount Carmel National Park, destroying 7500 dunams (727ha) of forest in one reserve (Alon, 1990). Generally throughout the entire region the total area of forest burnt during 1985 was 1,476ha (causing US$ 1.84 million of damage) compared to 6,315ha in 1989 (US$ 2.24 million) (Anon., 1990). The whole region has remained a highly militarised country since 1967. Despite genuine efforts to conserve wildlife and landscape under conditions of extreme economic or strategic pressure, designated reserve areas have been brought into agricultural, industrial or military use. For example, when Israel returned land to Egyptian administration, the Israeli armed forces are reported to have requisitioned a number of nature reserve areas in the Negev for military activities (Phillips, *in litt.*, 1986). Concern has been voiced over the threat to build what has been described as one of the largest transmission stations in the world in the Negev Desert, posing a potentially serious threat to migrating birds (Frumkin, *in litt.*, 1990). In the 1990-1991 Iraq-Kuwait military conflict, which led to the occupation of Kuwait, a limited amount of environmental damage was caused when missiles were fired into parts of Negev Conservation Area. Concern that chemical or biological weapons would be used was proven unfounded (Hunter, 1991).

Other Relevant Information   National and international tourism is of major importance to the region, with up to 1.65 million visitors in 1988 (Hunter, 1991). Visitors are catered for at many of the nature reserves and national parks, indeed in the legislation for national parks they are described as being " first and foremost intended for the enjoyment of the visitor". Well over 200,000 visitors per year visit En Gedi. Ecotourism is a major element of the activities organised by SPNI and associated tourist companies.

Addresses

Ministry of the Environment, PO Box 6158, JERUSALEM 91061 (Tel: 2 701 606; FAX: 2 385 038; Tlx: 25629 ENVIR IL)

Nature Reserves Authority, 78 Yirmiyahu Street, JERUSALEM 94467 (Tel: 2 387471; FAX: 2 383405)

National Parks Authority, 4 M. Makleff Street, Rehov Daled, Ha-Kirya, PO Box 7028, TEL AVIV 61070 (Tel: 3 252281)

Forest Department, Land Development Authority, (Keren Kayemeth Leisrael), PO Box 45, 26013 Kiryat-Hayim, 32000 HAIFA (Tel: 4 411983/414463; FAX: 4 411971; Tlx: 26112 KLL)

Society for the Protection of Nature in Israel (SPNI), 4 Hashfela Street, 66183 TEL AVIV (Tel: 3 375063; FAX: 3 377695; Tlx: 371478)

References

Alon, A. (1990). True rehabilitation for the forests of Mount Carmel. *Israel land and nature* 15(3): 108-109.

Amir, S. (1987). Classification of coastal resources: a Mediterranean Case Study. *Landscape and Urban Planning* 14: 399-414.

Anon. (1972). *Nature reserves in Israel.* Nature Reserves Authority.

Anon. (1983). *Society for the Protection of Nature in Israel (SPNI).* Brochure. SPNI, Tel Aviv.

Anon. (1984). Israel. *Environment Bulletin* 9(1): 7.

Anon. (1985). Nature Reserves Authority News sheet (untitled). 1 July.

Anon. (1988). Israel. *UNEP Regional Bulletin for Europe* 6: 9.

Anon. (1989). Governments, Israel. *Brundtland Bulletin* 4: 18-19.

Anon. (1990). National report on forestry in Israel. Report for the Tenth World Forestry Congress by the Land Development Authority, Kiryat-Hayim. 19 pp.

Baharav, D. and Meiboom, U. (1981). The status of the nubian ibex *Capra ibex nubiana* in the Sinai desert. *Biological Conservation* 20: 91-97.

Bjorhlund, M.I. (1974). Achievements in Marine Conservation: I. Marine Parks. *Environmental Conservation* 1(3).

Carp, E. (1980). *Directory of Western Palearctic wetlands.* IUCN, Gland, Switzerland. 506 pp.

Clark, B. (1990). HAI-BAR: Israel's programme to bring their wildlife home. *Zoo's Print* 5(1): 23-24.

Dafni, A. and Moshe, A. (1976). Extinct plants of Israel. *Biological Conservation* 10: 49-52.

Davis, S.D., Droop, S.J.M., Gregerson, P., Henson, L., Leon, C.J., Lamlein Villa-Lobos, J., Synge, H. and Zantovska, J. (1986). *Plants in danger: what do we know?* IUCN, Gland, Switzerland and Cambridge, UK. 461 pp.

Dov Por, F. and Ortal, R. (1985). River Jordan – the survival and future of a very special river. *Environmental Conservation* 12(3): 264-268.

EPS (1983). Environmental Protection Service. *Israel Environment Bulletin.* 5744 8(3).

Fishelson, L. (1985). Littoral marine ecosystems and marine parks of Israel. *Atti del Convegno Internazionale, I Parchi costieri Mediterranei.* Salerno-Castellabate. 18-22 Giugno, 1973. Regione campania assessorato per il Turismo. Pp. 453-468.

Furth, D. (1975). Israel, a great biogeographic crossroads. *Discovery* 11(1): 3-13.

Gour-Tanguay, R. (Ed.) (1977). Israel. *Environmental policies in developing countries.* Erich Schmidt Verlag.

Gryn-Ambroes, P. (1980). Preliminary annotated lists of existing and potential Mediterranean protected areas. UNEP/IG.20/INF.5.

Hunter, B. (Ed.) (1991). *The Statesman's Year Book 1991-92.* The Macmillan Press Ltd, London and Basingstoke. 1692 pp.

Lowdermilk, W.C. (1960). The reclamation of a man-made desert. IV. On Management and Buying Time.

Luckhurst, C. (n.d.) Environmental conservation in Israel. Anglo-Israel Association. Pamphlet No. 52.

Marinov, U. (1983). Environmental Management. Environmental Protection Service. *Israel Environment Bulletin* 5744 8(3): 1-4.

Montague, K. and Bruun, B. (1987). *Biological diversity in North Africa, the Middle East and Southwest Asia. A directory of organisations and institutions.* Holy land Conservation Fund, New York.

Nature Reserves Authority (1977). *Nature reserves in Israel.* Nature Reserves Authority, Tel-Aviv.

Nature Reserves Authority (1983). Nature reserves in Israel, their legal status. Nature Reserves Authority, Tel-Aviv. 18 pp.

Phillips, N. (1986). Report on visits made to institutions in Israel, May 1986. Memorandum. 7 pp.

Rabinov, D. (1981). *Nature conservation and environmental protection in the Negev Desert, a challenge for Israel in the 1980s.* Anglo-Israel Association, London. Pamphlet. No. 62.

Sagi, Y. (1991). Protection of open space landscape in areas exposed to massive development pressure. Paper 1. Society for the Protection of Nature in Israel. P. 3.

Sagi, Y. (1991b). The Ramat Hanadiv Project: integrated research, planning, education and management in an open space landscape. Paper 2. Society for the Protection of Nature in Israel. P. 4.

SPNI (n.d.). Landscape, nature and historic site conservation projects. SPNI Project Proposals. Society for the Protection of Nature in Israel.

SPNI (1991). Open spaces principles for building and development. Think tank for the integration of building and conservation of natural and open space resources. Society for the Protection of Nature in Israel. P. 5.

Weitz, J. (1974). *Forests and afforestation in Israel.* Massada Press, Jerusalem.

Zohary, M. (1959). Wild life protection in Israel, flora and vegetation. IUCN 7th Technical Meeting. Vol. 5: 199-202.

Zohary, M. (1959). Changes in the country vegetation. *Teva Va'aretz* 1: 325-329 (in Hebrew).

ANNEX
Definitions of protected area designations, as legislated, together with authorities responsible for their administration

Title: National Parks and Nature Reserves Law No. 5723

Date: 1963

Brief description: Providing for the creation of a protected areas system, with an administrative authority. It empowers the Ministry of the Interior to declare sites, and the Ministry of Agriculture to create regulations concerning protected fauna.

Administrative authority: Reshut Ha Gannim Ha-Le'Umi'im (National Parks Authority (NPA), Reshut Shmorot Ha-Tev'a (Nature Reserves Authority (NRA)

Designations:

Gan elumi (National park) Under the jurisdiction of the NPA

Large natural or semi-natural areas which "are first and foremost intended for the enjoyment of the visitor" and may include a strong element or priority for nature conservation, such as within designated nature reserves inside the park bounds.

They include man influenced landscapes such as planted meadows and pine tree plantations, along with archaeological sites and recreational facilities.

Otisar hatava (Nature reserve) Under the jurisdiction of the NRA. The majority are terrestrial sites but a number of coastal and marine area have also been declared since 1965. Many have management plans.

May also be declared inside national parks. They are divided into:

- *Scientific reserve* Sites set up to safeguard and protect threatened plants and animals. They can be used for scientific research but tend to be closed to the general public, any management is limited to ensure conservation protection;
- *Managed nature reserve* Semi-natural or natural sites which are partly open to public access, undergo some form of management and may include a large element of education to acquaint the public with landscapes and the natural environment.

Gan yanii (Marine park) Legally protected and managed by the NRA and Scientific Council.

Wardens patrol the areas and have official powers in each site. The formation of marine parks is carried out in accordance with the specific nature conservation values of each site, taking into account such aspects as the surrounding landuse complexity and ecological stability.

Collection, fishing, exploitation and destruction of designated marine species, including coral, is strictly prohibited and punishable by law.

Sources: Fishelson, 1985; Gour-Tanguay, 1977; NRA, 1972

Title: Palestine Forest Ordinance; Israel Forest Edict; Forest Regulations

Date: Ordinance of 1926; edict of 1956; regulations of 1960

Brief description: The enactment of the present Forest Ordinance dates from British Mandate legislation, and empowers the Ministry of Agriculture to declare certain areas as forest reserves, to control these areas and to declare certain types of tree in any part of the country as "protected trees". This act was accepted as law with the establishment of the state of Israel and strengthened in 1956. this act has since been renewed every 20 years.

Administrative authority: Forest Department, Keren Kayemeth Leisrael (Land Development Authority); Ministry of Agriculture

Designations:

Forest reserve Major functions of environmental, soil and dune stabilisation, wind brake, landscape improvement, pollution amelioration, social, recreation and tourism, grazing and nature conservation.

Extensive felling is forbidden without express permission of the Forestry Department.

Permitted activities include pruning or coppicing for charcoal and limited opening of dense oak maquis to prevent damage by wildfire.

Sources: Anon, 1990; Weitz, 1974

444

SUMMARY OF PROTECTED AREAS

Map[†] ref.	*National/international designations* Name of area	IUCN management category	Area (ha)	Year notified
	National Park			
1	Mount Carmel	V	8,400	
	Nature Reserves			
2	Amasa Mont	IV	1,145	1981
3	Bashanit Ridge	IV	1,037	1972
4	Beth-Saida	IV	1,050	
5	Carmel (Asdot Yagur, Nahal Me'aist, Qeren complex)	II	3,090	1971
6	Dead Sea cliffs	IV	6,475	1979
7	Ein Gedi	IV	2,780	1972
8	Einot Tzukim (Ein Fesh'ha)	IV	1,640	1980
9	Hai Bar Yotvata	IV	3,000	1970
10	Judean desert	IV	45,000	1980
11	Mashabim dunes	IV	1,300	
12	Mount Meron	IV	9,600	1956
13	Nahal K'ziv (Wadi Qurein)	IV	1,000	
14	Odem Forest	IV	1,100	1972
15	Ramon (Negev Makheteshim)	IV	100,000	
16	Susita	IV	1,017	1973
17	Wadi Meitzr	IV	1,054	1972
18	Wadi Yeetar	IV	1,468	1980
19	Yahudia Forest	IV	6,620	1973
20	Yatrata	IV	3,200	1970

[†]Locations of most protected areas are shown on the accompanying map.

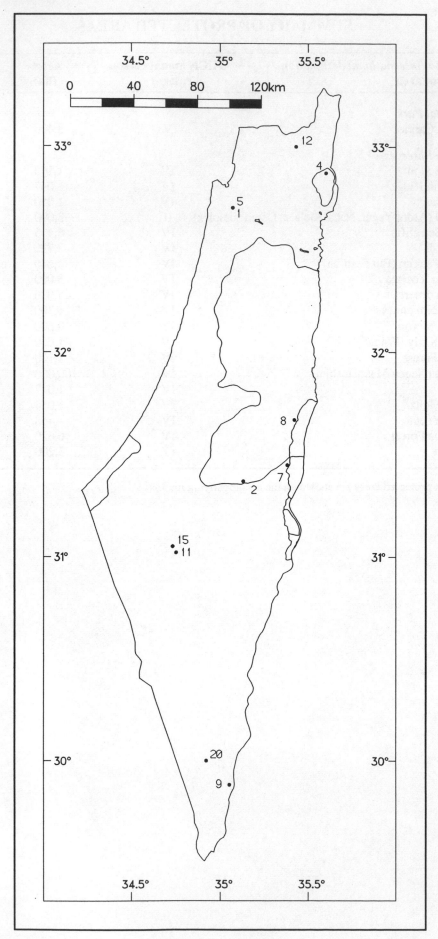

Protected Areas of Israel

JORDAN

Area 89,210 sq. km

Population 4,009,000 (1990)
Natural increase: 3.34% per annum

Economic Indicators
GDP: US$ 1,112 per capita (1987)
GNP: US$ 1,540 per capita (1987)

Policy and Legislation Jordan is a constitutional monarchy, with executive power vested in the King, who governs with the assistance of the Council of Ministers. Legislative power is vested in the national assembly. The Palestinian West Bank territory was placed under Jordanian rule in 1950 and occupied by Israel in 1967. Jordan relinquished all rights to the West Bank in July 1988.

Environmental protection has been included as a priority activity in the 1986-1990 development plan (McEachern, 1990). The existing network of areas protected specifically for nature conservation is covered under separate Royal proclamations. On 26 July 1965 the King issued a proclamation of intent to declare the first national park. Subsequently, the different categories of protected area, selected with the objective of protecting representative ecosystems with their characteristic fauna, flora and geomorphological features, were covered under Royal proclamation and include: national park, wildlife reserve, natural scenery area, game reserve, protected area and recreational area. Another category, marine nature reserve, has been established but legislation has yet to be approved (see Annex). National parks and historic monuments are proclaimed for their value as recreational or cultural wealth (see McEachern, 1990).

Provisions covering nature conservation in general are divided amongst the following laws: Woods and Forests Law of 1927 (amended 1951) covers protection of woods and forests and delimitation of protected forest boundaries; Law No. 18 of 1952 prohibits the grazing of goats; Law No. 20 of the Code of Agriculture (1973) relates to both state and private forests owned by individuals and corporate bodies. Legislation also relates to Ministry of Agriculture range reserves. In Article No. 180-186 of the Agricultural Act No. 20 (Part IV Aquatic Resources) there are declarations on marine or freshwater fishing areas, and areas and seasons in which fishing may be prohibited or specific kinds of fishing permitted. The Law of Hunting No. 28, 1957, Ordinance No. 1, 1958 relates to game protection and hunting of gazelle. This has been followed by Ordinance No. 2 1966 relating to general game protection. In 1979 the government declared a five-year ban on all hunting.

The National Environmental Strategy Project Steering Committee was formed in accordance with Cabinet Decision No. 7951 of 5 May 1988. A review of the existing legislation is currently being undertaken as part of preparation for the national environmental strategy, involving the Ministry of Municipal and Rural Affairs and Environment, Ministry of Energy and Mineral Resources, Ministry of Water and the University of Jordan. The proposed Law of Environment is currently under study at the Prime Ministry.

Deficiencies in prevailing conservation legislation have led to urgent requirements for the elaboration of a comprehensive laws on environmental protection (Anon., 1989; McEachern, 1990). In 1989 the Royal Letter of Designation to the government called for formulation and enactment of the appropriate legislation to protect the environment.

International Activities The Convention concerning the World Natural and Cultural Heritage (World Heritage Convention) was ratified on 5 May 1975, but no natural sites have been inscribed. On accession to the Convention on Wetlands of International Importance especially as Waterfowl Habitat (Ramsar Convention) on 10 January 1977 one site was listed. Jordan has ratified the UNEP Regional Convention for the Conservation of the Red Sea and Gulf of Aden Environment, 1982, and is a contracting party to the endangered species (CITES) Convention and the Hague Convention for the Protection of the Environment.

In 1986 discussions were proposed by WWF-International consultants on cooperation between Israeli and Jordanian authorities concerning a possible future transboundary or bi-lateral park including En Gedi Protected Area and Mujib Wildlife Reserve (Karpowicz, *in litt.*, 1986).

Administration and Management Protection of wildlife is the responsibility of the Forestry and Range Department of the Ministry of Agriculture. The Ministry of Agriculture, lacking expertise, delegates protected area establishment and management responsibilities to a private body, the Royal Society for the Conservation of Nature (RSCN) (formerly the Royal Jordanian Shooting Club). The RSCN, financed by both government and private donations, was set up in 1966 and is a nature conservation agency, handling wildlife conservation, management and control of hunting. From 1974 support was forthcoming from WWF and IUCN. The RSCN now also advises the government on hunting quotas, species and seasons, as well as issuing hunting licences (Science and Technology Division, 1979; Abu Jafar, *in litt.*, 1991).

The activities of the Department of National Parks of the Ministry of Tourism and Antiquities include restoration of antiquities and responsibility for the national parks and historic monuments system. Its operating costs in 1976 were JD 351,000, or 0.27% of the total annual budget (Clarke, 1976; McEachern, 1990; Science and Technology Division, 1979; Spangle, 1965).

The Ministry of Agriculture is the chief enforcement agency in state-owned forests and range reserves. Officers of the Ministry are authorised to seize forest products obtained without a licence and to arrest those illegally cutting timber within all state forest. The Forest Department controls about 131,500ha designated as forest land. The Forestry and Soil Conservation Directorate, under the Ministry of Agriculture, had an annual budget in 1976 of JD 367,800, or 0.27% of the total budget. The Directorate is composed of four divisions: Forestry, Investment and Protection, Soil Conservation and Nurseries.

The Natural Resources Authority (NRA), with an operating budget in 1976 of JD 1,575,000, or 1.2% of the total budget, was established to formulate a national water policy, as well as the utilisation and development of mineral resources. It cooperates with the Ministry of Agriculture in such matters as irrigation and reclamation. Its Water Resources Division is concerned with water pollution. The Jordan Valley Authority has responsibility for the economic development of the Jordan Valley, including water resources, irrigation and hydro-electric power stations. The Aqaba Regional Authority is directly involved in the management of Aqaba Marine Park and Nature Reserve (Abu Jafar, *in litt.*, 1989).

The Department of the Environment of the Ministry of Municipal and Rural Affairs and Environment, with collaboration from IUCN, has been managing the national environmental strategy project which includes elements for protected area designation, administration and management (McEachern, 1990; Fernando, pers. comm., 1991). The activities involve all other interested bodies including the Ministry of Agriculture, Ministry of Tourism and Antiquities, Royal Society for the Conservation of Nature, Ministry of Planning, Ministry of Water and Irrigation, Ministry of Energy and Mineral Resources, Aqaba Region Authority, and the University of Jordan, Yarmouk University, Jordan Armed Forces and Coast Guards (McEachern, 1990). Funding from IUCN and US-AID for the period to 1990 totalled US$ 123,798 and JD 32,636 (McEachern, 1990).

The Royal Society for the Conservation of Nature was established as a voluntary organisation in 1966 under the patronage of King Hussein Bin Talal (RSCN, 1987). Its chief goal is dedication to the conservation of nature and natural resources. It supervises and enforces many laws that are directly related to the conservation of nature, such as the enforcement of the hunting law. Following the Royal proclamation of protected areas, it has been establishing sites for wildlife conservation, undertaking activities including the reintroduction of globally endangered and locally extinct species to their natural habitat and protecting old buildings and sites that are considered part of the national heritage. It has also promoted the preparation of wildlife reserve

management plans, including those of Shaumari and Azraq reserves (Clarke, 1977, 1978; Conder, 1980). It is involved in nature conservation education, promoting public awareness of environmental issues, with special relevance to wildlife, by introducing them into the education programmes and the national school curriculum in cooperation with the Ministry of Education. The RSCN is governed by a central body in Amman which is responsible to the Director General. The RSCN is divided into three divisions: nature reserves, protection, information and public awareness. The Society planned to have 44 staff members by the end of 1988, eleven in administrative positions and the remainder in the field. By 1991 there were 45 employees directly employed in protected areas and six indirectly (Maher abou Jafer, 1991). The protected area staff includes an assistant director (wildlife reserves), below whom are chief wardens for each reserve managing the field staff. The RSCN budget comes from membership fees, government budget allocations and gifts, as well as donations and technical assistance offered by regional and international organisations such as IUCN, WWF and US-AID (Abu Jafar, *in litt.*, 1991). The RSCN is the largest non-governmental organisation in Jordan, and through its public awareness division promotes the establishment of wildlife conservation clubs at schools throughout the country. It publishes the quarterly *El-Reem* magazine in Arabic, which carries articles concentrating on wildlife conservation. By 1991, RSCN had established 150 clubs (Maher abou Jafer, *in litt.*, 1991).

In 1989 Crown Prince El-Hassan, chairman of the Higher Council for Science and Technology, declared the establishment of an environmental research centre (replacing the Environmental Pollution Studies division) as part of the Royal Scientific Society (RSS). Its priorities will be directed towards ecology and pollution control of water, soil and air (Mulki, *in litt.*, 1989).

Effectiveness of protected areas management is hampered by inadequate wildlife protection laws, by poor management of grazing land and insufficient financial support for wildlife conservation agencies. The national park category is further hampered by minimal regulations protecting the environment and none to prevent destruction of plant and animal species. It also lacks specialised and qualified management capable of bringing these sites up to the standard of national parks in the international sense (McEachern, 1990).

Systems Reviews The bioclimate is generally classed as Mediterranean, with prevailing winds and precipitation coming from the west. The country is divided into eight regions situated in the Irano-Turanian and Saharo-Sindian vegetation zones (Madany, 1978). The vegetation is classified into 13 divisions largely typified by dwarf shrubs, grassy plants and herbs (for lists see Madany, 1978; McEachern, 1990). The Gulf of Aqaba contains some of the most northern coral reefs and mangrove stands in the world. Millenia of human occupation in the Middle East has resulted in drastic changes to the environment and vegetation cover, leading to the replacement of natural vegetation by secondary species and the resulting altered plant associations over most of the country. Only some 10% of total land area is cultivable and only 4.2% can be considered as suitable for rainfed farming. Currently forests cover less than 1% of the total country (736,000 dunums) and are restricted to the northern and southern highlands (Willimott, 1978, quoted in Science and Technology, 1979). It is estimated that there are up to 2,300-2,400 species of vascular plant, of which 100 are endemic and 100-150 are threatened. There are 70 species of mammal and 360 species of bird (lists in McEachern, 1990).

The RSCN has encouraged the development of a national conservation strategy, promoted by the government following initial surveys by British consultants in 1963. In that year King Hussein contracted researchers to conduct an extensive survey of wildlife, with the intention of recommending the establishment of national parks and reserves for the protection of both wildlife resources and features of archaeological and geological interest. Three sites were recommended: Azraq Oasis, Petra in the southern highlands and Wadi Rum in the Rift Valley (Mountfort, 1969; Maher abou Jafar, *in litt.*, 1991).

Jordan is one of the first countries of the region to consider establishing a national strategy for the environment, the government instigating its national environmental strategy (NES) in 1988. The committee consists of eight specialist working groups including the Committee for the Wildlife and Habitat Sector. The strategy is a cooperative project between the government, IUCN and US-AID. It draws on the principles of the World Conservation Strategy and maps out long-term conservation planning in Jordan into the 21st century. Its preparation has involved experts from relevant governmental bodies as well as private agencies and organisations.

The Aqaba South Coast Master Plan, which was prepared under the auspices of the Aqaba Region Authority, involved preparing a coastal zone management plan for the entire Aqaba region. Within this framework environmental and ecological impact analysis has involved agricultural consultants. Three areas of coral habitat were designated as a coral reserve, Aqaba Marine Nature Reserve (Aqaba Region Authority, n.d.).

The first protected area declared by Royal statute was Shaumari Reserve near Azraq in 1965. Wildlife reserves have been selected with the objective of protecting representative ecosystems and their wildlife. By comparison historic national parks have been declared for their cultural interest, and range reserves managed for livestock grazing. In 1991 the reserves system included 12 wildlife reserve sites (3 designated sites; 3 under construction and 6 proposed), the largest of which totalled 54,000ha. The RSCN is in the process of establishing the six wildlife reserves, in order to achieve optimal protection of threatened ecosystems and their associated fauna and flora (Maher abou Jafer, *in litt.*, 1991). Sites based on the proposed list in the draft NES continue to be designated each year. The reserve system as a whole is intended to encompass 4.2% of the natural land area of the country by the end of the 1990s. In addition, proposals in the NES indicate that the area of protected range or grazing reserves will continue to expand under the auspices of the Ministry of Agriculture. By 1990 the total area of grazing reserves had risen to 20,360-50,000ha (McEachern, 1990).

WWF Project No. 3802, in collaboration with the RSCN and IUCN, involves establishment and management of Zubiya Reserve under the active involvement of an IUCN Jordan project manager (Fernando, pers. comm., 1991). Specific activities at these sites include those of the RSCN which undertakes release projects of Arabian oryx at Shaumari Reserve and Persian fallow deer at Zubiya Reserve (Abu Jafar, *in litt.*, 1991; Fernando, pers. comm., 1991). The RSCN also contributes to forest planting and establishment in order to prevent desertification. Public land is provided by the Department of Real Estate and the Ministry of Agriculture donates the saplings. Early attempts at reforestation were made in 1943, followed by systematic efforts from 1948 onwards. Areas of planted forest increased to 94,000ha in 1976 and to date five forest areas have been established by the RSCN (Science and Technology, 1979; Maher Abu Jafer, *in litt.*, 1991; Fernando, pers. comm., 1991). Other bodies interested in aiding environmental conservation include the World Bank which, following a 1991 mission, was reviewing the possibility of funding development of a number of projects in wildlife reserves (Scott, *in litt.*, 1991).

The main environmental problems relating specifically to protected areas include deforestation, reclamation of wetlands, soil salination, air pollution, overgrazing and hunting. Azraq Wetland is reported to have been seriously affected by water extraction and pollution, as well as by impact from refugee camps in the area (Ramsar Secretariat, 1991). In the 1970s a major environmental impact study, to assess the adverse effects on the human and natural environment of the Maqarin dam on the Yarmouk river (Jordan Valley irrigation system project stage II), was completed by US-AID (Little, 1979, cited in Science and Technology, 1979). River pollution is a major problem in the Zarqa, pollution sources being untreated domestic waste, phosphate mines, oil refineries and heavy industry (Ilani and Shalmon, 1985; Science and Technology, 1979). Other adverse environmental changes have included river diversion schemes, such as the construction of 96km of the East Ghar Canal to form the Ziglab Reservoir. Proposals exist to divert the Yarmnouk River to permit the extension of the canal by 14.5km to the Dead Sea.

Addresses

Director, National Parks and Historical Monuments Section, Ministry of Tourism and Antiquities,

PO Box 224, AMMAN (Tel: 44336/44320; Tlx: 21741)

Director of Forest and Range, Ministry of Agriculture, PO Box 2179, AMMAN

The Royal Society for the Conservation of Nature (RSCN) (Director General), PO Box 6354, AMMAN (Tel: 811689/814526; FAX: 009626/628258)

References

Anon. (1989). Protecting the environment. *Jordan Times.* 31 July. P. 3.

Aqaba Region Authority. (n.d.). The south coast tourist area, Aqaba Master Plan, Prospectus. Hashemite Kingdom of Jordan.

Bauman, F. (1979). *Draft Environmental Report on Jordan.* Science and Technology Division, Library of Congress Washington, DC.

Boyd, M. (1966). International Jordan Expedition 1966 Report. IBP/CT Section. London.

Clarke, J.E. (1976). A preliminary study of Jordan's proposed national parks. Unpublished document produced by the RSCN, Amman.

Clarke, J.E. (1977). Shaumari Wildlife Reserve Management Plan. RSCN, Amman.

Clarke, J.E. (1978). Azraq Desert Reserve, Jordan, Development Plan, RSCN, Amman.

Clarke, J.E. (1977). Reserve for Arabian oryx. *Oryx* 14(1): 31-35.

Clarke, J.E. (1979). Some personal experiences of conservation in dry land. *Black Lechwe* 13(1): 6-9.

Clarke, J.E. (1981). *A model wildlife program for developing countries.* Unpublished PhD Dissertation. Athens, Georgia, USA.

Condor, P.J. (1980). Proposed Management Plan for the Azraq Wetland reserve. Prepared for the RSCN by WWF/IUCN Consultant. January.

Fitter, M. (1967). New hope for wildlife in Jordan. *Oryx* 9: 35-38.

Hemsley, J.H. and George, M. (1966). Azraq desert national park, Jordan. Draft management plan. Unpublished report issued by IBP/CT Section, London.

Ilani, G. and Shalman, B. (1985). Nature protection in Jordan. Report.

Jafar, M.A. (1984). *National parks and nature reserves in the Arab World.* The Arab League Educational, Cultural, and Scientific Organization, Department of Sciences, Tunis.

Madany, M.H. (1978). *An ecological framework for a nature preserve system in Jordan.* Unpublished BSc Thesis. The University of Illinois, Urbana, Illinois, USA.

Matthews, M. (1986). Conservation news from Jordan. *Oryx* 20(3): 143-144.

McEachern, J. (1989). Report on project activities, National Environment Strategy Jordan (for the period June through August 1989). National Environment Strategy, c/o Department of Environment.

McEachern, J. (1990). Report on project activities, National Environment Strategy Jordan (September 1989 through January 1990). National Environment Strategy, c/o Department of Environment. IUCN Project Office, 31 January 1990.

McGregor, A. (1985). Bringing back the oryx and the ostrich. Nature conservation in Jordan: Part 1. *The Times.* 29 July. P. 5.

Montague, K. and Bruun, B. (1987). *Biological diversity in North Africa, the Middle East and Southwest Asia, a directory of organisations and institutions.* HLCF, New York, USA.

Mountfort, G. (1969). Jordan's National Parks. *Aramco World* 1(20): 34-37.

Nelson, J.B. (1973). *Azraq: desert oasis.* Allen Lane, London.

Ormond, R. (1978). A marine park for Jordan, report on the feasibility of establishing a marine park at Aqaba. Prepared for ALECSO, Red Sea and Gulf of Aden Marine Environmental Programme. Report.

Science and Technology Division (1979). Draft environmental report on Jordan. Contract AID/DS/ST No. SA/TOA 1-77. US MAB Secretariat. Library of Congress, Washington DC.

Spangle, P.F. (1965). Interpretation in the national parks and historic monuments of Jordan. Report to USAID/Jordan in accordance with PASA NESA (IF)-1-66. United States Department of the Interior, National Parks service.

ANNEX
Definitions of protected area designations, as legislated, together with authorities responsible for their administration

Title: Royal Proclamations on Wildlife Reserves

Date: Individually decreed, the first in 1965

Brief description: Wildlife reserves are individually decreed by Royal Proclamation and subsequently established under the administration and management of the RSCN in order to protect threatened wildlife and habitats.

Administrative authority: Royal Society for the Conservation of Nature

Designations:

The different categories of protected area include the following:

Wetland reserve Proclaimed to meet internationally recognised strict nature reserve criteria. The first site in this category was designated in 1965 under Royal proclamation.

Hunting, grazing, and other damaging activities are restricted or prohibited, although until 1979 widespread bird hunting was a major concern.

Wildlife reserve or reserve Proclaimed in order to meet internationally recognised managed nature reserve criteria. Sites in this category have been established since 1975 by Royal proclamation, each protected area being established under individual decrees.

Set up to protect indigenous fauna and flora and their natural habitats. The sites exclude trespass, hunting, grazing, and other major damaging activities.

Regulations identify that wildlife reserves exclude all agriculture, pastoralism, fishing, mining and industrial activity.

Under local regulations many sites are fenced and patrolled by wardens.

Marine park and nature reserve A category which has yet to be proclaimed by Royal Decree although one site has already been officially established. The site is managed by the Aqaba Regional Authority in Aqaba.

Regulations for this class of protected area include restriction of fishing and coral damage, restricting access (by fencing the reefs), and minimising the effects of pollution (by the use of suitable booms). Research is a key element of this category.

Title: Royal Proclamations on National Parks

Date: Individually decreed, the first in 1965

Brief description: National parks are established primarily for protection of the cultural heritage, for recreation and landscape although often encompass large buffer areas of natural environment. They are individually decreed and subsequently established under the administration and management of the Department of National Parks and Historic Monuments.

Administrative authority: Department of National Parks and Historic Monuments, Ministry of Tourism and Antiquities

Designations:

National park Set up to protect archaeological monuments. Regulations specify protection of the monuments, and include a significant element of tourist recreation. In certain parks buffer areas surround the monument and provide protection to nature, in others they encompass areas of forest.

There are no specific regulations protecting the environment or wildlife species within the parks.

Title: Woods and Forests Law and associated Code of Agriculture

Date: Law dated 1927 (amended 1951); Code dated 1973

Brief description: Covers protection of woods and forests and delimitation of protected forest boundaries.

Administrative authority: Ministry of Agriculture

Designations:

Protected forest land Law No. 20 of the Code of Agriculture (1973) relates to both state and private forests owned by individuals and corporate bodies.

Part X refers to the conservation of trees and provides for action to be taken against persons who raise or allow their livestock to cause damage to trees.

Part XI indicates that a licence is required for the cutting of wood from government or private forests.

The associated Law No. 18 of 1952 prohibits the grazing of goats in forest land.

Title: Natural Resources Authority Law No. 12

Date: 1968

Brief description: The law refers specifically to regulations within state forest.

Administrative authority: Ministry of Agriculture

Designations:

State forest The Law places prohibition on habitation within government forests, forcing those remaining to evacuation or liability to imprisonment; grazing on forested land is prohibited without authorization; cutting of forest trees of any kind is not permitted during the period March to end May.

In Article 144-155 of Act No. 20, the hunting of birds and wildlife is prohibited without authorization from the Ministry of Agriculture.

Marine area Articles 180-186 of the same Act, Part IV Aquatic Resources, makes declarations on marine or freshwater fishing areas, and areas and seasons in which fishing may be prohibited or specific kinds of fishing permitted.

SUMMARY OF PROTECTED AREAS

Map ref.	*National/international designations* Name of area	IUCN management category	Area (ha)	Year notified
	National Park			
1	Petra	V	20,000	
	Wildlife Reserves			
2	Dana	IV	15,000	1989
3	Shaumari	IV	2,200	1975
4	Wadi Mujib	IV	21,200	1985
5	Wadi Rum	IV	7,500	1989
6	Zubiya	IV	1,300	1987
	Wetland Reserve			
7	Azraq	I	1,200	1965
	Reserve			
8	Azraq Desert	IV	32,000	1987
	Ramsar Wetland Azraq Oasis	R	7,372	1977

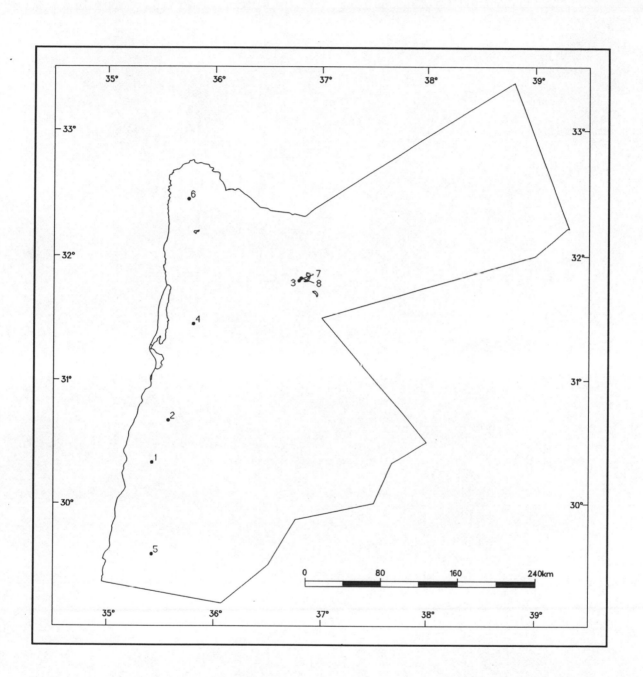

Protected Areas of Jordan

KUWAIT

Area 17,820 sq. km

Population 2.1 million (1989)
Natural increase: 2.8% per annum

Economic Indicators
GDP: US$ 9,751 per capita (1987)
GNP: US$ 14,870 per capita (1987)

Policy and Legislation In 1899 a treaty was signed with the United Kingdom recognising Kuwait as an independent government and state under British protection. In 1961, full independence and sovereignty was recognised with the ending of the 1899 Treaty. Kuwait is ruled by an Amir vesting executive authority in a Council of Ministers. Following invasion of Kuwait by Iraq on 2 August 1990, Iraq declared the annexation of Kuwait as part of the al-Basrah Governorate on the 8 August 1990. It withdrew unconditionally on the 28 February 1991 following military action authorised by United Nations Security Council Resolutions on 29 November 1990.

The Kuwaiti legal system subscribes to the Islamic law, Sharia, which is both state and religious. Traditional forms of nature protection in the region had their origins over 2,000 years ago and were subsequently adopted by the prophet Mohammed who established a legal system that continues to govern hema protected areas in a number of Gulf states. The territory of Kuwait has traditionally long been regarded as a vast hema. However, over the last two decades traditional practices have broken down as a consequence of urban development and industrialisation (Alsdirawi, *in litt.*, 1991).

Legislation relating to protected areas is based on Decree No. 18, 1968 which states that "Non-urban lands are government property and not permitted for public use, unless permission is authorised by the allocating agency". As such, Kuwait municipality has control of the land-use in all designated nature conservation areas and has the right to remove unauthorised users. The master plan of 1971 states "the Zor area should be considered for the enjoyment of many people...conservation should be given to designating a nature reserve in the area of Umm ar-Rimam" (KISR, 1986). Subsequent master plan reviews were undertaken in 1978 and 1983, stressing the need for protected area establishment (KISR, 1986).

The main piece of legislation governing protected areas and the protection of the environment is Decree Law No. 62/1980. Article 3 Item 1 indicates a general policy for the protection of the environment. This encompasses five main areas of which the conservation of nature and natural resources is one. This document is a general guideline or strategy and a detailed and comprehensive plan has still to be prepared and adopted. Section 2 of the general framework for environment protection deals with the preservation of nature and natural resources. Section 2a covers nature, it encompasses the necessary legislation, regulations and codes of practice, the provisions of adequate funds, manpower and legal capabilities to implement a comprehensive national plan. This plan should include the mode for preservation of the desert environment through: designation of certain areas and the means for designation, training manpower, surveys of flora and fauna to determine the species which are endangered, the use of experience of other countries to prepare management plans and environmental impact statement, and investigation of the possibilities of reinstating wildlife. Section G indicates the mode of protecting coral reefs. Section H includes the sentence "establish protected areas for plants and wildlife". Finally Section 5 deals with the "preservation of national heritage" and indicates the desirability to conserve historical buildings.

As a consequence of Decree Law No. 62/1980 Article 2, the Minister of Public Health was required to create a Council for Environment Protection, the Environment Protection Council (EPC), under the Minister. Under Article 3, the EPC is empowered to suggest a general policy for the protection of the environment and to propose protected areas, working with the municipality and other relevant agencies. Any recommendations have to be ratified and legislated for by the Council of Ministers.

Additional legislation or regulations on the environment in force prior to the August 1990 military occupation included the following: prohibition of commercial fishing of shrimp, including in important wetland areas, during the spawning season. Measures had also been taken to prevent the decline of marine turtles. By contrast, hunting was permitted throughout the country and there were no laws for its regulation (Maher abou Jaafer, 1984; Pilcher, pers. comm., 1991).

Under Decree No. 1964 oil discharge in territorial waters extending 50 miles from land and in the internal waters of Kuwait Bay is prohibited; fines and charges for clean-up of oil spills could be imposed on polluters. This Decree has particular relevance to the protection of the waters around coral islands. At the time of writing (1991), restrictions of movement in the Gulf continued to be restricted under military jurisdiction (Gwynne, pers. comm., 1991; Alsdirawi, *in litt.*, 1991).

Before the suspension of legislative activities in August 1990, as a result of Iraqi occupation, Kuwait was in the final stages of developing a detailed protected areas system.

International Activities Kuwait has not acceded to the Convention on Wetlands of International Importance especially as Waterfowl Habitat (Ramsar Convention), nor to the Convention concerning the Protection of the

World Cultural and Natural Heritage (World Heritage Convention).

Kuwait is a contracting part to the Kuwait Regional Convention for Cooperation on the Protection of the Marine Environment from Pollution (1978), and actively participates in meetings concerned with additional protocols and the Kuwait Action Plan (UNEP Regional Seas Programme for the Arabian Gulf). Coordination of the related action plan is by the Regional Organization for Protection of the Marine Environment (ROPME). The "Kuwait Regional Conference of Plenipotentiaries on the Protection and Development of the Marine Environment and the Coastal Areas" was convened by UNEP in Kuwait, 15-23 April 1978, and led to the adoption of the Action Plan (KAP) for the protection and development of the marine environment and the coastal areas of Bahrain, Iran, Iraq, Kuwait, Oman, Qatar, Saudi Arabia and United Arab Emirates (UNEP, 1983).

In 1986 the first Arabian Gulf conference on the marine environment and pollution was convened in Kuwait under the auspices of Kuwait University, the Kuwait Foundation for the Advancement of Sciences and the Kuwait Environment Protection Council, published proceeding were produced in 1986 (Halwagy *et al.*, 1986).

Following the hostilities arising from the occupation of Kuwait by Iraq from 2 August 1990 to February 1991, the UN Inter-Agency Consultation of Environmental Consequences of the Gulf War, convened by UNEP, stressed the serious potential consequences, especially for human health, of the introduction into the environment of chemical, biological and nuclear contaminants. Long-term monitoring of the environmental effects was identified as being necessary and, as a consequence, numerous governmental and non-governmental bodies have undertaken assessment programmes of the environmental situation in Kuwait. A consortium of UNEP-sponsored consultants is currently assisting in promoting and developing the ROPME Secretariat in Kuwait.

To protect the ecological integrity of the coastal and marine environment, a peace park was proposed by the World Conservation Monitoring Centre, incorporating the headwaters and north-east shore of the Arabian Gulf (WCMC, 1991b).

Administration and Management The protected areas system is under the management and direct supervision of the Public Authority for Agriculture and Fisheries (PAAF). By the 1980 Law, the Ministry of Public Health was obliged to create a Council, the Environment Protection Council (EPC) (Alsdirawi, 1991). The EPC was chaired by the Minister with membership of representatives of the ministries of Public Works, Commerce and Industry, Planning, Interior, Public Health, Electricity and Water, Communications and Oil, Kuwait Municipality, Directorate General of Shuaib Industrial area and

Kuwait Institute for Scientific Research (KISR). The EPC was established in 1980 and empowered by decree to propose a general policy for the protection of the environment, short and long-term integrated work plans, to coordinate activities, study pollution problems and prepare research policies, regulations and coordinate Kuwait's ratification of appropriate regional and international agreements. The EPC has also been empowered to carry out flora and faunal surveys and be involved in active protected area management.

Identification and subsequent allocation of land for any use, including parks and designated areas, is the sole responsibility of the Municipal Council, Kuwait Municipality. Development and management plans for these lands also have to be approved by the Ministry of Public Works, Ministry of Water and Electricity, Ministry of Petroleum, Ministry of Defence and Ministry of Interior.

The government has previously allocated over KD 2 million (KD 0.294 = US$ 1) for planning, research and assessment of renewable desert resources (1990). In the original proposals in 1986, the annual running budget for the first national park were estimated at KD 0.7-0.9 million with a fully functional administration and necessary maintenance (KISR, 1986). In the first year since establishment of the park in 1990, a total of KD 1 million was allocated for 2m-high galvanised fencing and for wardening (Alsdirawi, 1991). The first national park was established in part for habitat preservation, education and recreation; the park has become a favoured camping site. Efforts were being made, prior to fencing of the project in 1990, to educate the public regarding the importance of protection as a management tool for restoration of the natural vegetation. Implementation of master plans for protected areas have taken into consideration the primary objectives and functions of the park to preserve the natural and ecological components, provide education with proper land use, provide areas for environmental and ecological research, and provide facilities for education and training (KISR, 1986). Selection criteria for the various zones are listed by KISR: strict nature zone, managed nature zone, protected landscape, park headquarters and visitor centre, camping area, hiking trail and education and research areas (KISR, 1986). A number of reserves were established and fenced in May 1990 (Boulos, pers. comm., 1991; Pilcher, pers. comm., 1991).

The Kuwait Institute for Scientific Research (KISR), established in 1967, is involved in protection and management of the environment in addition to undertaking research on coastal ecosystems and in providing scientific support for the oil sector. In the 1980s, KISR was contracted to prepare the reports on the criteria for development and management of first national park of the country. KISR is in the process of preparing a plan for a living museum, with objectives to inform and entertain visitors (1991). In 1990 KISR had been collecting scientific information that could enhance

Failaka Island as a nature reserve for the breeding and reintroduction of locally eradicated endangered wildlife (Alsdirawi, 1991; KISR, 1986; Sardar, 1982).

The other bodies effectively undertaking protected area management include the Ministry of Petroleum and Kuwait Oil Company, which manages the oil fields of the country. Its six main exclusive right areas act as *de facto* protected areas, through prohibition of livestock grazing around oil fields (for the areas concerned see the National Physical Planning Strategy Map). Patrolling of areas is maintained by the military authorities. Designated military areas and reserve areas for exploitation of known underground water are also identified under the master plan, as are protected exclosures (Alsdirawi, *in litt.*, 1991). The Ministry of Water and Electricity has rights over the underground water areas. In all forms of environmental protection, police posts are used in coordination with protected area management (Pilcher, pers. comm., 1991). The Agriculture Affairs and Fish Resources Authority has undertaken various special protection measures, including fencing of Talha Acacia Enclosure, together with an integrated programme to set up a seedling nursery and replanting of this endangered plant species in protected areas (KISR, 1986; Boulos, pers. comm., 1991).

Amongst the many bodies, in addition to KISR, which undertake environmentally related research in protected areas is the Department of Agriculture of the Ministry of Public Works. It established an agricultural experimental station in 1953 to carry out research in plant protection, arid zone research, afforestation in protected areas and fisheries, amongst other disciplines (Sardar, 1982). The Regional Organisation for the Protection of the Marine Environment (ROPME), with offices based in Kuwait, has been actively involved in evaluating the action plan, including its marine pollution monitoring and research programme. This included organising the "coastal area development" workshop which concentrated on planning the development of a regional strategy for coastal zone management in the Arabian Gulf area. Subsequently, ROPME, in cooperation with UNEP, has been organising the preparation of draft plans for regional coastal zone management strategies. ROPME was also instrumental in the clean-up operation of the oil spills of the Iraq-Kuwait conflict of 1991.

Master plan reviews stressed the urgency of developing protection measures. Such areas would be fenced reserves where prime objectives would be protection of the natural environment. To promote an action plan for the development of Jal az Zor National Park, Kuwait Municipality and KISR collected detailed scientific information on the ecological components of the designated park and assessed and proposed management and administration plans (KISR, 1986). Various interested bodies were involved, including the Agriculture Affairs and Fish Resources Authority, Ministry of Electricity and Water, Ministry of Defence, Kuwait Oil Company, Environmental Protection Council, Ministry of Public Works, Ministry of Interior and the Touristic Enterprises Company. Proposals were then made with three administrative alternatives: a) to establish a new government body "the general authority for national parks" that would be attached to the offices of the Crown Prince to address policy issues and advise on park matters; b) to create a new department within the Agricultural Affairs and Fish Resources Authority. It was recommended that the office not be attached to any existing department; c) to establish an autonomous body to manage the park similar to the public share holding company concept, except that funding would be primarily from the government (KISR, 1986).

At the present time there are no private protected areas, although an individual is currently proposing to set up a reserve, and the government is reviewing its feasibility (Alsdirawi, *in litt.*, 1991). Non-governmental agencies involved in nature conservation and environmental assessment include the Ahmadi Natural History and Field Studies Group, which was formed in 1969 under the sponsorship of the Kuwait Oil Company, to encourage field studies, maintain contact with other institutions and help disseminate knowledge and to act as a conservation forum (Clayton and Pilcher, 1983; Tye, pers. comm., 1991). Ornithological material collected over 60 years has been computerised by volunteers (Pilcher, C.). Consultants (Pilcher, C.) coordinating with the EPC have produced habitat surveys, records of distribution and status of birds throughout the entire country in 1986 and 1987 (Pilcher, pers. comm., 1991; Tye, pers. comm., 1991).

Amongst the various management constraints identified, perhaps the chief concern is the poor practical coordination between the various administrative and management bodies. Although active within the country, the applied activities of non-governmental conservation bodies appear to provide little input into protected areas conservation.

Systems Reviews Kuwait is bounded in the east by the Arabian or Persian Gulf, north and west by Iraq and south and west by Saudi Arabia. Situated at the "crossroads" between the Palaearctic, Afro-Tropical and Indo-Malayan realms, Kuwait harbours a varied fauna and flora, but with relatively few species and a very low incidence of endemism. There are some 400 recorded species of plants, 28 mammalian species and over 300 bird species. The majority of Kuwait is desert plain covered in sparse scrub with perennial, and often salt tolerant, herbs and ephemerals (Daoud, 1985; Halwagy and Halwagy, 1974a, 1974b; Vessey-Fitzgerald, 1957). The Kuwaiti Gulf is represented by at least four critical marine habitats: coastal marsh and mudflat, coral reef, seagrass bed and mangrove. Several coral islands are major nesting areas for eight species of tern, Socotra cormorant and of two species of globally threatened turtle. Sublittoral rock habitats, rich in seaweed beds, are economically important for shrimps, pearl oysters and abalone fisheries (e.g. Kuwait Bay).

Of the large mammals four are already believed to be extinct (Asiatic cheetah, and Dorcas, mountain and Arabian sand gazelles), three are marine mammals, and two (grey wolf and caracal) have been recorded, but are probably only extremely rare vagrants from Iraq and Saudi Arabia. The region is important as a migration route for 2-3 million birds, involving up to 200 species (KISR, 1986; Tye, pers. comm., 1991). The reptile fauna is known to be relatively depauperate, with no endemic species, although 20 species have been recorded at Jal az Zor National Park (KISR, 1986).

Under studies for the National Physical Plan of 1971, prepared by the consultants Colin Buchanon and Partners, four national recreation areas, three national parks and two nature reserves were proposed (Anon., 1971, 1972). This was followed in 1976 by a UNEP report concerned with broad environmental issues (McMichael, 1976). The environmental plan outlined in the second five-year development plan (1977-1981) had as its objective the protection of all elements of the environment, and included policies on the formulation of a comprehensive plan for environmental protection, the drafting of an environmental law and the establishing of an agency for environmental protection (FAO, 1976). In 1980, KISR was requested by Kuwait Municipality to undertake a feasibility study on establishing national parks and nature reserves. This preliminary study identified areas in the north-east combining interests in varieties of animal and plant life with significant landscape features (KISR, 1986; Taha and Omar, 1982). The second phase of the project "Selection and criteria for establishment of national parks/nature reserves in Kuwait" was initiated in 1984 for a 22-month period (Omar *et al.*, 1984). The major emphasis was on identifying sizes and uses within designated areas. A result was the four-volume work *Criteria for development and management of Kuwait's first national park/nature reserve* (KISR, 1986). In this publication, details of other sites suitable as national parks were given following reconnaissance field surveys (KISR, 1986). The surveys were limited to areas delineated by Kuwait Municipality in its master plan second review (KMPR2, 1983). Three desert areas were investigated and proposed as national parks or equivalent reserves (Al Baytin, Um-Niqa and Al-Khiran) and five Kuwaiti islands were recommended as marine parks (Kubbar, Qaru, Bubiyan, Umm al-Muradum and part of Failaka) (KISR, 1986). The marine park designations were presented by the Department of Mariculture and Fisheries, Food Resources Division of KISR (KISR, 1986). In the spring seasons of 1986 and 1987, a countrywide survey of bird species and habitats was coordinated under the auspices of the EPC, with the intention of proposing important nature conservation areas for protection. The International Council for Bird Preservation coordinated further ornithological surveys in 1991 (Tye, pers. comm., 1991; Evans, *in litt.*, 1991). In 1980 an environmental sensitivity index (ESI) was undertaken by a joint team of the University of Kuwait and American consultants (Caulton and Keddie, 1990).

The purpose was to assess the possible impact of a major oil spillage in the Gulf reaching the Kuwait coastline, and to make recommendations for specific maritime habitats and their faunal and flora communities (Al-Sawari *et al.*, 1985).

Under the 1980 Law implications of activities on the environment are required. In April 1987, specialists visited Kuwait to undertake an environmental impact assessment in the south of the country for the consultants involved in planning Al Khiran new town. This area was of natural importance for Al Khiran Desert Park proposed in Kuwait Municipality master plans and for Khawr al Mufattah marshland (Caulton, 1987; Tye, pers. comm., 1991).

Programmes to establish further protected areas in the desert areas of southern Kuwait and to pass enabling protected area legislation were seriously affected by the Iraqi occupation of Kuwait during 1990 and early 1991 (Wells, 1991; Pilcher, pers. comm., 1991). Programmes to prevent desertification ("re-greening" programmes) were also well underway in the 1986/87 period. By 1986 a wildlife reintroduction programme had been officially recommended for the country, six habitats had been selected with recommendations for immediate protection; coastal mudflat, salt marsh and associated sand dunes, artificial oasis, escarpment and wadi, and gravel sandy area. Proposed introductions of wildlife included either locally threatened species of fauna or species which were regionally extinct (KISR, 1986; Wells, 1991).

By 1990 three terrestrial sites had been officially established under the Law of 1980, based on lists of nature conservation areas proposed in the master plan. The most advanced plans were for Jal az Zor National Park (30,000ha) near Kuwait city (Boulos, pers. comm., 1991; Pilcher, pers, comm., 1991). Other existing protected *de facto* areas included six main oil field exclusive rights areas, designated military areas and reserve areas for exploitation of known underground water and 10 protected exclosures (Kuwait Master Plan, 1977; Alsdirawi, *in litt.*, 1991). Three major marine islands are in the process of being declared protected (Alsdirawi, 1991; Pilcher, pers. comm. 1991). In 1988 the authorities launched a drive to establish "green" areas, for recreation and to prevent desertification, and to undertake massive planting projects to augment the 0.5 million trees already planted (Anon, 1988; Firmin, 1971; Gour-Tanguay, 1977; Boulos, pers. comm., 1991; Tye, pers. comm., 1991).

Environmental problems, due to a number of factors, have been identified, principally population growth, urban expansion, industrialisation, transport and recreation and climate. Natural renewable resources have long been heavily utilised, resulting in rapid environmental deterioration largely through such uncontrolled activities as overgrazing, uprooting or felling woody shrubs, hunting of wildlife from mammals through to reptiles and birds, off-road use of vehicles and heavy recreational pressure (Caulton and Keddie, 1989). Changing lifestyle had in part been a consequence of increased access to permanent water supplies, including the transportation of water tanks into the hinterland. Greater availability of water has led to an expansion of livestock numbers throughout the country and to stocks remaining the year round on rangeland without undergoing seasonal movements. This had resulted in livestock overgrazing by 1.3 million sheep, 0.3 million cattle and 0.6 million goats by 1987. Projects such as the sheep farm programme in the Jabed area of Sulaibiya would further increase the sheep population by 0.5 million head, increasing the threat to the environment if the livestock was permitted to roam unchecked. Aspects of conflict of land use include the relinquishing of oil rights areas by the Kuwait Oil Company, and of land allocated for military use and training. For example, the western part of Jal az Zor was appropriated by the Ministry of Defence for military training facilities through Municipal Council decision No. MC/320/18/83 of 12 December 1983 (KISR, 1986).

During the Iran-Iraq war of the mid 1980s, Kuwait was slightly affected by oil spills resulting from military activity. Following the Nowruz oil spill, there was an increase in algal cover on coral reefs which also led to an apparent reduction in invertebrate frequency. A secondary impact was increased sedimentation, resulting in complete or partial smothering of the coral polyps, killing the coral (WCMC, 1991a). Another consequence of the Iran-Iraq war was the increase in Iraqi bedouin and their camel and sheep herds which led to a serious overgrazing problem to the north of the country between 1980-88 (Tye, pers. comm., 1991). On 2 August 1990 Kuwait was occupied by Iraq military forces and placed under Iraqi law. As a consequence of United Nations resolutions, a military conflict lasted from 13 January to 27 February 1991. The environmental consequences were summarised in World Conservation Monitoring Centre Reports and by a United Nations mission following the end of hostilities (WCMC, 1991a, 1991b; Gwynne, *in litt.*, 1991). The sea and land-based hostilities are believed to have had a significant environmental impact that will affect the process of post-war reconstruction. A number of designated conservation areas are reported to have been adversely affected: Wadi Albattin Proposed Desert Park and Jal az Zor National Park have been identified as having been badly damaged by Iraqi troop emplacements, military manoeuvres and tank activities and by aerial bombing (Wells, 1991; Gwynne, *in litt.*, 1991). The burning of oil installations in Kuwait (the fires were finally all extinguished in November 1991) generated large smoke clouds which were reported to have had significant local and downwind effects upon species and habitats. The smoke was reported to have carried large amounts of pollutants into the atmosphere leading to soot fall-out, increased acid deposition, chemical contamination and shading causing reduced solar radiation. Depending upon its scale, this could have significant effects upon agriculture, the productivity of

terrestrial and marine ecosystems, and is already reported to have had a direct impact upon human health. KISR, UNEP and EPC have been monitoring pollution levels at various field stations (Gwynne, pers. comm., 1991). Inland oil slicks from uncapped oil wells have formed temporary lakes and may affect the soil horizons in the future. Large numbers of migratory birds had been trapped in these lakes of oil (ICBP, *in litt.*, 1991; Pilcher, pers. comm., 1991).

Other Relevant Information   Kuwait is rich in a number of natural resources including natural gas and oil, fish and shrimp. There is a total of 18 oil fields with 1,116 oil wells (oil reserve capacity of 94.5 billion barrels), of which about one-third was producing at the time of the Iraq invasion in August 1990. Within the neutral zone between Kuwait and Saudi Arabia are four oil fields with 337 wells, of which some 100 were producing prior to the 1990-1991 military conflict (WCMC, 1991b).

Tourism is not at all significant in Kuwait with just 116,000 visitors in 1985. However, the national parks are intended in part to be used for recreational use by visitors, the vast majority of which are nationals.

Addresses

Environment Protection Council, P O Box 24395, 13104 SAFAT (Tel: 456833, 452790; Tlx: 46408).
Kuwait Institute for Scientific Research, PO Box 24885, 13109 SAFAT (Tel: 4835034; FAX: 4830432; Tlx: 22299, 22616)
Public Authority for Agriculture and Fisheries (PAAF), KUWAIT
Ahmadi Natural History and Field Studies Group, Kuwait University, AHMADI-103
Kuwait Environment Protection Society, PO Box 1896, SAFAT

References

Alsdirawi, F. (1991). Protected areas in the state of Kuwait. Caracas Action Plan paper presented at the Third Man and Biosphere Meeting on Biosphere Reserves in the Mediterranean and the First IUCN-CNPPA Workshop on Protected Areas in the North Africa-Middle East Region, 14-19 October 1991, Tunis. 10 pp.
Al-Sawari, M., Gundlach, E.R. and Baca, B.J. (1985). *An atlas of shoreline types and resources, Kuwait.* University of Kuwait. (Unseen)
Anon. (1971). *Studies for National Physical Plan and Master Plan for Urban Areas, Second Report: The Short-Term Plan, Vol. I, Introduction and National Physical Plan.* Colin Buchanon and Partners.
Anon. (1972). Kuwait Environment. Kuwait National Report, Kuwait, 1971. In *Human Environment: Vol. 2: Summaries of National Reports on Environmental Problems' Environment Series 201.* Woodrow Wilson International Center for Scholars, Washington, DC.

Anon. (1980). Decree Law No. 62 for the year 1980 regarding protection of the environment and the general policy for the environment protection in the state of Kuwait. *Kuwait Al-Youm Edition No 1316 Twenty Sixth Year*. Environment Protection Council.

Anon. (1985). The management and conservation of renewable marine resources in the Indian Ocean region II KAP Region. Unpublished report.

Anon. (1988). Trees for the desert. *The Guardian*. 17 October 1988.

Baker, J.M. (1983). Impact of oil pollution on living resources. *Commission on Ecology Papers* No. 4. IUCN, Gland, Switzerland.

Basson, P.W. *et al*. (1977). *Biotopes of the Western Arabian Gulf*. Aramco Department of Loss Prevention and Environmental Affairs, Dhahran, Saudi Arabia.

Carp, E. (1980). *Directory of western Palaearctic wetlands*. UNEP/IUCN, Gland, Switzerland. 506 pp.

Carter, H.G. (1917). Some plants of the Zor hills, Koweit, Arabia. *Records of the Botanical Surveys of India* 6: 175-206.

Caulton, E. (1987). *Al Khiran New Town Working Paper No. 2. Environmental Impact Analysis*. Municipality of Kuwait.

Caulton, E. and Keddie, D. (1989). Environmental conservation problems in Kuwait. *The Environmentalist* 9: 219-228.

Child, G. and Grainger J. (1990). *A system plan for protected areas for wildlife conservation and sustainable rural development in Saudi Arabia*. NCWCD, Riyadh, Saudi Arabia.

Clayton, D. and Pilcher, C. (Eds.) (1983). *Kuwait's natural history*. Kuwait Oil Company, Kuwait.

Coral Reef and Tropical Marine Research Unit (1982). Management of critical habitats on the Arabian Gulf Coast of Saudi Arabia. Report to MEPA by Coral Reef and Tropical Marine Research Unit, University of York.

Daoud, H.S. (1985). *Flora of Kuwait: Volume 1*. KPI Ltd, London.

Davis, S.D., Droop, S.J.M., Gregerson, P., Henson, L., Leon, C.J., Lamlein Villa-Lobos, J., Synge, H. and Zantovska, J. (1986). *Plants in danger: what do we know?* IUCN, Gland, Switzerland and Cambridge, UK. 461 pp.

Downing, N. (1985). Coral reef communities in an extreme environment: the northwestern Arabian Gulf. *Proceedings of the Fifth International Coral Reef Congress. Tahiti. Volume 2*. Abstracts. 112 pp.

Dodson, M. (1982). Kuwait's wealth. *Wildlife* 24(5): 187-190.

Dryden, M. (1982). Kuwait's Wealth. *Wildlife* 24(5): 186-189.

FAO (1977). Conservation of wild plants and Animals. Report to the Government of Kuwait. Food And Agriculture Organization of the United Nations, Rome.

Firmin, R. (1971). Afforestation. Report to the government of Kuwait. FAO/KUW/TF-46, FAO, Rome (Revised by G.A.Booth).

Gour-Tanguay, R. (Ed.) (1977). Kuwait. Environmental policies in developing countries. *Beiträge zur Umweltgestaltung Heft A27*. Erich Schmidt Verlag.

Gwynne, M. (1991). Verbal report on the environmental situation of Kuwait following the Kuwait-Iraq conflict of 2 August 1990-27 February 1991. UN Secretary-General's Mission to Kuwait, March/April 1991.

Halwagy, R. and Halwagy, M. (1974a). Ecological studies on the desert of Kuwait I. The physical environment. *J. Univ Kuwait (Sci.)* 1: 75-86.

Halwagy, R. and Halwagy, M. (1974b). Ecological studies on the desert of Kuwait II. The vegetation. *J. Univ Kuwait (Sci.)* 1: 87-95.

Halwagy, R. and Halwagy, M. (1977). Ecological studies on the desert of Kuwait III. The vegetation of the coastal salt marshes. *J. Univ Kuwait (Sci.)* 4: 33-73.

Halwagy, R., Clayton, D. and Behbehani, M. (1986). Marine environment and pollution. Proceedings of the First Arabian Gulf Conference on environment and pollution. (Unseen)

Halwagy, R., Mustafa, A.F. and Kamel, S.M. (1982). On the ecology of the desert vegetation in Kuwait. *J. of Arid Environments* 5: 95-107.

Hamdan, I and Alzaidan, A. (1975). Summary of national report of Kuwait. In: Regional Seminar on de-desertification and arid-land ecology. Teheran, Iran. (Unseen)

Husain, N.A. (1976). Kuwait. In: IUCN Promotion of the Establishment of marine parks and reserves in the northern Indian Ocean including the Red Sea and Persian Gulf. *IUCN Publication New Series* 35: 84-85.

IUCN (1976). Ecological guidelines for the use of natural resources in the Middle East and South West Asia. *IUCN Publications New Series* No. 34.

KISR (1986). Criteria for development and management of Kuwait's first national park/nature reserve (Vol. I: Inventory and zoning; Vol. II: Reintroduction, management and legal land use; Vol III: Summary and recommendations). Kuwait Institute for Scientific Research, Safat.

McCarthy, M. (1991). Scientist's warning of Kuwait oil fires disaster rejected. *The Times*. 22 January. P. 2.

Maher Abu Jaafer (1984). *National parks and nature reserves in the Arab World*. Department of Sciences, the Arab League Educational, Cultural and Scientific Organisation, Tunis. 112 pp.

McMichael, D.F. (1976). Environmental management and administration in Kuwait. Report prepared for UNEP at the request of the Government of Kuwait. (Unseen)

Montague, K. and Bruun, B. (1987). *Biological diversity in North Africa, the Middle East and Southwest Asia: a directory of organisations and Institutions*. HLCF, New York, USA.

Perennou, C., Rose, P. and Poole, C. (1990). Asian Waterfowl Census 1990. IWRB, Slimbridge, UK.

Pearce, F. (1991). Desert fires cast a shadow over Asia. *New Scientist*. 12 January. Pp. 30-31.

Pearce, F. (1991). Gulf war could mean largest ever oil spill. *New Scientist* 19 January. P. 18.

Pilcher, C. (1990). Report on the environmental situation of coral islands of Kuwait. Adviser to the Environmental Protection Council, Kuwait.

Pilcher, C. (1991). Verbal report on the environmental situation in Kuwait. Adviser to the Environmental Protection Council, Kuwait.

Sardar, Z. (1982). *Science and Technology in the Middle East: a guide to issues, organisations and institutions.* Longman, London and New York.

Taha, F. K. and Omar, S.A. (1982). Selection and criteria for national parks/nature reserves in Kuwait's desert. *Kuwait Institute for Scientific Research Publication* No. KISR 729.

UNEP (1983). Action Plan for the protection of the marine environment and the coastal areas of Bahrain, Iran, Iraq, Kuwait, Oman, Qatar, Saudi Arabia and the United Arab Emirates. *UNEP Regional Seas Reports and Studies* No. 365.

UNEP/IUCN (1988). *Coral reefs of the world. Volume 2: Indian Ocean, Red Sea and Gulf. UNEP Regional Seas Directories and Bibliographies.* IUCN, Gland, Switzerland and Cambridge, UK/UNEP, Nairobi, Kenya. 440 pp.

UNESCO/ROPME/UPM/UNEP (1985). Proceedings of the symposium/workshop on oceanographic modelling of the Kuwait Action Plan (KAP) region. *UNEP Regional Seas Reports and Studies* No. 70.

UNESCO/ROPME/UNEP (1985). Combatting oil pollution in the Kuwait Action Plan region. *UNEP Regional Seas Reports and Studies* No. 44.

Vessey-Fitzgerald, D. F. (1957a) The vegetation of central and Eastern Arabia. *Journal of Ecology* 45: 779-798.

Vessey-Fitzgerald, D.F. (1957b). The vegetation of Central and Eastern Arabia. *Journal of Ecology* 45: 779-798.

WCMC (1991a). Gulf War Environmental Service: impact on the marine environment. World Conservation Monitoring Centre, Cambridge, UK. 37 pp.

WCMC (1991b). Gulf War Environmental Service: impact of atmospheric pollution on the terrestrial environment. World Conservation Monitoring Centre, Cambridge, UK. 37 pp.

Wells, K. (1991). Kuwait's environment suffers terrible irony as result of invasion. *Wall Street Journal.* 12/13 April.

ANNEX
Definitions of protected area designations, as legislated, together with authorities responsible for their administration

Title: Decree Law No 62, MC/73/7/80 15th SAFAR 140/H 22.12.1980 MC/299117/832rd SAFAR 1404 H 28.11.1983

Date: 22 December 1980

Brief Description: Regarding the general policy of the environment protection. Includes the decisions approving the allocation of the sites for national park and reserve activities (nature conservation areas). This law also relates to monitoring, pollution and water conditions.

Administrative authority: Environment Protection Council, Public Authority for Agriculture and Fisheries (PAAF)

Designations:

National park The primary objectives and functions of the park are to preserve natural and ecological components, provide education with proper land use, provide areas for environmental and ecological research, and provide facilities for education and training.

Livestock grazing is restricted by the use of fencing, hunting is not permitted.

Nature reserve The primary objectives and functions of this category of nature conservation area is to preserve all natural and ecological components of the desert environment and provide areas for environmental and ecological research.

The designated areas are established as protected areas primarily for plants and wildlife.

The National Plan (Master Plan) indicates that these areas are for investigation of the possibilities of restoring wildlife extinct from the region.

Livestock grazing is restricted by the use of fencing, hunting is not permitted.

Source: Master Plan; KISR, 1986

SUMMARY OF PROTECTED AREAS

Map ref.	*National/international designations* Name of area	IUCN management category	Area (ha)	Year notified
	National Park			
1	Jal az Zhor	V	30,000	1990

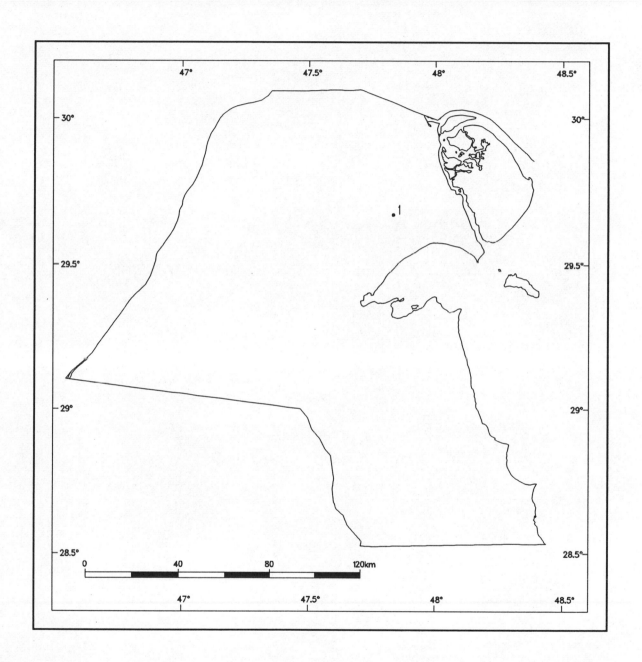

Protected Areas of Kuwait

LEBANON

Area 10,450 sq. km

Population 2,701,000 (1990)
Natural increase: 2.20% per annum

Economic Indicators
GDP: US$ 675 per capita (1987)
GNP: No information

Policy and Legislation Lebanon promulgated its first constitution on 23 May 1926 and it was last amended in 1991.

Land and habitat conservation has long been in existence in Lebanon. Cedar forest protection has been practised by local religious communities for many centuries, and a number continue to be maintained, such as the renowned Bshari Cedar Grove. Boundary stones, originating from the time of the Emperor Hadrian (138 AD), still demarcate the ancient protected forest domain (Drucker, *in litt.*, 1983; Mallett, *in litt.*, 1991).

The Ministry of Agriculture was set up with enabling legislation by Decree No. 8371 of 30 December 1961, Articles 17 and 19. The Society for the Protection of Nature and Natural Resources in Lebanon was established in accordance with acknowledgement No. 6/A of 8 January 1986 with express aims to construct and supervise national parks under Ministry of Agriculture Decree No. 1/60.

National parks are set up in compliance with a number of legislative decrees; Decree No. 8371 of 30 December 1961, entitled Organisation of the Ministry of Agriculture, Articles 17 and 19; Decree No. 1631 of 30 April 1984, Articles 111 and 130 of 12 June 1959 regarding the Organisation of Public Administration and the Functions of the Ministry of Agriculture; and specific enabling legislation for the establishment and naming of each protected area, such as for "Mashgara National Park" set up under compliance with Decree No. 1/60 of 1988 through the Ministry of Agriculture. Protected forests are covered under regulations of the Ministry of Agriculture.

International Activities Lebanon has entered a number of agreements and legal obligations relating to the environment. Lebanon is party to the Convention concerning the Protection of the World Cultural and Natural Heritage, World Heritage Convention, which was ratified on 3 February 1983. No natural sites have been inscribed to date. Lebanon does not participate in the Convention on Wetlands of International Importance especially as Waterfowl Habitat (Ramsar Convention). In February 1985 a proposal for Bentael National Park to be designated a biosphere reserve, under the Unesco Man and the Biosphere Programme, was submitted by the Lebanese Permanent Delegation to Unesco (Habib, *in litt.*, 1985). By September 1990 a national MAB committee had not been established. The Convention for the Protection of the Mediterranean Sea against Pollution, usually known as the Barcelona Convention, was ratified by Lebanon on 18 May 1983. The contracting parties to the Convention adopted the Protocol concerning Mediterranean Specially Protected Areas on 2 April 1982, and Lebanon has ratified the Protocol.

Administration and Management Protected areas are managed both privately and by the Ministry of Agriculture. National parks have been under the management of the Society for the Protection of Nature and Natural Resources (SPNC). The SPNC was created in 1984 and officially recognised by legislation in 1986, which embodied the requirement ensuring cooperation with the Ministry of Agriculture (General Secretary of the SPNC, *in litt.*, 1988). The main aims of the SPNC have included: conservation education; environmental planning; and establishing and subsequently managing a system of national parks and protected areas (Serhal, *in litt.*, 1986).

The main relevant government body with general remit for environmental issues throughout the country is the Ministry of the Environment (Ministère de l'environnement). The Environmental Protection Committee (Comité de protection de l'environnement), through its councillors to the Ministry, have specific interests in environmental protection. Other bodies include the Ministry of Agriculture, Green Plan Management and the Agricultural General Inspectorate (Montague and Bruun, 1987).

Administration and management of the remaining forests is under the jurisdiction of the Department of Forests and Natural Resources (Direction des Forêts et des Ressources Naturelles) of the Ministry of Agriculture. The National Council for Scientific Research of Lebanon (NCSR/CNRS) is concerned with science and technology and reports directly to the Prime Minister. It is responsible for natural science policy and oversees scientific research and promotion. It undertakes environmental studies, including research on fauna, flora, atmospheric pollution and protection (Tohme and Tohme, 1985). The National Hunting Council, established in 1974, is concerned with hunting and game management in coastal sites, deserts, forests, and wetlands, as well as with law enforcement (Montague and Bruun, 1987).

A number of privately-owned nature reserves have been established in the past including Khallet Khazem Farm and Natural Reserve, which had been protected for at least the last 50 years (Habib, *in litt.*, 1985).

Most research is conducted under the patronage of NCSR in independent universities or through international organisations. The International Council for Bird Preservation (ICBP) and the International Centre for Agricultural Research have been involved in the country as has the Ornithological Society of the Middle East (OSME).

Since the civil war and internal strife of 1978 the Development and Reconstruction Council was formed to coordinate reconstruction efforts (1991). The FAO is assisting in reconstruction by funding two projects; US$ 500,000 for institutional strengthening and US$ 150,000 for forestry (Child, *in litt.*, 1991).

Much of the territory has been occupied by the military forces of neighbouring countries since the civil war (Anon., 1983; Gour-Tanguay, 1977). Continued civil war and military conflict throughout the 1980s had forced an indefinite delay on many environmental programmes, including the establishment of an effective and wide-ranging protected area system, but at the same time had halted indefinitely at least eight environmentally damaging major dam projects (Anon., 1986).

Systems Reviews   Bordered by Syria to the north and east, the Mediterranean Sea in the west and Israel to the south, Lebanon is 193km long and a maximum of 56km wide. Steppes and scrub vegetation cover much of the country inland from the Mediterranean coastal oak maquis strip. The alluvial plains of the Bechar (Biqa) Valley separate the Lebanon mountains (3,086m) from the Anti-Lebanon mountains in the east (Mt Hermon at 2,814m). The mountain slopes are barren with only scattered surviving remnants of the once extensive stands of cedar *Cedrus*, fir *Abies* and juniper *Juniperus* renowned in biblical accounts. The western slopes up to 300m support oak maquis, with carob *Ceratonia*, oak *Quercus calliprinos* and *Pistacia*. Aleppo pine *Pinus halepensis* forest occurs from sea level to 1,200m; forests of cedar *Cedrus libani* are found between 1,400m and 1,800m in the north. The Anti-Lebanon mountains support *Amygdalus* and *Pistacia* scrub. Subalpine and alpine communities occur above 2,500m (Davis *et al.*, 1986). The greatest concentrations of woodland are in the Bechar Valley north-east of Bsharri, around Mt Qurnat as-Sawda (3,086m) to Hirmel, in the hills near Byblos and east of Beirut. The total remaining forest cover is 76,950ha, largely comprising scrub and degraded woodland and only 300ha of closed cedar forest (Beals, 1965). Documents from early Egyptian and Mesopotamian periods (*c.* 2600 BC) until the reign of Emperor Hadrian (138 AD), indicate that the mountains of Lebanon were known for their valuable timber. The Egyptian occupation of the Levant in the early-mid 19th century led to considerable logging operations. Uncontrolled use of wood as fuel for the Ottoman railroads continued into World War I.

A series of recommended national parks and natural reserves exists, although no systematic review has yet been undertaken. Recommended sites for future protection include the Ile du Palmier in the Mediterranean Sea, all the mountain conifer forests (cedar and fir) most notably in the remote areas of the north, and the remnant marshland of Ammik (Litani River Valley) which is of international importance as the only wetland of its type in the country and is on one of the principal bird migration routes in the Near East (Carp, 1980; Tohme, G. and Tohme, 1985; Habib, *in litt.*, 1985; H. Verheugt, pers. comm., 1987). In hill country near Beirut, the privately-owned slopes have successfully been planted with stone pine *Pinus pinea* from 1860 onwards, their survival being ensured by their use as a source for edible pine seeds, as well as industrial and fuel wood. From the 1950s, the FAO has been involved in reforestation programmes and more recently national activities have been underway to replant cedar areas (Mouterde, 1954; Hallah, *in litt.*, 1991).

In 1990 there were two major protected areas, of which Mashgara National Park totals 3,500ha. The first national park was created on 23 May 1987 to coincide with the 25th anniversary of the World Wildlife Fund (WWF). Protected forests are distributed throughout the country. There is at least one private protected area, Khallet Khazem Farm and Natural Reserve (202ha).

In medieval times, the central part of the Bechar Valley was occupied by lake and swamps, but during the early 20th century most of the area was drained and given over to agriculture, as were extensive areas of coastal plain swamps which were later planted with eucalyptus plantations. Reafforestation, including by the FAO, has been severely impeded by the continued presence of goat herds and illicit collection of fuelwood for charcoal, and more recently by civil unrest. Concern has also been voiced about the internationally renowned cedars being affected by insect pests, possibly as a consequence of atmospheric pollution. The internationally important remnant marshland of Ammik continues to be under threat from widespread indiscriminate and uncontrolled shooting of migratory birds. Raptors are particularly at threat, even though they are legally protected. Estimates indicate that up to 15-20 million birds are shot per year by some 0.5 million hunters (Carp, 1980; Mouterde, 1954; W. Verheugt, pers. comm., 1987).

Other Relevant Information   Parts of the country continue to be under military rule, including the so-called Israeli occupied security zone in the south. Syrian forces remain deployed in parts of Lebanon (Hunter, 1991). International tourism, once of major significance, is currently negligible. Ecotourism involving foreign visitors is non existent; by contrast national interest in recreation and wildlife continues in areas of natural interest throughout the country (Drucker, *in litt.*, 1991).

Addresses

Comité de protection de l'environnement (Environmental Protection Council), Ministère de l'environnement (Ministry of the Environment), BP 341, TRIPOLI

Directeur des Forêts et des Ressources Naturelles, Ministère de l'Agriculture, rue Sami Solh, BEIRUT

Conseil National de la Recherche Scientifique (National Council for Scientific Research), PO Box 123, JONIYE (Tel: 09 934763; Tlx: Public 29140 LE)

Society for Protection of Nature and Natural Resources in Lebanon (SPNL), PO Box 11-5665, BEIRUT (Tel: 343740)

References

Anon. (1983). Helping to hold the line: US troops and ships try to keep Lebanon from disintegrating. *Time* 40: 6-16.

Anon. (1986). Strife stops dams in Lebanon. *International Dams Newsletter* 1(6): 5.

Carp, E. (1980). *Directory of Western Palearctic Wetlands*. IUCN, Gland, Switzerland. 506 pp.

FAO (1952). Forestry in the Middle East. *Unasylva* 6: 104-123.

Gour-Tanguay, R. (Ed.) (1977). Lebanon. *Environmental Policies in developing countries*. Erich Schmidt Verlag.

Gryn-Ambroes, P. (1980). Preliminary annotated lists of existing and potential Mediterranean protected areas. UNEP/IG.20/INF.5. 108 pp.

Hunter, B. (Ed.) (1991). *The Statesman's Year Book 1991-92*. The Macmillan Press Ltd, London and Basingstoke, UK. 1692 pp.

Lakkis, S.H. (1985). Sur un projet d'établissement d'un Parc Marin dans i'ile du Palmier, au nord du Liban. *Atti del Convegno Internazionale: I parchi costieri Mediterranei*. Salerno-Castellabate, 18-22 Giugno 1973. Regione Campania Assessorato per il Turismo. Pp. 613-618.

Montague, K. and Bruun, B. (1987). *Biological diversity in North Africa, the Middle East and Southwest Asia. A directory of organisations and institutions*. Holy Land Conservation Fund, New York, USA. 134 pp.

Mouterde, P. (1954). Difficultés et possibilités de l'amélioration de la flore au Liban. In: *Unesco Symposium on the Protection and Conservation of Nature in the Near East*. Cairo. Pp. 112-117.

Serhal, Assad Adel (1983). Need for establishing a national park system in Lebanon. Unpublished report for the Holy Land Conservation Fund. 8 pp.

Tohme, G. and Tohme, H. (1985). Project de transformation de l'Ile du Palmier (Tripoli, Liban) en reserve naturelle. *Atti del Convegno Internazionale: I parchi costieri Mediterranei*. Salerno-Castellabate, 18-22 Giugno 1973. Regione Campania Assessorato per il Turismo. Pp. 613-618.

ANNEX
Definitions of protected area designations, as legislated, together with authorities responsible for their administration

Title: **Ministry of Agriculture Decree No. 1/60**

Date: 1988

Brief description: Relates specifically to the two designated national parks

Administrative authority: Ministry of Agriculture

Designations:

National park Article 2 defines parks as important nature conservation areas, where all fauna and flora must be preserved, and left in a natural undisturbed state in all except exceptional circumstances (Article 5)

Parks must have a zoning system whereby the public and tourists are only permitted to enter in limited areas, "accompanied by wardens and without weapons" (Article 9).

Special permission is required for scientific research (Article 8)

Agriculture and livestock are strictly prohibited (Article 7).

Source: Original legislation

SUMMARY OF PROTECTED AREAS

Map ref.	National/international designations Name of area	IUCN management category	Area (ha)	Year notified
	National Park			
1	Mashgara (Machgharah)	II	3,500	1988

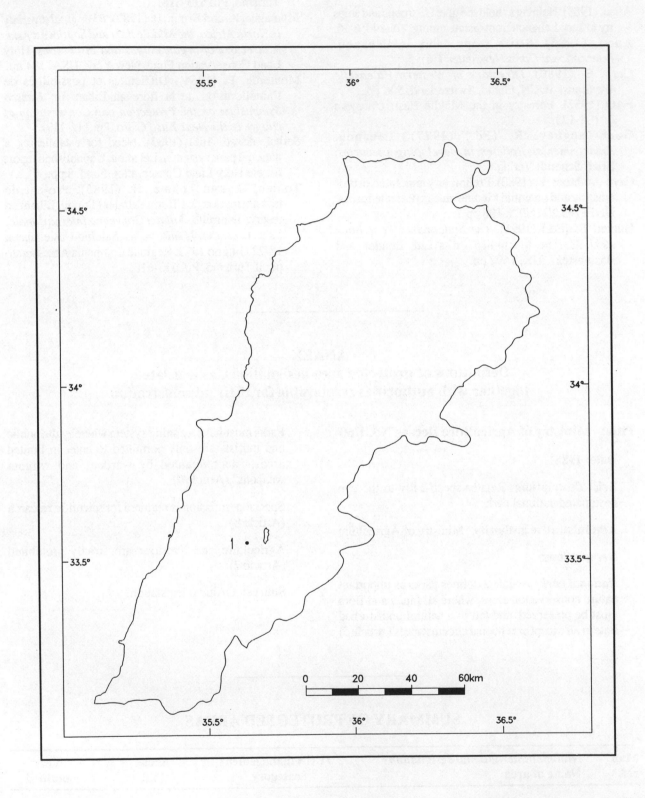

Protected areas of Lebanon

LIBYAN ARAB JAMAHIRIYAH
(LIBYA)

Area 1,759,540 sq. km

Population 4,545,000 (1990)
Natural increase: 3.62% per annum

Economic Indicators
GDP: US$ 5580 per capita (1987)
GNP: US$ 5500 per capita (1987)

Policy and Legislation The first conservation legislation came into existence in 1949, the Law on Forestry. The object was to give protection to forests and forest products, to soil, water sources and land under threat of desertification. Subsequently in 1970 the Law for the Protection of Agricultural Land introduced an ordinance on the protection of "green areas".

In 1977 the Secretariat of Agriculture passed an ordinance which in principal agreed to the establishment of a country-wide network of national parks. This was the basis for the Environmental Protection Law No. 2, 1982 which provides for the regulations on various forms of protection including hunting reserves, fishing zones and other forms of reserves (see below and Annex). As a result of the 1977 Ordinance a general technical agreement to develop natural resources was signed between the Secretariat and the Arab Centre for the Studies of Arid Zones and Drylands (ACSAD) in October 1977. A specific agreement to set up the first national park was signed and a special decree enacted in November 1978. The national park system was established with specific guidelines for the creation of protected areas, in order to "create meaningful national parks for the Libyan people and international tourism". It also aimed to take positive measures to restore native wild animals in reserves where they have been exterminated (Baccar, 1977; Child, 1978; Maaher abou Jaafer, 1984; El Gadi, pers. comm., 1987). National parks are declared by individual decree of the Council of Ministers after recommendation submitted by the General Secretariat of Agricultural Reclamation and Land Reform.

Law No. 2 provides for all other forms of protected area, including fishing zone, forest reserve, hunting reserve, protected area and nature reserve. Although this enabling legislation exists, sites have not been designated (see Annex). A number of forest reserves were designated from 1978 onwards and a series of nature reserves established in the north of the country prior to the enactment of the Law (Child, 1978; Maaher abou Jaafer, 1984). Marine areas have been proposed by the Secretariat of State for Marine Resources but none declared (El Gadi, pers. comm., 1987).

Reviews of protected area policy and legislation appear not to have been undertaken in the past five year period.

It is regarded to be still too short a period since the designation of the first park to identify whether these regulations are effective.

International Activities Libya has entered into a number of cooperative agreements and legal obligations. Libya is party to the Convention concerning the Protection of the World Cultural and Natural Heritage (World Heritage Convention) which was ratified on 13 October 1978. No natural sites have been inscribed to date. Libya does not participate in the Convention on Wetlands of International Importance especially as Waterfowl Habitat (Ramsar Convention). The Convention for the Protection of the Mediterranean Sea against Pollution, usually known as the Barcelona Convention, has formally been signed. The contracting parties to the Convention adopted the Protocol concerning Mediterranean Specially Protected Areas on 2 April 1982, and Libya has ratified the Protocol. One site, Kouf National Park, has been listed as a Mediterranean Specially Protected Area. Five sites have been recommended by the UNEP SPA Task Force following the first phase of the Coastal Resources Survey (Jeudy de Grissac, pers. comm., 1991).

Administration and Management Conservation activities are the technical and administrative responsibility of the General Secretariat of Agricultural Reclamation and Land Reform, also called the Secretariat for the General Popular Committee for Agricultural Reclamation and Land Development (formally the Secretariat of Agriculture). It is divided into a series of technical commissions, or committees, including that of Wildlife and National Parks (Technical Committee of Wildlife and National Parks, also called the National Commission on Wildlife Conservation and Protected Areas).

The main body with jurisdiction of protected areas is the Technical Committee of Wildlife and National Parks which was created in 1990. It oversees the administration of Kouf National Park, Hesha Proposed National Park and Garabulli Proposed National Park (Amnissi, *in litt.*, 1991). For a long period, Kouf National Park administration had a minimal number of park staff with specific wildlife conservation duties, although a director had been installed from inception (El Gadi, pers. comm., 1987). By 1991 park infrastructure consisted of a general director below whom there was an Administrative and Financial Department and a Technical Department. The Administrative Department is further subdivided into offices of administration, registration, photocopying, stores, general servicing and transportation. The Technical Department was subdivided into: wildlife office with various species units; natural vegetation office with forestry unit, range unit, herbarium and nurseries; marine life office; veterinary office; maintenance office with a firefighting unit, electrical unit and general maintenance unit; and a museum office. The Technical department currently consists of a maximum of ten staff (Amnissi, *in litt.*, 1991).

Previously, protected areas were administered by the Forests and Range Management and National Resources Department (renamed the Forestry Department) of the General Secretariat (El Gadi, pers. comm., 1987). The Forestry department continues to deal with forestry activities (FAO).

The Technical Centre for Environmental Protection was created in 1986 as part of the General Secretariat of Agricultural Reclamation and Land Reform. The centre was established according to the Environmental Protection Act of 1982. Its main objectives include: working as a consulting agency to solve all environmental problems; monitoring for violations of the law by all other agencies and administering authorities, governmental or private; provide and disseminate information to increase general awareness on the environment. It has headquarters in Tripoli and branches elsewhere in the country (Amnissi, *in litt.*, 1991).

Other bodies with interest in the environment include the Secretariat of Scientific Research in the Environmental Protection Programme, the National Academy for Scientific Research and the Agricultural Research Centre. The Arab Centre for the Studies of Arid Zones and Drylands has been instrumental in setting up the first national park and its administration (Maaher abou Jaafer, 1984). Research within protected areas is undertaken by a number of universities (El Gadi, pers. comm., 1987).

Management of the one existing national park is reported to have been hampered in the past by intensive settlement or by continued heavy grazing pressure and wood collecting rights of the local population, even though these activities were forbidden by law. To attempt to remedy this habitat degradation, the park authority has fenced off areas for increased protection (El Gadi, pers. comm., 1987; Amnissi, *in litt.*, 1991).

Systems Reviews   Libya is bounded on the north by the Mediterranean Sea, on the west by Algeria and Tunisia, east by Egypt and Sudan and in the south by Chad and Niger. It is represented by an arid terrain which has been exploited by man from well before the arrival of the Phoenicians and Carthaginians. The northern part of the country around the Jebel Akdar-Bengazi region is represented by a Mediterranean type flora and fauna; some areas still have wooded relict communities, as in the mountains and gorges of Jebel Akdar with its 1,800 plant species of which 109 are endemic (Davis *et al.*, 1986). Total forested areas cover 6,800 sq. km (Hunter, 1991). The Mediterranean zone is fringed by steppe habitats along the plains near Tripoli. To the south of Tripoli a Saharan desert type habitat is dominant and covers over three-quarters of the country. Much of the

coastline is of international importance for globally threatened reptile and marine mammal species and is of note for seagrass beds and coastal mudflats and marshes, which are internationally important for migratory birds and waders.

Comprehensive surveys of biological resources are severely lacking in a number of cases, although botanical surveys are extensive. There are approximately 1,600 plant species of which 90% occupy the coastal region (Ozenda, 1977; Davis *et al.*, 1986; El Gadi, pers. comm., 1987). In the late 1980s the UNEP-SPA Task Force undertook a habitat resource survey of the entire Libyan coastline (Jeudy de Grissac, pers. comm., 1991). A limited amount of work has also been undertaken on bird distribution (Bundy, 1976). To redress the balance from past destruction of larger animals, a widespread reintroduction programme of native and exotic species has been started (species include dorcas gazelle and barbary sheep).

An ongoing major environmental programme by the government is for arid land afforestation and sand dune fixation. This work is mainly undertaken by contractors, due to the lack of other on-site professionals and specialised man power. Other programmes being carried out in various regions tend to be mostly in agricultural areas. The Agricultural Development Authority plans to reclaim 60,000ha each year for agriculture (Hunter, 1991). In the 1970-1980 period there was a significant increase in the number of consultant activities providing management and technical advice, viz. the elaboration of a pilot forestry project in Jabal el Akhdar with Swedish aid (Khouzami, 1981; El Gadi, pers. comm., 1987). In 1990 a number of international companies were investigating the possibility of exploiting natural resources. Environmental impact assessments were regarded as a standard initial phase. In that year, international petroleum development companies prepared an assessment of the Hamada al Hamra region in western Libya using the resources of international conservation agencies (Smies and de Ligny, 1990). In January 1991, private environmental services began to investigate environmental impacts on the Gulf of Sirte region and Hammada Murzuq, south of Sabha (Harrison, *in litt.*, 1991).

A series of proposed or recommended sites has been identified by the authorities in an attempt to arrest habitat loss. In 1977 the Secretariat of Agriculture agreed in principal to the establishment of a country-wide network of national parks in different climatic and topographic regions in collaboration with ACSAD. In the late 1970s and early 1980s, the FAO coordinated assistance in project development of national parks and reserves (Child, 1978) and in 1980 Unesco consultants were invited to advise on the establishment of a national park and biosphere reserve under the Man and Biosphere Programme (MAB Project 8). In 1983 IUCN was invited by the authorities of Kouf National Park, through the Libyan National Bureau for Agricultural Consultation and Studies, to undertake a joint study on the avifauna of selected protected areas (Porter, *in litt.*, 1983; Scott, *in litt.*, 1983).

The greatest habitat loss in recent years has been through livestock over-grazing and wildlife hunting. Some of the most internationally important ecosystems are completely unprotected by legislation. Major potential changes affecting the environment include the "Great Man-Made River" project which has been under way since 1984. It intends to transport 2 million cu. m daily along a 2,000km pipeline from the Sahara Desert to the coastal plains. Not only is it tapping a finite amount of fossil water but is also inevitably causing disruption, sand compaction and erosion by construction machinery. It is regarded as the world's largest single civil engineering project and costs US$ 3.6 billion. Continued threat to many areas of desert exists where millions of land-mines were laid, and are still active, following the military conflict of World War II.

Other Information It was estimated that 100,000 tourists a year visited Kouf National Park in the early 1980s, rising to 300,000 in the five years leading to 1985 (Hemsley, *in litt.*, 1985). By 1991 numbers of national tourists was reported to be steadily increasing (Amnissi, *in litt.*, 1991).

Addresses

National Commission on Wildlife Conservation and Protected Areas Development (Technical Committee of Wildlife and National Parks), General Secretariat of Agricultural Reclamation and Land Reform (Secretariat for the General Popular Committee for Agricultural Reclamation and Land Development), Sidi Mesri, TRIPOLI

Technical Centre for Environmental Protection, PO Box 83618, TRIPOLI 20138 (Tel: 21 46868/48452; Tlx: 20138 TTEP LY)

Secretariat of Scientific Research, Environmental Protection Programme, PO Box 8004, TRIPOLI

National Academy for Scientific Research, PO Box 8004, TRIPOLI (Tlx: 20039)

References

Baccar, H. (1977). *A survey of existing and potential marine parks and reserves in the Mediterranean.* IUCN, Gland, Switzerland. 25 pp.

Bundy, G. (1976). *The birds of Libya, an annotated check-list.* British Ornithologists Union. Checklist No. 1. British Ornithologists Union, London. 83 pp.

Carp, E. (1980). *A directory of western Palearctic wetlands.* IUCN, Gland, Switzerland. 506 pp.

Child, G.S. (1978). Report on the establishment of national parks and reserves in the Libyan Arab Jamahiriyah. W/18401. FAO, Rome.

Davis, S.D., Droop, S.J.M., Gregerson, P., Henson, L., Leon, C.J., Lamlein Villa-Lobos, J., Synge, H. and Zantovska, J. (1986). *Plants in danger: what do we know?* IUCN, Gland, Switzerland and Cambridge, UK. 461 pp.

Grimmett, R. (1987). *A review of the problems affecting Palaearctic migratory birds in Africa.* International Council for Bird Preservation, Cambridge, UK.

Gryn-Ambroes, P. (1980). Preliminary annotated lists of existing and potential Mediterranean protected areas. UNEP/IUCN report. 108 pp.

Hunter, B. (Ed.) (1991). *The Statesman's Year Book 1991-92.* The Macmillan Press Ltd, London and Basingstoke, UK. 1692 pp.

Khouzami, M. (1981). Travel to Libya, 25-29 September. Report for the Forestry Department, FODO. 10 pp.

Maaher Abou Jaafar (1984). *National parks and natural reserves in the Arab World.* Report No. 80/001/1984/Science Division. Arab League of Education, Culture and Science Organisation (ALESCO), Tunis. 112 pp.

RAC/SPA (1986). *Proposed protected areas in the Mediterranean.* Special Protected Areas Center, Salammbo, Tunis. 196 pp.

Ozenda, P. (1977). *Flore du Sahara.* Centre National Recherche Scientifique, Paris.

Smies, M. and de Ligny, W. (1990). Environmental profile of Western Libya. Environmental impact assessment report prepared by Shell Petroleum. 6 pp.

ANNEX
Definitions of protected area designations, as legislated, together with authorities responsible for their administration

Title: Environment Protection Law No. 2

Date: 1982

Brief description: Provides for the regulations on various forms of protection on land and sea. Various categories of protected area are being designated under individual decree of the Council of Ministers.

Initially four categories were envisaged (national park, wildlife park, multi-purpose reserve and natural sanctuary)

Administrative authority: General Secretariat of Agricultural Reclamation and Land Reform

Designations:

Fishing zone   the law provided for the regulations on fishing zones and forbidding or limiting access to marine areas.

Forest reserve   A number of forest reserves were established in February 1978.

To protect specific sites for the remaining wildlife. In all cases habitat manipulation occurs, with a general policy to replant depleted woodland cover areas, reintroduce fauna and provide educational-visitor facilities and access.

Public forest protected areas seem to be established primarily for their recreational value.

The wildlife in these sites include exotic species as well as native fauna and flora (El Gadi, pers. comm. 1987).

Hunting reserve   shooting and fishing may be banned or restricted.

Protected area   No information

Nature reserve   Each area is established to protect specific sites for the remaining native wildlife and ecosystems.

Sources: General Secretariat of Agricultural Reclamation and Land Reform; Child, 1978; Maaher abou Jaafer, 1984; El Gadi, *in litt.*, 1987.

Title: National Park Decree of the Council of Ministers

Date: Individually declared by decree, the first in 1978

Brief description: The single national park was created prior to the Law of 1982 under Council of Ministers Decree.

Administrative authority   General Secretariat of Agricultural Reclamation and Land Reform

Designations:

National park   Declared by decree after recommendation submitted by the Secretariat. Legislation allows the authorities to restrict or stop grazing within protected areas; shooting and fishing may also be banned or restricted. Furthermore, there is also control over access, building development, agriculture, mining and pest control.

Source: General Secretariat of Agricultural Reclamation and Land Reform

---

SUMMARY OF PROTECTED AREAS

Map ref.	National/international designations Name of area	IUCN management category	Area (ha)	Year notified
	National Park			
1	Kouf	II	35,000	1979
	Nature Reserve			
2	Zellaf	IV	100,000	1978
	Protected Areas			
3	Garabulli	VIII	15,000	1982
4	Nefhusa	IV	20,000	1978

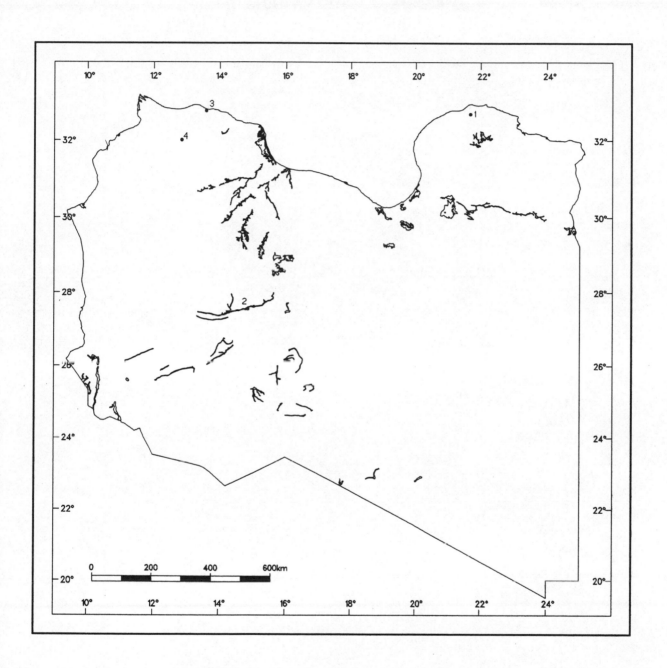

Protected Areas of Libya

MOROCCO
(KINGDOM OF MOROCCO)

Area 446,550 sq. km (710,000 sq. km including the province of Western Sahara)

Population 25,061,000 (1990)
Natural increase: 2.43% per annum

Economic Indicators
GDP: US$ 812 per capita (1987)
GNP: US$ 620 per capita (1987)

Policy and Legislation The kingdom is a constitutional monarchy. The king, as sovereign head of state, approves legislation (by royal edicts or Dahir). The Constitution was approved in March 1972 and amendments made in May 1980. A reunited Morocco became independent from its status as French and Spanish protectorates (set up in 1912) in March and April 1956, respectively, and from the Tangier International Zone which was abolished in October 1956. A tripartite agreement was announced on 14 November 1975 providing for the transfer of power of the former Spanish Province of West Sahara to the Moroccan and Mauritanian governments on 28 February 1976. On 14 April 1976 a Convention was signed by Mauritania and Morocco in which the two countries agreed to partition the territory, and on 14 August 1979 Mauritania renounced its claim to this region. Its territory was annexed as one of the four provinces of the Moroccan Sahara: Boujdour, Es Semara Laayoune and Oued el Dahab (for details see entry for Morocco Saharan provinces).

Traditional forms of protected rangeland, or land management control mechanisms on commonland, or hereditary lands (agdal, habous, guich), have early origins amongst the tribal systems of Morocco. Many common-land range areas are still respected by local tradition and maintained by the people as food reserves for crops, ploughing and livestock during periods of drought, and for controlled exploitation of firewood or timber. These areas are owned communally, with all members of the tribe having equal right to use the land, according to custom or tradition. Habous lands belong to religious foundations and Guich areas are hereditary lands permanently conceded by the state to individuals within the tribe. Such examples include the Agdal Escarpment Common Woodland Pasture between Imilchil and Aghbala (FAO, 1986; US-AID, 1986; Drucker, *in litt.*, 1990). These rangeland areas are covered under the ministerial Decree of 25 July 1969, as they are not administered under laws relating to state-owned land. There are also some indications that areas such as the cork oak forests near Rabat were first established as protected forest during the classic Roman period, 2,000 years ago. Caius Plinius Secondus (Pliny the Elder) wrote the *Natural History*, of which 37 volumes survive, recording everything known about the world. At that time throughout the Roman Empire there were forest administration structures, delimited forests, wardening systems and programmes of tree planting, along with areas set aside for wildlife (Drucker, *in litt.*, 1985; Mallett, *in litt.*, 1991).

The first forms of natural resource protection commenced with the forest policy initiated for jurisdiction in the French Protectorate and promulgated under the Royal Edict of 3 January 1916. The next relevant law was on 10 October 1917 in the Royal Edict defining the Conservation and Exploitation of Forests (see below). This was followed by the ministerial Decree of 21 May 1921 which regulated the rights of common pasture in state forests. In the former Spanish Protectorate, the Mountains Directorate was detailed to administer legislation on forestry, fishing and hunting in 1928. This body was incorporated into the Ministry of Agriculture in 1931. One of the more relevant pieces of Spanish legislation was the Decree of 7 June 1931 on the Protection of Natural Resources (Protección de los Recursos Naturales) which identified natural sites of national interest (Sitios naturales de interès nacional) (Poore and Gryn-Ambroes, 1980).

Currently the protected areas system consists of three classes of protected area: national park (parc national); permanent hunting reserve (réserve de chasse permanente) including the subclass royal hunting reserve (réserve de chasse royale); triennial hunting reserve (réserve de chasse triennale); and reserve (réserve), subdivided into three nature or natural reserve types: botanical, faunal and biological (réserve naturelle: réserve botanique, réserve de faune and réserve biologique). Wetland zones (zones humides) are included in the international Ramsar designation (see Annex).

The first protected areas ordinance was the Royal Edict (Dahir) of 11 September 1934, concerning the establishment of national parks. The original Grand Vizier, or ministerial order, of 24 September 1934 lays out the procedures to be followed. Under this order each protected area is created by ministerial decree, separate regulations being made for individual sites. Damaging activities, such as hunting and building would be vetted and authorisation come from the Administration of Water and Forests and of the Conservation of Soils (Administration des Eaux et Forêts et de la Conservation des Sols) of the Ministry of Agriculture and Agrarian Reform (Ministère de l'Agriculture et de la Réforme Agraire).

In each established national park, both the forest code law and hunting regulations are in force; restricted levels of livestock grazing and collection of dead wood are permitted, as defined in the ministerial Order of 21 May 1921 (see Annex). The recently declared Souss-Massa

National Park is intended as the first new national park in Morocco in which the government will attempt to develop, and benefit from, tourism and sports activities (cf tourism in Toubkal and Tazekka national parks) (Maghnouj, 1991; Posner and Edwards, 1987).

There are no specific Royal edicts for the establishment of nature reserves. As a consequence, the Ministry of Agriculture and Agrarian Reform is empowered to legislate the establishment of this form of protected area under local regulations. Acts from the Ministry of Agriculture and Agrarian Reform on 3 November 1962 and 6 March 1978 ensured the setting up the first few reserves. Legislation ensures that these reserves are totally protected from commercial exploitation, livestock grazing, building and hunting. A number of such reserves have been established within the existing and proposed national parks.

Various forms of protected area closed to all forms of hunting have been established under hunting legislation and forest ordinance. Hunting reserves (réserves de chasse) are set up under specific acts of the Waters and Forests Administration. Bokkoyas Permanent Hunting Reserve is closed to all forms of hunting, and is meant to serve as a buffer to the adjacent biological reserve (Duvall, 1988).

The Royal Edict of 21 July 1923 laid out the infrastructure for the policing of sites to prevent illegal hunting (last important modification on 30 June 1962). The 14 March 1955 Act of the Inspector General, Chief of the Water and Forests Administration, and Ministry of Agriculture and Agrarian Reform Act of 3 November 1962 identified the regulations and enforcement activities concerning hunting and hunting rights in rural areas (M'Hirit, 1990). Hunting regulations specify that one-third of all public domain be closed to hunting at any one time. These areas remain closed for two years, after which they are opened again and alternative areas closed (Duvall, 1988). In addition, a number of small permanent reserves have been established and covered under hunting reserve legislation to protect the five most important waldrapp *Geronticus eremita* colonies in Morocco. All are regularly visited and guarded by personnel from the Water and Forests Administration. The Royal Edict of 2 June 1950 created a Superior Council of Hunting, as well as a Hunting Fund (Fond de la Chasse) (Maghnouj, 1991).

Forest policy was first initiated by the Royal Edict of 3 January 1916 which delimited the boundaries of state forest land. In the following year, on 10 October 1917, a separate Royal Edict was decreed defining the Conservation and Exploitation of Forests. The 1917 Edict has been subsequently modified by the edicts of 17 July and 21 July 1960 and the acts of 4 September 1918 (prevention of forest fires), 15 January 1921 (regulating rights of passage through forest property), 16 April 1946 (sylvo-pastoral management of forestry areas) and 14 November 1949 (fixing modes of forest management of woods, forest and non-state land). Two classes of forest have been defined relating to the composition and the function of management objectives of the forest regime. Forests managed for forest conservation tend not to be specifically defined, sites protected for nature conservation are protected as nature reserves under the above mentioned legislation. Special legislation exists for a number of forest habitat types including the Royal Edict of 4 March 1925 on the protection and the definition of arganier forest boundaries and Act of 1 May 1938 on restocking arganier areas, together with the 8 September 1928 Royal Edict on the conservation and exploitation of walnut trees. The decree of 8 February 1949 relates to the functioning of the forestry research station and of experimental forestry. The Institut Scientifique was set up under Decree No. 2-75-662 on 17 October 1975 (Maghnouj, 1991).

Only one marine biological reserve has been established, Bokkoyas marine reserve, which extends one nautical mile into the sea (Duvall, 1988). The legislation is based on acts of the Ministry of Agriculture and Agrarian Reform and is under ministerial jurisdiction of the Ministry of Marine Fisheries and Merchant Marine. Other relevant pieces of legislation include the Royal Edict of the 11 April 1922 concerning the regulation of fishing in continental waters (last important amendment dated 23 January 1957) (M'Hirit, 1990). There are a number of wetland sites which are protected from seasonal hunting (for example, Affenourir) and considered to be of special importance to the nation (Eaux et Forêts, 1991).

A number of sites are listed as areas of national interest (périmètres d'intérêt national) (PIN), declared under decrees from the Ministry of Agriculture and Agrarian Reform after consultation with the Ministries of the Interior and Finance. Land and water use within such areas are to be regulated by ministerial order. They are limited to well defined areas of priority concern, such as watersheds upstream from dams or areas threatened by sand encroachment (Duvall, 1988; Eaux et Forêts, 1991).

Reviews of the protected areas legislation have been undertaken in 1986 by the National Park Service of the US Department of Interior. The review concluded that legislation at that time was outdated and inadequate and new pieces of legislation were hampered by conflicts between ministries. Recommendations to amend the legislation and increase effectiveness have been prepared and presented to the Administration of Waters and Forests (Duvall, 1988; NPS, 1987). International organisations, such as the IUCN-World Conservation Union and the FAO, have also recommended a review of the general laws for the protection of the environment, especially in respect to clarification and definition of protected areas and their management (Eaux et Forets, 1991; IUCN, 1987; Lemieux, *in litt.*, 1986).

International Activities   At the international level, Morocco has entered a number of cooperative agreements and legal obligations. The African

Convention on the Conservation of Nature and Natural Resources (1968) was ratified in November 1977. Morocco is party to the Convention concerning the Protection of the World Cultural and Natural Heritage, World Heritage Convention, which was ratified on 31 December 1975. No natural sites have been inscribed to date. Morocco became a contracting party to the Convention on Wetlands of International Importance especially as Waterfowl Habitat, Ramsar Convention, on 20 June 1980, at which time four sites were designated for the List of Wetlands of International Importance established under the terms of the Convention. Morocco participates in the Unesco Man and Biosphere Programme and in 1990 had a National Committee composed of nine representatives. To date no sites have been accepted as biosphere reserves.

The Convention for the Protection of the Mediterranean Sea against Pollution, usually known as the Barcelona Convention, was formally adopted on 16 February 1976, and ratified on 15 January 1980. The contracting parties to the Convention adopted the Protocol concerning Mediterranean Specially Protected Areas on 2 April 1982, which entered into force on 23 March 1986. One site has been identified by the Moroccan national focal point as being representative of the Mediterranean network.

The Commission of the European Communities has interests in Morocco through two complementary programmes for the protection of the Mediterranean environment: the Mediterranean Strategy and Action Plan (MEDSAP), which promotes community action for the protection of the environment in the region; and the Environmental Regional Programme (ENVIREG), for regional environmental measures undertaken on the initiative of the Commission. Under the Mediterranean Environmental Technical Assistance Programme (CY90-92 METAP), of the World Bank, European Investment Bank, United Nations Development Programme and Commission of the European Communities, environment project preparation includes one on coastal zone management. Under the CY91-93 programme one activity has been defined for implementation; project preparation activities of the proposed Al Hoceima National Park (Anon., 1991). Representatives from Morocco attended the first meeting of the Mediterranean Protected Areas Network (MEDPAN) meeting on 5-6 October 1990 in Monaco and the first technical meeting to discuss marine protection and economic impacts of protected areas creation was scheduled for September 1991 (Anon., 1990).

In the Tunis Declaration on the Environment on 19-23 April 1991 (conference of the Ministers of the Environment having in common the use of the French language) participating countries decided to work towards implementing the proposal of devoting at least 5% of their territories to safeguarding their natural heritage, putting the emphasis on the conservation of

ecosystems and the diversity of species, within the context of sustainable development (ACCT, 1991).

A transboundary park has been proposed that would incorporate wetland areas for migratory birds, extending from Tetuan in Morocco to Gibraltar and Spain across the Straits of Gibraltar (Eaux et Forêts, 1991; Cortes, *in litt.*, 1991). Another transboundary park is proposed at Al Hoceima, which would incorporate territory of the Spanish enclaves of Melilla. No known cooperative transfrontier initiatives are being planned between Morocco and its neighbouring countries of Algeria or Mauritania.

Administration and Management   The management of wildlife protected areas is under the technical and administrative responsibility of the Ministry of Agriculture and Agrarian Reform (Ministère de l'Agriculture et de la Réforme Agraire). The Administration of Water and Forests and of the Conservation of Soils (Direction des Eaux et Forêts et de la Conservation des Sols) of the Ministry of Agriculture and Agrarian Reform is in charge of general coordination, administration, and routine management. There are four divisions: Division for Public Domain, Division of Erosion Control and Reforestation; Division of Forest Economy and Division of Hunting, Fishing and the Protection of Nature. The Division of Hunting, Fishing and the Protection of Nature (Division de la Chasse, de la Pêche et de la Protection de la Nature) (CPN) deals specifically with administration and management of protected areas and wildlife as well as for issuing hunting and fishing permits. A number of administrative personnel, trained in American and European institutions and park authorities, have recently been appointed to head a new national park section within the CPN.

Day-to-day running of parks and other protected areas is undertaken by wardens of the regional forestry offices. The recently declared Souss-Massa National Park is unique in having a park director. In other sites wardens have general forestry duties as well as responsibility for reserves. The Division of Waters and Forests (Direction) is divided into 39 provincial regional forestry offices (services forestiers), each with an infrastructure of district offices (subdivisions forestières) and a network of forestry posts (postes forestières) to manage all forest land under their jurisdiction (Eaux et Forêts, 1991; Maghnouj, 1991). In total, 40 people (professional and support staff) were working permanently in protected areas, together with 88 gardes chasses and auxiliaries with the combined function of policing generally for hunting and protection of nature (Eaux et Forêts, 1991). It has been intended that future national park legislation will provide for a zoned system of protected areas. The proposed zone one will represent an integral reserve with complete protection; peripheral zones will have restrictions preventing building, hunting and livestock grazing. In the outer buffer zones human settlements would be permitted and hunting prohibited. The recently declared Souss-Massa National Park is the first to be divided into three zones, from core area to fringe zones (Eaux et Forêts, 1991).

In 1990 the Administration of Water and Forests was in the process of preparing management plans for wetlands in collaboration with the International Council for Bird Preservation (ICBP), the Ramsar Secretariat, International Waterfowl Research Bureau, Tour de Valat and a range of Moroccan institutes (Eaux et Forêts, 1991). In the Plan d'Orientation 1988-1992, prepared by the Sub-Commission on Natural Resources, protection of biological diversity has been highlighted as a key element, including the execution of a nation-wide extension programme for the protection of nature, and the drafting of management plans for two national parks and eight reserves (Duvall, 1988). The 1991-1993 plan indicated a need for expansion of the protected areas network, establishing management plans for five national parks, and then management plans to eventually develop eight national parks (Eaux et Forêts, 1991).

In 1987, up to 15% of the Ministry of Agriculture and Agrarian Reform budget went on the Water and Forests Administration (Duvall, 1988); 8% of the Water and Forests budget went towards parks and reserves administration and management (Duvall, 1988). In detail, funding went towards: maintaining roads, installing faunal reserve fencing, construction of warden accommodation, salaries to wardens, installing water points, transport acquisition, communication installation, reafforestation and soil protection, information dissemination to the public; a total for 1991 of DH 5 million (US$ 636,130). Entry into protected areas is currently free (Eaux et Forêts, 1991). Investment by the private sector is minimal.

Hunting reserves are managed by designated hunting wardens (gardes de chasse) of the Waters and Forests Administration with sole responsibility to patrol the reserves. In a number of cases rights are leased to private hunting societies or syndicates, such as to Sochatour (the Moroccan Hunting Society). Ten hunting reserves are managed by private hunting societies to provide "quality" hunting for tourists (Duvall, 1988). For example, Sochatour has hunting rights, amongst others, on the northern side of the Oued Drater, Merja Mellah and parts of Merja Zerga Reserve (Duvall, 1988; Drucker, *in litt.*, 1989). Many of these hunting reserves are frequented by wealthy Moroccan hunters and by foreign visitors (Duvall, 1988; Allaoui, pers. comm., 1988). A number of specific hunting reserves are managed by the Administration of Waters and Forests, and represent official hunting reserves for the King and official guests of the government and Royal family (réserves de chasse royales). They are protected from public interference, closed to any access by the public, and are havens for species protection (Haddane, pers. comm., 1991). They have voluntary hunting bans and are managed by the Administration of Waters and Forests (e.g. Merja Douyet, Ain el Johra-Mamora, Bouznika, Ouazzane, Amizmiz and Dunes d'Cereyse-Oued Souss) (Duvall, 1988).

The procedure for establishment of national parks includes previewing by consultative committees for each site, presided over by the Ministry of Agriculture and Agrarian Reform and by the following: Ministère de l'Intérieur, Autorité chargée de l'environnement, Gouverneur de province concerné par le parc, Ministère du Tourisme, Ministère du Plan, Ministre des Travaux Publiques, Ministre du Commerce et de l'Industrie, Ministère de la Justice, Ministre de l'Education Nationale, Ministre des Affaires Culturelles, Ministère des Finances, Ministère des Pêches Maritimes et de la Marine Marchande and relevant non-government organisations and individuals (Eaux et Forêts, 1991). At the local level the management committee will be established, presided by the governor of the region and by the director of the park. It will encompass representatives of different departments and presidents of the local interested communes. A scientific committee will be instituted at the national level, presided over by the Ministry of Agriculture and Agrarian Reform (Eaux et Forêts, 1991).

Traditional rangeland areas are owned communally, outside the forest domain, and management is the responsibility of the Range Management Service of the Division of Livestock Rearing (Direction de l'élevage, Service des parcours) established in 1981 (Duvall, 1988).

Due to the importance given to nature protection, a new national natural resources service was established within the Administration of Water and Forests in 1991. It is the Service of Terrestrial Ecology Flora and Fauna (Service d'écologie terrestre flore et faune) which has been created as part of the Division de recherches et d'experimentations forestières. Its function will be to work in close collaboration with other divisions, principally with the division of CPN. The principal mission of the Service will be the promotion of study and research on the flora, fauna, threatened species and the management of protected areas. Some of the most important initial activities will be to prepare a data bank of information about protected areas and to commence protected areas monitoring (Maghnouj, 1991).

Responsibilities for marine reserve designation is under the jurisdiction of the Administration of Waters and Forests and the Ministry of Marine Fisheries and Merchant Marine (Duvall, 1988). The Ministry is responsible for developing and executing the government's policy on marine fisheries and activities. The Marine Fisheries Scientific Institute is responsible for basic and applied research, and for monitoring purposes in order to permit the government to manage the resource (Duvall, 1988; UNDP, 1986).

Responsibilities of the Division of Urbanism, Territorial Management and the Environment (Direction Générale de l'Urbanisme, de l'Aménagement du Territoire et de l'Environnement (DGUATE) of the Ministry of the Interior (Ministère de l'intérieur) include identification of environmental policies for the Ministry. It prepared the journal *Ressources* as of November/December 1990, concerning the environmental situation in Morocco and abroad (DGUATE, 1990).

Between 1920 and 1975 research in protected areas was carried out by the Institut Scientifique Cherifien of Mohammed V University, Rabat, the official government scientific research organisation. In 1975 this institute was renamed the Institut Scientifique. It now has six departments: zoology and animal ecology, botany and vegetative ecology, geology, geography, physics and satellite imagery (Beaubrun et Thevenot, 1982). The Forestry Research Station in Rabat-Agdal has five sections including ecology, silviculture, tree improvement, range management and entomology (Duvall, 1988). In the Plan d'Orientation 1988-1992 there were proposals to establish a National Wildlife Research Centre (Duvall, 1988). The Centre was created in 1990 as the Unité d'écologie terrestre: flore et faune. Other research institutes which undertake activities within protected areas include the Ecole Nationale d'Ingénieurs Forestiers, Institut National Agronomique et Vétérinaire (INAV), Institut National de la Recherche Agronomique (INRA) and National Zoological Park of Rabat, with priority for conservation and research on wildlife and their biotopes. Research in and adjacent to protected areas has also been undertaken by various individuals or groups attached to Moroccan or foreign universities. Their work has included studies on threatened large mammals (such as threatened bird species, Barbary macaque, Barbary lion and Barbary sheep), on flora, palaeontology, palaeobotany, forestry, geology and on geography.

Cooperative agreements and projects between the Ministry of Agriculture and Agrarian Reform and foreign organisations include the development of national park management plans and information centres through the World Wide Fund for Nature (WWF), US National Park Service, the International Council for Bird Preservation (ICBP), US Peace Corps Service and the METAP programme (see above) (Anon., 1991). Also, there have been various IUCN-World Conservation Union/WWF projects relating to threatened species protection, together with development of coastal wetland parks and reserves by the International Waterfowl and Wetland Research Bureau (IWRB) and ICBP. The US Peace Corps has been involved in a parks and reserves and conservation education programme from 1985-1995, at the request of the Water and Forests Administration on a budget of US$ 250,000. Training involvement for Moroccan protected areas personnel is also undertaken by ICBP and by the Tour de Valat research station of the Camargue, France. Moroccan-French cooperation has included funding a nationwide study on wildlife (Duvall, 1988). The World Bank has been involved in funding a number of agricultural projects in Morocco which have also focused on environmental improvement, especially forestry projects in recommended protected areas (M'Hirit, 1990). The FAO has undertaken a range of

management projects and identification of potential protected areas (FAO, 1983, 1986; also see below).

Few active non-governmental organisations exist, and none owns protected areas. The main body involved in the protected area system is the Moroccan Association for Protection of the Environment (Association Marocaine pour la Protection de l'Environnement (ASMAPE) which was established in 1986 (Hassane, pers. comm., 1987). It is a small society composed largely of professional environmentalists, activities include the collection of data on the environment and on the status of species, an education and conservation programme, tree planting against erosion, anti-pollution activities and welfare of animals. It is seeking to collaborate with government agencies on the establishment of protected areas. The Society for the Protection of Animals in North Africa (SPANA) is active in Morocco as well as elsewhere in northern Africa. It has a centre in Rabat, and although largely concerned with the welfare of domestic animals it is also interested in Moroccan wildlife and its protection. The Moroccan Society for Environmental Rights (La Société Marocaine pour le droit de l'environnement) (SOMAD) produced the publication *La Forêt Marocaine, Droit, Economie, Ecologie* in 1989. The Committee for Environmental Liaison in Northwest Africa (Comité de liaison pour l'environnement au Maghreb) was created in 1990, with the intention of involving non-governmental organisations throughout north-west Africa in environmental concerns.

Various reviews of the protected areas system have been undertaken. In 1986 the National Park Service (Joint Evaluation Team) of the US Department of Interior conducted a brief review of existing legislation addressing national park designation and management (Duvall, 1988; NPS, 1987). Its review concluded that existing administration and management is outdated and inadequate (NPS, 1987). International organisations, such as the International Union for the Conservation of Nature and Natural Resources (IUCN) and the Food and Agriculture Organisation (FAO), have also recommended a review of the general laws for the protection of the environment, especially in respect to the clarification and definition of protected areas and their management, the clarification of responsibilities of the administrative bodies and the reinforcement of coordinated activities by the various ministerial departments (IUCN, 1987; Lemieux, *in litt.*, 1986).

The Division of Water and Forests Management is hampered by lack of financial resources, lack of qualified personnel, problems of management such as intensive settlement or continued heavy grazing pressure and wood collecting/grazing rights of the local population in forest land. Uncontrolled use of unprotected resources has frequently led to a situation where the population often will ignore restrictions, especially if there are no effective operational means for their enforcement due to limited manpower and financial resources. Imposition of regulations, without public consultation, has often led to a lack of cooperation and extreme public wariness of official activities. In traditionally protected areas there is evidence to indicate that people from all levels of society are grazing herds of livestock on common pastures, leading to overgrazing and a widespread breakdown of traditional systems of range management (Duvall, 1988; Eaux et Forêts, 1991a; FAO, 1986).

There are many specific management problems in the various designated protected areas. Grazing within reserves, especially during the dry season, is a countrywide problem; an estimated 13,000 head of livestock use Merja Zerga Reserve alone (Duvall, 1988). Other constraints include degradation of rangeland, drought, conflicting water use including dam construction, poaching and hunting of abundant as well as threatened species, implementation of regulations, difficulties of land ownership, administrative problems, and inadequate funding (Eaux et Forêts, n.d; FAO, 1986; Drucker, *in litt.*, 1990). Management responsibility is often split across administrative boundaries, such as between the chefs de service of different provinces, causing a reduction or complete lack of coordination in protected area management. In a number of localities tourism is a real threat and in a limited numbers of cases oil exploration and mineral extraction, including sand and soil extraction, are believed to be threatening sites (Duvall, 1988; Drucker *in litt.*, 1990). Throughout the country, local people or local authorities are often totally unaware of the existence of protected areas, or if they are cognizant of them, do not know what the restrictions are if any exist. In addition, because of long-term inadequate enforcement and general disregard of existing regulations and statutes, it would appear that ignoring legislation and other regulations pertaining to natural resources has become "institutionalised". In this situation, individuals of the administrative and management agencies are reported to have been continually disregarding or condoning such infractions (Duvall, 1988; Drucker, *in litt.*, 1990).

Recommendations for improvement were put forward by the US National Park Service, which identified the desirability to establish general natural policies for identification, designation and management of national parks throughout the country. It also recommended that a new agency be established in order to undertake this function, and that "the mission of this office be clearly defined and separated from Eaux et Forêts resource utilization functions" (NPS, 1987). It has been further recommended that nature-based tourism, ecotourism, receive higher priority (Duvall, 1988). One repeated recommendation is that in future developments it should be ensured that efforts are made to involve the local inhabitants in planning and implementation, and that they become voluntary participants whenever possible (Duvall, 1988). Reviews have proposed the reorganisation of the existing protected area designation and policy using international criteria (Drucker, 1986; Thevenot, 1987).

Systems Reviews   Morocco, located in the north-western corner of Africa, is bordered on the west by the Atlantic Ocean for 3,500km, on the north by the Mediterranean Sea (the Straits of Gibraltar), on the east by the steppe and mountains of the Atlas range leading to Algeria and in the south by the Sahara desert, Mauritania and the former province of Spanish Sahara ("Western Sahara"). There are four major mountain ranges (Rif, Moyen Atlas, Haut Atlas and Anti-Atlas) which influence the environment of the country, forming barriers separating the arid Saharan regions from the milder northern and western zones. Given its location, Morocco has always been the most isolated and remote of the North African countries and hence a major proportion of its natural resources, fauna and flora were not over-exploited at least until the beginning of this century. The cedar forests of the Middle Atlas plateau are a case in point, and were not even known to western science until the end of the 19th century. Still an important area for species diversity, there are as many as 3500 vascular plant species in the country, of which 650 are endemic (Davis *et al.*, 1986). The biogeography is represented by a Mediterranean and Macronesian type flora and fauna. One of the least damaged ecosystems, woodland, is situated primarily in the mountain ranges, yet there are also extensive areas of lowland forest such as the cork oak woodlands on the plains near Rabat. Forest cover represents 7-14% of the country, although it is regionally variable, rising to 28% cover in the High Atlas. Intensive cultivation tends to dominate at low altitudes, whilst pasture is generally predominant over 1,500m. The Atlas steppe habitats and other semi-arid communities total 106,000 sq. km of land. The south and extreme east of the country is dominated by the Sahara desert, 560,000 sq. km of land (Duvall, 1988). Wetlands of the Atlantic coast are considered to be of international importance as feeding and roosting sites for great numbers of migratory waterfowl en route between Northern Europe and West Africa.

A series of recommended sites for protection has been identified, including seven coastal and inland wetlands of international importance for migratory bird species. A number of other sites have been identified as of international or regional importance as the last known haunts of threatened bird species such as waldrapp and mammal species such as Barbary leopard. In the 1970s, a strategy was worked out for the protection of Moroccan fauna and flora, although the present status of many species of Morocco and the Maghreb as a whole is unknown. Priorities include assessing the status of species within existing parks and reserves, together with coastal zone management surveys (Duvall, 1988; Drucker, *in litt.*, 1990). Subsequent legislation on behalf of the Ministry of Agriculture and Agrarian Reform has identified a provisional list of protected species (see also lists by Duvall, 1988).

The establishment of protected areas dates back to the early years of the French Protectorate period when forest lands were placed under the jurisdiction of the protectorate government. The boundaries of forested areas were demarcated following the Royal edicts of 1916/1917. The first national park was designated by decree in 1942, followed by a second decree in 1950 for another park. The first reserve was established in 1946. There was a gap of 40 years before the next national park was established, in 1991. Currently, about 4,400,670ha of forest land are under the jurisdiction of the Water and Forests Service, of which 1,735,000ha are designated for forest protection (Eaux et Forêts, 1991; M'Hirit, 1990). In 1991 there was a total of 11 designated nature protection areas covering 97,220ha (0.2% of total surface area); comprising two special faunal permanent hunting reserves at 9,987ha, three biological reserves at 14,150ha, one botanical reserve at 2,603ha and three national parks totalling 70,480ha (Eaux et Forêts, 1991). Proposed national parks cover a total of 325,600ha; an official inquiry was being undertaken in September 1991 for the designation of the proposed Haut Atlas Oriental park (Eaux et Forêts, 1991). In addition, 148 permanent hunting reserves (réserves de chasse permanents) that are closed to hunting have been designated, totalling 3 million ha; and 143 réserves de chasse triennial covering a total area of 9 million ha (Eaux et Forêts, 1991).

Approximately 1,200 reserved areas, totalling 1.6 million ha, have been set aside by the Forestry Service for dune fixation, reforestation, soil erosion control, pasture improvement, protection around forestry posts and protected areas (Duvall, 1988; Eaux et Forêts, n.d.). Ten hunting reserves, totalling 350,000ha, are managed by private hunting societies and there are eight royal reserves closed to the public, of which four are managed for hunting (Duvall, 1988; Drucker, *in litt.*, 1987, 1990). Areas of national interest (PIN) range in size from 100ha to over 180,000ha. To 1988 there were 20 PINs up to 1,000ha in size and three major watershed PINs declared since 1980, with a total of 268,000ha (FAO, 1986; Duvall, 1988). Collective lands total 1.01 million ha, guich areas 319,000ha and habous areas 83,700ha (Duvall, 1988).

Other Relevant Information   Over the last two decades Morocco has become increasingly more developed, partly as a consequence of the phenomenal increase in tourism. In 1986 the Ministry of Tourism and US National Park Service undertook a technical assessment of national park/tourism potential. Tourism is now an important industry and may be important both for ecotourism and as a potential environmental threat; there were 189,000 visitors in 1962, 1.3 million in 1984 and 1.5 million in 1985 (Duvall, 1988). In 1986 the 1.5 million visitors to the country spent DH 6,200 million (Hunter, 1991). In 1990 the national parks of Toubkal, Souss-Massa and Haut Atlas Oriental (proposed) were frequented by an average of 10,000 tourists per park (Eaux et Forêts, 1991).

Addresses

Division de la Chasse, de la Pêche et de la Protection de la Nature, Direction des Eaux et Forêts et de la Conservation des Sols, Ministère de l'Agriculture et de la Réforme Agraire, 1 Rue Jaafer Essaddiq, RABAT-CHELLAH (Tel: 763166/762694/763946/764622; Tlx: 36696; FAX: 764446)

Direction Générale de l'Urbanisme, de l'amenagement du territoire et de l'Environnement, Ministère de l'interieur et de l'information, RABAT (Tel: 760262/763357 x 216)

Institut Scientifique, Charia (Avenue) Ibn Batouta, BP 703, RABAT (Tel: 774548)

Institut Scientifique de la Peche Maritime, Ministry of Marine Fisheries and Merchant Marine, CASABLANCA

Institut Agronomique et Veterinaire Hassan II (INAV Hassan II), BP 6202, Agdal, RABAT-INSTITUTES (Tel: 771545/771758/771759/770793; Tlx: 32089)

Association marocaine pour la protection de l'environnement, BP 6331, RABAT-INSTITUTES (Tel: 7761154; FAX: 7761153)

References

ACCT (1991). The Tunis Declaration on the Environment. Première Conférence des ministres chargés de l'environnement des pays ayant en commun l'usage du Français/First Conference of the Ministers of the Environment of Countries having in common the use of the French language. Agence de coopération culturelle et technique, Tunis, 19-23 April 1991. 2 pp.

Anon. (1991). Mediterranean Environmental Technical Assistance Program, activity report, Spring. World Bank, European Investment Bank, United Nations Development Programme and Commission of the European Communities. 24 pp.

Beaubrun, P. et Thevenot, M. (1982). Etude et Protection des zones humides aux Maroc, role de l'Institut Scientifique de Rabat. Deuxième reunion technique régionale sur les zones humides de l'ouest Africain, Nouhadibou, 9-14 December, 1982.

Carp, E. (1980). *A directory of western Palearctic wetlands.* IUCN, Gland, Switzerland. 506 pp.

Commission Nationale de l'Agriculture et des Barrages (1987). *Plan d'Orientation 1988-1992.* Commission Nationale de l'Agriculture et des Barrages, Sous Commission des Ressources Naturelles. 85 pp.

Conseil National de l'Environnement, 1985. Le phenomene de la desertification au Maroc. Ministere de l'habitat et de l'amenagement du territoire. 16 pp.

Drucker, G.R.F. (1986). Protected areas in Morocco. Unpublished report. Sussex, UK.

Drucker, G.R.F. (1987). Directory of the protected areas of North Africa, Draft. Protected Areas Data Unit, IUCN Conservation Monitoring Centre, Cambridge, UK.

Du Puy, A.R. (1986). La conservation de la nature au Maroc. *Le Courrier de la Nature* 104: 21-29.

Duvall, L. (1988). The status of biological resources in Morocco, constraints, and options for conserving biological diversity. Government of the United

States of America and the US Agency for International Development. 58 pp.

DGUATE (1990). *Ressources*. Journal of the Direction de l'Urbanisme, de l'Aménagement du Territoire et de l'Environnement (DGUATE) of the Ministry of the Interior in association with UNESCO/FNUAP. No. 1. 19 pp.

Eaux et Forêts (n.d.). Situation actuelle de la faune sauvage au Maroc. Mesures prises pour assurer sa protection. 4 pp.

Eaux et Forêts (n.d.). *Aperçu sur le Maroc forestier*. Ministère de l'Agriculture et de la Réforme Agraire. Royaume du Maroc. 55 pp.

Eaux et Forêts (n.d.). La mise en place de réserves et de parcs nationaux pour le sauvegarde des espèces menacées de disparition. Ministère de l'Agriculture et de la Réforme Agraire. Royaume du Maroc.

Eaux et Forêts (1991). Rapport sur les aires protégées au Maroc. Paper presented at the Third Man and Biosphere Meeting on Biosphere Reserves in the Mediterranean and the First IUCN-CNPPA Workshop on Protected Areas in the North Africa-Middle East Region, 14-19 October 1991, Tunis. 18 pp.

FAO (19830. Aménagement des parcs nationaux, Maroc. Rapport de la mission. FO: TCP/mor/2202. 27 pp.

FAO (1986). Plan national de lutte contre la désertification. Projet FAO/TCP/MOR/4506 (A). 149 pp.

Grimmett, R. (1987). *A review of the problems affecting Palearctic migratory birds in Africa*. International Council for Bird Preservation, Cambridge, UK.

Gryn-Ambroes, P. (1980). Preliminary annotated lists of existing and potential Mediterranean protected areas. UNEP/IUCN report. UNEP/IG.20/INF5.

Hunter, B. (Ed.) (1991). *The Statesman's Year Book 1991-92*. The Macmillan Press Ltd, London and Basingstoke, UK. 1692 pp.

IUCN (1987). Report on the status, the Mediterranean monk seal. IUCN/UNEP/MM-IC/1.3.

Maher abou Jaafar (1984). *National parks and natural reserves in the Arab world*. Arab League of Education, Culture and Science Organisation (ALECSO). 80/001/1984/Science Division. Tunis.

Mahnouj, M. (1991). Rapport sur l'Etat de la conservation de la nature au Maroc. Presented to the Third Man and Biosphere Meeting on Biosphere

Reserves in the Mediterranean, 14-19 October 1991, Tunis. Division de Recherches et d'Expérimentations Forestières, Direction des Eaux et Forêts et de la Conservation des Sols, Rabat. 18 pp.

Ministry of Tourism and US National Park Service (1986). A technical assessment of national park/tourism potential in Morocco. A joint study by the Moroccan Ministry of Tourism and the US National Park Service. 25 pp.

M'Hirit, Z.O. (1990). Evaluation des ressources forestières marocaines, 1990. Unpublished document prepared by the Division de Recherches et d'Expérimentation Forestières du Maroc.

NPS (1987). A proposal for development and management of Massa National Park. Report prepared for the Government of the Kingdom of Morocco, Ministry of Agriculture and Agrarian Reform, Department of Eaux et Forêts and the Ministry of Tourism and Commerce, Department of Tourism. National Park Service, US Department of the Interior. 110 pp.

Poore, D. and Gryn-Ambroes, P. (1980). *Nature conservation in Northern and Western Europe*. UNEP/IUCN/WWF, Gland, Switzerland. Pp. 291-314.

Posner, S.D. and Edwards, J.K. (1987). Compartment management recommendations. Massa National Park Project Morocco. Eaux et Forêts/US Peace Corps. 35 pp.

RAC/SPA (1986). Proposed protected areas in the Mediterranean. Special Protected Areas Center, Salambo, Tunis.

Scott, D.A. (1980). A preliminary inventory of wetlands of international importance for waterfowl in Western Europe and North-West Africa. *IWRB Special Publication* No. 2. 127 pp.

SOMAD (1989). *La Forêt Marocaine, Droit, Economie, Ecologie*. La Société Marocaine pour le droit de l'environnement. Editions Afrique Orient, Maroc. 200 pp.

Thevenot, M. (1987). Parc nationaux, réserves et autres sites protégés au Maroc. Report.

United Nations (1986). Rapport annuel sur l'assistance au développement pour l'année 1986, Royaume du Maroc. PNUD, Rabat. 70 pp.

UNDP (1986). Appui à l'Aménagement et au développement des pêches maritimes. Proj. Paper MOR/86/019/C/01/12. 48 pp.

ANNEX
Definitions of protected area designations, as legislated, together with authorities responsible for their administration

Title: Royal Edict (Dahir) on national parks

    Date: 11 September 1934

Brief description: Fixes the procedure to follow in view of the creation of national parks. Act of 20 March 1946 concerns the creation of a consultative committee for national parks.

Administrative authority: Direction des Eaux et Forêts et de la Conservation des Sols

Designations:

Parc national (National park) Article 1 states that national parks are natural regions which are established due to a) scientific or touristic purposes; b) protection of representative countryside; c) social utility; and d) ensuring that the environment is maintained without damage.

Article 2 states that existing rights for ownership of land in the national park must be exercised separately from land outside the park bounds. Those actions which result in the change of the park (tree felling, opening of new roads or highways, permanent or temporary buildings and intensive pasturage) are forbidden, and lesser damaging actions must be authorised by the Administration des Eaux et Forêts.

In each established national park, both the forest code law and the hunting regulations are in force; restricted livestock grazing and timber exploitation are permitted, as defined in the Ministerial order of 21 May 1921.

Activities in mine workings within the park, underground and surface, are covered under the Dahir of 1 November 1929 (Article No. 65). In Article 3 the creation of a national park is confirmed in the acts of the Grand Vizier with measures presented to protect or restore the fauna and flora in the national park and prohibit or restrict hunting, fishing and pasturage.

Article 4 states that the restrictions in the Dahir of 10 October 1917 (re the conservation and exploitation of forests) are valid within national parks. Infringements of these regulations will result in punishment by payment or imprisonment (six days to two months). The offence of hunting and fishing in the national park will be punished at the diligence of the Administration des Eaux et Forêts.

Article 5 states that the state can expropriate land, which is judged necessary to be incorporated into the national park domain. Article 6 recommends that a consultative committee would be created for national parks.

Sources: Eaux et Forêts, 1991; Maghnouj, 1991; SOMAD, 1989

Title: Nature Reserve Acts

Date: Individually declared

Brief Description:

Concerning the designation of reserves. Each reserve is individually declared by Ministry of Agriculture and Agrarian Reform order, and managed under specific regulations for these sites.

Administrative authority: Direction des Eaux et Forêts et de la Conservation des Sols of the Ministry of Agriculture and Agrarian Reform, Ministry of Marine Fisheries and Merchant Marine.

Designations:

Reserve (Reserve) Divided into three nature or natural reserve types: botanical, faunal and biological reserve and a number of sites can also be subclassed as marine reserve.

Botanical reserve (Réserve botanique) Regulations indicate that these reserves are natural regions which are established for their importance for: a) scientific purposes; b) protection of representative habitats and plant species. Those actions which result in the change of the reserve (tree felling, opening of new roads or highways, permanent or temporary buildings and intensive pasturage) are forbidden, and lesser damaging actions must be authorised by the Administration des Eaux et Forêts.

In each established reserve, both the forest code law and the hunting regulations are in force. Reportedly, special authorization is needed to enter into the reserves. Infringements of these regulations will result in punishment by payment or imprisonment (6 days to 2 months).

The offence of hunting and fishing in the reserve will be punished at the diligence of the Administration des Eaux et Forêts.

Faunal reserve (Réserve de faune) Regulations indicate that these reserves are natural regions which are established for their importance for: a) scientific purposes; b) protection of threatened animal species. Those actions which result in the change of the reserve (tree felling, opening of new roads or highways, permanent or temporary buildings and intensive pasturage) are forbidden, and lesser damaging actions must be authorised by the Administration des Eaux et Forêts.

In each established reserve habitat management is permitted, hunting is prohibited as is livestock grazing and timber exploitation. Infringements of these regulations will result in punishment by payment or imprisonment (6 days to 2 months). The offence of hunting and fishing in the reserve will be punished at the diligence of the Administration des Eaux et Forêts. Special permission is required to enter the reserve.

Biological reserve (Réserve biologique) Regulations indicate that these reserves are natural regions which are established for: a) scientific purposes; b) protection of representative habitats and species; and c) ensuring that the environment is maintained without damage. Those actions which result in the change of the reserve (tree felling, opening of new roads or highways, permanent or temporary buildings and intensive pasturage) are forbidden, and lesser damaging actions must be authorised by the Administration des Eaux et Forêts.

In each established reserve, both the forest code law and the hunting regulations are in force; livestock grazing and timber exploitation are permitted, as defined in the ministerial order of 21 May 1921. Infringements of these regulations will result in punishment by payment or imprisonment (six days to two months).

Marine reserve (Réserve marine) Regulations indicate that such reserves are natural regions which are established for their importance for: a) protection of representative marine and coastal habitats. Those actions which result in the change of the reserve (intensive fishing) are forbidden, and lesser damaging actions must be authorised by the Administration des Eaux et Forêts and the Ministry of Marine Fisheries and Merchant Marine. In established reserves, the Royal Edict of the 11 April 1922 concerning the regulation of fishing in continental waters is in force.

Sources: Drucker, 1987; Duvall, 1988; Eaux et Forêts, 1991; Maher Abu Jaafer, 1984; M'Hirit, 1990; Maghnouj, 1991

Title: Dahir Ordinance on Hunting

Date: Dahir of 21 July 1923, modified 30 June 1962; Dahir of 2 June 1950; Ministry of Agriculture and Agrarian Reform Act of 3 November 1962

Brief description: Governs hunting and hunting reserves

Administrative authority: Direction des Eaux et Forêts et de la Conservation des Sols

Designations:

Permanent hunting reserve (Réserve de chasse permanante) Established to provide a permanent area for the protection and breeding of indigenous wildlife, as well as to serve as a source from which the wildlife would spread out into the surrounding areas.

Closed to all forms of hunting. Policing and regulation of hunting areas is covered under the Dahir of 21 July 1923. Controlled grazing tends to be permitted as is forestry management. All forms of hunting are banned except under licence. Settlement tends to be permitted within hunting reserves as is cultivation and other rural activities.

In some cases act as buffer zones for strict protected areas. Regulations specify which species can be hunted in some reserves and during what period or periods of the year.

In a number of cases there are official Royal hunting reserves (réserves de chasse royal) for use by the King and official visitors; they are protected from public interference, closed to any access from the public, and are havens for species protection. They have voluntary hunting bans and are managed by the Administration of Waters and Forests.

Triennial hunting reserve (Réserve de chasse triennale) Established to provide a temporary area for the protection and breeding of indigenous wildlife.

Closed to all forms of hunting for three year periods. Policing and regulation of hunting areas is covered under the Dahir of 21 July 1923. Controlled grazing tends to be permitted as is forestry management. All forms of hunting are banned except under licence. Settlement tends to be permitted within hunting reserves as is cultivation and other rural activities.

In some cases temporary hunting reserves act as buffer zones for strict protected areas. Regulations specify which species can be hunted in some reserves and during what period or periods of the year.

Sources: Duvall, 1988; Eaux et Forêts, 1991; Maghnouj, 1991; M'Hirit, 1990

Title: Dahir concerning the Conservation and Exploitation of Forests, the Forest Ordinance

Date: 10 October 1917, amended by Dahirs of 25 November 1942, 15 April 1946, 10 October 1947, 17 April 1960 and 21 July 1960

Brief description: Concerns the conservation and the exploitation of forests and the regulation and exploitation of forest reserves and forest produce. It takes into account: Royal Edict (Dahir) of 3 January 1916 on delimitation of forest land; Act of 4 September 1918 regulating the conditions of the exploitation, peddling, selling, and the exportation of forestry products; Act of 15 January 1921 regulating the mode of exercise of the rights of travelling in the forestry estate; and Act of 15 April 1946 relating to the sylvo-pastoral management of forestry domain.

Administrative authority: Direction des Eaux et Forêts et de la Conservation des Sols

Designations:

State forest (Forêt Domainale) Areas which are divided into conservation and production forests as delimited under the law of 1916. Forests managed for forest conservation tend not to be specifically defined, sites protected for nature conservation are protected as nature reserves under the above mentioned legislation.

There are no specific forest reserves, management being based on administrative parcelles as declared by statuary order of the Ministry of Agriculture and Agrarian Reform. Licences may be issued for the cutting, taking and removal of forest products (see acts).

Prohibited activities include the erection of buildings or other dwellings, the felling of live trees without licences, hunting (usually only tourist hunting is allowed within these areas). Permitted activities include the taking of dead wood, passage of livestock through the forest. Up to 20 per cent of forested areas are to be closed to grazing at any one time.

Sources: Duvall, 1988; Eaux et Forêts, 1991; Maghnouj, 1991; M'Hirit, 1990

Title: Royal Edict (Dahir) on Communal lands (commune rural)

Date: 20 September 1976

Brief Description: Provides for communal participation in the management and exploitation of forest resources on communal lands.

Administrative authority: Communal council, Provincial Council and National Council of Forestry

Designations: Communal areas see text

Sources: Eaux et Forêts, 1991; Maghnouj, 1991

SUMMARY OF PROTECTED AREAS

Map ref.	National/international designations Name of area	IUCN management category	Area (ha)	Year notified
	National Parks			
1	Souss-Massa	V	33,800	1991
2	Toubkal	V	36,000	1942
	Biological Reserves			
3	Bokkoyas	I	43,000	1986
4	Khnifiss/Puerto Cansado	I	6,500	1962
5	Merja Zerga	IV	7,000	1978
	Botanical Reserve			
6	Talassantane	I	2,603	1972
	Permanent Hunting Reserves			
7	Bouarfa	IV	220,000	1967
8	Iriki	IV	10,000	1967
9	Sidi Boughaba	VIII	5,600	1946
10	Sidi Chiker (M'Sabih Talaa)	I	1,987	1952
11	Takherkhort	I	1,230	1967
	Ramsar Wetlands			
	Merja Zerga	R	3,500	1980
	Merja Sidi-Boughaba	R	200	1980
	Lac d'Affennourir	R	380	1980
	Khnifiss Bay or Puerto Cansado	R	6,500	1980

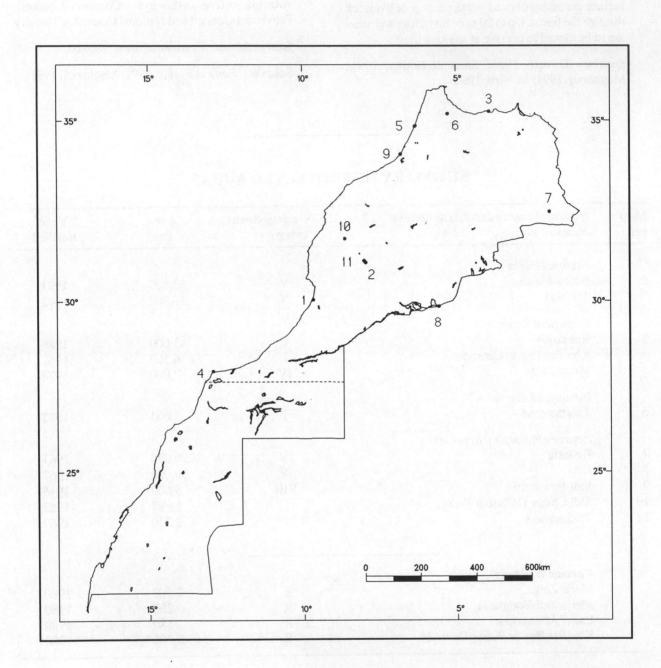

Protected Areas of Morocco

MOROCCO – SAHARAN PROVINCES OF BOUJDOUR, ES SEMARA LAAYOUNE AND DAKHLA OR OUED EL DAHAB (FORMERLY SPANISH SAHARA)

Area 266,769 sq. km (Hunter, 1991)

Population 180,000 (1986 estimate) (Hunter, 1991)

Economic Indicators
See main Morocco text

Policy and Legislation The colony of Spanish Sahara became a Spanish province (Western Sahara) in July 1958. A tripartite agreement was announced on 14 November 1975 providing for the transfer of power to the Moroccan and Mauritanian governments on 28 February 1976. On 14 April 1976 a Convention was signed in which Mauritania and Morocco agreed to partition the territory, and on 14 August 1979 Mauritania renounced its claim to this region. Its territory was annexed as one of the four provinces of Moroccan Sahara: Boujdour, Es Semara Laayoune and Oued el Dahab.

There has been continued civil unrest in parts of the former Spanish colony, and the Popular Front for the Liberation of Saguia el Hamra and Rio de Oro (Frente Popular para la Liberación de Seguia el Hamra y Rio de Oro) or Polisario Front (Frente Polisario) has unilaterally declared the whole territory as the Saharawi Arab Democratic Republic (SADR), although the region remains almost completely under Moroccan jurisdiction (Europa, 1984). Following United Nations Security Council Resolutions (690) for the recognition of the right to self-determination, a peace plan was accepted by all parties in August 1988. A ceasefire came into effect, and a referendum to determine the future of the area was due to take place in January 1992 under UN supervision (Dowden, 1991; Hunter, 1991).

Current nature conservation legislation is covered under the same laws as for the whole of Morocco: namely Royal Edict (Dahir) on National Parks of 11 September 1934, individual ministerial nature reserve acts whereby each reserve is individually declared by Ministry of Agriculture and Agrarian Reform orders, and the Dahir on Hunting of 21 July 1923 (modified 30 June 1962) which governs hunting and hunting reserves (Duvall, 1988; M'Hirit, 1990; Eaux et Forêts, 1991; Maghnouj, 1991).

At the time of the Spanish administration, the chief laws included the Spanish Hunting Law No. 1 of 4 April 1970 which was strengthened by strict control on gun ownership (Peris, *in litt.*, 1985). Other Spanish laws in force at that time included Law No. 37/1966 of 31 May 1966 concerning the creation of national hunting reserves (Ley sobre Creación de Reservas Nacionales de Caza) but no sites had been designated (Ortuño and Peña, 1976; ICONA, *in litt.*, 1988). The part of the former

Spanish colony ceded temporarily to Mauritania (Tiris el-Gharbiya, which was subsequently ceded as the Moroccan province of Oued El Dahab) was covered by Mauritanian Law No. 75-603 of 15 January 1975 concerning the hunting code and protection of fauna (Code Loi No. 75-603 portant Code de la Chasse et de la protection de la faune). No protected areas were designated at that time.

Deficiencies in legislation are reported to have been further hampered by disputes of ownership and associated military conflict in the region.

International Activities At the international level, Morocco has entered a number of cooperative agreements and legal obligations (see main Morocco text). At the international level some question has been made of the jurisdiction of Morocco over the four Saharan provinces: in the 4th meeting of the CITES Animal Committee in 1990 a proposal was put forward to export a CITES listed marine species from "Western Sahara". It was unclear whether the Moroccan authorities were the responsible body even though they were party to CITES. The conclusion was that Morocco did not have actual jurisdiction over the territory in question (CITES, 1990; Luxmoore, pers. comm., 1991).

Although not recognised as the legitimate government of an independent sovereign state by the United Nations, the self-proclaimed Sahrawi Arab Democratic Republic (SADR) has entered a number of cooperative agreements and legal obligations, although none specifically on the environment; it became a member of the Organization of African Unity in 1982 and holds an observer seat at the United Nations (Griffin, 1987; Shelley, 1989).

Potential transboundary protected areas include one between this region and Banc d'Arguin National Park in Mauritania, both areas renowned for possessing the last major colonies of Mediterranean monk seal left in the world.

Administration and Management No specific parks or reserves were established under the Spanish administration. All land was controlled by the Captain General of the Province of Spanish Sahara, effectively through the army which enforced hunting bans under Law No. 1 of 4 April 1970 (Peris, *in litt.*, 1985). Currently the administration and management of wildlife protected areas in all of Morocco is under the technical and administrative responsibility of the Ministry of Agriculture and Agrarian Reform (Ministère de l'Agriculture et de la Réforme Agraire). The Administration of Water and Forests and of the

Conservation of Soils (Direction des Eaux et Forêts et de la Conservation des Sols) is in charge of general coordination, administration, and routine management, and the Division of Hunting, Fishing and the Protection of Nature (Division de la Chasse, de la Pêche et de la Protection de la Nature) (CPN) deals specifically with administration and management of protected areas and wildlife as well as for issuing hunting and fishing permits. Siège de Service offices of the Administration of Waters and Forests are located at Ad-Dakhla and Layoun (DCFTT, 1987).

Nature protection related research is undertaken in the region by the Institut Scientifique of the Mohammed V University, Rabat, the official Government Scientific research organisation, together with that of the Institut National Agronomique et Vétérinaire (INAV) and Institut National de la Recherche Agronomique (INRA) (Beaubrun et Thevenot, 1982). The National Zoological Park of Rabat has undertaken surveys in the region with priority for conservation and research on wildlife and their biotopes, such as for the globally endangered monk seal and for the desert species of gazelle (Haddane, *in litt.*, 1991). Extensive research was also undertaken during the Spanish administrative period including by the Forestry and Experimental Research Institute (Forestal de Investigaciones y Experiencas) of Madrid, by the Botanical Gardens of Madrid, and the Institute of Scientific Studies (Istituto Estudios Africanos), as well as by the Centre for Saharan Fauna (Centro de Rescate de la Fauna Sahariana). Both the last two mentioned bodies were of the Superior Council of Scientific Research (Consejo Superior de Investigaciones Cientificas) based in Madrid. Throughout the 1980s the Centro de Rescate de la Fauna Sahariana has been undertaking research on gazelle reintroductions and breeding (Peris, *in litt.*, 1985).

Effectiveness of protected area management and wardening during the Spanish period was difficult, illegal hunting being undertaken by military personnel and others. Personnel from oil and mining companies had also been noted as having indiscriminately killed ungulates and ostriches. Currently, some areas in the east of the region are under partial control of the military and access is restricted in a number of sectors. In the areas where military conflicts are known to have occurred, management has been non-existent (Burgis and Symoens, 1987).

Systems Reviews The former province of Spanish Sahara was bounded in the west by the Atlantic, in the south by Mauritania, in the east by Algeria and in the north by Morocco. Since 1979 Morocco has claimed the Saharan Provinces of Boujdour, Es Semara, Laayoune and Dakhla or Oued el Dahab which occupy the former Spanish region.

The region mostly consists of desert with little or no perennial vegetation, divided into six biotopes: rhus/euphorbia matorral, Taljas *Acacia* woodland and wadi shrubs, reg vegetation, roquedos inselbergs, lagoons, and the coastal zone (Valverde, 1957). Along the 700km coastline a narrow band of atlantic coastal desert flora occurs where the vegetation cover is relatively dense, particularly in shallow depressions or grarat. In the extreme north the coastal area is occupied by sub-Mediterranean grassland and succulent shrubs composed of three species of euphorbia (Davis *et al.*, 1986). The low mountainous terrain includes Uarksis, El Zini, Zemmur and El Janfra; notable rock formations exist at Adrar Sutuf and El Tiris. The main seasonal rivers are the Seguiat, Itgui and Jat. The fauna is represented by typical desert communities (see Valverde, 1957). Cetaceans are numerous in the coastal waters and the globally endangered monk seal *Monachus monachus* is known to inhabit the area (Haddane, pers. comm., 1991). Green turtle *Chelonia mydas* is not uncommon in the area (Groombridge and Luxmoore, in press).

Important mineral deposits occur in the region, such as the Bou Craa phosphates (totalling 1 billion tonnes), as well as oil and iron-ore. Less than 19% of the terrain is in agricultural use; wooded land including scrub totals 1,011,000ha and in 1983 there were about 22,000 sheep and goat (DCFTT, 1987; Hunter, 1991).

Comprehensive surveys of biological resources were first undertaken during the provincial Spanish Sahara period, which included work on vegetation, geology, mineral and topographical surveys, fauna distributional and status surveys (Agacino, 1950; Berkes, 1980; Burgis and Symoens, 1987; Guinea, 1945a; Guinea Lopez, 1945; Guinea, 1948; Hernandez-Pacheco *et al.*, 1949; Murat, 1939; Peris, 1985; Valverde, 1957). Throughout the 1980s the Centro de Rescate de la Fauna Sahariana has been undertaking research on gazelle reintroductions and breeding and work is now being undertaken by a number of Moroccan agencies and institutes. In 1990 a French expedition proposed to capture and relocate Western Sahara monk seals to a commercial marine park in France (CITES, 1990).

Prior to 1973 the entire province of Spanish Sahara was regarded a "reserve subject" but no specific sites were designated with a protected status (Peris, *in litt.*, 1985). A limited number of sites have been recommended for protection as important haunts of globally threatened ungulate and bird species, including Edchera, Hagunia, Laadeim and Sebkhet Deboaa, as well as areas representing dense vegetation enclaves such as the Zemmur massif or the Roquedos rock outcrops with their relict Mediterranean flora of olive and juniper (Valverde, 1957; Peris, *in litt.*, 1985). A number of sites identified as monk seal beaches have also been identified for protection, including the Côte des Phoques, la Guera and Cap Boujadour (Berkes, 1980; Boulva, 1975; CITES, 1990; Trotignon, 1982; Haddane, *in litt.*, 1991). Notable wetlands recommended for protection include Guelta Zemmur and the Sebkhas Aghzoumalia, Dkhaciya and Lamhar Twil (Burgis and Symoens, 1987).

In 1991 there were no designated protected areas.

Environmental impact includes the ongoing but much reduced military conflict which continues in the eastern region, an area marked with numerous land mines and other explosives; fighting has been reported to have affected important nature conservation areas, including the wetland of Guelta Zemmur. In addition, major environmental impacts have resulted from the construction of military installations and a sand-wall line of defences 2,575km long from the Ourkziz to Dakhla. Transhumant population have also affected the natural vegetation and uncontrolled fishing still occurs offshore (Burgis and Symoens, 1987; Griffin, 1987).

Other Relevant Information Disruption as a result of the military conflict led to 40,000 refugees fleeing from the region into surrounding countries in the mid 1970s, a figure rising to 300,000 registered by the United Nations High Commission for Refugees in the mid 1980s. The impact on the environment of such population change has not been investigated (Griffin, 1987; Trotignon, 1982).

Addresses

See main Morocco entry for full lists

Siège de Service des Eaux et Forêts et de la Conservation des Sols, AD-DAKHLA

Siège de Service des Eaux et Forêts et de la Conservation des Sols, LAYOUN

References

Agacino, M. (1950). Notes sur les phoques-moines (*Monachus monachus*, herm.) du littoral Saharien Espagnol. *Mammalia* 1-2.

Agacino, M. (1950). Algunos datos sobre ciertos mamiferos del Sahara occidental. *Bulletin. R. Soc. Esp. Hist. Nat.* XLIII: 199-212.

Anon. (1962). XIII/1, Spain, Forest Regulations (Decree No. 485/1962) (Extracts: Preliminary Part and Book I (Forest Property). *Food and Agricultural Legislation*, Vol. XI – No. 2. Food and Agricultural Organisation, Rome. Pp. 1-16.

Berkes, F. (1980). Saharan coast. Monk seal, conservation of the Mediterranean population. Interim report to WWF/IUCN. Contract Reference: 1118. Pp. 7-8.

Burgis, M.J. and Symoens, J.J. (Eds.) (1987). *Directory of African wetlands and shallow water bodies*. Editions de l'ORSTOM, Paris, France. 650 pp.

Boulva, J. (1975). Spanish Sahara. Survey of the monk seal in the Western Mediterranean. A report presented to the International Fund for Animal Welfare and to IUCN. P. 13.

Conseil National de l'Environnement (1985). Le phénomène de la désertification au Maroc. Ministère de l'habitat et de l'aménagement du territoire. 16 pp.

CITES (1990). Monk seals. Minutes of the 4th Meeting of the CITES Animals Committee, 12-16 November 1990, Darwin, Australia. Point No. 13.

Davis, S.D., Droop, S.J.M., Gregerson, P., Henson, L., Leon, C.J., Lamlein Villa-Lobos, J., Synge, H. and Zantovska, J. (1986). *Plants in danger: what do we know?* IUCN, Gland, Switzerland and Cambridge, UK. 461 pp.

DCFTT (1987). *Le Maroc Forestier, echelle: 1/2,000,000.* Division de la Cartographie in collaboration with the Direction des Eaux et Forêts, Rabat, Morocco.

Dowden, R. (1991). Hassan accommodates only one side in Western Sahara. *Independent.* 7 November. P. 14.

Duvall, L. (1988). The status of biological resources in Morocco, constraints, and options for conserving biological diversity. Government of the United States of America and the US Agency for International Development. 58 pp.

Eaux et Forêts (1991). Rapport sur les aires protégées au Maroc. Paper presented at the Third Man and Biosphere Meeting on Biosphere Reserves in the Mediterranean and the First IUCN-CNPPA Workshop on Protected Areas in the North Africa-Middle East Region, 14-19 October 1991, Tunis. 18 pp.

Europa (1984). *The Middle East and North Africa, 1984-85.* Europa Publications Ltd, UK.

FAO (1986). Plan national de lutte contre la désertification. Project FAO/TCP/MOR/4506 (A). 149 pp.

Griffin, M. (1987). The divided desert. *Geographical Magazine* 59(8): 374-377.

Groombridge, B. and Luxmoore, R. (in press). The Green turtle and Hawksbill (Reptilia; Cheloniidae): World status, exploitation and trade: a report to the Cites Secretariat. World Conservation Monitoring Centre, Cambridge, UK.

Guinea, E. (1945a). Aspecto forestal del desierto. *La vegetation lenosa y los pastos del Sahara Español.* Instituto Forestal de Investigaciones y Experiencas, Madrid. 152 pp.

Guinea Lopez, E. (1945). España y el desierto. Impressiones Saharianas de un botanico Español. *Colección España ante el mundo.* Instituto de Estudios Politicos, Madrid. 279 pp.

Guinea, E. (1948). Catalogo razonado de las plantas del Sahara Español. *An. Jard. Bot. Madrid* 8: 357-442.

Hernandez-Pacheco, E *et al.* (Eds.) (1949). *El Sahara Español: Estudo Geologico, Geografico y Botanico.* Consejo Superior de Investigaciones Cientificas, Istituto Estudios Africanos, Madrid.

Hunter, B. (Ed.) (1991). *The Statesman's Year Book 1991-92.* The Macmillan Press Ltd, London and Basingstoke, UK. 1692 pp.

Mahnouj, M. (1991). Rapport sur l'Etat de la conservation de la Nature au Maroc. Presented to the Third Man and Biosphere Meeting on Biosphere Reserves in the Mediterranean, 14-19 October 1991, Tunis. Division de Recherches et d'Experimentations Forestières, Direction des Eaux et Forêts et de la Conservation des Sols, Rabat. 18 pp.

M'Hirit, Z.O. (1990). Evaluation des ressources forestières Marocaine, 1990. Unpublished document prepared by the Division de Recherches et d'Experimentation Forestières du Maroc.

Murat, M. (1939). La végétation du Sahara occidental en zone espagnole. *Compte Rendue Somm. Seanc. Soc. Biogeog.* Unpublished.

Ortuno, F. and Pena, J de la. (1976). *Reservas y cotos nacionales de Caza.* Region Pirenaica Vol. 1; Region Cantabrica, Vol. 2; Region Central, Vol. 3; Region Mediterranean, Vol. 4. INCAFO, Spain.

Poore, D. and Gryn-Ambroes, P. (1980). *Nature conservation in Northern and Western Europe.*

UNEP/IUCN/WWF, Gland, Switzerland. Pp. 291-314.

Saussey, Ch. du (1980). Legislation of wildlife, hunting and protected areas in some European countries. *Legislative Study* No. 20. FAO, Rome.

Shelley, T. (1989). Fighting for a desert home. *Geographical Magazine* 61(4): 46-48.

Trotignon, J. (1982). Les derniers phoques sahariens. *La Courrier de la Nature* 77: 14-20.

Valverde, J.A. (1957). *Aves del Sahara Español, estudio ecologico del desierto.* Instituto de Estudios Africanos, Consejo Superior de Investigaciones Cientificas, Madrid. 481 pp.

OMAN (SULTANATE OF OMAN)
(Formerly known as the Sultanate of Muscat and Oman)

Area 212,460 sq. km

Population 1.502 million (1990)
Natural increase: 3.75% per annum

Economic Indicators
GDP: US$ 5,635 per capita (1987)
GNP: US$ 5,780 per capita (1987)

Policy and Legislation Oman is an absolute monarchy and there is no formal constitution. All laws are issued by Royal Decree of the Sultan with assistance of the Council of Ministers. The Kuria Muria Islands ceded to the United Kingdom in 1854 were retroceded to the Sultanate on 30 November 1967, and the Gwadur enclave within Baluchistan was handed over to Pakistan in 1958 (Hunter, 1991).

The legal system subscribes to the Islamic law, Sharia, which is both state and religious. The Koran encourages great respect for the environment, embodied with the need for the traditional Islamic respect for nature. Nature conservation has a long tradition in the Arabian Peninsula. Traditional forms of protected area or range reserves (hema, hima, hujrah or ahmia) may have origins over 2,000 years ago in the pre-Islamic period and still occur to some extent in Oman as well as in the adjacent Republic of Yemen and in Saudi Arabia.

Existing legislation for wildlife and nature conservation is largely based on the following: Decree No. 26/79 of 15 May 1979 providing authority to establish national parks and nature reserves. The Decree calls for the establishment of a technical and consultative committee of members from specific ministries to prepare and study draft schemes for establishing protected areas. It also specifies the kinds of activities to be regulated in such areas (see Annex). A Ministerial Decision No. 4 of 6 April 1976 provides for a total prohibition of hunting, shooting, capture and molestation of "all species of birds in all parts of Oman's shores and islands, at all times". The shooting of birds of any kind and the taking of seabirds' eggs is forbidden along the entire coastline. Local authority regulations have been in force for some time and three sites have been granted protected area status. There are restrictions on visiting Daimaniyat islands between June and October. Other pieces of legislation include Royal Decree No. 53, 1981 entitled the "Law of Sea Fishing and the Preservation of Marine Biological Wealth", which regulates fishing. It also authorises the designation of areas where fishing will be permanently forbidden, and other areas where fishing will be allowed only within defined seasons and for specific species (Lausche, 1986). The Royal Decree was followed by Ministerial Decree No. 3/82, 1982 which includes executive regulations for law of marine fishing and conservation of aquatic resources. All capture of

turtles is prohibited during the nesting season, as determined by the appropriate authority. Specific areas are protected by law and collection of eggs within them is prohibited within a distance of the coast to be determined by the appropriate authority. Hunting of turtles on their way to lay eggs on the islands and coasts is prohibited during periods which are determined by the appropriate authorities.

In addition to specific protected area legislation is a whole series of planning controls which have evolved to include environmental protection. There are obligations of building developers to obtain a certificate of No Environmental Objection (NEO) from the Ministry of Environment and Water Resources, which is applicable to all areas of Oman. Important nature conservation areas can thus be protected by declining to grant NEO certificates (Munton, 1991). In addition, the Ministry of Environment and Water Resources is working on the principle of undertaking ecosystem conservation in wider areas extending beyond reserve boundaries: these are most finely tuned in the Development Plan for the Southern Region, where all areas are classified according to the degree of planning control in operation or category of use, and legislated through the authority of the PCDESR which was set up under Royal Decree No. 48 of 1984. Two classes of nature conservation area have been approved in 1991: reserve zone 1 and reserve zone 2 (Munton, 1991).

For a complete list and details of environmental legislation, including draft new legislation, see Appendix VIII in the IUCN report *Proposals for a system of nature conservation areas* (Lausche, 1986; Daly, *in litt*, 1991).

Decree No. 26/79 has not been implemented because of several factors. Concerns originally existed that a more complete scientific basis was needed before specific areas could be identified. Also the institutional arrangements within government had made some of the provisions outdated. Lausche 1986 felt that the decree was no longer adequate for the needs of the country and so a new draft law had been outlined. The Coastal Zone Management Plan, a joint project of IUCN and the Ministry of Commerce, also covers a number of these points (Salm, *in litt.*, 1991).

By 1991 responsibility for nature conservation was passing from the Diwan of Royal Court to the Ministry of Environment and Water Resources. With this change, the emphasis of ideas and activities has shifted from the conservation of high profile species through specification of protected areas to the development of a national conservation strategy (NCS), with its emphasis on ecosystem conservation. As a result of this evolution of ideas over the past 20 years, the Sultanate now has a variety of strategies and plans for conserving natural resources and a number of administrative measures that can be taken to conserve and ensure the sustainable use of resources. The NCS is broad, and if effectively implemented, will change both attitude towards nature and natural resources and action towards such resources by government agencies (Munton, 1991).

International Activities At the international level, the Sultanate of Oman has entered a number of cooperative agreements and legal obligations. Oman is party to the Convention concerning the Protection of the World Cultural and Natural Heritage (World Heritage Convention), which it accepted on 6 October 1981. No natural sites have been inscribed to date (see below). Oman does not participate in the Convention on Wetlands of International Importance especially as Waterfowl Habitat (Ramsar Convention), nor the Unesco Man and Biosphere (MAB) Programme. In 1979 the Sultanate of Oman ratified the Kuwait Regional Convention for Cooperation on the Protection of the Marine Environment from Pollution (Kuwait Action Plan). Oman actively participates in meetings concerned with additional protocols to the Kuwait Regional Agreement.

In 1990, the White Oryx Project and Nuquf, the Janaba Hills and Sahil al-Jazir were recommended as World Heritage sites, and a World Heritage funded assessment survey was due to take place in 1991 (Daly, *in litt.*, 1990; Ishwaran, pers. comm., 1991).

Administration and Management Seven government institutions currently have major responsibilities in matters of environmental protection: the Council on Conservation of the Environment and Water Resources (CCEWR), the Ministry of the Environment and Water Resources, the Office of the Adviser on Conservation of the Environment, the Planning Committee for Development and Environment in the Southern Region (PCDESR), the Ministry of Housing, the Ministry of Commerce and Industry (Director of Tourism) and the Ministry of Agriculture and Fisheries.

Throughout the 1970s and 1980s the ministries of Land Affairs and Municipalities, Agriculture, Education, Fisheries, Petroleum and Minerals, Communications, Commerce and Industry, Interior and Social Affairs and Labour and the Directorate General of Finance were required to provide members to set up a technical and consultative committee responsible for parks and nature reserves. The Committee was headed by a chairman and the Adviser for Conservation of the Environment acted as its secretary. The latter two positions were by Royal Decree. The Committee was required to draw up draft schemes and study schemes presented by the ministries (Daly, *in litt.*, 1982). As of 1986 the Royal Decree on National Parks and Nature Reserves of 1979 had not been used, chiefly because there was no single government entity to assume responsibility for parks and reserves. However, by 1991 responsibility for Nature Conservation was passing from the Diwan of Royal

Court to the Ministry of Environment and Water Resources. The main agencies currently involved with protected areas include the Office of the Adviser for Conservation of the Environment which was established by Royal Decree in 1974, with functions to acquire knowledge about the wild flora and fauna of Oman, and to ensure that wildlife and other natural resources would be protected and managed in harmony with other forms of development. It was set up in the Diwan of Royal Court Affairs and first undertook field surveys from 1975 onwards. It manages a number of nature reserves, the first of which, Wadi Serin Tahr Reserve, was set up and managed by a ranger force employed under this Office. Work has also been undertaken on species ecology in collaboration with IUCN and WWF. Under the authority and management of the Diwan of Royal Court Affairs is the Endangered Mammals Breeding Centre at Bait al Barakah. The Centre is involved in the support for the Adviser's field conservation projects such as the White Oryx Project, based at Ja'aluni on the Jiddat al Harasis. Arabian oryx was first reintroduced to the wild in the central desert of Oman in 1982. Since 1988, the population has increased from 37 to 109 in the 10,000 sq. km protected area. A monitoring programme has been developed and a new programme commenced on 1 April 1990 (Spalton, 1990). In 1986 a nature conservation strategy was completed in collaboration with IUCN consultants. "Proposals for a System of Nature Conservation Areas" (Child, 1986) identified a whole series of protected and nature conservation area categories. In this report (Appendix IX), a Directorate General for Wildlife and Nature Conservation in Oman had been proposed to supersede and restructure the then existing diverse administrative and management bodies. It was recommended that it would form part of the Ministry of the Environment and Water Resources. Two regional programmes (one for the Southern Region and the other for the rest of the Sultanate) were recommended, which were further sub-divided under a total of five regional directors (see below). By 1991 according to the Office of the Adviser for Conservation of the Environment the contents were still in the process of being sanctioned and implemented (Daly, *in litt.*, 1991).

The CCEWR, formally called the Council for Conservation of the Environment and Prevention of Pollution (CCEPP), was established by Royal Decree in 1979 (Law No. 68/79 superseded by Nos 46/84 and 105/85). It was set up to ensure cooperation between ministries so that their various projects could be undertaken without damaging the environment. The CCEWR has been instrumental in undertaking coastal surveys (see below). Its role is to ensure that the impact of all development projects upon the environment are studied, assessed and subsequently controlled. In the mid-1980s the council's policy-making technical and implementation roles were regarded as appearing to be well linked for dealing with national environmental problems (Lausche, 1986). In 1983 IUCN and the former

CCEPP instigated an ecological survey of the inter-tidal and sub-tidal regions (UNEP/IUCN, 1985).

The Ministry of Environment was set up under Royal Decree No. 45/84, 1984 and subsequently renamed the Ministry of Environment and Water Resources. Sections within the Ministry include the Division of Conservation Strategy with prime interests in conservation matters. Amongst others the activities of the Ministry include development of protected area management plans such as in the PCDESR and CZMP (see below). Since 1985 until completion in 1991 the Director of Tourism of the Ministry of Commerce and Industry has been working in collaboration with IUCN consultants to develop a coastal wildlife resource and tourism plan for the Sultanate, the Coastal Zone Management Project (CZMP). The CZMP has included basic management guidelines for protected areas and sets out responsibilities of government agencies for their part in maintaining the quality of the nearshore marine environment and coastal resources. Especial emphasis indicated ultimate coordination and administration through the Ministry of Environment and Water Resources, each agency making its contribution to the conservation of coastal zone resources (Munton, 1991; Salm, *in litt.*, 1991).

The PCDESR was set up under Royal Decree No. 48 of 1984 following the "Salalah workshop on environmental aspects of development in the Southern Region" which was convened in 1983. The technical secretariat became operational in 1985 following a second workshop. Its role is specifically to look into and address the environmental problems around Dhofar in the southern region. The regional development plan for the southern region was undertaken by consultants on behalf of the PCDESR. This project has reviewed all the major resources including woodland and wildlife resources, basing activities on a concept of renewable resources. The project included a complete review of all NCAs in the southern region. Some 32 NCAs have been incorporated into the plan, as compared to the original IUCN proposal of 30 (for details see Munton, 1991). The Ministry of Environment and Water Resources has the ultimate responsibility for management of these reserves, which include the categories of scenic reserve and nature reserve (reserves Zone 1 and 2). Management plans are under preparation for the important areas of Bar al Hikman and Masirah, and will be based on multiple resource use concepts derived from the NCR (Munton, 1991).

The Ministry of Agriculture and Fisheries is responsible for various pieces of legislation on the conservation of marine resources, starting with the Ministerial Decision of 1976. It is actively involved in species protection, restricting fishing by licences, preventing damage or destruction of various habitats, including coral reefs, and inhibiting hunting activities as well as maintaining fishing prohibitions and penalties. Work of the forest section of the Ministry of Agriculture and Fisheries, which was created in early 1980s, includes evaluating draft forest and rangeland legislation, such as provisions for rangeland and forest reserves. In 1991 a Technical Committee on Pastoral Lands and Nature Conservation Areas was convened (Munton, 1991). Also in 1991 a project was completed, in association with the University of Durham (UK), to map the woodlands (Munton, 1991).

Overall protected areas management currently includes staff wardening and monitoring in just four conservation areas; the turtle beaches between Khawr Jaramah and Ruwais (Ra'as al Hadd); Wadi Serin Nature Reserve and the Jiddat al Harasis; the Daimaniyat islands have a coastguard post and its staff monitors activities on the islands. In addition, the Ministry of Agriculture carries out some turtle tagging work on Masirah island (Munton, 1991).

No non-governmental groups are involved in protected areas. However, an active natural history group is based at the Natural History Museum, part of the Ministry of National Heritage and Culture. The museum was inaugurated in 1980 and natural history data has been collected since 1982. The Historical Association of Oman has a strong natural history section, which is actively involved in wildlife surveys such as collecting data on the birds of Masirah island (K. Bin Abdurredha Sultan, 1988, cited by Rogers, 1988; also contact the Oman Bird Record Committee).

Of the potential administrative and management constraints in the country, there is still no single government entity to assume coordinating responsibility for all nature protection activities, although this may change with the increasing activities of the Ministry of Environment and Water Resources. The response by government to the 1986 *Proposals for a System of Nature Conservation Areas* has shown that government agencies often misunderstand the concepts behind conservation of resources and the implications of designating an area for nature conservation. They have failed to show that it is necessary to illustrate that the emphasis on conservation management in a particular area does not mean that no development is possible in that area; the benefits to all of such management also need to be publicised (Munton, 1991). Specific reservations of the Ministry of Environment and Water Resources to the 1986 proposals concern the vast coverage and expense of the management systems proposed and the lack of details about the nature conservation value of some sites (for details see Munton, 1991).

In the present situation there continues to be a lack of on-the-ground monitoring and enforcement and a need for a strong educational component in the NCS to explain the basis of sustainable resource conservation. Therefore, for the NCS to be effective, funds need to be devoted both to an active educational programme and also to on-the-ground monitoring of natural resources and enforcement of their proper use. It has been indicated that such monitoring should take place in nature conservation areas where the natural resources has been identified as being of particular importance and outside such areas where particular ecosystems have to be conserved because of their value or sensitivity. At present, although there are many plans, provisions, legal and administrative measures available, there is a lack of application on the ground (Munton, 1991).

Systems Reviews   Oman is the second largest country in the Arabian Peninsula, bounded in the north-east by the Gulf of Oman and Straits of Hormuz opposite Iran, in the south-east by the Arabian Sea (Indian Ocean), in the south-west by the Republic of Yemen and north-west by Saudi Arabia and the United Arab Emirates. An enclave, the Musandam Peninsula, is surrounded by the United Arab Emirates (Hunter, 1991). Oman possesses about 1,800km of coastline bordering on the Indian Ocean. The climate varies considerably from region to region; humidity can reach 90% at Muscat. In the interior the climate is hot and dry throughout the year, whilst in the south the climate is more temperate, although heavy rains fall between June and October. Dhofar, the southern province, is the only part of the Arabian Peninsula to be touched by the south-west monsoon (Hunter, 1991).

Most of the country is desert to semi-desert, 80% lying at elevations ranging between 100m and 600m. In the extreme south of the country (Dhofar), on a coastal strip 150km long and up to 50km deep, the vegetation is rather atypical, consisting of grassland and scrub vegetation. Low juniper "forest" occurs on Jabal Akhdar in the north. The Musandam Peninsula in the north consists mostly of stony mountains with small patches of alluvium producing rich grassy pastures. The north is dominated by the Hajjar mountain range, which runs parallel to the coast, reaching 3,009m at the Jebel Akhdar (J. Shams). Between the Hajjar mountains and the coast is the Batinah plain, stretching from Muscat to the border. To the south and west of the mountains is an extensive desert of stony plain and sand dunes (for further details see Clarke *et al.*, 1986).

There is a provisional estimate of 1,100 plant species, with up to 50 endemic species of which most are concentrated in the southern part of Dhofar. Floristic affinities of southern Dhofar are Sudano-Deccanian, with Africa, Yemen and southern India elements. Affinities of northern Dhofar and the edge of the Empty Quarter are Saharo-Sindian, with Saharan and north-west Indian elements. Affinities of northern Oman are: low altitudes Irano-Turanian, with Iran; at higher altitudes western Himalayas (Davis *et al.*, 1986; Mandaville, 1977). The sublittoral region is represented by seagrass beds, mangrove and coral reefs, along with important planktonic and benthic algal resources (Daly, *in litt.*, 1982). In the Salalah region of Dhofar the unusual algal distribution, dominated by kelp, is the result of annual monsoon-driven coastal upwellings from the deep ocean. More than 200 algae, 200 mollusc, and 120 crustacean species have been recorded (UNEP/IUCN, 1985). Nutrient levels are so high that there is a large

population of fish, marine turtles and cetaceans. The Dhofar coastal algal communities are important resource areas for commercially important species including crayfish, abalone and many demersal fish. Only 41,000ha of the total land area is under cultivation; 0.12% arable, and goat grazing is widely distributed throughout Oman. Up to 80% of the country's revenue comes from oil production (Hunter, 1991; Papastavrou, 1990).

There are approximately 70 mammal species, 392 bird species, the latter of which are mainly migrants, 74 reptiles and 2 species of amphibians at least 58 marine fish species and 6 species of freshwater fish, 70 species of butterfly and 300 moths (for a more complete listing see review in Clarke *et al.*, 1986).

The Diwan of Royal Court, Adviser for Conservation of the Environment, was the first body to mount scientific surveys of flora and fauna (first in 1975, then in 1977 and 1980) (Government Adviser for the Conservation of the Environment, 1979; Clarke *et al.*, 1986). On-the-ground projects were initially aimed at specific, high profile species, commencing with Arabian tahr in 1976, four species of marine turtle from 1977 and on the reintroduction of Arabian oryx from 1978 (studies of wildlife have included joint enterprises of the government, IUCN and WWF). This in turn conserved some important scenic areas and their associated species, such as the relict *Ceratonia oreothauma*, *Acacia* and *Prosopis* vegetation in the Jiddat al Harasis (Green and Drucker, 1990: Munton, 1991). In 1983 as part of the marine conservation programme of the Kuwait action plan, IUCN and the former CCEPP instigated an ecological survey of the inter-tidal and sub-tidal regions. This was followed by the UNEP report of 1985, which outlined a strategy for protecting the important Dhofar algal communities and fish resources. This study identified means of protection through suitable zoning laws and recommended further research on species distribution, the impact of environmental factors, and ecological interactions (UNEP/IUCN, 1985). This was followed in 1986 by the preparation of the *Proposals for a system of nature conservation areas*, prepared by IUCN and the Sultanate (Clarke *et al.*, 1986), and the CZMP of IUCN, and the Ministry of Commerce and Industry (Salm, *in litt.*, 1991) (see below).

In October 1984 the government and IUCN set the 20-month project to prepare in-depth plans for a system of nature conservation areas (NCA) under the *Proposal for a system of nature conservation areas*, which was to form part of total land-use strategy. Plans included proposed details for policy and law, the designation of nature conservation area systems, and proposals for the structure and operation of a Directorate General of Wildlife and Nature Conservation within the Ministry of the Environment and Water Resources (Clarke *et al.*, 1986). Up to 43 different land classes and 12 marine habitats were identified, described and mapped, and populations of threatened and endemic wildlife of interest for conservation totalled 94 plant and 100 animal taxa. Exactly 89 sites of biotic or abiotic features, such as caves, and geomorphological sites were identified. A resultant 91 NCAs were identified for future protection, divided into 59 national nature reserves, 20 national scenic reserves, and 12 national resource reserves, representing about 37% of Oman (Clarke *et al.*, 1986).

Since 1985 the IUCN Marine Programme has been cooperating with the Ministry of Commerce and Industry to develop a tourist plan for the Sultanate, the Coastal Zone Management Project (CZMP). By 1990 the project leader had surveyed and mapped three major areas for potential tourism uses (Salm, *in litt.*, 1990). The resulting maps and management proposals have now been published by IUCN (1991). Elements of the management plan include establishment of touristic areas, protected areas such as turtle nesting beaches and areas of high scenic value, as well as areas that could be developed for urban or industrial purposes without causing serious damage to the environment. The project parallels the development of the national conservation strategy, and will form an integral part of it (Anon., 1989a; Salm, *in litt.*, 1991).

Between 1985 and 1987 the Royal Geographical Society of Great Britain instigated, together with the Office of the Adviser for Conservation of the Environment, the Oman Wahiba Sands Project, an integrated scientific survey of the entire Wahiba sands region (Dutton, 1988). Other recent projects include a seven-month coastal project identifying the environmental and wildlife situation of Masirah island and Bar Hikman, which was being undertaken by German Consultants under the PCDESR, with the final report due in December 1991 (Bauer, pers. comm., 1991).

By 1991 there were just four managed and wardened conservation areas in Oman. The first site was created in 1975 under authority of the Diwan of the Royal Court by Royal Decree. This site, Wadi Serin Tahr Reserve, initially covered an area of 240 sq. km and has since been extended from 530 sq. km to 800 sq. km. Jiddat al Harasis Protected Area covers a total which has increased from 10,000 sq. km to 27,500 sq. km (Spalton, 1990). By 1991 many of the 91 NCA proposals were still under review, although the full action plan had not been implemented (Daly, *in litt.*, 1991). Other areas include the turtle beaches between Khawr Jaramah and Ruwais (Ra'as al Hadd) and the Daimaniyat islands. In addition, the Ministry of Agriculture carries out some turtle tagging work on Masirah Island (Munton, 1991). The Law of Sea Fishing and the Preservation of Marine Biological Wealth authorises the designation of areas where fishing will be permanently forbidden, and other areas where fishing will be allowed only within defined seasons, in addition to sites for turtle protection and two classes of reserve zone (of PCDESR) approved in 1991. The areas of the White Oryx Project and the Nuquf, the Janaba Hills and Sahil al-Jazir were recommended as World Heritage sites in 1990 (Daly, *in litt.*, 1990; Ishwaran, pers. comm., 1991).

Major environmental problems include: natural water shortages, often worsened by prolonged drought; overpumping, leading to high salinity and oil spills along the coast. Following the cessation of war in the Dhofar, the number of cattle has risen sharply, leading to an imminent risk to the environment (Clarke *et al.*, 1986; Speece, 1981). Since about 1970 the pace of development and change in Oman has been marked, leading to widespread construction and rapid changes in lifestyle. Civil and military work in a number of cases is reported to have been undertaken without consideration of the environmental impact. Of the original conservation areas suggested by IUCN in 1986, a significant number have now been lost, for mineral extraction, grazing, industrial uses, military areas, tourism and agricultural development (Munton, 1991).

Other Relevant Information   As mentioned above, since 1985 the Ministry of Commerce and Industry has been developing a tourist plan. The CZMP includes mapping areas for potential tourist use, elements of which include establishing wildlife protected areas and areas of high scenic value (Munton, 1991; Salm, *in litt.*, 1990;). In 1989/90 tourist receipts for the country totalled US$ 44 million.

Addresses

Office of the Adviser for Conservation of the Environment, Diwan of Royal Court Affairs, PO Box 246, The Palace, MUSCAT (Tel: 736482, 722482/333; FAX: 740 550; Tlx: 5667 ace)

Division of Conservation Strategy, Ministry of Environment and Water Resources, PO Box 323, MUSCAT (Tel: 696458; FAX: 602320; Tlx: 5404)

Director of Tourism, Ministry of Commerce and Industry, PO Box 550, MUSCAT (Tel: 774 318; FAX: 794 238)

Ministry of Agriculture and Fisheries, Sultan Qaboos Street, PO Box 467 Al Khuwair, MUSCAT (Tel: 696312; Tlx: 3503 Agrifish on)

Council for Conservation of the Environment and Water Resources (CCEWR), PO Box 5310, RUWI

Ministry of National Heritage and Culture, Sultan Qaboos Street, Al Khuwair, PO Box 668, MUSCAT (Tel: 602555; Tlx: 5649 omnhcv on)

The Historical Association of Oman, PO Box 6941, RUWI

The Oman Bird Record Committee, PO Box 246, MUSCAT

References

Anon. (1985). The management and conservation of renewable marine resources in the Indian Ocean region II KAP Region. Unpublished report.

Anon. (1989a). Oman's coasts mapped. *IUCN Bulletin* 20(7-9): 13.

Anon. (1989b). NCS for Oman. *IUCN Bulletin* 20(7-9): 13-14.

Baker, J.M. (1983). Impact of oil pollution on living resources. *Commission on Ecology Papers Number 4*. IUCN, Gland, Switzerland.

Basson, P.W. *et al.* (1977). *Biotopes of the Western Arabian Gulf*. Aramco Department of Loss Prevention and Environmental Affairs, Dhahran, Saudi Arabia.

Bin Abdurredha Sultan, K. (1988). Foreword. In: Rogers, T.D. *A new list of the birds of Masirah Island, Sultanate of Oman*. Oman Bird Records Committee, Muscat.

Carp, E. (1980). *Directory of Western Palaearctic wetlands*. UNEP/IUCN, Gland, Switzerland. 506 pp.

Child, G. (1986). Proposed Directorate General for Wildlife and Nature Conservation in Oman. Appendix IX. In: Clarke, J.E., al-Lamki, F.M.S., Anderlini, V.C. and Shepperd, *Proposals for a system of nature conservation areas in the Sultanate of Oman*. Prepared by the International Union for Conservation of Nature and Natural Resources for the Diwan of Royal Court, Sultanate of Oman. Pp. 421-477.

Clarke, J.E., al-Lamki, F.M.S., Anderlini, V.C. and Shepperd, C.R.C. (1986). *Proposals for a system of nature conservation areas in the Sultanate of Oman*. Prepared by the International Union for Conservation of Nature and Natural Resources for the Diwan of Royal Court, Sultanate of Oman. 368 pp.

Davis, S.D., Droop, S.J.M., Gregerson, P., Henson, L., Leon, C.J., Lamlein Villa-Lobos, J., Synge, H. and Zantovska, J. (1986). *Plants in danger: what do we know?* IUCN, Gland, Switzerland and Cambridge, UK. 461 pp.

Downing, N. (1985). Coral reef communities in an extreme environment: the northwestern Arabian Gulf. *Proceedings of the Fifth International Coral Reef Congress. Tahiti. Volume 2*. Abstracts. 112 pp.

Dutton, R. (Ed.) (1986). Rapid Assessment Document. Oman Wahibi Sands Project 1985/1986.

Dutton, R. (Ed.) (1988). The Scientific Results of the Royal Geographical Society's Oman Wahiba Sands Project 1985-1987. Rapid Assessment Document. Oman Wahibi Sands Project 1985/1986. *Journal of Oman Studies Special Report* 3: 576.

Gour-Tanguay, R. (Ed.) (1977). Environmental policies in developing countries. *Beiträge zur Umweltgestaltung Heft A27*, Erich Schmidt Verlag.

Gallagher, M. D. (1977). The Oman flora and fauna survey, 1977, Dhofar. *Journal of Oman Studies* 3: 9-12.

Government Adviser for the Conservation of the Environment (1979). *Interim Report on the results of the Oman flora and fauna survey, Dhofar, 1977*. Al-Akidah Press, Muscat.

Green, M.J.B. and Drucker, G.R.F. (1990). Current status of protected areas and threatened mammal species in the Sahara-Gobian Region. World Conservation Monitoring Centre, Cambridge, UK.

Halwagy, R., Clayton, D. and Behbehani, M. (1986). Marine environment and pollution. Proceedings of the First Arabian Gulf Conference on environment and pollution. (Unseen)

Harrison, D.L. (1975). The Oman flora and fauna survey, 1975. *Journal of Oman Studies* 1: 181-186.

Harrison, D.L. and Gallagher, M.D. (1974). A park to save the Arabian Tahr. *Oryx* 12: 547-549.

Hunter, B. (Ed.) (1991). *The Statesman's Year Book 1991-92*. The Macmillan Press Ltd, London and Basingstoke, UK. 1692 pp.

IUCN (1976). Ecological guidelines for the use of natural resources in the Middle East and South West Asia. *IUCN Publications New Series* No. 34.

IUCN (1978). Promotion of the establishment of marine parks and reserves in the northern Indian Ocean including the Red Sea and Persian Gulf. *IUCN Publications New Series* No. 35.

Lausche, B. J. (1986). Legal Report Appendix VIII. In: Clarke, J.E., al- Lamki, F.M.S., Anderlini, V.C. and Shepperd, *Proposals for a System of Nature Conservation Areas in the Sultanate of Oman*. Prepared by the International Union for Conservation of Nature and Natural Resources for the Diwan of Royal Court, Sultanate of Oman. Pp. 377-420.

Loya, Y. and Rinkevich (1987). Effects of petroleum hydrocarbons on corals In: Salvat, B. (Ed.) Human impacts on coral reefs: facts and recommendations. *Antenne de Tahiti Museum, French Polynesia*. 253 pp.

Mandaville, J.P. (1977). Plants. In: Harrison, D.L. *et al.* (Eds), Scientific Results of the Oman Flora and Fauna Survey 1975. *J. Oman Studies, Scientific Report*. Ministry of Education and Culture. Pp. 229-267.

Mandaville, J.P. (1978). *Wild Flowers of Northern Oman*. Bartholomew Books, London. 64 pp.

Maher Abu Jaafer (1984). *National parks and nature reserves in the Arab World*. Department of Sciences, The Arab League Educational, Cultural and Scientific Organisation, Tunis. P. 112.

Montague, K. and Bruun, B. (1987). *Biological diversity in North Africa, the Middle East and Southwest Asia: a directory of organisations and Institutions*. HLCF, New York, USA.

Munton, P. (1991). Concept development in Oman for conservation of biological diversity. Paper for presentation at the Third Man and Biosphere Meeting on Biosphere Reserves in the Mediterranean and the First IUCN-CNPPA Workshop on Protected Areas in the North Africa-Middle East Region, 14-19 October 1991, Tunis. 14 pp.

Papastavrou, V. (1990). Oman's desert whale song. *Sonar (the magazine of the Whale and Dolphin Conservation Society)*. Spring. P. 18.

Perennou, C., Rose, P. and Poole, C. (1990). Asian Waterfowl Census 1990. International Wildfowl Research Bureau, Slimbridge, UK.

Radcliffe-Smith, A. (1979). Flora. In: *Interim Report on the results of the Oman flora and fauna survey, Dhofar, 1977*. Sultanate of Oman. Pp. 41-48.

Radcliffe-Smith, A. (1979). The vegetation of Dhofar. In: Scientific results of the Oman flora and fauna survey, 1977, Dhofar. *J. Oman Studies, Special Report* No. 2. Pp. 59-86.

Sardar, Z. (1982). *Science and Technology in the Middle East, a guide to issues, organisations and institutions.* Longman, London and New York.

Spalton, A. (1990). Recent developments in the re-introduction of the Arabian oryx (*Oryx leucoryx*) to Oman. *CBSG News* 2(1): 8.

Speece, M. W. (1981). Draft environmental profile of the Sultanate of Oman. US-AID Country Environmental Profiles. AID RSSA SA/TOA 77-1. 203 pp.

UNEP (1983). Action Plan for the protection of the marine environment and the coastal areas of Bahrain, Iran, Iraq, Kuwait, Oman, Qatar, Saudi Arabia and the United Arab Emirates. *UNEP Regional Seas Reports and Studies* No. 365.

UNEP/IUCN (1985). Ecological study of the rocky shores on the southern coast of Oman. Regional Seas Programme Studies and Reports. UNEP, Nairobi and IUCN, Gland, Switzerland. 14 pp.

UNEP/IUCN (1988). *Coral reefs of the world. Volume 2: Indian Ocean, Red Sea and Gulf. UNEP Regional Seas Directories and Bibliographies.*

IUCN, Gland, Switzerland and Cambridge, UK/UNEP, Nairobi, Kenya. 440 pp.

UNESCO/ROPME/UPM/UNEP (1985). Proceedings of the symposium/workshop on oceanographic modelling of the Kuwait Action Plan (KAP) region. *UNEP Regional Seas Reports and Studies* No. 70.

UNESCO/ROPME/UNEP (1985). Combatting oil pollution in the Kuwait Action Plan region. *UNEP Regional Seas Reports and Studies* No. 44.

Vessey-Fitzgerald, D. F. (1957a) The vegetation of central and Eastern Arabia. *Journal of Ecology* 45: 779-798.

Vessey-Fitzgerald, D.F. (1957b). The vegetation of Central and Eastern Arabia. *Journal of Ecology* 45:779-798.

WCMC (1991a). Gulf War Environmental Service: Impact on the marine environment. World Conservation Monitoring Centre, Cambridge, UK. 37 pp.

WCMC (1991b). Gulf War Environmental Service: Impact of atmospheric pollution on the terrestrial environment. World Conservation Monitoring Centre, Cambridge, UK. 37 pp.

ANNEX
Definitions of protected area designations, as legislated, together with authorities responsible for their administration

Title: Royal Decree 26/79

Date: 15 May 1979

Brief description: Article 3 states that private land may be designated as protected and Article 8 gives the responsible body the authority to employ guards.

Administrative authority: None specified

Designations:

National park Article 6 governs entry into reserves and national parks and their utilisation, listing prohibited activities and the fines governing this, it instigates entry fees and lists activities which are permitted only after permission is granted.

Areas allocated should be made available for "public benefit" but also "for the purpose of preserving animal or plant environment, or soil or subsoil or space or territorial waters" (Article 2).

Nature reserve Areas allocated should be made available for "public benefit" but also "for the purpose of preserving animal or plant environment, or soil or subsoil or space or territorial waters" (Article 2).

Source: Lausche, 1986.

Title: Ministerial Decision No. 4/76

Date: 6 April 1976

Brief description: Provides for protecting specified species of animals and birds from hunting, capture and molestation. It provides for specified closed season protected area status to islands and coastline.

Administrative authority: Ministry of Agriculture and Fisheries

Designation:

Protected shoreline provides for a total prohibition of hunting, shooting, capture and molestation of "all species of birds in all parts of Oman's shores and islands, at all times". The shooting of birds of any kind and the taking of seabirds' eggs is forbidden along the entire coastline.

There are restrictions on visiting specified islands between June and October.

Source: Lausche, 1986

Title: Royal Decree No. 53/81 Law of Sea Fishing and the Preservation of Marine Biological Wealth

Date: 1981

Brief description: Authorises the designation of areas where fishing will be permanently forbidden, and other areas where fishing will be allowed only within defined seasons and for specific species.

Administrative authority: Determined by the appropriate authority Ministry of Agriculture and Fisheries

Designations:

Protected fishing water As above. In addition, the decree prohibits the taking of marine resources during breeding periods. Penalties and enforcement measures are given.

Title: Ministerial Decision No. 3/82

Date: 1982

Brief description: Includes executive regulations for law of marine fishing and conservation of aquatic resources with details on species protection.

Administrative authority: Ministry of Agriculture and Fisheries

Designations:

Protected turtle area Certain marine resources are completely protected under the regulations, including sea turtles located along remote seashores as designated by the concerned authority.

All capture of turtles is prohibited during the nesting season. Collection of turtle and seabird eggs is prohibited within a distance of the coast which is to be determined by the appropriate authority. Hunting of turtles on their way to lay eggs on the islands and coasts is prohibited during periods which are determined by the appropriate authorities.

Source: Lausche, 1986

Title: Regional Development Plan for the Southern Region based on the authority of the PCDESR under Royal Decree No. 48 of 1984

Date: 1991 PCDESR acceptance

Brief description: Regional Development Plan which incorporates planning controls as part of environmental planning development, where all areas (including those for nature conservation) are classified according to the degree of planning control in operation or category of use.

Administrative authority: PCDESR, Ministry of Environment and Water Resources, Ministry of Housing

Designations:

Reserve zone 1 Large areas classed as natural resource reserves in the original IUCN proposals, in areas where it is thought there is insufficient information to decide which parts of the total area need special protection.

With the exception of new settlements and industry and other forms of development, such as tourism and agriculture would be permitted, subject to specific environmental control by the Ministry and PCDESR

Reserve zone 2 A status accorded to all remaining undesignated areas in the Southern Region:

Industry and housing should be in pre-designated areas but any proposals are considered on their merits by consultation with PCDESR and the Ministry of Housing.

Source: Munton, 1991

SUMMARY OF PROTECTED AREAS

Map ref.	*National/international designations* Name of area	IUCN management category	Area (ha)	Year notified
	(Managed) Nature Reserves			
1	Daymaniyat Islands	VI	20,300	1984
2	Qurum	IV	1,000	1986
3	Ra's al Jumayz	VI	4,000	1989
4	Wadi Serin (Arabian Tahr)	IV	80,000	
	Managed Reserve			
5	Ra's al Hadd (Turtle Reserve)	VI	8,000	1989
	Other area			
6	Jiddat al Harasis	VI	2,750,000	

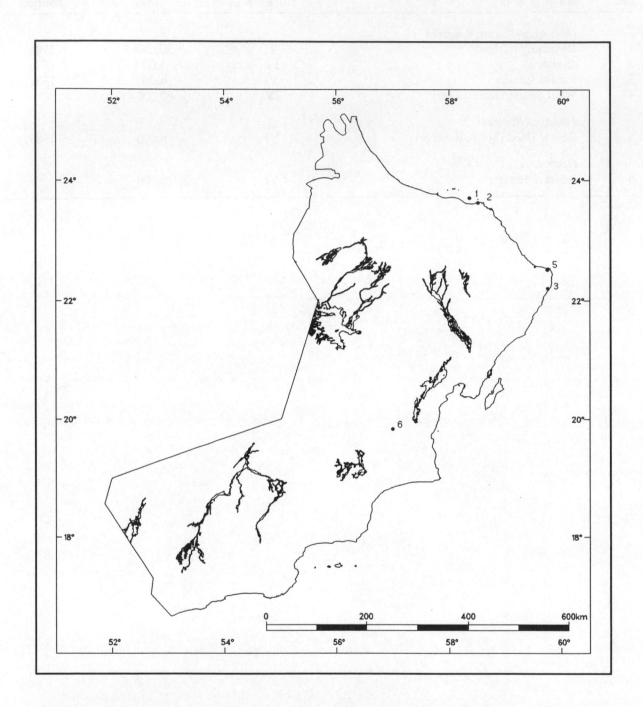

Protected Areas of Oman

QATAR

Area 10,360 sq. km

Population 368,000 (1990)
Natural increase: 3.41% per annum

Economic Indicators
GDP: US$ 15,783 per capita (1987)
GNP: US$ 21,880 per capita (1987)

Policy and Legislation Embodied in the Constitution, dated 2 April 1970, is the traditional Islamic respect for nature. The legal system subscribes to both state and religious Islamic law (Sharia). Under the Constitution, executive power is exercised by the Council of Ministers, and all laws have to be passed by the Head of State, the Emir (Amir).

Traditional forms of protected area or range reserves (hema, hima, hujrah or ahmia) may have their origins over 2,000 years ago in the pre-Islamic period. Insufficient information is available as to whether the hema system has survived to the present day.

In the strict sense, there is no specific protected area legislation. However, there is a class of game reserve or breeding station set up by state authorities and by members of the ruling family. These areas, or ranches, cover natural desert areas often over 100ha and are established to maintain breeding stocks of large game such as oryx and gazelle. One of the most renowned, the Shahaniyah ranch, was established in 1979 as a breeding station for Arabian oryx and gazelles (Maher abou Jaafer, 1984).

Environmental legislation is scarce, the environment being protected or buffered to some extent by the practice of industrial zoning (ERL, 1986). One of the earliest pieces of legislation which is still extant is Law No. 29, 1966 (amended 1982) concerning the environment of ports and pollution control. Decree Law No. 10, 1968 relates to the restrictions of pesticides for agriculture and this was followed in 1983 by Law No. 4, 1983 on the protection and utilisation of living sea resources. The Environment Protection Committee was established under Law No. 4, 1981 (ERL, 1986; UNEP/IUCN, 1988).

Effective environmental legislation, and protected area legislation specifically, continues to be lacking and may become of increasing concern if industry expands unchecked (1991). With the absence of legislation to protect natural habitats and species adequately, unregulated hunting, using falcons as well as guns, is rife throughout Qatar (ERL, 1986; Maher abou Jaafer, 1984).

International Activities Qatar has ratified the International Convention for the Prevention of Pollution of the Sea by Oil (1954) (ERL, 1986). The Kuwait Regional Convention for Cooperation on the Protection of the Marine Environment from Pollution, and Kuwait Action Plan, was adopted and subsequently ratified by Qatar on the 23 April 1978. The secretariat functions of the Kuwait Action Plan are carried out by the Regional Organisation for the Protection of the Marine Environment (ROPME). The Convention concerning the Protection of the World Cultural and Natural Heritage (World Heritage Convention) was accepted on 12 September 1984, but to date no sites have been inscribed. The Gulf Co-operation Council (GCC) takes an active interest in the marine environment and in other aspects of cooperation for environmental management throughout the region (ERL, 1986).

Administration and Management The ruling family is actively involved as one of the main forces in wildlife protection and has established a series of special wildlife ranches for wild fauna (Maher abou Jaafer, 1984). The main public body concerned with the protected areas system is the Ministry of Industry and Agriculture, although general environmental issues are the responsibility of the Environment Protection Committee (EPC). The remit of the Ministry of Industry and Agriculture includes administration, protection and management of flora, soils and fauna. It administers the state ranches or breeding stations on behalf of the members of the royal family. Day-to-day management, supervision and wardening is carried out by boards of veterinarians and agricultural engineers (Maher abou Jaafer, 1984). The ranches act as centres for breeding endangered game, for scientific research and for recreation.

The EPC, established in 1981, has broad environmental powers and responsibilities, including proposing and implementing environmental policy, drafting environmental laws and regulations, undertaking environmental analysis and assessment, coordinating environmental bodies and undertaking education programmes (ERL, 1986). The EPC consists of member ministries and agencies, including the Ministry of Municipal Affairs, IDTC, Ministry of Public Works and the Ministry of Electricity and Water. Its Secretariat produces the report *The State of the Environment* on an annual basis. The EPC has the power to issue regulations and demand information from any party practising any activity likely to cause environmental damage (ERL, 1986).

Other bodies involved in protected areas management includes the Ministry of Information, which has jurisdiction over the game reserve established by Sheikh Hamed al-Thani. Interested governmental bodies which play limited roles in area protection include the Ministry of Municipal Affairs, Ministry of Finance and Petroleum and the Ministry of Electricity and Water. General fishing restrictions are enforced by the Fisheries Department, which, amongst other duties, prohibits shrimp fishing during the growth period of February to June (UNEP/IUCN, 1988).

Non-governmental organisations concerned with nature conservation include the Qatar Natural History Society which has interests in a number of fields, most notably in ornithology. It has been involved in a series of bird censuses, in collaboration with the Ornithological Society of the Middle East (OSME). In the past it acted as a pressure group and has called on the authorities to control the shooting of wildlife. The Centre for Scientific and Applied Research, University of Qatar, has carried out studies of the flora, fauna and related topics, including human impacts on the environment (Batanouny, 1981; ERL, 1986). Collection, captive breeding and conservation of large game by members of the ruling family have been undertaken in collaboration with the Flora and Fauna Preservation Society, WWF and IUCN (Fitter, 1982). The establishment of Doha Zoo has been undertaken in collaboration with the Zoological Gardens of Regents Park, London (Fitter, 1982).

Reports dating from the early 1980s indicated that management of the environment was inadequate; the EPC lacked the ability to implement environmental management regulations, had a lack of technical and administrative capabilities, and was unable to ensure agreement between the various member ministries and agencies to put environmental control measures into action. To remedy some of these constraints consultants were contracted in 1986 to establish a series of proposals for the restructuring and recommended future plan of action of the EPC (ERL, 1986).

Systems Reviews   The Peninsula of Qatar, approximately 160km in length and up to 90km in width, projects out on the west coast of the Arabian (Persian) Gulf and is bounded by Saudi Arabia, the United Arab Emirates and Oman. It is predominantly a low-lying, stony desert landscape where natural vegetation is scarce, largely limited in abundance to the north where there are acacia and other scrub desert communities. Coral reefs, extensive seagrass beds and mangrove occur all around the coast (UNEP/IUCN, 1988). Species diversity is low and there are few, if any, endemics. Land use is divided into 4.5% pasture, 0.3% cropland and the rest semi-desert.

Surveys of seabird breeding colonies from several localities around the coast and islands have been undertaken by various independent bodies, including the Qatar Natural History Society and the OSME. Recommendations have been put forward by the Qatar Natural History Society for control of the indiscriminate shooting of wildlife. A national marine and coastal zone development and protection plan has been proposed for the marine resources, to control marine waste disposal, marine mining and transportation, coastal land use and marine fauna and flora resources (UNEP, 1984; cited in UNEP/IUCN, 1988). Further recommendations have been identified in the publication *Current status of protected areas and threatened mammal species in the Sahara-Gobian Region* prepared by WCMC (Green and Drucker, 1990). It was shown that at a national level protection of the Anatolian-Iranian desert in Qatar was a high priority.

Initial recommendations for protected area designation were made in 1986 for the investigation of practical arrangements for protecting sensitive coastal resources such as the mangroves north of Al Khawr (ERL, 1986). They also recommended that the EPC undertake a marine environment policy study, an essential element of which would be the establishment of a marine environment profile, environmental impact assessment of those marine and coastal habitats most vulnerable to pollution and prioritising a list of habitat types and proposed areas for future protected area designation (ERL, 1986). Part of this recommendation has been implemented following Canadian government funded airborne remote sensing surveys of coastal resources in April 1991 (Al-Midfa, *in litt.*, 1991; Reilly, *in litt.*, 1991).

In 1984 the number of protected areas, in the form of ranch wildlife reserves, totalled eight, varying widely in size, management and species diversity. The largest site, Shahaniyah ranch, covers 1,000ha and has been set up as a breeding station for Arabian oryx and gazelles (Maher abou Jaafer, 1984).

Threats to the environment include disturbance by cultivation, grazing and oil exploration. The spread of transport and the development of desert roads is steadily opening up the wilderness to hunters and semi-nomadic tribes. Bedouins especially prize the capture and training of falcons. Inevitably, pollution from the activities of the petroleum industry is affecting the environment. Oil pollution is reported to be putting at risk coral reefs and seagrass beds (ERL, 1986).

Other Relevant Information   The sovereign state of Qatar declared its independence from Britain on 3 September 1971. There is no parliament, but ministers are assisted by a nominated Consultative Council and ruled by an Emir who assumed power on independence. Ownership of the islands of Hawar and the Fasht al-Dibl reefs are disputed with Bahrain.

Addresses

Ministry of Industry and Agriculture, Agricultural Affairs Administration, PO Box 1966, DOHA (Tel: 433400; Tlx: 4751)

Environment Protection Committee, c/o Ministry of Public Health, PO Box 42, DOHA (Tel: 320825; FAX: 415246)

References

Anon. (1985). The management and conservation of renewable marine resources in the Indian Ocean region II KAP Region. Unpublished report.

Basson, P.W. *et al.* (1977). *Biotopes of the Western Arabian Gulf.* Aramco department of loss prevention and environmental affairs, Dhahran, Saudi Arabia.

Batanouny, K.H. (1981). *Ecology and Flora of Qatar*. University of Qatar, Doha. 245 pp.

Batanouny, K.H. and Turki, A.A. (1983). Vegetation of south-western Qatar. *Arab Gulf Journal of Scientific Research* 1(1): 5-19.

Carp, E. (1980). *Directory of Western Palaearctic wetlands*. UNEP/IUCN, Gland, Switzerland. 506 pp.

Coral Reef and Tropical Marine Research Unit (1982). Management of critical habitats on the Arabian Gulf Coast of Saudi Arabia. Report to MEPA by Coral Reef and Tropical Marine Research Unit, University of York.

Croxall, J.P., Evans, P.G.H. and Schreiber, R.W. (1984). Status and conservation of the World's Seabirds. *ICBP Technical Publication* No. 2.

Davis, S.D., Droop, S.J.M., Gregerson, P., Henson, L., Leon, C.J., Lamlein Villa-Lobos, J., Synge, H. and Zantovska, J. (1986). *Plants in danger: what do we know?* IUCN, Gland, Switzerland and Cambridge, UK. 461 pp.

Downing, N. (1985). Coral reef communities in an extreme environment: the northwestern Arabian Gulf. *Proceedings of the Fifth International Coral Reef Congress*. Tahiti. Volume 2. Abstracts. 112 pp.

Draz, O. (1969). The *hema* system of range management in the Arabian Peninsula. FAO/PL/PFC/13.11. 8 pp.

Draz, O. (1985). The *hema* system of range reserves in the Arabian Peninsula, its possibilities in range improvement and conservation projects in the Near East. In McNeely, J.A. and Pitt, D. (Eds.), *Culture and Conservation: The human dimension in environmental planning*. Pp. 109-121.

ERL (1986). Water and solid waste assessment report; Environmental Management Strategy. Report prepared for the Environment Protection Committee of the State of Qatar by Environmental Resources Ltd, London.

Fitter, R. (1982). Arabian oryx returns to the wild. *Oryx* 15(5): 406-410.

Ghabbour, S.I. (1975). National parks in Arab countries. *Environmental Conservation* 2(1): 45-46.

Gour-Tanguay, R. (Ed.) (1977). Saudi Arabia. *Environmental policies in developing countries*. Beiträge zur Umweltgestaltung Heft A27. Erich Schmidt Verlag.

Green, M.J.B. and Drucker, G.R.F. (1990). Current status of protected areas and threatened mammal species in the Sahara-Gobian Region. World Conservation Monitoring Centre, Cambridge, UK. 50 pp.

IUCN (1976). Promotion of the Establishment of marine parks and reserves in the northern Indian Ocean including the Red Sea and Persian Gulf. *IUCN Publication New Series* No. 35.

IUCN (1976). Ecological guidelines for the use of natural resources in the Middle East and South West Asia. *IUCN Publications New Series* No. 34.

IUCN/UNEP (1985a). The management and conservation of renewable resources in the Red Sea and Gulf of Aden Region. *UNEP Regional Seas Reports and Studies* No. 64. P. 106.

IUCN/UNEP (1985b) The management and conservation of renewable marine resources in the Kuwait Action Plan Region. *UNEP Regional Seas Reports and Studies* No. 56. P. 57.

Jungius, H. (1985). The role of indigenous flora and fauna in rangeland management systems of the arid zones in western Asia. *Journal of Arid Environments* 6: 75-85

Jungius, H. (1987). The establishment of national parks and protected areas in the arid zone: a contribution to conservation and rational utilization of natural resources. First symposium on the potential of wildlife conservation in Saudi Arabia. Held by the National Commission for Wildlife Conservation and Development, 15-18 February 1987. P. 11. (Unseen)

Jungius, H. (1988). The national parks and protected areas concept and its applications to the Arabian Peninsula. *Fauna of Saudi Arabia* 9:3-11.

Loya, Y. and Rinkevich (1987). Effects of petroleum hydrocarbons on corals. In: Salvat, B. (Ed.), *Human impacts on coral reefs: facts and recommendations*. Antenne de Tahiti Museum, French Polynesia. 253 pp.

Maher Abu Jaafer (1984). *National parks and nature reserves in the Arab World*. Department of Sciences, The Arab League Educational, Cultural and Scientific Organisation, Tunis. 112 pp.

Montague, K. and Bruun, B. (1987). *Biological Diversity in North Africa, the Middle East and Southwest Asia: a directory of organisations and institutions*. HLCF, New York, USA. 134 pp.

Perenou, C., Rose, P. and Poole, C. (1990). *Asian Waterfowl Census 1990*. International Waterfowl Research Bureau, Slimbridge, UK.

Pearce, F. (1991). Gulf war could mean largest ever oil spill. *New Scientist* 19 January 1991. P. 18.

Price, A.R.G. (1990). Rapid assessment of coastal zone management requirements: a case study from the Arabian Gulf. *Ocean and Shoreline Management* 13: 1-19.

Sardar, Z. (1982). *Science and technology in the Middle East, a guide to issues, organisations and institutions*. Longman, London and New York.

UNEP (1983). Action Plan for the protection of the marine environment and the coastal areas of Bahrain, Iran, Iraq, Kuwait, Oman, Qatar, Saudi Arabia and the United Arab Emirates. *UNEP Regional Seas Reports and Studies* No. 365.

UNEP (1984) *The state of the environment in Qatar*. UNEP Regional Office for Western Asia, Beirut, Lebanon.

UNEP/IUCN (1988). *Coral reefs of the world. Volume 2: Indian Ocean, Red Sea and Gulf*. UNEP Regional Seas Directories and Bibliographies. IUCN, Gland, Switzerland and Cambridge, UK/UNEP, Nairobi, Kenya. 440 pp.

UNESCO/ROMPE/UPM/UNEP (1985). Proceedings of the symposium/workshop on oceanographic modelling of the Kuwait Action Plan (KAP) region. *UNEP Regional Seas Reports and Studies* No. 70.

UNESCO/ROMPE/UNEP (1985). Combatting Oil Pollution in the Kuwait Action Plan region. *UNEP Regional Seas Reports and Studies* No. 44.

Vessey-Fitzgerald, D.F. (1957). The vegetation of Central and Eastern Arabia. *Journal of Ecology* 45:779-798.

ANNEX
Definitions of protected area designations, as legislated, together with authorities responsible for their administration

Title: Environment Protection Committee Law No. 4

Date: 1981

Brief Description: Provides for the establishment of the semi-governmental Environmental Protection Committee, for subsequent collecting of environmental data, and subsequent protection of the environment and habitats.

Administrative authority: Environmental Protection Committee

Designations:

No information

Sources: ERL, 1986; Maher Abu Jaafer, 1984

SAUDI ARABIA (KINGDOM OF)

Area 2,144,969 sq. km

Population 11.5 million (1988)
Natural increase: 3.6% per annum

Economic Indicators
GDP: US$ 5,757 per capita (1987)
GNP: US$ 6,930 per capita (1987)

Policy and Legislation By the Treaty of 20 May 1927 the United Kingdom recognised the independence of Hejaz, Nejd, Asir and Al-Hasa, which subsequently became the State of the Kingdom of Saudi Arabia by Decree of 23 September 1932 (Hunter, 1991). Constitutional practices are derived from the Koranic Sharia law. There is no formal constitution. As an absolute monarchy, all laws have to be passed by the King and all major initiatives come from the Royal family (Ba Kader *et al.*, 1983; Child and Grainger, 1990; Hunter, 1991).

Nature conservation has had a long tradition in the Arabian Peninsula. The Koran and Arabic poetic literature attach great importance to the value of man preserving his natural heritage, embodied with the need for the traditional Islamic respect for nature (Ba Kader *et al.*, 1883). Traditional forms of protected area or resource reserve (hema, hima, hujrah or ahmia) may have origins over 2,000 years ago in the pre-Islamic period, and developed as an ancient acknowledgement of the scarcity of renewable resources and the need to conserve and use them wisely in support of sustainable rural economic development. In their present form the Prophet Mohammed abolished private hemas belonging to powerful individuals and established a legal system that continues to govern these protected areas (Child and Grainger, 1990). The prophet Mohammed set up a protected area *hema alnaquia* near Medina in the 6th century AD and subsequent caliphs were very strict in keeping the hema system protected. The prophet stated "hema is only for God and His prophet", and as such the Islamic state protects hemas in the best interests of the community. The majority of hemas were abandoned in the 1960s, following the opening of lands to free grazing by Royal decree in 1953 (Abo Hassan, 1981; Abuzinada and Child, 1991; Dawood and Iskander, n.d.; Draz, 1985).

Existing hemas continue to be respected by local tradition (ourf) and are maintained under five types where: a) animal grazing is prohibited; b) grazing and/or cutting is permitted; c) grazing is allowed all the year round; d) beekeeping is undertaken; and e) forests are protected. The Royal Decree of 1953 permitted free grazing in Saudi Arabia including in hemas. This law was meant to replace the grazing rights of hemas only so long as they were protected by local amirs in different regions with government-owned grazing animals. This has now been modified to exclude tribal or personal ahmia (Draz, 1985; Child, 1982; Child and Grainger, 1990; Jungius, 1987).

Royal Decree No. M/22 of 20 June 1986 led to a public commitment by the government to the creation of an adequate representative system of protected areas (Child and Grainger, 1990). Article 3(4) entrusted the National Commission for Wildlife Conservation and Development (NCWCD) with the conservation of wildlife and creation and maintenance of the protected areas system (Child and Grainger, 1986). In 1990 a draft protected area legislation was prepared, providing for the management plan for each reserve to be the legal instrument guiding its control (see Child and Grainger, 1990 for full details). A system of five categories has been identified to which the traditional hema system could be added as a sixth class: special nature reserve, natural reserve, biological reserve, resource use reserve, and controlled hunting reserve (Child and Grainger, 1990) (see Annex). Existing NCWCD protected areas have all been effectively defined as controlled hunting reserves (Child and Grainger, 1990). In the draft protected areas legislation the process by which a protected area is created involves a range of methodical operations. Once candidate sites have been prioritised the list, together with supporting documentation, is passed to the Board of Governors for consideration. Sites approved by the Board should then be submitted to the Council of Ministers for ratification (Child and Grainger, 1990).

The only national park so far created is Asir National Park under directives issued by order of Prince Khaled Al-Faisal, governor of Asir province in 1978 and declared in 1981 (see Child and Grainger, 1990; Child, pers. comm., 1991) (see Annex).

Other legislation relating to protected areas includes the following: Council of Ministers Decision No. 271, 1984 ratifying approval of the designation of marine protectorates. This follows a list of resolutions presented by the Environmental Protection Coordination Committee (EPCCOM) to the Council of Ministers, providing a framework for conserving the coastal and offshore marine environment of the Saudi Arabian Red Sea and Gulf of Aden. Under this framework there would be a general moratorium on development pending the preparation of detailed conservation plans for each area (UNEP/IUCN, 1987). The Royal Forest Decree of 18 April 1978 lays down regulations for the protection of forests and wildlife, provides the basis for the delineation of forests and rangelands and establishes a framework for a national forestry and range policy. This Decree sets out criteria for defining the forests that shall be the property of the Kingdom and those that shall be the property of villages and individuals. National parks, recreation areas and forest and range reserves are defined within this Law (Child, 1982); regulations for the

National Hunting Law of 1977 were adequate to give protected area status to the island of Umm Al-Qamari (Child and Grainger, 1990).

In the two Royal Commission cities of Al Jubayl on the Gulf and Yanbu al Sinaiyah on the Red Sea, environmental responsibility lies with the Royal Commissions. Areas of protection were established within the jurisdiction of the Royal Commission at Yanbu in the early 1980s (UNEP/IUCN, 1987).

A draft law, Hema Law, has been proposed with the aim of preserving plant and animal species, natural biological communities or ecological processes or protecting areas of particular natural excellence. It is subdivided into the categories of strict natural hema, plant hema, resource use hema and hunting hema. As of October 1991 the law was still in the process of being refined (Child and Grainger, 1990; Child, pers. comm., 1991).

NCWCD proposals for the declaration of a minimum programme of 18 protected areas have been incorporated into the current five-year national development plan (Child and Grainger, 1990).

International Activities   Saudi Arabia accepted the Convention concerning the Protection of the World Cultural and Natural Heritage (World Heritage Convention) on 7 August 1978, but to date no sites have been inscribed. It has not acceded to the Convention on Wetlands of International Importance especially as Waterfowl Habitat (Ramsar Convention).

The Kuwait Regional conference of plenipotentiaries on the protection and development of the marine environment and the coastal areas convened by UNEP in Kuwait, 15-23 April 1978, led to the adoption of the Action Plan (KAP) for the protection and development of the marine environment and the coastal areas of Bahrain, Iran, Iraq, Kuwait, Oman, Qatar, Saudi Arabia and United Arab Emirates, and to the Kuwait Regional Convention for Cooperation on the Protection of the Marine Environment from Pollution (UNEP, 1983). Saudi Arabia is a participant in the Red Sea and Gulf of Aden Environment Programme (PERSGA) and has ratified the Regional Convention for the Conservation of the Red Sea and Gulf of Aden Environment.

To protect the ecological integrity of the coastal and marine environment, a peace park was proposed by the World Conservation Monitoring Centre in 1991 and subsequently developed further by UNEP, incorporating the headwaters and north-east shore of the Arabian Gulf. The park could include Shadegan Marshes, inland marshes adjacent to the Shatt al Arab waterway on the Iran/Iraq border, the mudflats and wetlands of Kuwait, the key ecological sites along the Saudi Arabian coast as far as Bahrain (WCMC, 1991b).

Recommendations have been made for transboundary protected areas in the security zones on the Jordanian border, in the eastern Rub al-Khali (Child and Grainger, 1990).

Administration and Management   The three main organisations concerned with conservation and the environment are the National Commission for Wildlife Conservation and Development (NCWCD), the Meteorology and Environmental Protection Agency (MEPA) and the Ministry of Agriculture and Water (MAW).

In 1976 a planning agreement was reached under the US-Saudi Arabia Joint Commission on Economic Cooperation (JECOR) and the US National Park Service which was asked to advise and develop a master plan for the Ministry of Agriculture and Water (MAW) on all phases of park management, including physical facilities, training, research and long-range goals and the establishment of a wide system of national parks (MAW, 1984). The MAW was responsible for the management and protection of public rangelands through the Department of Range and Forestry (DRF) and the General Department for National Parks which had responsibility for the establishment of national parks. In 1962 the MAW established a Forestry Branch under the plant production and protection division. In 1966 the Forestry Branch was transferred to the Department of Public Land Management and subsequently upgraded into the DRF. The range section of the DRF developed a programme to revive the hema system by fencing large enclosures in selected areas, including the 80 sq. km Abu Raklah at Taif (Al Dawood and Iskander, n.d.). From 1978 MAW has had responsibility for Asir National Park (declared 1981) (employing a superintendent and staff) and for the proposed Hima Huraymila National Park (Child, 1982; Child and Grainger, 1990). With bilateral assistance from the United States, a park headquarters and interpretive centre has been constructed at Asir National Park and four recreative sites developed (Child, 1982). The Ministry undertook water resources surveys in the mid-1970s as well as a complete land survey to determine the nature of soil and prepare an extensive agricultural development programme for the country (Gour-Tanguay, 1977). It has promoted studies and management plans for the establishment of other conservation areas (Jungius, 1988). The MAW has long been pursuing a goal of promoting the protective and productive capacity of woodlands.

The DRF from inception has been divided into sections on administration, development and improvement of forests and development and protection of rangelands. The Department for Improvement of Forests was further subdivided into forest sections, national parks, afforestation and dune fixation. The DRF was based in Riyadh and regional Directors of Agriculture located in the regional offices. The broad objectives of the DRF have been defined in decrees as: to ensure the proper protection and development of forest and range resources in the Kingdom; to supervise and administer the forest domain; to supervise private forests. In 1982 the Under Secretary of Agriculture in the Ministry of Agriculture and Water sought FAO assistance in the definition of a cooperative programme in priority areas of forestry. In response FAO sent a forestry mission to examine current forestry activities, assess the potential for forestry development and related constraints and identify technical assistance needs relevant to present and future development activities in the field of forestry, national parks and wildlife (Child, 1982).

Under the third plan of 1980-85 the Royal Forest Decree envisaged a substantial expansion of forestry activities, including the creation of nurseries, afforestation and sand dune fixation, the establishment of national parks, recreation areas and the rehabilitation of wildlife (Child, 1982). In 1981 Saudi Arabia signed a major agreement with the IUCN in a drive to conserve wildlife and other natural resources. Under the terms of the agreement, IUCN would provide expert guidance on how to go about protecting and managing its natural resources. The SAR 1 million (US$ 300,000) trust fund agreement was signed with MEPA. A plan for a national conservation strategy, a blueprint for a programme to protect endangered species, and legal and environmental education advice, were all included in the undertaking. Under the terms of the agreement IUCN would provide assistance on: setting up a network of protected areas; training Saudi Arabians in wildlife management; improving the government's legal capacity; establishing a department of natural resources; and incorporating conservation aims into development planning through the drawing up of a national conservation strategy; and conserving endangered species (see below for details).

The NCWCD was established in June 1986, charged with the responsibility of establishing and managing protected wildlife areas. Drawing on the experience of the MEPA and other agencies, the Commission provides a valuable focus for combined conservation efforts in Saudi Arabia. It is mainly concerned with the preservation, protection and development of wildlife population including marine and terrestrial life. The Commission's first action plan was dated from 1987-1990. Functions included a protected areas programme, management of wildlife outside protected areas, general environmental programme, monitoring and research, public awareness, administrative and technical support service. The NCWCD encourages and carries out scientific research in different fields of biology, promotes public interest in the environmental issues related to wildlife, and seeks proper solutions to problems through organising meetings, symposia and conferences; develop and implement plans and projects drawn up to preserve wildlife in its natural environment and to propose the establishment of protected areas and reserves for wildlife, and execute relevant laws and regulations.

One of the chief aims of the NCWCD is to draw up a national strategy to conserve and develop wildlife in accordance with Islamic laws and the international strategic attitudes for conservation of wildlife. The NCWCD has a Board of Directors consisting of the Head of Coordination Committee of Environment Protection, Minister of the Interior, Minister of Foreign Affairs,

Governor of Asir region, Minister of Agriculture and Water, President of the King Abdulaziz City for Sciences and Technology, President of MEPA and the Secretary General of the NCWCD. The elements of the Commission structure are the board of directors, managing director, the advisory committee, general secretariat, general director for financial and administrative affairs, general director for technical affairs and research, library and commission research centres.

The NCWCD budget comprises: funds appropriated from the state budget; revenues which it may earn from activities in its scope of work; grants, aid, donations and wills which are approved according to rules set by the board of directors; other revenues which the board of directors may decide to include in the funds of the Commission. The budget totals around US$ 9.06 million per year (Abuzinada and Child, 1991). The budget for IUCN support for two years was SAR 1,444,304 (US$ 380,000) (IUCN, 1987a). The NCWCD has instigated the development of a system plan for protected areas (Child and Grainger, 1990) with the assistance of IUCN consultants, and the final report was published in mid 1990. Its purpose was to develop a rationalised process for selecting and creating protected areas, based on the cultural concept of hemas, and to suggest and prioritise as many sites as possible. Of the 103 recommended sites, 2 are established and 16 are in the process of being recognised, with staff already established in 7 of the latter. In total during 1991 NCWCD employed 253 people of whom 169 were Saudis, including 34 with appropriate university degrees. Under the Director of Conservation, the ranger force stood at 102 staff (also see below) (Abuzinada and Child, 1991; Sulayem, *in litt.*, 1991). The NCWCD manages research stations including King Khalid Wildlife Research Centre near Riyadh and the National Wildlife Research Centre at Taif created in April 1986. The Commission is currently undertaking through its field centre in Taif captive breeding programmes for local birds and mammals as well as research, with the eventual aim of reintroducing birds and mammals to their natural habitat. The Centre is also involved in ecological studies on bustard, oryx and gazelle, including comparative studies relating to impact of grazing on vegetation, surveys of plants, birds and mammals in the area of the centre (Al-Faisal, 1986; NCWCD, n.d.; Williamson, pers. comm., 1991). NCWCD has responsibility for preparation of Red Lists of threatened and extinct species of plant and animal, to prepare distribution maps of species, to determine biogeographic provinces to be used in the studies of wildlife distribution, to establish and manage protected areas, to establish centres for preservation and development of marine life in the Arabian Gulf and Red Sea region and to establish a national natural history museum in Riyadh.

Throughout most of Saudi Arabia, marine conservation and environmental protection are the responsibility of the Meteorology and Environment Protection

Administration (MEPA) which was established in 1980 for the purpose of setting criteria, standards, guidelines and policies to protect the environment and to control pollution. MEPA initiated and is in charge of the development of a coastal zone management policy, the identification of protected areas, preparation of oil spill dispersant regulations and has promulgated a comprehensive set of air and water quality standards (UNEP/IUCN, 1988). By 1991 overall responsibility for a representative system of biological reserves had passed to NCWCD (Abuzinada and Child, 1991). The marine projects group of the MEPA Natural Resources Directorate is responsible for coordination of long-term monitoring programmes, to assess the state of marine and coastal environments and for the development of management strategies.

Additional bodies involved in protected areas management includes Riyadh Development Authority which has responsibility for Al Hair Wetland declared in 1988.

There is an absence of non-governmental agencies owning protected areas. Those involved in nature conservation and environmental assessment include the Saudi Biological Society, based at the College of Education at Abha, which was founded in 1976; with other institutions it helps to disseminate knowledge and to act as a conservation forum. The Society is chiefly responsible for documenting records and findings, including those of the main nature conservation areas of the region.

De facto protected areas also must be noted even though they are not designated for nature conservation. Examples exist in security zones on the Jordanian border, in the eastern Rub al-Khali. It has been recommended that these sites be officially designated with the assistance of the Ministry of Defence (Child and Grainger, 1990).

Recommendations have been made to revive traditional land-use based on the hema system, a concept which does not imply rebuilding old social structures (cf above for MAW activities). These would be replaced by modern administration within the context of the country's legislation. It has been recognised that it should transfer the positive elements of an ancient culture into the 20th century, for example by strengthening local participation in land-use planning (Child and Grainger, 1990).

It is reported that one of the main current complaints regarding the handling of management of protected areas is the lack of public participation (cf above activities). At the moment the conservation movement is entirely a governmental initiative and opposition from the rural population is reported when new sites are declared for nature protection. It is regarded that, if public opinion and cooperation is not taken into account, it is difficult to see how the progress made so far by various bodies such as the NCWCD, MAW and MEPA can be

maintained. They are reported to be further constrained in the face of increasing bureaucratic inertia (for a more extensive summary of management constraints see Thouless, 1991).

Systems Reviews Saudi Arabia lies within and encompasses 70% of the Arabian Peninsula, extending from the Red Sea to the Arabian or Persian Gulf, and borders Jordan, United Arab Emirates, Bahrain, Iraq, Kuwait, Republic of Yemen and Oman.

Saudi Arabia forms a part of the ancient northern section of the African shelf. The rift of the Red Sea separated the Peninsula from Africa about 50 million years ago. Situated at the "crossroads" between the Palaearctic, Afro-Tropical and Indo-Malayan realms, the Arabian Peninsula harbours a varied fauna and flora, with over 18% invertebrate endemism out of 3,027 recorded species. There are 25 endemic plant species (Miller and Nyberg, 1991). Partly this is due to relict flora and fauna which survived from the last Ice Age when the Arabian Peninsula was wetter and cooler than currently with a Mediterranean type climate. The country is divided into a number of regions: Tihama Red Sea coastal lowlands rise to the adjacent Sarawat mountains in the west; a plateau, the Najd in the centre from 600- 1,000m in altitude, gradually declines in the east towards the Arabian Gulf, to the Dahnaa desert and the eastern provinces; the Rub al Khali desert in the south and east; and the Nafud desert and northern province in the extreme north. The majority of land is desert plain, covered in sparse scrub with perennial, and often salt-tolerant, herbs and ephemerals, where the vegetation type and density is controlled primarily by the amount of precipitation. Forest covers 2.5 million ha but includes vast stretches of degraded scrub and remnant wood savanna (Child, 1982). Forest cover is centred in the Sarwat mountains in 0.5-1 million ha of *Juniperus procera*, together with *Olea chrysophylla*, *Pistacia palestina* and *Dodonia viscosa*, degrading to open savanna woodland of *Acacia* species and *Ziziphus spina-christi* at lower altitudes. The Arabian Gulf coastline largely consists of a system of low coastal dunes. The marshes show a distinct zonation (Child, 1982; Daoud, 1985; Halwagy and Halwagy, 1974; Vessey-Fitzgerald, 1957).

The Arabian Gulf is represented by at least four critical marine habitats: coastal marshes and mudflats, coral reefs, seagrass beds and mangroves (UNEP/IUCN, 1987). Tidal flats, sabkhas, hypersaline wetland areas are distributed particularly along the north and west Arabian Gulf; there are some 1,000 sq. km in Saudi Arabia. Important seaweed beds occur along the Arabian coast and bays. Sublittoral sand and mud habitats represent important shrimping and fishing grounds. Sublittoral rock habitats, abundant in seaweed beds, are economically important for shrimps, pearl oysters and abalone fisheries. According to UN figures for 1988, 0.56% of the total land area is wooded, and the remainder is largely various forms of desert habitat. 1% of the total land area is cultivated land, and 39.5% of the land is devoted to extensive livestock grazing.

As a large and topographically varied country, Saudi Arabia harbours many animal and plant species. Over 1,000 of the estimated 3,500 plant species of Arabia have either Mediterranean or Iranian affinities. The *Red Data Book* for rare and endangered mammals and birds, reptiles and amphibians lists a total of 59 terrestrial mammal species, 19 species of which are endangered, vulnerable or rare. There are 444 resident and migratory bird species, 11 species included in the Red Data Book, and 9 species of amphibian (7 of which are endemic). All the indigenous freshwater fish are full endemics. The region is important as a migration route for huge numbers of birds of a great variety of species. It has been estimated that some 2-3,000 million migrants move in a southerly direction across Arabia each autumn, involving up to 200 species (Child and Grainger, 1990).

A review of the development of nature conservation programmes include the following: a large-scale survey of water resources covering 1,248,000 sq. km in six regions undertaken in the mid-1970s (Gour-Tanguay, 1977); a survey in 1982 by MEPA recommended the protection of a number of sites, followed by another in 1986 to appraise coastal resources. A total of 74 sites along the Red Sea coast were recommended to the Environmental Protection Co-ordinating Committee in 1984 as marine protected areas. A review by MEPA and IUCN led to 46 marine and coastal sites being recommended for protection along the Red Sea coast and a further five coastal areas and six offshore areas in the Arabian Gulf (Child and Grainger, 1990; IUCN, 1987c, 1987d). Subsequent work by IUCN and NCWCD on the terrestrial ecosystems led to identification of a draft list of protected areas, with coverage of all key biological areas (for full details see Child and Grainger, 1990; Abuzinada and Child, 1991). Efforts have been made by MAW to delineate areas to be designated as forests. The first phase was to undertake aerial photographs and in subsequent phases prepare forest maps. A targetted maximum of 250ha a year was planted in the years 1980-85 (Child, 1982). Amongst projects still proposed is one for cooperation between the NCWCD protected areas programme, the MAW and local communities in locating, evaluating and registering all worthwhile traditional hemas throughout the country (Child and Grainger, 1990). In 1982 there were 19 proposed protected areas, represented by 16,450 sq. km of national park, 17,300 sq. km of nature reserves, 50 sq. km of national monuments and 100 sq. km of recreational areas (Buttiker, 1982). The 1990 system plan for protected areas identified 56 terrestrial and 47 marine and coastal sites for protection in one of five different reserve categories. Under this scheme 4% of the country would be fully protected, with another 4% partially protected (see Child and Grainger, 1990; Abuzinada and Child, 1991). By 1989, during the course of the fifth national five-year plan, the following designated and proposed sites were identified: 10 designated sites included one national park (415,000ha), one forest reserve (900ha), and eight protected areas (5,205,100ha) (totalling 5,621,000ha); eight proposed terrestrial sites totalling 1,083,000ha up to and including 1993, two sites to be declared each year and eight marine/coastal sites to be declared between 1990-1995 (totalling 330,900ha, two designated in 1990, one in 1991, one in 1992, three in 1993, and one in 1995) (Abuzinada, *in litt.*, 1989). NCWCD proposes a minimum programme of 18 protected areas to be declared during the current five-year national development plan 1990-1995 (Child and Grainger, 1990). In 1991 the actual protected areas system consisted of 15 sites totalling 514,300ha (excluding Asir) or 2.4% of the total land area (Abuzinada and Child, 1991). The total number of hemas has recently been reported to have been no less than 3,000 at its zenith – they vary in size from a few hectares to one with a diameter of 170km. The hema system and other areas of particular economic importance may approach *c.*10,000ha (Abuzinada and Child, 1991; Child and Grainger, 1990; Draz, 1985; Buttiker, *in litt.*, 1982; Child, pers. comm., 1991).

The first protected area was Umm al-Qamari Island (160ha) established in 1978 under the National Hunting Law), followed by Asir National Park (415,000ha) (MAW jurisdiction). A series of NCWCD-sponsored protected areas was initiated in 1987. The first two sites established were Harrat al Harrah and Al Khunfah. In 1991 only three sites, Asir, Umm al-Qamari and Majami' al-Hadh, are reported to have been notified and to have obtained legal status. The others are broadly covered under the general Royal Decree of 1986 for the establishment of the NCWCD (Abuzinada and Child, 1991). The MAW is currently proposing to designate Hima Huraymila (Hema Hureimla) as a national park (see Child and Grainger, 1990; Child, pers. comm., 1991).

Environmental problems due to a number of factors have been identified: principally population growth, industrialisation, transport, recreation, hunting and adverse climate. Natural renewable resources have long been heavily utilised, resulting in rapid environmental deterioration largely through such uncontrolled activities as overgrazing, uprooting or felling woody shrubs, hunting of wildlife from mammals through to reptiles and birds, off-road use of vehicles and heavy recreational pressure, extensive use of non-renewable ground water resources leading to an overall water deficit, decline in the water table, saltwater intrusion and subsidence of land (Al-Ibrahim, 1991; Child, 1982; Jungius, 1988; Woodford, 1978).

The last few decades of this century have brought about significant changes of lifestyle for rural peoples in arid lands. The most threatened biotopes in Saudi Arabia are wetlands such as seagrass beds, permanent and intermittent rivers and springs. The main threats come from over-large flocks, bedouin guns and axes, and vehicles and mobile water tanks giving them almost total freedom to range all over the landscape. Their traditional grazing rights over entire regions have also made the establishment of nature reserve or parks increasingly difficult. Over 30% of grazing land is seriously depleted due to unrestricted grazing and gathering of fuel wood (Woodford, 1978). During the Iran-Iraq war of 1980-86 Saudi Arabia was slightly affected by the oil spills as a result of military activity. Following the Nowruz oil spill, the increase in algal cover on coral reefs led to an apparent reduction in invertebrate frequency. A secondary impact was increased sedimentation, and resulted in complete or partial smothering of coral polyps, killing the coral (WCMC, 1991a). The Iraq-Kuwait land-based military hostilities in February 1991 took place in and around the important coral islands, wetlands and desert steppes and gravel plains habitats bordering Saudi Arabia, ecosystems which are regarded of international importance as identified in the World Conservation Strategy. Direct deleterious impacts have included extensive oil spills along the Arabian Gulf coastline, air pollution from burning Kuwaiti oil wells and extensive erosion from military manoeuvres; indirect impact included influx of Bedouin tribes and their livestock, putting a serious burden on the natural vegetation (Green and Drucker, 1989; WCMC, 1991b; Sulayem, pers. comm., 1991).

Other Relevant Information In 1989 nearly 774,560 pilgrims came to Mecca from abroad. According to the Tourism Development Department of Asir Principality in Abha and others, the approximate number of visitors in the first national park was 75,000 in 1981 rising to 300,000 in 1983 and approximately 3 million by 1991 (Al-Sayed, 1984; Child, pers. comm., 1991). Saudi Arabia is rich in a number of natural resources including natural gas and oil, fish and shrimp. Oil reserves are 255 billion barrels, supplying 16.6% of the world's crude oil. Within the neutral zone between Kuwait and Saudi Arabia there are four oil fields with 337 wells, of which some 100 were producing at the time of the Kuwait-Iraq war (WCMC, 1991b).

Addresses

National Commission for Wildlife Conservation and Development (NCWCD), PO Box 61681, RIYADH 11575 (Tel: 1 441 8700/0037; Tlx: 405930 SNCWCD SJl; FAX: 1 441 0797)

Meteorological and Environment Protection Administration (MEPA), PO Box 1358, JEDDAH

Directorate General for Forests and Range, Ministry of Agriculture and Water, RIYADH 11195

References

Abdulrahman, N. Al Dawood, Iskander, F. (n.d.). Resources and reserves of Saudi Arabia. Unpublished.

Abo Hassan, A.A. (1981). Rangeland management in Saudi Arabia. *Rangelands* 3(2): 51-53.

Abuzinada, A.H. (1989). Letter from the Secretary General of NCWCD concerning protected areas

system of Saudi Arabia. Ref: SG/175-10H/844. 10 October.

Abuzinada, A.H. and Child, G. (1991) Developing a system of protected areas in Saudi Arabia. National Commission for Wildlife Conservation and Development, Riyadh. Paper presented at the Third Man and Biosphere Meeting on Mediterranean Biosphere Reserves and the First IUCN-CNPPA meeting for the Middle East and North Africa, 14-19 October 1991, Tunis. 16 pp.

Abuzinada, A., Grainger, J. and Child, G. (1991). Planning a system of protected areas in Saudi Arabia. *Parks* 2: 12-17.

Al-Dawood, A.N. and Iskander, F. (n.d.). Resources and reserves of Saudi Arabia. Unpublished report.

Al-Faisal, S. (1986). Saudi Arabian National Commission for Wildlife Conservation and Development. *Environmental Conservation* 132(4): 367.

Al-Ibrahim, A.A. (1991). Excessive use of groundwater resources in Saudi Arabia: impact and policy options. *Ambio* 20(1): 34-37.

Al-Sayed, I. (1984). Nature Conservation in Saudi Arabia, The Asir National Park First Wildlife Refuge for Saudi Arabia. *Fauna of Saudi Arabia* 6: 5-8.

Anon. (1981). New desert park in Saudi Arabia. *Threatened Plant Committee Newsletter* 8: 15.

Anon. (1985). The management and conservation of renewable marine resources in the Indian Ocean region II KAP Region. Unpublished report.

Ba Kader, A.B.A., Al Sabbagh, A.L.T.S., Al Glenid, M.S. and Izzidien, M.Y.S. (1983). Islamic principles for the conservation of the natural environment. *IUCN Environmental Policy and Law Paper* No. 20. 47 pp.

Basson, P.W. *et al.* (1977). *Biotopes of the Western Arabian Gulf.* Aramco Department of Loss Prevention and Environmental Affairs, Dhahran.

Burhenne, W. (1989). Legal aspects of wildlife conservation in Saudi Arabia. In: Abuzinada, A.H., Goriup, P.D. and Nader, I.A. (Eds), *Wildlife conservation and development in Saudi Arabia.* Proceedings of the First Symposium, Riyadh, 1987. NCWCD Publication 3: 72-76.

Buttiker, W. (1982). Proposals for additional terrestrial national parks and nature reserves in Saudi Arabia. NUS corporation. Holliburton Company, Jeddah.

Buttiker, W. and Grainger, J. (1989). Possible sites for the protection and re-introduction of some wildlife species in Saudi Arabia. In: Abuzinada, A.H., Goriup, P.D. and Nader, I.A. (Eds), *Wildlife conservation and development in Saudi Arabia.* Proceedings of the First Symposium, Riyadh, 1987. NCWCD Publication 3: 287-297

Child, G.S. (1982). Forestry Project Identification Mission – Kingdom of Saudi Arabia. Food and Agriculture Organisation of the United Nations. Report UTFN/SAU/002.

Child, G. and Grainger J. (1990). *A system plan for protected areas for wildlife conservation and sustainable rural development in Saudi Arabia.* NCWCD, Riyadh. 389 pp.

Coral Reef and Tropical Marine Research Unit (1982). Management of critical habitats on the Arabian Gulf Coast of Saudi Arabia. Report to MEPA by Coral Reef and Tropical Marine Research Unit, University of York.

Downing, N. (1985). Coral reef communities in an extreme environment: the northwestern Arabian Gulf. *Proceedings of the Fifth International Coral Reef Congress. Tahiti. Volume 2.* Abstracts. 112 pp.

Draz, O. (1969). The *hema* system of range management in the Arabian Peninsula. FAO/PL/PFC/13.11. 8 pp.

Draz, O. (1985). The *hema* system of range reserves in the Arabian Peninsula, its possibilities in range improvement and conservation projects in the Near East. In: McNeely, J.A. and Pitt, D. (Eds.), *Culture and conservation: the human dimension in environmental planning.* Pp. 109-121.

Ghabbour, S.I. (1975). National parks in Arab countries. *Environmental Conservation* 2(1): 45-46.

Eighmy, J. and Ghanem, Y. (1982). The hima system: prospects for traditional subsistence systems in the Arabian peninsula. Working Paper No. 11, CID/FMES project. King Abdul Aziz university, Jeddah, Saudi Arabia. (Unseen)

Gour-Tanguay, R. (Ed.) (1977). Saudi Arabia. Environmental policies in developing countries. *Beiträge zur Umweltgestaltung* A27. Erich Schmidt Verlag.

Green, M.J.B. and Drucker, G.R.F. (1990). Current status of protected areas and threatened mammal species in the Sahara-Gobian Region. World Conservation Monitoring Centre, Cambridge, UK.

Habibi, K. (1985). Conservation and management of wildlife in Saudi Arabia. *FAO Technical Paper* No. 1.

Halwagy, R., Clayton, D. and Behbehani, M. (1986). *Marine environment and pollution.* Proceedings of the First Arabian Gulf Conference on environment and pollution.

Hunter, B. (Ed.) (1991). *The Statesman's Year Book 1991-92.* The Macmillan Press Ltd, London and Basingstoke, UK. 1692 pp.

IUCN (1976). Promotion of the establishment of marine parks and reserves in the northern Indian Ocean including the Red Sea and Persian Gulf. *IUCN Publication New Series* No. 35.

IUCN (1976). Ecological guidelines for the use of natural resources in the Middle East and South West Asia. *IUCN Publications New Series* No. 34.

IUCN (1987a). Providing IUCN Technical support to NCWCD in preparing its national protected areas system plan. Project proposal submitted to the National Commission for Wildlife Conservation and Development of Saudi Arabia. International Union for Conservation of Nature and Natural Resources, Gland, Switzerland.

IUCN (1987b). The Red Sea and Arabian Gulf. Saudi Arabia: a national coastal zone management programme to balance future growth with protection of coastal and marine resources. Report to MEPA, Jeddah. 54 pp.

IUCN (1987c). The Red Sea. Saudi Arabia: an assessment of management requirements for the Saudi Arabian Red Sea Coastal zone. Report to MEPA, Jeddah. 92 pp.

IUCN (1987d). The Red Sea. Saudi Arabia: an analysis of coastal and marine habitats of the Saudi Arabian Red Sea. Report of MEPA, Jeddah. 250 pp.

IUCN (1987c). The Arabian gulf. Saudi Arabia: an assessment of biotopes and management requirements for the Saudi Arabian Gulf coastal zone. Report to MEPA, Jeddah. 244 pp.

IUCN/UNEP (1985a) The management and conservation of renewable resources in the Red Sea and Gulf of Aden region. *UNEP Regional Seas Reports and Studies* No. 64. 106 pp.

IUCN/UNEP (1985b). The management and conservation of renewable marine resources in the Kuwait Action Plan region. *UNEP Regional Seas Reports and Studies* No 56. 57 pp.

Jungius, H. (1985). The role of indigenous flora and fauna in rangeland management systems of the arid zones in western asia. *Journal of Arid Environments* 6: 75-85.

Jungius, H. (1987). The establishment of national parks and protected areas in the arid zone: a contribution to conservation and rational utilization of natural resources. First symposium on the potential of wildlife conservation in Saudi Arabia, Riyadh, 15-18 February 1987. National Commission for Wildlife Conservation and Development. 11 pp.

Jungius, II. (1988). The national parks and protected areas concept and its applications to the Arabian peninsula. *Fauna of Saudi Arabia* 9: 3-11.

Khan, M. A. (1981). Asir national park. Khamis Mushayt and Abha handbook. US-SA Joint Commission on Economic Cooperation.

Kingdon, J. (1987). Wildlife conservation in Saudi Arabia – hope and despair. *Oryx* 21(3): 138-140.

Maher Abu Jaafer (1984). *National parks and nature reserves in the Arab World.* Department of Sciences, The Arab League Educational, Cultural and Scientific Organisation, Tunis.

MAW (1984). *Ministry of Agriculture and Water – National Parks.* Ministry of Agriculture and Water, National Parks Department. 40 pp.

MEPA (1987a). The Red Sea: An assessment of management requirements for the Saudi Arabian Red Sea Coastal Zone. *MEPA Coastal and Marine Management Series* No. 2.

MEPA (1987b). The Arabian Gulf Saudi Arabia. An assessment of biotopes and management requirements for the Saudi Arabian Gulf Coastal Zone. *MEPA Coastal and Marine Management Series* No. 3.

MEPA (1991). National Report on oil and air pollution. Presented by MEPA, Kingdom of Saudi Arabia to UNEP, Nairobi, Kenya. 12 pp.

McNeely, J.A. and Miller, K.R. (1987). Planning and management of terrestrial protected areas in Saudi Arabia. Contribution to the first symposium of wildlife conservation in Saudi Arabia, Riyadh, 15-18 February 1987.

Miller, A.G. and Nyberg, J.A. (1991). Pattern of endemism in Arabia. *Flora et Vegetatio Mundi* IX: 264-278.

NCWCD (n.d.). National Commission for Wildlife Conservation and Development in brief. NCWCD, King Saud University Press, Riyadh. 18 pp.

Porter, R.F. and Goriup, P.D. (1985). Recommendations for the conservation of the Arabian Bustard and Houbara Bustard in Saudi Arabia. Report for MEPA.

Price, A.R.G. (1990). Rapid assessment of coastal zone management requirements: a case study from the Arabian gulf. *Ocean and shoreline management* 13: 1-19.

Price, A.R.G.; Chiffings, T.W. Atkinson, M.A. and Wrathall, T.J. (1987). Appraisal of resources in the Saudi Arabian Gulf. Coastal Zone '87. WW Div./ASCE, Seattle, USA 26-29 May 1987. Pp. 1031-1045

Thouless, C. (1991). Conservation in Saudi Arabia. *Oryx* 25(4): 222-228.

UNEP (1983). Action Plan for the protection of the marine environment and the coastal areas of Bahrain, Iran, Iraq, Kuwait, Oman, Qatar, Saudi Arabia and the United Arab Emirates. *UNEP Regional Seas Reports and Studies* No. 365.

UNEP/IUCN (1988). *Coral reefs of the world. Volume 2: Indian Ocean, Red Sea and Gulf.* UNEP Regional Seas Directories and Bibliographies.

IUCN, Gland, Switzerland and Cambridge, UK/UNEP, Nairobi, Kenya. 440 pp.

UNESCO/ROPME/UPM/UNEP (1985). Proceedings of the symposium/workshop on oceanographic modelling of the Kuwait Action Plan (KAP) region. *UNEP Regional Seas Reports and Studies* No. 70.

UNESCO/ROPME/UNEP (1985). Combatting oil pollution in the Kuwait Action Plan region. *UNEP Regional Seas Reports and Studies* No. 44.

Vessey-Fitzgerald, D.F. (1957a). The vegetation of central and eastern Arabia. *Journal of Ecology* 45: 779-798.

Vincent-Barwood, A. (1980). A park for "Asir". *Aramco World* 31(5): 22-23.

WCMC (1991a). Gulf War Environmental Service: impact on the marine environment. World Conservation Monitoring Centre, Cambridge, UK. 37 pp.

WCMC (1991b). Gulf War Environmental Service: impact of atmospheric pollution on the terrestrial environment. World Conservation Monitoring Centre, Cambridge, UK. 37 pp.

Wittmer, W. and Buttiker, W. (Eds) (1979-82). *Fauna of Saudi Arabia.* MEPA, Jeddah and Pro-Entomologia, Basle, Switzerland.

Woodford, M.H. (1978). Consultancy on the restoration of the Kingdom's wildlife. Report to the Government of the Kingdom of Saudi Arabia. TF-SAU 117. FAO, Rome. 30 pp.

ANNEX
Definitions of protected area designations, as legislated, together with authorities responsible for their administration

Title: National Hunting law Decree Law No. 457

Date: 1977

Brief description: Includes details on permanent areas where hunting is banned.

Administrative authority: Administered centrally by the Ministry of Interior on advice from the National Commission for Wildlife Conservation and Development (NCWCD).

Designations:

Controlled hunting area Regulations have been promulgated relating to administration and management.

No person may hunt in a controlled hunting area without a permit.

Areas in which the NCWCD is solely concerned with the management of sustainable hunting in liaison with local people.

Source: Child and Grainger, 1990

Title: Royal Forest Decree Law No. 1392

Date: 11 April 1978 (1398) (incorporates National Park Law of 1977)

Brief description: Lays down regulations for the protection of forests and wildlife.

Administrative authority: General Directorate of Forests and Range, Ministry of Agriculture and Water.

Designations:

Recreation area Established for public recreation

Forest and range reserve The range section of the DRF had developed a programme to revive the hema system by fencing large enclosures in selected areas.

National park The General Department for National Parks has responsibility for the establishment of national parks which are subject to directives of the Governor of Asir Province.

Tree felling is prohibited and hunting restricted.

Tourism is a major element of park activities, construction and habitations are permitted as is livestock grazing.

Other activities include restoration of native wildlife and development of propagation centres for indigenous threatened species.

Source: Child, 1982; Al Dawood and Iskander, n.d.

Title: Royal Decree No. M/22

Date: 20 June 1986

Brief description: Led to a public commitment by the government to the creation of an adequate representative system of protected areas (Child and Grainger, 1990). Article 3(4) provided that the NWCWD was entrusted with conserving wildlife and creating and maintaining the managed system of protected areas. In 1991 a draft protected area legislation was being prepared, providing for a management plan for each reserve to be the legal instrument guiding its control (see Child and Grainger, 1990 for full details). A system of five categories have been identified to which the traditional hema or himas system could be added as a sixth class.

Administrative authority: National Commission for Wildlife Conservation and Development (NCWCD)

Designations:

Special nature reserve Covered under Article 3(4) and identified in the draft legal instrument of 1990.

Regarded as the prime sites of biological excellence and the focus of NCWCD activities.

Areas of great ecological excellence, fully protected from grazing and conflicting land use.

Natural reserve Covered under Article 3(4) and identified in the draft legal instrument of 1990.

Areas of great ecological excellence or small areas of ecological excellence protected from grazing and conflicting land use.

Areas that will include modified habitats, such as artificial wetlands and managed areas such as at field research stations.

Administered by NCWCD or a delegated authority.

Biological reserve Covered under Article 3(4) and identified in the draft legal instrument of 1990.

Generally small, for preserving local propagules or other conservation purposes. Amongst other objectives these areas are aimed at protecting seed stocks in strategically located sites from where seed can be dispersed by wind or water to help rehabilitate depleted rangeland.

Managed mainly by local authority.

Resource use reserve Covered under Article 3(4) and identified in the draft legal instrument of 1990

Large areas in which the emphasis will be on sound resource use, rather than conservation of biological resources.

Resource use is regulated by the NCWCD in consultation with appropriate government agencies and local resources.

Controlled hunting reserve Covered under Article 3(4) and identified in the draft legal instrument of 1990

Large areas in which the NCWCD is solely concerned with the management of sustainable hunting in liaison with local people.

Sources: Abuzinada and Grainger, 1991; Abuzinada, Grainger and Child, 1991; Child and Grainger, 1990

SUMMARY OF PROTECTED AREAS

Map[†] ref.	*National/international designations* Name of area	IUCN management category	Area (ha)	Year notified
	National Park			
1	Asir	V	450,000	1981
	Protected Areas (Controlled Hunting Areas)			
2	Farasan Islands	I	60,000	1989
3	Harrat al-Harrah	IV	1,377,500	1987
4	Hawtah Bani Tamin	IV	236,900	1988
5	Khunfah	IV	2,045,000	1987
6	Mahazat as Sayed	I	200,000	1988
7	Tubayq	IV	1,220,000	1989
8	Majami al-Hadb	IV	38,0000	1989
9	Remainder N. Wildlife Mgmt Zone	IV	15,228,000	1988
10	Umm al-Qamari Island	IV	160	1978

[†]Locations of most protected areas are shown on the accompanying map.

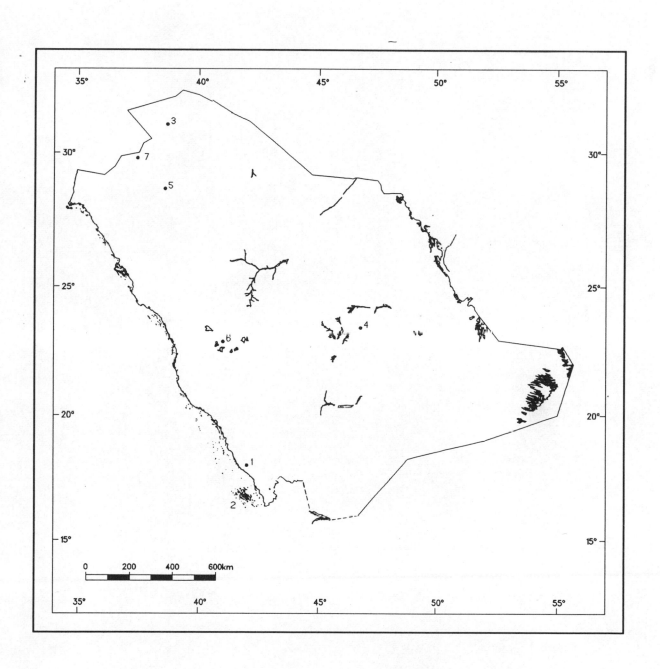

Protected Areas of Saudi Arabia

SPAIN – NORTH AFRICAN TERRITORIES

Area 32 sq. km
Ceuta 18 sq. km, Melilla 14 sq. km (Hunter, 1991)

Population 127,016 (1986) (Hunter, 1991)
Natural increase: 0.3% per annum

Economic Indicators
No information

Policy and Legislation Following independence of the former Spanish Protectorate of northern Morocco in 1956, a number of enclaves in Northern Africa were maintained under Spanish sovereignty. These territories include: Ceuta (Sebta), Melilla (El Melilla), Peñon de Velez de la Gomera (Bades), Peñon de Alhucemas (Al Hoceima island), Islas Chafarinas and also the offshore Alboran islands. Melilla has been a colony of Spain since 1497, Ceuta since 1580, Peñon de Alhucemas since 1673 and the Chafarinas since 1848 (Hureau, 1980; Michelin, 1982). The North African territories have been administrated as municipalities of the provinces of Cadiz (Ceuta) and Malaga (El Melilla), Andalucia region. However, they were due to gain full provincial status in 1991 (Hunter, 1991).

Being Sovereign Spanish territory, all the above mentioned areas are subject to Spanish law and policy (for full details see entry for Spain). The new Constitution for the whole of Spain came into force on 29 December 1978. This established a semi-federal system of regional administration, with the autonomous community (comunidad autonoma) as its basic element. There are 17 autonomous communities, each having a parliament, regional government and exclusive legislative rights to enact its own laws; Ceuta and Melilla were due to achieve this right in 1991. Article 45 Chapter III of the Constitution, entitled "Guidelines for Social and Economic Policy", embodies principles of conservation including rational use of resources, protection and restoration of the environment (Poore and Gryn-Ambroes, 1980).

In 1971 the National Institute for Nature Conservation (Instituto Nacional para la Conservación de la Naturaleza) (ICONA) was established by law. Under the Law on Protected Natural Areas (Espacios Naturales Protegidos) No. 15/1975 of 15 May 1975 protected areas were given legal status. Four categories of protected area are described in this Law: national park, natural park, natural area of national importance or interest and integral reserve of scientific interest (Rodriguez, 1985). A major new piece of legislation was enacted on 27 March 1989: Law No. 4 on the Conservation of Natural Spaces, Flora and Wildlife (Ley de Conservación de los Espacios Naturales, de la Flora y Fauna Silvestres). This Law was intended to comply with the 1978 constitution and lead to the regionalisation of many issues of nature conservation, including those relating to protected areas (Llorens and Rodriguez,

1991). Four categories of protected area are described: park, natural reserve, natural monument, and protected landscape (see Annex in the entry for Spain). The declaration of these protected areas is the responsibility of the autonomous communities which are also responsible for drawing up specific regulations for sites in their region. The state maintains the right to declare and manage natural areas that are a part of the "public domain", for example in marine and coastal areas and inland lakes. The state may also declare areas that fall under the jurisdiction of two or more autonomous communities (Llorens and Rodriguez, 1991).

Hunting legislation is particularly relevant to protected areas in the Spanish North African territories at the present time. Laws concerning the creation of national hunting reserves were declared on 31 May 1966 (Law No. 37/1966), on 4 April 1970 (Law No. 1/1970) and on 17 March 1973. There are three categories of hunting reserves: national hunting reserve, national hunting sanctuary and national hunting refuge (ICONA, *in litt.*, 1988) (see Annex). Faunal sanctuaries can be enacted under Articles 11 and 12 of the Hunting Act, following proposals of the Ministry of Agriculture (Poore and Gryn-Ambroes, 1980).

The protection of coastal areas, including all those of the Spanish Territories of North Africa, is covered by regulations within the Law on Coasts (Ley de Costas) of 28 July 1988 (Law No. 22/1988). This Law was approved by Royal Decree No. 1471 of 1 December 1989. It lists obligations for the protection of the sea up to 100m offshore (subject to extension); it restricts the number of traffic and access routes to the coast (including pedestrian); it also defines a 'zone of influence' which extends 500m from the waterline which may affect the land and urban planning; the disposal of solid waste and raw sewage is prohibited in this area (Cutrera, 1991).

There appears to be no adequate municipal legislation which relates specifically to the Spanish North African territories, although with the change in status of the territories in 1991 they may establish protected areas in the near future under Law No. 4 on the Conservation of Natural Spaces, Flora and Wildlife of 1989.

International Activities Spain acceded to the Convention Concerning the Protection of the World Cultural and Natural Heritage (World Heritage Convention) on 4 May 1982 and The Convention on Wetlands of International Importance Especially as Waterfowl Habitat (Ramsar Convention) also on 4 May 1982. No sites have been declared in the North African territories. Spain is party to the Barcelona Convention, and the Protocol Concerning Mediterranean Specially Protected Areas which was ratified on 22 January 1988, but no sites in the North African Territories have been listed. Spain joined the European Community (EC) in 1986 and is party to the 1979 Wild Birds Directive, one EC special protection area, Islas Chafarinas, has been designated close to Melilla (Grimmet and Jones, 1989). Spain ratified the Convention on the Conservation of European Wildlife and Natural Habitats (Bern Convention) in September 1986.

Under the Mediterranean Environmental Technical Assistance Programme (CY90-92 METAP), of the World Bank, European Investment Bank, United Nations Development Programme and Commission of the European Communities, environment project preparation includes one on coastal zone management and development of the proposed Al Hoceima National Park in Morocco which would have an immediate impact on the adjacent Spanish North African Territories (Anon., 1991).

A transboundary park has been proposed that would incorporate wetland areas for migratory birds, extending from Tetuan in Morocco, the Spanish North African Territories of Ceuta/Melilla to Gibraltar and Spain across the Straits of Gibraltar (Cortes, *in litt.*, 1991). Another transboundary park is proposed at Al Hoceima which could incorporate conservation management in adjacent territory under the jurisdiction of the Spanish enclave of Melilla.

Administration and Management The national body responsible for administration of protected areas is the National Institute for the Conservation of Nature (ICONA). Its functions in the North African territories are minimal, but include: the encouragement of renewable resource use and maintenance of ecological balance and the development and exploitation of inland fishing and hunting assets (Poore and Gryn-Ambroes, 1980). As a result of the decentralisation of the government in 1978, the responsibility for many conservation issues was handed over to the control of the 17 autonomous communities this has been further aided by the 1989 Law on the Conservation of Natural Areas, Flora and Wildlife. Some of the work originally performed by ICONA has thus, in subsequent years, been handed over to these authorities. ICONA remains responsible for the administration and management of hunting reserves within the region including the Chafarinas (the Wildlife Service, Servicio de Vidas Silvestre). ICONA consists of a central service and provincial network. The renewable natural resources division is responsible for hunting reserves amongst others, and is itself divided into two services: game, and parks and reserves.

The National Commission for the Protection of Nature (Comisión Nacional de Protección de la Natura) was established under the 1989 law as a consultant organisation, coordinating the activities of the central organisations and the autonomous communities within this Commission is the Committee for Natural Protected Areas (Comité Nacional d'Espacios Naturales Protegidos), comprising a representative of each of the autonomous communities and having the Director of ICONA as its President (Llorens and Rodriguez, 1991). It is thought that from 1991 Ceuta and Melilla will be able to provide their own representatives to this committee.

In practice routine wardening of sites such as the Chafarinas is under the jurisdiction of the Ministry of Defence through the Garrison commander, although conservation management is also undertaken by ICONA, and from 1991, with the new biological station constructed they will have a greater wardening capability (Bradley and Monaghan, 1986). The marine areas of the region, including proposed protected areas, come under the Ministry of Agriculture and would be managed through ICONA.

There are a number of non-governmental organisations concerned with conservation in Spanish North Africa, some of which are involved in the management of the few critical areas. Some of the more important of these organisations include the Federación Coordinadora para la Defensa da las Aves (CODA) and the Sociedad Española de Ornitología (SEO).

Systems Reviews Each of the Spanish territories is adjacent to, or enclaved within sovereign territory of Morocco and is found within various Mediterranean type bioclimates.

Ceuta The Spanish municipality of Ceuta, on mainland North Africa, is centred around a built-up town on Monte Hacho, a rocky promontory off the Rif coast. This peninsula is connected to the mainland by a narrow isthmus. It has a relatively undeveloped coastline extending for a number of kilometres westwards to Benzu, the border with Morocco. Inland on the slopes of Djebel Musa (apes hill) the landscape is rural in aspect with grazing land, fields, orchards, vineyards, pine and eucalyptus plantations, along with natural areas of maquis (sub humid bioclimate) consisting of wild olive *Olea europaea*, lentisc *Pistacia tentiscus* and dwarf palm *Chamaerops humilis*. The threatened North African endemic primate Barbary macaque *Macaca sylvanus* inhabits Djebel Musa, and is occasionally observed in the foothills above Ceuta (Drucker, pers. comm., 1987). The globally endangered Mediterranean monk seal *Monachus* is very occasionally observed passing along the coastline (Drucker, pers. comm., 1987; Haddane, pers. comm., 1991).

El Melilla This town is located in a sub arid bioclimate, and is situated on the North African coastline as an enclave within Morocco. It is largely built up around the old fortified peninsula of Medina Sidonia. There is pasture and arable land to the west of Melilla town and a relatively undeveloped coastline extending to the northern limits of its territorial border. Mediterranean monk seals are seen occasionally on the surrounding coastline (Drucker, pers. comm., 1987).

The remaining Spanish territories are all rocky islands or archipelagos off the Moroccan coastline (Boulva, 1975).

Peñon de Velez (or Peñon de la Gomera) is only a few hundred metres off the African continent, normally connected by a sandspit (east of the Moroccan town of Al Hoceima). It is a fortified rocky islet about 70km west of Alhucemas Bay.

Alboran is an isolated island some 53km north of the coastline from Cap des Trois Fourches near Melilla.

Chafarinas is a group of three islands 3.5km from Ras Kebdana, east of Melilla. Each of these sites has relatively sparse vegetation, largely dominated by chasmophytes and graminae. Chafarinas Island is the most important, with breeding colonies of Audouin's gull, Cory's shearwater and osprey. There is also a very small colony of the globally endangered Mediterranean monk seal in the archipelago, which were last seen in 1991 (Bradley and Monaghan, 1986; Carp, 1980; Grimmett and Jones, 1989; Serrada, *in litt.*, 1991).

Few comprehensive surveys of biological resources have been undertaken except concerning the ornithology of the Melilla area, although studies have also been undertaken on fish resources and sea mammals (Bradley and Monaghan, 1986). ICONA has undertaken or coordinated extensive work on the Chafarinas and in 1991 was building a permanent biological station there for future research.

Existing protection is limited to the Chafarinas which have been declared a national hunting reserve under Royal Decree (Bradley and Monaghan, 1986). The Peñon de Velez de Gomera is entirely surrounded by the Moroccan Ministry of Agriculture's biological terrestrial and marine reserve, Bokkoyas. It is presumed that the legislation will afford some protection to the Peñon, yet there are some doubts as to the degree of protection, as the immediate area is proposed for tourist development (BETURE/SETAME, 1985; Drucker, pers. comm. 1987). Recommendations have been put forward to station trained conservationists or wardens in these areas (see above) (Bradley and Monaghan, 1986).

The Chafarinas have been regarded as having a status which provides comparatively little protection for the fauna, as there have been no wardens to enforce the regulations (Bradley and Monaghan, 1986). Greatest threats to the areas concerned include disturbance to bird colonies by fishermen, military forces and egg collectors (Chafarinas), increasing accessibility and uncontrolled tourism (Peñon de Velez) and excessive or illicit boat excursions by tourists (Peñon de Alhucemas) (Drucker, pers. comm., 1987).

Addresses

Wildlife Service, National Institute for Nature Conservation, Instituto Nacional para la Conservacion de la Naturaleza (ICONA), Gran Via de San Francisco 35-41, 28005 MADRID (Tel: 1 347 6175; FAX: 1 265 8379; Tlx: 47591 aeico e)

Consejo Superior de Investigaciones Cientificas (CSIC), Serrano 117, 28005 MADRID

Sociedad Española de Ornitologia, Facultad de Biologia, Pl.9, 28040 MADRID (Tel: 91 449 35 54)

References

Anon. (1962). XIII/1, Spain, Forest Regulations (Decree No. 485/1962) (Extracts: Preliminary Part and Book I (Forest Property)) *Food and Agricultural Legislation*, Vol. XI – No. 2. Food and Agricultural Organisation, Rome. Pp. 1-16.

Anon. (1978). XIX/4 – National Parks and Nature Reserves, Spain – Crown Decree No. 2676/77 approving the Regulation for the enforcement of Act No. 15/1975, of 2 May 1975, on Protected Nature Areas. *Food and Agricultural Legislation*, Vol XXVII. Food and Agricultural Organisation, Rome. Pp. 91-100.

Anon. (1991). Mediterranean Environmental Technical Assistance Program, activity report Spring, 1991. World Bank, European Investment Bank, United Nations Development Programme and Commission of the European Communities. 24 pp.

Augier, H. (1985). *Protected marine areas. The example of France and appraisal and prospects*. European Committee for the Conservation of Nature and Natural Resources. Strasbourg.

BETURE/SETAME (1985). Protection des richesses naturelles de la côte méditerranéenne du Maroc: Réserve biologique des Bokoyas. Report.

Boulva, J. (1975). Survey of the monk seal in the Western Mediterranean. A report presented to the IFAW and IUCN.

Bradley, P.M. and Monaghan, P. (1986). Audouin's gull and the Chafarinas islands game reserve. *Oryx* 20(3): 161-164.

Carp, E. (1980). *A Directory of western Palearctic wetlands*. IUCN, Gland, Switzerland. 506 pp.

Eaux et Forets (1991). Rapport sur les Aires Protegees au Maroc. Paper presented at the Third Man and Biosphere Meeting on Biosphere Reserves in the Mediterranean and the First IUCN-CNPPA Workshop on Protected Areas in the North Africa-Middle East Region, 14-19 October 1991, Tunis. 18 pp.

Grimmett, R.F.A. and Jones, T.A. (1989). *Important Bird Areas of Europe*. International Council for Bird Preservation, Cambridge, UK.

Gryn-Ambroes, P. (1980). *Preliminary annotated lists of existing and potential Mediterranean protected areas*. IUCN UNEP/IG.20/INF. 5. GE. 80-3092.

Hunter, B. (Ed.) (1991). *The Statesman's Year Book 1991-92*. The Macmillan Press Ltd, London and Basingstoke, UK. 1692 pp.

ICONA (1984). XVI General Assembly of the IUCN. Conservation in Spain. Summary. 10 pp.

ICONA (1984b). Conservacionismo en España. Informacion No. 3 *Ambiental*. 47 pp.

Lillo, A.L. (1988). Protected natural areas in Spain. *Nature and national parks* 26(100): 24-26.

Llorens, V. and Rodriguez, J.A. (1991). *Els espais naturals protegits a espanya, legislació i inventari*.

Intitució Valenciana d'Estudis i Investigació, València. In Catalan. 165 pp.

Medina, F.O. (1977). Spain's national parks policy. *Parks* (2)1: 12-14.

Ortuño, F. and Jorge de la Peña (1976). *Reservas y cotos nacionales de Caza*. Region Pirenaica Vol. 1, Region Cantabrica, Vol. 2, Region Central, Vol. 3, Region Mediterranean, Vol. 4. INCAFO, Spain.

Poore, D. and Gryn-Ambroes, P. (1980). *Nature conservation in Northern and Western Europe*. UNEP/IUCN/WWF, Gland, Switzerland. Pp. 291-314.

Rodriguez, F. (1985). Administration of Protected Areas in Spain. In: Proceedings of Twenty-fourth Working Session of Commission on National Parks and Protected Areas, Madrid, Spain. 3-4 November 1984. IUCN, Gland, Switzerland.

ANNEX
Definitions of protected area designations, as legislated, together with authorities responsible for their administration

Title: Ley sobre Creación de Reservas Nacionales de Caza (Law on the creation of national hunting reserves) No. 37/1966 and Ley de Caza (Law on hunting) No. 1/1970

Date: 31 May 1966 and 4 April 1970

Brief description: The two laws contain the main legal provisions concerning the establishment and subsequent protection of the different categories of hunting reserves.

Administrative authority: Bodies set up in each of the 17 regional governments

Designations:

National hunting reserve (Reserva nacional de caza) May be publically or privately owned. They are areas which are considered important as core areas for hunting, and as important sites for the maintenance and regeneration of wild fauna, notably game species. The areas surrounding many of these sites have been destroyed or damaged through uncontrolled exploitation to such an extent that they have reached a critical situation or are in danger of disappearing. Hunting is a very important feature of these reserves, it is often considered a necessary form of management and actively encouraged, although it remains controlled.

National hunting sanctuary (Coto nacional de caza) Essentially very similar to the reserves in both the reasons for their designation and the restrictions imposed. Perhaps the major difference is that they may only be declared on nationally owned land. As a result, because there is no third party involved in the designation of sites, the legal formalities involved in declaring a site are less strict and complex.

National hunting refuge (Refugio nacional de caza) Areas where, for biological, scientific or educational reasons, it is necessary to ensure the conservation of determined species of game.

Sources: Ortuño and Peña, 1976; ICONA, *in litt.*, 1988

SYRIAN ARAB REPUBLIC (SYRIA)

Area 185,680 sq. km

Population 12,530,000 (1990)
Natural increase: 3.60% per annum

Economic Indicators
GDP: US$ 2,884 per capita (1987)
GNP: US$ 1,820 per capita (1987)

Policy and Legislation The constitution was promulgated on the 14 March 1973. Complete independence from France was achieved in April 1946.

Traditional forms of protection included range reserves (*Mahmeya*), which were not uncommon up to 30 or 40 years ago (cf Hema protection of the Arabian Peninsula). In the Badhia region, a diminishing number of such areas are found in steppe land (Khatib, *in litt.*, 1991). Whilst under Ottoman rule in the second half of the 19th century, the forests came under the jurisdiction of the Turkish forest administration. Forest legislation was primarily concerned with controlling tree felling by the issue of permits, and the transportation of wood for local industry and export to neighbouring countries. Limited legislation was covered under the Mejellah, Ottoman civil code within the body of Islamic law. Under Article 1243 of the civil code it was defined that land and associated trees growing wild in mountains could not be possessed and should remain ownerless. Under Article 1244 cutting wood on private forests was not permitted without authorisation, infringement resulting in payment for any damage caused. In 1935 the French mandate government issued a forest law providing for the protection of the few remaining forest areas (Science and Technology Division, 1981). From 1946, legislation was concerned with rectifying forest degradation and the need for its protection and management.

Extant nature conservation legislation concerns forest protection, hunting, protection of aquatic life and general care of the environment. The current law on forests, the Forest Code Legislative Decree No. 66 of 22 September 1953, includes a definition and provides for the establishment of state forests, defines the restrictions on forest usage rights and acts as general enabling legislation. Under Title IV of the Forest Code, the Directorate of Forests and Afforestation of the Ministry of Agriculture and Agrarian Reform has the jurisdiction to establish areas of state-owned protected forest as state forest protection zones (Science and Technology Division, 1981). Legislative Decree No. 86 of 22 September 1953, Law on the Forest Police, was enacted in order to establish a forest warden and policing system (Science and Technology Division, 1981).

Other laws relevant to nature conservation areas include: Law on Forest Goat Exclusion No. 128 of 23 August 1958, which concerns the protection of trees and plants from damage caused by goats and the implementation of this Law by the forest police force (Science and Technology Division, 1981); Legislative Decree No. 152 of 23 July 1970, Law on Hunting, which contains various acts including designation of the Hunting Council (Conseil Cynégétique) and areas where hunting is restricted. In Legislative Decree No. 50 of 5 April 1979, all hunting was banned for a five-year period, as a measure to preserve wildlife (penalties include fines and imprisonment terms of up to two years).

Legislative Decree No. 30 of 25 August 1964, and Law on the Protection of Aquatic Life include articles which covered the protection of public waters (protected public waters) and the regulation of fishing in sea water extending 12 miles from the coast (Science and Technology Division, 1981).

Following the Agrarian Reform Law, 1958, land reform was initiated in September 1959, such that private land holdings were restricted to 50ha of irrigated land or 300ha of rainfed land per person.

Reviews of the protected area legislation have not been undertaken, although in September/October 1991 the UNEP Mediterranean Specially Protected Areas Task Force proposed to undertake a mission to Syria to draft legal acts for the proclamation of coastal areas of special natural value, together with proposals for the management of protected areas, financing, operational and institutional reforms (Jeudy de Grissac, *in litt.*, 1991).

International Activities At the international level, the Syrian Arab Republic has entered a number of cooperative agreements and legal obligations. Syria is party to the Convention concerning the Protection of the World Cultural and Natural Heritage (World Heritage Convention), which it accepted on 13 August 1975. No natural sites have been inscribed to date. Syria does not participate in the Convention on Wetlands of International Importance especially as Waterfowl Habitat (Ramsar Convention), but does participate in the Unesco Man and Biosphere (MAB) Programme. The national MAB committee comprised 18 representatives in 1991. To date no biosphere reserves have been accepted under the Programme. The Convention for the Protection of the Mediterranean Sea against Pollution, usually known as the Barcelona Convention, was formally adopted in February 1976. The contracting parties to the Convention adopted the Protocol concerning Mediterranean Specially Protected Areas on 2 April 1982, which entered into force on 23 March 1986. No sites have been selected as specially protected areas, although a steering committee is studying the possibility of sites being listed. One site has been recommended by the UNEP SPA Task Force (Al Nimeh, *in litt.*, 1991).

Under the Mediterranean Environmental Technical Assistance Programme (CY90-92 METAP) of the World Bank, European Investment Bank, United Nations Development Programme and Commission of the European Community, representatives from Syria attended the first meeting of the Mediterranean Protected Areas Network (MEDPAN) meeting in Monaco from 5-6 October 1990 (Anon., 1990).

Administration and Management The main governmental body concerned with the environment, the Ministry of Agriculture and Agrarian Reform, was formed in 1967 from the Agrarian Reform Agency and the Ministry of Agriculture. The Ministry is responsible for agriculture, water pollution, hunting, fishing and management of protected areas. It is divided into sections including the Directorate of Forests and Afforestation, the Directorate of Rangeland and Countryside, and the Fisheries Office (concerned with inland water and marine matters).

The Directorate of Forests and Afforestation has responsibility for reafforestation, establishment of state forests, state forest protection zones and green belt areas. It has established a significant area of protected forest and by 1980 had undertaken extensive reafforestation work in an area covering some 60,000ha (Science and Technology Division, 1981). By law, forest police are detailed to patrol and manage state forests and forest protected areas.

The Directorate of Rangeland and Countryside has responsibility for the protected rangeland reserves, and works generally in the field of rangeland improvement.

The Ministry of State for Environmental Affairs in the Prime Ministry is concerned with the impact of air, water, chemical and noise pollution, although it also has interests in fauna, forest vegetation, coastal areas and deserts, botanical gardens, proposed wildlife areas and zoos. It provides public information and undertakes research on the future establishment of protected areas, preservation of individual species and environmental legislation (Montague and Bruun, 1987). Other ministries involved with environmental issues include the Ministry of Public Works and Water Resources, which has interests in water conservation and the construction of dams (also has responsibilities for water pollution control and in the drafting of legislation for the control of water pollution); the Ministry of Defence; the Ministry of the Euphrates Dam with its own special funds; and the Ministry of Local Administration which implements projects including the drainage and reclamation of swamps and ponds (Science and Technology Division, 1981).

Semi-governmental organisations with interests in wildlife conservation include the Department of Zoology, University of Damascus, which has undertaken surveys to identify important nature conservation areas. It is currently working closely with the UNEP SPA Task Force to identify marine and coastal protected areas

(Montague and Bruun, 1987; Al Nimeh, *in litt.*, 1991). Other bodies include the Arab Agronomists Union which was established in 1968 and is concerned with the impact of water pollution, as well as environmental threats posed by urban development and conservation of agricultural lands (Montague and Bruun, 1987). The Arab Centre for the Study of Arid Zones and Dry Lands (ACSAD) was established in 1971 as an autonomous intergovernmental organisation with activities covering Syria and assistance to 21 other Arab states. Its activities range from education and conferences to research on the impact of urban development, protected area surveys and data gathering on plants and natural vegetation in forests and deserts. ACSAD assists in the enhancement of natural vegetation, including the improvement of natural habitats utilised by wildlife (El Khash, *in litt.*, 1980). It promotes an integrated approach to the study of scientific, technological and human factors in regions where aridity is the main environmental constraint (Montague and Bruun, 1987).

Systems Reviews Syria is bounded on the west by the Mediterranean Sea, by Iraq on the east, Turkey in the north and Israel and Jordan in the south. The country is broadly divided by the Jebel el Ansariyah (1,550m), which separates the coastal Mediterranean type bioclimatic region, with its temperate and humid climate, from the dry steppe and desert country of the greater part of continental eastern Syria. Vegetation comprises Mediterranean, Irano-Turanian and Saharo-Sindian elements. However, virtually all natural vegetation has long since been altered and degraded by human activity. The surviving vegetation includes oak maquis along the narrow coastal plain, remnant coniferous forests on the slopes of the Jebel el Ansariyah and along the Anti-Lebanon mountains, inland Irano-Turanian steppe (and elements of Kurdo-Zagarosian steppe forest) and the Mediterranean subalpine and alpine communities in the southern mountains (found above 2,000m rising to Mt Hermo at 2,814m) (Davis *et al.*, 1986; Khatib, 1991; Khatib, *in litt.*, 1991).

About 32% of the land area is cultivated, 46% is steppe and 2.4% covered by forest (Science and Technology Division, 1981). Cultivation tends to be concentrated in the coastal zones and along the banks of the River Euphrates and its tributaries in the north-east (Carp, 1980). Loss of forest was probably at its mos' intense during the late 19th and early 20th centuries, brought about by increased human and livestock populations, increased access, technology and demands for additional sources of fuel.

In the early 1980s there was a strong desire by the Ministry of Agriculture and Agrarian Reform to reintroduce wildlife into the steppe regions of the country, particularly larger ungulates such as Syrian or Asiatic wild ass *Equus hemionus hemippus* and Saudi Arabian dorcas gazelle *Gazella dorcas saudiya* (Child, *in litt.*, 1978). This has led to the El Khelah Project releasing gazelle south of Palmyra (Khatib, *in litt.*, 1991). Attempts to improve the environment include the green belt programme which was launched in 1978 to restrict desertification.

Systems reviews or comprehensive surveys of selected biological resources have been undertaken on a countrywide basis, although not necessarily with the intention of setting up a network of protected areas. However, the UNEP SPA Task Force, in cooperation with the University of Damascus and the Ministry of Agriculture and Agrarian Reform, undertook a coastal resources survey in 1989 and proposed a coastal resources management plan and survey for 1991 (Jeudy de Grissac, *in litt.*, 1991). One site was recommended for protection. This site, Om'Attouyour near Lattakia, has also been proposed as a national park (Al Nimeh, *in litt.*, 1991). Botanical surveys of Syria and Lebanon have carried out by a number of organisations including the CNRS of France (see Davis *et al.*, 1986). For project AQUA, part of the International Biological Programme, the Ministry of Agriculture and Agrarian Reform undertook surveys of the wetlands of the country (Carp, 1980; Luther and Rzoska, 1971). In 1972 IWRB undertook an ornithological mission and identified two areas of importance (Koning and Dijksen, 1973). At present, a steering committee is studying the possibilities of designating protected areas specifically for wildlife (RACSPA, 1987/1988; Al Nimeh, *in litt.*, 1991; Director-General of ACSAD, *in litt.*, 1986; Jeudy de Grissac, *in litt.*, 1991).

Currently protected areas consist of state forest protection zones, green belts, enclosed rangeland and protected public waters. The first protected rangeland reserves (enclosed pasture areas) were established in 1968 to enrich the natural environment and prevent degradation. They total 22,000ha and in part were set up as green belts to ameliorate and develop vegetation cover in arid and desert conditions. Two were established in 1983 as animal sanctuaries or protection zones. There have been proposals to designate them as the first nature reserves, with nature conservation as the main management objective. Choula Protected Rangeland (governorate Dir Ezzour) covers 22,000ha, the other reserve is located on the border of the Oued Ghrib (Maaher Abou Jaafar, 1984; Science and Technology Division, 1981). Four wetland sites had been nominated by the Ministry of Agriculture and Agrarian Reform for Project AQUA (Carp, 1980; Luther and Rzoska, 1971).

The natural environment is under increasing threat from agriculture and technological developments. Deforestation has been the most striking form of vegetation loss. Although extensive forests once covered western Syria (as noted in the Bible and in ancient texts), only a few areas of high forest remain. A concomitant problem is that of desertification, the result of continuous cultivation and overgrazing (Science and Technology Division, 1981). Other constraints continue to include uncontrolled and excessive livestock grazing and illicit tree felling. A major dam on the Euphrates was constructed in 1968 to increase the irrigated area of the valley, but has had massive consequences for the environment as a whole. The resultant reservoir, Lake Bahret Assad, has flooded over 63,00ha of land and through the increased use of irrigation water, Syria is now bringing more of the arid eastern region under cultivation, leading to a dramatic decline in the area of natural steppe (Carp, 1980; Science and Technology Division, 1981). Oil pollution has become a major threat to the environment, following the discovery of oil at Karachuk, Suweida and Rumailan in the north-east of the country. Pipelines cross Syria to the Mediterranean coast at Homs, Baniyas and Tartus, where major pollution problems are attributable to a lack of sewage disposal systems and to industrial waste from petroleum processing and fertiliser production (Sardar, 1982; Science and Technology Division, 1981).

Other Relevant Information The Golan Heights of southern Syria continue to be occupied as part of the Israeli Military Administration Zone (1991).

Addresses

Directorate of Forests and Afforestation, Ministry of Agriculture and Agrarian Reform, Al-Jabri Street, DAMASCUS (Tel: 11 213613/6)

Ministry of State for Environmental Affairs, P O Box 3754, DAMASCUS (Tel: 11 226600; Tlx: 411930)

Faculty of Sciences, University of Damascus, DAMASCUS (Tel: 422103; Tlx: NR HAMAK 411971)

Faculty of Agriculture and Forestry, University of Aleppo, ALEPPO (Tel: 236130; Tlx: 331018)

Arab Center for Studies of Arid Zones and Dry Lands (ACSAD), PO Box 2440, DAMASCUS (Tel: 755713/755113; Tlx: 412697)

References

Anon. (1991). Mediterranean Environmental Technical Assistance Program, activity report Spring, 1991. World Bank/European Investment Bank/United Nations Development Programme/Commission of the European Communities. 24 pp.

Baccar, H. (1977). A survey of existing and potential marine parks and reserves in the Mediterranean. 25 pp.

Carp, E. (1980). *Directory of western Palaearctic wetlands*. UNEP and IUCN, Gland, Switzerland. 506 pp.

Glineur, N. (n.d). Environmental program for the Mediterranean: Conservation of biodiversity in the Mediterranean: Protection of coastal ecosystems. Working Paper No. 7. The World Bank and European Investment Bank. 35 pp.

Grimmett, R. (1987). *A review of the problems affecting Palearctic migratory birds in Africa*. ICBP, Cambridge, UK.

Gryn-Ambroes, P. (1980). Preliminary annotated lists of existing and potential Mediterranean protected areas. UNEP/IUCN report.

Khatib, A. (1991). Organisational report of the National MAB Committee for Syria. Presented at the Third

Man and Biosphere Meeting on Biosphere Reserves in the Mediterranean and the First IUCN-CNPPA Workshop on Protected Areas in the North Africa-Middle East Region, 14-19 October 1991, Tunis. 11 pp.

Koning, F.J. and Dijksen, L.J. (1977) IWRB Mission to Iraq and Syria, December 1972. *IWRB Bulletin* 35: 57-62

Luther, H. and Rzoska, J. (1971). *Project Aqua: a source book of inland waters proposed for conservation.* IBP Handbook No 21. IUCN Occasional Paper No 2. International Biological Programme, London.

Maaher Abou Jaafar (1984). *National parks and natural reserves in the Arab world.* Arab League of Education, Culture and Science Organisation (ALESCO). Report No. 80/001/1984/science division. Tunis. 112 pp.

Montague, K. and Bruun, B. (1987). *Biological diversity in North Africa, the Middle East and Southwest Asia: a directory of organizations and institutions.* HLCF, New York.

RAC/SPA (1987). Directory of marine and coastal protected areas of the Mediterranean Region. Regional Activity Center for Specially Protected Areas, Tunisia and International Union for Conservation of Nature and Natural Resources. 196 pp.

Sardar, Z. (1982). *Science and Technology in the Middle East.* Longman, London and New York.

Science and Technology Division (1981). Environmental Profile on Syria. Science and Technology Division, Library of Congress and US Man and the Biosphere Secretariat, Department of State, Washington, DC. Contract No. AID/S&T/ FNR SA/TOA 1-77. Draft.

ANNEX
Definitions of protected area designations, as legislated, together with authorities responsible for their administration

Title: Forest Code Legislative Decree No. 66

Date: 22 September 1953

Brief description: Supersedes all previous enabling forestry legislation. It concerns protected forest areas and green belt land. Protected rangeland is covered under related legislation.

Administrative authority: Directorate of Forests and Afforestation of the Ministry of Agriculture and Agrarian Reform

Designations:

State forest protection zone   Defines the restrictions on usage rights, management, and establishment legislation.

Acts within this law include:

- Title I (details about forests and forest products);
- Title II (definition and establishment of state forests);
- Title IV (details relating to creation of protected zones);
- Title V (particulars concerning delimitation and demarcation of private forests);
- Title VI (details concerning protection of forests)
- Title VII (precise details regarding infringement penalties).

Forest police and forest wardens are empowered by law to patrol the forest area.

Sources: Glineur, n.d; Science and Technology Division, 1981

Title: Law on Hunting, Legislative Decree No. 152

Date: 23 July 1970

Brief description: Relates to hunting and identifies regulations and areas for restricted hunting

Administrative authority: Hunting Council and Ministry of Agriculture and Agrarian Reform

Designations:

Contains various sections including:

- Chapter I – hunting and methods of hunting;
- Chapter II – hunting season;
- Chapter IV – hunting permits;
- Chapter IV – the hunting Council (Conseil Cynégétique).

In Legislative Decree No. 50 of 5 April 1979, all hunting has been banned for a five-year period as a measure to preserve wildlife (penalties include fines and imprisonment terms of up to two years).

Source: Science and Technology Division, 1981

Title: Law on the Protection of Aquatic Life Legislative Decree No. 30

Date: 25 August 1964

Brief description: Relates to marine and coastal forms of protection

Administrative authority: Fisheries Office, Ministry of Agriculture and Agrarian Reform

Designations:

Protected public water Chapter 6 (Articles 32 and 33) cover the protection of public waters (including inland waters, estuaries, marshland, lakes, rivers and the marine environment) and the regulation of fishing in seawater extending 12 miles from the coast.

Source: Science and Technology Division, 1981

Title: Law on Livestock Grazing and Rangeland

Date: No information

Brief description: Covering livestock ranging throughout the country and of rangeland reserves

Administrative authority: Directorate of Rangeland and Countryside, Ministry of Agriculture and Agrarian Reform

Designations:

Enclosed rangeland reserve To enrich the natural environment and prevent degradation, they are set up as green belts in part to ameliorate and develop vegetation cover in arid and desert conditions.

At least in the early 1980s, there was a strong desire by the Ministry of Agriculture and Agrarian Reform to reintroduce wildlife into these steppe regions.

Sources: Child, 1978; Maaher Abou Jaafar, 1984; Science and Technology Division, 1981

TERRITORIES OF THE WEST BANK AND GAZA STRIP ("OCCUPIED TERRITORIES OF THE WEST BANK AND GAZA STRIP")

Area West Bank 9,800 sq. km; Gaza Strip 361 sq. km

Population 1,484,000 (1988) (Hunter, 1991)
895,000 West Bank (1988) (Hunter, 1991)
589,000 Gaza Strip (1988) (Hunter, 1991)

Economic Indicators
No information

Policy and Legislation In November 1947 the United Nations called for the establishment of both a Jewish and an Arab state (Resolution 242) in the former British mandate state of Palestine (Hunter, 1991). The Jewish community proclaimed the state of Israel on 14 May 1948, but an Arab state was not established. Subsequently in 1967, the Palestinian areas, the West Bank and Gaza Strip, which had been under Jordanian and Egyptian administration respectively since 1950, became occupied by Israeli military forces.

Up to July 1988, Jordan continued to maintain West Bank civil administration and civil service, as well as West Bank members in the Lower House of its parliament (Anon., 1988e). However, on 31 July 1988 Jordan renounced its claim to the West Bank and dissolved the West Bank membership to its parliament (Anon., 1988d). On 15 November 1988 the Palestine leader of the Palestine Liberation Organisation (PLO), proclaimed the independent state of Palestine; the Palestinian National Council (PNC) in Algiers (Algeria) accepting the UN Security Council Resolutions 242 and 338, acknowledging the rights of existence and of security for all states of the region (Anon., 1988b). In 1991 the territories continue to be occupied by Israel.

At present the protected areas system in the West Bank and Gaza Strip is regarded by the Israeli government as being fully integrated into its protected areas network. However, it is thought that this may contribute to the contravention of the right to the existence of an Arab state under UN Resolutions. The Israeli protected area authorities have administered the nature reserves in the territories since 1979. They claim to act on the jurisdiction vested in them through the nature conservation laws enacted by the Israeli government (see Israel Policy and Legislation): the National Parks and Nature Reserves Law of 1963 (No. 5723-1963) which empowers the National Parks Authority (NPA) and Nature Reserves Authority (NRA) to administer and protect two categories of protected area: national parks and nature reserves; it empowers the Ministry of the Interior to declare protected natural areas; and to empower the Ministry of Agriculture to promulgate regulations defining fauna to be given special protection by law (Gour-Tanguay, 1977). The Forest Department claims no responsibility for administering any forest reserves in the Gaza Strip (Bonneh, *in litt.*, 1990). The Palestine Forest Ordinance of 1926 is still in force throughout the territories and has jurisdiction over forest reserves (Weitz, 1974) (see Annex).

Reviews of protected areas policy and legislation have not been not identified in this report.

International Activities The UNEP Regional Convention for the Conservation of the Red Sea and Gulf of Aden and the Protocol concerning Regional Co-operation in combatting pollution by oil and other harmful substances in cases of emergency, has been signed for Palestine by the Palestine Liberation Organization on 14 February 1982.

A bi-lateral park, Jordan Valley Park, has been recommended in Zor between Jordan and the occupied territories (Dov Por and Ortal, 1985).

Administration and Management The Occupied Territories Affairs Ministry of Israel claims responsibility for the territories. However, up to July 1988, Jordan continued to maintain West Bank administration and civil service (Anon., 1988e). Jordan did not begin to establish nature reserves until 1975 and was not instrumental in setting up protected areas in the occupied territories (Science and Technology Division, 1979).

The NRA of Israel (part of the Israeli Ministry of Agriculture) has been vested by Israeli law with responsibility for all topics concerning the preservation of nature in Israel and the occupied territories. Its tasks include: a) setting up and administering reserves; b) protecting designated plants, animals and geological features; and c) maintaining responsibility for hunting licences and supervision (Gour-Tanguay, 1977). The NRA is based on a regional system, with defined districts each of which has a ranger; the rangers responsibilities include the development of reserves and the control of poaching and plant collecting in the district. At the local level, each reserve has a small team responsible for estate management and wardening tasks including site protection and biological survey work (Phillips, *in litt.*, 1986).

Systems Reviews The Gaza Strip lies along the Mediterranean coastline; the West Bank is situated in the Jordan valley on the west bank of the River Jordan next to Jordan. The region has predominantly a Mediterranean climate. The hilly West Bank terrain in the upper Jordan valley consists of hammada (stony) desert supporting sparse thorn scrub. Millenia of human occupation in the entire region has resulted in drastic change to the environment and vegetation cover, leading to replacement of natural species by secondary vegetation. Farmland covers 193 sq. km of the 361 sq. km of the Gaza Strip (Hunter, 1991).

Two identified categories of protected area occur: nature reserve and forest reserve. Forest reserves were set up under the British Mandate prior to 1948. The first nature reserves were established from 1979 onwards and by the mid 1980s there were 13 declared reserves, two forest reserves and 36 proposed protected sites in the West Bank, and one non-forested reserve in the Gaza Strip. The single site in the Gaza Strip had a total area of 1200ha (Survey of Israel, 1985; Bonneh, *in litt.*, 1990). The forest reserves included Reihan Forest (Umm-Ri'han) west of the village of Ya'bad (West Bank) and the non-forested reserve near Beit Lahiya village in the Gaza Strip (Bonneh, *in litt.*, 1990).

Potential environmental problems originally included the 1980s development of the West Bank with limited environmental impact assessment. However, these plans were cancelled in July 1988 (Anon., 1988d). In 1988 unrest by the population of the Gaza strip apparently led to the setting fire to plantations and protected woodland (forest reserves) as a form of protest.

Addresses

Nature Reserves Authority of Israel, 78 Yirmiyahu Street, JERUSALEM 94467 (Tel: 2 387471; FAX: 2 383405)

Forest Department, Land Development Authority of Israel (Keren Kayemeth Leisrael), PO Box 45, 26013 Kiryat-Hayim, 32000 HAIFA (Tel: 4 411983/ 414463; FAX: 4 411971; Tlx: 26112 KLL)

Society for the Protection of Nature in Israel (SPNI), 4 Hashfela Street, 66183 TEL AVIV (Tel: 3 375063; FAX: 3 377695; Tlx: 371478)

References

Anon. (1988). The year of living dangerously. *The Economist.* 10 December P. 84.

Anon. (1988b). EC Declaration on Palestine. European Community. *Newsletter of the Delegation of the Commission of the European Communities in Kenya* 11: 3.

Anon. (1988c). Palestine, the birth of a phantom state. *The Economist.* 19 November. P. 95.

Anon. (1988d). A king bows out, maybe. *The Economist.* 6 August. Pp. 49-50.

Anon. (1988e). Two half-Palestines that don't fit. *The Economist.* 12 November. Pp. 93-94.

Anon. (1990). National report on forestry in Israel. Report for the Tenth World Forestry Congress by the Land Development Authority, Kiryat-Hayim. 19 pp.

Davis, S.D., Droop, S.J.M., Gregerson, P., Henson, L., Leon, C.J., Lamlein Villa-Lobos, J., Synge, H. and Zantovska, J. (1986). *Plants in danger: what do we know?* IUCN, Gland, Switzerland and Cambridge, UK. 461 pp.

Gour-Tanguay, R. (Ed.) (1977). Israel. *Environmental policies in developing countries.* Erich Schmidt Verlag.

Hunter, B. (Ed.) (1991). *The Statesman's Year Book 1991-92.* The Macmillan Press Ltd, London and Basingstoke, UK. 1692 pp.

Montague, K. and Bruun, B. (1987). *Biological diversity in North Africa, the Middle East and Southwest Asia. A directory of organisations and institutions.* Holy land Conservation Fund, New York.

Nature Reserves Authority (1977). *Nature reserves in Israel.* Nature Reserves Authority, Tel-Aviv.

Nature Reserves Authority (1983). *Nature Reserves in Israel; their legal status.* Nature Reserves Authority of Israel.

Palumbo, M. (1987). *The Palestinian Catastrophe.* Faber and Faber, London.

Por, F.D. and Ortal, R. (1985). River Jordan – The survival and future of a very special river. *Environmental Conservation* 12(3): 264-268.

Science and Technology Division (1979). Draft Environmental Report on Jordan. Science and Technology Division, Library of Congress, Washington, D.C. Contract AID/DS/ST contract No. SA/TOA 1-77. US Man and Biosphere Secretariat.

Sherman, S. (1988). Gaza, a history of conflict. *Geographical magazine.* December. Pp. 18-23.

The Survey of Israel (1985). *Nature reserves.* Map to the scale 1:400,000. Survey of Israel.

ANNEX
Definitions of protected area designations, as legislated, together with authorities responsible for their administration

Title: National Parks and Nature Reserves Law No. 5723

Date: 1963

Brief description: An Israeli law providing for the creation of a protected areas system. It empowers the Israeli Ministry of the Interior to declare sites, and the Israeli Ministry of Agriculture to create regulations concerning protected fauna.

Administrative authority: Nature Reserves Authority

Designations:

Nature reserve (subdivisions include):

Scientific reserve class Sites set up to safeguard and protect threatened plants and animals. They can be used for scientific research but tend to be closed to the general public, any management is limited to ensure conservation protection.

Managed nature reserve Semi-natural or natural sites which are partly open to public access, undergo some form of management and may include a large element of education to acquaint the public with landscapes and the natural environment.

Sources: Gour-Tanguay, 1977; NRA, 1977

Title: Palestine Forest Ordinance; Israel Forest Edict; Forest Regulations

Date: Ordinance of 1926; edict of 1956; regulations of 1960

Brief description: The enactment of the present Forest Ordinance dates from British Mandate legislation, and empowers the Israeli Ministry of Agriculture to declare certain areas as forest reserves, to control these areas and to declare certain types of tree in any part of the country as "protected trees".

Administrative authority: Israeli Minister of Agriculture

Designations:

Forest reserve Major functions of environmental, soil and dune stabilization, wind brake, landscape improvement, pollution amelioration, social, recreation and tourism, grazing and nature conservation.

Extensive felling is forbidden without express permission.

Permitted activities include pruning or coppicing for charcoal and limited opening of dense oak maquis to prevent damage by wildfire.

Sources: Anon., 1990

TUNISIA

Area 164,150 sq. km

Population 8,180,000 (1990)
Natural increase: 2.08% per annum

Economic Indicators
GDP: US$ 1,301 per capita (1987)
GNP: US$ 1,210 per capita (1987)

Policy and Legislation Tunisia was a French protectorate from 1883 and achieved independence on 20 March 1956, and the monarchy of the Bey of Tunis was abolished on 25 July 1957. The Constitution was promulgated on 1 June 1959.

A detailed understanding of the environment was well known 2,000 years ago at the height of the Carthaginian and Roman periods (the ancient city of Carthage was situated near modern day Tunis) (Fradier, 1989). Some of the first scientific expeditions were undertaken by the Carthaginian Hanno over 2,500 BP, and Herodotus described the ecology of the region sometime between 484-425 BC. At the time of Caius Plinius Secondus (Pliny the Elder) in the first century AD, throughout the Roman Empire there were forest administration structures, delimited forests, wardening systems and programmes of tree planting, along with areas set aside for wildlife (Drucker, *in litt.*, 1985; Mallatt, *in litt.*, 1991). Some of the earliest recorded forms of nature conservation protection were in 1240 under the reign of Abdallah Abou Zakaria, Hafside dynasty, who maintained hunting reserves at Ichkeul, management which continued through the Ottoman empire period into the 20th century (Anon., 1988a). During the Ottoman period until the end of the last century, limited environmental legislation was covered under the Ottoman civil code (Mejellah), within the body of Islamic law. Under Article 1243 it was defined that land and the associated trees growing wild in mountains were not allowed to be possessed and should remain ownerless.

The first of the more recent conservation legislation in Tunisia came into existence on 12 December 1884. The object of this Ordinance was to regulate hunting throughout the country (Kacem, 1985). Subsequently, the Forestry Service of the French administration set up a network of legal provisions for the protection of the environment, such as those for the "Defence des végétaux" on 11 July 1932 and Ordinance on national parks of 17 March 1936. In 1936 Ahmed Pacha Bey decreed that Bou Hedma be declared a state park of 5,000ha in order to protect its unique forest ecosystem (Anon., 1988b). This series of acts has been largely repealed after independence, and either reenacted or superseded in subsequent presidential and Ministry of Agriculture legislation.

The current legal provision for protected areas is based on the new Forestry Code (Code Forestier) Law No. 88-20 of 13 April 1988 (superseding Law No. 66-60 of 4 July 1966 and revisions of 9 August 1974). Title II of Law No. 88-20 concerns Hunting and the Conservation of Game Species and Title III concerns Protection of Nature, of Flora and Fauna. Chapter III of Title III is concerned with enabling legislation for national parks, natural reserves and recreation forests. Chapter IV concerns the protection of wetland zones and Chapter V defines the activities of the National Council of Nature Protection (Bel Hadj Kacem, 1991) (see Annex).

The complete list of existing protected areas designations covered under this law include: national park (parc national), recreational forest and a series of reserves set up to protect wildlife as natural or nature reserve (réserve naturelle) or wild fauna reserve (réserve de faune sauvage). In the past the reserves were subdivided into integral natural or nature reserve (réserve naturelle intégrale); integral marine reserve (réserve marine intégrale), permanent hunting reserve (réserve de chasse permanence); gazelle reserve (réserve à gazelle); deer enclosure (enclos à cerf) and breeding enclosure (enclos à reproduction). The reserve category currently includes the category integral marine reserve (réserve marine intégrale), two sites of which were established under the Ministry of Agriculture Order of 9 November 1973. Protection of these sites is devolved to military personnel, and hunting, fishing and all forms of development are banned.

Protection of wetland zones of national importance (Protection des zones humides d'importance nationale) is covered under Chapter IV (Title III) of the Law (see Annex). The Convention on Wetlands of International Importance Especially as Waterfowl Habitat (Ramsar Convention) was been signed following authorisation under National Law No. 80-9 of 3 March 1980.

National parks are declared by presidential decree after recommendations submitted by the Ministry of Agriculture. The first national parks were designated after the 1977 and 1980 presidential decrees. The enabling legislation and general management policies of national parks are published in the Official Journal *JORT* No. 44 on 24 and 27 July 1984. The legislation states that the Direction des Forêts is empowered to monitor or stop grazing within protected areas, and Articles 58-60 "textes législatives forestières" stipulate a series of regulations by order of the Council established by the Ministry of Agriculture.

In the past reserves were generally covered under Law No. 66-60 and the annual renewed decree of the Ministre de l'Agriculture "Rélatif à l'organisation de la chasse", and their protection mentioned site by site in Article 11. Temporary hunting reserve (réserve de chasse) required annual renewal of legislation or otherwise their protected status lapsed. Each reserve could be declared or altered by the Ministry with district/regional approval (University of Arizona, 1980).

Forest reserves and recreational forests were originally established under the Forest Ordinance No. 66-60 and subsequently under Forestry Code No. 88-20 of 1988 under Titre III, Chapitre III (for hunting regulations see also Bel Hadj Kacem, 1991; Direction Générale des Forêts, 1990).

By Decree No. 85-57 of 12 January 1985 an annual prize was instituted for the promotion of Nature Protection and the Environment (Grand Prix du Président de la République pour la Protection de la Nature et de l'Environnement).

With the near completion of the seventh (VII) national development plan (1987-1991), which envisaged investment of TD 8,000 million, on 9 August 1991 there was a Ministerial Council meeting with the President of the Republic to review the incorporation of environmental protection policies into the preparatory phases of the eighth development plan due to commence in 1992. This was based on directives following the preparation of a report on the ecological situation (Anon., 1991).

There appears to have been no major review of the protected areas policy and legislation following the Law of 1988, although deficiencies in prevailing provisions have been highlighted by the authorities. Prior to that date the apparent greatest deficiency had been the inadequate system of annually renewing legislation as a method for protecting reserves. Their legislation provided no control on land use and were widely regarded as largely ineffective as a conservation measure due to financial, administrative, demographic and sociological problems (Posner, 1988; IWRB, *in litt.*, 1990). Some authors had even gone as far as stating that legislation for the nature reserve system was effectively non-existent prior to the 1988 law (FAO, 1985; Smart, *in litt.*, 1987).

International Activities Tunisia ratified the Convention Concerning the Protection of the World Cultural and Natural Heritage (World Heritage Convention) on 10 March 1975 with one site inscribed and acceded to the Convention on Wetlands of International Importance Especially as Waterfowl Habitat (Ramsar Convention) on 24 November 1980 with one site inscribed on accession. The African Convention for the Conservation of Nature and Natural Resources was ratified under Law No. 76-91 on 4 November 1976. Four biosphere reserves were accepted in 1977 under the Unesco Man and Biosphere Programme. Tunisia is party to the Barcelona Convention, and the Protocol Concerning Mediterranean Specially Protected Areas and three specially protected areas have been listed. Tunisia is also party to the Washington Convention and the Bonn Convention.

In the Tunis Declaration on the Environment on 19-23 April 1991 (Conference of the Ministers of the Environment having in common the use of the French language) countries decided to work towards implementing the proposal of devoting at least 5% of their territories to safeguarding their natural heritage, putting the emphasis on the conservation of ecosystems and the diversity of species, within the context of sustainable development (ACCT, 1991).

Transboundary cooperative agreements are in the proposed form covering El Kala National Park/Annaba (Algeria) and a proposed park near Tabarka (Tunisia). Discussions have been under way between the two countries since the late 1980s to organise joint management and administrative programmes for the site (Djellouli, pers. comm., 1991; El Hili, *in litt.*, 1991).

Administration and Management Protected areas are under the technical and administrative responsibility of the Ministry of Agriculture, which was first formed at the end of the 19th century, and are managed on a day-to-day basis through the Sub Directorate of Hunting and National Parks (Sous Direction de la Chasse et Parcs Nationaux, CPN) under the Director of Conservation (Directeur de la Conservation) in the Directorate General of Forests (Direction Générale des Forêts).

In 1986/87 the Ministry of Agriculture was subdivided into two new bodies, one covering agricultural production and the other covering advisory and ancillary services including the environment. The principal departments of the Ministry of Agriculture deal with conservation matters, forests and the environment and remain largely unaffected by this recent division, although the Environment section had been promoted from sub-directorate to directorate level (Smart, 1987). The Sub-Directorate of Environment and Agriculture (Sous-Direction de l'Environnement et Agricole) was given charge of general coordination, whilst the Sub-Directorate of CPN of the Directorate of Forests undertook administration and routine management (1989), followed by the recently established National Agency for Protection of the Environment (Agence Nationale de Protection de l'Environnement) (ANPE) within the Prime Ministry (Premier Ministère). The Law establishing the ANPE stated that the Agency should represent Tunisia at the international level on environmental matters, as well as coordinate overall activities within the country. Since its establishment a new Secrétariat d'Etat auprès du Premier Ministre chargé de la Recherche Scientifique has been created and ANPE has become responsible to this Secretariat. In 1990 ANPE was receiving tenders for management work in Ichkeul national park. The amount available from government for management work at Ichkeul National Park will not exceed TD 500,000. In addition, DM 20 million are to be made available for park management *via* the KfW Bank, Frankfurt.

The infrastructure under the Director of Conservation in the Sub-Directorate of Hunting and National Parks (CPN) includes a scientific and administrative team in Tunis and a network of park directors (conservateurs) and support staff, technicians, vehicles and accommodation in the parks themselves. Park directors have authority for the day-to-day running of the areas under their administration. In major reserves such as Kechem el-Kelb wardens undertake general forestry duties, as well as being responsible for their protected area. Management plans have been prepared for a number of national parks and proposed areas (El Aloui, Sakouhi, Taieb and Zoghlami Dkhil, pers. comm., 1991).

The management of marine areas is under the jurisdiction of the General Commission of Fishing (Commissariat Général à la Pêche) and the Ministry of Defence (Ministère de la Défense). The Police de la Pêche Maritime patrol the Galite-Galiton area and Zembra Park; such policing has effectively limited all non-military activities in the area (RAC/SPA, 1987).

To redress the balance from past destruction of larger animal populations, a reintroduction programme for globally endangered species has been started by the Direction des Forêts (species include scimitar-horned oryx, ostrich, addax, Barbary sheep and Barbary stag). Technical assistance comes from the WWF and various European zoological establishments, such as Marwell Zoo in the United Kingdom. Other projects with international cooperation include the development of national park eco-museums and information centres (WWF/British Museum). Also, various IUCN/WWF projects have been undertaken in association with the International Wildfowl Research Bureau to study coastal wetlands and wintering waterfowl (IUCN/WWF Project No. 1258 "Conservation des zones d'importance internationale en Tunisie"). University College London has been carrying out a long-term programme of research and monitoring at Lake Ichkeul with the financial support of the EC.

An ensemble of non-governmental organisations contributes greatly to research and the conservation of fauna and flora. One of the most important is the Tunisian Association for the Protection of nature and Environment (Association Tunisienne pour la Protection de la Nature et de l'Environnement) (ATPNE) which is actively involved in surveying different environments and their ecology, disseminating information, publishing material and acting as an environmental advisory group (Abroughi, *in litt.*, 1991). Other conservation-oriented institutes include the Association des Amis des Oiseaux, Association Nationale des Fauconniers Tunisiens, Fédération Nationale des Associations de Chasseurs, Conseil Supérieur de la Chasse, Institut de Recherches Scientifiques et Techniques (University of Tunis) and the Institut National de Recherches Forestières (FAO, 1985).

Hunting associations have long been involved in protected area management largely under the auspices of the Federation of Regional Hunting Associations (Fédération des Associations Régionales de Chasse). Close collaborative work with University College London, WWF, the British Museum, the German GTZ, UNEP Regional Seas Programme SPA/RAC, the French Ministry of the Environment (SRETIE), CNRS, SOGREAH and the European Community has resulted in a whole series of programmes involving national park management plan development, site protection and interpretation. The World Bank has also been involved through environmentally-related loans (Posner, 1988).

A private reserve, Rocher à Mérou, has been established off the coast of western Tunisia by the Yachting Club of Tabarka, a site protected by voluntary fishing bans in order to promote international diving tourism in the area by ensuring that there is abundant marine wildlife to be seen. Management includes controlling entry into the area, and permitting foreign divers to see the fish and feed them. Fishing is totally prohibited in the area which is approximately 1km long and closely regulated by the Tabarka community which works in close association with the Tunisian Diving Club (Fédération des activités subaquatiques de Tunisie) (FAST) through its Responsable de la Commission biologie et environnement sous-marin (Djellouli, pers. comm., 1991).

Administrative and management constraints on effective conservation programmes at least in the past have included an almost complete lack of communication and cooperation between ministries and even sub-directional offices. In both the Environment Directorate and the Sub-Directorate of CPN of the Directorate of Forests there were reports of limited finance and only a minimal number of staff with wildlife conservation experience and duties. The authorities have long been reported to pay little heed to the concerns of non-governmental groups (RAC/SPA, 1987; Abroughi, pers. comm., 1991). Lack of funding and the lack of liaison between the forestry park service and ministry departments are resulting in potential loss of even existing protected areas. At least one national park (Ichkeul) is threatened by dams being built on the feeding rivers of the lake. Other sites under threat include the Lac de Tunis, a former reserve which has been partly filled in for building development, and Bou Kournine under threat from mineral extraction (FAO, 1985; Posner, 1988; Kacem, pers. comm., 1987).

Systems Reviews Tunisia is bounded in the north and east by the Mediterranean Sea, in the south-east by Libya and in the south and west by Algeria, and has a coastline of over 1,200km. Even though the country has been exploited by man since well before the arrival of the Phoenicians and Carthaginians, the wildlife has remained very diverse. Seven major ecosystems are represented: wetland, coastal, marine island, mountain (five main chains), steppe (Kasserine high steppe), desert (Eastern grand erg) and oasis. The northern part of the country is represented by a Mediterranean type flora and fauna. Many areas are still wooded except in the east where intensive cultivation occurs. Forested land is reported to cover 3.2% of the total land surface. Atlas steppe habitat is found along plains, hills and mountain chains in the centre of the country, whilst the south and extreme east is dominated by the Sahara desert. Mediterranean sclerophyllous forest (mixed oak) survives along the north-west coast and adjacent mountainous regions and contains many rare species. These mixed oak forests are important for the cork industry. Evergreen conifers are exploited further south in the region around Kasserine. The Sahara desert or Eastern grand erg covers 2.5 million ha together with 1.5 million ha of desertic steppe. Oases represent 75,000ha, dispersed in the steppe and desert of the south of the country. Wetlands are represented by more than 100 major sites ranging from salt lakes, sebkhets and chotts to freshwater wetlands and isolated peat bogs (for full details see Nabli, 1989).

There are 2,200 species of plant, 75 species of mammal and well over 400 species of bird. Five recognised globally threatened mammal species and 12 globally threatened bird species are recorded (see report summary by the University of Arizona, 1980; Posner, 1988).

Systems reviews and comprehensive surveys of biological resources have been undertaken on a wide range of biotopes and species, including ecological surveys of standing waters (Morgan, 1982) and numerous works on vegetation ecosystems (see synthesis in Nabli, 1989), numerous ornithological surveys throughout the whole country by national and international bodies such as the IWRB, and botanical and geological surveys (for further details see University of Arizona, 1980). A summary of available material on biological diversity was prepared by the US Agency for International Development, Washington DC and Tunis in 1988 (Posner, 1988).

Some of the foremost nature conservation areas are the network of wetlands, wintering havens for significant numbers of Palaearctic birds. There are also unprotected marine and coastal sites such as the unique marine ecosystems of the Gulf of Gabes. A series of proposed or recommended sites has been submitted to the authorities in an attempt to arrest significant habitat loss, if only to protect a few of the most representative of these ecosystems. It has been pointed out that even Saharan habitats are threatened if fairly drastic conservation action were not to be taken (Drucker, 1987). Chief amongst the conservation needs is to draw up and establish an integrated system of protected areas. A series of proposed natural parks (parcs naturels) and biospheres reserves was proposed by the Tunisian National MAB Committee in the Action Plan for Biosphere Reserves Workshop of Florac, France, 9-12 September 1986 (El Hamrouni, 1986) and the recommendations of the combined meeting of the Third Man and Biosphere Workshop on Biosphere Reserves in the Mediterranean and the First IUCN-CNPPA Workshop on Protected Areas in the North Africa-Middle East Region, 14-19 October 1991, held in Tunis.

A goal of the protected areas programme has been to designate major protected areas representing each of the major ecosystems of the country. Policy of the forestry division is to designate 20% of all forest as regeneration forest, thus prohibiting grazing and harvesting of forest products. In addition, Law No. 66-256 of 23 December 1986 requires that at least 2% of the area of each property be reforested.

In 1988 the protected areas network included five national parks, two proposed national parks and nine reserves. By 1991 the network had increased to six national parks (70,778ha), six natural or faunal reserves (1537ha), one marine biological zone (3639ha), one integral marine reserve (450ha) and 12 protection of wetland zones of national importance (130,800ha). In 1988 there were recommendations for the establishment of 19 additional protected areas, in 1991 three reserves and two national parks, totalling over 156,315ha, were in the process of being designated (Bel Hadj Kacem, 1991). In addition, a number of recreational forest reserves and mountain areas are protected from hunting, and special zones exist where grazing is prohibited or severely restricted. At least one community protected area, a marine site 1km in length, is known (Djellouli, pers. comm., 1991).

The greatest habitat losses in recent years have been through draining of internationally important wetlands and also through conversion of grazing land, especially Atlas steppe, to arable land. An estimated 18,000ha of potentially productive land is lost to desertification every year and Tunisia has lost one-third of its forest cover in the last 60 years (University of Arizona, 1980). Some of the most internationally important habitats have at least until recently been found to be completely unprotected by legislation. National parks are disturbed by intensive settlement or by continued heavy grazing pressure and wood collecting rights of the local population (even if these activities are actually forbidden by law). To remedy this habitat degradation, the Forestry Department is currently studying the problems and has kept a number of national parks closed to visitors until management plans were in force (FAO, 1985; Kacem, pers. comm., 1987).

Other Relevant Information   Tourism plays an important part in the national economy, representing TD 68.7 million in 1977 rising to TD 855 million by 1989 with 3.2 million tourists (Hunter, 1991; University of Arizona, 1980). The intention of the Ministry of Agriculture has long been to expand interest in ecotourism in its national parks. Three ecomuseums have been constructed, and the first in Ichkeul was opened in February 1989. Visitors to Ichkeul National Park number 20,000 annually and an average of 4,000 tourists visit the other parks each year (Bel Hadj Kacem, 1991).

Addresses

Agence Nationale de Protection de l'Environnement, Premier Ministère, 15 Rue 800, Montplaisir, 1002 TUNIS-BELVÉDERE (Tel: 785 618/782 281; FAX: 789 844)

Directeur de la Conservation, Direction Générale des forêts, Ministry de l'Agriculture, 30 rue Alain Savary, 1002 TUNIS (Tel: 1 282681/891926; Tlx: 13378 minagr tn)

Direction de l'environnement agricole, Ministère de l'Agriculture, 30 rue Alain Savary, TUNIS

Association Tunisienne pour la Protection de la Nature et de l'Environnement, Direction de l'Environnement et du Milieu, 12 Rue Tantaoui el Jawhari, 1005 TUNIS (Tel: 288141; FAX: 797295)

References

ACCT (1991). The Tunis Declaration on the Environment. Première Conférence des ministres chargés de l'environnement des pays ayant en commun l'usage du Français/First Conference of the Ministers of the Environment of Countries having in common the use of the French language. Agence de coopération culturelle et technique, Tunis, 19-23 April 1991. 2 pp.

Anon. (1988a). Le Parc National de l'Ichkeul. Parcs Nationaux de Tunisie. Sous Direction de la Chasse et des Parcs Nationaux, Direction Générale des Forets, Tunis.

Anon. (1988b). Le Bou Hedma. Parcs Nationaux de Tunisie. Sous Direction de la Chasse et des Parcs Nationaux, Direction Générale des Forets, Tunis.

Anon. (1991). Protection de l'Environnement: coordination et efficience sur le terrain écologique. *Le Temps.* 10 August 1991. P. 2

Bel Hadk Kacem, S. (1985). La conservation de la faune et de la flore sauvages en Tunisie. Séminaire sur la conservation du patrimoine forestier national, 30-31 octobre 1985 à l'INPPSA de Sidi-Thabet.

Bel Hadj Kacem, S. (1991). Liste des parcs nationaux et aires protégées Tunisie 1991. Direction Générale des Forêts, Ministère de l'Agriculture, Tunis. Paper presented to the Third Man and Biosphere Meeting on Biosphere Reserves in the Mediterranean, 14-19 October 1991, Tunis. 7 pp.

Carp, E. (1980). *A Directory of western Palaearctic wetlands.* IUCN, Gland, Switzerland. 506 pp.

Direction Générale des Forêts (c1990). *Guide du Chasseur.* Direction Générale des Forêts, Ministère de l'Agriculture, Tunis. 31 pp.

Drucker, G.R.F. (1987). Protected areas in Tunisia. Unpublished report. 30 pp.

El Hamrouni, A. (1986). Parcs naturels et réserves de la biosphère en Tunisie. Plan d'action pour les réserves de la biosphère dans la région Méditerranéenne. Atelier de Florac (MAB) 9-12 September 1986.

FAO (1985). Tunisie, projet de dévéloppement forestier, conservation du patrimoine naturel. FAO, Rome. 99/85 CP-TUN 48.

Fradier, G. (1989). Mosaïques romaines of Tunisie. Ceres Productions, Tunis. 188 pp.

Grimmett, R. (1987). *A review of the problems affecting Palaearctic migratory birds in Africa.* International Council for Bird Preservation, Cambridge, UK.

Gryn-Ambroes, P. (1980). *Preliminary annotated lists of existing and potential Mediterranean protected areas.* UNEP/IUCN report. UNEP/IG.20/INF5.

Johnson, A.R. and Hafner, H. (1972). *Dénombrement de sauvagine en automne sur des zones humides de Tunisie et d'Algérie.* Station Biologique de la Tour du Valat, Le Sambuc, France. Report. 15 pp.

Maaher Abou Jaafar (1984). *National parks and natural reserves in the Arab world.* Arab League of Education, Culture and Science Organisation (ALECSO). Report order number 80/001/1984/ science division. Tunis.

Morgan, N.C. (1982). An ecological survey of standing waters in North-east Africa: II Site descriptions for Tunisia and Algeria. *Biological Conservation* 24: 83-113.

Nabli, M.A. (Ed.)(1989). Essai de synthèse sur la végétation et la phyto-écologie tunisiennes. 1. Elements de Botanique et de Phyto-Ecologie. Faculté des Sciences de Tunis, Laboratoire de Botanique Fondamentale et Appliquée. *Programme Flore et Vegetation Tunisiennes.* Vol. 4A6. 247 pp.

Posner, S. (1988). Biological diversity and tropical forests in Tunisia. Report prepared for the Washington DC and Tunis offices of the US Agency for International Development. 206 pp.

RAC/SPA (1987). Proposed protected areas in the Mediterranean. Special Protected Areas Center, Salammbo, Tunis.

Riney, T. (1964). Potential of the wildlife resource on Tunisian forest lands. Report to the Government of Tunisia. FAO, Rome. 21 pp.

Riney, T. (1965). Les possibilités d'utilisation de la faune sauvage dans les zones forestières. Organisation des Nations Unies pour l'Alimentation et l'Agriculture, Rome, 1965. Report No. 1983.

Scott, D.A. (1980). A preliminary inventory of wetlands of international importance for waterfowl in Western Europe and North-west Africa. International Wildfowl Research Bureau, Slimbridge, UK. *Special Publication* No. 2. 127 pp.

Smart, M. (1974). *The wetlands of North Africa and their importance to waterfowl.* International Wildfowl Research Bureau, Slimbridge, UK.

Smart, M. (1975). Recensement des oiseaux d'eau en Tunisie. International Wildfowl Research Bureau, Slimbridge, UK.

University of Arizona (1980). Draft Environmental Profile on Tunisia. US MAB Secretariat. Prepared by the Arid Lands Information Center Office of Arid Lands Studies, Tucson, Arizona.

ANNEX
Definitions of protected area designations, as legislated, together with authorities responsible for their administration

Title: Code forestier (Forestry Code) Law No. 88-20, superseding Law No. 66-60 and Law No. 74-5

Date: 13 April 1988; superseding Law of 4 July 1966 (and revisions of 9 August 1974).

Brief description: The current legal provision for protected areas is based on the forestry code. Various categories of protected area are being designated under individual decree or by forestry regulations. Title II of the Forest Code is concerned with Hunting and the Conservation of Game and Title III is concerned with Protection of Nature, Flora and Wild Fauna. Chapter III of Title III comprises of matters on National Parks, Natural Reserves and Recreation Forests. Regulations are identified within the Law, sites are generally covered under Ministry of Agriculture orders. The policing and penalties for infringement of regulations are identified in Chapitre VI for Titre III and Chapitre VIII for Titre II. In addition Decree No. 1903 delimits state forests, Decree No. 1948 verifies forestry regulations. Law No. 59-96 of 1959 concerns regulations covering state forests, the forest administration and forest conservation. National parks are individually declared by decrees based on the forestry code.

Administrative authority: Ministry of Agriculture

Designations:

National park (Parc national) Covered under Titre III and Chapitre III.

Designated by presidential decree, legislation based upon the forestry code, using internationally recognised criteria for national park establishment. The general management policies of national parks were published in the Official Journal *JORT*.

The objectives of national parks are for the "protection and management of the physical and biological features" and "to develop both education and the appreciation of nature through increased tourism".

Additional objectives of the parks include regeneration of plant species which have become rare and reintroduction of animal species; scientific research relative to the natural environment; education and information dissemination about the environment; ecotourism; and development of socio-economic activities.

Legislation allows the Direction des Forêts to check on or prohibit grazing within protected areas and Article 58-60 "textes legislatives forestières"

stipulates that livestock grazing, shooting and fishing may be restricted. This can be done by order of the council established by the Ministry of Agriculture.

Access, building development, agriculture, mining and pests are controlled.

Natural or Nature Reserve (Réserve Naturelle) (also called wild fauna reserve (réserve de faune sauvage))

Covered under Chapter III and subdivided into different categories depending upon management requirements.

Integral natural or nature reserve (réserve naturelle intégrale) Wild fauna reserve (réserve de faune sauvage). Essentially these sites have been designated for strict nature protection and are natural habitats, managed or left undisturbed to maintain the fauna and flora. In a number of cases wild animals have been released to restock reserves.

Gazelle reserve (réserve à gazelle) Deer enclosure (enclos à cerf). Essentially these sites have been designated for strict nature protection and are natural habitats, managed or left undisturbed to maintain the fauna and flora. In a number of cases wild animals have been released to restock reserves.

Breeding enclosure (enclos à reproduction) Essentially these sites have been designated for strict nature protection and are natural habitats, managed or left undisturbed to maintain the fauna and flora. In a number of cases wild animals have been released to restock reserves.

Under Law No. 66-60 reserve protection was mentioned site by site in Article 11, which stated that "hunting in the following reserves is forbidden".

Under mineral orders exploitation and permanent settlement are forbidden.

Wardening is covered under ministerial orders.

Hunting reserve (réserve de chasse) Covered under Titre II, details in eight different chapters. The previous Law required sites to be either permanent or temporary hunting reserves (réserves de chasse permanentes ou temporaires), the latter requiring annual renewal of legislation or their protected status lapsed.

Hunting is only allowed with written permission; activities such as licensed hunting, fishing and logging are strictly controlled. Each reserve can be declared or altered by the Ministry with district/regional approval.

Recreation forest (Forêt récréative) State forest set up for recreational purposes.

In the original Law No. 66-60 usually only tourist hunting permitted.

In Regulations of 1966 statutes were established for the Regional Associations of Hunters and provided for hunting guards, superseded by the Law on 1888 and Ministerial Orders of 18 June 1988.

Protection of wetland zones of national importance (Protection des zones humides d'importance nationale):

Covered under Chapter IV (Title III)

Listed wetland areas which are protected from seasonal hunting and are regarded as wetlands of special importance to the nation.

One site is also covered under the Convention on Wetlands of International Importance especially as Waterfowl Habitat (Ramsar Convention) signed by Tunisia (1980), following authorisation under National Law No. 80-9 of 3 March 1980.

Sources: Bel Hadj Kacem, 1991; Direction Générale des Forets, *c.* 1990

SUMMARY OF PROTECTED AREAS

Map[†] ref.	National/international designations Name of area	IUCN management category	Area (ha)	Year notified
	National Parks			
1	Bou Kornine	II	1,939	1987
2	Djebel Bou-Hedma	II	16,488	1980
3	Djebel Chambi	II	6,723	1980
4	El Feidja	II	2,637	1990
5	Ichkeul	II	12,600	1980
6	Zembra and Zembretta (Protection Zone)	I	4,030	1973
	Natural Reserves			
7	Lac de Tunis	IV	3,000	1973
8	Galiton (Integral Marine Zone)	IV	450	1980
	Wetland Zones of National Importance			
9	Sebkhet Ariana	VIII	3,200	
10	Bahira el-Bibabe	VIII	30,000	
11	Sebkhet Halk-el-Menzel	VIII	2,400	
12	Sebkhet Kelbia	VIII	14,400	
13	Iles Kneiss	VIII	14,600	
14	Lac de Rades et Salines	VIII	2,000	
15	Sebkhet Sedjoumi	VIII	3,600	
16	Sebkhet Sidi-el-Hani	VIII	54,400	
17	Lac de Tunis (see above)	VIII	3,000	
18	Salines de Tyna	VIII	1,500	
	Biosphere Reserves			
	Djebel Bou-Hedma National Park	IX	11,625	1977
	Djebel Chambi National Park	IX	6,000	1977
	Ichkeul National Park	IX	10,770	1977
	Iles Zembra et Zembretta National Park	IX	4,030	1977
	Ramsar Wetland			
	Ichkeul	R	12,600	1980
	World Heritage Site			
	Ichkeul National Park	X	12,600	1980

[†]Locations of some protected areas are shown on the accompanying map.

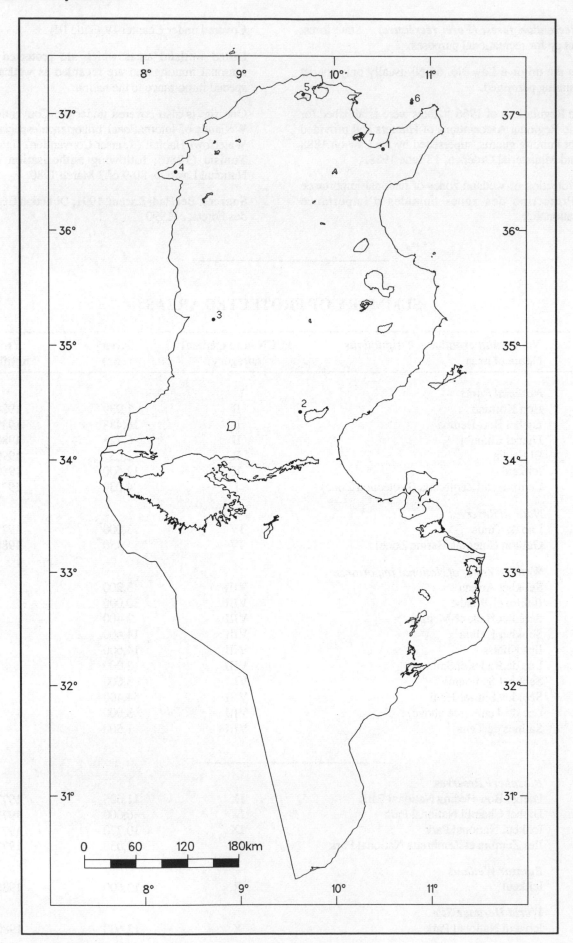

Protected Areas of Tunisia

TURKEY

Area 778,000 sq. km

Population 55,868,000 (1990)
Natural increase: 1.95% per annum

Economic Indicators
GDP: US$ 1,295 per capita (1987)
GNP: US$ 1,200 per capita (1987)

Policy and Legislation In 2 October 1923 the National Assembly declared Turkey a republic, effectively dissolving the former Ottoman Empire. The present Constitution dates from 7 November 1982.

Asia Minor was the cradle for one of the great ancient civilisations of the Mediterranean and has over the millennia been settled by ancient Egyptians, Phoenicians, Carthaginians, Romans, Byzantines and more recently by the Selcuk and other eastern dynasties. A detailed understanding of the environment was well known 5,000 years ago and the ancient Egyptians and subsequent civilisations carefully protected mountain forest resources as valuable timber reserves, imperative for constructing their vast navies. Between 370 and 285BC Theophrastus of Erosos was the first great botanical writer of classical antiquity and his works on botany, plant ecology and the environment were known throughout Asia Minor. Pedanios Dioscorides of the first century AD, a native of Cilicia near present day Adana, was renowned for his work on botany. The Byzantine emperors inherited and developed the agricultural and environmental practices developed throughout the Roman Empire, almost certainly maintaining forest administration structures and wardening systems right up till the Mediaeval period (Drucker, *in litt.*, 1985; Mallatt, *in litt.*, 1991). Traditional forms of protection continue to include a limited number of "sacred groves" and trees which are still protected in Turkey, including at Harbiya near Antakya, and traditional forms of rangeland protection which were prevalent amongst the nomadic steppe and mountain tribes (cf the Mahmeya of Syria and the Hema protection of the Arabian Peninsula) (Drucker, *in litt.*, 1991; Khatib *in litt.*, 1991).

Under Ottoman law, forests came under the jurisdiction of a forest administration. Forest legislation was primarily concerned with controlling tree felling by the issue of permits, and the transportation of wood for local industry and export to neighbouring countries. Environmental legislation was covered under the Ottoman civil code (Mejellah), within the body of Islamic law. Under Article 1243 it was defined that land and the associated trees growing wild in mountains could not be possessed and should remain ownerless. Under Article 1244 cutting wood on private forests was not permitted without authorisation, infringement resulting in payment for damage caused. The Land Law was enacted in 1856, and the Forest Regulations in 1869. These laws have been incorporated into Forest Law No.

3116 and Hunting Law No. 3167, which came into force in 1937 (General Directorate of Forestry, 1987; Drucker, *in litt.*, 1985).

The modern concept of the protected nature conservation area was introduced in 1949, with legal establishment of national parks coming into being on 5 September 1956, under Forest Law No. 6831. The law categorised forest ownership into state forest, forests of public institutes and private forests; being further sub-divided into protection forests, national parks and production forests. Articles 3, 23 and 25 gave the Ministry of Forestry the authority to designate areas as national parks and national forests, as well as to provide for the inclusion of privately-owned lands (the Forest Law was amended in 1983 Act No. 2896 with sole emphasis on forests).

Protected area designations include national park (milli park), nature park (tabiat parklari), natural monument (tabiat aniti), natural reserve area (tabiati korum alani) and special protected area, in addition to game breeding and protection area, game breeding station, game reintroduction area, biogenetic or nature conservation area (Forestry Defence Property) and recreation area (see Annex).

In 1983 the Ministry of Agriculture, Forestry and Rural Affairs (Tarim Orman ve Koyisleri Bakanliği) enacted the current National Park Law No. 2873 in order to establish the principles governing the selection and designation of national parks, natural monuments and nature reserve areas; a law concerned with the protection, development and management of such protected areas without spoiling their natural characteristics. In the same year the Environment Law No. 2872/1983, with prime objectives of general protection of the environment and the prevention of pollution, enacted by the Ministry of Environment. Under this Law zones of special protection of the environment, special protected areas, can be declared. An enabling act of 19 October 1989 provided for protected zonation within these areas (see Annex).

The purposes of the present National Park Law are: a) to establish the principles governing the selection and designation of protected areas of national and international value; and b) ensure protection, development and management of such places without spoiling their natural characteristics. There are 25 articles cited in the Law: Article 2 defines the four main protected area categories; Article 5 specifies that land can be nationalised in accordance with the Law on Expropriation No. 6830; Article 7 states that permissions for all activities are granted through the Ministry of Agriculture and Forestry, except for historic and archaeological sites (which come under the jurisdiction of the Ministry of Culture and Tourism); Article 8 concerns land-lease permits which expire after 49 years, after which time all facilities should be transferred to the Treasury. It is possible to extend the lease of land to 99 years; however, Article 10 states that no land-use permission may be granted in areas of national monuments and nature reserve areas; Article 16 refers to protection services and prosecution by forest guards in accordance with Forest Law No. 6831. Articles 17, 18 and 19 deal with the national park fund (see below). Penalties are dealt with in Articles 20-23 (see Annex).

National forests (state forests) are established to preserve nature and some urban and/or agricultural land from erosion. Many types of management are prohibited according to Item 23 of the Forest Law. Forest recreation areas are established for touristic, cultural and public recreational purposes (General Directorate of Forestry, 1987).

In addition to the protected areas governed by the National Park Law, a series of game forest sites is established on state forest and notified under Hunting Law No. 3167, 1937: game breeding and protection areas, game breeding stations, game reintroduction areas and biogenetic or nature conservation areas (General Directorate of Forestry, 1987) (see Annex).

Additional laws relating to protected areas include Law No. 1380, 1971 for the protection of water resources, management and improvement; Culture and Natural Resources Protection Law No. 2863, 1983 for the protection of natural and cultural sites and resources (administered by the Ministry of Culture and Tourism). In 18 November 1988 the Law of the Bosphorus was enacted in order to protect the cultural, historic and scenic beauty of the Bosphorus region. In 1990 a coastal law was adopted which would delimit the coastal zone and prohibit building within this area.

International Activities   At the international level, Turkey has entered a number of cooperative agreements and legal obligations. Turkey is party to the Convention concerning the Protection of the World Cultural and Natural Heritage (World Heritage Convention), which was ratified on 16 March 1983. One natural site and one mixed cultural and natural site have been inscribed on the World Heritage list. In 1989 Turkey has gave its intention that it will sign the Convention on Wetlands of International Importance especially as Waterfowl Habitat (Ramsar Convention). The Convention for the Protection of the Mediterranean Sea against Pollution, usually known as the Barcelona Convention, has been formally adopted by Turkey. The contracting parties to the Convention adopted the Protocol concerning Mediterranean Specially Protected Areas on 2 April 1982, which entered into force on 23 March 1986. By 1989 three sites had been listed as representative of the Mediterranean network.

Although Turkey is not a member state of the European Community and not party to the 1979 EC Wild Birds Directive, 79 important bird areas (cf EC special protection areas) have been identified (Grimmett and Jones, 1989). Turkey is a member of the Council of Europe: two sites have been designated as biogenetic reserves and one site has been awarded the Council of Europe European Diploma. In 1976 Bird Paradise (Kuscenetti) National Park was awarded the European Diploma Site award; the diploma was renewed in 1981, 1986 and 1991. Turkey ratified the Convention on the Conservation of European Wildlife and Natural Habitats (Bern Convention) in 1984.

Under the Mediterranean Environmental Technical Assistance Programme (CY90-92 METAP) of the World Bank, European Investment Bank, United Nations Development Programme and Commission of the European Communities, representatives from Turkey attended the first meeting of the Mediterranean Protected Areas Network (MEDPAN) meeting on 5-6 October 1990 in Monaco (Anon., 1990). Assistance has come through the Global Environment Facility (GEF) fund, METAP financing for project preparation and GEF financing for investment of the Menderes Wetland programme (Anon., 1990).

There is one transboundary park: Gala Golu Proposed Reserve and Evros Delta Reserve in Greece, but there is little or no interaction or cooperation between the countries in either of these areas. An initiative where Turkey is taking the lead is towards the development of an UNEP-sponsored regional seas programme for the Black Sea, for which Turkey has already sponsored a technical meeting with the other circum-Black Sea countries, the USSR, Romania and Bulgaria (Jeudy de Grissac, *in litt.*, 1991).

Administration and Management   Responsibility for the main protected areas lies with the Ministry of Agriculture, Forestry and Rural Affairs (Tarim Orman ve Koyisleri Bakanliği), General Directorate of Forestry (Orman Genel Müdürlüğü). It is headed by a Director General and four assistant general directors. Of the eight main service units, those that deal directly with protected areas are the Department of National Parks (Milli Parklar Dairesi Baskanliği), the departments of Forest Protection and Fire Control and the Department of Forest Management and Planning. The duties of the Department of National Parks include: a) to select, protect, plan, develop, administer and operate the various categories of protected area indicated in the National Parks Law, as well as to undertake work relating to the National Park Fund; b) to conserve and develop wildlife and game resources, to manage hunting, and to undertake work relating to undertaking inventories, project preparation, planning and application (General Directorate of Forestry, 1991).

The General Forest Directorate is divided into a provincial organisational network, with regional national park directorate offices either based within the provincial forest establishments, such as at Antalya Bolge, or as separate entities such as at Dilek Milli Park. These can be further subdivided into chief offices for

540

each national park (General Directorate of Forestry, 1987).

Research activities are undertaken primarily by the Forestry Research Institute at Ankara and the Forestry School at Istanbul, which are involved in projects throughout Turkey. An investigation and survey team has been set up by the National Park Office at Ankara to investigate new proposed protected areas. Subsequent work is to prepare management plans for each nature reserve once established. All proposed reserves are on state forest property (Karakurum, pers. comm., 1987).

The National Parks Fund has been established under the authority of the Ministry of Agriculture and Forestry, to meet the expenditures incurred in the protection, repair, maintenance, publicity and operation of the facilities located in areas covered by the National Park Law, 1983. In 1985 approximately TL 300 million was expended on park management (General Directorate of Forestry, 1987). The National Park Fund consists of: allocations made from the budget of the Ministry of Agriculture and Forestry; proceeds obtained from the use and operation of areas covered by the Law; as well as entrance fees and revenues obtained from the sale of all kinds of publications. The Fund has been granted an annual budget (see National Park Law No. 2873, Articles 17-19). In National Park Law No. 2873 the views of the Ministry of Culture and Tourism and the Defence Ministry must be taken into account (Article 4). The ministries of Education, Tourism and Information and State Planning Organisation are also given some responsibilities, both directly and indirectly, for management of national parks.

Master management plans for two major national parks were drawn up with the assistance of the US National Park Service in the 1960s and early 1970s. These plans are still used and tend to concentrate on recreation management with a limited amount of information about fauna and flora or habitat conservation and management (General Directorate of Forestry, 1987).

From early 1988 the Authority for the Protection of Special Areas (Özel Çevre Koruma Kurumu Baskanliği) of the Ministry of Environment (Çevre Bakanliği) has had jurisdiction over the newly-created designation of special protected area, based on the orders within the Environment Law (Vurdu, *in litt.*, 1991).

There are approximately one million registered hunters, providing up to TL 200 million in revenue each year (Karakurum, pers. comm., 1987).

The principal active non-governmental conservation organisations include the Society for the Protection of Wildlife (Dogal Hayati Koruma Dernegi) (DHKD) and the Environmental Problems Foundation of Turkey (Türkiye Çevre Sorunlari Vakfi). The former, funded partly by the International Council for Bird Preservation (ICBP), is largely involved with conservational education, and the latter with environmental issues and legislation. Other smaller organisations include the Environment and Woodlands Protection Society (Çevre Koruma ve Yesillendirme Dernegi) and the Turkish Association for Conservation of Nature and Natural Resources (Türkiye Tobiatini Koruma Dernegi).

The greatest management constraints have included the lack of adequate nature conservation skills and technical support within the General Directorate of Forestry. Although the major national parks have master management plans, they tend to be inadequate as they were drawn up in the 1960s, with an emphasis on tourism rather than nature protection. Lack of coordination between government agencies and of cooperation of government bodies with NGO groups tends to be a major problem.

Systems Reviews Consisting of Turkey in Europe (western Thrace and Istanbul) and Turkey in Asia (comprising the whole of Asia minor or Anatolia), the country extends from Greece and Bulgaria in the west, across the Aegean Sea to the western frontiers of Iran, Soviet Armenia and Georgia and from the Black Sea to the Mediterranean and the northern boundaries of Syria and Iraq.

Turkey is renowned as an important centre of floristic diversity. There are up to 2,400 endemic plant species in a country which is the meeting point of three phytogeographical regions: Euro-Siberian, Mediterranean and Irano-Turanian elements. There are also Balkan and Alpine elements in the flora. Endemism is lowest in Turkey in Europe where endemic species are almost absent. Endemism is highest in the Irano-Turanian region, especially near Erzincan, Erzurum, the mountains south of Lake Van and on gypsacaceous chalk near Cankiri and Sivas; also the Lycian and Cilician Taurus in the Mediterranean region. Boreal and Tertiary relicts are abundant east of the Melet River in the north-east. The three regions consist of a) the Irano-Turanian, which comprises two sub-phytogeographical areas; degraded sub-Mediterranean scrub and forest and a treeless steppe in central Anatolia and an *Artemisia* steppe which gives way to black pine forest and cistus scrub; b) Euro-Siberian or Euxine, a northern belt of broad-leaved deciduous forest of oriental beech and oak extending at greater altitudes into fir and scots pine forest, ranging from the Black sea to above 1,500m; and c) Mediterranean, consisting of maquis, degraded maquis (phrygana), through cedar forest to spiny cushion communities above 1,000m in the Taurus mountains and Aegean coast (Davis *et al.*, 1986; Green and Drucker, 1990).

Wetlands are an important feature. Approximately 60% are freshwater (1,343 million ha). The most important sites include Meric tributary, Gala Lake, Manyas Lake, Apolyont Lake, Sultansazligi marshland, Eber Lake, Aksehir Lake, Karamuk Lake, Beysehir Lake, Eğridir Lake, Menderes, Tuz golu, Seyfe Lake, Akyatan Lagoon, Yumurtalik Lagoon, Goksu, Bafra and Homtamis Lake (Grimmett, 1986; Karakurum, pers. comm., 1988).

Land-use is divided into forests with a total of 20.2 million ha (25.9%), meadows and pasture 25 million ha (32.2%) and wetlands 1.3 million (1.7%). Agricultural areas represent 27,699,000ha (35%) of the country (General Directorate of Forestry, 1986). The total area of forest is divided into 8.9 million ha (44%) of productive forest and 11.3 million ha (56%) of low grade or no yield status (General Directorate of Forestry, 1987).

An investigation and survey team has been set up by the National Park Office at Ankara to investigate new proposed protected areas (Karakurum, pers. comm., 1988). Emphasis is on establishing nature reserve areas, on state forest land, from an original short list of approximately 90 proposed sites (Karakurum, pers. comm., 1987). A total of 81 proposed nature reserves was identified by 1987, with the intention of designating sites over forthcoming years at a rate of approximately seven sites per year (Orman Genel Baskanliği, 1987; *Official Gazette* No. 18132; Karakurum, pers. comm., 1987).

Studies on the selection and establishment of nature protection areas began in 1956, and by 1987 eleven natural, one historic, two landscape, one reserve and one natural monument were set aside as national parks covering a total of over 250,000ha. This rose to a total of 21 national parks in 1990 with a total area of 263,575ha. By autumn 1987 five natural reserve area sites had been designated and a further two were in the process of being approved by the Ministry. This had risen to 18 sites totalling 25,492 ha in 1991. In 1988 the first two special protected areas were declared, rising to 11 by 1991. In 1981 at least 295,759ha were protected in 36 national forests (Orman Genel Baskanliği, 1987; *Official Gazette* No. 18132; Karakurum, pers. comm., 1987).

In 1990, in addition to the protected areas governed by the National Park Law, there were 83 game breeding and protection areas totalling 1.1 million ha; 27 game breeding stations; 20 game reintroduction areas; seven biogenetic or nature conservation areas set up on Forestry Defence Property (General Directorate of Forestry, 1987). Approximately 180 recreation areas were established between 1956-68 and 1968-1979. By the late 1980s there was a total of 260 recreation areas (General Directorate of Forestry, 1987).

Environmental problems include a lack of legal regulations relating to effective conservation in national parks. There has been no monitoring of the protection status of game reserves or breeding stations (General Directorate of Forestry, 1986). The prime management and environmental problems in Turkey are believed to be: a) "improved" agriculture and the resultant loss of wetland ecosystems and former grazing land; b) pollution from pesticides and fertilisers; c) building development, especially due to the manifold increase in tourism since the early 1980s along the entire Mediterranean coastline; and d) hunting of threatened species such as ibex, brown bear, wolf and some of the large cats, even though hunting is regulated and their status is largely unknown (Grimmett and Jones, 1989).

Other Relevant Information   In the 1960s the numbers of visitors to national parks approached 500,000. In 1985 about 10 million visitors made use of the national parks. Forest recreation areas are established for touristic, cultural and public recreational purposes and by 1987 there had been 30 million visitors to these areas (General Directorate of Forestry, 1987, 1991).

Addresses

Milli Parklar Dairesi (National Parks Department), Orman Genel Müdürlüğü, (General Directorate of Forestry), Tarim Orman ve Koyisleri Bakanliği (Ministry of Agriculture, Forestry and Rural Affairs), 11 No. lu Bina, Gazi, ANKARA (Tel: 4 212 6300; FAX: 4 222 5140)

Kultur ve tabiat varliklanni Koruma Genel Müdürlüğü (General Directorate for Preservation of Natural and Cultural Heritage), Kultur Bakanliği (Ministry of Culture), II TBMM Ulus, ANKARA (Tel: 4 310 6338/324 3049; FAX: 4 310 9112)

Özel Çevre Koruma Kurumu Baskanliği (The Authority for the Protection of Special Areas), Çevre Bakanliği (Ministry of Environment), Koza Sokak 32, GOP 06700, ANKARA (Tel: 4 140 6919/140 855152; FAX: 4 140 8553/6914)

Dogal Hayati Koruma Dernegi (DHKD) (Society for the protection of wildlife), PK 18, Bebek 80812, ISTANBUL (Tel: 1 163 6324; FAX: 1 163 6324; Tlx: 26534 rada tr)

The Environmental Problems Foundation of Turkey (EPFT), Kennedy Cad 33/3, Kavaklidere, 06660 ANKARA (Tel: 4 1 255508; FAX: 4 118 5118)

Turkiye Tabiatini Koruma Dernegi (TTKD) (Turkish Society for the Protection of Nature and its Resources), Menekse Sokak No 29/4, Kizilay, ANKARA

References

Anon. (1970-71). National park concept in Turkey and its development. Miméo. 17 pp.

Anon. (1991). Mediterranean Environmental Technical Assistance Program, activity report Spring, 1991. World Bank, European Investment Bank, United Nations Development Programme and Commission of the European Communities. 24 pp.

Bayer, Z. (1970). Nature Conservation and National Parks in Turkey. *Natur- und Nationalparke* 8(29): 33-35.

Bayer, Z. (n.d.). Turkey. Unpublished report. 7 pp.

Canakeioglu, H. (1987). Effects of pesticides on bird populations. *Uluslararasi Simpozyum – Turkiye ve Balkan Ulkelerinde Yaban Hayati* 16-20 September.

Environmental Problems Foundation of Turkey (1987). *Environmental law and its application in Turkey.* EPFT, Ankara.

General Directorate of Forestry (1980). *Forest recreation areas of Turkey*. General Directorate of National Parks and Wildlife, Ministry of Forestry, Ankara.

General Directorate of Forestry (1986). *Hunting and wildlife in Turkey (Turkiye'de av ve yaban hayati)*. Tarim Orman ve Koyisleri Bakanligi (Forest and Village Affairs), Orman Genel Müdürlügü, Ankara.

General Directorate of Forestry (1987). *Forestry in Turkey*. General Directorate of Forestry, Ministry of Agriculture, Forest and Rural Affairs, Ankara.

General Directorate of Forestry (1980). The protected areas situation in Turkey. General Directorate of National Parks and Wildlife, Ministry of Forestry, Ankara. Paper prepared by M. Savas for presentation to the Third Man and Biosphere Meeting on Mediterranean Biosphere Reserves and the First IUCN-CNPPA meeting for the Middle East and North Africa, 14-19 October 1991, Tunis. 3 pp.

Green, M.J.B. and Drucker, G.R.F. (1990). *Current status of protected areas and threatened mammal species in the Sahara-Gobian Region*. World Conservation Monitoring Centre, Cambridge, UK. 50 pp.

Grimmett, R. (1986). *Preliminary inventory of important bird areas in Turkey*. International Council for Bird Preservation, Cambridge, UK. 888 pp.

Grimmett, R.F.A. and Jones, T.A. (1989). *Important bird areas of Europe*. International Council for Bird Preservation, Cambridge, UK.

Hunter, B. (Ed.) (1991). *The Statesman's Year Book 1991-92*. The Macmillan Press Ltd, London and Basingstoke, UK. 1692 pp.

Istanbullu, T. (1976). Some aspects of national parks as a result of Nature Conservation in Turkey. *Natur-und Nationalparke* 15(52): 31-32.

Kettaneh, M. and Ozbaykal, N. (1980). National parks and protected areas of Turkey. Report prepared for the 17th meeting of IUCN Commission on National Parks and Protected Areas. Garoua, Cameroon, 17-23 November 1980.

Mursaloglu, B. (1987). The effects of pesticides and fertilizers on wildlife in Turkey. *Uluslararasi Simpozyum – Turkiye ve Balkan Ulkelerinde Yaban Hayati*. 16-20 September.

Official Gazette (1983). Milli Parklar Kanunu. *Official Gazette*, 11 August 1983, No. 18132.

Orman Genel Müdürlügü (1987). *Milli Parklar Kanunu*. Tarim Orman ve Koyisleri Bakanligi, Milli Parklar Dairesi Baskanligi, Orman Genel Müdürlügü, Ankara, Turkey.

Orman Genel Müdürlügü (1987). *Av Mevsimi Merkez Av Komisyonu Karari, 1987-1988*. Tarim Orman ve Koyisleri Bakanliği, Orman Genel Müdürlüğü, Ankara, Turkey.

Packard, F.M. (1958). Report on a survey of potential national parks and recreational areas in Turkey. IUCN, Morges, Switzerland.

Turan, S. (1987). The works of animal protection propagation and management of hunting. *Uluslararasi Simpozyum – Turkiye ve Balkan Ulkelerinde Yaban Hayati*. 16-20 September 1987.

Zengingonul, I. (1987). Tourism and hunting in Turkey. *Uluslararasi Simpozyum – Turkiye ve Balkan Ulkelerinde Yaban Hayati*. 16-20 September 1987.

ANNEX
Definitions of protected area designations, as legislated, together with authorities responsible for their administration

Title: National Park Law No. 2873

Date: 11 August 1983; 5 September 1956 (Forest Law No. 6831)

Brief description: Also concerned with the protection, development and management of such protected areas without spoiling their natural characteristics.

Administrative authority: General Directorate of Forestry (Orman Genel Müdürlüğü)

Designations:

National park (Milli park) By definition, a national park is principally state-owned land of at least 500ha that carries high natural, historical, archaeological, recreational, scientific and aesthetic values and in which wood gathering, timber cutting, mining, and hunting is prohibited. Zonation within the parks include: 1) protection zone, where at least one third of the total land is protected against all usage except for scientific research; 2) buffer zone, areas adjacent to the protection zone which can be used for touristic and/or recreational purposes (up to one third of total land); and 3) settlement zone, areas where settlement may take place if the existence of such constructions improves the park's characteristics or, at least, does not destroy them.

Article 13 states that the following activities shall not be permitted: a) the spoiling of the natural and ecological equilibrium; b) the destruction of wildlife; c) interference of any kind which would cause change of natural character or appearance of the park (or pollute soil, water or air or cause other similar environmental problems); d) extraction of forest products, hunting, grazing which will spoil the natural equilibrium may not be carried out; e) except for facilities specified in approved plans or for the requirements of the Turkish General Defence Staff, no facilities may be built.

Article 4 concerns the preparation of a development plan for each site and its implementation by the Ministry of Agriculture and Forestry;

Article 5 specifies that land can be nationalised in accordance with the Law on Expropriation No. 6830 and Article 6 concerns expropriation of governmental land or acquisition of Ministry of National Defence land;

Article 7 states that permissions for all activities are granted through the Ministry of Agriculture and Forestry, except for historic and archaeological sites (which come under the jurisdiction of the Ministry of Culture and Tourism); Article 8 concerns permission required to build touristic complexes in national parks and nature parks. Article 11 is concerned with exploration for oil and minerals; Article 13 concerns management to ensure continuation of multi-purpose usage: production, hunting and domestic livestock grazing may be permitted in certain areas; Article 14 identifies prohibited activities (see Annex). Article 15 concerns the occupation and utilisation of property belonging to public administration and public institutions. Article 16 refers to protection services and prosecution by forest guards in accordance with Forest Law No. 6831. Articles 17, 18 and 19 deal with the national park fund (see below). Penalties are dealt with in Articles 20-23.

Nature Park (Tabiat parklari)   Natural area containing characteristic vegetation and wildlife features, and is also suitable for recreational activities. Two sites have been designated, those of Corum city-Catak and Olüdeniz-Kidrak. In both cases special tourist facilities but no other buildings are permitted.

Natural monument (Tabiat aniti)   Natural area of scientific value, which was created by nature or natural phenomena and now protected within the framework of the principles on national parks. Article 10 states that no land-use permission may be granted in areas of monuments and nature reserve areas (see provisions of Law No. 2863 for the protection of cultural and natural assets); there have not yet been any specific studies on this class of protected area.

Natural reserve area (Tabiati korum alani) Natural area designated for use only for scientific and educational purposes, containing rare, threatened or endangered ecosystems and/or species and outstanding natural landscape or geological features. Article 10 states that no land-use permission may be granted in areas of monuments and nature reserve areas (see provisions of Law No. 2863 for the protection of cultural and natural assets);

Sources: Original legislation; Karakurum, pers. comm., 1987

Title: Environment Law No. 2872/1983

Date: 9 August 1983; enabling decree of 19 October 1989

Brief description: Also concerned with the protection, development and management of such protected areas without spoiling their natural characteristics.

Administrative authority: Özel Çevre Koruma Kurumu Baskanliği (The Authority for the Protection of Special Areas), Çevre Bakanliği (Ministry of Environment)

Designations:

Specially protected area   Declared with the objective of protecting the environment, with its rich diversity of natural and historic variety as well as for the protection of flora and fauna of national importance. Regulations ensure that development projects including tourist activities, are stopped pending re-evaluation by environmental impact assessments. These sites are selected to include only those which are of international importance. The 1989 decree ensures the designation of zonation within these areas.

Source: Özel Çevre Koruma Kurumu Baskanliği, *in litt.*, 1991

Title: Hunting Law No. 3167

Date: 1937

Brief description: Also concerned with hunting and the protection, development and management of areas for hunting and breeding of game on state forest-land

Administrative authority: Orman Genel Müdürlüğü

Designations:

Game breeding and protection areas   Areas for the protection of game and endangered species

Game breeding stations   Areas for the purpose of breeding game and wild animals

Game reintroduction areas   Areas where game has been reintroduced into habitats where the species has disappeared or has a very small population

Biogenetic or nature conservation areas   Areas established for protection of endemic, endangered or internationally important fauna and flora on Forestry Defence Property

Source: General Directorate of Forestry, 1987

SUMMARY OF PROTECTED AREAS

Map[†] ref.	*National/international designations* Name of area	IUCN management category	Area (ha)	Year notified
	National Parks			
1	Dilek Yarimadisi	II	10,985	1966
2	Gelibolu Yarimadisi (Galipoli)	V	33,000	1973
3	Goreme	V	9,576	1986
4	Ilgaz Daği	II	1,088	1976
5	Karatepe-Aslantas	V	7,715	1958
6	Koprulu Kanyon	II	36,614	1973
7	Kovada Golu	II	6,534	1970
8	Munzur	II	42,800	1971
9	Olimpos-Beydağlari	II	69,800	1972
10	Soguksu	II	1,050	1959
11	Spildağ	II	5,505	1968
12	Termessos	II	6,702	1970
13	Uludağ	II	11,338	1961
14	Yedigoller	II	2,019	1965
	Nature Reserve Areas			
15	Sultan Sazligi	IV	9,000	1988
16	Yukarigokdere	I	1,300	1987
	Game Reserves			
17	Akdağ	VI	7,500	1970
18	Bozdağ	VI	42,000	1966
19	Catacik	VI	25,000	1969
20	Cocak Cehennemdere	VI	15,000	1969
21	Coruh	VI	8,500	1971
22	Duzlercami	VI	14,000	1966
23	Golardi Sulun	VI	25,000	1969
24	Karacabey-Karadağ	VI	14,828	1968
25	Karadag	VI	6,000	
26	Karamanbayiri	VI	14,000	1967
27	Pos-Catalan	VI	9,000	1969
28	Sultan Sazligi	VI	9,000	1980
29	Turan-Emeksiz	VI	16,000	1969
30	Van Ozalp	VI	5,500	1971
	Special Protection Areas			
31	Goksu Delta	IV	13,000	1989
32	Koycegiz-Dalyan	IV	1,150	1988
	World Heritage Sites			
	Goreme National Park	X	9,576	1988
	Hierapolis-Pamukkale	X	n/a	1988

[†]Locations of some protected areas are shown on the accompanying map.

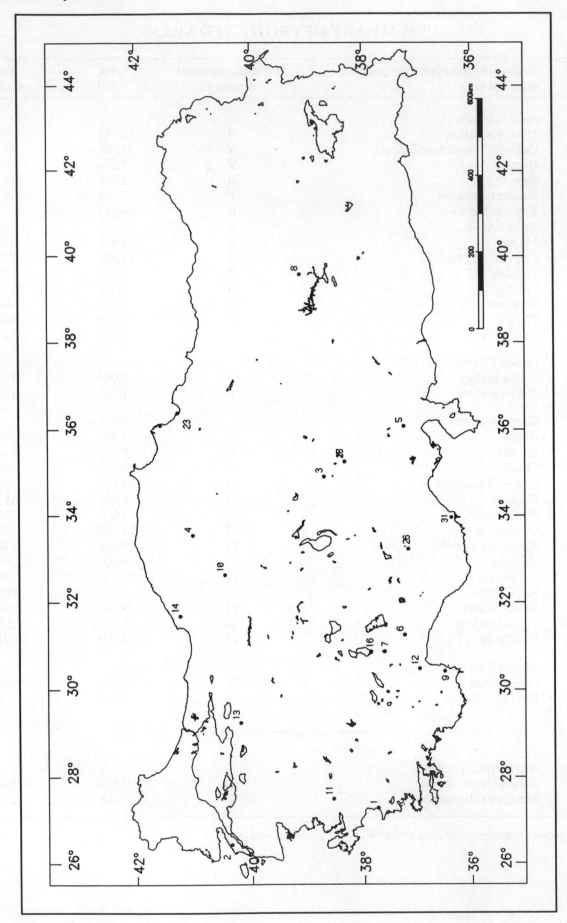

Protected Areas of Turkey

UNITED ARAB EMIRATES (UAE)
(States of Abu Dhabi, Dubai, Sharjah, Ajman, Umm al Qawain, Ras al Khaimah and Fujairah)

Area 86,449 sq. km

Population 1,589,000 (1990)
Natural increase: 2.24% per annum

Economic Indicators
GDP: US$ 15,889 per capita (1990)
GNP: US$ 15,680 per capita (1990)

Policy and Legislation The United Arab Emirates consists of a federation of the seven trucial states: Abu Dhabi, Dubai, Sharjah (including former Kalba), Ajman, Umm al Qawain, Ras al Khaimah and Fujairah. The trucial states formed the federation on 2 December 1971 which is headed by a Supreme Council composed of the seven rulers. A federal Council of Ministers drafts legislation for the whole of UAE. Embodied in the Constitution is the traditional Islamic respect for nature. The legal system subscribes to the Islamic law (Sharia).

Traditional forms of nature conservation have had a long history in the Arabian Peninsula, in the form of range reserves or hema (hima or ahmia). Variations of the hema survive in the UAE in the form of hunting reserves, such as at Jebel Hafit (Jacobson, 1985; Maher abou Jaafer, 1984).

Enabling legislation for nature reserves and national parks does not exist in the technical sense. Individual sites are established under private initiative of the ruling families or under hunting legislation. Under the Hunting Law seasonal protection is provided to a number of bird colonies, in addition to restrictions applying to at least one turtle beach and the Jebel Hafit Tahr Reserve area (see Annex). Khor Dubai Wildlife Sanctuary was established in 1985 (Carp, 1976; Maher abou Jaafer, 1984; Richardson, 1990; Savage, 1976). In addition, the Dubai government has designated a single national park, a combination of natural woodland and recreational area (Richardson, 1990). The only other forms of protection include Al Ayn Wildlife Enclosure and Zoological Garden and a municipal nursery in Ra's al-Khaymah (Richardson, 1990).

It is widely regarded that there is a lack of legislation relevant to protected areas. Indeed, in 1982 a recommendation was put forward for a comprehensive forest law for the country as a whole, envisaging a technically trained and suitably constituted forest service to apply and enforce the provisions of the proposed law (Khan, 1982). It was recommended that a study be made of existing forest laws in other parts of the Middle East. It was further suggested that subsequent phases could involve the United Nations Food and Agriculture Organisation to provide suitable consultancy services in drafting the outlines of the proposed forest law (Khan, 1982).

International Activities The UAE acceded to CITES on 1 July 1975 but withdrew from the Convention in 1988. It reacceded on 12 May 1990. The Kuwait Regional conference of plenipotentiaries on the protection and development of the marine environment and the coastal areas was convened by UNEP in Kuwait, 15-23 April 1978; this led to the adoption of the Kuwait Action Plan (KAP) for the protection and development of the marine environment and the coastal areas of Bahrain, Iran, Iraq, Kuwait, Oman, Qatar, Saudi Arabia and United Arab Emirates (UNEP, 1983).

Administration and Management The Ministry of Agriculture has jurisdiction over matters concerning the conservation of nature and the environment and is directly involved in the administration of the Hunting Law. The Ministry is also obliged to manage and protect the various hunting areas, bird sanctuaries and turtle beaches. Khor Dubai Flamingo Colony has 24-hour police protection (Richardson, 1990).

Other main state bodies with interests in protected areas are the Permanent Committee for Conservation and Ecology at the Presidential Court of Abu Dhabi and the Higher Environmental Committee (HEC) of the Ministry of Health. The HEC is concerned with aquatic life in coastal and marine areas and the impact of water pollution, as well as environmental threats posed by oil and gas development. In addition, both bodies undertake monitoring of marine pollution (Montague and Bruun, 1987). The Dubai Wildlife Research Centre, established by the son of the ruler of Dubai, is a semi-governmental organisation. Its sphere of interests include fauna and flora surveys, habitat studies including of wetlands and shorebird areas and the establishment and development of wildlife preserves and zoos, the latter leading to the conservation, through captive breeding, of individual native fauna species such as oryx, bustard and falcon. It has been closely involved in identifying important nature conservation areas of Dubai (DSP, 1987; Montague and Bruun, 1987). In 1986 a project to locate areas of importance for coastal birds was undertaken by the Dubai Wildlife Research Centre and members of the University of Durham (DSP, 1987).

The Fisheries Section of the Department of Agriculture undertakes research on the marine environment, although as far as is known there are no marine conservation areas (Carp, 1976).

Desert afforestation has long been accorded high priority, planting being undertaken by the authorities for amenity and for future establishment of wildlife parks (Satchell, 1978).

The main non-governmental body involved in protected areas and nature conservation in general is the Emirates Natural History Group based in Abu Dhabi. It is interested in all fields of natural history and is involved in the recommendation and establishment of wildlife reserves and zoos, as well as in surveys and identification of species and important habitats throughout the UAE (Montague and Bruun, 1987). The group publishes a bulletin three times a year and reports on the status of mangroves (Khan, 1982). Other bodies include: the Dubai Natural History Group, which publishes the *Gazelle* magazine monthly and distributes the *Emirates Bird Report Quarterly*; the United Arab Emirates University (Science College) which concentrates on pollution, environmental threats and on recommendations for future protected areas (Montague and Bruun, 1987; Richardson, 1990).

Agencies involved in environmental activities in the UAE include the Environmental Department within the Abu Dhabi National Oil Company which assists with EIAs (IUCN/UNEP, 1985; UNEP/IUCN, 1988). Surveys have also been undertaken by the Ornithological Society of the Middle East (OSME). Additional surveys have been undertaken by consultants for IUCN and IWRB to identify significant marine habitats and wetlands of international importance (Carp, 1976). The IUCN/IWRB report recommended the forbidding of hunting of dugong and turtles and the need to declare their feeding and breeding areas as protected (Carp, 1976). Surveys have also been undertaken by the Emirates Natural History Group and the British Trust for Ornithology. An artificial island was built to encourage nesting on Khor Dubai Wildlife Sanctuary (Richardson, 1990).

Systems Reviews   The United Arab Emirates, situated on the Arabian (Persian) Gulf coast of the Arabian Peninsula, is bounded by Oman, Saudi Arabia and Qatar. The terrain consists mostly of desert with little or no vegetation; some wooded steppes occur between the desert and the Hajar Mountains in the east on the border with Oman. Dry scrub and occasional trees occur in the Hajar mountains. Woodland areas are restricted to *Acacia* and *Prosopis* steppe and patchy coastal mangrove forests distributed in limited areas along 450km of the Arabian Gulf coast and 100km of the Gulf of Oman (Kahn, 1982; Ramadan-Jaradi, 1985; Satchell, 1978). Numerous offshore islands and banks are favourable for sea-grass beds and coral reef development (Carp, 1976; UNEP/IUCN, 1988). The wetlands, mudflats and saltmarshes of the UAE states such as Dubai are important migration stopover and wintering sites for several species of wader (Ramadan-Jaradi, 1985; Smart *et al.*, 1983) (information on the ecology and environment in the United Arab Emirates is summarised by Satchell, 1978; also see Richardson, 1990).

Comprehensive surveys of a number of biological resources have been undertaken, such as on ornithological sites, mangrove sites and marine habitats (Carp, 1976; Khan, 1982; Ramadan-Jaradi, 1985; Richardson, 1990). No major systems review exists, activities having been on restricted levels. For example, a master plan exists for the development of agriculture in Al Ain and its region (Anon., 1989). In the mid 1970s IUCN consultants undertook a survey of marine habitats and wetlands of international standard, and seven sites were recommended for protection (Carp, 1976). Subsequently, IUCN proposed a critical marine habitats programme to identify marine and coastal resources in urgent need of protection and analyse the action priorities required for their management. The proposal was put to the Ministry of Agriculture and Fisheries in 1981 (Al-Mutawa, *in litt.*, 1981; Jungius, *in litt.*, 1981).

The UAE authorities have shown an interest in the protected natural areas reserve system and intend to designate Al Ayn and Ra's al-Khaymah sites with some modifications and additions. The proposal to establish a reserve (110ha) in the area of Al Ayn (al-'Ayn) has met with preliminary agreement, since the zoo already holds a number of species of threatened wildlife, including Arabian oryx, Arabian wolf, Beisa oryx, Nubian ibex and scimitar oryx (Maher abou Jaafer, 1984).

At least 38,300ha has been recommended for protection, including Al Ayn, Ra's al Khaymah, a 1,500ha restricted zone at Jebel Ali, a 300ha wildlife sanctuary at Khor Dubai and at least two major private reserves, Ummal Qaiwain being at least 1,000ha. In addition, there is a 30ha protected wooded landscape, Mushrif National Park.

Environmental problems include expansion of cities such as Abu Dhabi, leading to reclamation of shallow waters and saltmarshes in order to provide more space for building, port installations and industry (Carp, 1976; Satchell, 1978). During the 1991 Iraq-Kuwait war oil slicks were reported to threaten the coastal and marine habitats all along the Arabian coastline.

Other Relevant Information   In 1820 the rulers signed a treaty prescribing peace with the British government. In 1971 the treaties whereby Britain had been responsible for foreign relations were terminated and replaced on 2 December 1971 by a treaty of friendship.

Addresses

Ministry of Agriculture and Fisheries, PO Box 213, ABU DHABI (Tel: 2 662781)
Higher Environmental Committee, Ministry of Health, PO Box 848, ABU DHABI (Tel: 2 341 444; FAX: 2 313 525)
Permanent Committee for Conservation and Ecology, ADFCF Presidential Court PO Box 2380, ABU DHABI
Emirates Natural History Group, PO Box 2380, ABU DHABI

References

Anon. (1989). Rural Development Programmes. Project Experience. Pamphlet. Minster Agriculture Ltd, Thame, UK.

Anon. (1989). Sharper lines in Arabia's sands. *The Economist.* 21 January 1989. P. 82.

Carp, E. (1976). United Arab Emirates: report of a survey of marine habitats carried out during 3-15 February 1975. In: Promotion of the establishment of marine parks and reserves in the Northern Indian Ocean including the Red Sea and Persian Gulf. Papers and proceedings of the Regional Meeting held at Tehran, Iran, 6-10 March 1975. *IUCN Publications New Series* 35: 107-114.

DSP (1987). Shorebirds of Khor Dubai: Dubai shorebird project report 1987. University of Durham, UK. 59 pp.

Groombridge, B. and Luxmoore, R. (in prep.). The green turtle and hawksbill (Reptilia; Cheloniidae): World status, exploitation and trade, a report to the Cites secretariat. World Conservation Monitoring Centre, Cambridge, UK.

IUCN/UNEP (1985). Management and conservation of renewable marine resources in the Kuwait Action Plan region. *UNEP Regional Seas Reports and Studies* 63: 1-63.

Jacobson, P. (1985). Ready to take on all comers; Sheikh Mohammed al Maktoum. *The Sunday Times*, 21 July 1985. P. 8.

Kahn, M.I.R. (1982). Status of the mangrove forests in the United Arab Emirates. *Bulletin of the Emirates Natural History Group (Abu Dhabi)* 17: 15-17

Kahn, M.I.R. (1982). Mangrove forest in the U.A.E. *Pakistan Journal of Forestry* 32(2): 36-39.

Maher abou Jaafer (1984). *National parks and nature reserves in the Arab World.* The Arab League Educational, Cultural and Scientific Organization, Tunis. 112 pp.

Montague, K. and Bruun, B. (1987). *Biological Diversity in North Africa, the Middle East and Southwest Asia; a directory of organizations and institutions.* HLCF, New York, USA.

Ramadan-Jaradi, G. (1985). Les oiseaux non nicheurs observes en migration dans les Emirats Arabes Unis. *L'Oiseau et la Revue Francaise d'Ornithologie* 55: 3-52.

Richardson, C. (1990). *The birds of the United Arab Emirates.* Hobby Publications, Dubai and Warrington, Cheshire, UK. 204 pp.

Satchell, J.E. (1978). Ecology and environment in the United Arab Emirates. *Journal of Arid Environments* 1:201-226.

Smart, I, Miles, G.A. and West, M. (1983). Waders and waterbirds on Dubai Creek. *Wader Study Group Bulletin* 37: 29-30.

UNEP (1987). Clearing house developments. *UNEP Regional Bulletin for Europe* 4: 9.

UNEP/IUCN (1988). *Coral Reefs of the World. Volume 2: Indian Ocean, Red Sea and Gulf. UNEP Regional Seas Directories and Bibliographies.* IUCN, Gland, Switzerland and Cambridge, UK/UNEP, Nairobi, Kenya. 440 pp.

Vessey-Fitzgerald, D.F. (1957). The vegetation of central and eastern Arabia. *Journal of Ecology* 45: 779-798.

Western, R.A. (1989). *The Flora of the United Arab Emirates an introduction.* United Arab Emirates University.

ANNEX
Definitions of protected area designations, as legislated, together with authorities responsible for their administration

Title: Hunting Law

Date: No information

Brief description: Throughout the Emirates the hunting of rabbits, hare, wood pigeon and partridge is banned. A law covering Abu Dhabi only prohibits the hunting of almost all birds and animals. Restricted hunting areas exist and are covered under specific hunting regulations for those sites. Contravening the Hunting law may result in jail sentences from 3-6 months and fines from a minimum of £140 to a maximum of £700, a figure which may be doubled on further convictions.

Administrative Authority: Ministry of Agriculture

Designations:

Seasonal bird sanctuary/Wildlife sanctuary Restrictions on disturbing nesting bird colonies imposed on a seasonal basis. At a number of sites protection by guards is undertaken on a 24-hour basis

Sea turtle beach Restricted area 400m above highwater to 4km offshore.

Sources: Richardson, 1990; Savage, 1976

Title: Mushrif National Park Decree

Date: No information

Brief description: Individual designation by the Dubai government

Administrative Authority: Dubai authorities

Designations:

National park Nationally important area of natural vegetation

Site management is permitted, restricted access to areas prevent damage to the natural vegetation. Recreation, tourism, vehicular use are permitted.

The area is fenced and access is restricted to certain times of the day. There is an entrance fee.

Source: Richardson, 1990

REPUBLIC OF YEMEN
unifying the former Yemen Arab Republic (YAR) and
The People's Democratic Republic of Yemen (PDRY)

Area 531,000 sq. km (Hunter, 1991); 195,000 sq. km (former YAR); 290,273 sq. km (former PDRY)
Area not incorporating undefined boundary with Saudi Arabia and Oman

Population 11.5 million (1990); 9.2 million (former YAR); 2.5 million (former PDRY)
Natural increase: 3.7% per annum (former YAR); 3.2% per annum (former PDRY)

Economic Indicators
GDP: US$ 579 per capita (YAR); US$ 513 per capita (PDRY) (1987)
GNP: US$ 580 per capita (YAR); US$ 420 per capita (PDRY) (1987)

Policy and Legislation On 22 May 1990 the Yemen Arab Republic (northern) and the People's Democratic Republic of Yemen (southern) were unified as the Republic of Yemen. The first Constitution for the unified republic was passed in 1991, however, at that date legislation enacted under the former republics was still at a review stage (Herzog, *in litt.*, 1991). The 42 ministries of the unified country have been concentrated in Sana'a, the former capital of YAR, in an attempt to establish a strong central administration. Tribal authority continues to be a dominant feature of the north-east. Rural communities are governed by sheikhs and aqilks who rule the communities by consent based on the Koran, the Islamic law Sharia and the traditional or tribal law Urf. Urf laws or customs, which include a significant element of environmental land-use, clearly dominate rural life to a greater extent than would legislation of central government (Herzog, *in litt.*, 1991).

Traditional forms of rangeland protected area (mahjour or mahjur) are still practised in the Yemens, often maintained by local communities over centuries for the production of hay, and as food reserves for livestock during periods of drought, or for firewood (Kessler, 1988; Herzog, pers. comm., 1991). Other forms of traditional land protection include Waqf land or property donation to religious institutions (Awqaf or Auqaf); Jebel Bura Forest was donated in 1309AH by Sheikh Bajil Beit al Fakih and Begeli landowner to the religious community, after which it has been under continual protection (Herzog, in press). Under the tribal jurisdiction of local sheikhs, administrators and local development councils there are cases of local forest felling and entry bans into certain areas to protect the environment; fines are levied in the case of infringements (Varisco *et al.*, in press; Wood, 1982; Herzog, *in litt.*, 1991).

Prior to unification there was no specific wildlife conservation nor protected areas legislation in either of the two republics. In the former PDRY, legislation concerning the environment included laws on hunting; activities being regulated in accordance with Law No. 14, 1970. PDRY Law No. 13, 1976 established the National Environment Council. The only environment-related legislation in the former YAR included a decree of the former Ministry of Agriculture requiring each regional project to include a forest component (FAO, *in litt.*, 1991) and Law No. 13, 1975 concerning environmental conditions of harbours and airports (UNEP, 1980; UNEP/IUCN, 1988). Former YAR Resolution No. 83, 1977 established a central committee and local committees for the protection of the environment, superseded by Prime Ministerial Decree No. 7 establishing the Environmental Protection Council (EPC) in 1987. Law No. 20, 1978 related to fisheries, with articles on the instigation of a permit/licence system and identification of fishing restrictions.

A YAR Forest Law was adopted in 1986, following drafting of the law by the FAO forest adviser at the Ministry of Agriculture between 1979-82. The law had not been ratified up to the time of unification in 1990. The law is to be applied to all forests or shrub-covered land, whether owned by government, communities or individuals (see Annex) (Herzog, in press).

Reviews of protected areas and general environmental policy include the need for a development policy able to respond to environmental degradation, the need for protected areas, species and general environment legislation, definition of the mechanisms for establishing legislation and implementing protection, and development of environmental policy with the appropriate bodies. In the mid 1980s the Ministry of Agriculture of the YAR proposed major wildlife conservation legislation relating to species and areas but this was rejected by the People's Constituent Assembly on the grounds of it being outside the development priorities of the government. It is thought that the central authorities will have great difficulty in enforcing any nature protection laws because of the present infrastructure of the country, and it is believed that the only way to continue nature protection policies is through arrangements with the local population.

International Activities Prior to unification at the international level, the former Yemen Arab Republic (YAR) and the People's Democratic Republic of Yemen (PDRY) entered a number of cooperative agreements and legal obligations. Confirmation of succession of obligations from the Republic of Yemen (RAY) have yet to be confirmed. Yemen does not participate in the

Unesco Man and Biosphere (MAB) Programme and does not have a National MAB Committee. The former Yemen republics were party to the Convention concerning the Protection of the World Cultural and Natural Heritage (World Heritage Convention), ratified on 25 January 1984 by YAR and on 7 October 1980 by PDRY. No sites had been inscribed on the World Heritage list up to unification. The former Yemen republics had not signed the Convention on Wetlands of International Importance especially as Waterfowl Habitat, Ramsar Convention. Both former Yemen republics participated in the Programme for the Environment of the Red Sea and the Gulf of Aden (PERSGA) and signed the Regional Convention for the Conservation of the Red Sea and Gulf of Aden Environment on 14 February 1982, and have made enquiries about the Tropical Forest Action Plan.

Cooperation with Saudi Arabia has been recommended for protection of transboundary juniper forests, and with Oman over the biologically rich transboundary area of the Dhofar region adjoining the Omani frontier.

Administration and Management   Although there are a number of governmental bodies involved in policy and overseeing of proposed protected areas administration and management, many initiatives have been undertaken at the private, village or tribal level, as government-owned land is minimal. Land rights are not at the national level but at the level of traditional land owners. The sole large government-owned area which is also of importance for nature conservation is the mangrove coastline which is under the jurisdiction of the army.

Jurisdiction and management at the private initiative level is largely through restrictions to maintain the land for sustainable production and development, basically by controlling forest infringement activities and grazing, and patrolled by the communities themselves. Tribal areas under the jurisdiction of local sheikhs or administrators such as in local development councils have in recent years imposed local forest felling bans and entry into certain areas in order to protect the environment. For example, such community initiatives have been functioning for a number of years in Jebel Lawz and Wadi Zabid catchment. A fine of YR 1,000 (YR12.05 = US$ 1) was to be levied on anyone cutting trees in the latter area (Varisco *et al.*, in press; Wood, 1982). Similar local laws can be found in many other villages including Hamil/Bet Na'ami both near Sana'a (Herzog, *in litt.*, 1991).

Management of religious land and protection of donated waqf land to the religious institution Awqaf results in strong adherence and protection observed by the local community (Herzog, in press).

By 1991 the Republic of Yemen government had largely reformed its ministries. The main ministry concerned with wildlife conservation, fisheries and forestry since unification has been the Ministry of Agriculture and

Water Resources, combining the former YAR Ministry of Agriculture and Fisheries based in Sana'a and the PDRY Ministry of Agriculture and Agrarian Reform based in Aden. The unified Ministry of Agriculture and Water Resources consists of general directorates of forestry and fisheries, including the General Directorate of Forests and Range (established in 1990 from the former General Directorate of Forests). A YAR Directorate of Forestry was established in 1975 with two professional staff and in 1980 was renamed the General Directorate of Forestry with seven named forest officials.

In 1991 the General Directorate of Forests and Range included national directors for natural forests, desertification and afforestation, nurseries, services and coordination and officer directors for botanic gardens and forest extension among women. Programmes include the Forest Development Project set up in 1986 and organised in association with FAO and financed by the Swiss authorities (see Herzog, in press for full list of forestry activities). The Ministry has identified two sites, Jebel Lawz and Jebel Bura. With the assistance of the FAO, the Ministry has identified the boundaries and drafted management plans. No staff members are currently involved in protected areas, although in 1992 there are intentions for one professional staff member and two wardens (Herzog, pers. comm., 1991). Funding will be obtained centrally and through international aid. Forestry funding generally in 1988 (former YAR) included a budget of YR 2 million (YR12.05 = US$ 1) towards conservation programmes, including a national tree planting campaign. For the period 1990-92 US$ 1 million has been budgeted for training of forest technicians (FAO, *in litt.*, 1991).

Other bodies involved in protected areas include the Ministry of Tourism and various private tourist development companies. Since 1990 the Ministry of Tourism has been involved in development plans which include an element of nature protection. It is currently investigating the possibility of aiding conservation activities in the Bura region (Herzog, pers. comm., 1991). Another initiative underway is that of a private tourist company which has already bought a coastal site at al Zuhrah with the intention of maintaining part of it as a nature preserve (Evans *et al.*, 1987; Varisco *et al.*, in press; Herzog, *in litt.*, 1991). Kumran island Reserve, a recommended protected area, has been the responsibility of the Office of Animal Resources Administration of the Ministry of Agriculture (Maher abou Jaafer, 1984; UNEP, 1987).

The Environmental Protection Council (EPC), established in 1987 in YAR, continued after unification to develop and coordinate environmental policy throughout the entire country, and currently has as its main interests pollution and pesticide contamination control. Pre-unification, the EPC was part of the Department of Environmental Health of the Ministry of Municipalities and Housing. Six committees were formed to establish EPC work plans; those relevant to wildlife conservation included the Agriculture Committee, the Land-Use Committee and the Marine Environment Committee. Funding assistance comes from UNEP, FAO and UNDP. Funding assistance from the government of the Netherlands, due to start in 1989, was fixed at DFl 1.6 million for a two-year period (Anon., 1987). Prior to unification, the YAR government institution specifically detailed to take responsibility of wildlife conservation issues was the Department of Wildlife and Zoos, of the Ministry of Agriculture and Fisheries. The department was not operational in 1987 and by 1990 was still nascent, although the Ministry was attempting to pass legislation through parliament in that year to strengthen the role of the proposed department (Varisco, 1987). Organisations and government agencies responsible for wildlife protection, conservation of nature, and genetic resources in the former PDRY included the Department of Forestry of the Ministry of Agriculture; the National Environment Council and the Ministry of Culture and Tourism. The National Environment Council was established in 1976 to advise on environmental and marine matters (UNEP, 1980; UNEP/IUCN, 1980; UNEP/IUCN, 1988). The Ministry of Fish Wealth had also been detailed during this period to be involved in the development of marine research and conservation matters (UNEP/IUCN, 1988).

Little conservation management research had been carried out in the past by the government bodies in either of the two former countries, although FAO had assisted, and continues to aid, the Ministry of Agriculture and Water Resources in undertaking forest inventories and management proposals, investigating indigenous knowledge and undertaking research on sample observation plots such as in the proposed Jebel Bura Reserve (Herzog, *in litt.*, 1991). Training includes programmes on forest ecology and sustainable management, with assistance from FAO and the World Bank, amongst others. Although it has been reported that there is an almost total lack of environmental awareness and of trained personnel involved in conservation, this has been rectified partly by extension courses being held (or planned), such as for schools, and by workshops to improve the understanding of environmental processes. Since unification the Faculty of Science at Sana'a University has continued to conduct research on biological resources. The University of Aden had faculties of Agriculture, Medicine, Engineering and Technology which have undertaken limited environmentally related activities. The El Kod research centre has been involved in botanical survey work and herbarium research. A marine science and resources research centre was established by the government in 1983 with the assistance of Unesco and the Islamic Development Bank.

Non-governmental organisations concerned with environmental issues have for long been lacking. One was founded in 1990/91, however, with interests in environmental protection, waste oil disposal and the safe storage and removal of pesticides. A private group called the Nature and Ornithological Society of Yemen existed in the former YAR and was totally dependent on the individual activities of non-Yemenis.

In the unified Yemen there is reported to be an almost total lack of attempts to set up protected areas at the national level, extremely limited funding, lack of trained personnel in conservation issues, and an apparent lack of coordination between government institutions. Since unification the EPC has been set up to coordinate environmental activities, but by 1991 it still had no capability to deal with all aspects of environmental issues throughout the country (Varisco *et al.*, in press; Herzog, *in litt.*, 1991). A WWF-US backed project in 1987 identified the long-term wildlife conservation needs of YAR. The report recommended coordination of conservation efforts and development of institutions addressing conservation issues. It was proposed that the first step should be affiliation of a Yemeni institution with IUCN, to link with countries on the Arabian Peninsula (Barratt *et al.*, 1987; IUCN, 1986).

Systems Reviews   Situated at the southern end of the Arabian Peninsula, Yemen is bounded in the north by Saudi Arabia, in the east by Oman, in the south by the Gulf of Aden and west by the Red Sea. The territory includes the islands of Kamaran and Perim in the Red Sea and the island of Socotra in the Gulf of Aden (Hunter, 1991). Yemen is located at the boundary between the Palaearctic, Afrotropical and Asiatic biogeographical zones, resulting in a biodiversity reported to be the highest in the Middle East. Generally, on the south Arabian Peninsula there is 5-10% plant endemism. There is an absence of dense forest cover (except at J. Bura), open woodland or succulent scrub being prevalent on the montane plains at 2,000m, and at lower altitudes thickets and woods being largely of *Acacia*, and coastal mangrove. The flora is dominated by desert and semi-desert vegetation throughout the country. Fringing coral and seagrass communities occur off the 765km-long Red Sea coast. Mangroves have developed along 17% of the coast.

The wildlife has affinities to tropical Africa, montane flora of the East African Highlands and the eastern desert flora with the Sahara-Sindian region. The highlands support the majority of endemic or near-endemic species of plants and animals. High escarpment ravines contain remnant natural, juniper vegetation such as at Jebel Lawz (Khawlan), Jebel Saba (Taiz) and Kubbeitah (south of Taiz) (Herzog, *in litt.*, 1991). In the high mountain tops are unique flora assemblages including alpine type vegetation. An estimated 1,700 plant species have been identified. The flora of Socotra is of particular botanical significance, including 215 endemic species, representing Somalia-Masai flora type communities (Anon., 1986; Cronk, pers. comm., 1991). Over 220 species of migrant and wintering passerines have been recorded on migration, of a total species count of 350. There are 55 species of mammal, 65 species of reptile and 43 species of freshwater fish. In total, there are five species of globally threatened mammals, 18 of birds, four of reptiles and two of freshwater fish. Critical habitats under threat include mangrove areas affected by coastal development (Hepper and Wood, 1979).

The coast of northern Yemen is one of the most significant fishery areas in the Red Sea, providing important sources of food and income. Domestic livestock totals are high, with 1.2 million head. There is virtually no large-scale industry. Agriculture is the main economy, occupying some 80% of the population. Arable land represents only 2% of the total area of the country and is largely confined to fertile valleys and flood plains. Irrigation schemes are in project stage.

Systems reviews and comprehensive surveys of biological resources have been undertaken in a number of fields: a national vegetation mapping survey of the former YAR, in association with the Range and Livestock Improvement Project based at Dhamar; a 1991 report on the vegetation of the Republic of Yemen (Scholte *et al.*, 1991) by consultants; extensive flora collections, botanical surveys and forestry programmes (Hepper, 1977; Hepper and Wood, 1979; Herzog, in press); WWF programmes surveying Socotra (Project 3324) (Anon., 1986); birds and wildlife studies particularly at Socotra, Mahra and Abian (Obadi, N.), airborne photographic surveys (Steffen *et al.*, 1978); preliminary work on coastal zone management plans, including comprehensive surveys of ecosystems and status of species (IUCN, 1986; Barratt *et al.*, 1987); and short-term expeditions to survey species (Rands *et al.*, 1987; for a summary see Varisco, *et al.*, in press).

Following a 1989 project proposal, the US-AID prepared a biological diversity assessment of the former YAR in 1990, backed by the US-Fish and Wildlife Service. Other reports have been undertaken on general environmental topics, for example by UNEP, UNDP, the Netherlands government, independent consultants and US-AID (Anon., 1987; Gubara, 1985; Speece, 1982; UNEP, 1980; Varisco *et al.*, in press). In March 1989, the UNDP, Central Planning Organisation and the Ministry of Municipalities and Housing sponsored an environmental protection workshop in Sana'a. Subsequently, the UNDP has prepared a document with the intention of the future integration of environmental protection into project planning (FAO, *in litt.*, 1991). Recommended conservation priorities include development policies to respond to environmental degradation and the development. In the period 1986-91 development planning in YAR provided for investment of US$ 3,776 million and concentrated principally on agricultural development (cf in PDRY over the same period the expenditure was D 998.2 million at the rate of D 0.46 = US$ 1).

IUCN has recommended the need for correcting intensification of fishing resources, tourism sites and unplanned coastal development, and identification of the location and extent of critical marine habitats along the Yemen Red Sea coast (Barratt *et al.*, 1987; IUCN, 1986). Other recommendations included the need for national

botanical surveys, surveys of land vertebrate fauna and insects, as identified by the Biology Department of the Sana'a University. The importance of involving local communities in self-policing programmes, to protect trees and the environment from over-development, has been stressed. Projects are underway to investigate the role of Yemeni tribal society in conservation activities and habitat restoration, by using agro-sylvo-pastoral tribal management systems. A case study is being undertaken at Jebel Bura (Herzog, in press).

A number of major recommendations exist, arising from reviews and surveys identifying critical areas in need of protection, although there has not been a nature conservation review to prioritise sites. One of the most detailed surveys was the IUCN coastal zone management plan, under the PERSGA environmental programme, which initiated a preliminary survey of key marine habitats, to develop management plans and provide relevant training to yemeni nationals. Up to eight sites have been short-listed for nature reserve status by IUCN, UNEP and WWF consultants, and 16 coastal sites recommended for special management (Anon., 1986; Barratt *et al.*, 1987; Ghadaf and Stirn, 1983; Maher abou Jaafer, 1984). A list of key areas for the conservation of sites of international importance for birds was prepared during a short 1985 visit to YAR by OSME members (Rands *et al.*, 1987). The 1985 WWF botanical survey of Socotra made a number of recommendations, including the future establishment of at least four nature reserves as centres for the conservation of endemic flora (Anon., 1986; Cronk, pers. comm., 1991). The recommended areas included Socotra island, Jabal al-Arais and the Eastern Region reserves, Socotra islands alone totalling 362,500ha (Maher abou Jaafer, 1984). In 1990/91 independent technical services began mapping the forests of Yemen, producing data which it is hoped will act as the basis for identifying new priority areas for protection.

Preliminary inventories and management plans of the recommended sites of Jebel Lawz (264ha) and Jebel Bura (300ha) have been drafted by FAO, Ministry of Agriculture and Water Resources and Ministry of Tourism consultants (Herzog, *in litt.*, 1991). A project is in hand to establish a national reserve on Socotra (Cronk, *in litt.*, 1991; Herzog, *in litt.*, 1991). Of all the recommended sites, FAO personnel report that the highest priorities for protection are J. Bura, J. ar Reis (Abyan), Jal (Mahra) and Socotra (Evans *et al.*, 1987; Varisco *et al.*, in press; FAO, *in litt.*, 1991; Herzog, *in litt.*, 1991).

By 1991 there were no nationally designated protected areas in the country, although a series of alternative well-established areas exists, including community areas such as at J. Lawz and Wadi Zabid catchment, as well as a series of Waqf and Majhur traditionally-protected rangeland and religious lands (Wood, 1982). *De facto* protected areas also exist in a number of restricted military areas, including the Red sea islands and the area south of Mawza and in the Tihama plain between Mocha and Bab al Mandib (Varisco *et al.*, in press).

Due to past civil unrest, the poor economic situation has led to environmental protection generally being given a low priority. However, in the case of fisheries, conservation has been recognised by the authorities by actively assisting in maintaining resources (Karpowicz, *in litt.*, 1985). Due to a lack of integrated environmental policies, the threat to the largely unsurveyed resources of wildlife in the country, through the proposed development and expansion of agriculture, industry and tourism, is extreme. Details of the current environmental situation and recent surveys of the status of fauna and flora are almost completely lacking. Some of the greatest environmental problems include the fuel wood trade, the charcoal industry and degradation caused by overgrazing of free-ranging livestock. The endemic flora of Socotra is under particular threat from the conflict of agricultural development and plant conservation. Oil exploration is taking place off the northern coast and there are potential threats from pollution. Land-use changes, as a consequence of increasing mechanisation of agriculture from the 1980s onwards, has led to serious problems of erosion through deep ploughing on former rangeland and of pollution from fertilizers and pesticides (J. Karpowicz, *in litt.*, 1985).

Other Relevant Information Tourism is gradually developing in the Yemen, with an estimated 43,500 entries in 1986-87. There are proposals to incorporate nature conservation and ecotourism into future tourism programmes. Since 1990 the Ministry of Tourism has been involved in developing plans for landscape protection and is currently investigating potential activities in the Bura region (Herzog, pers. comm., 1991). Other nature protection initiatives are reported as being undertaken by a private company in the al Zuhrah coastal area (Evans *et al.*, 1987; Varisco *et al.*, in press; Herzog, *in litt.*, 1991).

Addresses

General Directorate of Forest and Range, Ministry of Agriculture and Water Resources, PO Box 1867, SANA'A (Tel: 2 242910; FAX: 2 208852; Tlx: 2435 Foodag YE)

Environmental Protection Council, Department of Environmental Health, Ministry of Municipalities and Housing, SANA'A

Environmental Protection (President), c/o SANA'A (Tel: 2 215 832 (residence); 2 217 401 (work))

References

Anon. (1986). Plant protection for Socotra. Project 3324. *WWF Monthly Report.*
Anon. (1987). Environmental aspects of Yemen Arab Republic Netherlands Development Cooperation. Department of Development Co-operation, Ministry of Foreign Affairs, Netherlands. 60 pp.
Anon. (1989). Sharper lines in Arabia's sands. *The Economist.* 21 January. P. 82.
Barratt, L., Dawson-Shepherd, A., Ormond, R. and McDowell, R. (1987). Yemen Arab Republic Marine Conservation Survey II. Preliminary coastal zone management recommendations for the Yemen Arab Republic. IUCN, Gland, Switzerland and PERSGA, Jeddah, Saudi Arabia.
Evans, M., Newland, P. and Thompson, T. (1987). Flora and Fauna of Wadi Hudayn, Jabal Bura. Unpublished report submitted to IUCN-CMC, Cambridge, UK. 15 pp.
Ghadaf, A. and Stirn, J. (1983). A draft proposal for the UNEP research and development project: fisheries resource assessment and protection of marine environment, its shores and living resources in PDR of Yemen waters. Report.
Grimwood, I.R. (1974). Notes on birds seen in eastern Aden protectorate. A bibliography of the avifauna of the Arabian peninsula, the Levant and Mesopotamia. *Bulletin B.O.C.* 83: 50-52.
Gubara, E.M. (1985). The State of the environment in Yemen Arab Republic. UNEP Regional Office for West Asia.
Haskoning (1990). Support to the Secretariat of the Environmental Protection Council, Republic of Yemen. Report prepared by Haskoning Royal Dutch Consulting Engineers and Architects to the Government of the Netherlands. 39 pp.
Hepper, F.N. (1977). Outline of the vegetation of the Yemen Arab Republic. *Publications of the Cairo University Herbarium* 7/8: 307-322.
Hepper, F.N. and Wood, J.R.I. (1979). Were there forests in the Yemen? *Proc. Seminar for Arabian Studies* 9: 65-69.
Herzog, M. (1989). Jebel Burra. Inventory and technical management proposals. FAO, Sana'a.
Herzog, M. (1990). Jebel Lawz. Inventory and technical management proposals. FAO, Sana'a.
Herzog, M. (in press). The possibility of introducing trees (amenity) and agro-sylvo-pastoral tree management systems into tribal society. A case study at Jebel Bura's Forest, Yemen. Thesis in preparation. 66 pp.
Hunter, B. (Ed.) (1991). *The Statesman's Year Book 1991-92.* The Macmillan Press Ltd, London and Basingstoke, UK. 1692 pp.
IUCN (1986). Yemen Arab Republic Marine Conservation Survey. Draft Final Report. Tropical Marine Research Unit, York, UK.
Kessler, J.J. (1988). Mahjur areas: traditional rangeland reserves in the Dhamar Montane Plains (Yemen Arab Republic). Yemen Arab Republic: Range and Livestock Improvement Project Communication No. 16. (Unseen)
Loulou, H. (1976). Yemen Arab Republic. Country report 11. In: Promotion of the establishment of marine parks and reserves in the Northern Indian ocean including the Red Sea and Persian Gulf. Papers and proceedings of the Regional Meeting held at Tehran, Iran, 6-10 March 1975. *IUCN Publications New Series* 35: 101-102.

Maher abou Jaafer (1984). *National parks and nature reserves in the Arab world*. The Arab League Educational, Cultural and Scientific Organization, Tunis.

Montague, K. and Bruun, B. (1987). *Biological diversity in North Africa, the Middle East and Southwest Asia; a directory of organizations and institutions*. HLCF, New York, USA.

Ormond, R.F.G. (1980). Management and conservation of Red Sea habitats. *The coastal and marine environment of the Red Sea, Gulf of Aden and Tropical Western Indian Ocean* 2: 137-162.

Popov, G.B. (1957). The vegetation of Socotra. *Journal of the Linnaean Society. Botany* 55: 706-720.

Rahim, M.A. (1979). *Biology of the Arabian Peninsula, a bibliographic study*. Saudi Biological Society Publication No. 3.

Rands, M., Rands, G and Porter, R. (1987). Birds in the Yemen Arab Republic: A Report of the Ornithological Society of the Middle East Expedition, October-December, 1985. International Council for Bird Preservation, Cambridge, UK. 38 pp.

Sardar, Z. (1982). Yemen Arab Republic/People's Democratic Republic of Yemen. *Science and technology in the Middle East, a guide to issues, organisations and institutions*. Longman, London and New York.

Scholte, P., Al Khulaidi, A.W. and Kessler, J.J. (1991). The vegetation of the Republic of Yemen. DHV Consultants. 23 pp.

Speece, M. (1982). Draft Environmental report on Yemen (Yemen Arab Republic). Arid Lands Information Center, Tucson, USA.

Steffen, H. *et al.*, 1978. Yemen Arab Republic. Final report on the airphoto interpretation project. Swiss Technical Cooperation Services, Berne, Switzerland.

UNEP (1980). *State of the environment report for the People's Democratic Republic of Yemen*. United Nations Environment Programme. 50 pp.

UNEP Regional Bulletin for Europe (1987). Clearing house developments. *UNEP Regional Bulletin for Europe* 4: 9.

UNEP/IUCN (1988) *Coral Reefs of the World. Volume 2: Indian Ocean, Red Sea and Gulf*. UNEP Regional Seas Directories and Bibliographies. IUCN, Gland, Switzerland and Cambridge, UK/UNEP, Nairobi, Kenya. 440 pp.

Varisco, D.M. (1987). Horns and hilts, wildlife conservation for North Yemen (YAR). A report prepared for Asia/Near East Bureau, Agency for International Development, Washington, DC under a cooperative agreement with World Wildlife Fund - US Project No. 6298.

Varisco, D.M. (1989). Beyond rhino horn wildlife conservation for North Yemen. *Oryx* 23: 215-219.

Varisco, D.M., Ross, J.P. and Milroy, A. (in press). Biological diversity assessment of the Republic of Yemen. Draft report prepared for US-AID, International Council for Bird Preservation and the Government of the Republic of Yemen. Unpublished.

Wood, J.R.I. (1982). The Jabal Bura' Valley Forest Community. Report to the Gesellschaft für Technische Zusammenarbeit and YAR Ministry of Agriculture. Unpublished.

Zohary, M. (1973). *Geobotanical foundations of the Middle East*. G. Fischer, Stuttgart/Sweets and Zeitlinger, Amsterdam. 610 pp.

ANNEX
Definitions of protected area designations, as legislated, together with authorities responsible for their administration

Title: Forest Law (non ratified)

Date: Draft law of 1986 but not ratified up to unification in 1990

Brief description: To be applied to all forests or shrub-covered land, whether owned by government, communities or individual as, all man-made forests, and all land that is considered would benefit from afforestation such as sand dunes.

Administrative authority: No information

Designations: Any action calculated to damage the forest is forbidden and utilisation of forests for any purposes is to be regulated by licences.

Source: Herzog, in press
